THE
GREAT
CRITICS

An Anthology of Literary Criticism

THIRD EDITION

THE
GREAT
CRITICS

An Anthology of Literary Criticism

COMPILED AND EDITED BY

JAMES HARRY SMITH
and
EDD WINFIELD PARKS

THIRD EDITION REVISED AND ENLARGED

W · W · NORTON & COMPANY

New York · London

W. W. Norton & Company, Inc., 500 Fifth Avenue, New York, N.Y. 10110
W. W. Norton & Company Ltd., 37 Great Russell Street, London WC1B 3NU

ISBN 0 393 09074 4

PRINTED IN THE UNITED STATES OF AMERICA
FOR THE PUBLISHERS BY THE VAIL-BALLOU PRESS
3 4 5 6 7 8 9 0

CONTENTS

v

CONTENTS

SUPPLEMENT

CONTENTS

CONTENTS

PREFACE
TO THE THIRD EDITION

IN their revisions of *The Great Critics,* the Editors have not attempted to rebuild or drastically to change the form of the book. They have, however, made extensive alterations and additions to the selections. The result is a much wider and more representative anthology of critical writings, based on the suggestions and requests of many teachers. The Introductions have been lengthened, and some of them made to serve almost as miniature anthologies, in the attempt to give better representation to minor criticism which led up to the more important treatises, and to restore some flavor of diversity to the more important critical disputes. In this second revision, added scope has been given to criticism of fiction, and representation has been given to the work of recent and contemporary critics. In including the work of modern writers the Editors have been aware of the difficulties inherent in making selections and rendering judgments. However, we have checked our final impressions against those which we entertained eighteen and again eleven years ago, and have thoughtfully reviewed the suggestions made by many critics and scholars.

Acknowledgment is gratefully repeated to the following publishers who granted permission for the reprinting in the 1939 edition of material on which they held copyrights: The Macmillan Company, New York and London; The Clarendon Press, Oxford, England; Dominican Fathers, St. Dominic's Priory, and Burns, Oates & Washburn, Ltd., London; Cambridge University Press; E. P. Dutton & Co., Inc., New York; Princeton University Press, Princeton, N.J.; and Charles Scribner's Sons, New York. We wish also to acknowledge the co-operation of publishers and individuals who have granted permissions for the reprinting of material in the present edition: Faber and Faber, Ltd., for use in Canada of "Religion and Literature," from *Essays Ancient and Modern,* by T. S. Eliot; Methuen & Company, Ltd., for use in Canada of "Tradition and the Individual Talent," from *The Sacred Wood,* by T. S. Eliot; Harcourt, Brace and Company for use of selections from *Selected Essays 1917–1932,* by T. S. Eliot, and from *Essays Ancient and Modern,* by T. S. Eliot; Charles Scribner's Sons for use of "Poetry: A Note in Ontology," from *The World's Body,* by John Crowe Ransom; The Clarendon Press for use of *The Defense of Poetry,* by Benedetto Croce; Thomas Y. Crowell Company for use of selections from *What Is Art?* by Leo Tolstoi; J. M. Dent & Sons, Ltd., for use of the Preface to *The Nigger of the Narcissus,* by Joseph Conrad; Mr. C. D. Medley, London, for use of selections from *An Anthology of Pure Poetry,* by George Moore; Mr. Ludwig Lewisohn, Waltham, Mass., for use of his translation of *The Literary Life,* by Anatole France.

It is a pleasure to record here our indebtedness to the men who have aided by their counsel in both revisions. For their assistance on the 1939 edition we reiterate our sense of gratitude to Richmond P. Bond of North Carolina, Calvin S. Brown, Jr., of Georgia, Philo M. Buck, Jr., of Wisconsin, Hoyt Hudson of Princeton, the late William A. Neilson, C. D. Thorpe of Michigan, Henry Nash Smith of Minnesota, Austin Warren of Michigan, Herbert F. West of Dartmouth, C. S. Young of Culver, and Messrs. Robert E. Farlow and Addison C. Burnham of W. W. Norton and Company. For help in producing the 1950 edition we wish to thank Professor Donald A. Stauffer of Princeton and Professor Edwin R. Clapp of the University of Utah for analyses of the earlier editions and detailed suggestions, Miss Alice Dean Kelly of Florida State University, and the library staffs of the University of Georgia and Southwestern College for assistance in the securing of material for research, and Addison C. Burnham of W. W. Norton and Company for his patient and wise co-ordination of everyone's efforts. In all phases of the work we have had the constant and scholarly assistance of Sara Catron Smith and Aileen Wells Parks.

E. W. P.
J. H. S.

September, 1950

PREFACE

The numerous anthologies of poetry which have been brought out during recent years have made it readily possible for the student, though without large library facilities at his hand, to compare the accomplishments of different poets and periods. Unable to afford or to locate editions of many important authors, any reader can now find those things which "bear the force of universal tradition" in a purchasable collection. Anthologies of prose, though necessarily less catholic, more arbitrary, than those of verse, have done much toward the same purpose. Both types have made themselves important parts of the formal course in college and school.

Throughout this collecting, one department of *belles lettres* has had but scant attention. Criticism, at present much the study and practice of our best writers, and the expanding method of initiation to literature in colleges, has heretofore had little of that treatment by which poetry and artistic prose have so thoroughly been canvassed. There are those who will think it better so. Anthologies, indeed, have limitations and disadvantages: the translated *Poetics* of Aristotle printed here does not have the Greek on the opposite page; nor does it have Mr. Butcher's valuable outline and notes attached; but a sentence from it can quickly and with entire facility be placed beside its quotation in Dryden's *Essay of Dramatic Poesy,* or beside its restatement by Coleridge.

The purpose of the book has been to assemble, in a resourceful and convenient single volume, the most important pieces of criticism for English literature. This must include those which all times have declared greatest, and others which, though perhaps in discredit among our contemporaries, have yet moved men mightily at some former time. It is intended that these selections mark out a highway, though not of uniformly paved surface, yet leading generally through the central and most populous areas of our literature.

No critical essays of the present or of the recent past are included. This is not from the traditional heresy that nothing great is ever being done in the present; but from a recognition of the impossibility of gauging the present along with the past. Two recent collections of essays, by Mr. Lewisohn and by Mr. Burgum, serve as charts through the heavy growth of our contemporary thinking; with regard to which we could wish for no more than that our collection might to some degree map toward their boundaries. We propose to join to those *Defences* and *Arts of Poetry* in other languages which are always being quoted and are seldom read, the *Apologies* and *Prefaces* and *Essays* which have formulated what might be called the English tradition, and then to give sufficient scope to that period and those treaties in which the first community of critical doctrine established and then destroyed itself. After Wordsworth and Coleridge came such multiplicity and complexity of ideas that one whole anthology could hardly hope to represent them all. There is the further circumstance that these works are for the most part accessible to the general reader or to the student; certainly so as compared with such criticism as Young's *Conjectures* or Boileau's *Art of Poetry*. We have accordingly chosen what Nineteenth Century essays seemed the most significant issues from the disruption of neo-classicism, or the most productive of ideas for the readjustment.

Beside the securing for texts of the nearest available approaches to the originals, we have cherished as the first principle in this work the giving of selections in their entirety. Since the purpose of this collection is largely to increase the ease of various comparative studies, it has seemed desirable that completeness make no sacrifice to compactness, even though occasionally some waste land be walled in with the good estates. One seeing Sidney's *Apologie* among the contents may be sure of finding any sentence of it to which he may wish to refer. The same will be true of single chapters of the *Biographia Literaria*. Only in cases of obvious necessity has this rule been broken. To have included Samuel Johnson's entire *Life of Dryden* or *Life of Pope* would have required the omission of other pieces which are of value and are not easy of access; and three quarters of either of the *Lives* is more properly biographical or textual rather than critical. The aim of the supplement is to give expansion to numerous ideas which appear in the greater criticism, and, in some cases, to illustrate positions which did not have expression in the masterpieces.

We are happy to make acknowledgments to the following for permissions to use selections from their publications: The Macmillan Company for the Aristotle, Longinus, and Arnold; the Yale University Press and the translator, F. M. Padelford, for the Scaliger; J. M.

Dent & Co. for the Dante; the Manchester University Press for the Castelvetro. Professors D. C. Cabeen and W. C. Curry of Vanderbilt, who read portions of the original manuscript, have greatly assisted the editors with their scholarship and counsel, and Professors Clyde Pharr, H. C. Sanborn, and Edwin Mims, of Vanderbilt, Howard Mumford Jones of Michigan, and Alan D. McKillop of Rice, have contributed valuable suggestions. Miss Elizabeth Wenning, who translated the Goethe selection, and Miss Aileen Wells, Dr. Leota S. Driver, and Mrs. E. W. Ryan, who so kindly assisted in reading the proof, are likewise due our especial thanks. We wish to express the highest sense of indebtedness to the Vanderbilt library staff, notably to Miss Isabel Howell, Mrs. D. C. Cabeen, and Mrs. Brainerd Cheney, for their efficiency in providing and securing much needed material. There must be omitted, in any list of acknowledgments, many whose assistance, too indirect to be named, have had a part for which no editor could effectually thank them.

JAMES HARRY SMITH
EDD WINFIELD PARKS

INTRODUCTION

To take a wider and more removed view of any subject, after long engrossment in its details, is almost always to discover questions of the first importance which were not apparent on close examination. It is not possible to write a history of criticism in a brief survey of a collection: but the collection, regarded in its entirety, may present questions which do not occur to the strict historian or to the student of a special field. Among these are the *raison d'etre* of criticism itself, the Why of its existence; the peculiarities which distinguish it as a literary form; the chronological position which it holds to pure literature in various civilizations; the mutable nature of its power and of its respectability. It becomes fascinating to consider that the ancient masterpieces in this genre were the after-results of masterpieces in poetry, drama, oratory, while the modern literatures were theory-conscious by the time they were art-conscious; and that the Renaissance formulated nearly all the rules for neo-classicism, and wrote by none of them.

The *Poetics* of Aristotle is in a class to itself among critical works. One never feels that the philosopher relished the course of lectures which he gave on the subject of poetry. But there the subject was confronting him, as certainly a *thing* as marine biology or legal codification, and nothing could he pass by without giving it its classifications and asserting its laws. The *Poetics* proceeds to discuss the specimens known to its author. It does not interest itself with possibilities of the future. The declarations of laws seem aimed rather at explaining how the dramatists had worked than how they might or should work. It is an effort to understand literature as physiology might be understood. Aristotle alone has this attitude in its completeness. Scaliger has it to a degree. Longinus, Horace, Vida, and Ronsard are explaining *how to write;* Du Bellay and Sidney are defending the privilege of writing.

This distinction completely escaped the Renaissance and neo-classical critics. The observations which Aristotle made on Aeschylus and Sophocles thus became the rules for Ben Jonson and Corneille. The last century and a half has gained a freedom from them, though it has not escaped from the general principles and definitions of the *Poetics.*

The earliest criticism has for subject matter poetry and oratory. Prose other than oratory was not reckoned among the fine arts until a much later time; and from the point of view of criticism, at least, it grew out of oratory. Longinus and Quintilian interested themselves with the problems of the speaker, whose aim, in their opinion, was to persuade. Persuading and pleasing might often be achieved by the same means, and so criticism of oratory appeared in a parallel position to that of poetry, and as the only representative of prose. The ancient types of poetry have many of them been lost to the sway of verse, and we should read the critics from Aristotle even to Ben Jonson remembering that what they speak of as "poetry" is for us *belles lettres,* and that "oratory" is the only pure prose.

It is not easy to evaluate ancient criticism. We read much of Aristotle and Horace in disgust. We feel prone to resent what their influence, though misdirected, did to the Seventeenth and Eighteenth Centuries. We wonder whether poetizing was indeed so rife among the Greeks and Romans as to require such curbing. But our indebtedness to them becomes more apparent when we detach ourselves from smaller considerations, and hear poetry defined as the representation of nature in the ideal. For good or for ill, modern criticism has based itself upon antiquity as completely as modern literature has done.

The problems of Renaissance criticism are twofold, to justify the existence of fiction and to establish the vernaculars as fit modes of expression. The objections to "poetry" proceed largely from two sources, the Church and the neo-Platonic philosophers. In casting about for authorities in their support, the defenders rediscover Horace, and on the basis of his *aut prodesse aut delectare,* assert that poetry's aim is to please *and* instruct. Scaliger makes "the giving of instruction" the end, and puts himself to considerable pains to show that this is the supreme end, as distinguished from the subsidiary end, namely pleasing. The best summary of the objections is in Sidney's *Defense,* and this document remains the Magna Charta for poetry in England.

The importance of this moral condemnation is far-reaching. The dread of enthusiasm which inhibits the Eighteenth Century shows its influence. For those dangers which the Puritans attributed to poetry, the neo-classicists attributed to imagination. Fear of being deceived by fiction gave place to fear of going insane from an unrestricted exercise of the fancy.

For the establishment of the vernacular languages, the treatises of Dante and of Du Bellay hold the place of inspired Scriptures. With them begins, too, the cry for nationalism in literature, and, in an age of strong patriotic tendencies, it is not surprising to find critics demanding a "French Homer and Pindar," or indulging in such encomiums as "the English Virgil," "the English Horace": another tendency to bind the new literatures with the requirements of the new "imitation." An interesting matter for study is the influence which literary patriotism had in the development of the theory that excellence came from following the ancients. Vida's injunction to steal, to despoil, is a parallel to military aggrandisement. And the high honor given to translation, particularly in English, proceeds in great measure from this same tendency to hurry the young literature into preeminence.

The culmination of the two questions of the Renaissance is reached in Sidney's *Apologie for Poetrie*. The grounds on which the art had been condemned are reviewed, and the prerogatives of the imaginative faculty of the mind are asserted. "His 'Defense of Poesy' is a veritable epitome of the literary criticism of the Italian Renaissance;" says Mr. Spingarn; "and so thoroughly is it imbued with this spirit, that no other work, Italian, French, or English, can be said to give so complete and so noble a conception of the temper and the principles of Renaissance criticism." [*Hist. of Lit. Crit. in the Renaissance*, 268.]

There is found, too, the will to pattern English forms after the classic. Spenser is rebuked on the example of Virgil and Theocritus; *Gorboduc* is compared with Seneca as to style, and censured by the precepts of Aristotle. It is surprising to observe in what degree the cardinal principles of neo-classical doctrine were current before and during the Elizabethan period; in how many instances Du Bellay, Sidney, and Daniel, the liberals, formulated ideas that were to become infallible rules among writers and critics so unlike them. Discard our own old poets, and imitate the Greek and Latin, says Du Bellay; give our poets no prerogatives that the ancients did not have, implies Sidney.

The part had by the Renaissance in the development of criticism is comparable to formal education in the life of an individual. As we have seen men, often authors, who forgot what had been taught them long enough to gain great achievements without it, and who then returned fearfully to absolute compliance and safe mediocrity, so the productions of the Restoration and Eighteenth Century poets seem to us conscious illustrations of what the great Elizabethans had, without doing, taught should be done. We have for too long damned the French influence, without sufficiently considering Ben Jonson and Sidney as important teachers, and without looking carefully at the French writings themselves.

Literary historians have told of a malignant French influence in the Seventeenth Century, an influence which blighted the French lyric for nearly two centuries, and cast its baleful power, though to a lesser degree, over England also. But this mischievous terror, though it has been named and described, no one has seemed to think ought to be given to popular sight. It has been a companion with the marine octopus and the monsters of hell: a Cerberus of whom every professor and critic has spoken like a Hercules. With the bitterest of French accents, they have summoned up fiends whose very appellations could affright the startled listeners round: Malherbe; and Rapin; and Racin; and Nicolas Boileau-Desprèaux.

These critics have been, for the most part, set in their proper relationships to literature, and are generally quoted, thanks to a few good historians of criticism, with reasonable accuracy. But no one has thought it proper to expose the very monsters themselves; no one has thought it would make a truly entertaining sideshow, where he could set out Macduff's scoff as a signboard, "Here may you see the tyrant." And among the shades the fabled Cerberus has growled, but to no ear that heard.

A careful perusal of the Soame and Dryden translation of Boileau will change the popular conception of him materially. He is the exponent of *les trois unités,* and he insists that each literary genre has its peculiar rules. But his "common sense" is not more of a destructive influence than the wise cautions of many English liberals.

In Dryden, as in Sidney, the disputes of his time are gathered. The controversy regarding rhyme, which had engaged the attention of Campion and Daniel, Jonson, and Milton; the relative importance of the ancients and the moderns; the place of the unities in dramatic composition; the nature and uses of wit; all these are treated many times, and from many angles. And while Dryden's judgments remain generally within the pale of neo-classicism, he himself is beyond it. One of the great critics of the world, he advocates the tenets of his century with saneness, not with dogma, and he represents a liberalism which was lost in the century that followed.

It has been the fortune of a score of poets to be accepted and esteemed wherever known, and in whatever time. In criticism, for reasons readily apparent, very few indeed are they whose glories have outreached the controversies of a period. All critics have oriented themselves upon Aristotle, oftentimes grudgingly. From antiquity, Longinus has been good, and must ever be,

> To all that wander in that perilous flood.

But after Longinus, while many have cast long shadows into the future, or conjointly shaded a century, it frequently strains our attention to discover what precise object intercepted so much sunlight. Dryden is unique; his shadow falls not so much at his feet as farther away from him. He is, in criticism, a presence to be felt in all times—and not a staker of temporary boundaries.

In the unanimity of doctrine which prevailed throughout the Eighteenth Century, criticism dealt principally with terminology. Little originality showed itself, the orthodox and the rebellious being alike conventional in their arguments. Interest descends chiefly to the use of special words, the catch-words of neo-classicism: nature, imitation, invention, wit, imagination. All the effort is expended in deciding what is meant by terms the authority of which is beyond dispute. It is as though men had agreed to statements in a foreign language and were busy looking up the definitions of their words. So entangled became the situation at last that one might safely aver that "original genius" might disregard the "rules" if he also said that "nature" should be "followed." He might judge that "imitation" alone could not make a writer great if he also decreed that only "original genius" might dare disregard "ancient" "example" and "rule." Presently, in Johnson, the very antithesis of neo-classicism emerges from his own arguments, like an unaccountable result on an adding machine.

In the meantime, those young men who are generally termed the pre-Romanticists, came forward with a variety of new subject matter for poetry and the novel. The Wartons and Walpoles never vitally affected criticism, however. Neo-classicism died at the hands of its defenders. While the valiant young rebel bachelors questioned Pope and elevated Spenser, and sent up the medieval war-cry from the fields, the old widowers, deaf and secure within their fortress, argued themselves out of supremacy, using their own logic.

However it be with poetry, with criticism an old era ends and a new begins with Wordsworth. For the merits of his outstanding Preface of 1800 we must look in many places. It stands in a unique position to all Nineteenth Century literature. It passes sentence upon the century just closing. But the most amazing element in it, over and above the enshrinement of emotion, the attempt to reform diction, the flamboyant democracy, is the absence of the old terminology. With it gone, one senses immediately that there has been a revolution.

Of Nineteenth Century criticism it is most hard to judge. In this volume are included chiefly those writers who sought to achieve a healthy balance of the old and the new. There can be no greater praise of Coleridge than that he avoided being extremely Romantic after the manner in which Dryden avoided being extremely neo-classical, that his dicta bore the marks of a judgment that was independent of the doctrines of his time. The estimates of classical literatures in comparison with our own were part of Ruskin's and of Arnold's purposes. Goethe and Sainte-Beuve showed similar attitudes, in their literatures. The tendency toward "democratization" which began with Wordsworth's stressing of "incidents from common life" has had a wide influence: no one differs more from him perhaps, as a critic or as a poet, than does Whitman, the ultimate democrat. "The spontaneous overflow of powerful feelings" summarizes poetry's tendency toward the shorter lyric form which Poe advocates. So Wordsworth may aptly be called the father of Nineteenth Century criticism.

The Twentieth Century has seen wider divergencies from purely artistic considerations. Not only for the common man, but likewise for the scientist, the educator, the economist, and the searcher after religious truths, the critic has appointed himself the guide as well as the guardian. Amid the new interests, the importance of criticism as a literary kind, in addition to a methodizing of judgments, has gained in recognition. What has been well written, well thought, whether for causes that were lost or that triumphed, must always be a light unto our feet, even on roads newly found. "We may," says Mr. Saintsbury, "we must, we ought sometimes to differ with Aristotle and Longinus, with Quintilian and Scaliger, with Patrizzi and Castelvetro, with Dryden and Johnson, with Sainte-Beuve and Arnold. But what is good in them—and even what, though not so intrinsically good, is injured only by system and point of view, by time and chance and fatality—remains a possession for ever."

THE
GREAT
CRITICS

PLATO

(c. 427 B. C.–c. 347 B. C.)

PLATO was probably born in 427 B. C., of distinguished Athenian parentage. Ariston, his father, traced his descent from the god Poseidon; his mother's family was related to the law-giver Solon. His stepfather, Pyrilampes, was a prominent supporter of Pericles; his relatives were friends of Socrates, and through them Plato may, as a boy, have known the philosopher. One tradition has it, however, that after falling under the sway of Socrates (when Plato was about twenty), he destroyed his poems and dramas, and turned to philosophy and mathematics. His early ambitions were political (*7th Epistle*), but he abandoned this field after the execution of Socrates in 399 B. C. and went into temporary exile at Megara. Plato saw brief service in several of the Athenian wars, and traveled extensively, at different times, in Egypt, North Africa, Sicily, and Italy.

About 387 B. C., Plato founded the Academy, in the grove of Academus, and for the remainder of his life presided over this institute, where important work on philosophy, mathematics, natural sciences, jurisprudence, and practical legislation was done under his supervision. Here Plato wrote most, if not all, of his works: to list only a few of them, such early dialogues as *Ion, Lysis,* and *Gorgias;* the great achievements of his prime, the *Symposium, Phaedo, Phaedrus,* and *Republic;* in his old age, the *Laws.* At the request of Dion of Syracuse, in 367, Plato attempted to train the tyrant's successor, Dionysius, to rule as a wise constitutional monarch, and went to Syracuse for that purpose; but Dionysius drove out tutor and ruler, endangering their lives. Plato returned to Athens, but continued to travel widely and to send his pupils as advisers and writers of laws to many states. He died in 347 B. C., over eighty years of age, and widely loved and honored; his Academy continued to exist as a corporate body until 529 A. D.

Before Aristotle, there was no critical treatment of literature as literature by European writers. Suggestive hints were given by Homer, Hesiod, Xenophanes, Pindar, and Gorgias, and there may have been written in this earlier period treatises now lost. This fragmentary early criticism is well worth reviewing. J. W. H. Atkins [*Literary Criticism in Antiquity,* I, 12] indicates the pre-Platonic concern with the nature and function of poetry: "That the theory of inspiration was already current in connexion with poetry is suggested in the first place by the opening lines of the Homeric poems. Both the *Iliad* and the *Odyssey* begin with an appeal to the Muse for inspiration to utter the truth of things; and this is confirmed by Hesiod, who, in his Preface to the *Theogony,* explains how the Muse breathed into him the art of divine music. . . . Then, too, each poet pronounces indirectly on the function of poetry; but with some amount of difference. To Homer, on the one hand, the end of poetry was pleasure, produced by some sort of enchantment (θέλξις); and this point he stresses in more than one place. To Hesiod, on the other hand, the poetic function was that of teaching or conveying a divine message." Equally important is Homer's comment on the quality of illusion in art [*Iliad,* xviii, 548–49] when on the shield of Achilles "the earth looked dark behind the plough, and like to ground that had been ploughed, although it was made of gold; that was a marvellous piece of work."

What Plato describes in the *Republic* as "the quarrel of long standing between philosophy and poetry" began in the sixth century, B. C., with the criticism and defense of poetry on an ethical basis. The complaint of Xenophanes is typical: that "Homer and Hesiod attributed to the gods all that is a reproach and scandal among men." Theagenes and Anaxagoras answered by declaring poetry an allegory which veiled moral and scientific truths. In the fifth century, Pindar returned to a direct consideration of poetry, contrasting "the man who knows by nature" with "the man who learns," and placing the greatest value on natural genius, or on inspiration which becomes a conscious effort of genius. He recognizes the value of technique: "to know the paths that shorten the road"; also the value of brevity: "to say much in few words." The occasional remarks of the poet Pindar suggest that a considerable body of poetic theory existed; and from two speeches by the fifth-century rhetorician Gorgias, Mr. E. E. Sikes [*The Greek View of Poetry,* 32–33] has reconstructed, by combining miscellaneous comments, an early definition of tragedy which anticipates Aristotle: "a form of metrical composition (poetry), which aims at charming and persuading the audience, who willingly submit to the magic of fiction, and feel awe and pity for the fortunes of others represented by the poet."

Writers of comedy found a ready and popular subject in satires of literary men and works. With Aristophanes, this satire and parody becomes excellent criticism, the "part of a larger criticism of contemporary life" in the *Acharnians, Clouds,* and *Thesmophoriazusae,* but rounding into something of wholeness in the *Frogs* (405 B. C.). Here can be found the lament of Dionysius that "good poets are dead; only the false live on" [l. 72, Murray's trans.], and Aristophanes' objection to lack of content: modern poets are "leaves without fruit: trills in the empty air, and starling chatter mutilating art" [l. 92]. The dramatist has a keen eye for textual weaknesses, and great delight in parodying the florid, the affected, the frigid; as a judicial critic, he is frequently devastating. In the *Frogs,* with his comparison of Aeschylus and Euripides, he also presents indirectly his test for art: in answer to the question, "Tell me on what particular ground a poet should claim admiration?" he has Euripides answer, "If his art is true, and his counsel sound" [l. 1009]. But Aeschylus, whose counsel is proved greater than his art, is selected as victor on aesthetic rather than critical grounds: "My choice shall fall on him my soul desires" [l. 1468]. Frequently, Aristophanes' criticism has an ethical basis: in the *Clouds* [ll. 95 ff.], he attacks the "thinking-shop" of Socrates, blaming the philosopher-teacher with hastening the end of the old discipline and accusing him of being a charlatan. In the *Symposium,* Plato presents Aristophanes as concealing a serious purpose under a comic mask; although the disguise makes impossible the easy collection of his remarks on literature, it does not lessen their value.

The general wisdom of Plato is undeniable; his remarks on literature, however, have proved puzzling and most provocative to succeeding generations. The attempt, as Sidney phrases it, "to construe Plato justly" has led to many interpretations and contradictions, some of which can be traced in this anthology; the fact that Plato's *Republic* is itself a work of imitative art, noted by Aristotle as "between a poem and ordinary prose," has called forth such protests as Milton's: "Surely you will recall the poets exiled from your State, for you are the greatest of them all; or, founder though you be, you must yourself go forth" [*De Idea Platonica*, ll. 37–9, MacKellar's trans.]. Atkins [*op. cit.,* 50] attempts a vindication by presenting him as a special pleader, making "a case for the plaintiff (philosophy) without concern, for the time being, for the rightful claims of the defendant (epic and dramatic poetry)." This seems to impugn Plato's intellectual honesty, as does Lane Cooper's remark [*Plato,* 280] that "the unfavorable references to comic poets, including Aristophanes and the older comedy in the *Apology,* and to comic writers generally in the *Republic* and the *Laws,* may be in part explained by Plato's treatment at the hands of writers like Alexis and Epicrates." Possibly more pertinent is Cooper's warning [*ibid.,* xvii] that Plato is always an objective writer, effacing himself and working always to "the effect that he aims to produce in the mind and heart of an audience or observer."

No one of Plato's extant writings is primarily concerned with literature. He notices it constantly yet incidentally, but he "valued Art chiefly, it is true, for its moral effect on conduct in the city state. But he valued it too for its own sake and, if he was frightened of its fascination, that at any rate proves him aware of it. His aesthetic theory, culled from several dialogues, may be roughly summed up thus: All the arts are 'imitative,' but the objects which they represent are not the deceptive phenomena of sense (αἰσθητά) but essential truths apprehended by the mind (νοητά) and dimly descried in phenomena. The process by which the artist apprehends such truths is not the method, slow and sure, of dialectic. It is the ecstasy of inspiration. . . . Inspired therewith by God, the poet in turn inspires his interpreter, the 'rhapsodist' [Ion, for example], and through the interpreter the magnetic current passes to the audience" [W. H. Fyfe, *Aristotle,* x–xi]. This conception appears also in the *Phaedrus* [244, Jowett's trans.]: "The third kind is the madness of those who are possessed by the Muses; which taking hold of a delicate and virgin soul, and there inspiring frenzy, awakens lyrical and all other numbers; with these adorning the myriad actions of ancient heroes for the instruction of posterity. But he who, having no touch of the Muses' madness in his soul, comes to the door and thinks that he will get into the temple by the help of art—he, I say, and his poetry are not admitted; the sane man disappears and is nowhere when he enters into rivalry with the madman."

Unless the *Ion* and *Phaedrus* are to be considered as sustained irony, this belief in the mad or irresponsible poet has led naturally to Plato's treatment of poetry. He provides for a strict regulation as to subject matter, with a rigid censorship which would destroy utterly the validity of art: to cite one example [*Laws,* VII, 801, Cooper's trans.], "No poet shall write any poem that conflicts with what, in accordance with the public standard, is right and lawful, beautiful and good; nor show his compositions to any private individual until they have been submitted to the appointed judges in these matters, and to the guardians of the law, and been officially approved." Yet the spirit of Plato's own writing does not jibe with these theories; a conscious artist, he recognized the principle of organic unity [*Phaedrus,* 264c]: "Every discourse ought to be constructed like a living creature, having a body of its own as well as a head and feet, and with a middle and extremities also in perfect keeping with one another and the whole." Also, Dionysius of Halicarnassus [*De Compositione Verborum,* 264–67, R. W. Roberts' edition] and Demetrius [*On Style,* # 21, pp. 310–13, Roberts' edition] call attention to Plato's great care with the selection and arrangement of words. But this disciplined artistry Plato would not allow to poets. Not from them, but from philosophers could truth be gained; in the *Protagoras* [347c–348a], he suggests that educated men should not discuss poetry but attempt to find truth by "putting one another to the proof of conversation."

For the poets spoke falsehoods, and "Any one was a better interpreter of their writings than they were themselves" [*Apology,* 22b]; they appealed to emotion rather than to reason, and thus were guilty, along with those persuasive rhetoricians who had Socrates put to death (see the *Gorgias*), of endangering the ideals of citizenship. To him, "art does not deal in truth. It is content to represent the data of sense which are themselves a distorted image of reality. It is three removes from truth" [*Republic* X, 597e, Fyfe]. Plato's preoccupation with the ethical teachings of literature coincides with his view that "the real world is a weak or imperfect repetition of an ideal archetype [which] led to the world of reality being regarded in a special sense, and on a still lower plane, as a world of mere imitation" [Butcher, 115–16].

Plato's ideas on imitation and irresponsibility led to many rebuttals. The answers of Aristotle, especially the theory of catharsis, can be found in the *Poetics.* Xenophon [*Memorabilia,* III], indeed, indicates that Socrates himself had anticipated such a view, when he laid stress on the artist's power to select and combine objects for imitation, and thus virtually to create. Hellenistic critics went beyond this: Dio Chrysostom (50–117 A. D.) in his lecture "On Knowing God" wrote that "painters and sculptors invest the God with the human body, the vessel of wisdom and reason, seeking to manifest the imageless and unseen in the visible, which can be portrayed" [Bosanquet's trans.]. Philostratus (*c.* 170–250 A. D.), likewise speaking of sculpture, adds: "It was imagination that wrought these forms, a more cunning artist than imitation. Imitation will make what it has seen, but imagination will make what it has not seen" [Bosanquet's trans.]. The finest argument is presented by the neo-Platonist Plotinus (205–270 A. D.), who defends art boldly against Plato's attack: "We must bear in mind that the arts do not simply imitate the visible, but go back to the reasons from which nature comes; and further that they create much out of themselves, and add to that which is defective, as being themselves in possession of beauty" [Bosanquet's trans.]. The answer of Plotinus was not final; critics continued through the centuries and continue today to answer the original questions, or their equivalents phrased to fit contemporary conditions and immediate problems.

From

ION *

(*c.* 390 B. C.)

SOCRATES: I perceive, Ion; and I will proceed to explain to you what I imagine to be the reason of this. The gift which you possess of speaking excellently about Homer is not an art, but, as I was just saying, an inspiration; there is a divinity moving you, like that contained in the stone which Euripides calls a magnet, but which is commonly known as the stone of Heraclea. This stone not only attracts iron rings, but also imparts to them a similar power of attracting other rings; and sometimes you may see a number of pieces of iron and rings suspended from one another so as to form quite a long chain: and all of them derive their power of suspension from the original stone. In like manner the Muse first of all inspires men herself; and from these inspired persons a chain of other persons is suspended, who take the inspiration. For all good poets, epic as well as lyric, compose their beautiful poems not by art, but because they are inspired and possessed. And as the Corybantian revellers when they dance are not in their right mind, so the lyric poets are not in their right mind when they are composing their beautiful strains: but when falling under the power of music and metre they are inspired and possessed; like Bacchic maidens who draw milk and honey from the rivers when they are under the influence of Dionysus but not when they are in their right mind. And the soul of the lyric poet does the same, as they themselves say; for they tell us that they bring songs from honeyed fountains, culling them out of the gardens and dells of the Muses; they, like the bees, winging their way from flower to flower. And this is true. For the poet is a light and winged and holy thing, and there is no invention in him until he has been inspired and is out of his

* Translated by B. Jowett.

senses, and the mind is no longer in him: when he has not attained to this state, he is powerless and is unable to utter his oracles. Many are the noble words in which poets speak concerning the actions of men; but like yourself when speaking about Homer, they do not speak of them by any rules of art: they are simply inspired to utter that to which the Muse impels them, and that only; and when inspired, one of them will make dithyrambs, another hymns of praise, another choral strains, another epic or iambic verses—and he who is good at one is not good at any other kind of verse: for not by art does the poet sing, but by power divine. Had he learned by rules of art, he would have known how to speak not of one theme only, but of all; and therefore God takes away the minds of poets, and uses them as his ministers, as he also uses diviners and holy prophets, in order that we who hear them may know them to be speaking not of themselves who utter these priceless words in a state of unconsciousness, but that God himself is the speaker, and that through them he is conversing with us. And Tynnichus the Chalcidian affords a striking instance of what I am saying: he wrote nothing that any one would care to remember but the famous paean which is in every one's mouth, one of the finest poems ever written, simply an invention of the Muses, as he himself says. For in this way the God would seem to indicate to us and not allow us to doubt that these beautiful poems are not human, or the work of man, but divine and the work of God; and that the poets are only the interpreters of the Gods by whom they are severally possessed. Was not this the lesson which the God intended to teach when by the mouth of the worst of poets he sang the best of songs? Am I not right, Ion?

From

THE REPUBLIC *

(*c.* 373 B. C.)

BOOK X

Steph. 595
Socrates,
Glaucon. OF the many excellences which I perceive in the order of our State, there is none which upon reflection pleases me better than the rule about poetry.

* Translated by B. Jowett (Oxford University Press).

To what do you refer?

To the rejection of imitative poetry, which certainly ought not to be received; as I see far more clearly now that the parts of the soul have been distinguished.

What do you mean?

Speaking in confidence, for I should not like to have my words repeated to the tragedians and the rest of the imitative tribe—but I do not mind saying to you, that all poetical imitations are ruinous to the understanding of the hearers, and that the knowledge of their true nature is the only antidote to them.

Explain the purport of your remark.

Well, I will tell you, although I have always from my earliest youth had an awe and love of Homer, which even now makes the words falter on my lips, for he is the great captain and teacher of the whole of that charming tragic company; but a man is not to be reverenced more than the truth, and therefore I will speak out.

Very good, he said.

Listen to me then, or rather, answer me.

Put your question.

Can you tell me what imitation is? for I really do not know.

A likely thing, then, that I should know.

Why not? for the duller eye may often see a thing sooner than the keener.

Very true, he said; but in your presence, even if I had any faint notion, I could not muster courage to utter it. Will you enquire yourself?

Well then, shall we begin the enquiry in our usual manner: Whenever a number of individuals have a common name, we assume them to have also a corresponding idea or form:—do you understand me?

I do.

Let us take any common instance; there are beds and tables in the world—plenty of them, are there not?

Yes.

But there are only two ideas or forms of them—one the idea of a bed, the other of a table.

True.

Republic
X
Socrates,
Glaucon.

596

And the maker of either of them makes a bed or he makes a table for our use, in accordance with the idea— that is our way of speaking in this and similar instances— but no artificer makes the ideas themselves: how could he?

Impossible.

And there is another artist,—I should like to know what you would say of him.

Who is he?

One who is the maker of all the works of all other workmen.

What an extraordinary man!

Wait a little, and there will be more reason for your saying so. For this is he who is able to make not only vessels of every kind, but plants and animals, himself and all other things—the earth and heaven, and the things which are in heaven or under the earth; he makes the gods also.

He must be a wizard and no mistake.

Oh! you are incredulous, are you? Do you mean that there is no such maker or creator, or that in one sense there might be a maker of all these things but in another not? Do you see that there is a way in which you could make them all yourself?

What way?

An easy way enough; or rather, there are many ways in which the feat might be quickly and easily accomplished, none quicker than that of turning a mirror round and round—you would soon enough make the sun and the heavens, and the earth and yourself, and other animals and plants, and all the other things of which we were just now speaking, in the mirror.

Yes, he said; but they would be appearances only.

Very good, I said, you are coming to the point now. And the painter too is, as I conceive, just such another—a creator of appearances, is he not?

Of course.

But then I suppose you will say that what he creates is untrue. And yet there is a sense in which the painter also creates a bed?

Yes, he said, but not a real bed.

And what of the maker of the bed? were you not saying that he too makes, not the idea which, according to our view, is the essence of the bed, but only a particular bed?

Yes, I did.

597
Republic
X
Socrates,
Glaucon.

Then if he does not make that which exists he cannot make true existence, but only some semblance of existence; and if any one were to say that the work of the maker of the bed, or of any other workman, has real existence, he could hardly be supposed to be speaking the truth.

At any rate, he replied, philosophers would say that he was not speaking the truth.

No wonder, then, that his work too is an indistinct expression of truth.

No wonder.

Suppose now that by the light of the examples just offered we enquire who this imitator is?

If you please.

Well, then, here are three beds: one existing in nature, which is made by God, as I think that we may say—for no one else can be the maker?

No.

There is another which is the work of the carpenter?

Yes.

And the work of the painter is a third?

Yes.

Beds, then, are of three kinds, and there are three artists who superintend them: God, the maker of the bed, and the painter?

Yes, there are three of them.

God, whether from choice or from necessity, made one bed in nature and one only; two or more such ideal beds neither ever have been nor ever will be made by God.

Why is that?

Because even if He had made but two, a third would still appear behind them which both of them would have for their idea, and that would be the ideal bed and not the two others.

Very true, he said.

God knew this, and He desired to be the real maker

PLATO

of a real bed, not a particular maker of a particular bed, and therefore He created a bed which is essentially and by nature one only.

So we believe.

Shall we, then, speak of Him as the natural author or maker of the bed?

Yes, he replied; inasmuch as by the natural process of creation He is the author of this and of all other things.

And what shall we say of the carpenter—is not he also the maker of the bed?

Yes.

But would you call the painter a creator and maker?

Certainly not.

Yet if he is not the maker, what is he in relation to the bed?

I think, he said, that we may fairly designate him as the imitator of that which the others make.

Good, I said; then you call him who is third in the descent from nature an imitator?

Certainly, he said.

And the tragic poet is an imitator, and therefore, like all other imitators, he is thrice removed from the king and from the truth?

That appears to be so.

Then about the imitator we are agreed. And what about the painter?—I would like to know whether he may be thought to imitate that which originally exists in nature, or only the creations of artists?

The latter.

As they are or as they appear? you have still to determine this.

What do you mean?

I mean, that you may look at a bed from different points of view, obliquely or directly or from any other point of view, and the bed will appear different, but there is no difference in reality. And the same of all things.

Yes, he said, the difference is only apparent.

Now let me ask you another question: Which is the art of painting designed to be—an imitation of things as they are, or as they appear—of appearance or of reality?

Of appearance.

Then the imitator, I said, is a long way off the truth, and can do all things because he lightly touches on a small part of them, and that part an image. For example: A painter will paint a cobbler, carpenter, or any other artist, though he knows nothing of their arts; and, if he is a good artist, he may deceive children or simple persons, when he shows them his picture of a carpenter from a distance, and they will fancy that they are looking at a real carpenter.

Certainly.

And whenever any one informs us that he has found a man who knows all the arts, and all things else that anybody knows, and every single thing with a higher degree of accuracy than any other man—whoever tells us this, I think that we can only imagine him to be a simple creature who is likely to have been deceived by some wizard or actor whom he met, and whom he thought all-knowing, because he himself was unable to analyse the nature of knowledge and ignorance and imitation.

Most true.

And so, when we hear persons saying that the tragedians, and Homer, who is at their head, know all the arts and all things human, virtue as well as vice, and divine things too, for that the good poet cannot compose well unless he knows his subject, and that he who has not this knowledge can never be a poet, we ought to consider whether here also there may not be a similar illusion. Perhaps they may have come across imitators and been deceived by them; they may not have remembered when they saw their works that these were but imitations thrice removed from the truth, and could easily be made without any knowledge of the truth, because they are appearances only and not realities? Or, after all, they may be in the right, and poets do really know the things about which they seem to the many to speak so well?

The question, he said, should by all means be considered.

Now do you suppose that if a person were able to make the original as well as the image, he would seriously de-

599

vote himself to the image-making branch? Would he allow imitation to be the ruling principle of his life, as if he had nothing higher in him?

I should say not.

The real artist, who knew what he was imitating, would be interested in realities and not in imitations; and would desire to leave as memorials of himself works many and fair; and, instead of being the author of encomiums, he would prefer to be the theme of them.

Yes, he said, that would be to him a source of much greater honour and profit.

Then, I said, we must put a question to Homer; not about medicine, or any of the arts to which his poems only incidentally refer: we are not going to ask him, or any other poet, whether he has cured patients like Asclepius, or left behind him a school of medicine such as the Asclepiads were, or whether he only talks about medicine and other arts at second-hand; but we have a right to know respecting military tactics, politics, education, which are the chiefest and noblest subjects of his poems, and we may fairly ask him about them. 'Friend Homer,' then we say to him, 'if you are only in the second remove from truth in what you say of virtue, and not in the third—not an image maker or imitator—and if you are able to discern what pursuits make men better or worse in private or public life, tell us what State was ever better governed by your help? The good order of Lacedaemon is due to Lycurgus, and many other cities great and small have been similarly benefited by others; but who says that you have been a good legislator to them and have done them any good? Italy and Sicily boast of Charondas, and there is Solon who is renowned among us; but what city has anything to say about you?' Is there any city which he might name?

I think not, said Glaucon; not even the Homerids themselves pretend that he was a legislator.

600

Well, but is there any war on record which was carried on successfully by him, or aided by his counsels, when he was alive?

There is not.

Or is there any invention of his, applicable to the arts or to human life, such as Thales the Milesian or Anacharsis the Scythian, and other ingenious men have conceived, which is attributed to him?

There is absolutely nothing of the kind.

But, if Homer never did any public service, was he privately a guide, or teacher of any? Had he in his lifetime friends who loved to associate with him, and who handed down to posterity an Homeric way of life, such as was established by Pythagoras who was so greatly beloved for his wisdom, and whose followers are to this day quite celebrated for the order which was named after him?

Nothing of the kind is recorded of him. For surely, Socrates, Creophylus, the companion of Homer, that child of flesh, whose name always makes us laugh, might be more justly ridiculed for his stupidity, if, as is said, Homer was greatly neglected by him and others in his own day when he was alive?

Yes, I replied, that is the tradition. But can you imagine, Glaucon, that if Homer had really been able to educate and improve mankind—if he had possessed knowledge and not been a mere imitator—can you imagine, I say, that he would not have had many followers, and been honoured and loved by them? Protagoras of Abdera, and Prodicus of Ceos, and a host of others, have only to whisper to their contemporaries: 'You will never be able to manage either your own house or your own State until you appoint us to be your ministers of education'—and this ingenious device of theirs has such an effect in making men love them that their companions all but carry them about on their shoulders. And is it conceivable that the contemporaries of Homer, or again of Hesiod, would have allowed either of them to go about as rhapsodists, if they had really been able to make mankind virtuous? Would they not have been as unwilling to part with them as with gold, and have compelled them to stay at home with them? Or, if the master would not stay, then the disciples would have followed him about everywhere, until they had got education enough?

Yes, Socrates, that, I think, is quite true.

Then must we not infer that all these poetical individuals, beginning with Homer, are only imitators; they copy images of virtue and the like, but the truth they never reach? The poet is like a painter who, as we have already observed, will make a likeness of a cobbler though he understands nothing of cobbling; and his picture is good enough for those who know no more than he does, and judge only by colours and figures.

Quite so.

In like manner the poet with his words and phrases * may be said to lay on the colours of the several arts, himself understanding their nature only enough to imitate them; and other people, who are as ignorant as he is, and judge only from his words, imagine that if he speaks of cobbling, or of military tactics, or of anything else, in metre and harmony and rhythm, he speaks very well—such is the sweet influence which melody and rhythm by nature have. And I think that you must have observed again and again what a poor appearance the tales of poets make when stripped of the colours which music puts upon them, and recited in simple prose.

Yes, he said.

They are like faces which were never really beautiful, but only blooming; and now the bloom of youth has passed away from them?

Exactly.

Here is another point: The imitator or maker of the image knows nothing of true existence: he knows appearances only. Am I not right?

Yes.

Then let us have a clear understanding, and not be satisfied with half an explanation.

Proceed.

Of the painter we say that he will paint reins, and he will paint a bit?

Yes.

And the worker in leather and brass will make them?

Certainly.

* Or, 'with his nouns and verbs.'

But does the painter know the right form of the bit and reins? Nay, hardly even the workers in brass and leather who make them; only the horseman who knows how to use them—he knows their right form.

Most true.

And may we not say the same of all things?

What?

That there are three arts which are concerned with all things: one which uses, another which makes, a third which imitates them?

Yes.

And the excellence or beauty or truth of every structure, animate or inanimate, and of every action of man, is relative to the use for which nature or the artist has intended them.

True.

Then the user of them must have the greatest experience of them, and he must indicate to the maker the good or bad qualities which develop themselves in use; for example, the flute-player will tell the flute-maker which of his flutes is satisfactory to the performer; he will tell him how he ought to make them, and the other will attend to his instructions?

Of course.

The one knows and therefore speaks with authority about the goodness and badness of flutes, while the other, confiding in him, will do what he is told by him?

True.

The instrument is the same, but about the excellence or badness of it the maker will only attain to a correct belief; and this he will gain from him who knows, by talking to him and being compelled to hear what he has to say, whereas the user will have knowledge?

602

True.

But will the imitator have either? Will he know from use whether or no his drawing is correct or beautiful? or will he have right opinion from being compelled to associate with another who knows and gives him instructions about what he should draw?

Neither.

Then he will no more have true opinion than he will have knowledge about the goodness or badness of his imitations?

I suppose not.

The imitative artist will be in a brilliant state of intelligence about his own creations?

Nay, very much the reverse.

And still he will go on imitating without knowing what makes a thing good or bad, and may be expected therefore to imitate only that which appears to be good to the ignorant multitude?

Just so.

Thus far we are pretty well agreed that the imitator has no knowledge worth mentioning of what he imitates. Imitation is only a kind of play or sport, and the tragic poets, whether they write in Iambic or in Heroic verse, are imitators in the highest degree?

Very true.

And now tell me, I conjure you, has not imitation been shown by us to be concerned with that which is thrice removed from the truth?

Certainly.

And what is the faculty in man to which imitation is addressed?

What do you mean?

I will explain: The body which is large when seen near, appears small when seen at a distance?

True.

And the same objects appear straight when looked at out of the water, and crooked when in the water; and the concave becomes convex, owing to the illusion about colours to which the sight is liable. Thus every sort of confusion is revealed within us; and this is that weakness of the human mind on which the art of conjuring and of deceiving by light and shadow and other ingenious devices imposes, having an effect upon us like magic.

True.

And the arts of measuring and numbering and weighing come to the rescue of the human understanding—there is the beauty of them—and the apparent greater or less, or more or heavier, no longer have the mastery over us, but give way before calculation and measure and weight?

Most true.

And this, surely, must be the work of the calculating and rational principle in the soul?

To be sure.

And when this principle measures and certifies that some things are equal, or that some are greater or less than others, there occurs an apparent contradiction?

True.

But were we not saying that such a contradiction is impossible—the same faculty cannot have contrary opinions at the same time about the same thing?

603

Very true.

Then that part of the soul which has an opinion contrary to measure is not the same with that which has an opinion in accordance with measure?

True.

And the better part of the soul is likely to be that which trusts to measure and calculation?

Certainly.

And that which is opposed to them is one of the inferior principles of the soul?

No doubt.

This was the conclusion at which I was seeking to arrive when I said that painting or drawing, and imitation in general, when doing their own proper work, are far removed from truth, and the companions and friends and associates of a principle within us which is equally removed from reason, and that they have no true or healthy aim.

Exactly.

The imitative art is an inferior who marries an inferior, and has inferior offspring.

Very true.

And is this confined to the sight only, or does it extend to the hearing also, relating in fact to what we term poetry?

Probably the same would be true of poetry.

Do not rely, I said, on a probability derived from the analogy of painting; but let us examine further and see whether the faculty with which poetical imitation is concerned is good or bad.

By all means.

We may state the question thus:—Imitation imitates the actions of men, whether voluntary or involuntary, on which, as they imagine, a good or bad result has ensued, and they rejoice or sorrow accordingly. Is there anything more?

No, there is nothing else.

But in all this variety of circumstances is the man at unity with himself—or rather, as in the instance of sight there was confusion and opposition in his opinions about the same things, so here also is there not strife and inconsistency in his life? Though I need hardly raise the question again, for I remember that all this has been already admitted; and the soul has been acknowledged by us to be full of these and ten thousand similar oppositions occurring at the same moment?

And we were right, he said.

Yes, I said, thus far we were right; but there was an omission which must now be supplied.

What was the omission?

Were we not saying that a good man, who has the misfortune to lose his son or anything else which is most dear to him, will bear the loss with more equanimity than another?

Yes.

But will he have no sorrow, or shall we say that although he cannot help sorrowing, he will moderate his sorrow?

The latter, he said, is the truer statement.

604

Tell me: will he be more likely to struggle and hold out against his sorrow when he is seen by his equals, or when he is alone?

It will make a great difference whether he is seen or not.

When he is by himself he will not mind saying or doing many things which he would be ashamed of any one hearing or seeing him do?

True.

There is a principle of law and reason in him which bids him resist, as well as a feeling of his misfortune which is forcing him to indulge his sorrow?

True.

But when a man is drawn in two opposite directions, to and from the same object, this, as we affirm, necessarily implies two distinct principles in him?

Certainly.

One of them is ready to follow the guidance of the law?

How do you mean?

The law would say that to be patient under suffering is best, and that we should not give way to impatience, as there is no knowing whether such things are good or evil; and nothing is gained by impatience; also, because no human thing is of serious importance, and grief stands in the way of that which at the moment is most required.

What is most required? he asked.

That we should take counsel about what has happened, and when the dice have been thrown order our affairs in the way which reason deems best; not, like children who have had a fall, keeping hold of the part struck and wasting time in setting up a howl, but always accustoming the soul forthwith to apply a remedy, raising up that which is sickly and fallen, banishing the cry of sorrow by the healing art.

Yes, he said, that is the true way of meeting the attacks of fortune.

Yes, I said; and the higher principle is ready to follow this suggestion of reason?

Clearly.

And the other principle, which inclines us to recollection of our troubles and to lamentation, and can never have enough of them, we may call irrational, useless, and cowardly?

Indeed, we may.

And does not the latter—I mean the rebellious principle—furnish a great variety of materials for imitation? Whereas the wise and calm temperament, being always nearly equable, is not easy to imitate or to appreciate when imitated, especially at a public festival when a promiscuous crowd is assembled in a theatre. For the feeling represented is one to which they are strangers.

Certainly.

Then the imitative poet who aims at being popular is not by nature made, nor is his art intended, to please or to affect the rational principle in the soul; but he will prefer the passionate and fitful temper, which is easily imitated?

Clearly.

And now we may fairly take him and place him by the side of the painter, for he is like him in two ways: first, inasmuch as his creations have an inferior degree of truth—in this, I say, he is like him; and he is also like him in being concerned with an inferior part of the soul; and therefore we shall be right in refusing to admit him into a well-ordered State, because he awakens and nourishes and strengthens the feelings and impairs the reason. As in a city when the evil are permitted to have authority and the good are put out of the way, so in the soul of man, as we maintain, the imitative poet implants an evil constitution, for he indulges the irrational nature which has no discernment of greater and less, but thinks the same thing at one time great and at another small—he is a manufacturer of images and is very far removed from the truth.

Exactly.

But we have not yet brought forward the heaviest count in our accusation:—the power which poetry has of harming even the good (and there are very few who are not harmed), is surely an awful thing?

Yes, certainly, if the effect is what you say.

Hear and judge: The best of us, as I conceive, when we listen to a passage of Homer, or one of the tragedians, in which he represents some pitiful hero who is drawling out his sorrows in a long oration, or weeping, and smiting his breast—the best of us, you know, delight in giving way to sympathy, and are in raptures at the excellence of the poet who stirs our feelings most.

Yes, of course I know.

But when any sorrow of our own happens to us, then

you may observe that we pride ourselves on the opposite quality—we would fain be quiet and patient; this is the manly part, and the other which delighted us in the recitation is now deemed to be the part of a woman.

Very true, he said.

Now can we be right in praising and admiring another who is doing that which any one of us would abominate and be ashamed of in his own person?

No, he said, that is certainly not reasonable.

Nay, I said, quite reasonable from one point of view.   606

What point of view?

If you consider, I said, that when in misfortune we feel a natural hunger and desire to relieve our sorrow by weeping and lamentation, and that this feeling which is kept under control in our own calamities is satisfied and delighted by the poets;—the better nature in each of us, not having been sufficiently trained by reason or habit, allows the sympathetic element to break loose because the sorrow is another's; and the spectator fancies that there can be no disgrace to himself in praising and pitying any one who comes telling him what a good man he is, and making a fuss about his troubles; he thinks that the pleasure is a gain, and why should he be supercilious and lose this and the poem too? Few persons ever reflect, as I should imagine, that from the evil of other men something of evil is communicated to themselves. And so the feeling of sorrow which has gathered strength at the sight of the misfortunes of others is with difficulty repressed in our own.

How very true!

And does not the same hold also of the ridiculous? There are jests which you would be ashamed to make yourself, and yet on the comic stage, or indeed in private,[1] when you hear them, you are greatly amused by them, and are not at all disgusted at their unseemliness; —the case of pity is repeated;—there is a principle in human nature which is disposed to raise a laugh, and this which you once restrained by reason, because you were

---

[1] Lane Cooper (*Aristotelian Theory of Comedy,* 108) translates this: "when you hear them in comedy, or in prose, you are greatly amused. . . ."

afraid of being thought a buffoon, is now let out again, and having stimulated the risible faculty at the theatre, you are betrayed unconsciously to yourself into playing the comic poet at home.[2]

Quite true, he said.

And the same may be said of lust and anger and all the other affections, of desire and pain and pleasure, which are held to be inseparable from every action—in all of them poetry feeds and waters the passions instead of drying them up; she lets them rule, although they ought to be controlled, if mankind are ever to increase in happiness and virtue.

I cannot deny it.

Therefore, Glaucon, I said, whenever you meet with any of the eulogists of Homer declaring that he has been the educator of Hellas, and that he is profitable for education and for the ordering of human things, and that you should take him up again and again and get to know him and regulate your whole life according to him, we may love and honour those who say these things—they are excellent people, as far as their lights extend; and we are ready to acknowledge that Homer is the greatest of poets and first of tragedy writers; but we must remain firm in our conviction that hymns to the gods and praises of famous men are the only poetry which ought to be admitted into our State. For if you go beyond this and allow the honeyed muse to enter, either in epic or lyric verse, not law and the reason of mankind, which by common consent have ever been deemed best, but pleasure and pain will be the rulers in our State.

607

[2] Pertinent here are Plato's remarks on comedy in the *Philebus* (48–50, Jowett's trans.): "And you remember also how at the sight of tragedies the spectators smile through their tears? . . . And are you aware that even at a comedy the soul experiences a mixed feeling of pain and pleasure? . . . And the three kinds of vain conceit in our friends which we enumerated—the vain conceit of beauty, of wisdom, and of wealth, are ridiculous if they are weak, and detestable when they are powerful: May we not say, as I was saying before, that our friends who are in this state of mind, when harmless to others, are simply ridiculous? . . . Then the argument shows that when we laugh at the folly of our friends, pleasure, in mingling with envy, mingles with pain, for envy has been acknowledged by us to be mental pain, and laughter is pleasant; and so we envy and laugh at the same instant. . . . And the argument implies that there are combinations of pleasure and pain in lamentations, and in tragedy and comedy, not only on the stage, but on the greater stage of human life; and so in endless other cases."

That is most true, he said.

And now since we have reverted to the subject of poetry, let this our defence serve to show the reasonableness of our former judgment in sending away out of our State an art having the tendencies which we have described; for reason constrained us. But that she may not impute to us any harshness or want of politeness, let us tell her that there is an ancient quarrel between philosophy and poetry; of which there are many proofs, such as the saying of 'the yelping hound howling at her lord,' or of one 'mighty in the vain talk of fools,' and 'the mob of sages circumventing Zeus,' and the 'subtle thinkers who are beggars after all'; and there are innumerable other signs of ancient enmity between them. Notwithstanding this, let us assure our sweet friend and the sister arts of imitation, that if she will only prove her title to exist in a well-ordered State we shall be delighted to receive her—we are very conscious of her charms; but we may not on that account betray the truth. I dare say, Glaucon, that you are as much charmed by her as I am, especially when she appears in Homer?

Yes, indeed, I am greatly charmed.

Shall I propose, then, that she be allowed to return from exile, but upon this condition only—that she make a defence of herself in lyrical or some other metre?

Certainly.

And we may further grant to those of her defenders who are lovers of poetry and yet not poets the permission to speak in prose on her behalf: let them show not only that she is pleasant but also useful to States and to human life, and we will listen in a kindly spirit; for if this can be proved we shall surely be the gainers—I mean, if there is a use in poetry as well as a delight?

Certainly, he said, we shall be the gainers.

If her defence fails, then, my dear friend, like other persons who are enamoured of something, but put a restraint upon themselves when they think their desires are opposed to their interests, so too must we after the manner of lovers give her up, though not without a struggle. We too are inspired by that love of poetry which the education of noble States has implanted in us, and therefore we would have her appear at her best and truest; but so long as she is unable to make good her defence, this argument of ours shall be a charm to us, which we will repeat to ourselves while we listen to her strains; that we may not fall away into the childish love of her which captivates the many. At all events we are well aware that poetry being such as we have described is not to be regarded seriously as attaining to the truth; and he who listens to her, fearing for the safety of the city which is within him, should be on his guard against her seductions and make our words his law.

Yes, he said, I quite agree with you.

Yes, I said, my dear Glaucon, for great is the issue at stake, greater than appears, whether a man is to be good or bad. And what will any one be profited if under the influence of honour or money or power, aye, or under the excitement of poetry, he neglect justice and virtue?

Yes, he said; I have been convinced by the argument, as I believe that any one else would have been.

ARISTOTLE

(384–322 B. C.)

ARISTOTLE was born at Stagira, on the northwestern Aegean, in 384 B. C. His father, Nicomachus, was a doctor who had acted as court physician to Amyntas II, the father of Philip. At the age of 17 Aristotle became a disciple of Plato at Athens, and here he remained until his master's death (347 B. C.). He then removed to Assus in Asia Minor, where there was a colony of Platonists, and taught for three years. Here he married Pythias, the daughter of Hermes, whose wealth and influence had won him the title of "prince" among the Persians and elevated him to the position of "tyrant" of Atarneus. The two years following this marriage were spent in Lesbos, occupied largely with the study of marine biology, and then Aristotle was invited by Philip of Macedon to come to Pella. In 342 B. C. the period of instructorship to Alexander began, and it lasted until the pupil's accession to power in 336.

The life of Aristotle is often divided into three periods: the discipleship to Plato, the temporary residences at Assus, Lesbos, and Pella, and finally, the establishment at Athens. From 335 B. C. until 323 flourished the Peripatetic School of his founding. Here, as lectures, most of his works now extant were given to the world, though their composition often dates back into the earlier periods. In the confusion which followed Alexander's death in 323, Aristotle fled to Chalcis, in Euboea, and here, in 322 B. C. he died.

Whether the *Poetics* is an original work of the master or a summary by another hand or merely a body of notes compiled from lectures by some auditor, authorities do not agree. Of its influence in ancient times we know little, and it was strangely neglected during the Middle Ages, when Aristotle's philosophy was universally studied. The Greek text was first printed in the Aldine *Rhetores Graeci* (1508) [See D. L. Clark: *Rhetoric and Poetry in the Renaissance, 70*.], although there had been a Latin translation by Giorgio Valla in 1498. By the middle of the Sixteenth Century the work had become well known and generally accepted as undeniable doctrine. "From the time of Petrarch," says Mr. Spingarn, "Aristotle, identified in the minds of the humanists with the mediaeval scholasticism so obnoxious to them, had lost somewhat of his supremacy. . . . The beginning of the Aristotelian influence on modern literary theory may be said to date from the year 1536, in which year Trincaveli published a Greek text of the *Poetics*, Pazzi his edition and Latin version, and Daniello his own *Poetics*. . . . It marks the beginning of his supremacy in literature, and the decline of his dictatorial authority in philosophy." [*Literary Criticism in the Renaissance,* 136-37]. The first critical edition of the *Poetics* was that of Robortelli in 1548.

Though fragmentary and at times less well connected than are Artistotle's works generally, it presents the text of a consistent theory. It has nevertheless been regarded by some critics as primarily an answer to the strictures of Plato. Mr. J. W. H. Atkins, for instance, in a chapter which excellently summarizes the contents of the *Poetics* and, on careful appraisal, gives it a "place among the great world-books," finds Aristotle "merely careful to frame a reply to Plato's indictment; and with this he is apparently for the most part content." [*Literary Criticism in Antiquity,* I, 117] . . . "Plato . . . had challenged both tragedy and the epic on account of their nature and effects; he had demanded a poetry of a philosophical kind, produced in the light of ideal knowledge. And the nature of the attack determined the line of defence." [*Ibid.,* I, 78] Such a theory as that of "catharsis," to take only one specific item of the *Poetics,* is thus, from Mr. Atkins' point of view, of primary importance as a defensive argument. "It is . . . in the light of the circumstances that produced it that the doctrine of Aristotle is perhaps best understood. Plato had complained of the disturbing, debilitating effects of the drama; Aristotle's defence is that the effects are really hygienic, curative in kind. And herein probably lies the true explanation of Aristotle's argument. He had a case to answer, a defence to make; and his theory of 'catharsis,' thus conditioned, is to some extent at least a piece of special pleading." [*Ibid.,* I, 86.]

Now some relationship between the treatises of Aristotle and his master must be evident to anyone who has carefully read both of them. It is inconceivable that the author of the *Poetics* did not have the author of the *Republic* in mind as he framed his critical theories. But the variety of matters treated which are unrelated to mere defense brings into question any attempt to explain Aristotle's work as only a reply to Plato's. The obvious lack of completeness of the *Poetics* seems due to other causes than a satisfaction with having answered an opposing argument: indeed, it is probable that the entire treatise has not come down to us, that a section on comedy, in particular, has been lost; too, the piece is no more incomplete than the *Ars Poetica* of Horace, and it may reasonably be assumed that the earliest writers on poetic theory were not aware of such vacua in their designs as we, with some knowledge of later critical problems, may feel are obvious.

The major divisions of his treatise on poetry deal with Aristotle's theories on "Imitation" and Nature, the origin of poetry, its types then in existence, and the principles of tragedy. Poetry is taken to mean the literary art in general; the two branches of drama and the epic, being the most highly developed forms among the Greeks, are the centers of attention.

On "Imitation" Prof. Butcher has rendered perhaps the clearest exposition in his chapter on " 'Imitation' as an Aesthetic Term": " 'Imitation,' in the sense in which Aristotle applies the word to poetry, is thus seen to be equivalent to 'producing' or 'creating according to a true idea,' which forms part of the definition of art in general. The 'true idea' for fine art is derived from the εἶδος, the general concept which the intellect spontaneously abstracts from the details of sense. There is an ideal form which is present in each individual phenomenon but imperfectly manifested. This form impresses itself as a sensuous appearance on the mind of the artist; he seeks to give it a more complete expression, to bring to light the ideal which is only half revealed in the world of reality. His distinctive work as an artist consists in stamping the given material with the impress of the form which is universal. . . . 'Imitation,' so understood, is a creative act." [*Aristotle's Theory of Poetry and Fine Art*, 153]

This paragraph of Prof. Butcher's touches the core of Aristotle's philosophy of art. It becomes clearer when viewed alongside the metaphysic to which the Peripatetic School, as well as the Academy, subscribed: the phenomena of the world perceived through the physical senses were held to be imperfect manifestations of an ultimate reality; the forms of the physical world were copies of divine and perfect forms, copies distorted by the accidents of the material world. The task of the philosopher was to discover the ultimate reality behind the fortuitous forms, to seek with thought the pure forces which actuated and motivated all existence.

Aristotle's concept of "Poetic Imitation" gives the poet his place in this exalted function of philosophy; and it introduces, too, his concept of "Nature," which was so debated and misunderstood throughout later criticism; "for nature in Aristotle is not the outward world of created things," writes Mr. Butcher: "it is the creative force, the productive principle of the universe. . . . Fine art . . . passes beyond the bare reality given by nature, and expresses a purified form of reality disengaged from accident, and freed from conditions which thwart its development." [*Op. cit.* 116 and 150.]

Aristotle was the first to distinguish the fine arts from the useful, and to fix the purpose of them, above the service of necessities, in the mind's enjoyment alone. "At first he who invented any art that went beyond the common perceptions of man was naturally admired by men, not only because there was something useful in the inventions, but because he was thought wise and superior to the rest. But as more arts were invented, and some were directed to the necessities of life, *others to its recreation,* the inventors of the latter were naturally always regarded as wiser than the inventors of the former, because their branches of knowledge did not aim at utility." [*Metaphysics* I 981 b 13; trans. Smith and Ross.]

And so it is that he derives the origin of poetry from the human instinct to imitate, at the same time keeping the objects of imitation in a sphere removed from the plain realities of the physical world.

Elsewhere [*Rhetoric* I xi 23], he states that "as the acquisition of knowledge is pleasant, and the feeling admiration, and such things; that, too, must necessarily be pleasant which has been expressed in imitation, as in painting, sculpture, and poetry: also, every thing is pleasant which has been correctly imitated, although the original object, of which it is the imitation, may not in itself be pleasant; for one does not feel pleasure on that account; but there is an inference that 'this means that': and thus it happens that we learn something." [trans. Buckley.]

Types of Greek literature interest only the specialist in that field. But Aristotle's insistence upon classification, and his demand that each type please and satisfy in its own peculiar way, are found permeating much of Renaissance and all of Seventeenth and Eighteenth Century criticism. The *Poetics* discusses only Tragedy in any detail.

The aim of tragedy is declared to be the "purging" of the soul by exciting and then exhausting the passions of terror and pity. To this end a plot of proper magnitude and completeness, and characters, diction, thoughts, spectacle, and song, of appropriateness, are necessary. Unity, poetic truth, and probability, inadequate captions for three of the ideas advanced under this heading, are equally applicable to other forms of poetry, and were so considered from the first of the Aristotle revival during the Renaissance. Efforts to clarify these and other theories of the *Poetics*, and passages which significantly parallel them, compose a large body of critical literature, and illustrate, in their distribution through the centuries, Aristotle's undiminishing importance. One will find of particular interest Scaliger's section entitled "Tragedy" from his *Poetics* and Boileau's Canto III ("Tragedy") in his *Art of Poetry*, which are in the main body of this book; and, in the Supplement, the selections from Corneille's *Discourses*, Castelvetro's *Poetics*, Schiller's *On the Use of the Chorus in Tragedy*, and Goethe's *Supplement to Aristotle's Poetics*.

POETICS *

(*c.* 335–322 B. C.)

I

I PROPOSE to treat of Poetry in itself and of its various kinds, noting the essential quality of each; to inquire into the structure of the plot as requisite to a good poem; into the number and nature of the parts of which a poem is composed; and similarly into whatever else falls within the same inquiry. Following, then, the order of nature, let us begin with the principles which come first.

2. Epic poetry and Tragedy, Comedy also and Dithyrambic poetry, and the music of the flute and of the lyre in most of their forms, are all in their general conception modes of imitation.[1] 3. They dif-

---

* Translated by S. H. Butcher.

[1] "The explanation of μίμησις, as Aristotle uses the word, demands a treatise," Mr. Hamilton Fyfe has remarked. Translations of the term [Latin, *Mimesis*] have varied but little. Mr. Bywater follows Mr. Butcher with "modes of imitation." Mr. Fyfe translates, "representations of life," and Mr. Buckley, "imitations."

fer, however, from one another in three respects,—the medium, the objects, the manner or mode of imitation, being in each case distinct.

4. For as there are persons who, by conscious art or mere habit, imitate and represent various objects through the medium of colour and form, or again by the voice; so in the arts above mentioned, taken as a whole, the imitation is produced by rhythm, language, or "harmony," either singly or combined.

Thus in the music of the flute and of the lyre, "harmony" and rhythm alone are employed; also in other arts, such as that of the shepherd's pipe, which are essentially similar to these. 5. In dancing, rhythm alone is used without "harmony"; for even dancing imitates character, emotion, and action, by rhythmical movement.

6. There is another art which imitates by means of language alone, and that either in prose or verse—which verse, again, may either combine different metres or consist of but one kind—but this has hitherto been without a name. 7. For there is no common term we could apply to the mimes of Sophron and Xenarchus and the Socratic dialogues on the one hand; and, on the other, to poetic imitations in iambic, elegiac, or any similar metre. People do, indeed, add the word "maker" or "poet" to the name of the metre, and speak of elegiac poets, or epic (that is, hexameter) poets, as if it were not the imitation that makes the poet, but the verse that entitles them all indiscriminately to the name. 8. Even when a treatise on medicine or natural science is brought out in verse, the name of poet is by custom given to the author; and yet Homer and Empedocles have nothing in common but the metre, so that it would be right to call the one poet, the other physicist rather than poet. 9. On the same principle, even if a writer in his poetic imitation were to combine all metres, as Chaeremon did in his Centaur, which is a medley composed of metres of all kinds, we should bring him too under the general term poet. So much then for these distinctions.

10. There are, again, some arts which employ all the means above mentioned,—namely, rhythm, tune and metre. Such are Dithyrambic and Nomic poetry, and also Tragedy and Comedy; but between them the difference is, that in the first two cases these means are all employed in combination, in the latter, now one means is employed, now another.

Such, then, are the differences of the arts with respect to the medium of imitation.

II

Since the objects of imitation are men in action, and these men must be either of a higher or a lower type (for moral character mainly answers to these divisions, goodness and badness being the distinguishing marks of moral differences), it follows that we must represent men either as better than in real life, or as worse, or as they are. It is the same in painting. Polygnotus depicted men as nobler than they are, Pauson as less noble, Dionysius drew them true to life.

2. Now it is evident that each of the modes of imitation above mentioned will exhibit these differences, and become a distinct kind in imitating objects that are thus distinct. 3. Such diversities may be found even in dancing, flute-playing, and lyre-playing. So again in language, whether prose or verse unaccompanied by music. Homer, for example, makes men better than they are; Cleophon as they are; Hegemon the Thasian, the inventor of parodies, and Nicochares, the author of the Deiliad, worse than they are. 4. The same thing holds good of Dithyrambs and Nomes; here too one may portray different types, as Timotheus and Philoxenus differed in representing their Cyclopes. The same distinction marks off Tragedy from Comedy; for Comedy aims at representing men as worse, Tragedy as better than in actual life.

III

There is still a third difference—the manner in which each of these objects may be imitated. For the medium being the same, and the objects the same, the poet may imitate by narration—in which case he can either take another personality as Homer does, or speak in his own person, unchanged—or he may present all his characters as living and moving before us.

2. These, then, as we said at the beginning, are the three differences which distinguish artistic imitation—the medium, the objects and the manner. So that from one point of view, Sophocles is an imitator of the same kind as Homer—for both imitate higher types of character; from another point of view, of the same kind as Aristophanes—for both imitate persons acting and doing. 3. Hence, some say, the name of "drama" is given to such poems, as representing action. For the same reason the Dorians claim the invention both of Tragedy and Comedy. The claim to Comedy is put forward by the Megarians,— not only by those of Greece proper, who allege that it originated un-

der their democracy, but also by the Megarians of Sicily, for the poet
Epicharmus, who is much earlier than Chionides and Magnes, belonged to that country. Tragedy too is claimed by certain Dorians
of the Peloponnese. In each case they appeal to the evidence of language. Villages, they say, are by them called κῶμαι, by the Athenians
δῆμοι: and they assume that Comedians were so named not from
κωμάζειν, "to revel," but because they wandered from village to village (κατὰ κώμας), being excluded contemptuously from the city. They
add also that the Dorian word for "doing" is δρᾶν, and the Athenian,
πράττειν.

4. This may suffice as to the number and nature of the various
modes of imitation.

IV

Poetry in general seems to have sprung from two causes, each of
them lying deep in our nature. 2. First, the instinct of imitation is
implanted in man from childhood, one difference between him and
other animals being that he is the most imitative of living creatures;
and through imitation he learns his earliest lessons; and no less universal is the pleasure felt in things imitated. 3. We have evidence of
this in the facts of experience. Objects which in themselves we view
with pain, we delight to contemplate when reproduced with minute
fidelity: such as the forms of the most ignoble animals and of dead
bodies. 4. The cause of this again is, that to learn gives the liveliest
pleasure, not only to philosophers but to men in general; whose
capacity, however, of learning is more limited. 5. Thus the reason
why men enjoy seeing a likeness is, that in contemplating it they find
themselves learning or inferring, and saying perhaps, "Ah, that is he."
For if you happen not to have seen the original, the pleasure will
be due not to the imitation as such, but to the execution, the colouring, or some such other cause.

6. Imitation, then, is one instinct of our nature. Next, there is the
instinct for "harmony" and rhythm, metres being manifestly sections
of rhythm. Persons, therefore, starting with this natural gift developed
by degrees their special aptitudes, till their rude improvisations gave
birth to Poetry.

7. Poetry now diverged in two directions, according to the individual character of the writers. The graver spirits imitated noble actions,
and the actions of good men. The more trivial sort imitated the actions of meaner persons, at first composing satires, as the former did

hymns to the gods and the praises of famous men. 8. A poem of the satirical kind cannot indeed be put down to any author earlier than Homer; though many such writers probably there were. But from Homer onward, instances can be cited,—his own Margites, for example, and other similar compositions. The appropriate metre was also here introduced; hence the measure is still called the iambic or lampooning measure, being that in which people lampooned one another. 9. Thus the older poets were distinguished as writers of heroic or of lampooning verse.

As, in the serious style, Homer is pre-eminent among poets, for he alone combined dramatic form with excellence of imitation, so he too first laid down the main lines of Comedy, by dramatising the ludicrous instead of writing personal satire. His Margites bears the same relation to Comedy that the Iliad and Odyssey do to Tragedy. 10. But when Tragedy and Comedy came to light, the two classes of poets still followed their natural bent: the lampooners became writers of Comedy, and the Epic poets were succeeded by Tragedians, since the drama was a larger and higher form of art.

11. Whether Tragedy has as yet perfected its proper types or not; and whether it is to be judged in itself, or in relation also to the audience,—this raises another question. 12. Be that as it may, Tragedy—as also Comedy—was at first mere improvisation. The one originated with the leaders of the Dithyramb, the other with those of the phallic songs, which are still in use in many of our cities. Tragedy advanced by slow degrees; each new element that showed itself was in turn developed. Having passed through many changes, it found its natural form, and there it stopped.

13. Aeschylus first introduced a second actor; he diminished the importance of the Chorus, and assigned the leading part to the dialogue. Sophocles raised the number of actors to three, and added scene-painting. 14. Moreover, it was not till late that the short plot was discarded for one of greater compass, and the grotesque diction of the earlier satyric form for the stately manner of Tragedy. The iambic measure then replaced the trochaic tetrameter, which was originally employed when the poetry was of the satyric order, and had greater affinities with dancing. Once dialogue had come in, Nature herself discovered the appropriate measure. For the iambic is, of all measures, the most colloquial: we see it in the fact that conversational speech runs into iambic form more frequently than into any other kind of verse; rarely into hexameters, and only when we drop

the colloquial intonation. 15. The additions to the number of "episodes" or acts, and the other improvements of which tradition tells, must be taken as already described; for to discuss them in detail would, doubtless, be a large undertaking.

V

Comedy is, as we have said, an imitation of characters of a lower type—not, however, in the full sense of the word bad, the Ludicrous being merely a subdivision of the ugly. It consists in some defect or ugliness which is not painful or destructive. To take an obvious example, the comic mask is ugly and distorted, but does not imply pain.

2. The successive changes through which Tragedy passed, and the authors of these changes, are well known, whereas Comedy has had no history, because it was not at first treated seriously. It was late before the Archon granted a comic chorus to a poet; the performers were till then voluntary. Comedy had already taken definite shape when comic poets, distinctively so called, are heard of. 3. Who introduced masks, or prologues, or increased the number of actors—these and other similar details remain unknown. As for the plot, it came originally from Sicily; but of Athenian writers Crates was the first who, abandoning the "iambic" or lampooning form, generalised his themes and plots.

4. Epic poetry agrees with Tragedy in so far as it is an imitation in verse of characters of a higher type. They differ, in that Epic poetry admits but one kind of metre, and is narrative in form. They differ, again, in their length: for Tragedy endeavours, as far as possible, to confine itself to a single revolution of the sun, or but slightly to exceed this limit; whereas the Epic action has no limits of time. This, then, is a second point of difference; though at first the same freedom was admitted in Tragedy as in Epic poetry.

5. Of their constituent parts some are common to both, some peculiar to Tragedy. Whoever, therefore, knows what is good or bad Tragedy, knows also about Epic poetry: for all the elements of an Epic poem are found in Tragedy, but the elements of a Tragedy are not all found in the Epic poem.

VI

Of the poetry which imitates in hexameter verse, and of Comedy, we will speak hereafter. Let us now discuss Tragedy, resuming its formal definition, as resulting from what has been already said.

2. Tragedy then, is an imitation of an action that is serious, complete, and of a certain magnitude; in language embellished with each kind of artistic ornament, the several kinds being found in separate parts of the play; in the form of action, not of narrative; through pity and fear effecting the proper purgation of these emotions. 3. By "language embellished," I mean language into which rhythm, "harmony," and song enter. By "the several kinds in separate parts," I mean, that some parts are rendered through the medium of verse alone, others again with the aid of song.

4. Now as tragic imitation implies persons acting, it necessarily follows, in the first place, that Spectacular equipment will be a part of Tragedy. Next, Song and Diction, for these are the medium of imitation. By "Diction" I mean the mere metrical arrangement of the words: as for "Song," it is a term whose sense every one understands.

5. Again, Tragedy is the imitation of an action; and an action implies personal agents, who necessarily possess certain distinctive qualities both of character and thought; for it is by these that we qualify actions themselves, and these—thought and character—are the two natural causes from which actions spring, and on actions again all success or failure depends. 6. Hence, the Plot is the imitation of the action:—for by plot I here mean the arrangement of the incidents. By Character I mean that in virtue of which we ascribe certain qualities to the agents. Thought is required wherever a statement is proved, or, it may be, a general truth enunciated. 7. Every Tragedy, therefore, must have six parts, which parts determine its quality—namely, Plot, Character, Diction, Thought, Spectacle, Song. Two of the parts constitute the medium of imitation, one the manner, and three the objects of imitation. And these complete the list. 8. These elements have been employed, we may say, by the poets to a man; in fact, every play contains Spectacular elements as well as Character, Plot, Diction, Song, and Thought.

9. But most important of all is the structure of the incidents. For Tragedy is an imitation, not of men, but of an action and of life, and life consists in action, and its end is a mode of action, not a quality. 10. Now character determines men's qualities, but it is by their actions that they are happy or the reverse. Dramatic action, therefore, is not with a view to the representation of character: character comes in as subsidiary to the actions. Hence the incidents and the plot are the end of a tragedy; and the end is the chief thing of all. 11. Again, without action there cannot be a tragedy; there may be without char-

acter. The tragedies of most of our modern poets fail in the rendering of character; and of poets in general this is often true. It is the same in painting; and here lies the difference between Zeuxis and Polygnotus. Polygnotus delineates character well: the style of Zeuxis is devoid of ethical quality. 12. Again, if you string together a set of speeches expressive of character, and well finished in point of diction and thought, you will not produce the essential tragic effect nearly so well as with a play which, however deficient in these respects, yet has a plot and artistically constructed incidents. 13. Besides which, the most powerful elements of emotional interest in Tragedy —Peripeteia or Reversal of Intention, and Recognition scenes—are parts of the plot. 14. A further proof is, that novices in the art attain to finish of diction and precision of portraiture before they can construct the plot. It is the same with almost all the early poets.

The Plot, then, is the first principle, and, as it were, the soul of a tragedy: Character holds the second place. 15. A similar fact is seen in painting. The most beautiful colours, laid on confusedly, will not give as much pleasure as the chalk outline of a portrait. Thus Tragedy is the imitation of an action, and of the agents, mainly with a view to the action.

16. Third in order is Thought,—that is, the faculty of saying what is possible and pertinent in given circumstances. In the case of oratory, this is the function of the political art and of the art of rhetoric: and so indeed the older poets make their characters speak the language of civic life; the poets of our time, the language of the rhetoricians.

17. Character is that which reveals moral purpose, showing what kind of things a man chooses or avoids. Speeches, therefore, which do not make this manifest, or in which the speaker does not choose or avoid anything whatever, are not expressive of character. Thought, on the other hand, is found where something is proved to be or not to be, or a general maxim is enunciated.

18. Fourth among the elements enumerated comes Diction; by which I mean, as has been already said, the expression of the meaning in words; and its essence is the same both in verse and prose.

19. Of the remaining elements Song holds the chief place among the embellishments.

The Spectacle has, indeed, an emotional attraction of its own, but, of all the parts, it is the least artistic, and connected least with the art of poetry. For the power of Tragedy, we may be sure, is felt even apart from representation and actors. Besides, the production of spectacular effects depends more on the art of the stage machinist than on that of the poet.

VII

These principles being established, let us now discuss the proper structure of the Plot, since this is the first and most important part of Tragedy.

2. Now, according to our definition, Tragedy is an imitation of an action that is complete, and whole, and of a certain magnitude; for there may be a whole that is wanting in magnitude. 3. A whole is that which has a beginning, a middle, and an end. A beginning is that which does not itself follow anything by causal necessity, but after which something naturally is or comes to be. An end, on the contrary, is that which itself naturally follows some other thing, either by necessity, or as a rule, but has nothing following it. A middle is that which follows something as some other thing follows it. A well constructed plot, therefore, must neither begin nor end at haphazard, but conform to these principles.

4. Again, a beautiful object, whether it be a picture of a living organism or any whole composed of parts, must not only have an orderly arrangement of parts, but must also be of a certain magnitude; for beauty depends on magnitude and order. Hence an exceedingly small picture cannot be beautiful; for the view of it is confused, the object being seen in an almost imperceptible moment of time. Nor, again, can one of vast size be beautiful; for as the eye cannot take it all in at once, the unity and sense of the whole is lost for the spectator; as for instance if there were a picture a thousand miles long. 5. As, therefore, in the case of animate bodies and pictures a certain magnitude is necessary, and a magnitude which may be easily embraced in one view; so in the plot, a certain length is necessary, and a length which can be easily embraced by the memory. 6. The limit of length in relation to dramatic competition and sensuous present-ment, is no part of artistic theory. For had it been the rule for a hundred tragedies to compete together, the performance would have been regulated by the water-clock—as indeed we are told was formerly done. 7. But the limit as fixed by the nature of the drama itself is this:—the greater the length, the more beautiful will the piece be by reason of its size, provided that the whole be perspicuous. And

to define the matter roughly, we may say that the proper magnitude is comprised within such limits, that the sequence of events, according to the law of probability or necessity, will admit of a change from bad fortune to good, or from good fortune to bad.

VIII

Unity of plot does not, as some persons think, consist in the unity of the hero. For infinitely various are the incidents in one man's life, which cannot be reduced to unity; and so, too, there are many actions of one man out of which we cannot make one action. 2. Hence the error, as it appears, of all poets who have composed a Heracleid, a Theseid, or other poems of the kind. They imagine that as Heracles was one man, the story of Heracles must also be a unity. 3. But Homer, as in all else he is of surpassing merit, here too—whether from art or natural genius—seems to have happily discerned the truth. In composing the Odyssey he did not include all the adventures of Odysseus—such as his wound on Parnassus, or his feigned madness at the mustering of the host—incidents between which there was no necessary or probable connexion: but he made the Odyssey, and likewise the Iliad, to centre round an action that in our sense of the word is one. 4. As therefore, in the other imitative arts, the imitation is one when the object imitated is one, so the plot, being an imitation of an action, must imitate one action and that a whole, the structural union of the parts being such that, if any one of them is displaced or removed, the whole will be disjointed and disturbed. For a thing whose presence or absence makes no visible difference, is not an organic part of the whole.

IX

It is, moreover, evident from what has been said, that it is not the function of the poet to relate what has happened, but what may happen —what is possible according to the law of probability or necessity. 2. The poet and the historian differ not by writing in verse or in prose. The work of Herodotus might be put into verse, and it would still be a species of history, with metre no less than without it. The true difference is that one relates what has happened, the other what may happen. 3. Poetry, therefore, is a more philosophical and a higher thing than history: for poetry tends to express the universal, history the particular.

4. By the universal I mean how a person of a certain type will on occasion speak or act, according to the law of probability or necessity; and it is this universality at which poetry aims in the names she attaches to the personages. The particular is—for example—what Alcibiades did or suffered. 5. In Comedy this is already apparent: for here the poet first constructs the plot on the lines of probability, and then inserts characteristic names;—unlike the lampooners who write about particular individuals. 6. But tragedians still keep to real names, the reason being that what is possible is credible: what has not happened we do not at once feel sure to be possible: but what has happened is manifestly possible: otherwise it would not have happened. 7. Still there are some tragedies in which there are only one or two well known names, the rest being fictitious. In others, none are well known,—as in Agathon's Antheus, where incidents and names alike are fictitious, and yet they give none the less pleasure. 8. We must not, therefore, at all costs keep to the received legends, which are the usual subjects of Tragedy. Indeed, it would be absurd to attempt it; for even subjects that are known are known only to a few, and yet give pleasure to all. 9. It clearly follows that the poet or "maker" should be the maker of plots rather than of verses; since he is a poet because he imitates, and what he imitates are actions. And even if he chances to take an historical subject, he is none the less a poet; for there is no reason why some events that have actually happened should not conform to the law of the probable and possible, and in virtue of that quality in them he is their poet or maker.

10. Of all plots and actions the epeisodic are the worst. I call a plot "epeisodic" in which the episodes or acts succeed one another without probable or necessary sequence. Bad poets compose such pieces by their own fault, good poets, to please the players; for, as they write show pieces for competition, they stretch the plot beyond its capacity, and are often forced to break the natural continuity.

11. But again, Tragedy is an imitation not only of a complete action, but of events terrible and pitiful. Such an effect is best produced when the events come on us by surprise; and the effect is heightened when, at the same time, they follow as cause and effect. 12. The tragic wonder will then be greater than if they happened of themselves or by accident; for even coincidences are most striking when they have an air of design. We may instance the statue of Mitys at Argos, which fell upon his murderer while he was a spectator at a festival, and killed him. Such events seem not to be due to mere chance. Plots, therefore, constructed on these principles are necessarily the best.

X

Plots are either Simple or Complex, for the actions in real life, of which the plots are an imitation, obviously show a similar distinction. 2. An action which is one and continuous in the sense above defined, I call Simple, when the change of fortune takes place without Reversal of Intention and without Recognition.

A Complex action is one in which the change is accompanied by such Reversal, or by Recognition, or by both. 3. These last should arise from the internal structure of the plot, so that what follows should be the necessary or probable result of the preceding action. It makes all the difference whether any given event is a case of *propter hoc* or *post hoc*.

XI

Reversal of Intention is a change by which the action veers round to its opposite, subject always to our rule of probability or necessity. Thus in the Oedipus, the messenger comes to cheer Oedipus and free him from his alarms about his mother, but by revealing who he is, he produces the opposite effect. Again in the Lynceus, Lynceus is being led away to his death, and Danaus goes with him, meaning to slay him; but the outcome of the action is, that Danaus is killed and Lynceus saved.

2. Recognition, as the name indicates, is a change from ignorance to knowledge, producing love or hate between the persons destined by the poet for good or bad fortune. The best form of recognition is coincident with a Reversal of Intention, as in the Oedipus. 3. There are indeed other forms. Even inanimate things of the most trivial kind may sometimes be objects of recognition. Again, we may recognise or discover whether a person has done a thing or not. But the recognition which is most intimately connected with the plot and action is, as we have said, the recognition of persons. 4. This recognition, combined with Reversal, will produce either pity or fear; and actions producing these effects are those which, by our definition, Tragedy represents. Moreover, it is upon such situations that the issues of good or bad fortune will depend. 5. Recognition, then, being between persons, it may happen that one person only is recognised by the other—when the latter is already known —or it may be necessary that the recognition should be on both sides. Thus Iphigenia is revealed to Orestes by the sending of the letter; but

another act of recognition is required to make Orestes known to Iphigenia.

6. Two parts, then, of the Plot—Reversal of Intention and Recognition—turn upon surprises. A third part is the Tragic Incident. The Tragic Incident is a destructive or painful action, such as death on the stage, bodily agony, wounds, and the like.

XII

[The parts of Tragedy which must be treated as elements of the whole, have been already mentioned. We now come to the quantitative parts—the separate parts into which Tragedy is divided—namely, Prologue, Episode, Exodos, Choric song; this last being divided into Parodos and Stasimon. These are common to all plays: peculiar to some are the songs of actors from the stage and the Commoi.

2. The Prologos is that entire part of a tragedy which precedes the Parodos of the Chorus. The Episode is that entire part of a tragedy which is between complete choric songs. The Exodos is that entire part of a tragedy which has no choric song after it. Of the Choric part the Parodos is the first undivided utterance of the Chorus: the Stasimon is a Choric ode without anapaests or trochaic tetrameters: the Commos is a joint lamentation of Chorus and actors. 3. The parts of Tragedy which must be treated as elements of the whole have been already mentioned. The quantitative parts—the separate parts into which it is divided—are here enumerated.]

XIII

As the sequel to what has already been said, we must proceed to consider what the poet should aim at, and what he should avoid, in constructing his plots; and by what means the specific effect of Tragedy will be produced.

2. A perfect tragedy should, as we have seen, be arranged not on the simple but on the complex plan. It should, moreover, imitate actions which excite pity and fear, this being the distinctive mark of tragic imitation. It follows plainly, in the first place, that the change of fortune presented must not be the spectacle of a virtuous man brought from prosperity to adversity: for this moves neither pity nor fear; it merely shocks us. Nor, again, that of a bad man passing from adversity to

prosperity: for nothing can be more alien to the spirit of Tragedy; it possesses no single tragic quality; it neither satisfies the moral sense, nor calls forth pity or fear. Nor, again, should the downfall of the utter villain be exhibited. A plot of this kind would, doubtless, satisfy the moral sense, but it would inspire neither pity nor fear; for pity is aroused by unmerited misfortune, fear by the misfortune of a man like ourselves. Such an event, therefore, will be neither pitiful nor terrible. 3. There remains, then, the character between these two extremes,— that of a man who is not eminently good and just, yet whose misfortune is brought about not by vice or depravity, but by some error or frailty. He must be one who is highly renowned and prosperous,—a personage like Oedipus, Thyestes, or other illustrious men of such families.

4. A well constructed plot should, therefore, be single in its issue, rather than double as some maintain. The change of fortune should be not from bad to good, but, reversely, from good to bad. It should come about as the result not of vice, but of some great error or frailty, in a character either such as we have described, or better rather than worse. 5. The practice of the stage bears out our view. At first the poets recounted any legend that came in their way. Now, the best tragedies are founded on the story of a few houses,—on the fortunes of Alcmaeon, Oedipus, Orestes, Meleager, Thyestes, Telephus, and those others who have done or suffered something terrible. A tragedy, then, to be perfect according to the rules of art should be of this construction. 6. Hence they are in error who censure Euripides just because he follows this principle in his plays, many of which end unhappily. It is, as we have said, the right ending. The best proof is that on the stage and in dramatic competition, such plays, if well worked out, are the most tragic in effect; and Euripides, faulty though he may be in the general management of his subject, yet is felt to be the most tragic of the poets.

7. In the second rank comes the kind of tragedy which some place first. Like the Odyssey, it has a double thread of plot, and also an opposite catastrophe for the good and for the bad. It is accounted the best because of the weakness of the spectators; for the poet is guided in what he writes by the wishes of his audience. 8. The pleasure, however, thence derived is not the true tragic pleasure. It is proper rather to Comedy, where those who, in the piece, are the deadliest enemies— like Orestes and Aegisthus—quit the stage as friends at the close, and no one slays or is slain.

XIV

Fear and pity may be aroused by spectacular means; but they may also result from the inner structure of the piece, which is the better way, and indicates a superior poet. For the plot ought to be so constructed that, even without the aid of the eye, he who hears the tale told will thrill with horror and melt to pity at what takes place. This is the impression we should receive from hearing the story of the Oedipus. 2. But to produce this effect by the mere spectacle is a less artistic method, and dependent on extraneous aids. Those who employ spectacular means to create a sense not of the terrible but only of the monstrous, are strangers to the purpose of Tragedy; for we must not demand of Tragedy any and every kind of pleasure, but only that which is proper to it. 3. And since the pleasure which the poet should afford is that which comes from pity and fear through imitation, it is evident that this quality must be impressed upon the incidents.

Let us then determine what are the circumstances which strike us as terrible or pitiful.

4. Actions capable of this effect must happen between persons who are either friends or enemies or indifferent to one another. If an enemy kills an enemy, there is nothing to excite pity either in the act or the intention,—except so far as the suffering in itself is pitiful. So again with indifferent persons. But when the tragic incident occurs between those who are near or dear to one another—if, for example, a brother kills, or intends to kill, a brother, a son his father, a mother her son, a son his mother, or any other deed of the kind is done—these are the situations to be looked for by the poet. 5. He may not indeed destroy the framework of the received legends—the fact, for instance, that Clytemnestra was slain by Orestes and Eriphyle by Alcmaeon—but he ought to show invention of his own, and skilfully handle the traditional material. Let us explain more clearly what is meant by skilful handling.

6. The action may be done consciously and with knowledge of the persons, in the manner of the older poets. It is thus too that Euripides makes Medea slay her children. Or, again, the deed of horror may be done, but done in ignorance, and the tie of kinship or friendship be discovered afterwards. The Oedipus of Sophocles is an example. Here, indeed, the incident is outside the drama proper; but cases occur where it falls within the action of the play: one may cite the Alcmaeon of Astydamas, or Telegonus in the Wounded Odysseus. 7. Again, there

is a third case,—<to be about to act with knowledge of the persons and then not to act. The fourth case is> when some one is about to do an irreparable deed through ignorance, and makes the discovery before it is done. These are the only possible ways. For the deed must either be done or not done,—and that wittingly or unwittingly. But of all these ways, to be about to act knowing the persons, and then not to act, is the worst. It is shocking without being tragic, for no disaster follows. It is, therefore, never, or very rarely, found in poetry. One instance, however, is in the Antigone, where Haemon threatens to kill Creon. 8. The next and better way is that the deed should be perpetrated. Still better, that it should be perpetrated in ignorance, and the discovery made afterwards. There is then nothing to shock us, while the discovery produces a startling effect. 9. The last case is the best, as when in the Cresphontes Merope is about to slay her son, but, recognising who he is, spares his life. So in the Iphigenia, the sister recognises the brother just in time. Again in the Helle, the son recognises the mother when on the point of giving her up. This, then, is why a few families only, as has been already observed, furnish the subjects of tragedy. It was not art, but happy chance, that led poets to look for such situations and so impress the tragic quality upon their plots. They are compelled, therefore, to have recourse to those houses whose history contains moving incidents like these.

Enough has now been said concerning the structure of the incidents, and the proper constitution of the plot.

XV

In respect of Character there are four things to be aimed at. First, and most important, it must be good. Now any speech or action that manifests moral purpose of any kind will be expressive of character: the character will be good if the purpose is good. This rule is relative to each class. Even a woman may be good, and also a slave; though the woman may be said to be an inferior being, and the slave quite worthless. 2. The second thing to aim at is propriety. There is a type of manly valour; but valour in a woman, or unscrupulous cleverness, is inappropriate. 3. Thirdly, character must be true to life: for this is a distinct thing from goodness and propriety, as here described. 4. The fourth point is consistency: for though the subject of the imitation, who suggested the type, be inconsistent, still he must be consistently inconsistent. 5. As an example of motiveless degradation of character, we have Menelaus in the Orestes: of character indecorous and inappropriate, the lament of Odysseus in the Scylla, and the speech of Melanippe: of inconsistency, the Iphigenia at Aulis,—for Iphigenia the suppliant in no way resembles her later self.

6. As in the structure of the plot, so too in the portraiture of character, the poet should always aim either at the necessary or the probable. Thus a person of a given character should speak or act in a given way, by the rule either of necessity or of probability; just as this event should follow that by necessary or probable sequence. 7. It is therefore evident that the unravelling of the plot, no less than the complication, must arise out of the plot itself, it must not be brought about by the *Deus ex Machina*—as in the Medea, or in the Return of the Greeks in the Iliad. The *Deus ex Machina* should be employed only for events external to the drama,—for antecedent or subsequent events, which lie beyond the range of human knowledge, and which require to be reported or foretold; for to the gods we ascribe the power of seeing all things. Within the action there must be nothing irrational. If the irrational cannot be excluded, it should be outside the scope of the tragedy. Such is the irrational element in the Oedipus of Sophocles.

8. Again, since Tragedy is an imitation of persons who are above the common level, the example of good portrait-painters should be followed. They, while reproducing the distinctive form of the original, make a likeness which is true to life and yet more beautiful. So too the poet, in representing men who are irascible or indolent, or have other defects of character, should preserve the type and yet ennoble it. In this way Achilles is portrayed by Agathon and Homer.

9. These then are rules the poet should observe. Nor should he neglect those appeals to the senses, which, though not among the essentials, are the concomitants of poetry; for here too there is much room for error. But of this enough has been said in the published treatises.

XVI

What Recognition is has been already explained. We will now enumerate its kinds.

First, the least artistic form, which, from poverty of wit, is most commonly employed—recognition by signs. 2. Of these some are congenital, —such as "the spear which the earth-born race bear on their bodies," or the stars introduced by Carcinus in his Thyestes. Others are acquired after birth; and of these some are bodily marks, as scars; some external tokens, as necklaces, or the little ark in the Tyro by which the discovery is effected. 3. Even these admit of more or less skilful treatment. Thus in the recognition of Odysseus by his scar, the discovery is made in one way by the nurse, in another by the herdsmen. The use of tokens for the express purpose of proof—and, indeed, any formal proof with or without tokens—is a less artistic mode of recognition. A better kind is that which comes about by a turn of incident, as in the Bath Scene in the Odyssey.

4. Next come the recognitions invented at will by the poet, and on that account wanting in art. For example, Orestes in the Iphigenia reveals the fact that he is Orestes. She, indeed, makes herself knówn by the letter; but he, by speaking himself, and saying what the poet, not what the plot requires. This, therefore, is nearly allied to the fault above mentioned:—for Orestes might as well have brought tokens with him. Another similar instance is the "voice of the shuttle" in the Tereus of Sophocles.

5. The third kind depends on memory when the sight of some object awakens a feeling: as in the Cyprians of Dicaeogenes, where the hero breaks into tears on seeing the picture; or again in the "Lay of Alcinous," where Odysseus, hearing the minstrel play the lyre, recalls the past and weeps; and hence the recognition.

6. The fourth kind is by process of reasoning. Thus in the Choëphori: —"Some one resembling me has come: no one resembles me but Orestes: therefore Orestes has come." Such too is the discovery made by Iphigenia in the play of Polyidus the Sophist. It was a natural reflexion for Orestes to make, "So I too must die at the altar like my sister." So, again, in the Tydeus of Theodectes, the father says, "I came to find my son, and I lose my own life." So too in the Phineidae: the women, on seeing the place, inferred their fate:—"Here we are doomed to die, for here we were cast forth." 7. Again, there is a composite kind of recognition involving false inference on the part of one of the characters, as in the Odysseus Disguised as a Messenger. A said $<$ that no one else was able to bend the bow; . . . hence B (the disguised Odysseus) imagined that A would $>$ recognise the bow which, in fact, he had not seen; and to bring about a recognition by this means—the expectation that A would recognise the bow—is false inference.

8. But, of all recognitions, the best is that which arises from the incidents themselves, where the startling discovery is made by natural means. Such is that in the Oedipus of Sophocles, and in the Iphigenia; for it was natural that Iphigenia should wish to dispatch a letter. These

recognitions alone dispense with the artificial aid of tokens or amulets. Next come the recognitions by process of reasoning.

XVII

In constructing the plot and working it out with the proper diction, the poet should place the scene, as far as possible, before his eyes. In this way, seeing everything with the utmost vividness, as if he were a spectator of the action, he will discover what is in keeping with it, and be most unlikely to overlook inconsistencies. The need of such a rule is shown by the fault found in Carcinus. Amphiaraus was on his way from the temple. This fact escaped the observation of one who did not see the situation. On the stage, however, the piece failed, the audience being offended at the oversight.

2. Again, the poet should work out his play, to the best of his power, with appropriate gestures; for those who feel emotion are most convincing through natural sympathy with the characters they represent; and one who is agitated storms, one who is angry rages, with the most life-like reality. Hence poetry implies either a happy gift of nature or a strain of madness. In the one case a man can take the mould of any character; in the other, he is lifted out of his proper self.

3. As for the story, whether the poet takes it ready made or constructs it for himself, he should first sketch its general outline, and then fill in the episodes and amplify in detail. The general plan may be illustrated by the Iphigenia. A young girl is sacrificed; she disappears mysteriously from the eyes of those who sacrificed her; she is transported to another country, where the custom is to offer up all strangers to the goddess. To this ministry she is appointed. Some time later her own brother chances to arrive. The fact that the oracle for some reason ordered him to go there, is outside the general plan of the play. The purpose, again, of his coming is outside the action proper. However, he comes, he is seized, and, when on the point of being sacrificed, reveals who he is. The mode of recognition may be either that of Euripides or of Polyidus, in whose play he exclaims very naturally:—"So it was not my sister only, but I too, who was doomed to be sacrificed"; and by that remark he is saved.

4. After this, the names being once given, it remains to fill in the episodes. We must see that they are relevant to the action. In the case of Orestes, for example, there is the madness which led to his capture, and his deliverance by means of the purificatory rite. 5. In the drama,

the episodes are short, but it is these that give extension to Epic poetry. Thus the story of the Odyssey can be stated briefly. A certain man is absent from home for many years; he is jealously watched by Poseidon, and left desolate. Meanwhile his home is in a wretched plight—suitors are wasting his substance and plotting against his son. At length, tempest-tost, he himself arrives; he makes certain persons acquainted with him; he attacks the suitors with his own hand, and is himself preserved while he destroys them. This is the essence of the plot; the rest is episode.

XVIII

Every tragedy falls into two parts,—Complication and Unravelling or *Dénouement*. Incidents extraneous to the action are frequently combined with a portion of the action proper, to form the Complication; the rest is the Unravelling. By the Complication I mean all that extends from the beginning of the action to the part which marks the turning-point to good or bad fortune. The Unravelling is that which extends from the beginning of the change to the end. Thus, in the Lynceus of Theodectes, the Complication consists of the incidents presupposed in the drama, the seizure of the child, and then again * * <The Unravelling> extends from the accusation of murder to the end.

2. There are four kinds of Tragedy, the Complex, depending entirely on Reversal and Recognition; the Pathetic (where the motive is passion),—such as the tragedies on Ajax and Ixion; the Ethical (where the motives are ethical),—such as the Phthiotides and the Peleus. The fourth kind is the Simple. <We here exclude the purely spectacular element>, exemplified by the Phorcides, the Prometheus, and scenes laid in Hades. 3. The poet should endeavour, if possible, to combine all poetic merits; or failing that, the greatest number and those the most important; the more so, in face of the cavilling criticism of the day. For whereas there have hitherto been good poets, each in his own branch, the critics now expect one man to surpass all others in their several lines of excellence.

In speaking of a tragedy as the same or different, the best test to take is the plot. Identity exists where the Complication and Unravelling are the same. Many poets tie the knot well, but unravel it ill. Both arts, however, should always be mastered.

4. Again, the poet should remember what has been often said, and not make a Tragedy into an Epic structure. By an Epic structure I mean

one with a multiplicity of plots: as if, for instance, you were to make a tragedy out of the entire story of the Iliad. In the Epic poem, owing to its length, each part assumes its proper magnitude. In the drama the result is far from answering to the poet's expectation. 5. The proof is that the poets who have dramatised the whole story of the Fall of Troy, instead of selecting portions, like Euripides; or who have taken the whole tale of Niobe, and not a part of her story, like Aeschylus, either fail utterly or meet with poor success on the stage. Even Agathon has been known to fail from this one defect. In his Reversals of Intention, however, he shows a marvellous skill in the effort to hit the popular taste,—to produce a tragic effect that satisfies the moral sense. 6. This effect is produced when the clever rogue, like Sisyphus, is outwitted, or the brave villain defeated. Such an event is probable in Agathon's sense of the word: "it is probable," he says, "that many things should happen contrary to probability."

7. The Chorus too should be regarded as one of the actors; it should be an integral part of the whole, and share in the action, in the manner not of Euripides but of Sophocles. As for the later poets, their choral songs pertain as little to the subject of the piece as to that of any other tragedy. They are, therefore, sung as mere interludes,—a practice first begun by Agathon. Yet what difference is there between introducing such choral interludes, and transferring a speech, or even a whole act, from one play to another?

XIX

It remains to speak of Diction and Thought, the other parts of Tragedy having been already discussed. Concerning Thought, we may assume what is said in the Rhetoric, to which inquiry the subject more strictly belongs. 2. Under Thought is included every effect which has to be produced by speech, the subdivisions being,—proof and refutation; the excitation of the feelings, such as pity, fear, anger, and the like; the suggestion of importance or its opposite. 3. Now, it is evident that the dramatic incidents must be treated from the same points of view as the dramatic speeches, when the object is to evoke the sense of pity, fear, importance, or probability. The only difference is, that the incidents should speak for themselves without verbal exposition; while the effects aimed at in speech should be produced by the speaker, and as a result of the speech. For what were the business of a speaker, if the Thought were revealed quite apart from what he says?

4. Next, as regards Diction. One branch of the inquiry treats of the Modes of Expression. But this province of knowledge belongs to the art of Delivery, and to the masters of that science. It includes, for instance,—what is a command, a prayer, a narrative, a threat, a question, an answer, and so forth. 5. To know or not to know these things involves no serious censure upon the poet's art. For who can admit the fault imputed to Homer by Protagoras,—that in the words, "Sing, goddess, of the wrath," he gives a command under the idea that he utters a prayer? For to tell some one to do a thing or not to do it is, he says, a command. We may, therefore, pass this over as an inquiry that belongs to another art, not to poetry.

XX

[Language in general includes the following parts:—Letter, Syllable, Connecting word, Noun, Verb, Inflexion or Case, Sentence or Phrase.

2. A Letter is an indivisible sound, yet not every such sound, but only one which can form part of a group of sounds. For even brutes utter indivisible sounds, none of which I call a letter. 3. The sound I mean may be either a vowel, a semi-vowel, or a mute. A vowel is that which without impact of tongue or lip has an audible sound. A semi-vowel, that which with such impact has an audible sound, as S and R. A mute, that which with such impact has by itself no sound, but joined to a vowel sound becomes audible, as G and D. 4. These are distinguished according to the form assumed by the mouth, and the place where they are produced; according as they are aspirated or smooth, long or short; as they are acute, grave, or of an intermediate tone; which inquiry belongs in detail to a treatise on metre.

5. A Syllable is a non-significant sound, composed of a mute and a vowel: for GR without A is a syllable, as also with A,—GRA. But the investigation of these differences belongs also to metrical science.

6. A Connecting word is a non-significant sound, which neither causes nor hinders the union of many sounds into one significant sound; it may be placed at either end or in the middle of a sentence. Or, a non-significant sound, which out of several sounds, each of them significant, is capable of forming one significant sound,—as ἀμφί, περί, and the like. 7. Or, a non-significant sound, which marks the beginning, end, or division of a sentence; such, however, that it cannot correctly stand by itself at the beginning of a sentence,—as μέν, ἤτοι, δέ.

8. A Noun is a composite significant sound, not marking time, of

which no part is in itself significant: for in double or compound words we do not employ the separate parts as if each were in itself significant. Thus in Theodorus, "god-given," the δῶρον or "gift" is not in itself significant.

9. A Verb is a composite significant sound, marking time, in which, as in the noun, no part is in itself significant. For "man," or "white" does not express the idea of "when"; but "he walks," or "he has walked" does connote time, present or past.

10. Inflexion belongs both to the noun and verb, and expresses either the relation "of," "to," or the like; or that of number, whether one or many, as "man" or "men"; or the modes or tones in actual delivery, e. g. a question or a command. "Did he go?" and "go" are verbal inflexions of this kind.

11. A Sentence or Phrase is a composite significant sound, some at least of whose parts are in themselves significant; for not every such group of words consists of verbs and nouns—"the definition of man," for example—but it may dispense even with the verb. Still it will always have some significant part, as "in walking," or "Cleon son of Cleon." A sentence or phrase may form a unity in two ways,—either as signifying one thing, or as consisting of several parts linked together. Thus the Iliad is one by the linking together of parts, the definition of man by the unity of the thing signified.]

XXI

Words are of two kinds, simple and double. By simple I mean those composed of non-significant elements, such as γῆ. By double or compound, those composed either of a significant and non-significant element (though within the whole word no element is significant), or of elements that are both significant. A word may likewise be triple, quadruple, or multiple in form, like so many Massilian expressions, e. g. "Hermo-caico-xanthus <who prayed to Father Zeus.>"

2. Every word is either current, or strange, or metaphorical, or ornamental, or newly-coined, or lengthened, or contracted, or altered.

3. By a current or proper word I mean one which is in general use among a people; by a strange word, one which is in use in another country. Plainly, therefore, the same word may be at once strange and current, but not in relation to the same people. The word σίγυνον, "lance," is to the Cyprians a current term but to us a strange one.

4. Metaphor is the application of an alien name by transference either

from genus to species, or from species to genus, or from species to species, or by analogy, that is, proportion. 5. Thus from genus to species, as: "There lies my ship"; for lying at anchor is a species of lying. From species to genus, as: "Verily ten thousand noble deeds hath Odysseus wrought"; for ten thousand is a species of large number, and is here used for a large number generally. From species to species, as: "With blade of bronze drew away the life," and "Cleft the water with the vessel of unyielding bronze." Here ἀρύσαι, "to draw away," is used for ταμεῖν, "to cleave," and ταμεῖν again for ἀρύσαι, —each being a species of taking away. 6. Analogy or proportion is when the second term is to the first as the fourth to the third. We may then use the fourth for the second, or the second for the fourth. Sometimes too we qualify the metaphor by adding the term to which the proper word is relative. Thus the cup is to Dionysus as the shield to Ares. The cup may, therefore, be called "the shield of Dionysus," and the shield, "the cup of Ares." Or, again, as old age is to life, so is evening to day. Evening may therefore be called "the old age of the day," and old age, "the evening of life," or, in the phrases of Empedocles, "life's setting sun." 7. For some of the terms of the proportion there is at times no word in existence; still the metaphor may be used. For instance, to scatter seed is called sowing: but the action of the sun in scattering his rays is nameless. Still this process bears to the sun the same relation as sowing to the seed. Hence the expression of the poet "sowing the god-created light." 8. There is another way in which this kind of metaphor may be employed. We may apply an alien term, and then deny of that term one of its proper attributes; as if we were to call the shield, not "the cup of Ares," but "the wineless cup."

<An ornamental word . . .>

9. A newly-coined word is one which has never been even in local use, but is adopted by the poet himself. Some such words there appear to be: as ἐρνύγες, "sprouters," for κέρατα, "horns," and ἀρητήρ, "supplicator," for ἱερεύς, "priest."

10. A word is lengthened when its own vowel is exchanged for a longer one, or when a syllable is inserted. A word is contracted when some part of it is removed. Instances of lengthening are,—πόληος for πόλεως, and Πηληιάδεω for Πηλείδου: of contraction,—κρῖ, δῶ and ὄψ as in μία γίνεται ἀμφοτέρων ὄψ.

11. An altered word is one in which part of the ordinary form is left unchanged, and part is re-cast; as in δεξιτερὸν κατὰ μαζόν, δεξιτερόν is for δεξιόν.

12. [Nouns in themselves are either masculine, feminine, or neuter. Masculine are such as end in ν, ρ, ς, or in some letter compounded with ς,—these being two, ψ and ξ. Feminine, such as end in vowels that are always long, namely η and ω and—of vowels that admit of lengthening —those in α. Thus the number of letters in which nouns masculine and feminine end is the same; for ψ and ξ are equivalent to endings in ς. No noun ends in a mute or vowel short by nature. Three only end in ι,— μέλι, κόμμι, πέπερι: five end in υ. Neuter nouns end in these two latter vowels; also in ν and ς.]

XXII

The perfection of style is to be clear without being mean. The clearest style is that which uses only current or proper words; at the same time it is mean:—witness the poetry of Cleophon and of Sthenelus. That diction, on the other hand, is lofty and raised above the commonplace which employs unusual words. By unusual, I mean strange (or rare) words, metaphorical, lengthened,—anything, in short, that differs from the normal idiom. 2. Yet a style wholly composed of such words is either a riddle or a jargon; a riddle, if it consists of metaphors; a jargon, if it consists of strange (or rare) words. For the essence of a riddle is to express true facts under impossible combinations. Now this cannot be done by any arrangement of ordinary words, but by the use of metaphor it can. Such is the riddle:—"A man I saw who on another man had glued the bronze by aid of fire," and others of the same kind. A diction that is made up of strange (or rare) terms is a jargon. 3. A certain infusion, therefore, of these elements is necessary to style; for the strange (or rare) word, the metaphorical, the ornamental, and the other kinds above mentioned, will raise it above the commonplace and mean, while the use of proper words will make it perspicuous. 4. But nothing contributes more to produce a clearness of diction that is remote from commonness than the lengthening, contraction, and alteration of words. For by deviating in exceptional cases from the normal idiom, the language will gain distinction; while, at the same time, the partial conformity with usage will give perspicuity. 5. The critics, therefore, are in error who censure these licenses of speech, and hold the author up to ridicule. Thus Eucleides, the elder, declared that it would be an easy matter to be a poet if you might lengthen syllables at will. He caricatured the practice in the very form of his diction, as in the verse:

Ἐπιχάρην εἶδον Μαραθῶνάδε βαδίζοντα,
or,
οὐκ ἄν γ' ἐράμενος τὸν ἐκείνου ἐλλέβορον.

6. To employ such license at all obtrusively is, no doubt, grotesque; but in any mode of poetic diction there must be moderation. Even metaphors, strange (or rare) words, or any similar forms of speech, would produce the like effect if used without propriety, and with the express purpose of being ludicrous. 7. How great a difference is made by the appropriate use of lengthening, may be seen in Epic poetry by the insertion of ordinary forms in the verse. So, again, if we take a strange (or rare) word, a metaphor, or any similar mode of expression, and replace it by the current or proper term, the truth of our observation will be manifest. For example Aeschylus and Euripides each composed the same iambic line. But the alteration of a single word by Euripides, who employed the rarer term instead of the ordinary one, makes one verse appear beautiful and the other trivial. Aeschylus in his Philoctetes says:

φαγέδαινα <δ'> ἥ μου σάρκας ἐσθίει ποδός.[2]

Euripides substitutes θοινᾶται "feasts on" for ἐσθίει "feeds on." Again, in the line,

νῦν δέ μ' ἐὼν ὀλίγος τε καὶ οὐτιδανὸς καὶ ἀεικής,[3]

the difference will be felt if we substitute the common words,

νῦν δέ μ' ἐὼν μικρός τε καὶ ἀσθενικὸς καὶ ἀειδής.[4]

Or, if for the line,

δίφρον ἀεικέλιον καταθεὶς ὀλίγην τε τράπεζαν,[5]

we read,

δίφρον μοχθηρὸν καταθεὶς μικράν τε τράπεζαν.[6]

Or, for ἠιόνες βοόωσιν,[7] ἠιόνες κράζουσιν.[8]

8. Again, Ariphrades ridiculed the tragedians for using phrases which no one would employ in ordinary speech: for example, δωμάτων ἄπο instead of ἀπὸ δωμάτων, σέθεν, ἐγὼ δέ νιν, Ἀχιλλέως πέρι instead of περὶ Ἀχιλλέως, and the like. It is precisely because such phrases are not part of the current idiom that they give distinction to the style. This, however, he failed to see.

9. It is a great matter to observe propriety in these several modes of expression—compound words, strange (or rare) words, and so

[2] "The cancer, which feeds upon the flesh of his foot."
[3] "But now being of slight consequence, and a weakling, and in disgrace."
[4] "And now being little, and feeble, and shamed."
[5] "Having placed a simple chair and a small table."
[6] "Having placed an ugly chair and a tiny table."
[7] "Shores roar."
[8] "Shores scream."

forth. But the greatest thing by far is to have a command of metaphor. This alone cannot be imparted by another; it is the mark of genius, —for to make good metaphors implies an eye for resemblances.

10. Of the various kinds of words, the compound are best adapted to dithyrambs, rare words to heroic poetry, metaphors to iambic. In heroic poetry, indeed, all these varieties are serviceable. But in iambic verse, which reproduces, as far as may be, familiar speech, the most appropriate words are those which are found even in prose. These are,—the current or proper, the metaphorical, the ornamental.

Concerning Tragedy and imitation by means of action this may suffice.

XXIII

As to that poetic imitation which is narrative in form and employs a single metre, the plot manifestly ought, as in a tragedy, to be constructed on dramatic principles. It should have for its subject a single action, whole and complete, with a beginning, a middle, and an end. It will thus resemble a single and coherent picture of a living being, and produce the pleasure proper to it. It will differ in structure from historical compositions, which of necessity present not a single action, but a single period, and all that happened within that period to one person or to many, little connected together as the events may be. 2. For as the sea-fight at Salamis and the battle with the Carthaginians in Sicily took place at the same time, but did not tend to any one result, so in the sequence of events, one thing sometimes follows another, and yet no single result is thereby produced. Such is the practice, we may say, of most poets. 3. Here again, then, as has been already observed, the transcendent excellence of Homer is manifest. He never attempts to make the whole war of Troy the subject of his poem, though that war had a beginning and an end. It would have been too vast a theme, and not easily embraced in a single view. If, again, he had kept it within moderate limits, it must have been over-complicated by the variety of the incidents. As it is, he detaches a single portion, and admits as episodes many events from the general story of the war—such as the Catalogue of the ships and others— thus diversifying the poem. All other poets take a single hero, a single period, or an action single indeed, but with a multiplicity of parts. Thus did the author of the Cypria and of the Little Iliad. 4. For this reason the Iliad and the Odyssey each furnish the subject of one tragedy, or, at most, of two; while the Cypria supplies materials for many, and the Little Iliad for eight—the Award of the Arms, the Philoctetes, the Neoptolemus, the Eurypylus, the Mendicant Odysseus, the Laconian Women, the Fall of Ilium, the Departure of the Fleet.

XXIV

Again, Epic poetry must have as many kinds as Tragedy: it must be simple, or complex, or "ethical," or "pathetic." The parts also, with the exception of song and scenery, are the same; for it requires Reversals of Intention, Recognitions, and Tragic Incidents. 2. Moreover, the thoughts and the diction must be artistic. In all these respects Homer is our earliest and sufficient model. Indeed each of his poems has a twofold character. The Iliad is at once simple and "pathetic," and the Odyssey complex (for Recognition scenes run through it), and at the same time "ethical." Moreover, in diction and thought he is supreme.

3. Epic poetry differs from Tragedy in the scale on which it is constructed, and in its metre. As regards scale or length, we have already laid down an adequate limit:—the beginning and the end must be capable of being brought within a single view. This condition will be satisfied by poems on a smaller scale than the old epics, and answering in length to the group of tragedies presented at a single sitting.

4. Epic poetry has, however, a great—a special—capacity for enlarging its dimensions, and we can see the reason. In Tragedy we cannot imitate several lines of actions carried on at one and the same time; we must confine ourselves to the action on the stage and the part taken by the players. But in Epic poetry, owing to the narrative form, many events simultaneously transacted can be presented; and these, if relevant to the subject, add mass and dignity to the poem. The Epic has here an advantage, and one that conduces to grandeur of effect, to diverting the mind of the hearer, and relieving the story with varying episodes. For sameness of incident soon produces satiety, and makes tragedies fail on the stage.

5. As for the metre, the heroic measure has proved its fitness by the test of experience. If a narrative poem in any other metre or in many metres were now composed, it would be found incongruous. For of all measures the heroic is the stateliest and the most massive; and hence it most readily admits rare words and metaphors, which

is another point in which the narrative form of imitation stands alone. On the other hand, the iambic and the trochaic tetrameter are stirring measures, the latter being akin to dancing, the former expressive of action. 6. Still more absurd would it be to mix together different metres, as was done by Chaeremon. Hence no one has ever composed a poem on a great scale in any other than heroic verse. Nature herself, as we have said, teaches the choice of the proper measure.

7. Homer, admirable in all respects, has the special merit of being the only poet who rightly appreciates the part he should take himself. The poet should speak as little as possible in his own person, for it is not this that makes him an imitator. Other poets appear themselves upon the scene throughout, and imitate but little and rarely. Homer, after a few prefatory words, at once brings in a man, or woman, or other personage; none of them wanting in characteristic qualities, but each with a character of his own.

8. The element of the wonderful is admitted in Tragedy. The irrational, on which the wonderful depends for its chief effects, has wider scope in Epic poetry, because there the person acting is not seen. Thus, the pursuit of Hector would be ludicrous if placed upon the stage—the Greeks standing still and not joining in the pursuit, and Achilles waving them back. But in the Epic poem the absurdity passes unnoticed. Now the wonderful is pleasing: as may be inferred from the fact that, in telling a story, every one adds something startling of his own, knowing that his hearers like it. 9. It is Homer who has chiefly taught other poets the art of telling lies skilfully. The secret of it lies in a fallacy. For, assuming that if one thing is or becomes, a second is or becomes, men imagine that, if the second is, the first likewise is or becomes. But this is a false inference. Hence, where the first thing is untrue, it is quite unnecessary, provided the second be true, to add that the first is or has become. For the mind, knowing the second to be true, falsely infers the truth of the first. There is an example of this in the Bath Scene of the Odyssey.

10. Accordingly, the poet should prefer probable impossibilities to improbable possibilities. The tragic plot must not be composed of irrational parts. Everything irrational should, if possible, be excluded; or, at all events, it should lie outside the action of the play (as, in the Oedipus, the hero's ignorance as to the manner of Laius' death); not within the drama,—as in the Electra, the messenger's account of the Pythian games; or, as in the Mysians, the man who comes from Tegea to Mysia without speaking. The plea that otherwise the plot

would have been ruined, is ridiculous; such a plot should not in the first instance be constructed. But once the irrational has been introduced and an air of likelihood imparted to it, we must accept it in spite of the absurdity. Take even the irrational incidents in the Odyssey, where Odysseus is left upon the shore of Ithaca. How intolerable even these might have been would be apparent if an inferior poet were to treat the subject. As it is, the absurdity is veiled by the poetic charm with which the poet invests it.

11. The diction should be elaborated in the pauses of the action, where there is no expression of character or thought. For, conversely, character and thought are merely obscured by a diction that is over brilliant.

XXV

With respect to critical difficulties and their solutions, the number and nature of the sources from which they may be drawn may be thus exhibited.

The poet being an imitator, like a painter or any other artist, must of necessity imitate one of three objects,—things as they were or are, things as they are said or thought to be, or things as they ought to be. 2. The vehicle of expression is language,—either current terms or, it may be, rare words or metaphors. There are also many modifications of language, which we concede to the poets. 3. Add to this, that the standard of correctness is not the same in poetry and politics, any more than in poetry and any other art. Within the art of poetry itself there are two kinds of faults,—those which touch its essence, and those which are accidental. 4. If a poet has chosen to imitate something, <but has imitated it incorrectly> through want of capacity, the error is inherent in the poetry. But if the failure is due to a wrong choice—if he has represented a horse as throwing out both his off legs at once, or introduced technical inaccuracies in medicine, for example, or in any other art—the error is not essential to the poetry. These are the points of view from which we should consider and answer the objections raised by the critics.

5. First as to matters which concern the poet's own art. If he describes the impossible, he is guilty of an error; but the error may be justified, if the end of the art be thereby attained (the end being that already mentioned),—if, that is, the effect of this or any other

part of the poem is thus rendered more striking. A case in point is the pursuit of Hector. If, however, the end might have been as well, or better, attained without violating the special rules of the poetic art, the error is not justified: for every kind of error should, if possible, be avoided.

Again, does the error touch the essentials of the poetic art, or some accident of it? For example,—not to know that a hind has no horns is a less serious matter than to paint it inartistically.

6. Further, if it be objected that the description is not true to fact, the poet may perhaps reply,—"But the objects are as they ought to be": just as Sophocles said that he drew men as they ought to be; Euripides, as they are. 7. In this way the objection may be met. If, however, the representation be of neither kind, the poet may answer, —"This is how men say the thing is." This applies to tales about the gods. It may well be that these stories are not higher than fact nor yet true to fact: they are, very possibly, what Xenophanes says of them. But anyhow, "this is what is said." Again a description may be no better than the fact: "still, it was the fact"; as in the passage about the arms: "Upright upon their butt-ends stood the spears." This was the custom then, as it now is among the Illyrians.

8. Again, in examining whether what has been said or done by some one is poetically right or not, we must not look merely to the particular act or saying, and ask whether it is poetically good or bad. We must also consider by whom it is said or done, to whom, when, in whose interest, or for what end; whether, for instance, it be to secure a greater good, or avert a greater evil.

9. Other difficulties may be resolved by due regard to the usage of language. We may note a rare word, as in οὐρῆας μὲν πρῶτον, where the poet perhaps employs οὐρῆας not in the sense of mules, but of sentinels. So, again, of Dolon: "ill-favoured indeed he was to look upon." It is not meant that his body was ill-shaped, but that his face was ugly; for the Cretans use the word εὐειδές, "well-favoured," to denote a fair face. Again, ζωρότερον δὲ κέραιε, "mix the drink livelier," does not mean "mix it stronger" as for hard drinkers, but "mix it quicker."

10. Sometimes an expression is metaphorical, as "Now all gods and men were sleeping through the night,"—while at the same time the poet says: "Often indeed as he turned his gaze to the Trojan plain, he marvelled at the sound of flutes and pipes." "All" is here

used metaphorically for "many," all being a species of many. So in the verse,—"alone she hath no part . . ," οἴη, "alone," is metaphorical; for the best known may be called the only one.

11. Again, the solution may depend upon accent or breathing. Thus Hippias of Thasos solved the difficulties in the line,—δίδομεν (διδόμεν) δέ οἱ, and τὸ μὲν οὗ (οὐ) καταπύθεται ὄμβρῳ.

12. Or again, the question may be solved by punctuation, as in Empedocles,—"Of a sudden things became mortal that before had learnt to be immortal, and things unmixed before mixed."

13. Or again, by ambiguity of construction,—as in παρῴχηκεν δὲ πλέω νύξ, where the word πλέω is ambiguous.

14. Or by the usage of language. Thus any mixed drink is called οἶνος, "wine." Hence Ganymede is said "to pour the wine to Zeus," though the gods do not drink wine. So too workers in iron are called χαλκέας, or workers in bronze. This, however, may also be taken as a metaphor.

15. Again, when a word seems to involve some inconsistency of meaning, we should consider how many senses it may bear in the particular passage. 16. For example: "there was stayed the spear of bronze"—we should ask in how many ways we may take "being checked there." The true mode of interpretation is the precise opposite of what Glaucon mentions. Critics, he says, jump at certain groundless conclusions; they pass adverse judgment and then proceed to reason on it; and, assuming that the poet has said whatever they happen to think, find fault if a thing is inconsistent with their own fancy. The question about Icarius has been treated in this fashion. The critics imagine he was a Lacedaemonian. They think it strange, therefore, that Telemachus should not have met him when he went to Lacedaemon. But the Cephallenian story may perhaps be the true one. They allege that Odysseus took a wife from among themselves, and that her father was Icadius not Icarius. It is merely a mistake, then, that gives plausibility to the objection.

17. In general, the impossible must be justified by reference to artistic requirements, or to the higher reality, or to received opinion. With respect to the requirements of art, a probable impossibility is to be preferred to a thing improbable and yet possible. Again, it may be impossible that there should be men such as Zeuxis painted. "Yes," we say, "but the impossible is the higher thing; for the ideal type must surpass the reality." To justify the irrational, we appeal to what is commonly said to be. In addition to which, we urge that

the irrational sometimes does not violate reason; just as "it is probable that a thing may happen contrary to probability."

18. Things that sound contradictory should be examined by the same rules as in dialectical refutation—whether the same thing is meant, in the same relation, and in the same sense. We should therefore solve the question by reference to what the poet says himself, or to what is tacitly assumed by a person of intelligence.

19. The element of the irrational, and, similarly, depravity of character, are justly censured when there is no inner necessity for introducing them. Such is the irrational element in the Aegeus of Euripides, and the badness of Menelaus in the Orestes.

20. Thus, there are five sources from which critical objections are drawn. Things are censured either as impossible, or irrational, or morally hurtful, or contradictory, or contrary to artistic correctness. The answers should be sought under the twelve heads above mentioned.

XXVI

The question may be raised whether the Epic or Tragic mode of imitation is the higher. If the more refined art is the higher, and the more refined in every case is that which appeals to the better sort of audience, the art which imitates anything and everything is manifestly most unrefined. The audience is supposed to be too dull to comprehend unless something of their own is thrown in by the performers, who therefore indulge in restless movements. Bad flute-players twist and twirl, if they have to represent "the quoit-throw," or hustle the coryphaeus when they perform the "Scylla." 2. Tragedy, it is said, has this same defect. We may compare the opinion that the older actors entertained of their successors. Mynniscus used to call Callippides "ape" on account of the extravagance of his action, and the same view was held of Pindarus. Tragic art, then, as a whole, stands to Epic in the same relation as the younger to the elder actors. So we are told that Epic poetry is addressed to a cultivated audience, who do not need gesture; Tragedy, to an inferior public. 3. Being then unrefined, it is evidently the lower of the two.

Now, in the first place, this censure attaches not to the poetic but to the histrionic art; for gesticulation may be equally overdone in epic recitation, as by Sosistratus, or in lyrical competition, as by Mnasitheus the Opuntian. Next, all action is not to be condemned—

any more than all dancing—but only that of bad performers. Such was the fault found in Callippides, as also in others of our own day, who are censured for representing degraded women. Again, Tragedy like Epic poetry produces its effect even without action; it reveals its power by mere reading. If, then, in all other respects it is superior, this fault, we say, is not inherent in it.

4. And superior it is, because it has all the epic elements—it may even use the epic metre—with the music and scenic effects as important accessories; and these produce the most vivid of pleasures. Further, it has vividness of impression in reading as well as in representation. 5. Moreover, the art attains its end within narrower limits; for the concentrated effect is more pleasurable than one which is spread over a long time and so diluted. What, for example, would be the effect of the Oedipus of Sophocles, if it were cast into a form as long as the Iliad? 6. Once more, the Epic imitation has less unity; as is shown by this, that any Epic poem will furnish subjects for several tragedies. Thus if the story adopted by the poet has a strict unity, it must either be concisely told and appear truncated; or, if it conform to the Epic canon of length, it must seem weak and watery. <Such length implies some loss of unity,> if, I mean, the poem is constructed out of several actions, like the Iliad and the Odyssey, which have many such parts, each with a certain magnitude of its own. Yet these poems are as perfect as possible in structure; each is, in the highest degree attainable, an imitation of a single action.

7. If, then, Tragedy is superior to Epic poetry in all these respects, and, moreover, fulfils its specific function better as an art—for each art ought to produce, not any chance pleasure, but the pleasure proper to it, as already stated—it plainly follows that Tragedy is the higher art, as attaining its end more perfectly.

8. Thus much may suffice concerning Tragic and Epic poetry in general; their several kinds and parts, with the number of each and their differences; the causes that make a poem good or bad; the objections of the critics and the answers to these objections. * * *

*L*ONGINUS

THE true author of *On the Sublime,* and even its approximate date of composition, remain unknown. Francis Robortelli (or Robortello), when he re-published the treatise at Basle (1554), attributed it to Dionysius Longinus. But the oldest known manuscript, belonging to the Tenth Century, attributes the work to "Dionysius or Longinus": i. e., Dionysius of Halicarnassus, First Century rhetorician, or Cassius Longinus of Palmyra, counsellor of Queen Zenobia of Syria, in the Third Century. Internal evidence discloses too little to strengthen the right of either man. Other works of Dionysius reveal little similarity in his thought and expression, and in that of the treatise. But, against Longinus, no author is mentioned who wrote after the First Century, A. D.—a striking omission if Longinus was the author. Also, the treatise sets out to controvert a book *On the Sublime,* written in the First Century by the rhetorician Caecilius, of Sicily. Yet here, too, the path is far from straight. Another rhetorician named Caecilius lived in the reign of Hadrian, though we have no record that he wrote a treatise on the sublime. Many other possible authors have been suggested (Vaucher attributed the work to Plutarch), but with as little reason as men have from time to time ascribed the plays of Shakespeare to Bacon.

This treatise received no mention in ancient records. It was almost unknown until Robortelli published it at Basle (1554). But not until its translation and publication by Boileau (1674) did it receive adequate attention. From that time, it became the bible of neo-classicists, who praised it while disregarding its rules. It taught criticism a new language, but it did not breathe into creative writing the sublimity which the critic praised.

The English title, *On the Sublime,* carries with it a connotation of misty, yet calm, elevation which the author hardly intended. Hall (1652) translated the title "Of the Height of Eloquence;" Pulteney (1680), "A Treatise of the Loftiness or Elegancy of Speech." These clumsy translations are hardly more accurate than the expression *sublime,* nor is there any word that carries the meaning. As Saintsbury [History of Criticism, I, 154] remarks, "it is well to keep it [sublime], with a very careful preliminary explanation that the Longinian Sublime is not sublimity in its narrower sense, but all that quality, or combination of qualities, which creates *enthusiasm* in literature, all that gives consummateness to it, all that deserves the highest critical encomium either in prose or poetry."

This quality of enthusiasm Longinus added to the coldly logical precepts of Aristotle. "Till now," the historian Gibbon wrote in his *Journal,* "I was acquainted only with two ways of criticizing a beautiful passage, the one to show by an exact anatomy of it the distinct beauties of it and whence they sprung; the other an idle exclamation or general encomium, which leaves nothing behind it. Longinus has shown me that there is a third. He tells me his own feelings upon reading it, and tells them with such energy that he communicates them."

This, together with the fact that for the first time a great critic admits, gladly and without qualification, that pleasure is the end of literature, a worthy end in itself, is most striking to modern readers. But Longinus was writing a text-book to a young friend, Postumus, and his criticism was aimed at a practical end. With that aim in mind, he gives five sources of the Sublime, ably summarized by Rhys Roberts [*Longinus on the Sublime*, (1899),]: "The first and most important of these is grandeur of thought—the power of forming great conceptions. This power is founded on nobility of character. Elevated thoughts are also, we are told, the result of the imitation of great models, of imaginative power, and of the choice and grouping of the most striking circumstances. The second source is vehement and inspired passion. While affirming that there is no tone so lofty as that of genuine passion, the author does not treat of this topic in detail, but reserves it for a separate work. Third in order come figures of speech, such as adjuration, rhetorical question, asyndeton, and lastly hyperbaton or inverted order. The writer makes the general remark that a figure is at its best when the very fact that it is a figure escapes attention. The fourth source of sublimity is noble phrasing or diction. The chief element in this is the choice of proper and striking words, a choice which, he says, wonderfully attracts and enthralls the hearer, and breathes into dead things a kind of living voice. Other elements are metaphors, and similes, and hyperbole. Fifthly and finally comes elevation in the arrangement of words. Of this examples are given, and some remarks are added on such specific vices of style as arise from the use of too few words or too many, of too much rhythm or too little. The author concludes with the notable passage in which he endeavours to trace the causes of the dearth of great literature in his own day."

When considered narrowly, *On the Sublime* (or περὶ ὕψους) can be treated as stating simply, as S. H. Monk writes [*The Sublime*, 10–11], "the rhetorical conception of the grand style. . . . The idea that rhetoric is an instrument of emotional transport was dominant among the ancients, and the grand style, the purpose of which was to move, was an integral part of their rhetoric." Aristotle had made a rough distinction [*Rhetoric* III, xii, 1–6, R. C. Jebb's trans.]: "It must not be forgotten that each branch of Rhetoric has its fitting style. There is a difference between the literary and the agonistic style; and, in the latter, between the parliamentary and the forensic style. It is necessary to know both styles. A knowledge of the agonistic style means simply the power of speaking good Greek; a knowledge of the literary style means not being tongue-tied. . . . The literary style is the most accurate; the agonistic is the best adapted to delivery. This fitness depends upon one of two things: expression of character, or expression of emotion." The Roman and Hellenistic critics tended to divide style into set divisions; this tendency is also indicated, more philosophically, in

Cicero's well-known definition (here quoted from *De Optimo Genere Oratorum*) of the best orator: he "teaches, delights, and moves the minds of his hearers; to teach them is his duty, to delight them is creditable to him, to move them is indispensable." In the same manner, the scholastic critics decided, most frequently, on three rhetorical styles: perhaps the work of Dionysius of Halicarnassus [*On Literary Composition,* ed. W. R. Roberts] best illustrates this type of work: ". . . in poetry and in prose, though we all use the same words, we do not put them together in the same manner. I hold, however, that the essentially different varieties of composition are the three following only, to which any one who likes may assign the appropriate names, when he has heard their characteristics and their differences. For my own part, since I cannot find recognised names for them, inasmuch as none exist, I call them by metaphorical terms—the first *austere,* the second *smooth* (or *florid*), the third *harmoniously blended.*" Demetrius [*On Style,* ed. W. R. Roberts] adds a fourth style—the Forcible; another critic, Philodemus, preferred to call it the Vehement. It is worth noting that this attempt to divide rhetoric into rather mechanical styles is traced far back; Dionysius himself regarded Theophrastus (*c.* third century B. C.) as the originator.

Longinus pays little attention to the three styles; he is concerned only with the sublime or elevated. To quote Monk again [*op. cit.,* 12]: "The subject that he wrote on was an old question in rhetoric, and he might easily have repeated the old formulae and illustrated the old figures that were conventionally regarded as conducive to sublimity. . . . But he was at the same time rhetorician and critic, and as a critic he saw more deeply into the nature of art than did most of his fellows." It is this breaking away from the conventional, which had grown mechanical, that attests the superiority of Longinus: he worked with an old critical medium, but he gave to it a new life.

The various lacunae are indicated in the text. At the conclusion, Longinus has stated that he would next discuss the passions—and the loss of this passage is great, for the subject was never honestly treated by the ancients. For all the omissions, he has given us the first example of the application of criticism of literature by the comparative method, in addition to the enthusiasm and the able precepts that characterize his work. Though the treatise has been sadly mutilated, it remains among the greatest—classed by many as the greatest—of early critical works.

ON THE SUBLIME *

I

You will remember, my dear Postumius Terentianus,[1] that when we examined together the treatise of Caecilius on the Sublime, we found that it fell below the dignity of the whole subject, while it failed signally to grasp the essential points, and conveyed to its readers but little of that practical help which it should be a writer's principal aim to give. In every systematic treatise two things are required. The first is a statement of the subject; the other, which although second in order ranks higher in importance, is an indication of the methods by which we may attain our end. Now Caecilius seeks to show the nature of the sublime by countless instances as though our ignorance demanded it, but the consideration of the means whereby we may succeed in raising our own capacities to a certain pitch of elevation he has, strangely enough, omitted as unnecessary. 2. However, it may be that the man ought not so much to be blamed for his shortcomings as praised for his happy thought and his enthusiasm. But since you have urged me, in my turn, to write a brief essay on the sublime for your special gratification, let us consider whether the views I have formed contain anything which will be of use to public men. You will yourself, my friend, in accordance with your nature and with what is fitting, join me in appraising each detail with the utmost regard for truth; for he answered well who, when asked in what qualities we resemble the Gods, declared that we do so in benevolence and truth. 3. As I am writing to you, my good friend, who are well versed in literary studies, I feel almost absolved from the necessity of premising at any length that sublimity is a certain distinction and excellence in expression, and that it is from no other source than this that the greatest poets and writers have derived their eminence and gained an immortality of renown. 4. The effect of elevated language upon an audience is not persuasion but transport. At every time and in every way imposing speech, with the spell it throws over us, prevails over that which aims at persuasion and gratification. Our persuasions we can usually control, but the influences of the sublime bring power and irresistible might to bear,

---

* Trans. by W. Rhys Roberts.
[1] Probably this name (together with another which has disappeared) underlies the reading of P.

and reign supreme over every hearer. Similarly, we see skill in invention, and due order and arrangement of matter, emerging as the hard-won result not of one thing nor of two, but of the whole texture of the composition, whereas Sublimity flashing forth at the right moment scatters everything before it like a thunderbolt, and at once displays the power of the orator in all its plenitude. But enough; for these reflexions, and others like them, you can, I know well, my dear Terentianus, yourself suggest from your own experience.

II

First of all, we must raise the question whether there is such a thing as an art of the sublime or lofty. Some hold that those are entirely in error who would bring such matters under the precepts of art. A lofty tone, says one, is innate, and does not come by teaching; nature is the only art that can compass it. Works of nature are, they think, made worse and altogether feebler when wizened by the rules of art. 2. But I maintain that this will be found to be otherwise if it be observed that, while nature as a rule is free and independent in matters of passion and elevation, yet is she wont not to act at random and utterly without system. Further, nature is the original and vital underlying principle in all cases, but system can define limits and fitting seasons, and can also contribute the safest rules for use and practice. Moreover, the expression of the sublime is more exposed to danger when it goes its own way without the guidance of knowledge,—when it is suffered to be unstable and unballasted,—when it is left at the mercy of mere momentum and ignorant audacity. It is true that it often needs the spur, but it is also true that it often needs the curb. 3. Demosthenes expresses the view, with regard to human life in general, that good fortune is the greatest of blessings, while good counsel, which occupies the second place, is hardly inferior in importance, since its absence contributes inevitably to the ruin of the former. This we may apply to diction, nature occupying the position of good fortune, art that of good counsel. Most important of all, we must remember that the very fact that there are some elements of expression which are in the hands of nature alone, can be learnt from no other source than art. If, I say, the critic of those who desire to learn were to turn these matters over in his mind, he would no longer, it seems to me, regard the discussion of the subject as superfluous or useless. . . .

III

> Quell they the oven's far-flung splendour-glow!
> Ha, let me but one hearth-abider mark—
> One flame-wreath torrent-like I'll whirl on high;
> I'll burn the roof, to cinders shrivel it!—
> Nay, now my chant is not of noble strain.[2]

Such things are not tragic but pseudo-tragic—"flame-wreaths," and "belching to the sky," and Boreas represented as a "flute-player," and all the rest of it. They are turbid in expression and confused in imagery rather than the product of intensity, and each one of them, if examined in the light of day, sinks little by little from the terrible into the contemptible. But since even in tragedy, which is in its very nature stately and prone to bombast, tasteless tumidity is unpardonable, still less, I presume, will it harmonise with the narration of fact. 2. And this is the ground on which the phrases of Gorgias of Leontini are ridiculed when he describes Xerxes as the "Zeus of the Persians" and vultures as "living tombs." So is it with some of the expressions of Callisthenes which are not sublime but high-flown, and still more with those of Cleitarchus, for the man is frivolous and blows, as Sophocles has it,

On pigmy hautboys: mouthpiece have they none.[3]

Other examples will be found in Amphicrates and Hegesias and Matris, for often when these writers seem to themselves to be inspired they are in no true frenzy but are simply trifling. 3. Altogether, tumidity seems particularly hard to avoid. The explanation is that all who aim at elevation are so anxious to escape the reproach of being weak and dry that they are carried, as by some strange law of nature, into the opposite extreme. They put their trust in the maxim that "failure in a great attempt is at least a noble error." 4. But evil are the swellings, both in the body and in diction, which are inflated and unreal, and threaten us with the reverse of our aim; for nothing, say they, is drier than a man who has the dropsy. While tumidity desires to transcend the limits of the sublime, the defect which is termed puerility is the direct antithesis of elevation, for it is utterly low and mean and in real truth the most ignoble vice of style. What, then, is this puerility? Clearly, a pedant's thoughts, which begin in

[2] *Aeschvlus.*—Translated by A. S. Way.   [3] *Sophocles.*—-Translated by A. S. Way.

learned trifling and end in frigidity. Men slip into this kind of error because, while they aim at the uncommon and elaborate and most of all at the attractive, they drift unawares into the tawdry and affected. 5. A third, and closely allied, kind of defect in matters of passion is that which Theodorus used to call *parenthyrsus*. By this is meant unseasonable and empty passion, where no passion is required, or immoderate, where moderation is needed. For men are often carried away, as if by intoxication, into displays of emotion which are not caused by the nature of the subject, but are purely personal and wearisome. In consequence they seem to hearers who are in no wise affected to act in an ungainly way. And no wonder; for they are beside themselves, while their hearers are not. But the question of the passions we reserve for separate treatment.

IV

Of the second fault of which we have spoken—frigidity—Timaeus supplies many examples. Timaeus was a writer of considerable general ability, who occasionally showed that he was not incapable of elevation of style. He was learned and ingenious, but very prone to criticise the faults of others while blind to his own. Through his passion for continually starting novel notions, he often fell into the merest childishness. 2. I will set down one or two examples only of his manner, since the greater number have been already appropriated by Caecilius. In the course of a eulogy on Alexander the Great, he describes him as "the man who gained possession of the whole of Asia in fewer years than it took Isocrates to write his *Panegyric* urging war against the Persians." [4] Strange indeed is the comparison of the man of Macedon with the rhetorician. How plain it is, Timaeus, that the Lacedaemonians, thus judged, were far inferior to Isocrates in prowess, for they spent thirty years in the conquest of Messene, whereas he composed his *Panegyric* in ten. 3. Consider again the way in which he speaks of the Athenians who were captured in Sicily. "They were punished because they had acted impiously towards Hermes and mutilated his images, and the infliction of punishment was chiefly due to Hermocrates the son of Hermon, who was descended, in the paternal line, from the outraged god." [4] I am surprised, beloved Terentianus, that he does not write with regard to the despot Dionysius that "Dion and Heracleides deprived him of his sover-

[4] *Timaeus.*

eignty because he had acted impiously towards Zeus and Heracles."
4. But why speak of Timaeus when even those heroes of literature,
Xenophon and Plato, though trained in the school of Socrates, nevertheless sometimes forget themselves for the sake of such paltry pleas-
antries? Xenophon writes in the *Polity of the Lacedaemonians:* "You
would find it harder to hear their voice than that of busts of marble,
harder to deflect their gaze than that of statues of bronze; you would
deem them more modest than the very maidens in their eyes." [5]

It was worthy of an Amphicrates and not of a Xenophon to call
the pupils of our eyes "modest maidens." Good heavens, how strange
it is that the pupils of the whole company should be believed to be
modest notwithstanding the common saying that the shamelessness
of individuals is indicated by nothing so much as the eyes! "Thou
sot, that hast the eyes of a dog," as Homer has it.[6] 5. Timaeus, however, has not left even this piece of frigidity to Xenophon, but clutches
it as though it were hid treasure. At all events, after saying of
Agathocles that he abducted his cousin, who had been given in marriage to another man, from the midst of the nuptial rites, he asks,
"Who could have done this had he not had wantons, in place of
maidens, in his eyes?" 6. Yes, and Plato (usually so divine) when he
means simply *tablets* says, "They shall write and preserve *cypress
memorials* in the temples." [7]

And again, "As touching walls, Megillus, I should hold with Sparta
that they be suffered to lie asleep in the earth and not summoned to
arise." [8] 7. The expression of Herodotus to the effect that beautiful
women are "eye-smarts" is not much better.[9] This, however, may
be condoned in some degree since those who use this particular phrase
in his narrative are barbarians and in their cups, but not even in
the mouths of such characters is it well that an author should suffer,
in the judgment of posterity, from an unseemly exhibition of triviality.

V

All these ugly and parasitical growths arise in literature from a
single cause, that pursuit of novelty in the expression of ideas which
may be regarded as the fashionable craze of the day. Our defects
usually spring, for the most part, from the same sources as our good

[5] Xen. *de Rep. Laced.* III. 5.
[6] *Iliad* I. 225.
[7] Plato, *Legg.* V. 741 C.

[8] Plato, *Legg.* VI. 778 D.
[9] Herod. V. 18.

points. Hence, while beauties of expression and touches of sublimity, and charming elegances withal, are favourable to effective composition, yet these very things are the elements and foundation, not only of success, but also of the contrary. Something of the kind is true also of variations and hyperboles and the use of the plural number, and we shall show subsequently the dangers to which these seem severally to be exposed. It is necessary now to seek and to suggest means by which we may avoid the defects which attend the steps of the sublime.

VI

The best means would be, my friend, to gain, first of all, clear knowledge and appreciation of the true sublime. The enterprise is, however, an arduous one. For the judgment of style is the last and crowning fruit of long experience. None the less, if I must speak in the way of precept, it is not impossible perhaps to acquire discrimination in these matters by attention to some such hints as those which follow.

VII

You must know, my dear friend, that it is with the sublime as in the common life of man. In life nothing can be considered great which it is held great to despise. For instance, riches, honours, distinctions, sovereignties, and all other things which possess in abundance the external trappings of the stage, will not seem, to a man of sense, to be supreme blessings, since the very contempt of them is reckoned good in no small degree, and in any case those who could have them, but are high-souled enough to disdain them, are more admired than those who have them. So also in the case of sublimity in poems and prose writings, we must consider whether some supposed examples have not simply the appearance of elevation with many idle accretions, so that when analysed they are found to be mere vanity—objects which a noble nature will rather despise than admire. 2. For, as if instinctively, our soul is uplifted by the true sublime; it takes a proud flight, and is filled with joy and vaunting, as though it had itself produced what it has heard. 3. When, therefore, a thing is heard repeatedly by a man of intelligence, who is well versed in literature, and its effect is not to dispose the soul to high thoughts, and it does not leave in the mind more food for reflexion than the words seem to convey, but falls, if examined carefully through and through, into disesteem, it cannot rank as true sublimity because it does not survive a first hearing. For that is really great which bears a repeated examination, and which it is difficult or rather impossible to withstand, and the memory of which is strong and hard to efface. 4. In general, consider those examples of sublimity to be fine and genuine which please all and always. For when men of different pursuits, lives, ambitions, ages, languages, hold identical views on one and the same subject, then that verdict which results, so to speak, from a concert of discordant elements makes our faith in the object of admiration strong and unassailable.

VIII

There are, it may be said, five principal sources of elevated language. Beneath these five varieties there lies, as though it were a common foundation, the gift of discourse, which is indispensable. First and most important is the power of forming great conceptions, as we have elsewhere explained in our remarks on Xenophon. Secondly, there is vehement and inspired passion. These two components of the sublime are for the most part innate. Those which remain are partly the product of art. The due formation of figures deals with two sorts of figures, first those of thought and secondly those of expression. Next there is noble diction, which in turn comprises choice of words, and use of metaphors, and elaboration of language. The fifth cause of elevation—one which is the fitting conclusion of all that have preceded it—is dignified and elevated composition. Come now, let us consider what is involved in each of these varieties, with this one remark by way of preface, that Caecilius has omitted some of the five divisions, for example, that of passion. 2. Surely he is quite mistaken if he does so on the ground that these two, sublimity and passion, are a unity, and if it seems to him that they are by nature one and inseparable. For some passions are found which are far removed from sublimity and are of a low order, such as pity, grief and fear; and on the other hand there are many examples of the sublime which are independent of passion, such as the daring words of Homer with regard to the Aloadae, to take one out of numberless instances,

Yea, Ossa in fury they strove to upheave on Olympus on high,
With forest-clad Pelion above, that thence they might step to the sky.[10]

[10] *Odyss.* XI. 315, 316.

And so of the words which follow with still greater force:—

Ay, and the deed had they done.[11]

3. Among the orators, too, eulogies and ceremonial and occasional addresses contain on every side examples of dignity and elevation, but are for the most part void of passion. This is the reason why passionate speakers are the worst eulogists, and why, on the other hand, those who are apt in encomium are the least passionate. 4. If, on the other hand, Caecilius thought that passion never contributes at all to sublimity, and if it was for this reason that he did not deem it worthy of mention, he is altogether deluded. I would affirm with confidence that there is no tone so lofty as that of genuine passion, in its right place, when it bursts out in a wild gust of mad enthusiasm and as it were fills the speaker's words with frenzy.

IX

Now the first of the conditions mentioned, namely elevation of mind, holds the foremost rank among them all. We must, therefore, in this case also, although we have to do rather with an endowment than with an acquirement, nurture our souls (as far as that is possible) to thoughts sublime, and make them always pregnant, so to say, with noble inspiration. 2. In what way, you may ask, is this to be done? Elsewhere I have written as follows: "Sublimity is the echo of a great soul." Hence also a bare idea, by itself and without a spoken word, sometimes excites admiration just because of the greatness of soul implied. Thus the silence of Ajax in the Underworld is great and more sublime than words.[12] 3. First, then, it is absolutely necessary to indicate the source of this elevation, namely, that the truly eloquent must be free from low and ignoble thoughts. For it is not possible that men with mean and servile ideas and aims prevailing throughout their lives should produce anything that is admirable and worthy of immortality. Great accents we expect to fall from the lips of those whose thoughts are deep and grave. 4. Thus it is that stately speech comes naturally to the proudest spirits. [You will remember the answer of] Alexander to Parmenio when he said "For my part I had been well content."[13] . . .

[11] *Odyss.* XI. 317.   [13] Quotation from Arrian.
[12] *Odyss.* XI. 543.

... the distance from earth to heaven; and this might well be considered the measure of Homer no less than of Strife. 5. How unlike to this the expression which is used of Sorrow by Hesiod, if indeed the *Shield* is to be attributed to Hesiod:

> Rheum from her nostrils was trickling.[14]

The image he has suggested is not terrible but rather loathsome. Contrast the way in which Homer magnifies the higher powers:

> And far as a man with his eyes through the sea-line haze may discern,
> On a cliff as he sitteth and gazeth away o'er the wine-dark deep,
> So far at a bound do the loud-neighing steeds of the Deathless leap.[15]

He makes the vastness of the world the measure of their leap. The sublimity is so overpowering as naturally to prompt the exclamation that if the divine steeds were to leap thus twice in succession they would pass beyond the confines of the world. 6. How transcendent also are the images in the Battle of the Gods:—

> Far round wide heaven and Olympus echoed his clarion of thunder;
> And Hades, king of the realm of shadows, quaked thereunder.
> And he sprang from his throne, and he cried aloud in the dread of his heart
> Lest o'er him earth-shaker Poseidon should cleave the ground apart,
> And revealed to Immortals and mortals should stand those awful abodes,
> Those mansions ghastly and grim, abhorred of the very Gods.[16]

You see, my friend, how the earth is torn from its foundations, Tartarus itself is laid bare, the whole world is upturned and parted asunder, and all things together—heaven and hell, things mortal and things immortal—share in the conflict and the perils of that battle! 7. But although these things are awe-inspiring, yet from another point of view, if they be not taken allegorically, they are altogether impious, and violate our sense of what is fitting. Homer seems to me, in his legends of wounds suffered by the gods, and of their feuds, reprisals, tears, bonds, and all their manifold passions, to have made, as far as lay within his power, gods of the men concerned in the Siege of Troy, and men of the gods. But whereas we mortals have death as the destined haven of our ills if our lot is miserable, he por-

---

[14] Hesiod, *Scut.* 267.
[15] *Il.* v. 770.
[16] *Il.* XXI. 388, XX. 61–65.

trays the gods as immortal not only in nature but also in misfortune.
8. Much superior to the passages respecting the Battle of the Gods
are those which represent the divine nature as it really is—pure and
great and undefiled; for example, what is said of Poseidon in a passage fully treated by many before ourselves:

> Her far-stretching ridges, her forest-trees, quaked in dismay,
> And her peaks, and the Trojans' town, and the ships of Achaia's array,
> Beneath his immortal feet, as onward Poseidon strode.
> Then over the surges he drave: leapt sporting before the God
> Sea-beasts that uprose all around from the depths, for their king they knew,
> And for rapture the sea was disparted, and onward the car-steeds flew.[17]

9. Similarly, the legislator of the Jews, no ordinary man, having
formed and expressed a worthy conception of the might of the Godhead, writes at the very beginning of his Laws, "God said,"—what?
"Let there be light, and there was light; let there be land, and there
was land." [18] 10. Perhaps I shall not seem tedious, my friend, if I
bring forward one passage more from Homer—this time with regard
to the concerns of *men*—in order to show that he is wont himself
to enter into the sublime actions of his heroes. In his poem the battle
of the Greeks is suddenly veiled by mist and baffling night. Then
Ajax, at his wits' end, cries:

> Zeus, Father, yet save thou Achaia's sons from beneath the gloom,
> And make clear day, and vouchsafe unto us with our eyes to see!
> So it be but in light, destroy us! [19]

That is the true attitude of an Ajax. He does not pray for life, for
such a petition would have ill beseemed a hero. But since in the
hopeless darkness he can turn his valour to no noble end, he chafes
at his slackness in the fray and craves the boon of immediate light,
resolved to find a death worthy of his bravery, even though Zeus
should fight in the ranks against him. 11. In truth, Homer in these
cases shares the full inspiration of the combat, and it is neither more
nor less than true of the poet himself that

> Mad rageth he as Arês the shaker of spears, or as mad flames leap
> Wild-wasting from hill unto hill in the folds of a forest deep,
> And the foam-froth fringeth his lips.[20]

[17] *Il.* XIII. 18, XX. 60, XIII. 19, XIII. 27–29.
[18] *Moses.*

[19] *Il.* XVII. 645–647.
[20] *Il.* XV. 605–607.

He shows, however, in the Odyssey (and this further observation deserves attention on many grounds) that, when a great genius is declining, the special token of old age is the love of marvellous tales. 12. It is clear from many indications that the Odyssey was his second subject. A special proof is the fact that he introduces in that poem remnants of the adventures before Ilium as episodes, so to say, of the Trojan War. And indeed, he there renders a tribute of mourning and lamentation to his heroes as though he were carrying out a long-cherished purpose. In fact, the Odyssey is simply an epilogue to the Iliad:—

There lieth Ajax the warrior wight, Achilles is there,
There is Patroclus, whose words had weight as a God he were;
There lieth mine own dear son.[21]

13. It is for the same reason, I suppose, that he has made the whole structure of the Iliad, which was written at the height of his inspiration, full of action and conflict, while the Odyssey for the most part consists of narrative, as is characteristic of old age. Accordingly, in the Odyssey Homer may be likened to a sinking sun, whose grandeur remains without its intensity. He does not in the Odyssey maintain so high a pitch as in those poems of Ilium. His sublimities are not evenly sustained and free from the liability to sink; there is not the same profusion of accumulated passions, nor the supple and oratorical style, packed with images drawn from real life. You seem to see henceforth the ebb and flow of greatness, and a fancy roving in the fabulous and incredible, as though the ocean were withdrawing into itself and were being laid bare within its own confines. 14. In saying this I have not forgotten the tempests in the Odyssey and the story of the Cyclops and the like. If I speak of old age, it is nevertheless the old age of Homer. The fabulous element, however, prevails throughout this poem over the real. The object of this digression has been, as I said, to show how easily great natures in their decline are sometimes diverted into absurdity, as in the incident of the wine-skin and of the men who were fed like swine by Circe (*whining porkers*, as Zoilus called them), and of Zeus like a nestling nurtured by the doves, and of the hero who was without food for ten days upon the wreck, and of the incredible tale of the slaying of the suitors.[22] For what else can we term these things than veritable dreams of Zeus?

[21] *Odyss.* III. 109–111.   XII. 447, XXII. 79.
[22] *Odyss.* IX. 182, X. 17, X. 237, XII. 62.

15. These observations with regard to the Odyssey should be made for another reason—in order that you may know that the genius of great poets and prose-writers, as their passion declines, finds its final expression in the delineation of character. For such are the details which Homer gives, with an eye to characterisation, of life in the home of Odysseus; they form as it were a comedy of manners.

X

Let us next consider whether we can point to anything further that contributes to sublimity of style. Now, there inhere in all things by nature certain constituents which are part and parcel of their substance. It must needs be, therefore, that we shall find one source of the sublime in the systematic selection of the most important elements, and the power of forming, by their mutual combination, what may be called one body. The former process attracts the hearer by the choice of the ideas, the latter by the aggregation of those chosen. For instance, Sappho everywhere chooses the emotions that attend delirious passion from its accompaniments in actual life. Wherein does she demonstrate her supreme excellence? In the skill with which she selects and binds together the most striking and vehement circumstances of passion:—

> 2. Peer of Gods he seemeth to me, the blissful
>   Man who sits and gazes at thee before him,
>   Close beside thee sits, and in silence hears thee
>   Silverly speaking,
>
>   Laughing love's low laughter. Oh this, this only
>   Stirs the troubled heart in my breast to tremble!
>   For should I but see thee a little moment,
>   Straight is my voice hushed;
>
>   Yea, my tongue is broken, and through and through me
>   'Neath the flesh impalpable fire runs tingling;
>   Nothing see mine eyes, and a noise of roaring
>   Waves in my ear sounds;
>
>   Sweat runs down in rivers, a tremor seizes
>   All my limbs, and paler than grass in autumn,
>   Caught by pains of menacing death, I falter,
>   Lost in the love-trance.[23]

[23] *Sappho.*

3. Are you not amazed how at one instant she summons, as though they were all alien from herself and dispersed, soul, body, ears, tongue, eyes, colour? Uniting contradictions, she is, at one and the same time, hot and cold, in her senses and out of her mind, for she is either terrified or at the point of death. The effect desired is that not one passion only should be seen in her, but a concourse of the passions. All such things occur in the case of lovers, but it is, as I said, the selection of the most striking of them and their combination into a single whole that has produced the singular excellence of the passage. In the same way Homer, when describing tempests, picks out the most appalling circumstances. 4. The author of the *Arimaspeia* thinks to inspire awe in the following way:—

A marvel exceeding great is this withal to my soul—
Men dwell on the water afar from the land, where deep seas roll.
Wretches are they, for they reap but a harvest of travail and pain,
Their eyes on the stars ever dwell, while their hearts abide in the main.
Often, I ween, to the Gods are their hands upraised on high,
And with hearts in misery heavenward-lifted in prayer do they cry.[24]

It is clear, I imagine, to everybody that there is more elegance than terror in these words. 5. But what says Homer? Let one instance be quoted from among many:—

And he burst on them like as a wave swift-rushing beneath black clouds,
Heaved huge by the winds, bursts down on a ship, and the wild foam
    shrouds
From the stem to the stern her hull, and the storm-blast's terrible breath
Roars in the sail, and the heart of the shipmen shuddereth
In fear, for that scantly upborne are they now from the clutches of death.[25]

6. Aratus has attempted to convert this same expression to his own use:—

And a slender plank averteth their death.[26]

Only, he has made it trivial and neat instead of terrible. Furthermore, he has put bounds to the danger by saying *A plank keeps off death*. After all, it *does* keep it off. Homer, however, does not for one moment set a limit to the terror of the scene, but draws a vivid picture

---

[24] *Aristeas.*   [26] *Aratus.*
[25] *Il.* xv. 624–628.

of men continually in peril of their lives, and often within an ace of perishing with each successive wave. Moreover, he has in the words ὑπὲκ θανάτοιο, forced into union, by a kind of unnatural compulsion, prepositions not usually compounded. He has thus tortured his line into the similitude of the impending calamity, and by the constriction of the verse has excellently figured the disaster, and almost stamped upon the expression the very form and pressure of the danger, ὑπὲκ θανάτοιο φέρονται. 7. This is true also of Archilochus in his account of the shipwreck, and of Demosthenes in the passage which begins "It was evening," where he describes the bringing of the news.[27] The salient points they selected, one might say, according to merit and massed them together, inserting in the midst nothing frivolous, mean, or trivial. For these faults mar the effect of the whole, just as though they introduced chinks or fissures into stately and co-ordered edifices, whose walls are compacted by their reciprocal adjustment.

XI

An allied excellence to those already set forth is that which is termed *amplification*. This figure is employed when the narrative or the course of a forensic argument admits, from section to section, of many starting-points and many pauses, and elevated expressions follow, one after the other, in an unbroken succession and in an ascending order. 2. And this may be effected either by way of the rhetorical treatment of commonplaces, or by way of intensification (whether events or arguments are to be strongly presented), or by the orderly arrangement of facts or of passions; indeed, there are innumerable kinds of amplification. Only, the orator must in every case remember that none of these methods by itself, apart from sublimity, forms a complete whole, unless indeed where pity is to be excited or an opponent to be disparaged. In all other cases of amplification, if you take away the sublime, you will remove as it were the soul from the body. For the vigour of the amplification at once loses its intensity and its substance when not resting on a firm basis of the sublime. 3. Clearness, however, demands that we should define concisely how our present precepts differ from the point under consideration a moment ago, namely the marking-out of the most striking conceptions and the unification of them; and wherein, generally, the sublime differs from amplification.

[27] Demosth. *De Cor.*, 169.

XII

Now the definition given by the writers on rhetoric does not satisfy me. Amplification is, say they, discourse which invests the subject with grandeur. This definition, however, would surely apply in equal measure to sublimity and passion and figurative language, since they too invest the discourse with a certain degree of grandeur. The point of distinction between them seems to me to be that sublimity consists in elevation, while amplification embraces a multitude of details. Consequently, sublimity is often comprised in a single thought, while amplification is universally associated with a certain magnitude and abundance. 2. Amplification (to sum the matter up in a general way) is an aggregation of all the constituent parts and topics of a subject, lending strength to the argument by dwelling upon it, and differing herein from proof that, while the latter demonstrates the matter under investigation. . . .

With his vast riches Plato swells, like some sea, into a greatness which expands on every side. 3. Wherefore it is, I suppose, that the orator in his utterance shows, as one who appeals more to the passions, all the glow of a fiery spirit. Plato, on the other hand, firm-planted in his pride and magnificent stateliness, cannot indeed be accused of coldness, but he has not the same vehemence. 4. And it is in these same respects, my dear friend Terentianus, that it seems to me (supposing always that we Greeks are allowed to have an opinion upon the point) that Cicero differs from Demosthenes in elevated passages. For the latter is characterised by sublimity which is for the most part rugged, Cicero by profusion. Our orator,[28] owing to the fact that in his vehemence,—aye, and in his speed, power and intensity,—he can as it were consume by fire and carry away all before him, may be compared to a thunderbolt or flash of lightning. Cicero, on the other hand, it seems to me, after the manner of a wide-spread conflagration, rolls on with all-devouring flames, having within him an ample and abiding store of fire, distributed now at this point now at that, and fed by an unceasing succession. 5. This, however, you [29] will be better able to decide; but the great opportunity of Demosthenes' high-pitched elevation comes where intense utterance and vehement passion are in question, and in passages in which the audience is to be utterly enthralled. The profusion of Cicero is in place where the hearer must be flooded with words, for it is appropriate

[28] Sc. Demosthenes.   [29] Sc. "you Romans."

to the treatment of commonplaces, and to perorations for the most part and digressions, and to all descriptive and declamatory passages, and to writings on history and natural science, and to many other departments of literature.

XIII

To return from my digression. Although Plato thus flows on with noiseless stream, he is none the less elevated. You know this because you have read the *Republic* and are familiar with his manner. "Those," says he, "who are destitute of wisdom and goodness and are ever present at carousals and the like are carried on the downward path, it seems, and wander thus throughout their life. They never look upwards to the truth, nor do they lift their heads, nor enjoy any pure and lasting pleasure, but like cattle they have their eyes ever cast downwards and bent upon the ground and upon their feeding-places, and they graze and grow fat and breed, and through their insatiate desire of these delights they kick and butt with horns and hoofs of iron and kill one another in their greed." [30]

2. This writer shows us, if only we were willing to pay him heed, that another way (beyond anything we have mentioned) leads to the sublime. And what, and what manner of way, may that be? It is the imitation and emulation of previous great poets and writers. And let this, my dear friend, be an aim to which we steadfastly apply ourselves. For many men are carried away by the spirit of others as if inspired, just as it is related of the Pythian priestess when she approaches the tripod, where there is a rift in the ground which (they say) exhales divine vapour. By heavenly power thus communicated she is impregnated and straightway delivers oracles in virtue of the afflatus. Similarly from the great natures of the men of old there are borne in upon the souls of those who emulate them (as from sacred caves) what we may describe as *effluences,* so that even those who seem little likely to be possessed are thereby inspired and succumb to the spell of the others' greatness. 3. Was Herodotus alone a devoted imitator of Homer? No, Stesichorus even before his time, and Archilochus, and above all Plato, who from the great Homeric source drew to himself innumerable tributary streams. And perhaps we should have found it necessary to prove this, point by point, had not Ammonius and his followers selected and recorded the particu-

[30] Pl. *Rep.* ix. 586 A.

lars. 4. This proceeding is not plagiarism; it is like taking an impression from beautiful forms or figures or other works of art. And it seems to me that there would not have been so fine a bloom of perfection on Plato's philosophical doctrines, and that he would not in many cases have found his way to poetical subject-matter and modes of expression, unless he had with all his heart and mind struggled with Homer for the primacy, entering the lists like a young champion matched against the man whom all admire, and showing perhaps too much love of contention and breaking a lance with him as it were, but deriving some profit from the contest none the less. For, as Hesiod says, "This strife is good for mortals." [81] And in truth that struggle for the crown of glory is noble and best deserves the victory in which even to be worsted by one's predecessors brings no discredit.

XIV

Accordingly it is well that we ourselves also, when elaborating anything which requires lofty expression and elevated conception, should shape some idea in our minds as to how perchance Homer would have said this very thing, or how it would have been raised to the sublime by Plato or Demosthenes or by the historian Thucydides. For those personages, presenting themselves to us and inflaming our ardour and as it were illumining our path, will carry our minds in a mysterious way to the high standards of sublimity which are imaged within us. 2. Still more effectual will it be to suggest this question to our thoughts, "What sort of hearing would Homer, had he been present, or Demosthenes have given to this or that when said by me, or how would they have been affected by the other?" For the ordeal is indeed a severe one, if we presuppose such a tribunal and theatre for our own utterances, and imagine that we are undergoing a scrutiny of our writings before these great heroes, acting as judges and witnesses. 3. A greater incentive still will be supplied if you add the question, "In what spirit will each succeeding age listen to me who have written thus?" But if one shrinks from the very thought of uttering aught that may transcend the term of his own life and time, the conceptions of his mind must necessarily be incomplete, blind, and as it were untimely born, since they are by no means brought to the perfection needed to ensure a futurity of fame.

[81] Hes. *Op. et D.* 24.

XV

Images, moreover, contribute greatly, my young friend, to dignity, elevation, and power as a pleader. In this sense some call them mental representations. In a general way the name of *image* or *imagination* is applied to every idea of the mind, in whatever form it presents itself, which gives birth to speech. But at the present day the word is predominantly used in cases where, carried away by enthusiasm and passion, you think you see what you describe, and you place it before the eyes of your hearers. 2. Further, you will be aware of the fact that an image has one purpose with the orators and another with the poets, and that the design of the poetical image is enthralment, of the rhetorical—vivid description. Both, however, seek to stir the passions and the emotions.

> Mother!—'beseech thee, hark not thou on me
> Yon maidens gory-eyed and snaky-haired!
> Lo there!—lo there!—they are nigh—they leap on me! [32]

And:

> Ah! she will slay me! whither can I fly? [33]

In these scenes the poet himself saw Furies, and the image in his mind he almost compelled his audience also to behold. 3. Now, Euripides is most assiduous in giving the utmost tragic effect to these two emotions—fits of love and madness. Herein he succeeds more, perhaps, than in any other respect, although he is daring enough to invade all the other regions of the imagination. Notwithstanding that he is by nature anything but elevated, he forces his own genius, in many passages, to tragic heights, and everywhere in the matter of sublimity it is true of him (to adopt Homer's words) that

The tail of him scourgeth his ribs and his flanks to left and to right,
And he lasheth himself into frenzy, and spurreth him on to the fight.[34]

4. When the Sun hands the reins to Phaethon, he says

> "Thou, driving, trespass not on Libya's sky,
>   Whose heat, by dews untempered, else shall split
>   Thy car asunder."

[32] Eurip. *Orest.* 255.
[33] Eurip. *Iph. in T.* 291.
[34] *Il.* xx. 170. l.

And after that,

> "Speed onward toward the Pleiads seven thy course."
> Thus far the boy heard; then he snatched the reins:
> He lashed the flanks of that wing-wafted team;
> Loosed rein; and they through folds of cloudland soared.
> Hard after on a fiery star his sire
> Rode, counselling his son—"Ho! thither drive!
> Hither thy car turn—hither!" [85]

Would you not say that the soul of the writer enters the chariot at the same moment as Phaethon and shares in his dangers and in the rapid flight of his steeds? For it could never have conceived such a picture had it not been borne in no less swift career on that journey through the heavens. The same is true of the words which Euripides attributes to his Cassandra:—

> O chariot-loving Trojans. [86]

5. Aeschylus, too, ventures on images of a most heroic stamp. An example will be found in his *Seven against Thebes,* where he says

> For seven heroes, squadron-captains fierce,
> Over a black-rimmed shield have slain a bull,
> And, dipping in the bull's blood each his hand,
> By Ares and Enyo, and by Panic
> Lover of blood, have sworn. [87]

In mutual fealty they devoted themselves by that joint oath to a relentless doom. Sometimes, however, he introduces ideas that are rough-hewn and uncouth and harsh; and Euripides, when stirred by the spirit of emulation, comes perilously near the same fault, even in spite of his own natural bent. 6. Thus in Aeschylus the palace of Lycurgus at the coming of Dionysus is strangely represented as *possessed:*—

> A frenzy thrills the hall; the roofs are bacchant
> With ecstasy: [88]

an idea which Euripides has echoed, in other words, it is true, and with some abatement of its crudity, where he says:—

> The whole mount shared their bacchic ecstasy. [89]

---

[85] *Euripides.*
[86] *Euripides.*
[87] *Aesch. S. c. Th.* 42.

[88] *Aeschylus.*
[89] Eurip. *Bacchae,* 726.

7. Magnificent are the images which Sophocles has conceived of the death of Oedipus, who makes ready his burial amid the portents of the sky.[40] Magnificent, too, is the passage where the Greeks are on the point of sailing away and Achilles appears above his tomb to those who are putting out to sea—a scene which I doubt whether anyone has depicted more vividly than Simonides.[41] But it is impossible to cite all the examples that present themselves. 8. It is no doubt true that those which are found in the poets contain, as I said, a tendency to exaggeration in the way of the fabulous and that they transcend in every way the credible, but in oratorical imagery the best feature is always its reality and truth. Whenever the form of a speech is poetical and fabulous and breaks into every kind of impossibility, such digressions have a strange and alien air. For example, the clever orators forsooth of our day, like the tragedians, see Furies, and—fine fellows that they are—cannot even understand that Orestes when he cries

> Unhand me!—of mine Haunting Fiends thou art—
> Dost grip my waist to hurl me into hell![42]

has these fancies because he is mad. 9. What, then, can oratorical imagery effect? Well, it is able in many ways to infuse vehemence and passion into spoken words, while more particularly when it is combined with the argumentative passages it not only persuades the hearer but actually makes him its slave. Here is an example. "Why, if at this very moment," says Demosthenes, "a loud cry were to be heard in front of the courts, and we were told that the prison-house lies open and the prisoners are in full flight, no one, whether he be old or young, is so heedless as not to lend aid to the utmost of his power; aye, and if anyone came forward and said that yonder stands the man who let them go, the offender would be promptly put to death without a hearing."[43] 10. In the same way, too, Hyperides on being accused, after he had proposed the liberation of the slaves subsequently to the great defeat, said "This proposal was framed, not by the orator, but by the battle of Chaeroneia."[44] The speaker has here at one and the same time followed a train of reasoning and indulged a flight of imagination. He has, therefore, passed the bounds of mere persuasion by the boldness of his conception. 11. By a sort of natural law in all such matters we always attend to whatever possesses superior force; whence it is that we are

[40] Soph. *Oed. Col.* 1586.
[41] *Simonides.*
[42] Eurip. *Orest.* 264.

[43] Demosth. *c. Timocr.* 208.
[44] *Hyperides.*

drawn away from demonstration pure and simple to any startling image within whose dazzling brilliancy the argument lies concealed. And it is not unreasonable that we should be affected in this way, for when two things are brought together, the more powerful always attracts to itself the virtue of the weaker. 12. It will be enough to have said thus much with regard to examples of the sublime in thought, when produced by greatness of soul, imitation, or imagery.

XVI

Here, however, in due order comes the place assigned to Figures; for they, if handled in the proper manner, will contribute, as I have said, in no mean degree to sublimity. But since to treat thoroughly of them all at the present moment would be a great, or rather an endless task, we will now, with the object of proving our proposition, run over a few only of those which produce elevation of diction. 2. Demosthenes is bringing forward a reasoned vindication of his public policy. What was the natural way of treating the subject? It was this. "You were not wrong, you who engaged in the struggle for the freedom of Greece. You have domestic warrant for it. For the warriors of Marathon did no wrong, nor they of Salamis, nor they of Plataea." [45] When, however, as though suddenly inspired by heaven and as it were frenzied by the God of Prophecy, he utters his famous oath by the champions of Greece ("assuredly ye did no wrong; I swear it by those who at Marathon stood in the forefront of the danger"), in the public view by this one Figure of Adjuration, which I here term *Apostrophe,* he deifies his ancestors. He brings home the thought that we ought to swear by those who have thus nobly died as we swear by Gods, and he fills the mind of the judges with the high spirit of those who there bore the brunt of the danger, and he has transformed the natural course of the argument into transcendent sublimity and passion and that secure belief which rests upon strange and prodigious oaths. He instils into the minds of his hearers the conviction—which acts as a medicine and an antidote— that they should, uplifted by these eulogies, feel no less proud of the fight against Philip than of the triumph at Marathon and Salamis. By all these means he carries his hearers clean away with him through the employment of a single figure. 3. It is said, indeed, that the germ of the oath is found in Eupolis:—

[45] Dem. *de Cor.* 208.

For, by the fight I won at Marathon,
No one shall vex my soul and rue it not.[46]

But it is not sublime to swear by a person in any chance way; the sub-limity depends upon the place and the manner and the circumstances and the motive. Now in the passage of Eupolis there is nothing but the mere oath, addressed to the Athenians when still prosperous and in no need of comfort. Furthermore, the poet in his oath has not made divinities of the men in order so to create in his hearers a worthy con-ception of their valour, but he has wandered away from those who stood in the forefront of the danger to an inanimate thing—the fight. In Demosthenes the oath is framed for vanquished men, with the in-tention that Chaeroneia should no longer appear a failure to the Athenians. He gives them at one and the same time, as I remarked, a demonstration that they have done no wrong, an example, the sure evidence of oaths, a eulogy, an exhortation. 4. And since the orator was likely to be confronted with the objection, "You are speaking of the *defeat* which has attended your administration, and yet you swear by *victories*," in what follows he consequently measures even individ-ual words, and chooses them unerringly, showing that even in the revels of the imagination sobriety is required. "Those," he says, "who stood in the forefront of the danger at Marathon, and those who fought by sea at Salamis and Artemisium, and those who stood in the ranks at Plataea." Nowhere does he use the word "conquered," but at every turn he has evaded any indication of the result, since it was fortunate and the opposite of what happened at Chaeroneia. So he at once rushes forward and carries his hearer off his feet. "All of whom," says he, "were accorded a public burial by the state, Aeschines, and not *the successful only.*"

XVII

I ought not, my dear friend, to omit at this point an observation of my own, which shall be most concisely stated. It is that, by a sort of natural law, figures bring support to the sublime, and on their part derive sup-port in turn from it in a wonderful degree. Where and how, I will explain. The cunning use of figures is peculiarly subject to suspicion, and produces an impression of ambush, plot, fallacy. This is so when the plea is addressed to a judge with absolute powers, and particularly to despots, kings, and leaders in positions of superiority. Such an one

[46] *Eupolis.*

at once feels resentment if, like a foolish boy, he is tricked by the paltry figures of the oratorical craftsman. Construing the fallacy into a personal affront, sometimes he becomes quite wild with rage, or if he controls his anger, steels himself utterly against persuasive words. Wherefore a figure is at its best when the very fact that it is a figure escapes attention. 2. Accordingly, sublimity and passion form an antidote and a wonderful help against the mistrust which attends upon the use of figures. The art which craftily employs them lies hid and escapes all future suspicion, when once it has been associated with beauty and sublimity. A sufficient proof is the passage already adduced, "By the men of Marathon I swear." By what means has the orator here concealed the figure? Clearly, by the very excess of light. For just as all dim lights are extinguished in the blaze of the sun, so do the artifices of rhetoric fade from view when bathed in the pervading splendour of sublimity. 3. Something like this happens also in the art of painting. For although light and shade, as depicted in colours, lie side by side upon the same surface, light nevertheless meets the vision first, and not only stands out, but also seems far nearer. So also with the manifestations of passion and the sublime in literature. They lie nearer to our minds through a sort of natural kinship and through their own radiance, and always strike our attention before the figures, whose art they throw into the shade and as it were keep in concealment.

XVIII

But what are we next to say of questions and interrogations? Is it not precisely by the visualizing qualities of these figures that Demosthenes strives to make his speeches far more effective and impressive? "Pray tell me,—tell me, you sir,—do you wish to go about and inquire of one another, Is there any news? Why, what greater news could there be than this, that a Macedonian is subduing Greece? Is Philip dead? No; but he is ill. Dead or ill, what difference to you? Should anything happen to him, you will speedily create another Philip." [47] Again he says, "Let us sail against Macedonia. Where shall we find a landing-place? someone asks. The war itself will discover the weak places in Philip's position." [48] All this, if stated plainly and directly, would have been altogether weaker. As it is, the excitement, and the rapid play of question and answer, and the plan of meeting his own objections as though they were urged by another, have by the help of the figure made

[47] Dem. *Philipp.* I. 10.   [48] Dem. *Philipp.* I. 44.

the language used not only more elevated but also more convincing.
2. For an exhibition of passion has a greater effect when it seems not to
be studied by the speaker himself but to be inspired by the occasion;
and questions asked and answered by oneself simulate a natural outburst of passion. For just as those who are interrogated by others experience a sudden excitement and answer the inquiry incisively and with
the utmost candour, so the figure of question and answer leads the
hearer to suppose that each deliberate thought is struck out and uttered on the spur of the moment, and thus beguiles his reason. We may
further quote that passage of Herodotus which is regarded as one of
the most elevated: "if thus . . ."

XIX

The words issue forth without connecting links and are poured out
as it were, almost outstripping the speaker himself. "Locking their
shields," says Xenophon, "they thrust fought slew fell." [49] 2. And so
with the words of Eurylochus:—

We passed, as thou badst, Odysseus, midst twilight of oak-trees round.
There amidst of the forest-glens a beautiful palace we found. [50]

For the lines detached from one another, but none the less hurried
along, produce the impression of an agitation which interposes obstacles and at the same time adds impetuosity. This result Homer has
produced by the omission of conjunctions.

XX

A powerful effect usually attends the union of figures for a common
object, when two or three mingle together as it were in partnership,
and contribute a fund of strength, persuasiveness, beauty. Thus, in the
speech against Meidias, examples will be found of *asyndeton*,[51] interwoven with instances of *anaphora* [52] and *diatyposis*.[53] "For the smiter
can do many things (some of which the sufferer cannot even describe
to another) by attitude, by look, by voice." [54] 2. Then, in order that the
narrative may not, as it advances, continue in the same groove (for

---

[49] Xen. *Hellen.* IV. 3, 19.
[50] *Odyss.* X. 251, 2.
[51] *Broken sentences.*

[52] *Repetition of words.*
[53] *Vivid description.*
[54] Demosth. *in Mid.* 72.

continuance betokens tranquillity, while passion—the transport and commotion of the soul—sets order at defiance), straightway he hurries off to other *Asyndeta* and *Repetitions.* "By attitude, by look, by voice, when he acts with insolence, when he acts like an enemy, when he smites with his fists, when he smites you like a slave." By these words the orator produces the same effect as the assailant—he strikes the mind of the judges by the swift succession of blow on blow. 3. Starting from this point again, as suddenly as a gust of wind, he makes another attack. "When smitten with blows of fists," he says, "when smitten upon the cheek. These things stir the blood, these drive men beyond themselves, when unused to insult. No one can, in describing them, convey a notion of the indignity they imply." So he maintains throughout, though with continual variation, the essential character of the *Repetitions* and *Asyndeta.* In this way, with him, order is disorderly, and on the other hand disorder contains a certain element of order.

XXI

Come now, add, if you please, in these cases connecting particles after the fashion of the followers of Isocrates. Furthermore, this fact too must not be overlooked that the smiter may do many things, first by attitude, then by look, then again by the mere voice. You will feel, if you transcribe the passage in this orderly fashion, that the rugged impetuosity of passion, once you make it smooth and equable by adding the copulatives, falls pointless and immediately loses all its fire. 2. Just as the binding of the limbs of runners deprives them of their power of rapid motion, so also passion, when shackled by connecting links and other appendages, chafes at the restriction, for it loses the freedom of its advance and its rapid emission as though from an engine of war.

XXII

Hyperbata, or *inversions,* must be placed under the same category. They are departures in the order of expressions or ideas from the natural sequence; and they bear, it may be said, the very stamp and impress of vehement emotion. Just as those who are really moved by anger, or fear, or indignation, or jealousy, or any other emotion (for the passions are many and countless, and none can give their number), at times turn aside, and when they have taken one thing as their subject often leap to another, foisting in the midst some irrelevant matter, and then again wheel round to their original theme, and driven by their vehemence, as by a veering wind, now this way now that with rapid changes, transform their expressions, their thoughts, the order suggested by a natural sequence, into numberless variations of every kind; so also among the best writers it is by means of *hyperbaton* that imitation approaches the effects of nature. For art is perfect when it seems to be nature, and nature hits the mark when she contains art hidden within her. We may illustrate by the words of Dionysius of Phocaea in Herodotus. "Our fortunes lie on a razor's edge, men of Ionia; for freedom or for bondage, and that the bondage of runaway slaves. Now, therefore, if you choose to submit to hardships, you will have toil for the moment, but you will be able to overcome your foes." [55] 2. Here the natural order would have been: "Men of Ionia, now is the time for you to meet hardships; for our fortunes lie on a razor's edge." But the speaker postpones the words "Men of Ionia." He starts at once with the danger of the situation, as though in such imminent peril he had no time at all to address his hearers. Moreover, he inverts the order of ideas. For instead of saying that they ought to endure hardships, which is the real object of his exhortation, he first assigns the reason because of which they ought to endure hardships, in the words "our fortunes lie on a razor's edge." The result is that what he says seems not to be premeditated but to be prompted by the necessities of the moment. 3. In a still higher degree Thucydides is most bold and skilful in disjoining from one another by means of transpositions things that are by nature intimately united and indivisible. Demosthenes is not so masterful as Thucydides, but of all writers he most abounds in this kind of figure, and through his use of hyperbata makes a great impression of vehemence, yes and of unpremeditated speech, and moreover draws his hearers with him into all the perils of his long inversions. 4. For he will often leave in suspense the thought which he has begun to express, and meanwhile he will heap, into a position seemingly alien and unnatural, one thing upon another parenthetically and from any external source whatsoever, throwing his hearer into alarm lest the whole structure of his words should fall to pieces, and compelling him in anxious sympathy to share the peril of the speaker; and then unexpectedly, after a long interval, he adds the long-awaited conclusion at the right place, namely the end, and produces a far greater effect by this very use, so bold and hazardous, of hyperbaton. Examples may be spared because of their abundance.

[55] Herod. vi. 11.

XXIII

The figures which are termed *polyptota*—accumulations, and variations, and climaxes—are excellent weapons of public oratory, as you
are aware, and contribute to elegance and to every form of sublimity
and passion. Again, how greatly do changes of cases, tenses, persons,
numbers, genders, diversify and enliven exposition. 2. Where the use
of numbers is concerned, I would point out that style is not adorned
only or chiefly by those words which are, as far as their forms go, in the
singular but in meaning are, when examined, found to be plural: as
in the lines

> A countless crowd forthright
> Far-ranged along the beaches were clamouring "Thunny in sight!" [56]

The fact is more worthy of observation that in certain cases the use of
the plural (for the singular) falls on the ear with still more imposing
effect and impresses us by the very sense of multitude which the number conveys. 3. Such are the words of Oedipus in Sophocles:

> O nuptials, nuptials,
> Ye gendered me, and, having gendered, brought
> To light the selfsame seed, and so revealed
> Sires, brothers, sons, in one—all kindred blood!—
> Brides, mothers, wives, in one!—yea, whatso deeds
> Most shameful among humankind are done. [57]

The whole enumeration can be summed up in a single proper name—
on the one side Oedipus, on the other Jocasta. None the less, the expansion of the number into the plural helps to pluralise the misfortunes as well. There is a similar instance of multiplication in the line:—

> Forth Hectors and Sarpedons marching came, [58]

and in that passage of Plato concerning the Athenians which we have
quoted elsewhere. 4. "For no Pelopes, nor Cadmi, nor Aegypti and
Danai, nor the rest of the crowd of born foreigners dwell with us, but
ours is the land of pure Greeks, free from foreign admixture," etc. [59]
For naturally a theme seems more imposing to the ear when proper
names are thus added, one upon the other, in troops. But this must

[56] *Scriptor Incertus,* writer of uncertain
identity.
[57] Soph. *Oed. T.* 1403.

[58] *Scr. Inc.*
[59] Plat. *Menex.* 245 D.

only be done in cases in which the subject admits of amplification or redundancy or exaggeration or passion—one or more of these—since we all know that a richly caparisoned style is extremely pretentious.

XXIV

Further (to take the converse case) particulars which are combined from the plural into the singular are sometimes most elevated in appearance. "Thereafter," says Demosthenes, "all Peloponnesus was at variance." [60] "And when Phrynichus had brought out a play entitled the *Capture of Miletus,* the whole theatre burst into tears." [61] For the compression of the number from multiplicity into unity gives more fully the feeling of a single body. 2. In both cases the explanation of the elegance of expression is, I think, the same. Where the words are singular, to make them plural is the mark of unlooked-for passion; and where they are plural, the rounding of a number of things into a fine-sounding singular is surprising owing to the converse change.

XXV

If you introduce things which are past as present and now taking place, you will make your story no longer a narration but an actuality. Xenophon furnishes an illustration. "A man," says he, "has fallen under Cyrus' horse, and being trampled strikes the horse with his sword in the belly. He rears and unseats Cyrus, who falls." [62] This construction is specially characteristic of Thucydides.

XXVI

In like manner the interchange of persons produces a vivid impression, and often makes the hearer feel that he is moving in the midst of perils:—

Thou hadst said that with toil unspent, and all unwasted of limb,
They closed in the grapple of war, so fiercely they rushed to the fray; [63]

and the line of Aratus:—

Never in that month launch thou forth amid lashing seas.[64]

2. So also Herodotus: "From the city of Elephantine thou shalt sail upwards, and then shalt come to a level plain; and after crossing this

[60] Dem. *de Cor.* 18.
[61] Herod. VI. 21.
[62] Xen. *Cyrop.* VII. I. 37.
[63] *Il.* XV. 697, 8.
[64] *Aratus.*

tract, thou shalt embark upon another vessel and sail for two days, and then shalt thou come to a great city whose name is Meroe." [65] Do you observe, my friend, how he leads you in imagination through the region and makes you *see* what you hear? All such cases of direct personal address place the hearer on the very scene of action. 3. So it is when you seem to be speaking, not to all and sundry, but to a single individual:—

> But Tydeides—thou wouldst not have known him, for whom that
> hero fought.[66]

You will make your hearer more excited and more attentive, and full of active participation, if you keep him on the alert by words addressed to himself.

XXVII

There is further the case in which a writer, when relating something about a person, suddenly breaks off and converts himself into that selfsame person. This species of figure is a kind of outburst of passion:—

> Then with a far-ringing shout to the Trojans Hector cried,
> Bidding them rush on the ships, bidding leave the spoils blood-dyed—
> And whomso I mark from the galleys aloof on the farther side,
> I will surely devise his death.[67]

The poet assigns the task of narration, as is fit, to himself, but the abrupt threat he suddenly, with no note of warning, attributes to the angered chief. It would have been frigid had he inserted the words, "Hector said so and so." As it is, the swift transition of the narrative has outstripped the swift transitions of the narrator. 2. Accordingly this figure should be used by preference when a sharp crisis does not suffer the writer to tarry, but constrains him to pass at once from one person to another. An example will be found in Hecataeus: "Ceyx treated the matter gravely, and straightway bade the descendants of Heracles depart; for I am not able to succour you. In order, therefore, that ye may not perish yourselves and injure me, get you gone to some other country." [68] 3. Demosthenes in dealing with Aristogeiton has, somewhat differently, employed this variation of person to betoken the quick play of emotion. "And will none of you," he asks, "be found to

[65] Herod. II. 29.
[66] *Il.* v. 85.
[67] *Il.* xv. 346.
[68] *Hecataeus.*

be stirred by loathing or even by anger at the violent deeds of this vile and shameless fellow, who—you whose licence of speech, most abandoned of men, is not confined by barriers nor by doors, which might perchance be opened!" [69] With the sense thus incomplete, he suddenly breaks off and in his anger almost tears asunder a single expression into two persons,—"he who, O thou most abandoned!" Thus, although he has turned aside his address and seems to have left Aristogeiton, yet through passion he directs it upon him with far greater force. 4. Similarly with the words of Penelope:—

Herald, with what behest art thou come from the suitor-band?
To give to the maids of Odysseus the godlike their command
To forsake their labours, and yonder for them the banquet to lay?
I would that of all their wooing this were the latest day,
That this were the end of your banquets, your uttermost revelling-hour,
Ye that assemble together and all our substance devour,
The wise Telemachus' store, as though ye never had heard,
In the days overpast of your childhood, your fathers' praising word,
How good Odysseus was.[70]

XXVIII

As to whether or no Periphrasis contributes to the sublime, no one, I think, will hesitate. For just as in music the so-called accompaniments bring out the charm of the melody, so also periphrasis often harmonises with the normal expression and adds greatly to its beauty, especially if it has a quality which is not inflated and dissonant but pleasantly tempered. 2. Plato will furnish an instance in proof at the opening of his Funeral Oration. "In truth they have gained from us their rightful tribute, in the enjoyment of which they proceed along their destined path, escorted by their country publicly, and privately each by his kinsmen." [71] Death he calls "their destined path," and the tribute of accustomed rites he calls "being escorted publicly by their fatherland." Is it in a slight degree only that he has magnified the conception by the use of these words? Has he not rather, starting with unadorned diction, made it musical, and shed over it like a harmony the melodious rhythm which comes from periphrasis? 3. And Xenophon says, "You regard toil as the guide to a joyous life. You have garnered in your souls the goodliest of all possessions and the fittest

[69] Demosth. *c. Aristog.* I. 27.　　　　[71] Plato, *Menex.* 236 D.
[70] *Odyss.* IV. 681–689.

for warriors. For you rejoice in praise more than in all else." [72] In using, instead of "you are willing to toil," the words "you deem toil the guide to a joyous life," and in expanding the rest of the sentence in like manner, he has annexed to his eulogy a lofty idea. 4. And so with that inimitable phrase of Herodotus: "The goddess afflicted with an unsexing malady those Scythians who had pillaged the temple." [73]

XXIX

A hazardous business, however, eminently hazardous is periphrasis, unless it be handled with discrimination; otherwise it speedily falls flat, with its odour of empty talk and its swelling amplitude. This is the reason why Plato (who is always strong in figurative language, and at times unseasonably so) is taunted because in his *Laws* he says that "neither gold nor silver treasure should be allowed to establish itself and abide in the city." [74] The critic says that, if he had been forbidding the possession of cattle, he would obviously have spoken of ovine and bovine treasure. 2. But our parenthetical disquisition with regard to the use of figures as bearing upon the sublime has run to sufficient length, my dear Terentianus; for all these things lend additional passion and animation to style, and passion is as intimately allied with sublimity as sketches of character with entertainment.

XXX

Since, however, it is the case that, in discourse, thought and diction are for the most part developed one through the other, come let us proceed to consider any branches of the subject of diction which have so far been neglected. Now it is, no doubt, superfluous to dilate to those who know it well upon the fact that the choice of proper and striking words wonderfully attracts and enthralls the hearer, and that such a choice is the leading ambition of all orators and writers, since it is the direct agency which ensures the presence in writings, as upon the fairest statues, of the perfection of grandeur, beauty, mellowness, dignity, force, power, and any other high qualities there may be, and breathes into dead things a kind of living voice. All this it is, I say, needless to mention, for beautiful words are in very truth the peculiar light of thought. 2. It may, however, be pointed out that stately lan-

[72] Xen. *Cyrop.* I. 5. 12.   [74] Plato, *Leges,* 801 B.
[73] Herod. I. 105.

guage is not to be used everywhere, since to invest petty affairs with great and high-sounding names would seem just like putting a full-sized tragic mask upon an infant boy. But in poetry and . . .

XXXI

. . . full of vigour and racy; and so is Anacreon's line, "That Thracian mare no longer do I heed." [75] In this way, too, that original expression of Theopompus merits praise. Owing to the correspondence between word and thing it seems to me to be highly expressive; and yet Caecilius for some unexplained reason finds fault with it. "Philip," says Theopompus, "had a genius for *stomaching* things." [76] Now a homely expression of this kind is sometimes much more telling than elegant language, for it is understood at once since it is drawn from common life, and the fact that it is familiar makes it only the more convincing. So the words "stomaching things" are used most strikingly of a man who, for the sake of attaining his own ends, patiently and with cheerfulness endures things shameful and vile. 2. So with the words of Herodotus. "Cleomenes," he says, "went mad, and with a small sword cut the flesh of his own body into strips, until he slew himself by making mincemeat of his entire person." [77] And, "Pythes fought on shipboard, until he was utterly hacked to pieces." [78] These phrases graze the very edge of vulgarity, but they are saved from vulgarity by their expressiveness.

XXXII

Further, with regard to the number of metaphors to be employed, Caecilius seems to assent to the view of those who lay it down that not more than two, or at the most three, should be ranged together in the same passage. Demosthenes is, in fact, the standard in this as in other matters. The proper time for using metaphors is when the passions roll like a torrent and sweep a multitude of them down their resistless flood. 2. "Men," says he, "who are vile flatterers, who have maimed their own fatherlands each one of them, who have toasted away their liberty first to Philip and now to Alexander, who measure happiness by their belly and their lowest desires, and who have overthrown that liberty and that freedom from despotic mastery which

[75] *Anacreon.*
[76] *Theopompus.*
[77] Herod. vi. 75.
[78] Herod. vii. 181.

to the Greeks of an earlier time were the rules and standards of good." [79]
Here the orator's wrath against the traitors throws a veil over the number of the tropes. 3. In the same spirit, Aristotle and Theophrastus point out that the following phrases serve to soften bold metaphors—"as if," and "as it were," and "if one may so say," and "if one may venture such an expression"; for the qualifying words mitigate, they say, the audacity of expression.[80] 4. I accept that view, but still for number and boldness of metaphors I maintain, as I said in dealing with figures, that strong and timely passion and noble sublimity are the appropriate palliatives. For it is the nature of the passions, in their vehement rush, to sweep and thrust everything before them, or rather to demand hazardous turns as altogether indispensable. They do not allow the hearer leisure to criticise the number of the metaphors because he is carried away by the fervour of the speaker. 5. Moreover, in the treatment of commonplaces and in descriptions there is nothing so impressive as a number of tropes following close one upon the other. It is by this means that in Xenophon the anatomy of the human tabernacle is magnificently depicted, and still more divinely in Plato. Plato says that its head is a citadel; in the midst, between the head and the breast, is built the neck like some isthmus. The vertebrae, he says, are fixed beneath like pivots. Pleasure is a bait which tempts men to ill, the tongue the test of taste; the heart is the knot of the veins and the wellspring of the blood that courses round impetuously, and it is stationed in the guard-house of the body. The passages by which the blood races this way and that he names alleys. He says that the gods, contriving succour for the beating of the heart (which takes place when dangers are expected, and when wrath excites it, since it then reaches a fiery heat), have implanted the lungs, which are soft and bloodless and have pores within, to serve as a buffer, in order that the heart may, when its inward wrath boils over, beat against a yielding substance and so escape injury. The seat of the desires he compared to the women's apartments in a house, that of anger to the men's. The spleen he called the napkin of the inward parts, whence it is filled with secretions and grows to a great and festering bulk. After this, the gods canopied the whole with flesh, putting forward the flesh as a defence against injuries from without, as though it were a hair-cushion. The blood he called the fodder of the flesh. "In order to promote nutrition," he continues, "they irrigated the body, cutting conduits as in gardens, in order that, with the body forming a set of tiny channels, the streams of the veins

[79] Dem. *de Cor.* 296. [80] *Aristotle.*

might flow as from a never-failing source." When the end comes, he says that the cables of the soul are loosed like those of a ship, and she is allowed to go free.[81] 6. Examples of a similar nature are to be found in a never-ending series. But those indicated are enough to show that figurative language possesses great natural power, and that metaphors contribute to the sublime; and at the same time that it is impassioned and descriptive passages which rejoice in them to the greatest extent. 7. It is obvious, however, even though I do not dwell upon it, that the use of tropes, like all other beauties of expression, is apt to lead to excess. On this score Plato himself is much criticised, since he is often carried away by a sort of frenzy of words into strong and harsh metaphors and into inflated allegory. "For it is not readily observed," he says, "that a city ought to be mixed like a bowl, in which the mad wine seethes when it has been poured in, though when chastened by another god who is sober, falling thus into noble company, it makes a good and temperate drink." [82] For to call water "a sober god," and mixing "chastening," is—the critics say—the language of a poet, and one who is in truth far from sober. 8. Fastening upon such defects, however, Caecilius ventured, in his writings in praise of Lysias, to make the assertion that Lysias was altogether superior to Plato. In so doing he gave way to two blind impulses of passion. Loving Lysias better even than himself, he nevertheless hates Plato more perfectly than he loves Lysias. In fact, he is carried away by the spirit of contention, and even his premises are not, as he thought, admitted. For he prefers the orator as faultless and immaculate to Plato as one who has often made mistakes. But the truth is not of this nature, nor anything like it.

XXXIII

Come, now, let us take some writer who is really immaculate and beyond reproach. Is it not worth while, on this very point, to raise the general question whether we ought to give the preference, in poems and prose writings, to grandeur with some attendant faults, or to success which is moderate but altogether sound and free from error? Aye, and further, whether a greater number of excellences, or excellences higher in quality, would in literature rightly bear away the palm? For these are inquiries appropriate to a treatise on the sublime, and they imperatively demand a settlement. 2. For my part, I am well aware that lofty genius is far removed from flawlessness; for invariable ac-

[81] Plato, *Tim.* 65 c.–85 e.   [82] Plato, *Leges*, 773 c.

curacy incurs the risk of pettiness, and in the sublime, as in great fortunes, there must be something which is overlooked. It may be necessarily the case that low and average natures remain as a rule free from failing and in greater safety because they never run a risk or seek to scale the heights, while great endowments prove insecure because of their very greatness. 3. In the second place, I am not ignorant that it naturally happens that the worse side of human character is always the more easily recognised, and that the memory of errors remains indelible, while that of excellences quickly dies away. 4. I have myself noted not a few errors on the part of Homer and other writers of the greatest distinction, and the slips they have made afford me anything but pleasure. Still I do not term them wilful errors, but rather oversights of a random and casual kind, due to neglect and introduced with all the heedlessness of genius. Consequently I do not waver in my view that excellences higher in quality, even if not sustained throughout, should always on a comparison be voted the first place, because of their sheer elevation of spirit if for no other reason. Granted that Apollonius in his *Argonautica* shows himself a poet who does not trip, and that in his pastorals Theocritus is, except in a few externals, most happy, would you not, for all that, choose to be Homer rather than Apollonius? 5. Again: does Eratosthenes in the *Erigone* (a little poem which is altogether free from flaw) show himself a greater poet than Archilochus with the rich and disorderly abundance which follows in his train and with that outburst of the divine spirit within him which it is difficult to bring under the rules of law? Once more: in lyric poetry would you prefer to be Bacchylides rather than Pindar? And in tragedy to be Ion of Chios rather than—Sophocles? It is true that Bacchylides and Ion are faultless and entirely elegant writers of the polished school, while Pindar and Sophocles, although at times they burn everything before them as it were in their swift career, are often extinguished unaccountably and fail most lamentably. But would anyone in his senses regard all the compositions of Ion put together as an equivalent for the single play of the *Oedipus?*

XXXIV

If successful writing were to be estimated by number of merits and not by the true criterion, thus judged Hyperides would be altogether superior to Demosthenes. For he has a greater variety of accents than Demosthenes and a greater number of excellences, and like the pentathlete he falls just below the top in every branch. In all the contests he has to resign the first place to his rivals, while he maintains that place as against all ordinary persons. 2. Now Hyperides not only imitates all the strong points of Demosthenes with the exception of his composition, but he has embraced in a singular degree the excellences and graces of Lysias as well. For he talks with simplicity, where it is required, and does not adopt like Demosthenes one unvarying tone in all his utterances. He possesses the gift of characterisation in a sweet and pleasant form and with a touch of piquancy. There are innumerable signs of wit in him—the most polished raillery, high-bred ease, supple skill in the contests of irony, jests not tasteless or rude after the well-known Attic manner but naturally suggested by the subject, clever ridicule, much comic power, biting satire with well-directed fun, and what may be termed an inimitable charm investing the whole. He is excellently fitted by nature to excite pity; in narrating a fable he is facile, and with his pliant spirit he is also most easily turned towards a digression (as for instance in his rather poetical presentation of the story of Leto), while he has treated his Funeral Oration in the epideictic vein with probably unequalled success. 3. Demosthenes, on the other hand, is not an apt delineator of character, he is not facile, he is anything but pliant or epideictic, he is comparatively lacking in the entire list of excellences just given. Where he forces himself to be jocular and pleasant, he does not excite laughter but rather becomes the subject of it, and when he wishes to approach the region of charm, he is all the farther removed from it. If he had attempted to write the short speech about Phryne or about Athenogenes, he would have all the more commended Hyperides to our regard. 4. The good points of the latter, however, many though they be, are wanting in elevation; they are the staid utterances of a sober-hearted man and leave the hearer unmoved, no one feeling terror when he reads Hyperides. But Demosthenes draws—as from a store—excellences allied to the highest sublimity and perfected to the utmost, the tone of lofty speech, living passions, copiousness, readiness, speed (where it is legitimate), and that power and vehemence of his which forbid approach. Having, I say, absorbed bodily within himself these mighty gifts which we may deem heaven-sent (for it would not be right to term them *human*), he thus with the noble qualities which are his own routs all comers even where the qualities he does not possess are concerned, and overpowers with thunder and with lightning the orators of every age. One could sooner face with unflinching eyes a descending thunderbolt than meet with steady gaze his bursts of passion in their swift succession.

XXXV

But in the case of Plato and Lysias there is, as I said, a further point of difference. For not only in the degree of his excellences, but also in their number, Lysias is much inferior to Plato; and at the same time he surpasses him in his faults still more than he falls below him in his excellences. 2. What fact, then, was before the eyes of those super-human writers who, aiming at everything that was highest in composition, contemned an all-pervading accuracy? This besides many other things, that Nature has appointed us men to be no base or ignoble animals; but when she ushers us into life and into the vast universe as into some great assembly, to be as it were spectators of the mighty whole and the keenest aspirants for honour, forthwith she implants in our souls the unconquerable love of whatever is elevated and more divine than we. 3. Wherefore not even the entire universe suffices for the thought and contemplation within the reach of the human mind, but our imaginations often pass beyond the bounds of space, and if we survey our life on every side and see how much more it everywhere abounds in what is striking, and great, and beautiful, we shall soon discern the purpose of our birth. 4. This is why, by a sort of natural impulse, we admire not the small streams, useful and pellucid though they be, but the Nile, the Danube or the Rhine, and still more the Ocean. Nor do we view the tiny flame of our own kindling (guarded in lasting purity as its light ever is) with greater awe than the celestial fires though they are often shrouded in darkness; nor do we deem it a greater marvel than the craters of Etna, whose eruptions throw up stones from its depths and great masses of rock, and at times pour forth rivers of that pure and unmixed subterranean fire. 5. In all such matters we may say that what is useful or necessary men regard as commonplace, while they reserve their admiration for that which is astounding.

XXXVI

Now as regards the manifestations of the sublime in literature, in which grandeur is never, as it sometimes is in nature, found apart from utility and advantage, it is fitting to observe at once that, though writers of this magnitude are far removed from faultlessness, they none the less all rise above what is mortal; that all other qualities prove their possessors to be men, but sublimity raises them near the majesty of God; and that, while immunity from errors relieves from censure, it is grandeur that excites admiration. 2. What need to add thereto that each of these supreme authors often redeems all his failures by a single sublime and happy touch, and (most important of all) that if one were to pick out and mass together the blunders of Homer, Demosthenes, Plato, and all the rest of the greatest writers, they would be found to be a very small part, nay an infinitesimal fraction, of the triumphs which those heroes achieve on every hand? This is the reason why the judgment of all posterity—a verdict which envy itself cannot convict of perversity—has brought and offered those meeds of victory which up to this day it guards intact and seems likely still to preserve,

Long as earth's waters shall flow, and her tall trees burgeon and bloom.[88]

3. In reply, however, to the writer who maintains that the faulty Colossus is not superior to the Spearman of Polycleitus, it is obvious to remark among many other things that in art the utmost exactitude is admired, grandeur in the works of nature; and that it is by nature that man is a being gifted with speech. In statues likeness to man is the quality required; in discourse we demand, as I said, that which transcends the human. 4. Nevertheless—and the counsel about to be given reverts to the beginning of our memoir—since freedom from failings is for the most part the successful result of art, and excellence (though it may be unevenly sustained) the result of sublimity, the employment of art is in every way a fitting aid to nature; for it is the conjunction of the two which tends to ensure perfection.

Such are the decisions to which we have felt bound to come with regard to the questions proposed; but let every man cherish the view which pleases him best.

XXXVII

Closely related to Metaphors (for we must return to our point) are comparisons and similes, differing only in this respect. . . .

88 *Scr. Inc.*

XXXVIII

. . . such Hyperboles as: "unless you carry your brains trodden down in your heels." [84] It is necessary, therefore, to know where to fix the limit in each case; for an occasional overshooting of the mark ruins the hyperbole, and such expressions, when strained too much, lose their tension, and sometimes swing round and produce the contrary effect. 2. Isocrates, for example, fell into unaccountable puerility owing to the ambition which made him desire to describe everything with a touch of amplification. The theme of his *Panegyric* is that Athens surpasses Lacedaemon in benefits conferred upon Greece, and yet at the very outset of his speech he uses these words: "Further, language has such capacity that it is possible thereby to debase things lofty and invest things small with grandeur, and to express old things in a new way, and to discourse in ancient fashion about what has newly happened.[85] "Do you then, Isocrates," it may be asked, "mean in that way to interchange the facts of Lacedaemonian and Athenian history?" For in his eulogy of language he has, we may say, published to his hearers a preamble warning them to distrust himself. 3. Perhaps, then, as we said in dealing with figures generally, those hyperboles are best in which the very fact that they are hyperboles escapes attention. This happens when, through stress of strong emotion, they are uttered in connexion with some great crisis, as is done by Thucydides in the case of those who perished in Sicily. "The Syracusans," he says, "came down to the water's edge and began the slaughter of those chiefly who were in the river, and the water at once became polluted, but none the less it was swallowed although muddy and mixed with blood, and to most it was still worth fighting for." [86] That a draught of blood and mud should still be worth fighting for, is rendered credible by the intensity of the emotion at a great crisis. 4. So with the passage in which Herodotus tells of those who fell at Thermopylae. "On this spot," he says, "the barbarians buried them as they defended themselves with daggers— those of them who had daggers still left—and with hands and mouths." [87] Here you may be inclined to protest against the expressions "fight with their very mouths" against men in armour, and "being buried" with darts. At the same time the narrative carries conviction; for the event does not seem to be introduced for the sake of the hyper-

[84] [Demosth.] *de Halonneso* 45.—Demosthenes.
[85] Isocr. *Paneg.* 8.

[86] Thucyd. VII. 84.
[87] Herod. VII. 225.

bole, but the hyperbole to spring naturally from the event. 5. For (as I never cease to say) the deeds and passions which verge on transport are a sufficient lenitive and remedy for every audacity of speech. This is the reason why the quips of comedy, although they may be carried to the extreme of absurdity, are plausible because they are so amusing. For instance,

Smaller his field was than a Spartan letter.[88]

For mirth, too, is an emotion, an emotion which has its root in pleasure. 6. Hyperboles are employed in describing things small as well as great, since exaggeration is the common element in both cases. And, in a sense, ridicule is an amplification of the paltriness of things.

XXXIX

The fifth of those elements contributing to the sublime which we mentioned, my excellent friend, at the beginning, still remains to be dealt with, namely the arrangement of the words in a certain order. In regard to this, having already in two treatises sufficiently stated such results as our inquiry could compass, we will add, for the purpose of our present undertaking, only what is absolutely essential, namely the fact that harmonious arrangement is not only a natural source of persuasion and pleasure among men but also a wonderful instrument of lofty utterance and of passion. 2. For does not the flute instil certain emotions into its hearers and as it were make them beside themselves and full of frenzy, and supplying a rhythmical movement constrain the listener to move rhythmically in accordance therewith and to conform himself to the melody, although he may be utterly ignorant of music? Yes, and the tones of the harp, although in themselves they signify nothing at all, often cast a wonderful spell, as you know, over an audience by means of the variations of sounds, by their pulsation against one another, and by their mingling in concert. 3. And yet these are mere semblances and spurious copies of persuasion, not (as I have said) genuine activities of human nature. Are we not, then, to hold that composition (being a harmony of that language which is implanted by nature in man and which appeals not to the hearing only but to the soul itself), since it calls forth manifold shapes of words, thoughts, deeds, beauty, melody, all of them born at our birth and growing with

[88] *Scr. Inc.*

our growth, and since by means of the blending and variation of its own tones it seeks to introduce into the minds of those who are present the emotion which affects the speaker and since it always brings the audience to share in it and by the building of phrase upon phrase raises a sublime and harmonious structure: are we not, I say, to hold that harmony by these selfsame means allures us and invariably disposes us to stateliness and dignity and elevation and every emotion which it contains within itself, gaining absolute mastery over our minds? But it is folly to dispute concerning matters which are generally admitted, since experience is proof sufficient. 4. An example of a conception which is usually thought sublime and is really admirable is that which Demosthenes associates with the decree: "This decree caused the danger which then beset the city to pass by just-as a cloud." [89] But it owes its happy sound no less to the harmony than to the thought itself. For the thought is expressed throughout in dactylic rhythms, and these are most noble and productive of sublimity; and therefore it is that they constitute the heroic, the finest metre that we know. For if you derange the words of the sentence and transpose them in whatever way you will, as for example "This decree just-as a cloud caused the danger of the time to pass by"; nay, if you cut off a single syllable only and say "caused to pass by as a cloud," you will perceive to what an extent harmony is in unison with sublimity. For the very words "just-as a cloud" begin with a long rhythm, which consists of four metrical beats; but if one syllable is cut off and we read "as a cloud," we immediately maim the sublimity by the abbreviation. Conversely, if you elongate the word and write "caused to pass by just-as-if a cloud," it means the same thing, but no longer falls with the same effect upon the ear, inasmuch as the abrupt grandeur of the passage loses its energy and tension through the lengthening of the concluding syllables.

XL

Among the chief causes of the sublime in speech, as in the structure of the human body, is the collocation of members, a single one of which if severed from another possesses in itself nothing remarkable, but all united together make a full and perfect organism. So the constituents of grandeur, when separated from one another, carry with them sublimity in distraction this way and that, but when formed into a body by association and when further encircled in a chain of harmony they

[89] Demosth. *de Cor.* 188.

become sonorous by their very rotundity; and in periods sublimity is, as it were, a contribution made by a multitude. 2. We have, however, sufficiently shown that many writers and poets who possess no natural sublimity and are perhaps even wanting in elevation have nevertheless, although employing for the most part common and popular words with no striking associations of their own, by merely joining and fitting these together, secured dignity and distinction and the appearance of freedom from meanness. Instances will be furnished by Philistus among many others, by Aristophanes in certain passages, by Euripides in most. 3. In the last-mentioned author, Heracles, after the scene in which he slays his children, uses the words:—

> Full-fraught am I with woes—no space for more.[90]

The expression is a most ordinary one, but it has gained elevation through the aptness of the structure of the line. If you shape the sentence in a different way, you will see this plainly, the fact being that Euripides is a poet in virtue of his power of composition rather than of his invention. 4. In the passage which describes Dirce torn away by the bull:—

> Whitherso'er he turned
> Swift wheeling round, he haled and hurled withal
> Dame, rock, oak, intershifted ceaselessly,[91]

the conception itself is a fine one, but it has been rendered more forcible by the fact that the harmony is not hurried or carried as it were on rollers, but the words act as buttresses for one another and find support in the pauses, and issue finally in a well-grounded sublimity.

XLI

There is nothing in the sphere of the sublime, that is so lowering as broken and agitated movement of language, such as is characteristic of pyrrhics and trochees and dichorees, which fall altogether to the level of dance-music. For all over-rhythmical writing is at once felt to be affected and finical and wholly lacking in passion owing to the monotony of its superficial polish. 2. And the worst of it all is that, just as petty lays draw their hearer away from the point and compel his

---

[90] Eurip. *Herc. Fur.* 1245.   [91] *Euripides.*

attention to themselves, so also over-rhythmical style does not communicate the feeling of the words but simply the feeling of the rhythm. Sometimes, indeed, the listeners knowing beforehand the due terminations stamp their feet in time with the speaker, and as in a dance give the right step in anticipation. 3. In like manner those words are destitute of sublimity which lie too close together, and are cut up into short and tiny syllables, and are held together as if with wooden bolts by sheer inequality and ruggedness.

XLII

Further, excessive concision of expression tends to lower the sublime, since grandeur is marred when the thought is brought into too narrow a compass. Let this be understood not of proper compression, but of what is absolutely petty and cut into segments. For concision curtails the sense, but brevity goes straight to the mark. It is plain that, *vice versa,* prolixities are frigid, for so is everything that resorts to unseasonable length.

XLIII

Triviality of expression is also apt to disfigure sublimity. In Herodotus, for example, the tempest is described with marvellous effect in all its details, but the passage surely contains some words below the dignity of the subject. The following may serve as an instance—"when the sea seethed." [92] The word "seethed" detracts greatly from the sublimity because it is an ill-sounding one. Further, "the wind," he says, "grew fagged," and those who clung to the spars met "an unpleasant end." [93] The expression "grew fagged" is lacking in dignity, being vulgar; and the word "unpleasant" is inappropriate to so great a disaster. 2. Similarly, when Theopompus had dressed out in marvellous fashion the descent of the Persian king upon Egypt, he spoilt the whole by some petty words. "For which of the cities (he says) or which of the tribes in Asia did not send envoys to the Great King? Which of the products of the earth or of the achievements of art was not, in all its beauty or preciousness, brought as an offering to his presence? Consider the multitude of costly coverlets and mantles, in purple or white or embroidery; the multitude of pavilions of gold furnished with all things useful; the multitude, too, of tapestries and costly couches.

[92] Herod. VII. 188.   [93] Herod. VII. 191 and VIII. 13.

Further, gold and silver plate richly wrought, and goblets and mixing-bowls, some of which you might have seen set with precious stones, and others finished with care and at great price. In addition to all this, countless myriads of Greek and barbaric weapons, and beasts of burden beyond all reckoning and victims fattened for slaughter, and many bushels of condiments, and many bags and sacks and sheets of papyrus and all other useful things, and an equal number of pieces of salted flesh from all manner of victims, so that the piles of them were so great that those who were approaching from a distance took them to be hills and eminences confronting them." [94] 3. He runs off from the more elevated to the more lowly, whereas he should, on the contrary, have risen higher and higher. With his wonderful description of the whole outfit he mixes bags and condiments and sacks, and conveys the impression of a confectioner's shop! For just as if, in the case of those very adornments, between the golden vessels and the jewelled mixing-bowls and the silver plate and the pavilions of pure gold and the goblets, a man were to bring and set in the midst paltry bags and sacks, the proceeding would have been offensive to the eye, so do such words when introduced out of season constitute deformities and as it were blots on the diction. 4. He might have described the scene in broad outline just as he says that hills blocked their way, and with regard to the preparations generally have spoken of "waggons and camels and the multitude of beasts of burden carrying everything that ministers to the luxury and enjoyment of the table," or have used some such expression as "piles of all manner of grain and things which conduce preeminently to good cookery and comfort of body," or if he must necessarily put it in so uncompromising a way, he might have said that "all the dainties of cooks and caterers were there." 5. In lofty passages we ought not to descend to sordid and contemptible language unless constrained by some overpowering necessity, but it is fitting that we should use words worthy of the subject and imitate nature the artificer of man, for she has not placed in full view our grosser parts or the means of purging our frame, but has hidden them away as far as was possible, and as Xenophon says has put their channels in the remotest background, so as not to sully the beauty of the entire creature. 6. But enough; there is no need to enumerate, one by one, the things which produce triviality. For since we have previously indicated those qualities which render style noble and lofty, it is evident that their opposites will for the most part make it low and base.

[94] *Theopompus.*

XLIV

It remains however (as I will not hesitate to add, in recognition of your love of knowledge) to clear up, my dear Terentianus, a question which a certain philosopher has recently mooted. "I wonder," he says, "as no doubt do many others, how it happens that in our time there are men who have the gift of persuasion to the utmost extent, and are well fitted for public life, and are keen and ready, and particularly rich in all the charms of language, yet there no longer arise really lofty and transcendent natures unless quite exceptionally. So great and world-wide a dearth of high utterance attends our age." 2. "Can it be," he continued, "that we are to accept the trite explanation that democracy is the kind nursing-mother of genius, and that literary power may be said to share its rise and fall with democracy and democracy alone? For freedom, it is said, has power to feed the imaginations of the lofty-minded and to inspire hope, and where it prevails there spreads abroad the eagerness of mutual rivalry and the emulous pursuit of the foremost place. 3. Moreover, owing to the prizes which are open to all under popular government, the mental excellences of the orator are continually exercised and sharpened, and as it were rubbed bright, and shine forth (as it is natural they should) with all the freedom which inspires the doings of the state. To-day," he went on, "we seem in our boyhood to learn the lessons of a righteous servitude, being all but enswathed in its customs and observances, when our thoughts are yet young and tender, and never tasting the fairest and most productive source of eloquence (by which," he added, "I mean freedom), so that we emerge in no other guise than that of sublime flatterers." 4. This is the reason, he maintained, why no slave ever becomes an orator, although all other faculties may belong to menials. In the slave there immediately burst out signs of fettered liberty of speech, of the dungeon as it were, of a man habituated to buffetings. 5. "For the day of slavery," as Homer has it, "takes away half our manhood." [95] "Just as," he proceeded, "the cages (if what I hear is true) in which are kept the Pygmies, commonly called *nani*, not only hinder the growth of the creatures confined within them, but actually attenuate them through the bonds which beset their bodies, so one has aptly termed all servitude (though it be most righteous) the cage of the soul and a public prison-house." 6. I answered him thus: "It is easy, my good sir, and characteristic of human nature, to find fault with the age in which one lives. But consider

[95] *Odyss.* XVII. 322.

whether it may not be true that it is not the world's peace that ruins great natures, but far rather this war illimitable which holds our desires in its grasp, aye, and further still those passions which occupy as with troops our present age and utterly harry and plunder it. For the love of money, (a disease from which we all now suffer sorely) and the love of pleasure make us their thralls, or rather, as one may say, drown us body and soul in the depths, the love of riches being a malady which makes men petty, and the love of pleasure one which makes them most ignoble. 7. On reflexion I cannot discover how it is possible for us, if we value boundless wealth so highly, or (to speak more truly) deify it, to avoid allowing the entrance into our souls of the evils which are inseparable from it. For vast and unchecked wealth is accompanied, in close conjunction and step for step as they say, by extravagance, and as soon as the former opens the gates of cities and houses, the latter immediately enters and abides. And when time has passed the pair build nests in the lives of men, as the wise say, and quickly give themselves to the rearing of offspring, and breed ostentation, and vanity, and luxury, no spurious progeny of theirs, but only too legitimate. If these children of wealth are permitted to come to maturity, straightway they beget in the soul inexorable masters—insolence, and lawlessness, and shamelessness. 8. This must necessarily happen, and men will no longer lift up their eyes or have any further regard for fame, but the ruin of such lives will gradually reach its complete consummation and sublimities of soul fade and wither away and become contemptible, when men are lost in admiration of their own mortal parts and omit to exalt that which is immortal. 9. For a man who has once accepted a bribe for a judicial decision cannot be an unbiassed and upright judge of what is just and honourable (since to the man who is venal his own interests must seem honourable and just), and the same is true where the entire life of each of us is ordered by bribes, and huntings after the death of others, and the laying of ambushes for legacies, while gain from any and every source we purchase—each one of us—at the price of life itself, being the slaves of pleasure. In an age which is ravaged by plagues so sore, is it possible for us to imagine that there is still left an unbiassed and incorruptible judge of works that are great and likely to reach posterity, or is it not rather the case that all are influenced in their decisions by the passion for gain? 10. Nay, it is perhaps better for men like ourselves to be ruled than to be free, since our appetites, if let loose without restraint upon our neighbours like beasts from a cage, would set the world on fire with deeds of evil. 11. Summing up, I maintained that among the banes of the natures which our age produces must be reckoned that half-heartedness in which the life of all of us with few exceptions is passed, for we do not labour or exert ourselves except for the sake of praise and pleasure, never for those solid benefits which are a worthy object of our own efforts and the respect of others. 12. But " 'tis best to leave these riddles unresolved," [96] and to proceed to what next presents itself, namely the subject of the Passions, about which I previously undertook to write in a separate treatise. These form, as it seems to me, a material part of discourse generally and of the Sublime itself. . . .

[96] Eurip. *Electra* 379.

HORACE

(65 B.C.–8 B.C.)

QUINTUS HORATIUS FLACCUS was born near Venusia in 65 B. C.,
the son of a freedman whose unusual thrift enabled him to educate
the poet in Rome's best academies. After completing the usual course
at the capital, where his father constantly attended him, Horace went to
Athens and took up the study of philosophy, the customary educational
procedure in his time. Hither in 44 B. C. came Brutus, eager for recruits
for the republican cause, and the student joined his legions. Following
the defeat at Phillippi, he returned to Rome under the general amnesty,
to find the estate of his father, who had died in the meantime, confiscated.
He began work as clerk in the quaestor's office, and wrote, while in this
employment, the earliest of the *Epodes* and the *Satires.*

From his desperation during this period he was rescued by Virgil and
Varius, who had been attracted by his verses, and who introduced him
to the exemplary star of all patrons, Maecenas. Subsequently came recognition, assistance, friendship, to the poet, and then the gift of the famous
Sabine farm. To it Horace retired, and while his future years were
punctuated by frequent visits to Rome he chiefly led the easy, meditative
life which the *Odes* describe for us.

The first book of the *Satires,* and the *Epodes* appeared in the 30's, the
second about 29 B. C. The *Odes,* which he had already begun to write,
were privately circulated, but the first three books of them did not reach
publication until 23 B. C. They immediately established him as the greatest
of Latin lyric poets, just as the satires had secured his reputation in that form
which most nearly corresponds to our essay. During this time he had begun the literary epistles. These were subsequently published in two books.
In them we find the mature sentiments of an author who had come to
be recognized as the greatest living man of letters (Virgil had died in
19 B. C.), and who discourses on all matters with authority but without
tyranny. The *Ars Poetica,* or *Epistle to the Pisos,* is the last placed of these,
though not necessarily the last in time of composition.

Horace did not regard the *Satires,* nor could he have the *Epistles,* as
poetry. In *Satires* I, 4, he declares that the making of verses is not sufficient
to give one the exalted name of poet, when only the alteration of rhythm
would reduce them to prose. He here proceeds to give his definition:

Ingenium cui sit, cui mens divinior atque os
Magna sonaturam, des nominis huius honorem.

"Who has genius, the divine mind, and the tongue skilled to resound mighty things, him honor with the name of poet."

Whether the Piso family to whom the *Ars Poetica* was addressed was that of L. Calpurnius Piso, whose eldest son would have been maturing in Horace's last years, or the family of the earlier Cn. Calpurnius Piso, is of no moment for the understanding of the treatise. The poet's authoritative manner is more in keeping with the later period of his life, and so persuades toward the right of the first mentioned family.

The style is familiar and discursive. Horace follows no set design, and mixes maxims in a manner which makes the treatise hard to follow and to retain. As in all of Horace's work, the phrases and lines are individually masterpieces, carvings in the small; not only does he lay down doctrines, but he stations indestructible mile-posts, which throughout criticism become watchwords, mottoes, countersigns, shibboleths: *Purpureus pannus* (the purple patch), *labor limae* (the labor of the file), *aut prodesse aut delectare* (either to be of profit or to please), *ut pictura poesis* (the poem, like the picture), *Decipimur specie recti* (we are deceived by the appearance of truth), *dormitat Homerus* (Homer sometimes sleeps), *Parturiunt montes, nascetur ridiculus mus* (mountains are in labor, for the birth of a ridiculous mouse). The admirable conciseness with which critical observations are made and advices given, the extremely quotable quality of his lines, is destined later to make for a misunderstanding of Horace's real position: to the Renaissance and later periods his dicta became, in the words of Mr. J. W. H. Atkins, "none other than a frigid formalism, a body of conventions and rules which were binding on all poets; so that with him, indirectly, began the reign of authority and rule, as well as the constriction of literature in accordance with pre-established schemes of the past." [*Literary Criticism in Antiquity*, II, 102.] "This is what our master Horace tells us," says Dante innocently; and Vida, Boileau, and Pope, both by formal acknowledgment and by obvious adaptation of the Roman's lines, credit his authority as lawgiver. But if one reads the *Ars Poetica* not only for content but also for the spirit that never quite leaves it, the natural modesty, the consolingly sensible "utilitarian views on literature and life," (to use a phrase of Mr. Atkins'), the never-for-long-absent humor—he will realize that these lines of Horace are not merely for a school, but are for all literature.

The matter of the treatise requires little clarification after being understood, but it may be given emphasis by outline and summary.

After a brief and humorous exhortation to unity of design in writing, and a dissertation on the life of words which itself rises to the level of pure poetry, the critic discusses at length the division into types, stressing the necessity of observing what rules pertain to each. This leads naturally to an emphasis of types in character, and a conventionalizing, which is from our point of view unfortunate, of the personae. Achilles, Orestes, Ino, Ixion, are to be always the same; not even a Piso may discover a new characteristic in them. Deploring the unlearned and the mercenary attitudes of his contemporary versifiers, Horace passes to the aim of poetry—either to please or to instruct—urges the judgment of common sense and the wisdom of philosophy, and closes with a characterization, in his best satiric style, of the mad rhymester.

The lack of a clear, logical order in the epistle has led numerous commentators and at least one translator (Ben Jonson) to try to find a better arrangement. Indeed, the manner in which Horace leaps, without any warning to his reader, from one idea to another defies explanation, and receives but slight justification from the attempt to show a threefold division in the treatise. [See Atkins, *op. cit.*, II, 70, quoting E. Norden: "Die Composition und Litteraturgattung der Hor. Epistula ad Pisones."] For even though it be granted that the scheme honored by earlier Hellenistic critics was followed by Horace, and the *Ars Poetica* planned and executed in three parts, "(a) *poesis* or subject matter (ll. 1–41), (b) *poema* or form (ll. 42–294), (c) *poeta* or the poet (ll. 295–476)" [*ibid.*, II, 73], the last two of these divisions reveal within themselves a disconcerting lack of continuity. One is at last led to guess either that the poem never received the final form intended for it, or that its author felt sufficiently close to the Pisos to present to them a group of rather loosely united observations on his subject.

The present translators have divided the treatise in accordance with what appear the main sections of thought, and have introduced captions for each: the lines which are thus grouped together make satisfactorily unified short chapters or sections. There have been introduced as footnotes passages from the poetic translations of Ben Jonson (1640), the Earl of Roscommon (1680), and Francis Howes (1845).

EPISTLE TO THE PISOS

Or *The Art of Poetry* *

[The Importance of Unity]

SHOULD some painter take the fancy to draw the neck of a horse joined to a human head, and to overlay with varicolored plumage limbs gathered from anywhere and everywhere, making what appeared at the top a beautiful woman to end below as a foul fish, when you were admitted to the spectacle, should you, even though his friends, restrain your laughter? Believe me, dear Pisos, most similar to such a picture would be a book which figured forth, like the dreams of one in a fever, mad imaginings wherein neither foot nor head could be attributed to any one shape.

"But to painters and to poets the right has always been conceded of daring what they willed." Granted, and this privilege we ask for our-

* Translated by James Harry and Sara Catron Smith.

selves and allow to others: but not to the extent that wild animals should unite with tame, that serpents should be mated with birds, or lambs with tigers.*

Poems very often begin sonorously, making great promises; then, as they proceed, one widely gleaming purple patch [1] after another is sewn on, when there are described the grove and altar of Diana and the winding stream that rushes through the goodly fields, or the River Rhine, or the rainbow. But here was not the place for these descriptions. Furthermore, perhaps you (a painter) are particularly adept at sketching a cypress tree: what of it, if he who pays you to paint him is to be represented swimming in despair from a wrecked fleet? When a wine jar has been begun, on what excuse is a small pitcher brought from the potter's wheel? In short, whatever you design, let it have, if nothing else, simplicity and unity.

Noble sire and worthy sons, most of us poets are deceived by the semblance of excellence. I endeavor to be brief and become obscure; sinew and spirit desert the searcher after polish; one striving for grandeur becomes bombastic; whosoever is excessively cautious and fearful of the tempest crawls along the ground; and he who yearns after too prodigal a variety in his theme—he paints a dolphin in the forest, or a wild boar amid the waves. If the poet not have genuine artistry, the effort to avoid an imperfection leads him into graver botchery.

The poorest artificer who dwells near the Aemelian School will model the nails and imitate the flowing hair in bronze, but he will fail in the prime essential of his work, because he will not know how to order it as a whole. If I were taking pains to compose anything, I should no more wish to be this fellow than I should to go through life with a misshapen nose, at the same time much admired for comely black eyes and hair.

Choose material proportionate to your powers, you who write, and long consider what your shoulders can carry, what they cannot. Neither command of language nor perspicuous arrangement will fail the author who has chosen his subject wisely. The excellence and charm of arrangement, if I be not much mistaken, consists in this,—to say at each and every time just what should at that time be said, and to defer a very great

---

* Jonson:

If to a woman's head a painter would
Set a horse-neck, and divers feathers fold
On every limb, ta'en from a several creature,
Presenting upwards a fair female feature,
Which in some swarthy fish uncomely ends:
Admitted to the sight, although his friends,
Could you contain your laughter? Credit me,
This piece, my Pisos, and that book agree,
Whose shapes, like sick men's dreams, are feign'd so vain,
As neither head, nor feet, one form retain.

[1] *Purpureus pannus:* purple patch.

part of what might be said, and for the nonce omit it. The author must choose and reject as he pushes forward with his poem.*

[Words]

Respecting words,—though discerning and careful in your groupings of them, you will have spoken excellently if a happy phrasing gives a quite familiar word an air of novelty. If perchance it becomes necessary to relate abstruse matters in novel terms, it will be allowable to coin words unheard of by the (ancient) girded Cethegi, and the license will be granted to do this discreetly. And new or recently formed words will find acceptance if they proceed from a Greek source, only moderately altered. For why should Virgil and Varius be denied what was granted Caecilius and Plautus? Or why should I be criticized if I can add a few new words, since the speech of Cato and of Ennius enriched the language of our ancestors and brought forward new names for things. It has been and always must be permissible to give currency to words that bear the stamp of present usage.

As fall the earliest of forest leaves, changing with the autumnal seasons, so words perish of old age; the newborn ones flourish and grow strong, in the manner of things young. To death we owe ourselves and all that is ours, whether (a work worthy of a king) an artificial harbor that shelters ships from the north winds, whether a drained swamp, once worthless and navigable by oars, that now feeds towns and cities, and bears the heavy plow, whether a river that, better directed, has quit the course so destructive to the crops: the achievements of men pass; still less may endure the repute and charm of modes of speech.

Many expressions will be born again which now have perished, and many will die which now enjoy distinction, if it be so willed by usage, within whose sway rest the arbitrament, and the law, and the standard, of speech.**

* Roscommon:

As well the force as ornament of verse,
Consists in choosing a fit time for things,
And knowing when a muse should be indulg'd
In her full flight, and when she should be curb'd.

** Roscommon:

Words are like leaves, some wither ev'ry year,
And ev'ry year a younger race succeeds;

Death is a tribute all things owe to fate;
The Lucrine mole (Caesar's stupendous work)
Protects our navies from the raging north;
And (since Cethegus drain'd the Pontine Lake)
We plough and reap where former ages row'd.
See how the Tiber (whose licentious waves
So often overflow'd the neighb'ring fields,)
Now runs a smooth and inoffensive course,
Confin'd by our great emperor's command:
Yet this, and they, and all, will be forgot:

[Meters and their Appropriateness]

Homer has shown us in what meter may best be written the deeds of kings and great captains, and somber war. Verses of unequal length [a couplet of one hexameter line and one pentameter] were first used for laments, later also for the sentiment that attends granted beseechings. But who the author was of these shortened elegiac verses, critics dispute, and the altercation remains unsettled. His rage armed Archilochus with his iambic: comedy and tragedy have adopted it, as being natural for dialogue, able to drown out the noise of the audience, and suited to action. The Muse has given to the lyre the celebration of the gods and their off-spring, the victorious boxer, the horse first in the race, the amorous yearnings of youth, and the unrestrained pleasures of wine. If I do not know and cannot observe the conventions and forms of poems, why am I called by the name of poet? Why should I, through a false sense of modesty, choose rather not to know than to learn? Comic material is not to be treated in the verses of tragedy; similarly, it would be outrageous to narrate the feast of Thyestes in verses proper to common daily life and almost to comedy. Each particular *genre* should keep the place allotted to it. And yet occasionally Comedy exalts her style, and angered Chremes scolds with excited voice; and frequently the tragic figure expresses his grief in more lowly speech: Telephus and Peleus, poverty-stricken and in exile, put aside their bluster and their words a foot and a half long if their plaintive cries are meant to touch the spectator's heart.

[Characters: Consistency and Conventionality]

It is not enough that poems be beautiful: they must be charming too, and must lead the hearer's mind in whatsoever direction they will. As human countenances smile on those who are smiling, so too they show sympathy with those who weep. If you wish me to weep, you must first grieve yourself. Then your misfortunes will sadden me, Telephus and Peleus. If you speak your part badly, I shall either go to sleep or laugh. Sad words become the sad face, threatening words the angry one, sportive jests the frolicsome, grave precepts the mien of austerity. For

---

Why then should words challenge Eternity, When greatest men, and greatest actions die? Use may revive the obsoletest words.

And banish those that now are most in vogue; Use is the judge, and law, and rule of speech.

nature fashions us within to the various states of fortune: she makes us glad, drives us to anger, tortures and bends us to the ground under weighty sorrow; then she publishes in our speech the passions of our spirits. If the actor's words be not in keeping with his fortune, the Roman gentry will laugh jeeringly, and the commoners too.

It will make a great difference whether a god is speaking or a hero, whether a seasoned old man or a hot-headed, impetuous youth, whether an influential matron or an officious nurse, whether a wandering merchant or the farmer of a small, flourishing estate, whether a Colchian or an Assyrian, a Theban or an Argive.

Either follow established tradition or make your invention consistent. If perchance you write of the famed Achilles, make him energetic, wrathful, inexorable, fierce; no laws will he grant to have application to himself; there is nothing which he will not think must be associated with arms. Make your Medea savage and unsubdued, your Ino tearful, Ixion perfidious, Io a wanderer, Orestes melancholy.

If you introduce into your scene anything not previously tried, and presume to create a new character, keep him to the very end as he was at the beginning, and make him consistent. It is difficult to treat general material individualistically, and you will do better to turn the *Iliad* into drama than to produce matter not known and not previously composed upon. What is public property will become your private own if you not linger upon the trite, commonly trodden path, nor take pains to be an overly careful, word-for-word translator, nor plunge headlong into narrow straits of imitation, to take one step out of which, shame or the rules of the work will prevent.

[A Digression on Beginnings]

Do not begin your poem after the manner of that Cyclic author of a former time: "The destiny of Priam I shall sing, and heroic war." What will this promiser produce worthy of such a wide-mouthed boast? Mountains are in labor: there is born a ridiculous mouse. How much more rectitude an author has who does not set himself to his work with an absurdity: "Speak to me, O Muse, of the man who, after Troy was captured, viewed 'cities of men, and manners.' " [2] He expects to give you—not smoke after a lightning flash, but rather clear light after smoke, presently to unfold his shining wonders: Antiphates, Scylla, the

---

[2] The beginning of *The Odyssey*.

Cyclops, Charybdis. Nor does he begin the narration of Diomedes' return with the death of Meleager, nor the story of the Trojan war with the twin egg.[3] Always he pushes on toward the outcome, and he rushes his audience into the midst of things [4] as though they were already well known; he leaves out what on trial he has despaired of making shine; and he so coins his fables, so mixes the fictitious with the true, that the middle of the story is not incongruous with the first, nor the end with the middle.

[Characters: "the Types"]

Heed what I, and the public with me, desire, if your wish is for an enthusiastic spectator who will remain until the dropping of the curtain, and until the actor at the last calls, "Applaud": you must observe the manners of each age, presenting what is seemly for the varying natures and degrees of advancement in years. The lad just beginning to repeat words, just old enough to leave a footprint, longs to play with his chums, acquires and loses his anger causelessly, changes by the hour. The beardless youth, when at last his tutor or attendant is away, takes his pleasure with dogs and horses and in the sunny, grassy field: he is like wax, when an evil exists that he might be turned to; is rude to those who would instruct him; is slow to make useful provision, wasteful of money, soaring and ambitious, quick to forsake what he was formerly devoted to. With different enthusiasms, the older and manly mind desires affluence and friendships; he is ambition's slave; guards against doing what he might shortly strive to change. Many misfortunes beset the old man, whether because he is avaricious and miserly with what he has, and fearful in the use of it, or because he manages all his affairs faintheartedly and indifferently—is dilatory, slow to hope, sluggish, greedy of life, obstinate—is a praiser of times past, when he was a boy, and a reprover and critic of his juniors. The years to come bring many blessings with them; the passing years take many away. And so, lest the role of senility be allotted to a youth, or that of maturity to a child, we must always give attention to what belongs and is fitting to each age.

---

[3] Meleager, one of the Argonauts, was uncle of the hero Diomedes; his life and death would be unrelated to the return from Troy of his famous nephew. Yet a poem on the latter is alleged to have been begun with Meleager's death.

The "twin egg" (*gemino ab ovo*) is a reference to the birth of Helen, who was sister to the twins Castor and Pollux, and who, according to legend, was the issue of one of two eggs resulting from Leda's union with Jupiter disguised as a swan, the brothers being the product of the other.

[4] *In medias res.*

[Specific Advices on Tragedy, with a Digression on Satyric Drama]

Events are either performed on the stage or related as having occurred. Matters communicated by ear excite the mind more slowly than those which are brought before the faithful eyes, and which the spectator takes in for himself. Yet you must not produce on the stage actions which should be carried on behind the scenes, and must keep from the eyes certain incidents which presently one who viewed them will eloquently narrate. Do not have Medea slaughter her children before the audience, or wicked Atreus cook openly organs of a human body, or Procne be changed into a bird, Cadmus into a serpent. Whatever you show me thus, I disbelieve and despise.

The play which one hopes to have called for and reproduced after it has once been seen should have no more or less than five acts; nor should a god intervene unless there occurs a knot worthy of such an untier; nor should a fourth actor strive to speak. Let the chorus spiritedly sustain an actor's part and purpose, nor sing between the acts anything which is not conducive or contributory to the main design. Let it favor good men and counsel them in a friendly manner, restrain the wrathful, and show affection for those who fear to sin; let it praise temperance in feasts, sound laws and justice, and peace with the gates standing open; let it keep secret whatever matters are entrusted to it; let it pray to the gods and beseech them that fortune return to the wretched and forsake the haughty.

In former times the tibia, not (as now) brass bound and a rival of the tuba, but a slender and simple instrument with few stops on it, served the useful purposes of accompanying and assisting the chorus and of filling with its sound the sparsely filled benches, whither was wont to gather a crowd very easily numbered, inasmuch as it was small, and a temperate, virtuous, and modest crowd. Later, when there began the victorious expansion of domain, when the more extensive walls began to encircle the cities, and in broad daylight and with impunity men satisfied their appetites with wine on festal days, greater license entered into the (dramatic) meters and harmonies. For what discernment would the unlettered have, or the fellow free from his job, peasant mingled with city man, base individual with respected? So to his art of former times the flute-player added gesture and extravagance of manner, and trailed a train as he walked across the stage; so, too, new tones swelled from the sober strings, and the headlong fluency brought into being a new, unfamiliar sort of eloquence, which for shrewdness in practical

counsel and divination of things to come was hardly different from the
oracular utterances of Delphi.

The class of tragic poet who competed (in earlier days) for the prize
merely of a goat very shortly exposed to view the rustic satyrs naked and,
with safety to his dignity, tried out the coarse joke, since only by entice-
ments and by diverting novelty was he to hold the attention of a spectator who, with the sacrifices finished, was drunken and lawless. It will
nevertheless be proper to introduce these banterers and loose spoken
satyrs, and to pass from serious matters to merry, provided that no god
or hero brought upon the stage shall, though seen but a moment before
in regal gold and purple, depart into dingy taverns amid low conversation; nor shall, while shunning what is low, grasp at cloudy unrealities.
Tragedy, which is not the proper form for babbling verses of levity, may
be likened to a matron who, urged to dance on festival days, will move
for a little while amongst the pert satyrs, but will do so with becoming
modesty. I should not be the one, dear Pisos, to choose only unvarnished
and usual words in writing of satyrs; but I should not so exert myself to
achieve variation from the tragic tone that there remained no distinction
between the speech of (the slave) Davus and that of bold Pythias, who
had swindled Simo out of a talent, or that of Silenus, the guardian and
servant of a divine ward. I should take for my poem well known material, of such sort as anyone might hope to make his; but whoever
dared to attempt the same should sweat a-plenty and labor in vain,—so
strong would be the sequence and the connection of the parts, of such
distinction the treatment given to things which were but ordinary. If
the fauns are brought in from their forests, they should not, in my
judgment, as though the public streets and almost the very forum were
their habitat, make a display of the indiscretions of youth in their
shallow verses, or prattle obscenely and disgustingly; men of rank,
family, and means are offended by such faults, nor do they, even
though the purchaser of parched peas and nuts does approve this behavior, accept it in like spirit or present it with a crown.

[The Meter of Drama]

The long syllable preceded by a short is called an iambus,—a rapidly
moving foot: its swiftness fixed the name of iambic trimeter upon verse
which has six beats and is without variation first or last. Not so long
ago, in order that it might fall more slowly and a little more weightily
upon the ears, this iambic meter took under its paternal care the steady

marching spondee, doing so as though in kindness and tolerance, but not accommodatingly yielding to it the second or fourth places in the line. The iambus appears rarely in the famed trimeters of Accius; and the verses of Ennius, which were given to the stage in all their ponderosity, are to be taxed with the shameful fault either of careless haste or of indifference to art.

Not every critic recognizes unrhythmical verses, and undeserved indulgence has been given to the Roman poets. For that reason shall I ramble without restraint in my writing? Or shall I expect that my faults will be seen, and cautiously stay out of danger and within limits where I may hope for indulgence? If I do that, I have avoided blame, but have not merited praise.

The great Greek models, my friends, turn through by night, turn through by day.* But your fathers praised the numbers and the witticisms of Plautus? They admired both qualities too submissively (I shall not say stupidly)—if you and I can distinguish inurbane language from charming, or can tell proper rhythm by ear or by counting on the fingers.

[Early Greek Drama]

Thespis is credited with the origination of the tragic form, and is reported to have drawn about on wagons these (early) dramas, which were sung and performed by actors with faces smeared with wine lees. After him came Aeschylus, inventor of the mask and of the tragedian's garb, who constructed a stage of small timbers and taught his actors lofty diction and the stateliness of the buskin. There followed the old comedy, which was not without merit; but its freedom of style descended into faultiness and a violence deserving of legal restraint: the law was acknowledged and the chorus silenced, its power to do shameful injury removed.

[The Necessity of Art in Poetry]

Our poets have left none of the forms untried, nor have the authors either of tragedy or of comedy merited less by their daring to forsake Grecian tracks and to celebrate the achievements of their own country. Nor would Latium be any mightier in the realm of shining arms and

---

* Roscommon:
Consider well the Greek originals,

Read them by day, and think of them by night.

valor than in that of literature, if the labor of the file [5] and the tedium of revision were not irksome to each and every one of her poets. Repress, O descendants of Pompilius, any poem which many a day and many a blot have not gone to correcting and to polishing tenfold and in extremest detail.

Because Democritus holds that temperament is of more importance than despised art, and excludes from Mount Helicon all sober poets, a great tribe of the bards do not take care of their fingernails, do not shave, seek out secluded places, avoid the baths. For anyone will get the distinction and title of poet who does not entrust his head to the barber Licinus, a head which could not be made rational by three Anticyra purgings. How stupid I am to purge myself in the spring season. Otherwise, nobody would surpass me in poetry. But it is not worth while. Therefore I shall serve as a whetstone, which, itself incapable of cutting, is able to render steel sharp. Though I write nothing myself, I shall instruct the poet in his function and duty,—shall show him whence his resources come to hand, what nourishes and fashions him, what becomes him and what does not, whither skill will lead him, and whither error.

In good writing, the prime essential, the fountain source, is wisdom. The Socratic writings can give you matter, and the words will follow without difficulty once the material has been provided. He who has learned what he owes to his country, and what to his friends, in what affection a parent should be held, or a brother, or a guest, what a senator's duty is, or a judge's, what the position is of a leader sent into war,—such a one will know how to ascribe to each person whatever is appropriate to him. I should instruct the creative artist who has learned these relationships to look long at the pattern of life and customs, and thence to draw living expressions. Sometimes a play which is brilliant in places and has sound characterization is lacking in beauty, depth, or art; yet it delights the people more and better entertains them than do verses which are devoid of dramatic material and are mere trifles of song.

To the Greeks, desirous only of glory, the Muse gave genius; to them she gave true largeness of utterance. The Romans learn in childhood how by working out long calculations to divide the monetary unit into a hundred parts:—

"Let Albinus' son answer: if one uncia is taken from a quincunx, how much remains? — — you used to be able to answer that."

[5] *Limae labor.*

"A triens."

"That's right. You will be able to take care of your business. If one uncia is added, what will the sum be?"

"A semis." [6]

When once this desire for gain, this avarice, has tainted minds, shall we hope to have poetry written worthy of being preserved with oil of cedar and in cypress cases?

[The Aim of Poetry]

The aim of poets is either to be beneficial or to delight,[7] or in their phrases to combine charm and high applicability to life.[*] Be brief about whatever precepts you give, that receptive minds may readily take them in and faithfully retain them: whatever is to no purpose flows away from the full mind. Whatever you invent for the sake of pleasing, let it be not too distant from truth, and do not in your drama call for belief of just anything you fancy—do not have you a living child dragged from the stomach of the glutted Lamia. The elders' class scorn poetry devoid of useful precept; the knightly caste have little regard for what is austere. By at once delighting and teaching the reader, the poet who mixes the sweet with the useful has everybody's approval. His book earns money for the booksellers' firm of the Sosii; it crosses seas; it extends the literary life of its author.

[6] It has seemed undesirable to try to translate these untranslatable monetary terms; the attempt made by Howes to do so is included below. The dialogue as printed will, it is hoped, sufficiently well convey the impression of an arithmetic lesson.

Howes:

Genius to Greece, to Greece the pride of phrase
Heaven gave, of nothing covetous but praise.
Not so our youth, who, cramped by hopeful drilling,
Learn into fifty parts to split one shilling.
Let young Albinus solve the problem sought:

'Take one from five-pence; what results?'
—'A groat.'
'Good! you're the boy to thrive! But come, explain,
If added, what?'—'A tester.'—'Good again.'—
Where hearts thus trained to petty pelf we find,
And rust like this has cankered o'er the mind,
Who'd look for finished poems, wrought with toil,
Worthy the cypress case and cedar oil?
[7] *Aut prodesse aut delectare.*
[*] Roscommon:

A poet should instruct, or please, or both.

[Of Faults in Poetry]

There are faults, however, for which we wish to make allowance; for the string does not always give back the tone which the mind and hand had willed, and the effort to strike bass very often results in treble; the archer cannot always hit what he aims at. Indeed, when there is much that shines in a poem, I shall not be offended by a few blemishes, which either negligence permitted or human frailty could not avoid. How, then, may we sum up? As a copyist who makes the same mistake repeatedly in spite of warnings loses our indulgence, and as a singer is laughed at if he always falters on the same note, so the author who consistently blunders becomes for me another Choerilus, whose two or three *bon mots* cause amused amazement; and likewise I am irked when on occasion the worthy Homer nods.[8] Indeed, in a long work occasional sleep is bound to creep upon one. As with painting, so with poetry: [9] one picture you will find more captivating the nearer you stand, another, the farther away; one is preferable in shadow, another, for which the acute keenness of the critic need not be feared, wants to be viewed in the light. This one pleases once; that, visited ten times, will still please.*

Elder youth, although I am aware that you have been guided in the way of rectitude by your father's counsel, and that you have good discernment of your own, heed and keep ever in mind this concept: in certain fields of endeavor, moderately good, passable achievement may properly be granted recognition; a lawyer who prosecutes ordinary suits is far below the astute Messalla in ability, nor does he know as much as Cascellius Aulus, and yet he is held in esteem; but that poets may be mediocre neither man, nor gods, nor booksellers have granted.

Offensive, between the enjoyable courses of a banquet, are discordant music, heavy perfume, and poppy-seed with Sardinian honey, since the feast could have dispensed with these: likewise a poem, which is brought into being and designed for the delight of the spirit, if it depart ever so little from the highest in quality, sinks toward the lowest.

One who is ignorant about sports lets athletic equipment alone, and if

---

[8] *Bonus dormitat Homerus.*
[9] *Ut pictura poesis.*
* Roscommon:

But in long works sleep will sometimes surprise,
Homer himself hath been observ'd to nod.

Poems, like pictures, are of diff'rent sorts,
Some better at a distance, others near,
Some love the dark, some choose the clearest light,
And boldly challenge the most piercing eye,
Some please for once, some will for ever please.

he has no skill with quoits, balls, or trundling hoops he takes no part in the games, lest throngs of spectators indulge in justifiable laughter; but the ignoramus about poetry composes verses. Why not? He is freeborn and gentle, and, more to the point, has knightly rank, money, and a character above suspicion! But as for you, you will not speak or perform anything which is contrary to the natural bent of your own mind; such is your judgment, such your intelligence. If at any future time you write something, bring it to the attention of the critic Maecus, to your father's, to mine; and put your manuscript away and keep it for nine years. You can always destroy what you have not published; there is no art to unsay what you have once let go of.

[The High Office of Poetry]

The savage dwellers in the woods were deterred from slaughter and foul living by Orpheus, the priest and messenger of the gods, on which account it was fabled that he tamed tigers and ferocious lions; likewise Amphion, the founder of Thebes, was bruited to move rocks by the sound of his lyre, and with soft entreaty to lead them where he wished. It was the office of wisdom, in that former time, to set the bounds of public and private property, and the limits of the sacred and the secular, to prohibit promiscuous concubinage, and found the rite of marriage; to establish the civic order and record the laws: it was in these performances that the honor and renown of the divine bards and poems came into being. Following these, Homer achieved distinction and Tyrtaeus inspired masculine minds to war with his verses; prophecies were told in verse, the course of life taught, the good will of kings cultivated, and diversion and the victorious achievement of great tasks unfolded: so you need not feel shame for the Muse skillful at the lyre and for Apollo, the god of singers.

[Art or Nature?]

It has been questioned whether a poem achieves worthy distinction through nature or through art. I do not see that either avails alone, application without abundant natural bent or genius untrained, so much does each demand the help of the other, and amicably combine with it. He who yearns to reach the desired goal as a runner takes great pains and does much work as a boy, recoils not from sweat or from cold, abstains from wine and women; any flutist who plays at the Pythian games has first bowed to and trembled under a master. And it is not pardonable to take such an attitude as this: "A marvelous poet am I; [and in our little game ¹⁰] 'scurf take the hindmost'; to me it is disgraceful to be last, and is especially so to admit ignorance of whatever I do not know." *

[Of Insincere Critics and Mad Poets]

Like an auctioneer who urges the crowd to purchase his wares, a poet rich in lands or invested capital bids his fawning abjects to come and seek their profit. Again, if such a one can set you a lavish meal, go surety for some creditless insolvent, or deliver a poor fellow from the entanglements of hopeless litigation, I wonder whether, in his magnificence, he will know how to distinguish between a pretended and a true friend. As for yourself, if you have given or intend to give a present to anyone, do not get the idea of bringing him, filled with grateful pleasure, to hear verses which you have composed. "Beautiful!" he will exclaim, "Fine! Excellently done." He will grow pale over some of the lines; teardrops will bedew his sympathetic eyes; he will leap up, will stamp the ground with his foot. As the hired mourners at a funeral weep, talk, and do more, almost, than the true mourners, so the mocker is more moved than he who honestly praises. There is a saying that when great men attempt to find out whether someone is worthy of their trusting friendship they get him into his cups and rack him with wine; if you write verses, never be deceived by someone's foxlike cunning.

If you recited anything to Quintilius, "Correct this, if you will," he would say, "and this." If you insisted that you were not able after two or three vain attempts to better a passage, he advised that you break it up and return your badly wrought verses to be rehammered. If you preferred to defend rather than alter your faults, he expended no further word or useless exertion to hinder you from your solitary and unrivaled affection for yourself and your work. An honest and prudent man will

---

¹⁰ This is entirely the translators' interpolation, there being no equivalent for it in the Latin text. Annotators both ancient and modern have generally identified the expression *Occupet extremum scabies* (scurf take the hindmost) as a childish exclamation in games like tag; its significance here would therefore seem to be that the hypothetical poet is speaking of poetry as though it were mere play.

* Jonson:

He that's ambitious in the race to touch
The wished goal, both did, and suffer'd much

While he was young; he sweat, and freez'd again,
And both from wine and women did abstaine.
Who since to sing the Pythian rites is heard,
Did learn them first, and once a master fear'd.
But now it is enough to say, I make
An admirable verse. The great scurf take
Him that is last, I scorn to come behind,
Or of the things that ne'er came in my mind
To say, I'm ignorant.

find fault with unskillful verses, will condemn rough ones, will smear the artless with black pen-lines; he will lop off excessive ornaments, will insist that you throw light on what is not clear, will censure ambiguous phrasing, will mark down things to be changed; he will become an Aristarchus. He will not say, "Why shall I offend a friend with trifles?" These trifles will bring the poet to grief if sometime they cause him to be unfavorably exposed and laughed at.

Just as those who are wise flee from and fear to touch a man ravaged by scurf or jaundice, or obsessed with some insane delusion or lunacy, so they fear and avoid a mad poet. Children taunt him and reckless persons dog his steps. While he walks about belching forth lofty verses, if he, like a fowler watching blackbirds, falls into a well or pit, let no man take the pains to answer his prolonged cry of "Help! Quick, fellow citizens." If anyone does care to give him aid and to let down a rope, "Who knows," I would say, "but that he deliberately threw himself there and does not wish to be saved?" And I should relate the story of the Sicilian poet's finish: "Empedocles, because he longed to be considered an immortal god, coolly leapt into burning Aetna. Your poet should be allowed the prerogative of destroying himself. Whoever saves someone against his will is no better than a murderer. Not just once has he done this, nor will he, if pulled out this time, become like other men and put by this desire for a notorious death. Nor is it satisfactorily clear why he persistently continues to write verses, whether he committed a nuisance on his father's grave, or impiously violated some consecrated place. But 'tis certain he is crazy, and, like a bear that has broken the bars of his cage, he puts to flight both the learned and the unlearned with his violent declaiming. And when he succeeds in catching someone, he holds fast the poor victim and reads him to death, a very leech that will not let go the skin until sated with blood."

DANTE ALIGHIERI

(1265-1321)

DANTE ALIGHIERI was born in Florence in 1265; his father is said to have been a notary, and his family belonged to the minor nobility. The young Dante had no regular occupation, but devoted himself to studying, verse-making, and drawing. By the time he was eighteen he had gained some distinction as a lyric poet, and numbered among his friends the poets Guido Cavalcanti and Cino da Pistoia, the painter Giotto (whose surviving portrait of Dante seems the only authentic one), and the musician Casella. And he had seen Beatrice, whom, in Grandgent's phrase [*Dante*, 5], "he ardently worship but never wooed. . . . She was to him, in all likelihood, both a real being and a symbol; but her allegorical value, as it ever became more distinct, progressively etherealized his image of her human self, until at last her bodily form served only to lend visible beauty to an abstract principle." After her death in 1290, Dante immersed himself in study, but some four years later he collected his poems to her, connected them with a prose narrative, and published the autobiographic story under the title *Vita Nuova*.

Apparently affianced in boyhood to Gemma Donati, Dante married her at some time in his young manhood; two sons and two daughters were born to them. He also served as a soldier, fighting as a horseman in the Battle of Campaldino, and he became a member of the Guild of Doctors and Apothecaries (important civic offices were restricted to members of guilds, but there is no record as to Dante's qualifications for membership). Before 1300, he had served on municipal councils; after that date, he gained a quick and disastrous prominence as champion of domestic order and freedom from papal control. His kinsman, Corso Donati, was leader of the aristocratic Black party; his friend Guido Cavalcanti of the White. A moderate, Dante was caught between two extremes: he served as ambassador to San Gemignano, was elected one of the six Priors who were in executive authority (Cavalcanti was banished for inciting riots during Dante's term of office), served as member of an electoral commission, and as supervisor of street-making; but after the capture of Florence by Charles of Valois (brother of the French king and sponsored by the Pope), Dante was exiled in January, 1302, and his sentence was changed in March to death by fire.

A wanderer from this time on, Dante was in Bologna in 1303, plotting with the Whites to gain control of Florence; when that failed, he traveled to Verona, to northwest Italy, and possibly on to Paris. His *Convivio* was probably written between 1304 and 1308; his *De Vulgari Eloquentia*, left unfinished, was probably begun during this period. *The Divine Comedy* (or *Commedia*) and the *Monarchia* are generally assigned, on no certain evidence, to his later years, although the concluding sentences of the *Vita Nuova* indicate that he was planning the *Commedia* as early as 1294. Dante was expressly excepted in 1311 from a general amnesty by the officials of Florence, and in 1315 his sentence was renewed. He spent some time with the Scaligieri in Verona, where his patron was the young Can Grande della Scala, and to him Dante dedicated the *Paradiso,* with an epistle in Latin explaining his work (the authenticity of this letter is disputed). From Verona he went on to Ravenna, at the invitation of Guido Novella de Polenta; he perhaps gave public lectures there, engaged in a scholarly dispute over an invitation to write an epic in Latin verse, and went on an embassy to Venice in the attempt to prevent an attack on Ravenna. He died in 1321, and was buried in Ravenna.

Early in his career as a writer, Dante begins his defense of the vernacular as a medium for poetry, although his early statement is closely qualified. Poems of love [*Vita Nuova*, D. G. Rossetti's trans.] are properly written in the vulgar tongue: "the first was moved to the writings of such verses by the wish to make himself understood of a certain lady, unto whom Latin poetry was difficult." This curiously practical reason for writing in Italian may have led Dante, as Rossetti thinks [*ibid.,* p. 71], to "put such of his lyrical poems as related to philosophy into the form of love-poems"; Dante himself cautions in the same passage that "This thing is against such as rhyme concerning other matters than love." Gradually he worked out a complete defense for the vulgar tongue, a bold innovation which contemporary scholars protested against, both in the theory and in the practice.

In the *Convivio,* Dante grants [W. W. Jackson's trans.] that "Latin is stable and not subject to decay, while the vulgar tongue is unfixed and is subject to decay." Latin is admitted, here, to be "the more beautiful, the more excellent, and the more noble," but it is not used, and Dante's generous admission of superiority seems to be more dialectical than real. The poet gives three reasons why he used the vernacular: "I was moved to this course through natural affection for my own native speech . . . firstly, to magnify the object loved; secondly, to be jealous for it; thirdly, to defend it." For this mother tongue "shall be a new light and a new sun, which shall rise when the old sun shall set, and shall shine on those who are in darkness and mist because of the old sun which gives no light to them."

These are high words, over-weighing the earlier qualifications, and probably expressing Dante's inherent belief. The same ideas had been expressed indirectly by St. Augustine (354–430 A. D.) when he described his love for Latin poetry and his hatred for the Greek [*Confessions,* I: xiii–xvi, Pusey's trans.]: Latin "I learned without fear of suffering, by mere observation," but Virgil would seem equally unpleasant to Greek children, "when forced to learn him as I was Homer. Difficulty, in truth, the difficulty of a foreign tongue, dashed, as it were, with gall all the sweetness of Grecian fable." To Dante, in turn, Latin seemed a formal, not a natural, language; it had lost its living roots and its reality. For this reason, Boccaccio notes [*The Life of Dante*, 67–68, J. R. Smith's trans.], Dante abandoned his first attempts to write the *Commedia* in Latin (Boccaccio quotes the three opening Latin lines) and put it into "the Florentine idiom . . . in order to be of the most general use to his fellow-citizens and to other Italians. For he knew that if he wrote in Latin metre, as previous poets had done, he would have been useful only to the learned, while by writing in the vernacular he would accomplish something that had never been done before, without preventing his being understood by men of letters."

Thus, Dante's use and defense of the vernacular leads over to a larger, less revolutionary, but at the time no less important task: the defense of poetry itself, or, more broadly, the justification of imaginative literature. Poetry had long been under severe attack. Mr. Saintsbury [*History of Criticism*, I, 380] finds in the writings of St. Augustine the "appearance of what we may call the Puritan attitude to literature, in its earliest and perhaps almost its greatest exponent." To the criteria by which Plato judged poetry—the tests of reality and morality—the Christian writers of the Middle Ages may have added little, but they changed the point of emphasis. Imaginative literature was seen as a temptation away from God, a false and pagan fable. St. Augustine, once a professor of rhetoric and author of a lost treatise *De Apto et Proprio,* makes the attack, and indicates in connection with his remarks on the Bible the line of defense which was later taken by the poets themselves; after quoting from Terence he writes [*Confessions,* I, xv–xvi]: "Not one whit more easily are the words learnt for all this vileness; but by their means the vileness is committed with less shame." Words in themselves may be good, but they may also contain "the wine of error"; from books he had learned "many a useful word, but these may as well be learned in things not vain." Somewhat later, Augustine writes of drama [*op. cit.,* III, ii]: "Stage-plays also carried me away, full of images of my miseries, and of fuel to my fire." (This clerical objection to the psychological unrest caused by fiction is a fundamental one; in beauty, notes Aquinas, desire is quiet, or is quieted; but Tertullian [*De Spectat,* xxii–xxv, Spingarn's trans. 5–6] sees fiction, especially drama, as leading to spiritual agitation, and adds: "the Author of Truth hates all the false. . . . He never will approve pretended loves, and wraths, and groans, and tears.") Augustine objects to poets assigning vices to the Gods, and he tends to read an exact meaning into what the poet has said; yet he commends the symbolical or allegorical interpretation of the Bible: the Catholic faith could be maintained [*op. cit.,* V, xiv], "especially after I had heard one or two places of the Old Testament resolved, and ofttimes '*in a figure*' which when I understood literally, I was slain spiritually"; and he commends Ambrose for recommending [*op. cit.,* VI, iv] "this text for a rule, *The letter killeth, but the spirit giveth life;* whilst he drew aside the mystic veil, laying open spiritually what according to the letter, seemed to teach something unsound." (For the full statement of this allegorical interpretation of the Bible, consult the selection from Aquinas; for its application to poetry, the selections from Dante and Boccaccio.)

By drawing aside the mystic veil from pagan and contemporary poetry, by separating the letter from the spirit, the humanistic defenders of creative literature could present an impressive, if not a clear-cut, defense. Mr. Spin-garn [*op. cit.,* 7–8] notes: "The first instance of the systematic application of the method to the pagan myths occurs in the *Mythologicon* of Fulgentius, who probably flourished in the first half of the sixth century; and in his *Virgiliana Continentia,* the *Aeneid* is treated as an image of life, and the travels of Aeneas as the symbol of the progress of the human soul, from nature, through wisdom, to final happiness. ¶ From this period, the allegorical method became the recognized mode of interpreting literature, whether sacred or profane. Petrarch, in his letter, *De quibusdam fictionibus Virgilij,* treats the *Aeneid* after the manner of Fulgentius. . . ." This method led naturally to the interpretation of Scriptures as recommended by Aquinas (see the Supplement), a method which Dante took over without qualms and applied to his own poetry. Philosophic justification for these interpretations of sacred and profane work can be found in such a remark as that of Scotus Erigena [*De Divisione Mundi,* # 3, Bosanquet's trans.]: "there is nothing, as I think, of visible and corporeal objects which does not signify something incorporeal and [purely] intelligible."

To Dante, Petrarch, and Boccaccio, as to the Middle Ages generally, "symbolism was something more than an artistic device: it represented a habit of mind, a belief in mystic correspondences." [Grandgent, *Dante,* 272]. Criticism never departs far from a consideration of this symbolism, and the method used is the Scholastic: Dante absorbed from Aquinas more than the meanings of allegory. And it may not be without pertinence here that Boccaccio digresses, in his *Life of Dante,* to write a chapter "On the Difference Between Poetry and Theology." His conclusions (p. 54) show in brief compass the attempt to reconcile the Scholastic and the Humanistic points of view:

"I say that theology and poetry can be considered as almost one and the same thing when their subject is the same. Indeed I go further, and assert that theology is simply the poetry of God. What is it but poetic fiction to say in one place of Scripture that Christ is a lion and in another a lamb, now that He is a serpent and now a dragon, and in still another place that He is a rock? And He is called by many other names, to repeat all of which would take too long. What else signify the words of the Savior in the Gospel, if not a teaching different from the outward sense, which manner of speaking we term, using a more common word, allegory. It is clear, then, that not only is poetry theology, but also that theology is poetry. And truly if my words, in so great a matter, merit little credence, I shall not be disturbed; at least let Aristotle, a most worthy authority on all great questions, be believed, who affirmed that he found the poets were the first theologians. Let this suffice for this part, and let us turn to show why poets alone among learned men have been granted the honor of the laurel crown."

This, basically, is the point of view which Boccaccio maintains throughout his *Genealogia Deorum Gentilium.* But this represents only one phase of Dante's critical position, and is stated in the *Convivio* and *Epistle to Can Grande* rather than in the *De Vulgari.* Possibly he had reserved this matter for later treatment; even today, we can hardly go beyond Boccaccio's state-ment [*Life of Dante,* 70] that "when already near his death, he wrote a little book in Latin prose which he entitled *De Vulgari Eloquentia.* . . . Though he seems to have had in mind to compose four parts to this little book . . . only two remain." Even before its intrinsic worth is considered, writes Saintsbury [*op. cit.,* I, 418], the book is of the highest value: "In the first place, there is the importance of date, which gives us in it the first critical treatise on the literary use of the vernacular, at exactly the point when the various vernaculars of Europe had finished, more or less, their first stage. Secondly, there is the importance of authorship, in that we have, as is hardly anywhere else the case, the greatest creative writer, not merely of one literature but of a whole period of the European world, betaking himself to criticism."

From

DE VULGARI ELOQUENTIA *

(1304?)

BOOK I

CHAPTER I

SINCE we do not find that any one before us has treated of the science of the vernacular language, while in fact we see that this language is highly necessary for all, inasmuch as not only men, but even women and children, strive, in so far as nature allows them, to acquire it; and since it is our wish to enlighten to some little extent the discernment of those who walk through the streets like blind men, generally fancying that those things which are [really] in front of them are behind them, we will endeavour, the Word aiding us from heaven, to be of service to the vernacular speech; not only drawing the water of our own wit for such a drink, but mixing with it the best of what we have taken or compiled from others, so that we may thence be able to give draughts of the sweet-est hydromel. But because the business of every science is not to prove but to explain its subject, in order that men may know what that is with which the science is concerned, we say (to come quickly to the point) that what we call the vernacular speech is that to which children are accustomed by those who are about them when they first begin to dis-tinguish words; or to put it more shortly, we say that the vernacular

* Translated by A. G. Ferrers Howell (New York City: E. P. Dutton & Co., Inc.).

speech is that which we acquire without any rule, by imitating our nurses. There further springs from this another secondary speech, which the Romans called grammar.[1] And this secondary speech the Greeks also have, as well as others, but not all. Few, however, acquire the use of this speech, because we can only be guided and instructed in it by the expenditure of much time, and by assiduous study. Of these two kinds of speech also, the vernacular is the nobler, as well because it was the first employed by the human race, as because the whole world makes use of it, though it has been divided into forms differing in pronunciation and vocabulary. It is also the nobler as being natural to us, whereas the other is rather of an artificial kind; and it is of this our nobler speech that we intend to treat.

[Dante explains (chapters II–VII), in scholastic fashion, that man alone was endowed with speech, that Adam was the first speaker, using the Hebraic language, which prevailed until the confusion of tongues sent on man by God at the building of Babel. Dante then (VIII) confines his attention to Europe, which he divides according to language into Northern, Eastern, and Southern; in IX, he limits himself to the three-fold languages of the South, which were at first uniform and are still similar: roughly, the Italians, Provençals, and Spaniards, or those who say *yes,* respectively, by *sì, oïl,* and *oc.* Dante restricts himself (X) to the Italian, examining and rejecting (XI–XV) the dialects of Rome, Ancona, Spoleto, Milan, Bergamo, Sardinia; after more consideration, the dialects of Sicily and Apulia, Tuscany and Florence (although the Illustrious Vernacular is, in Dante's usage if not in his theory, closely related to the Tuscan), Romagna, Brescia, Verona, Padua, Venice, and Bologna.]

CHAPTER XVI

AFTER having scoured the heights and pastures of Italy, without having found that panther which we are in pursuit of, in order that we may be able to find her, let us now track her out in a more rational manner, so that we may with skilful efforts completely enclose within our toils her who is fragrant everywhere but nowhere apparent.

Resuming, then, our hunting-spears, we say that in every kind of

---

[1] By grammar Dante here means a literary language of conventional origin, artificial construction, and permanent character; with special reference to Latin. . . . In *Convivio,* I, ii: 95 ff., he talks of 'the Grammar of the Greeks,' meaning their literary language, and alludes also to the literary language of Provence.—Howell's note.

things there must be one thing by which all the things of that kind may be compared and weighed, and which we may take as the measure of all the others; just as in numbers all are measured by unity and are said to be more or fewer according as they are distant from or near to unity; so also in colours all are measured by white, for they are said to be more or less visible according as they approach or recede from it. And what we say of the predicaments which indicate quantity and quality, we think may also be said of any of the predicaments and even of substance; namely, that everything considered as belonging to a kind becomes measurable by that which is simplest in that kind. Wherefore in our actions, however many the species into which they are divided may be, we have to discover this standard by which they may be measured. Thus, in what concerns our actions as human beings simply, we have virtue, understanding it generally; for according to it we judge a man to be good or bad; in what concerns our actions as citizens, we have the law, according to which a citizen is said to be good or bad; in what concerns our actions as Italians, we have certain very simple standards of manners, customs, and language, by which our actions as Italians are weighed and measured. Now the supreme standards of those activities which are generically Italian are not peculiar to any one town in Italy, but are common to all; and among these can now be discerned that vernacular language which we were hunting for above, whose fragrance is in every town, but whose lair is in none. It may, however, be more perceptible in one than in another, just as the simplest of substances, which is God, is more perceptible in a man than in a brute, in an animal than in a plant, in a plant than in a mineral, in a mineral than in an element, in fire than in earth. And the simplest quantity, which is unity, is more perceptible in an odd than in an even number; and the simplest colour, which is white, is more perceptible in orange than in green.

Having therefore found what we were searching for, we declare the illustrious, cardinal, courtly, and curial vernacular language in Italy to be that which belongs to all the towns in Italy but does not appear to belong to any one of them, and by which all the municipal dialects of the Italians are measured, weighed, and compared.

CHAPTER XVII

WE must now set forth why it is that we call this language we have found by the epithets illustrious, cardinal, courtly, and curial; and by doing this we disclose the nature of the language itself more clearly.

First, then, let us lay bare what we mean by the epithet illustrious, and why we call the language illustrious. Now we understand by this term "illustrious" something which shines forth illuminating and illuminated. And in this way we call men illustrious either because, being illuminated by power, they illuminate others by justice and charity; or else because, having been excellently trained, they in turn give excellent training, like Seneca and Numa Pompilius. And the vernacular of which we are speaking has both been exalted by training and power, and also exalts its followers by honour and glory.

Now it appears to have been exalted by training, inasmuch as from amid so many rude Italian words, involved constructions, faulty expressions, and rustic accents we see that it has been chosen out in such degree of excellence, clearness, completeness, and polish as is displayed by Cino of Pistoja and his friend in their canzoni.

And that it has been exalted by power is plain; for what is of greater power than that which can sway the hearts of men, so as to make an unwilling man willing, and a willing man unwilling, just as this language has done and is doing?

Now that it exalts by honour is evident. Do not they of its household surpass in renown kings, marquises, counts, and all other magnates? This has no need at all of proof.

But how glorious it makes its familiar friends we ourselves know, who for the sweetness of this glory case our exile behind our back. Wherefore we ought deservedly to proclaim this language illustrious.

CHAPTER XVIII

NOR is it without reason that we adorn this illustrious vernacular language with a second epithet, that is, that we call it cardinal: for as the whole door follows its hinge, so that whither the hinge turns the door also may turn, whether it be moved inward or outward, in like manner also the whole herd of municipal dialects turns and returns, moves and pauses according as this illustrious language does, which really seems to be the father of the family. Does it not daily root out the thorny bushes from the Italian wood? Does it not daily insert grafts or plant young trees? What else have its foresters to do but to take away and bring in, as has been said? Wherefore it surely deserves to be adorned with so great a name as this.

Now the reason why we call it "courtly" is that if we Italians had a court it would be spoken at court. For if a court is a common home of all the realm, it is fitting that whatever is of such a character as to be common to all (parts) without being peculiar to any, should frequent this court and dwell there; nor is any other abode worthy of so great an inmate. Such in fact seems to be that vernacular language of which we are speaking; and hence it is that those who frequent all royal palaces always speak the illustrious vernacular. Hence also it is that our illustrious language wanders about like a wayfarer, and is welcomed in humble shelters, seeing we have no court.

This language is also deservedly to be styled "curial," because "curiality" is nothing else but the justly balanced rule of things which have to be done; and because the scales required for this kind of balancing are only wont to be found in the most excellent courts of justice, it follows that whatever in our actions has been well balanced is called curial. Wherefore since this illustrious language has been weighed in the balances of the most excellent court of justice of the Italians, it deserves to be curial. But it seems mere trifling to say that it has been weighed in the balances of the most excellent court of justice of the Italians, because we have no (Imperial) court of justice. To this the answer is easy. For though there is no court of justice of Italy in the sense of a single (supreme) court, like the court of the king of Germany, still the members of such a court are not wanting. And just as the members of the German court are united under one prince, so the members of ours have been united by the gracious light of Reason. Wherefore, though we have no prince, it would be false to assert that the Italians have no (such) court of justice, because we have a court, though in the body it is scattered.

BOOK II

CHAPTER I

URGING on once more the nimbleness of our wit, which is returning to the pen of useful work, we declare in the first place that the illustrious Italian vernacular is equally fit for use in prose and in verse. But because prose writers rather get this language from poets, and because poetry seems to remain a pattern to prose writers, and not the converse, which things appear to confer a certain supremacy, let us first disentangle this language as to its use in metre, treating of it in the order we set forth at the end of the first book.

Let us then first inquire whether all those who write verse in the

vernacular should use this illustrious language; and so far as a superficial consideration of the matter goes, it would seem that they should,
because every one who writes verse ought to adorn his verse as far as
he is able. Wherefore, since nothing affords so great an adornment as the
illustrious vernacular does, it would seem that every writer of verse
ought to employ it. Besides, if that which is best in its kind be mixed
with things inferior to itself, it not only appears not to detract anything
from them but even to improve them. Wherefore if any writer of verse,
even though his verse be rude in matter, mixes the illustrious vernacular
with his rudeness of matter, he not only appears to do well, but to be
actually obliged to take this course. Those who can do little need help
much more than those who can do much, and thus it appears that all
writers of verse are at liberty to use this illustrious language. But this is
quite false, because not even poets of the highest order ought always
to assume it, as will appear from a consideration of what is discussed
farther on. This illustrious language, then, just like our behaviour in
other matters and our dress, demands men of like quality to its own; for
munificence demands men of great resources, and the purple, men of
noble character, and in the same way this illustrious language seeks for
men who excel in genius and knowledge, and despises others, as will
appear from what is said below. For everything which is suited to us
is so either in respect of the genus, or of the species, or of the individual,
as sensation, laughter, war; but this illustrious language is not suited
to us in respect of our genus, for then it would also be suited to the
brutes; nor in respect of our species, for then it would be suited to all
men; and as to this there is no question; for no one will say that this
language is suited to dwellers in the mountains dealing with rustic
concerns: therefore it is suited in respect of the individual. But nothing
is suited to an individual except on account of his particular worth, as
for instance commerce, war, and government. Wherefore if things are
suitable according to worth, that is the worthy (and some men may be
worthy, others worthier and others worthiest), it is plain that good
things will be suited to the worthy, better things to the worthier, and
the best things to the worthiest. And since language is as necessary an
instrument of our thought as a horse is of a knight, and since the best
horses are suited to the best knights, as has been said, the best language
will be suited to the best thoughts. But the best thoughts cannot exist
except where knowledge and genius are found; therefore the best language is only suitable in those in whom knowledge and genius are
found; and so the best language is not suited to all who write verse,

since a great many write without knowledge and genius; and consequently neither is the best vernacular [suited to all who write verse]. Wherefore, if it is not suited to all, all ought not to use it, because no one ought to act in an unsuitable manner. And as to the statement that every one ought to adorn his verse as far as he can, we declare that it is true; but we should not describe an ox with trappings or a swine with a belt as adorned, nay rather we laugh at them as disfigured; for adornment is the addition of some suitable thing.

As to the statement that superior things mixed with inferior effect an improvement [in the latter], we say that it is true if the blending is complete, for instance when we mix gold and silver together; but if it is not, the inferior things appear worse, for instance when beautiful women are mixed with ugly ones. Wherefore, since the theme of those who write verse always persists as an ingredient distinct from the words, it will not, unless of the highest quality, appear better when associated with the best vernacular, but worse; like an ugly woman if dressed out in gold or silk.

CHAPTER II

AFTER having proved that not all those who write verse, but only those of the highest excellence, ought to use the illustrious vernacular, we must in the next place establish whether every subject ought to be handled in it, or not; and if not, we must set out by themselves those subjects that are worthy of it. And in reference to this we must first find out what we understand by that which we call *worthy*. We say that a thing which has worthiness is worthy, just as we say that a thing which has nobility is noble; and if when that which confers the habit is known, that on which the habit is conferred is [also] known, as such, then if we know what worthiness is, we shall know also what *worthy* is. Now worthiness is an effect or end of deserts; so that when any one has deserved well we say that he has arrived at worthiness of good; but when he has deserved ill, at worthiness of evil. Thus we say that a soldier who has fought well has arrived at worthiness of victory; one who has ruled well, at worthiness of a kingdom; also that a liar has arrived at worthiness of shame, and a robber at worthiness of death.

But inasmuch as [further] comparisons are made among those who deserve well, and also among those who deserve ill, so that some deserve well, some better, and some best; some badly, some worse, and some worst; while such comparisons are only made with respect to the end of deserts, which (as has been mentioned before) we call *worthiness,* it is plain that worthinesses are compared together according as they are greater or less, so that some are great, some greater, and some greatest; and, consequently, it is obvious that one thing is worthy, another worthier, and another worthiest. And whereas there can be no such comparison of worthinesses with regard to the same object [of desert] but [only] with regard to different objects, so that we call *worthier* that which is worthy of greater objects, and *worthiest* that which is worthy of the greatest, because no thing can be more worthy [than another] in virtue of the same qualification, it is evident that the best things are worthy of the best [objects of desert], according to the requirement of the things. Whence it follows that, since the language we call illustrious is the best of all the other forms of the vernacular, the best subjects alone are worthy of being handled in it, and these we call the *worthiest* of those subjects which can be handled; and now let us hunt out what they are. And, in order to make this clear, it must be observed that, as man has been endowed with a threefold life, namely, vegetable, animal, and rational, he journeys along a threefold road; for in so far as he is vegetable he seeks for what is useful, wherein he is of like nature with plants; in so far as he is animal he seeks for that which is pleasurable, wherein he is of like nature with the brutes; in so far as he is rational he seeks for what is right—and in this he stands alone, or is a partaker of the nature of the angels. It is by these three kinds of life that we appear to carry out whatever we do; and because in each one of them some things are greater, some greatest, within the range of their kind, it follows that those which are greatest appear the ones which ought to be treated of supremely, and consequently, in the greatest vernacular.

But we must discuss what things are greatest; and first in respect of what is useful. Now in this matter, if we carefully consider the object of all those who are in search of what is useful, we shall find that it is nothing else but safety. Secondly, in respect of what is pleasurable; and here we say that that is most pleasurable which gives pleasure by the most exquisite object of appetite, and this is love. Thirdly, in respect of what is right; and here no one doubts that virtue has the first place. Wherefore these three things, namely, safety, love, and virtue, appear to be those capital matters which ought to be treated of supremely, I mean the things which are most important in respect of them, as prowess in arms, the fire of love, and the direction of the will. And if we duly consider, we shall find that the illustrious writers have written poetry in the vulgar tongue on these subjects exclusively; namely, Bertran de Born on Arms, Arnaut Daniel on Love, Giraut de Borneil on Righteousness, Cino of Pistoja on Love, his friend on Righteousness. For Bertran says:—

> *'Non posc mudar c'un cantar non exparja.'* [2]
> Arnaut: *'L'aura amara fals bruols brancuz clairir.'* [3]
> Giraut: *'Per solaz reveillar*
>   *que s'es trop endormitz.'* [4]
> Cino: *'Digno sono eo de morte.'* [5]
> His friend: *'Doglia mi reca nello core ardire.'* [6]

I do not find, however, that any Italian has as yet written poetry on the subject of Arms.

Having then arrived at this point, we know what are the proper subjects to be sung in the highest vernacular language.

[In Chapter III, of Book II, Dante describes various forms of poems, and decides that the canzone is noblest and most worthy.]

CHAPTER IV

HAVING then laboured by a process of disentangling [to show] what persons and things are worthy of the courtly vernacular, as well as the form of verse which we deem worthy of such honour that it alone is fitted for the highest vernacular, before going off to other topics, let us explain the form of the canzone, which many appear to adopt rather at haphazard than with art; and let us unlock the workshop of the art of that form which has hitherto been adopted in a casual way, omitting the form of ballate and sonnets, because we intend to explain this in the fourth book of this work, when we shall treat of the middle vernacular language.

Reviewing, therefore, what has been said, we remember that we have frequently called those who write verse in the vernacular poets; and this we have doubtless ventured to say with good reason, because they are in fact poets, if we take a right view of poetry, which is nothing else but a rhetorical composition set to music. But these poets differ from the great poets, that is, the regular ones, for the language of the great poets was regulated by art, whereas these, as has been said, write at haphazard. It therefore happens that the more closely we copy the great

---

[2] 'I cannot choose but utter a song.'
[3] 'The bitter blast strips bare the leafy woods.'
[4] 'For the awakening of gallantry which is too fast asleep [I thought to labour].'

[5] 'Worthy am I of death.' Masson's translations.
[6] 'Grief makes me in the heart to burn.' Brown's translation. The friend is, of course, Dante.

poets, the more correct is the poetry we write; whence it behooves us, by devoting some trouble to the work of teaching, to emulate their poetic teaching.

Before all things therefore we say that each one ought to adjust the weight of the subject to his own shoulders, so that their strength may not be too heavily taxed, and he be forced to tumble into the mud. This is the advice our master Horace gives us when he says in the beginning of his 'Art of Poetry' ['Ye who write] take up a subject [suited to your strength'].

Next we ought to possess a discernment as to those things which suggest themselves to us as fit to be uttered, so as to decide whether they ought to be sung in the way of tragedy, comedy, or elegy. By tragedy we bring in (*sic*) the higher style, by comedy the lower style, by elegy we understand the style of the wretched. If our subject appears fit to be sung in the tragic style, we must then assume the illustrious vernacular language, and consequently we must bind up a canzone. If, however, it appears fit to be sung in the comic style, sometimes the middle and sometimes the lowly vernacular should be used; and the discernment to be exercised in this case we reserve for treatment in the fourth book. But if our subject appears fit to be sung in the elegiac style, we must adopt the lowly vernacular alone.

But let us omit the other styles and now, as is fitting, let us treat of the tragic style. We appear then to make use of the tragic style when the stateliness of the lines as well as the loftiness of the construction and the excellence of the words agree with the weight of the subject. And because, if we remember rightly, it has already been proved that the highest things are worthy of the highest, and because the style which we call tragic appears to be the highest style, those things which we have distinguished as being worthy of the highest song are to be sung in that style alone, namely, Safety, Love, and Virtue, and those other things, our conceptions of which arise from these; provided that they be not degraded by any accident.

Let every one therefore beware and discern what we say; and when he purposes to sing of these three subjects simply, or of those things which directly and simply follow after them, let him first drink of Helicon, and then, after adjusting the strings, boldly take up his *plectrum* and begin to ply it. But it is in the exercise of the needful caution and discernment that the real difficulty lies; for this can never be attained to without strenuous efforts of genius, constant practice in the art, and the habit of the sciences. And it is those [so equipped] whom the poet in the sixth book of the *Æneid* describes as beloved of God, raised by glowing virtue to the sky, and sons of the Gods, though he is speaking figuratively. And therefore let those who, innocent of art and science, and trusting to genius alone, rush forward to sing of the highest subjects in the highest style, confess their folly and cease from such presumption; and if in their natural sluggishness they are but geese, let them abstain from imitating the eagle soaring to the stars.

[Chapter V discusses the different lines admissible in canzoni, the line of eleven syllables being the stateliest; next come the lines of seven, five, and three syllables. Chapter VI takes up the arrangement of words in sentences: only the most excellent kind is suitable for canzoni.]

CHAPTER VII

THE next division of our progress now demands that an explanation be given as to those words which are of such grandeur as to be worthy of being admitted into that style to which we have awarded the first place. We declare therefore to begin with that the exercise of discernment as to words involves by no means the smallest labour of our reason, since we see that a great many sorts of them can be found. For some words are *childish*, some *feminine*, and some *manly;* and of these last some are *sylvan*, others *urban;* and of those we call urban we feel that some are *combed-out* and *glossy*, some *shaggy* and *rumpled.* Now among these urban words the combed-out and the shaggy are those which we call *grand;* whilst we call the glossy and the rumpled those whose sound tends to superfluity, just as among great works some are works of magnanimity, others of smoke; and as to these last, although when superficially looked at there may be thought to be a kind of ascent, to sound reason no ascent, but rather a headlong fall down giddy precipices will be manifest, because the marked-out path of virtue is departed from. Therefore look carefully, Reader, consider how much it behooves thee to use the sieve in selecting noble words; for if thou hast regard to the illustrious vulgar tongue which (as has been said above) poets ought to use when writing in the tragic style in the vernacular (and these are the persons whom we intend to fashion), thou wilt take care that the noblest alone are left in thy sieve. And among the number of these thou wilt not be able in any wise to place childish words, because of their simplicity, as *mamma* and *babbo, mate* and *pate;* nor feminine words, because of their softness, as *dolciada* and *placevole;* nor sylvan words, because of their roughness, as *greggia* and *cetra;* nor the glossy nor the rumpled urban words, as *femina* and *corpo.* Therefore thou wilt see that only the combed-out and the shaggy urban words will be left to thee, which are the noblest, and members of the illustrious vulgar tongue. Now we call those words *combed-out* which have three, or as nearly as possible three syllables; which are without aspirate, without acute or circumflex accent, without the double letters *z* or *x,* without double liquids, or a liquid placed immediately after a mute, and which, having been planed (so to say), leave the speaker with a certain sweetness, like *amore, donna, disio, vertute, donare, letitia, salute, securitate, defesa.*

We call *shaggy* all words besides these which appear either necessary or ornamental to the illustrious vulgar tongue. We call *necessary* those which we cannot avoid, as certain monosyllables like *sì, no, me, te, se, a, e, i, o, u,* the interjections, and many more. We describe as *ornamental* all polysyllables which when mixed with combed-out words produce a fair harmony of structure, though they may have the roughness of aspirate, accent, double letters, liquids, and length; as *terra, honore, speranza, gravitate, alleviato, impossibilità, impossibilitate, benaventuratissimo, inanimatissimamente, disaventuratissimamente, sovramagnificentissimamente,* which last has eleven syllables. A word might yet be found with more syllables still; but as it would exceed the capacity of all our lines it does not appear to fall into the present discussion; such is that word *honorificabilitudinitate,* which runs in the vernacular to twelve syllables, and in grammar to thirteen, in two oblique cases.

In what way shaggy words of this kind are to be harmonised in the lines with combed-out words, we leave to be taught farther on. And what has been said [here] on the pre-eminent nature of the words to be used may suffice for every one of inborn discernment.[1]

[Chapters VIII–XIV present a technical discussion of Canzoni, Stanzas and their arrangement, Rhyme, etc.]

---

[1] Saintsbury [*History of Criticism,* I, 436,] writes: "He [Dante] knows . . . that prosemen may have the treatment of the same subjects; but he knows that the poet's treatment is different, and he goes straight for the difference.

"And where does he find it? Exactly where Wordsworth five hundred years later refused to find it, in Poetic Diction and in Metre. The contrast of the *De Vulgari Eloquio* and of the *Preface* to *Lyrical Ballads* is so remarkable that it may be doubted whether there is any more remarkable thing of the kind in literature. . . . And, moreover, though in tendency the two tractates are diametrically opposed, he nowhere answers Dante; but, on the contrary, is answered by Dante."

From

EPISTOLA X *

[The letter to Can Grande della Scala]

(*c.* 1318)

.   .   .

6. Therefore if we desire to furnish some introduction to a part of any work, it behoves us to furnish some knowledge of the whole of which it is a part. Wherefore I too, desiring to furnish something by way of introduction to the above-named portion of the *Comedy,* have thought that something concerning the whole work should be premised, that the approach to the part should be the easier and more complete. There are six things then which must be inquired into at the beginning of any work of instruction; to wit, the *subject, agent, form,* and *end,* the *title of the work,* and the *branch of philosophy* it concerns. And there are three of these wherein this part which I purposed to design for you differs from the whole; to wit, *subject, form,* and *title;* whereas in the others it differs not, as is plain on inspection. And so, an inquiry concerning these three must be instituted specially with reference to the work as a whole; and when this has been done the way will be sufficiently clear to the introduction of the part. After that we shall examine the other three, not only with reference to the whole but also with reference to that special part which I am offering to you.

7. To elucidate, then, what we have to say, be it known that the sense of this work is not simple, but on the contrary it may be called polysemous, that is to say, 'of more senses than one'; [1] for it is one sense

---

* Translated by Philip H. Wicksteed (New York City: E. P. Dutton & Co., Inc.).
[1] Dante has explained this idea of allegory more completely in the Second Tractate of his *Convivio* (*c.* 1304–8; W. W. Jackson's trans.): . . . I say that, as is affirmed in the first chapter, it is meet for this exposition to be both literal and allegorical. And to make this intelligible, it should be known that writings can be understood and ought to be expounded chiefly in four senses. The first is called literal, and this is that sense which does not go beyond the strict limits of the letter; the second is called allegorical, and this is disguised under the cloak of such stories, and is a truth hidden under a beautiful fiction. Thus Ovid says that Orpheus with his lyre made beasts tame, and trees and stones move towards himself; that is to say that the wise man by the instrument of his voice makes cruel hearts grow mild and humble, and those who have not the life of Science and of Art move to his will, while they who have no rational life are as it were like stones. And wherefore this dis-

which we get through the letter, and another which we get through the thing the letter signifies; and the first is called literal, but the second allegorical or mystic. And this mode of treatment, for its better manifestation, may be considered in this verse: 'When Israel came out of Egypt, and the house of Jacob from a people of strange speech, Judæa became his sanctification, Israel his power.' For if we inspect the letter alone the departure of the children of Israel from Egypt in the time of Moses is presented to us; if the allegory, our redemption wrought by Christ; if the moral sense, the conversion of the soul from the grief and misery of sin to the state of grace is presented to us; if the anagogical, the departure of the holy soul from the slavery of this corruption to the liberty of eternal glory is presented to us. And although these mystic senses have each their special denominations, they may all in general be called allegorical, since they differ from the literal and historical; for *allegory* is derived from *alleon,* in Greek, which means the same as the Latin *alienum* or *diversum.*

8. When we understand this we see clearly that the *subject* round which the alternative senses play must be twofold. And we must therefore consider the subject of this work as literally understood, and then its subject as allegorically intended. The subject of the whole work, then, taken in the literal sense only, is 'the state of souls after death,' without qualification, for the whole progress of the work hinges on it and about it. Whereas if the work be taken allegorically the subject is 'man, as by good or ill deserts, in the exercise of the freedom of his choice, he becomes liable to rewarding or punishing justice.'

9. Now the *form* is twofold, the form of the treatise and the form of the treatment. The form of the treatise is threefold, according to its threefold division. The first division is that by which the whole work is

---

guise was invented by the wise will be shown in the last Tractate but one. Theologians indeed do not apprehend this sense in the same fashion as poets; but, inasmuch as my intention is to follow here the custom of poets, I will take the allegorical sense after the manner which poets use.

The third sense is called moral; and this sense is that for which teachers ought as they go through writings intently to watch for their own profit and that of their hearers; as in the Gospel when Christ ascended the Mount to be transfigured, we may be watchful of His taking with Himself the three Apostles out of the twelve; whereby morally it may be understood that for the most secret affairs we ought to have

few companions.

The fourth sense is called anagogic, that is, above the senses; and this occurs when a writing is spiritually expounded which even in the literal sense by the things signified likewise gives intimation of higher matters belonging to the eternal glory; as can be seen in that song of the prophet which says that, when the people of Israel went up out of Egypt, Judea was made holy and free. And although it be plain that this is true according to the letter, that which is spiritually understood is not less true, namely, that when the soul issues forth from sin she is made holy and free as mistress of herself.

divided into three *cantiche*; the second that whereby each *cantica* is divided into *cantos*; the third, that whereby each *canto* is divided into lines. The form or method of treatment is poetic, fictive, descriptive, digressive, transumptive; and likewise proceeding by definition, division, proof, refutation, and setting forth of examples.

10. The *title of the work* is, 'Here beginneth the *Comedy* of Dante Aligheri, a Florentine by birth, not by character.' To understand which, be it known that *comedy* is derived from *comus*, 'a village,' and *oda*, which is, 'song'; whence comedy is, as it were, 'rustic song.' So comedy is a certain kind of poetic narration differing from all others. It differs, then, from tragedy in its content, in that tragedy begins admirably and tranquilly, whereas its end or exit is foul and terrible; and it derives its name from *tragus*, which is a 'goat' and *oda*, as though to say 'goat-song,' that is fetid like a goat, as appears from Seneca in his tragedies; whereas comedy introduces some harsh complication, but brings its matter to a prosperous end, as appears from Terence, in his comedies. And hence certain writers, on introducing themselves, have made it their practice to give the salutation: 'I wish you a tragic beginning and a comic end.' They likewise differ in their mode of speech, tragedy being exalted and sublime, comedy lax and humble, as Horace has it in his *Poetica*, where he gives comedians leave sometimes to speak like tragedians and conversely:—

> *'Interdum tamen et vocem comœdia tollit,*
> *Iratusque Chremes tumido delitigat ore;*
> *Et tragicus plerumque dolet sermone pedestri.'* [2]

And hence it is evident that the title of the present work is *'the Comedy.'* For if we have respect to its content, at the beginning it is horrible and fetid, for it is hell; and in the end it is prosperous, desirable, and gracious, for it is *Paradise*. If we have respect to the method of speech the method is lax and humble, for it is the vernacular speech in which very women communicate. There are also other kinds of poetic narration, as the bucolic song, elegy, satire, and the utterance of prayer, as may also be seen from Horace in his *Poetica*. But concerning them nought need at present be said.

11. There can be no difficulty in assigning the *subject* of the part I am offering you; for if the subject of the whole, taken literally, is 'the state of souls after death,' not limited but taken without qualification, it

[2] 'Sometimes Comedy herself raises her voice, and wrathful Chremes denounces with tempestuous lips. And the tragedian often lowers his wail to pedestrian tone.

is clear that in this part that same state is the subject, but with a limitation, to wit, 'the state of blessed souls after death'; and if the subject of the whole work taken allegorically is 'man as by good or ill deserts, in the exercise of the freedom of his choice, he becomes liable to rewarding or punishing justice,' it is manifest that the subject in this part is contracted to 'man as by good deserts, he becomes liable to rewarding justice.'

12. And in like manner the *form* of the part is clear from the form assigned to the whole; for if the form of the treatise as a whole is threefold, in this part it is twofold only, namely, division of the cantiche and of the cantos. The first division cannot be a part of its special form, since it is itself a part under that first division.

13. The *title of the work* is also clear, for if the title of the whole work is 'Here beginneth the Comedy,' and so forth as set out above, the title of this part will be 'Here beginneth the third cantica of Dante's Comedy, which is entitled Paradise.'

14. Having investigated the three things in which the part differs from the whole, we must examine the other three, in which there is no variation from the whole. The *agent,* then, of the whole and of the part is the man already named, who is seen throughout to be such.

15. The *end* of the whole and of the part may be manifold, to wit, the proximate and the ultimate, but dropping all subtle investigation, we may say briefly that the end of the whole and of the part is to remove those living in this life from the state of misery and lead them to the state of felicity.

JULIUS CAESAR SCALIGER

(1484–1558)

BORN in 1484 at the castle of La Rocca, Scaliger early became a page to his kinsman, the Emperor Maximilian. He studied under Albrecht Dürer, meanwhile serving as an officer in the emperor's army. In 1514 he attended the university of Bologna, where he remained for five years. In 1525 he settled at Agen, in France, as a physician. Here he married Andiette Lobejac, and by her was the father of fifteen children. Joseph Justus, the tenth child, was destined to continue his father's name in scholarship.

Residing almost uninterruptedly at Agen the remainder of his life, Scaliger produced scientific commentaries, philosophical and general treatises, and Latin verse. Few of the works of science were published until his seventieth year, and the *Poetics* not until three years after his death, but he established a reputation for learning hardly equalled by any in Europe.

From the manner in which the *Poetics* begins, treating of the origin of language and its purposes, one may surmise that rhetoric is to be very much in evidence throughout the work, occasionally crowding criticism or poetics out. Like Aristotle, Scaliger is primarily a philosopher, and brings to this subject the same mental apparatus with which matters more scientific are treated. And so one is prepared for the expression of the serious purpose of poetry, an expression so important for Sidney and Jonson, and for the early French critics. Scaliger is following Horace part way, in averring that moral purpose increases poetry's effectiveness, but the close comparison with oratory as to scopes and ends makes it certain that Cicero and Quintilian are in his mind.

Scaliger quotes Horace to prove that the poet's purpose is "to teach and to please." Two years earlier, Minturno [*De Poeta*, 1559] had broadened the poet's purpose: "so to speak in his verses that he may teach, that he may delight, that he may move"—possibly in the Longinian sense of *transport*, though in his *Arte Poetica* (1564) he draws directly on Cicero's idea of oratorical persuasion, in much the same sense. The disagreement on this question was fundamental; H. B. Charlton [*Castelvetro's Theory of Poetry*, 66–70] considers that Castelvetro, alone, stood firm in the belief that poetry's purpose was "to delight and to recreate"; he adds, "to Castelvetro, art and morality, or art and political philosophy are quite separate spheres, each with its own functions and its own laws, in the one case aesthetic, in the other, moral or political." Castelvetro himself makes an even sharper distinction: "The aim of poetry is to give, by imitation, delight to its listeners, leaving the discovery of the hidden truth of natural philosophy to the philosopher and the scientist . . . [and, disagreeing with Aristotle on the theory of catharsis] Why is not delight sought here principally without meddling with utility, which ought to be of no account whatever." But few critics could make this separation; and Torquato Tasso [*Discorsi dell' Arte Poetica*, 1564], although he denies the utilitarian function of poetry, feels that the poet cannot be superior to the citizen: "he ought to have much regard to teaching if not in so far as he is a poet (since teaching is not the end of poetry) yet in so far as he is a citizen and a member of the state."

Scaliger, like most of his contemporaries, makes poetry the opposite of history. In probably the earliest critical treatise written in the Italian vernacular [*La Poetica*, 1536], Daniello had sanctioned the "mingling true things with false and feigned, because the poet is not bound, like the historian, to describe things as they are or have been, but as they ought to have been." Castelvetro is more explicit: "History, recording things happened, has not need to regard verisimilitude or necessity, but only truth of fact; poetry, describing things possible to happen, regards only verisimilitude or necessity, to establish the possibility, since it cannot regard truth to fact." Minturno, in Sidney's paraphrase, has it that "for the Poet, he nothing affirms, and therefore never lyeth."

When applied in another way, this distinction ceases to be one of function and purpose; it becomes a question of material. Scaliger identifies poetry with verse: "the name of poet is not . . . drawn from his being a maker in the sense of his using fiction, but from his being a maker of verses." Minturno [*De Poeta*] thinks "there is nothing impossible to write of with the poetic faculty," and G. Fracastoro [*Naugerius, sive de Poetica*, 1555] agrees: "everything is suitable for the poet's matter, if only it can be adorned." Castelvetro makes the material, not the meter, the test of poetry: "Verse does not distinguish poetry, but clothes and adorns it; and it is as improper for poetry to be written in prose, or history in verse, as it is for women to use the garments of men, and for men to wear the garments of women." By overtly limiting poetry to the imitation of human life, Castelvetro comes close to re-stating Aristotle's view. F. Patrizzi [*Della Poetica*, 1586] would set no limit on the choice of subject: "the matter of sciences, of arts, and of history can be fitting subject for poetry, provided it is poetically treated." But critics differed widely on whether or not the use of verse entitled a writer to be called a poet; a long controversy might have been avoided by the accepting of Scaliger's terminology and the invention of a term for "poetic prose." Not until the nineteenth century did the much needed term, *belles lettres*, become current, and through the centuries preceding, "poetry" had to answer for this meaning, as well as for composition in verse. (For résumé of this long dispute, and estimation of Scaliger's valuable position in it, see Gummere: *The Beginnings of Poetry*, 43 ff.)

Scaliger accepts Aristotle's theory of imitation and enlarges upon it. Mr. Spingarn's statement of the development of the neo-classical theory is deservedly well known: "This evolution may be traced . . . through three distinct stages, and these stages may be indicated by the doctrines respectively of Vida, Scaliger, and Boileau.

"Vida says that it is the first essential of literary art to imitate the classics. . . . In Scaliger this principle is carried one stage farther. The poet creates another nature and other fortunes as if he were another god. . . . Virgil especially has created another nature of such beauty and perfection that the poet need not concern himself with the realities of life, but can go to the second nature created by Virgil for the subject matter of his imitation. . . . Boileau carries the neo-classical ideal of nature and art to its ultimate perfection. According to him, nothing is beautiful that is not true, and nothing is true that is not in nature." [*Literary Criticism in the Renaissance,* 132 ff.] It is difficult not to read into Vida what is here ascribed to Scaliger; but the latter emphasizes his point successfully, and, more than any other critic, becomes responsible for an attitude toward poetical composition which was dominant in criticism until Wordsworth.

When he sets about his rule-making, especially for the epic, which he regards as the parent of other literary forms, this critic seems far less admirable to us than does Vida. He is among the first who contrive to reduce poetry to dogma, and his too great preoccupation with rhetoric and with forms takes away what value he might otherwise have. Likewise, when he writes of styles, one of his major subjects, the classification and naming of elements keeps him from ever coming to the heart of the matter.

It is questionable whether Scaliger or Castelvetro is the more responsible for fixing in Renaissance dramatic criticism the narrow interpretation of the three unities. Castelvetro, however, carries this point to its extreme implications, and for this see the selection from him in the *Supplement.*

POETICS *

(1561)

BOOK I CHAPTER I

THE INDISPENSABILITY OF LANGUAGE, ITS ORIGIN, USES, END, AND CULTIVATION

EVERYTHING that pertains to mankind may be classed as necessary, useful, or pleasure-giving, and by an inherent characteristic of all these classes the power of speech was implanted in man from the very beginning, or, as time went on, was acquired. Since man's development

---

* Translated by F. M. Padelford (1905).

depended upon learning, he could not do without that agency which was destined to make him the partaker of wisdom. Our speech is, as it were, the postman of the mind, through the services of whom civil gatherings are announced, the arts are cultivated, and the claims of wisdom intercede with men for man. It is of course necessary to secure from others those things which we need, to give orders to have things done, to prohibit, to propose, to dispose, to establish, and to abolish. Such were the functions of early speech.

Then the usefulness and effectiveness of language were increased by rules governing construction, dimensions, as it were, being given to a rude and formless body. Thus arose the established laws of speech. Later, language was adorned and embellished as with raiments, and then it appeared illustrious both in form and in spirit. As to an undefined body the metric science appoints breadth, angles, and length— the masters of harmony also add proportion, the ῥυθμοί of the Greeks —so to an unordered language law first gave the so-called rules. Next, more careful cultivation added knowledge of windings, of valleys and hills, of retreats, of light and shade. To speak figuratively, such cultivation afforded the soldier his necessary armor, the senator his useful toga, or the more elegant citizen his richer pleasure-robe. Not unlike these were the ends which language served, since necessity demanded language in the search of the philosophers after truth, utility dictated its cultivation in statesmanship, and pleasure drew it to the theatre. The language of the philosophers, confined to exact, logical reasoning, was necessarily concise and adapted to the subject-matter. On the other hand, in the forum and the camp less precise expression was permissible, governed by the subject, the place, the time, and the audience, and such speaking was called oratory. The third class contains two species, not very unlike, which in common employ narration, and use much embellishment. They differ, however, in that one professes to record the fixed truth, and employs a simple style of composition, while the other either adds a fictitious element to the truth, or imitates the truth by fiction, of course with more elaboration. While, as we have said, they are both equally narrative in character, the name History came to be applied to the former alone, since, I suppose, it was satisfied merely with that field of writing adapted to setting forth actual events. On the other hand, the latter was called Poetry, or Making, because it narrated not only actual events, but also fictitious events as if they were actual, and represented them as they might be or ought to be. Wherefore the basis of all poetry is imitation.

Imitation, however, is not the end of poetry, but is intermediate to the end. The end is the giving of instruction in pleasurable form, for poetry teaches, and does not simply amuse, as some used to think. Whenever language is used, the purpose, of course, is to acquaint the hearer with a fact or with the thought of the speaker, but because the primitive poetry was sung, its design seemed merely to please; yet underlying the music was that for the sake of which music was provided only as a sauce. In time this rude and pristine invention was enriched by philosophy, which made poetry the medium of its teaching. Let it be further said that when poetry describes military counsels, at one time open and frank, at another crafty—the στρατήγημα of the Greeks—when it tells of tempests, of wars, of routs, of various artifices, all is for one purpose: it imitates that it may teach. So in *The Frogs* of Aristophanes, to the one who asked him, "What merit in a poet can arouse the greatest admiration for him?" Euripides made a good answer when he replied, "The ability to impress adroitly upon citizens the need of being better men." Plato was less happy in the *Ion* in saying that a rhapsodist cannot satisfactorily represent military or nautical doings, because such arts are foreign to him. For the rhapsodist will say nothing worse about such things than the poet has written of them, since, as is very well remarked in the same passage, while the poet is the imitator of things, the rhapsodist is he who acts out the imitation, and according as the poet represents, the rhapsodist can reproduce.

Now is there not one end, and one only, in philosophical exposition, in oratory, and in the drama? Assuredly such is the case. All have one and the same end—persuasion; for, you see, just as we were saying above, whenever language is used it either expresses a fact or the opinion of the speaker. The end of learning is knowledge, that is, knowledge, of course, interpreted in no narrow sense. An accurate and simple definition of knowledge is as follows: Belief based either upon conclusive evidence, or upon a loose notion. Thus we say, "I know that Dido committed suicide because Aeneas departed." Now we do not know any such thing, but this is popularly accepted as the truth. Persuasion, again, means that the hearer accepts the words of the speaker. The soul of persuasion is truth, truth either fixed and absolute, or susceptible of question. Its end is to convince, or to secure the doing of something. Truth, in turn, is agreement between that which is said about a thing and the thing itself.

By no means are we to accept the popular idea that eloquent speaking, rather than persuasion, is the end of oratory, for the arguments of the grammarians on this point are not valid. Clearly, if a man does not persuade, this is due to no fault of the art, but either to the issue, which it is beyond the power of the orator to control, wherefore he does not cease to be an orator, or to some defect of his own, which may either reside in his speaking or in the bad cause which he espouses. In this last case he is either no orator, or else he is a knave.

Eloquent speaking certainly cannot be the end, for obviously it is the means to an end, or a mode of the means. An end is not that which serves another end, but that which all serves, and so one uses eloquence that he may persuade. Moreover, you are not the arbiter of your eloquence, but the judge is, and if he does not think you eloquent, not only is your eloquence fruitless, but it is not eloquence at all. Therefore you may go away frustrated in your purpose, even though you have spoken eloquently. Further, it is not possible that both the defendant and the plaintiff should be equally eloquent; in fact it is necessary that one or the other should lose his cause, or should merit losing it. Therefore he will not be your orator whom you have picked out as eloquent.

Finally, in that treatise entitled Εἰσαγωγικός, attributed to Galen, and in that other work on the science of medicine, the Σύστασις, which is more confidently attributed to him, two kinds of arts are recognized. If Quintilian, by the way, had run across this idea in Plato, from whom Galen borrowed it, he would have changed his theory about the end of oratory. Two kinds there are, then. Arts of the one kind can attain their ends in and of themselves, such as shoemaking, carpentry, and the like; the others are not thus able, as oratory, medicine, and navigation. The latter arts the Greeks denominate στοχαστικαί (*conjectural*), because, as is stated in the *Philebus,* they proceed, so to speak, by conjecture, not by fixed principle. Now, for my part, I take a different view. Medicine always cures curable diseases, but the physician does not always do so, because he is embarrassed by many obstacles; wherefore in that case he fails to be a doctor. In fact the physician does not accept an incurable case unless he be careless, or stupid, greedy for fees, or rash. Further, accidents are wont to befall the sick, either through their own instrumentality, or that of their servants, or through some chance happening, as of the atmosphere, the sun, dampness, anger, grief, fear, and the like. Here belong what Hippocrates and other physicians call external agencies—τὰ ἔξωθεν. Indeed, not even nature herself is a perfectly reliable workman, for occasionally she is embarrassed and fails of her end, as when she produces a monstrosity, or brings forth defective bodies.

The orator, then, speaks in the forum that good may be meted to good men, and punishment to evil men; in assemblies and councils that public affairs may be well administered; and in eulogies that we may be won from evil by good example, and may pursue and practice that which is set forth as honest. In this last class, the epideictic, certain invectives are to be included. Other kinds of invectives, however, belong to judicial bodies, such as those uttered in the presence of witnesses; still others to deliberative bodies, as the speeches against Antony and Catiline, and the addresses on consular provinces.

All of these different kinds of speaking have a common end. To be sure, there are those who contend that in judicial proceedings the end is justice; in deliberative proceedings, utility; and in eulogies, honesty; but such are properly rebuked by Quintilian. The ground of the rebuke should be noted rather carefully, for not only do these men reason superficially, but they even contradict themselves. In fact, in another passage they confound utility with honesty. But all that aside, be it observed that utility is the end of all the virtues, wherefore also of justice. And since justice is the righteous payment to a man of that which is his own or its equivalent, justice is the end of deliberative counsels. Justice is even the end of war, for the councils of war—they are very many—are held for the sake of justice. Finally, if the end of man is virtue, honesty is either a state of mind induced by virtue, or it is the soul of virtue. Of every human office, of every act and thought, honesty will be the end.

We must consider even more carefully than did Quintilian the basis for the classification of the different kinds of speaking. That he might simplify the threefold division, he classified as follows: cases either are subject for judicial investigation, or are outside of it. The latter relate either to the past or to the future. Those relating to the past are epideictic; those of the future, deliberative. But now who does not appreciate that in judicial proceedings the past is involved? Wherefore it is not possible for the latter to form a sub-species of the judicial. So I would have altered the statement as follows: a case is either in the past or in the future; the latter alone prescribes deliberation; the former divides into the forensic, or judicial, and the epideictic. Although that discerning man, the disciple of the first philosopher, classed them as forensic, deliberative, and epideictic, an accused man is never tried or defended without praise or censure either of a person, an event, an act, a word, or a policy, and in like manner never without deliberation. Indeed, it is deliberated whether to convict or to acquit the defendant. So you see that there cannot be species or genera of cases, because no species of one is able to be part of another species.

Finally, it is improper, as some do, to call speeches of a deliberative nature hortatory, for persuasion is the end of all speaking. What else does an orator do than create confidence, and this, to persuade? Quintilian makes an equally bad mistake when he interprets the word ἐπιδεικτικός to mean ostentatious speaking, on the ground that the word usually had this meaning among the Greeks. So far is this from the truth, that the philosophers used it to define the most simple and exact exposition.

Let it be observed, while we are on the subject, that in deliberative and judicial speaking the orator depends upon his audience. Indeed, the accomplishment of that purpose in behalf of which he essays to speak hinges upon the favor of his hearers. Let it be further noted, that in epideictic speaking the case is the opposite of this, inasmuch as the mind of the hearer is surrendered to the speaker. It is, indeed, as if he who adjudges praise were himself relieved from judgment. These points in which we differ from the recognized opinions of the rhetoricians must, from the very nature of my undertaking, be dwelt upon, just as we have dealt more accurately with various other matters. Thus we might say that the translative state could be subsumed under the conjectural, since in both, the fact being conceded, it is a question who is responsible for it. All kinds of speeches have this in common. The orator in the forum debates concerning life, vices, virtues, examining them in the state of quality, and in that in which inquiry is made concerning what is, just as in councils the question is what is to be preferred. But the philosopher and the poet deal with all such matters in the very same spirit, each in his own person or in that of another. As an illustration of the latter mode, Socrates introduces Diotimas or Aspasia, and Plato brings forward Socrates; and the orator in like manner interjects personifications. If he would eulogize a man, he must needs touch upon the story of his life, his family, his nation; and this allies him with the historian. The historian, on his part, frequently adds a characterization, such as we read of Camillus, Scipio, Hannibal, Jugurtha, and Cicero; and, as it were, intersperses his decrees. But it is only poetry which includes everything of this kind, excelling those other arts in this, that while they, as we have said above, represent things just as they are, in some sense like a speaking picture, the poet depicts quite another sort of nature, and a variety of fortunes; in fact, by so doing, he transforms himself almost into a second deity. Of those things which the Maker of all framed, the other sciences are, as it were, overseers; but since poetry fashions images of those things which are not, as well as images more beautiful than life of those things which are, it seems unlike other literary forms, such as history, which confine themselves to actual events, and rather to be another god, and to create. In view of this fact, its common title was furnished it, not by the agreement of men, but by the provident wisdom of nature. I must express my surprise that when the learned Greeks had most happily defined the poet as the *maker,* our ancestors should be so unfair to themselves as to limit the term to candle-makers, for though usage has sanctioned this practice, etymologically it is absurd.[1]

BOOK I CHAPTER VI

TRAGEDY

TRAGEDY, like comedy, is patterned after real life, but it differs from comedy in the rank of the characters, in the nature of the action, and in the outcome. These differences demand, in turn, differences in style. Comedy employs characters from rustic, or low city life, such as Chremes, Davus, and Thais. The beginning of a comedy presents a confused state of affairs, and this confusion is happily cleared up at the end. The language is that of every-day life. Tragedy, on the other hand, employs kings and princes, whose affairs are those of the city, the fortress, and the camp. A tragedy opens more tranquilly than a comedy, but the outcome is horrifying. The language is grave, polished, removed from the colloquial. All things wear a troubled look; there is a pervading sense of doom, there are exiles and deaths. Tradition has it that the Macedonian king, Archelaus, the intimate friend and patron of Euripides, asked the poet to make him the hero of a tragedy, but that Euripides replied: "Indeed I cannot do it; your life presents no adequate misfortune."

The name tragedy is derived from τράγος, the he-goat, for the simple reason that tragedy was acted in the honor of that divinity to whom the goat was wont to be sacrificed. Then, in turn, the goat was given

---

[1] Saintsbury, *Hist. of Crit.,* II, 71: "This joke requires a little explanation and adaptation to get it into English. The Latin is *miror majores nostros sibi tam iniquos* *fuisse ut factoris vocem maluerint* oleariorum cancellis *circumscribere.* In fact, *fattojo* and *fattojano,* if not *fattore,* do mean in Italian 'oil-press and oil-presser.'"

as a prize, that the victor might sacrifice it to the god. It is recorded as an assured fact that tragedies were first acted in the vintage season, and this gave the grammarians an opportunity to derive the name from τρύγημα, the vintage, just as if it were τρυγῳδία, a word which you actually find in the *Acharnians* of Aristophanes. It is not known who was the author of tragedy, but we know that Thespis refined it. He was the first to go about presenting scenes from a wagon, and to smear the mouth with lees, as a mask. As τρύξ means lees, just as τρύγημα, vintage, some would derive the name tragedy from this use of the dregs of the wine. But this is a false etymology, for the name tragedy is older than Thespis.

The grammarians blunder again here, for they say that the lees used were either from wine or from oil, and add, with their fatal predilection for blunders, that "lees" here means the watery liquid of the wine. Now, the lees of wine are anything but water, and are even subject to crystallization. The lees are the deposit which our physicians call tartar, known among the Arabs as *durdi,* a word which they use for the lees of wine, vinegar, and the like. For the lees of oil they have a different word, *thefal,* corresponding to our *amurca.* So much for the name and origin of tragedy.

The definition of tragedy given by Aristotle is as follows: "Tragedy is an imitation of an action that is illustrious, complete, and of a certain magnitude, in embellished language, the different kinds of embellishments being variously employed in the different parts, and not in the form of narration, but through pity and fear effecting the purgation of such like passions." I do not wish to attack this definition other than by adding my own: A tragedy is the imitation of the adversity of a distinguished man; it employs the form of action, presents a disastrous *dénouement,* and is expressed in impressive metrical language. Though Aristotle adds harmony and song, they are not, as the philosophers say, of the essence of tragedy; its one and only essential is acting. Then the phrase "of a certain magnitude" is put in to differentiate the tragedy from the epic, which is sometimes prolix. It is not always so, however, as the work of Musaeus illustrates. Further, the mention of "purgation" is too restrictive, for not every subject produces this effect. "A certain magnitude," to return to the phrase, means not too long and not too short, for a few verses would not satisfy the expectant public, who are prepared to atone for the disgusting prosiness of many a day by the enjoyment of a few hours. Prolixity, however, is just as bad, when you must say with Plautus: "My legs ache with sitting, and my eyes with looking."

BOOK III CHAPTER XXV

THE FOUR ATTRIBUTES OF THE POET

THUS far we have presented the *ideas* of things in examples drawn from Virgil, just as they might be taken from nature itself. Indeed, I think that the workmanship of his poetry finds an analogy in art, for sculptors and painters take from real life those conceptions which they use in imitating lines, light, shade, and background, and they embody in their own productions the peculiar excellencies of many objects, so that they do not seem to have been taught by nature, but to have vied with it, or even better to have given it its laws. Who, in fact, would say that nature ever produced a woman so beautiful that a connoisseur could not find some flaw in her beauty? For though the archetype of nature is altogether perfect in outline and proportions, the actual product suffers many hindrances through circumstances of parentage, climate, time, and place. So we have not been able to get from nature a single pattern such as the *ideas* of Virgil furnish us. Accordingly it now remains for us with acuteness and wisdom to consider in systematic order the elements in that divine power of his. This will be our next concern.

The early orators had only one end in view, to persuade and move their hearers, and their language was correspondingly rude; the poets sought only to please, and they whiled away their leisure simply with alluring songs. In due time, however, orator and poet secured from each other that which they lacked respectively. Isocrates is credited with having first given graceful movement to a hitherto rude diction, though deeper students of the literary monuments award this distinction to Thrasymachus, and add that his diligent efforts were furthered by Gorgias, while the work of Isocrates was to add the finishing touch. As to poetry, on the other hand, it was rendered more thoughtful by being transferred from the country to the town, where plots were added to furnish warning examples, and sentiments to furnish precepts.

Horace most aptly said, "He carries every vote who mingles the useful with the pleasing," for poetry bends all its energies to these two ends, to teach and to please. Now to realize these ends one's work must conform to certain principles. In the first place his poem must be deeply conceived, and be unvaryingly self-consistent. Then he must take pains to temper all with variety (*varietas*), for there is no worse mistake than to glut your hearer before you are done with him. What then are the dishes which would create distaste rather than pleasure? The third poetic quality is found in but few writers, and is what I would term vividness (*efficacia*); there is also a Greek name for it which will be given in the proper place. By vividness I mean a certain potency and force in thought and language which compels one to be a willing listener. The fourth is winsomeness (*suavitas*), which tempers the ardency of this last quality, of itself inclined to be harsh. Insight and foresight (*prudentia*), variety, vividness, and winsomeness, these, then, are the supreme poetic qualities.

BOOK III CHAPTER XCVI

REGULATIONS FOR THE VARIOUS KINDS OF POETRY: EPIC POETRY

WE have already remarked that for objects of every kind there exists one perfect original to which all the rest can be referred as their norm and standard. In epic poetry, which describes the descent, life, and deeds of heroes, all other kinds of poetry have such a norm, so that to it they turn for their regulative principles. Now our First Book has shown into what species poetry is divided. We shall therefore derive from the sovereignty of the epic the universal controlling rules for the composition of each other kind, according to its distinctive subject-matter and nature. Having thus found the laws common to all, we are to determine the privileges of each, making heroic poetry our point of departure.

After one has determined in a general way the events and characters of a poem, has adjusted them to times and places, and has deduced the sequence of action, there remains the composition according to a well-known principle. The precept of Horace to begin *ab ovo* [2] is by no means to be followed. Rather let the first rule be, to begin with something grand, cognate with the theme, and intimately related. This rule was observed by Lucan, who, in writing of the Civil War, begins with Caesar's crossing of the Rubicon, because for this act the senate adjudged him an enemy, and compelled him to make war. A second rule: Do not repeat and double on your tracks, lest you become tedious. If

---

[2] His misunderstanding of Horace on this point is beyond our comprehension. See *The Art of Poetry.*

the same event is often repeated, it is of necessity intrusively forced upon the attention, which is utterly contrary to the general rules heretofore established. The very thing, therefore, which you are going to take as your principal theme should not be placed first in the narrative, for the mind of the hearer is to be kept in suspense, awaiting that which is to develop. It is obviously a unique and chief virtue to hold the hearer captive. For this reason the greatest of poets so arranged his material that the end of the narrative of Aeneas was in reality the beginning of the action proper: "Thence me in my wanderings the God has driven to your shores." From this point the story moves on evenly. To be sure, it is interrupted by novel experiences, but these are constituent parts of it, or closely related. Thus the insertion of the story of Camilla looks to the fact that her death is atoned for by the death of Aruns. The critics have failed to note the nice variation in this passage, for though in this catalogue of warriors he gives the country, parents, and race of many, he only says of Camilla that she was fleet of foot, and the reason is that Diana was to tell the story of her life in a later book. In this instance, Virgil was acting in obvious conformity with the above principle. This principle of arrangement has a most admirable realization in the *Aethiopica* of Heliodorus, a book, I take it, that should be most carefully conned by the epic poet, as furnishing him the best model.

Another principle is that an author should divide his book into chapters in imitation of nature, which subdivides into parts of parts, all so related that they constitute an organic body. But in doing this, you should so assign each part to its proper place that the book shall seem to have shaped itself inevitably, an achievement perfectly realized only by the divine Maro. If one will read the *Aeneid* attentively, he will see that it conforms to this principle. To be sure, the *Georgics* does not, but this exception is due to the nature of the subject-matter. Now the epic story is wholly taken from civil life, and yet the more important parts are assigned to kings and heroes. With mortals, as already stated, the gods associate. Mingled with the affairs of peace, at intervals battles are waged. Variety dictates other usages. Now to some it has seemed that Sallust showed a vain ambition, because, poet-like, when he undertook to treat of Catiline he omitted the story of the man, but, instead, recalled history from the very beginning of Rome. But it seems to me that a man eminent and even peerless in his class, as was he, did this rightly and from necessity, in order thus to show the corruption of the state of which the worthless Catiline was himself a part, and where he had many confederates in his crime and wickedness. Nor is Musaeus

to be condemned because in his altogether charming story of Leander
he does not follow the same practice, for that story is, as it were, a tragedy, so that the narrative properly begins and ends with the immediate
tale of Leander.

BOOK IV CHAPTER II

THE GRAND STYLE

THOUGH Hermogenes classified *ideas* according to another principle,
and others propagated his system, we are constrained to consider certain precepts which might have hindered or helped in the education of
our poet. Let us then take up the different styles of poetic utterance, so
combining precept and illustration that we may become familiar with
the true theory of style.

We recognize three kinds of style, the grand or lofty (*altiloqua*), the
humble (*infima*), and the mean of the two, which I please to call the
moderate (*aequabilis*). Some properties are common to all of these,
some are particular. Common properties are perspicuity (*perspicuitas*),
refinement (*cultus*), propriety (*proprietas*), elegance or grace (*venus-
tas*), and rhythm (*numerositas*). These qualities should inhere in
every poem. Of the other common properties some are not invariably
used, but subject to occasion, as smoothness (*mollitia*), winsomeness
(*suavitas*), rapidity or spirit (*incitatio*), purity or unadornedness
(*puritas*), acumen (*acutum*), sharpness or raillery (*acre*), fulness
(*plenum*), and ornateness (*floridum*). As of the common properties,
so of the particular, some should be employed always, others only on
occasion. In the grand style those to be observed always are dignity
(*dignitas*) and sonorousness (*sonus*); those to be used on occasion,
ponderousness (*gravitas*) and fervency (*vehementia*). In the lowly
style that to be observed always is plainness or artless purity (*tenuitas*);
on occasion, simplicity (*simplicitas*) and negligence (*securitas*). Those
to be invariably observed in the moderate style are roundness (*rotundi-
tas*) and fluency (*volubilitas*). Such is our classification, and it is complete and invariable.

The grand style is that which portrays eminent characters and notable
events. The sentiments are correspondingly choice, and they are
couched in choice and euphonious diction. These eminent characters
are gods, heroes, kings, generals, and citizens. If inferior characters,
such as sailors, merchants, tradesmen, and hostlers are introduced, it is

because when men associate together they constitute a society which has, as it were, the character of an organism, the members of which, according to the nature and end of their functions, share in its nature and office. It is the nature of the kingly office to be superior to others; its end is to govern. So the king's share will be preëminent strength and wisdom, and his office to apply his strength in affording protection, and his wisdom in governing. Notable events are wars in behalf of peace and concord, deliberative counsels, judicial decisions, the pursuit of heroic deeds, and whatever else is attendant upon these. Choice sentiments are those which abhor vulgarity; choice diction, that which is not trite; and pleasing language, that which marries sense and sound. Now all this we shall treat in its proper place, after we have considered the properties of the various styles, a task upon which we now enter.

JOACHIM DU BELLAY

(1522?–1560)

BORN at the chateau of La Turmelière, near Lirè, Du Bellay lost both of his parents at an early age and was brought up under the neglectful custody of his brother. At the age of twenty-three he went to Poitiers to study law, where it is probable he first met Jacques Peletier, the publisher of a translation of Horace's *Ars Poetica,* and the well source of much of the critical theory for which Du Bellay and Ronsard have received credit.

Sometime later he met Ronsard, with whom he returned to the Collège de Coqueret to join the group of humanists who were studying there. He wrote the *Defense and Illustration* in 1549 as the Pleiade's reply to Thomas Sibilet's *Art Poétique* (1548), which upheld the cause of Marot and condemned the experiments being made with classical models. About this time Du Bellay's first important verse was published, in the sonnet sequences of *Recueil* and *Olive* (the latter name an anagram for that of his mistress Viole).

In 1550 he went to Italy with Cardinal Du Bellay, a cousin, and here lived as his secretary for several years, returning to Paris in 1557. *Les Regrets* and *Les Antiquités de Rome* were published soon after. Much time in his later years was spent seeking patronage, and the *Discourse au Roi* (1559), translated from a Latin original, secured him a pension. On Jan. 1, 1560, he died. His early intimacy with Ronsard does not seem to have been renewed after the return from Italy.

It has been aptly remarked that "what Dante's *De Vulgari Eloquentia* is for Italy, that and even more the *Défense et Illustration* is for France." [Nitze and Dargan: *A History of French Literature,* 170.] The treatise is primarily a declaration for the use of the vernacular for all purposes. An attack is made upon it in the anonymous *Quintil Horatian* (by Barthélemy Aneau, regent of the Collège de la Trinité at Lyons), on the ground that it despises what is native and traditional in French literature, while dedicating itself to the glorification of it. This point cannot be argued away by any reference to the weaknesses of the earlier French writers, and it is by a method similar to Du Bellay's that Malherbe is later to banish him and Ronsard, though working a greater harm.

The negligence of old French forms is readily comparable to the English attitude of the Seventeenth and Eighteenth Centuries, and constitutes a basis for neo-classicism.

C. H. C. Wright accuses Du Bellay of having "cribbed the main ideas" from the Italian Sperone Speroni; it is certain that he drew, in the customary fashion of the time, heavily upon the Italian critics, and directly from the *De Vulgari Eloquentia*. The ideal of Du Bellay, coming through Pelletier, is parallel with that of Dante, and the theories with those of Vida and the classical and neo-classical critics.

The importance of the French critic's theory of "imitation" is liable to be overlooked. He arrives at it by a revulsion from translation. The French, indeed, were never smitten with that notion which in English made Pope's translation of the *Iliad* the greatest poetical achievement of a century. The work of the translator remains with Du Bellay of a secondary nature: in the first place, it can never achieve the spirit of the original. But making translation his point of departure, he puts a unique significance upon the term "imitation," far from any Aristotelian sense, and very near to Vida's "stealing," thus abetting the confusing duality which the term has carried through criticism.

The *Defense* is the first selection met with thus far which gives specific attention to the lyric. Most of the ancient critics and many of those of the Renaissance had felt that it would take care of itself. "Pindar shows how," or "Copy Horace," had been the laconic maxims. Du Bellay makes no valid contribution, but the existence of the problem was coming to be felt.

THE DEFENSE AND ILLUSTRATION
OF THE
FRENCH LANGUAGE *

(1549)

BOOK I CHAPTER I

THE ORIGIN OF LANGUAGES

If Nature (of whom some famous person, not without reason, has expressed doubt whether she should be called mother or stepmother) had given to men a general will and assent, in addition to the numberless comforts that have come from her, the inconstancy of humans would not have needed to forge so many forms of speech. This diverse confusion may rightly be called a tower of Babel. For languages are not born out of themselves, like herbs, roots, trees, some frail and weak, others healthy and strong, and more able to carry the weight of human conceptions: but all their power is born in the world by the will and arbitrary act of man. This, it seems to me, is a good reason that one

* Translated by James Harry Smith and Edd Winfield Parks.

should not praise one language and condemn another, for all of them have the same origin, the imagination of man, and have been formed with the same judgment, for the same end: that we may signify to one another the concepts and thoughts of our minds. It is true that in course of time some, because they have been more carefully governed, have become richer than others; but that ought not to be attributed to the felicity of the languages, but solely to the ingenuity and industry of men. For all that nature has created, all the arts and sciences, in all quarters of the world, are in force to the same end; but, because men are of diverse wills, they speak and write differently. In this regard, I cannot enough blame the stupid arrogance and foolhardiness of some of our nation who, being anything but Greeks or Latins, disparage and reject with more than stoic scorn everything written in French; and I cannot marvel enough at the opinion of certain scholars who think that our vernacular is incapable of good literature and erudition, as if an invention ought to be judged good or bad on expression alone. I have not attempted to satisfy the former. As to the latter I am perfectly willing, if it be possible, to make them change their opinion, by certain considerations that I want briefly to set forth; not that I feel myself more "clair-voyant" in this, or in other matters, than they, but that the affection which they bear to alien languages does not allow them the desire to give sound and complete judgment to their own.

CHAPTER III

WHY THE FRENCH LANGUAGE IS NOT SO RICH
AS THE GREEK AND LATIN

AND if our language is not as copious and rich as the Greek or Latin, that ought not to be imputed to any fault of the language, as if it of itself could ever be other than poor and sterile: but the fault ought rather to be laid to the ignorance of our ancestors, who (as some one has said in speaking of the ancient Romans), holding in higher respect doing well than talking well, and preferring to leave to their posterity the examples, rather than the rules, of virtuous action, deprived themselves of the glory of their high deeds, and us of the fruit of the imitating of them: and in the same way have left us our language so impoverished and naked that it needs the ornaments and (if I may so speak) the pens of others. But who would say that Greek and Latin had always

been of that excellence which we see in the times of Homer, of Demosthenes, of Virgil, of Cicero? And if these authors had considered
that, for whatever diligence and cultivation might be expended, their
languages would never bear fruit, would they have striven so hard as
they have to bring them to the point where we now see them? I can
say the same thing of our language, which begins now to flower without
bearing fruit, or rather, like a plant stem, has not yet flowered, so far
is it from having brought forth all the fruit that it might very well
produce. This is certainly not the fault of its nature, which is as fertile
as are others, but the fault of those who have had it in charge and have
not cultivated it sufficiently: like a wild plant, in the very desert where
it had come to life, without watering or pruning, (or in any way protecting it from the brambles and thorns which overshadowed it), they
have left it to grow old and almost die. If the ancient Romans had
been as neglectful of the cultivation of their language, when it first
began to swarm, certain it is that in such a short time it could not have
grown so great. But they, like good farmers, first transplanted it from
a wild to a domestic soil; then, in order that it might the more quickly
and better bear fruit, cutting from around it the useless branches, they
replaced them with sound and serviceable ones; and, masterfully drawing upon Greek, they rapidly engrafted what they took and made it so
similar to their own trunk that thenceforth it appeared not adopted, but
natural. And so were produced in Latin flowers and fruits colored with
that high eloquence, with numbers, with the artful liaison, with all
those things which, not so much by its own nature as by artifice,
every language customarily produces. If the Greeks and Romans, more
diligent in the cultivation of their languages than we in that of ours,
did not find in theirs, except with great labor and application, any
grace, any number, finally, any eloquence, we ought not to wonder if
our vernacular is not as rich as it might be, nor to take occasion to
berate it as a low thing, and of little worth. The time will come, and I
hope for such a bright destiny for France, that this noble and puissant
kingdom will obtain in her turn the reins of monarchy, and that our
language—(if with Francis I the French language was not completely
buried) which now is beginning to throw out its roots, rise from the
ground, and lift itself with such pride and grandeur—may equal even
those of Greece and Rome, producing like them Homers, Demosthenes,
Virgils, Ciceros, as France has several times produced Pericles, Nicias,
Alcibiades, Themistocles, Caesars, Scipios.

CHAPTER IV

THAT THE FRENCH LANGUAGE IS NOT AS POOR AS MANY THINK IT

I DO not, nevertheless, think our vernacular, even as it is now, is so vile and abject as the ambitious admirers of Greek and Latin hold it, who do not think anything good, and who reckon even Pitho, goddess of Persuasion, unable to call anything good, except it be in a foreign tongue and one not understood by the common vulgar. And whoever will look well at it will find that our French language is not so poor that it cannot render faithfully what it borrows from others; so unproductive that it cannot, of itself, bear a fruit of good invention, through the industry and diligence of its cultivators, if any of them are found such friends to their country and to themselves that they are willing to devote themselves to it. But to whom, after God, are we to render thanks for such a blessing, but to our good king and sire, Francis, first of that name, and first in all virtues. I say first because he has, in his noble realm, been the first to restore all the arts and sciences in their ancient dignity: and he has carried our language from a rude and unpolished state into an elegant one, where, if not so ample as it might be, it is at least a faithful interpreter of all the others; the proof of which is that the Greek and Latin philosophers, historians, physicians, poets, orators, are all now in French. What shall I say of the Hebrews? The sacred letters bear sufficient witness to what I maintain. I shall lay by the ignorant arguments of those who contend that the mysteries of theology ought not to be uncovered, almost as though they were profaned by being put into the tongues, as those who sustain the contrary opinion assert. For this discussion is not germain to what I am trying to do, which is alone to show that our language did not have at its birth the gods and stars so hostile that it may not one day attain the excellence and perfection of the other languages, only provided that all the sciences can accurately and amply be negotiated in it, as one is able to see in such a large number of Greek and Latin books, nay more, even in Italian, Spanish, and others, translated into French by many an excellent pen, in our time.

CHAPTER V

THAT TRANSLATIONS ARE NOT ENOUGH TO GIVE PERFECTION TO THE FRENCH LANGUAGE

NEVERTHELESS this laudable toil of translating does not seem to me alone a sufficient means of raising our vernacular to be the equal and paragon of other more famous languages. I mean to prove this so clearly that no one, I think, will contradict it, without being manifestly a calumniator of the truth. In the first place, there is a close agreement between all the better writers on rhetoric, that there are five depart-ments of good speaking: invention, elocution, disposition, memory, and pronunciation. But since the last two of these are not acquired by the advantage of language so much as they are given to each according to the facility of his nature, augmented and supported by studious exercise and constant diligence; moreover, since "disposition" depends more upon the discretion and good judgment of the orator than upon particular rules and precepts (for the exigencies of time, the circum-stances of place, the situation of the audience, and the variety of occa-sions are numberless); I shall content myself with speaking of the first two, invention and elocution. The office then of the orator is to speak eloquently and at length of each thing proposed. But this faculty of speaking thus of all things can only be acquired by the perfect com-prehension of knowledge, which has been the first concern of their Roman imitators. It is necessary that these two languages be under-stood by those who wish to acquire that abundance and that richness of invention, the first and principal piece of harness for the orator. Once arrived at that point, the faithful translators can grandly serve and assist those who have not the unique accomplishment of devoting themselves to foreign languages. But the elocution is certainly the most difficult part, and without it all other things remain useless, similar to a sword still encased in its scabbard; elocution, by which principally an orator is judged most excellent, and one type of speaking better than another, as it is called eloquence itself; the virtue of which consists in using proper and ordinary words, and words not foreign to common usage, and in using metaphors, allegories, comparisons, similes, person-ification, and other figures and ornaments, without which all oratory and poems are bare, deficient and debilitated. I will never believe that one can learn all that from translations, because it is impossible to translate it with the same grace that the author has put into it: because each language has something indefinably individual only to itself; and if you make an effort to render its innate character into another language, observing the law of translation, so that it is not expanded at all beyond the limits of the author, your diction will be constrained, turgid, and without charm. This being so, if you read a Latin translation of Demosthenes or Homer, a French translation of Cicero or Virgil, in order to see if they will engender such sentiments, even as Proteus, they will transform you into diverse shapes from what you feel reading the authors in their own languages. You will think that you are crossing the heated Mountain of Aetna on the cold summit of the Caucasus. And what I say of the Greek and Latin tongues can reciprocally be said of all the vulgar tongues, of which I need cite only Petrarch, of whom I venture to say that, if Homer and Virgil came to life, and undertook to translate him, they could not do so with the same grace and naturalness that he has in his Tuscan dialect. Nevertheless men in our time have attempted to make him speak French. Here in brief are the reasons which have made me feel that the work and industry of translators, however useful to instruct those ignorant of languages foreign to their knowledge, is not sufficient to give to our own language that perfection and, as painters say of their pictures, that finishing touch, which we desire. And if the reasons that I have cited do not seem strong enough, I will produce, for my guarantors and defenders, the ancient Roman authors, principally poets and orators, who (since Cicero has translated some books of Xenophon and of Aratus, and Horace laid down the precepts for good translation) have attended to this part more for their own study and particular profit, rather than to give it to the world for the amplification of their language, to their own glory, and the profit of others. Whoever has seen works of that time in translation (I mean Cicero and Virgil, and that fortunate century of Augustus), cannot be able to give the lie to what I say.

CHAPTER VI

OF BAD TRANSLATORS AND OF NOT TRANSLATING THE POETS

Bur what shall I say of those who are truly more worthy of being called traducers than translators? Since they betray those whom they attempt to make known, defrauding them of their glory, and by the same means seducing the ignorant readers, showing them the white for the black: who, in order to acquire the name of scholars, credit themselves with translating from languages of which they have never understood the first elements, such as Hebrew and Greek: and still better to show themselves off, they seize upon the poets, the class that certainly, if I knew, or desired to translate, I would address myself to as little as possible because of that divine invention, which they have more than other authors, that grandeur of style, magnificence of words, gravity of sentences, audacity and variety of figures, and a thousand other splendors of poetry: in brief, that energy and incomparable spirit which is in their works, that the Latins call genius. All of which things can hardly be expressed in translation, any more than a painter can represent the soul with the body of the person whom he attempts to represent from nature. What I say is not addressed to those who, at the command of princes and great lords, translate the most famous Greek and Latin poets: because the obedience that one owes to such personages does not permit any excuse in such endeavors: but truly I desire to speak to those who, light-heartedly, undertake such tasks thoughtlessly, and acquit themselves in the same manner. O Apollo! O Muse! To profane thus the sacred relics of antiquity! But I shall not say another word. Those, however, who wish to do work worthy of a place in their own language, must leave this labor of translation, especially of poets, to those who inevitably distill more boredom than glory from a thing that is laborious and without profit, I dare to say useless, nay even pernicious, for the enrichment of their language.

CHAPTER VII

HOW THE ROMANS HAVE ENRICHED THEIR LANGUAGE

IF the Romans (some one will say), did not conquer by the labor of translation, by what means then did they so enrich their language, even almost to equality with the Greek? By imitating the better Greek authors, transforming themselves through them, devouring them; and, after having digested them well, converting them into blood and nurture; each taking to himself according to his nature and the argument which he wishes to choose, the best author, all of whose rarest and most exquisite virtues they observe diligently, appropriating and embodying these, like engraftments, as I have said before, to their language. That caused the Romans to build those sublime writings that we delight in and admire so greatly, counting some equal, others preferable, to the Greek. And what I say Cicero and Virgil well prove, whom gladly I always name among the Latins, of whom the one, as he was entirely given over to the imitation of the Greeks, so reproduced and truly expressed the meaning of Plato, the vehemency of Demosthenes, and the racy charm of Isocrates, that Molon of Rhodia, hearing him speak one time, exclaimed that he was introducing Greek eloquence to Rome. The other so well imitated Homer, Hesiod, and Theocritus, that it has since been said that he surpassed one of these three, equalled another, and approached so near to the third that if the felicity of the theme used had been equal, the palm would have been in doubt. I ask you then, you authors who busy yourselves only with translations, if those famous authors had trifled with translations, would they have raised their language to the excellence and eminence where we now see it? Do not think, then, that however much diligence and industry you may employ in that endeavor, you will be able to make our language, now prostrate, lift up its head and get up on its feet.

CHAPTER VIII

TO ENLARGE FRENCH LITERATURE BY IMITATION OF THE ANCIENT GREEK AND LATIN AUTHORS

WRITE himself, then, must he who wishes to enrich his language, write in imitation of the best Greek and Latin authors; at all their best qualities, as at a fair target, direct the aim of his style; for it cannot be doubted that the great part of the art is contained in imitation: and as it was for the ancients most praiseworthy to invent well, so it is most profitable well to imitate them, even for those whose language is not yet plentiful and rich. But he must understand, who wishes to imitate, that it is no easy thing to follow well the excellent qualities of a good author, as if to transform oneself with him, for nature has so wrought even those things which appeal, most similar, that by some mark or feature they can be distinguished. I say this because there are many in every literature who, without penetrating to the secret, innermost part of an author whom they have approached, adapt themselves solely to first appearances, and spend themselves rather on the beauty of words than on the might of the real content. And certainly, as it is not vicious, but greatly laudable, to borrow from another language sentences and words, and to appropriate them to one's own: so it is greatly reprehensible, and must seem odious to every reader of a liberal, cultivated nature, to see, in the same language, such an imitation, such a one as that of some of the learned, even, who think themselves better in proportion as they resemble an Heroet or a Marot. I charge you (O you who desire the enlargement of your literature and its excellence over the others) not to imitate headlong, as recently some one has said, its most famous authors, as ordinarily do the great part of our French poets, a practice certainly as faulty as it is of no worth to our vernacular: for that is not another thing but to give it (O tremendous liberality) what it already has. I would that our language were so rich in models of its own that we should have no need of recourse to others. But if Virgil and Cicero had been content to imitate the authors of their literature, what should we have had of Latin, beyond Ennius or Lucretius, beyond Crassus or Antonius?

BOOK II CHAPTER I

THE AUTHOR'S INTENTION

SINCE the poet and the orator are like the two pillars that support the edifice of a literature, I am eager, leaving that one which I perceive has been built by others,[1] for the duty that I owe to my country, to build that which yet waits: hoping that by mine, or by a more learned hand, it may have its perfection. But I do not wish, in this undertaking, to pretend, like a certain type of poet, that one perceives not with eyes, ears, or any of the senses, but comprehends only through abstract cogitation and thought: like those ideas which Plato says are in all things, to which, as to a certain imagined species, all that can be seen is referred. That certainly is greater knowledge than mine, and of greater leisure: I trust that I shall have well deserved, if to our writers I but point with a finger the road which they must follow to attain the excellence of the ancients; thereon some other, perhaps encouraged by our small labor, will lead them with his hand. Let us recall, then, to begin with, what we have, I believe, well enough proved in the first book. It is that without imitation we cannot give to our language the excellence and the lustre of those more famous ones. I know that many will censure me, who have dared, the first among the French, to introduce what seems a new poetry; or they will be dissatisfied, not so much with the brevity of the piece as with the variety of sentiments, of which

[1] *L'Orateur Francois* of Estienne Dolet   Book I.
had been mentioned at the conclusion of

some will think good what others will think faulty. Marot pleases me, one will say, because he is facile, and does not depart from the common manner of speech; another prefers Heroet, because all his verse is learned, weighty, elaborated; and some are pleased with yet other poets. As for me, such superstition does not retire me from my enterprise, because I have always believed that French poetry is capable of a greater height and a better style than those with which we have for so long contented ourselves. We shall give briefly our opinions of the French poets.

[Chapter II, "Des Poetes Francois," is highly specialized, and of interest only to such French Renaissance scholars as would require the original French text. Its argument is well enough deduced from the following chapter.]

CHAPTER III

THAT NATURAL TALENT IS NOT SUFFICIENT TO ONE WHO WISHES IN POETRY TO CREATE A WORK WORTHY OF IMMORTALITY

IN all literatures there are both good and bad authors. I caution the reader against fixing on one without due consideration and judgment. Certainly it is much better to write without imitation than to assimilate a poor author. It is a thing agreed among the wisest, that genius avails more without learning than learning does without genius. Since the broadening of our language (which is the thing I treat of) cannot be accomplished without principles and without learning, I recommend these to all who aspire to the glory of imitating the great Greeks and Romans, or even Italian, Spanish, and other literatures: else let them not write at all, unless for themselves, as some one has said, and for their own Muses. Let none urge that there have been some of our race who, without theory, or with but mediocre notions of the art, have been noised into reputation in our literature. Those willing to admire the smaller things, who disparage what is beyond their judgment, may make of this what they will: but I well know that the truly learned put them in no other class than that of those who speak French well, and who have (as Cicero said of the ancient Romans) admirable eagerness, but very little art. Nor let any urge that poets are born, for this is understood because of that ardor and alacrity of spirit which, in their natures, excites poets, and without which all theory would be imperfect and useless. Certainly it were an easy matter, and so beneath any pride, to become eternally renowned, if a happy faculty given by nature even to the unlearned, were sufficient to work a thing that deserved immortality. Whoever wishes his works to wing their ways about the hands and mouths of men, must delay long in his chamber; whoever wishes to live in the memory of posterity, must, dead to all thought of himself, sweat and tremble, and that many times; and unlike our libertine poets who drink, eat, sleep at their ease, he must endure hunger, thirst, long vigils. These are the pinions on which the writings of men mount to the sky. Once again I return to the beginning of this discourse, that our author take great care whom he shall desire to imitate, what in them he can imitate, and who is worthy of imitation; let him not be like some, who, wishing to appear like a great lord, will imitate rather an insignificant act or vicious fashion in him, than his virtues and gracious qualities. Above all things he must have the judgment to assess his powers, and to try what his shoulders can carry. Let him sound his nature with diligence, and apply himself to the imitation of that which he feels his nature approaches: otherwise his imitation will resemble that of a monkey.

CHAPTER IV

WHAT TYPES OF POEMS THE FRENCH POET SHOULD CHOOSE

READ then, and re-read, O future poet, handle lovingly, night and day, the exemplary Greek and Latin poets; then leave all those old French poets to the Jenix Floranx of Toulouse and to the Puy of Rouen; such as rondeaux, ballades, virelays, chants royal, chansons, and other such groceries, which corrupt the taste of our language and only serve to bear testimony to our ignorance. Devote yourself to pleasant epigrams, not as made today, by a mob of tellers of new tales, who, in a poem of ten lines, are content to have said nothing which gives value in the first nine lines, provided in the tenth there appear a laughable thing: but to the imitation of a Martial, or of some other excellent poet; if liveliness does not satisfy you, mingle the profitable with the pleasant. Distill with a pen flowing and not scabrous, these plaintive elegies, after the example of an Ovid, a Tibullus, and a Propertius, mingling into it sometimes some of these ancient fables, no small ornaments of poetry. Sing to me those odes, yet unknown to the French muse, on a lute well tuned to the sound of the Greek and Roman lyre, not without a single line in which appears some trace of rare but authentic lore. Material for that the praises of the gods and of great men will furnish you, and the deathward tread of earthly things, and the disquiet of youth: love, the unrestrained rites of wine, and all good cheer. Above all, take care that the type of poetry be far away from the vulgar, enriched and made illustrious with proper words and vigorous epithets, adorned with grave sentences, and varied with all manner of colorful and poetic ornaments: not as a *Laissez la Verde Couleur, Amour avecques Psyches, O Combien est Heureuse,* and other such works, more worthy of being called native chansons than odes or lyrical verse. For epistles are not a genre which greatly enriches our language, because they are concerned with familiar and domestic things, unless you wish to make them in imitation of elegies, like Ovid's, or sententious and grave poems, like Horace's. As much might I say to you of satires, which the French, I know not why, have labelled *cock-and-bull*[2] stories, and which I also advise you to avoid, as I desire you to be strangers to evil gossip; unless you desire to follow the example of the ancients in heroic verse, (that is to say, in verses varying from ten to eleven syllables, as well as from eight to nine), under the name of satire, and not of that inept appellation of *cock-and-bull* story, to censure with moderation the vices of our time, and not call by name vicious persons. You have for model Horace, who according to Quintillian held first place among satirists. Let me hear those beautiful sonnets, the learned and pleasant invention of the Italians, conforming to the ode, and differing from it only in that the sonnet has certain fixed and limited verse forms: whereas the ode can run through all manner of verse forms, even to the invention of new forms at will, as in Horace, who has sung, according to the grammarians, in nineteen forms of verse. For the sonnet, then, you have Petrarch and other modern Italians. Sing for me on a resonant musette and on a well-jointed flute some pleasant rustic eclogues, after the manner of Theocritus and of Virgil; poets of the sea can follow the example of a Sannazar, that delightful Neopolitan. If it please the Muses, may we have in all the kinds of poetry that I have named, many imitations such as the Eclogue on the birth of a son to Monsieur le Dauphin, to my mind, one of the best small works that Marot has ever written. Adopt also into the French family those easy-flowing and graceful hendecasyllabics as written by Catullus, by Pontano, and by Second, which you can write as in Latin, save for quantity, since French has not long and short syllables

[2] *Coqz a l'Asne.*

As to comedies and tragedies, if the king and the country desire them reestablished in their ancient dignity, which place the farces and moralities have usurped, I am indeed of the opinion that you should employ yourself on these, and if you wish to make for the enrichment of your language, you know where you can find the models.

PIERRE DE RONSARD

(1524–1585)

R ONSARD was born near the village of Couture, and received his early education at the Collège de Navarre, Paris. His father was *maître d'hotel du roi* to Francis I, and so the boy was introduced at court at an early age. Attached to several embassies of note, he retired from diplomatic service because of deafness, and settled at the Collège Coqueret to study. Here he was later joined by Du Bellay, and the famous Pleiade came into existence. Its seven members were Ronsard, Du Bellay, Baïf, Belleau, Pontus de Tyard, Jodelle, and Daurat.

The publications in 1550 of the first four books of the *Odes,* and in 1552 of the fifth book and of the *Amours de Cassandra,* established Ronsard's poetical fame immediately. There ensued a series of controversies with the poetic disciples of Clément Marot, who saw in the new poet's success with classical models the likelihood of their being relegated to obscurity. The calumny of the Huguenots because of Ronsard's strong Catholicism was added to this. Yet his position with the court party grew stronger constantly, and as the poet royal to Charles IX he passed the latter part of his life in eminence and honor. His *Françiade* (1572), which followed the king's request for a great French epic, in no wise approaches classical achievement. His lyrics remain his clear title to poetic pre-eminence.

The *Abregé,* or *Brief,* was addressed to Alphonse Delbene, a young poet of Italian parentage. Ronsard's compliment on the father's Italian and Latin writings is perhaps the only personal element of what is technically an epistle.

Written sixteen years after the *Defense* of Du Bellay, the *Abregé* is more self-confident, more authoritative, less argumentative, and less systematic. The main ideas of the Pleiade are incorporated in it, though treated in so little detail, sometimes so casually, as not to be evident except to a piercing examination. The divine nature of poetry, the requisite purity of the poets, and the desirableness of their comradeship, may not at first seem matters of criticism. Yet they are Platonic and Ciceronian echoes, reflected by the Italians, but nowhere more fervently championed than here; and they represent a plan which has not come nearer achievement than in the Pleiade. For to this group poetry was truly a religion, for which a certain revelation was necessary, and schooling, and an inspired leadership. While we may not think of the group at Coqueret as pursuing a monastic existence, they nevertheless parallel a religious sect, with Ronsard at their head. The *Abregé* has something of the tone of a divinely inspired epistle to one of the weaker brothers.

In his advices upon imitation, Ronsard unconsciously helps with the fetters which are later to be fastened upon French and English literature. The injunctions of such "horatianisms" as "file your verses" and "begin in the middle" are bestowed with pedantic unctuousness; the young poet is commanded to alternate his masculine and feminine rhymes, and the definitions of "invention," "disposition," and "elocution" are presumed to obviate any necessity in explaining them. There is, notwithstanding, a recognition of the place of the spirit and of individualism, and as fervent a desire as Du Bellay's to furnish French literature with the riches of antiquity, without all the latter's haughty disdain for the purely Gallic forms.

A BRIEF
ON THE ART OF FRENCH POETRY *

(1565)

ALTHOUGH the art of Poetry can be neither learned nor taught by precept, it being a thing more experiential than traditional,[1] yet, in so far as human art, attainment, and labor will permit, I wish to lay down some rules by which one day you may be able to reach the first order of skill in this happy calling, by my means, who confess myself reasonably learned in it. Always you will hold the Muses in reverence, in singular veneration, and not have them serve for any purpose dishonorable, ridiculous, or libelous; but you are to keep them beloved and sacramental, the daughters of Jupiter, which is to say, of God, who in his sacred grace, first through them made known to ignorant peoples the excellence of his majesty. For poetry was in the earliest time only an allegorical theology, to carry into men's coarse brains, by charming and prettily colored fables, the secret truths which they could not comprehend if openly declared. The Athenian Eumolpus, Linus the instructor of Hercules, Orpheus, Homer, Hesiod invented this excellent profession. So poets were called divine, not so much for the godlike soul which made them wonderful above others, as for the communion which they had with oracles, prophets, diviners, sibyls, interpreters of dreams, for of what these knew the poets had learned the

---

* Translated by James Harry Smith. [The technical sections at the end are omitted.]

[1] Mr. Saintsbury translates this phrase, *plus mental que tradatif,* "more native to the mind than communicable to it." [*Hist. Crit. II,* 120]

superior part: to what the oracles said in few words, these elevated persons gave expansion, color, commentary, being for the people what the sibyls and diviners were but for themselves. A long time afterward appeared in the same country the second school of poets, whom I call human, as being more filled with artifice and labor, than with divine inspiration. As an example of the latter, the Roman poets swarmed in abundance, with so many puffed out and artificial books that they brought to book-stores more burden than honor, except for five or six, whose understanding of their art, accompanied by perfect craftsmanship, has always held my admiration.

But since the Muses are not willing to reside in a soul unless it be kindly, saintly, virtuous, you should act always with kindness, never with meanness, sullenness, or chagrin; moved by a fine spirit, let nothing enter your soul which is not superhuman, divine. You are to bear in highest regard conceptions which are elevated, grand, beautiful— not those that lie round the earth. For the principal thing is invention, which comes as much from goodness of nature as from the lessons of the good ancient authors. If you attempt a great work, you should show yourself religious and God-fearing, beginning the poem either with his name or with another which will represent some effect of his majesty, as in the example of the Greek poets, "Sing, O Goddess, the wrath," "Tell me of the man, O Muse," "With Zeus let us begin," "Beginning from thee O Phoebus," [2] and of the Latin, "Great Mother of Rome," "Muse, relate to me the causes." [3] For the Muses, Apollo, Mercury, Pallas, Venus, and other such deities represent to us no other thing than powers of God, to which the earliest men gave various names, in accord with the different effects of his incomparable majesty. And it must also show you that nothing can be good or perfect, if the beginning not come of God. Then, you are to study the writings of the good poets, and learn by heart as many of them as you can. You are to take great pains to correct and file your verses, and are not to excuse faults in them any more than a good gardener neglects his poles when he sees them overburdened with branches useless or of little account. You are to hold sweet converse with the other poets of your time: you will honor the oldest among them as your fathers, those your age, as your brothers, the younger, as the children. And you will show to your fellow poets your writings, for you should let nothing

---

[2] Μῆνιν ἄειδε θεά; Ανδρα μοι ἔννεπε, Μοῦα; Εχ Διὸς αρχόμεσθα; Αρχόμενός σεὸ ζοῖβε: the beginnings of the Iliad, the Odyssey, the seventeenth idyl of Theocritus, and an unidentified work.

[3] *Aeneadum genetrix; Musa mihi causas memora:* the opening invocations of the *De Rerum Natura* and the *Aeneid.*

see the light which has not first been viewed and reviewed by your friends whom you think the best qualified on the matter; to the end that by such relationships and familiarities of your minds, with the learning and the talent that you have, you will arrive with ease at the height of all honor, having for local example the virtues of your father, who not only has surpassed in his, the Italian language, those in highest reputation in his time, but even has made the victory doubtful between himself and those who write today with most purity and learning the old language of the Romans.

But since you have denied recognition to Greek and Latin as mediums of composition, and only French remains, which ought to be the more readily commended to you, as it is your native language, I shall say a few things that seem expedient, and without losing you in a large and tedious forest, I shall conduct you straightway, and by the path which I have found shortest, so that you may easily overtake those who first set out on the road, and may find yourself not outstripped to any extent at all.

In the manner in which Latin verse has its feet, as you know, we have in our French poetry a certain measure of syllables, according to the kind of poem to be written; and this cannot be trespassed without offense to the law of our verse, the particular measures and numbers of which I treat more amply farther on. We have also a *cæsure* [4] on the vowel *e,* which is done away whenever it is encountered with another vowel or a diphthong, provided that the vowel which follows *e* not have the force of a consonant. In imitation of my precepts you will appoint the verses, masculine and feminine, as well as it be possible for you to do, to approach nearest music and the harmony of instruments, in the favor of which poetry seems to have been born: for poetry without instruments, or without the grace of one or more voices, is in no wise charming, any more than instruments unenlivened by a pleasing voice. If you happen to have composed the two first verses masculine in ending, make the next two feminine, and proceed in this manner for the remainder of your elegy or *chanson,* that the musicians may the more easily harmonize with it. As to lyric verse, you will build the first couplet as you desire, but the others must follow the plan of the first. If you make use of Greek and Roman proper names, you will, in so far as your tongue permits, give them French terminations; there are many which cannot so be changed. You ought not to disdain our old Latin words, but to choose them with prudence.

[4] For *elision.*

You will frequent the practitioners of all trades, seamanship, hunting, falconry, and especially those that owe the perfection in their craft to the furnace: goldsmiths, foundrymen, blacksmiths, metallurgists; and from them you will store up many good and lively semblances, along with the very names of the instruments, to enrich and beautify your work. For just as one may not call a body fair, comely, or gifted, unless it be made up of blood, veins, arteries, and tendons, and, above all, have a purely natural color, so Poetry cannot be charming, alive, or perfect without excellent inventions, descriptions, comparisons, which are the nerve and the life of books, which can force the centuries to leave them, in universal remembrance, victorious over time.

You are to learn to choose dexterously, and to appropriate to your work the most significant words of the dialects of our France, when those of your nation are not sufficiently proper or significant, not troubling yourself whether they be of Gascony, Poitou, Normandy, Manche, Lyonnais, or another province, provided only that they be good, and that they properly express what you want to say; without affecting too much the speech of the court, which is many times quite mediocre to be the language of courtly ladies and of gentlemen, who pursue more the practice of arms than of well chosen speech. You will observe that the Greek language would never have been so scattered and so full of dialects and varieties of words as it is, had not the majority of the republics that flourished in that time selfishly desired that their learned citizens write in their own particular dialects. And because of that there has come down an infinity of dialects, phrases, and manners of speaking, which even today carry on their foreheads the marks of their native countries, which are held indifferently good by the learned pens that write of that time. For a country can never be so entirely perfect that it may not borrow some something from its neighbor. And I doubt not that if there remained in France the Dukes of Burgundy, Picardy, Normandy, Brittany, Champaign, Gascony, they would yet desire the extreme honor of their subjects' writing in a provincial dialect. For princes must be no less eager to widen the bounds of their realms than, on the example of the Romans, to extend the language of their countries through all nations. But today, France under one king, we are compelled, if we wish to come to any honor, to speak the courtier's language; or our labor, however learned it may be, is liable to be estimated of little value, or may be totally scorned. And since the goods and favors come in from this source, it is often necessary to yield to the opinion of some court lady or some young courtier, who will often have as little knowledge of good and true poetry as they have skill in arms and other of the more honorable exercises.

OF INVENTION

Since I have mentioned invention before, it seems to me that it would be timely here to refresh your memory by a short notice of it. Invention is nothing other than the natural virtue of an imagination, conceiving the ideas and forms of all things that can be imagined, whether of heaven or of earth, living or inanimate, for the purpose of afterwards representing, describing, imitating: for just as the aim of the orator is to persuade, so that of the poet is to imitate, invent, and represent— things which are, or which may be—in a resemblance to truth. And it must not be doubted that after one have invented boldly and well, a "disposition" of verse which is effective will follow, for disposition follows invention, in all cases, just as the shadow does a body. When I bid you invent fair things and great, I do not mean inventions fantastic and melancholic; these do not more correspond to one another than do the broken dreams of one in a frenzy, or terribly tormented by a fever, to an imagination bruised or injured, in which a thousand monstrous forms, without order or connection, are represented. But your inventions, on which I cannot give you rules, as they are of the spirit, must be well ordered and appointed. And although they seem to pass those of the vulgar, they must nevertheless be such as can easily be conceived and understood by everyone.

OF DISPOSITION

As invention depends upon the refined state of the mind, so disposition depends upon sound invention, consisting in an elegant and consummate placing and ordering of the things invented; it does not permit what appertains to one place to be put in another, but, operating by artifice, study, and application, it disposes and sets each matter to its proper point. For examples of it you may take the ancient authors and those of the moderns who have during the last fifteen years illuminated our literature, now justly proud in this glorious achievement. Happy demi-gods, they who cultivate their own earth, nor strive after another, from which they could only return thankless and unhappy, unrecompensed, unhonored. The first to dare abandon the ancient Greek and Roman languages for the greater glory of their own truly must be good sons, not ungrateful citizens; worthy to be signalized in a public statue, wherein from age to age men shall encounter a lasting memorial of them and of their greatness: not that other languages should be ignored; for I counsel you to know them perfectly, and from them, as from an old treasure found under the earth, enrich your own nation. For it is very difficult to write well in the vernacular if one be not perfectly, or at least fairly, learned in those more honored and more famous languages.

OF ELOCUTION

Elocution is a propriety and splendor of words, properly chosen and adorned, in varying lengths of sentence, which make the verse glitter like precious stones on the fingers of some great lord. Under elocution I put choice of words, which Virgil and Horace so conscientiously observed. For you ought to strive to be well supplied with words, and to call the most appropriate and significant that you can to serve as the sinew and force of your song, which will shine in proportion as the words be significant, and chosen with judgment. You are not to forget the comparisons, the descriptions of places, streams, forests, mountains, of night, and of sunrise, of mid-day, of the winds, the sea, of gods and goddesses, with their proper attributes, dress, cars, horses: guiding yourself in this by imitation of Homer, whom you are to observe as a divine example, from whom you are to draw, as from life, the most perfect lineaments for your picture.

OF POETRY IN GENERAL

You are to know that great poems never begin at the first point of the action, nor are so completed as that the reader, taken with the de-light of it, may not still wish the end farther off; but the good literary craftsmen begin in the middle, and knowing so well how to join the beginning to the middle, and the middle to the end, make of the pieces so produced a body entire and perfect. Never begin a poem on a large scale unless its subject stretch back before the memory of men; and invoke the Muse, who remembers everything, being a goddess, to sing to you things of which men can remember nothing. The others, little poems, may be begun abruptly, the lyric odes, for example, in the composition of which I advise you to train yourself first, taking care above all against being more the versifier than the poet: for fable and fictions have furnished the material for the good poets, those who have been recommended to posterity from as far back as memory goes; and mere verse is but the aim of the ignorant versifier, who thinks that he has made great headway in his work when he has composed a great many rhyming verses which so smell of prose that I am amazed how our French publishers can print such drugs, to the confusion of authors, and of our nation as a whole. I should inform you of the proper subjects for each particular kind of poem, if you had not already read the *arts of poetry* of Horace and of Aristotle, in which I know you are fairly well versed.

I counsel you to avoid epithets relating to objects of nature, as they do not advance at all the sense of what you want to say; for example, *the flowing river, the green bough,* and infinite others. You should seek out epithets which mean something, not merely fill up your verse form, or trifle with your sense. Take this verse for an example:

> The vaulted sky encloses all the earth.

I have said "vaulted," and not "burning," "clear," "high," or "azure," because a vault appertains to the embracing and enclosing a thing. You may well say,

> The small boat goes along the running wave,

because the course of the water makes the boat to run. The Romans have been very cautious observers of this rule, Virgil and Horace among the others. The Greeks, as in all things pertaining to verse, have been freer about it, and have not regarded it so closely. You are also to avoid the manner of composition of the Italians in your language, who commonly put four or five epithets one after the other in the same verse, as for example, "dear, comely, angelic, rich gifts." You can see that such epithets are more to puff up and paint the verse than to fill any need in it. Content yourself with one epithet, or at most, with two, unless some time for amusement you make five or six, but if you follow my advice in the matter, that will happen as infrequently as you can manage.

OF RHYME

Rhyme is the correspondence and cadence of syllables, falling at the ends of the verses, which I wish you to observe as well for masculine as for feminine, in the two complete, perfect syllables, or at least in the masculine, provided that it be resonant, and of a sound perfect and entire. Examples of the feminine: *France, Esperance, despence, negligence, familiere, foumiliere, premiere, chere, mere.* Examples of the masculine: *surmonter, monter, donter, sauter, Juppiter.* Always you are to be more attentive to good invention and to the words, than to the rhyme, which comes easily enough of itself after some little practise and experience.

[The titles of the remaining sections indicate sufficiently their absorption with French phonetics and orthography, and are given here should anyone wish some idea of the remainder of the treatise: *De La Voyelle E. De L'H. Des Vers Alexandrins. Des Vers Communs. Des Autres Vers en Général. Des Personnes des Verbes François et de L'Ortographie.*]

SIR PHILIP SIDNEY

(1554–1586)

PHILIP SIDNEY was born at Penhurst in 1554, the eldest son of Sir Henry Sidney. At the age of nine he entered Shrewsbury School (where began the life-long friendship with Fulke Greville), and in 1568, Christ College, Oxford, where he studied for four years.

In 1572 came the first trip abroad, made for the purpose of studying. Sidney visited Paris, Vienna, Venice, and Prague, returning home in 1575. He became at once popular in the court, under the patronage of his uncle, the Earl of Leicester. In this same year came his meeting with Penelope Devereux, the "Stella" to whom the sonnets of the next five or six years were addressed. He met Spenser in 1578, and in the next year received the dedication of *The Shepherdes Calendar.*

In 1580 Sidney, along with his patron, took an active part in opposing the Queen's marrying the Duke of Anjou, and Leicester's disgrace involved him also. In virtual retirement at Wilton he wrote the *Arcadia.*

By 1583 he was reinstated at court, knighted, and married. Two years later he was appointed Governor of Flushing, and in 1586, at the battle of Zutphen, received the wound from which he died. A model of chivalry in his life and death, Sidney was eulogized in over two hundred elegies and poetic laments.

Before Sidney wrote *An Apologie for Poetrie,* there had been little of formal criticism written in England. Mr. Saintsbury praises the indirect criticism by Chaucer, in *Sir Thopas,* but [*Hist. of Crit.,* I, 452] "the whole is done by implication and unexpounded example, not in the very least by direct criticism." The modest printer and translator, William Caxton, imbedded in his Prefaces and Epilogues some attractive and not unimportant snippets: he encouraged and defended the use of prose on the ground that "divers men be of divers desires, some to read in metre and rhyme and some in prose"; it is impossible to estimate his part in helping to fix the language, but he plainly desired [Prologue to Virgil's *Eneydos,* 1490] "the common terms that be daily used," and disliked the "rude, and curious." In the Sixteenth Century there appeared several Arts of Rhetoric, variously titled, and containing some incidental criticism; possibly the most famous was Thomas Wilson's *Art of Rhetorique* (1553) with its strong injunction, "that we never affect any strange Inkhorn terms," and its disdainful mention of the Englishman who "chops in with English Italianated." The moral objection was put by Roger Ascham, who wrote [*The*

Scholemaster, 1570] that "Italian books are made English, to bring mischief enough openly and boldly to all states, great and meane, yong and old, every where." Ascham had no use, also, for books of chivalry, "as one for example, *Morte Arthure;* the whole pleasure of which book standeth in two speciall poyntes, in open mans slaughter and bold bawdrye." Yet Ascham was also a classicist, praising the study of Greek and Latin; in these "two onelie learned tonges . . . we find alwayes wisdome and elo-quence, good matter and good utterance, never or seldom asonder." There was thus a fundamental disagreement in their incidental criticism: a desire to keep English undefiled yet to encourage the imitation of classical models; to have the benefits of humanism yet avoid the iniquities of the Italian Renaissance; to have an English literature, but to disregard all the native work (usually with the exception of Chaucer's) written in earlier times.

The first technical treatise was George Gascoigne's *Certain Notes of In-struction Concerning the Making of Verse or Ryme in English* (1575). It is practical and sensible, written at the request of an Italian friend and modelled on Ronsard's work. Gascoigne begins well: "The first and most necessarie poynt that ever I founde meete to be considered in making of a delectable poeme is this, to grounde it upon some fine invention. For it is not inough to roll in pleasant woordes, nor yet to thunder in *Rym, Ram, Ruff* by letter (quoth my master *Chaucer*), nor yet to abounde in apt voca-bles or epythetes." But he is, mainly, giving technical advice, cautioning against irregular verse, wrenching of accents, "rime without reason," and regretting the tyranny of the iambic foot. Equally technical was the early Scottish treatise by King James VI [*Reulis and Cautelis to be observit and eschewit in Scottis Poesie,* 1584]. James drew heavily on Gascoigne and Du Bellay. To him, "airt is onely bot ane help and a remembrance to Na-ture," and he counsels the poet against translation because "ye not onely essay not your awin ingyne of *Invention,* bot be the same meanes ye are bound, as to a staik, to follow that buikis phrasis quhilk ye translate." These books are interesting as preliminaries in criticism, but it was left for Sidney, with some help from Minturno and Scaliger, to write philosophically of poetry

In the first of his famous letters to Harvey, Spenser remarked: "Newe bookes I heare of none, but only of one, that writing a certaine booke called *The Schoole of Abuse,* and dedicating it to Maister Sidney, was for hys labor scorned: if, at leaste, it be in the goodnesse of that nature to scorne." This attack upon poetry by Gosson was dedicated without permission. Its contentions, moral rather than critical, drew forth replies from Thomas Lodge and from Sidney. The latter's counter-arguments in the *Apologie* suggest Gosson's chief points, but the extent to which Sidney carries his discussion indicates that he was not writing merely to refute one insignificant document. *The Schoole of Abuse* was published in 1579, the year that saw *The Shepherdes Calendar,* and the date of the *Apologie's* composition can only be approximated by assignment to such time there-after as must be allowed for the establishment in fame of Spenser's work, which is treated seriously by Sidney. Though circulated for many years, it was not published until 1595, when there appeared, by different pub-lishers (Ponsonby and Olney), *The Defense of Poesie* and *An Apologie for Poetrie,* both attributed to Sidney. The text here used is the latter, following the reprint by Professor Arber.

With an advocate's shrewdness, Sidney approaches his argument. He refers to Plato's method of imaginative, even metaphorical, reasoning, and unobtrusively, without any show of defining, indicates the limits of his "Poetrie," which would for us more nearly signify "fiction." The phrase, "his poetical describing the circumstances" would equal in our conception "his describing the fictitious circumstances." A few pages later, having expounded the Greek term signifying "maker," he allows to the poet "making things either better than nature bringeth forth, or quite a newe formes such as never were in Nature. . . ." Aside from any question as to how Aristotelian this may be, it defines the ground for the defense against Puritanism.

Presently, following a generalization on all the arts, there begins the approach to the formal definition. Already have "imitation" and "Nature" brought such confusion that Sidney wisely qualifies for two pages before risking his definition.

In the expressed aims, "to teach and delight," he is not Aristotelian. The earliest form of this coupling of the *utile* with pleasure came, presumably, from the confusion of the commentators on Horace's *aut prodesse . . . aut delectare.* But the Renaissance critics generally champion it, and Sidney exalts poetry over moral philosophy in the service of ethics, over history in the service of culture.

Inasmuch as it is intellectual license for which he is contending, he anticipates somewhat the argument of the *Areopagitica,* and extends the domain of imaginative literature where not before Milton was anyone effectively to carry the claim even for argumentation: "whether it bee possible to finde any path so ready to leade a man to vertue, as that which teacheth what vertue is? and teacheth it not onely by delivering forth his very being, his causes, and effects: but also, by making known his enemie vice, which must be destroyed, and his combersome servant Passion, which must be maistered. . . ." Milton [*Areopagitica*]: "That virtue therefore which is but a youngling in the contemplation of evil, and knows not the utmost that vice promises to her followers, and rejects it, is but a blank virtue, not a pure . . ."

As Sidney himself has remained the ultimate in manners and chivalry, so this essay lifts far above everything written near it, in its attitude toward serious preparation for life. The passage beginning with the "waighing" of mental scopes, both for the Platonic ideal, and for the fervor with which it is expressed, calls to mind the educational purpose so debated in the Nineteenth Century: "Culture is then properly described not as having its origin in curiosity, but as having its origin in the love of perfection." [Arnold, "Sweetness and Light."] "Following our instincts for intellect and knowledge, we acquire pieces of knowledge; and presently, in the generality of men, there arises the desire to relate these pieces of knowledge to our sense for conduct, to our sense for beauty—" [Arnold, "Literature and Science."] It is on his contention that "Poetrie," more than any other branch of knowledge, aids toward "this purifying of wit, this enritching of memory, enabling of iudgment, and enlarging of conceyt," that Sidney logically bases his position; in short, on the educational value.

His careful divisions of poetry into types, and his "type criticism," must incur our censure. Unforgettable always in relation to all such is Shakespeare's quick satire: "The best actors in the world, either for tragedy, comedy, history, pastoral-comical, historical-pastoral, tragical-historical, tragical-comical-historical-pastoral, scene individable, or poem unlimited." [*Hamlet* II, 2.]

Likewise we are out of accord with the rigidity of his arguments from authority. "He 'looks merely at the stop-watch.' Theocritus did not do it; Virgil did not do it; Sannazar did not do it; therefore Spenser must not do it." [Saintsbury: *History of English Criticism*, Interchapter I, p. 100.]

But the scope and purpose which he assigns to *belles lettres* have not been broadened or displaced, nor can be, while the traditions of modern thought remain what they are. And where shall we find good humor and fervor and sound principle so mingled in the style of a critical writing?

AN APOLOGIE FOR POETRIE *

(1583)   (1595)

WHEN the right vertuous *Edward Wotton,* and I, were at the Emperors Court together, wee gave our selves to learne horsemanship of *John Pietro Pugliano:* one that with great commendation had the place of an Esquire in his stable. And hee, according to the fertilnes of the Italian wit, did not onely afoord us the demonstration of his practise, but sought to enrich our mindes with the contemplations therein, which hee thought most precious. But with none I remember mine eares were at any time more loden, then when (either angred with slowe paiment, or mooved with our learner-like admiration,) he exercised his speech in the prayse of his facultie. Hee sayd, Souldiours were the noblest estate of mankinde, and horsemen, the noblest of Souldiours. Hee sayde, they were the Maisters of warre, and ornaments of peace: speedy goers, and strong abiders, triumphers both in Camps and Courts. Nay, to so unbeleeved a poynt hee proceeded, as that no earthly thing bred such wonder to a Prince, as to be a good horseman. Skill of government, was but a Pedanteria [1] in comparison: then would hee adde certaine prayses, by telling what a peerlesse beast a horse was.

---

* The Arber reprint of the Olney text is used here.

[1] *Pedanteria,* Italian, pedantry.

The onely serviceable Courtier without flattery, the beast of most beutie, faithfulnes, courage, and such more, that if I had not beene a peece of a Logician before I came to him, I think he would have perswaded mee to have wished my selfe a horse. But thus much at least with his no fewe words hee drave into me, that selfe-love is better than any guilding to make that seeme gorgious, wherein our selves are parties. Wherein, if *Pugliano* his strong affection and weake arguments will not satisfie you, I wil give you a neerer example of my selfe, who (I knowe not by what mischance) in these my not old yeres and idelest times, having slipt into the title of a Poet, am provoked to say something unto you in the defence of that my unelected vocation, which if I handle with more good will then good reasons, beare with me, sith the scholler is to be pardoned that foloweth the steppes of his Maister. And yet I must say, that as I have just cause to make a pittiful defence of poore Poetry, which from almost the highest estimation of learning, is fallen to be the laughingstocke of children. So have I need to bring some more availeable proofes: sith the former is by no man barred of his deserved credite, the silly latter hath had even the names of Philosophers used to the defacing of it, with great danger of civill war among the Muses. And first, truly to al them that professing learning inveigh against Poetry, may justly be objected, that they goe very neer to ungratfulnes, to seek to deface that, which in the noblest nations and languages that are knowne, hath been the first light-giver to ignorance, and first Nurse, whose milk by little and little enabled them to feed afterwards of tougher knowledges: and will they now play the Hedghog, that being received into the den, drave out his host? or rather the Vipers, that with theyr birth kill their Parents? Let learned Greece in any of her manifold Sciences, be able to shew me one booke, before *Musæus, Homer,* and *Hesiodus,* all three nothing els but Poets. Nay, let any historie be brought, that can say any Writers were there before them, if they were not men of the same skil, as *Orpheus, Linus,* and some other are named: who having beene the first of that Country, that made pens deliverers of their knowledge to their posterity, may justly challenge to bee called their Fathers in learning: for not only in time they had this priority (although in it self antiquity be venerable) but went before them, as causes to drawe with their charming sweetnes, the wild untamed wits to an admiration of knowledge. So as *Amphion* was sayde to move stones with his Poetrie, to build Thebes. And *Orpheus* to be listened to by beastes, indeed, stony and beastly people. So among the Romans were *Livius, Andronicus,* and *Ennius.* So in the

Italian language, the first that made it aspire to be a Treasure-house of Science, where the Poets *Dante, Boccace,* and *Petrarch.* So in our English were *Gower* and *Chawcer.*

After whom, encouraged and delighted with theyr excellent foregoing, others have followed, to beautifie our mother tongue, as wel in the same kinde as in other Arts. This did so notably shewe it selfe, that the Phylosophers of Greece, durst not a long time appeare to the worlde but under the masks of Poets. So *Thales, Empedocles,* and *Parmenides,* sange their naturall Phylosophie in verses: so did *Pythagoras* and *Phocilides* their morrall counsells: so did *Tirteus* in war matters, and *Solon* in matters of policie: or rather, they beeing Poets, dyd exercise their delightful vaine in those points of highest knowledge, which before them lay hid to the world. For that wise *Solon* was directly a Poet, it is manifest, having written in verse, the notable fable of the Atlantick Iland, which was continued by *Plato.*

And truely, even *Plato,* whosoever well considereth, shall find, that in the body of his work, though the inside and strength were Philosophy, the skinne as it were and beautie, depended most of Poetrie: for all standeth upon Dialogues, wherein he faineth many honest Burgesses of Athens to speake of such matters, that if they had been sette on the racke, they would never have confessed them. Besides, his poetical describing the circumstances of their meetings, as the well ordering of a banquet, the delicacie of a walke, with enterlacing meere tales, as *Giges* Ring, and others, which who knoweth not to be flowers of Poetrie, did never walke into *Appolos* Garden.

And even Historiographers (although theyr lippes sounde of things doone, and veritie be written in theyr fore-heads,) have been glad to borrow both fashion, and perchance weight of Poets. So *Herodotus* entituled his Historie, by the name of the nine Muses: and both he and all the rest that followed him, either stole or usurped of Poetrie, their passionate describing of passions, the many particularities of battailes, which no man could affirme: or if that be denied me, long Orations put in the mouthes of great Kings and Captaines, which it is certaine they never pronounced. So that truely, neyther Phylosopher nor Historiographer, coulde at the first have entred into the gates of populer judgements, if they had not taken a great pasport of Poetry, which in all Nations at this day wher learning florisheth not, is plaine to be seene: in all which they have some feeling of Poetry. In Turky, besides their lawe-giving Divines, they have no other Writers but Poets. In our neighbour Countrey Ireland, where truelie learning goeth very bare, yet are theyr Poets held in a devoute reverence. Even among the most barbarous and simple Indians where no writing is, yet have they their Poets, who make and sing songs which they call *Areytos,* both of theyr Auncestors deedes, and praises of theyr Gods. A sufficient probabilitie, that if ever learning come among them, it must be by having theyr hard dull wits softened and sharpened with the sweete delights of Poetrie. For untill they find a pleasure in the exercises of the minde, great promises of much knowledge, will little perswade them, that knowe not the fruites of knowledge. In Wales, the true remnant of the auncient Brittons, as there are good authorities to shewe the long time they had Poets, which they called *Bardes:* so thorough all the conquests of Romaines, Saxons, Danes, and Normans, some of whom did seeke to ruine all memory of learning from among them, yet doo their Poets even to this day, last; so as it is not more notable in soone beginning then in long continuing. But since the Authors of most of our Sciences were the Romans, and before them the Greekes, let us a little stand uppon their authorities, but even so farre as to see, what names they have given unto this now scorned skill.

Among the Romans a Poet was called *Vates,* which is as much as a Diviner, Fore-seer, or Prophet, as by his conjoyned wordes *Vaticinium* and *Vaticinari,* is manifest: so heavenly a title did that excellent people bestow upon his hart-ravishing knowledge. And so farre were they carried into the admiration thereof, that they thought in the chaunce-able hitting uppon any such verses great fore-tokens of their following fortunes were placed. Whereupon grew the worde of *Sortes Virgilianæ,* when by suddaine opening *Virgils* booke, they lighted upon any verse of hys making, whereof the histories of the Emperors lives are full, as of *Albinus* the Governour of our Iland, who in his childehoode mette with this verse

Arma amens capio nec sat rationis in armis.[2]

And in his age performed it, which although it were a very vaine, and godles superstition, as also it was to think that spirits were commaunded by such verses, whereupon this word charmes, derived of *Carmina* commeth, so yet serveth it to shew the great reverence those wits were helde in. And altogether not without ground, since both the Oracles of *Delphos* and *Sibillas* prophecies, where wholy delivered in verses. For that same exquisite observing of number and measure in words,

[2] "Frenzied I take up arms, but judgment lies not in arms." *Aeneid* II, 314.

and that high flying liberty of conceit proper to the Poet, did seeme to have some dyvine force in it.

And may not I presume a little further, to shew the reasonablenes of this worde *Vates?* And say that the holy *Davids* Psalmes are a divine Poem? If I doo, I shall not do it without the testimonie of great learned men, both aunclent and moderne: but even the name Psalmes will speake for mee, which being interpreted, is nothing but songes Then that it is fully written in meeter, as all learned Hebricians agree, although the rules be not yet fully found. Lastly and principally, his handeling his prophecy, which is meerely poetical. For what els is the awaking his musicall instruments? The often and free changing of persons? His notable *Prosopopeias,*[3] when he maketh you as it were, see God comming in his Majestie. His telling of the Beastes joyfulnes and hills leaping, but a heavenlie poesie: wherein almost hee sheweth himself a passionate lover, of that unspeakable and everlasting beautie to be seene by the eyes of the minde, onely cleered by fayth. But truely nowe having named him, I feare mee I seeme to prophane that holy name, applying it to Poetrie, which is among us throwne downe to so ridiculous an estimation: but they that with quiet judgements will looke a little deeper into it, shall finde the end and working of it such, as beeing rightly applyed, deserveth not to bee scourged out of the Church of God.

But now, let us see how the Greekes named it, and howe they deemed of it. The Greekes called him a Poet, which name, hath as the most excellent, gone thorough other Languages. It commeth of this word *Poiein,* which is, to make: wherein I know not whether by lucke or wisedome, wee Englishmen have mette with the Greekes, in calling him a maker: which name, how high and incomparable a title it is, I had rather were knowne by marking the scope of other Sciences, then by my partiall allegation.

There is no Arte delivered to mankinde, that hath not the wordes of Nature for his principall object, without which they could not consist, and on which they so depend, as they become Actors and Players as it were, of what Nature will have set foorth. So doth the Astronomer looke upon the starres, and by that he seeth, setteth downe what order Nature hath taken therein. So doe the Geometrician, and Arithmetician, in their diverse sorts of quantities. So doth the Musitian in times, tel you which by nature agree, which not. The naturall Philosopher

[3] The Greek rhetorical figure for the in-　actually present.
troducing of a speech by someone not

thereon hath his name, and the Morrall Philosopher standeth upon the naturall vertues, vices, and passions of man; and followe Nature (saith hee) therein, and thou shalt not erre. The Lawyer sayth what men have determined. The Historian what men have done. The Grammarian speaketh onely of the rules of speech, and the Rethorician, and Logitian, considering what in Nature will soonest prove and perswade, thereon give artificiall rules, which still are compassed within the circle of a question, according to the proposed matter. The Phisition waigheth the nature of a mans bodie, and the nature of things helpeful, or hurtefull into it. And the Metaphisick, though it be in the seconde and abstract notions, and therefore be counted supernaturall: yet doth hee indeede builde upon the depth of Nature: onely the Poet, disdayning to be tied to any such subjection, lifted up with the vigor of his owne invention, dooth growe in effect, another nature, in making things either better then Nature bringeth forth, or quite a newe formes such as never were in Nature, as the *Heroes, Demigods, Cyclops, Chimeras, Furies,* and such like: so as hee goeth hand in hand with Nature, not inclosed within the narrow warrant of her guifts, but freely ranging onely within the Zodiack of his owne wit.

Nature never set forth the earth in so rich tapistry, as divers Poets have done, neither with plesant rivers, fruitful trees, sweet smelling flowers: nor whatsoever els may make the too much loved earth more lovely. Her world is brasen, the Poets only deliver a golden: but let those things alone and goe to man, for whom as the other things are, so it seemeth in him her uttermost cunning is imployed, and knowe whether shee have brought foorth so true a lover as *Theagines,* so constant a friende as *Pilades,* so valiant a man as *Orlando,* so right a Prince as *Xenophons Cyrus:* so excellent a man every way, as *Virgils Aeneas:* neither let this be jestingly conceived, because the works of the one be essentiall: the other, in imitation or fiction, for any understanding knoweth the skil of the Artificer: standeth in that *Idea* or fore-conceite of the work, and not in the work it selfe. And that the Poet hath that *Idea,* is manifest, by delivering them forth in such excellencie as hee hath imagined them. Which delivering forth also, is not wholie imaginative, as we are wont to say by them that build Castles in the ayre: but so farre substantially it worketh, not onely to make a *Cyrus,* which had been but a particuler excellencie, as Nature might have done, but to bestow a *Cyrus* upon the worlde, to make many *Cyrus's,* if they wil learne aright, why, and how that Maker made him.

Neyther let it be deemed too sawcie a comparison to ballance the highest poynt of mans wit with the efficacie of Nature: but rather give right honor to the heavenly Maker of that maker: who having made man to his owne likenes, set him beyond and over all the workes of that second nature, which in nothing hee sheweth so much as in Poetrie: when with the force of a divine breath, he bringeth things forth far surpassing her dooings, with no small argument to the incredulous of that first accursed fall of *Adam:* sith our erected wit, maketh us know what perfection is, and yet our infected will, keepeth us from reaching unto it. But these arguments wil by fewe be understood, and by fewer granted. Thus much (I hope) will be given me, that the Greekes with some probabilitie of reason, gave him the name above all names of learning. Now let us goe to a more ordinary opening of him, that the trueth may be more palpable: and so I hope, though we get not so unmatched a praise as the Etimologie of his names wil grant, yet his very description, which no man will denie, shall not justly be barred from a principall commendation.

Poesie therefore is an arte of imitation, for so *Aristotle* termeth it in his word *Mimesis,* that is to say, a representing, counterfetting, or figuring foorth: to speake metaphorically, a speaking picture: with this end, to teach and delight; of this have beene three severall kindes. The chiefe both in antiquitie and excellencie, were they that did imitate the inconceivable excellencies of GOD. Such were, *David* in his Psalmes, *Salomon* in his song of Songs, in his Ecclesiastes, and Proverbs: *Moses* and *Bebora* in theyr Hymnes, and the writer of *Job;* which beside other, the learned *Emanuell Tremilius* and *Franciscus Junius,* doe entitle the poeticall part of the Scripture. Against these none will speake that hath the holie Ghost in due holy reverence.

In this kinde, though in a full wrong divinitie, were *Orpheus, Amphion, Homer* in his hymes, and many other, both Greekes and Romaines: and this Poesie must be used, by whosoever will follow *S. James* his counsell, in singing Psalmes when they are merry: and I knowe is used with the fruite of comfort by some, when in sorrowfull pangs of their death-bringing sinnes, they find the consolation of the never-leaving goodnesse.

The second kinde, is of them that deale with matters Philosophicall; eyther morrall, as *Tirteus, Phocilides* and *Cato,* or naturall, as *Lucretius* and *Virgils Georgicks:* or Astronomicall, as *Manilius,* and *Pontanus:* or historical, as *Lucan:* which who mislike, the faulte is in their judgements quite out of taste, and not in the sweet foode of sweetly uttered knowledge. But because thys second sorte is wrapped within the folde of the proposed subject, and takes not the course of his owne invention, whether they properly be Poets or no, let Gramarians dispute: and goe to the thyrd, indeed right Poets, of whom chiefly this question ariseth; betwixt whom, and these second is such a kinde of difference, as betwixt the meaner sort of Painters, (who counterfet onely such faces as are sette before them) and the more excellent: who having no law but wit, bestow that in cullours upon you which is fittest for the eye to see: as the constant, though lamenting looke of *Lucrecia,* when she punished in her selfe an others fault.

Wherein he painteth not *Lucrecia* whom he never sawe, but painteth the outwarde beauty of such a vertue: for these third be they which most properly do imitate to teach and delight, and to imitate, borrow nothing of what is, hath been, or shall be: but range onely rayned with learned discretion, into the divine consideration of what may be, and should be. These bee they, that as the first and most noble sorte, may justly bee termed *Vates,* so these are waited on in the excellen[te]st languages and best understandings, with the fore described name of Poets: for these indeede doo meerely make to imitate: and imitate both to delight and teach: and delight to move men to take that goodnes in hande, which without delight they would flye as from a stranger. And teach, to make them know that goodnes whereunto they are mooved, which being the noblest scope to which ever any learning was directed, yet want there not idle tongues to barke at them. These be subdivided into sundry more speciall denominations. The most notable bee the *Heroick, Lirick, Tragick, Comick, Satirick, Iambick, Elegiack, Pastorall,* and certaine others. Some of these being termed according to the matter they deale with, some by the sorts of verses they liked best to write in, for indeede the greatest part of Poets have apparelled their poeticall inventions in that numbrous kinde of writing which is called verse: indeed but apparelled, verse being but an ornament and no cause to Poetry: sith there have beene many most excellent Poets, that never versified, and now swarme many versifiers that neede never aunswere to the name of Poets. For *Xenophon,* who did imitate so excellently, as to give us *effigiem justi imperij,* the portraiture of a just Empire under the name of *Cyrus,* (as *Cicero* sayth of him) made therein an absolute heroicall Poem.

So did *Heliodorus* in his sugred invention of that picture of love in *Theagines* and *Cariclea,* and yet both these writ in Prose: which I speak to shew, that it is not riming and versing that maketh a Poet, no more then a long gowne maketh an Advocate: who though he pleaded in armor should be an Advocate and no Souldier. But it is that fayning notable images of vertues, vices, or what els, with that delightfull teaching which must be the right describing note to know a Poet by: although indeed the Senate of Poets hath chosen verse as their fittest rayment, meaning, as in matter they passed all in all, so in maner to goe beyond them: not speaking (table talke fashion or like men in a dreame,) words as they chanceably fall from the mouth, but peyzing each sillable of each worde by just proportion according to the dignitie of the subject.

Nowe therefore it shall not bee amisse first to waigh this latter sort of Poetrie by his works, and then by his partes; and if in neyther of these Anatomies hee be condemnable, I hope wee shall obtaine a more favourable sentence. This purifing of wit, this enritching of memory, enabling of judgment, and enlarging of conceyt, which commonly we call learning, under what name soever it com forth, or to what immediat end soever it be directed, the final end is, to lead and draw us to as high a perfection, as our degenerate soules made worse by theyr clayey lodgings, can be capable of. This according to the inclination of the man, bred many formed impressions, for some that thought this felicity principally to be gotten by knowledge, and no knowledge to be so high and heavenly, as acquaintance with the starres, gave themselves to Astronomie; others, perswading themselves to be *Demigods* if they knewe the causes of things, became naturall and supernaturall Philosophers, some an admirable delight drew to Musicke: and some, the certainty of demonstration, to the Mathematickes. But all, one, and other, having this scope to knowe, and by knowledge to lift up the mind from the dungeon of the body, to the enjoying his owne divine essence. But when by the ballance of experience it was found, that the Astronomer looking to the starres might fall into a ditch, that the enquiring Philosopher might be blinde in himselfe, and the Mathematician might draw foorth a straight line with a crooked hart: then loe, did proofe the over ruler of opinions, make manifest, that all these are but serving Sciences, which as they have each a private end in themselves, so yet are they all directed to the highest end of the mistres Knowledge, by the Greekes called *Arkitecktonike,* which stands, (as I thinke) in the knowledge of a mans selfe, in the Ethicke and politick consideration, with the end of well dooing and not of well knowing onely; even as the Sadlers next end is to make a good saddle: but his farther end, to serve a nobler facultie, which is horsemanship, so the horsemans to souldiery, and the Souldier not onely to have the skill, but to performe the practise of a Souldier: so that the ending end of all earthly learning, being vertuous action, those skilles that most serve to bring forth that, have a most just title to bee Princes over all the rest: wherein if wee can shewe the Poets noblenes, by setting him before his other Competitors, among whom as principall challengers step forth the morrall Philosophers, whom me thinketh, I see comming towards me with a sullen gravity, as though they could not abide vice by day light, rudely clothed for to witnes outwardly their contempt of outward things, with bookes in their hands agaynst glory, whereto they sette theyr names, sophistically speaking against subtility, and angry with any man in whom they see the foule fault of anger: these men casting larges as they goe, of Definitions, Divisions, and Distinctions, with a scornefull interogative, doe soberly aske, whether it bee possible to finde any path, so ready to leade a man to vertue, as that which teacheth what vertue is? and teacheth it not onely by delivering forth his very being, his causes, and effects: but also, by making known his enemie vice, which must be destroyed, and his combersome servant Passion, which must be maistered, by shewing the generalities that contayneth it, and the specialities that are derived from it. Lastly, by playne setting downe, how it extendeth it selfe out of the limits of a mans own little world, to the government of families, and maintayning of publique societies.

The Historian, scarcely giveth leysure to the Moralist, to say so much, but that he loden with old Mouse-eaten records, authorising himselfe (for the most part) upon other histories, whose greatest authorities, are built upon the notable foundation of Heare-say, having much a-doe to accord differing Writers, and to pick trueth out of partiality, better acquainted with a thousande yeeres a goe, then with the present age: and yet better knowing how this world goeth, then how his owne wit runneth: curious for antiquities, and inquisitive of novelties, a wonder to young folkes, and a tyrant in table talke, denieth in a great chafe, that any man for teaching of vertue, and vertuous actions, is comparable to him. I am *Lux vitæ, Temporum Magistra, Vita memoriæ, Nuncia vetustatis, &c.*[4]

The Phylosopher (sayth hee) teacheth a disputative vertue, but I doe an active: his vertue is excellent in the dangerlesse Academie of *Plato*, but mine sheweth foorth her honorable face, in the battailes of *Marathon, Pharsalia, Poitiers,* and *Agincourt*. Hee teacheth vertue by cer-

[4] Inaccurately quoted from Cicero's *De Orat.* II 9, 36, "Historia vero testis temporum, lux veritatis, vita memoriae, magistra vitae, nuntia vetustatis . . . His- tory truly is the reporter of the times, the light of truth, the life of memory, the instructress to living, the messenger of old age."

taine abstract considerations, but I onely bid you follow the footing of them that have gone before you. Olde-aged experience, goeth beyond the fine-witted Phylosopher, but I give the experience of many ages. Lastly, if he make the Song-booke, I put the learners hande to the Lute: and if hee be the guide, I am the light.

Then woulde hee alledge you innumerable examples, conferring storie by storie, how much the wisest Senatours and Princes, have beene directed by the credite of history, as *Brutus, Alphonsus* of *Aragon,* and who not, if need bee? At length, the long lyne of theyr disputation maketh a poynt in thys, that the one giveth the precept, and the other the example.

Nowe, whom shall wee finde (sith the question standeth for the highest forme in the Schoole of learning) to bee Moderator? Trulie, as me seemeth, the Poet; and if not a Moderator, even the man that ought to carrie the title from them both, and much more from all other serving Sciences. Therefore compare we the Poet with the Historian, and with the Morrall Phylosopher, and, if hee goe beyond them both, no other humaine skill can match him. For as for the Divine, with all reverence it is ever to be excepted, not only for having his scope as far beyonde any of these, as eternitie exceedeth a moment, but even for passing each of these in themselves.

And for the Lawyer, though *Jus* bee the Daughter of Justice, and Justice the chiefe of Vertues, yet because hee seeketh to make men good, rather *Formidine pœnæ,* then *Virtutis amore,*[5] or to say righter, dooth not indevour to make men good, but that their evill hurt not others: having no care so hee be a good Cittizen; how bad a man he be. Therefore, as our wickedness maketh him necessarie, and necessitie maketh him honorable, so is hee not in the deepest trueth to stande in rancke with these; who all indevour to take naughtines away, and plant goodnesse even in the secretest cabinet of our soules. And these foure are all, that any way deale in that consideration of mens manners, which being the supreme knowledge, they that best breed it, deserve the best commendation.

The Philosopher therfore and the Historian, are they which would win the gole: the one by precept, the other by example. But both not having both, doe both halte. For the Philosopher, setting downe with thorny argument the bare rule, is so hard of utterance, and so mistie to bee conceived, that one that hath no other guide but him, shall wade

---

[5] "By fear of penalty," (rather than) "by   *Epist.* 1 16, 52-3.
love of good." The phrases are from Horace,

in him till hee be olde, before he shall finde sufficient cause to bee honest: for his knowledge standeth so upon the abstract and generall, that happie is that man who may understande him, and more happie, that can applye what hee dooth understand.

On the other side, the Historian wanting the precept, is so tyed, not to what shoulde bee, but to what is, to the particuler truth of things, and not to the general reason of things, that hys example draweth no necessary consequence and therefore a lesse fruitfull doctrine.

Nowe dooth the peerelesse Poet performe both: for whatsoever the Philosopher sayth should be doone, hee giveth a perfect picture of it in some one, by whom hee presupposeth it was done. So as hee coupleth the generall notion with the particuler example. A perfect picture I say, for hee yeeldeth to the powers of the minde, an image of that whereof the Philosopher bestoweth but a woordish description: which dooth neyther strike, pierce, nor possesse the sight of the soule, so much as that other dooth.

For as in outward things, to a man that had never seene an Elephant or a Rinoceros, who should tell him most exquisitely all theyr shapes, cullour, bignesse, and perticular markes: or of a gorgeous Pallace, the Architecture, with declaring the full beauties, might well make the hearer able to repeate as it were by rote, all hee had heard, yet should never satisfie his inward conceits, with being witnes to it selfe of a true lively knowledge: but the same man, as soone as hee might see those beasts well painted, or the house wel in moddel, should straightwaies grow without need of any description, to a judicial comprehending of them, so no doubt the Philosopher with his learned definition, bee it of vertue, vices, matters of publick policie, or privat government, replenisheth the memory with many infallible grounds of wisdom: which notwithstanding, lye darke before the imaginative and judging powre, if they bee not illuminated or figured foorth by the speaking picture of Poesie.

Tullie taketh much paynes and many times not without poeticall helpes, to make us knowe the force love of our Countrey hath in us Let us but heare old *Anchises* speaking in the middest of Troyes flames, or see *Ulisses* in the fulnes of all *Calipso's* delights, bewayle his absence from barraine and beggerly *Ithaca*. Anger the *Stoicks* say, was a short maddnes, let but *Sophocles* bring you *Ajax* on a stage, killing and whipping Sheepe and Oxen, thinking them the Army of Greeks, with theyr Chiefetaines *Agamemnon* and *Menelaus*, and tell mee if you have not a more familiar insight into anger, then finding in the Schoolemen

his *Genus* and difference. See whether wisdome and temperance in
Ulisses and *Diomedes,* valure in *Achilles,* friendship in *Nisus* and
Eurialus, even to an ignoraunt man, carry not an apparent shyning:
and contrarily, the remorse of conscience in *Oedipus,* the soone repent-
ing pride of *Agamemnon,* the selfe-devouring crueltie in his Father
Atreus, the violence of ambition in the two *Theban* brothers, the sowre-
sweetnes of revenge in *Medæa,* and to fall lower, the *Terentian Gnato,*
and our *Chaucers* Pandar, so exprest, that we nowe use their names to
signifie their trades. And finally, all vertues, vices, and passions, so in
their own naturall seates layd to the viewe, that wee seeme not to heare
of them, but cleerely to see through them. But even in the most excellent determination of goodnes, what Philosophers counsell can so
redily direct a Prince, as the fayned *Cyrus* in *Xenophon?* or a vertuous
man in all fortunes, as *Aeneas* in *Virgill?* or a whole Common-wealth,
as the way of Sir *Thomas Moores Eutopia?* I say the way, because
where Sir *Thomas Moore* erred, it was the fault of the man and
not of the Poet, for that way of patterning a Common-wealth was most
absolute, though hee perchaunce hath not so absolutely perfourmed it:
for the question is, whether the fayned image of Poesie, or the regular
instruction of Philosophy, hath the more force in teaching: wherein
if the Philosophers h. ˄ more rightly shewed themselves Philosophers,
then the Poets have obtained to the high top of their profession as in
truth.

> ———*Mediocribus esse poetis,*
> `ˋ˙˄n Diji, non homines, non concessere Columnæ:* [6]

It is I say againe, not the fault of the Art, but that by fewe men that
Arte can bee accomplished.

Certainly, even our Saviour Christ could as well have given, the
morrall common places of uncharitablenes and humblenes, as the
divine narration of *Dives* and *Lazarus:* or of disobedience and mercy,
as that heavenly discourse of the lost Child and the gratious Father; but
that hys through-searching wisdom, knewe the estate of *Dives* burning
in hell, and of *Lazarus* being in *Abrahams* bosome, would more constantly (as it were) inhabit both the memory and judgment. Truly, for
my selfe, mee seemes I see before my eyes the lost Childes disdainefull
prodigality, turned to envie a Swines dinner: which by the learned
Divines, are thought not historicall acts, but instructing Parables. **For**

---

[6] "Not men, nor gods, nor booksellers   poets." Horace *Ars Poetica,* 372–3.
grant any value or excuse for mediocre

conclusion, I say the Philosopher teacheth, but he teacheth obscurely, so as the learned onely can understande him: that is to say, he teacheth them that are already taught, but the Poet is the foode for the tenderest stomacks, the Poet is indeed the right Popular Philosopher, whereof *Esops* tales give good proofe: whose pretty Allegories, stealing under the formall tales of Beastes, make many, more beastly then Beasts, begin to heare the sound of vertue from these dumbe speakers.

But now may it be alledged, that if this imagining of matters be so fitte for the imagination, then must the Historian needs surpasse, who bringeth you images of true matters, such as indeede were doone, and not such as fantastically or falsely may be suggested to have been doone. Truely *Aristotle* himselfe in his discourse of Poesie, plainely determineth this question, saying, that Poetry is *Philosophoteron* and *Spoudaioteron,* that is to say, it is more Philosophicall, and more studiously serious, then history. His reason is, because Poesie dealeth with *Katholon,*[7] that is to say, with the universall consideration; and the history with *Kathekaston,* the perticuler; nowe sayth he, the universall wayes what is fit to bee sayd or done, eyther in likelihood or necessity, (which the Poesie considereth in his imposed names,) and the perticuler, onely mark's whether *Alcibiades* did, or suffered, this or that.[8] Thus farre *Aristotle*: which reason of his, (as all his) is most full of reason. For indeed. if the question were whether it were better to have a perticuler acte truly or falsly set down: there is no doubt which is to be chosen, no more then whether you had rather have *Vespasians* picture right as hee was, or at the Painters pleasure nothing resembling. But if the question be for your owne use and learning, whether it be better to have it set downe as it should be, or as it was: then certainely is more doctrinable the fained Cirus of *Xenophon* then the true *Cyrus* in *Justine*: and the fayned *Aeneas* in *Virgil,* then the right *Aeneas* in *Dares Phrigius.*

As to a Lady that desired to fashion her countenance to the best grace, a Painter should more benefite her to portraite a most sweet face, wryting *Canidia* upon it, then to paynt *Canidia* as she was, who *Horace* sweareth, was foule and ill favoured.

If the Poet doe his part a-right, he will shew you in *Tantalus, Atreus,* and such like, nothing that is not to be shunned. In *Cyrus, Aeneas, Ulisses,* each thing to be followed; where the Historian, bound to tell things as things were, cannot be liberall (without hee will be poeticall) of a perfect patterne: but as in *Alexander* or *Scipio* himselfe, shew doo-

---

[7] For *Katholou,* which is in the Sidney.   [8] *Poetics,* Chap. 9.

ings, some to be liked, some to be misliked. And then how will you discerne, what to followe but by your owne discretion, which you had without reading *Quintus Curtius?* And whereas a man may say, though in universall consideration of doctrine the Poet prevaileth; yet that the historie, in his saying such a thing was doone, doth warrant a man more in that hee shall follow.

The aunswere is manifest, that if hee stande upon that was; as if hee should argue, because it rayned yesterday, therefore it shoulde rayne to day, then indeede it hath some advantage to a grose conceite: but if he know an example onlie, informes a conjectured likelihood, and so goe by reason, the Poet dooth so farre exceede him, as hee is to frame his example to that which is most reasonable: be it in warlike, politick, or private matters; where the Historian in his bare *Was,* hath many times that which wee call fortune, to over-rule the best wisdome. Manie times, he must tell events, whereof he can yeelde no cause: or if hee doe, it must be poeticall; for that a fayned example, hath as much force to teach, as a true example: (for as for to moove, it is cleere, sith the fayned may bee tuned to the highest key of passion) let us take one example, wherein a Poet and a Historian doe concur.

Herodotus and *Justine* do both testifie, that *Zopirus,* King *Darius* faithful servaunt, seeing his Maister long resisted by the rebellious *Babilonians,* fayned himselfe in extreame disgrace of his King: for verifying of which, he caused his owne nose and eares to be cut off: and so flying to the *Babylonians,* was received: and for his knowne valour, so far credited, that hee did finde meanes to deliver them over to *Darius.* Much like matter doth *Livie* record of *Tarquinius* and his sonne. *Xenophon* excellently faineth such another stratageme, performed by *Abradates* in *Cyrus* behalfe. Now would I fayne know, if occasion bee presented unto you, to serve your Prince by such an honest dissimulation, why you doe not as well learne it of *Xenophons* fiction, as of the others verity: and truely so much the better, as you shall save your nose by the bargaine: for *Abradates* did not counterfet so far. So then the best of the Historian, is subject to the Poet; for whatsoever action, or faction, whatsoever counsell, pollicy, or warre stratagem, the Historian is bound to recite, that may the Poet (if he list) with his imitation make his own: beautifying it both for further teaching, and more delighting, as it pleaseth him: having all, from *Dante* his heaven, to hys hell, under the authoritie of his penne. Which if I be asked what Poets have done so, as I might well name some, yet say I, and say againe, I speak of the Arte, and not of the Artificer.

Nowe, to that which commonly is attributed to the prayse of histories, in respect of the notable learning is gotten by marking the successe, as though therein a man should see vertue exalted, and vice punished. Truely that commendation is peculiar to Poetrie, and farre of
from History. For indeede Poetrie ever setteth vertue so out in her best
cullours, making Fortune her wel-wayting hand-mayd, that one must
needs be enamored of her. Well may you see *Ulisses* in a storme, and
in other hard plights; but they are but exercises of patience and mag-
nanimitie, to make them shine the more in the neere-following pros-
peritie. And of the contrarie part, if evill men come to the stage, they
ever goe out (as the Tragedie Writer answered, to one that misliked
the shew of such persons) so manacled, as they little animate folkes to
followe them. But the Historian, beeing captived to the trueth of a
foolish world, is many times a terror from well dooing, and an incour-
agement to unbrideled wickednes.

For, see wee not valiant *Milciades* rot in his fetters? The just *Phocion,*
and the accomplished *Socrates,* put to death like Traytors? The cruell
Severus live prosperously? The excellent *Severus* miserably murthered?
Sylla and *Marius* dying in theyr beddes? *Pompey* and *Cicero* slaine
then, when they would have thought exile a happinesse?

See wee not vertuous *Cato* driven to kyll himselfe? and rebell *Cæsar*
so advaunced, that his name yet after 1600 yeares, lasteth in the highest
honor? And marke but even *Cæsars* own words of the fore-named
Sylla, (who in that onely did honestly, to put downe his dishonest tyran-
nie,) *Literas nescivit,*[9] as if want of learning caused him to doe well.
Hee meant it not by Poetrie, which not content with earthly plagues,
deviseth new punishments in hel for Tyrants; nor yet by Philosophie,
which teacheth *Occidendos esse,*[10] but no doubt by skill in Historie: for
that indeede can affoord your *Cipselus, Periander, Phalaris, Dionisius,*
and I know not how many more of the same kennell, that speede well
enough in theyr abhominable unjustice or usurpation. I conclude therefore, that hee excelleth Historie, not onely in furnishing the minde with
knowledge, but in setting it forward, to that which deserveth to be
called and accounted good: which setting forward, and mooving to
well dooing, indeed setteth the Lawrell crowne upon the Poet as victorious, not onely of the Historian, but over the Phylosopher: howso-
ever in teaching it may bee questionable.

For suppose it be granted, (that which I suppose with great reason

---

[9] *Literas nescivit:* "he was ignorant of
his very letters." (Suetonius. *Julius Cæsar*
LXXVII.)
[10] "That they ought to be killed."

may be denied,) that the Philosopher in respect of his methodical proceeding, doth teach more perfectly then the Poet: yet do I thinke, that no man is so much *Philophilosophos,* as to compare the Philosopher in mooving, with the Poet.

And that mooving is of a higher degree then teaching, it may by this appeare: that it is wel nigh the cause and the effect of teaching. For who will be taught, if hee bee not mooved with desire to be taught? and what so much good doth that teaching bring forth, (I speak still of morall doctrine) as that it mooveth one to doe that which it dooth teach? for as *Aristotle* sayth, it is not *Gnosis,* but *Praxis* must be the fruit. And howe *Praxis* cannot be, without being mooved to practise, it is no hard matter to consider.

The Philosopher sheweth you the way, hee informeth you of the particularities, as well of the tediousnes of the way, as of the pleasant lodging you shall have when your journey is ended, as of the many byturnings that may divert you from your way. But this is to no man but to him that will read him, and read him with attentive studious painfulnes. Which constant desire, whosoever hath in him, hath already past halfe the hardnes of the way, and therefore is beholding to the Philosopher but for the other halfe. Nay truely, learned men have learnedly thought, that where once reason hath so much overmastred passion, as that the minde hath a free desire to doe well, the inward light each minde hath in it selfe, is as good as a Philosophers booke; seeing in nature we know it is wel, to doe well, and what is well, and what is evill, although not in the words of Arte, which Philosophers bestowe upon us. For out of naturall conceit, the Philosophers drew it, but to be moved to doe that which we know, or to be mooved with desire to knowe, *Hoc opus: Hic labor est.*[11]

Nowe therein of all Sciences, (I speak still of humane, and according to the humane conceits) is our Poet the Monarch. For he dooth not only show the way, but giveth so sweete a prospect into the way, as will intice any man to enter into it. Nay, he dooth as if your journey should lye through a fayre Vineyard, at the first give you a cluster of Grapes: that full of that taste, you may long to passe further. He beginneth not with obscure definitions, which must blur the margent with interpretations, and load the memory with doubtfulnesse: but hee commeth to you with words sent in delightfull proportion, either accompanied with, or prepared for the well inchaunting skill of Musicke; and with a tale forsooth he commeth unto you: with a tale which holdeth children

[11] "In this the task and mighty labor lies." *Aeneid* VI 129. Dryden's trans.

from play, and old men from the chimney corner. And pretending no more, doth intende the winning of the mind from wickednesse to vertue: even as the childe is often brought to take most wholsom things, by hiding them in such other as have a pleasant tast: which if one should beginne to tell them, the nature of *Aloes,* or *Rubarb* they shoulde receive, woulde sooner take their Phisicke at their eares, then at their mouth. So is it in men (most of which are childish in the best things, till they bee cradled in their graves,) glad they will be to heare the tales of *Hercules, Achilles, Cyrus,* and *Aeneas:* and hearing them, must needs heare the right description of wisdom, valure, and justice; which, if they had been barely, that is to say, Philosophically set out, they would sweare they bee brought to schoole againe.

That imitation whereof Poetry is, hath the most conveniency to Nature of all other, in somuch, that as *Aristotle* sayth, those things which in themselves are horrible, as cruell battailes, unnaturall Monsters, are made in poeticall imitation delightfull.[12] Truely I have knowen men, that even with reading *Amadis de Gaule,* (which God knoweth wanteth much of a perfect Poesie) have found their harts mooved to the exercise of courtesie, liberalitie, and especially courage.

Who readeth *Aeneas* carrying olde *Anchises* on his back, that wisheth not it were his fortune to perfourme so excellent an acte? Whom doe not the words of *Turnus* moove? (the tale of *Turnus,* having planted his image in the imagination,)

> ——————————*Fugientem hæc terra videbit,*
> *Usque adeone mori miserum est?*——————[18]

Where the Philosophers, as they scorne to delight, so must they bee content little to moove: saving wrangling, whether Vertue bee the chiefe, or the onely good: whether the contemplative, or the active life doe excell: which *Plato* and *Boethius* well knew, and therefore made Mistres Philosophy, very often borrow the masking rayment of Poesie. For even those harde harted evill men, who thinke vertue a schoole name, and knowe no other good, but *indulgere genio,*[14] and therefore despise the austere admonitions of the Philosopher, and feele not the inward

[12] *Poetics,* Chap. 4.
[18] "Shall the earth see Turnus fleeing? Is to die even so wretched?" *Aeneid* xii 645–6.
[14] Persius: *Satires* v 151. An alteration from the imperative, *indulge,* as in many other quotations of Sidney, to fit the structure of the sentence; only that here he has been guilty also of changing the sense of the word. For Persius says, "Give scope to your genius (presumably the highest good) because tomorrow you will be but ashe and shadow and name." Sidney, with the other signification of *genius,* here disparages the petty good, "to indulge one's volition."

reason they stand upon; yet will be content to be delighted: which is all
the good felow Poet seemeth to promise: and so steale to see the forme
of goodnes (which seene they cannot but love) ere themselves be aware,
as if they tooke a medicine of Cherries. Infinite proofes of the strange
effects of this poeticall invention might be alledged, onely two shall
serve, which are so often remembred, as I thinke all men knowe them.

The one of *Menenius Agrippa,* who when the whole people of Rome
had resolutely devided themselves from the Senate, with apparant shew
of utter ruine: though hee were (for that time) an excellent Oratour,
came not among them, upon trust of figurative speeches, or cunning
insinuations: and much lesse, with farre set *Maximes* of Phylosophie,
which (especially if they were *Platonick,*) they must have learned
Geometrie before they could well have conceived: but forsooth he behaves himselfe, like a homely, and familiar Poet. Hee telleth them a tale,
that there was a time, when all the parts of the body made a mutinous
conspiracie against the belly, which they thought devoured the fruits of
each others labour: they concluded they would let so unprofitable a
spender starve. In the end, to be short, (for the tale is notorious, and as
notorious that it was a tale,) with punishing the belly, they plagued
themselves. This applied by him, wrought such effect in the people, as
I never read, that ever words brought forth but then, so suddaine and
so good an alteration: for upon reasonable conditions, a perfect reconcilement ensued. The other is of *Nathan* the Prophet, who when the
holie *David* had so far forsaken God, as to confirme adulterie with
murther: when hee was to doe the tenderest office of a friende, in laying
his owne shame before his eyes, sent by God to call againe so chosen a
servant: how doth he it? but by telling of a man, whose beloved Lambe
was ungratefullie taken from his bosome: the applycation most divinely true, but the discourse itselfe, fayned: which made *David,* (I
speake of the second and instrumentall cause) as in a glasse, to see his
own filthines, as that heavenly Psalme of mercie wel testifieth.

By these therefore examples and reasons, I think it may be manifest,
that the Poet with that same hand of delight, doth draw the mind more
effectually, then any other Arte dooth, and so a conclusion not unfitlie
ensueth: that as vertue is the most excellent resting place for all worldlie
learning to make his end of: so Poetrie, beeing the most familiar to
teach it, and most princelie to move towards it, in the most excellent
work, is the most excellent workman. But I am content, not onely to
decipher him by his workes, (although works in commendation or disprayse, must ever holde an high authority,) but more narrowly will ex-

amine his parts: so that (as in a man) though altogether may carry a presence ful of majestie and beautie, perchance in some one defectious peece, we may find a blemish: now in his parts, kindes, or *Species,* (as you list to terme them) it is to be noted that some Poesies have coupled together two or three kindes, as Tragicall and Comicall, wher-upon is risen, the Tragi-comicall. Some in the like manner have mingled Prose and Verse, as *Sanazzar* and *Boetius.* Some have mingled matters Heroicall and Pastorall. But that commeth all to one in this question, for if severed they be good, the conjunction cannot be hurtfull. Therefore perchaunce forgetting some, and leaving some as needlesse to be remembred, it shall not be amisse in a worde to cite the speciall kindes, to see what faults may be found in the right use of them.

Is it then the Pastorall Poem which is misliked? (for perchance, where the hedge is lowest, they will soonest leape over.) Is the poore pype disdained, which sometime out of *Melibeus* mouth, can shewe the miserie of people, under hard Lords, or ravening Souldiours? And again, by *Titirus,* what blessednes is derived to them that lye lowest from the goodnesse of them that sit highest? Sometimes, under the prettie tales of Wolves and Sheepe, can include the whole considerations of wrong dooing and patience. Sometimes shew, that contention for trifles, can get but a trifling victorie. Where perchaunce a man may see, that even *Alexander* and *Darius,* when they strave who should be Cocke of this worlds dunghill, the benefit they got, was, that the after-livers may say,

> *Hæc memini et victum frustra contendere Thirsin:*
> *Ex illo Coridon, Coridon est tempore nobis.*[15]

Or is it the lamenting Elegiack, which in a kinde hart would moove rather pitty then blame, who bewailes with the great Philosopher *Heraclitus,* the weakenes of man-kind, and the wretchednes of the world: who surely is to be praysed, either for compassionate accompanying just causes of lamentation, or for rightly paynting out how weake be the passions of wofulnesse. Is it the bitter, but wholsome Iambick, which rubs the galled minde, in making shame the trumpet of villanie, with bolde and open crying out against naughtines; Or the Satirick, who

> *Omne vafer vitium, ridenti tangit amico?* [16]

[15] These lines, as also the names above of Melibeus and Titirus, are from Virgil's *Eclogues.* Lines are from VII 69–70. "All this I remember, and that Thirsis competed, but competed in vain; and Coridon, from that time, has to us been—Coridon!"

[16] Horace, so described by Persius (*Sat.* I 116–17): "He in his craftiness touches every fault of his laughing friend."

Who sportingly never leaveth, until hee make a man laugh at folly, and
at length ashamed, to laugh at himselfe: which he cannot avoyd, without avoyding the follie. Who while

Circum præcordia ludit,[17]

giveth us to feele, how many head-aches a passionate life bringeth us
to. How when all is done,

Est ulubris animus si nos non deficit æquus? [18]

No perchance it is the Comick, whom naughtie Play-makers and Stage-
keepers, have justly made odious. To the argument of abuse, I will
answer after. Onely thus much now is to be said, that the Comedy is
an imitation of the common errors of our life, which he representeth, in
the most ridiculous and scornefull sort that may be. So as it is impossible, that any beholder can be content to be such a one.

Now, as in Geometry, the oblique must be knowne as wel as the
right: and in Arithmetick, the odde aswell as the even, so in the actions
of our life, who seeth not the filthines of evil, wanteth a great foile to
perceive the beauty of vertue. This doth the Comedy handle so in our
private and domestical matters, as with hearing it, we get as it were
an experience, what is to be looked for of a nigardly *Demea:* of a crafty
Danus: of a flattering *Gnato:* of a vaine glorious *Thraso:* and not onely
to know what effects are to be expected, but to know who be such, by
the signifying badge given them by the Comedian. And little reason
hath any man to say, that men learne evill by seeing it so set out: sith as
I sayd before, there is no man living, but by the force trueth hath in nature, no sooner seeth these men play their parts, but wisheth them in
Pistrinum: [19] although perchance the sack of his owne faults, lye so behinde his back, that he seeth not himselfe daunce the same measure:
whereto, yet nothing can more open his eyes, then to finde his own
actions contemptibly set forth. So that the right use of Comedy will (I
thinke) by no body be blamed, and much lesse of the high and excellent Tragedy, that openeth the greatest wounds, and sheweth forth
the Vlcers, that are covered with Tissue: that maketh Kinges feare to
be Tyrants, and Tyrants manifest their tirannicall humors: that with

---

[17] "He plays about the very fibres of the
heart." (Line following that of note 16).
[18] Horace, *Epist.* i 11, 30. (*nos* substituted for *te*) "(What we seek) is even at

Ulubrae, if we not lack a tranquil mind."
[19] *Pistrinum,* Lat., a pounding mill; by
later connotation, a drudgery.

stuiring the affects of admiration and commiseration, teacheth, the uncertainety of this world, and upon how weake foundations guilden roofes are builded. That maketh us knowe,

Qui sceptra sævus, duro imperio regit,
Timet timentes, metus in authorem redit.[20]

But how much it can moove, *Plutarch* yeeldeth a notable testimonie, of the abhominable Tyrant, *Alexander Pheræus;* from whose eyes, a Tragedy wel made, and represented, drewe aboundance of teares: who without all pitty, had murthered infinite nombers, and some of his owne blood. So as he, that was not ashamed to make matters for Tragedies, yet coulde not resist the sweet violence of a Tragedie.

And if it wrought no further good in him, it was, that he in despight of himselfe, withdrewe himselfe from harkening to that, which might mollifie his hardened heart. But it is not the Tragedy they doe mislike: For it were too absurd to cast out so excellent a representation of whatsoever is most worthy to be learned. Is it the Liricke that most displeaseth, who with his tuned Lyre, and wel accorded voyce, giveth praise, the reward of vertue, to vertuous acts? who gives morall precepts, and naturall Problemes, who sometimes rayseth up his voice to the height of the heavens, in singing the laudes of the immortall God. Certainly I must confesse my own barbarousnes, I never heard the olde song of *Percy* and *Duglas,* that I found not my heart mooved more then with a Trumpet: and yet is it sung but by some blinde Crouder, with no rougher voyce, then rude stile: which being so evill apparrelled in the dust and cobwebbes of that uncivill age, what would it worke trymmed in the gorgeous eloquence of *Pindar?* In *Hungary* I have seene it the manner at all Feasts, and other such meetings, to have songes of their Auncestours valour; which that right Souldier-like Nation thinck the chiefest kindlers of brave courage. The incomparable *Lacedemonians,* did not only carry that kinde of Musicke ever with them to the field, but even at home, as such songs were made, so were they all content to bee the singers of them, when the lusty men were to tell what they dyd, the olde men, what they had done, and the young men what they wold doe. And where a man may say, that *Pindar* many times prayseth highly victories of small moment, matters rather of sport then vertue: as it may be aunswered, it was the fault of the Poet, and

[20] Seneca, *Oedipus,* 705. "Who wields a sceptre with harsh might, and too severely, fears those who fear; dread turns back upon its author."

not of the Poetry; so indeede, the chiefe fault was in the tyme and custome of the Greekes, who set those toyes at so high a price, that *Phillip*
of *Macedon* reckoned a horse-race wonne at *Olimpus,* among hys three
fearefull felicities. But as the unimitable *Pindar* often did, so is that
kinde most capable and most fit, to awake the thoughts from the sleep
of idlenes, to imbrace honorable enterprises.

There rests the Heroicall, whose very name (I thinke) should daunt
all back-biters; for by what conceit can a tongue be directed to speak
evill of that, which draweth with it, no lesse Champions then *Achilles,*
Cyrus, Aeneas, Turnus, Tideus, and *Rinaldo?* who doth not onely teach
and move to a truth, but teacheth and mooveth to the most high and
excellent truth. Who maketh magnanimity and justice shine, throughout all misty fearefulnes and foggy desires. Who, if the saying of *Plato*
and *Tullie* bee true, that who could see Vertue, would be wonderfully
ravished with the love of her beauty: this man sets her out to make her
more lovely in her holyday apparell, to the eye of any that will daine,
not to disdaine, untill they understand. But if anything be already sayd
in the defence of sweete Poetry, all concurreth to the maintaining the
Heroicall, which is not onely a kinde, but the best, and most accomplished kinde of Poetry. For as the image of each action styrreth and
instructeth the mind, so the loftie image of such Worthies, most in-
flameth the mind with desire to be worthy, and informes with counsel
how to be worthy. Only let *Aeneas* be worne in the tablet of your
memory, how he governeth himselfe in the ruine of his Country, in the
preserving his old Father, and carrying away his religious ceremonies:
in obeying the Gods commandement to leave *Dido,* though not onely
all passionate kindenes, but even the humane consideration of vertuous
gratefulnes, would have craved other of him. How in storms, howe in
sports, howe in warre, howe in peace, how a fugitive, how victorious,
how besiedged, how besiedging, howe to strangers, howe to allyes, how
to enemies, howe to his owne: lastly, how in his inward selfe, and how
in his outward government. And I thinke, in a minde not prejudiced
with a prejudicating humor, hee will be found in excellencie fruitefull:
yea, even as *Horace* sayth

Melius Chrisippo et Crantore.[21]

[21] *Epist* 1 2, 4. "Better than Chrisippus
and Crantor (the rhetoricians)." Horace's
full context here, since it would have been
present in Sidney's mind, may pertinently
be quoted:

Troiani belli scriptorem, maxime Lolli,

Dum tu declamas Romae Praeneste relegi;
Qui quid sit pulchrum, quid turpe, quid
  utile, quid non,
Planius ac melius Chrysippo et Crantore
  dicit.

While you, great Lollius, have been de-

But truely I imagine, it falleth out with these Poet-whyppers, as with some good women, who often are sicke, but in fayth they cannot tel where. So the name of Poetrie is odious to them, but neither his cause, nor effects, neither the sum that containes him, nor the particularities descending from him, give any fast handle to their carping disprayse.

Sith then Poetrie is of all humane learning the most auncient, and of most fatherly antiquitie, as from whence other learnings have taken theyr beginnings: sith it is so universall, that no learned Nation dooth despise it, nor no barbarous Nation is without it: sith both Roman and Greek gave divine names unto it: the one of prophecying, the other of making. And that indeede, that name of making is fit for him; considering, that where as other Arts retaine themselves within their subject, and receive as it were, their beeing from it: the Poet onely, bringeth his owne stuffe, and dooth not learne a conceite out of a matter, but maketh matter for a conceite: Sith neither his description, nor his ende, contayneth any evill, the thing described cannot be evill: Sith his effects be so good as to teach goodnes and to delight the learners: Sith therein, (namely in morrall doctrine, the chiefe of all knowledges,) hee dooth not onely farre passe the Historian, but for instructing, is well nigh comparable to the Philosopher: and for moving, leaves him behind him: Sith the holy scripture (wherein there is no uncleannes) hath whole parts in it poeticall. And that even our Saviour Christ, vouchsafed to use the flowers of it: Sith all his kindes are not onlie in their united formes, but in their severed dissections fully commendable, I think, (and think I thinke rightly) the Lawrell crowne appointed for tryumphing Captaines, doth worthilie (of al other learnings) honor the Poets tryumph. But because wee have eares aswell as tongues, and that the lightest reasons that may be, will seeme to weigh greatly, if nothing be put in the counter-balance: let us heare, and aswell as wee can ponder, what objections may bee made against this Arte, which may be worthy, eyther of yeelding, or answering.

First truely I note, not onely in these *Mysomousoi* Poet-haters, but in all that kinde of people, who seek a prayse by dispraysing others, that they doe prodigally spend a great many wandering wordes, in quips, and scoffes; carping and taunting at each thing, which by styrring the Spleene, may stay the braine from a through beholding the worthines of the subject.

claiming (in the courts) at Rome, I at Praeneste have reread the poet of the Trojan war, who better than the rhetori-cians Chrisippus and Crantor, tells what is beautiful, what ugly, what useful, what not so.

Those kinde of objections, as they are full of very idle easines, sith there is nothing of so sacred a majestie, but that an itching tongue may rubbe it selfe upon it: so deserve they no other answer, but in steed of laughing at the jest, to laugh at the jester. Wee know a playing wit, can prayse the discretion of an Asse; the comfortablenes of being in debt, and the jolly commoditie of beeing sick of the plague. So of the contrary side, if we will turne *Ovids* verse,

Ut lateat virtus, proximitate mali,[22]

that good lye hid in neerenesse of the evill: *Agrippa* will be as merry in showing the vanitie of Science, as *Erasmus* was in commending of follie. Neyther shall any man or matter escape some touch of these smyling raylers. But for *Erasmus* and *Agrippa,* they had another foundation then the superficiall part would promise. Mary, these other pleasant Fault-finders, who wil correct the Verbe, before they understande the Noune, and confute others knowledge before they confirme theyr owne: I would have them onely remember, that scoffing commeth not of wisedom. So as the best title in true English they gette with their merriments, is to be called good fooles: for so have our grave Forefathers ever termed that humorous kinde of jesters: but that which gyveth greatest scope to their scorning humors, is ryming and versing. It is already sayde (and as I think, trulie sayde) it is not ryming and versing, that maketh Poesie. One may bee a Poet without versing, and a versifier without Poetry. But yet, presuppose it were inseparable (as indeede it seemeth *Scaliger* judgeth) truelie it were an inseparable commendation. For if *Oratio,* next to *Ratio,* Speech next to Reason, bee the greatest gyft bestowed upon mortalitie: that can not be praiselesse, which dooth most pollish that blessing of speech, which considers each word, not only (as a man may say) by his forcible qualitie, but by his best measured quantitie, carrying even in themselves, a Harmonie: (without (perchaunce) Number, Measure, Order, Proportion, be in our time growne odious.) But lay a side the just prayse it hath, by beeing the onely fit speech for Musick, (Musick I say, the most divine striker of the sences:) thus much is undoubtedly true, that if reading bee foolish, without remembring, memorie being the onely treasurer of knowled[g]e, those words which are fittest for memory, are likewise most convenient for knowledge.

[22] This verse, which Sidney translates in the clause following it, is an adaptation of *Et lateat vitium, proximitate boni. Artis Amatoriae* II 662.

Now, that Verse farre exceedeth Prose in the knitting up of the memory, the reason is manifest. The words, (besides theyr delight which hath a great affinitie to memory,) beeing so set, as one word cannot be lost, but the whole worke failes: which accuseth it selfe, calleth the remembrance backe to it selfe, and so most strongly confirmeth it; besides, one word so as it were begetting another, as be it in ryme or measured verse, by the former a man shall have a neere gesse to the follower: lastly, even they that have taught the Art of memory, have shewed nothing so apt for it, as a certaine roome devided into many places well and throughly knowne. Now, that hath the verse in effect perfectly; every word having his naturall seate, which seate, must needes make the words remembred. But what needeth more in a thing so knowne to all men? who is it that ever was a scholler, that doth not carry away some verses of *Virgill, Horace,* or *Cato,* which in his youth he learned, and even to his old age serve him for howrely lessons? but the fitnes it hath for memory, is notably proved by all delivery of Arts: wherein for the most part, from Grammar, to Logick, Mathematick, Phisick, and the rest, the rules chiefely necessary to bee borne away, are compiled in verses. So that, verse being in it selfe sweete and orderly, and beeing best for memory, the onely handle of knowledge, it must be in jest that any man can speake against it. Nowe then goe wee to the most important imputations laid to the poore Poets, for ought I can yet learne, they are these, first, that there beeing many other more fruitefull knowledges, a man might better spend his tyme in them, then in this. Secondly, that it is the mother of lyes. Thirdly, that it is the Nurse of abuse, infecting us with many pestilent desires: with a Syrens sweetnes, drawing the mind to the Serpents tayle of sinfull fancy. And heerein especially, Comedies give the largest field to erre, as *Chaucer* sayth: howe both in other Nations and in ours, before Poets did soften us, we were full of courage, given to martiall exercises; the pillers of manlyke liberty, and not lulled a sleepe in shady idlenes with Poets pastimes. And lastly, and chiefely, they cry out with an open mouth, as if they out shot *Robin Hood,* that *Plato* banished them out of hys Common-wealth. Truely, this is much, if there be much truth in it. First to the first: that a man might better spend his time, is a reason indeede: but it doth (as they say) but *Petere principium:* [23] for if it be as I affirme, that no learning is so good, as that which teacheth and mooveth to vertue; and that none can both teach and move thereto so much as Poetry: then is the conclusion manifest, that Incke and Paper cannot

---

[23] "Revert to the beginning," a logician's phrase.

be to a more profitable purpose employed. And certainly, though a man should graunt their first assumption, it should followe (me thinkes) very unwillingly, that good is not good, because better is better. But I still and utterly denye, that there is sprong out of earth a more fruitefull knowledge. To the second therefore, that they should be the principall lyars; I aunswere paradoxically, but truely, I thinke truely; that of all Writers under the sunne, the Poet is the least lier; and though he would, as a Poet can scarcely be a lyer, the Astronomer, with his cosen the Geometrician, can hardly escape, when they take upon them to measure the height of the starres.

How often, thinke you, doe the Phisitians lye, when they aver things, good for sicknesses, which afterwards send *Charon* a great number of soules drown[e]d in a potion before they come to his Ferry. And no lesse of the rest, which take upon them to affirme. Now, for the Poet, he nothing affirmes, and therefore never lyeth. For, as I take it, to lye, is to affirme that to be true which is false. So as the other Artists, and especially the Historian, affirming many things, can in the cloudy knowledge of mankinde, hardly escape from many lyes. But the Poet (as I sayd before) never affirmeth. The Poet never maketh any circles about your imagination, to conjure you to beleeve for true what he writes. Hee citeth not authorities of other Histories, but even for hys entry, calleth the sweete Muses to inspire into him a good invention: in troth, not labouring to tell you what is, or is not, but what should or should not be: and therefore, though he recount things not true, yet because hee telleth them not for true, he lyeth not, without we will say, that *Nathan,* lyed in his speech, before alledged to *David.* Which as a wicked man durst scarce say, so think I none so simple would say, that *Esope* lyed in the tales of his beasts: for who thinks that *Esope* writ it for actually true, were well worthy to have his name c[h]ronicled among the beastes hee writeth of.

What childe is there, that comming to a Play, and seeing *Thebes* written in great Letters upon an olde doore, doth beleeve that it is *Thebes?* If then, a man can arive, at that childs age, to know that the poets persons and dooings, are but pictures what should be, and not stories what have beene, they will never give the lye, to things not affirmatively, but allegorically, and figurativelie written. And therefore, as in Historie, looking for trueth, they goe away full fraught with falsehood: so in Poesie, looking for fiction, they shal use the narration. but as an imaginative groundplot of a profitable invention.

But heereto is replyed, that the Poets gyve names to men they write of, which argueth a conceite of an actuall truth, and so, not being true, prooves a falsehood. And doth the Lawyer lye then, when under the names of *John a stile* and *John a noakes*,[24] hee puts his case? But that is easily answered. Theyr naming of men, is but to make theyr picture the more lively, and not to builde any historie: paynting men, they cannot leave men namelesse. We see we cannot play at Chesse, but that wee must give names to our Chesse-men; and yet mee thinks, hee were a very partiall Champion of truth, that would say we lyed, for giving a peece of wood, the reverend title of a Bishop. The Poet nameth *Cyrus* or *Aeneas,* no other way, then to shewe, what men of theyr fames, fortunes, and estates, should doe.

Their third is, how much it abuseth mens wit, trayning it to wanton sinfulnes, and lustfull love: for indeed that is the principall, if not the onely abuse I can heare alledged. They say, the Comedies rather teach, then reprehend, amorous conceits. They say, the Lirick, is larded with passionate Sonnets. The Elegiack, weepes the want of his mistresse. And that even to the Heroicall, *Cupid* hath ambitiously climed. Alas Love, I would, thou couldest as well defende thy selfe, as thou canst offende others. I would those, on whom thou doost attend, could eyther put thee away, or yeelde good reason, why they keepe thee. But grant love of beautie, to be a beastlie fault, (although it be very hard, sith onely man, and no beast, hath that gyft, to discerne beauty.) Grant, that lovely name of Love, to deserve all hatefull reproches: (although even some of my Maisters the Phylosophers, spent a good deale of theyr Lamp-oyle, in setting foorth the excellencie of it.) Grant, I say, what soever they wil have granted; that not onely love, but lust, but vanitie, but, (if they list) scurrilitie, possesseth many leaves of the Poets bookes: yet thinke I, when this is granted, they will finde, theyr sentence may with good manners, put the last words foremost: and not say, that Poetrie abuseth mans wit, but that, mans wit abuseth Poetrie.

For I will not denie, but that mans wit may make Poesie, (which should be *Eikastike,* which some learned have defined, figuring foorth good things,) to be *Phantastike:* which doth contrariwise, infect the fancie with unworthy objects. As the Painter, that shoulde give to the eye, eyther some excellent perspective, or some fine picture, fit for building or fortification: or contayning in it some notable example, as *Abraham,* sacrificing his Sonne *Isaack, Judith* killing *Holofernes, David*

---

[24] Early "example" names: John who lives near the stile, and John who lives near the oaks.

fighting with *Goliah,* may leave those, and please an ill-pleased eye, with wanton shewes of better hidden matters. But what, shall the abuse of a thing, make the right use odious? Nay truely, though I yeeld, that Poesie may not onely be abused, but that beeing abused, by the reason of his sweete charming force, it can doe more hurt than any other Armie of words: yet shall it be so far from concluding, that the abuse, should give reproch to the abused, that contrariwise it is a good reason, that whatsoever being abused, dooth most harme, beeing rightly used: (and upon the right use each thing conceiveth his title) doth most good.

Doe wee not see the skill of Phisick, (the best rampire to our often-assaulted bodies) beeing abused, teach poyson the most violent de-stroyer? Dooth not knowledge of Law, whose end is, to even and right all things being abused, grow the crooked fosterer of horrible injuries? Doth not (to goe to the highest) Gods word abused, breed heresie? and his Name abused, become blasphemie? Truely, a needle cannot doe much hurt, and as truely, (with leave of Ladies be it spoken) it cannot doe much good. With a sword, thou maist kill thy Father, and with a sword thou maist defende thy Prince and Country. So that, as in their calling Poets the Fathers of lyes, they say nothing: so in this theyr argument of abuse, they proove the commendation.

They alledge heere-with, that before Poets beganne to be in price, our Nation, hath set their harts delight upon action, and not upon imagina-tion: rather doing things worthy to bee written, then writing things fitte to be done. What that before tyme was, I thinke scarcely *Sphinx* can tell: Sith no memory is so auncient, that hath the precedence of Poetrie. And certaine it is, that in our plainest homelines, yet never was the *Albion* Nation without Poetrie. Mary, thys argument, though it bee leaveld against Poetrie, yet is it indeed, a chaine-shot against all learning, or bookishnes, as they commonly tearme it. Of such minde were certaine *Goethes,* of whom it is written, that having in the spoile of a famous Citie, taken a fayre librarie: one hangman (bee like fitte to execute the fruites of their wits) who had murthered a great number of bodies, would have set fire on it: no sayde another, very gravely, take heede what you doe, for whyle they are busie about these toyes, wee shall with more leysure conquer their Countries.

This indeede is the ordinary doctrine of ignorance, and many wordes sometymes I have heard spent in it: but because this reason is generally against all learning, aswell as Poetrie; or rather, all learning but Poetry: because it were too large a digression, to handle, or at least, to superfluous: (sith it is manifest, that all government of action, is to be gotten by knowledg, and knowledge best, by gathering many knowledges, which is, reading,) I onely with *Horace,* to him that is of that opinion,

Iubeo stultum esse libenter; [25]

for as for Poetrie it selfe, it is the freest from thys objection. For Poetrie is the companion of the Campes.

I dare undertake, *Orlando Furioso,* or honest King *Arthur,* will never displease a Souldier: but the quiddity of *Ens,* and *Prima materia,* will hardly agree with a Corslet: and therefore, as I said in the beginning, even Turks and Tartares are delighted with Poets. *Homer* a Greek, florished, before Greece florished. And if to a slight conjecture, a conjecture may be opposed: truly it may seeme, that as by him, their learned men, tooke almost their first light of knowledge, so their active men, received their first notions of courage. Onlie *Alexanders* example may serve, who by *Plutarch* is accounted of such vertue, that Fortune was not his guide, but his foote-stoole: whose acts speake for him, though *Plutarch* did not: indeede, the Phœnix of warlike Princes. This *Alexander,* left his Schoole-maister, living *Aristotle* behinde him, but tooke deade *Homer* with him: he put the Philosopher *Calisthenes* to death, for his seeming philosophicall, indeed mutinous stubburnnes. But the chiefe thing he ever was heard to wish for, was, that *Homer* had been alive. He well found he received more braverie of minde, bye the patterne of *Achilles,* then by hearing the definition of Fortitude: and therefore, if *Cato* misliked *Fulvius,* for carying *Ennius* with him to the fielde, it may be aunswered, that if *Cato* misliked it, the noble *Fulvius* liked it, or els he had not doone it: for it was not the excellent *Cato Uticensis,* (whose authority I would much more have reverenced,) but it was the former: in truth, a bitter punisher of faults, but else, a man that had never wel sacrificed to the Graces. Hee misliked and cryed out upon all Greeke learning, and yet being 80. yeeres olde, began to learne it. Be-like, fearing that *Pluto* understood not Latine. Indeede, the Romaine lawes allowed, no person to be carried to the warres, but hee that was in the Souldiers role: and therefore, though *Cato* misliked his unmustered person, hee misliked not his worke. And if hee had, *Scipio Nasica* judged by common consent, the best Romaine, loved him. Both the other *Scipio* Brothers, who had by their vertues no lesse surnames, then of *Asia,* and *Affrick,* so loved him, that they caused his body to be

[25] "Cheerfully order him to be stupid." (*stultum* for *miserum*) *Satires* I i, 63.

buried in their Sepulcher. So as *Cato,* his authoritie being but against his person, and that aunswered, with so farre greater then himselfe, is heerein of no validitie. But now indeede my burthen is great; now *Plato* his name is layde upon mee, whom I must confesse, of all Philosophers, I have ever esteemed most worthy of reverence, and with great reason: Sith of all Philosophers, he is the most poeticall. Yet if he will defile the Fountaine, out of which his flowing streames have proceeded, let us boldly examine with what reasons hee did it. First truly, a man might maliciously object, that *Plato* being a Philosopher was a naturall enemie of Poets: for indeede, after the Philosophers, had picked out of the sweete misteries of Poetrie, the right discerning true points of knowledge, they forthwith putting it in method, and making a Schoole-arte of that which the Poets did onely teach, by a divine delightfulnes, beginning to spurne at their guides, like ungratefull Prentises, were not content to set up shops for themselves, but sought by all meanes to discredit their Maisters. Which by the force of delight being barred them, the lesse they could overthrow them, the more they hated them. For indeede, they found for *Homer,* seven Cities strove, who should have him for their Citizen: where many Citties banished Philosophers, as not fitte members to live among them. For onely repeating certaine of *Euripides* verses, many *Athenians* had their lyves saved of the *Siracusians:* when the *Athenians* themselves, thought many Philosophers, unwoorthie to live.

Certaine Poets, as *Simonides,* and *Pindarus* had so prevailed with *Hiero* the first, that of a Tirant they made him a just King, where *Plato* could do so little with *Dionisius,* that he himselfe, of a Philosopher, was made a slave. But who should doe thus, I confesse, should requite the objections made against Poets, with like cavillation against Philosophers, as likewise one should doe, that should bid one read *Phædrus,* or *Symposium* in *Plato,* or the discourse of love in *Plutarch,* and see whether any Poet doe authorize abhominable filthines, as they doe. Againe, a man might aske out of what Commonwealth *Plato* did banish them? insooth, thence where he himselfe alloweth communitie of women: So as belike, this banishment grewe not for effeminate wantonnes, sith little should poeticall Sonnets be hurtfull, when a man might have what woman he listed. But I honor philosophicall instructions, and blesse the wits which bred them: so as they be not abused, which is likewise stretched to Poetrie.

S. *Paule* himselfe, (who yet for the credite of Poets) alledgeth twise two Poets, and one of them by the name of a Prophet, setteth a watchword upon Philosophy, indeede upon the abuse. So dooth *Plato,* upon the abuse, not upon Poetrie. *Plato* found fault, that the Poets of his time, filled the worlde, with wrong opinions of the Gods, making light tales of that unspotted essence; and therefore, would not have the youth depraved with such opinions. Heerin may much be said, let this suffice: the Poets did not induce such opinions, but dyd imitate those opinions already induced. For all the Greek stories can well testifie, that the very religion of that time, stoode upon many, and many-fashioned Gods, not taught so by the Poets, but followed, according to their nature of imitation. Who list, may reade in *Plutarch,* the discourses of *Isis* and *Osiris,* of the cause why Oracles ceased, of the divine providence; and see, whether the Theologie of that nation, stood not upon such dreames, which the Poets indeed supersticiously observed, and truly, (sith they had not the light of Christ,) did much better in it then the Philosophers, who shaking off superstition, brought in Atheisme. *Plato* therefore, (whose authoritie I had much rather justly conster, then unjustly resist,) meant not in general of Poets, in those words of which *Julius Scaliger* saith *Qua authoritate, barbari quidam, atque hispidi, abuti velint, ad Poetas è republica exigendos;* [26] but only meant, to drive out those wrong opinions of the Deitie (whereof now, without further law, Christianity hath taken away all the hurtful beliefe,) perchance (as he thought) norished by the then esteemed Poets. And a man need goe no further then to *Plato* himselfe, to know his meaning: who in his Dialogue called *Ion,* giveth high, and rightly divine commendation to Poetrie.[27] So as *Plato,* banishing the abuse, not the thing, not banishing it, but giving due honor unto it, shall be our Patron, and not our adversarie. For indeed I had much rather, (sith truly I may doe it) shew theyr mistaking of *Plato,* (under whose Lyons skin they would make an Asselike braying against Poesie,) then goe about to overthrow his authority, whom the wiser a man is, the more just cause he shall find to have in admiration: especially, sith he attributeth unto Poesie, more then my selfe doe; namely, to be a very inspiring of a divine force, farre above mans wit; as in the aforenamed Dialogue is apparent.

Of the other side, who wold shew the honors, have been by the best sort of judgements granted them, a whole Sea of examples woulde

---

[26] "And this authority certain barbarians and crude peoples have wished wrongly to use to banish poets from the state." *Poetics* I 2.

[27] The passage is given earlier.

present themselves. *Alexanders, Cæsars, Scipios,* al favorers of Poets. *Lelius,* called the Romane *Socrates,* himselfe a Poet: so as part of *Heautontimorumenon* in *Terence,* was supposed to be made by him. And even the Greek *Socrates,* whom *Apollo* confirmed to be the onely wise man, is sayde to have spent part of his old tyme, in putting *Esops* fables into verses. And therefore, full evill should it become his scholler *Plato,* to put such words in his Maisters mouth, against Poets. But what need more? *Aristotle* writes the Arte of Poesie: and why if it should not be written? *Plutarch* teacheth the use to be gathered of them, and how if they should not be read? And who reades *Plutarchs* eyther historie or philosophy, shall finde, hee trymmeth both theyr garments, with gards of Poesie. But I list not to defend Poesie, with the helpe of her underling, Historiography. Let it suffise, that it is a fit soyle for prayse to dwell upon: and what dispraise may set upon it, is eyther easily overcome, or transformed into just commendation. So that, sith the excellencies of it, may be so easily, and so justly confirmed, and the low-creeping objections, so soone troden downe; it not being an Art of lyes, but of true doctrine: not of effeminatenes, but of notable stirring of courage: not of abusing mans witte, but of strengthning mans wit: not banished, but honored by *Plato:* let us rather plant more Laurels, for to engarland our Poets heads, (which honor of beeing laureat, as besides them, onely tryumphant Captaines weare, is a sufficient authority, to shewe the price they ought to be had in,) then suffer the ill-favouring breath of such wrong-speakers, once to blowe upon the cleere springs of Poesie.

But sith I have runne so long a careere in this matter, me thinks, before I give my penne a fulle stop, it shal be but a little more lost time, to inquire, why England, (the Mother of excellent mindes,) shoulde bee growne so hard a step-mother to Poets, who certainly in wit ought to passe all other: sith all onely proceedeth from their wit, being indeede makers of themselves, not takers of others. How can I but exclaime,

Musa mihi causas memora, quo numine læso.[28]

Sweete Poesie, that hath aunciently had Kings, Emperors, Senators, great Captaines, such, as besides a thousand others, *David, Adrian, Sophocles, Germanicus,* not onely to favour Poets, but to be Poets. And

[28] "O Muse, recount to me those causes: *Aeneid* I 8.
what   godhead   was   offended?"   Virgil,

of our neerer times, can present for her Patrons, a *Robert,* king of Sicil, the great king *Francis* of France, King *James* of Scotland. Such Cardinals as *Bembus,* and *Bibiena.* Such famous Preachers and Teachers, as *Beza* and *Melancthon.* So learned Philosophers, as *Fracastorius* and *Scaliger.* So great *Orators,* as *Pontanus* and *Muretus.* So piercing wits, as *George Buchanan.* So grave Counsellors, as besides many, but before all, that *Hospitall* of Fraunce: then whom, (I thinke) that Realme never brought forth a more accomplished judgement: more firmely builded upon vertue. I say these, with numbers of others, not onely to read others Poesies, but to poetise for others reading, that Poesie thus embraced in all other places, should onely finde in our time, a hard welcome in England, I thinke the very earth lamenteth it, and therefore decketh our Soyle with fewer Laurels then it was accustomed. For heertofore, Poets have in England also florished. And which is to be noted, even in those times, when the trumpet of *Mars* did sounde loudest. And now, that an overfaint quietnes should seeme to strew the house for Poets, they are almost in as good reputation, as the *Mountibancks* at *Venice.* Truly even that, as of the one side, it giveth great praise to Poesie, which like *Venus,* (but to better purpose) hath rather be troubled in the net with *Mars,* then enjoy the homelie quiet of *Vulcan:* so serves it for a peece of reason, why they are lesse gratefull to idle England, which nowe can scarce endure the payne of a pen. Upon this, necessarily followeth, that base men, with servile wits undertake it: who think it inough, if they can be rewarded of the Printer. And so as *Epaminondas* is sayd, with the honor of his vertue, to have made an office, by his exercising it, which before was contemptible, to become highly respected: so these, no more but setting their names to it, by their owne disgracefulnes, disgrace the most gracefull Poesie. For now, as if all the Muses were gotte with childe, to bring foorth bastard Poets, without any commission, they doe poste over the banckes of *Helicon,* tyll they make the readers more weary then Post-horses: while in the mean tyme, they

Queis meliore luto finxit præcordia Titan,[29]

are better content, to suppresse the out-flowing of their wit, then by publishing them, to bee accounted Knight of the same order. But I, that before ever I durst aspire unto the dignitie, am admitted into the

[29] Juvenal XIV 35 (*Queis* substituted for *et*); "whose soul [s] the Titan has fashioned . . . of a finer clay." [G. G. Ramsay, *Loeb Libr.*]

company of the Paper-blurers, doe finde the very true cause of our
wanting estimation, is want of desert: taking upon us to be Poets, in
despight of *Pallas*. Nowe, wherein we want desert, were a thanke-
worthy labour to expresse: but if I knew, I should have mended my
selfe. But I, as I never desired the title, so have I neglected the meanes
to come by it. Onely over-mastred by some thoughts, I yeelded an inckie
tribute unto them. Mary, they that delight in Poesie it selfe, should
seeke to knowe what they doe, and how they doe; and especially, looke
themselves in an unflattering Glasse of reason, if they bee inclinable
unto it. For Poesie, must not be drawne by the eares, it must bee gently
led, or rather, it must lead. Which was partly the cause, that made the
auncient-learned affirme, it was a divine gift, and no humaine skill:
sith all other knowledges, lie ready for any that hath strength of witte:
A Poet, no industrie can make, if his owne *Genius* bee not carried unto
it: and therefore is it an old Proverbe, *Orator fit; Poeta nascitur*. Yet
confesse I always, that as the firtilest ground must bee manured, so
must the highest flying wit, have a *Dedalus* to guide him. That *Dedalus,*
they say, both in this, and in other, hath three wings, to beare it selfe
up into the ayre of due commendation: that is, Arte, Imitation, and
Exercise. But these, neyther artificiall rules, nor imitative patterns, we
much cumber our selves withall. Exercise indeede wee doe, but that,
very fore-backwardly: for where we should exercise to know, wee
exercise as having knowne: and so is oure braine delivered of much
matter, which never was begotten by knowledge. For, there being two
principal parts, matter to be expressed by wordes, and words to expresse the matter, in neyther, wee use Arte, or Imitation, rightly. Our
matter is *Quodlibit* indeed, though wrongly perfourming *Ovids* verse,

Quicquid conabar dicere versus erit:[30]

never marshalling it into an assured rancke, that almost the readers
cannot tell where to finde themselves.

Chaucer, undoubtedly did excellently in hys *Troylus* and *Cresseid;*
of whom, truly I know not, whether to mervaile more, either that he in
that mistie time, could see so clearely, or that wee in this cleare age,
walke so stumblingly after him. Yet had he great wants, fitte to be forgiven, in so reverent antiquity. I account the *Mirrour of Magistrates,*
meetely furnished of beautiful parts; and in the Earle of Surries *Liricks,*

---

[30] *Tristia* IV x 26. (The future form,
erit, makes translation difficult, which
always before has proceeded upon the
assumption of the imperfect tense, *erat,*
which is in Ovid). "Whatever I tried to
say, was verse," if we assume *erat*

many things tasting of a noble birth, and worthy of a noble minde. The *Sheapheards Kalender,* hath much Poetrie in his Eglogues: indeede worthy the reading if I be not deceived. That same framing of his stile, to an old rustick language, I dare not alowe, sith neyther *Theocritus* in Greeke, *Virgill* in Latine, nor *Sanazar* in Italian, did affect it. Besides these, doe I not remember to have seene but fewe, (to speake boldely) printed, that have poeticall sinnewes in them: for proofe whereof, let but most of the verses bee put in Prose, and then aske the meaning: and it will be found, that one verse did but beget another, without ordering at the first, what should be at the last: which becomes a confused masse of words, with a tingling sound of ryme, barely accompanied with reason.

Our Tragedies, and Comedies, (not without cause cried out against,) observing rules, neyther of honest civilitie, nor of skilfull Poetrie, excepting *Gorboduck,* (againe, I say, of those that I have seen,) which notwithstanding, as it is full of stately speeches, and well sounding Phrases, clyming to the height of *Seneca* his stile, and as full of notable moralitie, which it doth most delightfully teach; and so obtayne the very end of Poesie: yet in troth it is very defectious in the circumstaunces; which greeveth mee, because it might not remaine as an exact model of all Tragedies. For it is faulty both in place, and time, the two necessary companions of all corporall actions. For where the stage should alwaies represent but one place, and the uttermost time presupposed in it, should be, both by *Aristotles* precept, and common reason, but one day: there is both many dayes, and many places, inartificially imagined. But if it be so in *Gorboduck,* how much more in al the rest? where you shal have *Asia* of the one side, and *Affrick* of the other, and so many other under-kingdoms, that the Player, when he commeth in, must ever begin with telling where he is: or els, the tale wil not be conceived. Now ye shal have three Ladies, walke to gather flowers, and then we must beleeve the stage to be a Garden. By and by, we heare newes of shipwracke in the same place, and then wee are to blame, if we accept it not for a Rock.

Upon the backe of that, comes out a hidious Monster, with fire and smoke, and then the miserable beholders, are bounde to take it for a Cave. While in the meantime, two Armies flye in, represented with foure swords and bucklers, and then what harde heart will not receive it for a pitched fielde? Now, of time they are much more liberall, for ordinary it is that two young Princes fall in love. After many traverces, she is got with childe, delivered of a faire boy, he is lost, groweth a man, falls in love, and is ready to get another child, and all this in two hours space: which how absurd it is in sence, even sence may imagine, and Arte hath taught, and all auncient examples justified: and at this day, the ordinary Players in Italie, wil not erre in. Yet wil some bring in an example of *Eunuchus* in *Terence,* that containeth matter of two dayes, yet far short of twenty yeeres. True it is, and so was it to be playd in two daies, and so fitted to the time it set forth. And though *Plautus* hath in one place done amisse, let us hit with him, and not misse with him. But they wil say, how then shal we set forth a story, which containeth both many places, and many times? And doe they not knowe, that a Tragedie is tied to the lawes of Poesie, and not of Historie? not bound to follow the storie, but having liberty, either to faine a quite newe matter, or to frame the history, to the most tragicall conveniencie. Againe, many things may be told, which cannot be shewed, if they knowe the difference betwixt reporting and representing. As for example, I may speake, (though I am heere) of *Peru,* and in speech, digresse from that, to the description of *Calicut:* but in action, I cannot represent it without *Pacolets* horse: and so was the manner the Auncients tooke, by some *Nuncius,* to recount thinges done in former time, or other place. Lastly, if they wil represent an history, they must not (as *Horace* saith) beginne *Ab ovo,*[31] but they must come to the principall poynt of that one action, which they wil represent. By example this wil be best expressed. I have a story of young *Polidorus,* delivered for safeties sake, with great riches, by his Father *Priamus* to *Polimnestor* king of *Thrace,* in the Troyan war time: Hee after some yeeres, hearing the over-throwe of *Priamus,* for to make the treasure his owne, murthereth the child: the body of the child is taken up [by] *Hecuba:* shee the same day, findeth a slight to bee revenged most cruelly of the Tyrant: where nowe would one of our Tragedy writers begin, but with the delivery of the childe? Then should he sayle over into *Thrace,* and so spend I know not how many yeeres, and travaile numbers of places. But where dooth *Euripides?* Even with the finding of the body, leaving the rest to be tolde by the spirit of *Polidorus.* This need no further to be inlarged, the dullest wit may conceive it. But besides these grosse absurdities, how all theyr Playes be neither right Tragedies, nor right Comedies: mingling Kings and Clownes, not because the matter so carrieth it: but thrust in Clownes by head and

---

[31] Horace, *Ars Poetica* 147. Literally, "from the egg"; by acquired connotation and by inference, "from the very origin." Horace has reference specifically to the conception of Castor and Pollox by Leda, who was also the mother of Helen.

shoulders, to play a part in majesticall matters, with neither decencie, nor discretion. So as neither the admiration and commiseration, nor the right sportfulnes, is by their mungrell Tragy-comedie obtained. I know *Apuleius* did some-what so, but that is a thing recounted with space of time, not represented in one moment: and I knowe, the Auntients have one or two examples of Tragy-comedies, as *Plautus* hath *Amphitrio:* But if we marke them well, we shall find, that they never, or very daintily, match Horn-pypes and Funeralls. So falleth it out, that having indeed no right Comedy, in that comicall part of our Tragedy, we have nothing but scurrility, unwoorthy of any chast eares: or some extreame shew of doltishnes, indeed fit to lift up a loude laughter, and nothing els: where the whole tract of a Comedy, shoulde be full of delight, as the Tragedy shoulde be still maintained, in a well raised admiration. But our Comedians, thinke there is no delight without laughter, which is very wrong, for though laughter may come with delight, yet commeth it not of delight: as though delight should be the cause of laughter, but well may one thing breed both together: nay, rather in themselves, they have as it were, a kind of contrarietie; for delight we scarcely doe, but in things that have a conveniencie to our selves, or to the general nature: laughter, almost ever commeth, of things most disproportioned to our selves, and nature. Delight hath a joy in it, either permanent, or present. Laughter, hath onely a scornful tickling.

For example, we are ravished with delight to see a faire woman, and yet are far from being moved to laughter. We laugh at deformed creatures, wherein certainely we cannot delight. We delight in good chaunces, we laugh at mischaunces; we delight to heare the happines of our friends, or Country; at which he were worthy to be laughed at, that would laugh; wee shall contrarily laugh sometimes, to finde a matter quite mistaken, and goe downe the hill agaynst the byas, in the mouth of some such men, as for the respect of them, one shal be hartely sorry, yet he cannot chuse but laugh; and so is rather pained, then delighted with laughter. Yet deny I not, but that they may goe well together, for as in *Alexanders* picture well set out, wee delight without laughter, and in twenty mad Anticks we laugh without delight: so in *Hercules,* painted with his great beard, and furious countenance, in womans attire, spinning at *Omphales* commaundement, it breedeth both delight and laughter. For the representing of so strange a power in love, procureth delight: and the scornefulnes of the action, stirreth laughter. But I speake to this purpose, that all the end of the comicall part, bee not upon such scornefull matters, as stirreth laughter onely: but mixt with it, that delightful teaching which is the end of Poesie. And the great fault even in that point of laughter, and forbidden plainely by *Aristotle,* is, that they styrre laughter in sinfull things; which are rather execrable then ridiculous: or in miserable, which are rather to be pittied than scorned. For what is it to make folkes gape at a wretched Begger, or a beggerly Clowne? or against lawe of hospitality, to jest at straungers, because they speake not English so well as wee doe? what do we learne, sith it is certaine

> *(Nil habet infœlix paupertas durius in se,)*
> *Quam quod ridiculos homines facit.——*[82]

But rather a busy loving Courtier, a hartles threatening *Thraso.* A selfe-wise-seeming schoolemaster. A awry-transformed Traveller. These, if we sawe walke in stage names, which wee play naturally, therein were delightfull laughter, and teaching delightfulnes: as in the other, the Tragedies of *Buchanan,* doe justly bring forth a divine admiration. But I have lavished out too many wordes of this play matter. I doe it because as they are excelling parts of Poesie, so is there none so much used in England, and none can be more pittifully abused. Which like an unmannerly Daughter, shewing a bad education, causeth her mother Poesies honesty, to bee called in question. Other sorts of Poetry almost have we none, but that Lyricall kind of Songs and Sonnets: which, Lord, if he gave us so good mindes, how well it might be imployed, and with howe heavenly fruite, both private and publique, in singing the prayses of the immortall beauty: the immortall goodnes of that God, who gyveth us hands to write, and wits to conceive, of which we might well want words, but never matter, of which, we could turne our eies to nothing, but we should ever have new budding occasions. But truely many of such writings, as come under the banner of unresistable love, if I were a Mistres, would never perswade mee they were in love: so coldely they apply fiery speeches, as men that had rather red Lovers writings; and so caught up certaine swelling phrases, which hang together, like a man which once tolde mee, the winde was at North, West, and by South, because he would be sure to name windes enowe: then that in truth they feele those passions, which easily (as I think) may be bewrayed, by that same forciblenes, or *Energia,* (as the

---

[82] Juvenal, *Sat.* III 152–3 "Nothing in   than this: that it makes men ridiculous." unfortunate poverty is harder to be endured

Greekes cal it) of the writer. But let this bee a sufficient, though short note, that wee misse the right use of the materiall point of Poesie.

Now, for the out-side of it, which is words, or (as I may tearme it) *Diction,* it is even well worse. So is that honny-flowing Matron Eloquence, apparelled, or rather disguised, in a Curtizan-like painted affectation: one time with so farre sette words, they may seeme Monsters: but must seeme straungers to any poore English man. Another tyme, with coursing of a Letter, as if they were bound to followe the method of a Dictionary: an other tyme, with figures and flowers, extreamelie winter-starved. But I would this fault were only peculier to Versifiers, and had not as large possession among Prose-printers; and, (which is to be mervailed) among many Schollers, and, (which is to be pittied) among some Preachers. Truly I could wish, if at least I might be so bold, to wish in a thing beyond the reach of my capacity, the diligent imitators of *Tullie,* and *Demosthenes,* (most worthy to be imitated) did not so much keep, *Nizolian* Paper-bookes of their figures and phrases, as by attentive translation (as it were) devoure them whole, and make them wholly theirs: For nowe they cast Sugar and Spice, upon every dish that is served to the table; Like those Indians, not content to weare eare-rings at the fit and naturall place of the eares, but they will thrust Jewels through their nose, and lippes because they will be sure to be fine.

Tullie, when he was to drive out *Cateline,* as it were with a Thunderbolt of eloquence, often used that figure of repitition, *Vivit vivit? imo Senatum venit &c.* Indeed, inflamed with a well-grounded rage, hee would have his words (as it were) double out of his mouth: and so doe that artificially, which we see men doe in choller naturally. And wee, having noted the grace of those words, hale them in sometime to a familier Epistle, when it were to too much choller to be chollerick. Now for similitudes, in certaine printed discourses, I thinke all Herbarists, all stories of Beasts, Foules, and Fishes, are rifled up, that they come in multitudes, to waite upon any of our conceits; which certainly is as absurd a surfet to the eares, as is possible: for the force of a similitude, not being to proove anything to a contrary Disputer, but onely to explane to a willing hearer, when that is done, the rest is a most tedious pratling: rather over-swaying the memory from the purpose whereto they were applyed, then any whit informing the judgement, already eyther satisfied, or by similitudes not to be satis-fied. For my part, I doe not doubt, when *Antonius* and *Crassus,* the great forefathers of *Cicero* in eloquence, the one (as *Cicero* testifieth of them)

pretended not to know Arte, the other, not to set by it: because with a
playne sensiblenes, they might win credit of popular eares; which
credit, is the neerest step to perswasion: which perswasion, is the chiefe
marke of Oratory; I doe not doubt (I say) but that they used these
tracks very sparingly, which who doth generally use, any man may
see doth daunce to his owne musick: and so be noted by the audience,
more careful to speake curiously, then to speake truly.

Undoubtedly, (at least to my opinion undoubtedly,) I have found
in divers smally learned Courtiers, a more sounde stile, then in some
professors of learning: of which I can gesse no other cause, but that
the Courtier following that which by practise hee findeth fittest to nature, therein, (though he know it not,) doth according to Art, though
not by Art: where the other, using Art to shew Art, and not to hide
Art, (as in these cases he should doe) flyeth from nature, and indeede
abuseth Art.

But what? me thinkes I deserve to be pounded, for straying from
Poetrie to Oratorie: but both have such an affinity in this wordish consideration, that I thinke this digression, will make my meaning receive
the fuller understanding: which is not to take upon me to teach Poets
howe they should doe, but onely finding my selfe sick among the rest,
to shewe some one or two spots of the common infection, growne
among the most part of Writers: that acknowledging our selves somewhat awry, we may bend to the right use both of matter and manner;
whereto our language gyveth us great occasion, beeing indeed capable
of any excellent exercising of it. I know, some will say it is a mingled
language. And why not so much the better, taking the best of both
the other? Another will say it wanteth Grammer. Nay truly, it hath
that prayse, that it wanteth not Grammer: for Grammer it might have,
but it needes it not; beeing so easie of it selfe, and so voyd of those
cumbersome differences of Cases, Genders, Moodes, and Tenses, which
I thinke was a peece of the Tower of *Babilons* curse, that a man should
be put to schoole to learne his mother-tongue. But for the uttering
sweetly, and properly the conceits of the minde, which is the end of
speech, that hath it equally with any other tongue in the world: and
is particulerly happy, in compositions of two or three words together,
neere the Greeke, far beyond the Latine: which is one of the greatest
beauties can be in a language.

Now, of versifying there are two sorts, the one Auncient, the other
Moderne: the Auncient marked the quantitie of each silable, and according to that, framed his verse: the Moderne, observing onely num-

ber, (with some regarde of the accent,) the chiefe life of it, standeth in that lyke sounding of the words, which we call Ryme. Whether of these be the most excellent, would beare many speeches. The Auncient, (no doubt) more fit for Musick, both words and tune observing quantity, and more fit lively to expresse divers passions, by the low and lofty sounde of the well-weyed silable. The latter likewise, with hys Ryme, striketh a certaine musick to the eare: and in fine, sith it dooth delight, though by another way, it obtaines the same purpose: there beeing in eyther sweetnes, and wanting in neither majestie. Truely the English, before any other vulgar language I know, is fit for both sorts: for, for the Ancient, the Italian is so full of Vowels, that it must ever be cumbred with *Elisions*. The Dutch, so of the other side with Consonants, that they cannot yeeld the sweet slyding, fit for a Verse. The French, in his whole language, hath not one word, that hath his accent in the last silable, saving two, called *Antepenultima,* and little more hath the Spanish: and therefore, very gracelesly may they use *Dactiles.* The English is subject to none of these defects.

Nowe, for the ryme, though wee doe not observe quantity, yet wee observe the accent very precisely: which other languages, eyther cannot doe, or will not doe so absolutely. That *Cæsura,* or breathing place in the middest of the verse, neither Italian nor Spanish have, the French, and we, never almost fayle of. Lastly, even the very ryme it selfe, the Italian cannot put in the last silable, by the French named the Masculine ryme, but still in the next to the last, which the French call the Female; or the next before that, which the Italians terme *Sdrucciola.* The example of the former, is *Buono, Suono,* of the *Sdrucciola, Femina, Semina.* The French, of the other side, hath both the Male, as *Bon, Son,* and the Female, as *Plaise, Taise.* But the *Sdrucciola,* hee hath not: where the English hath all three, as *Due, True, Father, Rather, Motion, Potion;* with much more which might be sayd, but that I finde already, the triflingnes of this discourse, is much too much enlarged. So that sith the ever-praise-worthy Poesie, is full of vertue-breeding delightfulnes, and voyde of no gyfte, that ought to be in the noble name of learning: sith the blames laid against it, are either false, or feeble: sith the cause why it is not esteemed in Englande, is the fault of Poet-apes, not Poets: sith lastly, our tongue is most fit to honor Poesie, and to bee honored by Poesie, I conjure you all, that have had the evill lucke to reade this incke-wasting toy of mine, even in the name of the nyne Muses, no more to scorne the sacred misteries of Poesie: no more to laugh at the name of Poets, as though they were next inheritours to

Fooles: no more to jest at the reverent title of a Rymer: but to beleeve with *Aristotle,* that they were the auncient Treasurers, of the Græcians Divinity. To beleeve with *Bembus,* that they were first bringers in of all civilitie. To beleeve with *Scaliger,* that no Philosophers precepts can sooner make you an honest man, then the reading of *Virgill.* To beleeve with *Clauserus,* the Translator of *Cornutus,* that it pleased the heavenly Deitie, by *Hesiod* and *Homer,* under the vayle of fables, to give us all knowledge, Logick, Rethorick, Philosophy, naturall, and morall; and *Quid non?* To beleeve with me, that there are many misteries contained in Poetrie, which of purpose were written darkely, least by prophane wits, it should bee abused. To beleeve with *Landin,* that they are so beloved of the Gods, that whatsoever they write, proceeds of a divine fury. Lastly, to beleeve themselves, when they tell you they will make you immortall, by their verses.

Thus doing, your name shal florish in the Printers shoppes; thus doing, you shall bee of kinne to many a poeticall Preface; thus doing, you shall be most fayre, most ritch, most wise, most all, you shall dwell upon Superlatives. Thus dooing, though you be *Libertino patre natus,*[33] you shall suddenly grow *Hercules proles:* [34]

Si quid mea carmina possunt.[35]

Thus doing, your soule shal be placed with *Dantes Beatrix,* or *Virgils Anchises.* But if, (fie of such a but) you be borne so neere the dull making *Cataphract of Nilus,* that you cannot heare the Plannet-like Musick of Poetrie, if you have so earth-creeping a mind, that it cannot lift it selfe up, to looke to the sky of Poetry: or rather, by a certaine rusticall disdaine, will become such a Mome, as to be a *Momus* of Poetry: then, though I will not wish unto you, the Asses eares of *Midas,* nor to bee driven by a Poets verses, (as *Bubonax* was) to hang himselfe, nor to be rimed to death, as is sayd to be doone in Ireland: yet thus much curse I must send you in the behalfe of all Poets, that while you live, you live in love, and never get favour, for lacking skill of a *Sonnet:* and when you die, your memory die from the earth, for want of an *Epitaph.*

[33] "The son of a freedman." Horace, *Satires* 1 6, 6.
[34] "Hercules' progeny."
[35] "If anything my poetry avails." Virgil, *Aeneid* IX, 446.

SAMUEL DANIEL

(1562–1619)

DANIEL was born in 1562 near Taunton. At the age of seventeen he entered Magdalen College, Oxford, but left without taking the degree and travelled in Italy. About 1590 he became tutor to William Herbert, and at Wilton found literary companionship with his pupil's mother, the Countess of Pembroke. The publication, with other papers, of the *Delia* sonnet sequence in 1592, of the *First Four Books of the Civil War* in 1595, and of *Poetical Essays* in 1599, brought him into a prominence which secured his elevation to the laureateship, an honor which he shortly resigned to Ben Jonson.

In 1602 Thomas Campion published his *Observations in the Art of English Poesie,* and Daniel's reply was written and published at some time between 1602 and 1607. His appointment in 1603 as Master of the Queen's Revels brought a seven year period of masque-writing, interrupted by other important publications, *Certain Small Poems* in 1605, the complete *Civil Wars* in 1609. Three years later, with the great prose *History of England,* he virtually closed his literary career, retired to a farm, the famous "Ridge," and died in 1619.

A Defence of Ryme was written in reply to Thomas Campion's *Observations in the Art of English Poesie,* published in 1602. The statement in the foreword "To all the Worthie . . ." that it had been composed as "a private letter . . . about a yeare since" would seem to put the date of its printing at least as late as 1603.

While numerous poets, great and small, have in the last three centuries gone about experiments and have sometimes allowed critical complainings to escape, none has assailed the dominance of our accentual verse. The debate on rhyme (in our present sense), ran on its way, quickening other times and critics.

From Ascham's *Schoolmaster,* through the rules of Thomas Drant, which are lost, to the Areopagus society of Sidney and Spenser, there was evident the high desire to frame English verse in classical metres. Webbe in his *Discourse of English Poesie* (1586) is yet in favor of "the new versifying," and the *Arte of English Poesie* (1589), ascribed to Puttenham, hedges on the matter. The last two decades of the Sixteenth Century established the practice of the verse most readily fitted to English, however, and the final critical flurry, that of Campion in 1602, had too little experimental support to be effective. The examples furnished in the treatise, when not improvisations, are, nevertheless, artless and artificial.

His thesis, however, is not as groping, nor is it as often mistaken, as were those that had preceded. He is not contending to displace the accentual prosody. He admits the inadequacy of the dactyl in English, and makes it his aim to ascertain what forms are indigenous to the language, and, by corresponding them to classical forms, to discover laws regarding them. A similarity to the technical rules on verse forms laid down by Ronsard and Du Bellay is apparent on examination. But Daniel observes that the "adversary" really has nothing new in his observations on verse. He points out that Campion is often merely stating under rule what all good poets assumed under licence.

The most dangerous objection of Campion is that made on the ground of difficulty: "But there is yet another fault in Rime altogether intollerable, which is, that it inforceth a man oftentimes to abiure his matter, and extend a short conceit beyond all bounds of arte." [Second Chapter].

Milton's mighty utterance is to this same effect, but came in a time when the right not to rhyme required fighting for. "The troublesome and modern bandage of riming" he held to be "the invention of a barbarous age, to set off wretched matter and lame metre; graced indeed since by the use of some famous modern poets, carried away by custom, but much to their own vexation, hindrance, and constraint to express many things otherwise, and for the most part worse, than else they would have expressed them." [Preface to *Paradise Lost*].

The young Dryden regrets but accepts, and in his statement there is perhaps a hint, heretofore unnoted, as to the reason for the predominance during the following years of the heroic couplet: it is just possible that the other verse forms died at the exaggerated difficulty of composing intricately in rhyme. "The learned languages," wrote Dryden, "have certainly a great advantage of us in not being tied to the slavery of any rhyme, and were less constrained in the quantity of every syllable, which they might vary with spondees and dactyls, besides so many other helps of grammatical figures for the lengthening or abbreviation of them, than the modern are in the close of that one syllable, which often confines, and more often corrupts, the sense of all the rest. But in this necessity of our rhymes, I have always found the couplet verse most easy . . . for there the work is sooner at an end, every two lines concluding the labour of the poet." [Preface to *Annus Mirabilis*]. Upon the restraint and guidance of rhyme has rested its chief praise in later times. Daniel, however, does not push his claim further than the barest refutation of Campion. There is furnished in the *Supplement* sufficient of Campion's treatise for comparison with Daniel's arguments against it.

In a manner which is not obvious to us until we look back at the *Defence* in the light of neo-classicism, Daniel prepares the way for bondage to the couplet. It can be seen how the Eighteenth Century must have read many of his sentences into their own doctrine, sentences which to us seem untainted by such subservience to a particular element of form. Recalling echoes, notably Gascoigne's injunction regarding "Poulter's measure" ("finish the sentence and meaning at the end of every staff"),

Daniel phrases an argument that is within twenty-five years to find such an expression as that of Sir John Beaumont:

> The relish of the muse consists in rhyme:
> One verse must meet another like a chime.
> ["Concerning the True Form of
> English Poetry"].

Far from such "tedious affectation," the very thing against which Campion had warned, would Daniel be in practice, whose numbers would never suggest "those continual cadences of couplets."

A DEFENCE OF RYME

Against a Pamphlet Entituled "Obseruations in the Art of English Poesie."

(1602?)

To all the Worthie Louers and Learned Professors of Ryme, within his Maiesties Dominions, S. D.

Worthie Gentlemen, about a yeare since, vpon the great reproach giuen to the Professors of Rime, and the vse therof, I wrote a priuate letter, as a defence of mine owne vndertakings in that kinde, to a learned Gentleman a great friend of mine, then in Court. VVhich I did, rather to confirm my selfe in mine owne courses, and to hold him from being wonne from vs, then with any desire to publish the same to the world.

But now, seeing the times to promise a more regarde to the present condition of our writings, in respect of our Soueraignes happy inclination this way; whereby wee are rather to expect an incoragement to go on with what we do, then that any innouation should checke vs, with a shew of what it would do in an other kinde, and yet doe nothing but depraue: I haue now giuen a greater body to the same Argument. And here present it to your view, vnder the patronage of a Noble Earle, who in bloud and nature is interested to take our parte in this cause, with others, who cannot, I know, but holde deare the monuments that haue beene left vnto the world in this manner of composition. And who I trust will take in good parte this my defence, if not as it is my particular, yet in respect of the cause I vndertake, which I heere inuoke you all to protect.

Sa: D.

To William Herbert Earle of Pembrooke

The Generall Custome, and vse of Ryme in this kingdome, Noble Lord, hauing beene so long (as if from a Graunt of Nature) held vnquestionable; made me to imagine that it lay altogither out of the way of contradiction, and was become so natural, as we should neuer haue had a thought to cast it off into reproch, or be made to thinke that it ill-became our language. But now I see, when there is opposition made to all things in the world by wordes, wee must nowe at length likewise fall to contend for words themselues; and make a question, whether they be right or not. For we are tolde how that our measures goe wrong, all Ryming is grosse, vulgare, barbarous, which if it be so, we haue lost much labour to no purpose: and for mine owne particular, I cannot but blame the fortune of the times and mine owne Genius that cast me vppon so wrong a course, drawne with the current of custome, and an vnexamined example. Hauing beene first incourag'd or fram'd thereunto by your most Worthy and Honourable Mother, receiuing the first notion for the formall ordering of those compositions at *Wilton,* which I must euer acknowledge to haue beene my best Schoole, and thereof alwayes am to hold a feeling and gratefull Memory. Afterward, drawne farther on by the well-liking and approbation of my worthy Lord, the fosterer of mee and my *Muse,* I aduentured to bestow all my whole powers therein, perceiuing it agreed so well, both with the complexion of the times, and mine owne constitution, as I found not wherein I might better imploy me. But yet now, vpon the great discouery of these new measures, threatning to ouerthrow the whole state of Ryme in this kingdom, I must either stand out to defend, or else be forced to forsake my selfe, and giue ouer all. And though irresolution and a selfe distrust be the most apparent faults of my nature, and that the least checke of reprehension, if it fauour of reason, will as easily shake my resolution as any mans liuing: yet in this case I know not how I am growne more resolued, and before I sinke, willing to examine what those powers of iudgement are, that must beare me downe, and beat me off from the station of my profession, which by the law of nature I am set to defend.

   And the rather for that this detractor (whose commendable Rymes albeit now himselfe an enemy to ryme, haue giuen heretofore to the world the best notice of his worth) is a man of faire parts, and good reputation, and therefore the reproach forcibly cast from such a hand may throw downe more at once then the labors of many shall in long time build vp againe, specially vpon the slippery foundation of opinion, and the worlds inconstancy, which knowes not well what it would haue, and:

Discit enim citius, meminitque libentius illud
Quod quis deridet quam quod probat & veneratur.[1]

And he who is thus, become our vnkinde aduersarie, must pardon vs if we be as iealous of our fame and reputation, as hee is desirous of credite by his new-old arte, and must consider that we cannot, in a thing that concernes vs so neere, but haue a feeling of the wrong done, wherein euery Rymer in this vniuersall Iland as well as my selfe, stands interressed. So that if his charitie had equally drawne with his learning hee would haue forborne to procure the enuie of so powerfull a number vpon him, from whom he cannot but expect the returne of a like measure of blame, and onely haue made way to his owne grace, by the proofe of his abilitie, without the disparaging of vs, who would haue bin glad to haue stood quietly by him, & perhaps commended his aduenture, seeing that euermore of one science an other may be borne, & that these Salies made out of the quarter of our set knowledges, are the gallant proffers onely of attemptiue spirits, and commendable though they worke no other effect than make a Brauado: and I know it were *Indecens, & morosum nimis, alienæ industriæ, modum ponere.*[2] We could well haue allowed of his numbers had he not disgraced our Ryme; Which both Custome and Nature doth most powerfully defend. Custome that is before all Law, Nature that is aboue all Arte. Euery language hath her proper number or measure fitted to vse and delight, which, Custome intertaining by the allowance of the Eare, doth indenize, and make naturall. All verse is but a frame of wordes confinde within certaine measure; differing from the ordinarie speach, and introduced, the better to expresse mens conceipts, both for delight and memorie. Which frame of wordes consisting of *Rithmus* or *Metrum*, Number or Measure, are disposed into diuers fashions, according to the humour of the Composer and the set of the time; And these *Rhythmi* as *Aristotle* saith are familiar amongst all Nations, and *è naturali & sponte fusa compositione:*[3] And they fall as naturally already in our language as euer Art can make them; being such as the Eare of it selfe doth marshall in their proper roomes, and they of themselues will not willingly be put out of their ranke; and that in such a verse as best comports with the Nature of our language. And for our Ryme (which is an excellencie added to this worke of measure, and

---

[1] "Learns more quickly and remembers more willingly what someone derides than that for which one shows approbation or reuerence." Horace, *Epist.* II 1 262–3.

[2] "Unseemly and captious to set bounds for the labors of another."

[3] "From composition that is natural and spontaneous." See *Poetics* IV, 6.

a Harmonie, farre happier than any proportion Antiquitie could euer shew vs) dooth adde more grace, and hath more of delight than euer bare numbers, howsoeuer they can be forced to runne in our slow language, can possibly yeeld. Which, whether it be deriu'd of *Rhythmus,* or of *Romance* which were songs the *Bards* & *Druydes* about Rymes vsed, & thereof were caled *Remensi,* as some Italians hold; or howsoeuer, it is likewise number and harmonie of words, consisting of an agreeing sound in the last silables of seuerall verses, giuing both to the Eare an Eccho of a delightfull report & to the Memorie a deeper impression of what is deliuered therein. For as Greeke and Latine verse consists of the number and quantitie of sillables, so doth the English verse of measure and accent. And though it doth not strictly obserue long and short sillables, yet it most religiously respects the accent: and as the short and the long make number, so the Acute and graue accent yeelde harmonie: And harmonie is likewise number, so that the English verse then hath number, measure and harmonie in the best proportion of Musike. Which being more certain & more resounding, works that effect of motion with as happy successe as either the Greek or Latin. And so naturall a melody is it, & so vniuersall as it seems to be generally borne with al the nations of the world, as an hereditary eloquence proper to all mankind. The vniuersallitie argues the generall power of it: for if the Barbarian vse it, then it shews that it swais th'affection of the Barbarian, if ciuil nations practise it, it proues that it works vpon the harts of ciuil nations: If all, then that it hath a power in nature on all. *Georgieuez de Turcarum moribus,* hath an example of the Turkish Rymes iust of the measure of our verse of eleuen sillables, in feminine Ryme: neuer begotten I am perswaded by any example in *Europe,* but borne no doubt in *Scythia,* and brought ouer *Caucasus* and *Mount Taurus.* The Sclauonian and Arabian tongs acquaint a great part of *Asia* and *Affrique* with it, the Moscouite, Polack, Hungarian, German, Italian, French, and Spaniard vse no other harmonie of words. The Irish, Briton, Scot, Dane, Saxon, English, and all the Inhabiters of this Iland, either haue hither brought, or here found the same in vse. And such a force hath it in nature, or so made by nature, as the Latine numbers notwithstanding their excellencie, seemed not sufficient to satitsfie the eare of the world thereunto accustomed, without this Harmonicall cadence: which made the most learned of all nations labour with exceeding trauaile to bring those numbers likewise vnto it: which many did with that happinesse, as neither their puritie of tongue, nor their materiall contemplations are thereby any way disgraced, but rather deserue to be reuerenced of all gratefull posteritie, with the due regard of their worth. And for *Schola Salerna,* and those *Carmina Prouerbialia,* who finds not therein more precepts for vse, concerning diet, health, and conuersation, then *Cato, Theognes,* or all the Greekes and Latines can shew vs in that kinde of teaching: and that in so few words, both for delight to the eare, and the hold of memorie, as they are to be imbraced of all modest readers that studie to know and not to depraue.

Me thinkes it is a strange imperfection, that men should thus ouer-runne the estimation of good things with so violent a censure, as though it must please none else, because it likes not them. Whereas *Oportet arbitratores esse non contradictores eos qui verum iudicaturi sunt,*[4] saith *Arist.* though he could not obserue it himselfe. And milde Char-itie tells vs:

> ——— *non ego paucis*
> *Offendor maculis quas aut incuria fudit*
> *Aut humana parum cauet natura.*[5]

For all men haue their errors, and we must take the best of their powers, and leaue the rest as not appertaining vnto vs.

Ill customes are to be left, I graunt it: but I see not howe that can be taken for an ill custome, which nature hath thus ratified, all nations receiued, time so long confirmed, the effects such as it performes those offices of motion for which it is imployed; delighting the eare, stirring the heart, and satisfying the iudgement in such sort as I doubt whether euer single numbers will do in our Climate, if they shew no more worke of wonder then yet we see. And if euer they prooue to become any thing, it must be by the approbation of many ages that must giue them their strength for any operation, or before the world will feele where the pulse, life, and enargie lies, which now we are sure where to haue in our Rymes, whose knowne frame hath those due staies for the minde, those incounters of touch as makes the motion certaine, though the varietie be infinite. Nor will the Generall sorte, for whom we write (the wise being aboue bookes) taste these laboured measures but as an orderly prose when wee haue all done. For this kinde ac-quaintance and continuall familiaritie euer had betwixt our eare and this cadence, is growne to so intimate a friendship, as it will nowe

---

[4] "Critics ought not to be contradictors if they are seeking the truth." *Met.* x 1.
[5] "I am not offended by little flaws which either negligence has dropped, or human nature has too little guarded against." Horace, *Ars Poetica,* 351–3.

hardly euer be brought to misse it. For be the verse neuer so good, neuer so full, it seemes not to satisfie nor breede that delight as when it is met and combined with a like sounding accents. Which seemes as the iointure without which it hangs loose, and cannot subsist, but runnes wildely on, like a tedious fancie without a close: suffer then the world to inioy that which it knowes, and what it likes. Seeing that whatsoeuer force of words doth mooue, delight and sway the affections of men, in what Scythian sorte soeuer it be disposed or vttered: that is true number, measure, eloquence, and the perfection of speach: which I said, hath as many shapes as there be tongues or nations in the world, nor can with all the tyrannicall Rules of idle Rhetorique be gouerned otherwise then custome, and present obseruation will allow. And being now the trym, and fashion of the times, to sute a man otherwise cannot but giue a touch of singularity, for when hee hath all done, hee hath but found other clothes to the same body, and per-aduenture not so fitting as the former. But could our Aduersary hereby set vp the musicke of our times to a higher note of iudgement and discretion, or could these new lawes of words better our imperfections, it were a happy attempt; but when hereby we shall but as it were change prison, and put off these fetters to receiue others, what haue we gained, as good still to vse ryme and a little reason, as neither ryme nor reason, for no doubt as idle wits will write, in that kinde, as do now in this, imitation wil after, though it breake her necke. *Scribimus indocti doctique poemata passim.*[6] And this multitude of idle writers can be no disgrace to the good, for the same fortune in one proportion or other is proper in a like season to all States in their turne: and the same vnmeasureable confluence of Scriblers hapned, when measures were most in vse among the Romanes, as we finde by this reprehension,

> *Mutauit mentem populus leuis, & calet vno*
> *Scribendi studio, pueri, patrésque seueri,*
> *Fronde comas vincti cænant, & carmina dictant.*

So that their plentie seemes to haue bred the same waste and con-tempt as ours doth now, though it had not power to disvalew what was worthy of posteritie, nor keep backe the reputation of excellencies,

---

[6] "Scribble alike, the unskilled and the skilled, poems at random." This line fol-lows (1 117) those quoted in Daniel's next sentence: "The disposition of the light-headed populace changes, grows hot in its zeal for versifying; boys, and men of discretion, dine with their hair bound with wreaths, and dictate off verses." Horace, *Epist.* ii 1 108–110.

destined to continue for many ages. For seeing it is matter that satisfies the iudiciall, appeare it in what habite it will, all these pretended proportions of words, howsoeuer placed, can be but words, and peraduenture serue but to embroyle our vnderstanding, whilst seeking to please our eare, we inthrall our iudgement: to delight an exterior sense, wee smoothe vp a weake confused sense, affecting sound to be vnsound, and all to seeme *Seruum pecus,*[7] onely to imitate the Greekes and Latines, whose felicitie, in this kind, might be something to themselues, to whome their owne *idioma* was naturall, but to vs it can yeeld no other commoditie then a sound. We admire them not for their smooth-gliding words, nor their measures, but for their inuentions: which treasure, if it were to be found in Welch, and Irish, we should hold those languages in the same estimation, and they may thanke their sword that made their tongues so famous and vniuersall as they are. For to say truth, their Verse is many times but a confused deliuerer of their excellent conceits, whose scattered limbs we are faine to looke out and ioyne together, to discerne the image of what they represent vnto vs. And euen the Latines, who professe not to be so licentious as the Greekes, shew vs many times examples but of strange crueltie, in torturing and dismembring of wordes in the middest, or disioyning such as naturally should be married and march together, by setting them as farre asunder, as they can possibly stand: that sometimes, vnlesse the kind reader, out of his owne good nature, wil stay them vp by their measure, they will fall downe into flatte prose, and sometimes are no other indeede in their naturall sound: and then againe, when you finde them disobedient to their owne Lawes, you must hold it to be *licentia poetica,* and so dispensable. The striuing to shew their changable measures in the varietie of their Odes, haue beene very painefull no doubt vnto them, and forced them thus to disturbe the quiet streame of their wordes, which by a naturall succession otherwise desire to follow in their due course.

But such affliction doth laboursome curiositie still lay vpon our best delights (which euer must be made strange and variable) as if Art were ordained to afflict Nature, and that we could not goe but in fetters. Euery science, euery profession, must be so wrapt vp in vnnecessary intrications, as if it were not to fashion, but to confound the vnderstanding, which makes me much to distrust man, and feare that our presumption goes beyond our abilitie, and our Curiositie is more than our Iudgement: laboring euer to seeme to be more than we are, or laying greater

---

[7] "Servile herd." Horace, *Epist.* 1 xix, 19.

burthens vpon our mindes, then they are well able to beare, because we would not appeare like other men.

And indeed I haue wished there were not that multiplicitie of Rymes as is vsed by many in Sonets, which yet we see in some so happily to succeed, and hath beene so farre from hindering their inuentions, as it hath begot conceit beyond expectation, and comparable to the best inuentions of the world: for sure in an eminent spirit whome Nature hath fitted for that mysterie, Ryme is no impediment to his conceit, but rather giues him wings to mount and carries him, not out of his course, but as it were beyond his power to a farre happier flight. Al excellencies being sold vs at the hard price of labour, it followes, where we bestow most thereof, we buy the best successe: and Ryme being farre more laborious then loose measures (whatsoeuer is obiected) must needs, meeting with wit and industry, breed greater and worthier effects in our language. So that if our labours haue wrought out a manumission from bondage, and that wee goe at libertie, notwithstanding these ties, wee are no longer the slaues of Ryme, but we make it a most excellent instrument to serue vs. Nor is this certaine limit obserued in Sonnets, any tyrannicall bounding of the conceit, but rather a reducing it in *girum,* and a iust forme, neither too long for the shortest proiect, nor too short for the longest, being but onely imployed for a present passion. For the body of our imagination, being as vnformed *Chaos* without fashion, without day, if by the diuine power of the spirit it be wrought into an Orbe of order and forme, is it not more pleasing to Nature, that desires a certaintie, and comports not with that which is infinite, to haue these clozes, rather than, not to know where to end, or how farre to goe, especially seeing our passions are often without measure: and wee finde the best of the latines many times, either not concluding, or els otherwise in the end then they began. Besides, is it not most delightfull to see much excellently ordred in a small-roome, or little, gallantly disposed and made to fill vp a space of like capacitie, in such sort, that the one would not appeare so beautifull in a larger circuite, nor the other do well in a lesse: which often we find to be so, according to the powers of nature, in the workeman. And these limited proportions, and rests of Stanzes: consisting of 6. 7. or 8. lines are of that happines, both for the disposition of the matter, the apt planting the sentence where it may best stand to hit, the certaine close of delight with the full body of a iust period well carried, is such, as neither the Greekes or Latines euer attained vnto. For their boundlesse running on, often so confounds the Reader, that hauing once lost himselfe, must either giue off vnsatisfied, or vncertainely cast backe to retriue the escaped sence, and to find way againe into his matter.

Me thinkes we should not so soone yeeld our consents captiue to the authoritie of Antiquitie, vnlesse we saw more reason: all our vnderstandings are not to be built by the square of *Greece* and *Italie.* We are the children of nature as well as they, we are not so placed out of the way of iudgement, but that the same Sunne of Discretion shineth vppon vs, wee haue our portion of the same vertues as well as of the same vices, *Et Catilinam Quocunque in populo videas, quocunque sub axe.*[8] Time and the turne of things bring about these faculties according to the present estimation: and, *Res temporibus non tempora rebus seruire opportet.*[9] So that we must neuer rebell against vse: *Quem penes arbitrium est, & vis & norma loquendi.*[10] It is not the obseruing of *Trochaicques* nor their *Iambicques,* that wil make our writings ought the wiser: All their Poesie, all their Philosophie is nothing, vnlesse we bring the discerning light of conceipt with vs to apply it to vse. It is not bookes, but onely that great booke of the world, and the allouerspreading grace of heauen that makes men truely iudiciall. Nor can it be but a touch of arrogant ignorance, to hold this or that nation Barbarous, these or those times grosse, considering how this manifold creature man, wheresoeuer hee stand in the world, hath alwayes some disposition of worth, intertaines the order of societie, affects that which is most in vse, and is eminent in some one thing or other, that fits his humour and the times. The Grecians held all other nations barbarous but themselues, yet *Pirrhus* when he saw the well ordered marching of the Romanes, which made them see their presumptuous errour, could say it was no barbarous maner of proceeding. The *Gothes, Vandales* and *Longobards,* whose comming downe like an inundation ouerwhelmed, as they say, al the glory of learning in *Europe,* haue yet left vs still their lawes and customes, as the originalls of most of the prouinciall constitutions of Christendome; which well considered with their other courses of gouernement, may serue to cleere them from this imputation of ignorance. And though the vanquished neuer yet spake well of the Conquerour: yet euen thorow the vnsound couerings of malediction appeare those monuments of trueth, as argue wel their worth and proues them not without iudgement, though without Greeke and Latine.

[8] "You may see a Catiline among any people you please, in any clime." Juvenal: *Satires* xiv 41.

[9] "Affairs ought to be subservient to times, not times to affairs."

[10] "Within whose power is the authority, is the force, is the pattern, of speech." Horace, *Ars Poetica,* 72.

Will not experience confute vs, if wee shoulde say the state of *China,* which neuer heard of Anapestiques, Trochies, and Tribracques, were grosse, barbarous, and vnciuile? And is it not a most apparant ignorance, both of the succession of learning in *Europe,* and the generall course of things, *to say, that all lay pittifully deformed in those lacke-lèarning times from the declining of the Romane Empire, till the light of the Latine tongue was reuiued by* Rewcline, Erasmus *and* Moore. When for three hundred yeeres before them about the comming downe of *Tamburlaine* into *Europe, Franciscus Petrarcha* (who then no doubt likewise found whom to imitate) shewed all the best notions of learning, in that degree of excellencie, both in Latin, Prose and Verse, and in the vulgare Italian, as all the wittes of posteritie haue not yet much ouer-matched him in all kindes to this day: his great Volumes written in Moral Philosophie, shew his infinite reading, and most happy power of disposition: his twelue Æglogues, his *Affrica* containing nine Bookes of the last Punicke warre, with his three Bookes of Epistles in Latine verse, shew all the transformations of wit and inuention, that a Spirite naturally borne to the inheritance of Poetrie & iudiciall knowledge could expresse: All which notwithstanding wrought him not that glory & fame with his owne Nation, as did his Poems in Italian, which they esteeme aboue al whatsoeuer wit could haue inuented in any other forme then wherein it is: which questionles they wil not change with the best measures, Greeks or Latins can shew them; howsoeuer our Aduersary imagines. Nor could this very same innouation in Verse, begun amongst them by *C. Tolomæi,* but die in the attempt, and was buried as soone as it came borne, neglected as a prodigious & vnnaturall issue amongst them: nor could it neuer induce *Tasso* the wonder of *Italy,* to write that admirable Poem of *Ierusalem,* comparable to the best of the ancients, in any other forme then the accustomed verse. And with *Petrarch* liued his scholer *Boccacius,* and neere about the same time, *Iohannis Rauenensis,* and from these *tanquam ex equo Troiano,* seemes to haue issued all those famous Italian Writers, *Leonardus Aretinus, Laurentius Valla, Poggius, Blondus,* and many others. Then *Emanuel Chrysolaras* a Constantinopolitan gentleman, renowmed for his learning and vertue, being imployed by *Iohn Paleologus* Emperour of the East, to implore the ayde of christian Princes, for the succouring of perishing *Greece:* and vnderstanding in the meane time, how *Baiazeth* was taken prisoner by *Tamburlan,* and his country freed from danger, stayed still at *Venice,* and there taught the Greeke tongue, discontinued before, in these parts the space of seauen hundred yeeres.

Him followed *Bessarion, George Trapezantius, Theodore Gaza,* & others, transporting Philosophie beaten by the Turke out of *Greece* into christendome. Hereupon came that mightie confluence of Learning in these parts, which returning, as it were *per postliminium,*[11] and heere meeting then with the new inuented stampe of Printing, spread it selfe indeed in a more vniuersall sorte then the world euer heeretofore had it. When *Pomponius Lætus, AEneas Syluius, Angelus Politianus, Hermolaus Barbarus, Iohannes Picus de Mirandula* the miracle & Phœnix of the world, adorned *Italie,* and wakened vp other Nations likewise with this desire of glory, long before it brought foorth, *Rewclen, Erasmus,* and *Moore,* worthy men I confesse, and the last a great ornament to this land, and a Rymer. And yet long before all these, and likewise with these, was not our Nation behind in her portion of spirite and worthinesse, but concurrent with the best of all this lettered worlde: witnesse venerable *Bede,* that flourished aboue a thousand yeeres since: *Aldelmus Durotelmus* that liued in the yeere 739. of whom we finde this commendation registred. *Omnium Poetarum sui temporis facilè primus, tantæ eloquentiæ, maiestatis & eruditionis homo fuit, vt nunquam satis admirari possim vnde illi in tam barbara ac rudi ætate facundia accreuerit, vsque adeo omnibus numeris tersa, elegans & rotunda, versus edidit cum antiquitate de palma contendentes.*[12] Witnesse *Iosephus Deuonius,* who wrote *de bello Troiano,* in so excellent manner, and so neere resembling Antiquitie, as Printing his Worke beyond the Seas, they haue ascribed it to *Cornelius Nepos,* one of the Ancients.

What should I name *Walterus Mape, Gulielmus Nigellus, Geruasius Tilburiensis, Bracton, Bacon, Ockam,* and an infinite Catalogue of excellent men, most of them liuing about foure hundred yeares since, and haue left behinde them monuments of most profound iudgement and learning in all sciences. So that it is but the clowds gathered about our owne iudgement that makes vs thinke all other ages wrapt vp in mists, and the great distance betwixt vs, that causes vs to imagine men so farre off, to be so little in respect of our selues. We must not looke vpon the immense course of times past, as men ouer-looke spacious and wide countries, from off high Mountaines and are neuer the neere to iudge of the true Nature of the soyle, or the particular syte and face of those territories they see. Nor must we thinke, viewing the superficiall figure of

---

11 "Through the right of reinstatement."
12 Of uncertain origin: "Of all the poets of his time easily the first, he was a man of such eloquence, sublimity, and erudition that I cannot but in amazement question whence came that superabundance to him in such an untutored and impoverished age, terseness in all his verses, ease and polish; he wrote poetry to engage with antiquity for the palm."

a region in a Mappe that wee know strait the fashion and place as it is. Or reading an Historie (which is but a Mappe of men, and dooth no otherwise acquaint vs with the true Substance of Circumstances, than a superficiall Card dooth the Sea-man with a Coast neuer seene, which always prooues other to the eye than the imagination forecast it) that presently wee know all the world, and can distinctly iudge of times, men and maners, iust as they were. When the best measure of man is to be taken by his owne foote, bearing euer the neerest proportion to himselfe, and is neuer so farre different and vnequall in his powers, that he hath all in perfection at one time, and nothing at an other. The distribution of giftes are vniuersall, and all seasons hath them in some sort. We must not thinke, but that there were *Scipioes, Cæsars, Catoes* and *Pompeies,* borne elsewhere then at *Rome,* the rest of the world hath euer had them in the same degree of nature, though not of state. And it is our weakenesse that makes vs mistake, or misconceiue in these deliniations of men the true figure of their worth. And our passion and beliefe is so apt to leade vs beyond truth, that vnlesse we try them by the iust compasse of humanitie, and as they were men, we shall cast their figures in the ayre when we should make their models vpon Earth. It is not the contexture of words, but the effects of Action that giues glory to the times: we finde they had *mercurium in pectore* [13] though not *in lingua,* and in all ages, though they were not Ciceronians, they knew the Art of men, which onely is, *Ars Artium,* the great gift of heauen, and the chiefe grace and glory on earth, they had the learning of Gouernement, and ordring their State, Eloquence inough to shew their iudgements. And it seemes the best times followed *Lycurgus* councell: *Literas ad vsum saltem discebant, reliqua omnis disciplina erat, vt pulchre parerent vt labores preferrent &c.* [14] Had not vnlearned *Rome* laide the better foundation, and built the stronger frame of an admirable state, eloquent *Rome* had confounded it vtterly, which we saw, ranne the way of all confusion, the plaine course of dissolution in her greatest skill: and though she had not power to vndoe her selfe, yet wrought she so that she cast her selfe quite away from the glory of a common-wealth, and fell vpon that forme of state she euer most feared and abhorred of all other: and then scarse was there seene any shadowe of pollicie vnder her first Emperours, but the most horrible and grosse confusion that could bee conceued, notwithstanding it stil indured, pre-

---

[13] "Eloquence in the heart [though not] on the tongue."
[14] "They learned enough in letters for their purpose, and the rest of their education was that they obey unquestioningly and perform their labors."

seruing not only a Monarchie, locked vp in her own limits, but there-withall held vnder her obedience, so many Nations so farre distant, so ill affected, so disorderly commanded & vniustly conquerd, as it is not to be attributed to any other fate but to the first frame of that common-wealth, which was so strongly ioynted and with such infinite combina-tions interlinckt, as one naile or other euer held vp the Maiestie thereof. There is but one learning, which *omnes gentes habent scriptum in cordi-bus suis,*[15] one and the selfe-same spirit that worketh in all. We haue but one body of Iustice, one body of Wisedome throughout the whole world, which is but apparaled according to the fashion of euery nation.

Eloquence and gay wordes are not of the Substance of wit, it is but the garnish of a nice time, the Ornaments that doe but decke the house of a State, *& imitatur publicos mores:* [16] Hunger is as well satisfied with meat serued in pewter as siluer. Discretion is the best measure, the right-est foote in what habit soeuer it runne. *Erasmus, Rewcline* and *More,* brought no more wisdome into the world with all their new reuiued wordes then we finde was before, it bred not a profounder Diuine than Saint *Thomas,* a greater Lawyer than *Bartolus,* a more accute Logician than *Scotus:* nor are the effects of all this great amasse of eloquence so ad-mirable or of that consequence, but that *impexa illa antiquitas* [17] can yet compare with them. Let vs go no further, but looke vpon the won-derfull Architecture of this state of *England,* and see whether they were deformed times, that could giue it such a forme. Where there is no one the least piller of Maiestie, but was set with most profound iudge-ment and borne vp with the iust conueniencie of Prince and people. No Court of Iustice, but laide by the Rule and Square of Nature, and the best of the best commonwealths that euer were in the world. So strong and substantial, as it hath stood against al the storms of factions, both of beliefe & ambition, which so powerfully beat vpon it, and all the tempestuous alterations of humorous times whatsoeuer. Being con-tinually in all ages furnisht with spirites fitte to maintaine the maiestie of her owne greatnes, and to match in an equall concurrencie all other kingdomes round about her with whome it had to incounter. But this innouation, like a Viper, must euer make way into the worlds opinion, thorow the bowelles of her owne breeding, & is always borne with re-proch in her mouth; the disgracing others is the best grace it can put on, to winne reputation of wit, and yet is it neuer so wise as it would seeme, nor doth the world euer get so much by it, as it imagineth:

---

[15] "All peoples have, written in their hearts."

[16] "Imitate the customs of the people."
[17] "The rude past."

which being so often deceiued, and seeing it neuer performes so much as it promises, me thinkes men should neuer giue more credite vnto it. For, let vs change neuer so often, wee can not change man, our imperfections must still runne on with vs. And therefore the wiser Nations haue taught menne alwayes to vse, *Moribus legibusque presentibus etiamsi deteriores sint.*[18] The Lacedemonians, when a Musitian, thincking to winne him-selfe credite by his new inuention, and be before his fellowes, had added one string more to his Crowde, brake his fiddle, and banished him the Cittie, holding the Innouator, though in the least things, dangerous to a publike societie. It is but a fantastike giddinesse to forsake the way of other men, especially where it lies tollerable: *Vbi nunc est respublica, ibi simus potius quam dum illam veterem sequimur, simus in nulla.*[19] But shal we not tend to perfection? Yes, and that euer best by going on in the course we are in, where we haue aduantage, being so farre onward, of him that is but now setting forth. For we shall neuer proceede, if wee be euer beginning, nor arriue at any certayne Porte, sayling with all windes that blow: *Non conualescit planta quæ sæpius transfertur,*[20] and therefore let vs hold on in the course wee haue vndertaken, and not still be wandring. Perfection is not the portion of man, and if it were, why may wee not as well get to it this way as an other? and suspect these great vndertakers, lest they haue conspired with enuy to betray our proceedings, and put vs by the honor of our attempts, with casting vs backe vpon an other course, of purpose to ouerthrow the whole action of glory when we lay the fairest for it, and were so neere our hopes? I thanke God that I am none of these great Schollers, if thus their hie knowledges doe but giue them more eyes to looke out into vncertaintie and confusion, accounting my selfe, rather beholding to my ignorance, that hath set me in so lowe an vnder-roome of conceipt with other men, and hath giuen me as much distrust, as it hath done hope, daring not aduenture to goe alone, but plodding on the plaine tract I finde beaten by Custome and the Time, contenting me with what I see in vse. And surely mee thinkes these great wittes should rather seeke to adorne, than to disgrace the present, bring something to it, without taking from it what it hath. But it is euer the misfortune of Learning, to be wounded by her owne hand. *Stimulos dat emula virtus,*[21] and when there is not abilitie to match what is, malice wil finde out ingines, either to disgrace or ruine it, with a peruerse incounter of

[18] "The contemporary customs and laws, even though they be meaner."
[19] "In the republic that now is, let us find our part, rather than, following after that old one, be in none at all."
[20] "A plant does not gain strength which too often is transplanted."
[21] "Emulation gives the stimulus."

some new impression: and which is the greatest misery, it must euer proceed from the powers of the best reputation, as if the greatest spirites were ordained to indanger the worlde, as the grosse are to dishonour it, and that we were to expect *ab optimis periculum, à pessimis dedecus publicum*.[22] Emulation the strongest pulse that beates in high mindes, is oftentimes a winde, but of the worst effect: For whilst the Soule comes disappoynted of the obiect it wrought on, it presently forges an other, and euen cozins it selfe, and crosses all the world, rather than it wil stay to be vnder hir desires, falling out with all it hath, to flatter and make faire that which it would haue. So that it is the ill successe of our longings that with *Xerxes* makes vs to whippe the Sea, and send a cartel of defiance to mount *Athos:* and the fault laide vpon others weakenesse, is but a presumptuous opinion of our owne strength, who must not seeme to be maistered. But had our Aduersary taught vs by his owne proceedings, this way of perfection, and therein fram'd vs a Poeme of that excellencie as should haue put downe all, and beene the maisterpeece of these times, we should all haue admired him. But to de-praue the present forme of writing, and to bring vs nothing but a few loose and vncharitable Epigrammes, and yet would make vs belieue those numbers were come to raise the glory of our language, giueth vs cause to suspect the performance, and to examine whether this new Arte, *constat sibi,* or, *aliquid sit dictum quod non sit dictum prius.*[23]

First we must heere imitate the Greekes and Latines, and yet we are heere shewed to disobey them, euen in their owne numbers and quanti-ties: taught to produce what they make short, and make short what they produce: made beleeue to be shewd measures in that forme we haue not seene, and no such matter: tolde that heere is the perfect Art of versifying, which in conclusion is yet confessed to be vnperfect, as if our Aduersary to be opposite to vs, were become vnfaithfull to him-selfe, and seeking to leade vs out of the way of reputation, hath ad-uentured to intricate and confound him in his owne courses, running vpon most vn-euen groundes, with imperfect rules, weake proofes, and vnlawfull lawes. Whereunto the world, I am perswaded, is not so vn-reasonable as to subscribe, considering the vniust authoritie of the Law-giuer. For who hath constituted him to be the *Radamanthus* thus to torture sillables, and adiudge them their perpetuall doome, setting his *Theta* or marke of condemnation vppon them, to indure the appoynted sentence of his crueltie, as hee shall dispose. As though there were that

---

[22] "From the best, danger, and from the worst. public shame."

[23] "Possesses consistency [or] says any-thing which has not been said previously."

disobedience in our wordes, as they would not be ruled or stand in order without so many intricate Lawes, which would argue a great peruersenesse amongst them, according to that, *in pessima republica plurimæ leges:* [24] or, that they were so farre gone from the quiet freedome of nature, that they must thus be brought backe againe by force. And now in what case were this poore state of words, if in like sorte another tyrant the next yeere should arise and abrogate these lawes and ordaine others cleane contrary according to his humor, and say that they were onely right, the others vniust, what disturbance were there here, to whome should we obey? Were it not farre better to hold vs fast to our old custome, than to stand thus distracted with vncertaine Lawes, wherein Right shal haue as many faces as it pleases Passion to make it, that wheresoeuer mens affections stand, it shall still looke that way. What trifles doth our vnconstant curiositie cal vp to contend for, what colours are there laid vpon indifferent things to make them seeme other then they are, as if it were but only to intertaine contestation amongst men; who standing according to the prospectiue of their owne humour, seeme to see the selfe same things to appeare otherwise to them, than either they doe to other, or are indeede in themselues, being but all one in nature. For what a doe haue we heere, what strange precepts of Arte about the framing of an Iambique verse in our language, which when all is done, reaches not by a foote, but falleth out to be the plaine ancient verse consisting of tenne sillables or fiue feete, which hath euer beene vsed amongst vs time out of minde. And for all this cunning and counterfeit name can or will be any other in nature then it hath beene euer heretofore: and this new *Dimeter* is but the halfe of this verse diuided in two, and no other then the *Cæsura* or breathing place in the middest thereof, and therefore it had bene as good to haue put two lines in one, but only to make them seeme diuerse. Nay it had beene much better for the true English reading and pronouncing thereof, without violating the accent, which now our Aduersarie hath heerein most vnkindely doone: for, being, as wee are to sound it, according to our Engglish March, we must make a rest, and raise the last sillable, which falles out very vnnaturall in *Desolate, Funerall, Elizabeth, Prodigall,* and in all the rest sauing the Monosillables. Then followes the English *Trochaicke,* which is saide to bee a simple verse, and so indeede it is, being without Ryme; hauing here no other grace then that in sound it runnes like the knowne measure of our former ancient Verse, ending (as we terme it according to the French) in a feminine foote, sauing that

---

[24] "In the worst state there are exceedingly many laws."

it is shorter by one sillable at the beginning, which is not much missed, by reason it falles full at the last. Next comes the *Elegiacke,* being the fourth kinde, and that likewise is no other than our old accustomed measure of fiue feete, if there be any difference, it must be made in the reading, and therein wee must stand bound to stay where often we would not, and sometimes either breake the accent, or the due course of the word. And now for the other foure kinds of numbers, which are to be employed for *Odes,* they are either of the same measure, or such as haue euer beene familiarly vsed amongst vs. So that of all these eight seuerall kindes of new promised numbers you see what we haue. Onely what was our owne before, and the same but apparelled in forraine Titles, which had they come in their kinde and naturall attire of Ryme, wee should neuer haue suspected that they had affected to be other, or sought to degenerate into strange manners, which now we see was the cause why they were turned out of their proper habite, and brought in as Aliens, onely to induce men to admire them as farre-commers. But see the power of Nature, it is not all the artificiall couerings of wit that can hide their natiue and originall condition which breakes out thorow the strongest bandes of affectation, and will be it selfe, doe Singularitie what it can. And as for those imagined quantities of sillables, which haue bin euer held free and indifferent in our language, who can inforce vs to take knowledge of them, being *in nullius verba iurati,*[25] & owing fealty to no forraine inuention; especially in such a case where there is no necessitie in Nature, or that it imports either the matter or forme, whether it be so, or otherwise. But euery Versifier that wel obserues his worke, findes in our language, without all these vnnecessary precepts, what numbers best fitte the Nature of her Idiome, and the proper places destined to such accents as she will not let in, to any other roomes then into those for which they were borne. As for example, you cannot make this fall into the right sound of a Verse.

> None thinkes reward rendred worthy his worth:

vnlesse you thus misplace the accent vppon *Rendrèd* and *Worthìe,* contrary to the nature of these wordes: which sheweth that two feminine numbers (or Trochies, if so you wil call them) will not succeede in the third and fourth place of the Verse. And so likewise in this case:

> Though Death doth consume, yet Virtue preserues,

[25] "Bound by oath to no one" [lit. "in the words of no one"]. Cf. Horace: *Epist.* I 1, 14, *nullius iurare in verba magistri.*

it will not be a Verse, though it hath the iust sillables, without the same number in the second, and the altering of the fourth place, in this sorte:

> Though Death doth ruine, Virtue yet preserues.

Againe, who knowes not that we cannot kindely answere a feminine number with a masculine Ryme, or (if you will so terme it) a *Trochei* with a *Sponde*, as *Weakenes* with *Confesse*, *Nature* and *Indure*, onely for that thereby wee shall wrong the accent, the chiefe Lord and graue Gouernour of Numbers. Also you cannot in a Verse of foure feete, place a *Trochei* in the first, without the like offence, as,

> Yearely out of his watry Cell,

for so you shall sound it *Yearelìè* which is vnnaturall. And other such like obseruations vsually occurre, which Nature and a iudiciall eare, of themselues teach vs readily to auoyde.

But now for whom hath our Aduersary taken all this paines? For the Learned, or for the Ignorant, or for himselfe, to shew his owne skill? If for the Learned, it was to no purpose, for euerie Grammarian in this land hath learned his *Prosodia*, and alreadie knowes all this Arte of Numbers: if for the Ignorant, it was vaine: For if they become Versifiers, wee are like to haue leane Numbers, instede of fat Ryme: and if *Tully* would haue his Orator skilld in all the knowledges appertaining to God and man, what should they haue, who would be a degree aboue Orators? Why then it was to shew his owne skill, and what himselfe had obserued: so he might well haue done, without doing wrong to the fame of the liuing, and wrong to *England*, in seeking to lay reproach vppon her natiue ornaments, and to turne the faire streame and full course of her accents, into the shallow current of a lesse vncertaintie, cleane out of the way of her knowne delight. And I had thought it could neuer haue proceeded from the pen of a Scholler (who sees no profession free from the impure mouth of the scorner) to say the reproach of others idle tongues is the curse of Nature vpon us, when it is rather her curse vpon him, that knowes not how to vse his tongue. What, doth he think himselfe is now gotten so farre out of the way of contempt, that his numbers are gone beyond the reach of obloquie, and that how friuolous, or idle soeuer they shall runne, they shall be protected from disgrace, as though that light rymes and light numbers

d:d not weigh all alike in the graue opinion of the wise. And that it is
not Ryme, but our ydle Arguments that hath brought downe to so base
a reckning, the price and estimation of writing in this kinde. When the
few good things of this age, by comming together in one throng and
presse with the many bad, are not discerned from them, but ouer-looked
with them, and all taken to be alike. But when after-times shall make a
quest of inquirie, to examine the best of this Age, peraduenture there
will be found in the now contemned recordes of Ryme, matter not vn-
fitting the grauest Diuine, and seuerest Lawyer in this kingdome. But
these things must haue the date of Antiquitie, to make them reuerend
and authentical: For euer in the collation of Writers, men rather weigh
their age then their merite, *& legunt priscos cum reuerentia, quando
coetaneos non possunt sine inuidia.*[26] And let no writer in Ryme be any
way discouraged in his endeuour by this braue allarum, but rather animated to bring vp all the best of their powers, and charge withall the
strength of nature and industrie vpon contempt, that the shew of their
reall forces may turne backe insolencie into her owne holde.
For, be sure that innouation neuer workes any ouerthrow, but
vpon the aduantage of a carelesse idlenesse. And let this make vs
looke the better to our feete, the better to our matter, better to our maners. Let the Aduersary that thought to hurt vs, bring more profit and
honor, by being against vs, then if he had stoode still on our side. For
that (next to the awe of heauen) the best reine, the strongst hand to
make men keepe their way, is that which their enemy beares vpon them:
and let this be the benefite wee make by being oppugned, and the
meanes to redeeme back the good opinion, vanitie and idlenesse haue
suffered to be wonne from vs; which, nothing but substance and matter
can effect, for,

Scribendi rectè sapere est & principium & fons.[27]

When we heare Musicke, we must be in our eare, in the vtter-roome
of sense, but when we intertaine iudgement, we retire into the cabinet
and innermost withdrawing chamber of the soule: And it is but as
Musicke for the eare,

[26] "Read the ancients with reverence, since they are not able to read contemporaries without invidiousness." In the margin opposite this had been inscribed, *Simplicius longè posita miramur*, "What is far removed naturally arouses our wonder."

[27] "Of good writing, To know is the beginning and the well-source." Horace, *Art Poetica*, 309.

Verba sequi fidibus modulanda Latinis.[28]

but it is a worke of power for the soule.

Numerósque modósque ediscere vitæ.[29]

The most iudiciall and worthy spirites of this Land are not so delicate, or will owe so much to their eare, as to rest vppon the out-side of wordes, and be intertained with sound: seeing that both Number, Measure, and Ryme, is but as the ground or seate, whereupon is raised the work that commends it, and which may be easily at the first found out by any shallow conceipt: as wee see some fantasticke to beginne a fashion, which afterward grauity it selfe is faine to put on, because it will not be out of the weare of other men, and *Recti apud nos locum tenet error vbi publicus factus est.*[30] And power and strength that can plant itselfe any where, hauing built within this compasse, and reard it of so high a respect, wee now imbrace it as the fittest dwelling for our inuention, and haue thereon bestowed all the substance of our vnderstanding to furnish it as it is: and therefore heere I stand foorth, onelie to make good the place we haue thus taken vp, and to defend the sacred monuments erected therein, which containe the honour of the dead, the fame of the liuing, the glory of peace, and the best power of our speach, and wherin so many honorable spirits haue sacrificed to Memorie their dearest passions, shewing by what diuine influence they haue beene moued, and vnder what starres they liued.

But yet now notwithstanding all this which I haue heere deliuered in the defence of Ryme, I am not so farre in loue with mine owne mysterie, or will seeme so froward, as to bee against the reformation, and the better setling these measures of ours. Wherein there be many things, I could wish were more certaine and better ordered, though my selfe dare not take vpon me to be a teacher therein, hauing so much neede to learne of others. And I must confesse, that to mine owne eare, those continuall cadences of couplets vsed in long and continued Poemes, are very tyresome, and vnpleasing, by reason that still, me thinks, they runne on with a sound of one nature, and a kinde of certaintie which stuffs the delight rather then intertaines it. But yet notwithstanding, I must not out of mine owne daintinesse, condemne this kinde of writing,

---

[28] "To follow words measured to the Latin lyre." Horace, *Epist.* ii 2, 143.
[29] "To learn by heart the measures and the harmonies of life." Horace, *Epist.* ii 2, 144.
[30] "Wrong, when it becomes popular, holds the place of right among us."

which peraduenture to another may seeme most delightfull, and many worthy compositions we see to haue passed with commendation in that kinde. Besides, me thinkes sometimes, to beguile the eare, with a running out, and passing ouer the Ryme, as no bound to stay vs in the line where the violence of the matter will breake thorow, is rather grace-full then otherwise. Wherein I finde my *Homer-Lucan*, as if he gloried to seeme to haue no bounds, albeit hee were confined within his meas-ures, to be in my conceipt most happy. For so thereby, they who care not for Verse or Ryme, may passe it ouer without taking notice thereof, and please themselues with a well-measured Prose. And I must confesse my Aduersary hath wrought this much vpon me, that I thinke a Tra-gedie would indeede best comporte with a blank Verse, and dispence with Ryme, sauing in the *Chorus* or where a sentence shall require a couplet. And to auoyde this ouerglutting the eare with that always certaine, and ful incounter of Ryme, I haue assaid in some of my Epistles to alter the vsuall place of meeting, and to sette it further off by one Verse, to trie how I could disuse my owne eare and to ease it of this continuall burthen, which indeede seemes to surcharge it a little too much, but as yet I cannot come to please my selfe therein: this alternate or crosse Ryme holding still the best place in my affection.

Besides, to me this change of number in a Poem of one nature fits not so wel, as to mixe vncertainly, feminine Rymes with masculine, which, euer since I was warned of that deformitie by my kinde friend and countriman Maister *Hugh Samford,* I haue alwayes so auoyded it, as there are not aboue two couplettes in that kinde in all my Poem of the Ciuill warres: and I would willingly if I coulde, haue altered it in all the rest, holding feminine Rymes to be fittest for Ditties, and either to be set certaine, or else by themselues. But in these things, I say, I dare not take vpon mee to teach that they ought to be so, in respect my selfe holdes them to be so, or that I thinke it right; for indeede there is no right in these things that are continually in a wandring motion, carried with the violence of our vncertaine likings, being but onely the time that giues them their power. For if this right, or truth, should be no other thing then that wee make it, we shall shape it into a thousand figures, seeing this excellent painter Man, can so well lay the colours which himselfe grindes in his owne affections, as that hee will make them serue for any shadow, and any counterfeit. But the greatest hin-derer to our proceedings, and the reformation of our errours, is this Selfe-loue, whereunto we Versifiers are euer noted to be especially sub-iect; a disease of all other, the most dangerous, and incurable, being once seated in the spirits, for which there is no cure, but onely by a spirituall remedy. *Multos puto, ad sapientiam potuisse peruenire, nisi putassent se peruenisse:* [31] and this opinion of our sufficiencie makes so great a cracke in our iudgement, as it wil hardly euer holde any thing of worth. *Cæcus amor sui,*[32] and though it would seeme to see all without it, yet certainely it discernes but little within. For there is not the simplest writer that will euer tell himselfe, he doth ill, but as if he were the parasite onely to sooth his owne doings, perswades him that his lines can not but please others, which so much delight himselfe:

> *Suffenus est quisque sibi.* ——— *neque idem vnquam.*
> *Æque est beatus, ac poema cum scribit,*
> *Tam gaudet in se tamque se ipse miratur.*[33]

And the more to shew that he is so, we shall see him euermore in all places, and to all persons repeating his owne compositions: and,

> *Quem vero arripuit, tenet occiditque legendo.*[34]

Next to this deformitie stands our affectation, wherein we always bewray our selues to be both vnkinde, and vnnaturall to our owne natiue language, in disguising or forging strange or vnvsuall wordes, as if it were to make our verse seeme an other kind of speach out of the course of our vsuall practise, displacing our wordes, or inuesting new, onely vpon a singularitie: when our owne accustomed phrase, set in the due place, would expresse vs more familiarly and to better delight, than all this idle affectation of antiquitie, or noueltie can euer doe. And I can not but wonder at the strange presumption of some men that dare so audaciously aduenture to introduce any whatsoeuer forraine wordes, be they neuer so strange; and of themselues as it were, without a Parliament, without any consent, or allowance, establish them as Freedenizens in our language. But this is but a Character of that perpetuall reuolution which wee see to be in all things that neuer remaine the same, and we must heerein be content to submit our selues to the law of time, which in few yeeres wil make al that, for which we now contend, *Nothing.*

---

[31] "Many, I think, would have been able to arrive at wisdom, had they not thought themselves already arrived there."

[32] "Blind love of self." Horace, *Odes* I 14, 18.

[33] Catullus, *Poems* XXII. The first sentence, not in Catullus, is evidently of Daniel's improvisation. "Everyone is a Suffenus. He is never so happy as when writing poems, so much does he delight in himself, and admire."

[34] "Upon whomever he has once fastened, him he clings to, and kills with his reading." Horace, *Ars Poetica.* 475.

BEN JONSON

(1573–1637)

BORN in 1573, probably at Wesminster, Jonson was sent to the famous school at that place. That he ever went to Cambridge is mere supposition. He was for a while a brick-layer apprentice to his stepfather, and later saw military service in the Low Countries.

By 1592 he was married, and by 1597 had begun his long occupation with the drama. At first an actor, and probably a poor one, he brought forward in 1598 the famous *Every Man in his Humour,* in the first production of which Shakespeare took a part. His imprisonment and near hanging for killing another actor in a duel, and his literary quarrels with Dekker and Marston, must here pass with mere mention.

In 1603, with the coming of James I, he became interested in masques and pageants, and eleven masques were written during the next thirteen years. This same period saw Jonson's dramatic genius at its height. *Catiline, Volpone, The Silent Woman, The Alchemist, Bartholomew Fair,* and *The Devil is an Ass,* all came in these years.

It was several years after the last mentioned play (acted in 1616) before Jonson again turned to the stage. And the plays of the later years, like *The Staple of News* (1625), are uneven, though sometimes containing excellences.

The forty years from his earliest known connection with the stage till his death in 1637, are marked off fairly clearly by the dramas which he wrote; his non-dramatic works, the lyrics, epigrams, translations, and, most important for us, the prose jottings, can seldom be dated. *Discoveries* was not written until late in life; was not published until 1641, four years after his death.

With immense erudition, keen critical judgment, fearlessness and good sense, Ben Jonson was admirably equipped to be a great critic. But the body of his critical works is small, and that little consists mainly of occasional prefaces, the records kept by Drummond of Hawthornden of Jonson's conversations, and the *Discoveries.* His notes perished in the fire of 1623, "twice-twelve-years stor'd up humanitie," and these notes could never be replaced. But Jonson continued to write brief critical comments on literature in general, and on specific authors. Selections from his notebooks were published in 1641, under the title *Timber: or, Discoveries,* and with alternative titles, *Sylva,* and *Explorata.* Apparently Jonson had never decided upon one title; the generous editors included all.

The attacks and defenses of poetry and the more limited controversy over rhyme led, naturally enough, to surveys of English poetry. If William Webbe [*A Discourse of English Poetrie*, 1586] and Puttenham [*The Arte of English Poesie*, 1589] added little to criticism, Webbe gave a freshly enthusiastic tribute to Spenser as "the rightest English Poet that ever I read," and Puttenham wrote a methodical though uninspired work which attempted to present the subject historically. Comparative ratings of modern and ancient poets were popular, such as that of Francis Meres in his *Palladis Tamia*, 1598, which set "mellifluous and hony-tongued Shakspeare" as "among the English . . . the most excellent in both kinds for the stage."

There was much critical activity, and much drawing upon ancient doctrine. The medieval ideas were less popular, although Sir John Harrington [Preface to his translation of *Orlando Furioso*, 1591] accepted the medieval concept of the three meanings of poetry: "First of all for the litterall sence . . . they set downe in manner of an historie the acts of some persons worthy memorie: then in the same fiction . . . they place the Morall sence profitable for the active life of man, approving vertuous actions and condemning the contrarie. Manie times also under the self same words they comprehend some true understanding of naturall Philosophie, or sometimes of politike governement, and now and then of divinitie. . . ." A year earlier, in his prefatory letter to the *Faerie Queene,* Spenser had written that it was "a continued allegory, or darke conceit"; he also justified allegory neatly: "so much more profitable and gratious is doctrine by ensample, than by rule." And Spenser anticipates, in part, Bacon's objection to poetry: "the method of a poet historical is not such as of an historiographer. For the historiographer discourseth of affayres orderly as they were donne, accounting as well the times as the actions; but a poet thrusteth into the middest, even where it most concerneth him."

Francis Bacon was equally given to neat divisions; he wrote that "The parts of human learning have reference to the three parts of man's understanding, which is the seat of learning: History to his memory, Poesy to his imagination, and Philosophy to his reason." By his definition [*Of the Advancement of Learning*, 1605] poetry "is nothing else but Feigned History, which may be styled as well in prose as in verse." But Bacon is doubtful of allegorical poetry, though he admits its existence; the fable, he notes dryly, "doth fall out sometimes with great felicity. . . . I do rather think that the fable was first, and the exposition devised, than that the moral was first, and thereupon the fable framed." Even more directly, Ben Jonson expresses distrust of this allegorical interpretation of poetry. Spingarn writes [*Lit. Crit. in the Renaissance*, 278]: "The reason for this is obvious. The allegorical critics regarded the plot . . . as a mere sweet and pleasant covering for the wholesome but bitter pill of moral doctrine. The neo-classicists, limiting the sense and application of Aristotle's definition of poetry as an imitation of life, regarded the fable as the medium of this imitation, and the more perfect according as it became more truly and more minutely an image of human life."

Discoveries owes much to the classics, to Quintilian, Horace, Seneca, and others. Jonson's instructions on how to form a good style are directly paraphrased from Quintilian [*De Institutione Oratio*, X, 3, 4, 5], and numerous other passages are freely translated or adapted. Jonson also knew, and used, the criticism of Minturno, Scaliger, and Jacobus Pontanus, in the abstract made by Joannes Buehler. Mr. Spingarn [*Modern Philology*, II, 451–460] writes that "the whole of Jonson's final essay, 'Of the Magnitude and Compass of any Fable, Epic or Dramatic,' is a literal translation of the fourth chapter of Heinsius's treatise," that "the Discoveries were merely a commonplace book, in which Jonson recorded jottings." This seems unduly strong, since Jonson apparently intended to weave his translations, paraphrases, and personal ideas into a whole, but it is useful in indicating the influence of Dutch and German critics. Moreover, Jonson undoubtedly would have expected his readers to know the source of most, if not all, of these borrowings.

The earlier part deals with ethics rather than with literature. Then Jonson, with his strong classical leanings, attacks diffusiveness and formlessness: Spenser and euphuisms, Montaigne and essays in general, the irregularities and carelessness even of Shakespeare. Similarly he attacked the "Tamerlanes, and Tamer-chams, of the late age, which had nothing in them but the scenicall strutting, and furious vociferation, to warrant them then to the ignorant gapers." Francis Bacon receives high praise: "him who hath filled up all numbers, and performed that in our tongue which may be compared or preferred to insolent Greece or haughty Rome."

The general critical position of Ben Jonson is made apparent from the selections given in the text. He did not escape the classical limitation by any means, but he tempered that limitation with strong and fearless common sense. Though he required "exactness of study and multiplicity of reading" for his poets, the first and indispensable requisite was *ingenium* —natural wit. And his remarks on style are as applicable today as in the time of King James. He preferred "pure and neat English . . . , yet plaine and customary." The best style combined clear thinking, close reasoning, and lucid expression: "the congruent, and harmonious fitting of parts in a sentence, hath almost the fastning, and force of knitting, and connection: As in stones well squar'd, which will rise strong a great way without mortar."

Jonson's critical ability, considerable though it was, seems less important in *Discoveries* than his philosophy of life. "The finest sayings of the *Discoveries* do not relate to books or theories of art. They deal with life and conduct, and they reflect Jonson's sterling honesty and fearlessness." (*Ben Jonson*, ed. Herford and Simpson, II, 450.)

Yet it was no small achievement, as Saintsbury points out, to anticipate the precepts of Dryden, Pope, and Samuel Johnson; to stand for unity, order, classicism, in an age that stood for liberty, variety, and romance.

From

TIMBER: or, DISCOVERIES

Made upon Men and Matter: as they have flow'd out of his daily Readings; or had their refluxe to his peculiar Notion of the Times.

(1641)

I REMEMBER, the Players have often mentioned it as an honour to Shakespeare, that in his writing, (whatsoever he penn'd) hee never blotted out line. My answer hath beene, would he had blotted a

De Shake-speare nostrat.

thousand. Which they thought a malevolent speech. I had not told posterity this, but for their ignorance, who choose that circumstance to commend their friend by, wherein he most faulted. And to justifie mine owne candor, (for I lov'd the man, and doe honour his memory (on this side Idolatry) as much as any.) Hee was (indeed) honest, and of an open, and free nature: had an excellent *Phantsie;* brave notions, and gentle expressions: wherein hee flow'd with that facility, that some-

Augustus in Hat.

time it was necessary he should be stop'd: *Sufflaminandus erat;* as *Augustus* said of *Haterius.* His wit was in his owne power; would the rule of it had beene so too. Many times hee fell into those things, could not escape laughter: As when hee said in the person of *Cæsar,* one speaking to him; *Cæsar thou dost me wrong.* Hee replyed: *Cæsar did never wrong, but with just cause:* and such like, which were ridiculous. But hee redeemed his vices, with his vertues. There was ever more in him to be praysed, then to be pardoned.

For a man to write well, there are required three Necessaries. To reade the best Authors, observe the best Speakers: and much exercise of his owne style. In style to consider, what ought to be

De stylo, et optimo scribendi genere.

written: and after what manner: Hee must first thinke, and excogitate his matter; then choose his words, and examine the weight of either. Then take care in placing, and ranking both matter, and words, that the composition be comely; and to doe this with diligence, and often. No matter how slow the style be at first, so it be labour'd, and accurate; seeke the best, and be not glad of the forward conceipts, or first words, that offer themselves to us, but judge of what wee invent; and order what wee approve. Repeat often, what wee have formerly written; which beside, that it helpes the consequence, and makes the juncture better, it quickens the heate of imagination, that often cooles in the time of setting downe, and gives it new strength, as if it grew lustier, by the going back. As wee see in the contention of leaping, they jumpe farthest, that fetch their race largest: or, as in throwing a Dart, or Iavelin, wee force back our armes, to make our loose the stronger. Yet, if we have a faire gale of wind, I forbid not the steering out of our sayle, so the favour of the gale deceive us not. For all that wee invent doth please us in the conception, or birth;

else we would never set it downe. But the safest is to returne to our Judgement, and handle over againe those things, the easinesse of which might make them justly suspected. So did the best Writers in their beginnings; they impos'd upon themselves care, and industry. They did nothing rashly. They obtain'd first to write well, and then custome made it easie, and a habit. By little and little, their matter shew'd it selfe to 'hem more plentifully; their words answer'd, their composition followed; and all, as in a well-order'd family, presented it selfe in the place. So that the summe of all is: Ready writing makes not good writing: but good writing brings on ready writing: Yet when wee thinke wee have got the faculty, it is even then good to resist it: as to give a Horse a check sometimes with bit, which doth not so much stop his course, as stirre his mettle. Againe, whether a mans *Genius* is best able to reach thither, it should more and more contend, lift and dilate it selfe, as men of low stature, raise themselves on their toes; and so oft times get even, if not eminent. Besides, as it is fit for grown and able Writers to stand of themselves, and worke with their owne strength, to trust and endeavour by their owne faculties: so it is fit for the beginner, and learner, to study others, and the best. For the mind, and memory are more sharply exercis'd in comprehending an other mans things, and are familiar with the best Authors, shall ever and anon find somewhat of them in themselves, and in the expression of their minds, even when they feele it not, be able to utter something like theirs, which hath an Authority above their owne. Nay, sometimes it is the reward of a mans study, the praise of quoting an other man fitly: And though a man be more prone, and able for one kind of writing, then another, yet hee must exercise all. For as in an Instrument, so in style, there must be a Harmonie, and consent of parts.

WHAT IS A POET?

Poeta.   *A Poet* is that, which by the *Greeks* is call'd ἐξοχὴν, ὁ ποιητὴς, a Maker, or a fainer: His Art, an Art of imitation, of faining; expressing the life of man in fit measure, numbers, and harmony, according to Aristotle: From the word ποιεῖν, which signifies to make or fayne. Hence, hee is call'd a *Poet,* not hee which writeth in measure only; but that fayneth and formeth a fable, and writes things like the Truth. For, the Fable and Fiction is (as it were) the forme and Soule of any Poeticall worke, or Poeme.

WHAT MEANE YOU BY A POEME?

Poema
Virgilius.
Aeneid. lib
3. Martial
lib 8. epig. 19

A Poeme is not alone any worke, or composition of the Poets in many, or few verses; but even one alone verse sometimes makes a perfect Poeme. As, when Aeneas hangs up, and consecrates the Armes of Abas, with this Inscription:

Æneas hæc de Danais victoribus arma.[1]

and calls it a *Poeme*, or *Carmen*. Such are those in *Martiall*.

Horatius.
Lucretius.

Omnia, Castor, emis: sic fiet, ut omnia vendas.[2] And, *Pauper videri Cinna vult, est pauper.*[3] So were *Horace* his *Odes* call'd *Carmina;* his *Lirik,* Songs. And Lucretius designes a whole booke, in his sixt:

Quod in primo quoque carmine claret.[4]

Epicum
Dramaticum.
Liricum.
Elegiacum.
Epigramat.
Poesis.

And anciently, all the Oracles were call'd, *Carmina;* or, what ever Sentence was express'd, were it much, or little, it was call'd, an *Epick, Dramatick, Lirike, Elegiake,* or *Epigrammatike Poeme.*

BUT, HOW DIFFERS A POEME FROM WHAT WEE CALL POESY?

A Poeme, as I have told you is the worke of the Poet; the end, and fruit of his labour, and studye. *Poesy* is his skill, or Crafte of making: the very Fiction it selfe, the reason, or forme of the worke. And these three voices differ, as the thing done, the doing, and the doer; the thing fain'd, the faining, and the fainer: so the *Poeme,* the Poesy, and the

Artium
Regina.

Poet. Now, the *Poesy* is the habit, or the Art: nay, rather the Queene of Arts: which had her Originall from heaven, received thence from the 'Ebrewes, and had in prime estimation with the Greeks, transmitted to the Latines, and all Nations, that profess'd Civility. The Study of it (if wee will trust

Aristotle.

Aristotle) offers to mankinde a certaine rule, and Patterne of living well, and happily; disposing us to all

M. T. Cicero.

Civill offices of Society. If wee will beleive Tully, it

---

[1] "Aeneas [here places] these arms [taken] from the victorious Greeks."

[2] "You buy everything, Castor; and it shall come to pass—that you sell everything."

[3] "He wishes to appear a pauper, does Cinna: and he is a pauper."

[4] " t what was clear in the Beginning, be so in my song."

nourisheth, and instructeth our Youth; delights our Age; adornes our prosperity; comforts our Adversity; entertaines us at home; keepes us company abroad, travailes with us; watches; divides the times of our earnest, and sports; shares in our Country recesses, and recreations; insomuch as the wisest, and best learned have thought her the absolute Mistresse of manners; and neerest of kin to Vertue. And, wheras they entitle *Philosophy* to bee a rigid, and austere *Poesie:* they have (on the contrary) stiled *Poesy,* a dulcet, and gentle *Philosophy,* which leades on, and guides us by the hand to Action, with a ravishing delight, and incredible Sweetnes. But, before wee handle the kindes of *Poems,* with

Poet: differentiae. Grammatica. Logic. Rhetoric. Ethica.
their speciall differences: or make court to the Art it selfe, as a Mistresse, I would leade you to the knowledge of our Poet, by a perfect Information, what he is, or should bee by nature, by exercise, by imitation, by Studie; and so bring him downe through the disciplines of Grammar, Logicke, Rhetoricke, and the Ethicks, adding somewhat, out of all, peculiar to himselfe, and worthy of your Admittance, or reception.

Ingenium.
First, wee require in our *Poet,* or maker, (for that Title our Language affordes him, elegantly, with the *Greeke*) a goodnes of naturall wit. For, wheras all other Arts consist of Doctrine, and Precepts; the *Poet* must bee able by nature, and in-

Seneca.
stinct, to powre out the Treasure of his minde; and, as *Seneca* saith, *Aliquando secundum Anacreontem insanire jucundum esse:* [5] by which hee understands, the *Poeticall Rapture.* And

Plato.
according to that of *Plato; Frustra Poeticas fores sui compos pulsavit:* [6] And of *Aristotle; Nullum magnum*

Aristotle.
ingenium sine mixtura dementiae fuit. Nec potest grande aliquid, & supra caeteros loqui, nisi mota mens. [7] Then it riseth higher, as by a devine Instinct, when it contemnes common, and knowne conceptions. It utters somewhat above a mortall mouth. Then it gets a loft, and flies away with his Ryder, whether, before, it was doubtfull to

Helicon. Pegasus. Parnassus. Ovidius.
ascend. This the Poets understood by their *Helicon, Pegasus,* or *Parnassus;* and this made *Ovid* to boast:

Est, Deus in nobis; agitante calescimus illo:
Sedibus æthereis spiritus ille venit. [8]

[5] "Sometimes it is delightful to rave, a second Anacreon."
[6] "One who is master of himself beats against the poetic doors in vain."
[7] "There has been no great genius without a mixture of madness. Nor can there be anything sublime [*grande*]—to name above other things, unless the mind be excited."
[8] "There is a god in us; we grow hot at his urging: from the ethereal abodes that spirit comes."

Lipsius. And *Lipsius*, to affirme; *Scio, Poetam neminem praestantem fuisse,sine parte quadam uberiore divinae aurae.*[9]
And, hence it is, that the comming up of good Poets, (for I minde not *mediocres*, or *imos*) is so thinne and rare among us; Every beggerly Corporation affoords the State a *Major*, or two *Bailiffs*, yearly: but, *solus Rex, aut Poeta, non quotannis nascitur.*[10] To this per-
Petron. in fragm. 2. Exercitatio. fection of Nature in our *Poet*, wee require Exercise of those parts, and frequent. If his wit will not arrive soddainly at the dignitie of the Ancients, let him not yet fall out with it, quarrell, or be over hastily Angry: offer, to turne it away from Study, in a humor; but come to it againe upon better cogitation; try an other time, with labour. If then it succeed not, cast not away the Quills, yet: nor scratch the Wainescott, beate not the poore Deske; but bring all to the forge, and file, againe; tourne it a newe. There is no Statute *Law* of the Kingdome bids you bee a Poet, against your will; or the first Quarter. If it come, in a yeare, or two, it is well. The common Rymers powre forth Verses, such as they are, (*ex tempore*) but there never come from them one Sense, worth the life of a Day. A Rymer, and a *Poet*, are two things. It is said of the incomparable
Virgill. Scaliger. *Virgil,* that he brought forth his verses like a Beare, and after form'd them with licking. *Scaliger,* the Father, writes it of him, that he made a quantitie of verses in the morning, which a fore night hee reduced to a lesse number. But, that which
Valer. Maximus. Euripides. Alcestis. *Valerius Maximus* hath left recorded of *Euripides, the tragicke Poet,* his answer to *Alcestis,* an other *Poet,* is as memorable, as modest: who, when it was told to Alcestis, that *Euripides* had in three daies brought forth, but three verses, and those with some difficultie, and throwes: *Alcestis,* glorying hee could with ease have sent forth a hundred in the space; *Euripides* roundly repl'd, like enough. But, here is the difference; Thy verses will not last those three daies; mine will to all time. Which was, as to tell him; he could not write a verse. I have met many of these Rattles, that made a noyse, and buz'de. They had their humme; and, no more. Indeed, things, wrote with labour, deserve to be so read, and will last their Age. The third requisite in our

---

[9] "I know that no poet has been illustrious who had not in him an abundant portion of the *divine breath." Divina aura* might correctly enough be translated "inspiration," the commonly accepted term for what the author means. But the literal rendering has seemed too interesting to be varied, revealing part of that course by which "inspiration" arrived out of *inspirare*, "to breathe into."

[10] "It is only King, or Poet, who is not born every year."

3. Imitatio.

Poet, or *Maker,* is *Imitation,* to bee able to convert the substance, or Riches of an other *Poet,* to his owne use. To make choise of one excellent man above the rest, and so to follow him, till he grow very *Hee:* or, so like him, as the Copie may be mistaken for the Principall. Not, as a Creature, that swallowes, what it takes in, crude, raw, or indigested; but, that feedes with an Appetite, and hath a Stomacke to concoct, devide, and turne all into nourishment. Not, to imitate servilely, as *Horace* saith, and catch at vices, for vertue: but, to draw forth out of the best, and choisest flowers, with the Bee, and turne all into Honey, worke it into one relish, and savour: make our *Imitation* sweet: observe, how the best writers have imitated, and follow them. How *Virgil,* and *Statius* have imitated *Homer:* how *Horace, Archilochus;* how *Alcaeus,* and the other *Liricks:* and so of the rest. But, that, which wee especially require in him is an exactness of Studie, and multiplicity of reading, which maketh a full man, not alone enabling him to know the *History,* or Argument of a *Poeme,* and to report it: but so to master the matter, and Stile, as to shew, hee knowes, how to handle, place, or dispose of either, with elegancie, when need shall bee. And not thinke, hee can leape forth suddainely a Poet, by dreaming hee hath been in *Parnassus,* or, having washt his lipps (as they say) in *Helicon.* There goes more to his making, then so. For to Nature, Exercise, Imitation, and Studie, *Art* must bee added, to make all these perfect. And, though these challenge to themselves much, in the making up of our Maker, it is Art only can lead him to perfection, and leave him there in possession, as planted by her hand.

Horatius.

Virgilius.
Statius.
Homer.
Horat.
Archil.
Alceus.
4. Lectio.

Parnassus.
Helicon.
Ars coron.

OF THE MAGNITUDE, AND COMPASSE OF ANY FABLE,
EPICKE, OR DRAMATICK

What the measure of a Fable is. The Fable, or Plott of a Poeme, defin'd.

To the resolving of this *Question,* wee must first agree in the definition of the Fable. The Fable is call'd the *Imitation* of one intire, and perfect Action; whose parts are so joyned, and knitt together, as nothing in the structure can be chang'd; or taken away, without imparing, or troubling the whole; of which there is a proportionable magnitude in the members. As for example; if a man would build a house, he would first appoint a place to build it in, which he would define within certaine bounds: So in the Constitution of a *Poeme,* the Action is aym'd at by the *Poet,* which answers Place in a building; and that Action hath his largenesse, compasse, and proportion. But, as a Court of Kings Palace requires other dimensions then a private house: So the *Epick* askes a magnitude, from other Poëms. Since, what is Place in the one, is Action in the other, the difference is in space. So that by this definition wee conclude the fable, to be the *imitation* of one perfect, and intire Action; as one perfect, and intire place is requir'd to a building. By perfect, wee understand that, to which nothing is wanting; as Place to the building, that is rais'd, and Action to the fable, that is form'd. It is perfect, perhaps, not for a Court, or Kings Palace, which requires a greater ground; but for the structure wee would raise, so the space of the Action, may not prove large enough for the *Epick Fable,* yet bee perfect for the *Dramatick,* and whole.

The Epick fable.

differing

from the Dramaticke. What wee understand by Whole.

Whole, wee call that, and perfect, which hath a *beginning,* a *mid'st,* and an *end.* So the place of any building may be whole, and intire, for that worke; though too little for a palace. As, to a *Tragedy* or a *Comedy,* the Action may be convenient, and perfect, that would not fit an *Epicke Poeme* in Magnitude. So a Lion is a perfect creature in himselfe, though it bee lesse, then that of a *Buffalo,* or a *Rhinocerote.* They differ, but in *specie:* either in the kinde is absolute. Both have their parts, and either the whole. Therefore, as in every body; so in every Action, which is the subject of a just worke, there is requir'd a certaine proportionable greatnesse, neither too vast, nor too minute. For that which happens to the Eyes, when wee behold a body, the same happens to the Memorie, when wee contemplate an action. I looke upon a monstrous Giant, as *Tityus,* whose body cover'd nine Acres of Land, and mine eye stickes upon every part; the whole that consists of those parts, will never be taken in at one intire view. So in a *Fable,* if the Action be too great wee can never comprehend the whole together in our Imagination. Againe, if it be too little, there ariseth no pleasure out of the object, it affords the view no stay: It is beheld and vanisheth at once. As if wee should looke upon an Ant or Pismyre, the parts fly the sight, and the whole considered is almost nothing. The same happens in Action, which is the object of Memory, as the body is of sight. Too vast oppresseth the Eyes, and exceeds the Memory: too little scarce admits either.

Now, in every Action it behooves the *Poet* to know
which is his utmost bound, how farre with fitnesse, and
a necessary proportion, he may produce, and determine
it. That is, till either good fortune change into the worse,
or the worse into the better. For as a body without proportion cannot
be goodly, no more can the Action, either in Comedy, or Tragedy without
his fit bounds. And every bound for the nature of the Subject, is
esteem'd the best that is largest, till it can increase no more: so it behooves the Action in *Tragedy,* or *Comedy,* to be let grow, till the
necessity aske a Conclusion: wherin two things are to be considered:
First, that it exceed not the compasse of one Day: Next, that there be
place left for digression, and Art. For the *Episodes,* and digressions in
a Fable, are the same that household stuffe, and other furniture are in
a house. And so farre for the measure, and extent of a *Fable Dramaticke.*

What the utmost bound of a fable.

Now, that it should be one, and intire. One is considerable two waies: either, as it is only separate, and by
it self: or as being compos'd of many parts, it beginnes
to be one, as those parts grow, or are wrought together. That it should
be one the first way alone, and by it self, no man that hath tasted letters
ever would say, especially having required before a just Magnitude, and
equall Proportion of the parts in themselves. Neither of which can
possibly bee, if the Action be single and separate, not compos'd of
parts, which laid together in themselves, with an equall and fitting
proportion, tend to the same end; which thing out of Antiquitie it
selfe, hath deceiv'd many; and more this Day it doth deceive.

What by one, and intire.

NICHOLAS BOILEAU-DESPRÉAUX

(1636-1711)

BORN in Paris in 1636, Nicholas Boileau was educated at the University of Beauvais for the legal profession. He soon deserted the law for the church, even more quickly deserted the church for literature. In 1660 a volume of his satires, *Adieus of a Poet to the City of Paris,* was published, quickly followed by other satires and parodies on Chapelain, Quinalt, Scuderi, and others. For these poems, he received a pension, and was made historiographer, along with Racine. His prose work, *Dialogue des heros de Roman* (1664), satirized the elaborate romances of the time. From 1669 on appeared the epistles; in 1674 *L'Art Poetique,* for which he is chiefly remembered today, and *Le Lutrin,* a mock heroic poem which furnished the model for *The Rape of the Lock.* Also in 1674 he published his translation of Longinus' *On the Sublime.* In his later years Boileau suffered much from ill health, and produced only occasional poems. He died in 1711.

The poet Boileau had little influence on English literature, hardly more influence on French; the critic Boileau vitally influenced the work of greater creative writers. He gave authority to critical catchwords, "reason and good sense," that were to dominate the minds of Eighteenth Century poets and critics. Though he translated *On the Sublime,* he has seemed to many critics to give the quality of sublimity little place in his creed, so little that Saintsbury [*Hist. of Crit.,* II, 281] has labelled the essay "that elaborately arranged code of neo-classic correctness." S. H. Monk [*The Sublime,* 28-32] disagrees completely; he writes that "the Longinus who is of value for this study is really the creation of Boileau. . . . He points out that by *sublime* Longinus did not mean what orators call the sublime style, but that extraordinary and marvellous quality . . . which strikes in a discourse, and which enables a work to elevate, ravish, and transport. . . . Thus at one blow the sublime is severed from rhetoric and becomes art, a matter of the revelation of a quality of thought and the emotions which that quality, vividly presented, evokes."

M. Ferdinand Brunetière has written of Boileau as being representative of French literary genius. From the historical point of view, at least, his work seems to catch up many diverse elements of French criticism, and to give a rounded statement of humanistic ideas. Some of these earlier and contemporary divergencies and similarities are worth noting. The sixteenth century critics had borrowed liberally from the Italians, and sometimes directly from Aristotle and Horace: Jodelle had imbedded in a speech in his tragedy *Cleopâtre* (1552) the unity of time ("Before the sun . . . has traced one day, Cleopatra dies"); Thomas Sibillet [*Art Poétique,* 1548] had daringly noted that the French Morality play "is in some ways like the Greek and Latin tragedy, mainly in that it treats grave and important subjects"; but Jean de la Taille [*Art de la tragédie,* 1572] takes as his final authority what "the great Aristotle in his *Poetics,* and after him Horace though not with the same subtlety, have said more amply and better than I"—though he borrowed his theory of the Unities from Castelvetro, and flatly denied that France had any real tragedies.

But this reliance on authority did not go unchallenged. Jacques Grévin [*Bref Discours pour l'intelligence de ce théâtre,* 1562] wrote that "Our tragedies have been so perfectly polished that they now leave nothing to be desired,—I speak of those which are composed according to the rules of Aristotle and Horace"; but Grévin substituted a group of soldiers for a chorus in his *Mort de Caesar,* on the amusing ground that singing at a tragedy is not true to life, and that "different nations require different ways of doing things." By 1598 Pierre de Laudun was arguing against the Unities, in his *Art Poétique;* and in 1601 Alexandre Hardy published an irregular drama, *Les Amours de Théagène et Cariclée,* with the prefatory defense that "everything which is approved by usage and public taste is legitimate." French theorists drew upon the Spanish, as did the dramatists; the most thoroughgoing defense of a free dramatic form is to be found in François Ogier's Preface to a play by Jean de Schélandre [*Tyr et Sidon,* 1628]. The play defied the rules, and Ogier defended the play vigorously; he appealed from the Ancients to Nature: "the putting off of no action to an imaginary tomorrow" led to implausible absurdities, and the constant use of messengers to explain happenings off-stage "is more suitable to a fair inn than to a good tragedy." By Ogier's time, however, Malherbe had come, to check the incipient romanticism.

Malherbe's criticism (especially in his *Commentaire sur Desportes,* 1606) is largely verbal and linguistic; he worked mainly through marginal notes, and by one line he would write "padding," by another "Will the reader believe," or "vieillard stupide." Literary historians have recognized his great influence without finding an adequate body of criticism to explain it; he was, as his contemporary Guez de Balzac described him, "a tyrant of words and of syllables." But his work was concrete and comprehensible; Spingarn writes justly of it [*Lit. Crit. in the Renaissance,* 238–39]: "His reforms were all in the direction of that verbal and mechanical perfection, the love of which is innate in the French nature. . . . He eliminated from French verse hiatus, enjambement, inversions, false and imperfect rhymes, and licenses or cacophonies of all kinds. He gave it, as has been said, mechanical perfection."

Even more powerful than Malherbe were Cardinal Richelieu and the newly formed French Academy (1634). Possibly because of Richelieu's jealousy of Corneille, the Academy was led into the notorious controversy over *Le Cid* (for Corneille's theories, see the Supplement). The play was violently attacked by Georges de Scudéry in his *Observations sur le Cid* for its violations of the rules; Corneille replied, and Jean Chapelain prepared for the Academy its official judgment, *Les Sentiments de l'Académie françoise sur la Tragi-Comédie du Cid* (1637), in which Chapelain—for the work seems to have been entirely his—stated "it is impossible that there can be pleasure contrary to reason, unless it be to a depraved taste." But Chapelain's criticism is, as Saintsbury puts it, "strictly *civil*"; and he defended the Arthurian romances: he would hold the drama, but not all of poetry, to the strictest rules. Pierre Mambrun [*De Poemate Epico*, 1652] extends this rigidity to the epic, although he makes some provision for poetic fury. The later critic René le Bossu [*Traité du poème épique*, 1680] extends this criticism without greatly extending its scope: "in the magnificent books of the Ancients we must seek the foundations" of the art of epic poetry; and he goes back to Aristotle and Horace for precepts, to Homer and Virgil for "the best models that have ever appeared in this genre." With Mambrun's work, in fact, the critical case for neo-classicism is extended to all phases of creative writing; only authority was lacking.

It remains a disputed point as to whether Rapin and Boileau gave final authority to this code, or represented the humanistic and therefore more liberal phase. In the quarrel between Ancients and Moderns they were definitely classicists. To René Rapin [*Réflexions sur la poétique*, 1672; his critical works were collected in an English edition in 1705] poetry is not bounded by rules: "There is a certain *Je ne sais quoi* in the numbers which is understood by few, and notwithstanding gives great delight in poetry . . . true poetry is not perceived but by the impression it makes on the soul; it is not as it should be unless it goes to the heart." To him the rules are founded on "good sense and sound reason," and "no man can be a poet without genius; the want of which no art or industry can repair." Rapin denied that madness was essential to the character of poetry, or of the poet, but he also stated that "there are no precepts to teach the hidden graces, the insensible charms, and all that secret power of poetry which passes to the heart." The ideas of Rapin are much like those of Boileau: basically, as Austin Warren has noted [*Alexander Pope*, 20] their "point of view attempts . . . to synthesize the doctrines of all the 'schools'—rationalism, classicism, and the cult of 'taste.'"

In common with all the early writers of *Arts of Poetry*, Boileau gave a rapid, and in many cases an inaccurate, history of his native literature. He attributed an ignorance to earlier French poets, especially with regard to prosody, which an examination of their work will not sustain. Villon, Marot, and others wrote in forms as strict as the classical models which Boileau desired French poets to use.

Early in the poem, Boileau advises poets to study themselves, to realize that genius for one mode of writing does not imply genius for every form. Good sense and reason must govern, and the wise poet must neither attempt to scale too great heights, nor descend to low vulgarities. For the various types of poetry, Boileau recommended the imitation of specific classic authors for specific types. Similarly, for the drama, he advised close adherence to the precepts of Aristotle, though he accepted the later and more rigorous interpretations of those precepts as truly Aristotelian.

The entire essay is in the tradition laid down by Aristotle, Horace, and Vida. Boileau adapted old tenets to fit his times, but those tenets were absolute. M. Brunetière (*L'Art Poétique*, edited F. Brunetière) considers that Boileau was not only "satirical and critical," but also "didactic," and that this both helped and hampered French authors. Professor Spingarn, relying partly on Brunetière, gives an excellent summary (Spingarn, *Literary Criticism in the Renaissance*, 134–35): "Boileau carried the neo-classical ideal of nature and art to its ultimate perfection. According to him, nothing is beautiful that is not true, and nothing is true that is not in nature. Truth, for classicism, is the final test of everything, including beauty; and hence to be beautiful poetry must be founded on nature. Nature should therefore be the poet's sole study, although for Boileau, as for Vida, nature is one with the court and the city. Now, in what way can we discover exactly how to imitate nature, and perceive whether or not we have imitated it correctly? Boileau finds the guide to the correct imitation of nature, and the very test of its correctness, in the imitation of the classics. The ancients are great, not because they are old, but because they are true, because they knew how to see and to imitate nature; and to imitate antiquity is therefore to use the best means the human spirit has ever found for expressing nature in its perfection. The advance of Boileau's theory on that of Vida and Scaliger is therefore that he founded the rules and literary practice of classical literature on reason and nature, and showed that there is nothing arbitrary in the authority of the ancients. For Vida, nature is to be followed on the authority of the classics; for Boileau, the classics are to be followed on the authority of nature and reason."

Later critics, perhaps too much influenced by romanticism, have almost invariably attacked Boileau's theories. Irving Babbitt (*New Laokoon*, 40–41) has written the ablest and most authoritative defense: ". . . Boileau, who under certain romantic obsessions has come to be looked on as an arch-formalist, was in reality the leader of a reaction against formalism. Few contrasts, indeed, are more surprising than that between the real Boileau and Boileau the romantic bugaboo. Boileau was simply a wit and man of the world, not especially logical or imaginative or profound, but with an admirable integrity of character and an extraordinarily keen and correct sensibility. . . . Boileau's message to the authors of his time was simple: It is proper and indeed necessary for you to obey the rules, but at best the rules have only a negative virtue: the really important matter is that you should interest us."

THE ART OF POETRY *

(1680) (1683)

CANTO I

RASH author, 'tis a vain presumptuous crime,
To undertake the sacred art of rhyme;
If at thy birth the stars that ruled thy sense
Shone not with a poetic influence,
In thy strait genius thou wilt still be bound,
Find Phoebus deaf, and Pegasus unsound.

   You, then, that burn with the desire to try
The dangerous course of charming poetry,
Forbear in fruitless verse to lose your time,
Or take for genius the desire of rhyme;   10
Fear the allurements of a specious bait,
And well consider your own force and weight.

   Nature abounds in wits of every kind,
And for each author can a talent find.
One may in verse describe an amorous flame,
Another sharpen a short epigram;
Waller [1] a hero's mighty acts extol,
Spenser [2] sing Rosalind in pastoral:
But authors, that themselves too much esteem,
Lose their own genius, and mistake their theme;   20
Thus in times past Dubartas [3] vainly writ,
Allaying sacred truth with trifling wit;
Impertinently, and without delight,
Described the Israelites triumphant flight;
And, following Moses o'er the sandy plain,
Perished with Pharaoh in the Arabian main.

    Whate'er you write of pleasant or sublime,
Always let sense accompany your rhyme.
Falsely they seem each other to oppose;
Rhyme must be made with reason's laws to close;   30

---

* Translated by Sir William Soame and John Dryden.

[1] Malherbe. This, and the following examples were drawn by Boileau from the French. Dryden has selected English poets who approximate somewhat the position of the French models. The original authors will be indicated in each case.

[2] Racan.

[3] Faret.

And when to conquer her you bend your force,
The mind will triumph in the noble course.
To reason's yoke she quickly will incline,
Which, far from hurting, renders her divine;
But if neglected, will as easily stray,
And master reason, which she should obey.
Love reason then; and let whate'er you write
Borrow from her its beauty, force, and light.
Most writers mounted on a resty muse,   40
Extravagant and senseless objects chuse;
They think they err, if in their verse they fall
On any thought that's plain or natural.
Fly this excess; and let Italians be
Vain authors of false glittering poetry.
All ought to aim at sense; but most in vain
Strive the hard pass and slippery path to gain;
You drown, if to the right or left you stray;
Reason to go has often but one way.
Sometimes an author, fond of his own thought,
Pursues its object till it's over wrought: 50
If he describes a house, he shews the face,
And after walks you round from place to place;
Here is a vista, there the doors unfold,
Balconies here are ballustred with gold;
Then counts the rounds and ovals in the halls,
"The festoons, freezes, and the astragals:"
Tired with his tedious pomp, away I run,
And skip o'er twenty pages, to be gone.
Of such descriptions the vain folly see,
And shun their barren superfluity.   60
All that is needless carefully avoid;
The mind once satisfied is quickly cloyed:
He cannot write, who knows not to give o'er;
To mend one fault, he makes a hundred more:
A verse was weak, you turn it much too strong,
And grow obscure for fear you should be long.
Some are not gaudy, but are flat and dry;
Not to be low, another soars too high.
Would you of every one deserve the praise?
In writing vary your discourse and phrase;   70

A frozen style, that neither ebbs nor flows,
Instead of pleasing, makes us gape and dose.
Those tedious authors are esteemed by none
Who tire us, humming the same heavy tone.
Happy who in his verse can gently steer,
From grave to light; from pleasant to severe:
His works will be admired wherever found,
And oft with buyers will be compassed round.
In all you write, be neither low nor vile;
The meanest theme may have a proper style.   80
   The dull burlesque appeared with impudence,
And pleased by novelty in spite of sense.
All, except trivial points, grew out of date;
Parnassus spoke the cant of Billingsgate; [4]
Boundless and mad, disordered rhyme was seen;
Disguised Apollo changed to Harlequin.
This plague, which first in country towns began,
Cities and kingdoms quickly over-ran;
The dullest scribblers some admirers found,
And the "Mock Tempest" was a while renowned.[5] 90
But this low stuff the town at last despised,
And scorned the folly that they once had prized;
Distinguished dull from natural and plain,
And left the villages to Flecknoe's reign.[6]
Let not so mean a style your muse debase,
But learn from Butler the buffooning grace; [7]
And let burlesque in ballads be employed,
Yet noisy bombast carefully avoid;
Nor think to raise, though on Pharsalia's plain,
"Millions of mourning mountains of the slain."   100
Nor with Dubartas bridle up the floods,
And periwig with wool the baldpate woods.
Chuse a just style; be grave without constraint,
Great without pride, and lovely without paint:
Write what your reader may be pleased to hear,
And for the measure have a careful ear.
   On easy numbers fix your happy choice;

---

[4] *le langage des halles.*
[5] D'Assouci. The English author of
"Mock Tempest" was Duffet.

[6] *Typhon*, by Scarron.
[7] Marot.

Of jarring sounds avoid the odious noise:
The fullest verse, and the most laboured sense,
Displease us, if the ear once take offence.   110
Our ancient verse, as homely as the times,
Was rude, unmeasured, only tagged with rhymes;
Number and cadence, that have since been shown,
To those unpolished writers were unknown.
Fairfax [8] was he, who, in that darker age,
By his just rules restrained poetic rage;
Spenser [9] did next in pastorals excel,
And taught the noble art of writing well;
To stricter rules the stanza did restrain,
And found for poetry a richer vein.   120
Then D'Avenant [10] came, who, with a new-found art,
Changed all, spoiled all, and had his way apart;
His haughty muse all others did despise,
And thought in triumph to bear off the prize,
'Till the sharp-sighted critics of the times,
In their Mock-Gondibert,[11] exposed his rhymes;
The laurels he pretended did refuse,
And dashed the hopes of his aspiring muse.
This headstrong writer falling from on high,
Made following authors take less liberty.   130
Waller came last,[12] but was the first whose art
Just weight and measure did to verse impart;
That of a well-placed word could teach the force,
And shewed for poetry a nobler course;
His happy genius did our tongue refine,
And easy words with pleasing numbers join;
His verses to good method did apply,
And changed hard discord to soft harmony.
All owned his laws; which, long approved and tried,
To present authors now may be a guide.   140
Tread boldly in his steps, secure from fear,
And be, like him, in your expressions clear.
If in your verse you drag, and sense delay,
My patience tires, my fancy goes astray;

[8] Villon.
[9] Marot.
[10] Ronsard.
[11] Work ridiculing D'Avenant's *Gondi-*bert. French originals, Desportes and Bertaut.
[12] *Enfin Malherbe vint.*

And from your vain discourse I turn my mind,
Nor search an author troublesome to find.
There is a kind of writer pleased with sound,
Whose fustian head with clouds is compassed round,
No reason can disperse them with its light:
Learn then to think ere you pretend to write.   156
As your idea's clear, or else obscure,
The expression follows perfect or impure:
What we conceive with ease we can express;
Words to the notions flow with readiness.

   Observe the language well in all you write,
And swerve not from it in your loftiest flight.
The smoothest verse, and the exactest sense,
Displease us, if ill English give offence:
A barbarous phrase no reader can approve;
Nor bombast, noise, or affectation love.   160
In short, without pure language, what you write
Can never yield us profit or delight.
Take time for thinking; never work in haste;
And value not yourself for writing fast.
A rapid poem, with such fury writ,
Shews want of judgement, not abounding wit.
More pleased we are to see a river lead
His gentle streams along a flowery mead,
Than from high banks to hear loud torrents roar,
With foamy waters on a muddy shore.   170
Gently make haste, of labour not afraid;
A hundred times consider what you've said:
Polish, repolish, every colour lay,
And sometimes add, but oftener take away.
'Tis not enough, when swarming faults are writ,
That here and there are scattered sparks of wit:
Each object must be fixed in the due place,
And differing parts have corresponding grace;
Till, by a curious art disposed, we find
One perfect whole, of all the pieces joined.   180
Keep to your subject close in all you say;
Nor for a sounding sentence ever stray.
The public censure for your writings fear,
And to yourself be critic most severe.

Fantastic wits their darling follies love;
But find you faithful friends that will reprove,
That on your works may look with careful eyes,
And of your faults be zealous enemies:
Lay by an author's pride and vanity,
And from a friend a flatterer descry,   190
Who seems to like, but means not what he says:
Embrace true counsel, but suspect false praise.
A sycophant will every thing admire;
Each verse, each sentence sets his soul on fire:
All is divine! there's not a word amiss!
He shakes with joy, and weeps with tenderness;
He overpowers you with his mighty praise.
Truth never moves in those impetuous ways;
A faithful friend is careful of your fame,
And freely will your heedless errors blame;   200
He cannot pardon a neglected line,
But verse to rule and order will confine;
Reprove of words the too-affected sound;—
Here the sense flags, and your expression's round,
Your fancy tires, and your discourse grows vain,
Your terms improper; make it just and plain.—
Thus 'tis a faithful friend will freedom use;
But authors, partial to their darling muse,
Think to protect it they have just pretence,
And at your friendly counsel take offence.—   210
Said you of this, that the expression's flat?
Your servant, sir, you must excuse me that,
He answers you.—This word has here no grace,
Pray leave it out;—that, sir's the properest place.—
This turn I like not;—'tis approved by all.
Thus, resolute not from one fault to fall,
If there's a syllable of which you doubt,
'Tis a sure reason not to blot it out.
Yet still he says you may his faults confute,
And over him your power is absolute.   220
But of his feigned humility take heed;
'Tis a bait laid to make you hear him read.
And when he leaves you happy in his muse,
Restless he runs some other to abuse,

And often finds; for in our scribbling times
No fool can want a sot to praise his rhymes.
The flattest work has ever in the court
Met with some zealous ass for its support;
And in all times a forward scribbling fop
Has found some greater fool to cry him up.   230

CANTO II

PASTORAL

As a fair nymph, when rising from her bed,
With sparkling diamonds dresses not her head,
But without gold, or pearl, or costly scents,
Gathers from neighbouring fields her ornaments;
Such, lovely in its dress, but plain withal,
Ought to appear a perfect Pastoral.
Its humble method nothing has of fierce,
But hates the rattling of a lofty verse;
There native beauty pleases, and excites,
And never with harsh sounds the ear affrights.   240
But in this style a poet often spent,
In rage throws by his rural instrument,
And vainly, when disordered thoughts abound,
Amidst the Eclogue makes the trumpet sound:
Pan flies alarmed into the neighbouring woods,
And frighted nymphs dive down into the floods,
Opposed to this, another, low in style,
Makes shepherds speak a language base and vile:
His writings, flat and heavy, without sound,
Kissing the earth, and creeping on the ground,   250
You'd swear that Randal,[18] in his rustic strains,
Again was quavering to the country swains,
And changing, without care of sound or dress,
Strephon and Phyllis, into Tom and Bess.
'Twixt these extremes 'tis hard to keep the right;
For guides take Virgil, and read Theocrite:
Be their just writings, by the Gods inspired,

[18] Ronsard.

Your constant pattern, practised and admired.
By them alone you'll easily comprehend
How poets, without shame, may condescend   260
To sing of gardens, fields, of flowers and fruit,
To stir up shepherds, and to tune the flute;
Of love's rewards to tell the happy hour,
Daphne a tree, Narcissus made a flower,
And by what means the Eclogue yet has power
To make the woods worthy a conqueror:
This of their writings is the grace and flight;
Their risings lofty, yet not out of sight.

ELEGY

  The Elegy, that loves a mournful style,
With unbound hair weeps at a funeral pile;   270
It paints the lover's torments and delights,
A mistress flatters, threatens, and invites:
But well these raptures if you'll make us see,
You must know love as well as poetry.
I hate those lukewarm authors, whose forced fire
In a cold style describes a hot desire;
That sigh by rule, and, raging in cold blood,
Their sluggish muse whip to an amorous mood:
Their feigned transports appear but flat and vain;
They always sigh, and always hug their chain,   280
Adore their prison, and their sufferings bless,
Make sense and reason quarrel as they please.
'Twas not of old in this affected tone,
That smooth Tibullus made his amorous moan;
Nor Ovid, when instructed from above,
By nature's rules he taught the art of love.
The heart in Elegies forms the discourse.

ODE

  The Ode is bolder, and has greater force;
Mounting to heaven in her ambitious flight,
Amongst the Gods and heroes takes delight;   290

Of Pisa's wrestlers tells the sinewy force,
And sings the dusty conqueror's glorious course;
To Simois' streams does fierce Achilles bring,
And makes the Ganges bow to Britain's king.[14]
Sometimes she flies like an industrious bee,
And robs the flowers by nature's chemistry,
Describes the shepherd's dances, feasts, and bliss,
And boasts from Phyllis to surprise a kiss,
When gently she resists with feigned remorse,
That what she grants may seem to be by force: 300
Her generous style at random oft will part,
And by a brave disorder shows her art.
Unlike those fearful poets, whose cold rhyme
In all their raptures keeps exactest time,
That sing the illustrious hero's mighty praise
(Lean writers!) by the terms of weeks and days;
And dare not from least circumstances part,
But take all towns by strictest rules of art:
Apollo drives those fops from his abode;
And some have said that once the humorous god   310
Resolving all such scribblers to confound,
For the short Sonnet ordered this strict bound;
Set rules for the just measure, and the time,
The easy running and alternate rhyme;
But above all, those licences denied
Which in these writings the lame sense supplied;
Forbade an useless line should find a place,
Or a repeated word appear with grace.
A faultless Sonnet, finished thus, would be
Worth tedious volumes of loose poetry.   320
A hundred scribbling authors without ground,
Believe they have this only phoenix found:
When yet the exactest scarce have two or three,
Among whole tomes from faults and censure free.
The rest, but little read, regarded less,
Are shovelled to the pastry from the press.
Closing the sense within the measured time,
'Tis hard to fit the reason to the rhyme.

14 *l'escaut sous le joug de Louis.*

EPIGRAM

The Epigram, with little art composed
Is one good sentence in a distich closed.   330
These points that by Italians first were prized,
Our ancient authors knew not, or despised:
The vulgar dazzled with their glaring light,
To their false pleasures quickly they invite;
But public favour so increased their pride,
They overwhelmed Parnassus with their tide.
The Madrigal at first was overcome,
And the proud Sonnet fell by the same doom;
With these grave Tragedy adorned her flights,
And mournful Elegy her funeral rites: 340
A hero never failed them on the stage,
Without his point a lover durst not rage;
The amorous shepherds took more care to prove
True to his point, than faithful to their love.
Each word, like Janus, had a double face;
And prose, as well as verse, allowed it place:
The lawyer with conceits adorned his speech,
The parson without quibbling could not preach.
At last affronted reason looked about,
And from all serious matters shut them out;   350
Declared that none should use them without shame,
Except a scattering in the Epigram;
Provided that by art, and in due time,
They turned upon the thought, and not the rhyme.
Thus in all parts disorders did abate:
Yet quibblers in the court had leave to prate;
Insipid jesters, and unpleasant fools,
A corporation of dull punning drolls.
'Tis not, but that sometimes a dexterous muse
May with advantage a turned sense abuse,   360
And on a word may trifle with address;
But above all avoid the fond excess,
And think not, when your verse and sense are lame,
With a dull point to tag your Epigram.
  Each poem his perfection has apart;

The British round [15] in plainness shows his art.
The Ballad,[16] though the pride of ancient time,
Has often nothing but his humorous rhyme;
The Madrigal may softer passions move,
And breathe the tender ecstasies of love.   37<
Desire to show itself, and not to wrong,
Armed Virtue first with Satire in its tongue.

SATIRE

Lucilius was the man, who, bravely bold,
To Roman vices did this mirror hold,
Protected humble goodness from reproach,
Showed worth on foot, and rascals in the coach.
Horace his pleasing wit to this did add,
And none uncensured could be fool or mad:
Unhappy was that wretch, whose name might be
Squared to the rules of their sharp poetry.   380
Persius obscure, but full of sense and wit,
Affected brevity in all he writ;
And Juvenal, learned as those times could be,
Too far did stretch his sharp hyperbole;
Though horrid truths through all his labours shine,
In what he writes there's something of divine,
Whether he blames the Caprean debauch,
Or of Sejanus' fall tells the approach,
Or that he makes the trembling senate come
To the stern tyrant to receive their doom;   390
Or Roman vice in coarsest habits shews,
And paints an empress reeking from the stews:
In all he writes appears a noble fire;
To follow such a master then desire.
Chaucer [17] alone, fixed on this solid base,
In his old style conserves a modern grace:
Too happy, if the freedom of his rhymes
Offended not the method of our times.
The Latin writers decency neglect;
But modern authors challenge our respect,   400
And at immodest writings take offence,

---

[15] *le rondeau.*   [16] ballade.   [17] Régnier.

If clean expression cover not the sense.
I love sharp Satire, from obsceneness free;
Not impudence, that preaches modesty:
Our English,[18] who in malice never fail,
Hence in lampoons and libels [19] learn to rail;
Pleasant detraction, that by singing goes
From mouth to mouth, and as it marches grows:
Our freedom in our poetry we see,
That child of joy begot by liberty.   410
But, vain blasphemer, tremble when you chuse
God for the subject of your impious muse:
At last, those jests which libertines invent,
Bring the lewd author to just punishment.
Even in a song there must be art and sense;
Yet sometimes we have seen that wine, or chance,
Have warmed cold brains, and given dull writers mettle,
And furnished out a scene for Mr Settle.[20]
But for one lucky hit, that made thee please,
Let not thy folly grow to a disease,   420
Nor think thyself a wit; for in our age
If a warm fancy does some fop engage,
He neither eats nor sleeps till he has writ,
But plagues the world with his adulterate wit.
Nay 'tis a wonder, if, in his dire rage,
He prints not his dull follies for the stage;
And in the front of all his senseless plays,
Makes David Logan [21] crown his head with bays.

CANTO III

TRAGEDY

There's not a monster bred beneath the sky,
But well-disposed by art, may please the eye: 430
A curious workman by his skill divine,
From an ill object makes a good design.
Thus to delight us, Tragedy, in tears

---

[18] *Le François.*
[19] *Vaudeville* (earliest French satire).
[20] *un couplet a Linière.*

[21] Should be spelled Loggan, an English engraver; French original, Nanteuil.

For Oedipus, provokes our hopes and fears;
For parricide Orestes asks relief,
And, to encrease our pleasure, causes grief.
You then that in this noble art would rise,
Come, and in lofty verse dispute the prize.
Would you upon the stage acquire renown,
And for your judges summon all the town?   440
Would you your works for ever should remain,
And after ages past be sought again?
In all you write, observe with care and art
To move the passions, and incline the heart.
If in a laboured act, the pleasing rage
Cannot our hopes and fears by turns engage,
Nor in our mind a feeling pity raise,
In vain with learned scenes you fill your plays:
Your cold discourse can never move the mind
Of a stern critic, naturally unkind,   450
Who, justly tired with your pedantic flight,
Or falls asleep, or censures all you write.
The secret is, attention first to gain;
To move our minds, and then to entertain;
That from the very opening of the scenes,
The first may show us what the author means.
I'm tired to see an actor on the stage,
That knows not whether he's to laugh or rage;
Who, an intrigue unravelling in vain,
Instead of pleasing keeps my mind in pain.   460
I'd rather much the nauseous dunce should say
Downright, my name is Hector in the play;
Than with a mass of miracles, ill-joined,
Confound my ears, and not instruct my mind.
The subject's never soon enough exprest;
Your place of action must be fixed, and rest.
A Spanish poet may with good event,
In one day's space whole ages represent;
There oft the hero of a wandering stage
Begins a child, and ends the play of age: 470
But we, that are by reason's rules confined,
Will, that with art the poem be designed;
That unity of action, time, and place,

Keep the stage full, and all our labours grace.
Write not what cannot be with ease conceived;
Some truths may be too strong to be believed.
A foolish wonder cannot entertain;
My mind's not moved if your discourse be vain.
You may relate what would offend the eye:
Seeing, indeed, would better satisfy;   480
But there are objects that a curious art
Hides from the eyes, yet offers to the heart.
The mind is most agreeably surprised,
When a well-woven subject, long disguised,
You on a sudden artfully unfold,
And give the whole another face and mould.
At first the Tragedy was void of art;
A song, where each man danced and sung his part,
And of God Bacchus roaring out the praise,
Sought a good vintage for their jolly days: 490
Then wine and joy were seen in each man's eyes,
And a fat goat was the best singer's prize.
Thespis was first, who, all besmeared with lee,
Began this pleasure for posterity:
And with his carted actors, and a song,
Amused the people as he passed along.
Next Aeschylus the different persons placed,
And with a better mask his players graced:
Upon a theatre his verse expressed,
And showed his hero with a buskin dressed.   500
Then Sophocles, the genius of his age,
Encreased the pomp and beauty of the stage,
Engaged the chorus song in every part,
And polished rugged verse by rules of art:
He in the Greek did those perfections gain,
Which the weak Latin never could attain.
Our pious fathers, in their priest-rid age,
As impious and prophane, abhorred the stage:
A troop of silly pilgrims, as 'tis said,
Foolishly zealous, scandalously played,   510
Instead of heroes, and of love's complaints,
The angels, God, the Virgin, and the saints.
At last, right reason did his laws reveal,

And showed the folly of their ill-placed zeal,
Silenced those noncomformists of the age,
And raised the lawful heroes of the stage:
Only the Athenian mask was laid aside,
And chorus by the music was supplied.
Ingenious love, inventive in new arts,
Mingled in plays, and quickly touched our hearts: 520
This passion never could resistance find,
But knows the shortest passage to the mind.
Paint then, I'm pleased my hero be in love;
But let him not like a tame shepherd move;
Let not Achilles be like Thyrsis seen,
Or for a Cyrus show an Artamen;
That struggling oft, his passions we may find,
The frailty, not the virtue of his mind.
Of romance heroes shun the low design;
Yet to great hearts some human frailties join: 530
Achilles must with Homer's heat engage;
For an affront I'm pleased to see him rage.
Those little failings in your hero's heart
Show that of man and nature he has part.
To leave known rules you cannot be allowed;
Make Agamemnon covetous and proud,
Aeneas in religious rites austere.
Keep to each man his proper character.
Of countries and of times the humours know;
From different climates different customs grow: 540
And strive to shun their fault, who vainly dress
An antique hero like some modern ass;
Who make old Romans like our English [22] move,
Show Cato sparkish, or make Brutus love.
In a romance those errors are excused:
There 'tis enough that, reading, we're amused:
Rules too severe would there be useless found;
But the strict scene must have a juster bound;
Exact decorum we must always find.
If then you form some hero in your mind,   550
Be sure your image with itself agree;
For what he first appears, he still must be,

[22] François.

Affected wits will naturally incline
To paint their figures by their own design;
Your bully poets, bully heroes write;   ⎫
Chapman in Bussy D'Ambois [23] took delight, ⎬
And thought perfection was to huff and fight. ⎭
Wise nature by variety does please;
Clothe differing passions in a differing dress.
Bold anger, in rough haughty words appears;   560
Sorrow is humble, and dissolves in tears.
Make not your Hecuba with fury rage,
And show a ranting grief upon the stage;
Or tell in vain how the rough Tanais bore
His sevenfold waters to the Euxine shore:
These swoln expressions, this affected noise,
Shows like some pedant that declaims to boys.
In sorrow you must softer methods keep;
And, to excite our tears, yourself must weep.
Those noisy words with which ill plays abound,   570
Come not from hearts that are in sadness drowned.
   The theatre for a young poet's rhymes
Is a bold venture in our knowing times:
An author cannot easily purchase fame;
Critics are always apt to hiss, and blame:
You may be judged by every ass in town,
The privilege is bought for half-a-crown.
To please, you must a hundred changes try;
Sometimes be humble, then must soar on high;
In noble thoughts must everywhere abound,   580
Be easy, pleasant, solid, and profound;
To these you must surprising touches join,
And show us a new wonder in each line;
That all, in a just method well-designed,
May leave a strong impression in the mind.
These are the arts that tragedy maintain:

THE EPIC

But the Heroic claims a loftier strain.
In the narration of some great design,

[23] La Calprenède made his hero, Juba, in *Cleopatre*, resemble himself.

Invention, art, and fable, all must join:
Here fiction must employ its utmost grace;   590
All must assume a body, mind, and face:
Each virtue a divinity is seen;
Prudence is Pallas, Beauty, Paphos' queen.
'Tis not a cloud from whence swift lightnings fly,
But Jupiter, that thunders from the sky;
Nor a rough storm that gives the sailor pain,
But angry Neptune plowing up the main;
Echo's no more an empty airy sound,
But a fair nymph that weeps her lover drowned.
Thus in the endless treasure of his mind,   600
The poet does a thousand figures find;
Around the work his ornaments he pours,
And strows with lavish hand his opening flowers.
'Tis not a wonder if a tempest bore
The Trojan fleet against the Libyan shore;
From faithless fortune this is no surprise,
For every day 'tis common to our eyes:
But angry Juno, that she might destroy,
And overwhelm the rest of ruined Troy;
That Aeolus, with the fierce goddess joined,   610
Opened the hollow prisons of the wind;
Till angry Neptune, looking o'er the main,
Rebukes the tempest, calms the waves again,
Their vessels from the dangerous quicksands steers.
These are the springs that move our hopes and fears:
Without these ornaments before our eyes,
The unsinewed poem languishes and dies:
Your poet in his art will always fail,
And tell you but a dull insipid tale.
In vain have our mistaken authors tried   620
To lay these ancient ornaments aside,
Thinking our God, and prophets that he sent,
Might act like those the poets did invent,
To fright poor readers in each line with hell,
And talk of Satan, Ashtaroth, and Bel.
The mysteries which Christians must believe,
Disdain such shifting pageants to receive:
The gospel offers nothing to our thoughts

But penitence, or punishment for faults;
And mingling falsehoods with those mysteries,   630
Would make our sacred truths appear like lies.
Besides, what pleasure can it be to hear
The howlings of repining Lucifer,
Whose rage at your imagined hero flies,
And oft with God himself disputes the prize?
Tasso, you'll say, has done it with applause:—
It is not here I mean to judge his cause:
Yet though our age has so extolled his name,
His works had never gained immortal fame,
If holy Godfrey in his ecstasies   640
Had only conquered Satan on his knees;
If Tancred and Armida's pleasing form
Did not his melancholy theme adorn.
'Tis not, that Christian poems ought to be
Filled with the fictions of idolatry;
But, in a common subject, to reject
The gods, and heathern ornaments neglect;
To banish Tritons, who the seas invade,
To take Pan's whistle, or the fates degrade,
To hinder Charon in his leaky boat   650
To pass the shepherd with the man of note,
Is with vain scruples to disturb your mind,
And search perfection you can never find:
As well they may forbid us to present
Prudence or Justice for an ornament,
To paint old Janus with his front of brass,
And take from Time his scythe, his wings, and glass,
And everywhere, as 'twere idolatry,
Banish descriptions from our poetry.
Leave them their pious follies to pursue;   660
But let our reason such vain fears subdue:
And let us not, amongst our vanities,
Of the true God create a god of lies.
In fable we a thousand pleasures see,
And the smooth names seem made for poetry;
As Hector, Alexander, Helen, Phyllis,
Ulysses, Agamemnon, and Achilles:
In such a crowd, the poet were to blame

To chuse king Chilperic for his hero's name.
Sometimes the name, being well or ill applied,   670
Will the whole fortune of your work decide.
Would you your reader never should be tired,
Chuse some great hero, fit to be admired,
In courage signal, and in virtue bright;
Let even his very failings give delight;
Let his great actions our attention bind,
Like Caesar, or like Scipio, frame his mind,
And not like Oedipus his perjured race;
A common conqueror is a theme too base.
Chuse not your tale of accidents too full;   680
Too much variety may make it dull:
Achilles' rage alone, when wrought with skill,
Abundantly does a whole Iliad fill.
Be your narrations lively, short, and smart;
In your descriptions show your noblest art:
There 'tis your poetry may be employed.
Yet you must trivial accidents avoid,
Nor imitate that fool, who, to describe
The wondrous marches of the chosen tribe,
Placed on the sides, to see their armies pass,   690
The fishes staring through the liquid glass;
Described a child, who, with his little hand,
Picked up the shining pebbles from the sand.
Such objects are too mean to stay our sight;
Allow your work a just and nobler flight.
Be your beginning plain; and take good heed
Too soon you mount not on the airy steed;
Nor tell your reader, in a thundering verse,
"I sing the conqueror of the universe."
What can an author after this produce?   700
The labouring mountain must bring forth a mouse.
Much better are we pleased with his address,
Who, without making such vast promises,
Says, in an easier style and plainer sense,
"I sing the combats of that pious prince,
Who from the Phrygian coasts his armies bore,
And landed first on the Lavinian shore."
His opening muse sets not the world on fire,

And yet performs more than we can require:
Quickly you'll hear him celebrate the fame, 710
And future glory of the Roman name;
Of Styx and Acheron describe the floods,
And Caesar's wandering in the Elysian woods;
With figures numberless his story grace,
And every thing in beauteous colours trace.
At once you may be pleasing and sublime:
I hate a heavy melancholy rhyme:
I'd rather read Orlando's comic tale,
Than a dull author always stiff and stale,
Who thinks himself dishonoured in his style, 720
If on his works the Graces do but smile.
'Tis said, that Homer, matchless in his art,
Stole Venus' girdle to engage the heart:
His works indeed vast treasures do unfold,
And whatsoe'er he touches turns to gold:
All in his hands new beauty does acquire;
He always pleases, and can never tire.
A happy warmth he every where may boast;
Nor is he in too long digressions lost:
His verses without rule a method find, 730
And of themselves appear in order joined;
All without trouble answers his intent;
Each syllable is tending to the event.
Let his example your endeavours raise;
To love his writings is a kind of praise.
 A poem, where we all perfections find,
Is not the work of a fantastic mind;
There must be care, and time, and skill, and pains;
Not the first heat of inexperienced brains.
Yet sometimes artless poets, when the rage 740
Of a warm fancy does their minds engage,
Puffed with vain pride, presume they understand,
And boldly take the trumpet in their hand:
Their fustian muse each accident confounds;
Nor can she fly, but rise by leaps and bounds,
Till, their small stock of learning quickly spent,
Their poem dies for want of nourishment.
In vain mankind the hot-brained fool decries,

No branding censures can unvail his eyes;
With impudence the laurel they invade,   750
Resolved to like the monsters they have made.
Virgil, compared to them, is flat and dry;
And Homer understood not poetry:
Against their merit if this age rebel,
To future times for justice they appeal.
But waiting till mankind shall do them right,
And bring their works triumphantly to light,
Neglected heaps we in bye-corners lay,
Where they become to worms and moths a prey.
Forgot, in dust and cobwebs let them rest,   760
Whilst we return from whence we first digrest.
   The great success which tragic writers found,
In Athens first the comedy renowned.
The abusive Grecian there, by pleasing ways,
Dispersed his natural malice in his plays:
Wisdom and virtue, honour, wit, and sense,
Were subject to buffooning insolence:
Poets were publicly approved, and sought,
That vice extolled, and virtue set at nought;
A Socrates himself, in that loose age,   770
Was made the pastime of a scoffing stage.
At last the public took in hand the cause,
And cured this madness by the power of laws;
Forbade at any time, or any place,
To name the person, or describe the face.
The stage its ancient fury thus let fall,
And comedy diverted without gall:
By mild reproofs recovered minds diseased,
And, sparing persons, innocently pleased.
Each one was nicely shewn in this new glass,   780
And smiled to think he was not meant the ass:
A miser oft would laugh at first, to find
A faithful draught of his own sordid mind;
And fops were with such care and cunning writ,
They liked the piece for which themselves did sit.
You, then, that would the comic laurels wear,
To study nature be your only care.
Whoe'er knows man, and by a curious art

Discerns the hidden secrets of the heart;
He who observes, and naturally can paint   790
The jealous fool, the fawning sycophant,
A sober wit, an enterprising ass,
A humorous Otter, or a Hudibras,—[24]
May safely in those noble lists engage,
And make them act and speak upon the stage.
Strive to be natural in all you write,
And paint with colours that may please the sight.
Nature in various figures does abound,
And in each mind are different humours found;
A glance, a touch, discovers to the wise,   800
But every man has not discerning eyes.
All-changing time does also change the mind,
And different ages different pleasures find;
Youth, hot and furious, cannot brook delay,
By flattering vice is easily led away;
Vain in discourse, inconstant in desire,
In censure, rash; in pleasures, all on fire.
The manly age does steadier thoughts enjoy;
Power and ambition do his soul employ;
Against the turns of fate he sets his mind;   810
And by the past the future hopes to find.
Decrepit age, still adding to his stores,
For others heaps the treasure he adores;
In all his actions keeps a frozen pace;
Past times extols, the present to debase:
Incapable of pleasures youth abuse,
In others blames what age does him refuse.
Your actors must by reason be controuled;
Let young men speak like young, old men like old,
Observe the town, and study well the court;   820
For thither various characters resort.
Thus 'twas great Jonson[25] purchased his renown,
And in his art had borne away the crown,
If, less desirous of the people's praise,
He had not with low farce debased his plays;
Mixing dull buffoonry with wit refined,
And Harlequin with noble Terence joined.

[24] There are no French parallels.   [25] Molière.

When in the Fox [26] I see the tortoise hist,
I lose the author of the Alchemist.[27]
The comic wit, born with a smiling air,   830
Must tragic grief and pompous verse forbear;
Yet may he not, as on a market-place,
With bawdy jests amuse the populace;
With well-bred conversation you must please,
And your intrigue unravelled be with ease;
Your action still should reason's rules obey,
Nor in an empty scene may lose its way.
Your humble style must sometimes gently rise;
And your discourse sententious be, and wise:
The passions must to nature be confined;   840
And scenes to scenes with artful weaving joined.
Your wit must not unseasonably play;
But follow business, never lead the way.
Observe how Terence does this error shun:
A careful father chides his amorous son;
Then see that son, whom no advice can move,
Forget those orders, and pursue his love:
'Tis not a well-drawn picture we discover;
'Tis a true son, a father, and a lover.
I like an author that reforms the age,   850
And keeps the right decorum of the stage;
That always pleases by just reason's rule:
But for a tedious droll, a quibbling fool,
Who with low nauseous bawdry fills his plays,
Let him be gone, and on two tressels raise
Some Smithfield [28] stage, where he may act his pranks,
And make Jack-Puddings [29] speak to mountebanks.

CANTO IV

In Florence dwelt a doctor of renown,
The scourge of God, and terror of the town,
Who all the cant of physic had by heart,   860
And never murdered but by rules of art.
The public mischief was his private gain:

---

[26] Molière's *Les Fourberies de Scapin.*   [28] *Pont Neuf.*
[27] Molière's *Misanthrope.*   [29] *Mascarades* (unknown form of verse).

Children their slaughtered parents sought in vain;
A brother here his poisoned brother wept,
Some bloodless died, and some by opium slept;
Colds, at his presence, would to phrenzies turn,
And agues, like malignant fevers, burn.
Hated, at last, his practice gives him o'er;
One friend, unkilled by drugs, of all his store,
In his new country-house affords him place;   870
('Twas a rich abbot, and a building ass.)
Here first the doctor's talent came in play;
He seems inspired, and talks like Wren or May; [30]
Of this new portico condemns the face,
And turns the entrance to a better place;
Designs the stair-case at the other end:
His friend approves, does for his mason send.
He comes; the doctor's arguments prevail;
In short, to finish this our humorous tale,
He Galen's dangerous science does reject,   880
And from ill doctor turns good architect.

    In this example we may have our part;
Rather be mason, ('tis a useful art,)
Than a dull poet; for that trade accurst,
Admits no mean betwixt the best and worst.
In other sciences, without disgrace,
A candidate may fill a second place;
But poetry no medium can admit,
No reader suffers an indifferent wit:
The ruined stationers against him bawl,   890
And Herringman degrades him from his stall.
Burlesque at least our laughter may excite;
But a cold writer never can delight.
The Counter-scuffle has more wit and art,
Than the stiff formal style of Gondibert. [31]
Be not affected with that empty praise
Which your vain flatterers will sometimes raise;
And when you read, with ecstasy will say,
"The finished piece! the admirable play!"
Which, when exposed to censure and to light,   900
Cannot endure a critic's piercing sight.

[30] Mansard.   [31] Motin.

A hundred authors fates have been foretold,
And Shadwell's [32] works are printed, but not sold.
Hear all the world; consider every thought;
A fool by chance may stumble on a fault:
Yet, when Apollo does your muse inspire,
Be not impatient to expose your fire;
Nor imitate the Settles of our times,
Those tuneful readers of their own dull rhymes,
Who seize on all the acquaintance they can meet,   910
And stop the passengers that walk the street:
There is no sanctuary you can chuse
For a defence from their pursuing muse.
I've said before, be patient when they blame;
To alter for the better is no shame.
Yet yield not to a fool's impertinence;
Sometimes conceited sceptics, void of sense,
By their false taste condemn some finished part,
And blame the noblest flights of wit and art.
In vain their fond opinions you deride,   920
With their loved follies they are satisfied;
And their weak judgement, void of sense and light,
Thinks nothing can escape their feeble sight;
Their dangerous counsels do not cure, but wound; ⎫
To shun the storm they run your verse aground, ⎬
And thinking to escape a rock, are drowned. ⎭
Chuse a sure judge to censure what you write,
Whose reason leads, and knowledge gives you light,
Whose steady hand will prove your faithful guide,
And touch the darling follies you would hide: 930
He, in your doubts, will carefully advise,
And clear the mist before your feeble eyes.
'Tis he will tell you, to what noble height
A generous muse may sometimes take her flight;
When too much fettered with the rules of art,
May from her stricter bounds and limits part:
But such a perfect judge is hard to see,
And every rhymer knows not poetry;
Nay some there are for writing verse extolled,
Who know not Lucan's dross from Virgil's gold.   940

[32] Gombant.

Would you in this great art acquire renown?
Authors, observe the rules I here lay down.
In prudent lessons every where abound;
With pleasant join the useful and the sound:
A sober reader a vain tale will slight;
He seeks as well instruction as delight.
Let all your thoughts to virtue be confined,
Still offering nobler figures to our mind:
I like not those loose writers, who employ
Their guilty muse, good manners to destroy;   950
Who with false colours still deceive our eyes,
And show us vice dressed in a fair disguise.
Yet do I not their sullen muse approve,
Who from all modest writings banish love;
That stript the play-house of its chief intrigue,
And make a murderer of Roderigue:
The lightest love, if decently exprest,
Will raise no vitious motions in our breast.
Dido in vain may weep, and ask relief;
I blame her folly, whilst I share her grief.   960
A virtuous author, in his charming art,
To please the sense needs not corrupt the heart:
His heat will never cause a guilty fire:
To follow virtue then be your desire.
In vain your art and vigour are exprest;
The obscene expression shows the infected breast.
But, above all, base jealousies avoid,
In which detracting poets are employed.
A noble wit dares liberally commend,
And scorns to grudge at his deserving friend.   970
Base rivals, who true wit and merit hate,
Caballing still against it with the great,
Maliciously aspire to gain renown,
By standing up, and pulling others down.
Never debase yourself by treacherous ways,
Nor by such abject methods seek for praise:
Let not your only business be to write;
Be virtuous, just, and in your friends delight.
'Tis not enough your poems be admired;
But strive your conversation be desired: 980

Write for immortal fame; nor ever chuse
Gold for the object of a generous muse.
I know a noble wit may, without crime,
Receive a lawful tribute for his time:
Yet I abhor those writers, who despise
Their honour, and alone their profits prize;
Who their Apollo basely will degrade,
And of a noble science make a trade.
Before kind reason did her light display,
And government taught mortals to obey, 990
Men, like wild beasts, did nature's laws pursue,
They fed on herbs, and drink from rivers drew;
Their brutal force, on lust and rapine bent,
Committed murder without punishment:
Reason at last, by her all-conquering arts,
Reduced these savages, and tuned their hearts;
Mankind from bogs, and woods, and caverns calls,
And towns and cities fortifies with walls:
Thus fear of justice made proud rapine cease,
And sheltered innocence by laws and peace. 1000
    These benefits from poets we received;
From whence are raised those fictions since believed,
That Orpheus, by his soft harmonious strains,
Tamed the fierce tygers of the Thracian plains;
Amphion's notes, by their melodious powers,
Drew rocks and woods, and raised the Theban towers:
These miracles from numbers did arise;
Since which, in verse heaven taught his mysteries,
And by a priest, possessed with rage divine,
Apollo spoke from his prophetic shrine. 1010
Soon after, Homer the old heroes praised,
And noble minds by great examples raised;
Then Hesiod did his Grecian swains incline
To till the fields, and prune the bounteous vine.
Thus useful rules were, by the poet's aid,
In easy numbers to rude men conveyed,
And pleasingly their precepts did impart;
First charmed the ear, and then engaged the heart;
The muses thus their reputation raised,
And with just gratitude in Greece were praised. 1020

With pleasure mortals did their wonders see,
And sacrificed to their divinity;
But want, at last, base flattery entertained,
And old Parnassus with this vice was stained;
Desire of gain dazzling the poets' eyes,
Their works were filled with fulsome flatteries.
Thus needy wits a vile revenue made,
And verse became a mercenary trade.
Debase not with so mean a vice thy art;
If gold must be the idol of thy heart,   1030
Fly, fly the unfruitful Heliconian strand!
Those streams are not enriched with golden sand;
Great wits, as well as warriors, only gain
Laurels and honours for their toil and pain.
But what? an author cannot live on fame,
Or pay a reckoning with a lofty name:
A poet, to whom fortune is unkind,
Who when he goes to bed has hardly dined,
Takes little pleasure in Parnassus' dreams,
Or relishes the Heliconian streams;   1040
Horace had ease and plenty when he writ, ⎫
And free from cares for money or for meat, ⎬
Did not expect his dinner from his wit. ⎭
'Tis true; but verse is cherished by the great,
And now none famish who deserve to eat:
What can we fear, when virtue, arts, and sense,
Receive the stars' propitious influence:
When a sharp-sighted prince, by early grants,
Rewards your merits, and prevents your wants?
Sing then his glory, celebrate his fame;   1050
Your nobelest theme is his immortal name.
Let mighty Spenser [33] raise his reverend head,
Cowley [34] and Denham start up from the dead;
Waller his age renew, and offerings bring,
Our monarch's praise let bright-eyed virgins sing:
Let Dryden with new rules our stage refine,
And his great models form by this design.
But where's a second Virgil to rehearse

[33] Corneille.   Cowley, Denham, and Waller.
[34] Racine is the only French parallel for

Our hero's glories in his epic verse?
What Orpheus sing his triumphs o'er the main, 1060
And make the hills and forest move again;
Shew his bold fleet on the Batavian shore,
And Holland trembling as his cannons roar;
Paint Europe's balance in his steady hand,
Whilst the two worlds in expectation stand
Of peace or war, that wait on his command?
But, as I speak, new glories strike my eyes,
Glories, which heaven itself does give, and prize,
Blessings of peace; that with their milder rays
Adorn his reign, and bring Saturnian days. 1070
Now let rebellion, discord, vice, and rage,
That have in patriots' forms debauched our age,
Vanish with all the ministers of hell;
His rays their poisonous vapours shall dispel:
'Tis he alone our safety did create,
His own firm soul secured the nation's fate,
Opposed to all the boutefeus [35] of the state.
Authors, for him your great endeavours raise;
The loftiest numbers will but reach his praise.
For me, whose verse in satire has been bred, 1080
And never durst heroic measures tread;
Yet you shall see me, in that famous field,
With eyes and voice, my best assistance yield;
Offer you lessons, that my infant muse
Learnt, when she Horace for her guide did chuse;
Second your zeal with wishes, heart, and eyes,
And afar off hold up the glorious prize.
But pardon too, if zealous for the right,
A strict observer of each noble flight,
From the fine gold I separate the allay, 1090
And show how hasty writers sometimes stray;
Apter to blame, than knowing how to mend;
A sharp, but yet a necessary friend.

[35] Incendiaries.

JOHN DRYDEN

(1631–1700)

DRYDEN was born at Aldwinkle, in Northamptonshire, in 1631. He studied at Westminster school under the famous Dr. Busby, and later attended Cambridge, where he took the degree of A. B. in 1654. He remained at the university for three years longer, and then went to London to make his way with his pen. His earliest poems, negligible exercises in the manner of the metaphysical poets, were followed by the *Heroic Stanzas* on Cromwell, and the *Astrea Redux* and *Panegyric on the Restoration,* illustrative of his first sudden switching of parties. The *Annus Mirabilis,* published in 1666, is his earliest excellent poem, and brought him into the first rank of contemporary writers.

Before this, in 1663, he had begun his career as a dramatist with the unsuccessful *Wild Gallant.* From the *Annus Mirabilis* until, in 1681, he turned his chief attention to satire, he wrote no significant poetry except in his plays, the chief of which were *Marriage à la Mode* (1672), *The Conquest of Granada* (two parts, 1669–70), *Aurengzebe* (1675), *All for Love, or the World Well Lost* (1678).

Dryden had married, in 1663, Lady Elizabeth Howard. During the years that he was writing for the stage, his fortunes increased, and in 1668 on the death of Davenant he had been made laureate. This greater responsibility to the crown was further cause for his taking up the weapon of satire in 1681.

Absalom and Achitophel appeared while the Earl of Shaftesbury was awaiting trial for treason, and *The Medall* (1682) was written to ridicule the medal which the Whigs had struck in celebration of his acquittal. *MacFlecknoe* (1682), often appraised the most brilliant satire in the language, had the smaller occasion of Dryden's quarrel with Shadwell to prompt it. In the same year appeared the second part of *Absalom and Achitophel,* and the didactic poem, *Religio Laici.*

With the accession of James II to the throne in 1685, Dryden turned to the Roman Catholic religion, to which he remained faithful until his death. *The Hind and the Panther* is the literary result of this change, and Dryden doubtless hoped to be the chief mouth-piece of the throne. The revolution of 1688 took away his laureateship and left him generally destitute. Most important in the later years are his translations, done, in part, to make his living, but bearing few traces of declining powers. *The Works of Virgil* (1697) and the *Fables* (1700) give splendid evidence of his vigorous and far-ranging style.

For over thirty-five years, from the *Epistle Dedicatory* of *The Rival Ladies* (1664) to the *Preface to the Fables* (1700), Dryden wrote criticism. His works of this kind are chiefly in the form of prefaces to plays and poems, but this circumstance did not confine the critic in respect to either variety of subject or manner of treatment.

The student of Dryden's prose learns somewhat of the cavils of Restoration critical controversy and discovers one of the largest sources in literature of critical good sense. Pages on pages debate the ephemeral question of rhyme on the stage, in which Dryden took the position which has seemed to later generations, as it subsequently did to him, the wrong one; whole essays are devoted to defending and explaining such long dead forms as the heroic play, which he wished defined as "an imitation, in little, of an heroic poem" [*An Essay of Heroic Plays*, Ker collection, I, 150]; there are accounts, which seem the inevitable second theme of preface after preface, of the pusillanimity of petty detractors, at whom Dryden apparently took space to sneer only because he could sneer so devastatingly and with such apparent probity of character. But when he deals with the undying questions of criticism, he both stirs emotion and gratifies reason by his essential rightness. The character of true art he understood, and the concept of nature, which later the neo-classicists so misunderstood. And his judgments on the great poets of former times, on Chaucer, Shakespeare, and Milton, contain admirable verdicts upon which later critics have built and which they have been fearful to disannul.

This essential rightness the too frequent engrossment with the controversies of his period cannot entirely obscure. Even in the debates of the Restoration problems mentioned above there appear arguments which show Dryden holding fast to critical realities. He defends rhyme in plays, for instance, by explaining what he holds to be the essential condition of all drama: "the work of the poet, imitating or representing the conversation of several persons. . . . 'Tis true, that to imitate well is a poet's work; but to affect the soul, and excite the passions, and, above all, to move admiration (which is the delight of serious plays), a bare imitation will not serve. The converse, therefore, which a poet is to imitate, must be heightened with all the arts and ornaments of poesy; and must be such as, strictly considered, could never be supposed spoken by any without premeditation. . . . But I will be bolder, and do not doubt to make it good, though a paradox, that one great reason why prose is not to be used in serious plays, is, because it is too near the nature of converse: there may be too great a likeness; as the most skilful painters affirm, that there may be too near a resemblance in a picture." [*Defence of an Essay of Dramatic Poesy*, Ker collection, I, 113–14.] And the apologia for heroic plays turns in at least one place into a liberal defense of poetic license and an illuminating comment upon "Nature": "Some men think they have raised a great argument against the use of spectres and magic in heroic poetry, by saying they are unnatural; but whether they or I believe there are such things, is not material; 'tis enough that, for aught we know, they may be in Nature; and whatever is, or may be, is not properly unnatural. . . . 'Tis enough that, in all ages and religions, the greatest part of mankind have believed the power of magic, and that there are spirits or spectres which have appeared.

This, I say, is foundation enough for poetry." [*An Essay of Heroic Plays,* Ker collection, I, 153–154, 153.]

Even when he shows through the duration of a preface that he has stumbled into the camp of Rapin, "my friend Mr. Rymer," and Bossu, "the best of modern critics," he maintains an equitable temper, and never totally forgets his directions. In the "Preface to Troilus and Cressida, Containing the Grounds of Criticism in Tragedy," which is for the most part a truer digest of the accepted doctrine of tragedy than any other in his time, Dryden goes through the whole category of classical tenets from plot to manners, setting up the principles which he and his contemporaries have abstracted from Aristotle and Horace and the Renaissance critics. Everywhere there is deference shown to the interpretations of Bossu, Rapin, and Rymer. The plays of Shakespeare, Jonson, and Fletcher are examined in terms of the rules, in the most approved neo-classical manner. But it must be observed, in due justice to Dryden, that he does not allow his instinctive and rational conviction of the excellence of Shakespeare to be beclouded by specious syllogism. Nor is there any of that condescension, so prevalent during the next century, which denominated the greatest of dramatists "an unlettered genius," a child of Nature who knew nothing of Art.

The justice done to Shakespeare in the *Essay of Dramatic Poesy* is paralleled by the genuine reverence paid to Milton in the *Apology for Heroic Poetry and Poetic Licence* prefixed to *The State of Innocence and Fall of Man, an Opera,* which was based on *Paradise Lost.* This essay is, in one sense, the first authoritative appreciation of *Paradise Lost,* whose author is further complimented by the fact that Dryden takes this occasion to give his fullest and most liberal exposition of the rights of the poet. By the most classical of arguments, by an eloquent appeal to the supremacy of taste such as we do not have from another critic before Reynolds, by a shrewd application of common sense to well-chosen examples, he carries poetical prerogative outside the prison of critical rules, and places upon it but the one check which he considers valid: effect. He thus gives to the troublesome question of imitating nature an interpretation which might, had it been followed, have saved later neo-classicism from falling into its narrow slough. One central passage from the *Apology* deserves quotation:

Virgil and Horace, the severest writers of the severest age, have made frequent use of the hardest metaphors, and of the strongest hyperboles; and in this case the best authority is the best argument; for generally to have pleased, and through all ages, must bear the force of universal tradition. And if you would appeal from thence to right reason, you will gain no more by it in effect, than, first, to set up your reason against those authors; and, secondly, against all those who have admired them. You must prove, why that ought not to have pleased, which has pleased the most learned, and the most judicious; and, to be thought knowing, you must first put the fool upon all mankind. If you can enter more deeply, than they have done, into the causes and resorts of that which moves pleasure in a reader, the field is open, you may be heard: but those springs of human nature are not so easily discovered by every superficial judge: it requires Philosophy, as well as Poetry, to sound the depth of all the passions; what they are in themselves, and how they are to be provoked: and in this science the best poets have excelled. Aristotle raised the fabric of his *Poetry* from observation of those things in which Euripides, Sophocles, and Aeschylus pleased: he considered how they raised the passions, and thence has drawn rules for our imitation. From hence have sprung the tropes and figures, for which they wanted a name, who first practiced them, and succeeded in them. Thus I grant you, that the knowledge of Nature was the original rule; and that all poets ought to study her, as well as Aristotle and Horace, her interpreters. But then this also undeniably follows, that those things, which delight all ages, must have been an imitation of Nature; which is all I contend.

The defense of boldness in figurative language leads him to another significant declaration. The license which he grants "to give voice and thought to things inanimate" anticipates part of the critical thought of the Nineteenth Century and in particular Ruskin's treatment of the pathetic fallacy. [Cf. the selection from Ruskin in the Supplement.] "The poet," says Dryden, "must put on the passion he endeavors to represent: a man in such an occasion is not cool enough, either to reason rightly, or to talk calmly. Aggravations are then in their proper places; interrogations, exclamations, hyperbata, or a disordered connexion of discourse, are graceful there, because they are natural." [Ker collection, I, 185–86.]

The two essays included in this volume illustrate both Dryden's frequent preoccupation with the particular problems of his age and his pronouncements on literature in general. The *Essay of Dramatic Poesy* discusses rhyme in plays, the unities [cf. the Corneille selections in the Supplement], and the "Ancients and Moderns" controversy. But from each of the arguments come flashes of insight which transcend Restoration quibblings and leave us enduring abstracts of a liberal Classicism. Among these are the definition of a play, sound judgments on the comparative virtues of regularity and variety in drama, the preference of strongly drawn characters to types and of artful complexity in plots to rule-ridden unity, and the famous inlaid critiques on Shakespeare, Beaumont and Fletcher, and Jonson.

The *Essay* is in the form of the Socratic dialogue. The speakers are to be identified with actual persons as follows: Eugenius, Lord Buckhurst, Dryden's patron and friend to whom the work was dedicated; Crites, Sir Robert Howard, Dryden's brother-in-law, with whom he waged a critical war concerning the propriety of rhymed plays for some time both before and after the *Essay;* Lisideius, Sir Charles Sedley; Neander, Dryden himself.

Dryden's last prose work, *The Preface to the Fables,* written a few months before his death, is, in the words of Mr. Ker, "more full of life than anything else in Dryden's prose." "It winds up," says Mr. Saintsbury, "as the *Essay* had practically begun, a volume of critical writing which, if not for pure, yet for applied, mixed, and sweetened criticism, deserves to be put on the shelf—no capacious one—reserved for the best criticism of the world." [*Hist. of Crit.,* ii, 386.]

Dryden's liberalism is nowhere better illustrated. The examination of Chaucer, just, to the highest critical degree, inaccurate only after the manner of seventeenth century scholarship, is yet so daring as to prefer the Englishman to his Roman prototype, Ovid. His explanation of Chaucer's method gives a new and healthful turn to the fast ossifying formula about "following nature"; his examples of Ovid's weakness bring to light and to ridicule that false wit which had so misled a multitude of his contemporaries. Nowhere in criticism do we find the faculty better displayed of teaching general truths by examining specific materials.

AN ESSAY OF DRAMATIC POESY

(1668)

It was that memorable day, in the first summer of the late war, when our navy engaged the Dutch; a day wherein the two most mighty and best appointed fleets which any age had ever seen, disputed the command of the greater half of the globe, the commerce of nations, and the riches of the universe: while these vast floating bodies, on either side, moved against each other in parallel lines, and our countrymen, under the happy conduct of his Royal Highness, went breaking, by little and little, into the line of the enemies; the noise of the cannon from both navies reached our ears about the City, so that all men being alarmed with it, and in a dreadful suspense of the event, which they knew was then deciding, every one went following the sound as his fancy led him; and leaving the town almost empty, some took towards the park, some cross the river, others down it; all seeking the noise in the depth of silence.

Among the rest, it was the fortune of Eugenius, Crites, Lisideius, and Neander, to be in company together; three of them persons whom their wit and quality have made known to all the town; and whom I have chose to hide under these borrowed names, that they may not suffer by so ill a relation as I am going to make of their discourse.

2. Taking then a barge, which a servant of Lisideius had provided for them, they made haste to shoot the bridge, and left behind them that great fall of waters which hindered them from hearing what they desired: after which, having disengaged themselves from many vessels which rode at anchor in the Thames, and almost blocked up the passage towards Greenwich, they ordered the watermen to let fall their oars more gently; and then, every one favouring his own curiosity with a strict silence, it was not long ere they perceived the air to break about them like the noise of distant thunder, or of swallows in a chimney: those little undulations of sound, though almost vanishing before they reached them, yet still seeming to retain somewhat of their first horror, which they had betwixt the fleets. After they had attentively listened till such time as the sound by little and little went from them, Eugenius, lifting up his head, and taking notice of it, was the first who congratulated to the rest that happy omen of our Nation's victory: adding, that we had but this to desire in confirmation of it, that we might hear no more of that noise, which was

now leaving the English coast. When the rest had concurred in the same opinion, Crites, a person of a sharp judgment, and somewhat too delicate a taste in wit, which the world have mistaken in him for ill-nature, said, smiling to us, that if the concernment of this battle had not been so exceeding great, he could scarce have wished the victory at the price he knew he must pay for it, in being subject to the reading and hearing of so many ill verses as he was sure would be made on that subject. Adding, that no argument could scape some of those eternal rhymers, who watch a battle with more diligence than the ravens and birds of prey; and the worst of them surest to be first in upon the quarry: while the better able, either out of modesty writ not at all, or set that due value upon their poems, as to let them be often desired and long expected. "There are some of those impertinent people of whom you speak," answered Lisideius, "who to my knowledge are already so provided, either way, that they can produce not only a Panegyric upon the victory, but, if need be, a Funeral Elegy on the Duke; wherein, after they have crowned his valour with many laurels, they will at last deplore the odds under which he fell, concluding that his courage deserved a better destiny." All the company smiled at the conceipt of Lisideius; but Crites, more eager than before, began to make particular exceptions against some writers, and said, the public magistrate ought to send betimes to forbid them; and that it concerned the peace and quiet of all honest people, that ill poets should be as well silenced as seditious preachers. "In my opinion," replied Eugenius, "you pursue your point too far; for as to my own particular, I am so great a lover of poesy, that I could wish them all rewarded who attempt but to do well; at least, I would not have them worse used than one of their brethren was by Sylla the Dictator:— *Quem in concione vidimus* (says Tully), *cum ei libellum malus poeta de populo subjecisset, quod epigramma in eum fecisset tantummodo alternis versibus longiusculis, statim ex iis rebus quas tunc vendebat jubere ei praemium tribui, sub ea conditione ne quid postea scriberet.*" [1] "I could wish with all my heart," replied Crites, "that many whom we know were as bountifully thanked upon the same condition,—that they would never trouble us again. For amongst others, I have a mortal apprehension of two poets, whom this victory, with the

---

[1] "We may note that in a gathering once, when a bad poet handed up to him, from the concourse of people, a book in which he had composed elegiacs on the general, he promptly ordered the poet to be given, out of what was then being sold [the plunders of war], a reward, on the condition that he not afterwards write anything." Cicero: *Pro Archia* 10, 25.

help of both her wings, will never be able to escape." " 'Tis easy to guess whom you intend," said Lisideius; "and without naming them, I ask you, if one of them does not perpetually pay us with clenches upon words, and a certain clownish kind of railery? if now and then he does not offer at a catachresis or Clevelandism, wresting and torturing a word into another meaning: in fine, if he be not one of those whom the French would call *un mauvais buffon;* one who is so much a well-willer to the satire, that he intends at least to spare no man; and though he cannot strike a blow to hurt any, yet he ought to be punished for the malice of the action, as our witches are justly hanged, because they think themselves to be such; and suffer deservedly for believing they did mischief, because they meant it." "You have described him," said Crites, "so exactly, that I am afraid to come after you with my other extremity of poetry. He is one of those who, having had some advantage of education and converse, knows better than the other what a poet should be, but puts it into practice more unluckily than any man; his style and matter are every where alike: he is the most calm, peaceable writer you ever read: he never disquiets your passions with the least concernment, but still leaves you in as even a temper as he found you; he is a very Leveller in poetry: he creeps along with ten little words in every line, and helps out his numbers with *For to,* and *Unto,* and all the pretty expletives he can find, till he drags them to the end of another line; while the sense is left tired half way behind it: he doubly starves all his verses, first for want of thought, and then of expression; his poetry neither has wit in it, nor seems to have it; like him in Martial:

Pauper videri Cinna *vult, et est pauper.*[2]

"He affects plainness, to cover his want of imagination: when he writes the serious way, the highest flight of his fancy is some miserable antithesis, or seeming contradiction; and in the comic he is still reaching at some thin conceit, the ghost of a jest, and that too flies before him, never to be caught; these swallows which we see before us on the Thames are the just resemblance of his wit: you may observe how near the water they stoop, how many proffers they make to dip, and yet how seldom they touch it; and when they do, it is but the surface:

[2] "He wishes to appear a pauper, does Cinna: and he is a pauper." *Martial* VIII. 19.

they skim over it but to catch a gnat, and then mount into the air and leave it."

3. "Well, gentlemen," said Eugenius, "you may speak your pleasure of these authors; but though I and some few more about the town may give you a peaceable hearing, yet assure yourselves, there are multitudes who would think you malicious and them injured: especially him whom you first described; he is the very Withers of the city: they have bought more editions of his works than would serve to lay under all their pies at the Lord Mayor's Christmas. When his famous poem first came out in the year 1660, I have seen them reading it in the midst of 'Change time; nay so vehement they were at it, that they lost their bargain by the candles' ends; but what will you say if he has been received amongst great persons? I can assure you he is, this day, the envy of one who is lord in the art of quibbling, and who does not take it well that any man should intrude so far into his province." "All I would wish," replied Crites, "is, that they who love his writings, may still admire him, and his fellow poet: *Qui Bavium non odit, etc.*, [3] is curse sufficient." "And farther," added Lisideius, "I believe there is no man who writes well, but would think he had hard measure, if their admirers should praise anything of his: *Nam quos contemnimus, eorum quoque laudes contemnimus.*" [4] "There are so few who write well in this age," says Crites, "that methinks any praises should be welcome; they neither rise to the dignity of the last age, nor to any of the Ancients: and we may cry out of the writers of this time, with more reason than Petronius of his, *Pace vestrâ liceat dixisse, primi omnium eloquentiam perdidistis:* [5] you have debauched the true old poetry so far, that Nature, which is the soul of it, is not in any of your writings."

4. "If your quarrel," said Eugenius, "to those who now write, be grounded only on your reverence to antiquity, there is no man more ready to adore those great Greeks and Romans than I am: but on the other side, I cannot think so contemptibly of the age in which I live, or so dishonourably of my own country, as not to judge we equal the Ancients in most kinds of poesy, and in some surpass them; neither know I any reason why I may not be as zealous for the reputation of our age as we find the Ancients themselves were in reference to those who lived before them. For you hear your Horace saying,

[3] "Who does not hate Bavius." Virgil, *Eclogues* III. 90.
[4] "For we despise the praise of people whom we despise."

[5] "By your leave, let me say that you were the first to lose that eloquence, which all before you had had." Petronius, *Satyr.* 2.

*Indignor quidquam reprehendi, non quia crassé
Compositum, illepidève putetur, sed quia nuper.*[6]

And after:

*Si meliora dies, ut vina, poemata reddit,
Scire velim, pretim chartis quotus arroget annus?*[7]

"But I see I am engaging in a wide dispute, where the arguments
are not like to reach close on either side; for Poesy is of so large an
extent, and so many both of the Ancients and Moderns have done well
in all kinds of it, that in citing one against the other, we shall take up
more time this evening than each man's occasions will allow him:
therefore I would ask Crites to what part of Poesy he would confine
his arguments, and whether he would defend the general cause of the
Ancients against the Moderns, or oppose any age of the Moderns
against this of ours?"

5. Crites, a little while considering upon this demand, told Eugenius, that if he pleased, he would limit their dispute to Dramatic Poesy;
in which he thought it not difficult to prove, either that the Ancients
were superior to the Moderns, or the last age of this of ours.

Eugenius was somewhat surprised, when he heard Crites make
choice of that subject. "For ought I see," said he, "I have undertaken
a harder province than I imagined; for though I never judged the
plays of the Greek or Roman poets comparable to ours, yet, on the
other side, those we now see acted come short of many which were
written in the last age: but my comfort is, if we are overcome, it will
be only by our own countrymen: and if we yield to them in this one
part of poesy, we more surpass them in all the other: for in the epic
or lyric way, it will be hard for them to show us one such amongst
them, as we have many now living, or who lately were: they can
produce nothing so courtly writ, or which expresses so much the conversation of a gentleman, as Sir John Suckling; nothing so even, sweet,
and flowing as Mr. Waller; nothing so majestic, so correct, as Sir John
Denham; nothing so elevated, so copious, and full of spirit as Mr.
Cowley; as for the Italian, French, and Spanish plays, I can make it
evident, that those who now write surpass them; and that the Drama
is wholly ours."

---

[6] "My indignation rises when any piece
is censured not because it is considered
written without clarity or wit, but simply
because it is recent." Horace, *Epist.* ii. i. 76.

[7] "If time betters books, like wines, let
me ask what year of their age bestows
value upon them?" *Ibid.* 34.

All of them were thus far of Eugenius his opinion, that the sweetness of English verse was never understood or practised by our fathers; even Crites himself did not much oppose it; and every one was willing to acknowledge how much our poesy is improved by the happiness of some writers yet living; who first taught us to mould our thoughts into easy and significant words,—to retrench the superfluities of expression,—and to make our rhyme so properly a part of the verse, that it should never mislead the sense, but itself be led and governed by it.

6. Eugenius was going to continue this discourse, when Lisideius told him that it was necessary, before they proceeded further, to take a standing measure of their controversy; for how was it possible to be decided who writ the best plays, before we know what a play should be? But, this once agreed on by both parties, each might have recourse to it, either to prove his own advantages, or to discover the failings of his adversary.

He had no sooner said this, but all desired the favour of him to give the definition of a play; and they were the more importunate, because neither Aristotle, nor Horace, nor any other, who had writ of that subject, had ever done it.

Lisideius, after some modest denials, at last confessed he had a rude notion of it; indeed, rather a description than a definition; but which served to guide him in his private thoughts, when he was to make a judgment of what others writ: that he conceived a play ought to be, *A just and lively image of human nature, representing its passions and humours, and the changes of fortune to which it is subject, for the delight and instruction of mankind.*

This definition, though Crites raised a logical objection against it— that it was only *a genere et fine*,[8] and so not altogether perfect, was yet well received by the rest; and after they had given order to the watermen to turn their barge, and row softly, that they might take the cool of the evening in their return, Crites, being desired by the company to begin, spoke on behalf of the Ancients, in this manner:—

"If confidence presage a victory, Eugenius, in his own opinion, has already triumphed over the Ancients: nothing seems more easy to him, than to overcome those whom it is our greatest praise to have imitated

---

[8] That is, set forth only "by general classification and by purpose," without sufficient *differentia*. "The description might be used of a narrative poem, or of a novel, as well as of a play. Dryden thought that the specific difference between drama and narrative was not likely to be mistaken, and was therefore of less importance than the points here described." (W. P. Ker, note in *Essays of John Dryden*.)

well; for we do not only build upon their foundations, but by their models. Dramatic Poesy had time enough, reckoning from Thespis (who first invented it) to Aristophanes, to be born, to grow up, and to flourish in maturity. It has been observed of arts and sciences, that in one and the same century they have arrived to great perfection; and no wonder, since every age has a kind of universal genius, which inclines those that live in it to some particular studies: the work then, being pushed on by many hands, must of necessity go forward.

"Is it not evident, in these last hundred years, (when the study of philosophy has been the business of all the Virtuosi in Christendom), that almost a new nature has been revealed to us? That more errors of the school have been detected, more useful experiments in philosophy have been made, more noble secrets in optics, medicine, anatomy, astronomy, discovered, than in all those credulous and doting ages from Aristotle to us?—so true it is, that nothing spreads more fast than science, when rightly and generally cultivated.

"Add to this, the more than common emulation that was in those times of writing well; which though it be found in all ages and all persons that pretend to the same reputation, yet Poesy, being then in more esteem than now it is, had greater honours decreed to the professors of it, and consequently the rivalship was more high between them; they had judges ordained to decide their merit, and prizes to reward it; and historians have been diligent to record of Eschylus, Euripides, Sophocles, Lycophron, and the rest of them, both who they were that vanquished in these wars of the theatre, and how often they were crowned: while the Asian kings and Grecian commonwealths scarce afforded them a nobler subject than the unmanly luxuries of a debauched court, or giddy intrigues of a factious city:—*Alit æmulatio ingenia* (says Paterculus), *et nunc invidia, nunc admiratio incitatio nem accendit*: Emulation is the spur of wit; and sometimes envy, sometimes admiration, quickens our endeavours.

"But now, since the rewards of honour are taken away, that virtuous emulation is turned into direct malice; yet so slothful, that it contents itself to condemn and cry down others, without attempting to do better: it is a reputation too unprofitable, to take the necessary pains for it; yet, wishing they had it, that desire is incitement enough to hinder others from it. And this, in short, Eugenius, is the reason why you have now so few good poets, and so many severe judges. Certainly, to imitate the Ancients well, much labour and long study is required; which pains, I have already shown, our poets would want encouragement to take, if yet they had ability to go through the work. Those Ancients have been faithful imitators and wise observers of that Nature which is so torn and ill represented in our plays; they have handed down to us a perfect resemblance of her; which we, like ill copiers, neglecting to look on, have rendered monstrous, and disfigured. But, that you may know how much you are indebted to those your masters, and be ashamed to have so ill requited them, I must remember you, that all the rules by which we practise the Drama at this day (either such as relate to the justness and symmetry of the plot, or the episodical ornaments, such as descriptions, narrations, and other beauties, which are not essential to the play,) were delivered to us from the observations which Aristotle made, of those poets, who either lived before him, or were his contemporaries: we have added nothing of our own, except we have the confidence to say our wit is better; of which, none boast in this our age, but such as understand not theirs. Of that book which Aristotle has left us, περὶ τῆς Ποιητικῆς, Horace his Art of Poetry is an excellent comment, and, I believe, restores to us that Second Book of his concerning *Comedy,* which is wanting in him.

"Out of these two have been extracted the famous Rules, which the French call *Des Trois Unitez,* or, The Three Unities, which ought to be observed in every regular play; namely, of Time, Place, and Action.

"The Unity of Time they comprehend in twenty-four hours, the compass of a natural day, or as near as it can be contrived; and the reason of it is obvious to every one,—that the time of the feigned action, or fable of the play, should be proportioned as near as can be to the duration of that time in which it is represented: since, therefore, all plays are acted on the theatre in the space of time much within the compass of twenty-four hours, that play is to be thought the nearest imitation of nature, whose plot or action is confined within that time; and, by the same rule which concludes this general proportion of time, it follows, that all the parts of it are (as near as may be) to be equally subdivided; namely, that one act take not up the supposed time of half a day, which is out of proportion to the rest; since the other four are then to be straitened within the compass of the remaining half: for it is unnatural that one act, which being spoke or written is not longer than the rest, should be supposed longer by the audience; it is therefore the poet's duty, to take care that no act should be imagined to exceed the time in which it is represented on the stage; and that the intervals and inequalities of time be supposed to fall out between the acts.

"This rule of time, how well it has been observed by the Ancients, most of their plays will witness; you see them in their tragedies (wherein to follow this rule is certainly most difficult), from the very beginning of their plays, falling close into that part of the story which they intend for the action or principal object of it, leaving the former part to be delivered by narration: so that they set the audience, as it were, at the post where the race is to be concluded; and, saving them the tedious expectation of seeing the poet set out and ride the beginning of the course, they suffer you not to behold him, till he is in sight of the goal, and just upon you.

"For the second Unity, which is that of Place, the Ancients meant by it, that the scene ought to be continued through the play, in the same place where it was laid in the beginning: for, the stage on which it is represented being but one and the same place, it is unnatural to conceive it many,—and those far distant from one another. I will not deny but, by the variation of painted scenes, the fancy, which in these cases will contribute to its own deceit, may sometimes imagine it several places, with some appearance of probability; yet it still carries the greater likelihood of truth if those places be supposed so near each other as in the same town or city; which may all be comprehended under the larger denomination of one place; for a greater distance will bear no proportion to the shortness of time which is allotted, in the acting, to pass from one of them to another; for the observation of this, next to the Ancients, the French are to be most commended. They tie themselves so strictly to the Unity of Place that you never see in any of their plays a scene changed in the middle of an act: if the act begins in a garden, a street, or chamber, 'tis ended in the same place; and that you may know it to be the same, the stage is so supplied with persons, that it is never empty all the time: he who enters second, has business with him who was on before; and before the second quits the stage, a third appears who has business with him. This Corneille calls *la liaison des scenes,* the continuity or joining of the scenes; and 'tis a good mark of a well-contrived play, when all the persons are known to each other, and every one of them has some affairs with all the rest.

"As for the third Unity, which is that of Action, the Ancients meant no other by it than what the logicians do by their *finis,* the end or scope of any action; that which is the first in intention, and last in execution: now the poet is to aim at one great and complete action, to the carrying on of which all things in his play, even the very obstacles, are to be subservient; and the reason of this is as evident as any of the former. For two actions, equally laboured and driven on by the writer, would destroy the unity of the poem; it would be no longer one play, but two: not but that there may be many actions in a play, as Ben Jonson has observed in his *Discoveries;* but they must be all subservient to the great one, which our language happily expresses in the name of *under-plots:* such as in Terence's *Eunuch* is the difference and reconcilement of Thais and Phædria, which is not the chief business of the play, but promotes the marriage of Chærea and Chremes's sister, principally intended by the poet. There ought to be but one action, says Corneille, that is, one complete action, which leaves the mind of the audience in a full repose; but this cannot be brought to pass but by many other imperfect actions, which conduce to it, and hold the audience in a delightful suspence of what will be.

"If by these rules (to omit many other drawn from the precepts and practice of the Ancients) we should judge our modern plays, 'tis probable that few of them would endure the trial: that which should be the business of a day, takes up in some of them an age; instead of one action, they are the epitomes of a man's life; and for one spot of ground, which the stage should represent, we are sometimes in more countries than the map can show us.

"But if we allow the Ancients to have contrived well, we must acknowledge them to have written better. Questionless we are deprived of a great stock of wit in the loss of Menander among the Greek poets, and of Cæcilius, Afranius, and Varius, among the Romans; we may guess at Menander's excellency by the plays of Terence, who translated some of his; and yet wanted so much of him, that he was called by C. Cæsar the half-Menander; and may judge of Varius, by the testimonies of Horace, Martial, and Velleius Paterculus. 'Tis probable that these, could they be recovered, would decide the controversy; but so long as Aristophanes and Plautus are extant, while the tragedies of Euripides, Sophocles, and Seneca, are in our hands, I can never see one of those plays which are now written but it increases my admiration of the Ancients. And yet I must acknowledge further, that to admire them as we ought, we should understand them better than we do. Doubtless many things appear flat to us, the wit of which depended on some custom or story, which never came to our knowledge; or perhaps on some criticism in their language, which being so long dead, and only remaining in their books, 'tis not possible they should make us understand perfectly. To read Macrobius, explaining the propriety and elegancy of many words in Virgil, which I had before passed over without consideration as common things, is enough to assure me that I ought to think the same of Terence; and that in the purity of his style (which Tully so much valued that he ever carried his works about him) there is yet left in him great room for admiration, if I knew but where to place it. In the meantime I must desire you to take notice that the greatest man of the last age (Ben Jonson) was willing to give place to them in all things: he was not only a professed imitator of Horace, but a learned plagiary of all the others; you track him everywhere in their snow: if Horace, Lucan, Petronius Arbiter, Seneca, and Juvenal, had their own from him, there are few serious thoughts which are new in him: you will pardon me, therefore, if I presume he loved their fashion, when he wore their clothes. But since I have otherwise a great veneration for him, and you, Eugenius, prefer him above all other poets, I will use no farther argument to you than his example: I will produce before you Father Ben, dressed in all the ornaments and colours of the Ancients; you will need no other guide to our party, if you follow him; and whether you consider the bad plays of our age, or regard the good plays of the last, both the best and worst of the modern poets will equally instruct you to admire the Ancients."

Crites had no sooner left speaking, but Eugenius, who had waited with some impatience for it, thus began:

"I have observed in your speech, that the former part of it is convincing as to what the Moderns have profited by the rules of the Ancients; but in the latter you are careful to conceal how much they have excelled them; we own all the helps we have from them, and want neither veneration nor gratitude, while we acknowledge that, to overcome them, we must make use of the advantages we have received from them: but to these assistances we have joined our own industry; for, had we sat down with a dull imitation of them, we might then have lost somewhat of the old perfection, but never acquired any that was new. We draw not therefore after their lines, but those of Nature; and having the life before us, besides the experience of all they knew, it is no wonder if we hit some airs and features which they have missed. I deny not what you urge of arts and sciences, that they have flourished in some ages more than others; but your instance in philosophy makes for me: for if natural causes be more known now than in the time of Aristotle, because more studied, it follows that poesy and other arts may, with the same pains, arrive still nearer to perfection; and, that granted, it will rest for you to prove that they wrought more perfect images of human life than we; which seeing in your discourse you have avoided to make good, it shall now be my task to show you some part of their defects, and some few excellencies of the Moderns. And I think there is none among us can imagine I do it enviously, or with purpose to detract from them; for what interest of fame or profit can the living lose by the reputation of the dead? On the other side, it is a great truth which Velleius Paterculus affirms: *Audita visis libentius laudamus; et præsentia invidia præterita admiratione prosequimur; et his nos obrui, illis instrui credimus:* [9] that praise or censure is certainly the most sincere, which unbribed posterity shall give us.

"Be pleased then in the first place to take notice that the Greek poesy, which Crites has affirmed to have arrived to perfection in the reign of the Old Comedy, was so far from it that the distinction of it into acts was not known to them; or if it were, it is yet so darkly delivered to us that we cannot make it out.

"All we know of it is from the singing of their Chorus; and that too is so uncertain, that in some of their plays we have reason to conjecture they sung more than five times. Aristotle indeed divides the integral parts of a play into four. First, the *Protasis,* or entrance, which gives light only to the characters of the persons, and proceeds very little into any part of the action. Secondly, the *Epitasis,* or working up of the plot; where the play grows warmer, the design or action of it is drawing on, and you see something promising that it will come to pass. Thirdly, the *Catastasis,* called by the Romans, *Status,* the height and full growth of the play: we may call it properly the counter-turn, which destroys that expectation, imbroils the action in new difficulties, and leaves you far distant from that hope in which it found you; as you may have observed in a violent stream resisted by a narrow passage,—it runs round to an eddy, and carries back the waters with more swiftness than it brought them on. Lastly, the *Catastrophe,* which the Grecians called λύσις, the French *le dénouement,* and we the discovery, or unravelling of the plot: there you see all things settling again upon their first foundations; and, the ob-

---

[9] "We praise things heard more freely than things seen; and we accompany envy for the present with admiration for the past; we believe ourselves oppressed by the former and by the latter strengthened."

stacles which hindered the design or action of the play once removed, it ends with that resemblance of truth and nature, that the audience are satisfied with the conduct of it. Thus this great man delivered to us the image of a play; and I must confess it is so lively, that from thence much light has been derived to the forming it more perfectly into acts and scenes: but what poet first limited to five the number of the acts, I know not; only we see it so firmly established in the time of Horace, that he gives it for a rule in comedy,—*Neu brevior quinto, neu sit productior actu.*[10] So that you see the Grecians cannot be said to have consummated this art; writing rather by entrances than by acts, and having rather a general indigested notion of a play, than knowing how and where to bestow the particular graces of it.

"But since the Spaniards at this day allow but three acts, which they call *Jornadas,* to a play, and the Italians in many of theirs follow them, when I condemn the Ancients, I declare it is not altogether because they have not five acts to every play, but because they have not confined themselves to one certain number: it is building an house without a model; and when they succeeded in such undertakings, they ought to have sacrificed to Fortune, not to the Muses.

"Next, for the plot, which Aristotle called τὸ μῦθος, and often τῶν πραγμάτων σύνθεσις,[11] and from him the Romans *Fabula;* it has already been judiciously observed by a late writer, that in their tragedies it was only some tale derived from Thebes or Troy, or at least something that happened in those two ages; which was worn so threadbare by the pens of all the epic poets, and even by tradition, itself of the talkative Greeklings (as Ben Jonson calls them), that before it came upon the stage it was already known to all the audience: and the people, so soon as ever they heard the name of Œdipus, knew as well as the poet, that he had killed his father by a mistake, and committed incest with his mother, before the play; that they were now to hear of a great plague, an oracle, and the ghost of Laius: so that they sat with a yawning kind of expectation, till he was to come with his eyes pulled out, and speak a hundred or more verses in a tragic tone, in complaint of his misfortunes. But one Œdipus, Hercules, or Medea, had been tolerable: poor people, they escaped not so good cheap; they had still the *chapon bouille* [12] set before them, till their

[10] "Let it be neither shorter nor longer than five acts." Horace: *Ars Poetica,* 189.

[11] Lit., "the placing together of the actions."

[12] (*Fr.*) "sop of bread."

appetites were cloyed with the same dish, and, the novelty being gone, the pleasure vanished; so that one main end of Dramatic Poesy in its definition, which was to cause delight, was of consequence destroyed.

"In their comedies, the Romans generally borrowed their plots from the Greek poets; and theirs was commonly a little girl stolen or wandered from her parents, brought back unknown to the city, there [falling into the hands of] some young fellow, who, by the help of his servant, cheats his father; and when her time comes, to cry,— *Juno Lucina, fer opem*,[18]—one or other sees a little box or cabinet which was carried away with her, and so discovers her to her friends, if some god do not prevent it, by coming down in a machine, and taking the thanks of it to himself.

"By the plot you may guess much of the characters of the persons. An old father, who would willingly, before he dies, see his son well married; his debauched son, kind in his nature to his mistress, but miserably in want of money; a servant or slave, who has so much wit to strike in with him, and help to dupe his father; a braggadocio captain, a parasite, and a lady of pleasure.

"As for the poor honest maid, on whom the story is built, and who ought to be one of the principal actors in the play, she is commonly a mute in it: she has the breeding of the old Elizabeth way, which was for maids to be seen and not to be heard; and it is enough you know she is willing to be married, when the fifth act requires it.

"These are plots built after the Italian mode of houses,—you see through them all at once: the characters are indeed the imitation of Nature, but so narrow, as if they had imitated only an eye or an hand, and did not dare to venture on the lines of a face, or the proportion of a body.

"But in how strait a compass soever they have bounded their plots and characters, we will pass it by, if they have regularly pursued them, and perfectly observed those three Unities of Time, Place, and Action; the knowledge of which you say is derived to us from them. But in the first place give me leave to tell you, that the Unity of Place, however it might be practised by them, was never any of their rules: we neither find it in Aristotle, Horace, or any who have written of it, till in our age the French poets first made it a precept of the stage. The Unity of Time, even Terence himself, who was the best and most regular of them, has neglected: his *Heautontimorumenos*,

<hr>

[18] "O Juno, goddess of childbirth, help me." Terence: *Andr.* III, i.

or Self-Punisher, takes up visibly two days, says Scaliger; the two first acts concluding the first day, the three last the day ensuing; and Euripides, in tying himself to one day, has committed an absurdity never to be forgiven him; for in one of his tragedies he has made Theseus go from Athens to Thebes, which was about forty English miles, under the walls of it to give battle, and appear victorious in the next act; and yet, from the time of his departure to the return of the Nuntius, who gives the relation of his victory, Æthra and the Chorus have but thirty-six verses; which is not for every mile a verse.

"The like error is as evident in Terence his *Eunuch*, when Laches, the old man, enters by mistake into the house of Thais; where, betwixt his exit and the entrance of Pythias, who comes to give ample relation of the disorders he has raised within, Parmeno, who was left upon the stage, has not above five lines to speak. *C'est bien employer un temps si court*,[14] says the French poet, who furnished me with one of the observations: and almost all their tragedies will afford us examples of the like nature.

"It is true, they have kept the continuity, or, as you called it, *liaison des scenes,* somewhat better: two do not perpetually come in together, talk, and go out together; and other two succeed them, and do the same throughout the act, which the English call by the name of single scenes; but the reason is, because they have seldom above two or three scenes, properly so called, in every act; for it is to be accounted a new scene, not only every time the stage is empty; but every person who enters, though to others, makes it so; because he introduces a new business. Now the plots of their plays being narrow, and the persons few, one of their acts was written in a less compass than one of our well-wrought scenes; and yet they are often deficient even in this. To go no further than Terence; you find in the *Eunuch*, Antipho entering single in the midst of the third act, after Chremes and Pythias were gone off; in the same play you have likewise Dorias beginning the fourth act alone; and after she had made a relation of what was done at the Soldier's entertainment (which by the way was very inartificial, because she was presumed to speak directly to the audience, and to acquaint them with what was necessary to be known, but yet should have been so contrived by the poet as to have been told by persons of the drama to one another, and so by them to have come to the knowledge of the people), she quits the stage, and

---

[14] "It is well to employ so short a time." Corneille: *Troisième Discours.*

Phædria enters next, alone likewise: he also gives you an account of himself, and of his returning from the country, in monologue; to which unnatural way of narration Terence is subject in all his plays. In his *Adelphi,* or Brothers, Syrus and Demea enter after the scene was broken by the departure of Sostrata, Geta, and Canthara; and indeed you can scarce look unto any of his comedies, where you will not presently discover the same interruption.

"But as they have failed both in laying of their plots, and in the management, swerving from the rules of their own art by misrepresenting Nature to us, in which they have ill satisfied one intention of a play, which was delight; so in the instructive part they have erred worse: instead of punishing vice and rewarding virtue, they have often shewn a prosperous wickedness, and an unhappy piety: they have set before us a bloody image of revenge in Medea, and given her dragons to convey her safe from punishment; a Priam and Astyanax murdered, and Cassandra ravished, and the lust and murder ending in the victory of him who acted them: in short, there is no indecorum in any of our modern plays, which if I would excuse, I could not shadow with some authority from the Ancients.

"And one farther note of them let me leave you: tragedies and comedies were not writ then as they are now, promiscuously, by the same person; but he who found his genius bending to the one, never attempted the other way. This is so plain, that I need not instance to you, that Aristophanes, Plautus, Terence, never any of them writ a tragedy; Æschylus, Euripides, Sophocles, and Seneca, never meddled with comedy: the sock and buskin were not worn by the same poet. Having then so much care to excel in one kind, very little is to be pardoned them, if they miscarried in it; and this would lead me to the consideration of their wit, had not Crites given me sufficient warning not to be too bold in my judgment of it; because, the languages being dead, and many of the customs and little accidents on which it depended lost to us, we are not competent judges of it. But though I grant that here and there we may miss the application of a proverb or a custom, yet a thing well said will be wit in all languages; and though it may lose something in the translation, yet to him who reads it in the original, 'tis still the same: he has an idea of its excellency, though it cannot pass from his mind into any other expression or words than those in which he finds it. When Phædria, in the *Eunuch,* had a command from his mistress to be absent two days, and, encouraging himself to go through with it, said, *Tandem ego non illa caream, si sit opus, vel totum triduum?* [15]—Parmeno, to mock the softness of his master, lifting up his hands and eyes, cries out, as it were in admiration, *Hui! universum triduum!* [16] the elegancy of which *universum*, though it cannot be rendered in our language, yet leaves an impression on our souls: but this happens seldom in him; in Plautus oftener, who is infinitely too bold in his metaphors and coining words, out of which many times his wit is nothing; which questionless was one reason why Horace falls upon him so severely in those verses:

> *Sed proavi nostri Plautinos et numeros et*
> *Laudavere sales, nimium patienter utrumque.*
> *Ne dicam stolidè.* [17]

For Horace himself was cautious to obtrude a new word on his readers, and makes custom and common use the best measure of receiving it into our writings:

> *Multa renascentur quæ nunc cecidere, cadentque*
> *Quæ nunc sunt in honore vocabula, si volet usus,*
> *Quem penes arbitrium est, et jus, et norma loquendi.* [18]

"The not observing this rule is that which the world has blamed in our satirist, Cleveland: to express a thing hard and unnaturally, is his new way of elocution. 'Tis true, no poet but may sometimes use a catachresis: Virgil does it—

> *Mistaque ridenti colocasia fundet acantho—* [19]

in his eclogue of *Pollio;* and in his 7th *Æneid:*

> *mirantur et undæ,*
> *Miratur nemus insuetum fulgentia longe*
> *Scuta virum fluvio pictasque innare carinas.* [20]

[15] "Shall I not do without her, if there be need of it, even for three days?" *Eunuchus* II i. 18.

[16] "Alas, the entirety of three days." *Ibid.*

[17] Incorrectly quoted from Horace: *Ars Poetica,* 270–72. "But our forefathers praised both the numbers and witticisms of Plautus; too tolerantly, I will not say stupidly, admiring [*mirati*] each of them."

[18] "Many words shall revive, which now have fallen off; and many which are now in esteem shall fall off, if it be the will of custom, in whose power is the decision and right and standard of language." *Ars Poetica.* 70. Smart trans.

[19] "And the colocasia [an Egyptian bean; trans. T. F. Royds, 'odorous arum'] shall spread forth, mingled with the laughing acanthus." *Eclogues* IV 20. Whether the catachresis Dryden sees be on *ridenti, mista,* or *fundit,* who can say?

[20] "The woods and waters wonder at the gleam
Of shields, and painted ships, that stem the stream."
Aeneid VIII 91. Dryden trans.

And Ovid once so modestly, that he asks leave to do it:

> *quem, si verbo audacia detur,*
> *Haud metuam summi dixisse Palatia cæli.*[21]

calling the court of Jupiter by the name of Augustus his palace; though in another place he is more bold, where he says,—*et longas visent Capitolia pompas.*[21a] But to do this always, and never be able to write a line without it, though it may be admired by some few pedants, will not pass upon those who know that wit is best conveyed to us in the most easy language; and is most to be admired when a great thought comes dressed in words so commonly received, that it is understood by the meanest apprehensions, as the best meat is the most easily digested: but we cannot read a verse of Cleveland's without making a face at it, as if every word were a pill to swallow: he gives us many times a hard nut to break our teeth, without a kernel for our pains. So that there is this difference betwixt his Satires and doctor Donne's; that the one gives us deep thoughts in common language, though rough cadence; the other gives us common thoughts in abstruse words: 'tis true, in some places his wit is independent of his words, as in that of the rebel Scot:

> Had *Cain* been *Scot*, God would have chang'd his doom;
> Not forc'd him wander, but confin'd him home.

"*Si sic omnia dixisset!*[22] This is wit in all languages: it is like Mercury, never to be lost or killed:—and so that other—

> For beauty, like white powder, makes no noise,
> And yet the silent hypocrite destroys.

You see the last line is highly metaphorical, but it is so soft and gentle, that it does not shock us as we read it.

"But, to return from whence I have digressed, to the consideration of the Ancients' writing, and their wit (of which by this time you will grant us in some measure to be fit judges). Though I see many excellent thoughts in Seneca, yet he of them who had a genius most proper for the stage, was Ovid; he had a way of writing so

---

[21] "Which, if a verbal licence may be granted, I shall not fear to call the Palatia [Caesar's palace] of the sky." a. "The capitol sees long processionals." *Metam.* I, 175 & 561.

[22] "If only he had spoken all things after this manner!" Juvenal, *Sat.* 10, 123.

fit to stir up a pleasing admiration and concernment, which are the objects of a tragedy, and to show the various movements of a soul combating betwixt two different passions, that, had he lived in our age, or in his own could have writ with our advantages, no man but must have yielded to him; and therefore I am confident the *Medea* is none of his: for, though I esteem it for the gravity and sententiousness of it, which he himself concludes to be suitable to a tragedy,— *Omne genus scripti gravitate tragœdia vincit,*[23]—yet it moves not my soul enough to judge that he, who in the epic way wrote things so near the drama as the story of Myrrha, of Caunus and Biblis, and the rest, should stir up no more concernment where he most endeavoured it. The masterpiece of Seneca I hold to be that scene in the *Troades,* where Ulysses is seeking for Astyanax to kill him: there you see the tenderness of a mother so represented in Andromache, that it raises compassion to a high degree in the reader, and bears the nearest resemblance of anything in the tragedies of the ancients to the excellent scenes of passion in Shakspeare, or in Fletcher: for love-scenes, you will find few among them; their tragic poets dealt not with that soft passion, but with lust, cruelty, revenge, ambition, and those bloody actions they produced; which were more capable of raising horror than compassion in an audience: leaving love untouched, whose gentleness would have tempered them; which is the most frequent of all the passions, and which, being the private concernment of every person, is soothed by viewing its own image in a public entertainment.

"Among their comedies, we find a scene or two of tenderness, and that where you would least expect it, in Plautus; but to speak generally, their lovers say little, when they see each other, but *anima mea vita mea;* Ζωὴ καὶ ψυχῇ,[24] as the women in Juvenal's time used to cry out in the fury of their kindness. Any sudden gust of passion (as an ecstasy of love in an unexpected meeting) cannot better be expressed than in a word and a sigh, breaking one another. Nature is dumb on such occasions; and to make her speak would be to represent her unlike herself. But there are a thousand other concernments of lovers, as jealousies, complaints, contrivances, and the like, where not to open their minds at large to each other, were to be wanting to their own love, and to the expectation of the audience; who watch

---

[23] "In gravity tragedy surpasses every genre of writing." Ovid, *Tristia* II, 381.
[24] "My soul, my life." [The Greek phrases, with the same meanings, are in the reverse order.]

the movements of their minds, as much as the changes of their fortunes. For the imaging of the first is properly the work of a poet; the latter he borrows from the historian."

Eugenius was proceeding in that part of his discourse, when Crites interrupted him. "I see," said he, "Eugenius and I are never like to have this question decided betwixt us; for he maintains, the Moderns have acquired a new perfection in writing; I can only grant they have altered the mode of it. Homer described his heroes men of great appetites, lovers of beef broiled upon the coals, and good fellows; contrary to the practice of the French Romances, whose heroes neither eat, nor drink, nor sleep, for love. Virgil makes Æneas a bold avower of his own virtues:

Sum pius Æneas, fama super æthera notus; [25]

which, in the civility of our poets is the character of a fanfaron or Hector: for with us the knight takes occasion to walk out, or sleep, to avoid the vanity of telling his own story, which the trusty 'squire is ever to perform for him. So in their love-scenes, of which Eugenius spoke last, the ancients were more hearty, were more talkative: they writ love as it was then the mode to make it; and I will grant thus much to Eugenius, that perhaps one of their poets had he lived in our age, *si foret hoc nostrum fato delapsus in ævum* [26] (as Horace says of Lucilius), he had altered many things; not that they were not natural before, but that he might accommodate himself to the age in which he lived. Yet in the meantime, we are not to conclude anything rashly against those great men, but preserve to them the dignity of masters, and give that honour to their memories, *quos Libitina sacravit,*[27] part of which we expect may be paid to us in future times."

This moderation of Crites, as it was pleasing to all the company, so it put an end to that dispute; which Eugenius, who seemed to have the better of the argument, would urge no farther: but Lisideius, after he had acknowledged himself of Eugenius his opinion concerning the Ancient, yet told him, he had forborne, till his discourse were ended, to ask him why he preferred the English plays above those of other nations? and whether we ought not to submit our stage to the exactness of our next neighbours?

[25] "I am that dutiful Aeneas, famed above the heavens." This line is constructed from parts of two, *Aeneid* I, 378–79.

[26] "If he had been dropped by the fates into this age of ours." *Sat.* I 10, 68.

[27] "Which Libitina [goddess of funerals] has hallowed." Horace: *Epist.* II 1, 49.

"Though," said Eugenius, "I am at all times ready to defend the honour of my country against the French, and to maintain, we are as well able to vanquish them with our pens, as our ancestors have been with their swords; yet, if you please," added he, looking upon Neander, "I will commit this cause to my friend's management; his opinion of our plays is the same with mine, and besides, there is no reason, that Crites and I, who have now left the stage, should re-enter so suddenly upon it; which is against the laws of comedy."

"If the question had been stated," replied Lisideius, "who had writ best, the French or English, forty years ago, I should have been of your opinion, and adjudged the honour to our own nation; but since that time" (said he, turning towards Neander), "we have been so long together bad Englishmen that we had not leisure to be good poets. Beaumont, Fletcher, and Jonson (who were only capable of bringing us to that degree of perfection which we have), were just then leaving the world; as if in an age of so much horror, wit, and those milder studies of humanity, had no farther business among us. But the Muses, who ever follow peace, went to plant in another country: it was then that the great Cardinal Richelieu began to take them into his protection; and that, by his encouragement, Corneille, and some other Frenchmen, reformed their theatre (which before was as much below ours, as it now surpasses it and the rest of Europe). But because Crites in his discourse for the Ancients has prevented me, by observing many rules of the stage which the Moderns have borrowed from them, I shall only, in short, demand of you, whether you are not convinced that of all nations the French have best observed them? In the Unity of Time you find them so scrupulous that it yet remains a dispute among their poets, whether the artificial day of twelve hours, more or less, be not meant by Aristotle, rather than the natural one of twenty-four; and consequently, whether all plays ought not to be reduced into that compass. This I can testify, that in all their dramas writ within these last twenty years and upwards, I have not observed any that have extended the time to thirty hours: in the Unity of Place they are full as scrupulous; for many of their critics limit it to that very spot of ground where the play is supposed to begin; none of them exceed the compass of the same town or city. The Unity of Action in all plays is yet more conspicuous; for they do not burden them with under-plots, as the English do: which is the reason why many scenes of our tragi-comedians carry on a design that is nothing of kin to the main plot; and that we see two distinct webs in a play, like those in ill-wrought stuffs; and two actions, that is, two plays, carried on together, to the confounding of the audience; who, before they are warm in their concernments for one part, are diverted to another; and by that means espouse the interest of neither. From hence likewise it arises that the one half of our actors are not known to the other. They keep their distances, as if they were Montagues and Capulets, and seldom begin an acquaintance till the last scene of the fifth act, when they are all to meet upon the stage. There is no theatre in the world has anything so absurd as the English tragi-comedy; 'tis a drama of our own invention, and the fashion of it is enough to proclaim it so; here a course of mirth, there another of sadness and passion, and a third of honour and a duel: thus, in two hours and a half, we run through all the fits of Bedlam. The French affords you as much variety on the same day, but they do it not so unseasonably, or *mal à propos,* as we: our poets present you the play and the farce together; and our stages still retain somewhat of the original civility of the Red Bull:

Atque ursum et pugiles media inter carmina poscunt.[28]

The end of tragedies or serious plays, says Aristotle, is to beget admiration, compassion, or concernment; but are not mirth and compassion things incompatible? and is it not evident that the poet must of necessity destroy the former by intermingling of the latter? that is, he must ruin the sole end and object of his tragedy, to introduce somewhat that is forced into it, and is not of the body of it. Would you not think that physician mad, who, having prescribed a purge, should immediately order you to take restringents?

"But to leave our plays, and return to theirs. I have noted one great advantage they have had in the plotting of their tragedies; that is, they are always grounded upon some known history: according to that of Horace, *Ex noto fictum carmen sequar;* [29] and in that they have so imitated the Ancients that they have surpassed them. For the Ancients, as was observed before, took for the foundation of their plays some poetical fiction, such as under that consideration could move but little concernment in the audience, because they already knew the event of it. But the French goes farther:

[28] . . . *media inter carmina poscunt Aut ursum aut pugiles:*
"In the middle of plays call for a bear or boxers."
Horace: *Epist.* II 1, 185.
[29] "I should construct a poem founded on a well known story." Horace, *Ars Poet.* 240.

*Atque ita mentitur, sic veris falsa remiscet
Primo ne medium, medio ne discrepet imum.*[30]

He so interweaves truth with probable fiction that he puts a pleasing fallacy upon us; mends the intrigues of fate, and dispenses with the severity of history, to reward that virtue which has been rendered to us there unfortunate. Sometimes the story has left the success so doubtful that the writer is free, by the privilege of a poet, to take that which of two or more relations will best suit with his design: as for example, in the death of Cyrus, whom Justin and some others report to have perished in the Scythian war, but Xenophon affirms to have died in his bed of extreme old age. Nay more, when the event is past dispute, even then we are willing to be deceived, and the poet, if he contrives it with appearance of truth, has all the audience of his party; at least during the time his play is acting: so naturally we are kind to virtue, when our own interest is not in question, that we take it up as the general concernment of mankind. On the other side, if you consider the historical plays of Shakspeare, they are rather so many chronicles of kings, or the business many times of thirty or forty years, cramped into a representation of two hours and a half; which is not to imitate or paint Nature, but rather to draw her in miniature, to take her in little; to look upon her through the wrong end of a perspective, and receive her images not only much less, but infinitely more imperfect than the life: this, instead of making a play delightful, renders it ridiculous:—

Quodcunque ostendis mihi sic, incredulus odi.[31]

For the spirit of man cannot be satisfied but with truth, or at least verisimility; and a poem is to contain, if not τὰ ἔτυμα, yet ἐτύμοισιν ὁμοῖα,[32] as one of the Greek poets has expressed it.

"Another thing in which the French differ from us and from the Spaniards, is that they do not embarrass, or cumber themselves with too much plot; they only represent so much of a story as will constitute one whole and great action sufficient for a play; we, who undertake more, do but multiply adventures which, not being produced from one another, as effects from causes, but rarely following, con-

---

[30] "And he so lies, so mixes the false with the true, that the middle part is not discernible from the first, or the last part from the middle." *Ibid.* 151.
[31] "Whatever you thus show me, I hold incredible and odious." Horace: *Ars Poet.* 188.
[32] "True things" (Hesiod: *Theogonia* 27); [yet] "things like the truth" (Homer: *Od.* XIX, 203).

stitute many actions in the drama, and consequently make it many plays.

"But by pursuing closely one argument, which is not cloyed with many turns, the French have gained more liberty for verse, in which they write; they have leisure to dwell on a subject which deserves it; and to represent the passions (which we have acknowledged to be the poet's work), without being hurried from one thing to another, as we are in the plays of Calderon, which we have seen lately upon our theatres under the name of Spanish plots. I have taken notice but of one tragedy of ours whose plot has that uniformity and unity of design in it, which I have commended in the French; and that is *Rollo*, or rather, under the name of Rollo, the Story of Bassianus and Geta in Herodian: there indeed the plot is neither large nor intricate, but just enough to fill the minds of the audience, not to cloy them. Besides, you see it founded upon the truth of history, —only the time of the action is not reduceable to the strictness of the rules; and you see in some places a little farce mingled, which is below the dignity of the other parts, and in this all our poets are extremely peccant: even Ben Jonson himself, in *Sejanus* and *Catiline*, has given us this oleo of a play, this unnatural mixture of comedy and tragedy; which to me sounds just as ridiculously as the history of David with the merry humours of Golias. In *Sejanus* you may take notice of the scene betwixt Livia and the physician which is a pleasant satire upon the artificial helps of beauty: in *Catiline* you may see the parliament of women; the little envies of them to one another; and all that passes betwixt Curio and Fulvia: scenes admirable in their kind, but of an ill mingle with the rest.

"But I return again to the French writers, who, as I have said, do not burden themselves too much with plot, which has been reproached to them by an *ingenious person* of our nation as a fault; for, he says, they commonly make but one person considerable in a play; they dwell on him, and his concernments, while the rest of the persons are only subservient to set him off. If he intends this by it,—that there is one person in the play who is of greater dignity than the rest, he must tax, not only theirs, but those of the Ancients, and which he would be loth to do, the best of ours; for it is impossible but that one person must be more conspicuous in it than any other, and consequently the greatest share in the action must devolve on him. We see it so in the management of all affairs; even in the most equal aristocracy, the balance cannot be so justly poised but some one will be superior to the rest, either in parts, fortune, interest, or the consideration of some glorious exploit; which will reduce the greatest part of business into his hands.

"But, if he would have us to imagine, that in exalting one character the rest of them are neglected, and that all of them have not some share or other in the action of the play, I desire him to produce any of Corneille's tragedies, wherein every person, like so many servants in a well-governed family, has not some employment, and who is not necessary to the carrying on of the plot, or at least to your understanding it.

"There are indeed some protatic persons in the Ancients, whom they make use of in their plays, either to hear or give the relation: but the French avoid this with great address, making their narrations only to, or by such, who are some way interested in the main design. And now I am speaking of relations, I cannot take a fitter opportunity to add this in favour of the French, that they often use them with better judgment and more *à propos* than the English do. Not that I commend narrations in general,—but there are two sorts of them. One, of those things which are antecedent to the play, and are related to make the conduct of it more clear to us. But 'tis a fault to choose such subjects for the stage as will force us on that rock because we see they are seldom listened to by the audience and that is many times the ruin of the play; for, being once let pass without attention, the audience can never recover themselves to understand the plot: and indeed it is somewhat unreasonable that they should be put to so much trouble, as that, to comprehend what passes in their sight, they must have recourse to what was done, perhaps, ten or twenty years ago.

"But there is another sort of relations, that is, of things happening in the action of the play, and supposed to be done behind the scenes; and this is many times both convenient and beautiful; for by it the French avoid the tumult to which we are subject in England, by representing duels, battles, and the like; which renders our stage too like the theatres where they fight prizes. For what is more ridiculous than to represent an army with a drum and five men behind it; all which the hero of the other side is to drive in before him; or to see a duel fought, and one slain with two or three thrusts of the foils, which we know are so blunted that we might give a man an hour to kill another in good earnest with them.

"I have observed that in all our tragedies, the audience cannot forbear laughing when the actors are to die; it is the most comic part of the whole play. All *passions* may be lively represented on the stage, if to the well-writing of them the actor supplies a good commanded voice, and limbs that move easily, and without stiffness; but there are many *actions* which can never be imitated to a just height: dying especially is a thing which none but a Roman gladiator could naturally perform on the stage, when he did not imitate or represent, but do it; and therefore it is better to omit the representation of it.

"The words of a good writer, which describe it lively, will make a deeper impression of belief in us than all the actor can insinuate into us, when he seems to fall dead before us; as a poet in the description of a beautiful garden, or a meadow, will please our imagination more than the place itself can please our sight. When we see death represented, we are convinced it is but fiction; but when we hear it related, our eyes, the strongest witnesses, are wanting, which might have undeceived us; and we are all willing to favour the sleight, when the poet does not too grossly impose on us. They therefore who imagine these relations would make no concernment in the audience, are deceived, by confounding them with the other, which are of things antecedent to the play: those are made often in cold blood, as I may say, to the audience; but these are warmed with our concernments, which were before awakened in the play. What the philosophers say of motion, that, when it is once begun, it continues of itself, and will do so to eternity, without some stop put to it, is clearly true on this occasion: the soul being already moved with the characters and fortunes of those imaginary persons, continues going of its own accord; and we are no more weary to hear what becomes of them when they are not on the stage, than we are to listen to the news of an absent mistress. But it is objected, that if one part of the play may be related, then why not all? I answer, some parts of the action are more fit to be represented, some to be related. Corneille says judiciously that the poet is not obliged to expose to view all particular actions which conduce to the principal: he ought to select such of them to be seen, which will appear with the greatest beauty, either by the magnificence of the show, or the vehemence of passions which they produce, or some other charm which they have in them; and let the rest arrive to the audience by narration. 'Tis a great mistake in us to believe the French present no part of the action on the stage; every alteration or crossing of a design, every new-sprung passion, and turn of it, is a part of the action, and much the noblest, except we conceive nothing to be action till the players come to blows; as if the painting of the hero's mind were not more properly the poet's work than the strength of his body. Nor does this anything contradict the opinion of Horace, where he tells us,

> *Segnius irritant animos demissa per aurem,*
> *Quam quæ sunt oculis subjecta fidelibus.*[33]

For he says immediately after,

> *Non tamen intus*
> *Digna geri promes in scenam; multaq; tolles*
> *Ex oculis, quæ mox narret facundia præsens.*

Among which many he recounts some:

> *Nec pueros coram populo Medea trucidet,*
> *Aut in avem Progne mutetur, Cadmus in anguem, etc.*

That is, those actions which by reason of their cruelty, will cause aversion in us, or by reason of their impossibility, unbelief, ought either wholly to be avoided by a poet, or only delivered by narration. To which we may have leave to add, such as, to avoid tumult (as was before hinted), or to reduce the plot into a more reasonable compass of time, or for defect of beauty in them, are rather to be related than presented to the eye. Examples of all these kinds are frequent, not only among all the Ancients, but in the best received of our English poets. We find Ben Jonson using them in his *Magnetic Lady,* where one comes out from dinner, and relates the quarrels and disorders of it, to save the undecent appearance of them on the stage, and to abbreviate the story; and this in express imitation of Terence, who had done the same before him in his *Eunuch,* where Pythias makes the like relation of what had happened within at the Soldier's entertainment. The relations likewise of Sejanus's death, and the prodigies before it, are remarkable; the one of which was hid from

[33] "What things are given through the ears stir the mind less forcibly than what are put before the faithful eyes." Horace: *Ars Poet.* 180–81. He continues with the lines which Dryden next quotes: "Things worthy to be done off stage should not be brought to pass upon it; you must keep many events from sight and presently contrive to narrate them."

"Medea should not carve up the children in front of the audience; nor should Progne be changed into a bird there, nor Cadmus into a snake."

sight, to avoid the horror and tumult of the representation; the other, to shun the introducing of things impossible to be believed. In that excellent play, *The King and no King,* Fletcher goes yet farther; for the whole unravelling of the plot is done by narration in the fifth act, after the manner of the ancients; and it moves great concernment in the audience, though it be only a relation of what was done many years before the play. I could multiply other instances, but these are sufficient to prove that there is no error in choosing a subject which requires this sort of narrations; in the ill management of them, there may.

"But I find I have been too long in this discourse, since the French have many other excellencies not common to us; as that you never see any of their plays end with a conversion, or simple change of will, which is the ordinary way which our poets use to end theirs. It shows little art in the conclusion of a dramatic poem, when they who have hindered the felicity during the four acts, desist from it in the fifth, without some powerful cause to take them off their design; and though I deny not but such reasons may be found, yet it is a path that is cautiously to be trod, and the poet is to be sure he convinces the audience that the motive is strong enough. As for example, the conversion of the Usurer in *The Scornful Lady* seems to me a little forced; for, being an Usurer, which implies a lover of money to the highest degree of covetousness,—and such the poet has represented him,—the account he gives for the sudden change is, that he has been duped by the wild young fellow; which in reason might render him more wary another time, and make him punish himself with harder fare and coarser clothes, to get up again what he had lost: but that he should look on it as a judgment, and so repent, we may expect to hear in a sermon, but I should never endure it in a play.

"I pass by this; neither will I insist on the care they take that no person after his first entrance shall ever appear, but the business which brings him upon the stage shall be evident; which rule, if observed, must needs render all the events in the play more natural; for there you see the probability of every accident, in the cause that produced it; and that which appears chance in the play, will seem so reasonable to you, that you will there find it almost necessary: so that in the exit of the actor you have a clear account of his purpose and design in the next entrance (though, if the scene be well wrought, the event will commonly deceive you); for there is nothing so absurd, says

Corneille, as for an actor to leave the stage only because he has no more to say.

"I should now speak of the beauty of their rhyme, and the just reason I have to prefer that way of writing in tragedies before ours in blank verse; but because it is partly received by us, and therefore not altogether peculiar to them, I will say no more of it in relation to their plays. For our own, I doubt not but it will exceedingly beautify them; and I can see but one reason why it should not generally obtain, that is, because our poets write so ill in it. This indeed may prove a more prevailing argument than all others which are used to destroy it, and therefore I am only troubled when great and judicious poets, and those who are acknowledged such, have writ or spoke against it: as for others, they are to be answered by that one sentence of an ancient author:—*Sed ut primo ad consequendos eos quos priores ducimus, accendimur, ita ubi aut proeteriri, aut æquari eos posse desperavimus, studium cum spe senescit: quod, scilicet, assequi non potest, sequi desinit; . . . praeteritoque eo in quo eminere non possumus, aliquid in quo nitamur, conquirimus.*" [34]

Lisideius concluded in this manner; and Neander, after a little pause, thus answered him:

"I shall grant Lisideius, without much dispute, a great part of what he has urged against us; for I acknowledge that the French contrive their plots more regularly, and observe the laws of comedy, and decorum of the stage (to speak generally), with more exactness than the English. Farther, I deny not but he has taxed us justly in some irregularities of ours, which he has mentioned; yet, after all, I am of opinion that neither our faults nor their virtues are considerable enough to place them above us.

"For the lively imitation of Nature being in the definition of a play, those which best fulfil that law ought to be esteemed superior to the others. 'Tis true, those beauties of the French poesy are such as will raise perfection higher where it is, but are not sufficient to give it where it is not: they are indeed the beauties of a statue, but not of a man, because not animated with the soul of Poesy, which is imitation of humour and passions: and this Lisideius himself, or any other, however biassed to their party, cannot but acknowledge, if he will

---

[34] "But as we are fired to the following of those whom we consider foremost, so when we despair either of surpassing or equalling them, our zeal wanes with our hope; indeed, because it cannot excel, it ceases to follow. That being past in which we cannot be foremost, we seek for something on which to strive." Velleius 1 17.

either compare the humours of our comedies, or the characters of our serious plays, with theirs. He who will look upon theirs which have been written till these last ten years, or thereabouts, will find it a hard matter to pick out two or three passable humours amongst them. Corneille himself, their arch-poet, what has he produced except *The Liar*, and you know how it was cried up in France; but when it came upon the English stage, though well translated, and that part of Dorant acted to so much advantage as I am confident it never received in its own country, the most favourable to it would not put it in competition with many of Fletcher's or Ben Jonson's. In the rest of Corneille's comedies you have little humour; he tells you himself, his way is, first to show two lovers in good intelligence with each other; in the working up of the play to embroil them by some mistake, and in the latter end to clear it, and reconcile them.

"But of late years Molière, the younger Corneille, Quinault, and some others, have been imitating afar off the quick turns and graces of the English stage. They have mixed their serious plays with mirth, like our tragi-comedies, since the death of Cardinal Richelieu; which Lisideius and many others not observing, have commended that in them for a virtue which they themselves no longer practise. Most of their new plays are, like some of ours, derived from the Spanish novels. There is scarce one of them without a veil, and a trusty Diego, who drolls much after the rate of *The Adventures*. But their humours, if I may grace them with that name, are so thin-sown, that never above one of them comes up in any play. I dare take upon me to find more variety of them in some one play of Ben Jonson's than in all theirs together; as he who has seen *The Alchemist, The Silent Woman,* or *Bartholomew-Fair,* cannot but acknowledge with me.

"I grant the French have performed what was possible on the ground-work of the Spanish plays; what was pleasant before, they have made regular: but there is not above one good play to be writ on all those plots; they are too much alike to please often; which we need not the experience of our own stage to justify. As for their new way of mingling mirth with serious plot, I do not, with Lisideius, condemn the thing, though I cannot approve their manner of doing it. He tells us, we cannot so speedily recollect ourselves after a scene of great passion and concernment, as to pass to another of mirth and humour, and to enjoy it with any relish: but why should he imagine the soul of man more heavy than his senses? Does not the eye pass from an unpleasant object to a pleasant in a much shorter time than is required to this? and does not the unpleasantness of the first commend the beauty of the latter? The old rule of logic might have convinced him, that contraries, when placed near, set off each other. A continued gravity keeps the spirit too much bent; we must refresh it sometimes, as we bait in a journey that we may go on with greater ease. A scene of mirth, mixed with tragedy, has the same effect upon us which our music has betwixt the acts; which we find a relief to us from the best plots and language of the stage, if the discourses have been long. I must therefore have stronger arguments, ere I am convinced that compassion and mirth in the same subject destroy each other; and in the meantime cannot but conclude, to the honour of our nation, that we have invented, increased, and perfected a more pleasant way of writing for the stage, than was ever known to the ancients or moderns of any nation, which is tragicomedy.

"And this leads me to wonder why Lisideius and many others should cry up the barrenness of the French plots above the variety and copiousness of the English. Their plots are single; they carry on one design, which is pushed forward by all the actors, every scene in the play contributing and moving towards it. Our plays, besides the main design, have under-plots or by-concernments, of less considerable persons and intrigues, which are carried on with the motion of the main plot: as they say the orb of the fixed stars, and those of the planets, though they have motions of their own, are whirled about by the motion of the *primum mobile,* in which they are contained. That similitude expresses much of the English stage; for if contrary motions may be found in nature to agree; if a planet can go east and west at the same time;—one way by virtue of his own motion, the other by the force of the First Mover;—it will not be difficult to imagine how the under-plot, which is only different, not contrary to the great design, may naturally be conducted along with it.

"Eugenius has already shown us, from the confession of the French poets, that the Unity of Action is sufficiently preserved, if all the imperfect actions of the play are conducing to the main design; but when those petty intrigues of a play are so ill ordered, that they have no coherence with the other, I must grant that Lisideius has reason to tax that want of due connection; for co-ordination in a play is as dangerous and unnatural as in a state. In the meantime he must acknowledge, our variety, if well ordered, will afford a greater pleasure to the audience.

"As for his other argument, that by pursuing one single theme they gain an advantage to express and work up the passions, I wish any example he could bring from them would make it good; for I confess their verses are to me the coldest I have ever read. Neither, indeed, is it possible for them, in the way they take, so to express passion, as that the effects of it should appear in the concernment of an audience, their speeches being so many declamations, which tire us with the length; so that instead of persuading us to grieve for their imaginary heroes, we are concerned for our own trouble, as we are in tedious visits of bad company; we are in pain till they are gone. When the French stage came to be reformed by Cardinal Richelieu, those long harangues were introduced to comply with the gravity of a churchman. Look upon the *Cinna* and the *Pompey;* they are not so properly to be called plays, as long discourses of reason of state; and *Polieucte* in matters of religion is as solemn as the long stops upon our organs. Since that time it is grown into a custom, and their actors speak by the hour-glass, like our parsons; nay, they account it the grace of their parts, and think themselves disparaged by the poet, if they may not twice or thrice in a play entertain the audience with a speech of an hundred lines. I deny not but this may suit well enough with the French; for as we, who are a more sullen people, come to be diverted at our plays, so they, who are of an airy and gay temper, come thither to make themselves more serious: and this I conceive to be one reason why comedies are more pleasing to us, and tragedies to them. But to speak generally: it cannot be denied that short speeches and replies are more apt to move the passions and beget concernment in us, than the other; for it is unnatural for any one in a gust of passion to speak long together, or for another in the same condition to suffer him, without interruption. Grief and passion are like floods raised in little brooks by a sudden rain; they are quickly up; and if the concernment be poured unexpectedly in upon us, it overflows us: but a long sober shower gives them leisure to run out as they came in, without troubling the ordinary current. As for Comedy, repartee is one of its chiefest graces; the greatest pleasure of the audience is a chase of wit, kept up on both sides, and swiftly managed. And this our forefathers, if not we, have had in Fletcher's plays, to a much higher degree of perfection than the French poets can reasonably hope to reach.

"There is another part of Lisideius his discourse, in which he rather excused our neighbours than commended them; that is, for aiming only to make one person considerable in their plays. 'Tis very true what he has urged, that one character in all plays, even without the poet's care, will have advantage of all the others; and that the design of the whole drama will chiefly depend on it. But this hinders not that there may be more shining characters in the play: many persons of a second magnitude, nay, some so very near, so almost equal to the first, that greatness may be opposed to greatness, and all the persons be made considerable, not only by their quality, but their action. 'Tis evident that the more the persons are, the greater will be the variety of the plot. If then the parts are managed so regularly, that the beauty of the whole be kept entire, and that the variety become not a perplexed and confused mass of accidents, you will find it infinitely pleasing to be led in a labyrinth of design, where you see some of your way before you, yet discern not the end till you arrive at it. And that all this is practicable, I can produce for examples many of our English plays: as *The Maid's Tragedy, The Alchemist, The Silent Woman:* I was going to have named *The Fox,* but that the unity of design seems not exactly observed in it; for there appear two actions in the play; the first naturally ending with the fourth act; the second forced from it in the fifth; which yet is the less to be condemned in him, because the disguise of Volpone, though it suited not with his character as a crafty or covetous person, agreed well enough with that of a voluptuary; and by it the poet gained the end at which he aimed, the punishment of vice, and the reward of virtue, both which that disguise produced. So that to judge equally of it, it was an excellent fifth act, but not so naturally proceeding from the former.

"But to leave this, and pass to the latter part of Lisideius his discourse, which concerns relations: I must acknowledge with him, that the French have reason to hide that part of the action which would occasion too much tumult on the stage, and to choose rather to have it made known by narration to the audience. Farther, I think it very convenient, for the reasons he has given, that all incredible actions were removed; but whether custom has so insinuated itself into our countrymen, or nature has so formed them to fierceness, I know not; but they will scarcely suffer combats and other objects of horror to be taken from them. And indeed, the indecency of tumults is all which can be objected against fighting: for why may not our imagination as well suffer itself to be deluded with the probability of it, as with any other thing in the play? For my part, I can with as great ease persuade myself that the blows are given in good earnest, as I can that they who strike them are kings or princes, or those persons which they represent. For objects of incredibility,—I would be satisfied from Lisideius, whether we have any so removed from all appearance of truth, as are those of Corneille's *Andromede;* a play which has been frequented the most of any he has writ. If the Perseus, or the son of a heathen god, the Pegasus, and the Monster, were not capable to choke a strong belief, let him blame any representation of ours hereafter. Those indeed were objects of delight; yet the reason is the same as to the probability: for he makes it not a Ballette or masque, but a play, which is to resemble truth. But for death, that it ought not to be represented, I have, besides the arguments alleged by Lisideius, the authority of Ben Jonson, who has forborne it in his tragedies; for both the death of Sejanus and Catiline are related: though in the latter I cannot but observe one irregularity of that great poet; he has removed the scene in the same act from Rome to Catiline's army, and from thence again to Rome; and besides, has allowed a very inconsiderable time, after Catiline's speech, for the striking of the battle, and the return of Petreius, who is to relate the event of it to the senate: which I should not animadvert on him, who was otherwise a painful observer of τὸ πρέπον, or the *decorum* of the stage, if he had not used extreme severity in his judgment on the incomparable Shakspeare for the same fault.—To conclude on this subject of relations; if we are to be blamed for showing too much of the action, the French are as faulty for discovering too little of it: a mean betwixt both should be observed by every judicious writer, so as the audience may neither be left unsatisfied by not seeing what is beautiful, or shocked by beholding what is either incredible or undecent.

"I hope I have already proved in this discourse, that though we are not altogether so punctual as the French in observing the laws of Comedy, yet our errors are so few, and little, and those things wherein we excel them so considerable, that we ought of right to be preferred before them. But what will Lisideius say, if they themselves acknowledge they are too strictly bounded by those laws, for breaking which he has blamed the English? I will allege Corneille's words, as I find them in the end of his Discourse of the Three Unities: *Il est facile aux spéculatifs d'estre sévères, etc.* ' 'Tis easy for speculative persons to judge severely; but if they would produce to public view ten or twelve pieces of this nature, they would perhaps give more latitude to the rules than I have done, when by experience they had known how much we are limited and constrained by them, and how many beauties of the stage they banished from it.' To illustrate a little what he has said: By their servile observations of the Unities of Time and Place, and integrity of scenes, they have brought on themselves that dearth of plot, and narrowness of imagination, which may be observed in all their plays. How many beautiful accidents might naturally happen in two or three days, which cannot arrive with any probability in the compass of twenty-four hours? There is time to be allowed also for maturity of design, which, amongst great and prudent persons, such as are often represented in Tragedy, cannot, with any likelihood of truth, be brought to pass at so short a warning. Farther; by tying themselves strictly to the Unity of Place, and unbroken scenes, they are forced many times to omit some beauties which cannot be shown where the act began; but might, if the scene were interrupted, and the stage cleared for the persons to enter in another place; and therefore the French poets are often forced upon absurdities; for if the act begins in a chamber, all the persons in the play must have some business or other to come thither, or else they are not to be shown that act; and sometimes their characters are very unfitting to appear there: as, suppose it were the king's bed-chamber; yet the meanest man in the tragedy must come and dispatch his business there, rather than in the lobby or courtyard (which is fitter for him), for fear the stage should be cleared, and the scenes broken. Many times they fall by it in a greater inconvenience; for they keep their scenes unbroken, and yet change the place; as in one of their newest plays, where the act begins in the street. There a gentleman is to meet his friend; he sees him with his man, coming out from his father's house; they talk together, and the first goes out: the second, who is a lover, has made an appointment with his mistress; she appears at the window, and then we are to imagine the scene lies under it. This gentleman is called away, and leaves his servant with his mistress; presently her father is heard from within; the young lady is afraid the serving-man should be discovered, and thrusts him into a place of safety, which is supposed to be her closet. After this, the father enters to the daughter, and now the scene is in a house; for he is seeking from one room to another for this poor Philipin, or French Diego, who is heard from within, drolling and breaking many a miserable conceit on the subject of his sad condition. In this ridiculous manner the play goes forward, the stage being never empty all the while: so that the street, the window, the houses, and the closet, are made to walk about, and the persons to stand still. Now what, I beseech you, is more easy than to write a regular French play, or more difficult than to write an irregular English one, like those of Fletcher, or of Shakspeare?

"If they content themselves, as Corneille did, with some flat design, which, like an ill riddle, is found out ere it be half proposed, such plots we can make every way regular, as easily as they; but whenever they endeavour to rise to any quick turns and counterturns of plot, as some of them have attempted, since Corneille's plays have been less in vogue, you see they write as irregularly as we, though they cover it more speciously. Hence the reason is perspicuous why no French plays, when translated, have, or ever can succeed on the English stage. For, if you consider the plots, our own are fuller of variety; if the writing, ours are more quick and fuller of spirit; and therefore 'tis a strange mistake in those who decry the way of writing plays in verse, as if the English therein imitated the French. We have borrowed nothing from them; our plots are weaved in English looms: we endeavour therein to follow the variety and greatness of characters which are derived to us from Shakspeare and Fletcher; the copiousness and well-knitting of the intrigues we have from Jonson; and for the verse itself we have English precedents of elder date than any of Corneille's plays. Not to name our old comedies before Shakspeare, which were all writ in verse of six feet, or Alexandrines, such as the French now use,—I can show in Shakspeare many scenes of rhyme together, and the like in Ben Jonson's tragedies: in *Catiline* and *Sejanus* sometimes thirty or forty lines,—I mean besides the Chorus, or the monologues; which, by the way, showed Ben no enemy to this way of writing, especially if you read his *Sad Shepherd*, which goes sometimes on rhyme, sometimes on blank verse, like an horse who eases himself on trot and amble. You find him likewise commending Fletcher's pastoral of *The Faithful Shepherdess*, which is for the most part rhyme, though not refined to that purity to which it hath since been brought. And these examples are enough to clear us from a servile imitation of the French.

"But to return whence I have digressed: I dare boldly affirm these two things of the English drama;—First, that we have many plays of ours as regular as any of theirs, and which, besides, have more variety of plot and characters; and secondly, that in most of the irregular plays of Shakspeare or Fletcher (for Ben Jonson's are for the most part regular), there is a more masculine fancy and greater spirit in the writing than there is in any of the French. I could produce, even in Shakspeare's and Fletcher's works, some plays which are almost exactly formed; as *The Merry Wives of Windsor,* and *The Scornful Lady:* but because (generally speaking) Shakspeare, who writ first, did not perfectly observe the laws of comedy, and Fletcher, who came nearer to perfection, yet through carelessness made many faults; I will take the pattern of a perfect play from Ben Jonson, who was a careful and learned observer of the dramatic laws, and from all his comedies I shall select *The Silent Woman;* of which I will make a short examen, according to those rules which the French observe."

As Neander was beginning to examine *The Silent Woman,* Eugenius, earnestly regarding him; "I beseech you, Neander," said he, "gratify the company, and me in particular, so far, as before you speak of the play, to give us a character of the author; and tell us frankly your opinion, whether you do not think all writers, both French and English, ought to give place to him."

"I fear," replied Neander, "that in obeying your commands I shall draw some envy on myself. Besides, in performing them, it will be first necessary to speak somewhat of Shakspeare and Fletcher, his rivals in poesy; and one of them, in my opinion, at least his equal, perhaps his superior.

"To begin, then, with Shakspeare. He was the man who of all modern, and perhaps ancient poets, had the largest and most comprehensive soul. All the images of Nature were still present to him, and he drew them, not laboriously, but luckily; when he describes anything, you more than see it, you feel it too. Those who accuse him to have wanted learning, give him the greater commendation: he was naturally learned; he needed not the spectacles of books to read Nature; he looked inwards, and found her there. I cannot say he is everywhere alike; were he so, I should do him injury to compare him with the greatest of mankind. He is many times flat, insipid; his comic wit degenerating into clenches, his serious swelling into bombast. But he is always great, when some great occasion is presented to him; no man can say he ever had a fit subject for his wit, and did not then raise himself as high above the rest of poets,

Quantum lenta solent inter viburna cupressi.[35]

---

[35] "As cypresses usually do among bending shrubs." Virgil: *Eclogues* 1 26.

The consideration of this made Mr. Hales of Eaton say, that there was no subject of which any poet ever writ, but he would produce it much better done in Shakspeare; and however others are now generally preferred before him, yet the age wherein he lived, which had contemporaries with him Fletcher and Jonson, never equalled them to him in their esteem: and in the last King's court, when Ben's reputation was at highest, Sir John Suckling, and with him the greater part of the courtiers, set our Shakspeare far above him.

"Beaumont and Fletcher, of whom I am next to speak, had, with the advantage of Shakspeare's wit, which was their precedent, great natural gifts, improved by study: Beaumont especially being so accurate a judge of plays, that Ben Jonson, while he lived, submitted all his writings to his censure, and, 'tis thought, used his judgment in correcting, if not contriving, all his plots. What value he had for him, appears by the verses he writ to him; and therefore I need speak no farther of it. The first play that brought Fletcher and him in esteem was their *Philaster:* for before that, they had written two or three very unsuccessfully, as the like is reported of Ben Jonson, before he writ *Every Man in his Humour.* Their plots were generally more regular than Shakspeare's, especially those which were made before Beaumont's death; and they understood and imitated the conversation of gentlemen much better; whose wild debaucheries, and quickness of wit in repartees, no poet before them could paint as they have done. Humour, which Ben Jonson derived from particular persons, they made it not their business to describe: they represented all the passions very lively, but above all, love. I am apt to believe the English language in them arrived to its highest perfection: what words have since been taken in, are rather superfluous than ornamental. Their plays are now the most pleasant and frequent entertainments of the stage; two of theirs being acted through the year for one of Shakspeare's or Jonson's: the reason is, because there is a certain gaiety in their comedies, and pathos in their more serious plays, which suit generally with all men's humours. Shakspeare's language is likewise a little obsolete, and Ben Jonson's wit comes short of theirs.

"As for Jonson, to whose character I am now arrived, if we look upon him while he was himself (for his last plays were but his dotages), I think him the most learned and judicious writer which any theatre ever had. He was a most severe judge of himself, as well as others. One cannot say he wanted wit, but rather that he was frugal of it. In his works you find little to retrench or alter. Wit, and language, and humour also in some measure, we had before him; but something of art was wanting to the Drama till he came. He managed his strength to more advantage than any who preceded him. You seldom find him making love in any of his scenes, or endeavouring to move the passions; his genius was too sullen and saturnine to do it gracefully, especially when he knew he came after those who had performed both to such an height. Humour was his proper sphere; and in that he delighted most to represent mechanic people. He was deeply conversant in the Ancients, both Greek and Latin, and he borrowed boldly from them: there is scarce a poet or historian among the Roman authors of those times whom he has not translated in *Sejanus* and *Catiline*. But he has done his robberies so openly, that one may see he fears not to be taxed by any law. He invades authors like a monarch; and what would be theft in other poets is only victory in him. With the spoils of these writers he so represents old Rome to us, in its rites, ceremonies, and customs, that if one of their poets had written either of his tragedies, we had seen less of it than in him. If there was any fault in his language, 'twas that he weaved it too closely and laboriously, in his comedies especially: perhaps, too, he did a little too much Romanise our tongue, leaving the words which he translated almost as much Latin as he found them: wherein, though he learnedly followed their language, he did not enough comply with the idiom of ours. If I would compare him with Shakspeare, I must acknowledge him the more correct poet, but Shakspeare the greater wit. Shakspeare was the Homer, or father of our dramatic poets; Jonson was the Virgil, the pattern of elaborate writing; I admire him, but I love Shakspeare. To conclude of him; as he has given us the most correct plays, so in the precepts which he has laid down in his *Discoveries,* we have as many and profitable rules for perfecting the stage, as any wherewith the French can furnish us.

"Having thus spoken of the author, I proceed to the examination of his comedy, *The Silent Woman.*

EXAMEN OF THE SILENT WOMAN

"To begin first with the length of the action; it is so far from exceeding the compass of a natural day, that it takes not up an artificial one. 'Tis all included in the limits of three hours and a

half, which is no more than is required for the presentment on the
stage: a beauty perhaps not much observed; if it had, we should not
have looked on the Spanish translation of *Five Hours* with so much
wonder. The scene of it is laid in London; the latitude of place is
almost as little as you can imagine; for it lies all within the compass
of two houses, and after the first act, in one. The continuity of scenes
is observed more than in any of our plays, except his own *Fox* and
Alchemist. They are not broken above twice or thrice at most in
the whole comedy; and in the two best of Corneille's plays, the *Cid*
and *Cinna,* they are interrupted once. The action of the play is entirely one; the end or aim of which is the settling Morose's estate on
Dauphine. The intrigue of it is the greatest and most noble of any
pure unmixed comedy in any language; you see in it many persons
of various characters and humours, and all delightful. As first, Morose,
or an old man, to whom all noise but his own talking is offensive.
Some who would be thought critics, say this humour of his is forced:
but to remove that objection, we may consider him first to be naturally of a delicate hearing, as many are, to whom all sharp sounds
are unpleasant; and secondly, we may attribute much of it to the
peevishness of his age, or the wayward authority of an old man in
his own house, where he may make himself obeyed; and to this the
poet seems to allude in his name Morose. Besides this, I am assured
from divers persons, that Ben Jonson was actually acquainted with
such a man, one altogether as ridiculous as he is here represented.
Others say, it is not enough to find one man of such an humour; it
must be common to more, and the more common the more natural.
To prove this, they instance in the best of comical characters, Falstaff. There are many men resembling him; old, fat, merry, cowardly,
drunken, amorous, vain, and lying. But to convince these people, I
need but tell them that humour is the ridiculous extravagance of
conversation, wherein one man differs from all others. If then it be
common, or communicated to many, how differs it from other men's?
or what indeed causes it to be ridiculous so much as the singularity
of it? As for Falstaff, he is not properly one humour, but a miscellany
of humours or images, drawn from so many several men: that wherein
he is singular is his wit, or those things he says *præter expectatum,*
unexpected by the audience; his quick evasions, when you imagine
him surprised, which, as they are extremely diverting of themselves,
so receive a great addition from his person; for the very sight of such
an unwieldy old debauched fellow is a comedy alone. And here, hav-

ing a place so proper for it, I cannot but enlarge somewhat upon this subject of humour into which I am fallen. The ancients had little of it in their comedies; for the τὸ γελοῖον [36] of the old comedy, of which Aristophanes was chief, was not so much to imitate a man, as to make the people laugh at some odd conceit, which had commonly somewhat of unnatural or obscene in it. Thus, when you see Socrates brought upon the stage, you are not to imagine him made ridiculous by the imitation of his actions, but rather by making him perform something very unlike himself; something so childish and absurd, as by comparing it with the gravity of the true Socrates, makes a ridiculous object for the spectators. In their New Comedy which succeeded, the poets sought indeed to express the ἦθος, as in their tragedies the πάθος [37] of mankind. But this ἦθος contained only the general characters of men and manners; as old men, lovers, serving-men, courtezans, parasites, and such other persons as we see in their comedies; all which they made alike: that is, one old man or father, one lover, one courtezan, so like another, as if the first of them had begot the rest of every sort: *Ex homine hunc natum dicas.*[38] The same custom they observed likewise in their tragedies. As for the French, though they have the word *humeur* among them, yet they have small use of it in their comedies or farces; they being but ill imitations of the *ridiculum,* or that which stirred up laughter in the Old Comedy. But among the English 'tis otherwise: where by humour is meant some extravagant habit, passion, or affection, particular (as I said before) to some one person, by the oddness of which, he is immediately distinguished from the rest of men; which being lively and naturally represented, most frequently begets that malicious pleasure in the audience which is testified by laughter; as all things which are deviations from customs are ever the aptest to produce it: though by the way this laughter is only accidental, as the person represented is fantastic or bizarre; but pleasure is essential to it, as the imitation of what is natural. The description of these humours, drawn from the knowledge and observation of particular persons, was the peculiar genius and talent of Ben Jonson; to whose play I now return.

"Besides Morose, there are at least nine or ten different characters and humours in *The Silent Woman;* all which persons have several

[36] "The laughable."
[37] ἦθος, "character"; πάθος, "emotion."
[38] "You would say that this fellow was born from that man." Terence: *Eunuchus* III 2, 7. Mr. Ker translates more freely, "The one is the born image of the other."

concernments of their own, yet are all used by the poet to the conducting of the main design to perfection. I shall not waste time in commending the writing of this play; but I will give you my opinion, that there is more wit and acuteness of fancy in it than in any of Ben Jonson's. Besides that he has here described the conversation of gentlemen in the persons of True-Wit, and his friends, with more gaiety, air, and freedom, than in the rest of his comedies. For the contrivance of the plot, 'tis extreme, elaborate, and yet withal easy; for the λυσις, or untying of it, 'tis so admirable, that when it is done, no one of the audience would think the poet could have missed it; and yet it was concealed so much before the last scene, that any other way would sooner have entered into your thoughts. But I dare not take upon me to commend the fabric of it, because it is altogether so full of art, that I must unravel every scene in it to commend it as I ought. And this excellent contrivance is still the more to be admired, because 'tis comedy, where the persons are only of common rank, and their business private, not elevated by passions or high concernments, as in serious plays. Here every one is a proper judge of all he sees, nothing is represented but that with which he daily converses: so that by consequence all faults lie open to discovery, and few are pardonable. 'Tis this which Horace has judiciously observed:

> *Creditur, ex medio quia res arcessit, habere*
> *Sudoris minimum; sed habet Comedia tanto*
> *Plus oneris, quanto veniæ minus.*[39]

But our poet who was not ignorant of these difficulties has made use of all advantages; as he who designs a large leap takes his rise from the highest ground. One of these advantages is that which Corneille has laid down as the greatest which can arrive to any poem, and which he himself could never compass above thrice in all his plays; viz., the making choice of some signal and long-expected day, whereon the action of the play is to depend. This day was that designed by Dauphine for the settling of his uncle's estate upon him; which to compass, he contrives to marry him. That the marriage had been plotted by him long beforehand, is made evident by what he tells True-wit in the second act, that in one moment he had destroyed what he had been raising many months.

---

[39] "Comedy is believed to require the least pains, because it fetches its subjects from common life; but the less indulgence it meets with, the more labor it requires." Horace: *Epist.* II i, 168. Smart trans.

"There is another artifice of the poet, which I cannot here omit, because by the frequent practice of it in his comedies he has left it to us almost as a rule; that is, when he has any character or humour wherein he would show a *coup de Maistre,* or his highest skill, he recommends it to your observation by a pleasant description of it before the person first appears. Thus, in *Bartholomew-Fair* he gives you the pictures of Numps and Cokes, and in this those of Daw, Lafoole, Morose, and the Collegiate Ladies; all which you hear described before you see them. So that before they come upon the stage, you have a longing expectation of them, which prepares you to receive them favourably; and when they are there, even from their first appearance you are so far acquainted with them, that nothing of their humour is lost to you.

"I will observe yet one thing further of this admirable plot; the business of it rises in every act. The second is greater than the first; the third than the second; and so forward to the fifth. There too you see, till the very last scene, new difficulties arising to obstruct the action of the play; and when the audience is brought into despair that the business can naturally be effected, then, and not before, the discovery is made. But that the poet might entertain you with more variety all this while, he reserves some new characters to show you, which he opens not till the second and third act; in the second Morose, Daw, the Barber, and Otter; in the third the Collegiate Ladies: all which he moves afterwards in by-walks, or under-plots, as diversions to the main design, lest it should grow tedious, though they are still naturally joined with it, and somewhere or other subservient to it. Thus, like a skilful chess-player, by little and little he draws out his men, and makes his pawns of use to his greater persons.

"If this comedy and some others of his were translated into French prose (which would now be no wonder to them, since Molière has lately given them plays out of verse, which have not displeased them), I believe the controversy would soon be decided betwixt the two nations, even making them the judges. But we need not call our heroes to our aid. Be it spoken to the honour of the English, our nation can never want in any age such who are able to dispute the empire of wit with any people in the universe. And though the fury of a civil war, and power for twenty years together abandoned to a barbarous race of men, enemies of all good learning, had buried the muses under the ruins of monarchy; yet, with the restoration of our happiness, we see revived poesy lifting up its head, and already shaking off the rubbish which lay so heavy on it. We have seen since his majesty's return, many dramatic poems which yield not to those of any foreign nation, and which deserve all laurels but the English. I will set aside flattery and envy: it cannot be denied but we have had some little blemish either in the plot or writing of all those plays which have been made within these seven years; (and perhaps there is no nation in the world so quick to discern them, or so difficult to pardon them, as ours:) yet if we can persuade ourselves to use the candour of that poet, who, though the most severe of critics, has left us this caution by which to moderate our censures—

> *ubi plura nitent in carmine, non ego paucis*
> *Offendar maculis;—*[40]

if, in consideration of their many and great beauties, we can wink at some slight and little imperfections, if we, I say, can be thus equal to ourselves, I ask no favour from the French. And if I do not venture upon any particular judgment of our late plays, 'tis out of the consideration which an ancient writer gives me: *vivorum, ut magna admiratio, ita censura difficilis:*[41] betwixt the extremes of admiration and malice, 'tis hard to judge uprightly of the living. Only I think it may be permitted me to say, that as it is no lessening to us to yield to some plays, and those not many, of our own nation in the last age, so can it be no addition to pronounce of our present poets, that they have far surpassed all the Ancients, and the modern writers of other countries."

This was the substance of what was then spoken on that occasion; and Lisideius, I think, was going to reply, when he was prevented thus by Crites: "I am confident," said he, "that the most material things that can be said have been already urged on either side; if they have not, I must beg of Lisideius that he will defer his answer till another time: for I confess I have a joint quarrel to you both, because you have concluded, without any reason given for it, that rhyme is proper for the stage. I will not dispute how ancient it hath been among us to write this way; perhaps our ancestors knew no better till Shakspeare's time. I will grant it was not altogether left by him, and that Fletcher and Ben Jonson used it frequently in their Pastorals, and sometimes in other plays. Farther,—I will not argue

---

[40] "Where many beauties shine in a poem, I am not offended at little faults." Horace: *Ars Poet.* 351.

[41] "As admiration for the living [is apt to be] great, criticism of them is difficult." Velleius: *Res Gestae* II 36.

whether we received it originally from our own countrymen, or from the French; for that is an inquiry of as little benefit, as theirs who, in the midst of the late plague, were not so solicitous to provide against it, as to know whether we had it from the malignity of our own air, or by transportation from Holland. I have therefore only to affirm, that it is not allowable in serious plays; for comedies, I find you already concluding with me. To prove this, I might satisfy myself to tell you, how much in vain it is for you to strive against the stream of the people's inclination; the greatest part of which are prepossessed so much with those excellent plays of Shakspeare, Fletcher, and Ben Jonson, which have been written out of rhyme, that except you could bring them such as were written better in it, and those too by persons of equal reputation with them, it will be impossible for you to gain your cause with them, who will still be judges. This it is to which, in fine, all your reasons must submit. The unanimous consent of an audience is so powerful, that even Julius Cæsar (as Macrobius reports of him), when he was perpetual dictator, was not able to balance it on the other side; but when Laberius, a Roman Knight, at his request contended in the *Mime* with another poet, he was forced to cry out, *Etiam favente me victus es, Laberi.*[42] But I will not on this occasion take the advantage of the greater number, but only urge such reasons against rhyme, as I find in the writings of those who have argued for the other way. First, then, I am of opinion that rhyme is unnatural in a play, because dialogue there is presented as the effect of sudden thought: for a play is the imitation of Nature; and since no man, without premeditation, speaks in rhyme, neither ought he to do it on the stage. This hinders not but the fancy may be there elevated to an higher pitch of thought than it is in ordinary discourse; for there is a probability that men of excellent and quick parts may speak noble things *extempore:* but those thoughts are never fettered with the numbers or sound of verse without study, and therefore it cannot be but unnatural to present the most free way of speaking in that which is the most constrained. For this reason, says Aristotle, 'tis best to write tragedy in that kind of verse which is the least such, or which is nearest prose: and this amongst the Ancients was the Iambic, and with us is blank verse, or the measure of verse kept exactly without rhyme. These numbers therefore are fittest for a play; the others for a paper of verses, or a poem; blank verse being as much below them as rhyme is improper for the Drama.

[42] "Even with me favoring you, you are beaten, Laberius."

And if it be objected that neither are blank verses made *extempore,* yet, as nearest nature, they are still to be preferred.—But there are two particular exceptions, which many besides myself have had to verse; by which it will appear yet more plainly how improper it is in plays. And the first of them is grounded on that very reason for which some have commended rhyme; they say, the quickness of repartees in argumentative scenes receives an ornament from verse. Now what is more unreasonable than to imagine that a man should not only light upon the wit, but the rhyme too, upon the sudden? This nicking of him who spoke before both in sound and measure, is so great an happiness, that you must at least suppose the persons of your play to be born poets: *Arcades omnes, et cantare pares, et respondere parati:* [43] they must have arrived to the degree of *quicquid conabar dicere;* [44]—to make verses almost whether they will or no. If they are anything below this, it will look rather like the design of two, than the answer of one: it will appear that your actors hold intelligence together; that they perform their tricks like fortune-tellers, by confederacy. The hand of art will be too visible in it, against that maxim of all professions—*Ars est celare artem;* that it is the greatest perfection of art to keep itself undiscovered. Nor will it serve you to object, that however you manage it, 'tis still known to be a play; and, consequently, the dialogue of two persons understood to be the labour of one poet. For a play is still an imitation of Nature; we know we are to be deceived, and we desire to be so; but no man ever was deceived but with a probability of truth; for who will suffer a gross lie to be fastened on him? Thus we sufficiently understand that the scenes which represent cities and countries to us are not really such, but only painted on boards and canvas; but shall that excuse the ill painture or designment of them? Nay, rather ought they not be laboured with so much the more diligence and exactness, to help the imagination? since the mind of man does naturally tend to truth; and therefore the nearer anything comes to the imitation of it, the more it pleases.

"Thus, you see, your rhyme is incapable of expressing the greatest thoughts naturally, and the lowest it cannot with any grace: for what is more unbefitting the majesty of verse, than to call a servant, or bid a door be shut in rhyme? and yet you are often forced on this

---

[43] Virgil has *Arcades ambo* (both), which Dryden here changes to *omnes* (all). "Both young Arcadians, both alike inspired

To sing, and answer as the song requir'd." *Eclogues* VII 4. Dryden trans.
[44] "[Of] singing whatever they attempted." Cf. Ovid: *Trist.* IV 10. 25.

miserable necessity. But verse, you say, circumscribes a quick and luxuriant fancy, which would extend itself too far on every subject, did not the labour which is required to well-turned and polished rhyme, set bounds to it. Yet this argument, if granted, would only prove that we may write better in verse, but not more naturally. Neither is it able to evince that; for he who wants judgment to confine his fancy in blank verse, may want it as much in rhyme: and he who has it will avoid errors in both kinds. Latin verse was as great a confinement to the imagination of those poets as rhyme to ours; and yet you find Ovid saying too much on every subject. *Nescivit* (says Seneca) *quod bene cessit relinquere:* [45] of which he gives you one famous instance in his description of the deluge:

> *Omnia pontus erat, deerant quoque litora ponto.*
> Now all was sea, nor had that sea a shore.

Thus Ovid's fancy was not limited by verse, and Virgil needed not verse to have bounded his.

"In our own language we see Ben Jonson confining himself to what ought to be said, even in the liberty of blank verse; and yet Corneille, the most judicious of the French poets, is still varying the same sense an hundred ways, and dwelling eternally on the same subject, though confined by rhyme. Some other exceptions I have to verse; but since these I have named are for the most part already public, I conceive it reasonable they should first be answered."

"It concerns me less than any," said Neander (seeing he had ended), "to reply to this discourse; because when I should have proved that verse may be natural in plays, yet I should always be ready to confess, that those which I have written in this kind come short of that perfection which is required. Yet since you are pleased I should undertake this province, I will do it, though with all imaginable respect and deference, both to that person from whom you have borrowed your strongest arguments, and to whose judgment, when I have said all, I finally submit. But before I proceed to answer your objections, I must first remember you, that I exclude all Comedy from my defence; and next that I deny not but blank verse may be also used; and content myself only to assert, that in serious plays where the subject and characters are great, and the plot unmixed with mirth, which might allay or divert these concernments which are

[45] "He did not know how to leave off   *troverses* IX 5.
where it was proper to." Seneca: *Con-*

produced, rhyme is there as natural and more effectual than blank verse.

"And now having laid down this as a foundation,—to begin with Crites,—I must crave leave to tell him, that some of his arguments against rhyme reach no farther than, from the faults or defects of ill rhyme, to conclude against the use of it in general. May not I conclude against blank verse by the same reason? If the words of some poets who write in it are either ill chosen, or ill placed, which makes not only rhyme, but all kind of verse in any language unnatural, shall I, for their vicious affectation, condemn those excellent lines of Fletcher, which are written in that kind? Is there anything in rhyme more constrained than this line in blank verse?—*I heaven invoke, and strong resistance make;* where you see both the clauses are placed unnaturally, that is, contrary to the common way of speaking, and that without the excuse of a rhyme to cause it: yet you would think me very ridiculous, if I should accuse the stubbornness of blank verse for this, and not rather the stiffness of the poet. Therefore, Crites, you must either prove that words, though well chosen, and duly placed, yet render not rhyme natural in itself; or that, however natural and easy the rhyme may be, yet it is not proper for a play. If you insist on the former part, I would ask you, what other conditions are required to make rhyme natural in itself, besides an election of apt words, and a right disposition of them? For the due choice of your words expresses your sense naturally, and the due placing them adapts the rhyme to it. If you object that one verse may be made for the sake of another, though both the words and rhyme be apt, I answer, it cannot possibly so fall out; for either there is a dependence of sense betwixt the first line and the second, or there is none: if there be that connection, then in the natural position of the words the latter line must of necessity flow from the former; if there be no dependence, yet still the due ordering of words makes the last line as natural in itself as the other: so that the necessity of a rhyme never forces any but bad or lazy writers to say what they would not otherwise. 'Tis true, there is both care and art required to write in verse. A good poet never establishes the first line till he has sought out such a rhyme as may fit the sense, already prepared to heighten the second: many times the close of the sense falls into the middle of the next verse, or farther off, and he may often prevail himself of the same advantages in English which Virgil had in Latin, —he may break off in the hemistich, and begin another line. Indeed, the not observing these two last things makes plays which are writ in verse so tedious: for though, most commonly, the sense is to be confined to the couplet, yet nothing that does *perpetuo tenore fluere,* run in the same channel, can please always. 'Tis like the murmuring of a stream, which not varying in the fall, causes at first attention, at last drowsiness. Variety of cadences is the best rule; the greatest help to the actors, and refreshment to the audience.

"If then verse may be made natural in itself, how becomes it unnatural in a play? You say the stage is the representation of nature, and no man in ordinary conversation speaks in rhyme. But you foresaw when you said this, that it might be answered—neither does any man speak in blank verse, or in measure without rhyme. Therefore you concluded, that which is nearest nature is still to be preferred. But you took no notice that rhyme might be made as natural as blank verse, by the well placing of the words, etc. All the difference between them, when they are both correct, is, the sound in one, which the other wants; and if so, the sweetness of it, and all the advantage resulting from it, which are handled in the Preface to *The Rival Ladies,* will yet stand good. As for that place of Aristotle, where he says, plays should be writ in that kind of verse which is nearest prose, it makes little for you; blank verse being properly but measured prose. Now measure alone, in any modern language, does not constitute verse; those of the Ancients in Greek and Latin consisted in quantity of words, and a determinate number of feet. But when, by the inundation of the Goths and Vandals into Italy, new languages were introduced, and barbarously mingled with the Latin, of which the Italian, Spanish, French, and ours (made out of them and the Teutonic) are dialects, a new way of poesy was practised; new, I say, in those countries, for in all probability it was that of the conquerors in their own nations: at least we are able to prove, that the eastern people have used it from all antiquity. This new way consisted in measure or number of feet, and rhyme; the sweetness of rhyme, and observation of accent, supplying the place of quantity in words, which could neither exactly be observed by those Barbarians, who knew not the rules of it, neither was it suitable to their tongues, as it had been to the Greek and Latin. No man is tied in modern poesy to observe any farther rule in the feet of his verse, but that they be dissyllables; whether Spondee, Trochee, or Iambic, it matters not; only he is obliged to rhyme: neither do the Spanish, French, Italian, or Germans, acknowledge at all, or very rarely, any such kind of poesy as blank verse amongst them. Therefore, at most 'tis but a poetic prose, a *sermo pedestris;* and as such, most fit for comedies, where I acknowledge rhyme to be improper.—Farther; as to that quotation of Aristotle, our couplet verses may be rendered as near prose as blank verse itself, by using those advantages I lately named,—as breaks in an hemistich, or running the sense into another line,—thereby making art and order appear as loose and free as nature: or not tying ourselves to couplets strictly, we may use the benefit of the Pindaric way practised in *The Siege of Rhodes;* where the numbers vary, and the rhyme is disposed carelessly, and far from often chiming. Neither is that other advantage of the Ancients to be despised, of changing the kind of verse when they please, with the change of the scene, or some new entrance; for they confine not themselves always to iambics, but extend their liberty to all lyric numbers, and sometimes even to hexameter. But I need not go so far to prove that rhyme, as it succeeds to all other offices of Greek and Latin verse, so especially to this of plays, since the custom of nations at this day confirms it; the French, Italian, and Spanish tragedies are generally writ in it; and sure the universal consent of the most civilised parts of the world, ought in this, as it doth in other customs, to include the rest.

"But perhaps you may tell me, I have proposed such a way to make rhyme natural, and consequently proper to plays, as is unpracticable; and that I shall scarce find six or eight lines together in any play, where the words are so placed and chosen as is required to make it natural. I answer, no poet need constrain himself at all times to it. It is enough he makes it his general rule; for I deny not but sometimes there may be a greatness in placing the words otherwise; and sometimes they may sound better; sometimes also the variety itself is excuse enough. But if, for the most part, the words be placed as they are in the negligence of prose, it is sufficient to denominate the way practicable; for we esteem that to be such, which in the trial oftener succeeds than misses. And thus far you may find the practice made good in many plays: where you do not, remember still, that if you cannot find six natural rhymes together, it will be as hard for you to produce as many lines in blank verse, even among the greatest of our poets, against which I cannot make some reasonable exception.

"And this, Sir, calls to my remembrance the beginning of your discourse, where you told us we should never find the audience favourable to this kind of writing, till we could produce as good plays in rhyme as Ben Jonson, Fletcher, and Shakspeare had writ out of it. But it is to raise envy to the living, to compare them with the dead. They are honoured, and almost adored by us, as they deserve; neither do I know any so presumptuous of themselves as to contend with them. Yet give me leave to say thus much, without injury to their ashes; that not only we shall never equal them, but they could never equal themselves, were they to rise and write again. We acknowledge them our fathers in wit; but they have ruined their estates themselves, before they came to their children's hands. There is scarce an humour, a character, or any kind of plot, which they have not used. All comes sullied or wasted to us: and were they to entertain this age, they could not now make so plenteous treatments out of such decayed fortunes. This therefore will be a good argument to us, either not to write at all, or to attempt some other way. There is no bays to be expected in their walks: *tentanda via est, quà me quoque possum tollere humo.*[46]

"This way of writing in verse they have only left free to us; our age is arrived to a perfection in it, which they never knew; and which (if we may guess by what of theirs we have seen in verse, as *The Faithful Shepherdess*, and *Sad Shepherd*) 'tis probable they never could have reached. For the genius of every age is different; and though ours excel in this, I deny not but to imitate Nature in that perfection which they did in prose, is a greater commendation than to write in verse exactly. As for what you have added—that the people are not generally inclined to like this way,—if it were true, it would be no wonder, that betwixt the shaking off an old habit, and the introducing of a new, there should be difficulty. Do we not see them stick to Hopkins' and Sternhold's psalms, and forsake those of David, I mean Sandys his translation of them? If by the people you understand the multitude, the οἱ πολλοί, 'tis no matter what they think; they are sometimes in the right, sometimes in the wrong: their judgment is a mere lottery. *Est ubi plebs rectè putat, est ubi peccat.*[47] Horace says it of the vulgar, judging poesy. But if you mean the mixed audience of the populace and the noblesse, I dare confidently affirm that a great part of the latter sort are already favourable to verse; and that no serious plays written since the King's return have been more kindly received by them than *The Siege of Rhodes*, the *Mustapha*, *The Indian Queen*, and *Indian Emperor*.

"But I come now to the inference of your first argument. You said

---

[46] "New ways I must attempt, my grov'-
ling name
To raise aloft. . ."
Virgil: *Georgics* III 8. Dryden trans.

[47] "There are times when the people think rightly, times when they err." Cf. Horace: *Epist.* II i 63, *Interdum volgus rectum videt, est ubi peccat.*

that the dialogue of plays is presented as the effect of sudden thought, but no man speaks suddenly, or *extempore,* in rhyme; and you inferred from thence, that rhyme, which you acknowledge to be proper to epic poesy, cannot equally be proper to dramatic, unless we could suppose all men born so much more than poets, that verses should be made in them, not by them.

"It has been formerly urged by you, and confessed by me, that since no man spoke any kind of verse *extempore,* that which was nearest Nature was to be preferred. I answer you, therefore, by distinguishing betwixt what is nearest to the nature of Comedy, which is the imitation of common persons and ordinary speaking, and what is nearest the nature of a serious play: this last is indeed the representation of Nature, but 'tis Nature wrought up to a higher pitch. The plot, the characters, the wit, the passions, the descriptions, are all exalted above the level of common converse, as high as the imagination of the poet can carry them, with proportion to verisimility. Tragedy, we know, is wont to image to us the minds and fortunes of noble persons, and to portray these exactly; heroic rhyme is nearest Nature, as being the noblest kind of modern verse.

> *Indignatur enim privatis et prope socco*
> *Dignis carminibus narrari cœna Thyestæ* [48]

says Horace: and in another place,

> *Effutire leves indigna tragœdia versus.* [49]

Blank verse is acknowledged to be too low for a poem, nay more, for a paper of verses; but if too low for an ordinary sonnet, how much more for Tragedy, which is by Aristotle, in the dispute betwixt the epic poesy and the dramatic, for many reasons he there alleges, ranked above it?

"But setting this defence aside, your argument is almost as strong against the use of rhyme in poems as in plays; for the epic way is everywhere interlaced with dialogue, or discoursive scenes; and therefore you must either grant rhyme to be improper there, which is contrary to your assertion, or admit it into plays by the same title which

---

[48] "For the banquet of Thyestes should not be narrated in familiar verses, almost proper to comedy." Horace: *Ars Poet.* 90. *Enim* is substituted for the *item* of the original, an example of Dryden's clever fitting of his quotations into his sentences, without taking illegitimate liberties with their meanings.

[49] "Tragedy [is] unfit to babble forth light verses." *Ibid.* 231.

you have given it to poems. For though Tragedy be justly preferred above the other, yet there is a great affinity between them, as may easily be discovered in that definition of a play which Lisideius gave us. The *genus* of them is the same—a just and lively image of human nature, in its actions, passions, and traverses of fortune: so is the end—namely, for the delight and benefit of mankind. The characters and persons are still the same, viz., the greatest of both sorts; only the manner of acquainting us with those actions, passions, and fortunes, is different. Tragedy performs it *viva voce,* or by action, in dialogue; wherein it excels the Epic Poem, which does it chiefly by narration, and therefore is not so lively an image of human nature. However, the agreement betwixt them is such, that if rhyme be proper for one, it must be for the other. Verse, 'tis true, is not the effect of sudden thought; but this hinders not that sudden thought may be represented in verse, since those thoughts are such as must be higher than Nature can raise them without premeditation, especially to a continuance of them, even out of verse; and consequently you cannot imagine them to have been sudden either in the poet or in the actors. A play, as I have said, to be like Nature, is to be set above it; as statues which are placed on high are made greater than the life, that they may descend to the sight in their just proportion.

"Perhaps I have insisted too long on this objection; but the clearing of it will make my stay shorter on the rest. You tell us, Crites, that rhyme appears most unnatural in repartees, or short replies: when he who answers (it being presumed he knew not what the other would say, yet) makes up that part of the verse which was left incomplete, and supplies both the sound and measure of it. This, you say, looks rather like the confederacy of two, than the answer of one.

"This, I confess, is an objection which is in every man's mouth, who loves not rhyme: but suppose, I beseech you, the repartee were made only in blank verse, might not part of the same argument be turned against you? for the measure is as often supplied there as it is in rhyme; the latter half of the hemistich as commonly made up, or a second line subjoined as a reply to the former; which any one leaf in Jonson's plays will sufficiently clear to you. You will often find in the Greek tragedians, and in Seneca, that when a scene grows up into the warmth of repartees, which is the close fighting of it, the latter part of the trimeter is supplied by him who answers; and yet it was never observed as a fault in them by any of the ancient or modern critics. The case is the same in our verse, as it was in theirs;

rhyme to us being in lieu of quantity to them. But if no latitude is to be allowed a poet, you take from him not only his licence of *quidlibet audendi*,[50] but you tie him up in a straiter compass than you would a philosopher. This is indeed *Musas colere severiores*.[51] You would have him follow Nature, but he must follow her on foot: you have dismounted him from his Pegasus. But you tell us, this supplying the last half of a verse, or adjoining a whole second to the former, looks more like the design of two, than the answer of one. Suppose we acknowledge it: how comes this confederacy to be more displeasing to you, than in a dance which is well contrived? You see there the united design of many persons to make up one figure: after they have separated themselves in many petty divisions, they rejoin one by one into ˄ gross: the confederacy is plain amongst them, for chance could never produce anything so beautiful; and yet there is nothing in it that shocks your sight. I acknowledge the hand of art appears in repartee, as of necessity it must in all kind of verse. But there is also the quick and poignant brevity of it (which is an high imitation of Nature in those sudden gusts of passion) to mingle with it; and this, joined with the cadency and sweetness of the rhyme, leaves nothing in the soul of the hearer to desire. 'Tis an art which appears; but it appears only like the shadowings of painture, which being to cause the rounding of it, cannot be absent; but while that is considered, they are lost: so while we attend to the other beauties of the matter, the care and labour of the rhyme is carried from us, or at least drowned in its own sweetness, as bees are sometimes buried in their honey. When a poet has found the repartee, the last perfection he can add to it, is to put it into verse. However good the thought may be, however apt the words in which 'tis couched, yet he finds himself at a little unrest, while rhyme is wanting: he cannot leave it till that comes naturally, and then is at ease, and sits down contented.

"From replies, which are the most elevated thoughts of verse, you pass to those which are most mean, and which are common with the lowest of household conversation. In these, you say, the majesty of verse suffers. You instance in the calling of a servant, or commanding a door to be shut, in rhyme. This, Crites, is a good observation of yours, but no argument: for it proves no more but that such thoughts should be waived as often as may be, by the address of the poet. But suppose they are necessary in the places where he uses them, yet there

[50] "Of daring what he wills." Horace: *Ars Poet.* 10.   [51] "To bestow intense care upon the Muses."

is no need to put them into rhyme. He may place them in the beginning of a verse, and break it off, as unfit, when so debased, for any
other use: or granting the worst,—that they require more room than
the hemistich will allow, yet still there is a choice to be made of the
best words, and least vulgar (provided they be apt), to express such
thoughts. Many have blamed rhyme in general, for this fault, when
the poet with a little care might have redressed it. But they do it with
no more justice than if English Poesy should be made ridiculous for
the sake of the Water Poet's rhymes. Our language is noble, full, and
significant; and I know not why he who is master of it may not
clothe ordinary things in it as decently as the Latin, if he use the same
diligence in his choice of words: *delectus verborum origo est eloquentiæ*.[52] It was the saying of Julius Cæsar, one so curious in his,
that none of them can be changed but for a worse. One would think,
unlock the door, was a thing as vulgar as could be spoken; and yet
Seneca could make it sound high and lofty in his Latin:

> *Reserate clusos regii postes laris.*
> Set wide the palace gates.

"But I turn from this conception, both because it happens not above
twice or thrice in any play that those vulgar thoughts are used; and
then too (were there no other apology to be made, yet), the necessity
of them, which is alike in all kind of writing, may excuse them. For
if they are little and mean in rhyme, they are of consequence such in
blank verse. Besides that the great eagerness and precipitation with
which they are spoken, makes us rather mind the substance than the
dress; that for which they are spoken, rather than what is spoken.
For they are always the effect of some hasty concernment, and something of consequence depends on them.

"Thus, Crites, I have endeavoured to answer your objections; it
remains only that I should vindicate an argument for verse, which
you have gone about to overthrow. It had formerly been said that
the easiness of blank verse renders the poet too luxuriant, but that the
labour of rhyme bounds and circumscribes an over-fruitful fancy; the
sense there being commonly confined to the couplet, and the words
so ordered that the rhyme naturally follows them, not they the rhyme.
To this you answered, that it was no argument to the question in

---

[52] "Proper choice of words is the source   quoting Caesar.
of eloquence." Cicero: *Brutus* 72, 253.

hand; for the dispute was not which way a man may write best, but which is most proper for the subject on which he writes.

"First, give me leave, Sir, to remember you that the argument against which you raised this objection was only secondary: it was built on this hypothesis,—that to write in verse was proper for serious plays. Which supposition being granted (as it was briefly made out in that discourse, by showing how verse might be made natural), it asserted, that this way of writing was an help to the poet's judgment, by putting bounds to a wild overflowing fancy. I think, therefore, it will not be hard for me to make good what it was to prove on that supposition. But you add, that were this let pass, yet he who wants judgment in the liberty of his fancy, may as well show the defect of it when he is confined to verse; for he who has judgment will avoid errors, and he who has it not, will commit them in all kinds of writing.

"This argument, as you have taken it from a most acute person, so I confess it carries much weight in it: but by using the word judgment here indefinitely, you seem to have put a fallacy upon us. I grant, he who has judgment, that is, so profound, so strong, or rather so infallible a judgment, that he needs no helps to keep it always poised and upright, will commit no faults either in rhyme or out of it. And on the other extreme, he who has a judgment so weak and crazed that no helps can correct or amend it, shall write scurvily out of rhyme, and worse in it. But the first of these judgments is nowhere to be found, and the latter is not fit to write at all. To speak therefore of judgment as it is in the best poets; they who have the greatest proportion of it, want other helps than from it, within. As for example, you would be loth to say that he who is endued with a sound judgment has no need of History, Geography, or Moral Philosophy, to write correctly. Judgment is indeed the master-workman in a play; but he requires many subordinate hands, many tools to his assistance. And verse I affirm to be one of these; 'tis a rule and line by which he keeps his building compact and even, which otherwise lawless imagination would raise either irregularly or loosely; at least, if the poet commits errors with this help, he would make greater and more without it: 'tis, in short, a slow and painful, but the surest kind of working. Ovid, whom you accuse for luxuriancy in verse, had perhaps been farther guilty of it, had he writ in prose. And for your instance of Ben Jonson, who, you say, writ exactly without the help of rhyme; you are to remember, 'tis only an aid to a luxuriant fancy, which his was not: as he did not want imagination, so none ever said he had much to spare. Neither was verse then refined so much, to be an help to that age, as it is to ours. Thus then the second thoughts being usually the best, as receiving the maturest digestion from judgment and the last and most mature product of those thoughts being artful and laboured verse, it may well be inferred, that verse is a great help to a luxuriant fancy; and this is what that argument which you opposed was to evince."

Neander was pursuing this discourse so eagerly that Eugenius had called to him twice or thrice, ere he took notice that the barge stood still, and that they were at the foot of Somerset-stairs, where they had appointed it to land. The company were all sorry to separate so soon, though a great part of the evening was already spent; and stood a-while looking back on the water, upon which the moonbeams played, and made it appear like floating quicksilver: at last they went up through a crowd of French people, who were merrily dancing in the open air, and nothing concerned for the noise of guns which had alarmed the town that afternoon. Walking thence together to the Piazze, they parted there; Eugenius and Lisideius to some pleasant appointment they had made, and Crites and Neander to their several lodgings.

PREFACE TO FABLES, ANCIENT AND MODERN

(1700)

'Tis with a Poet, as with a man who designs to build, and is very exact, as he supposes, in casting up the cost beforehand; but, generally speaking, he is mistaken in his account, and reckons short of the expense he first intended. He alters his mind as the work proceeds, and will have this or that convenience more, of which he had not thought when he began. So has it happened to me; I have built a house, where I intended but a lodge; yet with better success than a certain nobleman, who, beginning with a dog kennel, never lived to finish the palace he had contrived.

From translating the First of Homer's *Iliads,* (which I intended as an essay to the whole work,) I proceeded to the translation of the Twelfth Book of Ovid's *Metamorphoses,* because it contains, among other things, the causes, the beginning, and ending, of the Trojan war. Here I ought in reason to have stopped; but the speeches of Ajax and Ulysses lying next in my way, I could not balk 'em. When I had compassed them, I was so taken with the former part of the Fifteenth Book, (which is the masterpiece of the whole *Metamorphoses,*) that I enjoined myself the pleasing task of rendering it into English. And now I found, by the number of my verses, that they began to swell into a little volume; which gave me an occasion of looking backward on some beauties of my author, in his former books: There occurred to me the *Hunting of the Boar, Cinyras and Myrrha,* the good-natured story of *Baucis and Philemon,* with the rest, which I hope I have translated closely enough, and given them the same turn of verse which they had in the original; and this, I may say without vanity, is not the talent of every poet. He who has arrived the nearest to it, is the ingenious and learned Sandys, the best versifier of the former age; if I may properly call it by that name, which was the former part of this concluding century. For Spenser and Fairfax both flourished in the reign of Queen Elizabeth; great masters in our language, and who saw much further into the beauties of our numbers than those who immediately followed them. Milton was the poetical son of Spenser, and Mr. Waller of Fairfax; for we have our lineal descents and clans as well as other families. Spenser more than once insinuates, that the soul of Chaucer was transfused into his body, and that he was begotten by him two hundred years after his decease. Milton has acknowledged to me, that Spenser was his original; and many besides myself have heard our famous Waller own that he derived the harmony of his numbers from the *Godfrey of Bulloign,* which was turned into English by Mr. Fairfax.

But to return: having done with Ovid for this time, it came into my mind that our old English poet, Chaucer, in many things resembled him, and that with no disadvantage on the side of the modern author, as I shall endeavor to prove when I compare them; and as I am, and always have been, studious to promote the honour of my native country, so I soon resolved to put their merits to the trial, by turning some of the *Canterbury Tales* into our language, as it is now refined; for by this means, both the poets being set in the same light, and dressed in the same English habit, story to be compared with story, a certain judgment may be made betwixt them by the reader, without obtruding my opinion on him. Or, if I seem partial to my countryman and predecessor in the laurel, the friends of antiquity are not few; and besides many of the learned, Ovid has almost all the

Beaux, and the whole Fair Sex, his declared patrons. Perhaps I have assumed somewhat more to myself than they allow me, because I have adventured to sum up the evidence; but the readers are the jury, and their privilege remains entire, to decide according to the merits of the cause; or, if they please, to bring it to another hearing before some other court. In the mean time, to follow the thrid of my discourse (as thoughts, according to Mr. Hobbes, have always some connection,) so from Chaucer I was led to think on Boccace, who was not only his contemporary, but also pursued the same studies; wrote novels in prose, and many works in verse; particularly is said to have invented the octave rhyme, or stanza of eight lines, which ever since has been maintained by the practice of all Italian writers who are, or at least assume the title of heroic poets. He and Chaucer, among other things, had this in common, that they refined their mother-tongues; but with this difference, that Dante had begun to file their language, at least in verse, before the time of Boccace, who likewise received no little help from his master Petrarch. But the reformation of their prose was wholly owing to Boccace himself, who is yet the standard of purity in the Italian tongue; tho' many of his phrases are become obsolete, as in process of time it must needs happen. Chaucer (as you have formerly been told by our learned Mr. Rymer) first adorned and amplified our barren tongue from the Provençal, which was then the most polished of all the modern languages; but this subject has been copiously treated by that great critic, who deserves no little commendation from us his countrymen. For these reasons of time, and resemblance of genius, in Chaucer and Boccace, I resolved to join them in my present work; to which I have added some original papers of my own; which whether they are equal or inferior to my other poems, an author is the most improper judge, and therefore I leave them wholly to the mercy of the reader. I will hope the best, that they will not be condemned; but if they should, I have the excuse of an old gentleman, who, mounting on horseback before some ladies, when I was present, got up somewhat heavily, but desired of the fair spectators that they would count fourscore and eight before they judged him. By the mercy of God, I am already come within twenty years of his number, a cripple in my limbs, but what decays are in my mind, the reader must determine. I think myself as vigorous as ever in the faculties of my soul, excepting only my memory, which is not impaired to any great degree; and if I lose not more of it, I have no great **reason** to complain. What judgment I had, increases rather than diminishes; and thoughts, such as they are, come crowding in so fast upon me, that my only difficulty is to choose or to reject; to run them into verse, or to give them the other harmony of prose: I have so long studied and practiced both, that they are grown into a habit, and become familiar to me. In short, tho' I may lawfully plead some part of the old gentleman's excuse, yet I will reserve it till I think I have greater need, and ask no grains of allowance for the faults of this my present work, but those which are given of course to human frailty. I will not trouble my reader with the shortness of time in which I writ it, or the several intervals of sickness. They who think too well of their own performances, are apt to boast in their prefaces how little time their works have cost them, and what other business of more importance interfered; but the reader will be as apt to ask the question, why they allowed not a longer time to make their works more perfect? and why they had so despicable an opinion of their judges as to thrust their indigested stuff upon them, as if they deserved no better?

With this account of my present undertaking, I conclude the first part of this discourse: in the second part, as at a second sitting, tho' I alter not the draught, I must touch the same features over again, and change the dead-colouring of the whole. In general, I will only say, that I have written nothing which savors of immorality or profaneness; at least, I am not conscious to myself of any such intention. If there happen to be found an irreverent expression, or a thought too wanton, they are crept into my verses thro' my inadvertency: if the searchers find any in the cargo, let them be staved or forfeited, like counterbanded goods; at least, let their authors be answerable for them, as being but imported merchandise, and not of my own manufacture. On the other side, I have endeavored to choose such fables, both ancient and modern, as contain in each of them some instructive moral; which I could prove by induction, but the way is tedious, and they leap foremost into sight, without the reader's trouble of looking after them. I wish I could affirm, with a safe conscience, that I had taken the same care in all my former writings; for it must be owned, that supposing verses are never so beautiful or pleasing, yet, if they contain anything which shocks religion or good manners, they are at best what Horace says of good numbers without good sense, *Versus inopes rerum, nugæque canoræ.*[1] Thus far, I hope, I am right in court, without renouncing to my other right of self-defense, where I have been

---

1 "Verses empty of material, trifles of song." Horace: *Ars Poet.* 322.

wrongfully accused, and my sense wire-drawn into blasphemy or bawdry, as it has often been by a religious lawyer, in a late pleading against the stage; in which he mixes truth with falsehood, and has not forgotten the old rule of calumniating strongly, that something may remain.

I resume the thrid of my discourse with the first of my translations, which was the first *Iliad* of Homer. If it shall please God to give me longer life, and moderate health, my intentions are to translate the whole *Ilias;* provided still that I meet with those encouragements from the public, which may enable me to proceed in my undertaking with some cheerfulness. And this I dare assure the world beforehand, that I have found, by trial, Homer a more pleasing task than Virgil, tho' I say not the translation will be less laborious; for the Grecian is more according to my genius than the Latin poet. In the works of the two authors we may read their manners, and natural inclinations, which are wholly different. Virgil was of a quiet, sedate temper; Homer was violent, impetuous, and full of fire. The chief talent of Virgil was propriety of thoughts, and ornament of words: Homer was rapid in his thoughts, and took all the liberties, both of numbers and of expressions, which his language, and the age in which he lived, allowed him. Homer's invention was more copious, Virgil's more confined; so that if Homer had not led the way, it was not in Virgil to have begun heroic poetry; for nothing can be more evident, than that the Roman poem is but the second part of the *Ilias;* a continuation of the same story, and the persons already formed. The manners of Æneas are those of Hector, superadded to those which Homer gave him. The adventures of Ulysses in the *Odysseis* are imitated in the first Six Books of Virgil's *Æneis;* and tho' the accidents are not the same, (which would have argued him of a servile copying, and total barrenness of invention,) yet the seas were the same, in which both the heroes wandered; and Dido cannot be denied to be the poetical daughter of Calypso. The six latter Books of Virgil's poem are the four-and-twenty *Iliads* contracted; a quarrel occasioned by a lady, a single combat, battles fought, and a town besieged. I say not this in derogation to Virgil, neither do I contradict anything which I have formerly said in his just praise; for his episodes are almost wholly of his own invention, and the form which he has given to the telling makes the tale his own, even tho' the original story had been the same. But this proves, however, that Homer taught Virgil to design; and if invention be the first virtue of an epic poet, then the Latin poem can only be allowed the second place. Mr. Hobbes, in the preface to his own bald translation of the *Ilias* (studying poetry as he did mathematics, when it was too late,) Mr. Hobbes, I say, begins the praise of Homer where he should have ended it. He tells us, that the first beauty of an epic poem consists in diction; that is, in the choice of words, and harmony of numbers; now the words are the colouring of the work, which, in the order of nature, is last to be considered. The design, the disposition, the manners, and the thoughts, are all before it: where any of those are wanting or imperfect, so much wants or is imperfect in the imitation of human life, which is in the very definition of a poem. Words, indeed, like glaring colours, are the first beauties that arise and strike the sight; but, if the draught be false or lame, the figures ill disposed, the manners obscure or inconsistent, or the thoughts unnatural, then the finest colours are but daubing, and the piece is a beautiful monster at the best. Neither Virgil nor Homer were deficient in any of the former beauties; but in this last, which is expression, the Roman poet is at least equal to the Grecian, as I have said elsewhere: supplying the poverty of his language by his musical ear, and by his diligence.

But to return: our two great poets being so different in their tempers, one choleric and sanguine, the other phlegmatic and melancholic; that which makes them excel in their several ways is, that each of them has followed his own natural inclination, as well in forming the design, as in the execution of it. The very heroes shew their authors: Achilles is hot, impatient, revengeful, *Impiger, iracundus, inexorabilis, acer,*[2] &c., Æneas patient, considerate, careful of his people, and merciful to his enemies; ever submissive to the will of Heaven—*Quo fata trahunt retrahuntque, sequamur.*[3]

I could please myself with enlarging on this subject, but am forced to defer it to a fitter time. From all I have said, I will only draw this inference, that the action of Homer, being more full of vigour than that of Virgil, according to the temper of the writer, is of consequence more pleasing to the reader. One warms you by degrees; the other sets you on fire all at once, and never intermits his heat. 'Tis the same difference which Longinus makes betwixt the effects of eloquence in Demosthenes and Tully; one persuades, the other commands. You never cool while you read Homer, even not in the Second Book (a

2 "Energetic, choleric, relentless, violent." Horace: *Ars Poet.* 121.

3 "Whither the fates in their round draw us, there let us follow." Virgil: *Aeneid* V 709.

graceful flattery to his countrymen); but he hastens from the ships, and concludes not that book till he has made you an amends by the violent playing of a new machine. From thence he hurries on his action with variety of events, and ends it in less compass than two months. This vehemence of his, I confess, is more suitable to my temper; and, therefore, I have translated his First Book with greater pleasure than any part of Virgil; but it was not a pleasure without pains. The continual agitations of the spirits must needs be a weakening of any constitution, especially in age; and many pauses are required for refreshment betwixt the heats; the *Iliad* of itself being a third part longer than all Virgil's works together.

This is what I thought needful in this place to say of Homer. I proceed to Ovid and Chaucer; considering the former only in relation to the latter. With Ovid ended the golden age of the Roman tongue; from Chaucer the purity of the English tongue began. The manners of the poets were not unlike. Both of them were well-bred, well-natured, amorous, and libertine, at least in their writings; it may be, also in their lives. Their studies were the same, philosophy and philology. Both of them were knowing in astronomy; of which Ovid's books of the *Roman Feasts,* and Chaucer's *Treatise of the Astrolabe,* are sufficient witnesses. But Chaucer was likewise an astrologer, as were Virgil, Horace, Persius, and Manilius. Both writ with wonderful facility and clearness; neither were great inventors: for Ovid only copied the Grecian fables, and most of Chaucer's stories were taken from his Italian contemporaries, or their predecessors. Boccace his *Decameron* was first published, and from thence our Englishman has borrowed many of his *Canterbury Tales:* yet that of *Palamon and Arcite* was written, in all probability, by some Italian wit, in a former age, as I shall prove hereafter. The tale of *Grizild* was the invention of Petrarch; by him sent to Boccace; from whom it came to Chaucer. *Troilus and Cressida* was also written by a Lombard author, but much amplified by our English translator, as well as beautified; the genius of our countrymen, in general, being rather to improve an invention than to invent themselves, as is evident not only in our poetry, but in many of our manufactures. I find I have anticipated already, and taken up from Boccace before I come to him: but there is so much less behind; and I am of the temper of most kings, who love to be in debt, are all for present money, no matter how they pay it afterwards: besides, the nature of a preface is rambling, never wholly out of the way, nor in it. This I have learned from the practice of honest Montaigne, and return at my pleasure to Ovid and Chaucer, of whom I have little more to say.

Both of them built on the inventions of other men; yet since Chaucer had something of his own, as *The Wife of Bath's Tale, The Cock and the Fox,* which I have translated, and some others, I may justly give our countryman the precedence in that part; since I can remember nothing of Ovid which was wholly his. Both of them understood the manners, under which name I comprehend the passions, and, in a larger sense, the descriptions of persons, and their very habits. For an example, I see Baucis and Philemon as perfectly before me, as if some ancient painter had drawn them; and all the pilgrims in the *Canterbury Tales,* their humours, their features, and the very dress, as distinctly as if I had supped with them at the *Tabard* in Southwark. Yet even there, too, the figures of Chaucer are much more lively, and set in a better light; which tho' I have not time to prove, yet I appeal to the reader, and am sure he will clear me from partiality. The thoughts and words remain to be considered in the comparison of the two poets, and I have saved myself one-half of that labour, by owning that Ovid lived when the Roman tongue was in its meridian; Chaucer, in the dawning of our language: therefore that part of the comparison stands not on an equal foot, any more than the diction of Ennius and Ovid, or of Chaucer and our present English. The words are given up, as a post not to be defended in our poet, because he wanted the modern art of fortifying. The thoughts remain to be considered; and they are to be measured only by their propriety; that is, as they flow more or less naturally from the persons described, on such and such occasions. The vulgar judges, which are nine parts in ten of all nations, who call conceits and jingles wit, who see Ovid full of them, and Chaucer altogether without them, will think me little less than mad for preferring the Englishman to the Roman. Yet, with their leave, I must presume to say, that the things they admire are only glittering trifles, and so far from being witty, that in a serious poem they are nauseous, because they are unnatural. Would any man, who is ready to die for love, describe his passion like Narcissus? Would he think of *inopem me copia fecit,*[4] and a dozen more of such expressions, poured on the neck of one another, and signifying all the same thing? If this were wit, was this a time to be witty, when the poor wretch was in the agony of death? This is just John Little-wit, in *Bartholomew Fair,* who had a conceit (as he tells you) left him in his

---

[4] "Abundance has made me impoverished." Ovid: *Metam.* III 466.

misery; a miserable conceit. On these occasions the poet should endeavour to raise pity; but, instead of this, Ovid is tickling you to laugh. Virgil never made use of such machines when he was moving you to commiserate the death of Dido: he would not destroy what he was building. Chaucer makes Arcite violent in his love, and unjust in the pursuit of it; yet, when he came to die, he made him think more reasonably: he repents not of his love, for that had altered his character; but acknowledges the injustice of his proceedings, and resigns Emilia to Palamon. What would Ovid have done on this occasion? He would certainly have made Arcite witty on his deathbed. He had complained he was farther off from possession, by being so near, and a thousand such boyisms, which Chaucer rejected as below the dignity of the subject. They who think otherwise, would, by the same reason, prefer Lucan and Ovid to Homer and Virgil, and Martial to all four of them. As for the turn of words, in which Ovid particularly excels all poets, they are sometimes a fault, and sometimes a beauty, as they are used properly or improperly; but in strong passions always to be shunned, because passions are serious, and will admit no playing. The French have a high value for them; and, I confess, they are often what they call delicate, when they are introduced with judgment; but Chaucer writ with more simplicity, and follow'd Nature more closely than to use them. I have thus far, to the best of my knowledge, been an upright judge betwixt the parties in competition, not meddling with the design nor the disposition of it; because the design was not their own; and in the disposing of it they were equal. It remains that I say somewhat of Chaucer in particular.

In the first place, as he is the father of English poetry, so I hold him in the same degree of veneration as the Grecians held Homer, or the Romans Virgil. He is a perpetual fountain of good sense; learn'd in all sciences; and, therefore, speaks properly on all subjects. As he knew what to say, so he knows also when to leave off; a continence which is practiced by few writers, and scarcely by any of the ancients, excepting Virgil and Horace. One of our late great poets is sunk in his reputation, because he could never forgive any conceit which came in his way; but swept like a drag-net, great and small. There was plenty enough, but the dishes were ill sorted; whole pyramids of sweetmeats for boys and women, but little of solid meat for men. All this proceeded not from any want of knowledge, but of judgment. Neither did he want that in discerning the beauties and faults of other poets, but only indulged himself in the luxury of writing; and perhaps knew it was a fault, but hoped the reader would not find it. For this reason, tho' he must always be thought a great poet, he is no longer esteemed a good writer; and for ten impressions, which his works have had in so many successive years, yet at present a hundred books are scarcely purchased once a twelve-month; for, as my last Lord Rochester said, tho' somewhat profanely, *Not being of God, he could not stand.*

Chaucer followed Nature everywhere, but was never so bold to go beyond her; and there is a great difference of being *poeta* and *nimis poeta,*[5] if we may believe Catullus, as much as betwixt a modest behaviour and affectation. The verse of Chaucer, I confess, is not harmonious to us; but 'tis like the eloquence of one whom Tacitus commends, it was *auribus istius temporis accommodata:*[6] they who lived with him, and some time after him, thought it musical; and it continued so, even in our judgment, if compared with the numbers of Lydgate and Gower, his contemporaries: there is the rude sweetness of a Scotch tune in it, which is natural and pleasing, tho' not perfect. 'Tis true, I cannot go so far as he who published the last edition of him; for he would make us believe the fault is in our ears, and that there were really ten syllables in a verse where we find but nine: but this opinion is not worth confuting; 'tis so gross and obvious an error, that common sense (which is a rule in everything but matters of Faith and Revelation) must convince the reader, that equality of numbers, in every verse which we call *heroic,* was either not known, or not always practiced, in Chaucer's age. It were an easy matter to produce some thousands of his verses, which are lame for want of half a foot, and sometimes a whole one, and which no pronunciation can make otherwise. We can only say, that he lived in the infancy of our poetry, and that nothing is brought to perfection at the first. We must be children before we grow men. There was an Ennius, and in process of time a Lucilius, and a Lucretius, before Virgil and Horace; even after Chaucer there was a Spenser, a Harrington, a Fairfax, before Waller and Denham were in being; and our numbers were in their nonage till these last appeared. I need say little of his parentage, life, and fortunes; they are to be found at large in all the editions of his works. He was employed abroad and favoured by Edward the Third, Richard the Second, and Henry the Fourth, and was poet, as I suppose, to all three of them. In Richard's time, I doubt, he was a little

[5] "Too much of a poet." Martial III 44. The reference to Catullus is an error.
[6] "Suited to the ears of that time."

Tacitus (Orat. C. 21) has *auribus iudicium accommodata.*

dipt in the rebellion of the Commons; and being brother-in-law to John of Ghant, it was no wonder if he followed the fortunes of that family; and was well with Henry the Fourth when he had deposed his predecessor. Neither is it to be admired, that Henry, who was a wise as well as a valiant prince, who claimed by succession, and was sensible that his title was not sound, but was rightfully in Mortimer, who had married the heir of York; it was not to be admired, I say, if that great politician should be pleased to have the greatest Wit of those times in his interests, and to be the trumpet of his praises. Augustus had given him the example, by the advice of Mæcenas, who recommended Virgil and Horace to him; whose praises helped to make him popular while he was alive, and after his death have made him precious to posterity. As for the religion of our poet, he seems to have some little bias towards the opinions of Wycliffe, after John of Ghant his patron; somewhat of which appears in the tale of *Piers Plowman:* Yet I cannot blame him for inveighing so sharply against the vices of the clergy in his age: their pride, their ambition, their pomp, their avarice, their worldly interest, deserved the lashes which he gave them, both in that, and in most of his *Canterbury Tales*. Neither has his contemporary Boccace spared them: Yet both those poets lived in much esteem with good and holy men in orders; for the scandal which is given by particular priests reflects not on the sacred function. Chaucer's *Monk,* his *Canon,* and his *Friar,* took not from the character of his *Good Parson*. A satirical poet is the check of the laymen on bad priests. We are only to take care, that we involve not the innocent with the guilty in the same condemnation. The good cannot be too much honoured, nor the bad too coarsely used; for the corruption of the best becomes the worst. When a clergyman is whipped, his gown is first taken off, by which the dignity of his order is secured. If he be wrongfully accused, he has his action of slander; and 'tis at the poet's peril if he transgress the law. But they will tell us, that all kind of satire, tho' never so well deserved by particular priests, yet brings the whole order into contempt. Is then the peerage of England anything dishonoured when a peer suffers for his treason? If he be libelled or any way defamed, he has his *scandalum magnatum* [7] to punish the offender. They who use this kind of argument, seem to be conscious to themselves of somewhat which has deserved the poet's lash, and are less concerned for their public capacity than for their private; at least there is pride at the bottom of their reasoning. If the faults of

[7] "[Law of] slander extraordinary."

men in orders are only to be judged among themselves, they are all in some sort parties; for, since they say the honour of their order is concerned in every member of it, how can we be sure that they will be impartial judges? How far I may be allowed to speak my opinion in this case, I know not; but I am sure a dispute of this nature caused mischief in abundance betwixt a King of England and an Archbishop of Canterbury; one standing up for the laws of his land, and the other for the honour (as he called it) of God's Church; which ended in the murther of the prelate, and in the whipping of his Majesty from post to pillar for his penance. The learned and ingenious Dr. Drake has saved me the labour of inquiring into the esteem and reverence which the priests have had of old; and I would rather extend than diminish any part of it: yet I must needs say, that when a priest provokes me without any occasion given him, I have no reason, unless it be the charity of a Christian, to forgive him: *prior læsit* [8] is justification sufficient in the civil law. If I answer him in his own language, self-defense, I am sure must be allowed me; and if I carry it further, even to a sharp recrimination, somewhat may be indulged to human frailty. Yet my resentment has not wrought so far, but that I have followed Chaucer, in his character of a holy man, and have enlarged on that subject with some pleasure; reserving to myself the right, if I shall think fit hereafter, to describe another sort of priests, such as are more easily to be found than the Good Parson; such as have given the last blow to Christianity in this age, by a practice so contrary to their doctrine. But this will keep cold till another time. In the mean while, I take up Chaucer where I left him.

He must have been a man of a most wonderful comprehensive nature, because, as it has been truly observed of him, he has taken into the compass of his *Canterbury Tales* the various manners and humours (as we now call them) of the whole English nation, in his age. Not a single character has escaped him. All his pilgrims are severally distinguished from each other; and not only in their inclinations, but in their very physiognomies and persons. Bapista Porta could not have described their natures better, than by the marks which the poet gives them. The matter and manner of their tales, and of their telling, are so suited to their different educations, humours, and callings, that each of them would be improper in any other mouth. Even the grave and serious characters are distinguished by their several sorts of gravity: their discourses are such as belong to their age, their calling,

_____
[8] "He gave the first offence."

and their breeding; such as are becoming of them, and of them only. Some of his persons are vicious, and some virtuous; some are un-learn'd, or (as Chaucer calls them) lewd, and some are learn'd. Even the ribaldry of the low characters is different: the Reeve, the Miller, and the Cook, are several men, and distinguished from each other as much as the mincing Lady-Prioress and the broad-speaking gap-toothed Wife of Bath. But enough of this; there is such a variety of game springing up before me, that I am distracted in my choice, and know not which to follow. 'Tis sufficient to say, according to the prov-erb, that *here is God's plenty*. We have our forefathers and great-grandames all before us, as they were in Chaucer's days: their general characters are still remaining in mankind, and even in England, tho' they are called by other names than those of Monks, and Friars, and Canons, and Lady Abbesses, and Nuns; for mankind is ever the same, and nothing lost out of Nature, tho' everything is altered. May I have leave to do myself the justice (since my enemies will do me none, and are so far from granting me to be a good poet, that they will not al-low me so much as to be a Christian, or a moral man), may I have leave, I say, to inform my reader, that I have confined my choice to such tales of Chaucer as savour nothing of immodesty. If I had de-sired more to please than to instruct, the *Reeve,* the *Miller,* the *Ship-man,* the *Merchant,* the *Sumner,* and, above all, the *Wife of Bath,* in the Prologue to her *Tale,* would have procured me as many friends and readers, as there are *beaux* and ladies of pleasure in the town. But I will no more offend against good manners: I am sensible as I ought to be of the scandal I have given by my loose writings; and make what reparation I am able, by this public acknowledgment. If anything of this nature, or of profaneness, be crept into these poems, I am so far from defending it, that I disown it. *Totum hoc indictum volo.*[9] Chaucer makes another manner of apology for his broad speak-ing, and Boccace makes the like; but I will follow neither of them. Our countryman, in the end of his *Characters,* before the *Canterbury Tales,* thus excuses the ribaldry, which is very gross in many of his novels—

> But firste, I pray you, of your courtesy,
> That ye ne arrete it not my villainy,
> Though that I plainly speak in this mattere,
> To tellen you her words, and eke her chere:

[9] "I wish the entirety of it unsaid."

Ne though I speak her words properly,
For this ye knowen as well as I,
Who shall tellen a tale after a man,
He mote rehearse as nye as ever he can:
Everich word of it ben in his charge,
All speke he, never so rudely, ne large:
Or else he mote tellen his tale untrue,
Or feine things, or find words new:
He may not spare, altho he were his brother,
He mote as well say o word as another.
Crist spake himself ful broad in holy Writ,
And well I wote no villainy is it,
Eke *Plato* saith, who so can him rede,
The words mote been cousin to the dede.

Yet if a man should have enquired of Boccace or of Chaucer, what need they had of introducing such characters, where obscene words were proper in their mouths, but very undecent to be heard; I know not what answer they could have made; for that reason, such tales shall be left untold by me. You have here a specimen of Chaucer's language, which is so obsolete, that his sense is scarce to be understood; and you have likewise more than one example of his unequal numbers, which were mentioned before. Yet many of his verses consist of ten syllables, and the words not much behind our present English: as for example, these two lines, in the description of the Carpenter's young wife—

Wincing she was, as is a jolly colt,
Long as a mast, and upright as a bolt.

I have almost done with Chaucer, when I have answered some objections relating to my present work. I find some people are offended that I have turned these tales into modern English; because they think them unworthy of my pains, and look on Chaucer as a dry, old-fashioned wit, not worth reviving. I have often heard the late Earl of Leicester say, that Mr. Cowley himself was of that opinion; who, having read him over at my Lord's request, declared he had no taste of him. I dare not advance my opinion against the judgment of so great an author; but I think it fair, however, to leave the decision to the public. Mr. Cowley was too modest to set up for a dictator; and being shocked perhaps with his old style, never examined into the depth of his good sense. Chaucer, I confess, is a rough diamond, and must first be polished, ere he shines. I deny not likewise, that, living in our early days of poetry, he writes not always of a piece; but sometimes mingles trivial things with those of greater moment. Sometimes also, tho' not often, he runs riot, like Ovid, and knows not when he has said enough. But there are more great wits beside Chaucer, whose fault is their excess of conceits, and those ill sorted. An author is not to write all he can, but only all he ought. Having observed this redundancy in Chaucer, (as it is an easy matter for a man of ordinary parts to find a fault in one of greater,) I have not tied myself to a literal translation; but have often omitted what I judged unnecessary, or not of dignity enough to appear in the company of better thoughts. I have presumed further, in some places, and added somewhat of my own where I thought my author was deficient, and had not given his thoughts their true luster, for want of words in the beginning of our language. And to this I was the more emboldened, because (if I may be permitted to say it of myself) I found I had a soul congenial to his, and that I had been conversant in the same studies. Another poet, in another age, may take the same liberty with my writings; if at least they live long enough to deserve correction. It was also necessary sometimes to restore the sense of Chaucer, which was lost or mangled in the errors of the press. Let this example suffice at present: in the story of *Palamon and Arcite,* where the temple of Diana is described, you find these verses, in all the editions of our author:—

> There saw I *Danè* turned unto a tree,
> I mean not the goddess *Diane,*
> But *Venus* daughter, which that hight *Danè.*

Which, after a little consideration, I knew was to be reformed into this sense, that *Daphne,* the daughter of Peneus, was turned into a tree. I durst not make thus bold with Ovid, lest some future Milbourne should arise, and say, I varied from my author, because I understood him not.

But there are other judges, who think I ought not to have translated Chaucer into English, out of a quite contrary notion: they suppose there is a certain veneration due to his old language; and that it is little less than profanation and sacrilege to alter it. They are farther of opinion, that somewhat of his good sense will suffer in this transfusion, and much of the beauty of his thoughts will infallibly be lost, which appear with more grace in their old habit. Of this opinion was that excellent person, whom I mentioned, the late Earl of Leicester, who valued Chaucer as much as Mr. Cowley despised him. My Lord dissuaded me from this attempt, (for I was thinking of it some years before his death,) and his authority prevailed so far with me, as to defer my undertaking while he lived, in deference to him: yet my reason was not convinced with what he urged against it. If the first end of a writer be to be understood, then, as his language grows ob-solete, his thoughts must grow obscure—

Multa renascentur, quæ nunc cecidere; cadentque
Quæ nunc sunt in honore vocabula, si volet usus,
Quem penes arbitrium est et jus et norma loquendi.[10]

When an ancient word, for its sound and significancy, deserves to be revived, I have that reasonable veneration for antiquity to restore it. All beyond this is superstition. Words are not like landmarks, so sacred as never to be removed; customs are changed, and even stat-utes are silently repealed, when the reason ceases for which they were enacted. As for the other part of the argument, that his thoughts will lose of their original beauty by the innovation of words; in the first place, not only their beauty, but their being is lost, where they are no longer understood, which is the present case. I grant that some-thing must be lost in all transfusion, that is, in all translations; but the sense will remain, which would otherwise be lost, or at least be maimed, when it is scarce intelligible, and that but to a few. How few are there, who can read Chaucer so as to understand him perfectly? And if imperfectly, then with less profit, and no pleasure. It is not for the use of some old Saxon friends, that I have taken these pains with him: let them neglect my version, because they have no need of it. I made it for their sakes, who understand sense and poetry as well as they, when that poetry and sense is put into words which they understand. I will go farther, and dare to add, that what beauties I lose in some places, I give to others which had them not originally: but in this I may be partial to myself; let the reader judge, and I submit to his decision. Yet I think I have just occasion to complain of them, who because they understand Chaucer, would deprive the greater part of their countrymen of the same advantage, and hoard him up, as misers do their grandam gold, only to look on it themselves, and hinder others from making use of it. In sum, I seriously protest, that no man ever had, or can have, a greater veneration for Chaucer than myself. I have

[10] "Many words shall revive, which now have fallen off, and many which are now in esteem shall fall off, if it be the will of custom, in whose power is the decision and right and standard of language." Horace, *Ars Poet*. 70, trans. Smart.

translated some part of his works, only that I might perpetuate his memory, or at least refresh it, amongst my countrymen. If I have altered him anywhere for the better, I must at the same time acknowledge, that I could have done nothing without him. *Facile est inventis addere* [11] is no great commendation; and I am not so vain to think I have deserved a greater. I will conclude what I have to say of him singly, with this one remark: A lady of my acquaintance, who keeps a kind of correspondence with some authors of the fair sex in France, has been informed by them, that Mademoiselle de Scudery, who is as old as Sibyl, and inspired like her by the same God of Poetry, is at this time translating Chaucer into modern French. From which I gather, that he has been formerly translated into the old Provençal; for how she should come to understand old English, I know not. But the matter of fact being true, it makes me think that there is something in it like fatality; that, after certain periods of time, the fame and memory of great Wits should be renewed, as Chaucer is both in France and England. If this be wholly chance, 'tis extraordinary; and I dare not call it more, for fear of being taxed with superstition.

Boccace comes last to be considered, who, living in the same age with Chaucer, had the same genius, and followed the same studies. Both writ novels, and each of them cultivated his mother tongue. But the greatest resemblance of our two modern authors being in their familiar style, and pleasing way of relating comical adventures, I may pass it over, because I have translated nothing from Boccace of that nature. In the serious part of poetry, the advantage is wholly on Chaucer's side; for tho' the Englishman has borrowed many tales from the Italian, yet it appears, that those of Boccace were not generally of his own making, but taken from authors of former ages, and by him only modelled; so that what there was of invention, in either of them, may be judged equal. But Chaucer has refined on Boccace, and has mended the stories, which he has borrowed, in his way of telling; tho' prose allows more liberty of thought, and the expression is more easy when unconfined by numbers. Our countryman carries weight, and yet wins the race at disadvantage. I desire not the reader should take my word; and, therefore, I will set two of their discourses, on the same subject, in the same light, for every man to judge betwixt them. I translated Chaucer first, and, amongst the rest, pitched on *The Wife of Bath's Tale;* not daring, as I have said, to adventure on her Prologue, because 'tis too licentious. There Chaucer introduces an old woman, of mean

---

[11] "It is easy to add ··hat has already been invented."

parentage, whom a youthful knight, of noble blood, was forced to marry, and consequently loathed her. The crone being in bed with him on the wedding-night, and finding his aversion, endeavours to win his affection by reason, and speaks a good word for herself, (as who could blame her?) in hope to mollify the sullen bridegroom. She takes her topics from the benefits of poverty, the advantages of old age and ugliness, the vanity of youth, and the silly pride of ancestry and titles, without inherent virtue, which is the true nobility. When I had closed Chaucer, I returned to Ovid, and translated some more of his fables; and, by this time, had so far forgotten *The Wife of Bath's Tale,* that, when I took up Boccace, unawares I fell on the same argument, of preferring virtue to nobility of blood and titles, in the story of *Sigismonda;* which I had certainly avoided, for the resemblance of the two discourses, if my memory had not failed me. Let the reader weigh them both; and, if he thinks me partial to Chaucer, 'tis in him to right Boccace.

I prefer, in our countryman, far above all his other stories, the noble poem of *Palamon and Arcite,* which is of the epic kind, and perhaps not much inferior to the *Ilias,* or the *Æneis.* The story is more pleasing than either of them, the manners as perfect, the diction as poetical, the learning as deep and various, and the disposition full as artful: only it includes a greater length of time, as taking up seven years at least; but Aristotle has left undecided the duration of the action; which yet is easily reduced into the compass of a year, by a narration of what preceded the return of Palamon to Athens. I had thought, for the honour of our nation, and more particularly for his, whose laurel, tho' unworthy, I have worn after him, that this story was of English growth, and Chaucer's own: but I was undeceived by Boccace; for, casually looking on the end of his seventh *Giornata,* I found Dioneo, (under which name he shadows himself,) and Fiametta, (who represents his mistress, the natural daughter of Robert, King of Naples,) of whom these words are spoken: *Dioneo e Fiametta gran pezza cantarono insieme d' Arcita, e di Palamone;* [12] by which it appears, that this story was written before the time of Boccace; but the name of its author being wholly lost, Chaucer is now become an original; and I question not but the poem has received many beauties, by passing thro' his noble hands. Besides this tale, there is another of his own invention, after the manner of the Provençals, called *The Flower and the Leaf,* with which I was so particularly pleased, both for the inven-

---

[12] "Dioneo and Fiametta sang together for a long while of Arcite and of Palamon."

tion and the moral, that I cannot hinder myself from recommending it to the reader.

As a corollary to this preface, in which I have done justice to others, I owe somewhat to myself; not that I think it worth my time to enter the lists with one M——, or one B——, but barely to take notice, that such men there are, who have written scurrilously against me, without any provocation. M——, who is in orders, pretends, amongst the rest, this quarrel to me, that I have fallen foul on priesthood: if I have, I am only to ask pardon of good priests, and am afraid his part of the reparation will come to little. Let him be satisfied that he shall not be able to force himself upon me for an adversary. I contemn him too much to enter into competition with him. His own translations of Virgil have answered his criticisms on mine. If, (as they say, he has declared in print), he prefers the version of Ogleby to mine, the world has made him the same compliment; for 'tis agreed, on all hands, that he writes even below Ogleby. That, you will say, is not easily to be done; but what cannot M—— bring about? I am satisfied, however, that, while he and I live together, I shall not be thought the worst poet of the age. It looks as if I had desired him underhand to write so ill against me; but upon my honest word I have not bribed him to do me this service, and am wholly guiltless of his pamphlet. 'Tis true, I should be glad if I could persuade him to continue his good offices, and write such another critique on anything of mine; for I find, by experience, he has a great stroke with the reader, when he condemns any of my poems, to make the world have a better opinion of them. He has taken some pains with my poetry; but nobody will be persuaded to take the same with his. If I had taken to the Church, as he affirms, but which was never in my thoughts, I should have had more sense, if not more grace, than to have turned myself out of my benefice, by writing libels on my parishioners. But his account of my manners and my principles are of a piece with his cavils and his poetry; and so I have done with him for ever.

As for the City Bard, or Knight Physician, I hear his quarrel to me is, that I was the author of *Absalom and Achitophel*, which, he thinks, is a little hard on his fanatic patrons in London.

But I will deal the more civilly with his two poems, because nothing ill is to be spoken of the dead; and therefore peace be to the *manes* of his *Arthurs*. I will only say, that it was not for this noble Knight that I drew the plan of an epic poem on *King Arthur,* in my preface to the translation of *Juvenal.* The Guardian Angels of kingdoms were machines too ponderous for him to manage; and therefore he rejected them, as Dares did the whirl-bats of Eryx when they were thrown before him by Entellius: Yet from that preface, he plainly took his hint; for he began immediately upon the story, tho' he had the baseness not to acknowledge his benefactor, but instead of it, to traduce me in a libel.

I shall say the less of Mr. Collier, because in many things he has taxed me justly; and I have pleaded guilty to all thoughts and expressions of mine, which can be truly argued of obscenity, profaneness, of immorality, and retract them. If he be my enemy, let him triumph; if he be my friend, as I have given him no personal occasion to be otherwise, he will be glad of my repentance. It becomes me not to draw my pen in the defense of a bad cause, when I have so often drawn it for a good one. Yet it were not difficult to prove, that in many places he has perverted my meaning by his glosses, and interpreted my words into blasphemy and bawdry, of which they were not guilty. Besides that, he is too much given to horse-play in his raillery, and comes to battle like a dictator from the plow. I will not say, *the zeal of God's house has eaten him up;* but I am sure it has devoured some part of his good manners and civility. It might also be doubted, whether it were altogether zeal which prompted him to this rough manner of proceeding; perhaps, it became not one of his function to rake into the rubbish of ancient and modern plays: a divine might have employed his pains to better purpose, than in the nastiness of Plautus and Aristophanes, whose examples, as they excuse not me, so it might be possibly supposed that he read them not without some pleasure. They who have written commentaries on those poets, or on Horace, Juvenal, and Martial, have explained some vices, which, without their interpretation, had been unknown to modern times. Neither has he judged impartially betwixt the former age and us.

There is more bawdry in one play of Fletcher's, called *The Custom of the Country,* than in all ours together. Yet this has been often acted on the stage, in my remembrance. Are the times so much more reformed now, than they were five-and-twenty years ago? If they are, I congratulate the amendment of our morals. But I am not to prejudice the cause of my fellow poets, tho' I abandon my own defence: they have some of them answered for themselves; and neither they nor I can think Mr. Collier so formidable an enemy, that we should shun him. He has lost ground, at the latter end of the day, by pursuing his point too far, like the Prince of Condé, at the battle of Senneph: from immoral plays to no plays, *ab abusu ad usum, non valet consequentia.*[13] But, being a party, I am not to erect myself into a judge. As for the rest of those who have written against me, they are such scoundrels, that they deserve not the least notice to be taken of them. B——— and M——— are only distinguished from the crowd by being remembered to their infamy:—

> . . . *Demetri, teque Tigelli,*
> *Discipulorum inter jubeo plorare cathedras.*[14]

[13] "From the abuse to the [proper] use of a thing you can't argue validly."

[14] "I bid you, Demetrius and Tigellius, lament among the chairs of your scholars."

ALEXANDER POPE

(1688–1744)

BORN in 1688 in London, of Catholic parents, Pope had his earliest academic instruction under the tutorage of a Catholic priest, William Bannister. He attended two schools of his sect, studied under another tutor, and completed his education by his own reading. About 1700 his father left London for Binfield, in Windsor Forest. Here the youth began his writing. A childhood epic which he later destroyed, the *Ode to Solitude,* and some satires were among these earliest compositions. Before he was twenty, the *Pastorals* (published 1709), part of *Windsor Forest,* and a translation of one book of Statius' *Thebias* had been written. This work was done in spite of his physical deformity and delicate health; he hardly exaggerates when he writes [*Epistle to Dr. Arbuthnot*] that the muse has eased him "through this long disease, my Life." Early he gained wise and influential friends, and from William Walsh the advice that "though we had several great poets, we never had any one great poet that was *correct.*" And the value which Pope set on Walsh can be seen in the tribute at the end of the *Essay on Criticism.*

It is at this early stage in his career, before any of the great works upon which his reputation as a poet rests had been published, that he assumes the role of critic. Mr. Courthope believes the *Essay on Criticism* was written in 1709, Pope having so stated at first, although he later indicated 1707 as the year of composition, claiming that the first date had been taken erroneously. The piece was published in 1711.

The next year he published the first version of *The Rape of the Lock,* later revising and enlarging it (1714) to the form now usually read. The time between this and 1720 was occupied with the translation of the *Iliad,* on which Pope made his fortune. He had removed in 1719 to Twickenham, and here he resided the rest of his life, the acknowledged arbiter of literary taste for his age and friend of Swift, Bolingbroke, and Atterbury. The translation of the *Odyssey,* in which he was assisted by Broome and Fenton, was completed in 1725; and in 1728 appeared, after the stage had been properly set for it, the *Dunciad.* The first of the *Imitations from Horace* came out of his attempt to justify himself in the literary war waged against him.

Pope was strongly desirous, because of the unrivaled position in which he emerged from the controversy, to be the lawgiver for manners and morals to his time; the *Essay on Man* (1733) and the *Moral Epistles* which were scattered through the seventeen thirties were his means. In

1742, following an attack by the poet laureate Cibber, he added the fourth book to his *Dunciad,* which appeared in its final form the next year. It was the last work of the poet, who died in 1744.

An Essay on Criticism, in its first section, expands the chief rule, "Follow nature," in the light of imitation of the ancients; the second, with the discussion of "wit," commends unity and regularity, and cautions against extremes of various kinds; the third sketches the qualifications of a good critic.

Pope drew his material from a variety of sources: from the *Institutes* of Quintilian, the treatises by Horace, Vida, Boileau, Rapin, and Le Bossu, and from English predecessors in criticism, notably Dryden. John Dennis charged that Pope had "borrowed from living and dead, and particularly from the authors of the two famous Essays upon Poetry and Translated Verse"—works by Lord Mulgrave and Lord Roscommon, which have been well characterized as "sensible but both brief and casual." One element of originality there is: Pope was writing for critics, not poets. And "Pope's work, on the whole, lives up to its title, which states that it is an essay (that is, a tentative effort) at outlining the principles a good *critic* ought to follow; *not* a poetic art for the *poet.*" [A. F. B. Clark, *Boileau and the French Classical Critics in England,* 193]. Undoubtedly, Pope would have looked upon originality of precepts as [Austin Warren, *Alexander Pope,* 1–2] "an impertinence. The humanistic conception of culture, which Pope most decidedly held, is that it constitutes a continuum: each generation does not begin all over again; it carries on the thoughts and art of the past generations." Johnson's high praise of the *Essay* rests on proper grounds: "selection of matter, novelty of arrangement, justice of precept, splendour of illustration, and propriety of digression." [*Lives of the Poets:* "Pope"].

In general, Pope's use of the term "nature" is clear: as Austin Warren notes [*op. cit.,* 26–29], it is "derived from three points of view, of a regular and ordered world, with the emphasis commonly on human nature, the microcosm." But the phrase "follow nature" did not mean "to abandon yourself to your instincts—that would be to allow a 'false' or individual nature—but to subordinate yourself to the commands of the one thing which was the same in all men—the reason. . . . Nature had, too, its social implications . . . the classics afforded a third approach." It is in attempting to reconcile this relationship between the classics and nature that Pope confuses the reader, when he finds "Nature and Homer . . . the same." Pope's contemporary and enemy, John Dennis, was quick to point out this confusion [*Reflections upon a Late Rhapsody,* 222–23]: in lines 88–89, "the Rules are nothing but Nature"; in lines 130–34, "the Rules and Nature are two different things"; while "in the last Line of this very Paragraph they are the same things again." Dennis (in language strange for one who is usually called a neo-classicist) objects also to "the servile Deference which he pays to the Ancients." As Mr. Spingarn has pointed out (see the Introduction to Scaliger), there were definite stages in the development of neo-classicism, culminating in Boileau's theory that the Ancients were to be followed because they were true to Nature, showing the best way to imitate her. Pope argues, generally, from reason; a few times he appeals only to authority, and he has paid heavily in reputation, since the first attack by Dennis, for such flaws in his logical armor.

The opposition which he keeps in mind throughout the *Essay* between nature and wit helps somewhat to clarify what he means by the former term, and serves, if we but forget the one paragraph wherein he identifies the ancients with nature, to restore his position to soundness. (This idea is the basis of Mr. Courthope's reply to Mr. Saintsbury's contention that by "follow nature" Pope meant "stick to the usual, the ordinary, the commonplace." See *History of English Poetry* V, 164 ff.) What Pope or anyone else meant by Nature it is never safe to dismiss briefly. Some understanding of it comes with a wide reading of Eighteenth Century literature, and an observation of what was selected for material. To this there must be added, what has often-times been overlooked, that Nature signifies adherence to design or to type, and frequently refers rather to the manner than to the material, to consistency than to propriety of selection.

Pope's codification, though it contains little original matter, is enormously important because of its definiteness. Dryden's criticism had licenced outlets for the romantic temperament: Pope's fixed an inescapable limit to it, and one which, though battered, was not effectively done away during the remainder of his century. Yet Pope himself, in his later work, did not hesitate to go beyond his doctrines; although he qualifies somewhat according to his own regular tastes, he unhesitatingly recognizes [Preface to *Shakespear*] that "If ever any Author deserved the name of an *Original*, it was *Shakespear*. *Homer* himself drew not his art so immediately from the fountains of Nature. . . . His *Characters* are so much Nature her self, that 'tis a sort of injury to call them by so distant a name as Copies of her." Where the ordinarily admired rules are insufficient, Pope abandons them: "To judge therefore of *Shakespear* by *Aristotle's* rules, is like trying a man by the Laws of one Country, who acted under those of another. . . . I will conclude by saying of Shakespear, that with all his faults, and with all the irregularity of his *Drama,* one may look upon his works, in comparison with those that are more finish'd and regular, as upon an ancient majestick piece of *Gothick* Architecture, compar'd with a neat Modern building: The latter is more elegant and glaring, but the former is more strong and more solemn. It must be allow'd, that in one of these there are materials enough to make many of the other. It has much the greater variety, and much the nobler apartments; tho' we are often conducted to them by dark, odd, and uncouth passages. Nor does the Whole fail to strike us with greater reverence. . . ."

In the *Essay on Criticism,* Pope mentions invention or the role of the imagination but once, although he makes that mention forcible. In his Preface to the translation of Homer's *Iliad,* however, he expresses his concept in more detail:

"Homer is universally allow'd to have had the greatest Invention of any Writer whatever. The Praise of Judgment *Virgil* has justly contested with him, and others may have their Pretensions as to particular Excellencies;

but his Invention remains yet unrival'd. Nor is it a Wonder if he has ever been acknowledg'd the greatest of Poets, who most excell'd in That which is the very Foundation of Poetry. It is the Invention that in different degrees distinguishes all great Genius's: The utmost Stretch of human Study, Learning, and Industry, which masters every thing besides, can never attain to this. It furnishes Art with all her Materials, and without it Judgment itself can at best but *steal wisely:* For Art is only like a prudent Steward that lives on managing the Riches of Nature. Whatever Praises may be given to Works of Judgment, there is not even a single Beauty in them but is owing to the Invention: As in the most regular Gardens, however Art may carry the greatest Appearance, there is not a Plant or Flower but is the Gift of Nature. The first can only reduce the Beauties of the latter into a more obvious Figure, which the common Eye may better take in, and is therefore more entertain'd with. And perhaps the reason why most Criticks are inclin'd to prefer a judicious and methodical Genius to a great and fruitful one, is, because they find it easier for themselves to pursue their Observations through an uniform and bounded Walk of Art, than to comprehend the vast and various Extent of Nature."

AN ESSAY ON CRITICISM

(1711)

PART I

'Tis hard to say, if greater want of skill
Appear in writing or in judging ill;
But, of the two, less dang'rous is th' offence
To tire our patience, than mislead our sense:
Some few in that, but numbers err in this,
Ten censure wrong for one who writes amiss;
A fool might once himself alone expose;
Now one in verse makes many more in prose.
    'Tis with our judgments as our watches, none
Go just alike, yet each believes his own.   10
In poets as true genius is but rare,
True taste as seldom is the critic's share;
Both must alike from heav'n derive their light,
These born to judge, as well as those to write.
Let such teach others who themselves excel,
And censure freely, who have written well.
Authors are partial to their wit, 'tis true,
But are not critics to their judgment too?
    Yet, if we look more closely, we shall find
Most have the seeds of judgment in their mind.   20
Nature affords at least a glimm'ring light;
The lines, tho' touch'd but faintly are drawn right:
But as the slightest sketch, if justly trac'd,
Is by ill colouring but the more disgrac'd,
So by false learning is good sense defac'd:
Some are bewilder'd in the maze of schools,
And some made coxcombs Nature meant but fools:
In search of wit, these lose their common sense,
And then turn critics in their own defence:
Each burns alike, who can, or cannot write,   30
Or with a rival's, or an eunuch's spite.
All fools have still an itching to deride,
And fain would be upon the laughing side.

If Maevius scribble in Apollo's spite,
There are who judge still worse than he can write.
  Some have at first for wits, then poets past,
Turn'd critics next, and prov'd plain fools at last.
Some neither can for wits nor critics pass,
As heavy mules are neither horse nor ass.
Those half-learn'd witlings, num'rous in our isle,   40
As half-form'd insects on the banks of Nile;
Unfinish'd things, one knows not what to call,
Their generation's so equivocal;
To tell them would a hundred tongues require,
Or one vain wit's, that might a hundred tire.
  But you who seek to give and merit fame,
And justly bear a Critic's noble name,
Be sure yourself and your own reach to know,
How far your genius, taste, and learning go;
Launch not beyond your depth, but be discreet,   50
And mark that point where sense and dulness meet.
  Nature to all things fix'd the limits fit,
And wisely curb'd proud man's pretending wit.
As on the land while here the ocean gains,
In other parts it leaves wide sandy plains;
Thus in the soul while memory prevails,
The solid pow'r of understanding fails;
Where beams of warm imagination play,
The memory's soft figures melt away.
One science only will one genius fit;   60
So vast is art, so narrow human wit:
Not only bounded to peculiar arts,
But oft' in those confin'd to single parts.
Like kings we lose the conquests gain'd before,
By vain ambition still to make them more:
Each might his sev'ral province well command,
Would all but stoop to what they understand.
  First follow Nature, and your judgment frame
By her just standard, which is still the same:
Unerring Nature! still divinely bright,   70
One clear, unchang'd, and universal light,
Life, force, and beauty, must to all impart,
At once the source, and end, and test of art.

Art from that fund each just supply provides;
Works without show, and without pomp presides:
In some fair body thus th' informing soul
With spirits feeds, with vigour fills the whole;
Each motion guides, and ev'ry nerve sustains,
Itself unseen, but in th' effects remains.
Some, to whom Heav'n in wit has been profuse,   80
Want as much more, to turn it to its use;
For wit and judgment often are at strife,
Tho' meant each other's aid, like man and wife.
'Tis more to guide, than spur the Muse's steed;
Restrain his fury, than provoke his speed:
The winged courser, like a gen'rous horse,
Shows most true mettle when you check his course.
    Those Rules of old discover'd, not devis'd,
Are Nature still, but Nature methodiz'd:
Nature, like liberty, is but restrain'd   90
By the same laws which first herself ordain'd.
    Hear how learn'd Greece her useful rules indites,
When to repress, and when indulge our flights:
High on Parnassus' top her sons she show'd,
And pointed out those arduous paths they trod;
Held from afar, aloft, th' immortal prize,
And urg'd the rest by equal steps to rise.
Just precepts thus from great examples giv'n,
She drew from them what they deriv'd from Heav'n;
The gen'rous critic fann'd the poet's fire,   100
And taught the world with reason to admire.
Then Criticism the Muse's handmaid prov'd,
To dress her charms, and make her more belov'd:
But following wits from that intention stray'd;
Who could not win the mistress, woo'd the maid;
Against the poets their own arms they turn'd,
Sure to hate most the men from whom they learn'd
So modern 'pothecaries, taught the art
By doctors' bills to play the doctor's part,
Bold in the practice of mistaken rules,   110
Prescribe, apply, and call their masters fools.
Some on the leaves of ancient authors prey;
Nor time nor moths e'er spoil'd so much as they:

Some dryly plain, without invention's aid,
Write dull receipts how poems may be made;
These leave the sense, their learning to display,
And those explain the meaning quite away.
   You then whose judgment the right course would steer,
Know well each ancient's proper character;
His fable, subject, scope in ev'ry page;   120
Religion, country, genius of his age:
Without all these at once before your eyes,
Cavil you may, but never criticise.
Be Homer's works your study and delight,
Read them by day, and meditate by night;
Thence form your judgment, thence your maxims bring,
And trace the Muses upward to their spring.
Still with itself compar'd, his text peruse;
And let your comment be the Mantuan Muse.
   When first young Maro in his boundless mind   130
A work t' outlast immortal Rome design'd,
Perhaps he seem'd above the critic's law,
And but from Nature's fountain scorn'd to draw:
But when t' examine every part he came,
Nature and Homer were, he found, the same.
Convinc'd, amaz'd, he checks the bold design,
And rules as strict his labour'd work confine
As if the Stagyrite o'erlook'd each line.
Learn hence for ancient rules a just esteem;
To copy Nature is to copy them.   140
   Some beauties yet no precepts can declare,
For there's a happiness as well as care.
Music resembles poetry; in each
Are nameless graces which no methods teach,
And which a master-hand alone can reach.
If, where the rules not far enough extend,
(Since rules were made but to promote their end)
Some lucky licence answer to the full
Th' intent propos'd, that licence is a rule.
Thus Pegasus, a nearer way to take,   150
May boldly deviate from the common track.
Great wits sometimes may gloriously offend,
And rise to faults true critics dare not mend;

From vulgar bounds with brave disorder part,
And snatch a grace beyond the reach of art,
Which, without passing thro' the judgment, gains
The heart, and all its end at once attains.
In prospects thus some objects please our eyes,
Which out of Nature's common order rise,
The shapeless rock, or hanging precipice.   160
But tho' the Ancients thus their rules invade,
(As kings dispense with laws themselves have made)
Moderns, beware! or if you must offend
Against the precept, ne'er transgress its end;
Let it be seldom, and compell'd by need;
And have, at least, their precedent to plead;
The critic else proceeds without remorse,
Seizes your fame, and puts his laws in force.
   I know there are, to whose presumptuous thoughts
Those freer beauties, ev'n in them, seem faults.   170
Some figures monstrous and mis-shap'd appear,
Consider'd singly, or beheld too near,
Which, but proportion'd to their light, or place,
Due distance reconciles to form and grace.
A prudent chief not always must display
His pow'rs in equal ranks, and fair array,
But with th' occasion and the place comply,
Conceal his force, nay, seem sometimes to fly.
Those oft' are stratagems which errors seem,
Nor is it Homer nods but we that dream.   180
   Still green with bays each ancient altar stands,
Above the reach of sacrilegious hands;
Secure from flames, from envy's fiercer rage,
Destructive war, and all-involving age.
See, from each clime, the learn'd their incense bring;
Hear, in all tongues consenting Pæans ring!
In praise so just let ev'ry voice be join'd,
And fill the gen'ral chorus of mankind.
Hail, Bards triumphant! born in happier days;
Immortal heirs of universal praise!   190
Whose honours with increase of ages grow,
As streams roll down, enlarging as they flow;
Nations unborn your mighty names shall sound,

And worlds applaud, that must not yet be found!
O may some spark of your celestial fire,
The last, the meanest of your sons inspire,
(That on weak wings, from far, pursues your flights;
Glows while he reads, but trembles as he writes,)
To teach vain wits a science little known,
T' admire superior sense, and doubt their own!   200

PART II

Of all the causes which conspire to blind
Man's erring judgment, and misguide the mind,
What the weak head with strongest bias rules,
Is pride, the never-failing vice of fools.
Whatever Nature has in worth deni'd,
She gives in large recruits of needful pride;
For as in bodies, thus in souls, we find
What wants in blood and spirits, swell'd with wind:
Pride, where wit fails, steps in to our defence,
And fills up all the mighty void of sense: 210
If once right reason drives that cloud away,
Truth breaks upon us with resistless day.
Trust not yourself; but, your defects to know,
Make use of ev'ry friend—and ev'ry foe.
    A little learning is a dang'rous thing;
Drink deep, or taste not the Pierian spring:
There shallow draughts intoxicate the brain,
And drinking largely sobers us again.
Fir'd at first sight with what the Muse imparts,
In fearless youth we tempt the heights of arts,   220
While from the bounded level of our mind,
Short views we take, nor see the lengths behind;
But more advanc'd, behold with strange surprise,
New distant scenes of endless science rise!
So pleas'd at first the tow'ring Alps we try,
Mount o'er the vales, and seem to tread the sky,
Th' eternal snows appear already past,
And the first clouds and mountains seem the last:
But those attain'd, we tremble to survey
The growing labours of the lengthen'd way;   230

Th' increasing prospect tires our wand'ring eyes,
Hills peep o'er hills, and Alps on Alps arise!
   A perfect judge will read each work of wit
With the same spirit that its author writ;
Survey the whole, nor seek slight faults to find
Where Nature moves, and rapture warms the mind;
Nor lose for that malignant dull delight,
The gen'rous pleasure to be charm'd with wit.
But in such lays as neither ebb nor flow,
Correctly cold, and regularly low,   240
That, shunning faults, one quiet tenour keep,
We cannot blame indeed—but we may sleep.
In wit, as nature, what affects our hearts
Is not th' exactness of peculiar parts;
'Tis not a lip, or eye, we beauty call,
But the joint force and full result of all.
Thus when we view some well-proportion'd dome,
(The world's just wonder, and ev'n thine, O Rome!)
No single parts unequally surprise,
All comes united to th' admiring eyes;   250
No monstrous height, or breadth, or length, appear;
The whole at once is bold, and regular.
   Whoever thinks a faultless piece to see,
Thinks what ne'er was, nor is, nor e'er shall be.
In ev'ry work regard the writer's end,
Since none can compass more than they intend;
And if the means be just, the conduct true,
.Applause, in spite of trivial faults, is due.
As men of breeding, sometimes men of wit,
T' avoid great errors, must the less commit;   260
Neglect the rules each verbal critic lays,
For not to know some trifles is a praise.
Most critics, fond of some subservient art,
Still make the whole depend upon a part:
They talk of principles, but notions prize,
And all to one lov'd folly sacrifice.
   Once on a time, La Mancha's Knight, they say,
A certain bard encount'ring on the way,
Discours'd in terms as just, with looks as sage,
As e'er could Dennis, of the Grecian stage;   270

Concluding all were desp'rate sots and fools,
Who durst depart from Aristotle's rules.
Our author, happy in a judge so nice,
Produc'd his play, and begg'd the Knight's advice;
Made him observe the subject, and the plot,
The manners, passions, unities; what not?
All which, exact to rule, were brought about,
Were but a combat in the lists left out.
"What! leave the combat out?" exclaims the Knight.
"Yes, or we must renounce the Stagyrite." 280
"Not so, by Heav'n!" (he answers in a rage)
"Knights, squires, and steeds, must enter on the stage."
"So vast a throng, the stage can ne'er contain."
"Then build a new, or act it in a plain."
   Thus critics of less judgment than caprice,
Curious, not knowing, not exact but nice,
Form short ideas, and offend in arts
(As most in manners) by a love to parts.
   Some to Conceit alone their taste confine,
And glitt'ring thoughts struck out at ev'ry line; 290
Pleas'd with a work where nothing's just or fit;
One glaring chaos and wild heap of wit.
Poets, like painters, thus unskill'd to trace
The naked nature, and the living grace,
With golds and jewels cover ev'ry part,
And hide with ornaments their want of art.
True wit is Nature to advantage dress'd;
What oft' was thought, but ne'er so well express'd;
Something, whose truth convinc'd at sight we find,
That gives us back the image of our mind. 300
As shades more sweetly recommend the light,
So modest plainness sets off sprightly wit:
For works may have more wit than does them good,
As bodies perish thro' excess of blood.
   Others for Language all their care express,
And value books, as women men, for dress:
Their praise is still,—the style is excellent;
The sense, they humbly take upon content.
Words are like leaves, and where they most abound,
Much fruit of sense beneath is rarely found. 310

False eloquence, like the prismatic glass,
Its gaudy colours spreads on ev'ry place;
The face of Nature we no more survey,
All glares alike, without distinction gay;
But true expression, like th' unchanging sun,
Clears and improves whate'er it shines upon,
It gilds all objects, but it alters none.
Expression is the dress of thought, and still
Appears more decent, as more suitable:
A vile conceit in pompous words express'd   320
Is like a clown in regal purple dress'd:
For diff'rent styles with diff'rent subjects sort,
As several garbs with country, town, and court.
Some by old words to fame have made pretence,
Ancients in praise, mere Moderns in their sense;
Such labour'd nothings, in so strange a style,
Amaze th' unlearn'd, and make the learned smile.
Unlucky, as Fungoso in the play,
These sparks with aukward vanity display
What the fine gentleman wore yesterday;   330
And but so mimic ancient wits at best,
As apes our grandsires, in their doublets drest.
In words, as fashions, the same rule will hold;
Alike fantastic, if too new, or old:
Be not the first by whom the new are try'd,
Nor yet the last to lay the old aside.
　　But most by Numbers judge a poet's song,
And smooth or rough, with them, is right or wrong:
In the bright Muse, tho' thousand charms conspire,
Her voice is all these tuneful fools admire;   340
Who haunt Parnassus but to please their ear,
Not mend their minds; as some to church repair
Not for the doctrine, but the music there.
These equal syllables alone require,
Tho' oft' the ear the open vowels tire;
While expletives their feeble aid do join,
And ten low words oft' creep in one dull line:
While they ring round the same unvary'd chimes,
With sure returns of still expected rhymes;
Where'er you find "the cooling western breeze,"   350

In the next line, it "whispers thro' the trees:"
If crystal streams "with pleasing murmurs creep,"
The reader's threaten'd (not in vain) with "sleep:"
Then, at the last and only couplet, fraught
With some unmeaning thing they call a thought,
A needless Alexandrine ends the song,
That, like a wounded snake, drags its slow length along.
Leave such to tune their own dull rhymes, and know
What's roundly smooth, or languishingly slow;
And praise the easy vigour of a line   360
Where Denham's strength, and Waller's sweetness join.
True ease in writing comes from art, not chance,
As those move easiest who have learn'd to dance.
'Tis not enough no harshness gives offence;
The sound must seem an echo to the sense.
Soft is the strain when zephyr gently blows,
And the smooth stream in smoother numbers flows;
But when loud surges lash the sounding shore,
The hoarse, rough verse should like the torrent roar:
When Ajax strives some rock's vast weight to throw,   370
The line too labours, and the words move slow:
Not so when swift Camilla scours the plain,
Flies o'er th' unbending corn, and skims along the main.
Hear how Timotheus' vary'd lays surprise,
And bid alternate passions fall and rise,
While at each change, the son of Libyan Jove
Now burns with glory, and then melts with love;
Now his fierce eyes with sparkling fury glow,
Now sighs steal out, and tears begin to flow:
Persians and Greeks like turns of Nature found,   380
And the world's victor stood subdu'd by sound!
The pow'r of music all our hearts allow,
And what Timotheus was, is Dryden now.
     Avoid extremes, and shun the fault of such
Who still are pleas'd too little or too much.
At ev'ry trifle scorn to take offence,
That always shews great pride, or little sense:
Those heads, as stomachs, are not sure the best,
Which nauseate all, and nothing can digest.
Yet let not each gay turn thy rapture move: 390

For fools admire, but men of sense approve:
As things seem large which we thro' mists descry,
Dulness is ever apt to magnify.
   Some foreign writers, some our own despise;
The Ancients only, or the moderns prize.
Thus wit, like faith, by each man is apply'd
To one small sect, and all are damn'd beside.
Meanly they seek the blessing to confine,
And force that sun but on a part to shine,
Which not alone the southern wit sublimes,   400
But ripens spirits in cold northern climes;
Which, from the first has shone on ages past,
Enlights the present, and shall warm the last;
Tho' each may feel increases and decays,
And see now clearer and now darker days;
Regard not then if wit be old or new,
But blame the false, and value still the true.
   Some ne'er advance a judgment of their own,
But catch the spreading notion of the town;
They reason and conclude by precedent,   410
And own stale nonsense which they ne'er invent.
Some judge of authors' names, not works, and then
Nor praise nor blame the writings, but the men.
Of all this servile herd, the worst is he
That in proud dulness joins with quality;
A constant critic at the great man's board,
To fetch and carry nonsense for my Lord.
What woful stuff this madrigal would be,
In some starv'd hackney sonnetteer, or me!
But let a lord once own the happy lines,   420
How the wit brightens! how the style refines!
Before his sacred name flies ev'ry fault,
And each exalted stanza teems with thought!
   The vulgar thus thro' imitation err,
As oft the learn'd by being singular;
So much they scorn the crowd, that if the throng
By chance go right, they purposely go wrong:
So schismatics the plain believers quit,
And are but damn'd for having too much wit.
Some praise at morning what they blame at night,   430

But always think the last opinion right.
A muse by these is like a mistress us'd,
This hour she's idoliz'd, the next abus'd;
While their weak heads, like towns unfortify'd,
'Twixt sense and nonsense daily change their side.
Ask them the cause; they're wiser still they say;
And still to-morrow's wiser than to-day.
We think our fathers fools, so wise we grow;
Our wiser sons, no doubt, will think us so.
Once school-divines this zealous isle o'erspread;   440
Who knew most Sentences, was deepest read:
Faith, gospel, all, seem'd made to be disputed,
And none had sense enough to be confuted.
Scotists and Thomists, now in peace remain,
Amidst their kindred cobwebs in Duck Lane.
If faith itself has diff'rent dresses worn,
What wonder modes in wit should take their turn?
Oft' leaving what is natural and fit,
The current folly proves the ready wit;
And authors think their reputation safe,   450
Which lives as long as fools are pleas'd to laugh.
  Some, valuing those of their own side or mind,
Still make themselves the measure of mankind:
Fondly we think we honour merit then,
When we but praise ourselves in other men.
Parties in wit attend on those of state,
And public faction doubles private hate.
Pride, malice, folly, against Dryden rose,
In various shapes of parsons, critics, beaus;
But sense surviv'd when merry jests were past;   460
For rising merit will buoy up at last.
Might he return, and bless once more our eyes,
New Blackmores and new Milbourns must arise:
Nay, should great Homer lift his awful head,
Zoilus again would start up from the dead.
Envy will merit, as its shade, pursue;
But like a shadow, proves the substance true:
For envy'd wit, like Sol eclips'd, makes known
Th' opposing body's grossness, not its own.
When first that sun too pow'rful beams displays,   470

It draws up vapours which obscure its rays;
But ev'n those clouds at last adorn its way,
Reflect new glories, and augment the day.
  Be thou the first true merit to befriend;
His praise is lost, who stays till all commend.
Short is the date, alas! of modern rhymes,
And 'tis but just to let them live betimes.
No longer now that golden age appears,
When patriarch wits surviv'd a thousand years;
Now length of fame (our second life) is lost,   480
And bare threescore is all ev'n that can boast;
Our sons their fathers' failing language see,
And such as Chaucer is, shall Dryden be.
So when the faithful pencil has design'd
Some bright idea of the master's mind,
Where a new world leaps out at his command,
And ready Nature waits upon his hand;
When the ripe colours soften and unite,
And sweetly melt into just shade and light;
When mellowing years their full perfection give,   490
And each bold figure just begins to live,
The treach'rous colours the fair art betray,
And all the bright creation fades away!
  Unhappy wit, like most mistaken things,
Atones not for that envy which it brings;
In youth alone its empty praise we boast,
But soon the short-liv'd vanity is lost;
Like some fair flow'r the early spring supplies,
That gaily blooms, but ev'n in blooming dies.
What is this wit, which must our cares employ?   500
The owner's wife, that other men enjoy;
Then most our trouble still when most admir'd,
And still the more we give, the more requir'd;
Whose fame with pains we guard, but lose with ease,
Sure some to vex, but never all to please;
'Tis what the vicious fear, the virtuous shun,
By fools 'tis hated, and by knaves undone!
  If wit so much from ign'rance undergo,
Ah let not learning too commence its foe!
Of old, those met rewards who could excel,   510

And such were prais'd who but endeavour'd well:
Tho' triumphs were to gen'rals only due,
Crowns were reserv'd to grace the soldiers too.
Now, they who reach Parnassus' lofty crown,
Employ their pains to spurn some others down;
And while self-love each jealous writer rules,
Contending wits become the sport of fools;
But still the worst with most regret commend,
For each ill author is as bad a friend.
To what base ends, and by what abject ways,   520
Are mortals urg'd thro' sacred lust of praise!
Ah ne'er so dire a thirst of glory boast,
Nor in the critic let the man be lost.
Good nature and good sense must ever join;
To err is human, to forgive, divine.
   But if in noble minds some dregs remain
Not yet purg'd off, of spleen and sour disdain,
Discharge that rage on more provoking crimes,
Nor fear a dearth in these flagitious times.
No pardon vile obscenity should find,   530
Tho' wit and art conspire to move your mind;
But dulness with obscenity must prove
As shameful sure as impotence in love.
In the fat age of pleasure, wealth, and ease,
Sprung the rank weed, and thriv'd with large increase:
When love was all an easy monarch's care;
Seldom at council, never in a war,
Jilts rul'd the state, and statesmen farces writ;
Nay, wits had pensions, and young lords had wit;
The fair sat panting at a courtier's play,   540
And not a mask went unimprov'd away;
The modest fan was lifted up no more,
And virgins smil'd at what they blush'd before.
The foll'wing licence of a foreign reign
Did all the dregs of bold Socinus drain;
Then unbelieving priests reform'd the nation,
And taught more pleasant methods of salvation;
Where Heaven's free subjects might their rights dispute,
Lest God himself should seem too absolute:
Pulpits their sacred satire learn'd to spare,   550

And Vice admir'd to find a flatt'rer there!
Encourag'd thus, Wit's Titans braved the skies,
And the press groan'd with licens'd blasphemies.
These monsters, Critics! with your darts engage,
Here point your thunder, and exhaust your rage!
Yet shun their fault, who, scandalously nice,
Will needs mistake an author into vice:
All seems infected that th' infected spy,
As all looks yellow to the jaundic'd eye.

PART III

Learn then what morals critics ought to show,   560
For 'tis but half a judge's task, to know.
'Tis not enough, taste, judgment, learning, join;
In all you speak, let truth and candour shine,
That not alone what to your sense is due
All may allow, but seek your friendship too.
Be silent always when you doubt your sense,
And speak, tho' sure, with seeming diffidence:
Some positive, persisting fops we know,
Who, if once wrong, will needs be always so;
But you with pleasure own your errors past,   570
And make each day a critique on the last.
'Tis not enough your counsel still be true;
Blunt truths more mischief than nice falsehoods do;
Men must be taught as if you taught them not,
And things unknown propos'd as things forgot.
Without good-breeding truth is disapprov'd;
That only makes superior sense belov'd.
Be niggards of advice on no pretence,
For the worst avarice is that of sense.
With mean complaisance ne'er betray your trust,   580
Nor be so civil as to prove unjust.
Fear not the anger of the wise to raise;
Those best can bear reproof, who merit praise.
'Twere well might critics still this freedom take,
But Appius reddens at each word you speak,
And stares, tremendous, with a threat'ning eye,
Like some fierce tyrant in old tapestry.

Fear most to tax an Honourable fool,
Whose right it is, uncensur'd, to be dull:
Such, without wit, are poets when they please,   590
As without learning they can take degrees.
Leave dang'rous truths to unsuccessful satires,
And flattery to fulsome dedicators,
Whom, when they praise, the world believes no more,
Than when they promise to give scribbling o'er.
'Tis best sometimes your censure to restrain,
And charitably let the dull be vain;
Your silence there is better than your spite,
For who can rail so long as they can write?
Still humming on, their drowsy course they keep,   600
And lash'd so long, like tops, are lash'd asleep.
False steps but help them to renew the race,
As, after stumbling, jades will mend their pace.
What crowds of these, impenitently bold,
In sounds and jingling syllables grown old,
Still run on poets in a raging vein,
Ev'n to the dregs and squeezing of the brain,
Strain out the last dull droppings of their sense,
And rhyme with all the rage of impotence.
   Such shameless bards we have; and yet, 'tis true,   610
There are as mad, abandon'd critics too.
The bookful blockhead, ignorantly read,
With loads of learned lumber in his head,
With his own tongue still edifies his ears,
And always list'ning to himself appears:
All books he reads, and all he reads assails,
From Dryden's Fables down to Durfey's Tales.
With him most authors steal their works, or buy;
Garth did not write his own Dispensary.
Name a new play, and he's the poet's friend,   620
Nay, show'd his faults—but when would poets mend?
No place so sacred from such fops is barr'd,
Nor is Paul's church more safe than Paul's churchyard:
Nay, fly to altars, there they'll talk you dead;
For fools rush in where angels fear to tread.
Distrustful sense with modest caution speaks,
It still looks home, and short excursions makes;

But rattling nonsense in full volleys breaks,
And never shock'd, and never turn'd aside,
Bursts out, resistless, with a thund'ring tide.   630
    But where's the man, who counsel can bestow,
Still pleas'd to teach, and yet not proud to know?
Unbiass'd, or by favour, or by spite,
Not dully prepossess'd, nor blindly right;
Tho' learn'd, well-bred; and tho' well-bred, sincere;
Modestly bold, and humanly severe;
Who to a friend his faults can freely show,
And gladly praise the merit of a foe?
Bles'd with a taste exact, yet unconfin'd;
A knowledge both of books and human-kind;   640
Gen'rous converse; a soul exempt from pride;
And love to praise, with reason on his side?
    Such once were Critics; such the happy few
Athens and Rome in better ages knew.
The mighty Stagyrite first left the shore,
Spread all his sails, and durst the deeps explore;
He steer'd securely, and discover'd far,
Led by the light of the Maeonian star.
Poets, a race long unconfin'd and free,
Still fond and proud of savage liberty,   650
Receiv'd his laws, and stood convinc'd 'twas fit,
Who conquer'd Nature, should preside o'er wit.
    Horace still charms with graceful negligence,
And without method talks us into sense;
Will, like a friend, familiarly convey
The truest notions in the easiest way.
He, who supreme in judgment, as in wit,
Might boldly censure, as he boldly writ,
Yet judg'd with coolness, tho' he sung with fire;
His precepts teach but what his works inspire.   660
Our critics take a contrary extreme,
They judge with fury, but they write with phlegm:
Nor suffers Horace more in wrong translations
By wits, than critics in as wrong quotations.
    See Dionysius Homer's thoughts refine,
And call new beauties forth from ev'ry line!
    Fancy and art in gay Petronius please,

The scholar's learning, with the courtier's ease.
In grave Quintilian's copious work, we find
The justest rules, and clearest method join'd. 670
Thus useful arms in magazines we place,
All rang'd in order, and dispos'd with grace;
But less to please the eye, than arm the hand,
Still fit for use, and ready at command.
Thee, bold Longinus! all the Nine inspire,
And bless their critic with a poet's fire:
An ardent judge, who, zealous in his trust,
With warmth gives sentence, yet is always just;
Whose own example strengthens all his laws;
And is himself that great Sublime he draws. 680
Thus long succeeding critics justly reign'd,
Licence repress'd, and useful laws ordain'd.
Learning and Rome alike in empire grew,
And arts still follow'd where her Eagles flew;
From the same foes, at last, both felt their doom,
And the same age saw Learning fall, and Rome.
With Tyranny, then Superstition join'd,
As that the body, this enslav'd the mind;
Much was believ'd, but little understood,
And to be dull was constru'd to be good; 690
A second deluge Learning thus o'er-run,
And the Monks finish'd what the Goths begun.
At length Erasmus, that great injur'd name,
(The glory of the priesthood, and the shame!)
Stemm'd the wild torrent of a barb'rous age,
And drove those holy Vandals off the stage.
But see! each Muse, in Leo's golden days,
Starts from her trance, and trims her wither'd bays;
Rome's ancient Genius, o'er its ruins spread,
Shakes off the dust, and rears his rev'rend head. 700
Then Sculpture and her sister arts revive;
Stones leap'd to form, and rocks began to live;
With sweeter notes each rising temple rung;
A Raphael painted, and a Vida sung.
Immortal Vida: on whose honour'd brow
The poet's bays and critic's ivy grow:
Cremona now shall ever boast thy name,

As next in place to Mantua, next in fame!
  But soon by impious arms from Latium chas'd,
Their ancient bounds the banish'd Muses pass'd: 710
Thence arts o'er all the northern world advance,
But critic learning flourish'd most in France;
The rules a nation, born to serve, obeys;
And Boileau still in right of Horace sways.
But we, brave Britons, foreign laws despis'd,
And kept unconquer'd, and unciviliz'd;
Fierce for the liberties of wit, and bold,
We still defy'd the Romans, as of old.
Yet some there were, among the sounder few
Of those who less presum'd, and better knew,   720
Who durst assert the juster ancient cause,
And here restor'd Wit's fundamental laws.
Such was the Muse, whose rules and practice tell
"Nature's chief master-piece is writing well."
Such was Roscommon, not more learn'd than good,
With manners gen'rous as his noble blood;
To him the wit of Greece and Rome was known,
And ev'ry author's merit, but his own.
Such late was Walsh—the Muse's judge and friend,
Who justly knew to blame or to commend;   730
To failings mild, but zealous for desert;
The clearest head, and the sincerest heart.
Thus humble praise, lamented Shade! receive;
This praise at least a grateful Muse may give:
The Muse, whose early voice you taught to sing,
Prescrib'd her heights, and prun'd her tender wing,
(Her guide now lost) no more attempts to rise,
But in low numbers short excursions tries;
Content, if hence th' unlearn'd their wants may view,
The learn'd reflect on what before they knew: 740
Careless of censure, nor too fond of fame;
Still pleas'd to praise, yet not afraid to blame;
Averse alike to flatter, or offend;
Not free from faults, nor yet too vain to mend.

EDWARD YOUNG

(1683-1765)

YOUNG was born at Upham in 1683, the son of the rector of the parish, who was later dean of Salisbury and chaplain to William and Mary. He became a scholar at Winchester in 1695, and in 1702 entered New College, Oxford, but transferred to Corpus Christi within the year. He later secured a fellowship in law, and worked in this subject at various times for a number of years, taking degrees in 1714 and 1719. He meanwhile became associated with the literary groups in London. In 1713 appeared his *Epistle to Lord Lansdowne,* and the *Poem on the Last Day,* his best known early poem, was brought out the next year. Various works of a similar character were written in the succeeding years, but the tragedies *Busiris* (1719) and *Revenge* (1721) are chiefly important. In 1725 he began the satires included in *The Universal Passion* (completed three years later). This series of poems brought him poetic reputation second only to Pope's, considerable money, and a government pension, which was procured through Walpole. He had taken orders at some time prior to this, and was now made one of the chaplains to the king.

At the age of forty-eight, he married Lady Elizabeth Lee. While he had been given the college living of Welwyn, he complained bitterly in these later years because of his lack of preferment. Nothing of any merit was written until the *Night Thoughts,* the first of which appeared in 1742. Young's popularity because of them was immediate, and the remainder of his life was passed in comfortable and dignified retirement at Welwyn, where he died in 1765. The only significant fact of these years is the composition of the *Conjectures.*

Prof. Alan D. McKillop, in his review of the Richardson-Young correspondence relative to the *Conjectures* (in *Modern Philology* for May, 1925), gives a summary of this essay's inception which reveals the large part that Samuel Richardson had in it. The skeleton of the *Conjectures* is first observable in a letter from Richardson to Young in 1757, suggesting a large number of revisions in the manuscript which had been sent to him. Two years later the piece was published, and from the letters one may infer that criticism on Richardson's part and indecisive revising on Young's were responsible for the lapse. The two friends were in steady correspondence, and, as Mr. McKillop illustrates, the novelist's squeamish moral position definitely intruded upon Young's critical plan. The "Letter" was published anonymously, though the authorship was readily guessed, and was declared, within the month, by *The Gentleman's Magazine.* The list of criticism and reference in the Bibliography to Edith J. Morley's edition of the *Conjectures* gives an idea of the manner in which the work was received. Warburton's attribute of "nonsense" takes the opposite extreme to Johnson's remark that "he was surprised to find Young receive as novelties what he thought very common maxims." [Boswell: *Journal of a Tour to the Hebrides.*]

It seems one of the unhappy traits of the Eighteenth Century critics that they wish never to change their terms, but always to reform the definitions of them: so Addison on "Taste"; so Reynolds on "Imitation"; so everyone on "Nature." It is for this very reason that the shock of revolt was not truly felt until new critical terms replaced the old ones, in Wordsworth's Preface. Nearly everyone from Addison to Johnson declared against servility, "hampering rules," dogmatic criticism; Pope's and Swift's accusations against the Dunces (in the *Bathos*) contain many of the criticisms later to be directed against the entire Eighteenth Century school. But the protests so made were, before 1800, made under the standards which no one dared to challenge. Young appeared to Johnson to be saying nothing new. Likewise, statements such as occur in the letters of Shenstone, in Thomson's earliest preface, in Warton's examen of Pope, seem to represent no revolutionary doctrine. The contradiction implied in all of these to the generally accepted neo-classical theory, the theory that novelty could be achieved only by arrangement and selection of material, does not seem to have been apparent to contemporaries of Johnson and Young.

It has become a commonplace of criticism upon the *Conjectures* that the principal idea is a very old one. The *furor poeticus* of the ancients and the "enthusiasm" of the Eighteenth Century are not far apart. So venerable an ancestor of neo-classicism as Ben Jonson, collecting the statements of antiquity on the subject, restated the idea, and every critic for a century and a half following him did lip service to "genius" and "inspiration." Young identifies himself with those critics and poets of all ages who have asserted the divine origin of poetry. He is declaring, in an age less imbued with a belief in spiritualistic influences, much of what people like Ronsard had intended when they advised the invariable address to the Muse.

He asserts that the miracle of genius, of which Shakespeare is the prime example, is often within the reach of the individual poet who will free himself from the encumbrances of custom and outworn rule; and on this ground he takes occasion to condemn Pope much after the fashion of Warton, though in more certain terms. For Warton taxes the poetry of Pope with the lack of sublimity. But Young accuses the man himself, damns him for his "idolatry," and deplores the shadow of what might have been a great and original poet. "Where then," asks Warton, "according to the question proposed at the *beginning of this Essay,* shall we with justice be authorized to place our admired Pope? Not, assuredly, in the same rank with *Spenser, Shakespeare,* and *Milton;* however justly we may applaud the *Eloisa* and *Rape of the Lock;* but, considering the correctness, elegance, and utility of his works, the weight of sentiment, and the knowledge of man they contain, we may venture to assign him a place, *next* to *Milton*, and *just* above *Dryden*. Yet, to bring our minds steadily to make this decision, we must forget, for a moment, the divine *Music Ode* of *Dryden;* and may, perhaps, then be compelled to confess, that though *Dryden* be the greater genius, yet *Pope* is the better artist.

"The preference here given to Pope above other modern English poets, it must be remembered, is founded on the excellencies of his works *in general*, and *taken all together;* for there are *parts* and *passages* in other modern authors, in *Young* and in *Thomson*, for instance, equal to any of POPE; and he has written nothing in a strain so truly sublime, as the *Bard of Gray*." [*An Essay on the Genius and Writings of Pope*, the concluding paragraph.] But Young says of him that "his taste partook the error of his religion; it denied not worship to saints and angels."

Something should be said of Young's use of the word "imitation." His meaning was perfectly understandable to his contemporaries, referring only to imitation of authors. He probably did not comprehend the Aristotelian use of the word. There is, of course, throughout the entire century a duality in the usage of this term.

CONJECTURES ON ORIGINAL COMPOSITION

In a Letter to the Author of Sir Charles Grandison.

(1759)

DEAR SIR—We confess the follies of youth without a blush; not so, those of age. However, keep me a little in countenance, by considering, that age wants amusements more, tho' it can justify them less, than the preceding periods of life. How you may relish the pastime here sent you, I know not. It is miscellaneous in its nature, somewhat licentious in its conduct; and, perhaps, not over important in its end. However, I have endeavoured to make some amends, by digressing into subjects more important, and more suitable to my season of life. A serious thought standing single among many of a lighter nature, will sometimes strike the careless wanderer after amusement only, with useful awe: as monumental marbles scattered in a wide pleasure-garden (and such there are) will call to recollection those who would never have sought it in a churchyard-walk of mournful yews.

To one such monument I may conduct you, in which is a hidden lustre, like the sepulchral lamps of old; but not like those will This be extinguished, but shine the brighter for being produced, after so long concealment, into open day.

You remember that your worthy patron, and our common friend, put some questions on the *Serious Drama,* at the same time when he desired our sentiments on *Original,* and on *Moral* Composition. Tho' I despair of breaking thro' the frozen obstructions of age, and care's incumbent cloud, into that flow of thought, and brightness of expression, which subjects so polite require; yet will I hazard some conjectures on them.

I begin with *Original* Composition; and the more willingly, as it seems an original subject to me, who have seen nothing hitherto written on it: But, first, a few thoughts on Composition in general. Some are of opinion, that its growth, at present, is too luxuriant; and that the Press is overcharged. Overcharged, I think, it could never be, if none were admitted, but such as brought their Imprimatur from *sound Understanding,* and the *Public Good.* Wit, indeed, however brilliant, should not be permitted to gaze self-enamoured on its useless Charms, in that Fountain of Fame (if so I may call the Press), if beauty is all that it has to boast; but, like the first *Brutus,* it should sacrifice its most darling offspring to the sacred interests of virtue, and real service of mankind.

This restriction allowed, the more composition the better. To men of letters, and leisure, it is not only a noble amusement, but a sweet refuge; it improves their parts, and promotes their peace: It opens a back-door out of the bustle of this busy, and idle world, into a delicious garden of moral and intellectual fruits and flowers; the key of which is denied to the rest of mankind. When stung with idle anxieties, or teazed with fruitless impertinence, or yawning over insipid diversions, then we perceive the blessing of a letter'd recess. With what a gust do we retire to our disinterested, and immortal friends in our closet, and find our minds, when applied to some favourite theme, as naturally, and as easily quieted, and refreshed, as a peevish child (and peevish children are we all till we fall asleep) when laid to the breast? Our happiness no longer lives on charity; nor bids fair for a fall, by leaning on that most precarious, and thorny pillow, another's pleasure, for our repose. How independent of the world is he, who can daily find new acquaintance, that at once entertain, and improve him, in the little world, the minute but fruitful creation, of his own mind?

These advantages *Composition* affords us, whether we write ourselves, or in more humble amusement peruse the works of others. While we bustle thro' the thronged walks of public life, it gives us a respite, at least, from care; a pleasing pause of refreshing recollection. If the country is our choice, or fate, there it rescues us from *sloth* and *sensuality,* which, like obscene vermin, are apt gradually to creep unperceived into the delightful bowers of our retirement, and to poison all its sweets. Conscious guilt robs the rose of its scent, the lilly of its lustre; and makes an *Eden* a deflowered, and dismal scene.

Moreover, if we consider life's endless evils, what can be more prudent, than to provide for consolation under them? A consolation under them the wisest of men have found in the pleasures of the pen. Witness, among many more, *Thucydides, Xenophon, Tully, Ovid, Seneca, Pliny* the younger, who says *In uxoris infirmitate, & amicorum periculo, aut morte turbatus, ad studia, unicum doloris levamentum, confugio.*[1] And why not add to these their modern equals, *Chaucer, Rawleigh, Bacon, Milton, Clarendon,* under the same shield, unwounded by misfortune, and nobly smiling in distress?

Composition was a cordial to these under the frowns of fortune; but evils there are, which her smiles cannot prevent, or cure. Among these are the languors of old age. If those are held honourable, who in a hand benumbed by time have grasped the just sword in defence of their country; shall they be less esteemed, whose unsteady pen vibrates to the last in the cause of religion, of virtue, of learning? Both These are happy in *this,* that by fixing their attention on objects most important, they escape numberless little anxieties, and that *tedium vitae* which often hangs so heavy on its evening hours. May not this insinuate some apology for my spilling ink, and spoiling paper, so late in life?

But there are, who write with vigor, and success, to the world's delight, and their own renown. These are the glorious fruits where genius prevails. The mind of a man of genius is a fertile and pleasant field, pleasant as *Elysium,* and fertile as *Tempe;* it enjoys a perpetual spring. Of that spring, *Originals* are the fairest flowers: *Imitations* are of quicker growth, but fainter bloom. *Imitations* are of two kinds; one of nature, one of authors: The first we call *Originals,* and confine the term *Imitation* to the second. I shall not enter into the curious enquiry of what is, or is not, strictly speaking, *Original,* content with what all must allow, that some compositions are more so than others; and the more they are so, I say, the better. *Originals* are, and ought

[1] "My wife sick, my friends in danger, or myself troubled with the threat of death, I flee to my studies, the sole comfort for sorrow."

to be, great favourites, for they are great benefactors; they extend the republic of letters, and add a new province to its dominion: *Imitators* only give us a sort of duplicates of what we had, possibly much better, before; increasing the mere drug of books, while all that makes them valuable, *knowledge* and *genius,* are at a stand. The pen of an *original* writer, like *Armida's* wand, out of a barren waste calls a blooming spring: Out of that blooming spring an *Imitator* is a transplanter of laurels, which sometimes die on removal, always languish in a foreign soil.

But suppose an *Imitator* to be most excellent (and such there are), yet still he but nobly builds on another's foundation; his debt is, at least, equal to his glory; which therefore, on the balance, cannot be very great. On the contrary, an *Original,* tho' but indifferent (its *Originality* being set aside), yet has something to boast; it is something to say with him in *Horace,*

Meo sum Pauper in aere; [2]

and to share ambition with no less than *Cæsar,* who declared he had rather be the first in a village, than the second at *Rome.*

Still farther: An *Imitator* shares his crown, if he has one, with the chosen object of his imitation; an *Original* enjoys an undivided applause. An *Original* may be said to be of a *vegetable* nature; it rises spontaneously from the vital root of genius; it *grows,* it is not *made: Imitations* are often a sort of *manufacture* wrought up by those *mechanics, art,* and *labour,* out of pre-existent materials not their own.

Again: We read *Imitation* with somewhat of his languor, who listens to a twice-told tale: Our spirits rouze at an *Original; that is* a perfect stranger, and all throng to learn what news from a foreign land: And tho' it comes, like an *Indian* prince, adorned with feathers only, having little of weight; yet of our attention it will rob the more solid, if not equally new: Thus every telescope is lifted at a new-discovered star; it makes a hundred astronomers in a moment, and denies equal notice to the sun. But if an *Original,* by being as excellent, as new, adds admiration to surprize, then are we at the writer's mercy; on the strong wing of his imagination, we are snatched from *Britain* to *Italy,* from climate to climate, from pleasure to pleasure; we have no home, no thought, of our own; till the magician drops his pen: And then falling down into ourselves, we awake to

---

[2] "Poor though I be, I am in debt to no one." Lit., "I am poor in my own money."

flat realities, lamenting the change, like the beggar who dreamt him-self a prince.

It is with thoughts, as it is with words; and with both, as with men; they may grow old, and die. Words tarnished, by passing thro' the mouths of the vulgar, are laid aside as inelegant, and obsolete. So thoughts, when become too common, should lose their currency; and we should send new metal to the mint, that is, new meaning to the press. The division of tongues at *Babel* did not more effectually debar men from *making themselves a name* (as the Scripture speaks,) than the too great concurrence, or union of tongues will do for ever. We may as well grow good by another's virtue, or fat by another's food, as famous by another's thought. The world will pay its debt of praise but once; and instead of applauding, explode a second de-mand, as a cheat.

If it is said, that most of the *Latin* classics, and all the *Greek,* ex-cept, perhaps, *Homer, Pindar,* and *Anacreon,* are in the number of *Imitators,* yet receive our highest applause; our answer is, That they tho' not *real,* are *accidental Originals;* the works they imitated, few excepted, are lost: They, on their father's decease, enter as lawful heirs, on their estates in fame: The fathers of our copyists are still in possession; and secured in it, in spite of *Goths,* and Flames, by the perpetuating power of the Press. Very late must a modern *Imita-tor's* fame arrive, if it waits for their decease.

An *Original* enters early on reputation: *Fame,* fond of new glories, sounds her trumpet in triumph at its birth; and yet how few are awaken'd by it into the noble ambition of like attempts? Ambition is sometimes no vice in life; it is always a virtue in Composition. High in the towering *Alps* is the fountain of the *Po;* high in fame, and in antiquity, is the fountain of an *Imitator's* undertaking; but the river, and the imitation, humbly creep along the vale. So few are our *Origi-nals,* that, if all other books were to be burnt, the letter'd world would resemble some metropolis in flames, where a few incombustible build-ings, a fortress, temple, or tower, lift their heads, in melancholy grandeur, amid the mighty ruin. Compared with this conflagration, old *Omar* lighted up but a small bonfire, when he heated the baths of the Barbarians, for eight months together, with the famed *Alexan-drian* library's inestimable spoils, that no prophane book might ob-struct the triumphant progress of his holy *Alcoran* round the globe.

But why are *Originals* so few? not because the writer's harvest is over, the great reapers of antiquity having left nothing to be gleaned after them; nor because the human mind's teeming time is past, or because it is incapable of putting forth unprecedented births; but because illustrious examples *engross, prejudice,* and *intimidate.* They *engross* our attention, and so prevent a due inspection of ourselves: they *prejudice* our judgment in favour of their abilities, and so lessen the sense of our own; and they *intimidate* us with the splendor of their renown, and thus under diffidence bury our strength. Nature's impossibilities, and those of diffidence lie wide asunder.

Let it not be suspected, that I would weakly insinuate any thing in favour of the moderns, as compared with antient authors; no, I am lamenting their great inferiority. But I think it is no *necessary* inferiority; that it is not from divine destination, but from some cause far beneath the moon: I think that human souls, thro' all periods, are equal; that due care, and exertion, would set us nearer our immortal predecessors than we are at present; and he who questions and confutes this, will show abilities not a little tending toward a proof of that equality, which he denies.

After all, the first antients had no merit in being *Originals:* They could *not* be *Imitators.* Modern writers have a *choice* to make; and therefore have a merit in their power. They may soar in the regions of *liberty,* or move in the soft fetters of easy *imitation;* and *imitation* has as many plausible reasons to urge, as *Pleasure* had to offer to *Hercules. Hercules* made the choice of an hero, and *so* became immortal.

Yet let not assertors of classic excellence imagine, that I deny the tribute it so well deserves. He that admires not antient authors, betrays a secret he would conceal, and tells the world, that he does not understand them. Let us be as far from neglecting, as from copying, their admirable compositions; Sacred be their rights, and inviolable their fame. Let our understanding feed on theirs; they afford the noblest nourishment; But let them nourish, not annihilate, our own. When we read, let our imagination kindle at their charms; when we write, let our judgment shut them out of our thoughts; treat even *Homer* himself as his royal admirer was treated by the cynic; bid him stand aside, nor shade our Composition from the beams of our own genius; for nothing *Original* can rise, nothing immortal, can ripen, in any other sun.

Must we then, you say, not imitate antient authors? Imitate them, by all means; but imitate aright. He that imitates the divine *Iliad,* does not imitate *Homer;* but he who takes the same method, which

Homer took, for arriving at a capacity of accomplishing a work so great. Tread in his steps to the sole fountain of immortality; drink where he drank, at the true *Helicon,* that is, at the breast of nature: Imitate; but imitate not the *Composition,* but the *Man.* For may not this paradox pass into a maxim? *viz.* "The less we copy the renowned antients, we shall resemble them the more."

But possibly you may reply, that you must either imitate *Homer,* or depart from nature. Not so: For suppose you was to change place, in time, with *Homer;* then, if you write naturally, you might as well charge *Homer* with an imitation of you. Can you be said to imitate *Homer* for writing *so,* as you would have written, if *Homer* had never been? As far as a regard to nature, and sound sense, will permit a departure from your great predecessors; so far, ambitiously, depart from them; the farther from them in *similitude,* the nearer are you to them in *excellence;* you rise by it into an *Original;* become a noble collateral, not an humble descendant from them. Let us build our Compositions with the spirit, and in the taste, of the antients; but not with their materials: Thus will they resemble the structures of *Pericles* at *Athens,* which *Plutarch* commends for having had an air of antiquity as soon as they were built. All eminence, and distinction, lies out of the beaten road; excursion, and deviation, are necessary to find it; and the more remote your path from the highway, the more reputable; if, like poor *Gulliver* (of whom anon) you fall not into a ditch, in your way to glory.

What glory to come near, what glory to reach, what glory (presumptuous thought!) to surpass, our predecessors? And is that then in nature absolutely impossible? Or is it not, rather, contrary to nature to fail in it? Nature herself sets the ladder, all wanting is our ambition to climb. For by the bounty of nature we are as strong as our predecessors; and by the favour of time (which is but another round in nature's scale) we stand on higher ground. As to the *first,* were *they* more than men? Or are *we* less? Are not our minds cast in the same mould with those before the flood? The flood affected matter; mind escaped. As to the *second;* though we are moderns, the world is an antient; more antient far, than when they, whom we most admire, filled it with their fame. Have we not their beauties, as stars, to guide; their defects, as rocks, to be shunn'd; the judgment of ages on both, as a chart to conduct, and a sure helm to steer us in our passage to greater perfection than theirs? And shall we be stopt in our rival pretensions to fame by this just reproof?

Stat contra, dicitque tibi tua pagina, fur es.[3]
Mart.

It is by a sort of noble contagion, from a general familiarity with their writings, and not by any particular sordid theft, that we can be the better for those who went before us. Hope we, from plagiarism, any dominion in literature; as that of *Rome* arose from a nest of thieves?

Rome was a powerful ally to many states; antient authors are our powerful allies; but we must take heed, that they do not succour, till they enslave, after the manner of *Rome*. Too formidable an idea of their superiority, like a spectre, would fright us out of a proper use of our wits; and dwarf our understanding, by making a giant of theirs. Too great awe for them lays genius under restraint, and denies it that free scope, that full elbow-room, which is requisite for striking its most masterly strokes. Genius is a master-workman, learning is but an instrument; and an instrument, tho' most valuable, yet not always indispensable. Heaven will not admit of a partner in the accomplishment of some favourite spirits; but rejecting all human means, assumes the whole glory to itself. Have not some, tho' not famed for erudition, *so* written, as almost to persuade us, that they shone brighter, and soared higher, for escaping the boasted aid of that proud ally?

Nor is it strange; for what, for the most part, mean we by genius, but the power of accomplishing great things without the means generally reputed necessary to that end? A *genius* differs from a *good understanding,* as a magician from a good architect; *that* raises his structure by means invisible; *this* by the skilful use of common tools. Hence genius has ever been supposed to partake of something divine. *Nemo unquam vir magnus fuit, sine aliquo afflatu divino.*[4]

Learning, destitute of this superior aid, is fond, and proud, of what has cost it much pains; is a great lover of rules, and boaster of famed examples: As beauties less perfect, who owe half their charms to cautious art, learning inveighs against natural unstudied graces, and small harmless inaccuracies, and sets rigid bounds to that liberty, to which genius often owes its supreme glory; but the no-genius its frequent ruin. For unprescribed beauties, and unexampled excellence, which are characteristics of *genius,* lie without the pale of *learning's* authorities, and laws; which pale, genius must leap to come at them:

[3] "Your page stands in court against you, and says to you, 'You are a thief.'"

[4] "No one was ever a great man without some divine inspiration."

But by that leap, if genius is wanting, we break our necks; we lose that little credit, which possibly we might have enjoyed before. For rules, like crutches, are a needful aid to the lame, tho' an impediment to the strong. A *Homer* casts them away; and, like his *Achilles,*

Jura negat sibi nata, nihil non arrogat,[5]

by native force of mind. There is something in poetry beyond prose-reason; there are mysteries in it not to be explained, but admired; which render mere prose-men infidels to their divinity. And here pardon a second paradox; *viz. "Genius* often then deserves most to be praised, when it is most sure to be condemned; that is, when its excellence, from mounting high, to weak eyes is quite out of sight."

If I might speak farther of learning, and genius, I would compare genius to virtue, and learning to riches. As riches are most wanted where there is least virtue; so learning where there is least genius. As virtue without much riches can give happiness, so genius without much learning can give renown. As it is said in *Terence, Pecuniam negligere interdum maximum est lucrum;* [6] so to neglect of learning, genius sometimes owes its greater glory. Genius, therefore, leaves but the second place, among men of letters, to the learned. It is their merit, and ambition, to fling light on the works of genius, and point out its charms. We most justly reverence their informing radius for that favour; but we must much more admire the radiant stars pointed out by them.

A star of the first magnitude among the moderns was *Shakespeare;* among the antients, *Pindar;* who (as *Vossius* tells us) boasted of his no-learning, calling himself the eagle, for his flight above it. And such genii as these may, indeed, have much reliance on their own native powers. For genius may be compared to the natural strength of the body; learning to the super-induced accoutrements of arms: if the first is equal to the proposed exploit, the latter rather encumbers, than assists; rather retards, than promotes, the victory. *Sacer nobis inest Deus,*[7] says *Seneca.* With regard to the moral world, *conscience,* with regard to the intellectual, *genius,* is that god within. Genius can set us right in Composition, without the rules of the learned; as con-science sets us right in life, without the laws of the land: *This,* singly,

---

[5] "He denies that laws were made for him; there is nothing he does not arrogate to himself."

[6] "To neglect money, at times is the greatest gain."

[7] "Holy is the God within us."

can make us good, as men: *that,* singly, as writers, can, sometimes, make us great.

I say, sometimes, because there is a genius, which stands in need of learning to make it shine. Of genius there are two species, an earlier, and a later; or call them *infantine,* and *adult.* An adult genius comes out of nature's hand, as *Pallas* out of *Jove's* head, at full growth, and mature: *Shakespeare's* genius was of this kind; On the contrary, *Swift* stumbled at the threshold, and set out for distinction on feeble knees: His was an infantine genius; a genius, which, like other infants, must be nursed, and educated, or it will come to nought: Learning is its nurse, and tutor; but this nurse may overlay with an indigested load, which smothers common sense; and this tutor may mislead, with pedantic prejudice, which vitiates the best understanding: As too great admirers of the fathers of the church have sometimes set up their authority against the true sense of Scripture; so too great admirers of the classical fathers have sometimes set up their authority, or example, against reason.

Neve minor, neu sit quinto productior actu Fabula.[8]

So says *Horace,* so says antient example. But reason has not subscribed. I know but one book that can justify our implicit acquiescence in it: And (by the way) on that book a noble disdain of undue deference to prior opinion has lately cast, and is still casting, a new and inestimable light.

But, superstition for our predecessors set aside, the classics are for ever our rightful and revered masters in *Composition;* and our understandings bow before them: But when? When a master is wanted; which, sometimes, as I have shown, is not the case. Some are pupils of nature only, nor go farther to school: From such we reap often a double advantage; they not only rival the reputation of the great antient authors, but also reduce the number of mean ones among the moderns. For when they enter on subjects which have been in former hands, such is their superiority, that, like a tenth wave, they overwhelm, and bury in oblivion all that went before: And thus not only enrich and adorn, but remove a load, and lessen the labour, of the letter'd world.

"But, you say, since *Originals* can arise from genius only, and since genius is so very rare, it is scarce worth while to labour a point so

---

[8] "Let your play be not shorter, nor longer, than five acts."

much, from which we can reasonably expect so little." To show that genius is not so very rare as you imagine, I shall point out strong instances of it, in a far distant quarter from that mentioned above. The minds of the schoolmen were almost as much cloistered as their bodies; they had but little learning, and few books; yet may the most learned be struck with some astonishment at their so singular natural sagacity, and most exquisite edge of thought. Who would expect to find *Pindar* and *Scotus, Shakespeare* and *Aquinas,* of the same party? Both equally shew an *original,* unindebted, energy; the *vigor igneus,* and *cælestis origo,* burns in both; and leaves us in doubt whether genius is more evident in the sublime flights and beauteous flowers of poetry, or in the profound penetrations, and marvelously keen and minute distinctions, called the thorns of the schools. There might have been more able consuls called from the plough, than ever arrived at that honour: Many a genius, probably, there has been, which could neither write, nor read. So that genius, that supreme lustre of literature, is less rare than you conceive.

By the praise of genius we detract not from learning; we detract not from the value of gold, by saying that diamond has greater still. He who disregards learning, shows that he wants its aid; and he that overvalues it, shows that its aid has done him harm. Overvalued indeed it cannot be, if genius, as to Composition, is valued more. Learning we thank, genius we revere; That gives us pleasure, This gives us rapture; That informs, This inspires; and is itself inspired; for genius is from heaven, learning from man: *This* sets us above the low, and illiterate; *That,* above the learned, and polite. Learning is borrowed knowledge; genius is knowledge innate, and quite our own. Therefore, as *Bacon* observes, it may take a nobler name, and be called Wisdom; in which sense of wisdom, some are born wise.

But here a caution is necessary against the most fatal of errors in those automaths, those self-taught philosophers of our age, who set up genius, and often, mere *fancied* genius, not only above human learning, but divine truth. I have called genius wisdom; but let it be remembered, that in the most renowned ages of the most refined heathen wisdom (and theirs is not Christian) *"the world by wisdom knew not God, and it pleased God by the foolishness of preaching to save those that believed."* In the fairyland of fancy, genius may wander wild; there it has a creative power, and may reign arbitrarily over its own empire of chimeras. The wide field of nature also lies open before it, where it may range unconfined, make what discoveries it can, and sport with its infinite objects uncontrouled, as far as visible nature extends, painting them as wantonly as it will: But what painter of the most unbounded and exalted genius can give us the true portrait of a seraph? He can give us only what by his own or others' eyes, has been seen; tho' that indeed infinitely compounded, raised, burlesqued, dishonoured, or adorned: In like manner, who can give us divine truth unrevealed? Much less should any presume to set aside divine truth when revealed, as incongruous to their own sagacities— Is this too serious for my subject? I shall be more so before I close.

Having put in a caveat against the most fatal of errors, from the too great indulgence of genius, return we now to that too great suppression of it, which is detrimental to Composition; and endeavour to rescue the writer, as well as the man. I have said, that some are born wise; but they, like those that are born rich, by neglecting the cultivation and produce of their own possessions, and by running in debt, may be beggared at last; and lose their reputations, as younger brothers' estates, not by being born with less abilities than the rich heir, but at too late an hour.

Many a great man has been lost to himself, and the publick, purely because great ones were born before him. *Hermias,* in his collections on *Homer's* blindness, says, that *Homer* requesting the gods to grant him a sight of *Achilles,* that hero rose, but in armour so bright, that it struck *Homer* blind with the blaze. Let not the blaze of even *Homer's* muse darken us to the discernment of our own powers; which may possibly set us above the rank of *Imitators;* who, though most excellent, and even immortal (as some of them are) yet are still but *Dii minorum gentium,*[9] nor can expect the largest share of incense, the greatest profusion of praise, on their secondary altars.

But farther still: a spirit of *Imitation* hath many ill effects; I shall confine myself to three. *First,* It deprives the liberal and politer arts of an advantage which the mechanic enjoy: In these, men are ever endeavouring to go beyond their predecessors; in the former, to follow them. And since copies surpass not their *Originals,* as streams rise not higher than their spring, rarely so high; hence, while arts mechanic are in perpetual progress, and increase, the liberal are in retrogradation, and decay. *These* resemble pyramids, are broad at bottom, but lessen exceedingly as they rise; *Those* resemble rivers which, from a small fountain-head, are spreading ever wider and wider, as they

⁹ "Gods of lesser tribes."

run. Hence it is evident, that different portions of understanding are not (as some imagine) allotted to different periods of time; for we see, in the same period, understanding rising in one set of artists, and declining in another. Therefore *nature* stands absolved, and our inferiority in Composition must be charged on ourselves.

Nay, so far are we from complying with a necessity, which nature lays us under, that, *Secondly,* by a spirit of *Imitation* we counteract nature, and thwart her design. She brings us into the world all *Originals:* No two faces, no two minds, are just alike; but all bear nature's evident mark of separation on them. Born *Originals,* how comes it to pass that we die *Copies?* That meddling ape *Imitation,* as soon as we come to years of *Indiscretion* (so let me speak), snatches the pen, and blots out nature's mark of separation, cancels her kind intention, destroys all mental individuality; the letter'd world no longer consists of singulars, it is a medly, a mass; and a hundred books, at bottom, are but One. Why are Monkies such masters of mimickry? Why receive they such a talent at imitation? Is it not as the *Spartan* slaves received a licence for ebriety; that their betters might be ashamed of it?

The *Third* fault to be found with a spirit of *Imitation* is, that with great incongruity it makes us poor, and proud: makes us think little, and write much; gives us huge folios, which are little better than more reputable cushions to promote our repose. Have not some sevenfold volumes put us in mind of *Ovid's* sevenfold channels of the *Nile* at the conflagration?

> *Ostia septem*
> *Pulverulenta vacant septem sine flumine valles.*[10]

Such leaden labours are like *Lycurgus's* iron money, which was so much less in value than in bulk, that it required barns for strongboxes, and a yoke of oxen to draw five hundred pounds.

But notwithstanding these disadvantages of *Imitation,* imitation must be the lot (and often an honourable lot it is) of most writers. If there is a famine of *invention* in the land, like *Joseph's* brethren, we must travel far for food; we must visit the remote, and rich, Antients; but an inventive genius may safely stay at home; that, like the widow's cruse, is divinely replenished from within; and affords us a miraculous delight. Whether our own genius be such, or not, we

---

[10] "Its seven mouths are dusty and empty, seven riverless valleys."

diligently should inquire; that we may not go a begging with gold in our purse. For there is a mine in man, which must be deeply dug ere we can conjecture its contents. Another often sees that in us, which we see not ourselves; and may there not be that in us which is unseen by both? That there may, chance often discovers, either by a luckily chosen theme, or a mighty premium, or an absolute necessity of exertion, or a noble stroke of emulation from another's glory; as that on *Thucydides* from hearing *Herodotus* repeat part of his history at the *Olympic* games: Had there been no *Herodotus,* there might have been no *Thucydides,* and the world's admiration might have begun at *Livy* for excellence in that province of the pen. *Demosthenes* had the same stimulation on hearing *Callistratus;* or *Tully* might have been the first of consummate renown at the bar.

Quite clear of the dispute concerning *antient and modern learning,* we speak not of performance, but powers. The modern powers are equal to those before them; modern performance in general is deplorably short. How great are the names just mentioned? Yet who will dare affirm, that as great may not rise up in some future, or even in the present age? Reasons there are why talents may not *appear,* none why they may not *exist,* as much in one period as another. An evocation of vegetable fruits depends on rain, air, and sun; an evocation of the fruits of genius no less depends on externals. What a marvellous crop bore it in *Greece,* and *Rome?* And what a marvellous sunshine did it there enjoy? What encouragement from the nature of their governments, and the spirit of their people? *Virgil* and *Horace* owed their divine talents to Heaven; their immortal works, to men; thank *Maecenas* and *Augustus* for them. Had it not been for these, the genius of those poets had lain buried in their ashes. *Athens* expended on her theatre, painting, sculpture, and architecture, a tax levied for the support of a war. *Caesar* dropt his papers when *Tully* spoke; and *Philip* trembled at the voice of *Demosthenes:* And has there arisen but one *Tully,* one *Demosthenes,* in so long a course of years? The powerful eloquence of them both in one stream, should never bear me down into the melancholy persuasion, that several have not been born, tho' they have not emerged. The sun as much exists in a cloudy day, as in a clear; it is outward, accidental circumstances that with regard to genius either in nation, or age,

Collectas fugat nubes, solemque reducit.[11]
Virg.

[11] "Puts to flight the gathered clouds, and brings back the sun."

As great, perhaps, greater than those mentioned (presumptuous as it may sound) may, possibly, arise; for who hath fathomed the mind of man? Its bounds are as unknown, as those of the creation; since the birth of which, perhaps, not One has so far exerted, as not to leave his possibilities beyond his attainments, his powers beyond his exploits. Forming our judgements altogether by what *has* been done, without knowing, or at all inquiring, what possibly *might* have been done, we naturally enough fall into too mean an opinion of the human mind. If a sketch of the divine *Iliad* before Homer wrote, had been given to mankind, by some superior being, or otherwise, its execution would, probably, have appeared beyond the power of man. Now, to surpass it, we think impossible. As the first of these opinions would evidently have been a mistake, why may not the second be so too? Both are founded on the same bottom; on our ignorance of the possible dimensions of the mind of man.

Nor are we only ignorant of the dimensions of the human mind in general, but even of our own. That a man may be scarce less ignorant of his own powers, than an oyster of its pearl, or a rock of its diamond; that he may possess dormant, unsuspected abilities, till awakened by loud calls, or stung up by striking emergencies, is evident from the sudden eruption of some men, out of perfect obscurity, into publick admiration, on the strong impulse of some animating occasion; not more to the world's great surprize, than their own. Few authors of distinction but have experienced something of this nature, at the first beamings of their yet unsuspected genius on their hitherto dark Composition: The writer starts at it, as at a lucid meteor in the night; is much surprized; can scarce believe it true. During his happy confusion, it may be said to him, as to Eve at the lake,

What there thou seest, fair creature, is thyself.
Milt.

Genius, in this view, is like a dear friend in our company under disguise; who, while we are lamenting his absence, drops his mask, striking us, at once, with equal surprize and joy. This sensation, which I speak of in a writer, might favour, and so promote, the fable of poetic inspiration: A poet of a strong imagination, and stronger vanity, on feeling it, might naturally enough realize the world's mere compliment, and think himself truly inspired. Which is not improbable; for enthusiasts of all kinds do no less.

Since it is plain that men may be strangers to their own abilities;

and by thinking meanly of them without just cause, may possibly lose a name, perhaps a name immortal; I would find some means to prevent these evils. Whatever promotes virtue, promotes something more, and carries its good influence beyond the *moral* man: To prevent these evils, I borrow two golden rules from *ethics,* which are no less golden in *Composition,* than in life. 1. *Know thyself;* 2dly, *Reverence thyself:* I design to repay ethics in a future letter, by two rules from rhetoric for its service.

1st. *Know thyself.* Of ourselves it may be said, as *Martial* says of a bad neighbour,

Nil tam prope, proculque nobis.[12]

Therefore dive deep into thy bosom; learn the depth, extent, bias, and full fort of thy mind; contract full intimacy with the stranger within thee; excite and cherish every spark of intellectual light and heat, however smothered under former negligence, or scattered through the dull, dark mass of common thoughts; and collecting them into a body, let thy genius rise (if a genius thou hast) as the sun from chaos; and if I should then say, like an *Indian, Worship it,* (though too bold) yet should I say little more than my second rule enjoins, (*viz.*) *Reverence thyself.*

That is, let not great examples, or authorities, browbeat thy reason into too great a diffidence of thyself: Thyself so reverence, as to prefer the native growth of thy own mind to the richest import from abroad; such borrowed riches make us poor. The man who thus reverences himself, will soon find the world's reverence to follow his own. His works will stand distinguished; his the sole property of them; which property alone can confer the noble title of an *author;* that is, of one who (to speak accurately) *thinks,* and *composes;* while other invaders of the press, how voluminous, and learned soever, (with due respect be it spoken) only *read,* and *write.*

This is the difference between those two luminaries in literature, the well-accomplished scholar, and the divinely-inspired enthusiast; the *first* is, as the bright morning star; the *second,* as the rising sun. The writer who neglects those two rules above will never stand alone; he makes one of a group, and thinks in wretched unanimity with the throng: Incumbered with the notions of others, and impoverished by their abundance, he conceives not the least embryo of new thought;

---

[12] "Nothing so near, and yet so far from us."

opens not the least vista thro' the gloom of ordinary writers, into the bright walks of rare imagination, and singular design; while the true genius is crossing all publick roads into fresh untrodden ground; he, up to the knees in antiquity, is treading the sacred footsteps of great examples, with the blind veneration of a bigot saluting the papal toe; comfortably hoping full absolution for the sins of his own understanding, from the powerful charm of touching his idol's infallibility.

Such meanness of mind, such prostration of our own powers, proceeds from too great admiration of others. Admiration has, generally, a degree of two very bad ingredients in it; of ignorance, and of fear; and does mischief in Composition, and in life. Proud as the world is, there is more superiority in it *given,* than *assumed:* And its grandees of all kinds owe more of their elevation to the littleness of others' minds, than to the greatness of their own. Were not prostrate spirits their voluntary pedestals, the figure they make among mankind would not stand so high. *Imitators* and *Translators* are somewhat of the pedestal-kind, and sometimes rather raise their *Original's* reputation, by showing him to be by them inimitable, than their own. *Homer* has been translated into most languages; *Aelian* tells us, that the *Indians,* (hopeful tutors!) have taught him to speak their tongue. What expect we from them? Not *Homer's Achilles,* but something, which, like *Patroclus,* assumes his name, and, at its peril, appears in his stead; nor expect we *Homer's Ulysses,* gloriously bursting out of his cloud into royal grandeur, but an *Ulysses* under disguise, and a beggar to the last. Such is that inimitable father of poetry, and oracle of all the wise, whom *Lycurgus* transcribed; and for an annual public recital of whose works *Solon* enacted a law; that it is much to be feared, that his so numerous translations are but as the publish'd testimonials of so many nations, and ages, that this author so divine is untranslated still.

But here,

> *Cynthius aurem*
> *Vellit,—*[18]
> *Virg.*

and demands justice for his favourite, and ours. Great things he has done; but he might have done greater. What a fall is it from *Homer's*

---

[18] "Apollo plucks my ear."

numbers, free as air, lofty and harmonious as the spheres, into childish shackles, and tinkling sounds! But, in his fall, he is still great—

> Nor appears
> Less than archangel ruin'd, and the excess
> Of glory obscur'd.—
>
> *Milt.*

Had *Milton* never wrote, *Pope* had been less to blame: But when in *Milton's* genius, *Homer*, as it were, personally rose to forbid *Britons* doing him that ignoble wrong; it is less pardonable, by that *effeminate* decoration, to put *Achilles* in petticoats a second time: How much nobler had it been, if his numbers had rolled on in full flow, through the various modulations of *masculine* melody, into those grandeurs of solemn sound, which are indispensably demanded by the native dignity of heroick song? How much nobler, if he had resisted the temptation of that *Gothic* daemon, which modern poesy tasting, became mortal? O how unlike the deathless, divine harmony of three great names (how justly join'd), of *Milton, Greece,* and *Rome?* His verse, but for this little speck of mortality, in its extreme parts, as his hero had in his heel; like him, had been invulnerable, and immortal. But, unfortunately, *that* was undipt in *Helicon;* as *this,* in *Styx.* Harmony as well as eloquence is essential to poesy; and a murder of his musick is putting half *Homer* to death. *Blank* is a term of diminution; what we mean by blank verse, is, verse unfallen, uncurst; verse reclaim'd, reinthron'd in the true *language of the gods;* who never thunder'd nor suffer'd their *Homer* to thunder, in rhime; and therefore, I beg you, my Friend, to crown it with some nobler term; nor let the greatness of the thing lie under the defamation of such a name.

But supposing *Pope's Iliad* to have been perfect in its kind; yet it is a *Translation* still; which differs as much from an *Original,* as the moon from the sun.

> —*Phoeben alieno jusserat igne*
> *Impleri, solemque suo.*[14]
>
> *Claud.*

But as nothing is more easy than to write originally wrong; Originals are not here recommended, but under the strong guard of my first

---

[14] "He had commanded Phoebe to shine with light from another, the sun with its own."

rule—*Know thyself*. *Lucian*, who was an Original, neglected not this rule, if we may judge by his reply to one who took some freedom with him. He was, at first, an apprentice to a statuary; and when he was reflected on as such, by being called *Prometheus*, he replied, "I am indeed the inventor of new work, the model of which I owe to none; and, if I do not execute it well, I deserve to be torn by twelve vulturs, instead of one."

If so, O *Gulliver!* dost thou not shudder at thy brother *Lucian's* vulturs hovering o'er thee? Shudder on! they cannot shock thee more, than decency has been shock'd by thee. How have thy *Houyhnhunms* thrown thy judgment from its seat, and laid thy imagination in the mire? In what ordure hast thou dipt thy pencil? What a monster hast thou made of the

Human face divine?
Milt.

This writer has so satirised human nature, as to give a demonstration in himself, that it deserves to be satirised. But, say his wholesale admirers, Few could *so* have written; true, and Fewer *would*. If it required great abilities to commit the fault, greater still would have saved him from it. But whence arise such warm advocates for such a performance? From hence, *viz.* before a character is established, merit makes fame; afterwards fame makes merit. *Swift* is not commended for this piece, but this piece for *Swift*. He has given us some beauties which deserve all our praise; and our comfort is, that his faults will not become common; for none can be guilty of them, but who have wit as well as reputation to spare. His wit had been less wild, if his temper had not jostled his judgment. If his favourite *Houyhnhunms* could write, and *Swift* had been one of them, every horse with him would have been an ass, and he would have written a penegyrick on mankind, saddling with much reproach the present heroes of his pen: On the contrary, being born amongst men, and, of consequence, piqued by many, and peevish at more, he has blasphemed a nature little lower than that of angels, and assumed by far higher than they: But surely the contempt of the world is not a greater virtue, that the contempt of mankind is a vice. Therefore I wonder that, though forborn by others, the laughter-loving *Swift* was not reproved by the venerable Dean, who could sometimes be very grave.

For I remember, as I and others were taking with him an evening's walk, about a mile out of *Dublin,* he stopt short; we passed on; but perceiving that he did not follow us, I went back; and found him fixed as a statue, and earnestly gazing upward at a noble elm, which in its uppermost branches was much withered, and decayed. Pointing at it, he said, "I shall be like that tree, I shall die at top." As in this he seemed to prophesy like the Sybils; if, like one of them, he had burnt part of his works, especially *this* blasted branch of a noble genius, like her too, he might have risen in his demand for the rest.

Would not his friend *Pope* have succeeded better in an *original* attempt? Talents untried are talents unknown. All that I know, is that, contrary to these sentiments, he was not only an avowed professor of imitation, but a zealous recommender of it also. Nor could he recommend any thing better, except emulation, to those who write. One of these all writers must call to their aid; but aids they are of unequal repute. Imitation is inferiority confessed; emulation is superiority contested, or denied; imitation is servile, emulation generous; that fetters, this fires; that may give a name; this, a name immortal: This made *Athens* to succeeding ages the rule of taste, and the standard of perfection. Her men of genius struck fire against each other; and kindled, by conflict, into glories, which no time shall extinguish. We thank *Eschylus* for *Sophocles;* and *Parrhasius* for *Zeuxis; emulation,* for both. That bids us fly the general fault of *imitators;* bids us not be struck with the loud report of former fame, as with a knell, which damps the spirits; but, as with a trumpet, which inspires ardour to rival the renown'd. Emulation exhorts us, instead of learning our discipline for ever, like raw troops, under antient leaders in composition, to put those laurel'd veterans in some hazard of losing their superior posts in glory.

Such is emulation's high-spirited advice, such her immortalizing call. *Pope* would not hear, pre-engaged with imitation, which blessed him with all her charms. He chose rather, with his namesake of *Greece,* to triumph in the old world, than to look out for a new. His taste partook the error of his religion; it denied not worship to saints and angels; that is, to writers, who, canonized for ages, have received their apotheosis from established and universal fame. True poesy, like true religion, abhors idolatry; and though it honours the memory of the exemplary, and takes them willingly (yet cautiously) as guides in the way to glory; real, though unexampled, excellence is its only aim; nor looks it for any inspiration less than divine.

Though *Pope's* noble muse may boast her illustrious descent from *Homer, Virgil, Horace,* yet is an *Original* author more nobly born. As *Tacitus* says of *Curtius Rufus,* an *Original* author is born of himself, is his own progenitor, and will probably propagate a numerous offspring of imitators, to eternize his glory; while mule-like imitators die without issue. Therefore, though we stand much obliged for his giving us an *Homer,* yet had he doubled our obligation, by giving us—a *Pope.* Had he a strong imagination, and the true sublime? That granted, we might have had two *Homers* instead of one, if longer had been his life; for I heard the dying swan talk over an epic plan a few weeks before his decease.

Bacon, under the shadow of whose great name I would shelter my present attempt in favour of *Originals,* says, "Men seek not to know their own stock, and abilities; but fancy their possessions to be greater, and their abilities less, than they really are." Which is, in effect, saying, "That we ought to exert more than we do; and that, on exertion, our probability of success is greater than we conceive."

Nor have I *Bacon's* opinion only, but his assistance too, on my side. His mighty mind travelled round the intellectual world; and, with a more than eagle's eye, saw, and has pointed out, blank spaces, or dark spots in it, on which the human mind never shone: Some of these have been enlightened since; some are benighted still.

Moreover, so boundless are the bold excursions of the human mind, that, in the vast void beyond real existence, it can call forth shadowy beings, and unknown worlds, as numerous, as bright, and, perhaps, as lasting, as the stars; such quite-original beauties we may call paradisaical.

> *Natos sine semine flores.*[15]
> *Ovid.*

When such an ample area for renowned adventure in *original* attempts lies before us, shall we be as mere leaden pipes, conveying to the present age small streams of excellence from its grand reservoir in antiquity; and those too, perhaps, mudded in the pass? *Originals* shine, like comets; have no peer in their path; are rival'd by none, and the gaze of all: All other compositions (if they shine at all) shine in clusters; like the stars in the galaxy; where, like bad neighbours, all suffer from all; each particular being diminished, and almost lost in the throng.

15 "Flowers generated without seed."

If thoughts of this nature prevailed; if antients and moderns were no longer considered as masters and pupils, but as hard-matched rivals for renown; then moderns, by the longevity of their labours, might, one day, become antients themselves: And old time, that best weigher of merits, to keep his balance even, might have the golden weight of an *Augustan* age in both his scales: Or rather our scale might descend; and that of antiquity (as a modern match for it strongly speaks) might *kick the beam.*

And why not? For, consider, *since* an impartial Providence scatters talents indifferently, as thro' all orders of persons, so thro' all periods of time; *since,* a marvellous light, unenjoy'd of old, is pour'd on us by revelation, with larger prospects extending our understanding, with brighter objects enriching our imagination, with an inestimable prize setting our passions on fire, thus strengthening every power that enables composition to shine; *since,* there has been no fall in man on this side *Adam,* who left no works, and the works of all other antients are our auxiliars against themselves, as being perpetual spurs to our ambition, and shining lamps in our path to fame; *since,* this world is a school, as well for intellectual, as moral, advance; and the longer human nature is at school, the better scholar it should be; *since,* as the moral world expects its glorious millennium, the world intellectual may hope, by the rules of analogy, for some superior degrees of excellence to crown her later scenes; nor may it only hope, but must enjoy them too; for *Tully, Quintilian,* and all true critics allow, that virtue assists genius, and that the writer will be more able, when better is the man— All these particulars, I say, considered, why should it seem altogether impossible, that heaven's latest editions of the human mind may be the most correct, and fair; that the day may come, when the moderns may proudly look back on the comparative darkness of former ages, on the children of antiquity; reputing *Homer* and *Demosthenes,* as the dawn of divine genius; and *Athens* as the cradle of infant fame; what a glorious revolution would this make in the rolls of renown?

What a rant, say you, is here?—I partly grant it: Yet, consider, my friend! knowledge physical, mathematical, moral, and divine, increases; all arts and sciences are making considerable advance; with them, all the accommodations, ornaments, delights, and glories of human life; and these are new food to the genius of a polite writer; these are as the root, and composition, as the flower; and as the root spreads, and thrives, shall the flower fail? As well may a flower flourish, when the root is dead. It is prudence to read, genius to relish, glory to surpass, antient authors; and wisdom to try our strength, in an attempt in which it would be no great dishonour to fail.

Why condemn'd *Maro* his admirable epic to the flames? Was it not because his discerning eye saw some length of perfection beyond it? And what he saw, may not others reach? And who bid fairer than our country-men for that glory? Something new may be expected from *Britons* particularly; who seem not to be more sever'd from the rest of mankind by the surrounding sea, than by the current in their veins; and of whom little more appears to be required, in order to give us *Originals,* than a consistency of character, and making their compositions of a piece with their lives. May our genius shine; and proclaim us in that nobler view!

> . . . *minimâ contentos nocte Britannos.*[16]
> *Virg.*

And so it does; for in polite composition, in natural, and mathematical, knowledge, we have great *Originals* already—*Bacon, Boyle, Newton, Shakespeare, Milton,* have showed us, that all the winds cannot blow the *British* flag farther, than an original spirit can convey the *British* fame; their names go round the world; and what foreign genius strikes not as they pass? Why should not their posterity embark in the same bold bottom of new enterprize, and hope the same success? Hope it they may; or you must assert, either that those *Originals,* which we already enjoy, were written by angels, or deny that we are men. As *Simonides* said to *Pausanias,* reason should say to the writer, "Remember thou art a man." And for man not to grasp at all which is laudable within his reach, is a dishonour to human nature, and a disobedience to the divine; for as heaven does nothing in vain, its gift of talents implies an injunction of their use.

A friend of mine has obeyed that injunction; he has relied on himself, and with a genius, as well *moral,* as *original* (to speak in bold terms), has cast out evil spirits; has made a convert to virtue of a species of composition, once most its foe. As the first christian emperors expell'd daemons, and dedicated their temples to the living God.

But you, I know, are sparing in your praise of this author; there-

---

[16] "Britons content with their exceedingly short night."

fore I will speak of one, which is sure of your applause. *Shakespeare* mingled no water with his wine, lower'd his genius by no vapid imitation. *Shakespeare* gave us a *Shakespeare*, nor could the first in antient fame have given us more! *Shakespeare* is not their son, but brother; their equal; and that, in spite of all his faults. Think you this too bold? Consider, in those antients what is it the world admires? Not the fewness of their faults, but the number and brightness of their beauties; and if *Shakespeare* is their equal (as he doubtless is) in that, which in them is admired, then is *Shakespeare* as great as they; and not impotence, but some other cause, must be charged with his defects. When we are setting these great men in competition, what but the comparative size of their genius is the subject of our inquiry? And a giant loses nothing of his size, tho' he should chance to trip in his race. But it is a compliment to those heroes of antiquity to suppose *Shakespeare* their equal only in dramatic powers; therefore, though his faults had been greater, the scale would still turn in his favour. There is at least as much genius on the *British* as on the *Grecian* stage, tho' the former is not swept so clean; so clean from violations not only of the *dramatic,* but *moral* rule; for an honest heathen, on reading some of our celebrated scenes, might be seriously concerned to see, that our obligations to the religion of nature were cancel'd by Christianity.

Johnson, in the serious drama, is as much an imitator, as *Shakespeare* is an original. He was very learned, as *Sampson* was very strong, to his own hurt: Blind to the nature of tragedy, he pulled down all antiquity on his head, and buried himself under it; we see nothing of *Johnson,* nor indeed, of his admired (but also murdered) antients; for what shone in the historian is a cloud on the poet; and *Cataline* might have been a good play, if *Salust* had never writ.

Who knows whether *Shakespeare* might not have thought less, if he had read more? Who knows if he might not have laboured under the load of *Johnson's* learning, as *Enceladus* under *Aetna?* His mighty genius, indeed, through the most mountainous oppression would have breathed out some of his inextinguishable fire; yet, possibly, he might not have risen up into that giant, that much more than common man, at which we now gaze with amazement, and delight. Perhaps he was as learned as his dramatic province required; for whatever other learning he wanted, he was master of two books, unknown to many of the profoundly read, though books, which the last conflagration alone can destroy; the book of nature, and that of man. These he had by heart, and has transcribed many admirable pages of them, into his immortal works. These are the fountain-head, whence the *Castalian* streams of *original* composition flow; and these are often mudded by other waters, tho' waters in their distinct chanel, most wholesome and pure: As two chymical liquors, separately clear as crystal, grow foul by mixture, and offend the sight. So that he had not only as much learning as his dramatic province required, but, perhaps, as it could safely bear. If *Milton* had spared some of his learning, his muse would have gained more glory, than he would have lost, by it.

Dryden, destitute of *Shakespeare's* genius, had almost as much learning as *Johnson,* and, for the buskin, quite as little taste. He was a stranger to the pathos, and by numbers, expression, sentiment, and every other dramatic cheat, strove to make amends for it; as if a saint could make amends for the want of conscience; a soldier, for the want of valour; or a vestal, of modesty. The noble nature of tragedy disclaims an equivalent; like virtue, it demands the heart; and *Dryden* had none to give. Let epic poets *think,* the tragedian's point is rather to feel; such distant things are a tragedian and a poet, that the latter indulged, destroys the former. Look on *Barnwell,* and *Essex,* and see how as to these distant characters *Dryden* excells, and is excelled. But the strongest demonstration of his no-taste for the buskin, are his tragedies fringed with rhyme; which, in epic poetry, is a sore disease, in the tragic, absolute death. To *Dryden's* enormity, *Pope's* was a light offence. As lacemen are foes to mourning, these two authors, rich in rhyme, were no great friends to those solemn ornaments, which the noble nature of their works required.

Must rhyme then, say you, be banished? I wish the nature of our language could bear its intire expulsion; but our lesser poetry stands in need of a toleration for it; it raises that, but sinks the great; as spangles adorn children, but expose men. Prince *Henry* bespangled all over in his oylet-hole suit, with glittering pins; and an *Achilles,* or an *Almanzor,* in his *Gothic* array; are very much on a level, as to the majesty of the poet, and the prince. *Dryden* had a great, but a general capacity; and as for a general genius, there is no such thing in nature: A genius implies the rays of the mind concenter'd, and determined to some particular point; when they are scatter'd widely, they act feebly, and strike not with sufficient force, to fire, or dissolve, the heart. As what comes from the writer's heart, reaches ours; so what comes from his head, sets our brains at work, and our hearts at ease. It makes a circle of thoughtful critics, not of distressed patients; and a passive audience, is what tragedy requires. Applause is not to be given, but extorted; and the silent lapse of a single tear, does the writer more honour, than the rattling thunder of a thousand hands. Applauding hands, and dry eyes (which during *Dryden's* theatrical reign often met) are a satire on the writer's talent, and the spectator's taste. When by such judges the laurel is blindly given, and by such a poet proudly received, they resemble an intoxicated hoste, and his tasteless guests, over some sparkling adulteration, commending their Champaign.

But *Dryden* has his glory, tho' not on the stage; What an inimitable *original* is his ode? A small one, indeed, but of the first lustre, and without a flaw; and, amid the brightest boasts of antiquity, it may find a foil.

Among the brightest of the moderns, Mr. *Addison* must take his place. Who does not approach his character with great respect? They who refuse to close with the public in his praise, refuse at their peril. But, if men will be fond of their own opinions, some hazard must be run. He had, what *Dryden* and *Johnson* wanted, a warm, and feeling heart; but, being of a grave and bashful nature, thro' a philosophic reserve, and a sort of moral prudery, he conceal'd it, where he should have let loose all his fire, and have show'd the most tender sensibilities of heart. At his celebrated *Cato,* few tears are shed, but *Cato's* own; which, indeed, are truly great, but unaffecting, except to the noble few, who love their country better than themselves. The bulk of mankind want virtue enough to be touched by them. His strength of genius has reared up one glorious image, more lofty, and truly golden, than that in the plains of *Dura,* for cool admiration to gaze at, and warm patriotism (how rare!) to worship; while those two throbbing pulses of the drama, by which alone it is shown to live, *terror* and *pity,* neglected thro' the whole, leave our unmolested hearts at perfect peace. Thus the poet, like his hero, thro' mistaken excellence, and virtue overstrain'd, becomes a sort of suicide; and that which is most dramatic in the drama, dies. All his charms of poetry are but as funeral flowers, which adorn; all his noble sentiments but as rich spices, which embalm, the tragedy deceased.

Of tragedy, pathos is not only the life and soul, but the soul inextinguishable; it charms us thro' a thousand faults. Decorations, which in this author abound, tho' they might immortalize other poesy, are the *splendida peccata* [17] which damn the drama; while, on the contrary, the murder of all other beauties is a venial sin, nor plucks

[17] "Glittering sins."

the laurel from the tragedian's brow. Was it otherwise, *Shakespeare* himself would run some hazard of losing his crown.

Socrates frequented the plays of *Euripides;* and, what living *Socrates* would decline the theatre, at the representation of *Cato? Tully's* assassins found him in his litter, reading the *Medea* of the *Grecian* poet, to prepare himself for death. Part of *Cato* might be read to the same end. In the weight and dignity of moral reflection, *Addison* resembles that poet, who was called the dramatic philosopher; and is himself, as he says of *Cato, ambitiously sententious.* But as to the singular talent so remarkable in *Euripides,* at melting down hearts into the tender streams of grief and pity, there the resemblance fails. His beauties sparkle, but do not warm; they sparkle as stars in a frosty night. There is, indeed, a constellation in his play; there is the philosopher, patriot, orator, and poet; but where is the tragedian? And, if that is wanting,

> *Cur in theatrum Cato severe venisti?* [18]
> *Mart.*

And, when I recollect what passed between him and *Dryden* in relation to this drama, I must add the next line,

> *An ideo tantum veneras, ut exires?* [19]

For, when *Addison* was a student at *Oxford,* he sent up this play to his friend *Dryden,* as a proper person to recommend it to the theatre, if it deserved it; who returned it, with very great commendation; but with his opinion, that, on the stage, it could not meet with its deserved success. But tho' the performance was denied the theatre, it brought its author on the public stage of life. For persons in power inquiring soon after of the head of his college for a youth of parts, *Addison* was recommended, and readily received, by means of the great reputation which *Dryden* had just then spread of him above.

There is this similitude between the poet and the play; as this is more fit for the closet than the stage; so, that shone brighter in private conversation than on the public scene. They both had a sort of *local* excellency, as the heathen gods a local divinity; beyond such a bound *they,* unadmired; and *these,* unadored. This puts me in mind of *Plato,* who denied *Homer* to the public; that *Homer,* which, when in his

[18] "Why, austere Cato, came you into the theatre?"

[19] "Or had you come only that you might go out?"

closet, was rarely out of his hand. Thus, tho' *Cato* is not calculated to signalize himself in the warm emotions of the theatre, yet we find him a most amiable companion, in our calmer delights of recess.

Notwithstanding what has been offered, this, in many views, is an exquisite piece. But there is so much more of art, than nature in it, that I can scarce forbear calling it, an exquisite piece of statuary,

> Where the smooth chisel all its skill has shown,
> To soften into flesh the rugged stone.
>
> *Addison.*

That is, where art has taken great pains to labour undramatic matter into dramatic life; which is impossible. However, as it is, like *Pygmalion,* we cannot but fall in love with it, and wish it was alive. How would a *Shakespeare,* or an *Otway,* have answered our wishes? They would have outdone *Prometheus,* and, with their heavenly fire, have given him not only life, but immortality. At their dramas (such is the force of nature) the poet is out of sight, quite hid behind his *Venus,* never thought of, till the curtain falls. Art brings our author forward, he stands before his piece; splendidly indeed, but unfortunately; for the writer must be forgotten by his audience, during the representation, if for ages he would be remembered by posterity. In the theatre, as in life, delusion is the charm; and we are undelighted, the first moment we are undeceived. Such demonstration have we, that the theatre is not yet opened, in which solid happiness can be found by man; because none are more than comparatively good; and folly has a corner in the heart of the wise.

A genius fond of *ornament* should not be wedded to the tragic muse, which is in *mourning:* We want not to be diverted at an entertainment, where our greatest pleasure arises from the depth of our concern. But whence (by the way) this odd generation of pleasure from pain? The movement of our melancholy passions is pleasant, when we ourselves are safe: We love to be at once, miserable, and unhurt: So are we made; and so made, perhaps, to show us the divine goodness; to show that none of our passions were designed to give us pain, except when being pain'd is for our advantage on the whole; which is evident from this instance, in which we see, that passions the most painful administer greatly, sometimes, to our delight. Since great names have accounted otherwise for this particular, I wish this solution, though to me probable, may not prove a mistake.

To close our thoughts on *Cato:* He who sees not much beauty in it, has no taste for poetry; he who sees nothing else, has no taste for the stage. Whilst it justifies censure, it extorts applause. It is much to be admired, but little to be felt. Had it not been a tragedy, it had been immortal; as it is a tragedy, its uncommon fate somewhat resembles his, who, for conquering gloriously, was condemn'd to die. Both shone, but shone fatally; because in breach of their respective laws, the laws of the drama, and the laws of arms. But how rich in reputation must that author be, who can spare a *Cato*, without feeling the loss?

That loss by our author would scarce be felt; it would be but dropping a single feather from a wing, that mounts him above his contemporaries. He has a more refined, decent, judicious, and extensive genius, than *Pope*, or *Swift*. To distinguish this triumvirate from each other, and, like *Newton*, to discover the different colours in these genuine and meridian rays of literary light, *Swift* is a singular wit, *Pope* a correct poet, *Addison* a great author. *Swift* looked on wit as the *jus divinum* to dominion and sway in the world; and considered as usurpation, all power that was lodged in persons of less sparkling understandings. This inclined him to tyranny in wit; Pope was somewhat of his opinion, but was for softening tyranny into lawful monarchy; yet were there some acts of severity in his reign. *Addison's* crown was elective, he reigned by the public voice:

> . . . *Volentes*
> *Per populos dat jura, viamque affectat Olympo.*[20]
> *Virg.*

But as good books are the medicine of the mind, if we should dethrone these authors, and consider them, not in their royal, but their medicinal capacity, might it not then be said, that *Addison* prescribed a wholesome and pleasant regimen, which was universally relished, and did much good; that *Pope* preferred a purgative of satire, which, tho' wholesome, was too painful in its operation; and that *Swift* insisted on a large dose of ipecacuanha, which, tho' readily swallowed from the fame of the physician, yet, if the patient had any delicacy of taste, he threw up the remedy, instead of the disease?

Addison wrote little in verse, much in sweet, elegant, *Virgilian*, prose; so let me call it, since *Longinus* calls *Herodotus* most *Homeric*, and *Thucydides* is said to have formed his style on *Pindar*. *Addison's* compositions are built with the finest materials, in the taste of the

[20] "He gives laws to a willing people, and thus makes his way to Olympus."

antients, and (to speak his own language) on truly *Classic ground:*
And tho' they are the delight of the present age, yet am I persuaded
that they will receive more justice from posterity. I never read him,
but I am struck with such a disheartening idea of perfection, that I
drop my pen. And, indeed, far superior writers should forget his compositions, if they would be greatly pleased with their own.

And yet (perhaps you have not observed it) what is the common
language of the world, and even of his admirers, concerning him?
They call him an *elegant* writer: That elegance which shines on the
surface of his compositions, seems to dazzle their understanding, and
render it a little blind to the depth of sentiment, which lies beneath:
Thus (hard fate!) he loses reputation with them, by doubling his title
to it. On subjects the most interesting, and important, no author of
his age has written with greater, I had almost said, with equal weight:
And they who commend him for his elegance, pay him such a sort of
compliment, by their abstemious praise, as they would pay to *Lucretia,*
if they should commend her only for her beauty.

But you say, that you know his value already— You know, indeed,
the value of his writings, and close with the world in thinking them
immortal; but, I believe, you know not, that his name would have
deserved immortality, tho' he had never written; and that, by a better
title than the pen can give: You know too, that his life was amiable;
but, perhaps, you are still to learn, that his death was triumphant:
That is a glory granted to very few: And the paternal hand of Providence, which, sometimes, snatches home its beloved children in a
moment, must convince us, that it is a glory of no great consequence
to the dying individual; that, when it is granted, it is granted chiefly
for the sake of the surviving world, which may profit by his pious
example, to whom is indulged the strength, and opportunity to make
his virtue shine out brightest at the point of death: And, here, permit
me to take notice, that the world will, probably, profit more by a
pious example of lay-extraction, than by one born of the church; the
latter being, usually, taxed with an abatement of influence by the bulk
of mankind: Therefore, to smother a bright example of this superior
good influence, may be reputed a sort of murder injurious to the
living, and unjust to the dead.

Such an example have we in *Addison:* which, tho' hitherto suppressed, yet, when once known, is insuppressible, of a nature too rare,
too striking to be forgotten. For, after a long, and manly, but vain
struggle with his distemper, he dismissed his physicians, and with

them all hopes of life: But with his hopes of life he dismissed not his concern for the living, but sent for a youth nearly related, and finely accomplished, yet not above being the better for good impressions from a dying friend: He came; but life now glimmering in the socket, the dying friend was silent: After a decent, and proper pause, the youth said, "Dear Sir! you sent for me: I believe, and I hope, that you have some commands; I shall hold them most sacred:" May distant ages not only hear, but feel, the reply! Forcibly grasping the youth's hand, he softly said, "See in what peace a Christian can die." He spoke with difficulty, and soon expired. Thro' grace divine, how great is man! Thro' divine mercy, how stingless death! Who would not thus expire?

What an inestimable legacy were those *few dying words* to the youth beloved? What a glorious supplement to his own valuable fragment on the truth of Christianity? What a full demonstration, that his fancy could not feign beyond what his virtue could reach? For when he would strike us most strongly with the grandeur of *Roman* magnanimity, his dying hero is ennobled with this sublime sentiment,

> While yet I live, let me not live in vain.
> *Cato.*

But how much more sublime is that sentiment when realized in life; when dispelling the languors, and appeasing the pains of a last hour; and brightening with illustrious action the dark avenue, and all-awful confines of an eternity? When his soul scarce animated his body, strong faith, and ardent charity, animated his soul into divine ambition of saving more than his own. It is for our honour, and our advantage, to hold him high in our esteem: For the better men are, the more they will admire him; and the more they admire him, the better will they be.

By drawing the long closed curtain of his death-bed, have I not showed you a stranger in him whom you knew so well? Is not this of your favourite author,

> —*Notâ major imago?* [21]
> *Virg.*

His compositions are but a noble preface; the grand work is his death: That is a work which is read in heaven: How has it join'd the final

[21] "A greater image than the known one?"

approbation of angels to the previous applause of men? How gloriously has he opened a splendid path, thro' fame immortal, into eternal peace? How has he given religion to triumph amidst the ruins of his nature? And, stronger than death, risen higher in virtue when breathing his last?

If all our men of genius had *so* breathed their last; if all our men of genius, like him, had been men of genius for *eternals; then,* had we never been pained by the report of a latter end—oh! how unlike to this? But a little to balance our pain, let us consider, that such reports as make us, at once, adore, and tremble, are of use, when too many there are, who must tremble before they will adore; and who convince us, to our shame, that the surest refuge of our endanger'd virtue is in the fears and terrors of the disingenuous human heart.

"But reports, you say, may be false; and you farther ask me, If all reports were true, how came an anecdote of so much honour to human nature, as mine, to lie so long unknown? What inauspicious planet interposed to lay its lustre under so lasting and so surprising an eclipse?"

The fact is indisputably true; nor are you to rely on me for the truth of it: My report is but a second edition: It was published before, tho' obscurely, and with a cloud before it. As clouds before the sun are often beautiful; so, this of which I speak. How finely pathetic are those two lines, which this so solemn and affecting scene inspired?

> He taught us how to live; and, oh! too high
> A price for knowledge, taught us how to die.
> *Tickell.*

With truth wrapped in darkness, so sung our oracle to the public, but explained himself to me: He was present at his patron's death, and that account of it here given, he gave to me before his eyes were dry: By what means *Addison taught us how to die,* the poet left to be made known by a late, and less able hand; but one more zealous for his patron's glory: Zealous, and impotent, as the poor *Aegyptian,* who gather'd a few splinters of a broken boat, as a funeral pile for the great *Pompey,* studious of doing honour to so renown'd a name: Yet had not this poor plank (permit me, here, so to call this imperfect page) been thrown out, the chief article of his patron's glory would probably have been sunk for ever, and late ages have received but a fragment of his fame: A fragment glorious indeed, for his genius how bright! But to commend him for composition, tho' immortal, is detraction *now;* if there our encomium ends: Let us look farther to that concluding scene, which spoke human nature not unrelated to the divine. To that let us pay the long, and large arrear of our greatly posthumous applause.

This you will think a long digression; and justly; if that may be called a digression, which was my chief inducement for writing at all: I had long wished to deliver up to the public this sacred deposit, which by Providence was lodged in my hands; and I entered on the present undertaking partly as an introduction to that, which is more worthy to see the light; of which I gave an intimation in the beginning of my letter: For this is the *monumental marble* there mentioned, to which I promised to conduct you; this is the *sepulchral lamp,* the long-hidden lustre of our accomplished countryman, who now rises, as from his tomb, to receive the regard so greatly due to the dignity of his death; a death to be distinguished by tears of joy; a death which angels beheld with delight.

And shall that, which would have shone conspicuous amid the resplendent lights of Christianity's glorious morn, by these dark days be dropped into oblivion? Dropped it is; and dropped by our sacred, august, and ample register of renown, which has entered in its marble-memoirs the dim splendor of far inferior worth: Tho' so lavish of praise, and so talkative of the dead, yet is it silent on a subject, which (if any) might have taught its unletter'd stones to speak: If powers were not wanting, a monument more durable than those of marble, should proudly rise in this ambitious page, to the new, and far nobler *Addison,* than that which you, and the public, have so long, and so much admired: Nor this nation only; for it is *Europe's Addison,* as well as ours; tho' *Europe* knows not half his title to her esteem; being as yet unconscious that the *dying Addison* far outshines her *Addison Immortal:* Would we resemble him? Let us not limit our ambition to the least illustrious part of his character; heads, indeed, are crowned on earth; but hearts only are crowned in heaven: A truth, which, in such an *age of authors,* should not be forgotten.

It is piously to be hoped, that this narrative may have some effect, since all listen, when a death-bed speaks; and regard the person departing as an actor of a part, which the great master of the drama has appointed us to perform to-morrow: This was a *Roscius* on the stage of life; his exit how great? Ye lovers of virtue! *plaudite:* And let us, my friend! ever "remember his end, as well as our own, that we may never do amiss."—I am,

Dear Sir,

Your most obliged,

humble Servant.

P. S.—How far *Addison* is an *Original,* you will see in my next; where I descend from this consecrated ground into his sublunary praise; And great is the descent, tho' into noble heights of *intellectual* power.

SAMUEL JOHNSON

(1709–1784)

JOHNSON was born at Lichfield in 1709, the son of a bookseller. He attended schools at Lichfield and Stonebridge, where his precocity was admired, and in 1728 was enabled through the help of a friend to enter Pembroke College, Oxford. He returned to Lichfield, however, the next year. On his father's death in 1731 he received £20 from the estate, and faced the prospect of making his own fortune. He did some amount of hack writing and of tutoring to support himself, and after his marriage, in 1735, kept a small private school at Edial. David Garrick was one of the eight or so pupils that he had, and after the failure of the school venture, he went with Garrick up to London in 1737. The story of the next few years is one of poverty and unsuccess, Johnson making his way chiefly by contributing to the *Gentleman's Magazine,* for which he wrote the fictitious parliamentary debates which appeared, 1741–44. His publication in 1738 of "London" had won him some reputation and a kindly notice from Pope, and in 1744 appeared the notable *Life of Savage.*

But it was the *Dictionary* (1755) which made him his reputation. There followed a few years of struggle and poverty, but even during this time he was recognized and applauded. He had partly made his living while writing the *Dictionary* by his periodical, the *Rambler,* which circulated 1750–52. The *Idler,* its sequel, began in 1758 and continued for two years. During this period *Rasselas* was written, the notable novel of seven days' composition, written to defray the funeral expenses of his mother.

In 1762 came the great change in Johnson's life, and from the unexpected quarter of a government pension. He found himself independent for the first time in his life, and the remaining years were years of comparative ease and happiness. The famous "Club" was founded in 1764, and here and in the wider society of which he was a part, Johnson's conversation found its scope, and became, through Boswell's medium, part of Eighteenth Century literature, as no other mere conversation has ever been able to do.

In 1765 appeared the edition of Shakespeare, and in 1775 the *Journey to the Hebrides.* The edition of the *English Poets,* for which he wrote the *Lives,* appeared in 1779 and 1781, three years before his death.

Matthew Arnold reminds us that "Johnson was a strong force of conservatism and concentration, in an epoch which by its natural tendencies seemed to be moving towards expansion and freedom." [*Johnson's Chief Lives.*] This will serve as well as any remark which might be quoted, as a text for that long recognized importance of Johnson as a bolsterer for neo-classicism. He maintained a citadel for decades against the Wartons, Walpoles, Percys, those younger men toward whom he had what Mr. Saintsbury has so aptly characterized as "unfriendly dislike or friendly contempt." It is impossible to think of the *Lyrical Ballads* or their famous Preface being published during the lifetime of Johnson. Whatever critical truth or liberality may be found in his works, the first point which must be considered about him is that he continued the life of that literary theory with which are associated the names of Pope, Waller, Boileau.

Secondly, he was the last of the dictators. Jonson, Dryden, Pope, and Johnson, runs the line of the kings. We have had no sovereigns since him—only leaders.

But these are mainly external factors. If we ask after the laws of his reign, we find that the tyranny was a better government than might at first be suspected. It is true that he condemns imitation of Spenser, that he ridiculously decrees against blank verse, that he sentences masterpieces like *Lycidas* and *Samson Agonistes,* stooping to unfair quibbles and specious interpretations of the old laws, to gain his ends: "This [Samson's death] is undoubtedly a just and regular catastrophe, and the poem, there-fore, has a beginning and an end which Aristotle himself could not have disapproved; but it must be allowed to want a middle, since nothing passes between the first act and the last, that either hastens or delays the death of Samson. The whole drama, if its superfluities were cut off, would scarcely fill a single act; yet this is the tragedy which ignorance has ad-mired, and bigotry applauded."

But Johnson is capable of reversing his position when it becomes so prejudiced as this. He atones for the narrowness of principle, though not for the particular judgment: "The accidental prescriptions of authority, when time has procured them veneration, are often confounded with the laws of nature, and those rules are supposed coëval with reason of which the first rise cannot be discovered." [*Rambler* 156.] It is not hard to find inconsistencies in him: "In books which best deserve the name of originals, there is little new beyond the disposition of materials already provided; the same ideas and combinations of ideas have been long in the possession of other hands." [*Rambler* 143.] "No man ever yet became great by imi-tation. Whatever hopes for the veneration of mankind must have invention in the design or the execution; either the effect must itself be new, or the means by which it is produced. . . . That which hopes to resist the blast of malignity, and stand firm against the attacks of time, must contain in itself some original principle of growth. The reputation which arises from the detail or transportation of borrowed sentiments, may spread for a while like ivy on the rind of antiquity, but will be torn away by ac-cident or contempt, and suffered to rot unheeded on the ground." [*Rambler* 335.]

Nor does one easily reconcile all of the statements of the tenth chapter of *Rasselas* with Johnson's accepted position. It has been remarked, though this is something of an exaggeration, that he "states his conception of the poetic function in terms that may be compared with those of Shelley him-self." He declares that the poet's "character requires that he estimate the happiness and misery of every condition, observe the power of all the passions in all their combinations, and trace the changes of the human mind, as they are modified by various institutions and accidental influences of climate or custom, from the sprightliness of infancy to the despondency of decrepitude. . . . . He must write as the interpreter of Nature and the legislator of mankind, and consider himself as presiding over the thoughts and manners of future generations, as a being superior to time and place." There is that in it which reminds us that "Poets are the hierophants of an unapprehended inspiration; . . . Poets are the unacknowledged legislators of the world." But it partakes, too, of the ancient Horatian principle that the poet should know the characteristics of the various ages of man. And we know perfectly where we are when Imlac declares that "this business of a poet is to examine, not the individual, but the species; to remark general properties and large appearances. He does not number the streaks of the tulip, or describe the different shades of the verdure of the forest."

It is not to be forgotten that in his strenuous principles there is narrowness, even bigotry. One has only to read him on Thomson or Collins to realize this. But one has only to open the Shakespeare Preface to find that rules are with him but roads by which to reach his ends; when he cannot arrive by them, he does not hesitate to travel across the fields; one has but to read the *Rambler* essay on Tragi-comedy to find that roads are ridiculous, even though they be ancient highways, when they lead nowhere.

Indeed, after once recognizing Johnson's essential conservatism, it is difficult not to center attention on the fascinating lapses of it which are evident in him. Of these, there is none more spectacular than his attack on the unities in the Shakespeare Preface, an attack so "unclassical" that he confesses surprise at his own boldness. But he was too great a critic to tell himself, or his generation, that what was pleasing and moving ought not to have been so—because of some rules.

It has generally been the custom to think of the Romantic Movement as a rebellion whose cohorts stormed the walls of a feudal castle, and fought valiantly for rights that had been for centuries withheld. It is a question worth asking, whether the Romantic troops did not arrive to find the walled city of Neo-classicism ungarrisoned, and, entering, to discover that the liberties which they were demanding had long been legalized, though little used. Indeed, the first battles to attract our attention are the squabbles of the leaders over the spoils.

From

PREFACE TO SHAKESPEARE

(1765)

THAT praises are without reason lavished on the dead, and that the honours due only to excellence are paid to antiquity, is a complaint likely to be always continued by those, who, being able to add nothing to truth, hope for eminence from the heresies of paradox; or those, who, being forced by disappointment upon consolatory expedients, are willing to hope from posterity what the present age refuses, and flatter themselves that the regard which is yet denied by envy, will be at last bestowed by time.

Antiquity, like every other quality that attracts the notice of mankind, has undoubtedly votaries that reverence it, not from reason, but from prejudice. Some seem to admire indiscriminately whatever has been long preserved, without considering that time has sometimes co-operated with chance; all perhaps are more willing to honour past than present excellence; and the mind contemplates genius through the shades of age, as the eye surveys the sun through artificial opacity. The great contention of criticism is to find the faults of the moderns, and the beauties of the ancients. While an author is yet living we estimate his powers by his worst performance, and when he is dead, we rate them by his best.

To works, however, of which the excellence is not absolute and definite, but gradual and comparative; to works not raised upon principles demonstrative and scientifick, but appealing wholly to observation and experience, no other test can be applied than length of duration and continuance of esteem. What mankind have long possessed they have often examined and compared; and if they persist to value the possession, it is because frequent comparisons have confirmed opinion in its favour. As among the works of nature no man can properly call a river deep, or a mountain high, without the knowledge of many mountains, and many rivers; so in the productions of genius, nothing can be stiled excellent till it has been compared with other works of the same kind. Demonstration immediately displays its power, and has nothing to hope or fear from the flux of years; but works tentative and experimental must be estimated by their proportion to the general and collective ability of man, as it is discovered in a long succession of endeavours. Of the first building that was raised, it might be with certainty determined that it was round or square; but whether it was spacious or lofty must have been referred to time. The Pythagorean scale of numbers was at once discovered to be perfect; but the poems of *Homer* we yet know not to transcend the common limits of human intelligence, but by remarking, that nation after nation, and century after century, has been able to do little more than transpose his incidents, new-name his characters, and paraphrase his sentiments.

The reverence due to writings that have long subsisted arises therefore not from any credulous confidence in the superior wisdom of past ages, or gloomy persuasion of the degeneracy of mankind, but is the consequence of acknowledged and indubitable positions, that what has been longest known has been most considered, and what is most considered is best understood.

The Poet, of whose works I have undertaken the revision, may now begin to assume the dignity of an ancient, and claim the privilege of established fame and prescriptive veneration. He has long outlived his century, the term commonly fixed as the test of literary merit. Whatever advantages he might once derive from personal allusions, local customs, or temporary opinions, have for many years been lost; and every topick of merriment, or motive of sorrow, which the modes of artificial life afforded him, now only obscure the scenes which they once illuminated. The effects of favour and competition are at an end; the tradition of his friendships and his enemies has perished; his works support no opinion with arguments, nor supply any faction with invectives; they can neither indulge vanity nor gratify malignity; but are read without any other reason than the desire of pleasure, and are therefore praised only as pleasure is obtained; yet, thus unassisted by interest or passion, they have past through variations of taste and changes of manners, and, as they devolved from one generation to another, have received new honours at every transmission.

But because human judgment, though it be gradually gaining upon certainty, never becomes infallible; and approbation, though long continued, may yet be only the approbation of prejudice or fashion; it is proper to inquire, by what peculiarities of excellence *Shakespeare* has gained and kept the favour of his countrymen.

Nothing can please many, and please long, but just representations of general nature. Particular manner, can be known to few, and therefore few only can judge how nearly they are copied. The irregular combinations of fanciful invention may delight a-while, by that novelty of which the common satiety of life sends us all in quest; but the pleasures of sudden wonder are soon exhausted, and the mind can only repose on the stability of truth.

Shakespeare is above all writers, at least above all modern writers, the poet of nature; the poet that holds up to his readers a faithful mirrour of manners and of life. His characters are not modified by the customs of particular places, unpractised by the rest of the world; by the peculiarities of studies or professions, which can operate but upon small numbers; or by the accidents of transient fashions or temporary opinions: they are the genuine progeny of common humanity, such as the world will always supply, and observation will always find. His persons act and speak by the influence of those general passions and principles by which all minds are agitated, and the whole system of life is continued in motion. In the writings of other poets a character is too often an individual; in those of *Shakespeare* it is commonly a species.

It is from this wide extension of design that so much instruction is derived. It is this which fills the plays of *Shakespeare* with practical axioms and domestic wisdom. It was said of *Euripides,* that every verse was a precept; and it may be said of *Shakespeare,* that from his works may be collected a system of civil and oeconomical prudence. Yet his real power is not shewn in the splendour of particular passages, but by the progress of his fable, and the tenour of his dialogue; and he that tries to recommend him by select quotations, will succeed like the pedant in *Hierocles,* who, when he offered his house to sale, carried a brick in his pocket as a specimen.

It will not easily be imagined how much *Shakespeare* excells in accommodating his sentiments to real life, but by comparing him with other authors. It was observed of the ancient schools of declamation, that the more diligently they were frequented, the more was the student disqualified for the world, because he found nothing there which he should ever meet in any other place. The same remark may be applied to every stage but that of *Shakespeare.* The theatre, when it is under any other direction, is peopled by such characters as were never seen, conversing in a language which was never heard, upon topicks which will never rise in the commerce of mankind. But the dialogue of this author is often so evidently determined by the incident which produces it, and is pursued with so much ease and simplicity, that it seems scarcely to claim the merit of fiction, but to have been gleaned by diligent selection out of common conversation, and common occurrences.

Upon every other stage the universal agent is love, by whose power all good and evil is distributed, and every action quickened or retarded. To bring a lover, a lady and a rival into the fable; to entangle them in contradictory obligations, perplex them with oppositions of interest, and harrass them with violence of desires inconsistent with each other; to make them meet in rapture and part in agony; to fill their mouths with hyperbolical joy and outrageous sorrow; to distress them as nothing human ever was distressed; to deliver them as nothing human ever was delivered; is the business of a modern dramatist. For this probability is violated, life is misrepresented, and language is depraved. But love is only one of many passions; and as it has no great influence upon the sum of life, it has little operation in the dramas of a poet, who caught his ideas from the living world, and exhibited only what he saw before him. He knew, that any other passion, as it was regular or exorbitant, was a cause of happiness or calamity.

Characters thus ample and general were not easily discriminated and preserved, yet perhaps no poet ever kept his personages more distinct from each other. I will not say with *Pope,* that every speech may be assigned to the proper speaker, because many speeches there are which have nothing characteristical; but perhaps, though some may be equally adapted to every person, it will be difficult to find any that can be properly transferred from the present possessor to another claimant. The choice is right, when there is reason for choice.

Other dramatists can only gain attention by hyperbolical or aggravated characters, by fabulous and unexampled excellence or depravity, as the writers of barbarous romances invigorated the reader by a giant and a dwarf; and he that should form his expectations of human affairs from the play, or from the tale, would be equally deceived. *Shakespeare* has no heroes; his scenes are occupied only by men, who act and speak as the reader thinks that he should himself have spoken or acted on the same occasion: Even where the agency is supernatural the dialogue is level with life. Other writers disguise the most natural passions and most frequent incidents; so that he who contemplates them in the book will not know them in the world: *Shakespeare* approximates the remote, and familiarizes the wonderful; the event which he represents will not happen, but if it were possible, its effects would probably be such as he has assigned; and it may be said, that he has not only shewn human nature as it acts in real exigencies, but as it would be found in trials, to which it cannot be exposed.

This therefore is the praise of *Shakespeare,* that his drama is the mirrour of life; that he who has mazed his imagination, in following the phantoms which other writers raise up before him, may here be cured of his delirious extasies, by reading human sentiments in human language, by scenes from which a hermit may estimate the transactions of the world, and a confessor predict the progress of the passions.

His adherence to general nature has exposed him to the censure of criticks, who form their judgments upon narrow principles. *Dennis* and *Rhymer* think his Romans not sufficiently *Roman;* and *Voltaire* censures his kings as not completely royal. *Dennis* is offended, that *Menenius,* a senator of *Rome,* should play the buffoon; and *Voltaire* perhaps thinks decency violated when the *Danish* Usurper is represented as a drunkard. But *Shakespeare* always makes nature predominate over accident; and if he preserves the essential character, is not very careful of distinctions superinduced and adventitious. His story requires Romans or kings, but he thinks only on men. He knew that *Rome,* like every other city, had men of all dispositions; and wanting a buffoon, he went into the senate-house for that which the senate-house would certainly have afforded him. He was inclined to shew an usurper and a murderer not only odious but despicable, he therefore added drunkenness to his other qualities, knowing that kings love wine like other men, and that wine exerts its natural power upon kings. These are the petty cavils of petty minds; a poet overlooks the casual distinction of country and condition, as a painter, satisfied with the figure, neglects the drapery.

The censure which he has incurred by mixing comick and tragick scenes, as it extends to all his works, deserves more consideration. Let the fact be first stated, and then examined.

Shakespeare's plays are not in the rigorous and critical sense either tragedies or comedies, but compositions of a distinct kind; exhibiting the real state of sublunary nature, which partakes of good and evil, joy and sorrow, mingled with endless variety of proportion and innumerable modes of combination; and expressing the course of the world, in which the loss of one is the gain of another; in which, at the same time, the reveller is hasting to his wine, and the mourner burying his friend; in which the malignity of one is sometimes defeated by the frolick of another; and many mischiefs and many benefits are done and hindered without design.

Out of this chaos of mingled purposes and casualties the ancient poets, according to the laws which custom had prescribed, selected some the crimes of men, and some their absurdities; some the momentous vicissitudes of life, and some the lighter occurrences; some the terrours of distress, and some the gayeties of prosperity. Thus rose the two modes of imitation, known by the names of *tragedy* and *comedy,* compositions intended to promote different ends by contrary means, and considered as so little allied, that I do not recollect among the *Greeks* or *Romans* a single writer who attempted both.

Shakespeare has united the powers of exciting laughter and sorrow not only in one mind, but in one composition. Almost all his plays are divided between serious and ludicrous characters, and, in the successive evolutions of the design, sometimes produce seriousness and sorrow, and sometimes levity and laughter.

That this is a practice contrary to the rules of criticism will be readily allowed; but there is always an appeal open from criticism to nature. The end of writing is to instruct; the end of poetry is to instruct by pleasing. That the mingled drama may convey all the instruction of tragedy or comedy cannot be denied, because it includes both in its alterations of exhibition and approaches nearer than either to the appearance of life, by shewing how great machinations and slender designs may promote or obviate one another, and the high and the low co-operate in the general system by unavoidable concatenation.

It is objected, that by this change of scenes the passions are interrupted in their progression, and that the principal event, being not advanced by a due gradation of preparatory incidents, wants at last the power to move, which constitutes the perfection of dramatick poetry. This reasoning is so specious, that it is received as true even by those who in daily experience feel it to be false. The interchanges of mingled scenes seldom fail to produce the intended vicissitudes of passion. Fiction cannot move so much, but that the attention may be easily transferred; and though it must be allowed that pleasing melancholy be sometimes interrupted by unwelcome levity, yet let it be considered likewise, that melancholy is often not pleasing, and that the disturbance of one man may be the relief of another; that different auditors have different habitudes; and that, upon the whole, all pleasure consists in variety.

The players, who in their edition divided our authour's works into comedies, histories, and tragedies, seem not to have distinguished the three kinds by any very exact or definite ideas.

And action which ended happily to the principal persons, however serious or distressful through its intermediate incidents, in their opinion, constituted a comedy. This idea of a comedy continued long amongst us; and plays were written, which, by changing the catastrophe, were tragedies to-day, and comedies to-morrow.

Tragedy was not in those times a poem of more general dignity or elevation than comedy; it required only a calamitous conclusion, with which the common criticism of that age was satisfied, whatever lighter pleasure it afforded in its progress.

History was a series of actions, with no other than chronological succession, independent on each other, and without any tendency to introduce or regulate the conclusion. It is not always very nicely distinguished from tragedy. There is not much nearer approach to unity of action in the tragedy of *Antony and Cleopatra,* than in the history of *Richard the Second.* But a history might be continued through many plays; as it had no plan, it had no limits.

Through all these denominations of the drama, *Shakespeare's* mode of composition is the same; an interchange of seriousness and merriment, by which the mind is softened at one time, and exhilarated at another. But whatever be his purpose, whether to gladden or depress, or to conduct the story, without vehemence or emotion, through tracts of easy and familiar dialogue, he never fails to attain his purpose; as he commands us, we laugh or mourn, or sit silent with quiet expectation, in tranquillity without indifference.

When *Shakespeare's* plan is understood, most of the criticisms of *Rhymer* and *Voltaire* vanish away. The play of *Hamlet* is opened, without impropriety, by two sentinels; *Iago* bellows at *Brabantio's* window, without injury to the scheme of the play, though in terms which a modern audience would not easily endure; the character of *Polonius* is seasonable and useful; and the Grave-diggers themselves may be heard with applause.

Shakespeare engaged in dramatick poetry with the world open before him; the rules of the ancients were yet known to few; but publick judgment was unformed; he had no example of such fame as might force him upon imitation, nor criticks of such authority as might restrain his extravagance: He therefore indulged his natural disposition, and his disposition, as *Rhymer* has remarked, led him to comedy. In tragedy he often writes, with great appearance of toil and study, what is written at last with little felicity; but in his comick scenes, he seems to produce without labour what no labour can improve. In tragedy he is always struggling after some occasion to be comick; but in comedy he seems to repose, or to luxuriate, as in a mode of thinking congenial to his nature. In his tragick scenes there is always something wanting, but his comedy often surpasses expectation or desire. His comedy pleases by the thoughts and the language, and his tragedy for the greater part by incident and action. His tragedy seems to be skill, his comedy to be instinct.

The force of his comick scenes has suffered little diminution from the changes made by a century and a half, in manners or in words. As his personages act upon principles arising from genuine passion, very little modified by particular forms, their pleasures and vexations are communicable to all times and to all places; they are natural, and therefore durable; the adventitious peculiarities of personal habits, are only superficial dies, bright and pleasing for a little while, yet soon fading to a dim tinct, without any remains of former lustre; but the discriminations of true passion are the colours of nature; they pervade the whole mass, and can only perish with the body that exhibits them. The accidental compositions of heterogeneous modes are dissolved by the chance which combined them; but the uniform simplicity of primitive qualities neither admits increase, nor suffers decay. The sand heap by one flood is scattered by another, but the rock always continues in its place. The stream of time, which is continually washing the dissoluble fabricks of other poets, passes without injury by the adamant of *Shakespeare.*

If there be, what I believe there is, in every nation, a stile which never becomes obsolete, a certain mode of phraseology so consonant and congenial to the analogy and principles of its respective language as to remain settled and unaltered; this style is probably to be sought in the common intercourse of life, among those who speak only to be understood, without ambition of elegance. The polite are always catching modish innovations, and the learned depart from established forms of speech, in hope of finding or making better; those who wish for distinction forsake the vulgar, when the vulgar is right; but there is a conversation above grossness and below refinement, where propriety resides, and where this poet seems to have gathered his comick dialogue. He is therefore more agreeable to the ears of the present age than any other authour equally remote, and among his other excellencies deserves to be studied as one of the original masters of our language.

These observations are to be considered not as unexceptionally constant, but as containing general and predominant truth. *Shakespeare's* familiar dialogue is affirmed to be smooth and clear, yet not wholly without ruggedness or difficulty; as a country may be eminently fruitful, though it has spots unfit for cultivation: His characters are praised as natural, though their sentiments are sometimes forced, and their actions improbable; as the earth upon the whole is spherical, though its surface is varied with protuberances and cavities.

Shakespeare with his excellencies has likewise faults, and faults sufficient to obscure and overwhelm any other merit. I shall shew them in the proportion in which they appear to me, without envious malignity or superstitious veneration. No question can be more innocently discussed than a dead poet's pretensions to renown; and little regard is due to that bigotry which sets candour higher than truth.

His first defect is that to which may be imputed most of the evil in books or in men. He sacrifices virtue to convenience, and is so much more careful to please than to instruct, that he seems to write without any moral purpose. From his writings indeed a system of social duty may be selected, for he that thinks reasonably must think morally; but his precepts and axioms drop casually from him; he makes no just distribution of good or evil, nor is always careful to shew in the virtuous a disapprobation of the wicked; he carries his persons indifferently through right and wrong, and at the close dismisses them without further care, and leaves their examples to operate by chance. This fault the barbarity of his age cannot extenuate; for it is always a writer's duty to make the world better, and justice is a virtue independent on time or place.

The plots are often so loosely formed, that a very slight consideration may improve them, and so carelessly pursued, that he seems not always fully to comprehend his own design. He omits opportunities of instructing or delighting which the train of his story seems to force upon him, and apparently rejects those exhibitions which would be more affecting, for the sake of those which are more easy.

It may be observed, that in many of his plays the latter part is evidently neglected. When he found himself near the end of his work, and, in view of his reward, he shortened the labour to snatch the profit. He therefore remits his efforts where he should most vigorously exert them, and his catastrophe is improbably produced or imperfectly represented.

He had no regard to distinction of time or place, but gives to one age or nation, without scruple, the customs, institutions, and opinions of another, at the expence not only of likelihood, but of possibility. These faults *Pope* has endeavoured, with more zeal than judgment, to transfer to his imagined interpolators. We need not wonder to find *Hector* quoting *Aristotle,* when we see the loves of *Theseus* and *Hippolyta* combined with the *Gothick* mythology of fairies. *Shakespeare,* indeed, was not the only violator of chronology, for in the same age *Sidney,* who wanted not the advantages of learning, has, in his *Arcadia,* confounded the pastoral with the feudal times, the days of innocence, quiet and security, with those of turbulence, violence, and adventure.

In his comick scenes he is seldom very successful, when he engages his characters in reciprocations of smartness and contests of sarcasm; their jests are commonly gross, and their pleasantry licentious; neither his gentlemen nor his ladies have much delicacy, nor are sufficiently distinguished from his clowns by any appearance of refined manners. Whether he represented the real conversation of his time is not easy to determine; the reign of *Elizabeth* is commonly supposed to have been a time of stateliness, formality and reserve; yet perhaps the relaxations of that severity were not very elegant. There must, however, have been always some modes of gayety preferable to others, and a writer ought to chuse the best.

In tragedy his performance seems constantly to be worse, as his labour is more. The effusions of passion which exigence forces out are for the most part striking and energetick; but whenever he solicits his invention, or strains his faculties, the offspring of his throes is tumour, meanness, tediousness, and obscurity.

In narration he affects a disproportionate pomp of diction, and a wearisome train of circumlocution, and tells the incident imperfectly in many words, which might have been more plainly delivered in few. Narration in dramatick poetry is naturally tedious, as it is unanimated and inactive, and obstructs the progress of the action; it should therefore always be rapid, and enlivened by frequent interruption. *Shakespeare* found it an encumberance, and instead of lightening it by brevity, endeavoured to recommend it by dignity and splendour.

His declamations or set speeches are commonly cold and weak, for his power was the power of nature; when he endeavoured, like other tragick writers, to catch opportunities of amplification, and instead of inquiring what the occasion demanded, to show how much his stores of knowledge could supply, he seldom escapes without the pity or resentment of his reader.

It is incident to him to be now and then entangled with an unwieldy sentiment, which he cannot well express, and will not reject; he struggles with it a while, and if it continues stubborn, comprises it in words such as occur, and leaves it to be disentangled and evolved by those who have more leisure to bestow upon it.

Not that always where the language is intricate the thought is subtle, or the image always great where the line is bulky; the equality of words to things is very often neglected, and trivial sentiments and vulgar ideas disappoint the attention, to which they are recommended by sonorous epithets and swelling figures.

But the admirers of this great poet have never less reason to indulge their hopes of supreme excellence, than when he seems fully resolved to sink them in dejection, and mollify them with tender emotions by the fall of greatness, the danger of innocence, or the crosses of love. He is not long soft and pathetick without some idle conceit, or contemptible equivocation. He no sooner begins to move, than he counteracts himself; and terrour and pity, as they are rising in the mind, are checked and blasted by sudden frigidity.

A quibble is to *Shakespeare,* what luminous vapours are to the traveller; he follows it at all adventures; it is sure to lead him out of his way, and sure to engulf him in the mire. It has some malignant power over his mind, and its fascinations are irresistible. Whatever be the dignity or profundity of his disquisition, whether he be enlarging knowledge or exalting affection, whether he be amusing attention with incidents, or enchaining it in suspense, let but a quibble spring up before him, and he leaves his work unfinished. A quibble is the golden apple for which he will always turn aside from his career, or stoop from his elevation. A quibble, poor and barren as it is, gave him such delight, that he was content to purchase it, by the sacrifice of reason, propriety and truth. A quibble was to him the fatal *Cleopatra* for which he lost the world, and was content to lose it.

It will be thought strange, that, in enumerating the defects of this writer, I have not yet mentioned his neglect of the unities; his violation of those laws which have been instituted and established by the joint authority of poets and criticks.

For his other deviations from the art of writing I resign him to critical justice, without making any other demand in his favour, than that which must be indulged to all human excellence: that his virtues be rated with his failings: But, from the censure which this irregularity may bring upon him, I shall, with due reverence to that learning which I must oppose, adventure to try how I can defend him.

His histories, being neither tragedies nor comedies are not subject to any of their laws; nothing more is necessary to all the praise which they expect, than that the changes of action be so prepared as to be understood, that the incidents be various and affecting, and the characters consistent, natural, and distinct. No other unity is intended, and therefore none is to be sought.

In his other works he has well enough preserved the unity of action. He has not, indeed, an intrigue regularly perplexed and regularly unravelled: he does not endeavour to hide his design only to discover it, for this is seldom the order of real events, and *Shakespeare* is the poet of nature: But his plan has commonly what *Aristotle* requires, a beginning, a middle, and an end; one event is concatenated with another, and the conclusion follows by easy consequence. There are perhaps some incidents that might be spared, as in other poets there is much talk that only fills up time upon the stage; but the general system makes gradual advances, and the end of the play is the end of expectation.

To the unities of time and place he has shewn no regard; and perhaps a nearer view of the principles on which they stand will diminish their value, and withdraw from them the veneration which, from the time of *Corneille,* they have very generally received, by discovering that they have given more trouble to the poet, than pleasure to the auditor.

The necessity of observing the unities of time and place arises from the supposed necessity of making the drama credible. The criticks hold it impossible, that an action of months or years can be possibly believed to pass in three hours; or that the spectator can suppose himself to sit in the theatre, while ambassadors go and return between distant kings, while armies are levied and towns besieged, while an exile wanders and returns, or till he whom they saw courting his mistress, shall lament the untimely fall of his son. The mind revolts from evident falsehood, and fiction loses its force when it departs from the resemblance of reality.

From the narrow limitation of time necessarily arises the contraction of place. The spectator, who knows that he saw the first act at *Alexandria,* cannot suppose that he sees the next at *Rome,* at a distance to which not the dragons of *Medea* could, in so short a time, have transported him; he knows with certainty that he has not changed his place, and he knows that place cannot change itself; that what was a house cannot become a plain; that what was *Thebes* can never be *Persepolis.*

Such is the triumphant language with which a critick exults over the misery of an irregular poet, and exults commonly without resistance or reply. It is time therefore to tell him by the authority of

Shakespeare, that he assumes, as an unquestionable principle, a position, which, while his breath is forming it into words, his understanding pronounces to be false. It is false, that any representation is mistaken for reality; that any dramatick fable in its materiality was ever credible, or, for a single moment, was ever credited.

The objection arising from the impossibility of passing the first hour at *Alexandria,* and the next at *Rome,* supposes, that when the play opens, the spectator really imagines himself at *Alexandria,* and believes that his walk to the theatre has been a voyage to *Egypt,* and that he lives in the days of *Antony* and *Cleopatra.* Surely he that imagines this may imagine more. He that can take the stage at one time for the palace of the *Ptolemies,* may take it in half an hour for the promontory of *Actium.* Delusion, if delusion be admitted, has no certain limitation; if the spectator can be once persuaded, that his old acquaintance are *Alexander* and *Cæsar,* that a room illuminated with candles is the plain of *Pharsalia,* or the bank of *Granicus,* he is in a state of elevation above the reach of reason, or of truth, and from the heights of empyrean poetry, may despise the circumscriptions of terrestrial nature. There is no reason why a mind thus wandering in extacy should count the clock, or why an hour should not be a century in that calenture of the brains that can make the stage a field.

The truth is, that the spectators are always in their senses, and know, from the first act to the last, that the stage is only a stage, and that the players are only players. They came to hear a certain number of lines recited with just gesture and elegant modulation. The lines relate to some action, and an action must be in some place; but the different actions that complete a story may be in places very remote from each other; and where is the absurdity of allowing that space to represent first *Athens,* and then *Sicily,* which was always known to be neither *Sicily* nor *Athens,* but a modern theatre?

By supposition, as place is introduced, times may be extended; the time required by the fable elapses for the most part between the acts; for, of so much of the action as is represented, the real and poetical duration is the same. If, in the first act, preparations for war against *Mithridates* are represented to be made in *Rome,* the event of the war may, without absurdity, be represented, in the catastrophe, as happening in *Pontus;* we know that there is neither war, nor preparation for war; we know that we are neither in *Rome* nor *Pontus;* that neither *Mithridates* nor *Lucullus* are before us. The drama exhibits successive imitations of successive actions; and why may not the second imitation represent an action that happened years after the first, if it be so connected with it, that nothing but time can be supposed to intervene? Time is, of all modes of existence, most obsequious to the imagination; a lapse of years is as easily conceived as a passage of hours. In contemplation we easily contract the time of real actions, and therefore willingly permit it to be contracted when we only see their imitation.

It will be asked, how the drama moves, if it is not credited. It is credited with all the credit due to a drama. It is credited, whenever it moves, as a just picture of a real original; as representing to the auditor what he would himself feel, if he were to do or suffer what is there feigned to be suffered or to be done. The reflection that strikes the heart is not, that the evils before us are real evils, but that they are evils to which we ourselves may be exposed. If there be any fallacy, it is not that we fancy the players, but that we fancy ourselves unhappy for a moment; but we rather lament the possibility than suppose the presence of misery, as a mother weeps over her babe, when she remembers that death may take it from her. The delight of tragedy proceeds from our consciousness of fiction; if we thought murders and treasons real, they would please no more.

Imitations produce pain or pleasure, not because they are mistaken for realities, but because they bring realities to mind. When the imagination is recreated by a painted landscape, the trees are not supposed capable to give us shade, or the fountains coolness; but we consider, how we should be pleased with such fountains playing beside us, and such woods waving over us. We are agitated in reading the history of *Henry* the Fifth, yet no man takes his book for the field of *Agencourt.* A dramatick exhibition is a book recited with concomitants that encrease or diminish its effect. Familiar comedy is often more powerful in the theatre, than on the page; imperial tragedy is always less. The humour of *Petruchio* may be heightened by grimace; but what voice or what gesture can hope to add dignity or force to the soliloquy of *Cato.*

A play read, affects the mind like a play acted. It is therefore evident, that the action is not supposed to be real; and it follows, that between the acts a longer or shorter time may be allowed to pass, and that no more account of space or duration is to be taken by the auditor of a drama, than by the reader of a narrative, before whom may pass in an hour the life of a hero, or the revolutions of an empire.

Whether *Shakespeare* knew the unities, and rejected them by design, or deviated from them by happy ignorance, it is, I think, impossible to decide, and useless to enquire. We may reasonably suppose, that, when he rose to notice, he did not want the counsels and admonitions of scholars and criticks, and that he at last deliberately persisted in a practice, which he might have begun by chance. As nothing is essential to the fable, but unity of action, and as the unities of time and place arise evidently from false assumptions, and, by circumscribing the extent of the drama, lessen its variety, I cannot think it much to be lamented, that they were not known by him, or not observed: Nor, if such another poet could arise, should I very vehemently reproach him, that his first act passed at *Venice,* and his next in *Cyprus.* Such violations of rules merely positive, become the comprehensive genius of *Shakespeare,* and such censures are suitable to the minute and slender criticism of *Voltaire:*

> *Non usque adeo permiscuit imis*
> *Longus summa dies, ut non, si voce Metelli*
> *Serventur leges, malint a Cæsare tolli.*[1]

Yet when I speak thus slightly of dramatick rules, I cannot but recollect how much wit and learning may be produced against me; before such authorities I am afraid to stand, not that I think the present question one of those that are to be decided by mere authority, but because it is to be suspected, that these precepts have not been so easily received but for better reasons than I have yet been able to find. The result of my enquiries, in which it would be ludicrous to boast of impartiality, is, that the unities of time and place are not essential to a just drama, that though they may sometimes conduce to pleasure, they are always to be sacrificed to the nobler beauties of variety and instruction; and that a play, written with nice observation of critical rules, is to be contemplated as an elaborate curiosity, as the product of superfluous and ostentatious art, by which is shewn, rather what is possible, than what is necessary.

He that, without diminution of any other excellence, shall preserve all the unities unbroken, deserves the like applause with the architect, who shall display all the orders of architecture in a citadel, without any deduction from its strength; but the principal beauty of a citadel is to exclude the enemy; and the greatest graces of a play, are to copy nature and instruct life.

[1] "A long period of time does not so confuse the highest with the lowest but that laws made by Metellus may desire to be abolished by Caesar."

Perhaps what I have here not dogmatically but deliberatively written, may recal the principles of the drama to a new examination. I am almost frighted at my own temerity; and when I estimate the fame and the strength of those that maintain the contrary opinion, am ready to sink down in reverential silence; as *Æneas* withdrew from the defence of *Troy,* when he saw *Neptune* shaking the wall, and *Juno* heading the besiegers.

Those whom my arguments cannot persuade to give their approbation to the judgment of *Shakespeare,* will easily, if they consider the condition of his life, make some allowance for his ignorance.

Every man's performances, to be rightly estimated, must be compared with the state of the age in which he lived, and with his own particular opportunities; and though to the reader a book be not worse or better for the circumstances of the authour, yet as there is always a silent reference of human works to human abilities, and as the enquiry, how far man may extend his designs, or how high he may rate his native force, is of far greater dignity than in what rank we shall place any particular performance, curiosity is always busy to discover the instruments, as well as to survey the workmanship, to know how much is to be ascribed to original powers, and how much to casual and adventitious help. The palaces of *Peru* or *Mexico* were certainly mean and incommodious habitations, if compared to the houses of *European* monarchs; yet who could forbear to view them with astonishment, who remembered that they were built without the use of iron?

The *English* nation, in the time of *Shakespeare,* was yet struggling to emerge from barbarity. The philology of *Italy* had been transplanted hither in the reign of *Henry* the Eighth; and the learned languages had been successfully cultivated by *Lilly, Linacer,* and *More;* by *Pole, Cheke,* and *Gardiner;* and afterwards by *Smith, Clerk, Haddon,* and *Ascham.* Greek was now taught to boys in the principal schools; and those who united elegance with learning, read, with great diligence, the *Italian* and *Spanish* poets. But literature was yet confined to professed scholars, or to men and women of high rank. The publick was gross and dark; and to be able to read and write, was an accomplishment still valued for its rarity.

Nations, like individuals, have their infancy. A people newly awakened to literary curiosity, being yet unacquainted with the true state of things, knows not how to judge of that which is proposed as its resemblance. Whatever is remote from common appearances is always

welcome to vulgar, as to childish credulity; and of a country unen
lightened by learning, the whole people is the vulgar. . . .

From

LIVES OF THE ENGLISH POETS

(1779–81)

From *Abraham Cowley*

.   .   .

COWLEY, like other poets who have written with narrow views, and,
instead of tracing intellectual pleasures to the natural sources in the
mind of man, paid their court to temporary prejudices, has been at
one time too much praised, and too much neglected at another.

Wit, like all other things subject by their nature to the choice of
man, has its changes and fashions, and at different times takes different forms. About the beginning of the seventeenth century appeared
a race of writers that may be termed the metaphysical poets, of whom,
in a criticism on the works of Cowley, it is not improper to give some
account.

The metaphysical poets were men of learning, and to show their
learning was their whole endeavour; but unluckily resolving to show
it in rhyme, instead of writing poetry, they only wrote verses, and
very often such verses as stood the trial of the finger better than of
the ear; for the modulation was so imperfect, that they were only
found to be verses by counting the syllables.

If the father of criticism has rightly denominated poetry τέχνη
μιμητικὴ, *an imitative art,* these writers will, without great wrong, lose
their right to the name of poets, for they cannot be said to have imitated anything; they neither copied nature nor life; neither painted
the forms of matter, nor represented the operations of intellect.

Those, however who deny them to be poets, allow them to be
wits. Dryden confesses of himself and his contemporaries, that they
fall below Donne in wit, but maintains that they surpass him in
poetry.

If Wit be well described by Pope, as being "that which has been
often thought, but was never before so well expressed," they certainly never attained, nor ever sought it; for they endeavoured to
be singular in their thoughts, and were careless of their diction. But

Pope's account of wit is undoubtedly erroneous: he depresses it below its natural dignity, and reduces it from strength of thought to happiness of language.

If by a more noble and more adequate conception that be considered as Wit, which is at once natural and new, that which, though not obvious, is, upon its first production, acknowledged to be just; if it be that, which he that never found it, wonders how he missed; to wit of this kind the metaphysical poets have seldom risen. Their thoughts are often new, but seldom natural; they are not obvious, but neither are they just; and the reader, far from wondering that he missed them, wonders more frequently by what perverseness of industry they were ever found.

But wit, abstracted from its effects upon the hearer, may be more rigorously and philosophically considered as a kind of *discordia concors;* a combination of dissimilar images, or discovery of occult resemblances in things apparently unlike. Of wit, thus defined, they have more than enough. The most heterogeneous ideas are yoked by violence together; nature and art are ransacked for illustrations, comparisons, and allusions; their learning instructs, and their subtilty surprises; but the reader commonly thinks his improvement dearly bought, and, though he sometimes admires, is seldom pleased.

From this account of their compositions it will be readily inferred, that they were not successful in representing or moving the affections. As they were wholly employed on something unexpected and surprising, they had no regard to that uniformity of sentiment which enables us to conceive and to excite the pains and the pleasure of other minds: they never inquired what, on any occasion, they should have said or done; but wrote rather as beholders than partakers of human nature; as beings looking upon good and evil, impassive and at leisure; as Epicurean deities, making remarks on the actions of men, and the vicissitudes of life, without interest and without emotion. Their courtship was void of fondness, and their lamentation of sorrow. Their wish was only to say what they hoped had been never said before.

Nor was the sublime more within their reach than the pathetick; for they never attempted that comprehension and expanse of thought which at once fills the whole mind, and of which the first effect is sudden astonishment, and the second rational admiration. Sublimity is produced by aggregation, and littleness by dispersion. Great thoughts are always general, and consist in positions not limited by exceptions, and in descriptions not descending to minuteness. It is with great propriety that Subtlety, which in its original import means exility of particles, is taken in its metaphorical meaning for nicety of distinction. Those writers who lay on the watch for novelty could have little hope of greatness; for great things cannot have escaped former observation. Their attempts were always analytick; they broke every image into fragments; and could no more represent, by their slender conceits and laboured particularities, the prospects of nature, or the scenes of life, than he, who dissects a sunbeam with a prism, can exhibit the wide effulgence of a summer noon.

What they wanted however of the sublime, they endeavoured to supply by hyperbole; their amplification had no limits; they left not only reason but fancy behind them; and produced combinations of confused magnificence, that not only could not be credited, but could not be imagined.

Yet great labour, directed by great abilities, is never wholly lost: if they frequently threw away their wit upon false conceits, they likewise sometimes struck out unexpected truth; if their conceits were far-fetched, they were often worth the carriage. To write on their plan, it was at least necessary to read and think. No man could be born a metaphysical poet, nor assume the dignity of a writer, by descriptions copied from descriptions, by imitations borrowed from imitations, by traditional imagery, and hereditary similes, by readiness of rhyme, and volubility of syllables.

In perusing the works of this race of authors, the mind is exercised either by recollection or inquiry; either something already learned is to be retrieved, or something new is to be examined. If their greatness seldom elevates, their acuteness often surprises; if the imagination is not always gratified, at least the powers of reflection and comparison are employed; and in the mass of materials which ingenious absurdity has thrown together, genuine wit and useful knowledge may be sometimes found buried, perhaps in grossness of expression, but useful to those who know their value; and such as, when they are expanded to perspicuity, and polished to elegance, may give lustre to works which have more propriety though less copiousness of sentiment. . . .

From *John Dryden*

.   .   .

DRYDEN may be properly considered as the father of English criticism, as the writer who first taught us to determine upon principles the merit of composition. Of our former poets, the greatest dramatist wrote without rules, conducted through life and nature by a genius that rarely misled, and rarely deserted him. Of the rest, those who knew the laws of propriety had neglected to teach them.

Two "Arts of English Poetry" were written in the days of Elizabeth by Webb and Puttenham, from which something might be learned, and a few hints had been given by Jonson and Cowley; but Dryden's "Essay on Dramatick Poetry" was the first regular and valuable treatise on the art of writing.

He who, having formed his opinions in the present age of English literature, turns back to peruse this dialogue, will not perhaps find much increase of knowledge, or much novelty of instruction; but he is to remember that critical principles were then in the hands of a few, who had gathered them partly from the ancients, and partly from the Italians and French. The structure of dramatick poems was then not generally understood. Audiences applauded by instinct; and poets perhaps often pleased by chance.

A writer who obtains his full purpose loses himself in his own lustre. Of an opinion which is no longer doubted, the evidence ceases to be examined. Of an art universally practised, the first teacher is forgotten. Learning once made popular is no longer learning; it has the appearance of something which we have bestowed upon ourselves, as the dew appears to rise from the field which it refreshes.

To judge rightly of an author, we must transport ourselves to his time, and examine what were the wants of his contemporaries, and what were his means of supplying them. That which is easy at one time was difficult at another. Dryden at least imported his science, and gave his country what it wanted before; or rather, he imported only the materials, and manufactured them by his own skill.

The Dialogue on the Drama was one of his first essays of criticism, written when he was yet a timorous candidate for reputation, and therefore laboured with that diligence which he might allow himself somewhat to remit, when his name gave sanction to his positions, and his awe of the public was abated, partly by custom, and partly by success. It will not be easy to find, in all the opulence of our language, a treatise so artfully variegated with successive representations of opposite probabilities, so enlivened with imagery, so brightened with illustrations. His portraits of the English dramatists are wrought with great spirit and diligence. The account of Shakspeare may stand as a perpetual model of encomiastic criticism; exact without minuteness, and lofty without exaggeration. The praise lavished by Longinus, on the attestation of the heroes of Marathon, by Demosthenes, fades away before it. In a few lines is exhibited a character, so extensive in its comprehension, and so curious in its limitations, that nothing can be added, diminished, or reformed; nor can the editors and admirers of Shakspeare, in all their emulation of reverence, boast of much more than of having diffused and paraphrased this epitome of excellence, of having changed Dryden's gold for baser metal, of lower value though of greater bulk.

In this, and in all his other essays on the same subject, the criticism of Dryden is the criticism of a poet; not a dull collection of theorems, nor a rude detection of faults, which perhaps the censor was not able to have committed; but a gay and vigorous dissertation, where delight is mingled with instruction, and where the author proves his right of judgement by his power of performance. . . .

He who writes much, will not easily escape a manner, such a recurrence of particular modes as may be easily noted. Dryden is always *another and the same,* he does not exhibit a second time the same elegances in the same form, nor appears to have any art other than that of expressing with clearness what he thinks with vigour. His style could not easily be imitated, either seriously or ludicrously; for, being always equable and always varied, it has no prominent or discriminative characters. The beauty who is totally free from disproportion of parts and features, cannot be ridiculed by an overcharged resemblance.

From his prose, however, Dryden derives only his accidental and secondary praise; the veneration with which his name is pronounced by every cultivator of English literature, is paid to him as he refined the language, improved the sentiments, and tuned the numbers of English poetry.

After about half a century of forced thoughts, and rugged metre, some advances towards nature and harmony had been already made by Waller and Denham; they had shewn that long discourses in rhyme grew more pleasing when they were broken into couplets, and that verse consisted not only in the number but the arrangement of syllables.

But though they did much, who can deny that they left much to do? Their works were not many, nor were their minds of very ample comprehension. More examples of more modes of composition were necessary for the establishment of regularity, and the introduction of propriety in word and thought.

Every language of a learned nation necessarily divides itself into diction scholastick and popular, grave and familiar, elegant and gross; and from a nice distinction of these different parts, arises a great part of the beauty of style. But if we except a few minds, the favourites of nature, to whom their own original rectitude was in the place of rules, this delicacy of selection was little known to our authors; our speech lay before them in a heap of confusion, and every man took for every purpose what chance might offer him.

There was therefore before the time of Dryden no poetical diction, no system of words at once refined from the grossness of domestick use, and free from the harshness of terms appropriated to particular arts. Words too familiar, or too remote, defeat the purpose of a poet. From those sounds which we hear on small or on coarse occasions, we do not easily receive strong impressions, or delightful images: and words to which we are nearly strangers, whenever they occur, draw that attention on themselves which they should transmit to things.

Those happy combinations of words which distinguish poetry from prose, had been rarely attempted; we had few elegances or flowers of speech, the roses had not yet been plucked from the bramble, or different colours had not been joined to enliven one another.

It may be doubted whether Waller and Denham could have overborne the prejudices which had long prevailed, and which even then were sheltered by the protection of Cowley. The new versification, as it was called, may be considered as owing its establishment to Dryden; from whose time it is apparent that English poetry has had no tendency to relapse to its former savageness.

The affluence and comprehension of our language is very illustriously displayed in our poetical translations of Ancient Writers; a work which the French seem to relinquish in despair, and which we were long unable to perform with dexterity. Ben Jonson thought it necessary to copy Horace almost word by word; Feltham, his contemporary and adversary, considers it as indispensably requisite in a translation to give line for line. It is said that Sandys, whom Dryden calls the best versifier of the last age, has struggled hard to comprise every book of his English Metamorphoses in the same number of verses with the original. Holyday had nothing in view but to shew that he understood his author, with so little regard to the grandeur of his diction, or the volubility of his numbers, that his metres can hardly be called verses; they cannot be read without reluctance, nor will the labour always be rewarded by understanding them. Cowley saw that such *copyers* were a *servile race;* he asserted his liberty, and spread his wings so boldly that he left his authors. It was reserved for Dryden to fix the limits of poetical liberty, and give us just rules and examples of translation.

When languages are formed upon different principles, it is impossible that the same modes of expression should always be elegant in both. While they run on together, the closest translation may be considered as the best; but when they divaricate, each must take its natural course. Where correspondence cannot be obtained, it is necessary to be content with something equivalent. *Translation therefore,* says Dryden, *is not so loose as paraphrase, nor so close as metaphrase.*

All polished languages have different styles; the concise, the diffuse, the lofty, and the humble. In the proper choice of style consists the resemblance which Dryden principally exacts from the translator. He is to exhibit his author's thoughts in such a dress of diction as the author would have given them, had his language been English: rugged magnificence is not to be softened: hyperbolical ostentation is not to be repressed, nor sententious affectation to have its point blunted. A translator is to be like his author; it is not his business to excel him.

The reasonableness of these rules seems sufficient for their vindication; and the effects produced by observing them were so happy, that I know not whether they were ever opposed but by Sir Edward Sherburne, a man whose learning was greater than his powers of poetry; and who, being better qualified to give the meaning than the spirit of Seneca, has introduced his version of three tragedies by a defence of close translation. The authority of Horace, which the new translators cited in defence of their practice, he has, by a judicious explanation, taken fairly from them; but reason wants not Horace to support it. . . .

The occasional poet is circumscribed by the narrowness of his subject. Whatever can happen to man has happened so often, that little remains for fancy or invention. We have been all born; we have most of us been married; and so many have died before us, that our deaths can supply but few materials for a poet. In the fate of princes the publick has an interest; and what happens to them of good or evil, the poets have always considered as business for the Muse. But after so many inauguratory gratulations, nuptial hymns, and funeral dirges, he must be highly favoured by nature, or by fortune, who says anything not said before. Even war and conquest, however splendid, suggest no new images; the triumphal chariot of a victorious monarch can be decked only with those ornaments that have graced his predecessors.

Not only matter but time is wanting. The poem must not be delayed till the occasion is forgotten. The lucky moments of animated imagination cannot be attended; elegances and illustrations cannot be multiplied by gradual accumulation: the composition must be dispatched while conversation is yet busy, and admiration fresh; and haste is to be made, lest some other event should lay hold upon mankind.

Occasional composition may however secure to a writer the praise both of learning and facility; for they cannot be the effect of long study, and must be furnished immediately from the treasures of the mind. . . .

From *Alexander Pope*

.   .   .

OF genius, that power which constitutes a poet; that quality without which judgement is cold, and knowledge is inert; that energy which collects, combines, amplifies, and animates; the superiority must, with some hesitation, be allowed to Dryden. It is not to be inferred that of this poetical vigour Pope had only a little, because Dryden had more; for every other writer since Milton must give place to Pope; and even of Dryden it must be said, that if he has brighter paragraphs, he has not better poems. Dryden's performances were always hasty, either excited by some external occasion, or extorted by domestick necessity; he composed without consideration, and published without correction. What his mind could supply at call, or gather in one excursion, was all that he sought, and all that he gave. The dilatory caution of Pope enabled him to condense his sentiments, to multiply his images, and to accumulate all that study might produce, or chance might supply. If the flights of Dryden therefore are higher, Pope continues longer on the wing. If of Dryden's fire the blaze is brighter, of Pope's the heat is more regular and constant. Dryden often surpasses expectation, and Pope never falls below it. Dryden is read with frequent astonishment, and Pope with perpetual delight.

.   .   .

One of his greatest, though of his earliest works, is the "Essay on Criticism," which, if he had written nothing else, would have placed him among the first criticks and the first poets, as it exhibits every mode of excellence that can embellish or dignify didactick composition, selection of matter, novelty of arrangement, justness of precept, splendour of illustration, and propriety of digression. I know not whether it be pleasing to consider that he produced this piece at twenty, and never afterwards excelled it: he that delights himself with observing that such powers may be soon attained, cannot but grieve to think that life was ever after at a stand.

To mention the particular beauties of the Essay would be unprofitably tedious; but I cannot forbear to observe, that the comparison of a student's progress in the sciences with the journey of a traveller in the Alps, is perhaps the best that English poetry can shew. A simile, to be perfect, must both illustrate and ennoble the subject; must shew it to the understanding in a clearer view, and display it to the fancy with greater dignity; but either of these qualities may be sufficient to recommend it. In didactick poetry, of which the great purpose is instruction, a simile may be praised which illustrates, though it does not ennoble; in heroicks, that may be admitted which ennobles, though it does not illustrate. That it may be complete, it is required to exhibit, independently of its references, a pleasing image; for a simile is said to be a short episode. To this antiquity was so attentive, that circumstances were sometimes added, which, having no parallels, served only to fill the imagination, and produced what Perrault ludicrously called *comparisons with a long tail*. In their similes the greatest writers have sometimes failed; the ship-race, compared with the chariot-race, is neither illustrated nor aggrandised; land and water make all the difference: when Apollo, running after Daphne, is likened to a greyhound chasing a hare, there is nothing gained; the ideas of pursuit and flight are too plain to be made plainer, and a god and the daughter of a god are not represented much to their advantage, by a hare and dog. The simile of the Alps has no useless parts, yet affords a striking picture by itself; it makes the foregoing position better understood, and enables it to take faster hold on the attention; it assists the apprehension, and elevates the fancy.

Let me likewise dwell a little on the celebrated paragraph, in which it is directed that *the sound should seem an echo to the sense;* a precept which Pope is allowed to have observed beyond any other English poet.

This notion of representative metre, and the desire of covering frequent adaptations of the sound to the sense, have produced, in my opinion, many wild conceits and imaginary beauties. All that can furnish this representation are the sounds of the words considered singly, and the time in which they are pronounced. Every language has some words framed to exhibit the noises which they express, as *thump, rattle, growl, hiss.* These however are but few; and the poet cannot make them more, nor can they be of any use but when sound is to be mentioned. The time of pronunciation was in the dactylick measures of the learned languages capable of considerable variety; but that variety could be accommodated only to motion or duration, and different degrees of motion were perhaps expressed by verses rapid or slow, without much attention of the writer, when the image had full possession of his fancy; but our language having little flexibility, our verses can differ very little in their cadence. The fancied resemblances, I fear, arise sometimes merely from the ambiguity of words; there is supposed to be some relation between a *soft* line and *soft* couch, or between *hard* syllables and *hard* fortune. . . .

GOTTHOLD EPHRAIM LESSING

(1729–1781)

BORN at Kamenz, Saxony, in 1729, Gotthold Ephraim Lessing was early given strict training in theology and morals by his clergyman father. After training in the Latin School of Kamenz, Lessing was sent to the famous School of St. Afra, at Meissen; in 1746 to the University of Leipzig, to study theology. But he was less interested in theology than in philosophy and the drama. After five years of literary hackwork in Berlin, he studied at Wittenberg, and received the degree of M.A. (1752). In 1753–54 Lessing published four volumes of miscellaneous works: poetry, fables, plays, and reviews. The production (1755) of *Miss Sara Sampson,* one of the first great bourgeois tragedies, established Lessing, and led to offers of academic positions, but he preferred a place with the Leipzig theatre. In 1758 he returned to Berlin, to write the *Literaturbriefe,* and the prose tragedy *Philotus.* From 1760 to 1765, he acted as Secretary to General Tauentzien, and in addition wrote incessantly. *Laocoön* was published in 1766; *Minna Von Barnhelm,* his most successful play from the dramatic standpoint, in 1767. In that year Lessing settled in Hamburg, and his experiences with that theatre led to the writing and publication of the periodical, *Hamburgische Dramaturgie,* (first number, May 1, 1767; collected and published in book form, 1769). In 1770 he became librarian at Wolfenbüttel to the Prince of Brunswick, a position which he held the remainder of his life. The successful tragedy, *Emilia Galotta,* was published in 1772, and in 1779 appeared the last of his great works, *Nathan der Weise.* Lessing died in 1781.

The criticism of Lessing was firmly fixed upon Aristotelian precepts. His work, in the *Hamburgische Dramaturgie,* was of incalculable benefit to the German theatre, but it added little to theories of criticism. He attacked the French classical dramatists, and even proved, after a fashion, that Shakespeare was a follower of Aristotle. For the plays of Shakespeare are unified, as far as unity of action is concerned, and "Unity of action was the first dramatic law of the ancients; unity of time and place were mere consequences of the former which they would scarcely have observed more strictly than exigency required had not the combination with the chorus arisen." And "the only unpardonable fault of a tragic poet is this, that he leaves us cold; if he interests us he may do as he likes with the little mechanical rules." (*Hamburg Dramaturgy,* trans. Beasley and Zimmern.)

But in the *Laocoön* his criticism reached more universal ground. Confusion between the arts has been the subject of much critical writing, from the earliest days of criticism to the present. Plutarch (*Comm. Bellone an Pace Clariores fuerint Athenienses*, vol. 7, p. 366, ed. Reiske) writes: "Simonides addressed painting as silent poetry, and poetry as speaking painting." The fable of *Laocoön* is equally old, and Lessing found, made to hand, the poems by Homer and Virgil, and the Greek statue: a perfect springboard for his comparison of the two arts, and his refutation of the dictum of Simonides. Most critics, before Lessing, agreed with that early writer. Ben Jonson (*Discoveries*) thought: "*Poetry, and Picture, are Arts of a like nature; and both are busie about imitation.* It was excellently said of *Plutarch, Poetry* was a speaking Picture, and *Picture* a mute Poesie. For they both invent, faine, and devise many things, and accommodate all they invent to the use, and service of nature. Yet of the two, the Pen is more noble, then the Pencill. For the one can speake to the Understanding; the other, but to the Sense. They both behold pleasure, and profit, as their common Object; but should abstaine from all base pleasures, lest they should erre from their end: and while they seeke to better mens minds, destroy their manners."

Dryden (*Parallel of Poetry and Painting*, 1695) had written: "The imitation of nature is, therefore, justly constituted as the general, indeed the only, rule of pleasing both in *Poetry* and *Painting*." One differentiation he made: "the principal end of painting is to please, of Poetry to instruct." And Joseph Spence (*Polymetis*, 1747) took the extreme position that "there can be no room to doubt that some of the best comments we could have on the ancient poets, might be drawn from the works of the artists who were their contemporaries."

Other critics had observed the fallacy of this reasoning before Lessing. Sir Joshua Reynolds, who makes no reference to Lessing, later made the same point (*Discourse* IV): "A painter must compensate the natural deficiencies of art. He has but one sentence to utter, but one moment to exhibit." But criticism of the theory, and of Lessing's classicism, was not lacking, and his distinctions were disregarded by the Romantic School, and the Pre-Raphaelite movement might seem a literal attempt (which met with poor success) to contradict every precept in the *Laocoön*. In Germany, A. W. Schlegel objected to "anatomical ideas which have been stamped as rules," and much preferred the "original chaos of human nature."

For all these criticisms, the distinctions made with such definitiveness by Lessing remain valuable and, in most cases, valid.

From

LAOCOÖN *

(1766)

CHAPTER XVI

But I will try to consider the matter upon first principles. I reason in this way. If it be true that Painting, in its imitations, makes use of entirely different means and signs from those which Poetry employs; the former employing figures and colours in space, the latter articulate sounds in time,—if, incontestably, signs must have a proper relation to the thing signified, then co-existent, signs can only express objects which are co-existent, or the parts of which co-exist, but signs which are successive can only express objects which are in succession, or the parts of which succeed one another in time. Objects which co-exist, or the parts of which co-exist, are termed bodies. It follows that bodies, with their visible properties, are the proper objects of Painting. Objects which succeed, or the parts of which succeed to each other, are called generally actions. It follows that actions are the proper object of Poetry.

But all bodies do not exist only in space, but also in time. They have continued duration, and in every moment of their duration may assume a different appearance and stand in a different relation. Each of these momentary appearances and relations is the effect of a preceding, and the cause of a subsequent action, and so presents to us, as it were, a centre of action. It follows that Painting can imitate actions, but only by way of indication, and through the means of bodies.

On the other hand, actions cannot subsist by themselves, but must be dependent on certain beings. In so far, now, as these beings are bodies, or may be regarded as such, poetry also paints bodies, but only by way of indication, and through the means of actions.

Painting, with regard to compositions in which the objects are co-existent, can only avail itself of one moment of action, and must therefore choose that which is the most pregnant, and by which what has gone before and what is to follow will be most intelligible.

And even thus Poetry, in her progressive imitations, can only make use of one single property of bodies, and must therefore choose that

* Translated by Sir Robert Phillimore.

one which conveys to us the most sensible idea of the form of the body, from that point of view for which it employs it.

From this is derived the rule of the unity of picturesque epithets, and of frugality in the description of bodily objects.

I should put little confidence in this dry chain of argument did I not find it fully confirmed by the practice of Homer, or rather, I should say, if the practice of Homer had not introduced me to it. Upon these principles only the great manner of the Greek can be defined and explained, and the sentence which it deserves be passed on the directly opposite manner of so many modern poets who wish to rival the painter in a performance in which they must necessarily be surpassed by him. I find that Homer paints nothing but progressive actions, and paints all bodies and individual things only on account of their relation to these actions, and generally with a single trait. What wonder is it, then, that the painter, where Homer has painted, finds little or nothing for himself to do, and that his harvest is only to be gathered where history brings together a multitude of beautiful bodies, in beautiful attitudes, within a space favourable to art, while the poet himself may paint as little as he pleases bodies, these attitudes, and this space? Let any one go through the whole series of paintings, piece by piece, which Caylus has taken from him, and he will find a confirmation of this remark.

Here I leave the Count, who would make the colour-grinding stone of the painter the touchstone of the poet, in order that I may throw a greater light upon the manner of Homer.

I say that Homer usually makes use of one trait. A ship is to him at one time a dark ship, at another a hollow ship, at another a swift ship, at the most a well-rowed black ship. He goes no farther in the painting of a ship but the navigation, the departure, the arrival of the ship; out of these he makes a detailed picture, a picture out of which the painter must make five or six separate pictures if he wishes to place it entirely upon his canvas.

If particular circumstances compel Homer to fix our attention for a longer time upon one individual corporeal object, he nevertheless produces no picture which the painter can imitate with his pencil; but he knows how to use numberless expedients of art, so as to place this single object in a successive series of moments, in each of which it appears in a different form, and for the last of which the painter is obliged to wait, in order that he may show us completely formed that object, the gradual formation of which we have seen in the poet.

For example, when Homer wishes to show us the chariot of Juno, he makes Hebe put together every piece of it before our eyes. We see the spoles and the axletrees, and the driving-seat, the pole, the traces, and the straps, not brought together as a whole, but as they are separately put together by the hands of Hebe. Upon the wheels alone the poet lavishes more than one trait, and he shows us the eight brazen spokes, the golden fellies, the tires of bronze, the silver naves —each individual separate thing. One might almost say, that because there were more wheels than one, therefore he was obliged to spend much more time on their description than the putting on of each particular part would in reality have required.

'Ήβη δ' ἀμφ' ὀχέεσσι θοῶς βάλε καμπύλα κύκλα,
Χάλκεα ὀκτάκνημα, σιδηρέῳ ἄξονι ἀμφίς.
Τῶν ἦ τοι χρυσέη ἴτυς ἄφθιτος, αὐτὰρ ὕπερθε
Χάλκε' ἐπίσσωτρα προσαρηρότα, θαῦμα ἰδέσθαι·
Πλῆμναι δ' ἀργύρου εἰσὶ περίδρομοι ἀμφοτέρωθεν·
Δίφρος δὲ χρυσέοισι καὶ ἀργυρέοισιν ἱμᾶσιν
Ἐντέταται, δοιαὶ δὲ περίδρομοι ἄντυγές εἰσι.
Τοῦ δ' ἐξ ἀργύρεος ῥυμὸς πέλεν· αὐτὰρ ἐπ' ἄκρῳ
Δῆσε χρύσειον καλὸν ζυγόν, ἐν δὲ λέπαδνα
Κάλ' ἔβαλε χρύσεια.[1]

Does Homer wish to show us how Agememnon was clad? Then the king must put on his whole clothing piece by piece before our eyes— the soft under-garment, the great mantle, the beautiful sandals, the sword—and then he is ready, and grasps the sceptre. We see the raiment in which the poet paints the act of his being clothed; another would have painted the clothes in detail down to the smallest fringe, and we shall have seen nothing of the action of putting on the raiment.

[1] *Iliad*, E 722–731.

Her golden-bridled steeds
Then Saturn's daughter brought abroad;
and Hebe, she proceeds,
T' address her chariot instantly; she gives
it—either wheel
Beam'd with eight spokes of sounding
brass; the axle-tree was steel,
The fell'ffs incorruptible gold, their upper
bands of brass,
Their matter most unvalued, their work
of wondrous grace.
The naves in which the spokes were
driven, were all with silver bound;
The chariot's seat, two hoops of gold and
silver strength'ned round;
Edg'd with a gold and silver fringe; the
beam that look'd before,
Was massy silver; on whose top, geres all
of gold it wore,
And golden poitrils.—Chapman.

Μαλακὸν δ' ἔνδυνε χιτῶνα,
Καλὸν νηγάτεον, περὶ δὲ μέγα βάλλετο φᾶρος·
Ποσσὶ δ' ὑπὸ λιπαροῖσιν ἐδήσατο καλὰ πέδιλα,
'Αμφὶ δ' ἄρ' ὤμοισιν βάλετο ξίφος ἀργυρόηλον·
Εἵλετο δὲ σκῆπτρον πατρῷον, ἄφθιτον αἰεί.[2]

And as to that sceptre which here is only described as ancestral and immortal, as in another place one like it is described only as χρυσείοις ἥλοισι πεπαρμένον, *garnished with golden bosses*, when I say we are to have a more complete and more accurate picture of this mighty sceptre, what is it that Homer does? Does he paint for us, besides the golden bosses, the wood of which it is made, and the carved head? Yes, it would have been so in a description of heraldic art, in order that in future time it might be possible to make one exactly like it. And I am certain that many a modern poet would have given such an heraldic description, with the simple and honest notion that he himself was really painting because a painter could imitate him. But did Homer trouble himself with considering how far he should leave the painter behind him? Instead of a description he gives us the history of the sceptre: first we see it as worked by Vulcan; next it glitters in the hand of Jupiter; then it proclaims the dignity of Mercury; then it becomes the commander-staff of the warrior Pelops; and then it is the pastoral-staff of the peaceful Atreus.

Σκῆπτρον ἔχων, τὸ μὲν ῞Ηφαιστος κάμε τεύχων,
῞Ηφαιστος μεν δῶκε Διὶ Κρωνίωνι ἄνακτι·
Αὐτὰρ ἄρα Ζεὺς δῶκε διακτόρῳ 'Αργειφόντῃ·
'Ερμείας δὲ ἄναξ δῶκεν Πέλοπι πληξίππῳ·
Αὐτὰρ ὁ αὖτε Πέλοχ δῶκ' 'Ατρέϊ, ποιμένι λαῶν·
'Ατρεὺς δὲ θνήσκων ἔλιπεν πολύαρνι Θυέστῃ·
Αὐτὰρ ὁ αὖτε Θυέστ' 'Αγαμέμνονι λεῖπε φορῆναι,
Πολλῇσιν νήσοισι καὶ ῞Αργεϊ παντὶ ἀνάσσειν[3]

[2] *Iliad*, B 42–46:
The dream gone, his voice still murmured
About the king's ears: who sate up, put on him in his bed
His silken inner weed; fair, new, and then in haste arose;
Cast on his ample mantle, tied to his soft feet fair shoes;
His silver-hilted sword he hung about his shoulders. took

His father's sceptre never stain'd; which then abroad he shook.—Chapman.
[3] *Iliad*, B 101–108:
Then stood divine Atrides up, and in his hand compress'd
His sceptre, th' elaborate work of fiery Mulciber:
Who gave it to Saturnian Jove; Jove to his messenger;
His messenger, Argicides, to Pelops, skill'd in horse;

And thus, at last, I am better acquainted with this sceptre than if a painter had placed it before my eyes, or a second Vulcan delivered it into my hand. I should not be surprised to find that one of the ancient expositors of Homer had admired this passage, as containing the most perfect allegory of the origin, the progress, the establishment, and finally of the hereditary character of kingly authority among men. I should smile, indeed, if I were to read that Vulcan, who wrought the sceptre, represented fire, that thing which is most indispensable to the support of man, that relief of our necessities which had induced the first mortals to subject themselves to the rule of a single person; that the first king was a *son of Time* (Ζεὺς Κρονίων), a venerable old man, who wished to share his power with an *eloquent clever* man, with a Mercury (διακτόρῳ 'Αργειφόντῃ), or entirely to give it up to him; that the wise orator, at a time when the young state was threatened by foreign foes, had delivered up his supreme authority to the bravest warrior (Πέλοπι πληξίππῳ); [4] that the brave warrior, after he had subdued the enemy and secured the state, had found means to transfer it to his son, who, as a peace-loving ruler, as a beneficent pastor of his people, had made them acquainted with good living and abundance (ποιμὴν λαῶν); [5] whereby he had paved the way after his death for the wealthiest of his relations (πολύαρνι Θυέστῃ): [6] so that what hitherto confidence had bestowed and merit had considered rather as a burthen than a dignity, should not be obtained by presents and bribes, and secured for ever to the family, like any other acquired property. I should smile, but I should notwithstanding be confirmed in my esteem for the poet to whom so much could be attributed.

But this lies out of my path, and I consider the history of the sceptre merely as an artifice to induce us to contemplate for a while an individual thing without introducing us to a frigid description of its separate parts. Also, when Achilles swears by his sceptre to avenge the contumely with which Agamemnon has treated him, Homer gives us the history of this sceptre. We see it green and flourishing on the mountain, the steel severs it from the trunk, strips

Pelops to Atreus, chief of men: he dying,
    gave it course
To prince Thyestes, rich in herbs; Thyestes
    to the hand
Of Agamemnon render'd it, and with it
    the command

Of many isles, and Argos all.
              —Chapman.

[4] Pelops smiter of horses.
[5] Shepherd of his people.
[6] Thyestes rich in flocks.

off its leaves and bark, and makes it a fitting instrument to signify, in the hands of the judges of the people, their divine dignity.

Ναὶ μὰ τόδε σκῆπτρον, τὸ μὲν οὔ ποτε φύλλα καὶ ὄζους
Φύσει, ἐπεὶ δὴ πρῶτα τομὴν ἐν ὄρεσσι λέλοιπεν,
Οὐδ' ἀναθηλήσει· περὶ γάρ ῥά ἑ χαλκὸς ἔλεψε
Φύλλα τε καὶ φλοιόν· νῦν αὐτέ μιν υἶες 'Αχαιῶν
'Εν παλάμῃς φορέουσι δικασπόλοι, οἵ τε θέμιστας
Πρὸς Διὸς εἰρύαται.[7]

It was not so much the object of Homer to paint two sceptres of different materials and forms, as to make a clear and plain representation to us of the difference of power of which these sceptres were the emblems. The former, a work by Vulcan; the latter cut on the mountain by an unknown hand: the former, the ancient possession of a noble house; the latter destined for the strongest hand: the former in the hand of a monarch stretched over many islands and over the whole of Argos; the latter borne by one chosen out of the midst of the Greeks, to whom, with others, the administration of the laws was confided. This was really the distance at which Agamemnon and Achilles stood from each other; a distance which Achilles himself, in spite of all his blind wrath, could not do otherwise than confess.

But not only on those occasions when Homer combines with his descriptions of this kind ulterior objects, but also when he only desires to show us the picture, he will disperse, as it were, the picture in a kind of history of the object, in order that the different parts of it, which in nature we see combined together, may in his picture as naturally seem to follow upon each other, and to keep true step with the flow of his narrative. For example, he wishes to paint for us the bow of Pandarus: a bow of horn, of such-and-such a length, well polished, and tipped at both ends with beaten gold. What does he do? Does he give us a dry enumeration of all its properties, one after the other? No such thing: that would be to give an account of a bow,

---

[7] *Iliad*, A 234–239:
Yet I vow, and by a great oath swear,
Even by this sceptre, that as this never again shall bear,
Green leaves or branches, nor increase with any growth his size;

Nor did since first it left the hills, and had his faculties
And ornaments bereft with iron; which now to other end
Judges of Greece bear, and their laws, received from Jove, defend.--Chapman.

to enumerate its qualities; but not to paint one. He begins with the chase of the wild goat, out of whose horns the bow is made. Pandarus had lain in wait for him in the rocks, and had slain him: the horns were of extraordinary size, and on that account he destined them for a bow. They are brought to the workshop; the artist unites, polishes, decorates them. And so, as I have said, we see the gradual formation by the poet of that which we can only see in a completed form in the work of the painter.

> Τόξον ἔυξοον ἰξάλου αἰγὸς
> Ἀγρίου, ὅν ῥά ποτ' αὐτὸς ὑπὸ στέρνοιο τυχήσας
> Πέτρης ἐκβαίνοντα δεδεγμένος ἐν προδοκῇσι,
> Βεβλήκει πρὸς ·στῆθος· ὁ δ' ὕπτιος ἔμπεσε πέτρῃ·
> Τοῦ κέρα ἐκ κεφαλῆς ἐκκαιδεκάδωρα πεφύκει·
> Καὶ τὰ μὲν ἀσκήσας κε ραο ξόος ἤραρε τέκτων,
> Πᾶν δ' εὖ λειήνας, χρυσέην ἐπέθηκε κορώνην.[8]

I should never have done if I were to transcribe all the instances of this kind. They will occur in multitudes to him who really knows his Homer.

[8] *Iliad,* D 105–111:
Who instantly drew forth a bow most
  admirably made
Of th' antler of a jumping goat, bred in a
  steep up-land,
Which archer-like (as long before he took
  his hidden stand
The doom'd one skipping from a rock)
  into the breast he smote,

And headlong felled him from his cliff.
  The forehead of the goat
Held out a wondrous goodly palm, that
  sixteen branches brought,
Of all of which (join'd) an useful bow a
  skilful bowyer wrought,
Which piked and polished both the ends
  he hid with horns of gold.
  —Chapman.

SIR JOSHUA REYNOLDS

(1723-1792)

REYNOLDS was born at Plympton Earl, in Devonshire, in 1723. His father was a clergyman and schoolmaster, and from him Joshua received the formal part of his general education. At seventeen he was apprenticed to Thomas Hudson, a painter in London, with whom he worked for two years. There followed a short period of painting for himself, and then four years spent in Italy studying. His return to England in 1752 was to an immediate success and popularity. The years that followed brought rapid advancement in artistic achievement, fortune, and social position.

It was at Reynolds' suggestion that "The Club" of Johnson and his friends was formed, in 1764. The outcome of the art exhibitions which began in 1760 was the founding of the Royal Academy. This took place in 1768, with Reynolds the first president. A few months later he was knighted. Taking no active part in the instruction at the Academy, Reynolds delivered lectures (*The Discourses*) every one or two years on the occasions of the banquets. The danger of total blindness brought an end to his painting in 1790, and two years later he died. Burke's eulogy of him is famous: "The loss of no man of his time can be felt with more sincere, general, and unmixed sorrow"; Johnson had characteristically declared Sir Joshua "the most invulnerable man he knew; whom, if he should quarrel with him, he should find the most difficulty how to abuse."

No one who studies the *Discourses* for either style or matter will long credit the possibility, at one time insinuated, that Johnson wrote them, or part of them. For considering Burke there might, entirely on internal evidence, be argument, but there is not sufficient basis for serious debate. Mr. F. L. Hilles, in his *Literary Career of Sir Joshua Reynolds,* discusses the manner in which the painter assembled notes and planned his discourses; Johnson "corrected" the early drafts, and there remain manuscripts which clearly illustrate the amount of his casual contribution to Reynolds' literary achievement. No external evidence exists of Burke's having performed a similar service.

Although the *Discourses* were addressed to a society of artists, their author endeavored to make them applicable also to poetry, which often becomes the center of inquiry. Reynolds recognizes the distinction between the arts, and nowhere breaks over it. He contends that in certain matters poetry and painting learn from one another, and he discusses such topics as invention and imagination as qualities of the creative temperament which are much the same for every art.

With the notice taken by Prof. Arthur Beatty [*William Wordsworth*] of Reynolds' influence in Wordsworth's prefaces of 1798 and 1800, there has been a growing interest in the painter's position in criticism. It has nevertheless been customary to regard the *Discourses* as a simple document of the so-called School of Taste, a superior expression of the generally accepted doctrine held by the late Eighteenth Century theorists. Furthermore, it has usually been assumed that they have a clear unity of thesis, and that no material change or development of idea occurred between the First Discourse and the Fifteenth. Mr. E. N. S. Thompson ["The *Discourses* of Sir Joshua Reynolds," *P.M.L.A.*, XXXII] takes no account of the spread of nearly twenty-two years which their composition covered. Austin Warren [*Alexander Pope as Critic and Humanist*, 48] says that they are "throughout a development of the Aristotelian conception of art." One of the biographers (John Sime) finds that "considering that twenty years passed between the first and last Discourses, it is wonderful to find such consistency of thought running through them." [*Sir Joshua Reynolds*, 98.] These observations are of unquestionable soundness for the first twelve of the discourses. The Thirteenth, however, reveals a line of thought which, if not contradictory to the doctrines previously laid down, is at least outside them.

In the earlier papers Reynolds discusses at length and with admirable clarity the concepts of "Nature" and of "imitation." In the Third Discourse he lays down "the principle . . . that the perfection of this art [painting] does not consist in mere imitation," and substantiates this by quotation from Proclus (*Timaeum Platonis*, Lib. 2): "He . . . who takes for his model such forms as nature produces, and confines himself to an exact imitation of them, will never attain to what is perfectly beautiful. For the works of nature are full of disproportion, and fall very short of the true standard of beauty. So that Phidias, when he formed his Jupiter, did not copy any object ever presented to his sight; but contemplated only that image which he had conceived in his mind from Homer's description." Cicero's famous statement to the same effect is included: "Neither did this artist [Phidias], when he carved the image of Jupiter or Minerva, set before him any one human figure, as a pattern, which he was to copy; but having a more perfect idea of beauty fixed in his mind, this he steadily contemplated, and to the imitation of this all his skill and labour were directed." Reynolds further clarifies the means by which ideal Nature is to be discovered: the artist's "eye being enabled to distinguish the accidental deficiencies, excrescences, and deformities of things, from their general figures, he makes out an abstract idea of their forms more perfect than any one original. . . ." So the Third Discourse, and indeed all of the earlier ones, represent a true and accurate recapitulation of the Aristotelian doctrine.

The identification of Reynolds with the School of Taste has been due chiefly to his Seventh Discourse. Here, defining taste as "that act of the mind by which we like or dislike, whatever be the subject," he proceeds in a very logical manner to identify it with the artist's manner of investigating and following nature. In so doing, he broadens the scope of the latter term in a significant direction: "My notion of nature comprehends not only the forms which nature produces, but also the nature and internal fabrick and organization, as I may call it, of the human mind and imagination. The terms beauty, or nature, which are general ideas, are but different modes of expressing the same thing. . . . He who thinks nature, in the narrow sense of the word, is alone to be followed, will produce but a scanty entertainment for the imagination. . . . In short, whatever pleases has in it what is analogous to the mind, and is therefore, in the highest and best sense of the word, natural." From this it clearly follows that the province of taste includes examination not only of external things but also of the imagination and the passions. These latter two, however, are declared to have "principles . . . as invariable as the former, and are to be reasoned upon in the same manner, by an appeal to common sense deciding upon the common feelings of mankind. . . . We may therefore conclude, that the real substance, as it may be called, of what goes under the name of taste, is fixed and established in the nature of things; that there are certain and regular causes by which the imagination and passions of men are affected; and that the knowledge of these causes is acquired by a laborious and diligent investigation of nature."

The conception of nature as including the human mind thus enables the theory of taste to be brought into harmony with the older classical doctrine. It nevertheless necessitates an attention to the imagination and the feelings, and this attention is destined at last to be one of the rocks upon which neo-classicism wrecks itself. Too, it forces anyone adopting it either to take greater pains in distinguishing ideal nature from actual nature, or to run the risk of being misunderstood. Hugh Blair's recognition of this difficulty in his essay on "Taste" [*Lectures on Rhetoric and Belles Lettres,* 1783] drives him to the easier and safer position of regarding taste as possessing in itself standards which are independent of recourse to nature:

> When we say that nature is the standard of taste, we lay down a principle very true and just, as far as it can be applied. There is no doubt, that in all cases where an imitation is intended of some object that exists in nature, as in representing human characters or actions, conformity to nature affords a full and distinct criterion of what is truly beautiful. Reason hath in such cases full scope for exerting its authority; for approving or condemning; by comparing the copy with the original. But there are innumerable cases in which this rule cannot be at all applied; and conformity to nature, is an expression frequently used, without any distinct or determinate meaning. We must therefore search for somewhat that can be rendered more clear and precise, to be the standard of taste. . . . That which men concur the most in admiring, must be held to be beautiful. His taste must be esteemed just and true, which coincides with the general sentiments of men.

The significance, in the development of his own critical theory, of Reynolds' placing the faculties of the mind within nature is seen in the discourses which follow the Seventh. His emphasis is more and more upon "the passions and affections of the mind" (VIII), and less is said of "real forms of nature, distinct from accidental deformity" (III). Imagination, whatever precisely be meant by it, had been given a place of importance from the first. As early as the Third Discourse he had said that the "genuine painter . . . instead of seeking praise by deceiving the superficial sense of the spectator, . . . must strive for fame, by captivating the imagination." Similar injunctions occur repeatedly throughout the addresses. But the Thirteenth Discourse, delivered (1786) ten years after the Seventh, clearly shows a shift of emphasis in the ideas which Reynolds has been dealing with; "imagination" supersedes "nature": the importance accorded it provides a link between failing neo-classicism and the romanticism which is to follow.

One of the most startling facts about this Discourse is that no single mention of ideal nature occurs in it. There is not a passing reference to "genuine habits of nature" or "real forms of nature," although the entire essay is devoted to such "deviations" from ordinary nature as "it is natural for the imagination to be delighted with."

Reynolds sets out to demonstrate that the arts must sometimes have no recourse to actuality. He carefully modifies the word "nature" with such adjectives as "particular," "actual," "common," wishing his hearers and readers to think only of the accidental forms against the imitation of which he has from the first warned them. But as he expands his ideas with illustrations, one comes to feel that, even if deviations from ideal nature are not also countenanced, at least the term "nature" has lost any distinguishable significances. Formerly the important distinction had been between accidental nature and real nature; in the Thirteenth Discourse it is between nature and imagination.

DISCOURSE XIII

Delivered to the Students of the Royal Academy, on the Distribution of the Prizes, December 11, 1786.

Art not merely Imitation, but under the Direction of the Imagination. In what Manner Poetry, Painting, Acting, Gardening, and Architecture depart from Nature.

GENTLEMEN,

To discover beauties, or to point out faults, in the works of celebrated masters, and to compare the conduct of one artist with another, is certainly no mean or inconsiderable part of criticism; but this is still no more than to know the art through the artist. This test of investigation must have two capital defects; it must be narrow, and it must be uncertain. To enlarge the boundaries of the art of painting, as well as to fix its principles, it will be necessary, that *that* art and *those* principles should be considered in their correspondence with the principles of the other arts which, like this, address themselves primarily and principally to the imagination. When those connected and kindred principles are brought together to be compared, another comparison will grow out of this; that is, the comparison of them all with those of human nature, from whence arts derive the materials upon which they are to produce their effects.

When this comparison of art with art, and of all arts with the nature of man, is once made with success, our guiding lines are as well ascertained and established, as they can be in matters of this description.

This, as it is the highest style of criticism, is at the same time the soundest; for it refers to the eternal and immutable nature of things.

You are not to imagine that I mean to open to you at large, or to recommend to your research, the whole of this vast field of science. It is certainly much above my faculties to reach it; and though it may not be above yours to comprehend it fully, if it were fully and properly brought before you, yet perhaps the most perfect criticism requires habits of speculation and abstraction, not very consistent with the employment which ought to occupy and the habits of mind which ought to prevail in a practical artist. I only point out to you these things, that when you do criticise (as all who work on a plan will criticise more or less), your criticism may be built on the foundation of true principles; and that though you may not always travel a great way, the way that you do travel may be the right road.

I observe, as a fundamental ground, common to all the arts with which we have any concern in this discourse, that they address themselves only to two faculties of the mind, its imagination and its sensibility.

All theories which attempt to direct or to control the art, upon any principles falsely called rational, which we form to ourselves upon a supposition of what ought in reason to be the end or means of art, independent of the known first effect produced by objects on the imagination, must be false and delusive. For though it may appear bold to say it, the imagination is here the residence of truth. If the imagination be affected, the conclusion is fairly drawn; if it be not affected, the reasoning is erroneous, because the end is not obtained; the effect itself being the test, and the only test, of the truth and efficacy of the means.

There is in the commerce of life, as in art, a sagacity which is far from being contradictory to right reason, and is superior to any occasional exercise of that faculty; which supersedes it; and does not wait for the slow progress of deduction, but goes at once, by what appears a kind of intuition, to the conclusion. A man endowed with this faculty feels and acknowledges the truth, though it is not always in his power, perhaps, to give a reason for it; because he cannot recollect and bring before him all the materials that gave birth to his opinion; for very many and very intricate considerations may unite to form the principle, even of small and minute parts, involved in, or dependent on, a great system of things: though these in process of time are forgotten, the right impression still remains fixed in his mind.

This impression is the result of the accumulated experience of our whole life, and has been collected, we do not always know how, or when. But this mass of collective observation, however acquired, ought to prevail over that reason, which, however powerfully exerted on any particular occasion, will probably comprehend but a partial view of the subject; and our conduct in life as well as in the arts is, or ought to be, generally governed by this habitual reason: it is our happiness that we are enabled to draw on such funds. If we were obliged to enter into a theoretical deliberation on every occasion, before we act, life would be at a stand, and art would be impracticable.

It appears to me, therefore, that our first thoughts, that is, the effect which anything produces on our minds, on its first appearance, is never to be forgotten; and it demands for that reason, because it is the first, to be laid up with care. If this be not done, the artist may happen to impose on himself by partial reasoning; by a cold consideration of those animated thoughts which proceed, not perhaps from caprice or rashness (as he may afterwards conceit), but from the fulness of his mind, enriched with the copious stores of all the various inventions which he had ever seen, or had ever passed in his mind. These ideas are infused into his design, without any conscious effort; but if he be not on his guard, he may reconsider and correct them, till the whole matter is reduced to a commonplace invention.

This is sometimes the effect of what I mean to caution you against; that is to say, an unfounded distrust of the imagination and feeling, in favour of narrow, partial, confined, argumentative theories; and of principles that seem to apply to the design in hand; without considering those general impressions on the fancy in which real principles of *sound reason,* and of much more weight and importance, are involved, and, as it were, lie hid, under the appearance of a sort of vulgar sentiment.

Reason, without doubt, must ultimately determine everything; at this minute it is required to inform us when that very reason is to give way to feeling.

Though I have often spoken of that mean conception of our art which confines it to mere imitation, I must add, that it may be narrowed to such a mere matter of experiment, as to exclude from it the application of science, which alone gives dignity and compass to any art. But to find proper foundations for science is neither to narrow nor to vulgarise it; and this is sufficiently exemplified in the success of experimental philosophy. It is the false system of reasoning, grounded on a partial view of things, against which I would most earnestly guard you. And I do it the rather, because those narrow theories, so coincident with the poorest and most miserable practice, and which are adopted to give it countenance, have not had their origin in the poorest minds, but in the mistakes, or possibly in the mistaken interpretations, of great and commanding authorities. We are not therefore in this case misled by feeling, but by false speculation.

When such a man as Plato speaks of painting as only an imitative art, and that our pleasure proceeds from observing and acknowledging the truth of the imitation, I think he misleads us by a partial theory. It is in this poor, partial, and so far false view of the art, that Cardinal Bembo has chosen to distinguish even Raffaelle himself, whom our enthusiasm honours with the name of Divine. The same sentiment is adopted by Pope in his epitaph on Sir Godfrey Kneller; and he turns the panegyric solely on imitation, as it is a sort of deception.

I shall not think my time misemployed, if by any means I may contribute to confirm your opinion of what ought to be the object of your pursuit; because, though the best critics must always have exploded this strange idea, yet I know that there is a disposition towards a perpetual recurrence to it, on account of its simplicity and superficial plausibility. For this reason I shall beg leave to lay before you a few thoughts on this subject; to throw out some hints that may lead your minds to an opinion (which I take to be the truth), that painting is not only to be considered as an imitation, operating by deception, but that it is, and ought to be, in many points of view, and strictly speaking, no imitation at all of external nature. Perhaps it ought to be as far removed from the vulgar idea of imitation, as the refined civilised state in which we live, is removed from a gross state of nature; and those who have not cultivated their imaginations, which the majority of mankind certainly have not, may be said, in regard to arts, to continue in this state of nature. Such men will always prefer imitation to that excellence which is addressed to another faculty that they do not possess; but these are not the persons to whom a painter is to look, any more than a judge of morals and manners ought to refer controverted points upon those subjects to the opinions of people taken from the banks of the Ohio, or from New Holland.

It is the lowest style only of arts, whether of painting, poetry, or music, that may be said, in the vulgar sense, to be naturally pleasing. The higher efforts of those arts, we know by experience, do not affect minds wholly uncultivated. This refined taste is the consequence of education and habit; we are born only with a capacity of entertaining this refinement, as we are born with a disposition to receive and obey all the rules and regulations of society; and so far it may be said to be natural to us, and no further.

What has been said, may show the artist how necessary it is, when he looks about him for the advice and criticism of his friends, to make some distinction of the character, taste, experience, and observation in this art of those from whom it is received. An ignorant uneducated man may, like Apelles's critic, be a competent judge of the truth of the representation of a sandal; or to go somewhat higher, like Molière's old woman, may decide upon what is nature, in regard to comic humour; but a critic in the higher style of art ought to possess the same refined taste, which directed the artist in his work.

To illustrate this principle by a comparison with other arts, I shall now produce some instances to show, that they, as well as our own art, renounce the narrow idea of nature, and the narrow theories derived from that mistaken principle, and apply to that reason only which informs us not what imitation is,—a natural representation of a given object,—but what it is natural for the imagination to be delighted with. And perhaps there is no better way of acquiring this knowledge, than by this kind of analogy: each art will corroborate and mutually reflect the truth on the other. Such a kind of juxtaposition may likewise have this use, that whilst the artist is amusing himself in the contemplation of other arts, he may habitually transfer the principles of those arts to that which he professes; which ought to be always present to his mind, and to which everything is to be referred.

So far is art from being derived from, or having any immediate intercourse with, particular nature as its model, that there are many arts that set out with a professed deviation from it.

This is certainly not so exactly true in regard to painting and sculpture. Our elements are laid in gross common nature,—an exact imitation of what is before us: but when we advance to the higher state, we consider this power of imitation, though first in the order of acquisition, as by no means the highest in the scale of perfection.

Poetry addresses itself to the same faculties and the same dispositions as painting, though by different means. The object of both is to accommodate itself to all the natural propensities and inclinations of the mind. The very existence of poetry depends on the licence it assumes of deviating from actual nature, in order to gratify natural propensities by other means, which are found by experience full as capable of affording such gratification. It sets out with a language in the highest degree artificial, a construction of measured words, such as never is, nor ever was used by man. Let this measure be what it may, whether hexameter or any other metre used in Latin or Greek—or rhyme, or blank verse varied with pauses and accents, in modern languages,— they are all equally removed from nature, and equally a violation of common speech. When this artificial mode has been established as the vehicle of sentiment, there is another principle in the human mind, to which the work must be referred, which still renders it more artificial, carries it still further from common nature, and deviates only to render it more perfect. That principle is the sense of congruity, coherence, and consistency, which is a real existing principle in man; and it must be gratified. Therefore having once adopted a style and a measure not found in common discourse, it is required that the sentiments also should be in the same proportion elevated above common nature, from the necessity of there being an agreement of the parts among themselves, that one uniform whole may be produced.

To correspond therefore with this general system of deviation from nature, the manner in which poetry is offered to the ear, the tone in which it is recited, should be as far removed from the tone of conversation, as the words of which that poetry is composed. This naturally suggests the idea of modulating the voice by art, which I suppose may be considered as accomplished to the highest degree of excellence in the recitative of the Italian Opera; as we may conjecture it was in the chorus that attended the ancient drama. And though the most violent passions, the highest distress, even death itself, are expressed in singing or recitative, I would not admit as sound criticism the condemnation of such exhibitions on account of their being unnatural.

If it is natural for our senses, and our imaginations, to be delighted with singing, with instrumental music, with poetry, and with graceful action, taken separately (none of them being in the vulgar sense natural, even in that separate state); it is conformable to experience, and therefore agreeable to reason as connected with and referred to experience, that we should also be delighted with this union of music, poetry, and graceful action, joined to every circumstance of pomp and magnificence calculated to strike the senses of the spectator. Shall reason stand in the way, and tell us that we ought not to like what we know we do like, and prevent us from feeling the full effect of this complicated exertion of art? This is what I would understand by poets and painters being allowed to dare everything; for what can be more daring, than accomplishing the purpose and end of art, by a complication of means, none of which have their archetypes in actual nature?

So far therefore is servile imitation from being necessary, that whatever is familiar, or in any way reminds us of what we see and hear every day, perhaps does not belong to the higher provinces of art, either in poetry or painting. The mind is to be transported, as Shakspeare expresses it, *beyond the ignorant present* to ages past. Another and a higher order of beings is supposed; and to those beings everything which is introduced into the work must correspond. Of this conduct, under these circumstances, the Roman and Florentine schools afford sufficient examples. Their style by this means is raised and elevated above all others; and by the same means the compass of art itself is enlarged.

We often see grave and great subjects attempted by artists of another school; who, though excellent in the lower class of art, proceeding on the principles which regulate that class, and not recollecting, or not knowing, that they were to address themselves to another faculty of the mind, have become perfectly ridiculous.

The picture which I have at present in my thoughts is a sacrifice of Iphigenia, painted by Jan Steen, a painter of whom I have formerly had occasion to speak with the highest approbation; and even in this picture, the subject of which is by no means adapted to his genius, there is nature and expression; but it is such expression, and the countenances are so familiar, and consequently so vulgar, and the whole accompanied with such finery of silks and velvets, that one would be almost tempted to doubt, whether the artist did not purposely intend to burlesque his subject.

Instances of the same kind we frequently see in poetry. Parts of Hobbes's translation of Homer are remembered and repeated merely for the familiarity and meanness of their phraseology, so ill corresponding with the ideas which ought to have been expressed, and, as I conceive, with the style of the original.

We may proceed in the same manner through the comparatively inferior branches of art. There are in works of that class, the same distinction of a higher and a lower style; and they take their rank and degree in proportion as the artist departs more, or less, from common nature, and makes it an object of his attention to strike the imagination of the spectator by ways belonging specially to art,—unobserved and untaught out of the school of its practice.

If our judgments are to be directed by narrow, vulgar, untaught, or rather ill-taught reason, we must prefer a portrait by Denner or any other high finisher, to those of Titian or Vandyck; and a landscape of Vanderheyden to those of Titian or Rubens; for they are certainly more exact representations of nature.

If we suppose a view of nature represented with all the truth of the *camera obscura,* and the same scene represented by a great artist, how little and mean will the one appear in comparison of the other, where no superiority is supposed from the choice of the subject. The scene shall be the same, the difference only will be in the manner in which it is presented to the eye. With what additional superiority then will the same artist appear when he has the power of selecting his materials, as well as elevating his style? Like Nicolas Poussin, he transports us to the environs of ancient Rome, with all the objects which a literary education makes so precious and interesting to man: or, like Sebastian Bourdon, he leads us to the dark antiquity of the Pyramids of Egypt; or, like Claude Lorrain, he conducts us to the tranquillity of arcadian scenes and fairyland.

Like the history-painter, a painter of landscapes in this style and with this conduct sends the imagination back into antiquity; and, like the poet, he makes the elements sympathise with his subject; whether the clouds roll in volumes, like those of Titian or Salvator Rosa, or, like those of Claude, are gilded with the setting sun; whether the mountains have sudden and bold projections, or are gently sloped; whether the branches of his trees shoot out abruptly in right angles from their trunks, or follow each other with only a gentle inclination. All these circumstances contribute to the general character of the work, whether it be of the elegant, or of the more sublime kind. If we add to this the powerful materials of lightness and darkness, over which the artist has complete dominion, to vary and dispose them as he pleases; to diminish, or increase them, as will best suit his purpose, and correspond to the general idea of his work; a landscape thus conducted, under the influence of a poetical mind, will have the same superiority over the more ordinary and common views, as Milton's *Allegro* and *Penseroso* have over a cold prosaic narration or description; and such a picture would make a more forcible impression on the mind than the real scenes, were they presented before us.

If we look abroad to other arts, we may observe the same distinction, the same division into two classes; each of them acting under the influence of two different principles, in which the one follows nature, the other varies it, and sometimes departs from it.

The theatre, which is said *to hold the mirror up to nature,* comprehends both those sides. The lower kind of comedy or farce, like the inferior style of painting, the more naturally it is represented, the better; but the higher appears to me to aim no more at imitation, so far as it belongs to anything like deception, or to expect that the spectators should think that the events there represented are really passing before them, than Raffaelle in his cartoons, or Poussin in his sacraments, expected it to be believed, even for a moment, that what they exhibited were real figures.

For want of this distinction, the world is filled with false criticism. Raffaelle is praised for naturalness and deception, which he certainly has not accomplished, and as certainly never intended; and our late great actor, Garrick, has been as ignorantly praised by his friend Fielding; who doubtless imagined he had hit upon an ingenious device, by introducing in one of his novels (otherwise a work of the highest merit) an ignorant man, mistaking Garrick's representation of a scene in Hamlet for reality. A very little reflection will convince us, that there is not one circumstance in the whole scene that is of the nature of deception. The merit and excellence of Shakspeare, and of Garrick, when they were engaged in such scenes, is of a different and much higher kind. But what adds to the falsity of this intended compliment is that the best stage-representation appears even more unnatural to a person of such a character, who is supposed never to have seen a play before, than it does to those who have had a habit of allowing for those necessary deviations from nature which the art requires.

In theatric representation, great allowances must always be made for the place in which the exhibition is represented; for the surrounding company, the lighted candles, the scenes visibly shifted in your sight, and the language of blank verse, so different from common English; which merely as English must appear surprising in the mouths of Hamlet, and all the court and natives of Denmark. These allowances are made; but their being made puts an end to all manner of deception: and further, we know that the more low, illiterate, and vulgar any person is, the less he will be disposed to make these allowances, and of course to be deceived by any imitation; the things in which the trespass against nature and common probability is made in favour of the theatre being quite within the sphere of such uninformed men. Though I have no intention of entering into all the circumstances of unnaturalness in theatrical representations, I must observe, that even the expression of violent passion is not always the most excellent in proportion as it is the most natural; so great terror and such disagreeable sensations may be communicated to the audience, that the balance may be destroyed by which pleasure is preserved, and holds its predominance in the mind: violent distortion of action, harsh screamings of the voice, however great the occasion, or however natural on such occasion, are therefore not admissible in the theatric art. Many of these allowed deviations from nature arise from the necessity which there is, that everything should be raised and enlarged beyond its natural state; that the full effect may come home to the spectator, which otherwise would be lost in the comparatively extensive space of the theatre. Hence the deliberate and stately step, the studied grace of action, which seems to enlarge the dimensions of the actor, and alone to fill the stage. All this unnaturalness, though right and proper in its place, would appear affected and ridiculous in a private room; *quid enim deformius, quam scenam in vitam transferre?* [1]

And here I must observe, and I believe it may be considered as a general rule, that no art can be engrafted with success on another art. For though they all profess the same origin, and to proceed from the same stock, yet each has its own peculiar modes both of imitating nature, and of deviating from it, each for the accomplishment of its own particular purpose. These deviations, more especially, will not bear transplantation to another soil.

If a painter should endeavour to copy the theatrical pomp and parade of dress and attitude, instead of that simplicity, which is not a greater beauty in life than it is in painting, we should condemn such pictures, as painted in the meanest style.

So also gardening, as far as gardening is an art, or entitled to that appellation, is a deviation from nature; for if the true taste consists, as many hold, in banishing every appearance of art, or any traces of the footsteps of man, it would then be no longer a garden. Even though we define it, "Nature to advantage dress'd," and in some sense is such, and much more beautiful and commodious for the recreation of man; it is, however, when so dressed, no longer a subject for the pencil of a landscape-painter, as all landscape-painters know, who love to have

[1] For what [would be] more unbecoming than to carry a scene from drama over into actual life?

recourse to nature herself, and to dress her according to the principles of their own art; which are far different from those of gardening, even when conducted according to the most approved principles; and such as a landscape-painter himself would adopt in the disposition of his own grounds, for his own private satisfaction.

I have brought together as many instances as appear necessary to make out the several points which I wished to suggest to your consideration in this discourse, that your own thoughts may lead you further in the use that may be made of the analogy of the arts, and of the restraint which a full understanding of the diversity of many of their principles ought to impose on the employment of that analogy.

The great end of all those arts is, to make an impression on the imagination and the feeling. The imitation of nature frequently does this. Sometimes it fails, and something else succeeds. I think therefore the true test of all the arts is not solely whether the production is a true copy of nature, but whether it answers the end of art, which is to produce a pleasing effect upon the mind.

It remains only to speak a few words of architecture, which does not come under the denomination of an imitative art. It applies itself, like music (and I believe we may add poetry), directly to the imagination, without the intervention of any kind of imitation.

There is in architecture, as in painting, an inferior branch of art, in which the imagination appears to have no concern. It does not, however, acquire the name of a polite and liberal art, from its usefulness, or administering to our wants or necessities, but from some higher principle: we are sure that in the hands of a man of genius it is capable of inspiring sentiment, and of filling the mind with great and sublime ideas.

It may be worth the attention of artists to consider what materials are in their hands, that may contribute to this end; and whether this art has it not in its power to address itself to the imagination with effect, by more ways than are generally employed by architects.

To pass over the effect produced by that general symmetry and proportion, by which the eye is delighted, as the ear is with music, architecture certainly possesses many principles in common with poetry and painting. Among those which may be reckoned as the first is that of affecting the imagination by means of association of ideas. Thus, for instance, as we have naturally a veneration for antiquity, whatever building brings to our remembrance ancient customs and manners, such as the castles of the barons of ancient chivalry, is sure to give this delight. Hence it is that *towers and battlements* [2] are so often selected by the painter and the poet, to make a part of the composition of their ideal landscape; and it is from hence in a great degree, that in the buildings of Vanbrugh, who was a poet as well as an architect, there is a greater display of imagination than we shall find perhaps in any other, and this is the ground of the effect we feel in many of his works, notwithstanding the faults with which many of them are justly charged. For this purpose, Vanbrugh appears to have had recourse to some of the principles of the Gothic architecture; which, though not so ancient as the Grecian, is more so to our imagination, with which the artist is more concerned than with absolute truth.

The barbaric splendour of those Asiatic buildings, which are now publishing by a member of this Academy,[3] may possibly, in the same manner, furnish an architect, not with models to copy, but with hints of composition and general effect, which would not otherwise have occurred.

It is, I know, a delicate and hazardous thing (and as such I have already pointed it out), to carry the principles of one art to another, or even to reconcile in one object the various modes of the same art, when they proceed on different principles. The sound rules of the Grecian architecture are not to be lightly sacrificed. A deviation from them, or even an addition to them, is like a deviation or addition to, or from, the rules of other arts,—fit only for a great master, who is thoroughly conversant in the nature of man, as well as all combinations in his own art.

It may not be amiss for the architect to take advantage *sometimes* of that to which I am sure the painter ought always to have his eyes open, I mean the use of accidents; to follow when they lead, and to improve them, rather than always to trust to a regular plan. It often happens that additions have been made to houses, at various times, for use or pleasure. As such buildings depart from regularity, they now and then acquire something of scenery by this accident, which I should think might not unsuccessfully be adopted by an architect, in an original plan, if it does not too much interfere with convenience. Variety and intricacy is a beauty and excellence in every other of the arts which address the imagination; and why not in architecture?

The forms and turnings of the streets of London, and other old towns, are produced by accident, without any original plan or design; but they are not always the less pleasant to the walker or spectator, on that

[2] Towers and battlements it sees
Bosom'd high in tufted trees.—MILTON,
"L'Allegro." R.

[3] Mr. Hodges.

account. On the contrary, if the city had been built on the regular plan of Sir Christopher Wren, the effect might have been, as we know it is in some new parts of the town, rather unpleasing; the uniformity might have produced weariness, and a slight degree of disgust.

I can pretend to no skill in the detail of architecture. I judge now of the art, merely as a painter. When I speak of Vanbrugh, I mean to speak of him in the language of our art. To speak then of Vanbrugh in the language of a painter, he had originality of invention, he understood light and shadow, and had great skill in composition. To support his principal object he produced his second and third groups or masses; he perfectly understood in his art what is the most difficult in ours, the conduct of the background, by which the design and invention is set off to the greatest advantage. What the background is in painting, in architecture is the real ground on which the building is erected; and no architect took greater care than he that his work should not appear crude and hard: that is, it did not abruptly start out of the ground without expectation or preparation.

This is a tribute which a painter owes to an architect who composed like a painter; and was defrauded of the due reward of his merit by the wits of his time, who did not understand the principles of composition in poetry better than he; and who knew little or nothing of what he understood perfectly, the general ruling principles of architecture and painting. His fate was that of the great Perrault; both were the objects of the petulant sarcasms of factious men of letters; and both have left some of the fairest ornaments which to this day decorate their several countries; the façade of the Louvre, Blenheim, and Castle Howard.

Upon the whole, it seems to me, that the object and intention of all the arts is to supply the natural imperfection of things, and often to gratify the mind by realising and embodying what never existed but in the imagination.

It is allowed on all hands, that facts and events, however they may bind the historian, have no dominion over the poet or the painter. With us, history is made to bend and conform to this great idea of art. And why? Because these arts, in their highest province, are not addressed to the gross senses, but to the desires of the mind, to that spark of divinity which we have within, impatient of being circumscribed and pent up by the world which is about us. Just so much as our art has of this, just so much of dignity, I had almost said of divinity, it exhibits; and those of our artists who possessed this mark of distinction in the highest degree acquired from thence the glorious appellation of Divine.

WILLIAM WORDSWORTH

(1770–1850)

BORN at Cockermouth, Cumberland, Wordsworth lost both his parents before he was fourteen; he was educated under the guardianship of his two uncles. During his father's lifetime he had been sent to the Hawkshead grammar school, and in 1787, despite the impecunious condition of his family, he went to St. Johns College, Cambridge. The writing of verse, chiefly *The Evening Walk,* and a tour of France in 1790, are the significant aspects to a rather idle college career. He took his B.A. degree in 1791, and late in that year went again to France, where he remained until the end of 1792. Early in the next year were published *Descriptive Sketches* and *An Evening Walk,* in which the effect which he achieved first sickened Wordsworth on the poetic diction of the seventeen hundreds. There followed three years in which the poet, impassioned but inert, struggled under over-burdening philosophies, the influence of Godwin combating the influence of Rousseau. In 1795 he settled with his sister at Racedown, whence he moved, in 1797, to Alfoxden, in order to be nearer Coleridge, who was residing at Nether Stowey. These "neighbors" collaborated on the *Lyrical Ballads,* which were published in 1798. A second edition appeared in 1800, for which the famous Preface was written. In 1799, after a trip to the Rhine country with his sister Dorothy and Coleridge, Wordsworth settled at Grasmere, where he resided the rest of his life. No travelling other than occasional, no external struggles worthy of mention in so short a sketch as this, no sudden failures, changes, or successes, marked the latter half of the poet's long life. It would not be unsafe conjecture to call this circumstance most unfortunate: the life of the mind became almost his only life, and after the publication in 1807 of *Poems in Two Volumes,* Wordsworth might have died with no material hurt to his eventual poetic reputation. He married, in 1804, Mary Hutchinson; in 1843 he was appointed poet laureate; in 1850 he died and was buried at Grasmere.

After the *Poems* of 1807, his chief publications were the *Excursion* in 1814, the first collected edition of his poems, in 1815, *Peter Bell* and the *Wagoner* in 1819, *Ecclesiastical Sketches,* in 1822, and *Evening Voluntaries* in 1835.

The *Observations Prefixed to the Second Edition* of *Lyrical Ballads* has had a various treatment. It has been regarded in certain quarters as a declaration of literary rights, a powerful document in the liberating of letters from bondage; elsewhere it has been thought the pentateuch of the anarchists. But everybody has agreed on its importance. This fact has more significance than is at first obvious: whatever sort of *thing* the document was, it raised a wall between the Eighteenth and Nineteenth Centuries; it dated a new era—it served to make intelligible forever the dividing line between two regions in criticism that might otherwise have seemed to flow into one another. We do not often have such dividing walls.

An item of great significance in this critical Preface, though it has hardly been noted before, is the absence of the neo-classical jargon. With the abruptness of one who teaches with authority, Wordsworth dismisses the terms with which the critics from Jonson to Johnson have been concerned. And when they are gone, the refining disputations are gone, too: how far "rules" are to be allowed, whether they "cramp" or not, whether in learning to "imitate nature" more time ought to be spent with the "antients" or with the "moderns" or with "nature," whether "genius" needed to be "schooled," what form of "poesy" was the "highest"—these the Preface, like the stare of a king, condemns with silence.

This is not saying that Wordsworth is unrelated to the century preceding: on the contrary, his kinship is stronger than many have suspected. He went to school to the Eighteenth Century. He learned the practices and the theories of his time. And when he came to a systematic defence of his own theories, he used a method of reasoning, and a weapon, which no Johnsonian classicist could have criticized. The *Advertisement,* or foreword, to the volume of 1798 did indeed voice a spirit of revolt against the poetic practices of his contemporaries, but the argument advanced is not out of accord with late Eighteenth Century criticism. "An accurate taste in poetry," Wordsworth wrote, "and in all the other arts, Sir Joshua Reynolds has observed, is an acquired talent, which can only be produced by severe thought, and a long continued intercourse with the best models of composition." Prof. Arthur Beatty [*William Wordsworth,* 42–43] has well stated the relationship of the *Advertisement* to earlier critical theory:

> When Wordsworth defended his "experiments" in a new kind of poetry in the *Lyrical Ballads* of 1798, he did not use the arguments in favor of "genius," but those of imitation. . . . He first appeals to nature, and claims that these "attempts" must not be judged by a narrow definition of poetry but by truth to nature. I quote the entire passage:
>
> "Readers accustomed to the gaudiness and inane phraseology of many modern writers, if they persist in reading this book to its conclusion, will perhaps frequently have to struggle with feelings of strangeness and awkwardness: they will look round for poetry, and will be induced to enquire by what species of courtesy these attempts can be permitted to assume that title. It is desirable that such readers, for their own sakes, should not suffer the solitary word Poetry, a word of very disputed meaning, to stand in the way of their gratification; but that, while they are perusing this book, they should ask themselves if it contains a natural delineation of human passions, human characters, and human incidents; and if the answer be favorable to the author's wishes, that they should consent to be pleased in spite of that most dreadful enemy to our pleasures, our own pre-established codes of decision."

This is said in the very spirit of Sir Joshua Reynolds, who thus defines his main purpose in addressing the pupils of the Royal Academy: "The tendency of this Discourse [Eighth], with the instances which have been given, is not so much to place the artist above rules, as to teach him their reason; to prevent him from entertaining a narrow confined conception of art; to clear his mind from a perplexed variety of rules and their exceptions, by directing his attention to an intimate acquaintance with the passions and affections of the mind, from which all rules arise, and to which they are all referable."

It is therefore, in the words of Mr. Beatty, "by no 'romantic' argument, but by the most 'classical,' that Wordsworth defends these 'experiments' in the volume of 1798. He claims that he is in the great English tradition of 'the best models of composition'—Chaucer, Spenser, Shakespeare, Milton, —and he appeals to the educated taste of his readers for proper appreciation of the seriousness of his endeavors." [*Op. cit.*, p. 44.]

The fuller theory of poetry which is set forth in the *Observations* of 1800 is based, as were previous theories, on adherence to nature. It is Wordsworth's contention that "the primary laws of our nature" and the "beautiful and permanent forms of nature" are discernible through "incidents and situations from common life." To some thinkers this has appeared to be pure Rousseauistic doctrine and as illogically extreme in one direction as Eighteenth Century theory and practice had been in another. "He [Wordsworth] proceeds to set up a view of poetry," declares Mr. Irving Babbitt, "that is only the neo-classical view turned upside down. For the proper subjects and speech of poetry he would turn from the highest class of society to the lowest, from the aristocrat to the peasant. The peasant is more poetical than the aristocrat because he is closer to nature, for Wordsworth as he himself avows, is less interested in the peasant for his own sake than because he sees in him a sort of emanation from the landscape." [*Rousseau and Romanticism*, 145.] That Wordsworth had keenly felt the influence of Rousseau is not to be questioned. It nevertheless needs to be pointed out that the stress laid in various places throughout the Preface on "the language really used by men" has the primary purpose of making clear the cleavage between the "gaudiness and inane phraseology of many modern writers" and the critic's ideal of a free diction. Furthermore, this exaggeration of the importance of "humble and rustic life" is somewhat modified by his bringing forward as his chosen models "the earliest poets of all nations." There is no denying that the pieces of his own poetry which Wordsworth selects to exemplify what he argues are unhappy; but, in the succinct words of Mr. Garrod, he "was always ready to be ludicrous for the purpose of being perfectly truthful." [*William Wordsworth*, 28.]

Since Wordsworth's position is the starting point not only for the "democracy" but also for the emotional predominance in literature which have since developed, he has been accused, largely on the basis of poetical utterances, of complicity in perpetrating that "indolence of reverie"—to use an apt phrase of Prof. Babbitt's—which is one of the worst features of Romanticism. It is not difficult to understand how the poet who wrote "The Tables Turned" should excite such comment as the following:

Nature feeds our minds through our senses without any effort on our part!
This is that confusion of the world of sense and the world of intellect, utterly dis-
tinct, in reality, which has undermined the basis of thought in the last century. . . ."
[Barry Cerf: *P.M.L.A.,* XXXVII, 624.]

It is in freeing Wordsworth, even the Wordsworth of the *Lyrical Ballads,*
from such a current as this that the great Preface is alone powerful. For the
definition of poetry therein given both recognizes the importance of emotion
and modifies it. That a true poet must have "thought long and deeply," must
have developed "habits of meditation" and "habits of mind," and must allow "influxes of feelings" to be "modified and directed" by thoughts is not
carefully enough considered by those who diagnose "the spontaneous overflow of powerful feelings" as rank decadence. A Rousseauistic tendency was
present in these earlier moods. But that the disparagings of "our meddling
intellect" are overstatements, not normalcies, that they are modified in the
entirety of his thought, only the Preface, through this early period, can assure
us. His next great exposition of his art, the *Prelude,* expands the conception
of *mind* without inconsistency with the Preface: the "feeling intellect" [XIV,
226], which has been called "hybrid" [Cerf, *op. cit.,* 627], is but the essence of
those "thoughts, which are indeed the representatives of all our past feelings."

The *Appendix on Poetic Diction* (which was not included in the edition
of 1800) and the statements of the body of the Preface on the same subject need not be discussed at length. In setting his friend right on this
matter, Coleridge has left an explanation which makes us very willing
to forget Wordsworth's, except as an intellectual curiosity.

OBSERVATIONS PREFIXED TO "LYRICAL BALLADS"

(1800)

THE first volume of these Poems has already been submitted to general perusal. It was published, as an experiment, which, I hoped, might
be of some use to ascertain, how far, by fitting to metrical arrangement a selection of the real language of men in a state of vivid sensation, that sort of pleasure and that quantity of pleasure may be imparted, which a Poet may rationally endeavour to impart.

I had formed no very inaccurate estimate of the probable effect
of those Poems: I flattered myself that they who should be pleased
with them would read them with more than common pleasure: and,
on the other hand, I was well aware, that by those who should dislike
them, they would be read with more than common dislike. The result has differed from my expectation in this only, that a greater number have been pleased than I ventured to hope I should please.

Several of my Friends are anxious for the success of these Poems,
from a belief, that, if the views with which they were composed were

indeed realized, a class of Poetry would be produced, well adapted to interest mankind permanently, and not unimportant in the quality, and in the multiplicity of its moral relations: and on this account they have advised me to prefix a systematic defence of the theory upon which the Poems were written. But I was unwilling to undertake the task, knowing that on this occasion the Reader would look coldly upon my arguments, since I might be suspected of having been principally influenced by the selfish and foolish hope of *reasoning* him into an approbation of these particular Poems: and I was still more unwilling to undertake the task, because, adequately to display the opinions, and fully to enforce the arguments, would require a space wholly disproportionate to a preface. For, to treat the subject with the clearness and coherence of which it is susceptible, it would be necessary to give a full account of the present state of the public taste in this country, and to determine how far this taste is healthy or depraved; which, again, could not be determined, without pointing out in what manner language and the human mind act and re-act on each other, and without retracing the revolutions, not of literature alone, but likewise of society itself. I have therefore altogether declined to enter regularly upon this defence; yet I am sensible, that there would be something like impropriety in abruptly obtruding upon the Public, without a few words of introduction, Poems so materially different from those upon which general approbation is at present bestowed.

It is supposed, that by the act of writing in verse an Author makes a formal engagement that he will gratify certain known habits of association; that he not only thus apprises the Reader that certain classes of ideas and expressions will be found in his book, but that others will be carefully excluded. This exponent or symbol held forth by metrical language must in different eras of literature have excited very different expectations: for example, in the age of Catullus, Terence, and Lucretius, and that of Statius or Claudian; and in our own country, in the age of Shakespeare and Beaumont and Fletcher, and that of Donne and Cowley, or Dryden, or Pope. I will not take upon me to determine the exact import of the promise which, by the act of writing in verse, an Author in the present day makes to his reader: but it will undoubtedly appear to many persons that I have not fulfilled the terms of an engagement thus voluntarily contracted. They who have been accustomed to the gaudiness and inane phraseology of many modern writers, if they persist in reading this book to its conclusion, will, no doubt, frequently have to struggle with feelings of strangeness and awkwardness: they will look round for poetry, and will be induced to inquire by what species of courtesy these attempts can be permitted to assume that title. I hope therefore the reader will not censure me for attempting to state what I have proposed to myself to perform; and also (as far as the limits of a preface will permit) to explain some of the chief reasons which have determined me in the choice of my purpose: that at least he may be spared any unpleasant feeling of disappointment, and that I myself may be protected from one of the most dishonourable accusations which can be brought against an Author; namely, that of an indolence which prevents him from endeavouring to ascertain what is his duty, or, when his duty is ascertained, prevents him from performing it.

The principal object, then, proposed in these Poems was to choose incidents and situations from common life, and to relate or describe them, throughout, as far as was possible in a selection of language really used by men, and, at the same time, to throw over them a certain colouring of imagination, whereby ordinary things should be presented to the mind in an unusual aspect; and, further, and above all, to make these incidents and situations interesting by tracing in them, truly though not ostentatiously, the primary laws of our nature: chiefly, as far as regards the manner in which we associate ideas in a state of excitement. Humble and rustic life was generally chosen, because, in that condition, the essential passions of the heart find a better soil in which they can attain their maturity, are less under restraint, and speak a plainer and more emphatic language; because in that condition of life our elementary feelings coexist in a state of greater simplicity, and, consequently, may be more accurately contemplated, and more forcibly communicated; because the manners of rural life germinate from those elementary feelings, and, from the necessary character of rural occupations, are more easily comprehended, and are more durable; and, lastly, because in that condition the passions of men are incorporated with the beautiful and permanent forms of nature. The language, too, of these men has been adopted (purified indeed from what appear to be its real defects, from all lasting and rational causes of dislike or disgust) because such men hourly communicate with the best objects from which the best part of language is originally derived; and because, from their rank in society and the sameness and narrow circle of their intercourse, being less under the influence of social vanity, they convey their feelings and notions in simple and unelaborated expressions. Accordingly, such a language, arising out of repeated experience and regular feelings, is a more permanent, and a far more philosophical language, than that which is frequently substituted for it by Poets, who think that they are conferring honour upon themselves and their art, in proportion as they separate themselves from the sympathies of men, and indulge in arbitrary and capricious habits of expression, in order to furnish food for fickle tastes, and fickle appetites, of their own creation.[1]

I cannot, however, be insensible to the present outcry against the triviality and meanness, both of thought and language, which some of my contemporaries have occasionally introduced into their metrical compositions; and I acknowledge that this defect, where it exists, is more dishonourable to the Writer's own character than false refinement or arbitrary innovation, though I should contend at the same time, that it is far less pernicious in the sum of its consequences. From such verses the Poems in these volumes will be found distinguished at least by one mark of difference, that each of them has a worthy *purpose*. Not that I always began to write with a distinct purpose formerly conceived; but habits of meditation have, I trust, so prompted and regulated my feelings, that my descriptions of such objects as strongly excite those feelings, will be found to carry along with them a *purpose*. If this opinion be erroneous, I can have little right to the name of a Poet. For all good poetry is the spontaneous overflow of powerful feelings: and though this be true, Poems to which any value can be attached were never produced on any variety of subjects but by a man who, being possessed of more than usual organic sensibility, had also thought long and deeply. For our continued influxes of feeling are modified and directed by our thoughts, which are indeed the representatives of all our past feelings; and, as by contemplating the relation of these general representatives to each other, we discover what is really important to men, so, by the repetition and continuance of this act, our feelings will be connected with important subjects, till at length, if we be originally possessed of much sensibility, such habits of mind will be produced, that, by obeying blindly and mechanically the impulses of those habits, we shall describe objects, and utter sentiments, of such a nature, and in such connexion with each other, that the understanding of the Reader must

[1] It is worth while here to observe, that the affecting parts of Chaucer are almost always expressed in language pure and universally intelligible even to this day.

necessarily be in some degree enlightened, and his affections strengthened and purified.

It has been said that each of these poems has a purpose. Another circumstance must be mentioned which distinguishes these Poems from the popular Poetry of the day; it is this, that the feeling therein developed gives importance to the action and situation, and not the action and situation to the feeling.

A sense of false modesty shall not prevent me from asserting, that the Reader's attention is pointed to this mark of distinction, far less for the sake of these particular Poems than from the general importance of the subject. The subject is indeed important! For the human mind is capable of being excited without the application of gross and violent stimulants; and he must have a very faint perception of its beauty and dignity who does not know this, and who does not further know, that one being is elevated above another, in proportion as he possesses this capability. It has therefore appeared to me, that to endeavour to produce or enlarge this capability is one of the best services in which, at any period, a Writer can be engaged; but this service, excellent at all times, is especially so at the present day. For a multitude of causes, unknown to former times, are now acting with a combined force to blunt the discriminating powers of the mind, and, unfitting it for all voluntary exertion, to reduce it to a state of almost savage torpor. The most effective of these causes are the great national events which are daily taking place, and the increasing accumulation of men in cities, where the uniformity of their occupations produces a craving for extraordinary incident, which the rapid communication of intelligence hourly gratifies. To this tendency of life and manners the literature and theatrical exhibitions of the country have conformed themselves. The invaluable works of our elder writers, I had almost said the works of Shakespeare and Milton, are driven into neglect by frantic novels, sickly and stupid German Tragedies, and deluges of idle and extravagant stories in verse.—When I think upon this degrading thirst after outrageous stimulation, I am almost ashamed to have spoken of the feeble endeavour made in these volumes to counteract it; and, reflecting upon the magnitude of the general evil, I should be oppressed with no dishonourable melancholy, had I not a deep impression of certain inherent and indestructible qualities of the human mind, and likewise of certain powers in the great and permanent objects that act upon it, which are equally inherent and indestructible; and were there not added to this impression a belief, that the time is approaching when the evil will be systematically opposed, by men of greater powers, and with far more distinguished success.

Having dwelt thus long on the subjects and aim of these Poems, I shall request the Reader's permission to apprise him of a few circumstances relating to their *style,* in order, among other reasons, that he may not censure me for not having performed what I never attempted. The Reader will find that personifications of abstract ideas rarely occur in these volumes; and are utterly rejected, as an ordinary device to elevate the style, and raise it above prose. My purpose was to imitate, and, as far as possible, to adopt the very language of men; and assuredly such personifications do not make any natural or regular part of that language. They are, indeed, a figure of speech occasionally prompted by passion, and I have made use of them as such; but have endeavoured utterly to reject them as a mechanical device of style, or as a family language which Writers in metre seem to lay claim to by prescription. I have wished to keep the Reader in the company of flesh and blood, persuaded that by so doing I shall interest him. Others who pursue a different track will interest him likewise; I do not interfere with their claim, but wish to prefer a claim of my own. There will also be found in these volumes little of what is usually called poetic diction; as much pains has been taken to avoid it as is ordinarily taken to produce it; this has been done for the reason already alleged, to bring my language near to the language of men; and further, because the pleasure which I have proposed to myself to impart, is of a kind very different from that which is supposed by many persons to be the proper object of poetry. Without being culpably particular, I do not know how to give my Reader a more exact notion of the style in which it was my wish and intention to write, than by informing him that I have at all times endeavoured to look steadily at my subject; consequently, there is I hope in these Poems little falsehood of description, and my ideas are expressed in language fitted to their respective importance. Something must have been gained by this practice, as it is friendly to one property of all good poetry, namely, good sense: but it has necessarily cut me off from a large portion of phrases and figures of speech which from father to son have long been regarded as the common inheritance of Poets. I have also thought it expedient to restrict myself still further, having abstained from the use of many expressions, in themselves proper and beautiful, but which have been foolishly repeated by bad Poets, till such feelings of disgust are connected with them as it is scarcely possible by any art of association to overpower.

If in a poem there should be found a series of lines, or even a single line, in which the language, though naturally arranged, and according to the strict laws of metre, does not differ from that of prose, there is a numerous class of critics, who, when they stumble upon these prosaisms, as they call them, imagine that they have made a notable discovery, and exult over the Poet as over a man ignorant of his own profession. Now these men would establish a canon of criticism which the Reader will conclude he must utterly reject, if he wishes to be pleased with these volumes. And it would be a most easy task to prove to him, that not only the language of a large portion of every good poem, even of the most elevated character, must necessarily, except with reference to the metre, in no respect differ from that of good prose, but likewise that some of the most interesting parts of the best poems will be found to be strictly the language of prose when prose is well written. The truth of this assertion might be demonstrated by innumerable passages from almost all the poetical writings, even of Milton himself. To illustrate the subject in a general manner, I will here adduce a short composition of Gray, who was at the head of those who, by their reasonings, have attempted to widen the space of separation betwixt Prose and Metrical composition, and was more than any other man curiously elaborate in the structure of his own poetic diction.

> In vain to me the smiling mornings shine,
> And reddening Phœbus lifts his golden fire:
> The birds in vain their amorous descant join,
> Or cheerful fields resume their green attire.
> These ears, alas! for other notes repine;
> *A different object do these eyes require;*
> *My lonely anguish melts no heart but mine;*
> *And in my breast the imperfect joys expire;*
> Yet morning smiles the busy race to cheer,
> And new-born pleasure brings to happier men;
> The fields to all their wonted tribute bear;
> To warm their little loves the birds complain,
> *I fruitless mourn to him that cannot hear,*
> *And weep the more because I weep in vain.*

It will easily be perceived, that the only part of this Sonnet which is of any value is the lines printed in Italics; it is equally obvious, that, except in the rhyme, and in the use of the single word "fruitless" for fruitlessly, which is so far a defect, the language of these lines does in no respect differ from that of prose.

By the foregoing quotation it has been shown that language of Prose may yet be well adapted to Poetry; and it was previously asserted, that a large portion of the language of every good poem can in no respect differ from that of good Prose. We will go further. It may be safely affirmed, that there neither is, nor can be, any *essential* difference between the language of prose and metrical composition. We are fond of tracing the resemblance between Poetry and Painting, and, accordingly, we call them Sisters: but where shall we find bonds of connexion sufficiently strict to typify the affinity betwixt metrical and prose composition? They both speak by and to the same organs; the bodies in which both of them are clothed may be said to be of the same substance, their affections are kindred, and almost identical, not necessarily differing even in degree; Poetry [2] sheds no tears "such as Angels weep," but natural and human tears; she can boast of no celestial ichor that distinguishes her vital juices from those of prose; the same human blood circulates through the veins of them both.

If it be affirmed that rhyme and metrical arrangement of themselves constitute a distinction which overturns what has just been said on the strict affinity of metrical language with that of prose, and paves the way for other artificial distinctions which the mind voluntarily admits, I answer that the language of such Poetry as is here recommended is, as far as is possible, a selection of the language really spoken by men; that this selection, wherever it is made with true taste and feeling, will of itself form a distinction far greater than would at first be imagined, and will entirely separate the composition from the vulgarity and meanness of ordinary life; and, if metre be superadded thereto, I believe that a dissimilitude will be produced altogether sufficient for the gratification of a rational mind. What other distinction would we have? Whence is it to come? And where is it to exist? Not, surely, where the Poet speaks through the mouths of his characters: it cannot be necessary here, either for elevation of style, or any of its supposed ornaments: for, if the Poet's subject be judiciously chosen, it will naturally, and upon

[2] I here use the word "Poetry" (though against my own judgement) as opposed to the word Prose, and synonymous with metrical composition. But much confusion has been introduced into criticism by this contradistinction of Poetry and Prose, instead of the more philosophical one of Poetry and Matter of Fact, or Science. The only strict antithesis to Prose is Metre; nor is this, in truth, a *strict* antithesis, because lines and passages of metre so naturally occur in writing prose, that it would be scarcely possible to avoid them, even were it desirable.

fit occasion, lead him to passions the language of which, if selected truly and judiciously, must necessarily be dignified and variegated, and alive with metaphors and figures. I forbear to speak of an incongruity which would shock the intelligent Reader, should the Poet interweave any foreign splendour of his own with that which the passion naturally suggests: it is sufficient to say that such addition is unnecessary. And, surely, it is more probable that those passages, which with propriety abound with metaphors and figures, will have their due effect, if, upon other occasions where the passions are of a milder character, the style also be subdued and temperate.

But, as the pleasure which I hope to give by the Poems now presented to the Reader must depend entirely on just notions upon this subject, and, as it is in itself of high importance to our taste and moral feelings, I cannot content myself with these detached remarks. And if, in what I am about to say, it shall appear to some that my labour is unnecessary, and that I am like a man fighting a battle without enemies, such persons may be reminded, that, whatever be the language outwardly holden by men, a practical faith in the opinions which I am wishing to establish is almost unknown. If my conclusions are admitted, and carried as far as they must be carried if admitted at all, our judgements concerning the works of the greatest Poets both ancient and modern will be far different from what they are at present, both when we praise, and when we censure: and our moral feelings influencing and influenced by these judgements will, I believe, be corrected and purified.

Taking up the subject, then, upon general grounds, let me ask, what is meant by the word Poet? What is a Poet? To whom does he address himself? And what language is to be expected from him?—He is a man speaking to men: a man, it is true, endowed with more lively sensibility, more enthusiasm and tenderness, who has a greater knowledge of human nature, and a more comprehensive soul, than are supposed to be common among mankind; a man pleased with his own passions and volitions, and who rejoices more than other men in the spirit of life that is in him; delighting to contemplate similar volitions and passions as manifested in the goings-on of the Universe, and habitually impelled to create them where he does not find them. To these qualities he has added a disposition to be affected more than other men by absent things as if they were present; an ability of conjuring up in himself passions, which are indeed far from being the same as those produced by real events, yet (especially in those parts of the general sympathy which are pleasing and delightful) do more nearly resemble the passions produced by real events, than anything which, from the motions of their own minds merely, other men are accustomed to feel in themselves:—whence, and from practice, he has acquired a greater readiness and power in expressing what he thinks and feels, and especially those thoughts and feelings which, by his own choice, or from the structure of his own mind, arise in him without immediate external excitement.

But whatever portion of this faculty we may suppose even the greatest Poet to possess, there cannot be a doubt that the language which it will suggest to him, must often, in liveliness and truth, fall short of that which is uttered by men in real life, under the actual pressure of those passions, certain shadows of which the Poet thus produces, or feels to be produced, in himself.

However exalted a notion we would wish to cherish of the character of a Poet, it is obvious, that while he describes and imitates passions, his employment is in some degree mechanical, compared with the freedom and power of real and substantial action and suffering. So that it will be the wish of the Poet to bring his feelings near to those of the persons whose feelings he describes, nay, for short spaces of time, perhaps, to let himself slip into an entire delusion, and even confound and identify his own feelings with theirs; modifying only the language which is thus suggested to him by a consideration that he describes for a particular purpose, that of giving pleasure. Here, then, he will apply the principle of selection which has been already insisted upon. He will depend upon this for removing what would otherwise be painful or disgusting in the passion; he will feel that there is no necessity to trick out or to elevate nature: and, the more industriously he applies this principle, the deeper will be his faith that no words, which *his* fancy or imagination can suggest, will be to be compared with those which are the emanations of reality and truth.

But it may be said by those who do not object to the general spirit of these remarks, that, as it is impossible for the Poet to produce upon all occasions language as exquisitely fitted for the passion as that which the real passion itself suggests, it is proper that he should consider himself as in the situation of a translator, who does not scruple to substitute excellencies of another kind for those which are unattainable by him; and endeavours occasionally to surpass his original, in order to make some amends for the general inferiority to which he feels that he must submit. But this would be to encourage idleness and unmanly despair. Further, it is the language of men who speak of what they do not understand; who talk of Poetry as of a matter of amusement and idle pleasure; who will converse with us as gravely about a *taste* for Poetry, as they express it, as if it were a thing as indifferent as *r* taste for rope-dancing, or Frontiniac or Sherry. Aristotle, I have been told, has said, that Poetry is the most philosophic of all writing: it is so: its object is truth, not individual and local, but general, and operative; not standing upon external testimony, but carried alive into the heart by passion; truth which is its own testimony, which gives competence and confidence to the tribunal to which it appeals, and receives them from the same tribunal. Poetry is the image of man and nature. The obstacles which stand in the way of the fidelity of the Biographer and Historian, and of their consequent utility, are incalculably greater than those which are to be encountered by the Poet who comprehends the dignity of his art. The Poet writes under one restriction only, namely, the necessity of giving immediate pleasure to a human Being possessed of that information which may be expected from him, not as a lawyer, a physician, a mariner, an astronomer, or a natural philosopher, but as a Man. Except this one restriction, there is no object standing between the Poet and the image of things; between this, and the Biographer and Historian, there are a thousand.

Nor let this necessity of producing immediate pleasure be considered as a degradation of the Poet's art. It is far otherwise. It is an acknowledgement of the beauty of the universe, an acknowledgement the more sincere, because not formal, but indirect; it is a task light and easy to him who looks at the world in the spirit of love: further, it is a homage paid to the native and naked dignity of man, to the grand elementary principle of pleasure, by which he knows, and feels, and lives, and moves. We have no sympathy but what is propagated by pleasure: I would not be misunderstood; but wherever we sympathize with pain, it will be found that the sympathy is produced and carried on by subtle combinations with pleasure. We have no knowledge, that is, no general principles drawn from the contemplation of particular facts, but what has been built up by pleasure, and exists in us by pleasure alone. The Man of science, the Chemist and Mathematician, whatever difficulties and disgusts they may have had to struggle with, know and feel this. However painful may be the objects with which the Anatomist's knowledge is connected, he feels that his knowledge is pleasure; and where he has no pleasure he has no knowledge. What then does the Poet? He considers man and the objects that surround him as acting and reacting upon each other, so as to produce an infinite complexity of pain and pleasure; he considers man in his own nature and in his ordinary life as contemplating this with a certain quantity of immediate knowledge, with certain convictions, intuitions, and deductions, which from habit acquire the quality of intuitions; he considers him as looking upon this complex scene of ideas and sensations, and finding everywhere objects that immediately excite in him sympathies which, from the necessities of his nature, are accompanied by an overbalance of enjoyment.

To this knowledge which all men carry about with them, and to these sympathies in which, without any other discipline than that of our daily life, we are fitted to take delight, the Poet principally directs his attention. He considers man and nature as essentially adapted to each other, and the mind of man as naturally the mirror of the fairest and most interesting properties of nature. And thus the Poet, prompted by this feeling of pleasure, which accompanies him through the whole course of his studies, converses with general nature, with affections akin to those, which, through labour and length of time, the Man of science has raised up in himself, by conversing with those particular parts of nature which are the objects of his studies. The knowledge both of the Poet and the Man of science is pleasure; but the knowledge of the one cleaves to us as a necessary part of our existence, our natural and unalienable inheritance; the other is a personal and individual acquisition, slow to come to us, and by no habitual and direct sympathy connecting us with our fellow-beings. The Man of science seeks truth as a remote and unknown benefactor; he cherishes and loves it in his solitude: the Poet singing a song in which all human beings join with him, rejoices in the presence of truth as our visible friend and hourly companion. Poetry is the breath and finer spirit of all knowledge; it is the impassioned expression which is in the countenance of all Science. Emphatically may it be said of the Poet, as Shakespeare hath said of man, "that he looks before and after." He is the rock of defence for human nature; an upholder and preserver, carrying everywhere with him relationship and love. In spite of difference of soil and climate, of language and manners, of laws and customs: in spite of things silently gone out of mind, and things violently destroyed; the Poet binds together by passion and knowledge the vast empire of human society, as it is spread over the whole earth, and over all time. The objects of the Poet's thoughts are everywhere; though the eyes and senses of man are, it is true, his favourite guides, yet he will follow wheresoever he can find an atmosphere of sensation in which to move his wings. Poetry is the first and last of all knowledge—it is as immortal as the heart of man. If the labours of Men of science should ever create any material revolution, direct or indirect, in our condition, and in the impressions which we habitually receive, the Poet will sleep then no more than at present; he will be ready to follow the steps of the Man of science, not only in those general indirect effects, but he will be at his side, carrying sensation into the midst of the objects of the science itself. The remotest discoveries of the Chemist, the Botanist, or Mineralogist, will be as proper objects of the Poet's art as any upon which it can be employed, if the time should ever come when these things shall be familiar to us, and the relations under which they are contemplated by the followers of these respective sciences shall be manifestly and palpably material to us as enjoying and suffering beings. If the time should ever come when what is now called science, thus familiarized to men, shall be ready to put on, as it were, a form of flesh and blood, the Poet will lend his divine spirit to aid the transfiguration, and will welcome the Being thus produced, as a dear and genuine inmate of the household of man.—It is not, then, to be supposed that any one, who holds that sublime notion of Poetry which I have attempted to convey, will break in upon the sanctity and truth of his pictures by transitory and accidental ornaments, and endeavour to excite admiration of himself by arts, the necessity of which must manifestly depend upon the assumed meanness of his subject.

What has been thus far said applies to Poetry in general; but especially to those parts of composition where the Poet speaks through the mouths of his characters; and upon this point it appears to authorize the conclusion that there are few persons of good sense, who would not allow that the dramatic parts of composition are defective, in proportion as they deviate from the real language of nature, and are coloured by a diction of the Poet's own, either peculiar to him as an individual Poet or belonging simply to Poets in general; to a body of men who, from the circumstance of their compositions being in metre, it is expected will employ a particular language.

It is not, then, in the dramatic parts of composition that we look for this distinction of language; but still it may be proper and necessary where the Poet speaks to us in his own person and character. To this I answer by referring the Reader to the description before given of a Poet. Among the qualities there enumerated as principally conducing to form a Poet, is implied nothing differing in kind from other men, but only in degree. The sum of what was said is, that the Poet is chiefly distinguished from other men by a greater promptness to think and feel without immediate external excitement, and a greater power in expressing such thoughts and feelings as are produced in him in that manner. But these passions and thoughts and feelings are the general passions and thoughts and feelings of men. And with what are they connected? Undoubtedly with our moral sentiments and animal sensations, and with the causes which excite these; with the operations of the elements, and the appearances of the visible universe; with storm and sunshine, with the revolutions of the seasons, with cold and heat, with loss of friends and kindred, with injuries and resentments, gratitude and hope, with fear and sorrow. These, and the like, are the sensations and objects which the Poet describes, as they are the sensations of other men, and the objects which interest them. The Poet thinks and feels in the spirit of human passions. How, then, can his language differ in any material degree from that of all other men who feel vividly and see clearly? It might be *proved* that it is impossible. But supposing that this were not the case, the Poet might then be allowed to use a peculiar language when expressing his feelings for his own gratification, or that of men like himself. But Poets do not write for Poets alone, but for men. Unless therefore we are advocates for that admiration which subsists upon ignorance, and that pleasure which arises from hearing what we do not understand, the Poet must descend from this supposed height; and, in order to excite rational sympathy, he must express himself as other men express themselves. To this it may be added, that while he is only selecting from the real language of men, or, which amounts to the same thing, composing accurately in the spirit of such selection, he is treading upon safe ground, and we know what we are to expect from him. Our feelings are the same with respect to metre; for, as it may be proper to remind the Reader, the distinction of metre is regular and uniform, and not, like that which is produced by what is usually called POETIC DICTION, arbitrary, and subject to infinite caprices upon which no calculation whatever can be made. In the one case, the Reader is utterly at the mercy of the Poet, respecting what imagery or diction he may choose to connect with the passion; whereas, in the other, the metre obeys certain laws, to which the Poet and Reader both willingly submit because they are certain, and because no interference is made by them with the passion, but such as the concurring testimony of ages has shown to heighten and improve the pleasure which co-exists with it.

It will now be proper to answer an obvious question, namely, Why, professing these opinions, have I written in verse? To this, in addition to such answer as is included in what has been already said, I reply, in the first place, Because, however I may have restricted myself, there is still left open to me what confessedly constitutes the most valuable object of all writing, whether in prose or verse; the great and universal passions of men, the most general and interesting of their occupations, and the entire world of nature before me—to supply endless combinations of forms and imagery. Now, supposing for a moment that whatever is interesting in these objects may be as vividly described in prose, why should I be condemned for attempting to superadd to such description the charm which, by the consent of all nations, is acknowledged to exist in metrical language? To this, by such as are yet unconvinced, it may be answered that a very small part of the pleasure given by Poetry depends upon the metre, and that it is injudicious to write in metre, unless it be accompanied with the other artificial distinctions of style with which metre is usually accompanied, and that, by such deviation, more will be lost from the shock which will thereby be given to the Reader's associations than will be counterbalanced by any pleasure which he can derive from the general power of numbers. In answer to those who still contend for the necessity of accompanying metre with certain appropriate colours of style in order to the accomplishment of its appropriate end, and who also, in my opinion, greatly underrate the power of metre in itself, it might, perhaps, as far as relates to these Volumes, have been almost sufficient to observe, that poems are extant, written upon more humble subjects, and in a still more naked and simple style, which have continued to give pleasure from generation to generation. Now, if nakedness and simplicity be a defect, the fact here mentioned affords a strong presumption that poems somewhat less naked and simple are capable of affording pleasure at the present day; and, what I wish *chiefly* to attempt, at present, was to justify myself for having written under the impression of this belief.

But various causes might be pointed out why, when the style is manly and the subject of some importance, words metrically arranged will long continue to impart such a pleasure to mankind as he who proves the extent of that pleasure will be desirous to impart. The end of Poetry is to produce excitement in co-existence with an overbalance of pleasure; but, by the supposition, excitement is an unusual and irregular state of the mind; ideas and feelings do not, in that state, succeed each other in accustomed order. If the words, however, by which this excitement is produced be in themselves powerful, or the images and feelings have an undue proportion of pain connected with them, there is some danger that the excitement may be carried beyond its proper bounds. Now the co-presence of something regular, something to which the mind has been accustomed in various moods and in a less excited state, cannot but have great efficacy in tempering and restraining the passion by an inter-texture of ordinary feeling, and of feeling not strictly and necessarily connected with the passion. This is unquestionably true; and hence, though the opinion will at first appear paradoxical, from the tendency of metre to divest language, in a certain degree, of its reality, and thus to throw a sort of half-consciousness of unsubstantial existence over the whole composition, there can be little doubt but that more pathetic situations and sentiments, that is, those which have a greater proportion of pain connected with them, may be endured in metrical composition, especially in rhyme, than in prose. The metre of the old ballads is very artless; yet they contain many passages which would illustrate this opinion; and, I hope, if the following Poems be attentively perused, similar instances will be found in them. This opinion may be further illustrated by appealing to the Reader's own experience of the reluctance with which he comes to the re-perusal of the distressful parts of *Clarissa Harlowe,* or *The Gamester;* while Shakespeare's writings, in the most pathetic scenes, never act upon us, as pathetic, beyond the bounds of pleasure—an effect which, in a much greater degree than might at first be imagined, is to be ascribed to small, but continual and regular impulses of pleasurable surprise from the metrical arrangement.—On the other hand (what it must be allowed will much more frequently happen) if the Poet's words should be incommensurate with the passion, and inadequate to raise the Reader to a height of desirable excitement, then (unless the Poet's choice of his metre has been grossly injudicious), in the feelings of pleasure which the Reader has been accustomed to connect with metre in general, and in the feeling, whether cheerful or melancholy, which he has been accustomed to connect with that particular movement of metre, there will be found something which will greatly contribute to impart passion to the words, and to effect the complex end which the Poet proposes to himself.

If I had undertaken a SYSTEMATIC defence of the theory here maintained, it would have been my duty to develop the various causes upon which the pleasure received from metrical language depends. Among the chief of these causes is to be reckoned a principle which must be well known to those who have made any of the Arts the object of accurate reflection; namely, the pleasure which the mind derives from the perception of similitude in dissimilitude. This principle is the great spring of the activity of our minds, and their chief feeder. From this principle the direction of the sexual appetite, and all the passions connected with it, take their origin: it is the life of our ordinary conversation; and upon the accuracy with which similitude in dissimilitude, and dissimilitude in similitude are perceived, depend our taste and our moral feelings. It would not be a useless employment to apply this principle to the consideration of metre, and to show that metre is hence enabled to afford much pleasure, and to point out in what manner that pleasure is produced. But my limits will not permit me to enter upon this subject, and I must content myself with a general summary.

I have said that poetry is the spontaneous overflow of powerful feelings: it takes its origin from emotion recollected in tranquillity: the emotion is contemplated till, by a species of reaction, the tranquillity gradually disappears, and an emotion, kindred to that which was before the subject of contemplation, is gradually produced, and does itself actually exist in the mind. In this mood successful composition generally begins, and in a mood similar to this it is carried on; but the emotion, of whatever kind, and in whatever degree, from various causes, is qualified by various pleasures, so that in describing any passions whatsoever, which are voluntarily described, the mind will, upon the whole, be in a state of enjoyment. If Nature be thus cautious to preserve in a state of enjoyment a being so employed, the Poet ought to profit by the lesson held forth to him, and ought especially to take care, that, whatever passions he communicates to his Reader, those passions, if his Reader's mind be sound and vigorous, should always be accompanied with an overbalance of pleasure. Now the music of harmonious metrical language, the sense of difficulty overcome, and the blind association of pleasure which has been previously received from works of rhyme or metre of the same or similar construction, an indistinct perception perpetually renewed of language closely resembling that of real life, and yet, in the circumstance of metre, differing from it so widely— all these imperceptibly make up a complex feeling of delight, which is of the most important use in tempering the painful feeling always found intermingled with powerful descriptions of the deeper passions. This effect is always produced in pathetic and impassioned poetry; while, in lighter compositions, the ease and gracefulness with which the Poet manages his numbers are themselves confessedly a principal source of the gratification of the Reader. All that it is *necessary* to say, however, upon this subject, may be effected by affirming, what few persons will deny, that, of two descriptions, either of passions, manners, or characters, each of them equally well executed, the one in prose and the other in verse, the verse will be read a hundred times where the prose is read once.

Having thus explained a few of my reasons for writing in verse, and why I have chosen subjects from common life, and endeavoured to bring my language near to the real language of men, if I have been too minute in pleading my own cause, I have at the same time been treating a subject of general interest; and for this reason a few words shall be added with reference solely to these particular poems, and to some defects which will probably be found in them. I am sensible that my associations must have sometimes been particular instead of general, and that, consequently, giving to things a false importance, I may have sometimes written upon unworthy subjects; but I am less apprehensive on this account, than that my language may frequently have suffered from those arbitrary connexions of feelings and ideas with particular words and phrases, from which no man can altogether protect himself. Hence I have no doubt, that, in some instances, feelings, even of the ludicrous, may be given to my Readers by expressions which appeared to me tender and pathetic. Such faulty expressions, were I convinced they were faulty at present, and that they must necessarily continue to be so, I would willingly take all reasonable pains to correct. But it is dangerous to make these alterations on the simple authority of a few individuals, or even of certain classes of men; for where the understanding of an Author is not convinced, or his feelings altered, this cannot be done without great injury to himself: for his own feelings are his stay and support; and, if he set them aside in one instance, he may be induced to repeat this act till his mind shall lose all confidence in itself, and become utterly debilitated. To this it may be added, that the critic ought never to forget that he is himself exposed to the same errors as the Poet, and, perhaps, in a much greater degree: for there can be no presumption in saying of most readers, that it is not probable they will be so well acquainted with the various stages of meaning through which words have passed, or with the fickleness or stability of the relations of particular ideas to each other; and, above all, since they are so much less interested in the subject, they may decide lightly and carelessly.

Long as the Reader has been detained, I hope he will permit me to caution him against a mode of false criticism which has been applied to Poetry, in which the language closely resembles that of life and nature. Such verses have been triumphed over in parodies, of which Dr. Johnson's stanza is a fair specimen:—

> I put my hat upon my head
> And walked into the Strand,
> And there I met another man
> Whose hat was in his hand.

Immediately under these lines let us place one of the most justly admired stanzas of the "Babes in the Wood."

> These pretty Babes with hand in hand
> Went wandering up and down;
> But never more they saw the Man
> Approaching from the Town.

In both these stanzas the words, and the order of the words, in no respect differ from the most unimpassioned conversation. There are words in both, for example, "the Strand," and "the Town," connected with none but the most familiar ideas; yet the one stanza we admit as admirable, and the other as a fair example of the superlatively contemptible. Whence arises this difference? Not from the metre, not from the language, not from the order of the words; but the *matter* expressed in Dr. Johnson's stanza is contemptible. The proper method of treating trivial and simple verses, to which Dr. Johnson's stanza would be a fair parallelism, is not to say, this is a bad kind of poetry, or, this is not poetry; but, this wants sense; it is neither interesting in itself nor can *lead* to anything interesting; the images neither originate in that sane state of feeling which arises out of thought, nor can excite thought or feeling in the Reader. This is the only sensible manner of dealing with such verses. Why trouble yourself about the species till you have previously decided upon the genus? Why take pains to prove than an ape is not a Newton, when it is self-evident that he is not a man?

One request I must make of my reader, which is, that in judging these Poems he would decide by his own feelings genuinely, and not by reflection upon what will probably be the judgement of others. How common is it to hear a person say, I myself do not object to this style of composition, or this or that expression, but, to such and such classes of people it will appear mean or ludicrous! This mode of criticism, so destructive of all sound unadulterated judgement, is almost universal: let the Reader then abide, independently, by his own feelings, and, if

he finds himself affected, let him not suffer such conjectures to interfere with his pleasure.

If an Author, by any single composition, has impressed us with
respect for his talents, it is useful to consider this as affording a presumption, that on other occasions where we have been displeased, he, nevertheless, may not have written ill or absurdly; and further, to give him
so much credit for this one composition as may induce us to review
what has displeased us, with more care than we should otherwise have
bestowed upon it. This is not only an act of justice, but, in our decisions
upon poetry especially, may conduce, in a high degree, to the improvement of our own taste; for an *accurate* taste in poetry, and in all the
other arts, as Sir Joshua Reynolds has observed, is an *acquired* talent,
which can only be produced by thought and a long continued intercourse with the best models of composition. This is mentioned, not with
so ridiculous a purpose as to prevent the most inexperienced Reader
from judging for himself (I have already said that I wish him to judge
for himself), but merely to temper the rashness of decision, and to
suggest, that, if Poetry be a subject on which much time has not been
bestowed, the judgement may be erroneous; and that, in many cases,
it necessarily will be so.

Nothing would, I know, have so effectually contributed to further
the end which I have in view, as to have shown of what kind the pleasure is, and how that pleasure is produced, which is confessedly produced by metrical composition essentially different from that which
I have here endeavoured to recommend: for the Reader will say that
he has been pleased by such composition; and what more can be done
for him? The power of any art is limited; and he will suspect, that, if
it be proposed to furnish him with new friends, that can be only upon
condition of his abandoning his old friends. Besides, as I have said, the
Reader is himself conscious of the pleasure which he has received from
such composition, composition to which he has peculiarly attached the
endearing name of Poetry; and all men feel an habitual gratitude, and
something of an honourable bigotry, for the objects which have long
continued to please them: we not only wish to be pleased, but to be
pleased in that particular way in which we have been accustomed to
be pleased. There is in these feelings enough to resist a host of arguments; and I should be the less able to combat them successfully, as I
am willing to allow, that, in order entirely to enjoy the Poetry which I
am recommending, it would be necessary to give up much of what is
ordinarily enjoyed. But, would my limits have permitted me to point

out how this pleasure is produced, many obstacles might have been removed, and the Reader assisted in perceiving that the powers of language are not so limited as he may suppose; and that it is possible for poetry to give other enjoyments, of a purer, more lasting, and more exquisite nature. This part of the subject has not been altogether neglected, but it has not been so much my present aim to prove, that the interest excited by some other kinds of poetry is less vivid, and less worthy of the nobler powers of the mind, as to offer reasons for presuming, that if my purpose were fulfilled, a species of poetry would be produced, which is genuine poetry; in its nature well adapted to interest mankind permanently, and likewise important in the multiplicity and quality of its moral relations.

From what has been said, and from a perusal of the Poems, the Reader will be able clearly to perceive the object which I had in view: he will determine how far it has been attained; and, what is a much more important question, whether it be worth attaining: and upon the decision of these two questions will rest my claim to the approbation of the Public.

APPENDIX TO LYRICAL BALLADS

(1802)

PERHAPS, as I have no right to expect that attentive perusal, without which, confined, as I have been, to the narrow limits of a preface, my meaning cannot be thoroughly understood, I am anxious to give an exact notion of the sense in which the phrase poetic diction has been used; and for this purpose, a few words shall here be added, concerning the origin and characteristics of the phraseology, which I have condemned under that name.

The earliest poets of all nations generally wrote from passion excited by real events; they wrote naturally, and as men: feeling powerfully as they did, their language was daring, and figurative. In succeeding times, Poets, and Men ambitious of the fame of Poets, perceiving the influence of such language, and desirous of producing the same effect without being animated by the same passion, set themselves to a mechanical adoption of these figures of speech, and made use of them, sometimes with propriety, but much more frequently applied them to feelings and thoughts with which they had no natural connexion whatsoever. A language was thus insensibly produced, differing materially from the real language of men in *any situation*. The Reader or Hearer of this distorted language found himself in a perturbed and unusual state of mind: when affected by the genuine language of passion he had been in a perturbed and unusual state of mind also: in both cases he was willing that his common judgement and understanding should be laid asleep, and he had no instinctive and infallible perception of the true to make him reject the false; the one served as a passport for the other. The emotion was in both cases delightful, and no wonder if he confounded the one with the other, and believed them both to be produced by the same, or similar causes. Besides, the Poet spake to him in the character of a man to be looked up to, a man of genius and authority. Thus, and from a variety of other causes, this distorted language was received with admiration; and Poets, it is probable, who had before contented themselves for the most part with misapplying only expressions which at first had been dictated by real passion, carried the abuse still further, and introduced phrases composed apparently in the spirit of the original figurative language of passion, yet altogether of their own invention, and characterized by various degrees of wanton deviation from good sense and nature.

It is indeed true, that the language of the earliest Poets was felt to differ materially from ordinary language, because it was the language of extraordinary occasions; but it was really spoken by men, language which the Poet himself had uttered when he had been affected by the events which he described, or which he had heard uttered by those around him. To this language it is probable that metre of some sort or other was early superadded. This separated the genuine language of Poetry still further from common life, so that whoever read or heard the poems of these earliest Poets felt himself moved in a way in which he had not been accustomed to be moved in real life, and by causes manifestly different from those which acted upon him in real life. This was the great temptation to all the corruptions which have followed: under the protection of this feeling succeeding Poets constructed a phraseology which had one thing, it is true, in common with the genuine language of poetry, namely, that it was not heard in ordinary conversation; that it was unusual. But the first Poets, as I have said, spake a language which, though unusual, was still the language of men. This circumstance, however, was disregarded by their successors; they found that they could please by easier means: they became proud of modes of expression which they themselves had invented, and which were uttered only by themselves. In process of time metre became a symbol or promise of this unusual language, and whoever took upon him to write in metre, according as he possessed more or less of true poetic genius, introduced less or more of this adulterated phraseology into his compositions, and the true and the false were inseparately interwoven until, the taste of men becoming gradually perverted, this language was received as a natural language: and at length, by the influence of books upon men, did to a certain degree really become so. Abuses of this kind were imported from one nation to another, and with the progress of refinement this diction became daily more and more corrupt, thrusting out of sight the plain humanities of nature by a motley masquerade of tricks, quaintnesses, hieroglyphics, and enigmas.

It would not be uninteresting to point out the causes of the pleasure given by this extravagant and absurd diction. It depends upon a great variety of causes, but upon none, perhaps, more than its influence in impressing a notion of the peculiarity and exaltation of the Poet's character, and in flattering the Reader's self-love by bringing him nearer to a sympathy with that character; an effect which is accomplished by unsettling ordinary habits of thinking, and thus assisting the Reader to approach to that perturbed and dizzy state of mind in which if he does not find himself, he imagines that he is *balked* of a peculiar enjoyment which poetry can and ought to bestow.

The sonnet quoted from Gray, in the Preface, except the lines printed in italics, consists of little else but this diction, though not of the worst kind; and indeed, if one may be permitted to say so, it is far too common in the best writers both ancient and modern. Perhaps in no way, by positive example could more easily be given a notion of what I mean by the phrase *poetic diction* than by referring to a comparison between the metrical paraphrase which we have of passages in the Old and New Testament, and those passages as they exist in our common Translation. See Pope's *Messiah* throughout; Prior's "Did sweeter sounds adorn my flowing tongue," &c. &c. "Though I speak with the tongues of men and of angels," &c. &c., 1st Corinthians, ch. xiii. By way of immediate example take the following of Dr. Johnson:

> Turn on the prudent Ant thy heedless eyes,
> Observe her labours, Sluggard, and be wise;
> No stern command, no monitory voice,
> Prescribes her duties, or directs her choice;
> Yet, timely provident, she hastes away
> To snatch the blessings of a plenteous day;

When fruitful Summer loads the teeming plain,
She crops the harvest, and she stores the grain.
How long shall sloth usurp thy useless hours,
Unnerve thy vigour, and enchain thy powers?
While artful shades thy downy couch enclose,
And soft solicitation courts repose,
Amidst the drowsy charms of dull delight,
Year chases year with unremitted flight,
Till Want now following, fraudulent and slow,
Shall spring to seize thee, like an ambush'd foe.

From this hubbub of words pass to the original. "Go to the Ant, thou Sluggard, consider her ways, and be wise: which having no guide, overseer, or ruler, provideth her meat in the summer, and gathereth her food in the harvest. How long wilt thou sleep, O Sluggard? when wilt thou arise out of thy sleep? Yet a little sleep, a little slumber, a little folding of the hands to sleep. So shall thy poverty come as one that travelleth, and thy want as an armed man." Proverbs, ch. vi.

One more quotation, and I have done. It is from Cowper's Verses supposed to be written by Alexander Selkirk:

Religion! what treasure untold
Resides in that heavenly word!
More precious than silver and gold,
Or all that this earth can afford.
But the sound of the church-going bell
These valleys and rocks never heard,
Ne'er sighed at the sound of a knell,
Or smiled when a sabbath appeared.
Ye winds, that have made me your sport
Convey to this desolate shore
Some cordial endearing report
Of a land I must visit no more.
My Friends, do they now and then send
A wish or a thought after me?
O tell me I yet have a friend,
Though a friend I am never to see.

This passage is quoted as an instance of three different styles of composition. The first four lines are poorly expressed; some Critics would call the language prosaic; the fact is, it would be bad prose, so bad, that it is scarcely worse in metre. The epithet "church-going" applied to a bell, and that by so chaste a writer as Cowper, is an instance of the strange abuses which Poets have introduced into their language, till they and their Readers take them as matters of course, if they do not single them out expressly as objects of admiration. The two lines "Ne'er sighed at the sound," &c., are, in my opinion, an instance of the language of passion wrested from its proper use, and, from the mere circumstance of the composition being in metre, applied upon an occasion that does not justify such violent expressions; and I should condemn the passage, though perhaps few Readers will agree with me, as vicious poetic diction. The last stanza is throughout admirably expressed: it would be equally good whether in prose or verse, except that the Reader has an exquisite pleasure in seeing such natural language so naturally connected with metre. The beauty of this stanza tempts me to conclude with a principle which ought never to be lost sight of, and which has been my chief guide in all I have said,—namely, that in works of *imagination and sentiment,* for of these only have I been treating, in proportion as ideas and feelings are valuable, whether the composition be in prose or in verse, they require and exact one and the same language. Metre is but adventitious to composition, and the phraseology for which that passport is necessary, even where it may be graceful at all, will be little valued by the judicious.

SAMUEL TAYLOR COLERIDGE

(1772–1834)

COLERIDGE was born in 1772 at Ottery St. Mary, Devonshire. His father, the vicar of the town and master of the grammar school, was known for his kindliness and learning. After his death, in 1781, Samuel was sent to Christ Hospital as a charity student, and here he remained for eight years. Lamb, who knew him there, has left an interesting account in "Recollections of Christ's Hospital," and in one of the *Essays of Elia.* Coleridge entered Jesus College, Cambridge, in 1793, and here he continued the desultory reading which had become his habit, and won renown as a talker. For a cause not definitely known he went to London toward the end of 1793, and presently joined the dragoons. Four months later he had been discharged and was back at Cambridge. He had meanwhile met Southey and become a party to the "Pantisocracy" scheme. In 1794 he left Cambridge without a degree, and the next year married Sarah Fricker, of Bristol. Here he began lecturing, and published in 1796 a volume of *Poems.* He moved soon afterwards to Nether Stowey, and in 1797 Wordsworth and his sister took up their residence at Alfoxden in order to be near him. The two poets had met nearly two years before. There rapidly grew the intimacy between them which has become so famous. *Lyrical Ballads* was published in September, 1798, and in the same month the friends sailed together for the continent. Coleridge had received an annuity from his friends, the Wedgewoods, and was thereby enabled to study for some time in Germany, where his absorption with metaphysics became complete. He returned to England in 1799 and was for a time connected with the *Morning Post.*

His next few years involve many uncompleted schemes, a recognized flagging of his poetical impulse, one extended trip abroad, and an almost constant depression of spirits. In 1811 he gave in London a series of lectures on Shakespeare, and thereafter was better remunerated for his literary contributions. The kindnesses of his friends at all times had kept him from want.

From about the year 1803 he had been habitually addicted to opium. There had been some use of it prior to this time; "Kubla Khan," composed in his remarkable year of 1797, had been written under the influence of an "anodyne." But he was a slave to the drug from 1803 till 1816. In this year he settled in the house of the Gillmans, where he resided until his death. Here he gradually reduced the amount of the drug taken, but whether a complete cure was ever effected cannot be stated. "Christabel," "Kubla Khan," and "The Pains of Sleep" were published in 1816. The

following year appeared *Sibylline Leaves* and the *Biographia Literaria.*
The life at Gillman's was quiet and studious, with the great of the literary
world coming to see the poet-critic-theologian. His later published works
were the *Essay on Church and State* (1820), and his most famous religious
work, *Aids to Reflection* (1825). He gave his last series of lectures in
1818. A trip up the Rhine with the Wordsworths in 1828 and a visit
to Cambridge in 1833 represent almost the only travels of this romantic
figure, who in his early years scarce ever settled anywhere at all. He died
peacefully in the home of the Gillmans in 1834.

The principal posthumous publications were the *Table Talk* (1835) and
Confessions of an Inquiring Spirit (1840). These, with the works above
mentioned, contain the bulk of his important writing, although lectures,
pamphlets, newspaper articles, unfinished notes, scattered through the busy
years of his unresting spirit, make a complete listing impossible in a short
sketch.

In the arrangement of Coleridge selections in this book, the chronological order has not been followed. It seemed best, because of their relation to it, to place the selections from the *Biographia Literaria* next the
Preface of Wordsworth. They present, too, a more likely approach to
Coleridge's critical principles than do the lectures on Shakespeare.

It should not be forgotten that Coleridge dedicated this greatest of his
critical works to his friend, and that his refutations of Wordsworthian
theory are all made in such a spirit of friendship as no other critic has
ever exemplified for us. There is needed no comment on what Coleridge
says about poetic diction: he clarifies and dignifies Wordsworth's own
position before taking issue with it. Indeed, by their sympathy, as by their
comprehensiveness and soundness in judgment, these selections have become classic models as well as classic doctrine; so that one delights to turn
back to them, from any other critical writing whatsoever, and say, "Here
is how criticism should be written."

Coleridge's objections to Wordsworth's theory of rusticity and the ordinary are made on the earliest thesis defined by criticism, truth to nature,
that is, to nature freed from accident, nature in the ideal. Wordsworth's
"low" poems are censurable on exactly the same grounds as the Eighteenth
Century's "high" poems.

The account of the plan for the *Lyrical Ballads* given in Chapter XIV
contains the maxims, if not the theories, of two leading aspects of Romanticism. Most of the Nineteenth Century statements of poetry's function
have owed something to the paragraph which phrased "that willing suspension of disbelief for the moment, which constitutes poetic faith," and
"to give the charm of novelty to things of every day."

The best commentary on the "willing suspension of disbelief" is in the
lectures on Shakespeare; here he generalizes little, but he devotes a great
proportion of his time to the manner in which Shakespeare handles the
supernatural and the unbelievable. Of the character of Ariel he remarks
that "here, what is called poetic faith is required and created, and our

common notions of philosophy give way before it: this feeling may be said to be much stronger than historic faith, since for the exercise of poetic faith the mind is previously prepared" [*Lectures on Shakespeare and Milton,* IX]; and we gain an excellent insight into the meaning of poetic faith from the examination of *The Tempest,* of which this remark quoted is a part.

Coleridge felt that one of his chief contributions to criticism was the distinction which he made between imagination and fancy. His explanations of these terms are never satisfactory. He loses himself in metaphysical abstractions or departs too easily into considerations of specific poems. Two passages in the earlier chapters of the *Biographia* cover the characteristics of these qualities:

"I shall now proceed to the nature and *genesis* of the Imagination; but I must first take leave to notice, that after a more accurate perusal of Mr. Wordsworth's remarks on the Imagination, in his preface to the new edition of his poems, [1815] I find that my conclusions are not so consentient with his as, I confess, I had taken for granted. In an article contributed by me to Mr. Southey's Omniana, *On the soul and its organs of sense,* are the following sentences: 'These (the human faculties) I would arrange under the different senses and powers: as the eye, the ear, the touch, &c; the imitative power, voluntary and automatic; the imagination, or shaping and modifying power; the fancy, or the aggregative and associative power; the understanding, or the regulative, substantiating and realizing power; the speculative reason, *vis theoretica et scientifica,* [theorizing and scientific energy] or the power by which we produce or aim to produce unity, necessity, and universality in all our knowledge by means of principles *a priori;* the will, or practical reason; the faculty of choice (*Germanice,* Willkühr) and (distinct both from the moral will and the choice,) the *sensation* of volition, which I have found reason to include under the head of single and double touch.' [*Biog. Lit.* Chapter XII.]

"The imagination then I consider either as primary, or secondary. The primary Imagination I hold to be the living power and prime agent of all human perception, and as a repetition in the finite mind of the eternal act of creation in the infinite I AM. The secondary Imagination I consider as an echo of the former, co-existing with the conscious will, yet still as identical with the primary in the *kind* of its agency, and differing only in *degree,* and in the *mode* of its operation. It dissolves, diffuses, dissipates, in order to recreate: or where this process is rendered impossible, yet still at all events it struggles to idealize and to unify. It is essentially *vital,* even as all objects (as objects) are essentially fixed and dead.

"FANCY, on the contrary, has no other counters to play with, but fixities and definites. The fancy is indeed no other than a mode of memory emancipated from the order of time and space; while it is blended with, and modified by that empirical phenomenon of the will, which we express by the word Choice. But equally with the ordinary memory the Fancy must receive all its materials ready made from the law of association." [*Biog. Lit.* Chapter XIII.]

The lecture on Shakespeare included in this volume is from the 1818 series. Of the significance of his attitude on Shakespeare there is no better way of learning than by comparing the four critics on him whose statements are included in this volume: Jonson, Dryden, Johnson, and Coleridge. It has been said that the last named "set the sun in heaven;" perhaps the exaggeration bound up in this remark was not in the thought of its author. Coleridge's attitude, indeed, passes the bounds of that exactness and temperance which he so generally observed. We cannot accuse him of inaccuracies, but we have to remember that his feeling for Shakespeare approaches worship, and that the criticisms of Hazlitt and Lamb after him, though less inspired, have on the whole more of the *temper* which has endured. Yet, though it be uncritical to say so, one does better "to err slightly with *Coleridge* than to be exactly right with *Hazlitt* and *Lamb*."

From

BIOGRAPHIA LITERARIA

(1817)

CHAPTER XIV

OCCASION OF THE LYRICAL BALLADS, AND THE OBJECTS ORIGINALLY PROPOSED—PREFACE TO THE SECOND EDITION—THE ENSUING CONTROVERSY, ITS CAUSES AND ACRIMONY—PHILOSOPHIC DEFINITIONS OF A POEM AND POETRY WITH SCHOLIA

DURING the first year that Mr. Wordsworth and I were neighbours, our conversations turned frequently on the two cardinal points of poetry, the power of exciting the sympathy of the reader by a faithful adherence to the truth of nature, and the power of giving the interest of novelty by the modifying colours of imagination. The sudden charm, which accidents of light and shade, which moon-light or sunset diffused over a known and familiar landscape, appeared to represent the practicability of combining both. These are the poetry of nature. The thought suggested itself—(to which of us I do not recollect)—that a series of poems might be composed of two sorts. In the one, the incidents and agents were to be, in part at least, supernatural; and the excellence aimed at was to consist in the interesting of the affections by the dramatic truth of such emotions, as would naturally accompany such situations, supposing them real. And real in this sense they have been to every human being who, from whatever source of delusion, has at any time believed himself under supernatural agency. For the second class, subjects were to be chosen from ordinary life; the characters and incidents were to be such as will be found in every village and its vicinity, where there is a meditative and feeling mind to seek after them, or to notice them, when they present themselves.

In this idea originated the plan of the Lyrical Ballads; in which it was agreed, that my endeavours should be directed to persons and characters supernatural, or at least romantic; yet so as to transfer from our inward nature a human interest and a semblance of truth sufficient to procure for these shadows of imagination that willing suspension of disbelief for the moment, which constitutes poetic faith. Mr. Wordsworth, on the other hand, was to propose to himself as his object, to give the charm of novelty to things of every day, and to excite a feeling analogous to the supernatural, by awakening the mind's attention to the lethargy of custom, and directing it to the loveliness and the wonders of the world before us; an inexhaustible treasure, but for which, in consequence of the film of familiarity and selfish solicitude, we have eyes, yet see not, ears that hear not, and hearts that neither feel nor understand.

With this view I wrote The Ancient Mariner, and was preparing among other poems, The Dark Ladie, and the Christabel, in which I should have more nearly realized my ideal, than I had done in my first attempt. But Mr. Wordsworth's industry had proved so much more successful, and the number of his poems so much greater, that my compositions, instead of forming a balance, appeared rather an interpolation of heterogeneous matter. Mr. Wordsworth added two or three poems written in his own character, in the impassioned, lofty, and sustained diction, which is characteristic of his genius. In this form the Lyrical Ballads were published; and were presented by him, as an experiment, whether subjects, which from their nature rejected the usual ornaments and extra-colloquial style of poems in general, might not be so managed in the language of ordinary life as to produce the pleasurable interest, which it is the peculiar business of poetry to impart. To the second edition he added a preface of considerable length; in which, notwithstanding some passages of apparently a contrary import, he was understood to contend for the extension of this style to poetry of all kinds, and to reject as vicious and indefensible all phrases and forms of speech that were not included in what he (unfortunately, I think, adopting an equivocal expression) called the language of real life. From this preface, prefixed to poems in which it was impossible to deny the presence of original genius, however mistaken its direction might be deemed, arose the whole long-continued controversy. For from the conjunction of perceived power with supposed heresy I explain the inveteracy and in some instances, I grieve to say, the acrimonious passions, with which the controversy has been conducted by the assailants.

Had Mr. Wordsworth's poems been the silly, the childish things, which they were for a long time described as being: had they been really distinguished from the compositions of other poets merely by meanness of language and inanity of thought; had they indeed contained nothing more than what is found in the parodies and pretended imitations of them; they must have sunk at once, a dead weight, into the slough of oblivion, and have dragged the preface along with them. But year after year increased the number of Mr. Wordsworth's admirers. They were found too not in the lower classes of the reading public, but chiefly among young men of strong sensibility and meditative minds; and their admiration (inflamed perhaps in some degree by opposition) was distinguished by its intensity, I might almost say, by its religious fervour. These facts, and the intellectual energy of the author, which was more or less consciously felt, where it was outwardly and even boisterously denied, meeting with sentiments of aversion to his opinions, and of alarm at their consequences, produced an eddy of criticism, which would of itself have borne up the poems by the violence with which it whirled them round and round. With many parts of this preface in the sense attributed to them and which the words undoubtedly seem to authorize, I never concurred; but on the contrary objected to them as erroneous in principle, and as contradictory (in appearance at least) both to other parts of the same preface, and to the author's own practice in the greater part of the poems themselves. Mr. Wordsworth in his recent collection has, I find, degraded this prefatory disquisition to the end of his second volume, to be read or not at the reader's choice. But he has not, as far as I can discover, announced any change in his poetic creed. At all events, considering it as the source of a controversy, in which I have been honoured more than I deserve by the frequent conjunction of my name with his, I think it expedient to declare once for all, in what points I coincide with the opinions supported in that preface, and in what points I altogether differ. But in order to render myself intelligible I must previously, in as few words as possible, explain my views, first, of a Poem; and secondly, of Poetry itself, in kind, and in essence.

The office of philosophical disquisition consists in just distinction; while it is the privilege of the philosopher to preserve himself constantly aware, that distinction is not division. In order to obtain adequate notions of any truth, we must intellectually separate its distinguishable parts; and this is the technical process of philosophy. But having so done, we must then restore them in our conceptions to the unity, in which they actually co-exist; and this is the result of philosophy. A poem contains the same elements as a prose composition; the difference therefore must consist in a different combination of them, in consequence of a different object being proposed. According to the difference of the object will be the difference of the combination. It is possible, that the object may be merely to facilitate the recollection of any given facts or observations by artificial arrangement; and the composition will be a poem, merely because it is distinguished from prose by metre, or by rhyme, or by both conjointly. In this, the lowest sense, a man might attribute the name of a poem to the well-known enumeration of the days in the several months;

> "Thirty days hath September,
> April, June, and November," &c.

and others of the same class and purpose. And as a particular pleasure is found in anticipating the recurrence of sounds and quantities, all compositions that have this charm super-added, whatever be their contents, *may* be entitled poems.

So much for the superficial form. A difference of object and contents supplies an additional ground of distinction. The immediate purpose may be the communication of truths; either of truth absolute and demonstrable, as in works of science; or of facts experienced and recorded, as in history. Pleasure, and that of the highest and most permanent kind, may result from the attainment of the end; but it is not itself the immediate end. In other works the communication of pleasure may be the immediate purpose; and though truth, either moral or intellectual, ought to be the ultimate end, yet this will distinguish the character of the author, not the class to which the work belongs. Blest indeed is that state of society, in which the immediate purpose would be baffled by the perversion of the proper ultimate end; in which no charm of diction or imagery could exempt the BATHYLLUS even of an Anacreon, or the ALEXIS of Virgil, from disgust and aversion!

But the communication of pleasure may be the immediate object of a work not metrically composed; and that object may have been in a high degree attained, as in novels and romances. Would then the mere superaddition of metre, with or without rhyme, entitle these to the name of poems? The answer is, that nothing can permanently please, which does not contain in itself the reason why it is so, and not otherwise. If metre be superadded, all other parts must be made consonant with it. They must be such, as to justify the perpetual and distinct attention to each part, which an exact correspondent recurrence of accent and sound are calculated to excite. The final definition then, so deduced, may be thus worded. A poem is that species of composition, which is opposed to works of science, by proposing for its *immediate* object pleasure, not truth; and from all other species—(having *this* object in common with it)—it is discriminated by proposing to itself such delight from the *whole,* as is compatible with a distinct gratification from each component *part.*

Controversy is not seldom excited in consequence of the disputants attaching each a different meaning to the same word; and in few instances has this been more striking, than in disputes concerning the present subject. If a man chooses to call every composition a poem, which is rhyme, or measure, or both, I must leave his opinion uncontroverted. The distinction is at least competent to characterize the writer's intention. If it were subjoined, that the whole is likewise entertaining or affecting, as a tale, or as a series of interesting reflections, I of course admit this as another fit ingredient of a poem, and an additional merit. But if the definition sought for be that of a *legitimate* poem, I answer it must be one, the parts of which mutually support and explain each other; all in their proportion harmonizing with, and supporting the purpose and known influences of metrical arrangement. The philosophic critics of all ages coincide with the ultimate judgment of all countries, in equally denying the praises of a just poem, on the one hand, to a series of striking lines or distiches, each of which, absorbing the whole attention of the reader to itself, becomes disjoined from its context, and forms a separate whole, instead of a harmonizing part; and on the other hand, to an unsustained composition, from which the reader collects rapidly the general result unattracted by the component parts. The reader should be carried forward, not merely or chiefly by the mechanical impulse of curiosity, or by a restless desire to arrive at the final solution; but by the pleasureable activity of mind excited by the attractions of the journey itself. Like the motion of a serpent, which the Egyptians made the emblem of intellectual power; or like the path of sound through the air;—at every step he pauses and half recedes, and from the retrogressive movement collects the force which again carries him onward. *Præcipitandus est liber spiritus,*[1] says Petronius most happily. The epithet, *liber,* here balances the preceding verb; and it is not easy to conceive more meaning condensed in fewer words.

But if this should be admitted as a satisfactory character of a poem, we have still to seek for a definition of poetry. The writings of Plato, and Jeremy Taylor, and Burnet's Theory of the Earth, furnish undeniable proofs that poetry of the highest kind may exist without metre, and even without the contradistinguishing objects of a poem. The first chapter of Isaiah—(indeed a very large portion of the whole book) —is poetry in the most emphatic sense; yet it would be not less irrational than strange to assert, that pleasure, and not truth was the immediate object of the prophet. In short, whatever specific import we attach to the word, Poetry, there will be found involved in it, as a necessary consequence, that a poem of any length neither can be, nor ought to be, all poetry. Yet if an harmonious whole is to be produced, the remaining parts must be preserved in keeping with the poetry; and this can be no otherwise effected than by such a studied selection and artificial arrangement, as will partake of one, though not a peculiar property of poetry. And this again can be no other than the property of exciting a more continuous and equal attention than the language of prose aims at, whether colloquial or written.

My own conclusions on the nature of poetry, in the strictest use of the word, have been in part anticipated in some of the remarks on the Fancy and Imagination in the early part of this work. What is poetry? —is so nearly the same question with, what is a poet?—that the answer to the one is involved in the solution of the other. For it is a distinction resulting from the poetic genius itself, which sustains and modifies the images, thoughts, and emotions of the poet's own mind.

The poet, described in ideal perfection, brings the whole soul of man into activity, with the subordination of its faculties to each other according to their relative worth and dignity. He diffuses a tone and spirit of unity, that blends, and (as it were) *fuses,* each into each, by that synthetic and magical power, to which I would exclusively appropriate the name of Imagination. This power, first put in action by the will and understanding, and retained under their irremissive, though gentle and unnoticed, control, *laxis effertur habenis,*[2] reveals itself in the bal-

[1] "The free spirit must be brought down."   [2] "Is swept along with reins loose."

ance or reconcilement of opposite or discordant qualities: of sameness,
with difference; of the general with the concrete; the idea with the
image; the individual with the representative; the sense of novelty and
freshness with old and familiar objects; a more than usual state of
emotion with more than usual order; judgment ever awake and steady
self-possession with enthusiasm and feeling profound or vehement;
and while it blends and harmonizes the natural and the artificial, still
subordinates art to nature; the manner to the matter; and our admiration of the poet to our sympathy with the poetry. Doubtless, as Sir John
Davies observes of the soul—(and his words may with slight alteration
be applied, and even more appropriately, to the poetic Imagination)—

> Doubtless this could not be, but that she turns
> Bodies to *spirit* by sublimation strange,
> As fire converts to fire the things it burns,
> As we our food into our nature change.
>
> From their gross matter she abstracts *their* forms,
> And draws a kind of quintessence from things;
> Which to her proper nature she transforms
> To bear them light on her celestial wings.
>
> *Thus* does she, when from *individual states*
> She doth abstract the universal kinds;
> *Which then re-clothed in divers names and fates*
> *Steal access through the senses to our minds.*

Finally, Good Sense is the Body of poetic genius, Fancy its Drapery,
Motion its Life, and Imagination the Soul that is everywhere, and in
each; and forms all into one graceful and intelligent whole.

CHAPTER XVII

EXAMINATION OF THE TENETS PECULIAR TO MR. WORDSWORTH—RUSTIC LIFE
(ABOVE ALL, LOW AND RUSTIC LIFE) ESPECIALLY UNFAVOURABLE TO THE
FORMATION OF A HUMAN DICTION—THE BEST PARTS OF LANGUAGE THE
PRODUCT OF PHILOSOPHERS, NOT OF CLOWNS OR SHEPHERDS—POETRY ES-
SENTIALLY IDEAL AND GENERIC—THE LANGUAGE OF MILTON AS MUCH THE
LANGUAGE OF REAL LIFE, YEA, INCOMPARABLY MORE SO THAN THAT OF
THE COTTAGER

As far then as Mr. Wordsworth in his preface contended, and most ably
contended, for a reformation in our poetic diction, as far as he has

evinced the truth of passion, and the dramatic propriety of those figures and metaphors in the original poets, which, stripped of their justifying reasons, and converted into mere artifices of connection or ornament, constitute the characteristic falsity in the poetic style of the moderns; and as far as he has, with equal acuteness and clearness, pointed out the process by which this change was effected, and the resemblances between that state into which the reader's mind is thrown by the pleasurable confusion of thought from an unaccustomed train of words and images; and that state which is induced by the natural language of impassioned feeling; he undertook a useful task, and deserves all praise, both for the attempt and for the execution. The provocations to this remonstrance in behalf of truth and nature were still of perpetual recurrence before and after the publication of this preface. I cannot likewise but add, that the comparison of such poems of merit, as have been given to the public within the last ten or twelve years, with the majority of those produced previously to the appearance of that preface, leave no doubt on my mind, that Mr. Wordsworth is fully justified in believing his efforts to have been by no means ineffectual. Not only in the verses of those who have professed their admiration of his genius, but even of those who have distinguished themselves by hostility to his theory, and depreciation of his writings, are the impressions of his principles plainly visible. It is possible, that with these principles others may have been blended, which are not equally evident; and some which are unsteady and subvertible from the narrowness or imperfection of their basis. But it is more than possible, that these errors of defect or exaggeration, by kindling and feeding the controversy, may have conduced not only to the wider propagation of the accompanying truths, but that, by their frequent presentation to the mind in an excited state, they may have won for them a more permanent and practical result. A man will borrow a part from his opponent the more easily, if he feels himself justified in continuing to reject a part. While there remain important points in which he can still feel himself in the right, in which he still finds firm footing for continued resistance, he will gradually adopt those opinions, which were the least remote from his own convictions, as not less congruous with his own theory than with that which he reprobates. In like manner with a kind of instinctive prudence, he will abandon by little and little his weakest posts, till at length he seems to forget that they had ever belonged to him, or affects to consider them at most as accidental and "petty annexments," the removal of which leaves the citadel unhurt and unendangered.

My own differences from certain supposed parts of Mr. Wordsworth's theory ground themselves on the assumption, that his words had been rightly interpreted, as purporting that the proper diction for poetry in general consists altogether in a language taken, with due exceptions, from the mouths of men in real life, a language which actually constitutes the natural conversation of men under the influence of natural feelings. My objection is, first, that in any sense this rule is applicable only to certain classes of poetry; secondly, that even to these classes it is not applicable, except in such a sense, as hath never by any one (as far as I know or have read,) been denied or doubted; and lastly, that as far as, and in that degree in which it is practicable, it is yet as a rule useless, if not injurious, and therefore either need not, or ought not to be practised. The poet informs his reader, that he had generally chosen low and rustic life; but not as low and rustic, or in order to repeat that pleasure of doubtful moral effect, which persons of elevated rank and of superior refinement oftentimes derive from a happy imitation of the rude unpolished manners and discourse of their inferiors. For the pleasure so derived may be traced to three exciting causes. The first is the naturalness, in fact, of the things represented. The second is the apparent naturalness of the representation, as raised and qualified by an imperceptible infusion of the author's own knowledge and talent, which infusion does, indeed, constitute it an imitation as distinguished from a mere copy. The third cause may be found in the reader's conscious feeling of his superiority awakened by the contrast presented to him; even as for the same purpose the kings and great barons of yore retained, sometimes actual clowns and fools, but more frequently shrewd and witty fellows in that character. These, however, were not Mr. Wordsworth's objects. *He* chose low and rustic life, "because in that condition the essential passions of the heart find a better soil, in which they can attain their maturity, are less under restraint, and speak a plainer and more emphatic language; because in that condition of life our elementary feelings coexist in a state of greater simplicity, and consequently may be more accurately contemplated, and more forcibly communicated; because the manners of rural life germinate from those elementary feelings; and from the necessary character of rural occupations are more easily comprehended, and are more durable; and lastly, because in that condition the passions of men are incorporated with the beautiful and permanent forms of nature."

Now it is clear to me, that in the most interesting of the poems, in which the author is more or less dramatic, as THE BROTHERS, MICHAEL,

Ruth, The Mad Mother, and others, the persons introduced are by no means taken from low or rustic life in the common acceptation of those words! and it is not less clear, that the sentiments and language, as far as they can be conceived to have been really transferred from the minds and conversation of such persons, are attributable to causes and circumstances not necessarily connected with "their occupations and abode." The thoughts, feelings, language, and manners of the shepherd-farmers in the vales of Cumberland and Westmoreland, as far as they are actually adopted in those poems, may be accounted for from causes, which will and do produce the same results in every state of life, whether in town or country. As the two principal I rank that independence, which raises a man above servitude, or daily toil for the profit of others, yet not above the necessity of industry and a frugal simplicity of domestic life; and the accompanying unambitious, but solid and religious, education, which has rendered few books familiar, but the Bible, and the Liturgy or Hymn book. To this latter cause, indeed, which is so far accidental, that it is the blessing of particular countries and a particular age, not the product of particular places or employments, the poet owes the show of probability, that his personages might really feel, think, and talk with any tolerable resemblance to his representation. It is an excellent remark of Dr. Henry More's, that "a man of confined education, but of good parts, by constant reading of the Bible will naturally form a more winning and commanding rhetoric than those that are learned: the intermixture of tongues and of artificial phrases debasing *their* style."

It is, moreover, to be considered that to the formation of healthy feelings, and a reflecting mind, negations involve impediments not less formidable than sophistication and vicious intermixture. I am convinced, that for the human soul to prosper in rustic life a certain vantage-ground is pre-requisite. It is not every man that is likely to be improved by a country life or by country labours. Education, or original sensibility, or both, must pre-exist, if the changes, forms, and incidents of nature are to prove a sufficient stimulant. And where these are not sufficient, the mind contracts and hardens by want of stimulants: and the man becomes selfish, sensual, gross, and hard-hearted. Let the management of the Poor Laws in Liverpool, Manchester, or Bristol be compared with the ordinary dispensation of the poor rates in agricultural villages, where the farmers are the overseers and guardians of the poor. If my own experience have not been particularly unfortunate, as well as that of the many respectable country clergymen with whom I have conversed on the subject, the result would engender more than scepticism concerning the desirable influences of low and rustic life in and for itself. Whatever may be concluded on the other side, from the stronger local attachments and enterprising spirit of the Swiss, and other mountaineers, applies to a particular mode of pastoral life, under forms of property that permit and beget manners truly republican, not to rustic life in general, or to the absence of artificial cultivation. On the contrary the mountaineers, whose manners have been so often eulogized, are in general better educated and greater readers than men of equal rank elsewhere. But where this is not the case, as among the peasantry of North Wales, the ancient mountains, with all their terrors and all their glories, are pictures to the blind, and music to the deaf.

I should not have entered so much into detail upon this passage, but here seems to be the point, to which all the lines of difference converge as to their source and centre;—I mean, as far as, and in whatever respect, my poetic creed *does* differ from the doctrines promulgated in this preface. I adopt with full faith, the principle of Aristotle, that poetry, as poetry, is essentially ideal, that it avoids and excludes all accident; that its apparent individualities of rank, character, or occupation must be representative of a class; and that the persons of poetry must be clothed with generic attributes, with the common attributes of the class: not with such as one gifted individual might possbily possess, but such as from his situation it is most probable before-hand that he would possess. If my premises are right and my deductions legitimate, it follows that there can be no poetic medium between the swains of Theocritus and those of an imaginary golden age.

The characters of the vicar and the shepherd-mariner in the poem of THE BROTHERS, and that of the shepherd of Green-head Ghyll in the MICHAEL, have all the verisimilitude and representative quality, that the purposes of poetry can require. They are persons of a known and abiding class, and their manners and sentiments the natural product of circumstances common to the class. Take Michael for instance:

> An old man stout of heart, and strong of limb.
> His bodily frame had been from youth to age
> Of an unusual strength: his mind was keen,
> Intense, and frugal, apt for all affairs,
> And in his shepherd's calling he was prompt
> And watchful more than ordinary men.
> Hence he had learned the meaning of all winds,
> Of blasts of every tone; and oftentimes
> When others heeded not, He heard the South
> Make subterraneous music, like the noise

Of bagpipers on distant Highland hills.
The Shepherd, at such warning, of his flock
Bethought him, and he to himself would say,
"The winds are now devising work for me!"
And truly, at all times, the storm, that drives
The traveller to a shelter, summoned him
Up to the mountains: he had been alone
Amid the heart of many thousand mists,
That came to him and left him on the heights.
So lived he, until his eightieth year was past.
And grossly that man errs, who should suppose
That the green valleys, and the streams and rocks,
Were things indifferent to the Shepherd's thoughts.
Fields, where with cheerful spirits he had breathed
The common air; the hills, which he so oft
Had climbed with vigorous steps; which had impressed
So many incidents upon his mind
Of hardship, skill or courage, joy or fear;
Which, like a book, preserved the memory
Of the dumb animals, whom he had saved,
Had fed or sheltered, linking to such acts,
So grateful in themselves, the certainty
Of honourable gain; these fields, these hills
Which were his living Being, even more
Than his own blood—what could they less? had laid
Strong hold on his affections, were to him
A pleasurable feeling of blind love,
The pleasure which there is in life itself.

On the other hand, in the poems which are pitched in a lower key, as the HARRY GILL, and THE IDIOT BOY, the feelings are those of human nature in general; though the poet has judiciously laid the scene in the country, in order to place himself in the vicinity of interesting images, without the necessity of ascribing a sentimental perception of their beauty to the persons of his drama. In THE IDIOT BOY, indeed, the mother's character is not so much the real and native product of a "situation where the essential passions of the heart find a better soil, in which they can attain their maturity and speak a plainer and more emphatic language," as it is an impersonation of an instinct abandoned by judgment. Hence the two following charges seem to me not wholly groundless: at least, they are the only plausible objections, which I have heard to that fine poem. The one is, that the author has not, in the poem itself, taken sufficient care to preclude from the reader's fancy the disgusting images of ordinary morbid idiocy, which yet it was by no means his intention to represent. He has even by the "burr, burr, burr," uncounteracted by any preceding description of the boy's beauty, assisted in recalling them. The other is, that the idiocy of the boy is so evenly balanced by the folly of the mother, as to present to the general reader rather a laughable burlesque on the blindness of anile dotage, than an analytic display of maternal affection in its ordinary workings.

In THE THORN, the poet himself acknowledges in a note the necessity of an introductory poem, in which he should have portrayed the character of the person from whom the words of the poem are supposed to proceed: a superstitious man moderately imaginative, of slow faculties and deep feelings, "a captain of a small trading vessel, for example, who, being past the middle age of life, had retired upon an annuity, or small independent income, to some village or country town of which he was not a native, or in which he had not been accustomed to live. Such men having nothing to do become credulous and talkative from indolence." But in a poem, still more in a lyric poem—and the Nurse in ROMEO AND JULIET alone prevents me from extending the remark even to dramatic poetry, if indeed even the Nurse can be deemed altogether a case in point—it is not possible to imitate truly a dull and garrulous discourser, without repeating the effects of dullness and garrulity. However this may be, I dare assert, that the parts —(and these form the far larger portion of the whole)—which might as well or still better have proceeded from the poet's own imagination, and have been spoken in his own character, are those which have given, and which will continue to give, universal delight; and that the passages exclusively appropriate to the supposed narrator, such as the last couplet of the third stanza;[3] the seven last lines of the tenth;[4] and the

[3] "I've measured it from side to side;
'Tis three feet long, and two feet wide."

[4] "Nay, rack your brain—'tis all in vain,
I'll tell you every thing I know;
But to the Thorn, and to the Pond
Which is a little step beyond,
I wish that you would go:
Perhaps, when you are at the place,
You something of her tale may trace.

I'll give you the best help I can:
Before you up the mountain go,
Up to the dreary mountain-top,
I'll tell you all I know.
'Tis now some two-and-twenty years
Since she (her name is Martha Ray)
Gave, with a maiden's true good will,
Her company to Stephen Hill;
And she was blithe and gay,

And she was happy, happy still
Whene'er she thought of Stephen Hill.

And they had fixed the wedding-day,
The morning that must wed them both
But Stephen to another maid
Had sworn another oath;
And, with this other maid, to church
Unthinking Stephen went—
Poor Martha! on that woeful day
A pang of pitiless dismay
Into her soul was sent;
A fire was kindled in her breast,
Which might not burn itself to rest.

They say, full six months after this,
While yet the summer leaves were green,
She to the mountain-top would go,
And there was often seen,
'Tis said a child was in her womb,
As now to any eye was plain;

five following stanzas, with the exception of the four admirable lines at the commencement of the fourteenth, are felt by many unprejudiced and unsophisticated hearts, as sudden and unpleasant sinkings from the height to which the poet had previously lifted them, and to which he again re-elevates both himself and his reader.

If then I am compelled to doubt the theory, by which the choice of characters was to be directed, not only *a priori,* from grounds of reason, but both from the few instances in which the poet himself need be supposed to have been governed by it, and from the comparative inferiority of those instances; still more must I hesitate in my assent to the sentence which immediately follows the former citation; and which I can neither admit as particular fact, nor as general rule. "The language, too, of these men has been adopted (purified indeed from what appear to be its real defects, from all lasting and rational causes of dislike or disgust) because such men hourly communicate with the best objects from which the best part of language is originally derived; and because, from their rank in society and the sameness and narrow circle of their intercourse, being less under the action of social vanity, they convey their feelings and notions in simple and unelaborated expressions." To this I reply; that a rustic's language, purified from all provincialism and grossness, and so far reconstructed as to be made consistent with the rules of grammar—(which are in essence no other than the laws of universal logic, applied to psychological materials)—will not differ from the language of any other man of common sense, however learned or refined he may be, except as far as the notions, which the rustic has to convey, are fewer and more indiscriminate. This will become still clearer, if we add the consideration—(equally important though less obvious)—that the rustic, from the more imperfect development of his faculties, and from the lower state of their cultivation, aims almost solely to convey insulated facts, either those of his scanty experience or his traditional

She was with child, and she was mad;
Yet often she was sober sad
From her exceeding pain.
Oh me! ten thousand times I'd rather
That he had died, that cruel father!
*   *   *   *   *   *
*   *   *   *   *   *
*   *   *   *   *   *
*   *   *   *   *   *
Last Christmas when they talked of this,
Old Farmer Simpson did maintain,
That in her womb the infant wrought
About its mother's heart, and brought
Her senses back again:

And, when at last her time drew near,
Her looks were calm, her senses clear.

No more I know, I wish I did,
And I would tell it all to you:
For what became of this poor child
There's none that ever knew:
And if a child was born or no,
There's no one that could ever tell;
And if 'twas born alive or dead,
There's no one knows, as I have said:
But some remember well,
That Martha Ray about this time
Would up the mountain often climb."

belief; while the educated man chiefly seeks to discover and express those connections of things, or those relative bearings of fact to fact, from which some more or less general law is deducible. For facts are valuable to a wise man, chiefly as they lead to the discovery of the indwelling law, which is the true being of things, the sole solution of their modes of existence, and in the knowledge of which consists our dignity and our power.

As little can I agree with the assertion, that from the objects with which the rustic hourly communicates the best part of language is formed. For first, if to communicate with an object implies such an acquaintance with it, as renders it capable of being discriminately reflected on, the distinct knowledge of an uneducated rustic would furnish a very scanty vocabulary. The few things and modes of action requisite for his bodily conveniences would alone be individualized; while all the rest of nature would be expressed by a small number of confused general terms. Secondly, I deny that the words and combinations of words derived from the objects, with which the rustic is familiar, whether with distinct or confused knowledge, can be justly said to form the best part of language. It is more than probable, that many classes of the brute creation possess discriminating sounds, by which they can convey to each other notices of such objects as concern their food, shelter, or safety. Yet we hesitate to call the aggregate of such sounds a language, otherwise than metaphorically. The best part of human language, properly so called, is derived from reflection on the acts of the mind itself. It is formed by a voluntary appropriation of fixed symbols to internal acts, to processes and results of imagination, the greater part of which have no place in the consciousness of uneducated man; though in civilized society, by imitation and passive remembrance of what they hear from their religious instructors and other superiors, the most uneducated share in the harvest which they neither sowed, nor reaped. If the history of the phrases in hourly currency among our peasants were traced, a person not previously aware of the fact would be surprised at finding so large a number, which three or four centuries ago were the exclusive property of the universities and the schools; and, at the commencement of the Reformation, had been transferred from the school to the pulpit, and thus gradually passed into common life. The extreme difficulty, and often the impossibility, of finding words for the simplest moral and intellectual processes of the languages of uncivilized tribes has proved perhaps the weightiest obstacle to the progress of our most zealous and adroit missionaries. Yet these tribes are surrounded by the same nature as our peasants are; but in still more impressive forms; and they are, moreover, obliged to particularize many more of them. When, therefore, Mr. Wordsworth adds, "accordingly, such a language"—(meaning, as before, the language of rustic life purified from provincialism)—"arising out of repeated experience and regular feelings, is a more permanent, and a far more philosophical language, than that which is frequently substituted for it by Poets, who think that they are conferring honour upon themselves and their art in proportion as they indulge in arbitrary and capricious habits of expression;" it may be answered, that the language, which he has in view, can be attributed to rustics with no greater right, than the style of Hooker or Bacon to Tom Brown or Sir Roger L'Estrange. Doubtless, if what is peculiar to each were omitted in each, the result must needs be the same. Further, that the poet, who uses an illogical diction, or a style fitted to excite only the low and changeable pleasure of wonder by means of groundless novelty, substitutes a language of folly and vanity, not for that of the rustic, but for that of good sense and natural feeling.

Here let me be permitted to remind the reader, that the positions, which I controvert, are contained in the sentences—"a selection of the real language of men;"—"the language of these men" (that is, men in low and rustic life) "has been adopted; I have proposed to myself to imitate, and, as far as is possible, to adopt the very language of men."

"Between the language of prose and that of metrical composition, there neither is, nor can be, any *essential difference:*" it is against these exclusively that my opposition is directed.

I object, in the very first instance, to an equivocation in the use of the word "real." Every man's language varies, according to the extent of his knowledge, the activity of his faculties, and the depth or quickness of his feelings. Every man's language has, first, its individualities; secondly, the common properties of the class to which he belongs; and thirdly, words and phrases of universal use. The language of Hooker, Bacon, Bishop Taylor, and Burke differs from the common language of the learned class only by the superior number and novelty of the thoughts and relations which they had to convey. The language of Algernon Sidney differs not at all from that, which every well-educated gentleman would wish to write, and (with due allowances for the undeliberateness, and less connected train, of thinking natural and proper to conversation) such as he would wish to talk. Neither one nor the other differ half as much from the general language of cultivated society, as the language of Mr. Wordsworth's homeliest composition differs from that of a common peasant. For "real" therefore, we must substitute ordinary, or *lingua communis*. And this, we have proved, is no more to be found in the phraseology of low and rustic life than in that of any other class. Omit the peculiarities of each and the result of course must be common to all. And assuredly the omissions and changes to be made in the language of rustics, before it could be transferred to any species of poem, except the drama or other professed imitation, are at least as numerous and weighty, as would be required in adapting to the same purpose the ordinary language of tradesmen and manufacturers. Not to mention, that the language so highly extolled by Mr. Wordsworth varies in every county, nay in every village, according to the accidental character of the clergyman, the existence or non-existence of schools; or even, perhaps, as the exciseman, publican, and barber happen to be, or not to be, zealous politicians, and readers of the weekly newspaper *pro bono publico*. Anterior to cultivation the *lingua communis* of every country, as Dante has well observed, exists every where in parts, and no where as a whole.

Neither is the case rendered at all more tenable by the addition of the words, "in a state of excitement." For the nature of a man's words, where he is strongly affected by joy, grief, or anger, must necessarily depend on the number and quality of the general truths, conceptions and images, and of the words expressing them, with which his mind had been previously stored. For the property of passion is not to create; but to set in increased activity. At least, whatever new connections of thoughts or images, or—(which is equally, if not more than equally, the appropriate effect of strong excitement)—whatever generalizations of truth or experience the heat of passion may produce; yet the terms of their conveyance must have pre-existed in his former conversations, and are only collected and crowded together by the unusual stimulation. It is indeed very possible to adopt in a poem the unmeaning repetitions, habitual phrases, and other blank counters, which an unfurnished or confused understanding interposes at short intervals, in order to keep hold of his subject, which is still slipping from him, and to give him time for recollection; or, in mere aid of vacancy, as in the scanty companies of a country stage the same player pops backwards and forwards, in order to prevent the appearance of empty spaces, in the procession of Macbeth, or Henry VIII. But what assistance to the poet, or ornament to the poem, these can supply, I am at a loss to conjecture. Nothing assuredly can differ either in origin or in mode more widely from the apparent tautologies of intense and turbulent feeling, in which the passion is greater and of longer endurance than to be exhausted or satisfied by a single representation of the image or incident exciting it. Such repetitions I admit to be a beauty of the highest kind; as illustrated by Mr. Wordsworth himself from the song of Deborah. *At her feet he bowed, he fell, he lay down: at her feet he bowed, he fell: where he bowed, there he fell down dead.* Judges v. 27.

From

SHAKSPEARE LECTURES

(1818)

SHAKSPEARE, A POET GENERALLY

CLOTHED in radiant armour, and authorized by titles sure and manifold, as a poet, Shakspeare came forward to demand the throne of fame, as the dramatic poet of England. His excellences compelled even his contemporaries to seat him on that throne, although there were giants in those days contending for the same honour. Hereafter I would fain endeavour to make out the title of the English drama as created by, and existing in, Shakspeare, and its right to the supremacy of dramatic excellence in general. But he had shown himself a poet, previously to his appearance as a dramatic poet; and had no Lear, no Othello, no Henry IV., no Twelfth Night ever appeared, we must have admitted that Shakspeare possessed the chief, if not every, requisite of a poet,—deep feeling and exquisite sense of beauty, both as exhibited to the eye in the combinations of form, and to the ear in sweet and appropriate melody; that these feelings were under the command of his own will; that in his very first productions he projected his mind out of his own particular being, and felt, and made others feel, on subjects no way connected with himself, except by force of contemplation and that sublime faculty by which a great mind becomes that, on which it meditates. To this must be added that affectionate love of nature and natural objects, without which no man could have observed so steadily, or painted so truly and passionately, the very minutest beauties of the external world:—

> And when thou hast on foot the purblind hare,
> Mark the poor wretch; to overshoot his troubles,
> How he outruns the wind, and with what care,

He cranks and crosses with a thousand doubles:
The many musits through the which he goes
Are like a labyrinth to amaze his foes.

Sometimes he runs among the flock of sheep,
To make the cunning hounds mistake their smell;
And sometime where earth-delving conies keep,
To stop the loud pursuers in their yell;
And sometime sorteth with a herd of deer:
Danger deviseth shifts, wit waits on fear.

For there his smell with others' being mingled,
The hot scent-snuffing hounds are driven to doubt,
Ceasing their clamorous cry, till they have singled,
With much ado, the cold fault cleanly out,
Then do they spend their mouths; echo replies,
As if another chase were in the skies.

By this poor Wat far off, upon a hill,
Stands on his hinder legs with listening ear,
To hearken if his foes pursue him still:
Anon their loud alarums he doth hear,
And now his grief may be compared well
To one sore-sick, that hears the passing bell.

Then shalt thou see the dew-bedabbled wretch
Turn, and return, indenting with the way:
Each envious briar his weary legs doth scratch,
Each shadow makes him stop, each murmur stay.
For misery is trodden on by many,
And being low, never relieved by any.

                                   Venus and Adonis.

And the preceding description:—

> But lo! from forth a copse that neighbours by,
> A breeding jennet, lusty, young and proud, &c.

is much more admirable, but in parts less fitted for quotation.

Moreover Shakspeare had shown that he possessed fancy, considered
as the faculty of bringing together images dissimilar in the main by some
one point or more of likeness, as in such a passage as this:—

> Full gently now she takes him by the hand,
> A lily prisoned in a jail of snow,
> Or ivory in an alabaster band:
> So white a friend ingirts so white a foe! *Ib.*

And still mounting the intellectual ladder, he had as unequivocally proved the indwelling in his mind of imagination, or the power by which one image or feeling is made to modify many others, and by a sort of fusion to force many into one;—that which afterwards showed itself in such might and energy in Lear, where the deep anguish of a father spreads the feeling of ingratitude and cruelty over the very elements of heaven;—and which, combining many circumstances into one moment of consciousness, tends to produce that ultimate end of all human thought and human feeling, unity, and thereby the reduction of the spirit to its principle and fountain, who is alone truly one. Various are the workings of this the greatest faculty of the human mind, both passionate and tranquil. In its tranquil and purely pleasurable operation, it acts chiefly by creating out of many things, as they would have appeared in the description of an ordinary mind, detailed in unimpassioned succession, a oneness, even as nature, the greatest of poets, acts upon us, when we open our eyes upon an extended prospect. Thus the flight of Adonis in the dusk of the evening:—

> Look! how a bright star shooteth from the sky;
> So glides he in the night from Venus' eye!

How many images and feelings are here brought together without effort and without discord, in the beauty of Adonis, the rapidity of his flight, the yearning, yet hopelessness, of the enamoured gazer, while a shadowy ideal character is thrown over the whole! Or this power acts by impressing the stamp of humanity, and of human feelings, on inanimate or mere natural objects:—

> Lo! here the gentle lark, weary of rest,
> From his moist cabinet mounts up on high,
> And wakes the morning, from whose silver breast
> The sun ariseth in his majesty,
> Who doth the world so gloriously behold,
> The cedar-tops and hills seem burnish'd gold.

Or again, it acts by so carrying on the eye of the reader as to make him almost lose the consciousness of words,—to make him see every thing flashed, as Wordsworth has grandly and appropriately said,—

> *Flashed* upon that inward eye
> Which is the bliss of solitude;—

and this without exciting any painful or laborious attention, without any anatomy of description, (a fault not uncommon in descriptive poetry)—but with the sweetness and easy movement of nature. This energy is an absolute essential of poetry, and of itself would constitute a poet, though not one of the highest class;—it is, however, a most hopeful symptom, and the Venus and Adonis is one continued specimen of it.

In this beautiful poem there is an endless activity of thought in all the possible associations of thought with thought, thought with feeling, or with words, of feelings with feelings, and of words with words.

> Even as the sun, with purple-colour'd face,
> Had ta'en his last leave of the weeping morn,
> Rose-cheek'd Adonis hied him to the chase:
> Hunting he loved, but love he laughed to scorn.
> Sick-thoughted Venus makes amain unto him,
> And like a bold-faced suitor 'gins to woo him.

Remark the humanizing imagery and circumstances of the first two lines, and the activity of thought in the play of words in the fourth line. The whole stanza presents at once the time, the appearance of the morning, and the two persons distinctly characterized, and in six simple verses puts the reader in possession of the whole argument of the poem.

> Over one arm the lusty courser's rein,
> Under the other was the tender boy,
> Who blush'd and pouted in a dull disdain,
> With leaden appetite, unapt to toy,
> She red and hot, as coals of glowing fire,
> He red for shame, but frosty to desire:—

This stanza and the two following afford good instances of that poetic power, which I mentioned above, of making every thing present to the imagination—both the forms, and the passions which modify those forms, either actually, as in the representations of love, or anger, or other human affections; or imaginatively, by the different manner in which inanimate objects, or objects unimpassioned themselves, are caused to be seen by the mind in moments of strong excitement, and according to the kind of the excitement,—whether of jealousy, or rage, or love, in the only appropriate sense of the word, or of the lower impulses of our nature, or finally of the poetic feeling itself. It is, perhaps, chiefly in the power of producing and reproducing the latter that the poet stands distinct.

The subject of the Venus and Adonis is unpleasing; but the poem itself is for that very reason the more illustrative of Shakspeare. There are men who can write passages of deepest pathos and even sublimity on circumstances personal to themselves and stimulative of their own passions; but they are not, therefore, on this account poets. Read that magnificent burst of woman's patriotism and exultation, Deborah's song of victory; it is glorious, but nature is the poet there. It is quite another matter to become all things and yet remain the same,—to make the changeful god be felt in the river, the lion and the flame;—that it is, that is the true imagination. Shakspeare writes in this poem, as if he were of another planet, charming you to gaze on the movements of Venus and Adonis, as you would on the twinkling dances of two vernal butterflies.

Finally, in this poem and the Rape of Lucrece, Shakspeare gave ample proof of his possession of a most profound, energetic, and philosophical mind, without which he might have pleased, but could not have been a great dramatic poet. Chance and the necessity of his genius combined to lead him to the drama his proper province: in his conquest of which we should consider both the difficulties which opposed him, and the advantages by which he was assisted.

SHAKSPEARE'S JUDGMENT EQUAL TO HIS GENIUS

Thus then Shakspeare appears, from his Venus and Adonis and Rape of Lucrece alone, apart from all his great works, to have possessed all the conditions of the true poet. Let me now proceed to destroy, as far as may be in my power, the popular notion that he was a great dramatist by mere instinct, that he grew immortal in his own despite, and sank below men of second or third-rate power, when he attempted aught beside the drama—even as bees construct their cells and manufacture their honey to admirable perfection; but would in vain attempt to build a nest. Now this mode of reconciling a compelled sense of inferiority with a feeling of pride, began in a few pedants, who having read that Sophocles was the great model of tragedy, and Aristotle the infallible dictator of its rules, and finding that the Lear, Hamlet, Othello and other master-pieces were neither in imitation of Sophocles, nor in obedience to Aristotle,—and not having (with one or two exceptions) the courage to affirm, that the delight which their country received from generation to generation, was in defiance of the alterations of circumstances and habits, was wholly groundless,—took upon them, as a happy medium and refuge, to talk of Shakspeare as a sort of beautiful *lusus naturæ*, a delightful monster,—wild, indeed, and without taste or judgment, but like the inspired idiots so much venerated in the East, uttering, amid the strangest follies, the sublimest truths. In nine places out of ten in which I find his awful name mentioned, it is with some epithet of "wild," "irregular," "pure child of nature," &c. If all this be true, we must submit to it; though to a thinking mind it cannot but be painful to find any excellence, merely human, thrown out of all human analogy, and thereby leaving us neither rules for imitation, nor motives to imitate;—but if false, it is a dangerous falsehood;—for it affords a refuge to secret self-conceit,—enables a vain man at once to escape his reader's indignation by general swoln panegyrics, and merely by his *ipse dixit* to treat, as contemptible, what he has not intellect enough to comprehend, or soul to feel, without assigning any reason, or referring his opinion to any demonstrative principle;—thus leaving Shakspeare as a sort of grand Lama, adored indeed, and his very excrements prized as relics, but with no authority or real influence. I grieve that every late voluminous edition of his works would enable me to substantiate the present charge with a variety of facts one tenth of which would of themselves exhaust the time allotted to me. Every critic, who has or has not made a collection of black letter books—in itself a useful and respectable amusement—puts on the seven-league boots of self-opinion, and strides at once from an illustrator into a supreme judge, and blind and deaf, fills his three-ounce phial at the waters of Niagara; and determines positively the greatness of the cataract to be neither more nor less than his three-ounce phial has been able to receive.

I think this a very serious subject. It is my earnest desire—my passionate endeavour,—to enforce at various times and by various arguments and instances the close and reciprocal connexion of just taste with pure morality. Without that acquaintance with the heart of man, or that docility and childlike gladness to be made acquainted with it, which those only can have, who dare look at their own hearts—and that with a steadiness which religion only has the power of reconciling with sincere humility;—without this, and the modesty produced by it, I am deeply convinced that no man, however wide his erudition, however patient his antiquarian researches, can possibly understand, or be worthy of understanding, the writings of Shakspeare.

Assuredly that criticism of Shakspeare will alone be genial which is reverential. The Englishman, who without reverence, a proud and affectionate reverence, can utter the name of William Shakspeare, stands disqualified for the office of critic. He wants one at least of the very senses, the language of which he is to employ, and will discourse, at best, but as a blind man, while the whole harmonious creation of light and shade with all its subtle interchange of deepening and dissolving colours rises in silence to the silent *fiat* of the uprising Apollo. However inferior in ability I may be to some who have followed me, I own I am proud that I was the first in time who publicly demonstrated to the full extent of the position, that the supposed irregularity and extravagances of Shakspeare were the mere dreams of a pedantry that arraigned the eagle because it had not the dimensions of the swan. In all the successive courses of lectures delivered by me, since my first attempt at the Royal Institution, it has been, and it still remains, my object, to prove that in all points from the most important to the most minute, the judgment of Shakspeare is commensurate with his genius,—nay, that his genius reveals itself in his judgment, as in its most exalted form. And the more gladly do I recur to this subject from the clear conviction, that to judge aright, and with distinct consciousness of the grounds of our judgment, concerning the works of Shakspeare, implies the power and the means of judging rightly of all other works of intellect, those of abstract science alone excepted.

It is a painful truth that not only individuals, but even whole nations, are ofttimes so enslaved to the habits of their education and immediate circumstances, as not to judge disinterestedly even on those subjects, the very pleasure arising from which consists in its disinterestedness, namely, on subjects of taste and polite literature. Instead of deciding concerning their own modes and customs by any rule of reason, nothing appears rational, becoming, or beautiful to them, but what coincides with the peculiarities of their education. In this narrow circle, individuals may attain to exquisite discrimination, as the French critics have done in their own literature; but a true critic can no more be such without placing himself on some central point, from which he may command the whole, that is, some general rule, which, founded in reason, or the faculties common to all men, must therefore apply to each,—than an astronomer can explain the movements of the solar system without taking his stand in the sun. And let me remark, that this will not tend to produce despotism, but, on the contrary, true tolerance, in the critic. He will, indeed, require, as the spirit and substance of a work, something true in human nature itself, and independent of all circumstances; but in the mode of applying it, he will estimate genius and judgment according to the felicity with which the imperishable soul of intellect shall have adapted itself to the age, the place, and the existing manners. The error he will expose, lies in reversing this, and holding up the mere circumstances as perpetual to the utter neglect of the power which can alone animate them. For art cannot exist without, or apart from, nature; and what has man of his own to give to his fellow man, but his own thoughts and feelings, and his observations, so far as they are modified by his own thoughts or feelings?

Let me, then, once more submit this question to minds emancipated alike from national, or party, or sectarian prejudice:—Are the plays of Shakspeare works of rude uncultivated genius, in which the splendour of the parts compensates, if aught can compensate, for the barbarous shapelessness and irregularity of the whole?—Or is the form equally admirable with the matter, and the judgment of the great poet, not less deserving our wonder than his genius?—Or, again, to repeat the question in other words:—Is Shakspeare a great dramatic poet on account only of those beauties and excellences which he possesses in common with the ancients, but with diminished claims to our love and honour to the full extent of his differences from them?—Or are these very differences additional proofs of poetic wisdom, at once results and symbols of living power as contrasted with lifeless mechanism—or free and rival originality as contra-distinguished from servile imitation, or, more accurately, a blind copying of effects, instead of a true imitation, of the essential principles?—Imagine not that I am about to oppose genius to rules. No! the comparative value of these rules is the very cause to be tried. The spirit of poetry, like all other living powers, must of necessity circumscribe itself by rules, were it only to unite power with beauty. It must embody in order to reveal itself; but a living body is of necessity an organized one; and what is organization but the connection of parts in and for a whole, so that each part is at once end and means? —This is no discovery of criticism;—it is a necessity of the human mind; and all nations have felt and obeyed it, in the invention of metre, and measured sounds, as the vehicle and *involucrum* of poetry—itself a fellow-growth from the same life,—even as the bark is to the tree!

No work of true genius dares want its appropriate form, neither indeed is there any danger of this. As it must not, so genius cannot, be lawless; for it is even this that constitutes it genius—the power of acting creatively under laws of its own origination. How then comes it that not only single *Zoïli,* but whole nations have combined in unhesitating condemnation of our great dramatist, as a sort of African nature, rich in beautiful monsters—as a wild heath where islands of fertility look the greener from the surrounding waste, where the loveliest plants now shine out among unsightly weeds, and now are choked by their parasitic growth, so intertwined that we cannot disentangle the weed without snapping the flower?—In this statement I have had no reference to the vulgar abuse of Voltaire,[1] save as far as his charges are coincident with the decisions of Shakspeare's own commentators and (so they would tell you) almost idolatrous admirers. The true ground of the mistake lies in the confounding mechanical regularity with organic form. The form is mechanic, when on any given material we impress a pre-determined form, not necessarily arising out of the properties of the material;—as when to a mass of wet clay we give whatever shape we wish it to retain when hardened. The organic form, on the other hand, is innate; it shapes, as it developes, itself from within, and the fulness of its development is one and the same with the perfection of its outward form. Such as the life is, such is the form. Nature, the prime genial artist, inexhaustible in diverse powers, is equally inexhaustible in forms; —each exterior is the physiognomy of the being within,—its true image reflected and thrown out from the concave mirror;—and even such is the appropriate excellence of her chosen poet, of our own Shakspeare,— himself a nature humanized, a genial understanding directing self-consciously a power and an implicit wisdom deeper even than our consciousness.

I greatly dislike beauties and selections in general; but as proof positive of his unrivalled excellence, I should like to try Shakspeare by this criterion. Make out your amplest catalogue of all the human faculties, as reason or the moral law, the will, the feeling of the coincidence of the two (a feeling *sui generis et demonstratio demonstrationum*) called the conscience, the understanding or prudence, wit, fancy, imagination, judgment,—and then of the objects on which these are to be employed, as the beauties, the terrors, and the seeming caprices of nature, the reali-

---

[1] Take a slight specimen of it. Je suis bien loin assurément de justifier en tout la tragédie d'Hamlet: *c'est une pièce grossière et barbare, qui ne serait pas supportée par la plus vile populace de la France et de l'Italie.* Hamlet y devient fou au second acte, et sa maîtresse folle au troisième; le prince tue le père de sa maîtresse, feignant de tuer un rat, et l'héroïne se jette dans la rivière. On fait sa fosse sur le théâtre; des fossoyers disent des *quolibets* dignes d'eux, en tenant dans leurs mains des têtes de morts; le prince Hamlet répond à leurs *grossièretés abominables par des folies non moins dégoûtantes.* Pendant ce temps-là, un des acteurs fait la conquête de la Pologne. *Hamlet, sa mère, et son beau-père boivent ensemble sur le théâtre; on chante à table, on s'y querelle, on se bat, on se tue: on croirait que cet ouvrage est le fruit de l'imagination d'un sauvage ivre.* Dissertation before Semiramis.

ties and the capabilities, that is, the actual and the ideal, of the human mind, conceived as an individual or as a social being, as in innocence or in guilt, in a play-paradise, or in a war-field of temptation;—and then compare with Shakspeare under each of these heads all or any of the writers in prose and verse that have ever lived! Who, that is competent to judge, doubts the result?—And ask your own hearts,—ask your own common sense—to conceive the possibility of this man being—I say not, the drunken savage of that wretched sciolist, whom Frenchmen, to their shame, have honoured before their elder and better worthies,— but the anomalous, the wild, the irregular, genius of our daily criticism! What! are we to have miracles in sport?—Or, I speak reverently, does God choose idiots by whom to convey divine truths to man?

PERCY BYSSHE SHELLEY

(1792–1822)

SHELLEY was born at Field Place, near Horsham, Sussex, the son of Timothy Shelley, M.P., and heir to a baronetcy. After attending two schools, the boy entered Eton at the age of twelve, and in 1810 went up to Oxford. He had been known as "mad Shelley" and "the Atheist" at Eton, and at the end of five months of university life he was expelled for his publication "The Necessity of Atheism." He spent some time in London, where began his acquaintance with Harriet Westbrook, with whom he eloped in August of 1811. The couple did not, during their three years together, reside long anywhere.

In 1813 they were in London, and here their child Ianthe Eliza was born, and Shelley published *Queen Mab*. The next year he met Mary Wollstonecraft Godwin, daughter of the philosopher, and three months later he eloped with her to Switzerland. Returning to England they settled at Bishopgate, near Windsor Forest. With Harriet they seem to have resumed a friendly relationship, which lasted until her suicide, for causes not immediately connected with Shelley, in 1816. The poet and Mary Godwin were subsequently married.

Alastor had been published earlier in this year, which was eventful also in bringing the acquaintance of Lord Byron and Leigh Hunt. In 1818 *The Revolt of Islam* was brought out; Shelley and Mary shortly left for Italy, where the remainder of his life was spent.

In 1819, his year of greatest achievement, he produced *The Cenci* and *Prometheus Unbound*. *The Witch of Atlas* occupied most of 1820, and *Adonais* and *Hellas* followed in 1821. These years were without unusual incident, spent mainly in travel and visits with friends, notably Byron. Shelley was drowned while sailing with a friend near Leghorn in July, 1822.

Shelley's "Defence of Poetry" was first published in 1840, although it had been written nineteen years earlier. Thomas Love Peacock noted [*Memoirs of Shelley*, 208] that "the paper as it now stands is a defence without an attack." Shelley's Defence, in its original draft, was aimed at Peacock himself, and at his wittily ironic, skeptical views expressed in "The Four Ages of Poetry." Much amicable correspondence preceded and followed the publication of Peacock's essay; on March 20, 1821, Shelley wrote to his friend: "I dispatch by this post the first part of an essay intended to consist of three parts, which I design for an antidote to your *Four Ages of Poetry*. You will see that I have taken a more general view of what is poetry than you have, and will perhaps agree with several of my positions, without considering your

553

own touched." Only one part was written, although an outline of the scope of the proposed second part is given at the conclusion of the essay. Ollier's *Miscellany,* for which it was intended, failed; John Hunt prepared the manuscript for *The Liberal* (which also failed before publishing it) and omitted the allusions to Peacock's article, thus altering the Defence from a controversial to a general treatise on poetry. In fact, as H. F. B. Brett-Smith [*The Four Ages of Poetry, etc.,* xx] notes, although the "immediate spur of antagonism" is traceable to Peacock's article, "it exhibits very clearly two influences of deeper and more serious effect. Shelley had long been steeped in the work of Plato, and he studied Sidney's *Apologie* with peculiar care now that he had himself a similar task to perform." Shelley draws heavily upon the *Symposium* and *Ion,* two dialogues which he translated, but he makes effective use of Plato's adverse arguments to defend poetry and poets. This marked use of sources, however, does not keep Shelley's document from being a highly personal confession of poetic faith.

Although Shelley's ethical and philosophical ideas are based largely on intuition and imagination, the essential features of the Defence are clearly set forth. Most of them are the tenets of those contemporaries of Shelley's to whom we commonly refer as the Romanticists. The historical view of literature, the belief in the purity of what is primitive, the de-throning of reason and the exaltation of sensations, are but a few examples. In his earlier work, Shelley had thought of himself as teacher; in the Preface to *The Revolt of Islam* (1818) he wrote: "I have sought to enlist the harmony of metrical language, the ethereal combinations of the fancy, the rapid and subtle transitions of human passions, all those elements which essentially compose a Poem, in the cause of a liberal and comprehensive morality; and in the view of kindling within the bosoms of my readers a virtuous enthusiasm for those doctrines of liberty and justice, that faith and hope in something good, which neither violence nor misrepresentation nor prejudice can ever totally extinguish among mankind." The purpose of poetry was, partially at least, to reform mankind, but men simply did not read his poetic tracts; M. T. Solve [*Shelley: His Theory of Poetry,* 17] finds a key to his setting expression above communication in this: "Shelley's retirement into himself as a result of public neglect and repeated failure to find sympathy for his views is well illustrated in the following lines from Lionel's song in *Rosalind and Helen:*

> I wake to weep,
> And sit through the long day gnawing the core
> Of my bitter heart, and, like a miser, keep,
> Since none in what I feel take pain or pleasure,
> To my own soul its self-consuming treasure."
>
> —775–79.

Yet this advocacy of expression does not deny a moral and utilitarian purpose to art; in a note to *Hellas* (which was written after the Defence) he says: "it is the province of the poet to attach himself to those ideas which exalt and ennoble humanity." Shelley's metaphysic has a shifting ethical basis, a personal quality which is sometimes contradictory, as his "passion to reform the world" was grounded only in his own fancies, and never reasoned out or systematized.

It has ever been the unphilosophical habit of critics to attribute phases of the literary art to particular mental qualities, to trace carefully the dependence, and then to leave the qualities without anything more than a mystical analogy to explain them. So the neo-classicists did with "invention" and "imitation"; so the early Nineteenth Century critics did with "imagination." Shelley follows Coleridge's lead, accepts his use of the term, sets it opposite to reason, and never asks himself what it does. Even its connection with the rational element is explained only by saying that "Reason is to imagination as the instrument to the agent, as the body to the spirit, as the shadow to the substance." Although he speaks at times of "the just boundaries of art" and recognizes that "the source of poetry is native and involuntary, but requires severe labor in its development," there is little question that he preferred to think of the poet's work as inspired. In the Defence, he denies that the finest poetry is produced by labor and study, adding: "The toil and the delay recommended by the critics, can be justly interpreted to mean no more than a careful observation of the inspired moments. . . ." This dependence on inspiration Keats attacked as "self-concentration, selfishness, perhaps," and he advised Shelley to be "more of an artist"; it led Poe to write: "His rhapsodies are but the rough notes, the stenographic memoranda of poems —memoranda which, because they were all-sufficient for his own intelligence, he cared not to be put to the trouble of transcribing in full for mankind."

Shelley followed Plato in the theory that one cannot create poetry unless inspired by madness. Writing to Peacock, he says: "What a wonderful passage there is in the *Phaedrus* [quoted in Introduction to Plato], the beginning, I think, of one of the speeches of Socrates—in praise of poetic madness, and in definition of what poetry is, and how a man becomes a poet. Every man who lives in this age and desires to write poetry, ought . . . to impress himself with this sentence. . . ." This fine frenzy combines naturally with Shelley's Messianic complex; it leads him in criticism and poetry constantly to an idealized ethereal region which has but slight relation with the world of life. Possibly the Defence for this reason explains better than any other critical work the premises of romanticism, its failures and successes, and its heady transcendentalism. For Plato may have written ironically, but in the fine phrase of Robert Browning [*An Essay on Percy Bysshe Shelley*], "Whatever Shelley was, he was with an admirable sincerity. It was not always truth that he thought and spoke; but in the purity of truth he spoke and thought always." That purity was personal and private; but this testament records publicly the impassioned beliefs of a great romantic poet.

A DEFENCE OF POETRY

(1821) (1840)

ACCORDING to one mode of regarding those two classes of mental action, which are called reason and imagination, the former may be considered as mind contemplating the relations borne by one thought to another, however produced, and the latter, as mind acting upon those thoughts so as to colour them with its own light, and composing from them, as from elements, other thoughts, each containing within itself the principle of its own integrity. The one is the τὸ ποιεῖν, or the principle of synthesis, and has for its objects those forms which are common to universal nature and existence itself; the other is the τὸ λογιζειν, or principle of analysis, and its action regards the relations of things simply as relations; considering thoughts, not in their integral unity, but as the algebraical representations which conduct to certain general results. Reason is the enumeration of quantities already known; imagination is the perception of the value of those quantities, both separately and as a whole. Reason respects the differences, and imagination the similitudes of things. Reason is to imagination as the instrument to the agent, as the body to the spirit, as the shadow to the substance.

Poetry, in a general sense, may be defined to be "the expression of the imagination"; and poetry is connate with the origin of man. Man is an instrument over which a series of external and internal impressions are driven, like the alternations of an ever-changing wind over an Æolian lyre, which move it by their motion to ever-changing melody. But there is a principle within the human being, and perhaps within all sentient beings, which acts otherwise than in the lyre, and produces not melody alone, but harmony, by an internal adjustment of the sounds or motions thus excited to the impressions which excite them. It is as if the lyre could accommodate its chords to the motions of that which strikes them, in a determined proportion of sound; even as the musician can accommodate his voice to the sound of the lyre. A child at play by itself will express its delight by its voice and motions: and every inflexion of tone and every gesture will bear exact relation to a corresponding antitype in the pleasurable impressions which awakened it; it will be the reflected image of that impression; and as the lyre trembles and sounds after the wind has died away, so the child seeks, by prolonging in its voice and motions the duration of the effect, to prolong also a consciousness of the cause. In relation to the objects which delight a child, these expressions are, what poetry is to higher objects. The savage (for the savage is to ages what the child is to years) expresses the emotions produced in him by surrounding objects in a similar manner; and language and gesture, together with plastic or pictorial imitation, become the image of the combined effect of those objects, and of his apprehension of them. Man in society, with all his passions and his pleasures, next becomes the object of the passions and pleasures of man; an additional class of emotions produces an augmented treasure of expressions; and language, gesture, and the imitative arts, become at once the representation and the medium, the pencil and the picture, the chisel and the statue, the chord and the harmony. The social sympathies, or those laws from which, as from its elements, society results, begin to develop themselves from the moment that two human beings co-exist; the future is contained within the present, as the plant within the seed; and equality, diversity, unity, contrast, mutual dependence, become the principles alone capable of affording the motives according to which the will of a social being is determined to action, inasmuch as he is social; and constitute pleasure in sensation, virtue in sentiment, beauty in art, truth in reasoning, and love in the intercourse of kind. Hence men, even in the infancy of society, observe a certain order in their words and actions, distinct from that of the objects and the impressions represented by them, all expression being subject to the laws of that from which it proceeds. But let us dismiss those more general considerations which might involve an inquiry into the principles of society itself, and restrict our view to the manner in which the imagination is expressed upon its forms.

In the youth of the world, men dance and sing and imitate natural objects, observing in these actions, as in all others, a certain rhythm or order. And, although all men observe a similar, they observe not the same order, in the motions of the dance, in the melody of the song, in the combinations of language, in the series of their imitations of natural objects. For there is a certain order or rhythm belonging to each of these classes of mimetic representation, from which the hearer and the spectator receive an intenser and purer pleasure than from any other: the sense of an approximation to this order has been called taste by modern writers. Every man in the infancy of art, observes an order which approximates more or less closely to that from which this highest delight results: but the diversity is not sufficiently marked, as that its gradations should be sensible, except in those instances where the predominance of this faculty of approximation to the beautiful (for so we may be permitted to name the relation between this highest pleasure and its cause) is very great. Those in whom it exists in excess are poets, in the most universal sense of the word; and the pleasure resulting from the manner in which they express the influence of society or nature upon their own minds, communicates itself to others, and gathers a sort of reduplication from that community. Their language is vitally metaphorical; that is, it marks the before unapprehended relations of things and perpetuates their apprehension, until the words which represent them, become, through time, signs for portions or classes of thoughts instead of pictures of integral thoughts; and then if no new poets should arise to create afresh the associations which have been thus disorganized, language will be dead to all the nobler purposes of human intercourse. These similitudes or relations are finely said by Lord Bacon to be "the same footsteps of nature impressed upon the various subjects of the world" *—and he considers the faculty which perceives them as the storehouse of axioms common to all knowledge. In the infancy of society every author is necessarily a poet, because language itself is poetry; and to be a poet is to apprehend the true and the beautiful, in a word, the good which exists in the relation, subsisting, first between existence and perception, and secondly between perception and expression. Every original language near to its source is in itself the chaos of a cyclic poem: the copiousness of lexicography and the distinctions of grammar are the works of a later age, and are merely the catalogue and the form of the creations of poetry.

But poets, or those who imagine and express this indestructible order, are not only the authors of language and of music, of the dance, and architecture, and statuary, and painting: they are the institutors of laws, and the founders of civil society, and the inventors of the arts of life, and the teachers, who draw into a certain propinquity with the beautiful and the true, that partial apprehension of the agencies of the invisible world which is called religion. Hence all original religions are allegorical, or susceptible of allegory, and, like Janus, have a double face of false and true. Poets, according to the circumstances of the age and nation in which they appeared, were called, in the earlier epochs of the world, legislators, or prophets: a poet essentially comprises and unites both these characters. For he not only beholds intensely the present as it is, and discovers those laws according to which present things ought to be ordered, but he beholds the future in the present, and his thoughts are the germs of the flower and the fruit of latest time. Not that I assert poets to be prophets in the gross sense of the word, or that they can foretell the form as surely as they foreknow the spirit of events: such is the pretence of superstition, which would make poetry an attribute of prophecy, rather than prophecy an attribute to poetry. A poet participates in the eternal, the infinite, and the one; as far as

* *De Augment. Scient.,* cap. I, lib. iii.

relates to his conceptions, time and place and number are not. The grammatical forms which express the moods of time, and the difference of persons, and the distinction of place, are convertible with respect to the highest poetry without injuring it as poetry; and the choruses of Æschylus, and the Book of Job, and Dante's Paradise, would afford, more than any other writings, examples of this fact, if the limits of this essay did not forbid citation. The creations of sculpture, painting, and music are illustrations still more decisive.

Language, colour, form, and religious and civil habits of action, are all the instruments and materials of poetry; they may be called poetry by that figure of speech which considers the effect as a synonyme of the cause. But poetry in a more restricted sense expresses those arrangements of language, and especially metrical language, which are created by that imperial faculty, whose throne is curtained within the invisible nature of man. And this springs from the nature itself of language, which is a more direct representation of the actions and passions of our internal being, and is susceptible of more various and delicate combinations, than colour, form, or motion, and is more plastic and obedient to the control of that faculty of which it is the creation. For language is arbitrarily produced by the imagination, and has relation to thoughts alone; but all other materials, instruments, and conditions of art have relations among each other, which limit and interpose between conception and expression. The former is as a mirror which reflects, the latter as a cloud which enfeebles, the light of which both are mediums of communication. Hence the fame of sculptors, painters, and musicians, although the intrinsic powers of the great masters of these arts may yield in no degree to that of those who have employed language as the hieroglyphic of their thoughts, has never equalled that of poets in the restricted sense of the term; as two performers of equal skill will produce unequal effects from a guitar and a harp. The fame of legislators and founders of religions, so long as their institutions last, alone seems to exceed that of poets in the restricted sense; but it can scarcely be a question, whether, if we deduct the celebrity which their flattery of the gross opinions of the vulgar usually conciliates, together with that which belonged to them in their higher character of poets, any excess will remain.

We have thus circumscribed the word poetry within the limits of that art which is the most familiar and the most perfect expression of the faculty itself. It is necessary, however, to make the circle still narrower, and to determine the distinction between measured and unmeasured language; for the popular division into prose and verse is inadmissible in accurate philosophy.

Sounds as well as thoughts have relation both between each other and towards that which they represent, and a perception of the order of those relations has always been found connected with a perception of the order of the relations of thoughts. Hence the language of poets has ever affected a certain uniform and harmonious recurrence of sound, without which it were not poetry, and which is scarcely less indispensable to the communication of its influence, than the words themselves, without reference to that peculiar order. Hence the vanity of translation; it were as wise to cast a violet into a crucible that you might discover the formal principle of its colour and odour, as seek to transfuse from one language into another the creations of a poet. The plant must spring again from its seed, or it will bear no flower—and this is the burthen of the curse of Babel.

An observation of the regular mode of the recurrence of harmony in the language of poetical minds, together with its relation to music, produced metre, or a certain system of traditional forms of harmony and language. Yet it is by no means essential that a poet should accommodate his language to this traditional form, so that the harmony, which is its spirit, be observed. The practice is indeed convenient and popular, and to be preferred, especially in such composition as includes much action: but every great poet must inevitably innovate upon the example of his predecessors in the exact structure of his peculiar versification. The distinction between poets and prose writers is a vulgar error. The distinction between philosophers and poets has been anticipated. Plato was essentially a poet—the truth and splendour of his imagery, and the melody of his language, are the most intense that it is possible to conceive. He rejected the measure of the epic, dramatic, and lyrical forms, because he sought to kindle a harmony in thoughts divested of shape and action, and he forebore to invent any regular plan of rhythm which would include, under determinate forms, the varied pauses of his style. Cicero sought to imitate the cadence of his periods, but with little success. Lord Bacon was a poet.* His language has a sweet and majestic rhythm, which satisfies the sense, no less than the almost superhuman wisdom of his philosophy satisfies the intellect; it is a strain which distends, and then bursts the circumference of the reader's mind, and pours itself forth together with it into the universal element with which it

---

* See the *Filum Labyrinthi*, and the *Essay on Death* particularly.

has perpetual sympathy. All the authors of revolutions in opinion are not only necessarily poets as they are inventors, nor even as their words unveil the permanent analogy of things by images which participate in the life of truth; but as their periods are harmonious and rhythmical, and contain in themselves the elements of verse; being the echo of the eternal music. Nor are those supreme poets, who have employed traditional forms of rhythm on account of the form and action of their subjects, less capable of perceiving and teaching the truth of things, than those who have omitted that form. Shakspeare, Dante, and Milton (to confine ourselves to modern writers) are philosophers of the very loftiest power.

A poem is the very image of life expressed in its eternal truth. There is this difference between a story and a poem, that a story is a catalogue of detached facts, which have no other connection than time, place, circumstance, cause and effect; the other is the creation of actions according to the unchangeable forms of human nature, as existing in the mind of the Creator, which is itself the image of all other minds. The one is partial, and applies only to a definite period of time, and a certain combination of events which can never again recur; the other is universal, and contains within itself the germ of a relation to whatever motives or actions have place in the possible varieties of human nature. Time, which destroys the beauty and the use of the story of particular facts, stripped of the poetry which should invest them, augments that of poetry, and for ever develops new and wonderful applications of the eternal truth which it contains. Hence epitomes have been called the moths of just history; they eat out the poetry of it. A story of particular facts is as a mirror which obscures and distorts that which should be beautiful: poetry is a mirror which makes beautiful that which is distorted.

The parts of a composition may be poetical, without the composition as a whole being a poem. A single sentence may be considered as a whole, though it may be found in the midst of a series of unassimilated portions; a single word even may be a spark of inextinguishable thought. And thus all the great historians, Herodotus, Plutarch, Livy, were poets; and although the plan of these writers, especially that of Livy, restrained them from developing this faculty in its highest degree, they made copious and ample amends for their subjection, by filling all the interstices of their subjects with living images.

Having determined what is poetry, and who are poets, let us proceed to estimate its effects upon society.

Poetry is ever accompanied with pleasure: all spirits on which it falls open themselves to receive the wisdom which is mingled with its delight. In the infancy of the world, neither poets themselves nor their auditors are fully aware of the excellence of poetry: for it acts in a divine and unapprehended manner, beyond and above consciousness; and it is reserved for future generations to contemplate and measure the mighty cause and effect in all the strength and splendour of their union. Even in modern times, no living poet ever arrived at the fullness of his fame; the jury which sits in judgment upon a poet, belonging as he does to all time, must be composed of his peers: it must be impanelled by Time from the selectest of the wise of many generations. A poet is a nightingale, who sits in darkness and sings to cheer its own solitude with sweet sounds; his auditors are as men entranced by the melody of an unseen musician, who feel that they are moved and softened, yet know not whence or why. The poems of Homer and his contemporaries were the delight of infant Greece; they were the elements of that social system which is the column upon which all succeeding civilization has reposed. Homer embodied the ideal perfection of his age in human character; nor can we doubt that those who read his verses were awakened to an ambition of becoming like Achilles, Hector, and Ulysses: the truth and beauty of friendship, patriotism, and persevering devotion to an object, were unveiled to the depths in these immortal creations: the sentiments of the auditors must have been refined and enlarged by a sympathy with such great and lovely impersonations, until from admiring they imitated, and from imitation they identified themselves with the objects of their admiration. Nor let it be objected, that these characters are remote from moral perfection, and that they can by no means be considered as edifying patterns for general imitation. Every epoch, under names more or less specious, has deified its peculiar errors; Revenge is the naked idol of the worship of a semi-barbarous age; and Self-deceit is the veiled image of unknown evil, before which luxury and satiety lie prostrate. But a poet considers the vices of his contemporaries the temporary dress in which his creations must be arrayed, and which cover without concealing the eternal proportions of their beauty. An epic or dramatic personage is understood to wear them around his soul, as he may the ancient armour or the modern uniform around his body; whilst it is easy to conceive a dress more graceful than either. The beauty of the internal nature cannot be so far concealed by its accidental vesture, but that the spirit of its form shall communicate itself to the very disguise, and indicate the shape it hides from the manner in which it is worn. A majestic form and graceful motions will express themselves through the most barbarous and tasteless costume. Few poets of the highest class have chosen to exhibit the beauty of their conceptions in its naked truth and splendour; and it is doubtful whether the alloy of costume, habit, etc., be not necessary to temper this planetary music for mortal ears.

The whole objection, however, of the immorality of poetry rests upon a misconception of the manner in which poetry acts to produce the moral improvement of man. Ethical science arranges the elements which poetry has created, and propounds schemes and proposes examples of civil and domestic life: nor is it for want of admirable doctrines that men hate, and despise, and censure, and deceive, and subjugate one another. But poetry acts in another and diviner manner. It awakens and enlarges the mind itself by rendering it the receptacle of a thousand unapprehended combinations of thought. Poetry lifts the veil from the hidden beauty of the world, and makes familiar objects be as if they were not familiar; it reproduces all that it represents, and the impersonations clothed in its Elysian light stand thenceforward in the minds of those who have once contemplated them, as memorials of that gentle and exalted content which extends itself over all thoughts and actions with which it co-exists. The great secret of morals is love; or a going out of our nature, and an identification of ourselves with the beautiful which exists in thought, action, or person, not our own. A man, to be greatly good, must imagine intensely and comprehensively; he must put himself in the place of another and of many others; the pains and pleasures of his species must become his own. The great instrument of moral good is the imagination; and poetry administers to the effect by acting upon the cause. Poetry enlarges the circumference of the imagination by replenishing it with thoughts of ever new delight, which have the power of attracting and assimilating to their own nature all other thoughts, and which form new intervals and interstices whose void for ever craves fresh food. Poetry strengthens the faculty which is the organ of the moral nature of man, in the same manner as exercise strengthens a limb. A poet therefore would do ill to embody his own conceptions of right and wrong, which are usually those of his place and time, in his poetical creations, which participate in neither. By this assumption of the inferior office of interpreting the effect, in which perhaps after all he might acquit himself but imperfectly, he would resign a glory in a participation in the cause. There was little danger that Homer, or any of the eternal poets, should have so far misunderstood themselves as to have abdicated this throne of their widest dominion. Those in whom the poetical faculty, though great, is less intense, as Euripides, Lucan, Tasso, Spenser, have frequently affected a moral aim, and the effect of their poetry is diminished in exact proportion to the degree in which they compel us to advert to this purpose.

Homer and the cyclic poets were followed at a certain interval by the dramatic and lyrical poets of Athens, who flourished contemporaneously with all that is most perfect in the kindred expressions of the poetical faculty; architecture, painting, music, the dance, sculpture, philosophy, and we may add, the forms of civil life. For although the scheme of Athenian society was deformed by many imperfections which the poetry existing in chivalry and Christianity has erased from the habits and institutions of modern Europe; yet never at any other period has so much energy, beauty, and virtue been developed; never was blind strength and stubborn form so disciplined and rendered subject to the will of man, or that will less repugnant to the dictates of the beautiful and the true, as during the century which preceded the death of Socrates. Of no other epoch in the history of our species have we records and fragments stamped so visibly with the image of the divinity in man. But it is poetry alone, in form, in action, or in language, which has rendered this epoch memorable above all others, and the storehouse of examples to everlasting time. For written poetry existed at that epoch simultaneously with the other arts, and it is an idle inquiry to demand which gave and which received the light, which all, as from a common focus, have scattered over the darkest periods of succeeding time. We know no more of cause and effect than a constant conjunction of events: poetry is ever found to co-exist with whatever other arts contribute to the happiness and perfection of man. I appeal to what has already been established to distinguish between the cause and the effect.

It was at the period here adverted to, that the drama had its birth; and however a succeeding writer may have equalled or surpassed those few great specimens of the Athenian drama which have been preserved to us, it is indisputable that the art itself never was understood or practised according to the true philosophy of it, as at Athens. For the Athenians employed language, action, music, painting, the dance, and religious institutions, to produce a common effect in the representation of the highest idealisms of passion and of power; each division in the art was made perfect in its kind by artists of the most consummate skill, and was disciplined into a beautiful proportion and unity one towards the other. On the modern stage a few only of the elements capable of expressing the image of the poet's conception are employed at once. We have tragedy without music and dancing; and music and dancing without the highest impersonations of which they are the fit accompaniment, and both without religion and solemnity. Religious institution has indeed been usually banished from the stage. Our system of divesting the actor's face of a mask, on which the many expressions appropriated to his dramatic character might be moulded into one permanent and unchanging expression, is favourable only to a partial and inharmonious effect; it is fit for nothing but a monologue, where all the attention may be directed to some great master of ideal mimicry. The modern practice of blending comedy with tragedy, though liable to great abuse in point of practice, is undoubtedly an extension of the dramatic circle; but the comedy should be as in *King Lear,* universal, ideal, and sublime. It is perhaps the intervention of this principle which determines the balance in favour of *King Lear* against the *Œdipus Tyrannus* or the *Agamemnon,* or, if you will, the trilogies with which they are connected; unless the intense power of the choral poetry, especially that of the latter, should be considered as restoring the equilibrium. *King Lear,* if it can sustain this comparison, may be judged to be the most perfect specimen of the dramatic art existing in the world; in spite of the narrow conditions to which the poet was subjected by the ignorance of the philosophy of the drama which has prevailed in modern Europe. Calderon, in his religious *Autos,* has attempted to fulfil some of the high conditions of dramatic representation neglected by Shakespeare; such as the establishing a relation between the drama and religion, and the accommodating them to music and dancing; but he omits the observation of conditions still more important, and more is lost than gained by the substitution of the rigidly-defined and ever-repeated idealisms of a distorted superstition for the living impersonations of the truth of human passion.

But I digress.[1]—The connection of scenic exhibitions with the improvement or corruption of the manners of men, has been universally recognized; in other words, the presence or absence of poetry in its most perfect and universal form has been found to be connected with

---

[1] As an example of John Hunt's excisions, it may be useful to give here Shelley's original statement, from Mrs. Shelley's copy: But we digress.—The Author of the Four Ages of Poetry has prudently omitted to dispute on the effect of the Drama upon life and manners. For, if I know the knight by the devise of his shield, I have only to inscribe Philoctetes, or Agamemnon or Othello upon mine to put to flight the giant sophisms which have enchanted him, as the mirror of intolerable light, though on the arm of one of the weakest of the Paladins, could blind and scatter whole armies of Necromancers and pagans. The connection of scenic. . . .

good and evil in conduct or habit. The corruption which has been imputed to the drama as an effect, begins, when the poetry employed in its constitution ends: I appeal to the history of manners whether the periods of the growth of the one and the decline of the other have not corresponded with an exactness equal to any example of moral cause and effect.

The drama at Athens, or wheresoever else it may have approached to its perfection, ever co-existed with the moral and intellectual greatness of the age. The tragedies of the Athenian poets are as mirrors in which the spectator beholds himself, under a thin disguise of circumstance, stript of all but that ideal perfection and energy which every one feels to be the internal type of all that he loves, admires, and would become. The imagination is enlarged by a sympathy with pains and passions so mighty, that they distend in their conception the capacity of that by which they are conceived; the good affections are strengthened by pity, indignation, terror and sorrow; and an exalted calm is prolonged from the satiety of this high exercise of them into the tumult of familiar life: even crime is disarmed of half its horror and all its contagion by being represented as the fatal consequence of the unfathomable agencies of nature; error is thus divested of its wilfulness; men can no longer cherish it as the creation of their choice. In a drama of the highest order there is little food for censure or hatred; it teaches rather self-knowledge and self-respect. Neither the eye nor the mind can see itself, unless reflected upon that which it resembles. The drama, so long as it continues to express poetry, is as a prismatic and many-sided mirror, which collects the brightest rays of human nature and divides and reproduces them from the simplicity of these elementary forms, and touches them with majesty and beauty, and multiplies all that it reflects, and endows it with the power of propagating its like wherever it may fall.

But in periods of the decay of social life, the drama sympathizes with that decay. Tragedy becomes a cold imitation of the form of the great masterpieces of antiquity, divested of all harmonious accompaniment of the kindred arts, and often the very form misunderstood, or a weak attempt to teach certain doctrines, which the writer considers as moral truth; and which are usually no more than specious flatteries of some gross vice or weakness, with which the author, in common with his auditors, are infected. Hence what has been called the classical and domestic drama. Addison's *Cato* is a specimen of the one; and would it were not superfluous to cite examples of the other! To such purposes poetry cannot be made subservient. Poetry is a sword of lightning, ever unsheathed, which consumes the scabbard that would contain it. And thus we observe that all dramatic writings of this nature are un-imaginative in a singular degree; they affect sentiment and passion, which, divested of imagination, are other names for caprice and appetite. The period in our own history of the grossest degradation of the drama is the reign of Charles II, when all forms in which poetry had been accustomed to be expressed became hymns to the triumph of kingly power over liberty and virtue. Milton stood alone illuminating an age unworthy of him. At such periods the calculating principle pervades all the forms of dramatic exhibition, and poetry ceases to be expressed upon them. Comedy loses its ideal universality: wit succeeds to humour; we laugh from self-complacency and triumph, instead of pleasure; malignity, sarcasm, and contempt succeed to sympathetic merriment; we hardly laugh, but we smile. Obscenity, which is ever blasphemy against the divine beauty in life, becomes, from the very veil which it assumes, more active if less disgusting: it is a monster for which the corruption of society for ever brings forth new food, which it devours in secret.

The drama being that form under which a greater number of modes of expression of poetry are susceptible of being combined than any other, the connexion of poetry and social good is more observable in the drama than in whatever other form. And it is indisputable that the highest perfection of human society has ever corresponded with the highest dramatic excellence; and that the corruption or extinction of the drama in a nation where it has once flourished, is a mark of a corruption of manners, and an extinction of the energies which sustain the soul of social life. But, as Machiavelli says of political institutions, that life may be preserved and renewed, if men should arise capable of bringing back the drama to its principles. And this is true with respect to poetry in its most extended sense: all language, institution and form, require not only to be produced but to be sustained: the office and character of a poet participates in the divine nature as regards providence, no less than as regards creation.

Civil war, the spoils of Asia, and the fatal predominance first of the Macedonian, and then of the Roman arms, were so many symbols of the extinction or suspension of the creative faculty in Greece. The bucolic writers, who found patronage under the lettered tyrants of Sicily and Egypt, were the latest representatives of its most glorious reign. Their poetry is intensely melodious; like the odour of the tuberose, it overcomes and sickens the spirit with excess of sweetness; while the poetry of the preceding age was as a meadow-gale of June, which mingles the fragrance of all the flowers of the field, and adds a quickening and harmonizing spirit of its own which endows the sense with a power of sustaining its extreme delight. The bucolic and erotic delicacy in written poetry is correlative with that softness in statuary, music, and the kindred arts, and even in manners and institutions, which distinguished the epoch to which I now refer. Nor is it the poetic faculty itself, or any mis-application of it, to which this want of harmony is to be imputed. An equal sensibility to the influence of the senses and the affections is to be found in the writings of Homer and Sophocles: the former, especially, has clothed sensual and pathetic images with irresistible attractions. Their superiority over these succeeding writers consists in the presence of those thoughts which belong to the inner faculties of our nature, not in the absence of those which are connected with the external: their incomparable perfection consists in a harmony of the union of all. It is not what the erotic poets have, but what they have not, in which their imperfection consists. It is not inasmuch as they were poets, but inasmuch as they were not poets, that they can be considered with any plausibility as connected with the corruption of their age. Had that corruption availed so as to extinguish in them the sensibility to pleasure, passion, and natural scenery, which is imputed to them as an imperfection, the last triumph of evil would have been achieved. For the end of social corruption is to destroy all sensibility to pleasure; and, therefore, it is corruption. It begins at the imagination and the intellect as at the core, and distributes itself thence as a paralysing venom, through the affections into the very appetites, until all become a torpid mass in which hardly sense survives. At the approach of such a period, poetry ever addresses itself to those faculties which are the last to be destroyed, and its voice is heard, like the footsteps of Astræa departing from the world. Poetry ever communicates all the pleasure which men are capable of receiving: it is ever still the light of life; the source of whatever of beautiful or generous or true can have place in an evil time. It will readily be confessed that those among the luxurious citizens of Syracuse and Alexandria, who were delighted with the poems of Theocritus, were less cold, cruel, and sensual than the remnant of their tribe. But corruption must utterly have destroyed the fabric of human society before poetry can ever cease. The sacred links of that chain have never been entirely disjoined,[2] which

[2] See the selection from Plato's *Ion*.

descending through the minds of many men is attached to those great minds, whence as from a magnet the invisible effluence is sent forth, which at once connects, animates, and sustains the life of all. It is the faculty which contains within itself the seeds at once of its own and of social renovation. And let us not circumscribe the effects of the bucolic and erotic poetry within the limits of the sensibility of those to whom it was addressed. They may have perceived the beauty of those immortal compositions, simply as fragments and isolated portions: those who are more finely organized, or, born in a happier age, may recognize them as episodes to that great poem, which all poets, like the co-operating thoughts of one great mind, have built up since the beginning of the world.

The same revolutions within a narrower sphere had place in ancient Rome; but the actions and forms of its social life never seem to have been perfectly saturated with the poetical element. The Romans appear to have considered the Greeks as the selectest treasuries of the selectest forms of manners and of nature, and to have abstained from creating in measured language, sculpture, music, or architecture, anything which might bear a particular relation to their own condition, whilst it should bear a general one to the universal constitution of the world. But we judge from partial evidence, and we judge perhaps partially. Ennius, Varro, Pacuvius, and Accius, all great poets, have been lost. Lucretius is in the highest, and Virgil in a very high sense, a creator. The chosen delicacy of expressions of the latter, are as a mist of light which conceal from us the intense and exceeding truth of his conceptions of nature. Livy is instinct with poetry. Yet Horace, Catullus, Ovid, and generally the other great writers of the Virgilian age, saw man and nature in the mirror of Greece. The institutions also, and the religion of Rome, were less poetical than those of Greece, as the shadow is less vivid than the substance. Hence poetry in Rome seemed to follow, rather than accompany, the perfection of political and domestic society. The true poetry of Rome lived in its institutions; for whatever of beautiful, true, and majestic, they contained, could have sprung only from the faculty which creates the order in which they consist. The life of Camillus, the death of Regulus; the expectation of the senators, in their godlike state, of the victorious Gauls; the refusal of the republic to make peace with Hannibal, after the battle of Cannæ, were not the consequences of a refined calculation of the probable personal advantage to result from such a rhythm and order in the shows of life, to those who were at once the poets and the actors of these immortal dramas. The imagination beholding the beauty of this order, created it out of itself according to its own idea; the consequence was empire, and the reward ever-living fame. These things are not the less poetry, *quia carent vate sacro.*[3] They are the episodes of that cyclic poem written by Time upon the memories of men. The Past, like an inspired rhapsodist, fills the theatre of everlasting generations with their harmony.

At length the ancient system of religion and manners had fulfilled the circle of its revolutions. And the world would have fallen into utter anarchy and darkness, but that there were found poets among the authors of the Christian and chivalric systems of manners and religion, who created forms of opinion and action never before conceived; which, copied into the imaginations of men, became as generals to the bewildered armies of their thoughts. It is foreign to the present purpose to touch upon the evil produced by these systems: except that we protest, on the ground of the principles already established, that no portion of it can be attributed to the poetry they contain.

It is probable that the poetry of Moses, Job, David, Solomon, and Isaiah had produced a great effect upon the mind of Jesus and his disciples. The scattered fragments preserved to us by the biographers of this extraordinary person, are all instinct with the most vivid poetry. But his doctrines seem to have been quickly distorted. At a certain period after the prevalence of a system of opinions founded upon those promulgated by him, the three forms into which Plato had distributed the faculties of mind underwent a sort of apotheosis, and became the object of the worship of the civilized world. Here it is to be confessed that "Light seems to thicken," and

> The crow makes wing to the rooky wood,
> Good things of day begin to droop and drowse,
> And night's black agents to their preys do rouse.[4]

But mark how beautiful an order has sprung from the dust and blood of this fierce chaos! how the world, as from a resurrection, balancing itself on the golden wings of knowledge and of hope, has reassumed its yet unwearied flight into the heaven of time. Listen to the music, unheard by outward ears, which is as a ceaseless and invisible wind, nourishing its everlasting course with strength and swiftness.

The poetry in the doctrines of Jesus Christ, and the mythology and

---

[3] "Because they lack the divine bard." Horace's *Odes*, IV, ix, 28. [4] *Macbeth*, III, ii, 50.

institutions of the Celtic conquerors of the Roman empire, outlived the darkness and the convulsions connected with their growth and victory, and blended themselves in a new fabric of manners and opinion. It is an error to impute the ignorance of the dark ages to the Christian doctrines or the predominance of the Celtic nations.[5] Whatever of evil their agencies may have contained sprang from the extinction of the poetical principle, connected with the progress of despotism and super-stition. Men, from causes too intricate to be here discussed, had become insensible and selfish: their own will had become feeble, and yet they were its slaves, and thence the slaves of the will of others: lust, fear, avarice, cruelty, and fraud, characterized a race amongst whom no one was to be found capable of *creating* in form, language, or institution. The moral anomalies of such a state of society are not justly to be charged upon any class of events immediately connected with them, and those events are most entitled to our approbation which could dis-solve it most expeditiously. It is unfortunate for those who cannot dis-tinguish words from thoughts, that many of these anomalies have been incorporated into our popular religion.

It was not until the eleventh century that the effects of the poetry of the Christian and chivalric systems began to manifest themselves. The principle of equality had been discovered and applied by Plato in his *Republic,* as the theoretical rule of the mode in which the materials of pleasure and of power produced by the common skill and labour of human beings ought to be distributed among them. The limitations of this rule were asserted by him to be determined only by the sensibility of each, or the utility to result to all. Plato, following the doctrines of Timæus and Pythagoras, taught also a moral and intellectual system of doctrine, comprehending at once the past, the present, and the future condition of man. Jesus Christ divulged the sacred and eternal truths contained in these views to mankind, and Christianity, in its abstract purity, became the exoteric expression of the esoteric doctrines of the poetry and wisdom of antiquity. The incorporation of the Celtic nations with the exhausted population of the south, impressed upon it the figure of the poetry existing in their mythology and institutions. The result was a sum of the action and reaction of all the causes included in it; for it may be assumed as a maxim that no nation or religion can super-sede any other without incorporating into itself a portion of that which it supersedes. The abolition of personal and domestic slavery, and the

[5] I. e., Germanic nations.

emancipation of women from a great part of the degrading restraints of antiquity, were among the consequences of these events.

The abolition of personal slavery is the basis of the highest political hope that it can enter into the mind of man to conceive. The freedom of women produced the poetry of sexual love. Love became a religion, the idols of whose worship were ever present. It was as if the statues of Apollo and the Muses had been endowed with life and motion, and had walked forth among their worshippers; so that earth became peopled by the inhabitants of a diviner world. The familiar appearance and proceedings of life became wonderful and heavenly, and a paradise was created as out of the wrecks of Eden. And as this creation itself is poetry, so its creators were poets; and language was the instrument of their art: "Galeotto fù il libro, e chi lo scrisse." [6] The Provençal Trouveurs, or inventors, preceded Petrarch, whose verses are as spells, which unseal the inmost enchanted fountains of the delight which is in the grief of love. It is impossible to feel them without becoming a portion of that beauty which we contemplate: it were superfluous to explain how the gentleness and the elevation of mind connected with these sacred emotions can render men more amiable, more generous and wise, and lift them out of the dull vapours of the little world of self. Dante understood the secret things of love even more than Petrarch. His *Vita Nuova* is an inexhaustible fountain of purity of sentiment and language: it is the idealized history of that period, and those intervals of his life which were dedicated to love. His apotheosis of Beatrice in Paradise, and the gradations of his own love and her loveliness, by which as by steps he feigns himself to have ascended to the throne of the Supreme Cause, is the most glorious imagination of modern poetry. The acutest critics have justly reversed the judgment of the vulgar, and the order of the great acts of the *Divine Drama,* in the measure of the admiration which they accord to the Hell, Purgatory, and Paradise. The latter is a perpetual hymn of everlasting love. Love, which found a worthy poet in Plato alone of all the ancients, has been celebrated by a chorus of the greatest writers of the renovated world; and the music has penetrated the caverns of society, and its echoes still drown the dissonance of arms and superstition. At successive intervals, Ariosto, Tasso, Shakespeare, Spenser, Calderon, Rousseau, and the great writers of our own age, have celebrated the dominion of love, planting as it were trophies in the human mind of that sublimest victory

---

[6] "Galeotto was the book, and he that wrote it." Dante, *Inferno,* V, 137.

over sensuality and force. The true relation borne to each other by the sexes into which human kind is distributed has become less misunderstood; and if the error which confounded diversity with inequality of the powers of the two sexes has been partially recognized in the opinions and institutions of modern Europe, we owe this great benefit to the worship of which chivalry was the law, and poets the prophets.

The poetry of Dante may be considered as the bridge thrown over the stream of time, which unites the modern and ancient world. The distorted notions of invisible things which Dante and his rival Milton have idealized, are merely the mask and the mantle in which these great poets walk through eternity enveloped and disguised. It is a difficult question to determine how far they were conscious of the distinction which must have subsisted in their minds between their own creeds and that of the people. Dante at least appears to wish to mark the full extent of it by placing Riphæus, whom Virgil calls *justissimus unus,*[7] in Paradise, and observing a most heretical caprice in his distribution of rewards and punishments. And Milton's poem contains within itself a philosophical refutation of that system, of which, by a strange and natural antithesis, it has been a chief popular support. Nothing can exceed the energy and magnificence of the character of Satan as expressed in *Paradise Lost*. It is a mistake to suppose that he could ever have been intended for the popular personification of evil. Implacable hate, patient cunning, and a sleepless refinement of device to inflict the extremest anguish on an enemy, these things are evil; and, although venial in a slave, are not to be forgiven in a tyrant; although redeemed by much that ennobles his defeat in one subdued, are marked by all that dishonours his conquest in the victor. Milton's Devil as a moral being is as far superior to his God, as one who perseveres in some purpose which he has conceived to be excellent in spite of adversity and torture, is to one who in the cold security of undoubted triumph inflicts the most horrible revenge upon his enemy, not from any mistaken notion of inducing him to repent of a perseverance in enmity, but with the alleged design of exasperating him to deserve new torments. Milton has so far violated the popular creed (if this shall be judged to be a violation) as to have alleged no superiority of moral virtue to his God over his Devil. And this bold neglect of a direct moral purpose is the most decisive proof of the supremacy of Milton's genius. He mingled as it were the elements of human nature as colours upon a single pallet,

7 "The one most just." *Aeneid*, ii, 426–28.

and arranged them in the composition of his great picture according to the laws of epic truth; that is, according to the laws of that principle by which a series of actions of the external universe and of intelligent and ethical beings is calculated to excite the sympathy of succeeding generations of mankind. The *Divina Commedia* and *Paradise Lost* have conferred upon modern mythology a systematic form; and when change and time shall have added one more superstition to the mass of those which have arisen and decayed upon the earth, commentators will be learnedly employed in elucidating the religion of ancestral Europe, only not utterly forgotten because it will have been stamped with the eternity of genius.

Homer was the first and Dante the second epic poet: that is, the second poet, the series of whose creations bore a defined and intelligible relation to the knowledge and sentiment and religion of the age in which he lived, and of the ages which followed it, developing itself in correspondence with their development. For Lucretius had limed the wings of his swift spirit in the dregs of the sensible world; and Virgil, with a modesty that ill became his genius, had affected the fame of an imitator, even whilst he created anew all that he copied; and none among the flock of mock-birds, though their notes were sweet, Apollonius Rhodius, Quintus Calaber, Nonnus, Lucan, Statius, or Claudian, have sought even to fulfil a single condition of epic truth. Milton was the third epic poet. For if the title of epic in its highest sense be refused to the *Æneid,* still less can it be conceded to the *Orlando Furioso,* the *Gerusalemme Liberata,* the *Lusiad,* or the *Fairy Queen.*

Dante and Milton were both deeply penetrated with the ancient religion of the civilized world; and its spirit exists in their poetry probably in the same proportion as its forms survived in the unreformed worship of modern Europe. The one preceded and the other followed the Reformation at almost equal intervals. Dante was the first religious reformer, and Luther surpassed him rather in the rudeness and acrimony, than in the boldness of his censures of papal usurpation. Dante was the first awakener of entranced Europe; he created a language, in itself music and persuasion, out of a chaos of inharmonious barbarisms. He was the congregator of those great spirits who presided over the resurrection of learning; the Lucifer of that starry flock which in the thirteenth century shone forth from republican Italy, as from a heaven, into the darkness of the benighted world. His very words are instinct with spirit; each is as a spark, a burning atom of inextinguishable thought; and many yet lie covered in the ashes of their birth, and pregnant with the lightning which has yet found no conductor. All high poetry is infinite; it is as the first acorn, which contained all oaks potentially. Veil after veil may be undrawn, and the inmost naked beauty of the meaning never exposed. A great poem is a fountain for ever overflowing with the waters of wisdom and delight; and after one person and one age has exhausted all its divine effluence which their peculiar relations enable them to share, another and yet another succeeds, and new relations are ever developed, the source of an unforeseen and an unconceived delight.

The age immediately succeeding to that of Dante, Petrarch, and Boccaccio, was characterized by a revival of painting, sculpture, and architecture. Chaucer caught the sacred inspiration, and the superstructure of English literature is based upon the materials of Italian invention.

But let us not be betrayed from a defence into a critical history of poetry and its influence on society. Be it enough to have pointed out the effects of poets, in the large and true sense of the word, upon their own and all succeeding times.

But poets have been challenged [8] to resign the civic crown to reasoners and mechanists on another plea. It is admitted that the exercise of the imagination is most delightful, but it is alleged that that of reason is more useful. Let us examine as the grounds of this distinction what is here meant by utility. Pleasure or good, in a general sense, is that which the consciousness of a sensitive and intelligent being seeks, and in which, when found, it acquiesces. There are two kinds of pleasure, one durable, universal, and permanent; the other transitory and particular. Utility may either express the means of producing the former or the latter. In the former sense, whatever strengthens and purifies the affections, enlarges the imagination, and adds spirit to sense, is useful. But a narrower meaning may be assigned to the word utility, confining it to express that which banishes the importunity of the wants of our animal nature, the surrounding men with security of life, the dispersing the grosser delusions of superstition, and the conciliating such a degree of mutual forbearance among men as may consist with the motives of personal advantage.

Undoubtedly the promoters of utility, in this limited sense, have their appointed office in society. They follow the footsteps of poets, and copy the sketches of their creations into the book of common life. They make

[8] "This begins a definite reply to the four paragraphs with which Peacock's essay concludes." (Brett-Smith.) These paragraphs are printed in the Supplement.

space, and give time. Their exertions are of the highest value, so long as they confine their administration of the concerns of the inferior powers of our nature within the limits due to the superior ones. But whilst the sceptic destroys gross superstitions, let him spare to deface, as some of the French writers have defaced, the eternal truths charactered upon the imaginations of men. Whilst the mechanist abridges, and the political economist combines labour, let them beware that their speculations, for want of correspondence with those first principles which belong to the imagination, do not tend, as they have in modern England, to exasperate at once the extremes of luxury and want. They have exemplified the saying, "To him that hath, more shall be given; and from him that hath not, the little that he hath shall be taken away." [9] The rich have become richer, and the poor have become poorer; and the vessel of the state is driven between the Scylla and Charybdis of anarchy and despotism. Such are the effects which must ever flow from an unmitigated exercise of the calculating faculty.

It is difficult to define pleasure in its highest sense; the definition involving a number of apparent paradoxes. For, from an inexplicable defect of harmony in the constitution of human nature, the pain of the inferior is frequently connected with the pleasures of the superior portions of our being. Sorrow, terror, anguish, despair itself, are often the chosen expressions of an approximation to the highest good. Our sympathy in tragic fiction depends on this principle; tragedy delights by affording a shadow of the pleasure which exists in pain. This is the source also of the melancholy which is inseparable from the sweetest melody. The pleasure that is in sorrow is sweeter than the pleasure of pleasure itself. And hence the saying, "It is better to go to the house of mourning, than to the house of mirth." [10] Not that this highest species of pleasure is necessarily linked with pain. The delight of love and friendship, the ecstasy of the admiration of nature, the joy of the perception and still more of the creation of poetry, is often wholly unalloyed.

The production and assurance of pleasure in this highest sense is true utility. Those who produce and preserve this pleasure are poets or poetical philosophers.

The exertions of Locke, Hume, Gibbon, Voltaire, Rousseau,* and their disciples, in favour of oppressed and deluded humanity, are en-

---

[9] Mark, 4:25. An inexact quotation.
[10] Ecclesiastes, 7:2. Also inexact.

* Although Rousseau has been thus classed, he was essentially a poet. The others, even Voltaire, were mere reasoners.

titled to the gratitude of mankind. Yet it is easy to calculate the degree of moral and intellectual improvement which the world would have exhibited, had they never lived. A little more nonsense would have been talked for a century or two; and perhaps a few more men, women, and children burnt as heretics. We might not at this moment have been congratulating each other on the abolition of the Inquisition in Spain.[11] But it exceeds all imagination to conceive what would have been the moral condition of the world if neither Dante, Petrarch, Boccaccio, Chaucer, Shakespeare, Calderon, Lord Bacon, nor Milton, had ever existed; if Raphael and Michael Angelo had never been born; if the Hebrew poetry had never been translated; if a revival of the study of Greek literature had never taken place; if no monuments of ancient sculpture had been handed down to us; and if the poetry of the religion of the ancient world had been extinguished together with its belief. The human mind could never, except by the intervention of these excitements, have been awakened to the invention of the grosser sciences, and that application of analytical reasoning to the aberrations of society, which it is now attempted to exalt over the direct expression of the inventive and creative faculty itself.

We have more moral, political, and historical wisdom than we know how to reduce into practice; we have more scientific and economical knowledge than can be accommodated to the just distribution of the produce which it multiplies. The poetry in these systems of thought is concealed by the accumulation of facts and calculating processes. There is no want of knowledge respecting what is wisest and best in morals, government, and political economy, or at least, what is wiser and better than what men now practise and endure. But we let *"I dare not* wait upon *I would,* like the poor cat in the adage."[12] We want the creative faculty to imagine that which we know; we want the generous impulse to act that which we imagine; we want the poetry of life: our calculations have outrun conception; we have eaten more than we can digest. The cultivation of those sciences which have enlarged the limits of the empire of men over the external world, has, for want of the poetical faculty, proportionally circumscribed those of the internal world; and man, having enslaved the elements, remains himself a slave. To what but a cultivation of the mechanical arts in a degree disproportioned to the presence of the creative faculty, which is the basis of all knowledge, is to be attributed the abuse of all invention for abridging

---

[11] In 1820. [12] *Macbeth,* I, vii, 44.

and combining labour, to the exasperation of the inequality of mankind? From what other cause has it arisen that the discoveries which should have lightened, have added a weight to the curse imposed on Adam? Poetry, and the principle of Self, of which money is the visible incarnation, are the God and Mammon of the world.

The functions of the Poetical faculty are two-fold; by one it creates new materials of knowledge, and power, and pleasure; by the other it engenders in the mind a desire to reproduce and arrange them according to a certain rhythm and order which may be called the beautiful and the good. The cultivation of poetry is never more to be desired than at periods when, from an excess of the selfish and calculating principle, the accumulation of the materials of external life exceed the quantity of the power of assimilating them to the internal laws of human nature. The body has then become too unwieldy for that which animates it.

Poetry is indeed something divine. It is at once the centre and circumference of knowledge; it is that which comprehends all science, and that to which all science must be referred. It is at the same time the root and blossom of all other systems of thought; it is that from which all spring, and that which adorns all; and that which, if blighted, denies the fruit and the seed, and withholds from the barren world the nourishment and the succession of the scions of the tree of life. It is the perfect and consummate surface and bloom of all things; it is as the odour and the colour of the rose to the texture of the elements which compose it, as the form and splendour of unfaded beauty to the secrets of anatomy and corruption. What were virtue, love, patriotism, friendship—what were the scenery of this beautiful universe which we inhabit; what were our consolations on this side of the grave—and what were our aspirations beyond it, if poetry did not ascend to bring light and fire from those eternal regions where the owl-winged faculty of calculation dare not ever soar? Poetry is not like reasoning, a power to be exerted according to the determination of the will. A man cannot say, "I will compose poetry." The greatest poet even cannot say it; for the mind in creation is as a fading coal, which some invisible influence, like an inconstant wind, awakens to transitory brightness; this power arises from within, like the colour of a flower which fades and changes as it is developed, and the conscious portions of our natures are unprophetic either of its approach or its departure. Could this influence be durable in its original purity and force, it is impossible to predict the greatness of the results; but when composition begins, inspiration is already on the decline, and the most glorious poetry that has ever been communicated to the world is probably a feeble shadow of the original conceptions of the poet. I appeal to the greatest poets of the present day, whether it is not an error to assert that the finest passages of poetry are produced by labour and study. The toil and the delay recommended by critics can be justly interpreted to mean no more than a careful observation of the inspired moments, and an artificial connexion of the spaces between their suggestions by the intertexture of conventional expressions; a necessity only imposed by the limitedness of the poetical faculty itself: for Milton conceived the *Paradise Lost* as a whole before he executed it in portions. We have his own authority also for the muse having "dictated" to him the "unpremeditated song." [13] And let this be an answer to those who would allege the fifty-six various readings of the first line of the *Orlando Furioso*. Compositions so produced are to poetry what mosaic is to painting. This instinct and intuition of the poetical faculty is still more observable in the plastic and pictorial arts: a great statue or picture grows under the power of the artist as a child in the mother's womb; and the very mind which directs the hands in formation is incapable of accounting to itself for the origin, the gradations, or the media of the process.

Poetry is the record of the best and happiest moments of the happiest and best minds. We are aware of evanescent visitations of thought and feeling sometimes associated with place or person, sometimes regarding our own mind alone, and always arising unforeseen and departing unbidden, but elevating and delightful beyond all expression: so that even in the desire and the regret they leave, there cannot but be pleasure, participating as it does in the nature of its object. It is as it were the interpenetration of a diviner nature through our own; but its footsteps are like those of a wind over the sea, which the coming calm erases, and whose traces remain only as on the wrinkled sands which pave it. These and corresponding conditions of being are experienced principally by those of the most delicate sensibility and the most enlarged imagination; and the state of mind produced by them is at war with every base desire. The enthusiasm of virtue, love, patriotism, and friendship is essentially linked with such emotions; and whilst they last, self appears as what it is, an atom to a universe. Poets are not only subject to these experiences as spirits of the most refined organization, but they can

---

13 . . . my Celestial Patroness, who deignes
Her nightly visitation unimplor'd,
And dictates to me slumbring, or inspires
Easie my unpremeditated Verse:
Since first this Subject for Heroic Song
Pleas'd me. *Paradise Lost*, ix, 21–26.

colour all that they combine with the evanescent hues of this ethereal world; a word, a trait in the representation of a scene or a passion will touch the enchanted chord, and reanimate, in those who have ever experienced these emotions, the sleeping, the cold, the buried image of the past. Poetry thus makes immortal all that is best and most beautiful in the world; it arrests the vanishing apparitions which haunt the interluminations of life, and veiling them, or in language or in form, sends them forth among mankind, bearing sweet news of kindred joy to those with whom their sisters abide—abide, because there is no portal of expression from the caverns of the spirit which they inhabit into the universe of things. Poetry redeems from decay the visitations of the divinity in man.

Poetry turns all things to loveliness; it exalts the beauty of that which is most beautiful, and it adds beauty to that which is most deformed; it marries exultation and horror, grief and pleasure, eternity and change; it subdues to union under its light yoke all irreconcilable things. It transmutes all that it touches, and every form moving within the radiance of its presence is changed by wondrous sympathy to an incarnation of the spirit which it breathes: its secret alchemy turns to potable gold the poisonous waters which flow from death through life; it strips the veil of familiarity from the world, and lays bare the naked and sleeping beauty, which is the spirit of its forms.

All things exist as they are perceived: at least in relation to the percipient. "The mind is its own place, and of itself can make a heaven of hell, a hell of heaven." [14] But poetry defeats the curse which binds us to be subjected to the accident of surrounding impressions. And whether it spreads its own figured curtain, or withdraws life's dark veil from before the scene of things, it equally creates for us a being within our being. It makes us the inhabitants of a world to which the familiar world is a chaos. It reproduces the common universe of which we are portions and percipients, and it purges from our inward sight the film of familiarity which obscures from us the wonder of our being. It compels us to feel that which we perceive, and to imagine that which we know. It creates anew the universe, after it has been annihilated in our minds by the recurrence of impressions blunted by reiteration. It justifies the bold and true words of Tasso—*Non merita nome di creatore, se non Iddio ed il Poeta.*[15]

A poet, as he is the author to others of the highest wisdom, pleasure,

[14] *Paradise Lost*, I, 254–55.   God and the Poet."
[15] "None merits the name of creator but

virtue, and glory, so he ought personally to be the happiest, the best, the wisest, and the most illustrious of men. As to his glory, let time be challenged to declare whether the frame of any other institutor of human life be comparable to that of a poet. That he is the wisest, the happiest, and the best, inasmuch as he is a poet, is equally incontrovertible: the greatest poets have been men of the most spotless virtue, of the most consummate prudence, and, if we would look into the interior of their lives, the most fortunate of men: and the exceptions, as they regard those who possessed the poetic faculty in a high yet inferior degree, will be found on consideration to confine rather than destroy the rule. Let us for a moment stoop to the arbitration of popular breath, and usurping and uniting in our own persons the incompatible characters of accuser, witness, judge, and executioner, let us decide without trial, testimony, or form, that certain motives of those who are "there sitting where we dare not soar," [16] are reprehensible. Let us assume that Homer was a drunkard, that Virgil was a flatterer, that Horace was a coward, that Tasso was a madman, that Lord Bacon was a peculator, that Raphael was a libertine, that Spenser was a poet laureate. It is inconsistent with this division of our subject to cite living poets, but posterity has done ample justice to the great names now referred to. Their errors have been weighed and found to have been dust in the balance; if their sins "were as scarlet, they are now white as snow"; [17] they have been washed in the blood of the mediator and redeemer, Time. Observe in what a ludicrous chaos the imputations of real or fictitious crime have been confused in the contemporary calumnies against poetry and poets; consider how little is, as it appears—or appears, as it is; look to your own motives, and judge not, lest ye be judged.

Poetry, as has been said, differs in this respect from logic, that it is not subject to the control of the active powers of the mind, and that its birth and recurrence have no necessary connexion with the consciousness or will. It is presumptuous to determine that these are the necessary conditions of all mental causation, when mental effects are experienced unsusceptible of being referred to them. The frequent recurrence of the poetical power, it is obvious to suppose, may produce in the mind a habit of order and harmony correlative with its own nature and with its effects upon other minds. But in the intervals of inspiration, and

[16] Adapted from *Paradise Lost*, IV, 829:
Ye knew me once no mate
For you, there sitting where ye durst not
soar.

[17] Isaiah, I:18. Shelley also used phrases, in this passage, from Daniel, 5:27; Isaiah, 40:15; Revelation, 7:14; Matthew, 7:1.

they may be frequent without being durable, a poet becomes a man, and is abandoned to the sudden reflux of the influences under which others habitually live. But as he is more delicately organized than other men, and sensible to pain and pleasure, both his own and that of others, in a degree unknown to them, he will avoid the one and pursue the other with an ardour proportioned to this difference. And he renders himself obnoxious to calumny, when he neglects to observe the circumstances under which these objects of universal pursuit and flight have disguised themselves in one another's garments.

But there is nothing necessarily evil in this error, and thus cruelty, envy, revenge, avarice, and the passions purely evil, have never formed any portion of the popular imputations on the lives of poets.

I have thought it most favourable to the cause of truth to set down these remarks according to the order in which they were suggested to my mind, by a consideration of the subject itself, instead of observing the formality of a polemical reply; but if the view which they contain be just, they will be found to involve a refutation of the arguers against poetry, so far at least as regards the first division of the subject. I can readily conjecture what should have moved the gall of some learned and intelligent writers who quarrel with certain versifiers; I confess myself, like them, unwilling to be stunned by the Theseids of the hoarse Codri of the day.[18] Bavius and Mævius undoubtedly are, as they ever were, insufferable persons. But it belongs to a philosophical critic to distinguish rather than confound.

The first part of these remarks has related to poetry in its elements and principles; and it has been shown, as well as the narrow limits assigned them would permit, that what is called poetry, in a restricted sense, has a common source with all other forms of order and of beauty, according to which the materials of human life are susceptible of being arranged, and which is poetry in an universal sense.

The second part[19] will have for its object an application of these principles to the present state of the cultivation of poetry, and a defence of the attempt to idealize the modern forms of manners and opinions, and compel them into a subordination to the imaginative and creative faculty. For the literature of England, an energetic development of which has ever preceded or accompanied a great and free development of the national will, has arisen as it were from a new birth. In spite of

---

[18] Juvenal attacked the bad poetry of Codrus, *Satires* I, 1–2; Horace, *Epode* X, attacked Maevius; Virgil, *Eclogues*, III, 90–1, coupled Bavius and Maevius as bad poets.

[19] This was never written.

the low-thoughted envy which would undervalue contemporary merit, our own will be a memorable age in intellectual achievements, and we live among such philosophers and poets as surpass beyond comparison any who have appeared since the last national struggle for civil and religious liberty. The most unfailing herald, companion, and follower of the awakening of a great people to work a beneficial change in opinion or institution, is poetry. At such periods there is an accumulation of the power of communicating and receiving intense and impassioned conceptions respecting man and nature. The persons in whom this power resides, may often, as far as regards many portions of their nature, have little apparent correspondence with that spirit of good of which they are the ministers. But even whilst they deny and abjure, they are yet compelled to serve, the power which is seated on the throne of their own soul. It is impossible to read the compositions of the most celebrated writers of the present day without being startled with the electric life which burns within their words. They measure the circumference and sound the depths of human nature with a comprehensive and all-penetrating spirit, and they are themselves perhaps the most sincerely astonished at its manifestations; for it is less their spirit than the spirit of the age. Poets are the hierophants of an unapprehended inspiration; the mirrors of the gigantic shadows which futurity casts upon the present; the words which express what they understand not; the trumpets which sing to battle, and feel not what they inspire; the influence which is moved not, but moves. Poets are the unacknowledged legislators of the world.

$\mathcal{E}$DGAR $\mathcal{A}$LLAN $\mathcal{P}$OE

(1809–1849)

EDGAR POE was born in Boston, January 19, 1809, where his parents were acting in a stock company. In December, 1811, his mother died in Richmond; according to Poe, his father died a few weeks later. Edgar was taken into the family of John Allan, Scottish tobacco exporter, but was never legally adopted; when business expansion necessitated a trip to England, Edgar Allan Poe went with the family. From 1815 to 1820 he lived in London, attending the Manor House School in Stoke Newington. After returning to Richmond, Poe studied at private schools until, in 1826, he entered the University of Virginia, where he remained for one year. Reputedly, his excessive gambling debts caused Mr. Allan to withdraw Poe from the University and put him as a clerk in the counting room.

In 1827, Poe left without notice, going to Boston, where he published his first book, *Tamerlane and Other Poems, by a Bostonian;* in May he enlisted in the United States Army as Edgar A. Perry. After serving for two years—part of the time in Charleston, South Carolina—and gaining the rank of Sergeant Major, Poe was honorably discharged. The same year (1829), he published a second book of poems, and began negotiations for an appointment to West Point, which he secured; but he was soon dismissed for deliberate infractions of the rules. His third volume, *Poems,* appeared in 1831, but received little more attention than his earlier work. The poet lived in obscurity in Baltimore until his story "Ms. Found in a Bottle" won first prize in a contest held by the *Baltimore Saturday Visitor.* John Pendleton Kennedy, author of *Swallow Barn* and a judge in the contest, helped Poe to place other manuscripts, and secured for him the assistant editorship of the *Southern Literary Messenger* (1835–37). In September, 1835, Poe secretly married his thirteen-year-old cousin, Virginia Clemm; in May, 1836, he remarried her publicly.

A successful editor who increased the circulation of every magazine he edited, Poe was successively discharged from several positions; the reason generally given was his drinking. In 1838 he published *The Narrative of Arthur Gordon Pym;* in 1840, *Tales of the Grotesque and Arabesque.* Not until the appearance of *The Raven and Other Poems* (1845) was Poe widely known as a poet, his contemporaries valuing more highly his short stories and his criticisms. His critical articles and reviews appeared frequently in the *Southern Literary Messenger, Burton's Gentleman's Magazine,* and *Graham's Magazine;* they set a new standard in American criticism, but his outspoken comments gained for him the title of "the tomahawk critic." After the death of his wife (January 30, 1845), Poe for a time apparently drifted, writing pathetic letters to friends and engaging in equally pathetic and in-decisive love affairs with sentimental ladies; but he also wrote *Eureka* and several of his best poems and stories. He died in Baltimore, October 7, 1849.

Norman Foerster [*American Criticism*, 6–7] has given an excellent sum-mary of Poe's aesthetic beliefs: "The end of art is pleasure, not truth. In order that pleasure may be intense, the work of art must have unity and brevity. In poetry, the proper means of arousing pleasure is the creation of beauty; not the beauty of concrete things alone, but also a higher beauty—supernal beauty." Poe first expressed these ideas, in rudimentary form, in a prefatory letter to the 1831 poems; they were re-worked and elaborated until they formed a theory consistent in itself and remarkably consistent with Poe's own creative work. In part, his ideas were drawn from Schlegel, Kames, Blair, and, above all, from Coleridge, his chief master in criticism; in part, they were influenced by Poe's work as editor and by his interest in magazine writing. The age wanted brevity: "We now demand the light artillery of the intellect; we need the curt, the condensed, the pointed, the readily dif-fused." [*Marginalia*] Poe was among the first of critics to hammer out and refine his ideas through the medium of reviews of contemporary books; not the least valuable of his achievements was the setting of an aesthetic for a magazine age.

The opposing ideas on Americanism in literature are better represented in the work of Lowell and Whitman (see the Supplement). Poe's words, however, add something worth noting ["Nationality in American Litera-ture"]: "After all, the world at large is the only legitimate stage of the autorial *histrio*. ¶ But of the need of *that* nationality which defends our own literature, upholds our own dignity, and depends upon our own resources, there cannot be the shadow of a doubt."

Brevity and unity, to his mind, go hand in hand. The poet's first effort is to secure exaltation, which implies intensity, and "brevity must be in di-rect ratio to the intensity of the intended effect." A poem or story should produce a single effect, which requires a perfect unity secured by a har-monious arrangement of parts. In his earlier criticism, Poe placed almost his entire reliance on the imagination; by 1842, he had added [Alterton and Craig, *Poe*, lx–lxii] "to his former opinions the new one in respect to reason-ing imagination. This was the faculty . . . that signified to Poe 'poetic in-tellect' and analytic imagination, the latter distinguished by balance or equality. From this faculty arose in his mind a vision of heavenly beauty characterized by harmonious adjustments such as he had recognized in the perfect plan of the universe." This conception led naturally to Poe's attacks on didacticism in poetry. In reviewing Longfellow's *Voices of the Night* (1840), Poe wrote: "By truth, here, we mean that perfection which is the result only of the strictest proportion and adaptation in all the poetical requisites—these requisites being considered as each existing in the highest degree of beauty and strength." To these fundamental ideas in his criticism Poe re-turned time and again. In a review of Hawthorne's *Twice-Told Tales* (1842) he applied his basic thought to the short story, setting a foundation for much later work in that genre; in "The Philosophy of Composition" (1846) he analyzes his own poem "The Raven," and thus illustrates his principles concretely. But he gives in "The Poetic Principle" a final and rounded statement of his consistently held theories; these may, as Joseph Wood Krutch [*Edgar Allan Poe,* 234] argues, be "a rationalized defense of the limitations of his own critical taste," but they seem rather to belong integrally to the romantic movement.

THE POETIC PRINCIPLE

(1848) (1850)

In speaking of the Poetic Principle, I have no design to be either thorough or profound. While discussing, very much at random, the essentiality of what we call Poetry, my principal purpose will be to cite for consideration, some few of those minor English or American poems which best suit my own taste, or which, upon my own fancy, have left the most definite impression. By "minor poems" I mean, of course, poems of little length. And here, in the beginning, permit me to say a few words in regard to a somewhat peculiar principle which, whether rightfully or wrongfully, has always had its influence in my own critical estimate of the poem. I hold that a long poem does not exist. I maintain that the phrase, "a long poem," is simply a flat contradiction in terms.

I need scarcely observe that a poem deserves its title only inasmuch as it excites, by elevating the soul. The value of the poem is in the ratio of this elevating excitement. But all excitements are, through a psychal necessity, transient. That degree of excitement which would entitle a poem to be so called at all, cannot be sustained throughout a composition of any great length. After the lapse of half an hour, at the very utmost, it flags—fails—a revulsion ensues—and then the poem is, in effect, and in fact, no longer such.

There are, no doubt, many who have found difficulty in reconciling the critical dictum that the "Paradise Lost" is to be devoutly admired throughout, with the absolute impossibility of maintaining for it, during perusal, the amount of enthusiasm which that critical dictum would demand. This great work, in fact, is to be regarded as poetical, only when, losing sight of that vital requisite in all works of Art, Unity, we view it merely as a series of minor poems. If, to preserve its Unity—its totality of effect or impression—we read it (as would be necessary) at a single sitting, the result is but a constant alternation of excitement and depression. After a passage of what we feel to be true poetry, there follows, inevitably, a passage of platitude which no critical prejudgment can force us to admire; but if, upon completing the work, we read it again, omitting the first book (that is to say, commencing with the second), we shall be surprised at now finding that admirable which we before condemned—that damnable which we had previously so much admired. It follows from all this that the ultimate, aggregate, or absolute effect of even the best epic under the sun is a nullity;—and this is precisely the fact.

In regard to the "Iliad," we have, if not positive proof, at least very good reason for believing it intended as a series of lyrics; but, granting the epic intention, I can say only that the work is based in an imperfect sense of art. The modern epic is, of the supposititious ancient model, but an inconsiderate and blindfold imitation. But the day of these artistic anomalies is over. If, at any time, any very long poems *were* popular in reality—which I doubt—it is at least clear that no very long poem will ever be popular again.

That the extent of a poetical work is, *ceteris paribus,* the measure of its merit, seems undoubtedly, when we thus state it, a proposition sufficiently absurd—yet we are indebted for it to the Quarterly Reviews. Surely there can be nothing in mere size, abstractly considered—there can be nothing in mere bulk, so far as a volume is concerned which has so continuously elicited admiration from these saturnine pamphlets! A mountain, to be sure, by the mere sentiment of physical magnitude which it conveys, does impress us with a sense of the sublime—but no man is impressed after *this* fashion by the material grandeur of even "The Columbiad." Even the Quarterlies have not instructed us to be so impressed by it. *As yet,* they have not *insisted* on our estimating Lamartine by the cubic foot, or Pollok by the pound—but what else are we to *infer* from their continual prating about "sustained effort"? If, by "sustained effort," any little gentleman has accomplished an epic, let us frankly commend him for the effort,—if this indeed be a thing commendable,—but let us forbear praising the epic on the effort's account. It is to be hoped that common sense, in the time to come, will prefer deciding upon a work of Art, rather by the impression it makes—by the effect it produces—than by the time it took to impress the effect, or by the amount of "sustained effort" which had been found necessary in effecting the impression. The fact is, that perseverance is one thing and genius quite another:

nor can all the Quarterlies in Christendom confound them. By and by, this proposition, with many which I have been just urging, will be received as self-evident. In the mean time, by being generally con-demned as falsities they will not be essentially damaged as truths.

On the other hand, it is clear that a poem may be improperly brief. Undue brevity degenerates into mere epigrammatism. A *very* short poem, while now and then producing a brilliant or vivid, never pro-duces a profound or enduring, effect. There must be the steady press-ing down of the stamp upon the wax. Béranger has wrought innumer-able things, pungent and spirit-stirring; but, in general, they have been too imponderous to stamp themselves deeply into the public opinion, and thus, as so many feathers of fancy, have been blown aloft only to be whistled down the wind. . . .

[At this point, Poe quotes with almost no critical comment the follow-ing poems: Shelley's "The Indian Serenade," and N. P. Willis's "Un-seen Spirits," as examples of poems that suffer from undue brevity.]

While the epic mania—while the idea that, to merit in poetry, prolix-ity is indispensable—has, for some years past, been gradually dying out of the public mind, by mere dint of its own absurdity, we find it suc-ceeded by a heresy too palpably false to be long tolerated, but one which, in the brief period it has already endured, may be said to have accom-plished more in the corruption of our Poetical Literature than all its other enemies combined. I allude to the heresy of *The Didactic*. It has been assumed, tacitly and avowedly, directly and indirectly, that the ultimate object of all Poetry is Truth. Every poem, it is said, should inculcate a moral; and by this moral is the poetical merit of the work to be adjudged. We Americans especially have patronized this happy idea; and we Bostonians, very especially, have developed it in full. We have taken it into our heads that to write a poem simply for the poem's sake, and to acknowledge such to have been our design, would be to confess ourselves radically wanting in the true Poetic dignity and force: —but the simple fact is, that, would we but permit ourselves to look into our own souls, we should immediately there discover that under the sun there neither exists nor *can* exist any work more thoroughly dignified—more supremely noble than this very poem—this poem *per se*—this poem which is a poem and nothing more—this poem written solely for the poem's sake.

With as deep a reverence for the True as ever inspired the bosom of

man, I would, nevertheless, limit in some measure its modes of inculcation. I would limit to enforce them. I would not enfeeble them by
dissipation. The demands of Truth are severe; she has no sympathy
with the myrtles. All *that* which is so indispensable in Song, is precisely
all *that* with which *she* has nothing whatever to do. It is but making
her a flaunting paradox to wreathe her in gems and flowers. In enforc-
ing a truth we need severity rather than efflorescence of language. We
must be simple, precise, terse. We must be cool, calm, unimpassioned.
In a word, we must be in that mood, which, as nearly as possible, is the
exact converse of the poetical. He must be blind, indeed, who does not
perceive the radical and chasmal differences between the truthful and
the poetical modes of inculcation. He must be theory-mad beyond redemption who, in spite of these differences, shall still persist in attempting to reconcile the obstinate oils and waters of Poetry and Truth.

Dividing the world of mind into its three most immediately obvious
distinctions, we have the Pure Intellect, Taste, and the Moral Sense. I
place Taste in the middle, because it is just this position which in the
mind it occupies. It holds intimate relations with either extreme, but
from the Moral Sense is separated by so faint a difference that Aristotle
has not hesitated to place some of its operations among the virtues
themselves. Nevertheless, we find the *offices* of the trio marked with a
sufficient distinction. Just as the intellect concerns itself with Truth,
so Taste informs us of the Beautiful, while the Moral Sense is regard-
ful of Duty. Of this latter, while Conscience teaches the obligation, and
Reason the expediency, Taste contents herself with displaying the
charms:—waging war upon Vice solely on the ground of her deformity
—her disproportion—her animosity to the fitting, to the appropriate, to
the harmonious—in a word, to Beauty.

An immortal instinct, deep within the spirit of man, is thus, plainly,
a sense of the Beautiful. This it is which administers to his delight in the
manifold forms, and sounds, and odors, and sentiments, amid which
he exists. And just as the lily is repeated in the lake, or the eyes of
Amaryllis in the mirror, so is the mere oral or written repetition of
these forms, and sounds, and colors, and odors, and sentiments, a duplicate source of delight. But this mere repetition is not poetry. He who
shall simply sing, with however glowing enthusiasm, or with however
vivid a truth of description, of the sights, and sounds, and odors, and
colors, and sentiments, which greet *him* in common with all mankind
—he, I say, has yet failed to prove his divine title. There is still a something in the distance which he has been unable to attain. We have still a

thirst unquenchable, to allay which he has not shown us the crystal springs. This thirst belongs to the immortality of Man. It is at once a consequence and an indication of his perennial existence. It is the desire of the moth for the star. It is no mere appreciation of the Beauty before us, but a wild effort to reach the Beauty above. Inspired by an ecstatic prescience of the glories beyond the grave, we struggle, by multiform combinations among the things and thoughts of Time, to attain a portion of that Loveliness whose very elements, perhaps, appertain to eternity alone. And thus when by Poetry—or when by Music, the most entrancing of the Poetic moods—we find ourselves melted into tears not as the Abbate Gravia supposes through excess of pleasure, but through a certain petulant, impatient sorrow at our inability to grasp now, wholly, here on earth, at once and forever, those divine and rapturous joys, of which *through* the poem, or *through* the music, we attain to but brief and indeterminate glimpses.

The struggle to apprehend the supernal Loveliness—this struggle, on the part of souls fittingly constituted—has given to the world all that which it (the world) has ever been enabled at once to understand and to feel as poetic.

The Poetic Sentiment, of course, may develop itself in various modes —in Painting, in Sculpture, in Architecture, in the Dance—very especially in Music,—and very peculiarly and with a wide field, in the composition of the Landscape Garden. Our present theme, however, has regard only to its manifestation in words. And here let me speak briefly on the topic of rhythm. Contenting myself with the certainty that Music, in its various modes of metre, rhythm, and rhyme, is of so vast a moment in Poetry as never to be wisely rejected—is so vitally important an adjunct, that he is simply silly who declines its assistance, I will not now pause to maintain its absolute essentiality. It is in Music, perhaps, that the soul most nearly attains the great end for which, when inspired by the Poetic Sentiment, it struggles—the creation of supernal Beauty. It *may* be, indeed, that here this sublime end is, now and then, attained *in fact*. We are often made to feel, with a shivering delight, that from an earthly harp are stricken notes which *cannot* have been unfamiliar to the angels. And thus there can be little doubt that in the union of Poetry with Music in its popular sense, we shall find the widest field for the Poetic development. The old Bards and Minnesingers had advantages which we do not possess—and Thomas Moore, singing his own songs, was, in the most legitimate manner, perfecting them as poems.

To recapitulate, then:—I would define, in brief, the Poetry of words as *The Rhythmical Creation of Beauty*. Its sole arbiter is Taste. With the Intellect or with the Conscience, it has only collateral relations. Unless incidentally, it has no concern whatever either with Duty or with Truth.

A few words, however, in explanation. *That* pleasure which is at once the most pure, the most elevating, and the most intense, is derived, I maintain, from the contemplation of the Beautiful. In the contemplation of Beauty we alone find it possible to attain that pleasurable elevation, or excitement *of the soul,* which we recognize as the Poetic Sentiment, and which is so easily distinguished from Truth, which is the satisfaction of Reason, or from Passion, which is the excitement of the Heart. I make Beauty, therefore,—using the word as inclusive of the sublime, —I make Beauty the province of the poem, simply because it is an obvious rule of Art that effects should be made to spring as directly as possible from their causes:—no one as yet having been weak enough to deny that the peculiar elevation in question is at least *most readily* attainable in the poem. It by no means follows, however, that the incitements of Passion, or the precepts of Duty, or even the lessons of Truth, may not be introduced into a poem, and with advantage; for they may subserve, incidentally, in various ways, the general purposes of the work:—but the true artist will always contrive to tone them down in proper subjection to that *Beauty* which is the atmosphere and the real essence of the poem.

[Poe concludes the essay—originally delivered as a lecture—by quoting several poems: Longfellow's "The Day is Done"; Bryant's "June"; Pinkney's "A Health"; T. Moore's "Come, Rest in this Bosom"; T. Hood's "Fair Ines" and "Bridge of Sighs"; Byron's "Though the Day of my Destiny's Over"; Tennyson's "Tears, Idle Tears"; and Motherwell's "Song of the Cavalier." Only one sentence in this later section needs quoting: "It has been my purpose to suggest that, while this Principle itself is, strictly and simply, the Human Aspiration for Supernal Beauty, the manifestation of the Principle is always found in *an elevating excitement of the Soul*—quite independent of that passion which is the intoxication of the Heart—or of that Truth which is the satisfaction of the Reason."]

CHARLES-AUGUSTIN SAINTE-BEUVE

(1804–1869)

CHARLES-AUGUSTIN SAINTE-BEUVE was born in Boulogne-sur-Mer, France, December 23, 1804. His father, till his marriage at fifty-two a bachelor of scholarly interests, had died the previous October. His mother, forty when she married, was a pious middle-class woman, half English in descent, and with little intellectual interest. Till he was fourteen, Sainte-Beuve attended the local school, taught by a good humanist, and studied his father's richly annotated books. In the Collège Charlemagne (1818–21) and the Collège Bourbon (1821–23) in Paris, his early maturity and gifted mind enabled him to establish unusual and highly valued relations with various of his professors.

While a student in the medical school (1823–27), he began to contribute to the *Globe,* which was founded in 1824 by Dubois, a liberalist and one of his earlier professors. Literature, both creative and as material for criticism, absorbed his attention from then till his death in 1869. Briefly he was a teacher: in Lausanne in 1837–38, where he delivered the lectures which, during the next twenty years, he enlarged into the five-volume history of the Jansenists, *Port Royal;* in Liége (1848–49) where he lectured on Chateaubriand and his literary group; in the Collège de France (1855) for two lectures, before the students, incensed at his misunderstood monarchial sympathies, secured his resignation (*Étude sur Virgile,* 1857, had been prepared for this series of lectures); in the École Normale (1857–61). From 1840 to 1848 he was keeper of the Mazarin Library.

Sainte-Beuve won and maintained his place among his colleagues, and his later renown, by his independence of judgment and his breadth of knowledge. For many years, however, his work shows very definite influences. In 1827 two reviews praising Victor Hugo's *Odes et Ballades* led to a friendship with M. and Mme. Hugo and to a place in the inner circle of the loosely integrated group of writers termed the Cénacle. Sainte-Beuve became thoroughly imbued with the doctrines of romanticism and not only reviewed with a favorable eye the work of many of the group but himself wrote two books of "subtle, ingenious and rather morbid poetry": *Vie, poésie et pensées de Joseph Delorme* (1829) and *Les Consolations* (1830).

When the *Globe* became an organ of the Saint-Simonians in 1831, Sainte-Beuve wrote its "Profession of Faith" and for a brief while he was a strong upholder of their tenets. Obsessed with the need for a religious understanding and faith, he came strongly under the influence of Lamennais and of his circle; about the same time he began writing for the *National,* a paper of revolutionary tendencies. During this period of restlessness and mental agitation, he broke with the Hugoes. Although hard pressed financially, he made brief trips to England, Germany, and Italy and to visit friends in France and in Switzerland. He wrote reviews and articles for periodicals and published the autobiographical novel *Volupté* (1834) and the poems *Pensées d'Août* (1837) and *Livre d'Amour* (1843). In 1844 his cumulative writings and the esteem in which he was held in various salons won his election to the Academy.

After 1849, Sainte-Beuve's life became more integrated and he settled down in Paris as a regular contributor to the *Constitutionnel*. His weekly papers were collected into the *Causeries de Lundi* series (sixteen volumes, 1851–62) and the *Nouveaux lundis* (thirteen volumes, 1863–70).

Throughout his life, Sainte-Beuve devoted some five or six hours daily to diligent study. Through his literary, political, and journalistic connections, he knew most of the literary figures of France; with many he was for years on terms of formal intimacy. His nine volumes of *Portraits* (1862–71) grew naturally out of his keen interest in people and his humanistic belief that literature must be studied through the men who produced it. His appointment to the Senate in 1865 gave him, for the first time, a salary sufficient for his standard of living.

Although Sainte-Beuve divided his critical career into ten "literary campaigns . . . all of which need to be judged by themselves and as different wholes" [*Portraits lit.*, II, 526], the fundamental changes in critical outlook he reduces to three: the period of militant romanticism (1824–31); the comprehensive, impressionistic period (1831–48); the humanistic, judicial period which began with his essay "Chateaubriand and his Literary Group" in 1849 and continued to 1869. Thus in 1829 Sainte-Beuve attacks Boileau from the romantic point of view; in 1843 he makes a partial retraction with an examination to see what Boileau said; in 1852 he praises him without stint (cf. also his essay on Tartuffe). In these earlier periods, he thought of the critic as guide and interpreter; in 1835 he wrote ["Bayle and the Critical Spirit," Babbitt's trans.]: "The critical spirit is by nature facile, insinuating, mobile and comprehensive. It is a great and limpid stream which winds and bends its way about the works and monuments of poetry, as about so many rocks, fortresses, vine-clad hills and leafy valleys that border its shores. While each one of these objects remains fixed in the landscape and cares little for the others, while the feudal tower disdains the valley, and the valley knows nothing of the hillside, the stream goes from one to the other, bathes them without doing them violence, embraces them in its living waters, *comprehends* them, reflects them, and when the traveller is curious to know and visit these varied spots, it takes him in a boat, carries him smoothly along, and unfolds to him in succession all the changing spectacle of its course."
But this intermingling of romanticism and impressionism—later used as a motto by the impressionistic critic Lemaître—did not for long satisfy Sainte-Beuve. In *Portraits littéraires* [III, 550, 1864] he states this dissatisfaction: "I have played the part of an advocate long enough; let me now play that of judge." The essential kernel of judgment was the finding of truth: his motto, he notes, "would be the *true,* the true alone. As for the good and the beautiful,

they might fare as best they could." Yet his demand for truth is related rather to his scientific and naturalistic beliefs than to his religious or humanistic views and it was, as Babbitt notes [*Masters of Modern French Criticism,* 144], "as a naturalist rather than a humanist" that he has been most influential. In 1864 he could write, "I have but one pleasure left. I analyze, botanize; I am a naturalist of minds. What I should like to establish is the natural history of literature." [*Portraits lit.* III, 546].

Thus he answered a query as to his critical method; he went on: "One individual carefully observed is referred quickly to the species of which you knew only in a general way, and throws light on it." Sainte-Beuve had an insatiable anecdotal curiosity; he seems at times more interested in the man than in his book; he works for "a true likeness" of mind and spirit; he constantly relates the book to the man, the author to his times. As Babbitt writes [*op. cit.,* 161], "criticism in Sainte-Beuve is plainly moving away from its own centre towards something else; it is ceasing to be literary and becoming historical and biographical and scientific." Many times Sainte-Beuve states his desire that criticism be made an art and a science, but the preliminary steps are only incidentally concerned with art. MacClintock [*Sainte-Beuve's Critical Theory,* 44] thus summarizes his ideas: "To be a scientific critic is to study an author in his race, his native country, his epoch, his family, his education and early environment, his group of associates, his first success, his first moment of disintegration, his peculiarities of body and mind, especially his weaknesses. We must determine his *faculté-maîtresse;* we must glance at his imitators and disciples and learn of him from his friends and his enemies; and we must devise for him a formula and classify him in his *famille d'esprits."* The ease with which this criticism lapses into pseudo-science is more apparent in Sainte-Beuve's followers (Taine, for example) than in Sainte-Beuve; but this insistence on a family of spirits, or natural kindred of intellects (so excellently illustrated in his groupings in "What is a Classic"), and of a master faculty or passion continues the emphasis on the man rather than his work. This phase of his criticism needs emphasizing, for it has become increasingly prevalent with later writers; but in Sainte-Beuve's case, this phase was supposedly preliminary: the science of criticism led naturally into the art of criticism.

Ferdinand Brunetière, in his essay on Sainte-Beuve, has put these contrasting ideas: "In the eyes of many people Sainte-Beuve's remarkable originality consists of his having transformed criticism from a lifeless analysis of letters to a living biography of men. . . . But Sainte-Beuve was not the man to be blind to the fact that when this tendency is exaggerated the very purpose of criticism is lost . . . and if, in the history of the nineteenth century (one of its claims to originality is having applied criticism to all things, even where it was not required) the name of Sainte-Beuve remains representative of and synonymous with criticism itself, we may feel assured that he owes it to his constant and passionate love of literature." Fearing generalizations, or at least cautious of them, he stays close to the individual and the book; typical enough of his criticism is the remark, "To particularize Nicole is the greatest service one can render him." And in his review of

Taine's *History of English Literature,* Sainte-Beuve adds: "After every allowance is made for general and particular elements and circumstances, there remains place and space enough around men of talent to give them every freedom of moving and turning. Besides, however narrow the circle traced round them, each talent, each genius, by the very fact that it is in a way a magician and an enchanter, has its own secrets for working miracles and producing marvels, in this circle itself."

For to truth, as a touchstone of literary excellence, he joined taste and the spirit of the classical tradition. An aesthetic humanism tempered and restrained his naturalistic beliefs. The critic's work, as he saw it, has been excellently summarized by MacClintock [*op. cit.,* 15–16]: "The distinctive service of the critic to his age and his group is that of cultivating taste in literature and the other arts; of preserving and making operative in the social mind whatever of good taste and good usage has been handed down from former times; of protecting the best tradition, proclaiming the best models; of constantly indicating the path by which beauty and distinction may be reached." The emphasis on taste is Sainte-Beuve's own emphasis; it was the keystone of his critical arch. But he was careful to check it, careful to note that personal taste might be capricious and untrustworthy: Voltaire's attack on Shakespeare does not lessen the merit of Shakespeare's work. The inherent dangers of taste, when not restrained, as a standard become apparent in Anatole France's judgment of Zola [*La Vie lit.,* I, 233]: "He has not taste, and that I have finally come to believe is the mysterious sin spoken of in Holy Writ, the greatest of sins, the only one that will not be pardoned." This is far removed from the supremacy of judgment founded on taste and tradition which Sainte-Beuve advocated, though perhaps in the line of it; both tradition and "the consciousness of our own civilized nature," he notes, in "Of a Literary Tradition," tell us "even more plainly, reason always must preside, and does preside at least among these favorites and elect of the imagination." In this passage he places Shakespeare within the classical tradition, as part of the legacy which it is the critic's duty to defend and preserve. Most of all, in this classical legacy, he valued the clarity and restraint and universalized sane trueness which he found in Greek and Latin literature: "his life was a long endeavour to supplant the romantic elements of his taste by the classical." [Paul Elmer More, *Shelburne Essays,* III, 73]

After 1849, he worked more and more in this tradition; of his work during this period, Matthew Arnold wrote: "Something of fervour, enthusiasm, poetry, he may have lost, but he had become a perfect critic." "What is a Classic" is in one sense an introductory to this later work, though it shows strong traces of his earlier ideas; and it reveals also those parts of his criticism which later became most influential. Here he was, as G. M. Harper [*Sainte-Beuve,* 366] notes, "In spite of his skeptical habit, in spite of his distrust of theory and doctrine . . . seeking eternal law under the discordant contradictions of human history."

WHAT IS A CLASSIC? *

(1850)

A DELICATE question, to which somewhat diverse solutions might be
given according to times and seasons. An intelligent man suggests it
to me, and I intend to try, if not to solve it, at least to examine and
discuss it face to face with my readers, were it only to persuade them
to answer it for themselves, and, if I can, to make their opinion and
mine on the point clear. And why, in criticism, should we not, from
time to time, venture to treat some of those subjects which are not
personal, in which we no longer speak of some one but of some thing?
Our neighbours, the English, have well succeeded in making of it a
special division of literature under the modest title of "Essays." It is
true that in writing of such subjects, always slightly abstract and
moral, it is advisable to speak of them in a season of quiet, to make
sure of our own attention and of that of others, to seize one of those
moments of calm moderation and leisure seldom granted our amiable
France; even when she is desirous of being wise and is not making
revolutions, her brilliant genius can scarcely tolerate them.

A classic, according to the usual definition, is an old author canonised
by admiration, and an authority in his particular style. The word *classic*
was first used in this sense by the Romans. With them not all the citizens of the different classes were properly called *classici,* but only those
of the chief class, those who possessed an income of a certain fixed sum.
Those who possessed a smaller income were described by the term
infra classem, below the pre-eminent class. The word *classicus* was
used in a figurative sense by Aulus Gellius, and applied to writers: a
writer of worth and distinction, *classicus assiduusque scriptor,* a writer
who is of account, has real property, and is not lost in the proletariate
crowd. Such an expression implies an age sufficiently advanced to have
already made some sort of valuation and classification of literature.

At first the only true classics for the moderns were the ancients. The
Greeks, by peculiar good fortune and natural enlightenment of mind,
had no classics but themselves. They were at first the only classical authors for the Romans, who strove and contrived to imitate them. After
the great periods of Roman literature, after Cicero and Virgil, the Ro-

* Translated by Elizabeth Lee.

mans in their turn had their classics, who became almost exclusively the classical authors of the centuries which followed. The middle ages, which were less ignorant of Latin antiquity than is believed, but which lacked proportion and taste, confused the ranks and orders. Ovid was placed above Homer, and Boetius seemed a classic equal to Plato. The revival of learning in the fifteenth and sixteenth centuries helped to bring this long chaos to order, and then only was admiration rightly proportioned. Thenceforth the true classical authors of Greek and Latin antiquity stood out in a luminous background, and were harmoniously grouped on their two heights.

Meanwhile modern literatures were born, and some of the more precocious, like the Italian, already possessed the style of antiquity. Dante appeared, and, from the very first, posterity greeted him as a classic. Italian poetry has since shrunk into far narrower bounds; but, whenever it desired to do so, it always found again and preserved the impulse and echo of its lofty origin. It is no indifferent matter for a poetry to derive its point of departure and classical source in high places; for example, to spring from Dante rather than to issue laboriously from Malherbe.

Modern Italy had her classical authors, and Spain had every right to believe that she also had hers at a time when France was yet seeking hers. A few talented writers endowed with originality and exceptional animation, a few brilliant efforts, isolated, without following, interrupted and recommenced, did not suffice to endow a nation with a solid and imposing basis of literary wealth. The idea of a classic implies something that has continuance and consistence, and which produces unity and tradition, fashions and transmits itself, and endures. It was only after the glorious years of Louis XIV that the nation felt with tremor and pride that such good fortune had happened to her. Every voice informed Louis XIV of it with flattery, exaggeration, and emphasis, yet with a certain sentiment of truth. Then arose a singular and striking contradiction: those men of whom Perrault was the chief, the men who were most smitten with the marvels of the age of Louis the Great, who even went the length of sacrificing the ancients to the moderns, aimed at exalting and canonising even those whom they regarded as inveterate opponents and adversaries. Boileau avenged and angrily upheld the ancients against Perrault, who extolled the moderns—that is to say, Corneille, Molière, Pascal, and the eminent men of his age, Boileau, one of the first, included. Kindly La Fontaine, taking part in the dispute in behalf of the learned Huet, did not perceive that, in spite of his defects, he was in his turn on the point of being held as a classic himself.

Example is the best definition. From the time France possessed her age of Louis XIV and could contemplate it at a little distance, she knew, better than by any arguments, what to be classical meant. The eighteenth century, even in its medley of things, strengthened this idea through some fine works, due to its four great men. Read Voltaire's *Age of Louis XIV*, Montesquieu's *Greatness and Fall of the Romans*, Buffon's *Epochs of Nature*, the beautiful pages of reverie and natural description of Rousseau's *Savoyard Vicar*, and say if the eighteenth century, in these memorable works, did not understand how to reconcile tradition with freedom of development and independence. But at the beginning of the present century and under the Empire, in sight of the first attempts of a decidedly new and somewhat adventurous literature, the idea of a classic in a few resisting minds, more sorrowful than severe, was strangely narrowed and contracted. The first Dictionary of the Academy (1694) merely defined a classical author as "a much-approved ancient writer, who is an authority as regards the subject he treats." The Dictionary of the Academy of 1835 narrows that definition still more, and gives precision and even limit to its rather vague form. It describes classical authors as those "who have become *models* in any language whatever," and in all the articles which follow, the expression, *models, fixed rules* for composition and style, *strict rules* of art to which men must conform, continually recur. That definition of *classic* was evidently made by the respectable Academicians, our predecessors, in face and sight of what was then called *romantic*—that is to say, in sight of the enemy. It seems to me time to renounce those timid and restrictive definitions and to free our mind of them.

A true classic, as I should like to hear it defined, is an author who has enriched the human mind, increased its treasure, and caused it to advance a step; who has discovered some moral and not equivocal truth, or revealed some eternal passion in that heart where all seemed known and discovered; who has expressed his thought, observation, or invention, in no matter what form, only provided it be broad and great, refined and sensible, sane and beautiful in itself; who has spoken to all in his own peculiar style, a style which is found to be also that of the whole world, a style new without neologism, new and old, easily contemporary with all time.

Such a classic may for a moment have been revolutionary; it may at least have seemed so, but it is not; it only lashed and subverted whatever prevented the restoration of the balance of order and beauty.

If it is desired, names may be applied to this definition which I wish to make purposely majestic and fluctuating, or in a word, all-embracing. I should first put there Corneille of the *Polyeucte, Cinna,* and *Horaces.* I should put Molière there, the fullest and most complete poetic genius we have ever had in France. Goethe, the king of critics, said:—

"Molière is so great that he astonishes us afresh every time we read him. He is a man apart; his plays border on the tragic, and no one has the courage to try and imitate him. His *Avare,* where vice destroys all affection between father and son, is one of the most sublime works, and dramatic in the highest degree. In a drama every action ought to be important in itself, and to lead to an action greater still. In this respect *Tartuffe* is a model. What a piece of exposition the first scene is! From the beginning everything has an important meaning, and causes something much more important to be foreseen. The exposition in a certain play of Lessing that might be mentioned is very fine, but the world only sees that of *Tartuffe* once. It is the finest of the kind we possess. Every year I read a play of Molière, just as from time to time I contemplate some engraving after the great Italian masters."

I do not conceal from myself that the definition of the classic I have just given somewhat exceeds the notion usually ascribed to the term. It should, above all, include conditions of uniformity, wisdom, moderation, and reason, which dominate and contain all the others. Having to praise M. Royer-Collard, M. de Rémusat said—"If he derives *purity of taste, propriety of terms, variety of expression,* attentive care in *suiting the action to the thought,* from our classics, he owes to himself alone the distinctive character he gives it all." It is here evident that the part allotted to classical qualities seems mostly to depend on harmony and *nuances* of expression, on graceful and temperate style: such is also the most general opinion. In this sense the pre-eminent classics would be writers of a middling order, exact, sensible, elegant, always clear, yet of noble feeling and airily veiled strength. Marie-Joseph Chénier has described the poetics of those temperate and accomplished writers in lines where he shows himself their happy disciple:—

"It is good sense, reason which does all,—virtue, genius, soul, talent, and taste.—What is virtue? reason put in practice;—talent? reason expressed with brilliance;—soul? reason delicately put forth;—and genius is sublime reason."

While writing those lines he was evidently thinking of Pope, Boileau, and Horace, the master of them all. The peculiar characteristic of the theory which subordinated imagination and feeling itself to reason, of which Scaliger perhaps gave the first sign among the moderns, is, properly speaking, the *Latin* theory, and for a long time it was also by preference the *French* theory. If it is used appositely, if the term *reason* is not abused, that theory possesses some truth; but it is evident that it is abused, and that if, for instance, reason can be confounded with poetic genius and make one with it in a moral epistle, it cannot be the same thing as the genius, so varied and so diversely creative in its expression of the passions, of the drama or the epic. Where will you find reason in the fourth book of the *Æneid* and the transports of Dido? Be that as it may, the spirit which prompted the theory, caused writers who ruled their inspiration, rather than those who abandoned themselves to it, to be placed in the first rank of classics; to put Virgil there more surely than Homer, Racine in preference to Corneille. The masterpiece to which the theory likes to point, which in fact brings together all conditions of prudence, strength, tempered boldness, moral elevation, and grandeur, is *Athalie*. Turenne in his two last campaigns and Racine in *Athalie* are the great examples of what wise and prudent men are capable of when they reach the maturity of their genius and attain their supremest boldness.

Buffon, in his Discourse on Style, insisting on the unity of design, arrangement, and execution, which are the stamps of true classical works, said:—"Every subject is one, *and however vast it is, it can be comprised in a single treatise.* Interruptions, pauses, sub-divisions should only be used when many subjects are treated, when, having to speak of great, intricate, and dissimilar things, the march of genius is interrupted by the multiplicity of obstacles, and contracted by the necessity of circumstances: otherwise, far from making a work more solid, a great number of divisions destroys the unity of its parts; the book appears clearer to the view, but the author's design remains obscure." And he continues his criticism, having in view Montesquieu's *Spirit of Laws,* an excellent book at bottom, but sub-divided: the famous author, worn out before the end, was unable to infuse inspiration into all his ideas, and to arrange all his matter. However, I can scarcely believe that Buffon was not also thinking, by way of contrast, of Bossuet's *Discourse on Universal History,* a subject vast indeed, and yet of such an unity that the great orator was able to comprise it in a single treatise. When we open the first edition, that of 1681, before the division into chapters, which was introduced later, passed from the margin into the text, everything is developed in a single series, almost in one breath. It might be said that the orator has here acted like the nature of which Buffon speaks, that "he has worked on an eternal plan from which he has nowhere departed," so deeply does he seem to have entered into the familiar counsels and designs of providence.

Are *Athalie* and the *Discourse on Universal History* the greatest masterpieces that the strict classical theory can present to its friends as well as to its enemies? In spite of the admirable simplicity and dignity in the achievement of such unique productions, we should like, nevertheless, in the interests of art, to expand that theory a little, and to show that it is possible to enlarge it without relaxing the tension. Goethe, whom I like to quote on such a subject, said:—

"I call the classical *healthy,* and the romantic *sickly.* In my opinion the Nibelungen song is as much a classic as Homer. Both are healthy and vigorous. The works of the day are romantic, not because they are new, but because they are weak, ailing, or sickly. Ancient works are classical not because they are old, but because they are powerful, fresh, and healthy. If we regarded romantic and classical from those two points of view we should soon all agree."

Indeed, before determining and fixing the opinions on that matter, I should like every unbiased mind to take a voyage round the world and devote itself to a survey of different literatures in their primitive vigour and infinite variety. What would be seen? Chief of all a Homer, the father of the classical world, less a single distinct individual than the vast living expression of a whole epoch and a semi-barbarous civilisation. In order to make him a true classic, it was necessary to attribute to him later a design, a plan, literary invention, qualities of atticism and urbanity of which he had certainly never dreamed in the luxuriant development of his natural aspirations. And who appear by his side? August, venerable ancients, the Æschyluses and the Sophocles, mutilated, it is true, and only there to present us with a *débris* of themselves, the survivors of many others as worthy, doubtless, as they to survive, but who have succumbed to the injuries of time. This thought alone would teach a man of impartial mind not to look upon the whole of even classical literatures with a too narrow and restricted view; he would learn that the exact and well-proportioned order which has since so largely prevailed in our admiration of the past was only the outcome of artificial circumstances.

And in reaching the modern world, how would it be? The greatest names to be seen at the beginning of literatures are those which disturb and run counter to certain fixed ideas of what is beautiful and appropriate in poetry. For example, is Shakespeare a classic? Yes, now, for England and the world; but in the time of Pope he was not considered so. Pope and his friends were the only pre-eminent classics; directly after their death they seemed so for ever. At the present time they are still classics, as they deserve to be, but they are only of the second order, and are for ever subordinated and relegated to their rightful place by him who has again come to his own on the height of the horizon.

It is not, however, for me to speak ill of Pope or his great disciples, above all, when they possess pathos and naturalness like Goldsmith: after the greatest they are perhaps the most agreeable writers and the poets best fitted to add charm to life. Once when Lord Bolingbroke was writing to Swift, Pope added a postscript, in which he said—"I think some advantage would result to our age, if we three spent three years together." Men who, without boasting, have the right to say such things must never be spoken of lightly: the fortunate ages, when men of talent could propose such things, then no chimera, are rather to be envied. The ages called by the name of Louis XIV or of Queen Anne are, in the dispassionate sense of the word, the only true classical ages, those which offer protection and a favourable climate to real talent. We know only too well how in our untrammelled times, through the instability and storminess of the age, talents are lost and dissipated. Nevertheless, let us acknowledge our age's part and superiority in greatness. True and sovereign genius triumphs over the very difficulties that cause others to fail: Dante, Shakespeare, and Milton were able to attain their height and produce their imperishable works in spite of obstacles, hardships, and tempests. Byron's opinion of Pope has been much discussed, and the explanation of it sought in the kind of contradiction by which the singer of *Don Juan* and *Childe Harold* extolled the purely classical school and pronounced it the only good one, while himself acting so differently. Goethe spoke the truth on that point when he remarked that Byron, great by the flow and source of poetry, feared that Shakespeare was more powerful than himself in the creation and realisation of his characters. "He would have liked to deny it; the elevation so free from egoism irritated him; he felt when near it that he could not display himself at ease. He never denied Pope, because he did not fear him; he knew that Pope was only a *low wall* by his side."

If, as Byron desired, Pope's school had kept the supremacy and a sort of honorary empire in the past, Byron would have been the first and only poet in his particular style; the height of Pope's wall shuts out

Shakespeare's great figure from sight, whereas when Shakespeare reigns and rules in all his greatness, Byron is only second.

In France there was no great classic before the age of Louis XIV; the Dantes and Shakespeares, the early authorities to whom, in times of emancipation, men sooner or later return, were wanting. There were mere sketches of great poets, like Mathurin Regnier, like Rabelais, without any ideal, without the depth of emotion and the seriousness which canonises. Montaigne was a kind of premature classic, of the family of Horace; but for want of worthy surroundings, like a spoiled child, he gave himself up to the unbridled fancies of his style and humour. Hence it happened that France, less than any other nation, found in her old authors a right to demand vehemently at a certain time literary liberty and freedom, and that it was more difficult for her, in enfranchising herself, to remain classical. However, with Molière and La Fontaine among her classics of the great period, nothing could justly be refused to those who possessed courage and ability.

The important point now seems to me to be to uphold, while extending, the idea and belief. There is no receipt for making classics; this point should be clearly recognised. To believe that an author will become a classic by imitating certain qualities of purity, moderation, accuracy, and elegance, independently of the style and inspiration, is to believe that after Racine the father there is a place for Racine the son; dull and estimable *rôle,* the worst in poetry. Further, it is hazardous to take too quickly and without opposition the place of a classic in the sight of one's contemporaries; in that case there is a good chance of not retaining the position with posterity. Fontanes in his day was regarded by his friends as a pure classic; see how at twenty-five years' distance his star has set. How many of these precocious classics are there who do not endure, and who are so only for a while! We turn round one morning and are surprised not to find them standing behind us. Madame de Sévigné would wittily say they possessed but an *evanescent colour.* With regard to classics, the least expected prove the best and greatest: seek them rather in the vigorous genius born immortal and flourishing for ever. Apparently the least classical of the four great poets of the age of Louis XIV was Molière; he was then applauded far more than he was esteemed; men took delight in him without understanding his worth. After him, La Fontaine seemed the least classical: observe after two centuries what is the result for both. Far above Boileau, even above Racine, are they not now unanimously considered to possess in the highest degree the characteristics of an all-embracing morality?

Meanwhile there is no question of sacrificing or depreciating anything. I believe the temple of taste is to be rebuilt; but its reconstruction is merely a matter of enlargement, so that it may become the home of all noble human beings, of all who have permanently increased the sum of the mind's delights and possessions. As for me, who cannot, obviously, in any degree pretend to be the architect or designer of such a temple, I shall confine myself to expressing a few earnest wishes, to submit, as it were, my designs for the edifice. Above all I should desire not to exclude any one among the worthy, each should be in his place there, from Shakespeare, the freest of creative geniuses, and the greatest of classics without knowing it, to Andrieux, the last of classics in little. "There is more than one chamber in the mansions of my Father;" that should be as true of the kingdom of the beautiful here below, as of the kingdom of Heaven. Homer, as always and everywhere, should be first, likest a god; but behind him, like the procession of the three wise kings of the East, would be seen the three great poets, the three Homers, so long ignored by us, who wrote epics for the use of the old peoples of Asia, the poets Valmiki, Vyasa of the Hindoos, and Firdousi of the Persians: in the domain of taste it is well to know that such men exist, and not to divide the human race. Our homage paid to what is recognised as soon as perceived, we must not stray further; the eye should delight in a thousand pleasing or majestic spectacles, should rejoice in a thousand varied and surprising combinations, whose apparent confusion would never be without concord and harmony. The oldest of the wise men and poets, those who put human morality into maxims, and those who in simple fashion sung it, would converse together in *rare and gentle* speech, and would not be surprised at understanding each other's meaning at the very first word. Solon, Hesiod, Theognis, Job, Solomon, and why not Confucius, would welcome the cleverest moderns. La Rochefoucauld and La Bruyère, who, when listening to them, would say "they knew all that we know, and in repeating life's experiences, we have discovered nothing." On the hill, most easily discernible, and of most accessible ascent, Virgil, surrounded by Menander, Tibullus, Terence, Fénélon, would occupy himself in discoursing with them with great charm and divine enchantment: his gentle countenance would shine with an inner light, and be tinged with modesty; as on the day when entering the theatre at Rome, just as they finished reciting his verses, he saw the people rise with an unanimous movement and pay to him the same homage as to

Augustus. Not far from him, regretting the separation from so dear a friend, Horace, in his turn, would preside (as far as so accomplished and wise a poet could preside) over the group of poets of social life who could talk although they sang,—Pope, Boileau, the one become less irritable, the other less fault-finding. Montaigne, a true poet, would be among them, and would give the finishing touch that should deprive that delightful corner of the air of a literary school. There would La Fontaine forget himself, and becoming less volatile would wander no more. Voltaire would be attracted by it, but while finding pleasure in it would not have patience to remain. A little lower down, on the same hill as Virgil, Xenophon, with a simple bearing, looking in no way like a general, but rather resembling a priest of the Muses, would be seen gathering round him the Attics of every tongue and of every nation, the Addisons, Pellissons, Vauvenargues—all who feel the value of an easy persuasiveness, an exquisite simplicity, and a gentle negligence mingled with ornament. In the centre of the place, in the portico of the principal temple (for there would be several in the enclosure), three great men would like to meet often, and when they were together, no fourth, however great, would dream of joining their discourse or their silence. In them would be seen beauty, proportion in greatness, and that perfect harmony which appears but once in the full youth of the world. Their three names have become the ideal of art—Plato, Sophocles, and Demosthenes. Those demi-gods honoured, we see a numerous and familiar company of choice spirits who follow, the Cervantes and Molières, practical painters of life, indulgent friends who are still the first of benefactors, who laughingly embrace all mankind, turn man's experience to gaiety, and know the powerful workings of a sensible, hearty, and legitimate joy. I do not wish to make this description, which if complete would fill a volume, any longer. In the middle ages, believe me, Dante would occupy the sacred heights: at the feet of the singer of Paradise all Italy would be spread out like a garden; Boccaccio and Ariosto would there disport themselves, and Tasso would find again the orange groves of Sorrento. Usually a corner would be reserved for each of the various nations, but the authors would take delight in leaving it, and in their travels would recognise, where we should least expect it, brothers or masters. Lucretius, for example, would enjoy discussing the origin of the world and the reducing of chaos to order with Milton. But both arguing from their own point of view, they would only agree as regards divine pictures of poetry and nature.

Such are our classics; each individual imagination may finish the sketch and choose the group preferred. For it is necessary to make a choice, and the first condition of taste, after obtaining knowledge of all, lies not in continual travel, but in rest and cessation from wandering. Nothing blunts and destroys taste so much as endless journeyings; the poetic spirit is not the *Wandering Jew*. However, when I speak of resting and making choice, my meaning is not that we are to imitate those who charm us most among our masters in the past. Let us be content to know them, to penetrate them, to admire them; but let us, the latecomers, endeavour to be ourselves. Let us have the sincerity and naturalness of our own thoughts, of our own feelings; so much is always possible. To that let us add what is more difficult, elevation, an aim, if possible, towards an exalted goal; and while speaking our own language, and submitting to the conditions of the times in which we live, whence we derive our strength and our defects, let us ask from time to time, our brows lifted towards the heights and our eyes fixed on the group of honoured mortals: *what would they say of us?*

But why speak always of authors and writings? Maybe an age is coming when there will be no more writing. Happy those who read and read again, those who in their reading can follow their unrestrained inclination! There comes a time in life when, all our journeys over, our experiences ended, there is no enjoyment more delightful than to study and thoroughly examine the things we know, to take pleasure in what we feel, and in seeing and seeing again the people we love: the pure joys of our maturity. Then it is that the word classic takes its true meaning, and is defined for every man of taste by an irresistible choice. Then taste is formed, it is shaped and definite; then good sense, if we are to possess it at all, is perfected in us. We have neither more time for experiments, nor a desire to go forth in search of pastures new. We cling to our friends, to those proved by a long intercourse. Old wine, old books, old friends. We say to ourselves with Voltaire in these delightful lines:—"Let us enjoy, let us write, let us live, my dear Horace! . . . I have lived longer than you: my verse will not last so long. But on the brink of the tomb I shall make it my chief care—to follow the lessons of your philosophy—to despise death in enjoying life—to read your writings full of charm and good sense—as we drink an old wine which revives our senses."

In fact, be it Horace or another who is the author preferred, who reflects our thoughts in all the wealth of their maturity, of some one of those excellent and antique minds shall we request an interview at every moment; of some one of them shall we ask a friendship which never deceives, which could not fail us; to some one of them shall we appeal for that sensation of serenity and amenity (we have often need of it) which reconciles us with mankind and with ourselves.

ᴍATTHEW ᴀRNOLD

(1822–1888)

THE father of Matthew Arnold was Dr. Thomas Arnold, headmaster of Rugby. The scholarly and kindly character of his father remained throughout his life an influence and an example of the greatest importance.

In 1837, after a brief attendance at Winchester, Matthew Arnold entered Rugby, and in 1840, Balliol College, Oxford. Here he published his *Cromwell,* a poem which won the Newdigate prize. Graduating in 1844, he became a fellow of Oriel College, where he first became acquainted with A. H. Clough. He subsequently held numerous scholarly positions, becoming an inspector of schools in 1851. In this year he married Frances Lucy Wightman.

He had published prior to this *The Strayed Reveller, and other Poems,* and in 1852 appeared *Empedocles on Etna,* and in 1853, a volume of *Poems,* composed chiefly of selections from the other two publications. These early poems brought him election as professor of poetry at Oxford in 1857, and in this capacity he continued for ten years. *Merope* was published in 1858, the *New Poems* in 1867. These years (1857–67) saw the composition of many of his outstanding critical works, *On Translating Homer* (1861), the first series of *Essays in Criticism* (1865), *On the Study of Celtic Literature* (1867). The years from 1867 to 1888 were spent in his profession as inspector of schools and in the study and practice of criticism. He was commissioned on numerous investigations of the educational systems of the continental countries. His outstanding researches along these lines are embodied in *Schools and Universities on the Continent* (1868) and the *Special Report on . . . Elementary Education in Germany, Switzerland, and France* (1886).

The chief of his later critical publications were: *Culture and Anarchy* (1869); *Literature and Dogma* (1873); *Mixed Essays* (1879); *Irish Essays* (1882); *Essays in Criticism,* second series (1888). In 1875 appeared the collection called *God and the Bible,* and in 1877 the *Last Essays on Church and Religion.* "The Study of Poetry" was written in 1880 as the introduction to Ward's *English Poets.* The importance of Arnold as a lecturer during these last years should also be mentioned. He died suddenly in 1888.

In a higher degree than were most of the other major critics, Arnold was concerned in his theoretical writings with social, educational, and religious forces as well as with literary. His influence has therefore tended to broaden the whole scope of criticism; and the body of his critical essays, even when most definitely turned in a literary direction, keep alive in the reader an awareness that other problems are related to those under discussion. That literature is a "criticism of life" he asserts as early as the "Joubert" essay, and "The Function of Criticism at the Present Time" examines a variety of conditions which are far removed from any questions of purely literary significance. But it is this insistence upon criticism's application to all phases of life that enables him to state the new ideal for criticism, to give to it a scope not less wide than that of poetry.

Of prime importance in Arnold's view of the life of his time is the place which he insists upon for "culture" in a world moving to a rapidly accelerating tempo. Of "culture" we get his famous definition in the opening chapter of the book *Culture and Anarchy,* where it is explained as "a study of perfection," with an explanatory motto borrowed from Bishop Wilson, "to make reason and the will of God prevail;" its characteristics are "sweetness and light," or a broad human sympathy and a vigorous understanding. The purpose of culture must always be to clarify the worthiest ends of existence, and to distinguish between these ends and the means toward them —to discern in all movements what is permanent and perfect, and what only transitory and partial. Among the many isms of the Victorian period, amid the glorification of machinery and the agitation for political reform, Arnold discerned next to no sweetness and light.

Culture, however, shows its single-minded love of perfection, its desire simply to make reason and the will of God prevail, its freedom from fanaticism, by its attitude towards all this machinery, even while it insists that it *is* machinery. Fanatics, seeing the mischief men do themselves by their blind belief in some machinery or other,—whether it is wealth and industrialism, or whether it is the cultivation of bodily strength and activity, or whether it is a political organisation,—or whether it is a religious organisation,—oppose with might and main the tendency to this or that political and religious organisation, or to games and athletic exercises, or to wealth and industrialism, and try violently to stop it. But the flexibility which sweetness and light give, and which is one of the rewards of culture pursued in good faith, enables a man to see that a tendency may be necessary, and even, as a preparation for something in the future, salutary, and yet that the generations or individuals who obey this tendency are sacrificed to it, that they fall short of the hope of perfection by following it; and that its mischiefs are to be criticised, lest it should take too firm a hold and last after it has served its purpose. ["Sweetness and Light."]

In the light of this idealistic view of culture it is not hard to understand Arnold's insistence in "The Function of Criticism at the Present Time" that "criticism must maintain its independence of the practical spirit and its aims;" it is not to be sacrificed to gaining actions: "a disinterested endeavour to learn and propagate the best that is known and thought in the world" is above, free of, "alien, practical considerations;" its ends are not *things;* it achieves its purpose in the promotion of a "fresh current of ideas."

For such promulgation and furthering of ideas Arnold held that openness of mind was necessary: the insularity and conceitedness of contemporary

Englishmen he deplored. The remedy which he recommended was the study of the continental literatures, particularly that of France. "Of these . . . literatures [those of France and Germany]," he writes, "as of the intellect of Europe in general, the main effort for now many years, has been a *critical* effort; the endeavour, in all branches of knowledge, theology, philosophy, history, art, science,—to see the object as in itself it really is. But owing to the presence in English literature of this eccentric and arbitrary spirit, owing to the strong tendency of English writers to bring to the consideration of their object some individual fancy, almost the last thing for which one would come to English literature is just that very thing which now Europe most desires—*criticism.*" [*On Translating Homer*, II.] The will "to see the object as in itself it really is" Arnold observed to be excellently exemplified in Renan's research in comparative religions, in Sainte-Beuve's criticism; the reason for the general French superiority, he felt, lay in the factor responsible for Joubert's having in his country a greater influence than Coleridge in his: "There is . . . in France a sympathy with intellectual activity for its own sake, and for the sake of its inherent pleasurableness and beauty, keener than any which exists in England." ["Joubert; or a French Coleridge."]

A need which Arnold considered of hardly less importance for nineteenth century England than the influence of French disinterestedness, was the rediscovery of classicism. In the Preface to his *Poems*, 1853, often referred to as the essay on "The Choice of Subjects in Poetry," he recalls to his readers "the calm, the cheerfulness, the disinterested objectivity" possessed by the great Greeks, the "clearness of arrangement, rigour of development, simplicity of style," by which "the tone of the parts was to be perpetually kept down, in order not to impair the grandiose effect of the whole." He "fearlessly" asserts that "*Hermann and Dorothea, Childe Harold, Jocelyn, The Excursion,* leave the reader cold in comparison with the effect produced by the latter books of the *Iliad,* by the *Orestea,* or by the episode of Dido . . , because in the latter cases the action is greater, the personages nobler, the situations more intense: and this is the true basis of the interest in a poetical work, and this alone." It is for this reason that the great ancients should be regarded as the best models, that they, "although infinitely less suggestive than Shakespeare, are thus, to the artist, more instructive."

There is a true Aristotelianism in the insistence upon action in literary works, action as opposed to "the dialogue of the mind with itself," upon such actions as "most powerfully appeal to the great primary human affections: to those elementary feelings which subsist permanently in the race, and which are independent of time." One paragraph significantly directs this great tenet of the *Poetics* against the modern tendency toward pathos:

> What then are the situations, from the representation of which, though accurate, no poetical enjoyment can be derived? They are those in which the suffering finds no vent in action; in which a continuous state of mental distress is prolonged, unrelieved by incident, hope, or resistance; in which there is everything to be endured, nothing to be done. In such situations there is inevitably something morbid, in the description of them something monotonous. When they occur in actual

life, they are painful, not tragic; the representation of them in poetry is painful also.

To Arnold's critical method Mr. W. C. Brownell has devoted a good part of his essay on him in *Victorian Prose Masters*. The absence of a scientific, or philological, or psychological approach, as also the far remove from the impressionistic criticism which has developed under the influence of M. Anatole France, are quickly felt when one turns back to the *Essays in Criticism*. "Arnold's own theme is the personal element in the works of others, and its treatment is frankly the application to these of this element in himself. The report it gives is the result, though this personal report is, as I began by noting, very different from an impressionist report in being carefully controlled and corrected by culture, framed, in fact, in accordance with the express principle of classic comparisons that he eloquently advocates and specifically illustrates in his essay on 'The Study of Poetry,' and as far removed from irresponsibility as if it claimed scientific exactness." [*Victorian Prose Masters*, 166.]

From

THE FUNCTION OF CRITICISM AT THE PRESENT TIME *

(1865)

MANY objections have been made to a proposition which, in some remarks of mine on translating Homer, I ventured to put forth; a proposition about criticism, and its importance at the present day. I said that "of the literature of France and Germany, as of the intellect of Europe in general, the main effort, for now many years, has been a critical effort; the endeavour, in all branches of knowledge, theology, philosophy, history, art, science, to see the object as in itself it really is." I added, that owing to the operation in English literature of certain causes, "almost the last thing for which one would come to English literature is just that very thing which now Europe most desires,—criticism;" and that the power and value of English literature was thereby impaired. More than one rejoinder declared that the importance I here assigned to criticism was excessive, and asserted the inherent superiority of the creative effort of the human spirit over its critical effort. And the other day, having been led by an excellent notice of Wordsworth, published in the *North British Review,* to turn again to his biography, I found, in the words of this great man, whom I, for one,

* Published by E. P. Dutton & Co., Inc., New York, N. Y.

must always listen to with the profoundest respect, a sentence passed on the critic's business, which seems to justify every possible disparagement of it. Wordsworth says in one of his letters:—

"The writers in these publications" (the Reviews), "while they prosecute their inglorious employment, cannot be supposed to be in a state of mind very favourable for being affected by the finer influences of a thing so pure as genuine poetry."

And a trustworthy reporter of his conversation quotes a more elaborate judgment to the same effect:—

"Wordsworth holds the critical power very low, infinitely lower than the inventive; and he said to-day that if the quantity of time consumed in writing critiques on the works of others were given to original composition, of whatever kind it might be, it would be much better employed; it would make a man find out sooner his own level, and it would do infinitely less mischief. A false or malicious criticism may do much injury to the minds of others; a stupid invention, either in prose or verse, is quite harmless."

It is almost too much to expect of poor human nature, that a man capable of producing some effect in one line of literature, should, for the greater good of society, voluntarily doom himself to impotence and obscurity in another. Still less is this to be expected from men addicted to the composition of the "false or malicious criticism" of which Wordsworth speaks. However, everybody would admit that a false or malicious criticism had better never have been written. Everybody, too, would be willing to admit, as a general proposition, that the critical faculty is lower than the inventive. But is it true that criticism is really, in itself, a baneful and injurious employment? is it true that all time given to writing critiques on the works of others would be much better employed if it were given to original composition, of whatever kind this may be? Is it true that Johnson had better have gone on producing more *Irenes* instead of writing his *Lives of the Poets?* nay, is it certain that Wordsworth himself was better employed in making his Ecclesiastical Sonnets than when he made his celebrated Preface, so full of criticism, and criticism of the works of others? Wordsworth was himself a great critic, and it is to be sincerely regretted that he has not left us more criticism; Goethe was one of the greatest critics, and we may sincerely congratulate ourselves that he has left us so much criticism. Without wasting time over the exaggeration which Wordsworth's judgment on criticism clearly contains, or over an attempt to trace the causes,—not difficult, I think, to be traced,—which may have led Wordsworth to this exaggeration, a critic may with advantage seize an occasion for trying his own conscience, and for asking himself of what real service, at any given moment, the practice of criticism either is, or may be made, to his own mind and spirit, and to the minds and spirits of others.

The critical power is of lower rank than the creative. True; but in assenting to this proposition, one or two things are to be kept in mind. It is undeniable that the exercise of a creative power, that a free creative activity, is the true function of man; it is proved to be so by man's finding in it his true happiness. But it is undeniable, also, that men may have the sense of exercising this free creative activity in other ways than in producing great works of literature or art; if it were not so, all but a very few men would be shut out from the true happiness of all men; they may have it in well-doing, they may have it in learning, they may have it even in criticising. This is one thing to be kept in mind. Another is, that the exercise of the creative power in the production of great works of literature or art, however high this exercise of it may rank, is not at all epochs and under all conditions possible; and that therefore labour may be vainly spent in attempting it, and may with more fruit be used in preparing for it, in rendering it possible. This creative power works with elements, with materials; what if it has not those materials, those elements, ready for its use? In that case it must surely wait till they are ready. Now, in literature,—I will limit myself to literature, for it is about literature that the question arises,—the elements with which the creative power works are ideas; the best ideas on every matter which literature touches, current at the time; at any rate we may lay it down as certain that in modern literature no manifestation of the creative power not working with these can be very important or fruitful. And I say *current* at the time, not merely accessible at the time; for creative literary genius does not principally show itself in discovering new ideas, that is rather the business of the philosopher; the grand work of literary genius is a work of synthesis and exposition, not of analysis and discovery; its gift lies in the faculty of being happily inspired by a certain intellectual and spiritual atmosphere, by a certain order of ideas, when it finds itself in them; of dealing divinely with these ideas, presenting them in the most effective and attractive combinations, making beautiful works with them, in short. But it must have the atmosphere, it must find itself amidst the order of ideas, in order to work freely; and these it is not so easy to command. This is why great creative epochs in literature are so rare; this is why there is so much that is unsatisfactory in the productions of many men of real genius; because, for the creation of a master-work of literature two powers must concur, the power of the man and the power of the moment, and the man is not enough without the moment; the creative power has, for its happy exercise, appointed elements, and those elements are not in its own control.

Nay, they are more within the control of the critical power. It is the business of the critical power, as I said in the words already quoted, "in all branches of knowledge, theology, philosophy, history, art, science, to see the object as in itself it really is." Thus it tends, at last, to make an intellectual situation of which the creative power can profitably avail itself. It tends to establish an order of ideas, if not absolutely true, yet true by comparison with that which it displaces; to make the best ideas prevail. Presently these new ideas reach society, the touch of truth is the touch of life, and there is a stir and growth everywhere; out of this stir and growth come the creative epochs of literature.

Or, to narrow our range, and quit these considerations of the general march of genius and of society,—considerations which are apt to become too abstract and impalpable,—every one can see that a poet, for instance, ought to know life and the world before dealing with them in poetry; and life and the world being in modern times, very complex things, the creation of a modern poet, to be worth much, implies a great critical effort behind it; else it would be a comparatively poor, barren, and short-lived affair. This is why Byron's poetry had so little endurance in it, and Goethe's so much; both had a great productive power, but Goethe's was nourished by a great critical effort providing the true materials for it, and Byron's was not; Goethe knew life and the world, the poet's necessary subjects, much more comprehensively and thoroughly than Byron. He knew a great deal more of them, and he knew them much more as they really are.

It has long seemed to me that the burst of creative activity in our literature, through the first quarter of this century, had about it in fact something premature; and that from this cause its productions are doomed, most of them, in spite of the sanguine hopes which accompanied and do still accompany them, to prove hardly more lasting than the productions of far less splendid epochs. And this prematureness comes from its having proceeded without having its proper data, without sufficient materials to work with. In other words, the English poetry of the first quarter of this century, with plenty of energy, plenty of creative force, did not know enough. This makes Byron so empty of matter, Shelley so incoherent, Wordsworth even, profound as he is, yet so wanting in completeness and variety. Wordsworth cared little for books, and disparaged Goethe. I admire Wordsworth, as he is, so much that I cannot wish him different; and it is vain, no doubt, to imagine such a man different from what he is, to suppose that he could have been different; but surely the one thing wanting to make Wordsworth an even greater poet than he is,—his thought richer, and his influence of wider application,—was that he should have read more books, among them, no doubt, those of that Goethe whom he disparaged without reading him. But to speak of books and reading may easily lead to a misunderstanding here. It was not really books and reading that lacked to our poetry at this epoch; Shelley had plenty of reading, Coleridge had immense reading. Pindar and Sophocles—as we all say so glibly, and often with so little discernment of the real import of what we are saying—had not many books; Shakspeare was no deep reader. True; but in the Greece of Pindar and Sophocles, in the England of Shakspeare, the poet lived in a current of ideas in the highest degree animating and nourishing to the creative power; society was, in the fullest measure, permeated by fresh thought, intelligent and alive; and this state of things is the true basis for the creative power's exercise, in this it finds its data, its materials, truly ready for its hand; all the books and reading in the world are only valuable as they are helps to this. Even when this does not actually exist, books and reading may enable a man to construct a kind of semblance of it in his own mind, a world of knowledge and intelligence in which he may live and work; this is by no means an equivalent to the artist for the nationally diffused life and thought of the epochs of Sophocles or Shakspeare; but, besides that it may be a means of preparation for such epochs, it does really constitute, if many share in it, a quickening and sustaining atmosphere of great value. Such an atmosphere the many-sided learning and the long and widely-combined critical effort of Germany formed for Goethe, when he lived and worked. There was no national glow of life and thought there, as in the Athens of Pericles or the England of Elizabeth. That was the poet's weakness. But there was a sort of equivalent for it in the complete culture and unfettered thinking of a large body of Germans. That was his strength. In the England of the first quarter of this century there was neither a national glow of life and thought, such as we had in the age of Elizabeth, nor yet a culture and a force of learning and criticism such as were to be found in Germany. Therefore the creative power of poetry wanted, for success in the highest sense, materials and a basis; a thorough interpretation of the world was necessarily denied to it.

At first sight it seems strange that out of the immense stir of the French Revolution and its age should not have come a crop of works of genius equal to that which came out of the stir of the great productive time of Greece, or out of that of the Renaissance, with its powerful episode the Reformation. But the truth is that the stir of the French Revolution took a character which essentially distinguished it from such movements as these. These were, in the main, disinterestedly intellectual and spiritual movements; movements in which the human spirit looked for its satisfaction in itself and in the increased play of its own activity: the French Revolution took a political, practical character. This Revolution—the object of so much blind love and so much blind hatred,—found indeed its motive-power in the intelligence of men, and not in their practical sense;—this is what distinguishes it from the English Revolution of Charles the First's time; this is what makes it a more spiritual event than our Revolution, an event of much more powerful and world-wide interest, though practically less successful— it appeals to an order of ideas which are universal, certain, permanent. 1789 asked of a thing, Is it rational? 1642 asked of a thing, Is it legal? or, when it went furthest, Is it according to conscience? This is the English fashion, a fashion to be treated, within its own sphere, with the highest respect; for its success, within its own sphere, has been prodigious. But what is law in one place is not law in another; what is law here to-day is not law even here to-morrow; and as for conscience, what is binding on one man's conscience is not binding on another's, the old woman who threw her stool at the head of the surpliced minister in the Tron Church at Edinburgh obeyed an impulse to which millions of the human race may be permitted to remain strangers. But the prescriptions of reason are absolute, unchanging, of universal validity; *to count by tens is the easiest way of counting*—that is a proposition of which every one, from here to the Antipodes, feels the force; at least I should say so if we did not live in a country where it is not impossible that any morning we may find a letter in the *Times* declaring that a decimal coinage is an absurdity. That a whole nation should have been penetrated with an enthusiasm for pure reason, and with an ardent zeal for making its prescriptions triumph, is a very remarkable thing, when we consider how little of mind, or anything so worthy and quickening as mind, comes into the motives which alone, in general, *impel* great masses of men. In spite of the extravagant direction given to this enthusiasm, in spite of the crimes and follies in which it lost itself, the French Revolution derives from the force, truth, and uni-

versality of the ideas which it took for its law, and from the passion with
which it could inspire a multitude for these ideas, a unique and still
living power; it is—it will probably long remain—the greatest, the most
animating event in history. And as no sincere passion for the things of
the mind, even though it turn out in many respects an unfortunate
passion, is ever quite thrown away and quite barren of good, France
has reaped from hers one fruit, the natural and legitimate fruit, though
not precisely the grand fruit she expected: she is the country in Europe
where *the people* is most alive.

But the mania for giving an immediate political and practical application to all these fine ideas of the reason was fatal. Here an Englishman is in his element: on this theme we can all go for hours. And all
we are in the habit of saying on it has undoubtedly a great deal of truth.
Ideas cannot be too much prized in and for themselves, cannot be too
much lived with; but to transport them abruptly into the world of
politics and practice, violently to revolutionise this world to their bid-
ding,—that is quite another thing. There is the world of ideas and there
is the world of practice; the French are often for suppressing the one
and the English the other; but neither is to be suppressed. A member of
the House of Commons said to me the other day: "That a thing is an
anomaly, I consider to be no objection to it whatever." I venture to think
he was wrong; that a thing is an anomaly *is* an objection to it, but absolutely and in the sphere of ideas: it is not necessarily, under such and
such circumstances, or at such and such a moment, an objection to it in
the sphere of politics and practice. Joubert has said beautifully: "C'est
la force et le droit qui réglent toutes choses dans le monde; la force en
attendant le droit." Force and right are the governors of this world;
force till right is ready. *Force till right is ready;* and till right is ready,
force, the existing order of things, is justified, is the legitimate ruler. But
right is something moral, and implies inward recognition, free assent
of the will; we are not ready for right,—*right,* so far as we are concerned, *is not ready,*—until we have attained this sense of seeing it and
willing it. The way in which for us it may change and transform force,
the existing order of things, and become, in its turn, the legitimate ruler
of the world, will depend on the way in which, when our time comes,
we see it and will it. Therefore for other people enamoured of their
own newly discerned right, to attempt to impose it upon us as ours, and
violently to substitute their right for our force, is an act of tyranny,
and to be resisted. It sets at nought the second great half of our maxim,
force till right is ready. This was the grand error of the French Revolu-

tion; and its movement of ideas, by quitting the intellectual sphere and rushing furiously into the political sphere, ran, indeed, a prodigious and memorable course, but produced no such intellectual fruit as the movement of ideas of the Renaissance, and created, in opposition to itself, what I may call an *epoch of concentration.* The great force of that epoch of concentration was England; and the great voice of that epoch of concentration was Burke. It is the fashion to treat Burke's writings on the French Revolution as superannuated and conquered by the event; as the eloquent but unphilosophical tirades of bigotry and prejudice. I will not deny that they are often disfigured by the violence and passion of the moment, and that in some directions Burke's view was bounded, and his observation therefore at fault, but on the whole, and for those who can make the needful corrections, what distinguishes these writings is their profound, permanent, fruitful, philosophical truth, they contain the true philosophy of an epoch of concentration, dissipate the heavy atmosphere which its own nature is apt to engender round it, and make its resistance rational instead of mechanical.

But Burke is so great because, almost alone in England, he brings thought to bear upon politics, he saturates politics with thought; it is his accident that his ideas were at the service of an epoch of concentration, not of an epoch of expansion; it is his characteristic that he so lived by ideas, and had such a source of them welling up within him, that he could float even an epoch of concentration and English Tory politics with them. It does not hurt him that Dr. Price and the Liberals were displeased with him; it does not even hurt him that George the Third and the Tories were enchanted with him. His greatness is that he lived in a world which neither English Liberalism nor English Toryism is apt to enter;—the world of ideas, not the world of catchwords and party habits. So far is it from being really true of him that he "to party gave up what was meant for mankind," that at the very end of his fierce struggle with the French Revolution, after all his invectives against its false pretensions, hollowness, and madness, with his sincere conviction of its mischievousness, he can close a memorandum on the best means of combating it, some of the last pages he ever wrote,—the *Thoughts on French Affairs,* in December 1791,—with these striking words:—

"The evil is stated, in my opinion, as it exists. The remedy must be where power, wisdom, and information, I hope, are more united with good intentions than they can be with me. I have done with this subject, I believe, for ever. It has given me many anxious moments for the last two years. *If a great change is to be made in human affairs, the minds of men will be fitted to it; the general opinions and feelings will draw that way. Every fear, every hope will forward it; and then they who persist in opposing this mighty current in human affairs, will appear rather to resist the decrees of Providence itself, than the mere designs of men. They will not be resolute and firm, but perverse and obstinate."*

That return of Burke upon himself has always seemed to me one of the finest things in English literature, or indeed in any literature. That is what I call living by ideas: when one side of a question has long had your earnest support, when all your feelings are engaged, when you hear all round you no language but one, when your party talks this language like a steam-engine and can imagine no other,—still to be able to think, still to be irresistibly carried, if so it be, by the current of thought to the opposite side of the question, and, like Balaam, to be unable to speak anything *but what the Lord has put in your mouth.* I know nothing more striking, and I must add that I know nothing more un-English.

For the Englishman in general is like my friend the Member of Parliament, and believes, point-blank, that for a thing to be an anomaly is absolutely no objection to it whatever. He is like the Lord Auckland of Burke's day, who, in a memorandum on the French Revolution, talks of "certain miscreants, assuming the name of philosophers, who have presumed themselves capable of establishing a new system of society." The Englishman has been called a political animal, and he values what is political and practical so much that ideas easily become objects of dislike in his eyes, and thinkers "miscreants," because ideas and thinkers have rashly meddled with politics and practice. This would be all very well if the dislike and neglect confined themselves to ideas transported out of their own sphere, and meddling rashly with practice; but they are inevitably extended to ideas as such, and to the whole life of intelligence; practice is everything, a free play of the mind is nothing. The notion of the free play of the mind upon all subjects being a pleasure in itself, being an object of desire, being an essential provider of elements without which a nation's spirit, whatever compensations it may have for them, must, in the long run, die of inanition, hardly enters into an Englishman's thoughts. It is noticeable that the word *curiosity,* which in other languages is used in a good sense, to mean, as a high and fine quality of man's nature, just this disinterested love of a free play of the mind on all subjects, for its own sake,—it is noticeable, I say, that this word has in our language no sense of the kind, no sense but a rather bad and disparaging one. But criticism, real criticism, is essentially the exercise of this very quality; it obeys an instinct prompting it to try to know the best that is known and thought in the world, irrespectively of practice, politics, and everything of the kind; and to value knowledge and thought as they approach this best, without the intrusion of any other considerations whatever. This is an instinct for which there is, I think, little original sympathy in the practical English nature, and what there was of it has undergone a long benumbing period of check and suppression in the epoch of concentration which followed the French Revolution.

But epochs of concentration cannot well endure for ever; epochs of expansion, in the due course of things, follow them. Such an epoch of expansion seems to be opening in this country. In the first place all danger of a hostile forcible pressure of foreign ideas upon our practice has long disappeared; like the traveller in the fable, therefore, we begin to wear our cloak a little more loosely. Then, with a long peace the ideas of Europe steal gradually and amicably in, and mingle, though in infinitesimally small quantities at a time, with our own notions. Then, too, in spite of all that is said about the absorbing and brutalising influence of our passionate material progress, it seems to me indisputable that this progress is likely, though not certain, to lead in the end to an apparition of intellectual life; and that man, after he has made himself perfectly comfortable and has now to determine what to do with himself next, may begin to remember that he has a mind, and that the mind may be made the source of great pleasure. I grant it is mainly the privilege of faith, at present, to discern this end to our railways, our business, and our fortune-making; but we shall see if, here as elsewhere, faith is not in the end the true prophet. Our ease, our travelling, and our unbounded liberty to hold just as hard and securely as we please to the practice to which our notions have given birth, all tend to beget an inclination to deal a little more freely with these notions themselves, to canvass them a little, to penetrate a little into their real nature. Flutterings of curiosity, in the foreign sense of the word, appear amongst us, and it is in these that criticism must look to find its account. Criticism first; a time of true creative activity, perhaps,—which, as I have said, must inevitably be preceded amongst us by a time of criticism,—hereafter, when criticism has done its work.

It is of the last importance that English criticism should clearly discern what rules for its course, in order to avail itself of the field now opening to it, and to produce fruit for the future, it ought to take. The rules may be given in one word; by being *disinterested.* And how is it to be disinterested? By keeping aloof from practice; by resolutely following the law of its own nature, which is to be a free play of the mind on all subjects which it touches; by steadily refusing to lend itself to any of those ulterior, political, practical considerations about ideas, which plenty of people will be sure to attach to them, which perhaps ought often to be attached to them, which in this country at any rate are certain to be attached to them quite sufficiently, but which criticism has really nothing to do with. Its business is, as I have said, simply to know the best that is known and thought in the world, and by in its turn making this known, to create a current of true and fresh ideas. Its business is to do this with inflexible honesty, with due ability; but its business is to do no more, and to leave alone all questions of practical consequences and applications, questions which will never fail to have due prominence given to them. Else criticism, besides being really false to its own nature, merely continues in the old rut which it has hitherto followed in this country, and will certainly miss the chance now given to it. For what is at present the bane of criticism in this country? It is that practical considerations cling to it and stifle it; it subserves interests not its own; our organs of criticism are organs of men and parties having practical ends to serve, and with them those practical ends are the first thing and the play of mind the second; so much play of mind as is compatible with the prosecution of those practical ends is all that is wanted. An organ like the *Revue des Deux Mondes,* having for its main function to understand and utter the best that is known and thought in the world, existing, it may be said, as just an organ for a free play of the mind, we have not; but we have the *Edinburgh Review,* existing as an organ of the old Whigs, and for as much play of the mind as may suit its being that; we have the *Quarterly Review,* existing as an organ of the Tories, and for as much play of mind as may suit its being that; we have the *British Quarterly Review,* existing as an organ of the political Dissenters, and for as much play of mind as may suit its being that; we have the *Times,* existing as an organ of the common, satisfied, well-to-do Englishman, and for as much play of mind as may suit its being that. And so on through all the various fractions, political and religious, of our society; every fraction has, as such, its organ of criticism, but the notion of combining all fractions in the common pleasure of a free disinterested play of mind meets with no favour. Directly this play of mind wants to have more scope, and to forget the pressure of practical considerations a little, it is checked, it is made to feel the chain. We saw this the other day in the extinction, so much to be regretted, of the *Home and Foreign Review;* perhaps in no organ of criticism in this country was there so much knowledge, so much play of mind; but these could not save it. The *Dublin Review* subordinates play of mind to the practical business of Roman Catholicism, and lives. It must needs be that men should act in sects and parties, that each of these sects and parties should have its organ, and should make this organ subserve the interests of its action; but it would be well, too, that there should be a criticism, not the minister of these interests, not their enemy, but absolutely and entirely independent of them. No other criticism will ever attain any real authority or make any real way towards its end,—the creating a current of true and fresh ideas.

[Several sections that deal mainly with politics and religion are here omitted.]

If I have insisted so much on the course which criticism must take where politics and religion are concerned, it is because, where these burning matters are in question, it is most likely to go astray. In general, its course is determined for it by the idea which is the law of its being; the idea of a disinterested endeavour to learn and propagate the best that is known and thought in the world, and thus to establish a current of fresh and true ideas. By the very nature of things, as England is not all the world, much of the best that is known and thought in the world cannot be of English growth, must be foreign; by the nature of things, again, it is just this that we are least likely to know, while English thought is streaming in upon us from all sides, and takes excellent care that we shall not be ignorant of its existence; the English critic, therefore, must dwell much on foreign thought, and with particular heed on any part of it, which, while significant and fruitful in itself, is for any reason specially likely to escape him. Judging is often spoken of as the critic's one business, and so in some sense it is; but the judgment which almost insensibly forms itself in a fair and clear mind, along with fresh knowledge, is the valuable one; and thus knowledge, and ever fresh knowledge, must be the critic's great concern for himself; and it is by communicating fresh knowledge, and letting his own judgment pass along with it,—but insensibly, and in the second place, not the first, as a sort of companion and clue, not as an abstract lawgiver,— that he will generally do most good to his readers. Sometimes, no doubt, for the sake of establishing an author's place in literature, and his relation to a central standard (and if this is not done, how are we to get at our *best in the world?*) criticism may have to deal with a subject-matter so familiar that fresh knowledge is out of the question, and then it must be all judgment; an enunciation and detailed application of principles. Here the great safeguard is never to let oneself become abstract, always to retain an intimate and lively consciousness of the truth of what one is saying, and, the moment this fails us, to be sure that something is wrong. Still, under all circumstances, this mere judgment and application of principles is, in itself, not the most satisfactory work to the critic; like mathematics, it is tautological, and cannot well give us, like fresh learning, the sense of creative activity. To have this sense is, as I said at the beginning, the great happiness and the great proof of being alive, and it is not denied to criticism to have it; but then criticism must be sincere, simple, flexible, ardent, ever widening its knowledge. Then it may have, in no contemptible measure, a joyful sense of creative activity; a sense which a man of insight and conscience will prefer to what he might derive from a poor, starved, fragmentary, inadequate creation. And at some epochs no other creation is possible.

Still, in full measure, the sense of creative activity belongs only to genuine creation; in literature we must never forget that. But what true man of letters ever can forget it? It is no such common matter for a gifted nature to come into possession of a current of true and living ideas, and to produce amidst the inspiration of them, that we are likely to underrate it. The epochs of Æschylus and Shakspeare make us feel their pre-eminence. In an epoch like those is, no doubt, the true life of literature; there is the promised land, towards which criticism can only beckon. That promised land it will not be ours to enter, and we shall die in the wilderness: but to have desired to enter it, to have saluted it from afar, is already, perhaps, the best distinction among contemporaries; it will certainly be the best title to esteem with posterity.

THE STUDY OF POETRY

(1888)

"THE future of poetry is immense, because in poetry, where it is worthy of its high destinies, our race, as time goes on, will find an ever surer and surer stay. There is not a creed which is not shaken, not an accredited dogma which is not shown to be questionable, not a received tradition which does not threaten to dissolve. Our religion has materialised itself in the fact, in the supposed fact; it has attached its emotion to the fact, and now the fact is failing it. But for poetry the idea is everything; the rest is a world of illusion, of divine illusion. Poetry attaches its emotion to the idea; the idea *is* the fact. The strongest part of our religion to-day is its unconscious poetry."

Let me be permitted to quote these words of my own, as uttering the thought which should, in my opinion, go with us and govern us in all our study of poetry. In the present work it is the course of one great contributory stream to the world-river of poetry that we are invited to follow. We are here invited to trace the stream of English poetry. But whether we set ourselves, as here, to follow only one of the several streams that make the mighty river of poetry, or whether we seek to know them all, our governing thought should be the same. We should conceive of poetry worthily, and more highly than it has been the custom to conceive of it. We should conceive of it as capable of higher uses, and called to higher destinies, than those which in general men have assigned to it hitherto. More and more mankind will discover that we have to turn to poetry to interpret life for us, to console us, to sustain us. Without poetry, our science will appear incomplete; and most of what now passes with us for religion and philosophy will be replaced by poetry. Science, I say, will appear incomplete without it. For finely and truly does Wordsworth call poetry "the impassioned expression which is in the countenance of all science"; and what is a countenance without its expression? Again, Wordsworth finely and truly calls poetry "the breath and finer spirit of all knowledge"; our religion, parading evidences such as those on which the popular mind relies now; our philosophy, pluming itself on its reasonings about causation and finite and infinite being; what are they but the shadows and dreams and false shows of knowledge? The day will come when we shall wonder at ourselves for having trusted to them, for having taken them seriously; and the more we perceive their hollowness, the more we shall prize "the breath and finer spirit of knowledge" offered to us by poetry.

But if we conceive thus highly of the destinies of poetry, we must also set our standard for poetry high, since poetry, to be capable of fulfilling such high destinies, must be poetry of a high order of excellence. We must accustom ourselves to a high standard and to a strict judgment. Sainte-Beuve relates that Napoleon one day said, when somebody was spoken of in his presence as a charlatan: "Charlatan as much as you please; but where is there *not* charlatanism?"—"Yes," answers Sainte-Beuve, "in politics, in the art of governing mankind, that is perhaps true. But in the order of thought, in art, the glory, the eternal honour is that charlatanism shall find no entrance; herein lies the inviolableness of that noble portion of man's being." It is admirably said, and let us hold fast to it. In poetry, which is thought and art in one, it is the glory, the eternal honour, that charlatanism shall find no entrance; that this noble sphere be kept inviolate and inviolable. Charlatanism is for confusing or obliterating the distinctions between excellent and inferior, sound and unsound or only half-sound, true and untrue or only half-true. It is charlatanism, conscious or unconscious, whenever we confuse or obliterate these. And in poetry, more than anywhere else, it is unpermissible to confuse or obliterate them. For in poetry the distinction between excellent and inferior, sound and unsound or only half-sound, true and untrue or only half-true, is of paramount importance. It is of paramount importance because of the high destinies of poetry. In poetry, as in criticism of life under the conditions fixed for such a criticism by the laws of poetic truth and poetic beauty, the spirit of our race will find, we have said, as time goes on and as other helps fail, its consolation and stay. But the consolation and stay will be of power in proportion to the power of the criticism of life. And the criticism of life will be of power in proportion as the poetry conveying it is excellent rather than inferior, sound rather than unsound or half-sound, true rather than untrue or half-true.

The best poerty is what we want; the best poetry will be found to have a power of forming, sustaining, and delighting us, as nothing else can. A clearer, deeper sense of the best in poetry, and of the strength and joy to be drawn from it, is the most precious benefit which we can gather from a poetical collection such as the present. And yet in the very nature and conduct of such a collection there is inevitably something which tends to obscure in us the consciousness of what our benefit should be, and to distract us from the pursuit of it. We should therefore steadily set it before our minds at the outset, and should compel ourselves to revert constantly to the thought of it as we proceed.

Yes; constantly in reading poetry, a sense for the best, the really excellent, and of the strength and joy to be drawn from it, should be present in our minds and should govern our estimate of what we read. But this real estimate, the only true one, is liable to be superseded, if we are not watchful, by two other kinds of estimate, the historic estimate and the personal estimate, both of which are fallacious. A poet or a poem may count to us historically, they may count to us on grounds personal to ourselves, and they may count to us really. They may count to us historically. The course of development of a nation's language, thought, and poetry, is profoundly interesting; and by regarding a poet's work as a stage in this course of development we may easily bring ourselves to make it of more importance as poetry than in itself it really is, we may come to use a language of quite exaggerated praise in criticising it; in short, to over-rate it. So arises in our poetic judgments the fallacy caused by the estimate which we may call historic. Then, again, a poet or poem may count to us on grounds personal to ourselves. Our personal affinities, likings and circumstances, have great power to sway our estimate of this or that poet's work, and to make us attach more importance to it as poetry than in itself it really possesses, because to us it is, or has been, of high importance. Here also we over-rate the object of our interest, and apply to it a language of praise which is quite exaggerated. And thus we get the source of a second fallacy in our poetic judgments —the fallacy caused by an estimate which we may call personal.

Both fallacies are natural. It is evident how naturally the study of the history and development of poetry may incline a man to pause over reputations and works once conspicuous but now obscure, and to quarrel with a careless public for skipping, in obedience to mere tradition and habit, from one famous name or work in its national poetry to another, ignorant of what it misses, and of the reason for keeping what it keeps, and of the whole process of growth in its poetry. The French have become diligent students of their own early poetry, which they long neglected; the study makes many of them dissatisfied with their so-called classical poetry, the court-tragedy of the seventeenth century, a poetry which Pellisson long ago reproached with its want of the true poetic stamp, with its *politesse stérile et rampante,* but which nevertheless has reigned in France as absolutely as if it had been the perfection of classical poetry indeed. The dissatisfaction is natural; yet a lively and accomplished critic, M. Charles d'Héricault, the editor of Clément Marot, goes too far when he says that "the cloud of glory playing round a classic is a mist as dangerous to the future of a literature as it is intolerable for the purposes of history." "It hinders," he goes on, "it hinders us from seeing more than one single point, the culminating and exceptional point; the summary, fictitious and arbitrary, of a thought and of a work. It substitutes a halo for a physiognomy, it puts a statue where there was once a man, and hiding from us all trace of the labour, the attempts, the weaknesses, the failures, it claims not study but veneration; it does not show us how the thing is done, it imposes upon us a model. Above all, for the historian this creation of classic personages is inadmissible; for it withdraws the poet from his time, from his proper life, it breaks historical relationships, it blinds criticism by conventional admiration, and renders the investigation of literary origins unacceptable. It gives us a human personage no longer but a God seated immovable amidst His perfect work, like Jupiter on Olympus; and hardly will it be possible for the young student to whom such work is exhibited at such a distance from him, to believe that it did not issue ready made from that divine head."

All this is brilliantly and tellingly said, but we must plead for a distinction. Everything depends on the reality of a poet's classic character. If he is a dubious classic, let us sift him; if he is a false classic, let us explode him. But if he is a real classic, if his work belongs to the class of the very best (for this is the true and right meaning of the word *classic, classical*), then the great thing for us is to feel and enjoy his work as deeply as ever we can, and to appreciate the wide difference between it and all work which has not the same high character. This is what is salutary, this is what is formative; this is the great benefit to be got from the study of poetry. Everything which interferes with it, which hinders it, is injurious. True, we must read our classic with open eyes, and not with eyes blinded with superstition; we must perceive when his work comes short, when it drops out of the class of the very best, and we must rate it, in such cases, at its proper value. But the use of this negative criticism is not in itself, it is entirely in its enabling us to have a clearer sense and a deeper enjoyment of what is truly excellent. To trace the labour, the attempts, the weaknesses, the failures of a genuine classic, to acquaint oneself with his time and his life and his historical relationships, is mere literary dilettantism unless it has that clear sense and deeper enjoyment for its end. It may be said that the more we know about a classic the better we shall enjoy him; and, if we lived as long as Methuselah and had all of us heads of perfect clearness and wills of perfect steadfastness, this might be true in fact as it is plausible in theory. But the case here is much the same as the case with the Greek and Latin studies of our schoolboys. The elaborate philological ground-work which we require them to lay is in theory an admirable prepara-tion for appreciating the Greek and Latin authors worthily. The more thoroughly we lay the groundwork, the better we shall be able, it may be said, to enjoy the authors. True, if time were not so short, and schoolboys' wits not so soon tired and their power of attention ex-hausted; only, as it is, the elaborate philological preparation goes on, but the authors are little known and less enjoyed. So with the investi-gator of "historic origins" in poetry. He ought to enjoy the true classic all the better for his investigations; he often is distracted from the enjoyment of the best, and with the less good he overbusies him-self, and is prone to over-rate it in proportion to the trouble which it has cost him.

The idea of tracing historic origins and historical relationships can-not be absent from a compilation like the present. And naturally the poets to be exhibited in it will be assigned to those persons for exhibition who are known to prize them highly, rather than to those who have no special inclination towards them. Moreover, the very occupation with an author, and the business of exhibiting him, disposes us to affirm and amplify his importance. In the present work, therefore, we are sure of frequent temptation to adopt the historic estimate, or the personal esti-mate, and to forget the real estimate; which latter, nevertheless, we must employ if we are to make poetry yield us its full benefit. So high is that benefit, the benefit of clearly feeling and of deeply enjoying the really excellent, the truly classic in poetry, that we do well, I say, to set it fixedly before our minds as our object in studying poets and poetry, and to make the desire of attaining it the one principle to which, as the *Imitation* says, whatever we may read or come to know, we always return. *Cum multa legeris et cognoveris, ad unum semper oportet redire principium.*

The historic estimate is likely in especial to affect our judgment and our language when we are dealing with ancient poets; the personal estimate when we are dealing with poets our contemporaries, or at any rate modern. The exaggerations due to the historic estimate are not in themselves, perhaps, of very much gravity. Their report hardly enters the general ear; probably they do not always impose even on the liter-ary men who adopt them. But they lead to a dangerous abuse of language. So we hear Cædmon, amongst our own poets, compared to Milton. I have already noticed the enthusiasm of one accomplished French critic for "historic origins." Another eminent French critic, M. Vitet, comments upon that famous document of the early poetry of his nation, the *Chanson de Roland*. It is indeed a most interesting document. The *joculator* or *jongleur* Taillefer, who was with William the Conqueror's army at Hastings, marched before the Norman troops, so said the tradition, singing "of Charlemagne and of Roland and of Oliver, and of the vassals who died at Roncevaux"; and it is suggested that in the *Chanson de Roland* by one Turoldus or Théroulde, a poem preserved in a manuscript of the twelfth century in the Bodleian Library at Oxford, we have certainly the matter, perhaps even some of the words, of the chant which Taillefer sang. The poem has vigour and freshness; it is not without pathos. But M. Vitet is not satisfied with seeing in it a document of some poetic value, and of very high historic and linguistic value; he sees in it a grand and beautiful work, a monument of epic genius. In its general design he finds the grandiose conception, in its details he finds the constant union of simplicity with greatness, which are the marks, he truly says, of the genuine epic, and distinguish it from the artificial epic of literary ages. One thinks of Homer; this is the sort of praise which is given to Homer, and justly given. Higher praise there cannot well be, and it is the praise due to epic poetry of the highest order only, and to no other. Let us try, then, the *Chanson de Roland* at its best. Roland, mortally wounded, lay himself down under a pine-tree, with his face turned towards Spain and the enemy—

> "De plusurs choses à remembrer li prist,
> De tantes teres cume li bers cunquist,
> De dulce France, des humes de sun lign,
> De Carlemagne sun seignor ki l'nurrit." [1]

That is primitive work, I repeat, with an undeniable poetic quality of its own. It deserves such praise, and such praise is sufficient for it. But now turn to Homer—

> "Ὣς φάτο· τοὺς δ᾽ ἤδη κατέχεν φυσίζοος αἶα
> ἐν Λακεδαίμονι αὖθι, φίλῃ ἐν πατρίδι γαίῃ. [2]

---

[1] "Then began he to call many things to remembrance,—all the lands which his valour conquered, and pleasant France, and the men of his lineage, and Charlemagne his liege lord who nourished him." —*Chanson de Roland*, iii. 939–942.

[2] "So said she; they long since in Earth's soft arms were reposing, There, in their own dear land, their fatherland, Lacedæmon." —*Iliad*, iii. 243, 244 (translated by Dr. Hawtrey).

We are here in another world, another order of poetry altogether; here is rightly due such supreme praise as that which M. Vitet gives to the *Chanson de Roland.* If our words are to have any meaning, if our judgments are to have any solidity, we must not heap that supreme praise upon poetry of an order immeasurably inferior.

Indeed there can be no more useful help for discovering what poetry belongs to the class of the truly excellent, and can therefore do us most good, than to have always in one's mind lines and expressions of the great masters, and to apply them as a touchstone to other poetry. Of course we are not to require this other poetry to resemble them; it may be very dissimilar. But if we have any tact we shall find them, when we have lodged them well in our minds, an infallible touchstone for detecting the presence or absence of high poetic quality, and also the degree of this quality, in all other poetry which we may place beside them. Short passages, even single lines, will serve our turn quite sufficiently. Take the two lines which I have just quoted from Homer, the poet's comment on Helen's mention of her brothers;—or take his

<blockquote>
Ἄ δειλώ, τί σφῶϊ δόμεν Πηλῆϊ ἄνακτι
Θνητῷ; ὑμεῖς δ' ἐστὸν ἀγήρω τ' ἀθανάτω τε.
ἦ ἵνα δυστήνοισι μετ' ἀνδράσιν ἄλγε' ἔχητον; [3]
</blockquote>

the address of Zeus to the horses of Peleus;—or take finally his

<blockquote>
Καὶ σέ, γέρον, τὸ πρὶν μὲν ἀκούομεν ὄλβιον εἶναι· [4]
</blockquote>

the words of Achilles to Priam, a suppliant before him. Take that incomparable line and a half of Dante, Ugolino's tremendous words—

<blockquote>
"Io no piangeva; sì dentro impietrai.
Piangevan elli . . ." [5]
</blockquote>

take the lovely words of Beatrice to Virgil—

<blockquote>
"Io son fatta da Dio, sua mercè, tale,
Che la vostra miseria non mi tange,
Nè fiamma d'esto incendio non m'assale . . ." [6]
</blockquote>

take the simple, but perfect, single line—

<blockquote>
"In la sua volontade è nostra pace." [7]
</blockquote>

---

[3] "Ah, unhappy pair, why gave we you to King Peleus, to a mortal? but ye are without old age, and immortal. Was it that with men born to misery ye might have sorrow?"—*Iliad,* xvii. 443-445.

[4] "Nay, and thou too, old man, in former days wast, as we hear, happy."—*Iliad,* xxiv. 543.

[5] "I wailed not, so of stone grew I within; —*they* wailed."—*Inferno,* xxxiii. 39, 40.

[6] "Of such sort hath God, thanked be His mercy, made me, that your misery toucheth me not, neither doth the flame of this fire strike me."—*Inferno,* ii. 91-93.

[7] "In His will is our peace."—*Paradiso,* iii. 85.

Take of Shakespeare a line or two of Henry the Fourth's expostulation with sleep—

> "Wilt thou upon the high and giddy mast
> Seal up the ship-boy's eyes, and rock his brains
> In cradle of the rude imperious surge . . ."

and take, as well, Hamlet's dying request to Horatio—

> "If thou didst ever hold me in thy heart,
> Absent thee from felicity awhile,
> And in this harsh world draw thy breath in pain
> To tell my story . . ."

Take of Milton that Miltonic passage:

> "Darken'd so, yet shone
> Above them all the archangel; but his face
> Deep scars of thunder had intrench'd, and care
> Sat on his faded cheek . . ."

add two such lines as—

> "And courage never to submit or yield
> And what is else not to be overcome . . ."

and finish with the exquisite close to the loss of Proserpine, the loss

> ". . . which cost Ceres all that pain
> To seek her through the world."

These few lines, if we have tact and can use them, are enough even of themselves to keep clear and sound our judgments about poetry, to save us from fallacious estimates of it, to conduct us to a real estimate.

The specimens I have quoted differ widely from one another, but they have in common this: the possession of the very highest poetical quality. If we are thoroughly penetrated by their power, we shall find that we have acquired a sense enabling us, whatever poetry may be laid before us, to feel the degree in which a high poetical quality is present or wanting there. Critics give themselves great labour to draw out what in the abstract constitutes the characters of a high quality of poetry. It is much better simply to have recourse to concrete examples; —to take specimens of poetry of the high, the very highest quality, and to say: The characters of a high quality of poetry are what is expressed *there*. They are far better recognized by being felt in the verse of the master, than by being perused in the prose of the critic. Nevertheless if we are urgently pressed to give some critical account of them, we may safely, perhaps, venture on laying down, not indeed how and why the characters arise, but where and in what they arise. They are in the matter and substance of the poetry, and they are in its manner and style. Both of these, the substance and matter on the one hand, the style and manner on the other, have a mark, an accent, of high beauty, worth, and power. But if we are asked to define this mark and accent in the abstract, our answer must be: No, for we should thereby be darkening the question, not clearing it. The mark and accent are as given by the substance and matter of that poetry, by the style and manner of that poetry, and of all other poetry which is akin to it in quality.

Only one thing we may add as to the substance and matter of poetry, guiding ourselves by Aristotle's profound observation that the superiority of poetry over history consists in its possessing a higher truth and a higher seriousness ($\phi\iota\lambda o\sigma o\phi\acute{\omega}\tau\epsilon\rho o\nu$ $\chi\alpha\grave{\iota}$ $\sigma\pi o\upsilon\delta\alpha\iota\acute{o}\tau\epsilon\rho o\nu$). Let us add, therefore, to what we have said, this: that the substance and matter of the best poetry acquire their special character from possessing, in an eminent degree, truth and seriousness. We may add yet further, what is in itself evident, that to the style and manner of the best poetry their special character, their accent, is given by their diction, and, even yet more, by their movement. And though we distinguish between the two characters, the two accents, of superiority, yet they are nevertheless vitally connected one with the other. The superior character of truth and seriousness, in the matter and substance of the best poetry, is inseparable from the superiority of diction and movement marking its style and manner. The two superiorities are closely related, and are in steadfast proportion one to the other. So far as high poetic truth and seriousness are wanting to a poet's matter and substance, so far also, we may be sure, will a high poetic stamp of diction and movement be wanting to his style and manner. In proportion as this high stamp of diction and movement, again, is absent from a poet's style and manner, we shall find, also, that high poetic truth and seriousness are absent from his substance and matter.

So stated, these are but dry generalities; their whole force lies in their application. And I could wish every student of poetry to make the application of them for himself. Made by himself, the application would impress itself upon his mind far more deeply than made by me.

Neither will my limits allow me to make any full application of the generalities above propounded; but in the hope of bringing out, at any rate, some significance in them, and of establishing an important principle more firmly by their means, I will, in the space which remains to me, follow rapidly from the commencement the course of our English poetry with them in my view.

Once more I return to the early poetry of France, with which our own poetry, in its origins, is indissolubly connected. In the twelfth and thirteenth centuries, that seed-time of all modern language and literature, the poetry of France had a clear predominance in Europe. Of the two divisions of that poetry, its productions in the *langue d'oïl* and its productions in the *langue d'oc,* the poetry of the *langue d'oc,* of southern France, of the troubadours, is of importance because of its effect on Italian literature;—the first literature of modern Europe to strike the true and grand note, and to bring forth, as in Dante and Petrarch it brought forth, classics. But the predominance of French poetry in Europe, during the twelfth and thirteenth centuries, is due to its poetry of the *langue d'oïl,* the poetry of northern France and of the tongue which is now the French language. In the twelfth century the bloom of this romance-poetry was earlier and stronger in England, at the court of our Anglo-Norman kings, than in France itself. But it was a bloom of French poetry; and as our native poetry formed itself, it formed itself out of this. The romance-poems which took possession of the heart and imagination of Europe in the twelfth and thirteenth centuries are French; "they are," as Southey justly says, "the pride of French literature, nor have we anything which can be placed in competition with them." Themes were supplied from all quarters; but the romance-setting which was common to them all, and which gained the ear of Europe, was French. This constituted for the French poetry, literature, and language, at the height of the Middle Age, an unchallenged predominance. The Italian Brunetto Latini, the master of Dante, wrote his *Treasure* in French because, he says, "la parleure en est plus délitable et plus commune à toutes gens." In the same century, the thirteenth, the French romance-writer, Christian of Troyes, formulates the claims, in chivalry and letters, of France, his native country, as follows:—

> "Or vous ert par ce livre apris,
> Que Gresse ot de chevalerie
> Le premier los et de clergie;
> Puis vint chevalerie à Rome.

Et de la clergie la some,
  Qui ore est en France venue.
  Diex doinst qu'ele i soit retenue,
  Et que li lius li abelisse
  Tant que de France n'isse
  L'onor qui s'i est arestée!"

"Now by this book you will learn that first Greece had the renown for chivalry and letters: then chivalry and the primacy in letters passed to Rome, and now it is come to France. God grant it may be kept there; and that the place may please it so well, that the honour which has come to make stay in France may never depart thence!"

Yet it is now all gone, this French romance-poetry of which the weight of substance and the power of style are not unfairly represented by this extract from Christian of Troyes. Only by means of the historic estimate can we persuade ourselves now to think that any of it is of poetical importance.

But in the fourteenth century there comes an Englishman nourished on this poetry, taught his trade by this poetry, getting words, rhyme, metre from this poetry; for even of that stanza which the Italians used, and which Chaucer derived immediately from the Italians, the basis and suggestion was probably given in France. Chaucer (I have already named him) fascinated his contemporaries, but so too did Christian of Troyes and Wolfram of Eschenbach. Chaucer's power of fascination, however, is enduring; his poetical importance does not need the assistance of the historic estimate; it is real. He is a genuine source of joy and strength, which is flowing still for us and will flow always. He will be read, as time goes on, far more generally than he is read now. His language is a cause of difficulty for us; but so also, and I think in quite as great a degree, is the language of Burns. In Chaucer's case, as in that of Burns, it is a difficulty to be unhesitatingly accepted and overcome.

If we ask ourselves wherein consists the immense superiority of Chaucer's poetry over the romance-poetry—why it is that in passing from this to Chaucer we suddenly feel ourselves to be in another world, we shall find that his superiority is both in the substance of his poetry and in the style of his poetry. His superiority in substance is given by his large, free, simple, clear yet kindly view of human life,—so unlike the total want, in the romance-poets, of all intelligent command of it. Chaucer has not their helplessness; he has gained the power to survey the world from a central, a truly human point of view. We have only to call to mind the Prologue to *The Canterbury Tales.* The right comment upon it is Dryden's: "It is sufficient to say, according to the proverb, that *here is God's plenty.*" And again: "He is a perpetual fountain of good sense." It is by a large, free, sound representation of things, that poetry, this high criticism of life, has truth of substance; and Chaucer's poetry has truth of substance.

Of his style and manner, if we think first of the romance-poetry and then of Chaucer's divine liquidness of diction, his divine fluidity of movement, it is difficult to speak temperately. They are irresistible, and justify all the rapture with which his successors speak of his "gold dew-drops of speech." Johnson misses the point entirely when he finds fault with Dryden for ascribing to Chaucer the first refinement of our numbers, and says that Gower also can show smooth numbers and easy rhymes. The refinement of our numbers means something far more than this. A nation may have versifiers with smooth numbers and easy rhymes, and yet may have no real poetry at all. Chaucer is the father of our splendid English poetry; he is our "well of English undefiled," because by the lovely charm of his diction, the lovely charm of his movement, he makes an epoch and founds a tradition. In Spenser, Shakespeare, Milton, Keats, we can follow the tradition of the liquid diction, the fluid movement of Chaucer; at one time it is his liquid diction of which in these poets we feel the virtue, and at another time it is his fluid movement. And the virtue is irresistible.

Bounded as is my space, I must yet find room for an example of Chaucer's virtue, as I have given examples to show the virtue of the great classics. I feel disposed to say that a single line is enough to show the charm of Chaucer's verse; that merely one line like this—

"O martyr souded [8] in virginitee!"

has a virtue of manner and movement such as we shall not find in all the verse of romance-poetry;—but this is saying nothing. The virtue is such as we shall not find, perhaps, in all English poetry, outside the poets whom I have named as the special inheritors of Chaucer's tradition. A single line, however, is too little if we have not the strain of Chaucer's verse well in our memory; let us take a stanza. It is from *The Prioress's Tale,* the story of the Christian child murdered in a Jewry—

"My throte is cut unto my nekke-bone
    Saidè this child, and as by way of kinde

[8] The French *soudé;* soldered, fixed fast.

> I should have deyd, yea, longè time agone;
> But Jesu Christ, as ye in bookès finde,
> Will that his glory last and be in minde,
> And for the worship of his mother dere
> Yet may I sing *O Alma* loud and clere."

Wordsworth has modernised this Tale, and to feel how delicate and evanescent is the charm of verse, we have only to read Wordsworth's first three lines of this stanza after Chaucer's—

> "My throat is cut unto the bone, I trow,
> Said this young child, and by the law of kind
> I should have died, yea, many hours ago."

The charm is departed. It is often said that the power of liquidness and fluidity in Chaucer's verse was dependent upon a free, a licentious dealing with language, such as is now impossible; upon a liberty, such as Burns too enjoyed, of making words like *neck, bird,* into a dissyllable by adding to them, and words like *cause, rhyme,* into a dissyllable by sounding the *e* mute. It is true that Chaucer's fluidity is conjoined with this liberty, and is admirably served by it; but we ought not to say that it was dependent upon it. It was dependent upon his talent. Other poets with a like liberty do not attain to the fluidity of Chaucer; Burns himself does not attain to it. Poets, again, who have a talent akin to Chaucer's, such as Shakespeare or Keats, have known how to attain his fluidity without the like liberty.

And yet Chaucer is not one of the great classics. His poetry transcends and effaces, easily and without effort, all the romance-poetry of Catholic Christendom; it transcends and effaces all the English poetry contemporary with it, it transcends and effaces all the English poetry subsequent to it down to the age of Elizabeth. Of such avail is poetic truth of substance, in its natural and necessary union with poetic truth of style. And yet, I say, Chaucer is not one of the great classics. He has not their accent. What is wanting to him is suggested by the mere mention of the name of the first great classic of Christendom, the immortal poet who died eighty years before Chaucer,—Dante. The accent of such verse as

> *"In la sua volontage è nostra pace . . ."*

is altogether beyond Chaucer's reach; we praise him, but we feel that this accent is out of the question for him. It may be said that it was necessarily out of the reach of any poet in the England of that stage of growth. Possibly; but we are to adopt a real, not a historic, estimate of poetry. However we may account for its absence, something is wanting, then, to the poetry of Chaucer, which poetry must have before it can be placed in the glorious class of the best. And there is no doubt what that something is. It is the σπουδαιότης the high and excellent seriousness, which Aristotle assigns as one of the grand virtues of poetry. The substance of Chaucer's poetry, his view of things and his criticism of life, has largeness, freedom, shrewdness, benignity; but it has not this high seriousness. Homer's criticism of life has it, Dante's has it, Shakespeare's has it. It is this chiefly which gives to our spirits what they can rest upon; and with the increasing demands of our modern ages upon poetry, this virtue of giving us what we can rest upon will be more and more highly esteemed. A voice from the slums of Paris, fifty or sixty years after Chaucer, the voice of poor Villon out of his life of riot and crime, has at its happy moments (as, for instance, in the last stanza of *La Belle Heaulmière* [9]) more of this important poetic virtue of seriousness than all the productions of Chaucer. But its apparition in Villon, and in men like Villon, is fitful; the greatness of the great poets, the power of their criticism of life, is that their virtue is sustained.

To our praise, therefore, of Chaucer as a poet there must be this limitation; he lacks the high seriousness of the great classics, and therewith an important part of their virtue. Still, the main fact for us to bear in mind about Chaucer is his sterling value according to that real estimate which we firmly adopt for all poets. He has poetic truth of substance, though he has not high poetic seriousness, and corresponding to his truth of substance he has an exquisite virtue of style and manner. With him is born our real poetry.

For my present purpose I need not dwell on our Elizabethan poetry, or on the continuation and close of this poetry in Milton. We all of

[9] The name *Heaulmière* is said to be derived from a head-dress (helm) worn as a mark by courtesans. In Villon's ballad, a poor old creature of this class laments her days of youth and beauty. The last stanza of the ballad runs thus—

"*Ainsi le bon temps regretons
Entre nous, pauvres vieilles sottes,
Assises bas, à croppetons,
Tout en ung tas comme pelottes;*

*A petit feu de chenevottes
Tost allumées, tost estainctes.
Et jadis fusmes si mignottes!
Ainsi en prend à maintz et maintes.*"

"Thus amongst ourselves we regret the good time, poor silly old things, low-seated on our heels, all in a heap like so many balls; by a little fire of hemp-stalks, soon lighted, soon spent. And once we were such darlings! So fares it with many and many a one."

us profess to be agreed in the estimate of this poetry; we all of us recognise it as great poetry, our greatest, and Shakespeare and Milton as our poetical classics. The real estimate, here, has universal currency. With the next age of our poetry divergency and difficulty begin. An historic estimate of that poetry has established itself; and the question is, whether it will be found to coincide with the real estimate.

The age of Dryden, together with our whole eighteenth century which followed it, sincerely believed itself to have produced poetical classics of its own, and even to have made advance, in poetry, beyond all its predecessors. Dryden regards as not seriously disputable the opinion "that the sweetness of English verse was never understood or practised by our fathers." Cowley could see nothing at all in Chaucer's poetry. Dryden heartily admired it, and, as we have seen, praised its matter admirably; but of its exquisite manner and movement all he can find to say is that "there is the rude sweetness of a Scotch tune in it, which is natural and pleasing, though not perfect." Addison, wishing to praise Chaucer's numbers, compares them with Dryden's own. And all through the eighteenth century, and down even into our own times, the stereotyped phrase of approbation for good verse found in our early poetry has been, that it even approached the verse of Dryden, Addison, Pope, and Johnson.

Are Dryden and Pope poetical classics? Is the historic estimate, which represents them as such, and which has been so long established that it cannot easily give way, the real estimate? Wordsworth and Coleridge, as is well known, denied it; but the authority of Wordsworth and Coleridge does not weigh much with the young generation, and there are many signs to show that the eighteenth century and its judgments are coming into favour again. Are the favourite poets of the eighteenth century classics?

It is impossible within my present limits to discuss the question fully. And what man of letters would not shrink from seeming to dispose dictatorially of the claims of two men who are, at any rate, such masters in letters as Dryden and Pope; two men of such admirable talent, both of them, and one of them, Dryden, a man, on all sides, of such energetic and genial power? And yet, if we are to gain the full benefit from poetry, we must have the real estimate of it. I cast about for some mode of arriving, in the present case, at such an estimate without offence. And perhaps the best way is to begin, as it is easy to begin, with cordial praise.

When we find Chapman, the Elizabethan translator of Homer, ex-

pressing himself in his preface thus: "Though truth in her very nakedness sits in so deep a pit, that from Gades to Aurora and Ganges few
eyes can sound her, I hope yet those few here will so discover and
confirm that, the date being out of her darkness in this morning of
our poet, he shall now gird his temples with the sun,"—we pronounce
that such a prose is intolerable. When we find Milton writing: "And
long it was not after, when I was confirmed in this opinion, that he,
who would not be frustrate of his hope to write well hereafter in
laudable things, ought himself to be a true poem,"—we pronounce that
such a prose has its own grandeur, but that it is obsolete and inconvenient. But when we find Dryden telling us: "What Virgil wrote in
the vigour of his age, in plenty and at ease, I have undertaken to
translate in my declining years; struggling with wants, oppressed with
sickness, curbed in my genius, liable to be misconstrued in all I write,"
—then we exclaim that here at last we have the true English prose, a
prose such as we would all gladly use if we only knew how. Yet
Dryden was Milton's contemporary.

But after the Restoration the time had come when our nation felt
the imperious need of a fit prose. So, too, the time had likewise come
when our nation felt the imperious need of freeing itself from the
absorbing preoccupation which religion in the Puritan age had exercised. It was impossible that this freedom should be brought about
without some negative excess, without some neglect and impairment
of the religious life of the soul; and the spiritual history of the
eighteenth century shows us that the freedom was not achieved without them. Still, the freedom was achieved; the preoccupation, an undoubtedly baneful and retarding one if it had continued, was got rid
of. And as with religion amongst us at that period, so it was also with
letters. A fit prose was a necessity; but it was impossible that a fit
prose should establish itself amongst us without some touch of frost
to the imaginative life of the soul. The needful qualities for a fit prose
are regularity, uniformity, precision, balance. The men of letters,
whose destiny it may be to bring their nation to the attainment of
a fit prose, must of necessity, whether they work in prose or in verse,
give a predominating, an almost exclusive attention to the qualities of
regularity, uniformity, precision, balance. But an almost exclusive attention to these qualities involves some repression and silencing of
poetry.

We are to regard Dryden as the puissant and glorious founder, Pope
as the splendid high priest, of our age of prose and reason, of our ex-

cellent and indispensable eighteenth century. For the purposes of their mission and destiny their poetry, like their prose, is admirable. Do you ask me whether Dryden's verse, take it almost where you will, is not good?

> "A milk-white Hind, immortal and unchanged,
> Fed on the lawns and in the forest ranged."

I answer: Admirable for the purposes of the inaugurator of an age of prose and reason. Do you ask me whether Pope's verse, take it almost where you will, is not good?

> "To Hounslow Heath I point, and Banstead Down
> Thence comes your mutton, and these chicks my own."

I answer: Admirable for the purposes of the high priest of an age of prose and reason. But do you ask me whether such verse proceeds from men with an adequate poetic criticism of life, from men whose criticism of life has a high seriousness, or even, without that high seriousness, has poetic largeness, freedom, insight, benignity? Do you ask me whether the application of ideas to life in the verse of these men, often a powerful application, no doubt, is a powerful *poetic* application? Do you ask me whether the poetry of these men has either the matter or the inseparable manner of such an adequate poetic criticism; whether it has the accent of

> "Absent thee from felicity awhile . . ."

or of

> "And what is else not to be overcome . . ."

or of

> "O Martyr souded in virginitee!"

I answer: It has not and cannot have them; it is the poetry of the builders of an age of prose and reason. Though they may write in verse, though they may in a certain sense be masters of the art of versification, Dryden and Pope are not classics of our poetry, they are classics of our prose.

Gray is our poetical classic of that literature and age; the position of Gray is singular, and demands a word of notice here. He has not the volume or the power of poets who, coming in times more favourable, have attained to an independent criticism of life. But he lived with the great poets, he lived, above all, with the Greeks, through perpetually studying and enjoying them; and he caught their poetic point of view for regarding life, caught their poetic manner. The point of view and the manner are not self-sprung in him, he caught them of others; and he had not the free and abundant use of them. But, whereas Addison and Pope never had the use of them, Gray had the use of them at times. He is the scantiest and frailest of classics in our poetry, but he is a classic.

And now, after Gray, we are met, as we draw towards the end of the eighteenth century, we are met by the great name of Burns. We enter now on times where the personal estimate of poets begins to be rife, and where the real estimate of them is not reached without difficulty. But in spite of the disturbing pressures of personal partiality, of national partiality, let us try to reach a real estimate of the poetry of Burns.

By his English poetry Burns in general belongs to the eighteenth century, and has little importance for us.

> "Mark ruffian Violence, distain'd with crimes,
> Rousing elate in these degenerate times;
> View unsuspecting Innocence a prey,
> As guileful Fraud points out the erring way;
> While subtle Litigation's pliant tongue
> The life-blood equal sucks of Right and Wrong!"

Evidently this is not the real Burns, or his name and fame would have disappeared long ago. Nor is Clarinda's love-poet, Sylvander, the real Burns either. But he tells us himself: "These English songs gravel me to death. I have not the command of the language that I have of my native tongue. In fact, I think that my ideas are more barren in English than in Scotch. I have been at *Duncan Gray* to dress it in English, but all I can do is desperately stupid." We English turn naturally, in Burns, to the poems in our own language, because we can read them easily; but in those poems we have not the real Burns.

The real Burns is of course in his Scotch poems. Let us boldly say that of much of this poetry, a poetry dealing perpetually with Scotch drink, Scotch religion, and Scotch manners, a Scotchman's estimate is apt to be personal. A Scotchman is used to this world of Scotch drink, Scotch religion, and Scotch manners; he has a tenderness for it; he meets its poet half way. In this tender mood he reads pieces like the *Holy Fair* or *Halloween*. But this world of Scotch drink, Scotch religion, and Scotch manners is against a poet, not for him, when it is not a partial countryman who reads him; for in itself it is not a beautiful world, and no one can deny that it is of advantage to a poet to deal with a beautiful world. Burns's world of Scotch drink, Scotch religion, and Scotch manners, is often a harsh, a sordid, a repulsive world: even the world of his *Cotter's Saturday Night* is not a beautiful world. No doubt a poet's criticism of life may have such truth and power that it triumphs over its world and delights us. Burns may triumph over his world, often he does triumph over his world, but let us observe how and where. Burns is the first case we have had where the bias of the personal estimate tends to mislead; let us look at him closely, he can bear it.

Many of his admirers will tell us that we have Burns, convivial, genuine, delightful, here—

> "Leeze me on drink! it gies us mair
>   Than either school or college;
> It kindles wit, it waukens lair,
>   It pangs us fou o' knowledge.
> Be't whisky gill or penny wheep
>   Or ony stronger potion,
> It never fails, on drinking deep,
>   To kittle up our notion
>   By night or day.

There is a great deal of that sort of thing in Burns, and it is unsatisfactory, not because it is bacchanalian poetry, but because it has not that accent of sincerity which bacchanalian poetry, to do it justice, very often has. There is something in it of bravado, something which makes us feel that we have not the man speaking to us with his real voice; something, therefore, poetically unsound.

With still more confidence will his admirers tell us that we have the genuine Burns, the great poet, when his strain asserts the independence, equality, dignity, of men, as in the famous song *For a' that, and a' that*—

> "A prince can mak' a belted knight,
>   A marquis, duke, and a' that;

But an honest man's aboon his might,
   Guid faith he mauna fa' that!
For a' that, and a' that,
   Their dignities, and a' that,
The pith o' sense, and pride o' worth,
   Are higher rank than a' that."

Here they find his grand, genuine touches; and still more, when this
puissant genius, who so often set morality at defiance, falls moralis-
ing—

The sacred lowe o' weel-placed love
   Luxuriantly indulge it;
But never tempt th' illicit rove,
   Tho' naething should divulge it.
I waive the quantum o' the sin,
   The hazard o' concealing,
But och! it hardens a' within,
   And petrifies the feeling."

Or in a higher strain—

"Who made the heart, 'tis He alone
   Decidedly can try us;
He knows each chord, its various tone;
   Each spring, its various bias.
Then at the balance let's be mute,
   We never can adjust it;
What's *done* we partly may compute,
   But know not what's resisted."

Or in a better strain yet, a strain, his admirers will say, unsur-
passable—

"To make a happy fire-side clime
   To weans and wife,
That's the true pathos and sublime
   Of human life."

There is criticism of life for you, the admirers of Burns will say to
us; there is the application of ideas to life! There is, undoubtedly.
The doctrine of the last-quoted lines coincides almost exactly with
what was the aim and end, Xenophon tells us, of all the teaching of
Socrates. And the application is a powerful one; made by a man of
vigorous understanding, and (need I say?) a master of language.

But for supreme poetical success more is required than the powerful application of ideas to life; it must be an application under the conditions fixed by the laws of poetic truth and poetic beauty. Those laws fix as an essential condition, in the poet's treatment of such matters as are here in question, high seriousness;—the high seriousness which comes from absolute sincerity. The accent of high seriousness, born of absolute sincerity, is what gives to such verse as

"In la sua volontade è nostra pace . . ."

to such criticism of life as Dante's, its power. Is this accent felt in the passages which I have been quoting from Burns? Surely not; surely, if our sense is quick, we must perceive that we have not in those passages a voice from the very inmost soul of the genuine Burns; he is not speaking to us from these depths, he is more or less preaching. And the compensation for admiring such passages less, from missing the perfect poetic accent in them, will be that we shall admire more the poetry where that accent is found.

No; Burns, like Chaucer, comes short of the high seriousness of the great classics, and the virtue of matter and manner which goes with that high seriousness is wanting to his work. At moments he touches it in a profound and passionate melancholy, as in those four immortal lines taken by Byron as a motto for *The Bride of Abydos,* but which have in them a depth of poetic quality such as resides in no verse of Byron's own—

> "Had we never loved sae kindly,
> Had we never loved sae blindly,
> Never met, or never parted,
> We had ne'er been broken-hearted."

But a whole poem of that quality Burns cannot make; the rest, in the *Farewell to Nancy,* is verbiage.

We arrive best at the real estimate of Burns, I think, by conceiving his work as having truth of matter and truth of manner, but not the accent or the poetic virtue of the highest masters. His genuine criticism of life, when the sheer poet in him speaks, is ironic; it is not—

> "Thou Power Supreme, whose mighty scheme
> These woes of mine fulfil,
> Here firm I rest, they must be best
> Because they are Thy will!"

It is far rather: *Whistle owre the lave o't!* Yet we may say of him as
of Chaucer, that of life and the world, as they come before him, his
view is large, free, shrewd, benignant,—truly poetic therefore; and his
manner of rendering what he sees is to match. But we must note, at
the same time, his great difference from Chaucer. The freedom of
Chaucer is heightened, in Burns, by a fiery, reckless energy; the benignity of Chaucer deepens, in Burns, into an overwhelming sense of
the pathos of things;—of the pathos of human nature, the pathos, also,
of non-human nature. Instead of the fluidity of Chaucer's manner,
the manner of Burns has spring, boundless swiftness. Burns is by far
the greater force, though he has perhaps less charm. The world of
Chaucer is fairer, richer, more significant than that of Burns; but when
the largeness and freedom of Burns get full sweep, as in *Tam o'
Shanter,* or still more in that puissant and splendid production, *The
Jolly Beggars,* his world may be what it will, his poetic genius triumphs over it. In the world of *The Jolly Beggars* there is more than
hideousness and squalor, there is bestiality; yet the piece is a superb
poetic success. It has a breadth, truth, and power which make the
famous scene in Auerbach's Cellar, of Goethe's *Faust,* seem artificial
and tame beside it, and which are only matched by Shakespeare and
Aristophanes.

Here, where his largeness and freedom serve him so admirably, and
also in those poems and songs where to shrewdness he adds infinite
archness and wit, and to benignity infinite pathos, where his manner
is flawless, and a perfect poetic whole is the result,—in things like the
address to the mouse whose home he had ruined, in things like *Duncan Gray, Tam Glen, Whistle and I'll come to you my Lad, Auld
Lang Syne* (this list might be made much longer),—here we have the
genuine Burns, of whom the real estimate must be high indeed. Not a
classic, nor with the excellent σπουδαιότης of the great classics, nor with
a verse rising to a criticism of life and a virtue like theirs; but a poet
with thorough truth of substance and an answering truth of style,
giving us a poetry sound to the core. We all of us have a leaning
towards the pathetic, and may be inclined perhaps to prize Burns
most for his touches of piercing, sometimes almost intolerable, pathos;
for verse like—

> "We twa hae paidl't i' the burn
> From mornin' sun till dine;
> But seas between us braid hae **roar'd**
> Sin auld lang syne . . ."

where he is as lovely as he is sound. But perhaps it is by the perfection of soundness of his lighter and archer masterpieces that he is poetically most wholesome for us. For the votary misled by a personal estimate of Shelley, as so many of us have been, are, and will be,—of that beautiful spirit building his many-coloured haze of words and images

"pinnacled dim in the intense inane"—

no contact can be wholesomer than the contact with Burns at his archest and soundest. Side by side with the

"On the brink of the night and the morning
My coursers are wont to respire,
But the Earth has just whispered a warning
That their flight must be swifter than fire . . ."

of *Prometheus Unbound,* how salutary, how very salutary, to place this from *Tam Glen*—

"My minnie does constantly deave me
And bids me beware o' young men;
They flatter, she says, to deceive me;
But wha can think sae o' Tam Glen?"

But we enter on burning ground as we approach the poetry of times so near to us—poetry like that of Byron, Shelley, and Wordsworth—of which the estimates are so often not only personal, but personal with passion. For my purpose, it is enough to have taken the single case of Burns, the first poet we come to of whose work the estimate formed is evidently apt to be personal, and to have suggested how we may proceed, using the poetry of the great classics as a sort of touchstone, to correct this estimate, as we had previously corrected by the same means the historic estimate where we met with it. A collection like the present, with its succession of celebrated names and celebrated poems, offers a good opportunity to us for resolutely endeavouring to make our estimates of poetry real. I have sought to point out a method which will help us in making them so, and to exhibit it in use so far as to put any one who likes in a way of applying it for himself.

At any rate the end to which the method and the estimate are designed to lead, and from leading to which, if they do lead to it, they get their whole value,—the benefit of being able clearly to feel and deeply to enjoy the best, the truly classic, in poetry,—is an end, let me say it once more at parting, of supreme importance. We are often told that an era is opening in which we are to see multitudes of a common sort of readers, and masses of a common sort of literature; that such readers do not want and could not relish anything better than such literature, and that to provide it is becoming a vast and profitable industry. Even if good literature entirely lost currency with the world, it would still be abundantly worth while to continue to enjoy it by oneself. But it never will lose currency with the world, in spite of momentary appearances; it never will lose supremacy. Currency and supremacy are insured to it, not indeed by the world's deliberate and conscious choice, but by something far deeper,—by the instinct of self-preservation in humanity.

HENRY JAMES

(1843–1916)

HENRY JAMES was born in New York City on April 15, 1843. His father, Henry James, Sr., was independently wealthy, and independent almost to the point of eccentricity in his religious, economic, and social beliefs; he was constantly attempting to explain and define his religious doctrine, "the immanence of God in the unity of mankind," through such books as *Substance and Shadow* (1863) and *The Secret of Swedenborg* (1869). Henry's oldest brother, William (1842–1910), gained fame earlier than Henry, as one of the outstanding philosophers and psychologists of his time. The James children were given an informal, cosmopolitan education, first under governesses and tutors, then at a variety of schools in Geneva, London, Paris, and Newport, in line with their father's belief that his children should be citizens of the world. When an injury to his back kept him from army service, Henry in 1862 entered the Harvard Law School, but by 1864 he had decided on a literary career. He contributed reviews and stories to the *Atlantic Monthly* and other magazines; visited Europe and wrote numerous travel sketches; and in 1875 left the United States to reside permanently in Europe. In Paris he enjoyed particularly his associations with Ivan Turgeniev, Gustave Flaubert, and Guy de Maupassant; but after a year he moved to London and established a residence there. His early novels (*Roderick Hudson*, 1876, *The American*, 1877, *Daisy Miller*, 1879, *Washington Square*, 1881, among others) and his short stories and critical essays established his position as an international novelist, a detached spectator of life more interested in the reactions of his characters than in their actions, and as a pioneer in the fields of psychological realism and of fictional techniques. Always interested in writing and the arts, with little concern for business or politics, he wrote voluminously yet with infinite care for artistry and expression. After an interlude of writing for the theatre (1889–1895), he moved from London to Lamb House, Rye, Sussex, and returned to writing the novels and novelettes of his later, more involved manner: *The Spoils of Poynton* (1897), *The Turn of the Screw* (1898), *The Awkward Age* (1898), and the three major works, *The Wings of the Dove* (1902), *The Ambassadors* (1903), and *The Golden Bowl* (1904). In 1904–5 he made an extended visit to the United States, which he described in *The American Scene* (1907). After returning to England, he began a painstaking revision of his works for a collected edition, writing a preface for each volume; this body of critical writing was characterized by Ezra Pound as "The one extant great treatise on novel writing in English." James started other projects and wrote numerous short pieces, but

World War I, he felt, prevented his bringing many of them to completion. In 1915 he became a naturalized British subject; on February 28, 1916, he died at Chelsea, England.

The criticism of prose fiction developed late. The use of prose even in the comic drama was not sanctioned by many Renaissance critics, and its use in the romance was defended only on the ground that the romance was an entirely new form [see J. E. Spingarn, *Literary Criticism in the Renaissance,* 31ff. and 112–124]. There was a somewhat greater, though still a reluctant, willingness to admit that the epic could be written in prose. Cervantes [*Don Quixote,* Part I, ch. XLVII] states the opinion of many critics, including Sidney, when he writes that "epics may be as well writ in prose as in verse." The French critic Huet, in his *Lettre sur l'Origine des Romans,* makes a distinction between the poetic epic and the prose romance, but so many authors of romances called their works "prose epics" that the distinction was soon forgotten.

Instead, the critics began to distinguish between the novel and the romance. William Congreve, in the Preface to *Incognita,* defines his own work by drawing a contrast between the two terms: "Romances are generally composed of the Constant Loves and invincible Courages of Hero's, Heroins, Kings and Queens, Mortals of the first Rank, and so forth; where lofty performances, elevate and surprize the Reader into a giddy Delight, which leaves him flat upon the Ground whenever he gives off, and vexes him to think how he has suffer'd himself to be pleased and transported . . . Novels are of a more familiar nature; Come near us, and represent to us Intrigues in practice, delight us with Accidents and Odd Events, but not such as are wholly unusual or unpresidented, such which not being so distant from our Belief bring also the pleasure nearer us." Fielding accepted this distinction, but he tended to go back for authority for the genre to the earlier concept of the prose epic. He cited Aristotle, and claimed that his type of work lacked only metre; the Preface to *Joseph Andrews* is indeed an analysis of the prose and comic epic in the traditional terms of epic criticism. The introductory chapters to the eighteen books of *Tom Jones* elaborate on this view of the novel, but he also emphasizes the role of the novelist as historian [Book VIII]: "Nor is possibility alone sufficient to justify us; we must keep likewise within the rules of probability. It is, I think, the opinion of Aristotle; or if not, it is the opinion of some wise man, whose authority will be as weighty when he is as old, 'That it is no excuse for a poet who relates what is incredible, that the thing related is really a matter of fact.' This may perhaps be allowed true with regard to poetry, but it may be thought impracticable to extend it to the historian; for he is obliged to record matters as he finds them, though they may be of so extraordinary a nature as will require no small degree of historical faith to swallow them. . . ."

The novel was to deal with ordinary human life; the romance, as its last vigorous defender in the traditional epic terms, William Gilmore Simms, defined it in the Preface to *The Yemassee,* was "the substitute which the people of the present day offer for the ancient epic. The form is changed; the matter is very much the same; at all events, it differs much more seriously from the

English novel than it does from the epic and the drama, because the difference is one of material, even more than of fabrication. . . . The Romance is of loftier origin than the Novel. It approximates the poem. It may be described as an amalgam of the two. . . . It invests individuals with an absorbing interest—it hurries them rapidly through crowding and exacting events, in a narrow space of time—it requires the same unities of plan, of purpose, and harmony of parts, and it seeks for its adventures among the wild and wonderful." This was an extreme statement; in general, the author claimed for the romance only a somewhat greater freedom than for the novel. Hawthorne, in the Preface to *The House of the Seven Gables,* gave a reasoned and reasonable statement of this distinction: "When a writer calls his work a Romance, it need hardly be observed that he wishes to claim a certain latitude, both as to its fashion and material, which he would not have felt himself entitled to assume had he professed to be writing a Novel. The latter form of composition is presumed to aim at a very minute fidelity, not merely to the possible, but to the probable and ordinary course of man's experience. The former— while, as a work of art, it must rigidly subject itself to laws, and while it sins unpardonably so far as it may swerve aside from the truth of the human heart—has fairly a right to present that truth under circumstances, to a great extent, of the writer's own choosing or creation."

Traditionally, the novel lacked such freedom. Samuel Johnson called these works "familiar histories" [*Rambler* #4], and thought that their "province is to bring about natural events by easy means and to keep up curiosity without the help of wonder"; the authors were indeed so bound to actual life that "The chief advantage which these fictions have over real life is that their authors are at liberty, though not to invent, yet to select objects, and to cull from the mass of mankind those individuals upon which the attention ought most to be employed; as a diamond, though it cannot be made, may be polished by art, and placed in such situation as to display that luster which before was buried among common stones."

These somewhat artificial distinctions never attained the wide recognition in France that they held in England and the United States. Stendhal [in "Walter Scott and *The Princess of Cleves*"] briefly discussed the two genres, and noted that "it is infinitely less difficult to describe in picturesque fashion the costume of a character, than to say what he felt, or to make him speak." But French critics were generally content to let the word *roman* cover all types of the novel.

Henry James greatly preferred that prose fiction be considered simply as one inclusive genre. He felt the need for an aesthetic of fiction. As Morton D. Zabel noted [Preface to *Literary Opinion in America*], he was constantly looking for bases in art and criticism: "He studied Balzac and the realists, Eliot and the moral problem in fiction, George Sand for her imaginative and atmospheric methods, the new French naturalists for their inventories of contemporary society. In ten years more his European education was fairly complete. He had examined the contrasting purposes of the schools of Paris— romantic, symbolist, and realist. He listened to the counsels of Flaubert, Turgeniev, Daudet, and Zola; he wrote his book on Hawthorne and the essays on *French Poets and Novelists* and *Partial Portraits;* he formed his friendship with Stevenson and arrived at his own creative maturity. He was perhaps the first American man of letters to follow a complete course of literary and critical education, to compare European writers and doctrines, to impose on his own craft and conscience an unprejudiced critical detachment. He saw the modern creative problem in its two essential aspects: its oppression by social conflict and theories of scientific and moral determinism, and its acute subtilization by the defenses which the esthetic techniques of the modern sensibility had set up against these oppressions. He saw modern criticism confronting the task of reconciling the real and esthetic, human life in 'its unprejudiced identity' with the form and laws of art. That task was nowhere more urgent than in America, and during the eighties, when James still had the ambition of becoming the 'American Balzac,' he formulated his working principles as a critic. His critical doctrine had three clauses. He argued for subtlety and plasticity in the critic's sympathy as a first condition. As a second he demanded a tireless study of the vital experience upon which all art is based and its use as a test of material validity, since for him all art was 'in basis moral.' And he required finally a knowledge of how the intelligence of the artist stamps this material with its unmistakable impression of form and language, since that imprint constituted for James the 'quality of mind' he looked for in any valid work of art." *

These qualities in his criticism are seen at their best in "The Art of Fiction." In his later criticism his interest in form and structure increased until he could see little merit in writers who disregarded the demands of art. In the essay included in this book, however, he emphasizes the freedom of the novel, and its correspondence with life. Although he shied away equally from the "art-for-art's-sake" ideas of Gautier and the naturalism of Zola, he defended the right of the novelist to present any point of view as long as he recorded human life accurately and truly, interpreted and assessed human conduct wisely, and portrayed situations, manners, and people with artistry. He was the first great critic to argue that the novel is "the most magnificent form of art"; in his critical essays and in the prefaces to his own novels he went far toward establishing an art of fiction.

THE ART OF FICTION [1]

(1884)

I SHOULD not have affixed so comprehensive a title to these few remarks, necessarily wanting in any completeness upon a subject the full consideration of which would carry us far, did I not seem to discover a pretext for my temerity in the interesting pamphlet lately published under this name by Mr. Walter Besant. Mr. Besant's lecture at the

* Reprinted from the Preface to *Literary Opinion in America,* by Morton D. Zabel; copyright 1937 by Harper and Brothers. Used by permission of the author, whose revised and enlarged edition of *Literary Opinion in America* is scheduled for publication by Harper and Brothers in 1951.

[1] Originally published in *Longman's Magazine* (September, 1884); it was included in *Partial Portraits* (1888). The text is that of 1888.

Royal Institution—the original form of his pamphlet—appears to indicate that many persons are interested in the art of fiction, and are not indifferent to such remarks, as those who practice it may attempt to make about it. I am therefore anxious not to lose the benefit of this favorable association, and to edge in a few words under cover of the attention which Mr. Besant is sure to have excited. There is something very encouraging in his having put into form certain of his ideas on the mystery of storytelling.

It is a proof of life and curiosity—curiosity on the part of the brotherhood of novelists as well as on the part of their readers. Only a short time ago it might have been supposed that the English novel was not what the French call *discutable*. It had no air of having a theory, a conviction, a consciousness of itself behind it—of being the expression of an artistic faith, the result of choice and comparison. I do not say it was necessarily the worse for that: it would take much more courage than I possess to intimate that the form of the novel as Dickens and Thackeray (for instance) saw it had any taint of incompleteness. It was, however, *naïf* (if I may help myself out with another French word); and evidently if it be destined to suffer in any way for having lost its *naïveté* it has now an idea of making sure of the corresponding advantages. During the period I have alluded to there was a comfortable, good-humored feeling abroad that a novel is a novel, as a pudding is a pudding, and that our only business with it could be to swallow it. But within a year or two, for some reason or other, there have been signs of returning animation—the era of discussion would appear to have been to a certain extent opened. Art lives upon discussion, upon experiment, upon curiosity, upon variety of attempt, upon the exchange of views and the comparison of standpoints; and there is a presumption that those times when no one has anything particular to say about it, and has no reason to give for practice or preference, though they may be times of honor, are not times of development—are times, possibly even, a little of dullness. The successful application of any art is a delightful spectacle, but the theory too is interesting; and though there is a great deal of the latter without the former I suspect there has never been a genuine success that has not had a latent core of conviction. Discussion, suggestion, formulation, these things are fertilizing when they are frank and sincere. Mr. Besant has set an excellent example in saying what he thinks, for his part, about the way in which fiction should be written, as well as about the way in which it should be published; for his view of the "art," carried on into an appendix, covers that too. Other laborers in the same field will doubtless take up the argument, they will give it the light of their experience, and the effect will surely be to make our interest in the novel a little more what it had for some time threatened to fail to be—a serious, active, inquiring interest, under protection of which this delightful study may, in moments of confidence, venture to say a little more what it thinks of itself.

It must take itself seriously for the public to take it so. The old superstition about fiction being "wicked" has doubtless died out in England; but the spirit of it lingers in a certain oblique regard directed toward any story which does not more or less admit that it is only a joke. Even the most jocular novel feels in some degree the weight of the proscription that was formerly directed against literary levity: the jocularity does not always succeed in passing for orthodoxy. It is still expected, though perhaps people are ashamed to say it, that a production which is after all only a "make-believe" (for what else is a "story"?) shall be in some degree apologetic—shall renounce the pretension of attempting really to represent life. This, of course, any sensible, wide-awake story declines to do, for it quickly perceives that the tolerance granted to it on such a condition is only an attempt to stifle it disguised in the form of generosity. The old evangelical hostility to the novel, which was as explicit as it was narrow, and which regarded it as little less favorable to our immortal part than a stage play, was in reality far less insulting. The only reason for the existence of a novel is that it does attempt to represent life. When it relinquishes this attempt, the same attempt that we see on the canvas of the painter, it will have arrived at a very strange pass. It is not expected of the picture that it will make itself humble in order to be forgiven; and the analogy between the art of the painter and the art of the novelist is, so far as I am able to see, complete. Their inspiration is the same, their process (allowing for the different quality of the vehicle) is the same, their success is the same. They may learn from each other, they may explain and sustain each other. Their cause is the same, and the honor of one is the honor of another. The Mahometans think a picture an unholy thing, but it is a long time since any Christian did, and it is therefore the more odd that in the Christian mind the traces (dissimulated though they may be) of a suspicion of the sister art should linger to this day. The only effectual way to lay it to rest is to emphasize the analogy to which I just alluded—to insist on the fact that as the picture is reality, so the novel is history. That is the only general description (which does it justice) that we may give of the novel. But history also is allowed to represent life; it is not, any more than painting, expected to apologize. The subject matter of fiction is stored up likewise in documents and records, and if it will not give itself away, as they say in California, it must speak with assurance, with the tone of the historian. Certain accomplished novelists have a habit of giving themselves away which must often bring tears to the eyes of people who take their fiction seriously. I was lately struck, in reading over many pages of Anthony Trollope, with his want of discretion in this particular. In a digression, a parenthesis or an aside, he concedes to the reader that he and this trusting friend are only "making believe." He admits that the events he narrates have not really happened, and that he can give his narrative any turn the reader may like best. Such a betrayal of a sacred office seems to me, I confess, a terrible crime; it is what I mean by the attitude of apology, and it shocks me every whit as much in Trollope as it would have shocked me in Gibbon or Macaulay. It implies that the novelist is less occupied in looking for the truth (the truth, of course I mean, that he assumes, the premises that we must grant him, whatever they may be) than the historian, and in doing so it deprives him at a stroke of all his standing room. To represent and illustrate the past, the actions of men, is the task of either writer, and the only difference that I can see is, in proportion as he succeeds, to the honor of the novelist, consisting as it does in his having more difficulty in collecting his evidence, which is so far from being purely literary. It seems to me to give him a great character, the fact that he has at once so much in common with the philosopher and the painter; this double analogy is a magnificent heritage.

It is of all this evidently that Mr. Besant is full when he insists upon the fact that fiction is one of the *fine* arts, deserving in its turn of all the honors and emoluments that have hitherto been reserved for the successful profession of music, poetry, painting, architecture. It is impossible to insist too much on so important a truth, and the place that Mr. Besant demands for the work of the novelist may be represented, a trifle less abstractly, by saying that he demands not only that it shall be reputed artistic, but that it shall be reputed very artistic indeed. It is excellent that he should have struck this note, for his doing so indicates that there was need of it, that his proposition may be to many people a novelty. One rubs one's eyes at the thought; but the rest of Mr. Besant's essay confirms the revelation. I suspect in truth that it would be possible to confirm it still further, and that one would not be far wrong in saying that in addition to the people to whom it has never occurred that a novel ought to be artistic, there are a great many others who, if this principle were urged upon them, would be filled with an indefinable mistrust. They would find it difficult to explain their repugnance, but it would operate strongly to put them on their guard. "Art," in our Protestant communities, where so many things have got so strangely twisted about, is supposed in certain circles to have some vaguely injurious effect upon those who make it an important consideration, who let it weigh in the balance. It is assumed to be opposed in some mysterious manner to morality, to amusement, to instruction. When it is embodied in the work of the painter (the sculptor is another affair!) you know what it is: it stands there before you, in the honesty of pink and green and a gilt frame; you can see the worst of it at a glance, and you can be on your *guard*. But when it is introduced into literature it becomes more insidious—there is danger of its hurting you before you know it. Literature should be either instructive or amusing, and there is in many minds an impression that these artistic preoccupations, the search for form, contribute to neither end, interfere indeed with both. They are too frivolous to be edifying, and too serious to be diverting; and they are moreover priggish and paradoxical and superfluous. That, I think, represents the manner in which the latent thought of many people who read novels as an exercise in skipping would explain itself if it were to become articulate. They would argue, of course, that a novel ought to be "good," but they would interpret this term in a fashion of their own, which indeed would vary considerably from one critic to another. One would say that being good means representing virtuous and aspiring characters, placed in prominent positions; another would say that it depends on a "happy ending," on a distribution at the last of prizes, pensions, husbands, wives, babies, millions, appended paragraphs, and cheerful remarks. Another still would say that it means being full of incident and movement, so that we shall wish to jump ahead, to see who was the mysterious stranger, and if the stolen will was ever found, and shall not be distracted from this pleasure by any tiresome analysis or "description." But they would all agree that the "artistic" idea would spoil some of their fun. One would hold it accountable for all the description, another would see it revealed in the absence of sympathy. Its hostility to a happy ending would be evident, and it might even in some cases render any ending at all impossible. The "ending" of a novel is, for many persons, like that of a good dinner, a course of dessert and ices, and the artist in fiction is regarded as a sort of meddlesome doctor who forbids agreeable aftertastes. It is therefore true that this conception of Mr. Besant's of the novel as a superior form encounters not only a negative but a positive indifference. It matters little that as a work of art it should really be as little or as much of its essence to supply happy endings, sympathetic characters, and an objective tone, as if it were a work of mechanics: the association of ideas, however incongruous, might easily be too much for it if an eloquent voice were not sometimes raised to call attention to the fact that it is at once as free and as serious a branch of literature as any other.

Certainly this might sometimes be doubted in presence of the enormous number of works of fiction that appeal to the credulity of our generation, for it might easily seem that there could be no great character in a commodity so quickly and easily produced. It must be admitted that good novels are much compromised by bad ones, and that the field at large suffers discredit from overcrowding. I think, however, that this injury is only superficial, and that the superabundance of written fiction proves nothing against the principle itself. It has been vulgarized, like all other kinds of literature, like everything else today, and it has proved more than some kinds accessible to vulgarization. But there is as much difference as there ever was between a good novel and a bad one: the bad is swept with all the daubed canvases and spoiled marble into some unvisited limbo, or infinite rubbish yard beneath the back windows of the world, and the good subsists and emits its light and stimulates our desire for perfection. As I shall take the liberty of making but a single criticism of Mr. Besant, whose tone is so full of the love of his art, I may as well have done with it at once. He seems to me to mistake in attempting to say so definitely beforehand what sort of an affair the good novel will be. To indicate the danger of such an error as that has been the purpose of these few pages; to suggest that certain traditions on the subject, applied *a priori,* have already had much to answer for, and that the good health of an art which undertakes so immediately to reproduce life must demand that it be perfectly free. It lives upon exercise, and the very meaning of exercise is freedom. The only obligation to which in advance we may hold a novel, without incurring the accusation of being arbitrary, is that it be interesting. That general responsibility rests upon it, but it is the only one I can think of. The ways in which it is at liberty to accomplish this result (of interesting us) strike me as innumerable, and such as can only suffer from being marked out or fenced in by prescription. They are as various as the temperament of man, and they are successful in proportion as they reveal a particular mind, different from others. A novel is in its broadest definition a personal, a direct impression of life: that, to begin with, constitutes its value, which is greater or less according to the intensity of the impression. But there will be no intensity at all, and therefore no value, unless there is freedom to feel and say. The tracing of a line to be followed, of a tone to be taken, of a form to be filled out, is a limitation of that freedom and a suppression of the very thing that we are most curious about. The form, it seems to me, is to be appreciated after the fact: then the author's choice has been made, his standard has been indicated; then we can follow lines and directions and compare tones and resemblances. Then in a word we can enjoy one of the most charming of pleasures, we can estimate quality, we can apply the test of execution. The execution belongs to the author alone; it is what is most personal to him, and we measure him by that. The advantage, the luxury, as well as the torment and responsibility of the novelist, is that there is no limit to what he may attempt as an executant—no limit to his possible experiments, efforts, discoveries, successes. Here it is especially that he works, step by step, like his brother of the brush, of whom we may always say that he has painted his picture in a manner best known to himself. His manner is his secret, not necessarily a jealous one. He cannot disclose it as a general thing if he would; he would be at a loss to teach it to others. I say this with a due recollection of having insisted on the community of method of the artist who paints a picture and the artist who writes a novel. The painter *is* able to teach the rudiments of his practice, and it is possible, from the study of good work (granted the aptitude), both to learn how to paint and to learn how to write. Yet it remains true, without injury to the *rapprochement,* that the literary artist would be obliged to say to his pupil much more than the other, "Ah, well, you must do it as you can!" It is a question of degree, a matter of delicacy. If there are exact sciences, there are also exact arts, and the grammar of painting is so much more definite that it makes the difference.

I ought to add, however, that if Mr. Besant says at the beginning of his essay that the "laws of fiction may be laid down and taught with as much precision and exactness as the laws of harmony, perspective, and proportion," he mitigates what might appear to be an extravagance by applying his remark to "general" laws, and by expressing most of these rules in a manner with which it would certainly be unaccommodating to disagree. That the novelist must write from his experience, that his "characters must be real and such as might be met with in actual life"; that "a young lady brought up in a quiet country village should avoid descriptions of garrison life," and "a writer whose friends and personal experiences belong to the lower middle class should carefully avoid introducing his characters into society"; that one should enter one's notes in a common-place book; that one's figures should be clear in outline; that making them clear by some trick of speech or of carriage is a bad method, and "describing them at length" is a worse one; that English fiction should have a "conscious moral purpose"; that "it is almost impossible to estimate too highly the value of careful workmanship—that is, of style"; that "the most important point of all is the story," that "the story is everything": these are principles with most of which it is surely impossible not to sympathize. That remark about the lower middle-class writer and his knowing his place is perhaps rather chilling; but for the rest I should find it difficult to dissent from any one of these recommendations. At the same time, I should find it difficult positively to assent to them, with the exception, perhaps, of the injunction as to entering one's notes in a common-place book. They scarcely seem to me to have the quality that Mr. Besant attributes to the rules of the novelist—the "precision and exactness" of "the laws of harmony, perspective, and proportion." They are suggestive, they are even inspiring, but they are not exact, though they are doubtless as much so as the case admits of: which is a proof of that liberty of interpretation for which I just contended. For the value of these different injunctions—so beautiful and so vague—is wholly in the meaning one attaches to them. The characters, the situation, which strike one as real will be those that touch and interest one most, but the measure of reality is very difficult to fix. The reality of Don Quixote or of Mr. Micawber is a very delicate shade; it is a reality so colored by the author's vision that, vivid as it may be, one would hesitate to propose it as a model: one would expose one's self to some very embarrassing questions on the part of a pupil. It goes without saying that you will not write a good novel unless you possess the sense of reality; but it will be difficult to give you a recipe for calling that sense into being. Humanity is immense, and reality has a myriad forms; the most one can affirm is that some of the flowers of fiction have the odor of it, and others have not; as for telling you in advance how your nosegay should be composed, that is another affair. It is equally excellent and inconclusive to say that one must write from experience; to our suppositious aspirant such a declaration might savor of mockery. What kind of experience is intended, and where does it begin and end? Experience is never limited, and it is never complete; it is an immense sensibility, a kind of huge spiderweb of the finest silken threads suspended in the chamber of consciousness, and catching every air-borne particle in its tissue. It is the very atmosphere of the mind; and when the mind is imaginative—much more when it happens to be that of a man of genius—it takes to itself the faintest hints of life, it converts the very pulses of the air into revelations. The young lady living in a village has only to be a damsel upon whom nothing is lost to make it quite unfair (as it seems to me) to declare to her that she shall have nothing to say about the military. Greater miracles have been seen than that, imagination assisting, she should speak the truth about some of these gentlemen. I remember an English novelist, a woman of genius, telling me that she was much commended for the impression she had managed to give in one of her tales of the nature and way of life of the French Protestant youth. She had been asked where she learned so much about this recondite being, she had been congratulated on her peculiar opportunities. These opportunities consisted in her having once, in Paris, as she ascended a staircase, passed an open door where, in the household of a *pasteur,* some of the young Protestants were seated at table round a finished meal. The glimpse made a picture; it lasted only a moment, but that moment was experience. She had got her direct personal impression, and she turned out her type. She knew what youth was, and what Protestantism; she also had the advantage of having seen what it was to be French, so that she converted these ideas into a concrete image and produced a reality. Above all, however, she was blessed with the faculty which when you give it an inch takes an ell, and which for the artist is a much greater source of strength than any accident of residence or of place in the social scale. The power to guess the unseen from the seen, to trace the implication of things, to judge the whole piece by the pattern, the condition of feeling life in general so completely that you are well on your way to knowing any particular corner of it— this cluster of gifts may almost be said to constitute experience, and they occur in country and in town, and in the most differing stages of education. If experience consists of impressions, it may be said that impressions *are* experience, just as (have we not seen it?) they are the very air we breathe. Therefore, if I should certainly say to a novice, "Write from experience and experience only," I should feel that this was rather a tantalizing monition if I were not careful immediately to add, "Try to be one of the people on whom nothing is lost!"

I am far from intending by this to minimize the importance of exactness—of truth of detail. One can speak best from one's own taste, and I may therefore venture to say that the air of reality (solidity of specification) seems to me to be the supreme virtue of a novel—the merit on which all its other merits (including that conscious moral purpose of which Mr. Besant speaks) helplessly and submissively depend. If it be not there, they are all as nothing, and if these be there, they owe their effect to the success with which the author has produced the illusion of life. The cultivation of this success, the study of this exquisite process, form, to my taste, the beginning and the end of the art of the novelist. They are his inspiration, his despair, his reward, his torment, his delight. It is here in very truth that he competes with life; it is here that he competes with his brother the painter in *his* attempt to render the look of things, the look that conveys their meaning, to catch the color, the relief, the expression, the surface, the substance of the human spectacle. It is in regard to this that Mr. Besant is well inspired when he bids him take notes. He cannot possibly take too many, he cannot possibly take enough. All life solicits him, and to "render" the simplest surface, to produce the most momentary illusion, is a very complicated business. His case would be easier, and the rule would be more exact, if Mr. Besant had been able to tell him what notes to take. But this, I fear, he can never learn in any manual; it is the business of his life. He has to take a great many in order to select a few, he has to work them up as he can, and even the guides and philosophers who might have most to say to him must leave him alone when it comes to the application of precepts, as we leave the painter in communion with his palette. That his characters "must be clear in outline," as Mr. Besant says—he feels that down to his boots; but how he shall make them so is a secret between his good angel and himself. It would be absurdly simple if he could be taught that a great deal of "description" would make them so, or that on the contrary the absence of description and the cultivation of dialogue, or the absence of dialogue and the multiplication of "incident," would rescue him from his difficulties. Nothing, for instance, is more possible than that he be of a turn of mind for which this odd, literal opposition of description and dialogue, incident and description, has little meaning and light. People often talk of these things as if they had a kind of internecine distinctness, instead of melting into each other at every breath, and being intimately associated parts of one general effort of expression. I cannot imagine composition existing in a series of blocks, nor conceive, in any novel worth discussing at all, of a passage of description that is not in its intention narrative, a passage of dialogue that is not in its intention descriptive, a touch of truth of any sort that does not partake of the nature of incident, or an incident that derives its interest from any other source than the general and only source of the success of a work of art—that of being illustrative. A novel is a living thing, all one and continuous, like any other organism, and in proportion as it lives will it be found, I think, that in each of the parts there is something of each of the other parts. The critic who over the close texture of a finished work shall pretend to trace a geography of items will mark some frontiers as artificial, I fear, as any that have been known to history. There is an old-fashioned distinction between the novel of character and the novel of incident which must have cost many a smile to the intending fabulist who was keen about his work. It appears to me as little to the point as the equally celebrated distinction between the novel and the romance—to answer as little to any reality. There are bad novels and good novels, as there are bad pictures and good pictures; but that is the only distinction in which I see any meaning, and I can as little imagine speaking of a novel of character as I can imagine speaking of a picture of character. When one says picture one says of character, when one says novel one says of incident, and the terms may be transposed at will. What is character but the determination of incident? What is incident but the illustration of character? What is either a picture or a novel that is *not* of character? What else do we seek in it and find in it? It is an incident for a woman to stand up with her hand resting on a table and look out at you in a certain way; or if it be not an incident I think it will be hard to say what it is. At the same time it is an expression of character. If you say you don't see it (character in *that—allons donc!*), this is exactly what the artist who has reasons of his own for thinking he *does* see it undertakes to show you. When a young man makes up his mind that he has not faith enough after all to enter the church as he intended, that is an incident, though you may not hurry to the end of the chapter to see whether perhaps he doesn't change once more. I do not say that these are extraordinary or startling incidents. I do not pretend to estimate the degree of interest proceeding from them, for this will depend upon the skill of the painter. It sounds almost puerile to say that some incidents are intrinsically much more important than others, and I need not take this precaution after having professed my sympathy for the major ones in remarking that the only classification of the novel that I can understand is into that which has life and that which has it not.

The novel and the romance, the novel of incident and that of character—these clumsy separations appear to me to have been made by critics and readers for their own convenience, and to help them out of some of their occasional queer predicaments, but to have little reality or interest for the producer, from whose point of view it is of course that we are attempting to consider the art of fiction. The case is the same with another shadowy category which Mr. Besant apparently is disposed to set up—that of the "modern English novel"; unless indeed it be that in this matter he has fallen into an accidental confusion of standpoints. It is not quite clear whether he intends the remarks in which he alludes to it to be didactic or historical. It is as difficult to suppose a person intending to write a modern English as to suppose him writing an ancient English novel: that is a label which begs the question. One writes the novel, one paints the picture, of one's language and of one's time, and calling it modern English will not, alas! make the difficult task any easier. No more, unfortunately, will calling this or that work of one's fellow artist a romance—unless it be, of course, simply for the pleasantness of the thing, as for instance when Hawthorne gave this heading to his story of *Blithedale*. The French, who have brought the theory of fiction to remarkable completeness, have but one name for the novel, and have not attempted smaller things in it, that I can see, for that. I can think of no obligation to which the "romancer" would not be held equally with the novelist; the standard of execution is equally high for each. Of course it is of execution that we are talking—that being the only point of a novel that is open to contention. This is perhaps too often lost sight of, only to produce interminable confusions and cross purposes. We must grant the artist his subject, his idea, his *donnée:* our criticism is applied only to what he makes of it. Naturally I do not mean that we are bound to like it or find it interesting: in case we do not, our course is perfectly simple —to let it alone. We may believe that of a certain idea even the most sincere novelist can make nothing at all, and the event may perfectly justify our belief; but the failure will have been a failure to execute, and it is in the execution that the fatal weakness is recorded. If we pretend to respect the artist at all, we must allow him his freedom of choice, in the face, in particular cases, of innumerable presumptions that the choice will not fructify. Art derives a considerable part of its beneficial exercise from flying in the face of presumptions, and some of the most interesting experiments of which it is capable are hidden in the bosom of common things. Gustave Flaubert has written a story about the devotion of a servant girl to a parrot, and the production, highly finished as it is, cannot on the whole be called a success. We are perfectly free to find it flat, but I think it might have been interesting; and I, for my part, am extremely glad he should have written it; it is a contribution to our knowledge of what can be done—or what cannot. Ivan Turgenev has written a tale about a deaf and dumb serf and a lap dog, and the thing is touching, loving, a little masterpiece. He struck the note of life where Gustave Flaubert missed it—he flew in the face of a presumption and achieved a victory.

Nothing, of course, will ever take the place of the good old fashion of "liking" a work of art or not liking it: the most improved criticism will not abolish that primitive, that ultimate test. I mention this to guard myself from the accusation of intimating that the idea, the subject, of a novel or a picture, does not matter. It matters, to my sense, in the highest degree, and if I might put up a prayer it would be that artists should select none but the richest. Some, as I have already hastened to admit, are much more remunerative than others, and it would be a world happily arranged in which persons intending to treat them should be exempt from confusions and mistakes. This fortunate condition will arrive only, I fear, on the same day that critics become purged from error. Meanwhile, I repeat, we do not judge the artist with fairness unless we say to him, "Oh, I grant you your starting point, because if I did not I should seem to prescribe to you, and heaven forbid I should take that responsibility. If I pretend to tell you what you must not take, you will call upon me to tell you then what you must take; in which case I shall be prettily caught. Moreover, it isn't till I have accepted your data that I can begin to measure you. I have the standard, the pitch; I have no right to tamper with your flute and then criticize your music. Of course I may not care for your idea at all; I may think it silly, or stale, or unclean; in which case I wash my hands of you altogether. I may content myself with believing that you will not have succeeded in being interesting, but I shall, of course, not attempt to demonstrate it, and you will be as indifferent to me as I am to you. I needn't remind you that there are all sorts of tastes: who can know it better? Some people, for excellent reasons, don't like to read about carpenters; others, for reasons even better, don't like to read about courtesans. Many object to Americans. Others (I believe they are mainly editors and publishers) won't look at Italians. Some readers don't like quiet subjects; others don't like bustling ones. Some enjoy a complete illusion, others the consciousness of large concessions. They choose their novels accordingly, and if they don't care about your idea they won't, *a fortiori,* care about your treatment."

So that it comes back very quickly, as I have said, to the liking: in spite of M. Zola, who reasons less powerfully than he represents, and who will not reconcile himself to this absoluteness of taste, thinking that there are certain things that people ought to like, and that they can be made to like. I am quite at a loss to imagine anything (at any rate in this matter of fiction) that people *ought* to like or to dislike. Selection will be sure to take care of itself, for it has a constant motive behind it. That motive is simply experience. As people feel life, so they will feel the art that is most closely related to it. This closeness of relation is what we should never forget in talking of the effort of the novel. Many people speak of it as a factitious, artificial form, a product of ingenuity, the business of which is to alter and arrange the things that surround us, to translate them into conventional, traditional molds. This, however, is a view of the matter which carries us but a very short way, condemns the art to an eternal repetition of a few familiar *clichés,* cuts short its development, and leads us straight up to a dead wall. Catching the very note and trick, the strange irregular rhythm of life, that is the attempt whose strenuous force keeps Fiction upon her feet. In proportion as in what she offers us we see life *without* rearrangement do we feel that we are touching the truth; in proportion as we see it *with* rearrangement do we feel that we are being put off with a substitute, a compromise and convention. It is not uncommon to hear an extraordinary assurance of remark in regard to this matter of rearranging, which is often spoken of as if it were the last word of art. Mr. Besant seems to me in danger of falling into the great error with his rather unguarded talk about "selection." Art is essentially selection, but it is a selection whose main care is to be typical, to be inclusive. For many people art means rose-colored windowpanes, and selection means picking a bouquet for Mrs. Grundy. They will tell you glibly that artistic considerations have nothing to do with the disagreeable, with the ugly; they will rattle off shallow commonplaces about the province of art and the limits of art till you are moved to some wonder in return as to the province and the limits of ignorance. It appears to me that no one can ever have made a seriously artistic attempt without becoming conscious of an immense increase—a kind of revelation—of freedom. One perceives in that case—by the light of a heavenly ray—that the province of art is all life, all feeling, all observation, all vision. As Mr. Besant so justly intimates, it is all experience. That is a sufficient answer to those who maintain that it must not touch the sad things of life, who stick into its divine unconscious bosom little prohibitory inscriptions on the end of sticks, such as we see in public gardens—"It is forbidden to walk on the grass; it is forbidden to touch the flowers; it is not allowed to introduce dogs or to remain after dark; it is requested to keep to the right." The young aspirant in the line of fiction whom we continue to imagine will do nothing without taste, for in that case his freedom would be of little use to him; but the first advantage of his taste will be to reveal to him the absurdity of the little sticks and tickets. If he have taste, I must add, of course he will have ingenuity, and my disrespectful reference to that quality just now was not meant to imply that it is useless in fiction. But it is only a secondary aid; the first is a capacity for receiving straight impressions.

Mr. Besant has some remarks on the question of "the story" which I shall not attempt to criticize, though they seem to me to contain a singular ambiguity, because I do not think I understand them. I cannot see what is meant by talking as if there were a part of a novel which is the story and part of it which for mystical reasons is not—unless indeed the distinction be made in a sense in which it is difficult to suppose that anyone should attempt to convey anything. "The story," if it represents anything, represents the subject, the idea, the *donnée* of the novel; and there is surely no "school"—Mr. Besant speaks of a school—which urges that a novel should be all treatment and no subject. There must assuredly be something to treat; every school is intimately conscious of that. This sense of the story being the idea, the starting point, of the novel, is the only one that I see in which it can be spoken of as something different from its organic whole; and since in proportion as the work is successful the idea permeates and penetrates it, informs and animates it, so that every word and every punctuation point contribute directly to the expression, in that proportion do we lose our sense of the story being a blade which may be drawn more or less out of its sheath. The story and the novel, the idea and the form, are the needle and thread, and I never heard of a guild of tailors who recommended the use of the thread without the needle, or the needle without the thread. Mr. Besant is not the only critic who may be observed to have spoken as if there were certain things in life which constitute stories, and certain others which do not. I find the same odd implication in an entertaining article in the *Pall Mall Gazette*, devoted, as it happens, to Mr. Besant's lecture. "The story is the thing!" says this graceful writer, as if with a tone of opposition to some other idea. I should think it was, as every painter who, as the time for "sending in" his picture looms in the distance, finds himself still in quest of a subject—as every belated artist not fixed about his theme will heartily agree. There are some subjects which speak to us and others which do not, but he would be a clever man who should undertake to give a rule—an index expurgatorius— by which the story and the no-story should be known apart. It is impossible (to me at least) to imagine any such rule which shall not be altogether arbitrary. The writer in the *Pall Mall* opposes the delightful (as I suppose) novel of *Margot la Balafrée* to certain tales in which "Bostonian nymphs" appear to have "rejected English dukes for psychological reasons." I am not acquainted with the romance just designated, and can scarcely forgive the *Pall Mall* critic for not mentioning the name of the author, but the title appears to refer to a lady who may have received a scar in some heroic adventure. I am inconsolable at not being acquainted with this episode, but am utterly at a loss to see why it is a story when the rejection (or acceptance) of a duke is not, and why a reason, psychological or other, is not a subject when a cicatrix is. They are all particles of the multitudinous life with which the novel deals, and surely no dogma which pretends to make it lawful to touch the one and unlawful to touch the other will stand for a moment on its feet. It is the special picture that must stand or fall, according as it seem to possess truth or to lack it. Mr. Besant does not, to my sense, light up the subject by intimating that a story must, under penalty of not being a story, consist of "adventures." Why of adventures more than of green spectacles? He mentions a category of impossible things, and among them he places "fiction without adventure." Why without adventure, more than without matrimony, or celibacy, or parturition, or cholera, or hydropathy, or Jansenism? This seems to me to bring the novel back to the hapless little role of being an artificial, ingenious thing —bring it down from its large, free character of an immense and exquisite correspondence with life. And what *is* adventure, when it comes to that, and by what sign is the listening pupil to recognize it? It is an adventure—an immense one—for me to write this little article; and for a Bostonian nymph to reject an English duke is an adventure only less stirring, I should say, than for an English duke to be rejected by a Bostonian nymph. I see dramas within dramas in that, and innumerable points of view. A psychological reason is, to my imagination, an object adorably pictorial; to catch the tint of its complexion—I feel as if that idea might inspire one to Titianesque efforts. There are few things more exciting to me, in short, than a psychological reason, and yet, I protest, the novel seems to me the most magnificent form of art. I have just been reading, at the same time, the delightful story of *Treasure Island,* by Mr. Robert Louis Stevenson and, in a manner less consecutive, the last tale from M. Edmond de Goncourt, which is entitled *Chérie.* One of these works treats of murders, mysteries, islands of dreadful renown, hairbreadth escapes, miraculous coincidences, and buried doubloons. The other treats of a little French girl who lived in a fine house in Paris, and died of wounded sensibility because no one would marry her. I call *Treasure Island* delightful because it appears to me to have succeeded wonderfully in what it attempts; and I venture to bestow no epithet upon *Chérie,* which strikes me as having failed deplorably in what it attempts—that is, in tracing the development of the moral consciousness of a child. But one of these productions strikes me as exactly as much of a novel as the other, and as having a "story" quite as much. The moral consciousness of a child is as much a part of life as the islands of the Spanish Main, and the one sort of geography seems to me to have those "surprises" of which Mr. Besant speaks quite as much as the other. For myself (since it comes back in the last resort, as I say, to the preference of the individual), the picture of the child's experience has the advantage that I can at successive steps (an immense luxury, near to the "sensual pleasure" of which Mr. Besant's critic in the *Pall Mall* speaks) say Yes or No, as it may be, to what the artist puts before me. I have been a child in fact, but I have been on a quest for a buried treasure only in supposition, and it is a simple accident that with M. de Goncourt I should have for the most part to say No. With George Eliot, when she painted that country with a far other intelligence, I always said Yes.

The most interesting part of Mr. Besant's lecture is unfortunately the briefest passage—his very cursory allusion to the "conscious moral purpose" of the novel. Here again it is not very clear whether he be recording a fact or laying down a principle; it is a great pity that in the latter case he should not have developed his idea. This branch of the subject is of immense importance, and Mr. Besant's few words point to considerations of the widest reach, not to be lightly disposed of. He will have treated the art of fiction but superficially who is not prepared to go every inch of the way that these considerations will carry him. It is for this reason that at the beginning of these remarks I was careful to notify the reader that my reflections on so large a theme have no pretension to be exhaustive. Like Mr. Besant, I have left the question of the morality of the novel till the last, and at the last I find I have used up my space. It is a question surrounded with difficulties, as witness the very first that meets us, in the form of a definite question, on the threshold. Vagueness, in such a discussion, is fatal, and what is the meaning of your morality and your conscious moral purpose? Will you not define your terms and explain how (a novel being a picture) a picture can be either moral or immoral? You wish to paint a moral picture or carve a moral statue: will you not tell us how you would set about it? We are discussing the Art of Fiction; questions of art are questions (in the widest sense) of execution; questions of morality are quite another affair, and will you not let us see how it is that you find it so easy to mix them up? These things are so clear to Mr. Besant that he has deduced from them a law which he sees embodied in English fiction, and which is "a truly admirable thing and a great cause for congratulation." It is a great cause for congratulation indeed when such thorny problems become as smooth as silk. I may add that in so far as Mr. Besant perceives that in point of fact English fiction has addressed itself preponderantly to these delicate questions he will appear to many people to have made a vain discovery. They will have been positively struck, on the contrary, with the moral timidity of the usual English novelist; with his (or with her) aversion to face the difficulties with which on every side the treatment of reality bristles. He is apt to be extremely shy (whereas the picture that Mr. Besant draws is a picture of boldness), and the sign of his work, for the most part, is a cautious silence on certain subjects. In the English novel (by which of course I mean the American as well), more than in any other, there is a traditional difference between that which people know and that which they agree to admit that they know, that which they see and that which they speak of, that which they feel to be a part of life and that which they allow to enter into literature. There is the great difference, in short, between what they talk of in conversation and what they talk of in print. The essence of moral energy is to survey the whole field, and I should directly reverse Mr. Besant's remark and say not that the English novel has a purpose, but that it has a diffidence. To what degree a purpose in a work of art is a source of corruption I shall not attempt to inquire; the one that seems to me least dangerous is the purpose of making a perfect work. As for our novel, I may say lastly on this score that as we find it in England today it strikes me as addressed in a large degree to "young people," and that this in itself constitutes a presumption that it will be rather shy. There are certain things which it is generally agreed not to discuss, not even to mention, before young people. That is very well, but the absence of discussion is not a symptom of the moral passion. The purpose of the English novel—"a truly admirable thing, and a great cause for congratulation"—strikes me therefore as rather negative.

There is one point at which the moral sense and the artistic sense lie very near together; that is in the light of the very obvious truth that the deepest quality of a work of art will always be the quality of the mind of the producer. In proportion as that intelligence is fine will the novel, the picture, the statue partake of the substance of beauty and truth. To be constituted of such elements is, to my vision, to have purpose enough. No good novel will ever proceed from a superficial mind; that seems to me an axiom which, for the artist in fiction, will cover all needful moral ground: if the youthful aspirant take it to heart it will illuminate for him many of the mysteries of "purpose." There are many other useful things that might be said to him, but I have come to the end of my article, and can only touch them as I pass. The critic in the *Pall Mall Gazette,* whom I have already quoted, draws attention to the danger, in speaking of the art of fiction, of generalizing. The danger that he has in mind is rather, I imagine, that of particularizing, for there are some comprehensive remarks which, in addition to those embodied in Mr. Besant's suggestive lecture, might without fear of misleading him be addressed to the ingenuous student. I should remind him first of the magnificence of the form that is open to him, which offers to sight so few restrictions and such innumerable opportunities. The other arts, in comparison, appear confined and hampered; the various conditions under which they are exercised are so rigid and definite. But the only condition that I can think of attaching to the composition of the novel is, as I have already said, that it be sincere. This freedom is a splendid privilege, and the first lesson of the young novelist is to learn to be worthy of it. "Enjoy it as it deserves," I should say to him; "take possession of it, explore it to its utmost extent, publish it, rejoice in it. All life belongs to you, and do not listen either to those who would shut you up into corners of it and tell you that it is only here and there that art inhabits, or to those who would persuade you that this heavenly messenger wings her way outside of life altogether, breathing a superfine air, and turning away her head from the truth of things. There is no impression of life, no manner of seeing it and feeling it, to which the plan of the novelist may not offer a place; you have only to remember that talents so dissimilar as those of Alexandre Dumas and Jane Austen, Charles Dickens and Gustave Flaubert have worked in this field with equal glory. Do not think too much about optimism and pessimism; try and catch the color of life itself. In France today we see a prodigious effort (that of Emile Zola,[2] to whose solid and serious work no explorer of the capacity of the novel can allude without respect), we see an extraordinary effort vitiated by a spirit of pessimism on a narrow basis. M. Zola is magnificent, but he strikes an English reader as ignorant; he has an air of working in the dark; if he had as much light as energy, his results would be of the highest value. As for the aberrations of a shallow optimism, the ground (of English fiction especially) is strewn with their brittle particles as with broken glass. If you must indulge in conclusions, let them have the taste of a wide knowledge. Remember that your first duty is to be âs complete as possible—to make as perfect a work. Be generous and delicate and pursue the prize."

[2] See James's study of Zola, in *Notes on Novelists* (New York, 1914), pp. 26–64.

LEO TOLSTOY

(1828–1910)

COUNT LEO NIKOLAYEVICH TOLSTOY was born on the family's country estate, Yasnaya Polyana, August 1828. He was educated by French and German tutors until he entered the University of Kazan at the age of 16. In 1847 he left the University without taking a degree, and for several years he divided his time between social life in Moscow and St. Petersburg, and vague, ineffectual schemes to better the condition of his serfs. He volunteered for service in the Caucasus in 1851 and won a commission; in 1854 he served against the Turks but wearied of army life and returned to St. Petersburg in 1855. His first novel, *Childhood,* was published in 1852, but his stories of Sevastopol, emphasizing the horrors of war, first gained him wide literary attention. Sequels to his first novel enhanced his reputation.

In 1861, after traveling widely in western Europe, Tolstoy settled at Yasnaya, where he devoted himself to managing his estate and teaching the peasant children. In 1862 he married. He continued writing, and produced in the next fifteen years his greatest works: *War and Peace* (1865–69) and *Anna Karenina* (1875–77). After completing *Anna,* Tolstoy became more and more dissatisfied; finding the religion of the Russian Church inadequate, he evolved his own concept of Christianity, and described his conversion in *A Confession* (1879). His later writings were mainly an attempt to expound and defend his religious, ethical, and social beliefs. He condemned private property and the exploitation of man by man; he tried to live according to his new faith, to the disruption of his family life.

In 1886 he wrote *The Death of Ivan Ilyich,* based on his own experiences, and in 1889 the controversial novel on sex, *The Kreutzer Sonata.* His major work in criticism, *What Is Art?* (1898), was an attempt to define art in terms of his new faith; in it he condemned his own earlier works. His last years were saddened by opposition from his family to his socialistic beliefs. His health broke down, and in October 1910 he stole secretly away from home. On November 8, 1910, Tolstoy died.

During a stay in Russia in 1897, Aylmer Maude began translating *What Is Art?* before Tolstoy had completed revising it. Difficulties with the Russian Censor resulted in so many omissions and changes that Tolstoy wrote to Maude [*Life of Tolstoy: Later Years,* p. 540] that the book in its English edition "appears now for the first time in its true form." Maude, who apparently considers the book more important from a cultural than from a critical point of view, called it "one of Tolstoy's greatest contributions to the welfare of mankind." For Tolstoy was attempting to put art on a new basis: it should be judged by its usefulness to society. His doctrine was diametrically opposed to the "art-for-art's-sake" adherents; instead, "the business of art lies just in this,—to make that understood and felt which, in the form of an argument, might be incomprehensible and inaccessible. . . . People talk about incomprehensibility; but if art is the transmission of feelings flowing from man's religious perception, how can a feeling be incomprehensible which is founded on religion, *i.e.,* on man's relation to God? Such art should be, and has actually always been, comprehensible to everybody" (Ch. X).

The value of art is in its value to humanity. Tolstoy begins by rejecting artistic works intended for specific classes of people, or works which possess merit only because of their beauty. The second criterion is particularly unsatisfying because "There is no objective definition of beauty. The existing definitions (both the metaphysical and the experimental) amount only to one and the same subjective definition, which (strange as it seems to say so) is, that art is that which makes beauty manifest, and beauty is that which pleases (without exciting desire)." Beauty means "that which pleases"; but what pleases depends on taste and, since taste differs, can in any particular work please only "a certain class of people" (Ch. IV).

Tolstoy presents his own concept: "In order correctly to define art, it is necessary, first of all, to cease to consider it as a means of pleasure, and to consider it as one of the conditions of human life. Viewing it in this way, we cannot fail to observe that art is one of the means of intercourse between man and man. . . . Art is a human activity, consisting in this, that one man consciously, by means of certain external signs, hands on to others feelings he has lived through, and that other people are infected by these feelings, and also experience them" (Ch. V).

True art has been debased by class art, by false art, by spurious imitations and counterfeits which attract attention, but do harm to mankind. Shakespeare is dismissed because his work is meaningless when judged by Tolstoy's standards; Goethe's *Faust* "may be very well executed and be full of mind and every beauty, but because it lacks the chief characteristic of a work of art —completeness, oneness, the inseparable unity of form and contents expressing the feeling the artist has experienced—it cannot produce a really artistic impression" (Ch. XI); in the selection included here, Beethoven is dismissed because the "Ninth Symphony" does not "rank as Christian universal art."

Tolstoy believed that government, laws, customs, and manners depend ultimately on the minds and especially the feelings of the people; and that, next to religion, art is the most fundamental force in shaping the minds and feelings of men. He was not optimistic that his theory would be readily accepted: "I know that most men—not only those considered clever, but even those who are very clever, and capable of understanding most difficult scientific, mathematical, or philosophic problems—can very seldom discern even the simplest and most obvious truth if it be such as to oblige them to admit the falsity of conclusions they have formed, perhaps with much difficulty— conclusions of which they are proud, which they have taught to others, and on which they have built their lives. And therefore I have little hope that what

I adduce as to the perversion of art and taste in our society will be accepted or even seriously considered. Nevertheless, I must state fully the inevitable conclusion to which my investigation into the question of art has brought me. This investigation has brought me to the conviction that almost all that our society considers to be art, good art, and the whole of art, far from being real and good art, and the whole of art, is not even art at all, but only a counterfeit of it. This position, I know, will seem very strange and paradoxical; but if we once acknowledge art to be a human activity by means of which some people transmit their feelings to others (and not a service of Beauty, nor a manifestation of the Idea, and so forth), we shall inevitably have to admit this further conclusion also. If it is true that art is an activity by means of which one man, having experienced a feeling, intentionally transmits it to others, then we have inevitably to admit further, that of all that among us is termed the art of the upper classes—of all those novels, stories, dramas, comedies, pictures, sculptures, symphonies, operas, operettas, ballets, etc., which profess to be works of art—scarcely one in a hundred thousand proceeds from an emotion felt by its author, all the rest being but manufactured counterfeits of art, in which borrowing, imitating, effects, and interestingness replace the contagion of feeling" (Ch. XIV).

Art had been perverted, but it is "indispensable for the life and progress towards well-being of individuals and the community"; and the art which reaches multitudes is of more importance than the art which reaches a few. The ability to move, even to convert, ordinary human beings was of first importance: *Hamlet* caused Tolstoy to experience "that peculiar suffering which is caused by false imitations of works of art," but the description of a theatrical performance among a savage tribe (in which the audience is "paralyzed with suspense; deep groans and even weeping is heard among them") he felt to be a true work of art (Ch. XIV).

The art of the future would be and must be "completely distinct, both in subject-matter and in form, from what is now called art. The only subject-matter of the art of the future will be either feelings drawing men toward union, or such as already unite them; and the forms of art will be such as will be open to everyone—" (Ch. XIX).

As Edmund Wilson has noted: "Even the neo-Christian moralist Tolstoy, who pretends to be non-political, is as political in his implications as any because his preaching will inevitably embroil him with the Church, and the Church is an integral part of the tsardom. His pamphlet called *What Is Art?*, in which he throws overboard Shakespeare and a large part of modern literature, including his own novels, in the interests of his own intransigent morality, is the example which is most familiar to us of the moralizing Russian criticism; but it was only the most sensational expression of a kind of approach which had been prevalent since Belinsky and Chernyshevsky in the early part of the century." [1]

Tolstoy thought of his work not as sensational but as a document that had been slowly and carefully thought out. He said that he had pondered the

---

[1] Reprinted from Mr. Wilson's essay, "The Historical Interpretation of Literature," from *The Triple Thinkers*. Oxford University Press, 1948. Used by permission of Mr. Wilson.

subject for fifteen years, and he concluded his work (Ch. XX) with a powerful and explicit statement of his deepest belief: "Art is not a pleasure, a solace, or an amusement; art is a great matter. Art is an organ of human life, transmitting man's reasonable perception into feeling. In our age the common religious perception of men is the consciousness of the brotherhood of man—we know that the well-being of man lies in union with his fellowmen. True science should indicate the various methods of applying this consciousness to life. Art should transform this perception into feeling.

"The task of art is enormous. Through the influence of real art, aided by science guided by religion, that peaceful coöperation of man which is now obtained by external means—by our law-courts, police, charitable institutions, factory inspection, etc.—should be obtained by man's free and joyous activity. Art should cause violence to be set aside.

"And it is only art that can accomplish this."

WHAT IS ART? *

(1898)

CHAPTER XV

ART, in our society, has been so perverted that not only has bad art come to be considered good, but even the very perception of what art really is has been lost. In order to be able to speak about the art of our society, it is, therefore, first of all necessary to distinguish art from counterfeit art.

There is one indubitable indication distinguishing real art from its counterfeit, namely, the infectiousness of art. If a man, without exercising effort and without altering his standpoint, on reading, hearing, or seeing another man's work, experiences a mental condition which unites him with that man and with other people who also partake of that work of art, then the object evoking that condition is a work of art. And however poetical, realistic, effectual, or interesting a work may be, it is not a work of art if it does not evoke that feeling (quite distinct from all other feelings) of joy, and of spiritual union with another (the author) and with others (those who are also infected by it).

It is true that this indication is an *internal* one, and that there are people who have forgotten what the action of real art is, who expect something else from art (in our society the great majority are in this state), and that therefore such people may mistake for this aesthetic

* *What Is Art?* by Leo Tolstoy. Translated by Aylmer Maude. Copyright 1899 by Thomas Y. Crowell Company. Used by permission of the publisher.

feeling the feeling of divertisement and a certain excitement which they receive from counterfeits of art. But though it is impossible to undeceive these people, just as it is impossible to convince a man suffering from "Daltonism" that green is not red, yet, for all that, this indication remains perfectly definite to those whose feeling for art is neither perverted nor atrophied, and it clearly distinguishes the feeling produced by art from all other feelings.

The chief peculiarity of this feeling is that the receiver of a true artistic impression is so united to the artist that he feels as if the work were his own and not someone else's—as if what it expresses were just what he had long been wishing to express. A real work of art destroys, in the consciousness of the receiver, the separation between himself and the artist; nor that alone, but also between himself and all whose minds receive this work of art. In this freeing of our personality from its separation and isolation, in this uniting of it with others, lies the chief characteristic and the great attractive force of art.

If a man is infected by the author's condition of soul, if he feels this emotion and this union with others, then the object which has effected this is art; but if there be no such infection, if there be not this union with the same author and others who are moved by the same work—then it is not art. And not only is infection a sure sign of art, but the degree of infectiousness is also the sole measure of excellence of art.

The stronger the infection the better is the art, as art, speaking now apart from its subject-matter; *i.e.* not considering the quality of the feelings it transmits.

And the degree of the infectiousness of art depends on three conditions:—

(1) On the greater or lesser individuality of the feeling transmitted; (2) on the greater or lesser clearness with which the feeling is transmitted; (3) on the sincerity of the artist, *i.e.* on the greater or lesser force with which the artist himself feels the emotion he transmits.

The more individual the feeling transmitted the more strongly does it act on the receiver; the more individual the state of soul into which he is transferred the more pleasure does the receiver obtain, and therefore the more readily and strongly does he join in it.

The clearness of expression assists infection, because the receiver, who mingles in consciousness with the author, is the better satisfied the more clearly the feeling is transmitted, which, as it seems to him, he has long known and felt, and for which he has only now found expression.

But most of all is the degree of infectiousness of art increased by the degree of sincerity in the artist. As soon as the spectator, hearer, or reader feels that the artist is infected by his own production, and writes, sings, or plays for himself, and not merely to act on others, this mental condition of the artist infects the receiver; and, contrariwise, as soon as the spectator, reader, or hearer feels that the author is not writing, singing, or playing for his own satisfaction,—does not himself feel what he wishes to express,—but is doing it for him, the receiver, a resistance immediately springs up, and the most individual and the newest feelings and the cleverest technique not only fail to produce any infection, but actually repel.

I have mentioned three conditions of contagiousness in art, but they may be all summed up into one, the last, sincerity, *i.e.* that the artist should be impelled by an inner need to express his feeling. That condition includes the first; for if the artist is sincere he will express the feeling as he experienced it. And as each man is different from everyone else, his feeling will be individual for everyone else; and the more individual it is,—the more the artist has drawn it from the depths of his nature, —the more sympathetic and sincere will it be. And this same sincerity will impel the artist to find a clear expression of the feeling which he wishes to transmit.

Therefore this third condition—sincerity—is the most important of the three. It is always complied with in peasant art, and this explains why such art always acts so powerfully; but it is a condition almost entirely absent from our upper-class art, which is continually produced by artists actuated by personal aims of covetousness or vanity.

Such are the three conditions which divide art from its counterfeits, and which also decide the quality of every work of art apart from its subject-matter.

The absence of any one of these conditions excludes a work from the category of art and relegates it to that of art's counterfeits. If the work does not transmit the artist's peculiarity of feeling, and is therefore not individual, if it is unintelligibly expressed, or if it has not proceeded from the author's inner need for expression—it is not a work of art. If all these conditions are present, even in the smallest degree, then the work, even if a weak one, is yet a work of art.

The presence in various degrees of these three conditions—individuality, clearness, and sincerity—decides the merit of a work of art, as art, apart from subject-matter. All works of art take rank of merit according to the degree in which they fulfil the first, the second, and the third of these conditions. In one the individuality of the feeling transmitted may predominate; in another, clearness of expression; in a third, sincerity; while a fourth may have sincerity and individuality, but be deficient in clearness; a fifth, individuality and clearness, but less sincerity; and so forth, in all possible degrees and combinations.

Thus is art divided from not art, and thus is the quality of art, as art, decided, independently of its subject-matter, *i.e.* apart from whether the feelings it transmits are good or bad.

But how are we to define good and bad art with reference to its subject-matter?

CHAPTER XVI

How in art are we to decide what is good and what is bad in subject-matter?

Art, like speech, is a means of communication, and therefore of progress, *i.e.* of the movement of humanity forward toward perfection. Speech renders accessible to men of the latest generations all the knowledge discovered by the experience and reflection, both of preceding generations and of the best and foremost men of their own times; art renders accessible to men of the latest generations all the feelings experienced by their predecessors, and those also which are being felt by their best and foremost contemporaries. And as the evolution of knowledge proceeds by truer and more necessary knowledge dislodging and replacing what is mistaken and unnecessary, so the evolution of feeling proceeds through art,—feelings less kind and less needful for the well-being of mankind are replaced by others kinder and more needful for that end. That is the purpose of art. And, speaking now of its subject-matter, the more art fulfils that purpose the better the art, and the less it fulfils it the worse the art.

And the appraisement of feelings (*i.e.* the acknowledgment of these or those feelings as being more or less good, more or less necessary for the well-being of mankind) is made by the religious perception of the age.

In every period of history, and in every human society, there exists an understanding of the meaning of life which represents the highest level to which men of that society have attained,—an understanding defining the highest good at which that society aims. And this understanding is the religious perception of the given time and society. And this religious perception is always clearly expressed by some advanced men, and more or less vividly perceived by all the members of the society. Such a religious perception and its corresponding expression exists always in every society. If it appears to us that in our society there is no religious perception, this is not because there really is none, but only because we do not want to see it. And we often wish not to see it because it exposes the fact that our life is inconsistent with that religious perception.

Religious perception in a society is like the direction of a flowing river. If the river flows at all, it must have a direction. If a society lives, there must be a religious perception indicating the direction in which, more or less consciously, all its members tend.

And so there always has been, and there is, a religious perception in every society. And it is by the standard of this religious perception that the feelings transmitted by art have always been estimated. Only on the basis of this religious perception of their age have men always chosen from the endlessly varied spheres of art that art which transmitted feelings making religious perception operative in actual life. And such art has always been highly valued and encouraged; while art transmitting feelings already outlived, flowing from the antiquated religious perceptions of a former age, has always been condemned and despised. All the rest of art, transmitting those most diverse feelings by means of which people commune together, was not condemned, and was not tolerated, if only it did not transmit feelings contrary to religious perception. Thus, for instance, among the Greeks, art transmitting the feeling of beauty, strength, and courage (Hesiod, Homer, Phidias) was chosen, approved, and encouraged; while art transmitting feelings of rude sensuality, despondency, and effeminacy was condemned and despised. Among the Jews, art transmitting feelings of devotion and submission to the God of the Hebrews and to His will (the epic of Genesis, the prophets, the Psalms) was chosen and encouraged, while art transmitting feelings of idolatry (the golden calf) was condemned and despised. All the rest of art—stories, songs, dances, ornamentation of houses, of utensils, and of clothes—which was not contrary to religious perception, was neither distinguished nor discussed. Thus, in regard to its subject-matter, has art been appraised always and everywhere, and thus it should be appraised; for this attitude toward art proceeds from the fundamental characteristics of human nature, and those characteristics do not change.

I know that according to an opinion current in our times religion is a superstition which humanity has outgrown, and that it is therefore assumed that no such thing exists as a religious perception, common to us all, by which art, in our time, can be estimated. I know that this is the opinion current in the pseudo-cultured circles of to-day. People who do not acknowledge Christianity in its true meaning because it undermines all their social privileges, and who, therefore, invent all kinds of philosophic and aesthetic theories to hide from themselves the meaninglessness and wrongness of their lives, cannot think otherwise. These people intentionally, or sometimes unintentionally, confusing the conception of a religious cult with the conception of religious perception, think that by denying the cult they get rid of religious perception. But even the very attacks on religion, and the attempts to establish a life-conception contrary to the religious perception of our times, most clearly demonstrate the existence of a religious perception condemning the lives that are not in harmony with it.

If humanity progresses, *i.e.* moves forward, there must inevitably be a guide to the direction of that movement. And religions have always furnished that guide. All history shows that the progress of humanity is accomplished not otherwise than under the guidance of religion. But if the race cannot progress without the guidance of religion,—and progress is always going on, and consequently also in our own times, —then there must be a religion of our times. So that, whether it pleases or displeases the so-called cultured people of to-day, they must admit the existence of religion,—not of a religious cult, Catholic, Protestant, or another, but of a religious perception,—which, even in our times, is the guide always present where there is any progress. And if a religious perception exists amongst us, then our art should be appraised on the basis of that religious perception; and, as has always and everywhere been the case, art transmitting feelings flowing from the religious perception of our time should be chosen from all the indifferent art, should be acknowledged, highly esteemed, and encouraged; while art running counter to that perception should be condemned and despised, and all the remaining indifferent art should neither be distinguished nor discouraged.

The religious perception of our time, in its widest and most practical application, is the consciousness that our well-being, both material and spiritual, individual and collective, temporal and eternal, lies in the growth of brotherhood among all men—in their loving harmony with one another. This perception is not only expressed by Christ and all the best men of past ages, it is not only repeated in the most varied forms and from most diverse sides by the best men of our own times, but it already serves as a clue to all the complex labor of humanity, consisting as this labor does, on the one hand, in the destruction of physical and moral obstacles to the union of men, and, on the other hand, in establishing the principles common to all men which can and should unite them into one universal brotherhood. And it is on the basis of this perception that we should appraise all the phenomena of our life, and, among the rest, our art also; choosing from all realms whatever transmits feelings flowing from this religious perception, highly prizing and encouraging such art, rejecting whatever is contrary to this perception and not attributing to the rest of art an importance not properly pertaining to it.

The chief mistake made by people of the upper classes of the time of the so-called Renaissance—a mistake which we still perpetuate—was not that they ceased to value and to attach importance to religious art (people of that period could not attach importance to it, because, like our own upper classes, they could not believe in what the majority considered to be religion), but their mistake was that they set up in place of religious art, which was lacking, an insignificant art which aimed only at giving pleasure, *i.e.* they began to choose, to value, and to encourage, in place of religious art, something which, in any case, did not deserve such esteem and encouragement.

One of the Fathers of the Church said that the great evil is, not that men do not know God, but that they have set up, instead of God, that which is not God. So also with art. The great misfortune of the people of the upper classes of our time is not so much that they are without a religious art, as that, instead of a supreme religious art, chosen from all the rest as being specially important and valuable, they have chosen a most insignificant and, usually, harmful art, which aims at pleasing certain people, and which, therefore, if only by its exclusive nature, stands in contradiction to that Christian principle of universal union which forms the religious perception of our time. Instead of religious art, an empty and often vicious art is set up, and this hides from men's notice the need of that true religious art which should be present in life in order to improve it.

It is true that art which satisfies the demands of the religious perception of our time is quite unlike former art, but, notwithstanding this dissimilarity, to a man who does not intentionally hide the truth from himself, it is very clear and definite what does form the religious art of our age. In former times, when the highest religious perception united only some people (who, even if they formed a large society, were yet but one society surrounded by others—Jews, or Athenian or Roman citizens), the feelings transmitted by the art of that time flowed from a desire for the might, greatness, glory, and prosperity of that society, and the heroes of art might be people who contributed to that prosperity by strength, by craft, by fraud, or by cruelty (Ulysses, Jacob, David, Samson, Hercules, and all the heroes). But the religious perception of our times does not select any one society of men; on the contrary, it demands the union of all,—absolutely of all people without exception,—and above every other virtue it sets brotherly love to all men. And, therefore, the feelings transmitted by the art of our time not only cannot coincide with the feelings transmitted by former art, but must run counter to them.

Christian, truly Christian, art has been so long in establishing itself, and has not yet established itself, just because the Christian religious perception was not one of those small steps by which humanity advances regularly, but was an enormous revolution, which, if it has not already altered, must inevitably alter the entire life-conception of mankind, and, consequently, the whole internal organization of their life. It is true that the life of humanity, like that of an individual, moves regularly; but in that regular movement come, as it were, turning-points, which sharply divide the preceding from the subsequent life. Christianity was such a turning-point; such, at least, it must appear to us who live by the Christian perception of life. Christian perception gave another, a new, direction to all human feelings, and therefore completely altered both the contents and the significance of art. The Greeks could make use of Persian art and the Romans could use Greek art, or, similarly, the Jews could use Egyptian art,—the fundamental ideals were one and the same. Now the ideal was the greatness and prosperity of the Persians, now the greatness and prosperity of the Greeks, now that of the Romans. The same art was transferred into other conditions, and served new nations. But the Christian ideal changed and reversed everything, so that, as the gospel puts it, "That which was exalted among men has become an abomination in the sight of God." The ideal is no longer the greatness of Pharaoh or of a Roman emperor, not the beauty of a Greek, nor the wealth of Phoenicia, but humility, purity, compassion, love. The hero is no longer Dives, but Lazarus the beggar; not Mary Magdalene in the day of her beauty, but in the day of her repentance; not those who acquire wealth, but those who have abandoned it; not those who dwell in palaces, but those who dwell in catacombs and huts; not those who rule over others, but those who acknowledge no authority but God's. And the greatest work of art is no longer a cathedral of victory [1] with the statues of conquerors, but the representation of a human soul so transformed by love that a man who is tormented and murdered yet pities and loves his persecutors.

And the change is so great that men of the Christian world find it difficult to resist the inertia of the heathen art to which they have been accustomed all their lives. The subject-matter of Christian religious art is so new to them, so unlike the subject-matter of former art, that it seems to them as though Christian art were a denial of art, and they cling desperately to the old art. But this old art, having no longer, in our day, any source in religious perception, has lost its meaning, and we shall have to abandon it whether we wish to or not.

The essence of the Christian perception consists in the recognition by every man of his sonship to God, and of the consequent union of men with God and with one another, as is said in the gospel (John 17:21 [2]). Therefore the subject-matter of Christian art is such feeling as can unite men with God and with one another.

The expression *unite men with God and with one another* may seem obscure to people accustomed to the misuse of these words which is so customary, but the words have a perfectly clear meaning nevertheless. They indicate that the Christian union of man (in contradiction to the partial, exclusive union of only some men) is that which unites all without exception.

Art, all art, has this characteristic, that it unites people. Every art causes those to whom the artist's feeling is transmitted to unite in soul with the artist, and also with all who receive the same impression. But non-Christian art, while uniting some people together, makes that very union a cause of separation between these united people and others; so that union of this kind is often a source, not only of division, but even of enmity toward others. Such is all patriotic art, with its anthems, poems, and monuments; such is all Church art, *i.e.* the art of certain cults, with their images, statues, processions, and other local ceremonies. Such art is belated and non-Christian art, uniting the people of one cult only to separate them yet more sharply from the members of other cults, and even to place them in relations of hostility to each

---

[1] There is in Moscow a magnificent "Cathedral of Our Saviour," erected to commemorate the defeat of the French in the War of 1812.—Tr.

[2] "That they may be one; even as thou, Father, art in me, and I in thee, that they also may be in us."

other. Christian art is only such as tends to unite all without exception, either by evoking in them the perception that each man and all men stand in like relation toward God and toward their neighbor, or by evoking in them identical feelings, which may even be the very simplest, provided only that they are not repugnant to Christianity and are natural to everyone without exception.

Good Christian art of our time may be unintelligible to people because of imperfections in its form, or because men are inattentive to it, but it must be such that all men can experience the feelings it transmits. It must be the art, not of some one group of people, nor of one class, nor of one nationality, nor of one religious cult; that is, it must not transmit feelings which are accessible only to a man educated in a certain way, or only to an aristocrat, or a merchant, or only to a Russian, or a native of Japan, or a Roman Catholic, or a Buddhist, etc., but it must transmit feelings accessible to everyone. Only art of this kind can be acknowledged in our time to be good art, worthy of being chosen out from all the rest of art and encouraged.

Christian art, *i.e.* the art of our time, should be catholic in the original meaning of the word, *i.e.* universal, and therefore it should unite all men. And only two kinds of feeling do unite all men: first, feelings flowing from the perception of our sonship to God and of the brotherhood of man; and next, the simple feelings of common life, accessible to everyone without exception—such as the feeling of merriment, of pity, of cheerfulness, of tranquillity, etc. Only these two kinds of feelings can now supply material for art good in its subject-matter.

And the action of these two kinds of art, apparently so dissimilar, is one and the same. The feelings flowing from perception of our sonship to God and of the brotherhood of man—such as a feeling of sureness in truth, devotion to the will of God, self-sacrifice, respect for and love of man—evoked by Christian religious perception; and the simplest feelings—such as a softened or a merry mood caused by a song or an amusing jest intelligible to everyone, or by a touching story, or a drawing, or a little doll: both alike produce one and the same effect,—the loving union of man with man. Sometimes people who are together are, if not hostile to one another, at least estranged in mood and feeling, till perchance a story, a performance, a picture, or even a building, but oftenest of all, music, unites them all as by an electric flash, and, in place of their former isolation or even enmity, they are all conscious of union and mutual love. Each is glad that another feels what he feels;

glad of the communion established, not only between him and all present, but also with all now living who will yet share the same impression; and more than that, he feels the mysterious gladness of a communion which, reaching beyond the grave, unites us with all men of the past who have been moved by the same feelings, and with all men of the future who will yet be touched by them. And this effect is produced both by the religious art which transmits feelings of love to God and one's neighbor, and by universal art, transmitting the very simplest feelings common to all men.

The art of our time should be appraised differently from former art chiefly in this, that the art of our time, *i.e.* Christian art (basing itself on a religious perception which demands the union of man), excludes from the domain of art good in subject-matter everything transmitting exclusive feelings, which do not unite but divide men. It relegates such work to the category of art bad in its subject-matter, while, on the other hand, it includes in the category of art good in subject-matter a section not formerly admitted to deserve to be chosen out and respected, namely, universal art, transmitting even the most trifling and simple feelings if only they are accessible to all men without exception, and therefore unite them. Such art cannot, in our time, but be esteemed good, for it attains the end which the religious perception of our time, *i.e.* Christianity, sets before humanity.

Christian art either evokes in men those feelings which, through love of God and of one's neighbor, draw them to greater and ever greater union, and make them ready for and capable of such union; or evokes in them those feelings which show them that they are already united in the joys and sorrows of life. And therefore the Christian art of our time can be and is of two kinds: (1) art transmitting feelings flowing from a religious perception of man's position in the world in relation to God and to his neighbor—religious art in the limited meaning of the term; and (2) art transmitting the simplest feelings of common life, but such, always, as are accessible to all men in the whole world—the art of common life—the art of a people—universal art. Only these two kinds of art can be considered good art in our time.

The first, religious art,—transmitting both positive feelings of love to God and one's neighbor, and negative feelings of indignation and horror at the violation of love,—manifests itself chiefly in the form of words, and to some extent also in painting and sculpture; the second kind (universal art), transmitting feelings accessible to all, manifests itselt in words, in painting, in sculpture, in dances, in architecture, and, most of all, in music.

If I were asked to give modern examples of each of these kinds of art, then, as examples of the highest art, flowing from love of God and man (both of the higher, positive, and of the lower, negative kind), in literature I should name, "The Robbers," by Schiller; Victor Hugo's "Les Pauvres Gens" and "Les Misérables"; the novels and stories of Dickens,—"The Tale of Two Cities," "The Christmas Carol," "The Chimes," and others; "Uncle Tom's Cabin"; Dostoievsky's works—especially his "Memoirs from the House of Death"; and "Adam Bede," by George Eliot.

In modern painting, strange to say, works of this kind, directly transmitting the Christian feeling of love of God and of one's neighbor, are hardly to be found, especially among the works of the celebrated painters. There are plenty of pictures treating of the gospel stories; they, however, depict historical events with great wealth of detail, but do not, and cannot, transmit religious feeling not possessed by their painters. There are many pictures treating of the personal feelings of various people, but of pictures representing great deeds of self-sacrifice and of Christian love there are very few, and what there are, are principally by artists who are not celebrated, and are, for the most part, not pictures, but merely sketches. Such, for instance, is the drawing by Kramskoy (worth many of his finished pictures), showing a drawing-room with a balcony, past which troops are marching in triumph on their return from the war. On the balcony stands a wet-nurse holding a baby and a boy. They are admiring the procession of the troops, but the mother, covering her face with a handkerchief, has fallen back on the sofa, sobbing. Such also is the picture by Walter Langley, to which I have already referred, and such again is a picture by the French artist Morlon, depicting a lifeboat hastening, in a heavy storm, to the relief of a steamer that is being wrecked. Approaching these in kind are pictures which represent the hard-working peasant with respect and love. Such are the pictures by Millet, and, particularly, his drawing, "The Man with the Hoe"; also pictures in this style by Jules Breton, L'Hermitte, Defregger, and others. As examples of pictures evoking indignation and horror at the violation of love to God and man, Gay's picture, "Judgment," may serve, and also Leizen-Mayer's, "Signing the Death Warrant." But there are also very few of this kind. Anxiety about the technique and the beauty of the picture for the most part obscures the feeling. For instance, Gérôme's "Pollice Verso" expresses, not so much horror at what is being perpetrated as attraction by the beauty of the spectacle.[3]

To give examples, from the modern art of our upper classes, of art of the second kind, good universal art or even of the art of a whole people, is yet more difficult, especially in literary art and music. If there are some works which by their inner contents might be assigned to this class (such as "Don Quixote," Molière's comedies, "David Copperfield" and "The Pickwick Papers" by Dickens, Gogol's and Pushkin's tales, and some things of Maupassant's), these works are for the most part—from the exceptional nature of the feelings they transmit, and the superfluity of special details of time and locality, and, above all, on account of the poverty of their subject-matter in comparison with examples of universal ancient art (such, for instance, as the story of Joseph)—comprehensible only to people of their own circle. That Joseph's brethren, being jealous of his father's affection, sell him to the merchants; that Potiphar's wife wishes to tempt the youth; that having attained the highest station, he takes pity on his brothers, including Benjamin, the favorite,—these and all the rest are feelings accessible alike to a Russian peasant, a Chinese, an African, a child or an old man, educated or uneducated; and it is all written with such restraint, is so free from any superfluous detail, that the story may be told in any circle and will be equally comprehensible and touching to everyone. But not such are the feelings of Don Quixote or of Molière's heroes (though Molière is perhaps the most universal, and therefore the most excellent, artist of modern times), nor of Pickwick and his friends. These feelings are not common to all men, but very exceptional; and therefore, to make them infectious, the authors have surrounded them with abundant details of time and place. And this abundance of detail makes the stories difficult of comprehension to all people not living within reach of the conditions described by the author.

The author of the novel of Joseph did not need to describe in detail, as would be done nowadays, the blood-stained coat of Joseph, the dwelling and dress of Jacob, the pose and attire of Potiphar's wife, and how, adjusting the bracelet on her left arm, she said, "Come to me," and so on, because the subject-matter of feelings in this novel is so strong that all details, except the most essential,—such as that Joseph went out into another room to weep,—are superfluous, and would only hinder the

[3] In this picture the spectators in the Roman Amphitheater are turning down their thumbs to show that they wish the vanquished gladiator to be killed.—Tr.

transmission of feelings. And therefore this novel is accessible to all men, touches people of all nations and classes, young and old, and has lasted to our times, and will yet last for thousands of years to come. But strip the best novels of our times of their details, and what will remain?

It is therefore impossible in modern literature to indicate works fully satisfying the demands of universality. Such works as exist are, to a great extent, spoilt by what is usually called "realism," but would be better termed "provincialism," in art.

In music the same occurs as in verbal art, and for similar reasons. In consequence of the poorness of the feeling they contain, the melodies of the modern composers are amazingly empty and insignificant. And to strengthen the impression produced by these empty melodies, the new musicians pile complex modulations on to each trivial melody, not only in their own national manner, but also in the way characteristic of their own exclusive circle and particular musical school. Melody—every melody—is free, and may be understood of all men; but as soon as it is bound up with a particular harmony, it ceases to be accessible except to people trained to such harmony, and it becomes strange, not only to common men of another nationality, but to all who do not belong to the circle whose members have accustomed themselves to certain forms of harmonization. So that music, like poetry, travels in a vicious circle. Trivial and exclusive melodies, in order to make them attractive, are laden with harmonic, rhythmic, and orchestral complications, and thus become yet more exclusive; and, far from being universal, are not even national, *i.e.* they are not comprehensible to the whole people but only to some people.

In music, besides marches and dances by various composers, which satisfy the demands of universal art, one can indicate very few works of this class: Bach's famous violin *aria*, Chopin's nocturne in E-flat major, and perhaps a dozen bits (not whole pieces, but parts) selected from the works of Haydn, Mozart, Schubert, Beethoven, and Chopin.[4]

---

[4] While offering as examples of art those that seem to me the best, I attach no special importance to my selection; for, besides being insufficiently informed in all branches of art, I belong to the class of people whose taste has, by false training, been perverted. And therefore my old, inured habits may cause me to err, and I may mistake for absolute merit the impression a work produced on me in my youth. My only purpose in mentioning examples of works of this or that class is to make my meaning clearer, and to show how, with my present views, I understand excellence in art in relation to its subject-matter. I must, moreover, mention that I consign my own artistic productions to the category of bad art, excepting the story "God Sees the Truth," which seeks a place in the first class, and "The Prisoner of the Caucasus," which belongs to the second.

Although in painting the same thing is repeated as in poetry and music,—namely, that in order to make them more interesting, works weak in conception are surrounded by minutely studied accessories of time and place, which give them a temporary and local interest but make them less universal,—still, in painting, more than in the other spheres of art, may be found works satisfying the demands of universal Christian art; that is to say, there are more works expressing feelings in which all men may participate.

In the arts of painting and sculpture, all pictures and statues in so-called genre style, depictions of animals, landscapes and caricatures with subjects comprehensible to everyone, and also all kinds of ornaments, are universal in subject-matter. Such productions in painting and sculpture are very numerous (*e.g.* china dolls), but for the most part such objects (for instance, ornaments of all kinds) are either not considered to be art or are considered to be art of a low quality. In reality all such objects, if only they transmit a true feeling experienced by the artist and comprehensible to everyone (however insignificant it may seem to us to be) are works of real good Christian art.

I fear it will here be urged against me that having denied that the conception of beauty can supply a standard for works of art, I contradict myself by acknowledging ornaments to be works of good art. The reproach is unjust, for the subject-matter of all kinds of ornamentation consists not in the beauty, but in the feeling (of admiration of, and delight in, the combination of lines and colors) which the artist has experienced and with which he infects the spectator. Art remains what it was and what it must be: nothing but the infection by one man of another, or of others, with the feelings experienced by the infector. Among those feelings is the feeling of delight at what pleases the sight. Objects pleasing the sight may be such as please a small or a large number of people, or such as please all men. And ornaments for the most part are of the latter kind. A landscape representing a very unusual view, or a genre picture of a special subject, may not please everyone, but ornaments, from Yakutsk ornaments to Greek ones, are intelligible to everyone and evoke a similar feeling of admiration in all, and therefore this despised kind of art should, in Christian society, be esteemed far above exceptional, pretentious pictures and sculptures.

So that there are only two kinds of good Christian art: all the rest of art not comprised in these two divisions should be acknowledged to be bad art, deserving not to be encouraged, but to be driven out, denied, and despised, as being art not uniting but dividing people. Such, in literary art, are all novels and poems which transmit Church or patriotic feelings, and also exclusive feelings pertaining only to the class of the idle rich; such as aristocratic honor, satiety, spleen, pessimism, and refined and vicious feelings flowing from sex-love—quite incomprehensible to the great majority of mankind.

In painting we must similarly place in the class of bad art all the Church, patriotic, and exclusive pictures; all the pictures representing the amusements and allurements of a rich and idle life; all the so-called symbolic pictures, in which the very meaning of the symbol is comprehensible only to the people of a certain circle; and, above all, pictures with voluptuous subjects—all that odious female nudity which fills all the exhibitions and galleries. And to this class belongs almost all the chamber and opera music of our times,—beginning especially from Beethoven (Schumann, Berlioz, Liszt, Wagner), by its subject-matter devoted to the expression of feelings accessible only to people who have developed in themselves an unhealthy, nervous irritation, evoked by this exclusive, artificial, and complex music.

"What! the 'Ninth Symphony' not a good work of art!" I hear exclaimed by indignant voices.

And I reply, Most certainly it is not. All that I have written I have written with the sole purpose of finding a clear and reasonable criterion by which to judge the merits of works of art. And this criterion, coinciding with the indications of plain and sane sense, indubitably shows me that that symphony by Beethoven is not a good work of art. Of course, to people educated in the adoration of certain productions and of their authors, to people whose taste has been perverted just by being educated in such adoration, the acknowledgment that such a celebrated work is bad is amazing and strange. But how are we to escape the indications of reason and of common sense?

Beethoven's "Ninth Symphony" is considered a great work of art. To verify its claim to be such, I must first ask myself whether this work transmits the highest religious feeling. I reply in the negative, for music in itself cannot transmit those feelings; and therefore I ask myself next, Since this work does not belong to the highest kind of religious art, has it the other characteristic of the good art of our time,— the quality of uniting all men in one common feeling: does it rank as Christian universal art? And again I have no option but to reply in the negative; for not only do I not see how the feelings transmitted by this work could unite people not specially trained to submit themselves to its complex hypnotism, but I am unable to imagine to myself a crowd of normal people who could understand anything of this long, confused, and artificial production, except short snatches which are lost in a sea of what is incomprehensible. And therefore, whether I like it or not, I am compelled to conclude that this work belongs to the rank of bad art. It is curious to note in this connection, that attached to the end of this very symphony is a poem of Schiller's which (though somewhat obscurely) expresses this very thought, namely, that feeling (Schiller speaks only of the feeling of gladness) unites people and evokes love in them. But though this poem is sung at the end of the symphony, the music does not accord with the thought expressed in the verses; for the music is exclusive and does not unite all men, but unites only a few, dividing them off from the rest of mankind.

And just in this same way, in all branches of art, many and many works considered great by the upper classes of our society will have to be judged. By this one sure criterion we shall have to judge the celebrated "Divine Comedy" and "Jerusalem Delivered," and a great part of Shakespear's and Goethe's works, and in painting every representation of miracles, including Raphael's "Transfiguration," etc.

Whatever the work may be and however it may have been extolled, we have first to ask whether this work is one of real art or a counterfeit. Having acknowledged, on the basis of the indication of its infectiousness even to a small class of people, that a certain production belongs to the realm of art, it is necessary, on the basis of the indication of its accessibility, to decide the next question, Does this work belong to the category of bad, exclusive art, opposed to religious perception, or to Christian art, uniting people? And having acknowledged an article to belong to real Christian art, we must then, according to whether it transmits the feelings flowing from love to God and man, or merely the simple feelings uniting all men, assign it a place in the ranks of religious art or in those of universal art.

Only on the basis of such verification shall we find it possible to select from the whole mass of what, in our society, claims to be art, those works which form real, important, necessary spiritual food, and to separate them from all the harmful and useless art, and from the counterfeits of art which surround us. Only on the basis of such verification shall we be able to rid ourselves of the pernicious results of harmful art, and to avail ourselves of that beneficent action which is the purpose of true and good art, and which is indispensable for the spiritual life of man and of humanity.

BENEDETTO CROCE

(1866-1952)

IN HIS autobiography Croce wrote that "the chronicle of my life, so far
as it contains anything worth recording, is contained in the chronology
and bibliography of my written works." He was born February 25, 1866,
at Pescasseroli, Aquila, of a wealthy family of Abruzzese landowners and
Neapolitan magistrates. He was educated in an exclusive Catholic school in
Naples, until in 1883 most of his family was killed and he himself seriously
injured in the earthquake of Casamicciola. He lived in Rome with his uncle,
studied law at the University of Rome but never graduated, and in 1886 returned to Naples. Being financially independent, he devoted himself to the
study of local history, editing a magazine (*Napoli Nobilissima*, 1892-97),
and writing numerous essays. By 1893 he was attempting to define the nature of history and the method of literary criticism; in 1902 he began the systematic exposition of his theory, dividing the human faculties into the
aesthetic, the ethical, the economic, and the logical; the activities growing
out of these forms, he believed, complete the entire circle of the human
spirit.

In 1903 he founded the magazine *La Critica,* and edited it until 1944.
Through this magazine and through books and essays he acquired such an
authoritative position that he was able to attack fascism without reprisals,
although his official positions were limited to serving as a Senator in 1910 and
as Minister of Education, 1920-21.

J. E. Spingarn, in *The New Criticism,* has well indicated Croce's position
in literary criticism: "The theory of expression, the concept of literature as
an art of expression, is the common ground on which critics have met for
a century or more. Yet how many absurdities, how many complicated systems,
how many confusions have been superimposed on this fundamental idea;
and how slowly has its full significance become the possession of critics! To
accept the naked principle is to play havoc with these confusions and complications; and no one has seen this more clearly, or driven home its inevitable
consequences with more intelligence and vigor, than an Italian thinker and
critic of our own day, Benedetto Croce, who has been gaining ground in the
English-speaking world from the day when Mr. Balfour several years ago
gave him a kind of official introduction in his Romanes Lecture. But I for
one needed no introduction to his work; under his banner I enrolled myself
long ago, and here re-enroll myself in what I now say. He has led esthetic
thought inevitably from the concept that art is expression to the conclusion

that all expression is art. Time does not permit, nor reason ask, that we should follow this argument through all its pros and cons. If this theory of expression be once and for all accepted, as indeed it has been partly though confusedly accepted by all modern critics, the ground of Criticism is cleared of its dead lumber and its weeds."

This dead lumber which has been discarded consists of all the old rules; the genres, types, and kinds; the terms like comic, tragic, and sublime; the concern with style and rhetoric; the moral judgment as applied to art; with technique as separate from art; with race, time, and environment as an element in criticism; and with the evolution of literature. All of these, Spingarn claims, Croce has taught us to disregard: "When Criticism first propounded as its real concern the oft-repeated question: 'What has the poet tried to express and how has he expressed it?' Criticism prescribed for itself the only possible method. How can the critic answer this question without becoming (if only for a moment of supreme power) at one with the creator? That is to say, taste must reproduce the work of art within itself in order to understand and judge it; and at that moment esthetic judgment becomes nothing more nor less than creative art itself. The identity of genius and taste is the final achievement of modern thought on the subject of art, and it means that fundamentally, in their most significant moments, the creative and the critical instincts are one and the same."

Croce found the central idea of his critical theory in the words of Francesco De Sanctis: " . . . art is not a work of reflection and logic, nor yet a product of skill, but pure and spontaneous imaginative form" [*Autobiography*, p. 78–79]. Although he wrote his first book on the methods of literary criticism in 1894 (*La Critica Letteraria*), his work in criticism seems primarily an outgrowth of his aesthetic theories, and especially of his concepts of intuition and expression. He divides knowledge into two forms: ". . . it is either *intuitive* knowledge or *logical* knowledge; knowledge obtained through the *imagination* or knowledge obtained through the *intellect;* knowledge of the *individual* or knowledge of the *universal;* of *individual things* or of the *relations* between them; it is, in fact, productive either of *images* or of *concepts*" ["Intuition and Expression," *Aesthetic*, 2nd ed.].

Croce identifies intuitive knowledge with the aesthetic or artistic fact. He does not deny to the artist the use of concepts, but he argues that these are changed by the artist: "Those concepts which are found mingled and fused with the intuitions are no longer concepts, in so far as they are really mingled and fused, for they have lost all independence and autonomy. They have been concepts, but have now become simple elements of intuition. The philosophical maxims placed in the mouth of a personage of tragedy or of comedy, perform there the function, not of concepts, but of characteristics of such personage; in the same way as the red in a painted face does not there represent the red colour of the physicists, but is a characteristic element of the portrait. The whole is that which determines the quality of the parts. A work of art may be full of philosophical concepts; it may contain them in greater abundance and they may there be even more profound than in a philosophical dissertation, which in its turn may be rich to overflowing with descriptions and intuitions. But notwithstanding all these concepts the total effect of the work of art is an intuition; and notwithstanding all these intuitions, the total effect of the philosophical dissertation is a concept. The *Promessi Sposi* contains copious ethical observations and distinctions, but does not for that reason lose as a whole its character of simple story or intuition. In like manner the anecdotes and satirical effusions to be found in the works of a philosopher like Schopenhauer do not deprive those works of their character of intellectual treatises. The difference between an intellectual fact and an intuitive fact, lies in the difference of the total effect aimed at by their respective authors." [*Idem.*]

If the total effect of a work of art is an intuition, it is not dependent on intellectualism, perception, sensation, or synthesis. Being independent of these concepts, intuition exists in and of itself, and there is only one sure method of distinguishing true intuition "from that which is inferior to it: the spiritual fact from the mechanical, passive, natural fact. Every true intuition or representation is also expression. That which does not objectify itself in expression is not intuition or representation, but sensation and mere natural fact. The spirit only intuits in making, forming, expressing. He who separates intuition from expression never succeeds in reuniting them. . . . We may thus add this to the various verbal descriptions of intuition, noted at the beginning: intuitive knowledge is expressive knowledge. Independent and autonomous in respect to intellectual function; indifferent to later empirical discriminations, to reality and to unreality, to formations and apperceptions of space and time, which are also later: intuition or representation is distinguished as form from what is felt and suffered, from the flux or wave of sensation, or from psychic matter; and this form, this taking possession, is expression. To intuit is to express; and nothing else (nothing more, but nothing less) than to express." [*Idem.*]

In the chapter "Intuition and Art" [*Aesthetic,* 2nd ed.], Croce develops the basic idea that all pure intuition-expression is artistic. There are degrees of excellence only because some men collect "intuitions that are wider and more complex than those which we generally experience," but the intuition of the simplest love-song is the same qualitatively and intensively as the most complex drama. The difference is quantitative: "There is not a science of lesser intuition as distinct from a science of greater intuition, nor one of ordinary intuition as distinct from artistic intuition." On this basis Croce maintains that all men are born poets, and that all expression is art; the distinction he sets up is that "some men are born great poets, some small." There is an identity of nature between the imagination of the great poet and of the understanding reader: since the work of art is the expression, the reader who gets to the expression is temporarily the equal of the poet. But this creative reading is not easy: "No one can read Dante without adequate preparation and culture, without the necessary mediation of philology. But the mediation should lead to our finding ourselves with Dante as man to man, or to placing us in immediate relation with the poetry" [*The Poetry of Dante,* p. 29].

Criticism becomes an aid to re-creation. The artist produces; the critic reproduces. Where the artist starts with impressions, goes from those to an inner expression, and translates or externalizes the expression into the artistic form, the critic reverses this process: "In order to judge a work of art, it (criticism) knows of no other way except to interrogate the work itself directly and receive a living impression of it . . . This living impression once obtained, the further labor only consists in determining what, in the object under examination, is the pure product of art, and what in it appears to be not truly artistic . . . The critical estimate simply states (and in stating has thereby judged) *wie es ergentlich geschehen*, 'how it really happened' " [*La Critica*, July 1907]. When this is properly done, all art is contemporary art no matter how long ago it was produced, since to exist as art it must be re-created by "the critic's imagination, with the aid of minute knowledge of the circumstances of its composition, of the artist's personality and the age in which he lived" [A. E. Powell, *The Romantic Theory of Poetry*, p. 16].

In a brief article on Aesthetics [*Encyc. Britannica*, 14th ed.], Croce indicates his method of distinguishing poetry from non-poetry: "If we examine a poem in order to determine what it is that makes us feel it to be a poem, we at once find two constant and necessary elements: a complex of *images,* and a *feeling* that animates them." But true poetry "must be called neither feeling, nor image, nor yet the sum of the two, but 'contemplation of feeling' or 'lyrical intuition' or (which is the same thing) 'pure intuition'—pure, that is, of all historical and critical reference to the reality or unreality of the images of which it is woven and apprehending the pure throb of life in its ideality."

This does not deny the value of content. He treats it, however, as inseparable from form: "The relation between matter and form, or between content and form, as is generally said, is one of the most disputed questions in Æsthetics. Does the æsthetic fact consist of content alone, or of form alone, or of both together? This question has taken on various meanings, which we shall mention, each in its place. But when these words are taken as signifying what we have above defined, and matter is understood as emotionality not æsthetically elaborated, or impressions, and form as intellectual activity and expression, then our view cannot be in doubt. We must, that is to say, reject both the thesis that makes the æsthetic fact to consist of the content alone (that is, the simple impressions), and the thesis which makes it to consist of a junction between form and content, that is, of impressions plus expressions. In the æsthetic fact, expressive activity is not added to the fact of the impressions, but these latter are formed and elaborated by it. The impressions reappear as it were in expression, like water put into a filter, which reappears the same and yet different on the other side. The æsthetic fact, therefore, is form, and nothing but form" [*Idem.*].

Since each form is unique, there can be no useful cross-comparisons of works of art. Each must be examined purely on its own intrinsic merits. But the work of the critic does not stop with distinguishing the kinds of beauty and ugliness, the art and the non-art in a particular work; he must also give a characterization of it. In doing this, he must work within the individual reality of the poem, in order properly to determine "its content or fundamental moving force, and to assign what has been determined to the psychological class or type best suited to include it" [*La Poesia*, Bk. III, ch. iii, tr. A. H. Gilbert]. This characterization is never fully satisfactory, for there remains always a wide gulf between the poem and the formula of characterization. In fact, the formula is necessarily based upon a concept of art (*i.e.,* on intellectual knowledge), while the poem is a product of intuition-expression (*i.e.,* of the imagination). So the formula can never coincide with the poem. But it can serve as a workable method for separating the poetic from the non-poetic, and the greater voices from the smaller ones. The critic, in Croce's view, "must possess a concept of what is a work of Art, so that, turning to his imaginative recreation of the individual work, he may judge how far he finds in it other activities which have nothing to do with Art" [Powell, *op. cit.,* p. 15].

THE DEFENCE OF POETRY *
(1933)

In English literature the classical *Defence of Poetry* is that of Shelley, though to speak exactly there are two; for that of Philip Sidney, belonging to the Renaissance, sets out from a point of view very distant from our own. Shelley's work was written in 1821 to refute the assertion that poetry can no longer find a place in mature civilization; or, as Vico would have said, 'in fully developed mind.' The theory of the death of poetry, or of its superannuation in the modern world, was not peculiar to Hegel, who gave it its most extreme and most systematic form, but sprang up in many places in the early decades of the nineteenth century. There were various reasons for this, but the chief, and perhaps a fundamental one, was the habit of confusing, or too closely connecting, images of art with religious myths. Shelley pointed to poetry as the eternal source of all intellectual, moral, and civil vitality, and claimed that it was a specially necessary corrective for times when the selfish and mechanical principle, represented by Mammon, threatens to prevail, and when the body has become too unwieldy for that which animates it. In fact, it was for his own times that he sought the aid of poetry, times when, in spite of their splendid culture, he thought that the intellect was excessively honoured. He foresaw a dangerous disproportion between the accumulated growth of moral, historical, political, and economic science on the one hand and, on the other, the failing forces of imagination, with all those kindred generous impulses which alone can quicken abstract knowledge to a fruitful and beneficent activity.

Thirty years before Shelley, Friedrich Schiller had been moved in like manner to invoke the aid of art and poetry for the salvation of a

* *The Defence of Poetry,* by Benedetto Croce. Translated by E. F. Carritt. The Philip Maurice Deneke Lecture delivered at Lady Margaret Hall, Oxford, on October 17, 1933, reproduced by the permission of the Clarendon Press, Oxford.

humanity tossed unceasingly from the extreme of servitude to the extreme of anarchy, and unable to foresee any other end to its troubles than in some blind force, which might settle with a strong hand the dispute between these rival principles. While Schiller was writing, the crisis of the French Revolution was developing with terrible rapidity. The theoretical programme of that revolution was the triumph of reason and liberty; its actual achievement was to unbridle the fiercest passions and to trample all liberty under foot. The consequences, in countries not yet affected by the movement, were a growing hostility of governments to a liberty which seemed their obvious enemy, and a design to uphold and fortify tyranny and oppression; while, at the same time, among their subject peoples, the promised reign of liberty and reason raised an ever stronger enthusiasm and more irresistible agitation. How was it possible to avoid or to mitigate this ominous clash between the state of nature, where might is right, and the state of reason and liberty? The former was incapable of really rising to the latter, and, after spasmodic efforts, only relapsed into brutality. The latter was unable to stoop to the former or to assimilate it, and striving, consistently with its theory, to realize itself by uncompromising and impatient methods, became so violent, tyrannical, and bloody as to provoke reaction. Or, to ask the same question in terms of psychology, how could the sensuous, passionate man be raised to the level of the rational man, without a deterioration in which each party would rival the other, and finally both sink to the same depth of monstrosity and degradation? Schiller could see no solution except to set up, as a mediator between the sensuous and the rational man, a third, the artist.[1] Between the state of nature and the state of reason he set the state of art or poetry, which has gone beyond the first and not attained the second; which is no longer purely passive [2] or passionate, but is not yet ethically active; [3] which has gained aesthetic but not moral freedom. Such a state has escaped from nature but has not yet developed itself in any definite sphere; it covers rather the totality of human faculties, training and exercising them all as in some noble kind of play.

Do we too live in an age that might justify once more an appeal to poetry for the succour which Schiller and Shelley implored of it? I think all who heard such a question would, with one voice, eagerly answer: Yes.

In fact, no day passes without our all hearing the universal complaint

---

[1] *L'uomo estetico.*
[2] *passività.*

[3] *pratica attività.*

that lofty motives have now vanished from our world; that the only aim of life is victory in the fight for riches, the only pleasure that of the body; that the one spectacle which can stir us to excitement or admiration is the strange and reckless exhibition of physical force; that our only emulation is in the fierce struggle for pre-eminence between nations or classes. The sublime and sacred watchwords, which stirred the hearts of former ages, are either a mere laughingstock, or quite meaningless for a generation which knows not what to make of them, and which cannot comprehend the power and fascination that they exercised, or seem to have exercised, upon its fathers and grandfathers, who still mumble the tale. The dreams, the enthusiasms, the despondencies *de grands amants ou de grands citoyens,* as the poet calls them, have become a byword. Science interests us only when it can afford new methods of production; philosophy only when it lends itself to adorn the aims of particular classes, governments, and nations with sophistic formulas or shameless lies; art only when it panders to the mental and spiritual vacuity of its audience by elaborate staging, discordant imagery, or the vain promise of new and strange sensations. The old religion loses every day more of what respectability it still possessed as a practical institution, by making terms with the powers of this world and, in return for its services, pocketing a bribe or snatching a material advantage. As a spiritual institution it offers an asylum to those who through laziness or disillusion are weary of thinking and acting on their own responsibility. Our civilization is technically perfect and spiritually barbarous; ravenous of wealth and indifferent to good; utterly insensible to all that ought to move the human conscience. All its powers seem employed in selfish aggression or defence. This is the dense atmosphere in which we are stifled, which painfully chokes and crushes every freedom of heart, every delicate sensibility, every quickness of mind. But if some fresh rain of poetry should permeate it, what recreation would it bring, what ampler breath, what heightened spirits! Then we should renew our sense of the eternal human drama, of the tragedies and glories of our kind; we should see things once more in their true proportions and relations, in their harmonious hierarchy; we should fall in love again with love and with loving-kindness; we should renew our scorn for all that is base and abject, and vulgar; our hearts would re-open to hope and joy, to manly grief, to the relief of tears, to frank and cleansing laughter—the laughter so seldom heard in a world where it is outfaced by sarcasm, by sly leers, or by shameless ribaldry.

In point of objective truth it is easy to see how much exaggeration and illusion there is in such a picture of the modern world. That it is no historical portrait we have already hinted by borrowing the tones of the stricken and complaining hearts who bewail its character. Rather it is the vision which contemporaries have of a development in which they are actors, and which they endure in their own persons. Consequently, when they balance the necessary contrasts of new and old, the necessary losses and innovations, they are apt to see in the course of the struggle nothing but what offends them and arouses their protest, their opposition, and rebellion. It is from such hostile criticisms that they compose their picture, which accordingly, is the prejudiced portrayal of a dreaded enemy, coloured by the injuries received or feared from him. To paint a true picture of the whole process, they would obviously have to include themselves, and many like themselves, who resist it or work in an opposite and complementary sense, not to mention that mute, inglorious host of good and honest men who are the underlying fabric which holds human society together. Instead of this, in the strife and fury of passion they forget both themselves and these others; their imagination sees the whole field occupied by the triumphant and ravaging hordes of the enemy. That is why in every age almost identical complaints are heard, and the same gloomy pictures painted; just objects of irony, sometimes, to the cultivated and the reflective. But granting all this, every age, besides what all have in common, has its proper difficulties and problems. If it would be ingenuous to take for historic truth the pessimistic picture projected by the fears of a combatant, it would be stupid to overlook the peculiar physiognomy and character of every age. On the most calm and careful consideration, we have to admit two important points. The first is that the vast improvement in means of production and in economy of labour during the nineteenth and early twentieth centuries has left its mark on the general character, and has overshadowed other elements of human experience, which struggled painfully against its undue preponderance. The second is that the world war has further weakened the resistance of our higher spiritual powers by mowing down millions of young lives, by cutting short or hampering the education of millions more, by breaking the tradition of culture, and by elevating to power new classes ignorant or contemptuous of that tradition. All this suffices to prove that the crudity and barbarism complained of, if not the only characteristics of modern society, are yet, after all deductions, real enough; it suffices to justify our renewed appeal to poetry as a saviour of the world.

But, in such an appeal, what are we really asking? What do we in fact expect of poetry, and what can it give? Both Shelley and Schiller had pretty clear ideas on the nature of poetry and its function in individual and social life. They firmly grasped the disinterested nature of the aesthetic activity, which Schiller defined as free from any definite aim,[4] and spiritually effective precisely by this unpracticalness.[5] Shelley forbade art to pursue moral ends, but recognized its power to purge the human mind of base desires, to rouse our enthusiasm for love and for all that is good or noble, to enlarge the mind by rendering it the receptacle of a thousand unapprehended combinations of thought. He understood, moreover, the regeneration of truths which poetry effects in face of the intellectual algebra which tends to conventionalize them; poetry, he says, 'purges from our inward sight the film of familiarity which obscures from us the wonder of our being.' But both Schiller and Shelley, in developing the arguments of their discussions, either attributed to poetry a good deal more than it can really do, and thus lost sight of its true and simple nature, or assigned to it a particular task which is not appropriate to it. In neither of them is the scientific elaboration of the thesis worthy of its primary and fundamental idea.

Shelley, in fact, was carried away by his sense of the infinite value of this spiritual activity, and gave it absolute supremacy over all others, making it the first author of every human achievement and the source of all civilization. Poets are for him the unacknowledged legislators of the world, its 'true princes,' as Tommaso Campanella would have called them, in contrast to 'the pretenders,' who oppose them with physical force. Poets are not only the authors of language and of music, of the dance, and architecture, and statuary, and painting: they are the institutors of laws, and the founders of civil society, and the inventors of the arts of life, and the teachers who draw into a certain propinquity with the beautiful and the true, that partial apprehension of the agencies of the invisible world which is called religion. Poetry is indeed something divine. It is at once the centre and circumference of knowledge; it is that which comprehends all science, and that to which all science must be referred. Without the exertions of the philosophers, of Locke, Hume, Gibbon, Voltaire, and Rousseau, who put to flight the shades of slavish credulity and ignorance, and shook off the chains of tyrants, a little more nonsense would have been talked for a century or two, and a few more heretics might have been burnt. But if neither Dante, Petrarch, Boccaccio, Shakespeare nor Milton, had ever existed; if

---

[4] *particolare determinazione.*
[5] *indeterminazione.* Cf. Schiller, *Letters*   on the *Aesthetic Education of Mankind,* xxii.

Raphael and Michelangelo had never been born; if a revival of the study of Greek literature had never taken place; the human mind could never have been awakened to the invention of the grosser sciences or that application of analytical reasoning to the aberrations of society, which it is now attempted to exalt over the direct expression of the inventive and creative faculty itself. The dark ages were therefore the dark ages because in them the poetical principle decayed, and despotism and superstition proportionately flourished. Poetry is not only what is so called in the restricted sense, what is expressed in words and verses. The true poetry of Rome was fashioned in its institutions and in the deeds of its heroic history, in Camillus and Regulus, in the senators seated before the invading Gauls, in the stolid resistance of the republic after Cannae. Poetry is philosophy and philosophy is poetry. Plato and Bacon were great poets; Shakespeare, Dante, and Milton are great philosophers.

Such statements have, no doubt, an element of truth—without which they could not have issued from the mind of Shelley—namely that poetry, being an eternal category of the human spirit, can be discovered in every individual, in every achievement, and in every action of our life. Their element of error consists in overlooking or forgetting that the other categories also—logical thought, will, morality—must, like poetry, have their place in every person and in every act. Consequently a captious criticism might give the supremacy in turn to logical thought, will, and morality, thus making the whole world, which for Shelley revolved on the axis of poetry, revolve on the axis of any of these categories. Poetry, far from gaining by being expanded over the whole world, loses its proper and distinctive character, and therewith its proper strength and efficacy. Nor, in truth, can we say that this proper and distinctive character is comprised in Shelley's definition of poetry, so often re-echoed, as 'the record of the best and happiest moments of the happiest and best minds.' This is in fact rather a poetical or imaginative expression than a technical definition, and indeed the whole *Defence* has a movement which is a good deal more poetical than reasoned or critical.

Schiller, for his part, demanded from poetry, and in general from aesthetic education, the solution of the problem of development from a state of violence to a state of freedom, from sense and passion to reason. This was the problem which the eighteenth century had solved in its own way by its faith in the irresistible power of enlightenment through reason. Before reason all errors were to melt away; spiritual and temporal arms were to fall from the hands of priests and despots, and the natural goodness of men was to celebrate its final triumpL. It was the same problem as that offered by Kant's conception of an absolute, unyielding moral law which subdues and expels the passions with no aid save its own fearless and heroic strength. Schiller could no longer believe in the miracles of mere reason; he could not accept the hard and fast Kantian opposition between feeling and morality, between impulse and duty, nor the eradication and suppression of the former by the latter. To him the old problem appeared in a new guise, as the political problem of his own day, as the quest for a mediator between old and new, between the actual and the ideal. He was equally unable to satisfy himself with the solution of the Jacobins or with that of the reactionaries, both alike ruinous; he longed for a genuine and substantial progress towards reason and liberty. But, in inserting a third state between the two which he assumed, he was treating Kant's problem, which was really dialectical or metaphysical, psychologically. For in actual fact there is not first the state of nature or feeling and then the state of freedom or reason, nor is there an intermediate aesthetic state; but only the unceasing alternation from the one moment or factor to the other, from feeling to reason, from random impulse [6] to moral freedom. In such an alternation poetry can have no place, except in the sense, already explained, that poetry pervades all things as the unity of all-pervasive spirit does. Accordingly, the logical problem which Schiller had in mind reduced itself to the problem of the nature of development or evolution, and his political problem to that of finding in the actual some point of contact with the ideal, in the old some seed of the new. He had, therefore, both to criticize and to respect, both to abolish and to retain, the old and actual, if he would really achieve the new and ideal. A similar solution was in fact reached by the historically-minded liberal policy of the nineteenth century, among whose prophets Schiller, with his theory of Aesthetic Education, must be included. But poetry and art have a sphere both wider and narrower than this political principle, or, more truly, the aesthetic problem belongs to a different branch of inquiry. The education dreamed of by Schiller, which, by cultivating all man's various faculties harmoniously, should train him for life without engaging him in any one path of life leading to this or the other particular object, was evidently not pure poetry or aesthetic education. Rather it was liberal education and general culture, not narrowly intellectual or rationalistic, nor yet narrowly artistic and imaginative, but directed

[6] *l'arbitrio.*

alike on the reason and the imagination, on the will and the conscience, and harmonizing all together.

Having noted the varieties in the conception of poetry in two great minds, both exceptionally rich in poetic genius, if we now set ourselves to define that conception, it is certainly not, as might be suspected, with the idea of discovering and revealing it for the first time, *nondum auditum indictumque prius.* The conception of poetry, like the other fundamental conceptions, needs no discovery, because it has always been present in man's mind since his spirit first created poetry, which is as much as to say *ab eterno.* But from time to time it is useful in particular discussions to reaffirm it against new confusions and errors which tend to obscure it, though, at the same time, by stimulating it to a clearer consciousness and stronger emphasis, they keep it sound and vigorous. The subject of our discussion is the way in which poetry can help to preserve or refresh man's superior nature in its contest with his inferior, morality in its contest with expediency. And since the way suggested by Schiller and Shelley has been shown impossible, or their descriptions of it vague and loose, we must, for this purpose, reaffirm the true conception of poetry; not only in order to correct, in some degree, their aesthetic theories, but still more to contend against other current theories which confuse or replace it by conceptions of different nature and application.

It is certainly unnecessary to-day to attack 'oratorical' poetry. For more than a century and a half it has been condemned in theory by aesthetics or the philosophy of art, and attacked in practice by critics, both in its form of solemn poems or decorous odes designed to inculcate political, moral, and religious virtue, or to expound the great truths of philosophy and science, and also in its lighter, more palatable form of satire, epigram, and playful or 'occasional' verse. Such things have their uses, but, in spite of Aristotle's warning, they have been falsely called poetry because they were written in verse. Yet criticism distinguishes them from true poetry, and even in single poems distinguishes the poetical portions from the oratorical, which it dismisses from its consideration. The same aesthetic tendency has made itself felt in various ways in the plastic and pictorial arts, where sharp distinctions have been drawn between 'literature,' which is a subject edifying or in general 'oratorical,' and 'painting' which is the poetic element; between 'illustrative' and 'decorative' values, and many more. In Italy, at least, the same tendency begins to show itself also in musical criticism. The only proper object of aesthetic consideration to-day is the poetry which is nothing but poetry or, as it is also called, 'pure poetry.'

Unfortunately into this very conception of 'pure' poetry, as opposed to oratory, has been insinuated another, which is its opposite and its corruption, which might indeed be called a conception of a poetry that is 'impure' because contaminated with a questionable sensationalism. To avoid misunderstanding, it might be better to call the poetry thus set before us as our ideal, 'mystical-voluptuous,' since its mark is the union of sensual gratification with turgid emotion, as if in this sensuality we fathomed the mystery of the universe and attained a kind of beatific ecstasy. This ideal of poetry and of the arts is connected, in devious ways, with what is called 'decadence,' whose chief symptoms consist precisely in the confusion of matter with form, of the sensuous with the ideal, of pleasure with morality; so that the former are disguised and honoured as the latter, and a witches' banquet celebrated where the devil sits enthroned and worshipped.

Such an impure conception of pure poetry excludes, or pretends to exclude, from poetry all the meaning of words, concentrating on the mere sound. But people who have banished all meaning naturally cannot dwell in this night of not-being. They have to elaborate a kind of significance of their own out of the mere nervous titillation, or 'suggestion,' as they call it, which arouses no clear image, but only the possibility of innumerable images and thoughts, varying from reader to reader and from moment to moment, linked solely by threads of contiguity, contrast, and other forms of the so-called association of ideas.

We need not trouble to attack poets who boast of such doctrines, since there is no causal connexion between theories of poetry and poetic creation. Men of poetic genius, holding these or even worse doctrines, have done very beautiful work; and, on the other hand, men with the best theories and no genius write cold insipidities which naturally remain unread. The fact that our modern Maevius and Bavius, and Suffenus may generally be found under the banner of 'pure poetry' only means that this happens to be the fashion and that mediocrity always follows the fashion. But the theory concerns us for its own sake and as a theory, since, if we took it for true, it would destroy the very conception of poetry and annihilate the problem before us. As a principle of practical criticism it has, hitherto at least, had little or no importance, for it has occurred to nobody to apply it in a history of poetry. Past poetry, indeed, answers badly to the demands of this theory, and worst in the supreme poets, in Homer, Sophocles, Dante, and Shakespeare, who give it the lie direct. Accordingly, the so-called critics of this school usually either neglect all past art, as if it had been condemned by some peculiar law of its nature literally to pass away, or else they pronounce that all former poets were unfortunate, since, in the course of composition, they lost sight of that spark of inspiration which glimmers here and there in their verses. In practical criticism the theory has been little applied except for the consolation and honour of some beloved brother-artist, who is ready with mutual praise and admiration, instead of the laughter that would be more in place. Generally it is elaborated to serve as the criticism of the future for an art of the future, which, like so many futurisms, does not escape some suspicion of quackery.

Coming to the theory as such, if what it says were true, poetry would be nothing but a voluptuous thrill leading only to satiety, and comparable, as the name here suggested for it would imply, to barren sensuality, bearing no fruit in the life of the soul. It could receive nothing from thought or will and could give them nothing, nor could it compose with them the harmonious unity of the spirit. At best it would belong to that class of pleasures which satisfy physiological or pathological needs, like those of alcohol and tobacco, narcotics, stimulants, and aphrodisiacs. We need not exclude the possibility that the manufacturers and amateurs of these verbal or phonetic drugs labelled 'pure poems,' granting that their physical raptures are no affectation but as real as they are capable of feeling, may be some kind of erotic maniacs.

Pure poetry, in the pure sense of the term, is certainly 'sounds,' and certainly it is not sounds which have a logical meaning like the sounds of prose. That is to say, it does not communicate a conception, a judgement, or an inference, nor the story of particular facts. But to say it has no logical meaning is not to say it is a mere physical sound without a soul, an embodied soul which is one with its body as that is with it. In order to distinguish the soul of truth in poetry from the soul of truth in prose, aesthetic science has borrowed and employs the word 'intuition,' and asserts that poetic intuition and poetic expression are brought forth at a single birth. It maintains also that poetic intuition cannot be translated into logical terms; it is something infinite that has no other equivalent than the melody in which it is expressed, and that may be sung but never rendered into prose. It is impossible to see what people mean when, in their desire to confine poetry to pure sound which is nothing but sound, they so often say that it is or ought to be pure 'music': as if music could be mere sound and nothing more, and had not already a soul of its own, which would equally justify us in demanding that music should be poetry. It is a delusion to suppose that a verse delights us by any sounds with which it stimulates our ears to ecstasy. What it stimulates to ecstasy is our imagination, and thereby our emotion. There is a verse of Racine which Théophile Gautier used to scan and declaim with gusto, and which other disciples of preciosity are in the habit of citing as absolutely unmeaning and yet, or rather for that reason, the only beautiful verse which the poet ever succeeded in writing:

La fille de Minos et de Pasiphaé

That is certainly beautiful, but not in virtue of the physical combination of its sounds. One might make infinite other combinations of such sounds without producing any effect of beauty. It is beautiful because these sounds, these syllables and accents, bring before us, in an instantaneous imaginative fusion, all that was mysterious and sinister, all that was divine and fiendish, all that was majestic and perverted, both in the person and in the parentage of Phaedra. And this is expressed by two epic names, that of the royal Cretan legislator and that of his incestuous wife, at whose side rises, in our imagination, the brutal figure of the bull.

And while we are dealing with mistakes of this kind, I may perhaps be allowed to say that we should not lend too docile ears to similar errors of artists when they talk of their artistic aims and methods, or describe their inspired experience and the usual physical symptoms which precede, accompany, and follow it. Such accounts are not very weighty and do not deserve to be taken as philosophically or scientifically sound. Many years ago a man with one of the most purely poetic talents that I have ever intimately known—a poet of the Neapolitan dialect named Salvatore di Giacomo—told me that poetry always came to him in the shape of an overmastering stomach-ache; and, while he made the confession, his face exhibited every mark of agony and nausea. And lately, in a lecture given by an English poet this year at Cambridge,[7] I met with a mention of the same part of his anatomy. For there I read that poetry is a 'secretion,' like the resin which exudes from a pine-tree, or the pearl formed in a diseased oyster, and that its birth-place is in 'the pit of the stomach.' And this reminded me that Goethe too, in a like context, talked about the stomach: but his experience, on the contrary, was that if he were to conceive and bring forth good poetry this digestive organ must be in sound condition, and he concluded that, to judge from his extraordinary powers of creation, nobody ever had so fine a stomach as William Shakespeare. But whatever action poetic travail may have upon the stomach, or whatever the stomachic condition favourable for its com-

[7] *The Name and Nature of Poetry,* by A. E. Housman (Cambridge University Press, 1933).

pletion, we are, none the less, entitled to reject the conclusion drawn in the Cambridge lecture quoted above, that poetry 'is rather physical than intellectual,' or only to accept it, in the sense perhaps intended, as a curiosity of whimsical paradox.

If, then, poetry is intuition and expression, the fusion of sound and imagery, what is the material which takes on the form of sound and imagery? It is the whole man: the man who thinks and wills, and loves, and hates; who is strong and weak, sublime and pathetic, good and wicked; man in the exultation and agony of living; and together with the man, integral with him, it is all nature in its perpetual labour of evolution. But the thoughts and actions and emotions of life, when sublimated to the subject-matter of poetry, are no longer the thought that judges, the action effectually carried out, the good and evil, or the joy and pain actually done or suffered. They are all now simply passions and feelings immediately assuaged and calmed, and transfigured in imagery. That is the magic of poetry: the union of calm and tumult, of passionate impulse with the controlling mind which controls by contemplating. It is the triumph of contemplation, but a triumph still shaken by past battle, with its foot upon a living though vanquished foe. Poetic genius chooses a strait path in which passion is calmed and calm is passionate; a path that has on one side merely natural feeling, and on the other the reflection and criticism which is twice removed from nature; a path from which minor talents find it but too easy to slip into an art either convulsed and distorted by passion, or void of passion and guided by principles of the understanding. Then they are called 'romantic' or 'classical.' The man of poetic taste also treads this narrow path, in which he is permitted to share the delights of poetry. He knows how that delight is compounded: it is shot with pain; permeated by a strange sweetness and tenderness; torn between alternate impulses and repulsions, desires and renunciations, between the zest of life and the desire of death; yet always delight: the delight of perfect form and of beauty.

Is this enjoyment of poetry, this delight in beauty, rare or common? It is both: as a settled habit it is rare, reserved for select spirits who are born to it and trained by education; it is common, as the native tendency of all ingenuous minds. The place where it is hardest to find is precisely among the professional students of poetry and of its historical achievements. They seem gifted with a strange immunity, which lets them all their life handle the books of the poets, edit and annotate them, discuss their various interpretations, investigate their sources, furnish them with biographical introductions, and all without suffering so much contagion as to experience in their own persons the poetic fever. After all, it is much the same in religion, which is felt by lofty minds and by the humble plebs, but not by those who handle the sacred vessels, by the priests and sacristans, who go through their ritual unconcerned, and sometimes with little reverence.

If we call to mind the conception of poetry in its strict character, circumscribed within its proper limits, it must not only decline all those particular functions to which it has been invoked or bent against its nature, but also it must lose the supreme place of honour assigned to it by Shelley, when he called it the fountain of all the forms of civil life. We may indeed invoke it for the regeneration and refreshment and spiritual renewal of human society, but only in accordance with its own essence, not as if it could replace or spontaneously generate the other powers, capacities, and relations of man. In short, we must only look upon it as one among other paths leading to a single goal. Other paths lead there too: the paths of thought, of philosophy, of religion, of conscience, of political action. Not least, there is that path of activity which aims at the production of economic goods; an activity which, seriously carried on, is compelled to realize itself as part of the universal human activity on which all its own strength and permanence depend. Whichever of these paths we enter and pursue we must at least enter the others also, and we find in the end that they are not divergent nor even parallel, but join in a circle which is the rounded unity of the human spirit. And on every path there is the chance—though it is no chance when looked at in the contexture of the whole and as an incident of the world-drama—that an individual may stop half-way, as if exhausted, and never reach the goal that is set before him, but remain one-sided, incomplete, discordant. There is the philosopher who does not carry out the practical requirements of his philosophy but sees the better and follows the worse, or at least stands idle when he should be fulfilling his duties as a citizen and a soldier. There is the artistic genius who never effects the passage from the dreams of poetry to philosophic thought and consistent action. Both are half-men, *dimidiati viri*. But this stunting of life, this breach which the individual makes at some point in the integrity of the spiritual circle, revenges itself, and often in the very region which is dearest to him. The philosopher of easy virtue or of loose morals feels his philosophic enthusiasm gradually dry up, and loses faith in his own thinking; the creator and lover of poetry who has exhausted his early stock of human experience gradually degenerates into the mere stylist or purveyor of *belles-lettres*. For our part, in the meantime, let us try, as our aptitudes and attainments may permit, to introduce others to the path of poetry, by which they may reach one of the unfailing fountains of perennial youth. Will they be disposed to follow us or will they refuse? Will they exchange expressions of ready sympathy, or will they accompany us with reluctance and even disgust, and turn out bad companions? Certainly I will not conceal a feeling, perhaps not peculiar to myself, which I have had during the last twenty years: a feeling that if I recite aloud a line or stanza of Dante or Petrarch or Foscolo, their voices find no echo: a sense of a surrounding atmosphere strange, hostile, and contemptuous; a sense of sacrilege in bringing into it those gentle and exalted words, born in a different world and addressed to a different world. But does such an experience imply that we must withdraw into ourselves; that we must keep silence; that we must hold such communion only with our own hearts, shyly, as becomes us when we dream over lost happiness? Or is it rather simply the signal that here is a barrier to be broken down? Let me picture to you a mythical scene of very different character. We are in a gathering of men and youths on edge with mutually hostile passions. They are opponents who mistrust one another, alienated by conflicting aims; each of them aloof and angry, on the defensive of his own narrow circumference. Suddenly somebody opens a book of poetry and begins to read: as the music flows on, as the images float before their eyes, something mysterious moves in their hearts, their souls incline to it, their imagination awakes. They follow the expressive rhythm in its theme, in its modulations, in its final harmony; and in these modulations and that harmony they begin, with wonder and emotion, to remember something in themselves that was sleeping, cold or buried—their common humanity. After that discovery, can they still look at one another as before? Can they any longer see themselves as utterly divided, as mortal enemies, when a bond has been forged between them, when all have had a momentary glimpse into the world of beauty, and learned that in that world they are brothers? Can such a moment of divine augury vainly vanish and leave not a trace upon their minds? Must it not bring the need for other such moments, and for much else of the same kind; not only for verses and poems, and music, and pictures, but for thoughts which illuminate and for deeds that uplift the heart?

It may be said, in discouragement of vain hopes and over-confidence, that the world is hard and heavy, and needs more than individual goodwill and poetic fancies. But we know that, all the same, this hard and heavy world moves, or rather that it only exists in movement, and that it is moved by nothing but our united efforts; that each of us, great or small or tiny as he may be, in his relation to all the others is answerable for the world. If we too, as lovers of poetry, exert what strength we have, we shall have done the duty of our station.

THOMAS STEARNS ELIOT

(1888–1965)

THOMAS STEARNS ELIOT is descended from the New England family of distinguished divines and educators. He was born in St. Louis, Missouri, on September 26, 1888; he prepared for college at private schools, the Smith Academy in St. Louis and Milton in Massachusetts, and graduated from Harvard in 1909. For several years he studied literature and philosophy at the Sorbonne, Harvard, and Oxford. His first important poem, "The Love Song of J. Alfred Prufrock," appeared in Harriet Monroe's journal *Poetry* in 1915. At about this time he established residence in England, and during the next few years made contributions to English philosophical and literary reviews, notably *The Athenaeum*. From these grew his first volume of criticism, *The Sacred Wood* (1920), which contains "Tradition and the Individual Talent." In 1922 *The Waste Land* was published, and in the following year Eliot became editor of *The Criterion,* a quarterly which continued till 1939. Other key poetry has been "The Hollow Men" (1925), "Ash Wednesday" (1930), the *Collected Poems, 1909–35,* and *Four Quartets* (1943). His most significant criticism since *The Sacred Wood* has been gathered in *Selected Essays, 1917–32, The Use of Poetry and the Use of Criticism* (1933), *After Strange Gods* (1934), *Essays Ancient and Modern* (1936), *The Idea of a Christian Society* (1940), and *Notes towards the Definition of Culture* (1949).

Eliot is one of those critics who leave the systematizing of their work to others: most of his production has been articles on specific rather than abstract problems and for specific occasions. This fact has given special importance to "Tradition and the Individual Talent," one of his earliest essays but perhaps the nearest to a general statement of critical philosophy. Its concept of the "simultaneous existence" and "simultaneous order" of European literature emphasizes the necessity of a review and revaluation from time to time of the great names, a task which Eliot appropriated to himself insofar as English literature was concerned in *The Use of Poetry and the Use of Criticism*. In another direction the defining of tradition has led inevitably to unliterary searches, to the emphasis on sectional customs set out in *After Strange Gods,* to the high Toryism of *Notes towards the Definition of Culture,* to an insistence on parallels between literature and social activities and between literature and religion. His position that "the 'greatness' of literature cannot be determined solely by literary standards" orients him with respect to Arnold and to Pater and distinguishes him from contemporaries like Spender and Auden.

For Eliot the importance of form in literature is preponderant, and his basic concept of it reminds us at once of the French Symbolists and of the fourth section of Aristotle's *Poetics*. In the essay "Hamlet and His Problems" [1] he says:

> The only way of expressing emotion in the form of art is by finding an "objective correlative"; in other words, a set of objects, a situation, a chain of events which shall be the formula of that *particular* emotion; such that when the external facts, which must terminate in sensory experience, are given, the emotion is immediately invoked. . . . The artistic "inevitability" lies in this complete adequacy of the external to the emotion.

The "objective correlative" principle is used to illustrate the artistic deficiency of Shakespeare's play:

> Hamlet is up against the difficulty that his disgust is occasioned by his mother, but that his mother is not an adequate equivalent for it; his disgust envelops and exceeds her. . . . And it must be noticed that the very nature of the *données* of the problem precludes objective equivalence. To have heightened the criminality of Gertrude would have been to provide the formula for a totally different emotion in Hamlet; it is just *because* her character is so negative and insignificant that she arouses in Hamlet the feeling which she is incapable of representing.

The importance of this principle in understanding Eliot's own poetry has variously been pointed out by critics, notably by Professor F. O. Matthiessen in the third chapter of *The Achievement of T. S. Eliot*.

The relation of intellect and emotion in art is a vital one in Eliot's criticism. The poetical achievement is "the emotional equivalent of thought," and the intenser the poet's sensibility to the thought of his own time (together with his sense of his time's significance in the whole of intellectual history—the "tradition principle") the greater is his artistic performance. But the immediacy of the emotion's fusion of the thought makes a great difference in the poetry. For two centuries there has been evident an increasing "dissociation of sensibility" in English poetry, a fact which accounts for many of Eliot's judgments on single poets and literary periods:

> Tennyson and Browning are poets, and they think; but they do not feel their thought as immediately as the odour of a rose. A thought to Donne was an experience; it modified his sensibility. . . .

> We may express the difference by the following theory: The poets of the seventeenth century, the successors of the dramatists of the sixteenth, possessed a mechanism of sensibility which could devour any kind of experience. They are simple, artificial, difficult, or fantastic, as their predecessors were; no less nor more than Dante, Guido Cavalcanti, Guinizelli, or Cino. In the seventeenth century a dissociation of sensibility set in, from which we have never recovered; and this dissociation, as is natural, was aggravated by the influence of the two most powerful poets of the century, Milton and Dryden. Each of these men performed certain poetic functions so magnificently well that the magnitude of the

[1] Reprinted from *Selected Essays* by T. S. Eliot. Copyright 1932 by Harcourt, Brace and Company, Inc. Used by permission of the publishers.

effect concealed the absence of others. The language went on and in some respects improved; the best verse of Collins, Gray, Johnson, and even Goldsmith satisfies some of our fastidious demands better than that of Donne or Marvell or King. But while the language became more refined, the feeling became more crude. The feeling, the sensibility, expressed in the *Country Churchyard* (to say nothing of Tennyson and Browning) is cruder than that in the *Coy Mistress* [2] ["The Metaphysical Poets"].

And what of poetry and beliefs? The expression in poetry of philosophies which we cannot accept need not detract from our enjoyment (except when the view of life "is one which the reader rejects as childish or feeble," as in Shelley, for instance), but the philosophies must not go unheeded. There is a passage in the *Dante* which belongs with the major statements of Coleridge and Richards on the same subject.

> My point is that you cannot afford to *ignore* Dante's philosophical and theological beliefs, or to skip the passages which express them most clearly; but that on the other hand you are not called upon to believe them yourself. It is wrong to think that there are parts of the *Divine Comedy* which are of interest only to *Catholics* or to mediaevalists. For there is a difference (which here I hardly do more than assert) between philosophical *belief* and philosophical *assent*. I am not sure that there is not as great a difference between philosophical belief and scientific belief; but that is a difference only now beginning to appear, and certainly inapposite to the thirteenth century. In reading Dante you must enter the world of thirteenth-century Catholicism: which is not the world of modern Catholicism, as his world of physics is not the world of modern physics. You are not called upon to believe what Dante believed, for your belief will not give you a groat's worth more of understanding and appreciation; but you are called upon more and more to understand it. If you can read poetry as poetry, you will "believe" in Dante's theology exactly as you believe in the physical reality of his journey; that is, you suspend both belief and disbelief. [3]

To "read poetry as poetry" is one thing. To read poetry with an awareness of its moral and religious implications is another, and one which has increasingly taken Eliot's interest in later years. He earlier (Preface to the 1928 Edition of *The Sacred Wood*) reaffirmed his position in the *delectare* camp of critics by defining poetry as "a superior amusement," good poetry as "excellent words in excellent arrangement and excellent metre." He has repeatedly berated Arnold for "substituting" poetry for religion. "On the other hand," he continues in the 1928 Preface,

> . . . poetry . . . certainly has something to do with morals, and with religion, and even with politics perhaps, though we cannot say what. If I ask myself (to take a comparison on a higher plane) why I prefer the poetry of Dante to that of Shakespeare, I should have to say, because it

---

[2] Reprinted from *Selected Essays* by T. S. Eliot. Copyright 1932 by Harcourt, Brace and Company, Inc. Used by permission of the publisher.

[3] Reprinted from *Selected Essays* by T. S. Eliot. Copyright 1932 by Harcourt, Brace and Company, Inc. Used by permission of the publisher.

seems to me to illustrate a saner attitude towards the mystery of life. And in these questions, and others which we cannot avoid, we appear already to be leaving the domain of criticism of "poetry." So we cannot stop at any point. The best that we can hope to do is to agree upon a point from which to start, and that is, in part, the subject of this book." When we read in "Religion and Literature" six years later that "The 'greatness' of literature cannot be determined by literary standards; though we must remember that whether it is literature or not can be determined only by literary standards," and that "For literary judgment we need to be acutely aware of two things: of 'what we like,' and of 'what we *ought* to like,' " we perceive that the relationship of poetry to morals, religion, and politics has assumed increasing importance, as it did for Arnold, *within* "the domain of criticism of poetry."

Insofar as the importance of a literary figure may be gauged by controversy centered about him, T. S. Eliot must be regarded as the outstanding writer of his half-century. The recent anthology edited by Leonard Unger [*T. S. Eliot: A Selected Critique*] contains the reactions of thirty-one literary critics and a list totaling fifteen pages of bibliography. With but casual reading of his contemporary literati one finds Eliot condemned for "his horror of the common man" by Harold J. Laski; celebrated as the international "culture hero" by Delmore Schwartz; characterized as an intellectual "leading us in two directions at once" in his poetry and his prose, by Paul Elmer More; and by R. P. Blackmur declared to be (as Mr. Eliot said of Shakespeare) "himself the unity of his work." Nor is it surprising that within the individual mind there are strong approbations and reservations, that Edmund Wilson, admiring Eliot's "infinitely sensitive apparatus for aesthetic appreciation," finds that the effect of his literary criticism "is to impose upon us a conception of poetry as some sort of pure and rare aesthetic essence with no relation to any of the practical human uses . . . a quintessential distillation. . . ." And John Crowe Ransom, rejecting much of the Tradition theory as "very nearly a doctrine of poetic automatism," yet thinks it "likely that we have had no better critic than Eliot," even in Dryden or Johnson.

TRADITION AND THE INDIVIDUAL TALENT *

(1920)

I

In English writing we seldom speak of tradition, though we occasionally apply its name in deploring its absence. We cannot refer to "the tradition" or to "a tradition"; at most, we employ the adjective in saying that the poetry of So-and-so is "traditional" or even "too tradi-

* From *Selected Essays*, 1917–1932, by T. S. Eliot, copyright, 1932, by Harcourt, Brace & Company, Inc. Also from *The*   *Sacred Wood*, 1920, used by permission of Methuen & Co., Ltd., London.

tional." Seldom, perhaps, does the word appear except in a phrase of censure. If otherwise, it is vaguely approbative, with the implication, as to the work approved, of some pleasing archaeological reconstruction. You can hardly make the word agreeable to English ears without this comfortable reference to the reassuring science of archaeology.

Certainly the word is not likely to appear in our appreciations of living or dead writers. Every nation, every race, has not only its own creative, but its own critical turn of mind; and is even more oblivious of the shortcomings and limitations of its critical habits than of those of its creative genius. We know, or think we know, from the enormous mass of critical writing that has appeared in the French language the critical method or habit of the French; we only conclude (we are such unconscious people) that the French are "more critical" than we, and sometimes even plume ourselves a little with the fact, as if the French were the less spontaneous. Perhaps they are; but we might remind ourselves that criticism is as inevitable as breathing, and that we should be none the worse for articulating what passes in our minds when we read a book and feel an emotion about it, for criticizing our own minds in their work of criticism. One of the facts that might come to light in this process is our tendency to insist, when we praise a poet, upon those aspects of his work in which he least resembles anyone else. In these aspects or parts of his work we pretend to find what is individual, what is the peculiar essence of the man. We dwell with satisfaction upon the poet's difference from his predecessors, especially his immediate predecessors; we endeavour to find something that can be isolated in order to be enjoyed. Whereas if we approach a poet without this prejudice we shall often find that not only the best, but the most individual parts of his work may be those in which the dead poets, his ancestors, assert their immortality most vigorously. And I do not mean the impressionable period of adolescence, but the period of full maturity.

Yet if the only form of tradition, of handing down, consisted in following the ways of the immediate generation before us in a blind or timid adherence to its successes, "tradition" should positively be discouraged. We have seen many such simple currents soon lost in the sand; and novelty is better than repetition. Tradition is a matter of much wider significance. It cannot be inherited, and if you want it you must obtain it by great labour. It involves, in the first place, the historical sense, which we may call nearly indispensable to anyone who would continue to be a poet beyond his twenty-fifth year; and the historical sense involves a perception, not only of the pastness of the past, but of its presence; the historical sense compels a man to write not merely with his own generation in his bones, but with a feeling that the whole of the literature of Europe from Homer and within it the whole of the literature of his own country has a simultaneous existence and composes a simultaneous order. This historical sense, which is a sense of the timeless as well as of the temporal and of the timeless and of the temporal together, is what makes a writer traditional. And it is at the same time what makes a writer most acutely conscious of his place in time, of his contemporaneity.

No poet, no artist of any art, has his complete meaning alone. His significance, his appreciation is the appreciation of his relation to the dead poets and artists. You cannot value him alone; you must set him, for contrast and comparison, among the dead. I mean this as a principle of aesthetic, not merely historical, criticism. The necessity that he shall conform, that he shall cohere, is not one-sided; what happens when a new work of art is created is something that happens simultaneously to all the works of art which preceded it. The existing monuments form an ideal order among themselves, which is modified by the introduction of the new (the really new) work of art among them. The existing order is complete before the new work arrives; for order to persist after the supervention of novelty, the *whole* existing order must be, if ever so slightly, altered; and so the relations, proportions, values of each work of art toward the whole are readjusted; and this is conformity between the old and the new. Whoever has approved this idea of order, of the form of European, of English literature, will not find it preposterous that the past should be altered by the present as much as the present is directed by the past. And the poet who is aware of this will be aware of great difficulties and responsibilities.

In a peculiar sense he will be aware also that he must inevitably be judged by the standards of the past. I say judged, not amputated, by them; not judged to be as good as, or worse or better than, the dead; and certainly not judged by the canons of dead critics. It is a judgment, a comparison, in which two things are measured by each other. To conform merely would be for the new work not really to conform at all; it would not be new, and would therefore not be a work of art. And we do not quite say that the new is more valuable because it fits in; but its fitting in is a test of its value—a test, it is true, which can only be slowly and cautiously applied, for we are none of us infallible judges of conformity. We say: it appears to conform, and is perhaps individual, or it appears individual, and may conform; but we are hardly likely to find that it is one and not the other.

To proceed to a more intelligible exposition of the relation of the poet to the past: he can neither take the past as a lump, an indiscriminate bolus, nor can he form himself wholly on one or two private admirations, nor can he form himself wholly upon one preferred period. The first course is inadmissible, the second is an important experience of youth, and the third is a pleasant and highly desirable supplement. The poet must be very conscious of the main current, which does not at all flow invariably through the most distinguished reputations. He must be quite aware of the obvious fact that art never improves, but that the material of art is never quite the same. He must be aware that the mind of Europe—the mind of his own country—a mind which he learns in time to be much more important than his own private mind —is a mind which changes, and that this change is a development which abandons nothing *en route,* which does not superannuate either Shakespeare, or Homer, or the rock drawing of the Magdalenian draughtsmen. That this development, refinement perhaps, complication certainly, is not, from the point of view of the artist, any improvement. Perhaps not even an improvement from the point of view of the psychologist or not to the extent which we imagine; perhaps only in the end based upon a complication in economics and machinery. But the difference between the present and the past is that the conscious present is an awareness of the past in a way and to an extent which the past's awareness of itself cannot show.

Someone said: "The dead writers are remote from us because we *know* so much more than they did." Precisely, and they are that which we know.

I am alive to a usual objection to what is clearly part of my programme for the *métier* of poetry. The objection is that the doctrine requires a ridiculous amount of erudition (pedantry), a claim which can be rejected by appeal to the lives of poets in any pantheon. It will even be affirmed that much learning deadens or perverts poetic sensibility. While, however, we persist in believing that a poet ought to know as much as will not encroach upon his necessary receptivity and necessary laziness, it is not desirable to confine knowledge to whatever can be put into a useful shape for examinations, drawing-rooms, or the still more pretentious modes of publicity. Some can absorb knowledge, the more tardy must sweat for it. Shakespeare acquired more essential history from Plutarch than most men could from the whole British Museum. What is to be insisted upon is that the poet must develop or procure the consciousness of the past and that he should continue to develop this consciousness throughout his career.

What happens is a continual surrender of himself as he is at the moment to something which is more valuable. The progress of an artist is a continual self-sacrifice, a continual extinction of personality.

There remains to define this process of depersonalization and its relation to the sense of tradition. It is in this depersonalization that art may be said to approach the condition of science. I shall, therefore, invite you to consider, as a suggestive analogy, the action which takes place when a bit of finely filiated platinum is introduced into a chamber containing oxygen and sulphur dioxide.

II

Honest criticism and sensitive appreciation is directed not upon the poet but upon the poetry. If we attend to the confused cries of the newspaper critics and the susurrus of popular repetition that follows, we shall hear the names of poets in great numbers; if we seek not Bluebook knowledge but the enjoyment of poetry, and ask for a poem, we shall seldom find it. In the last article I tried to point out the importance of the relation of the poem to other poems by other authors, and suggested the conception of poetry as a living whole of all the poetry that has ever been written. The other aspect of this Impersonal theory of poetry is the relation of the poem to its author. And I hinted, by an analogy, that the mind of the mature poet differs from that of the immature one not precisely in any valuation of "personality," not being necessarily more interesting, or having "more to say," but rather by being a more finely perfected medium in which special, or very varied, feelings are at liberty to enter into new combinations.

The analogy was that of the catalyst. When the two gases previously mentioned are mixed in the presence of a filament of platinum, they form sulphurous acid. This combination takes place only if the platinum is present; nevertheless the newly formed acid contains no trace of platinum, and the platinum itself is apparently unaffected; has remained inert, neutral, and unchanged. The mind of the poet is the shred of platinum. It may partly or exclusively operate upon the experience of the man himself; but, the more perfect the artist, the more completely separate in him will be the man who suffers and the mind which creates;

the more perfectly will the mind digest and transmute the passions which are its material.

The experience, you will notice, the elements which enter the presence of the transforming catalyst, are of two kinds: emotions and feelings. The effect of a work of art upon the person who enjoys it is an experience different in kind from any experience not of art. It may be formed out of one emotion, or may be a combination of several; and various feelings, inhering for the writer in particular words or phrases or images, may be added to compose the final result. Or great poetry may be made without the direct use of any emotion whatever: composed out of feelings solely. Canto XV of the *Inferno* (Brunetto Latini) is a working up of the emotion evident in the situation; but the effect, though single as that of any work of art, is obtained by considerable complexity of detail. The last quatrain gives an image, a feeling attaching to an image, which "came," which did not develop simply out of what precedes, but which was probably in suspension in the poet's mind until the proper combination arrived for it to add itself to. The poet's mind is in fact a receptacle for seizing and storing up numberless feelings, phrases, images, which remain there until all the particles which can unite to form a new compound are present together.

If you compare several representative passages of the greatest poetry you see how great is the variety of types of combination, and also how completely any semi-ethical criterion of "sublimity" misses the mark. For it is not the "greatness," the intensity, of the emotions, the components, but the intensity of the artistic process, the pressure, so to speak, under which the fusion takes place, that counts. The episode of Paolo and Francesca employs a definite emotion, but the intensity of the poetry is something quite different from whatever intensity in the supposed experience it may give the impression of. It is no more intense, furthermore, than Canto XXVI, the voyage of Ulysses, which has not the direct dependence upon an emotion. Great variety is possible in the process of transmutation of emotion: the murder of Agamemnon, or the agony of Othello, gives an artistic effect apparently closer to a possible original than the scenes from Dante. In the *Agamemnon,* the artistic emotion approximates to the emotion of an actual spectator; in *Othello* to the emotion of the protagonist himself. But the difference between art and the event is always absolute; the combination which is the murder of Agamemnon is probably as complex as that which is the voyage of Ulysses. In either case there has been a fusion of elements. The ode of Keats contains a number of feelings which have nothing particular to do with the nightingale, but which the nightingale, partly, perhaps, because of its attractive name, and partly because of its reputation, served to bring together.

The point of view which I am struggling to attack is perhaps related to the metaphysical theory of the substantial unity of the soul: for my meaning is, that the poet has, not a "personality" to express, but a particular medium, which is only a medium and not a personality, in which impressions and experiences combine in peculiar and unexpected ways. Impressions and experiences which are important for the man may take no place in the poetry, and those which become important in the poetry may play quite a negligible part in the man, the personality.

I will quote a passage which is unfamiliar enough to be regarded with fresh attention in the light—or darkness—of these observations:

> And now methinks I could e'en chide myself
> For doating on her beauty, though her death
> Shall be revenged after no common action.
> Does the silkworm expend her yellow labours
> For thee? For thee does she undo herself?
> Are lordships sold to maintain ladyships
> For the poor benefit of a bewildering minute?
> Why does yon fellow falsify highways,
> And put his life between the judge's lips,
> To refine such a thing—keeps horse and men
> To beat their valours for her? . . .

In this passage (as is evident if it is taken in its context) there is a combination of positive and negative emotions: an intensely strong attraction toward beauty and an equally intense fascination by the ugliness which is contrasted with it and which destroys it. This balance of contrasted emotion is in the dramatic situation to which the speech is pertinent, but that situation alone is inadequate to it. This is, so to speak, the structural emotion, provided by the drama. But the whole effect, the dominant tone, is due to the fact that a number of floating feelings, having an affinity to this emotion by no means superficially evident, have combined with it to give us a new art emotion.

It is not in his personal emotions, the emotions provoked by particular events in his life, that the poet is in any way remarkable or interesting. His particular emotions may be simple, or crude, or flat. The emotion in his poetry will be a very complex thing, but not with the complexity of the emotions of people who have very complex or unusual emotions in life. One error, in fact, of eccentricity in poetry is to seek for new human emotions to express; and in this search for novelty in the wrong place it discovers the perverse. The business of the poet is not to find new emotions, but to use the ordinary ones and, in working them up into poetry, to express feelings which are not in actual emotions at all. And emotions which he has never experienced will serve his turn as well as those familiar to him. Consequently, we must believe that "emotion recollected in tranquillity" is an inexact formula. For it is neither emotion, nor recollection, nor, without distortion of meaning, tranquillity. It is a concentration, and a new thing resulting from the concentration, of a very great number of experiences which to the practical and active person would not seem to be experiences at all; it is a concentration which does not happen consciously or of deliberation. These experiences are not "recollected," and they finally unite in an atmosphere which is "tranquil" only in that it is a passive attending upon the event. Of course this is not quite the whole story. There is a great deal, in the writing of poetry, which must be conscious and deliberate. In fact, the bad poet is usually unconscious where he ought to be conscious, and conscious where he ought to be unconscious. Both errors tend to make him "personal." Poetry is not a turning loose of emotion, but an escape from emotion; it is not the expression of personality, but an escape from personality. But, of course, only those who have personality and emotions know what it means to want to escape from these things.

III

ὁ δὲ νοῦς ἴσως θειότερόν τι καὶ ἀπαθές ἐστιν.[1]

This essay proposes to halt at the frontier of metaphysics or mysticism, and confine itself to such practical conclusions as can be applied by the responsible person interested in poetry. To divert interest from the poet to the poetry is a laudable aim: for it would conduce to a juster estimation of actual poetry, good and bad. There are many people who appreciate the expression of sincere emotion in verse, and there is a smaller number of people who can appreciate technical excellence. But very few know when there is expression of *significant* emotion, emotion which has its life in the poem and not in the history of the poet. The emotion of art is impersonal. And the poet cannot

---

[1] From Aristotle's *On the Soul:* "Possibly the mind is too divine, and is therefore unaffected" (W. S. Hewitt, Trans.).

reach this impersonality without surrendering himself wholly to the work to be done. And he is not likely to know what is to be done unless he lives in what is not merely the present, but the present moment of the past, unless he is conscious, not of what is dead, but of what is already living.

RELIGION AND LITERATURE *
(1936)

WHAT I have to say is largely in support of the following propositions: Literary criticism should be completed by criticism from a definite ethical and theological standpoint. In so far as in any age there is common agreement on ethical and theological matters, so far can literary criticism be substantive. In ages like our own, in which there is no such common agreement, it is the more necessary for Christian readers to scrutinize their reading, especially of works of imagination, with explicit ethical and theological standards. The 'greatness' of literature cannot be determined solely by literary standards; though we must remember that whether it is literature or not can be determined only by literary standards.[1]

We have tacitly assumed, for some centuries past, that there is *no* relation between literature and theology. This is not to deny that literature—I mean, again, primarily works of imagination—has been, is, and probably always will be judged by some moral standards. But moral judgements of literary works are made only according to the moral code accepted by each generation, whether it lives according to that code or not. In any age which accepts some precise Christian theology, the common code may be fairly orthodox: though even in such periods the common code may exalt such concepts as 'honour', 'glory' or 'revenge' to a position quite intolerable to Christianity. The dramatic ethics of the Elizabethan Age offers an interesting study. But when the common code is detached from its theological background, and is consequently more and more merely a matter of habit, it is exposed both to prejudice and to change. At such times morals are open to being altered *by* literature; so that we find in practice that what is 'objectionable' in literature is merely what the present generation is not used to. It is a

* From *Essays Ancient and Modern*, by T. S. Eliot, copyright, 1932, 1936, by Harcourt, Brace & Company, Inc. Used in Canada by permission of Faber & Faber, Ltd., London.

[1] As an example of literary criticism given greater significance by theological interests, I would call attention to Theodor Haecker: *Virgil* (Sheed and Ward).

commonplace that what shocks one generation is accepted quite calmly by the next. This adaptability to change of moral standards is sometimes greeted with satisfaction as an evidence of human perfectibility: whereas it is only evidence of what unsubstantial foundations people's moral judgements have.

I am not concerned here with religious literature but with the application of our religion to the criticism of any literature. It may be as well, however, to distinguish first what I consider to be the three senses in which we can speak of 'religious literature'. The first is that of which we say that it is religious 'literature' in the same way that we speak of 'historical literature' or of 'scientific literature'. I mean that we can treat the Authorized translation of the Bible, or the works of Jeremy Taylor, as literature, in the same way that we treat the historical writing of Clarendon or of Gibbon—our two great English historians—as literature; or Bradley's *Logic,* or Buffon's *Natural History.* All of these writers were men who, incidentally to their religious, or historical, or philosophic purpose, had a gift of language which makes them delightful to read to all those who can enjoy language well written, even if they are unconcerned with the objects which the writers had in view. And I would add that though a scientific, or historical, or theological, or philosophic work which is also 'literature', may become superannuated as anything but literature, yet it is not likely to be 'literature' unless it had its scientific or other value for its own time. While I acknowledge the legitimacy of this enjoyment, I am more acutely aware of its abuse. The persons who enjoy these writings *solely* because of their literary merit are essentially parasites; and we know that parasites, when they become too numerous, are pests. I could easily fulminate for a whole hour against the men of letters who have gone into ecstasies over 'the Bible as literature', the Bible as 'the noblest monument of English prose'. Those who talk of the Bible as a 'monument of English prose' are merely admiring it as a monument over the grave of Christianity. I must try to avoid the by-paths of my discourse: it is enough to suggest that just as the work of Clarendon, or Gibbon, or Buffon, or Bradley would be of inferior literary value if it were insignificant as history, science and philosophy respectively, so the Bible has had a *literary* influence upon English literature *not* because it has been considered as literature, but because it has been considered as the report of the Word of God. And the fact that men of letters now discuss it as 'literature' probably indicates the *end* of its 'literary' influence.

The second kind of relation of religion to literature is that which is found in what is called 'religious' or 'devotional' poetry. Now what is the usual attitude of the lover of poetry—and I mean the person who is a genuine and first-hand enjoyer and appreciator of poetry, not the person who follows the admirations of others—towards this department of poetry? I believe, all that may be implied in his calling it a *department*. He believes, not always explicitly, that when you qualify poetry as 'religious' you are indicating very clear limitations. For the great majority of people who love poetry, *'religious* poetry' is a variety of *minor* poetry: the religious poet is not a poet who is treating the whole subject matter of poetry in a religious spirit, but a poet who is dealing with a confined part of this subject matter: who is leaving out what men consider their major passions, and thereby confessing his ignorance of them. I think that this is the real attitude of most poetry lovers towards such poets as Vaughan, or Southwell, or Crashaw, or George Herbert, or Gerard Hopkins.

But what is more, I am ready to admit that up to a point these critics are right. For there is a kind of poetry, such as most of the work of the authors I have mentioned, which is the product of a special religious awareness, which may exist without the general awareness which we expect of the major poet. In some poets, or in some of their works, this general awareness may have existed; but the preliminary steps which represent it may have been suppressed, and only the end-product presented. Between these, and those in which the religious or devotional genius represents the *special* and limited awareness, it may be very difficult to discriminate. I do not pretend to offer Vaughan, or Southwell, or George Herbert, or Hopkins as major poets: I feel sure that the first three, at least, are poets of this limited awareness. They are not great religious poets in the sense in which Dante, or Corneille, or Racine, even in those of their plays which do not touch upon Christian themes, are great Christian religious poets. Or even in the sense in which Villon and Baudelaire, with all their imperfections and delinquencies, are Christian poets. Since the time of Chaucer, Christian poetry (in the sense in which I shall mean it) has been limited in England almost exclusively to minor poetry.

I repeat that when I am considering Religion and Literature, I speak of these things only to make clear that I am not concerned primarily with Religious Literature. I am concerned with what should be the relation between Religion and all Literature. Therefore the third type of 'religious literature' may be more quickly passed over. I mean the literary works of men who are sincerely desirous of forwarding the cause of religion: that which may come under the heading of Propaganda. I am thinking, of course, of such delightful fiction as Mr. Chesterton's *Man Who Was Thursday,* or his *Father Brown.* No one admires and enjoys these things more than I do; I would only remark that when the same effect is aimed at by zealous persons of less talent than Mr. Chesterton the effect is negative. But my point is that such writings do not enter into any serious consideration of the relation of Religion and Literature: because they are conscious operations in a world in which it is assumed that Religion and Literature are not related. It is a conscious and limited relating. What I want is a literature which should be *un*consciously, rather than deliberately and defiantly, Christian: because the work of Mr. Chesterton has its point from appearing in a world which is definitely not Christian.

I am convinced that we fail to realize how completely, and yet how irrationally, we separate our literary from our religious judgements. If there could be a complete separation, perhaps it might not matter: but the separation is not, and never can be, complete. If we exemplify literature by the novel—for the novel is the form in which literature affects the greatest number—we may remark this gradual secularization of literature during at least the last three hundred years. Bunyan, and to some extent Defoe, had moral purposes: the former is beyond suspicion, the latter may be suspect. But since Defoe the secularization of the novel has been continuous. There have been three chief phases. In the first, the novel took the Faith, in its contemporary version, for granted, and omitted it from its picture of life. Fielding, Dickens and Thackeray belong to this phase. In the second, it doubted, worried about, or contested the Faith. To this phase belong George Eliot, George Meredith and Thomas Hardy. To the third phase, in which we are living, belong nearly all contemporary novelists except Mr. James Joyce. It is the phase of those who have never heard the Christian Faith spoken of as anything but an anachronism.

Now, do people in general hold a definite opinion, that is to say religious or anti-religious; and do they read novels, or poetry for that matter, with a separate compartment of their minds? The common ground between religion and fiction is behaviour. Our religion imposes our ethics, our judgement and criticism of ourselves, and our behaviour toward our fellow men. The fiction that we read affects our behaviour towards our fellow men, affects our patterns of ourselves. When we read of human beings behaving in certain ways, with the approval of the author, who gives his benediction to this behaviour by his attitude toward the result of the behaviour arranged by himself, we can be influenced towards behaving in the same way.[2] When the contemporary novelist is an individual thinking for himself in isolation, he may have something important to offer to those who are able to receive it. He who is alone may speak to the individual. But the majority of novelists are persons drifting in the stream, only a little faster. They have some sensitiveness, but little intellect.

We are expected to be broadminded about literature, to put aside prejudice or conviction, and to look at fiction as fiction and at drama as drama. With what is inaccurately called 'censorship' in this country —with what is much more difficult to cope with than an official censorship, because it represents the opinions of individuals in an irresponsible democracy, I have very little sympathy; partly because it so often suppresses the wrong books, and partly because it is little more effective than Prohibition of Liquor; partly because it is one manifestation of the desire that state control should take the place of decent domestic influence; and wholly because it acts only from custom and habit, not from decided theological and moral principles. Incidentally, it gives people a false sense of security in leading them to believe that books which are *not* suppressed are harmless. Whether there *is* such a thing as a harmless book I am not sure: but there very likely are books so utterly unreadable as to be incapable of injuring anybody. But it is certain that a book is not harmless merely because no one is consciously offended by it. And if we, as readers, keep our religious and moral convictions in one compartment, and take our reading merely for entertainment, or on a higher plane, for aesthetic pleasure, I would point out that the author, whatever his conscious intentions in writing, in practice recognizes no such distinctions. The author of a work of imagination is trying to affect us wholly, as human beings, whether he knows it or not; and we are affected by it, as human beings, whether we intend to be or not. I suppose that everything we eat has some other effect upon us than merely the pleasure of taste and mastication; it affects us during the process of assimilation and digestion; and I believe that exactly the same is true of anything we read.

The fact that what we read does not concern merely something called our *literary taste,* but that it affects directly, though only amongst many other influences, the whole of what we are, is best elicited, I think,

[2] Here and later I am indebted to Montgomery Belgion. *The Human Parrot* (chapter on The Irresponsible Propagandist).

by a conscientious examination of the history of our individual literary education. Consider the adolescent reading of any person with some literary sensibility. Everyone, I believe, who is at all sensible to the seductions of poetry, can remember some moment in youth when he or she was completely carried away by the work of one poet. Very likely he was carried away by several poets, one after the other. The reason for this passing infatuation is not merely that our sensibility to poetry is keener in adolescence than in maturity. What happens is a kind of inundation, of invasion of the undeveloped personality, the empty (swept and garnished) room, by the stronger personality of the poet. The same thing may happen at a later age to persons who have not done much reading. One author takes complete possession of us for a time; then another; and finally they begin to affect each other in our mind. We weigh one against another; we see that each has qualities absent from others, and qualities incompatible with the qualities of others: we begin to be, in fact, critical; and it is our growing critical power which protects us from excessive possession by any one literary personality. The good critic—and we should all try to be critics, and not leave criticism to the fellows who write reviews in the papers—is the man who, to a keen and abiding sensibility, joins wide and increasingly discriminating reading. Wide reading is not valuable as a kind of hoarding, an accumulation of knowledge, or what sometimes is meant by the term 'a well-stocked mind'. It is valuable because in the process of being affected by one powerful personality after another, we cease to be dominated by any one, or by any small number. The very different views of life, cohabiting in our minds, affect each other, and our own personality asserts itself and gives each a place in some arrangement peculiar to ourself.

It is simply not true that works of fiction, prose or verse, that is to say works depicting the actions, thoughts and words and passions of imaginary human beings, *directly* extend our knowledge of life. Direct knowledge of life is knowledge directly in relation to ourselves, it is our knowledge of *how* people behave in general, of *what* they are like in general, in so far as that part of life in which we ourselves have participated gives us material for generalization. Knowledge of life obtained through fiction is only possible by another stage of self-consciousness. That is to say, it can only be a knowledge of other people's knowledge of life, not of life itself. So far as we are taken up with the happenings in any novel in the same way in which we are taken up with what happens under our eyes, we are acquiring at least as much falsehood as truth. But when we are developed enough to say: 'This is the view of life of a person who was a good observer within his limits, Dickens, or Thackeray, or George Eliot, or Balzac; but he looked at it in a different way from me, because he was a different man; he even selected rather different things to look at, or the same things in a different order of importance, because he was a different man; so what I am looking at is the world as seen by a particular mind'—then we are in a position to gain something from reading fiction. We are learning *something* about life from these authors direct, just as we learn something from the reading of history direct; but these authors are only really helping us when we can see, and allow for, their differences from ourselves.

Now what we get, as we gradually grow up and read more and more, and read a greater diversity of authors, is a variety of views of life. But what people commonly assume, I suspect, is that we gain this experience of other men's views of life only by 'improving reading'. This, it is supposed, is a reward we get by applying ourselves to Shakespeare, and Dante, and Goethe, and Emerson, and Carlyle, and dozens of other respectable writers. The rest of our reading for amusement is merely killing time. But I incline to come to the alarming conclusion that it is just the literature that we read for 'amusement', or 'purely for pleasure' that may have the greatest, and least suspected influence upon us. It is the literature which we read with the least effort that can have the easiest and most insidious influence upon us. Hence it is that the influence of popular novelists, and of popular plays of contemporary life, requires to be scrutinized most closely. And it is chiefly *contemporary* literature that the majority of people ever read in this attitude of 'purely for pleasure', of pure passivity.

The relation of what I have been saying to the subject announced for my discourse should now be a little more apparent. Though we may read literature merely for pleasure, of 'entertainment' or of 'aesthetic enjoyment', this reading never affects simply a sort of special sense: it affects us as entire human beings; it affects our moral and religious existence. And I say that while individual modern writers of eminence can be improving, contemporary literature as a whole tends to be degrading. And that even the effect of the better writers, in an age like ours, may be degrading to some readers; for we must remember that what a writer does to people is not necessarily what he intends to do. It may be only what people are capable of having done to them. People exercise an unconscious selection, in being influenced. A writer like

D. H. Lawrence may be in his effect either beneficial or pernicious. I am not even sure that I have not had some pernicious influence myself.

At this point I anticipate a rejoinder from the liberal-minded, from all those who are convinced that if everybody says what he thinks, and does what he likes, things will somehow, by some automatic compensation and adjustment, come right in the end. 'Let everything be tried,' they say, 'and if it is a mistake, then we shall learn by experience.' This argument might have some value, if we were always the same generation upon earth; or if, as we know to be not the case, people ever learned much from the experience of their elders. These liberals are convinced that only by what is called unrestrained individualism, will truth ever emerge. Ideas, views of life, they think, issue distinct from independent heads, and in consequence of their knocking violently against each other, the fittest survive, and truth rises triumphant. Anyone who dissents from this view must be either a mediaevalist, wishful only to set back the clock, or else a fascist, and probably both.

If the mass of contemporary authors were really individualists, every one of them inspired Blakes, each with his separate vision, and if the mass of the contemporary public were really a mass of *individuals* there might be something to be said for this attitude. But this is not, and never has been, and never will be. It is not only that the reading individual to-day (or at any day) is not enough an individual to be able to absorb all the 'views of life' of all the authors pressed upon us by the publishers' advertisements and reviewers, and to be able to arrive at wisdom by considering one against another. It is that the contemporary authors are not individuals enough either. It is not that the world of separate individuals of the liberal democrat is undesirable; it is simply that this world does not exist. For the reader of contemporary literature is not, like the reader of the established great literature of all time, exposing himself to the influence of divers and contradictory personalities; he is exposing himself to a mass movement of writers who, each of them, think that they have something individually to offer, but are really all working together in the same direction. And there never was a time, I believe, when the reading public was so large, or so helplessly exposed to the influences of its own time. There never was a time, I believe, when those who read at all, read so many more books by living authors than books by dead authors; there never was a time so completely parochial, so shut off from the past. There may be too many publishers; there are certainly too many books published; and the journals ever incite the reader to 'keep up' with what is being published. Individualistic democracy has come to high tide: and it is more difficult to-day to be an individual than it ever was before.

Within itself, modern literature has perfectly valid distinctions of good and bad, better and worse: and I do not wish to suggest that I confound Mr. Bernard Shaw with Mr. Noel Coward, Mrs. Woolf with Miss Mannin. On the other hand, I should like it to be clear that I am not defending a 'high'-brow against a 'low'-brow literature. What I do wish to affirm is that the whole of modern literature is corrupted by what I call Secularism, that it is simply unaware of, simply cannot understand the meaning of, the primacy of the supernatural over the natural life: of something which I assume to be our primary concern.

I do not want to give the impression that I have delivered a mere fretful jeremiad against contemporary literature. Assuming a common attitude between you, or some of you, and myself, the question is not so much, what is to be done about it? as, how should we behave towards it?

I have suggested that the liberal attitude towards literature will not work. Even if the writers who make their attempt to impose their 'view of life' upon us were really distinct individuals, even if we as readers were distinct individuals, what would be the result? It would be, surely, that each reader would be impressed, in his reading, merely by what he was previously prepared to be impressed by; he would follow the 'line of least resistance', and there would be no assurance that he would be made a better man. For literary judgement we need to be acutely aware of two things at once: of 'what we like', and of 'what we *ought* to like'. Few people are honest enough to know either. The first means knowing what we really feel: very few know that. The second involves understanding our shortcomings; for we do not really know what we ought to like unless we also know why we ought to like it, which involves knowing why we don't yet like it. It is not enough to understand what we ought to be, unless we know what we are; and we do not understand what we are, unless we know what we ought to be. The two forms of self-consciousness, knowing what we are and what we ought to be, must go together.

It is our business, as readers of literature, to know what we like. It is our business, as Christians, *as well as* readers of literature, to know what we ought to like. It is our business as honest men not to assume that whatever we like is what we ought to like; and it is our business as honest Christians not to assume that we do like what we ought to like. And the last thing I would wish for would be the existence of two literatures, one for Christian consumption and the other for the pagan world. What I believe to be incumbent upon all Christians is the duty of maintaining consciously certain standards and criteria of criticism over and above those applied by the rest of the world; and that by these criteria and standards everything that we read must be tested. We must remember that the greater part of our current reading matter is written for us by people who have no real belief in a supernatural order, though some of it may be written by people with individual notions of a supernatural order which are not ours. And the greater part of our reading matter is coming to be written by people who not only have no such belief, but are even ignorant of the fact that there are still people in the world so 'backward' or so 'eccentric' as to continue to believe. So long as we are conscious of the gulf fixed between ourselves and the greater part of contemporary literature, we are more or less protected from being harmed by it, and are in a position to extract from it what good it has to offer us.

There are a very large number of people in the world to-day who believe that all ills are fundamentally economic. Some believe that various specific economic changes alone would be enough to set the world right; others demand more or less drastic changes in the social as well, changes chiefly of two opposed types. These changes demanded, and in some places carried out, are alike in one respect, that they hold the assumptions of what I call Secularism: they concern themselves only with changes of a temporal, material, and external nature; they concern themselves with morals only of a collective nature. In an exposition of one such new faith I read the following words:

'In our morality the one single test of any moral question is whether it impedes or destroys in any way the power of the individual to serve the State. (The individual) must answer the questions: "Does this action injure the nation? Does it injure other members of the nation? Does it injure my ability to serve the nation?" And if the answer is clear on all those questions, the individual has absolute liberty to do as he will.'

Now I do not deny that this is a kind of morality, and that it is capable of great good within limits; but I think that we should all repudiate a morality which had no higher ideal to set before us than that. It represents, of course, one of the violent reactions we are witnessing, against the view that the community is solely for the benefit of the individual; but it is equally a gospel of this world, and of this world alone. My complaint against modern literature is of the same kind. It is not that modern literature is in the ordinary sense 'immoral' or even 'amoral'; and in any case to prefer that charge would not be enough. It is simply that it repudiates, or is wholly ignorant of, our most fundamental and important beliefs; and that in consequence its tendency is to encourage its readers to get what they can out of life while it lasts, to miss no 'experience' that presents itself, and to sacrifice themselves, if they make any sacrifice at all, only for the sake of tangible benefits to others in this world either now or in the future. We shall certainly continue to read the best of its kind, of what our time provides; but we must tirelessly criticize it according to our own principles, and not merely according to the principles admitted by the writers and by the critics who discuss it in the public press.

IVOR ARMSTRONG RICHARDS

(1893-   )

IVOR ARMSTRONG RICHARDS was born in Sandbach, Cheshire, in 1893. He was educated at Clifton College and at Magdalene College, Cambridge, where he graduated in 1915. In 1921 he published, in collaboration with C. K. Ogden and J. Wood, *The Foundations of Aesthetics*. From 1922 to 1929 he taught literature and moral philosophy at Magdalene. During this time were published the works which established him as an important new force in criticism: *The Meaning of Meaning*, in collaboration with C. K. Ogden in 1923, *Principles of Literary Criticism*, 1924, *Science and Poetry*, 1925, and *Practical Criticism*, 1929. In 1926 he married Dorothy Eleanor Pilley, a writer. He taught abroad (at the Tsing Hua University) in Peiping in 1929–30 and at Harvard in 1931. *Mencius on the Mind* and *Experiments in Multiple Definition* appeared in 1931, *Basic Rules of Reason* in 1933, *Coleridge on Imagination* in 1934, *The Philosophy of Rhetoric* in 1936, *Interpretation and Teaching* in 1938, *How to Read a Page* in 1942, *Plato's Republic: a New Version Founded on Basic English* in 1942, and *The Wrath of Achilles* in 1950. Since returning to the Harvard staff in 1939, Mr. Richards has been much interested in propagation of his simplified version of English, known as Basic English, in the Western Hemisphere.

With the work of Richards, literary criticism adds a new but long predictable quality. The urge toward a scientific explanation of the arts, as old as Aristotle, and recognizable in modern form in certain passages of Wordsworth and Goethe and in the epistemological emphasis that unites Kant and Coleridge, naturally comes of age with the maturing of psychology as a science. Neurology accordingly supersedes metaphysics as the milieu of critical activity, and one may look forward confidently to typically scientific advances: "the knowledge which the men of A.D. 3000 will possess, if all goes well, may make all our aesthetics, all our psychology, all our modern theory of value, look pitiful." [Preface to *Practical Criticism*.]

Viewing criticism as a scientific psychologist, Richards sweeps aside, with a superiority equaling Croce's, the ancient terms of classical dispute, the nomenclatures and the types. Each poem is a thing of its own kind, answerable to no law but the requirement that it prove valuable as a record of experience. Not to ethics, or to the varied species of philosophical truth, nor to the illusory concept of the beautiful, does it owe allegiance. It has a duty to perform which, alas, we are not yet able to tell by laboratory means when it performs; but if we be persons of sensibility, if we possess the three requisites of the good critic, adeptness at experiencing "the state of mind relative to the work," ability to "distinguish experiences from one another as regards their less superficial features," and a sound judgment of values [*Principles of Literary Criticism*, p. 114], then we may know. The first two of these requisites are admirable indices of Mr. Richards' concern with the problems of artistic communication and receptivity; the third one is the subject for his justification of poetry.

The extensive study of semantics at the present time stems in large measure from the Ogden and Richards work, *The Meaning of Meaning* (1923), which established the terminology of the new science: referent, reference, symbol, complex reference, attitudes, the logical form of the symbol, the context theory of interpretation. The triangle introduced to illustrate the relations of the first three of these, and the distinctions emphasized between thing and word, or referent and symbol, in communication, have had very important expansions in contemporary theories of pedagogy and particularly of reading. A different concept of the correspondence of language to thought has developed. "The plasticity of speech material under symbolic conditions is less than the plasticity of human attitudes, ends and endeavors, *i.e.,* of the affective-volitional system; and therefore the same modifications in language are required for quite different reasons and may be due to quite different causes. Hence the importance of considering the sentence in the paragraph, the paragraph in the chapter, and the chapter in the volume, if our interpretations are not to be misleading, and our analysis arbitrary" [p. 226]. And again: "What is required is not only strictness of definition and rigidity of expression, but also plasticity, ease and freedom in rapid expansion when expansion is necessary. . . . A new Science, the Science of Symbolism, is now ready to emerge, and with it will come a new educational technique" [p. 242].

In the new science a distinction is repeatedly emphasized between scientifically exact symbols and emotive or evocative symbols and between the purposes of the two in communication. In *Principles of Literary Criticism* (Chapter XVI) the operation of emotive symbols is presented and explained by diagram (the analysis of "Westminster Bridge" in Section 2 of *Science and Poetry* is similar), from the incipient "visual sensations" through tied and free imagery and references ("thinkings of" various things) to the reader's emotions and attitudes, it being "the attitudes evoked which are the all-important part of any experience. Upon the texture and form of the attitudes involved its value depends" [p. 132]. In the evoking of these attitudes the importance of "reference"—that is to say, of plain prose sense is not to be overlooked, as some contemporary critics might do. The examination of readers' reactions in *Practical Criticism* establishes Richards' contention that an understanding of the intellectual content of verse is essential to fullness of experience. But "in poetry," as we are told in the second section of *Science and Poetry*, "it matters only *as a means;* it directs and excites" the interests which make up our attitudes.

Science and Poetry is devoted more particularly to the exposition of poetic values. Richards' relationship to Matthew Arnold cannot be escaped. The quotation from *The Study of Poetry* which he takes as a starting text shows that the two men accept similar data and look in the same direction for solutions. But when we read that "our thoughts are the servants of our interests" and that "People who are always winning victories over themselves might equally well be described as always enslaving themselves," we realize that "the study of perfection" as an end and "sweetness and light" as a guide for culture are of another temperament and time.

This absence of universals is the ground upon which Richards' rival contemporaries, Eliot and Ransom, most clearly delineate their differences with him. The latter's examination of "The Psychological Critic" in *The New Criticism* finds "the emotive and conative phases of poetic experience" insufficient for "the valid world view" or "realistic ontology" which poetry, as a means to knowledge, ought to give us. Eliot, with admiration for the psychological and linguistic equipment of "the scientific critic," states in *The Use of Poetry and the Use of Criticism,* "His ethics, or theory of value, is one which I cannot accept; or rather, I cannot accept any such theory which is erected upon purely individual-psychological foundations [p. 7]. . . . I only assert again that what he is trying to do is essentially the same as what Arnold wanted to do: to preserve emotions without the beliefs with which their history has been involved. It would seem that Mr. Richards, on his own showing, is engaged in a rear-guard religious action" [p. 127].

SCIENCE AND POETRY *

(1926)

The future of poetry is immense, because in poetry, where it is worthy of its high destinies, our race, as time goes on, will find an ever surer and surer stay. There is not a creed which is not shaken, not an accredited dogma which is not shown to be questionable, not a received tradition which does not threaten to dissolve. Our religion has materialised itself in the fact, in the supposed fact; it has attached its emotion to the fact, and now the fact is failing it. But for poetry the idea is everything.— MATTHEW ARNOLD

CHAPTER I

THE GENERAL SITUATION

MAN's prospects are not at present so rosy that he can neglect any means of improving them. He has recently made a number of changes in his customs and ways of life, partly with intention, partly by accident. These changes are involving such widespread further changes that the fairly near future is likely to see an almost complete reorganization of our lives, in their intimate aspects as much as in their public. Man himself is changing, together with his circumstances; he has changed in

* *Science and Poetry* by I. A. Richards. Company, Inc. Reprinted by permission Copyright 1926 by W. W. Norton and of the publisher.

the past, it is true, but never perhaps so swiftly. His circumstances are not known ever to have changed so much or so suddenly before, with psychological as well as with economic, social and political dangers. This suddenness threatens us. Some parts of human nature resist change more than others. We risk disaster if some of our customs change while others which should change with them stay as they are.

Habits that have endured for many thousands of years are not easy to throw off—least of all when they are habits of thought, and when they do not come into open conflict with changing circumstances, or do not clearly involve us in loss or inconvenience. Yet the loss may be great without our knowing anything about it. Before 1590 no one knew how inconvenient were our natural habits of thought about the ways in which a stone may fall; yet the modern world began when Galileo discovered what really happens. Before 1800 only persons thought to be crazy knew that ordinary traditional ideas as to cleanliness are dangerously inadequate. The infant's average 'expectation of life' has increased by about 30 years since Lister upset them. Nobody before Sir Ronald Ross knew what were the consequences of thinking about malaria in terms of influences and miasmas instead of in terms of mosquitoes. The Roman Empire might perhaps have still been flourishing if someone had found this out before A.D. 100.

With such examples all about us we can no longer, in any department of life, so easily accept what was good enough for our fathers as good enough for ourselves or for our children. We are forced to wonder whether our ideas, even upon subjects apparently of little practical importance, such as poetry, may not be dangerously inadequate. It becomes indeed somewhat alarming to recognize, as we must, that our habits of thought remain, as regards most of our affairs, much as they were 5,000 years ago. The Sciences are, of course, simply the exceptions to this rule. Outside the Sciences—and the greater part of our thinking still goes on outside the Sciences—we think very much as our ancestors thought a hundred or two hundred generations ago. Certainly this is so as regards official views about poetry. Is it not possible that these are wrong, as wrong as most ideas of an equally hoary antiquity? Is it not possible that to the men of the future our life to-day will seem a continual, ceaseless disaster due only to our own stupidity, to the nervelessness with which we accept and transmit ideas which do not apply and never have applied to anything?

The average educated man is growing more conscious, an extraordinarily significant change. It is probably due to the fact that his life is becoming more complex, more intricate, his desires and needs more varied and more apt to conflict. And as he becomes more conscious he can no longer be content to drift in unreflecting obedience to custom. He is forced to reflect. And if reflection often takes the form of inconclusive worrying, that is no more than might be expected in view of the unparalleled difficulty of the task. To live reasonably is much more difficult today than it was in Dr. Johnson's time, and even then, as Boswell shows, it was difficult enough.

To live reasonably is not to live by reason alone—the mistake is easy, and, if carried far, disastrous—but to live in a way of which reason, a clear full sense of the whole situation, would approve. And the most important part of the whole situation, as always, is ourselves, our own psychological make-up. The more we learn about the physical world, about our bodies, for example, the more points we find at which our ordinary behaviour is out of accord with the facts, inapplicable, wasteful, disadvantageous, dangerous or absurd. Witness our habit of boiling our vegetables. We have still to learn how to feed ourselves satisfactorily. Similarly, the little that is yet known about the mind already shows that our ways of thinking and feeling about very many of the things with which we concern ourselves are out of accord with the facts. This is pre-eminently true of our ways of thinking and feeling about poetry. We think and talk in terms of states of affairs which have never existed. We attribute to ourselves and to things, powers which neither we nor they possess. And equally we overlook or misuse powers which are all-important to us.

Day by day, in recent years, man is getting more out of place in Nature. Where he is going to he does not yet know, he has not yet decided. As a consequence he finds life more and more bewildering, more and more difficult to live coherently. Thus he turns to consider himself, his own nature. For the first step towards a reasonable way of life is a better understanding of human nature.

It has long been recognized that if only something could be done in psychology remotely comparable to what has been achieved in physics, practical consequences might be expected even more remarkable than any that the engineer can contrive. The first positive steps in the science of the mind have been slow in coming, but already they are beginning to change man's whole outlook.

CHAPTER II

THE POETIC EXPERIENCE

EXTRAORDINARY claims have often been made for poetry—Matthew Arnold's words quoted at the head of this essay are an example—claims which very many people are inclined to view with astonishment or with the smile which tolerance gives to the enthusiast. Indeed a more representative modern view would be that the future of poetry is *nil*. Peacock's conclusion in his *The Four Ages of Poetry* finds a more general acceptance. "A poet in our times is a semi-barbarian in a civilized community. He lives in the days that are past. . . . In whatever degree poetry is cultivated, it must necessarily be to the neglect of some branch of useful study: and it is a lamentable thing to see minds, capable of better things, running to seed in the specious indolence of these empty aimless mockeries of intellectual exertion. Poetry was the mental rattle that awakened the attention of intellect in the infancy of civil society: but for the maturity of mind to make a serious business of the playthings of its childhood, is as absurd as for a grown man to rub his gums with coral, and cry to be charmed asleep by the jingle of silver bells." And with more regret many others—Keats was among them —have thought that the inevitable effect of the advance of science would be to destroy the possibility of poetry.

What is the truth in this matter? How is our estimate of poetry going to be affected by science? And how will poetry itself be influenced? The extreme importance which has in the past been assigned to poetry is a fact which must be accounted for whether we conclude that it was rightly assigned or not, and whether we consider that poetry will continue to be held in such esteem or not. It indicates that the case for poetry, whether right or wrong, is one which turns on momentous issues. We shall not have dealt adequately with it unless we have raised questions of great significance.

Very much toil has gone to the endeavour to explain the high place of poetry in human affairs, with, on the whole, few satisfactory or convincing results. This is not surprising. For in order to show how poetry is important it is first necessary to discover to some extent what it is. Until recently this preliminary task could only be very incompletely carried out; the psychology of instinct and emotion was too little advanced; and, moreover, the wild speculations natural in prescientific enquiry definitely stood in the way. Neither the professional psychologist, whose interest in poetry is frequently not intense, nor the man of letters, who as a rule has no adequate ideas of the mind as a whole, has been equipped for the investigation. Both a passionate knowledge of poetry and a capacity for dispassionate psychological analysis are required if it is to be satisfactorily prosecuted.

It will be best to begin by asking 'What *kind of a thing,* in the widest sense, is poetry?' When we have answered this we shall be ready to ask 'How can we use and misuse it?' and 'What reasons are there for thinking it valuable?'

Let us take an experience, ten minutes of a person's life, and describe it in broad outline. It is now possible to indicate its general structure, to point out what is important in it, what trivial and accessory, which features depend upon which, how it has arisen, and how it is probably going to influence his future experience. There are, of course, wide gaps in this description, none the less it *is* at last possible to understand in general how the mind works in an experience, and what sort of stream of events the experience is.

A poem, let us say Wordsworth's *Westminster Bridge* sonnet, is such an experience, it is the experience the right kind of reader has when he peruses the verses. And the first step to an understanding of the place and future of poetry in human affairs is to see what the general structure of such an experience is. Let us begin by reading it very slowly, preferably aloud, giving every syllable time to make its full effect upon us. And let us read it experimentally, repeating it, varying our tone of voice until we are satisfied that we have caught its rhythm as well as we are able, and—whether our reading is such as to please other people or not—we ourselves at least are certain how it should 'go.'

> Earth has not anything to show more fair:
> Dull would he be of soul who could pass by
> A sight so touching in its majesty:
> This City now doth like a garment wear
> The beauty of the morning: silent, bare,
> Ships, towers, domes, theatres and temples lie
> Open to the fields, and to the sky;
> All bright and glittering in the smokeless air.
> Never did sun more beautifully steep
> In his first splendour valley, rock or hill;
> Ne'er saw I, never felt, a calm so deep!
> The river glideth at its own sweet will:
> Dear God! the very houses seem asleep
> And all that mighty heart is lying still!

We may best make our analysis of the experience that arises through reading these lines from the surface inwards, to speak metaphorically. The surface is the impression of the printed words on the retina. This sets up an agitation which we must follow as it goes deeper and deeper.

The first things to occur (if they do not, the rest of the experience will be gravely inadequate) are the sound of the words 'in the mind's ear' and the feel of the words imaginarily spoken.[1] These together give the *full body,* as it were, to the words, and it is with the full bodies of words that the poet works, not with their printed signs. But many people lose nearly everything in poetry through these indispensable parts escaping them.

Next arise various pictures 'in the mind's eye'; not of words but of things for which the words stand; perhaps of ships, perhaps of hills; and together with them, it may be, other images of various sorts. Images of what it feels like to stand leaning on the parapet of Westminster Bridge. Perhaps that odd thing an image of 'silence.' But, unlike the image-bodies of the words themselves, those other images of things are not vitally important. Those who have them may very well think them indispensable, and *for them* they may be necessary; but other people may not require them at all. This is a point at which differences between individual minds are very marked

Thence onwards the agitation which is the experience divides into a major and a minor branch, though the two streams have innumerable interconnections and influence one another intimately. Indeed it is only as an expositor's artifice that we may speak of them as two streams.

The minor branch we may call the intellectual stream; the other, which we may call the active, or emotional, stream, is made up of the play of our interests.

The intellectual stream is fairly easy to follow; it follows itself, so to speak; but it is the less important of the two. In poetry it matters only *as a means;* it directs and excites the active stream. It is made up of thoughts, which are not static little entities that bob up into consciousness and down again out of it, but fluent happenings, events, which reflect or point to the things the thoughts are of. Exactly how they do this is a matter which is still much disputed.

This pointing to or reflecting things is all that thoughts do. They appear to do much more; which is our chief illusion. The realm of

[1] The view of the mind-body problem assumed here is defended and maintained with references to the contemporary authorities who hold it, in *The Meaning of Psychology* by C. K. Ogden, Chapter II. (London, Kegan Paul; New York, Harpers; 1926.)

thought is never a sovereign state. Our thoughts are the servants of our interests, and even when they seem to rebel it is usually our interests that are in disorder. Our thoughts are pointers and it is the other, the active, stream which deals with the things which thoughts reflect or point to.

Some people who read verse (they do not often read much of it) are so constituted that very little more happens than this intellectual stream of thoughts. It is perhaps superfluous to point out that they miss the real poem. To exaggerate this part of the experience, and give it too much importance on its own account, is a notable current tendency, and for many people explains why they do not read poetry.

The active branch is what really matters; for from it all the energy of the whole agitation comes. The thinking which goes on is somewhat like the play of an ingenious and invaluable 'governor' run by, but controlling, the main machine. Every experience is essentially some interest or group of interests swinging back to rest.

To understand what an interest is we should picture the mind as a system of very delicately poised balances, a system which so long as we are in health is constantly growing. Every situation we come into disturbs some of these balances to some degree. The ways in which they swing back to a new equipoise are the impulses with which we respond to the situation. And the chief balances in the system are our chief interests.

Suppose that we carry a magnetic compass about in the neighbourhood of powerful magnets. The needle waggles as we move and comes to rest pointing in a new direction whenever we stand still in a new position. Suppose that instead of a single compass we carry an arrangement of many magnetic needles, large and small, swung so that they influence one another, some able only to swing horizontally, others vertically, others hung freely. As we move, the perturbations in this system will be very complicated. But for every position in which we place it there will be a final position of rest for all the needles into which they will in the end settle down, a general poise for the whole system. But even a slight displacement may set the whole assemblage of needles busily readjusting themselves.

One further complication. Suppose that while all the needles influence one another, some of them respond only to some of the outer magnets among which the system is moving. The reader can easily draw a diagram if his imagination needs a visual support.

The mind is not unlike such a system if we imagine it to be incredibly complex. The needles are our interests, varying in their importance, that is in the degree to which any movement they make involves movement in the other needles. Each new disequilibrium, which a shift of position, a fresh situation, entails, corresponds to a need; and the wagglings which ensue as the system rearranges itself are our responses, the impulses through which we seek to meet the need. Often the new poise is not found until long after the original disturbance. Thus states of strain can arise which last for years.

The child comes into the world as a comparatively simple arrangement. Few things affect him comparatively speaking, and his responses also are few and simple, but he very quickly becomes more complicated. His recurrent needs for food and for various attentions are constantly setting all his needles swinging. Little by little separate needs become departmentalized as it were, sub-systems are formed; hunger causes one set of responses, the sight of his toys another, loud noises yet another, and so on. But the sub-systems never become quite independent. So he grows up, becoming susceptible to ever more numerous and more delicate influences.

He grows more discriminating in some respects, he is thrown out of equilibrium by slighter differences in his situation. In other respects he becomes more stable. From time to time, through growth, fresh interests develop; sex is the outstanding example. His needs increase, he becomes capable of being upset by quite new causes, he becomes responsive to quite new aspects of the situation.

This development takes a very indirect course. It would be still more erratic if society did not mould and remould him at every stage, reorganising him incompletely two or three times over before he grows up. He reaches maturity in the form of a vast assemblage of major and minor interests, partly a chaos, partly a system, with some tracts of his personality fully developed and free to respond, others tangled and jammed in all kinds of accidental ways. It is this incredibly complex assemblage of interests to which the printed poem has to appeal. Sometimes the poem is itself the influence which disturbs us, sometimes it is merely the means by which an already existing disturbance can right itself. More usually perhaps it is both at once.

We must picture then the stream of the poetic experience as the swinging back into equilibrium of these disturbed interests. We are reading the poem in the first place only because we are in some way interested in doing so, only because some interest is attempting to regain its poise thereby. And whatever happens as we read happens only for a similar reason. We understand the words (the intellectual branch of the stream goes on its way successfully) only because an interest is reacting through that means, and all the rest of the experience is equally but more evidently our adaptation working itself out.

The rest of the experience is made up of emotions and attitudes. Emotions are what the reaction, with its reverberations in bodily changes, feels like. Attitudes are the impulses towards one kind of behaviour or another which are set ready by the response. They are, as it were, its outward going part.[2] Sometimes, as here in *Westminster Bridge,* they are very easily overlooked. But consider a simpler case—a fit of laughter which it is absolutely essential to conceal, in Church or during a solemn interview, for example. You contrive not to laugh; but there is no doubt about the activity of the impulses in their restricted form. The much more subtle and elaborate impulses which a poem excites are not different in principle. They do not show themselves as a rule, they do not come out into the open, largely because they are so complex. When they have adjusted themselves to one another and become organized into a coherent whole, the needs concerned may be satisfied. *In a fully developed man a state of readiness for action will take the place of action when the full appropriate situation for action is not present.* The essential peculiarity of poetry as of all the arts is that the full appropriate situation is *not* present. It is an *actor* we are seeing upon the stage, not Hamlet. So readiness for action takes the place of actual behaviour.

This is the main plan then of the experience. Signs on the retina, taken up by sets of needs (remember how many other impressions all day long remain entirely *unnoticed* because no interest responds to them); thence an elaborate agitation of impulses, one branch of which is *thoughts* of what the words mean, the other an emotional response leading to the development of *attitudes,* preparations, that is, for action which may or may not take place; the two branches being in intimate connection.

We must look now a little more closely at these connections. It may seem odd that we do not more definitely make the thoughts the rulers and causes of the rest of the response. To do just this has been in fact the grand error of traditional psychology. Man prefers to stress the features which distinguish him from monkey, and chief among these are his intellectual capacities. Important though they are, he has given them a rank to which they are not entitled. Intellect is an adjunct to the

---

[2] For a further discussion of attitudes see the author's *Principles of Literary Criticism,* Chapter XV (International Library of Psychology).

interests, a means by which they adjust themselves more successfully. Man is not in any sense primarily an intelligence; he is a system of interests. Intelligence helps man but does not run him.

Partly through this natural mistake, and partly because intellectual operations are so much easier to study, the whole traditional analysis of the working of the mind has been turned upside down. It is largely as a remedy from the difficulties which this mistake involves that poetry may have so much importance in the future. But let us look again more closely at the poetic experience.

In the first place, why is it essential in reading poetry to give the words their full imagined sound and body? What is meant by saying that the poet works with this sound and body? The answer is that even before the words have been intellectually understood and the thoughts they occasion formed and followed, the movement and sound of the words is playing deeply and intimately upon the interests. How this happens is a matter which has yet to be successfully investigated, but that it happens no sensitive reader of poetry doubts. A good deal of poetry and even some great poetry exists (*e.g.,* some of Shakespeare's Songs and, in a different way, much of the best of Swinburne) in which the sense of the words can be *almost* entirely missed or neglected without loss. Never perhaps entirely without effort, however; though sometimes with advantage. But the plain fact that the relative importance of grasping the sense of the words may vary (compare Browning's *Before* with his *After*) is enough for our purpose here.

In nearly all poetry the sound and feel of the words, what is often called the *form* of the poem in opposition to its *content,* get to work first, and the sense in which the words are taken is subtly influenced by this fact. Most words are ambiguous as regards their plain sense, especially in poetry. We can take them as we please in a variety of senses. The sense we are pleased to choose is the one which most suits the impulses already stirred through the form of the verse. The same thing can be noticed in conversation. Not the strict logical sense of what is said, but the tone of voice and the occasion are the primary factors by which we interpret. Science, it is worth noting, endeavours with increasing success to bar out these factors. We believe a scientist because he can substantiate his remarks, not because he is eloquent or forcible in his enunciation. In fact, we distrust him when he seems to be influencing us by his manner.

In its use of words poetry is just the reverse of science. Very definite thoughts do occur, but not because the words are so chosen as logically to bar out all possibilities but one. No. But because the manner, the tone of voice, the cadence and the rhythm play upon our interests and make *them* pick out from among an indefinite number of possibilities the precise particular thought which they need. This is why poetical descriptions often seem so much more accurate than prose descriptions. Language logically and scientifically used cannot describe a landscape or a face. To do so it would need a prodigious apparatus of names for shades and nuances, for precise particular qualities. These names do not exist, so other means have to be used. The poet, even when, like Ruskin or De Quincey, he writes in prose, makes the reader pick out the precise particular sense required from an indefinite number of possible senses which a word, phrase or sentence may carry. The means by which he does this are many and varied. Some of them have been mentioned above, but the way in which he uses them is the poet's own secret, something which cannot be taught. He knows how to do it, but he does not himself know how it is done.

Misunderstanding and under-estimation of poetry is mainly due to over-estimation of the thought in it. We can see still more clearly that thought is not the prime factor if we consider for a moment not the experience of the reader but that of the poet. Why does the poet use these words and no others? Not because they stand for a series of thoughts which in themselves are what he is concerned to communicate. It is never what a poem *says* which matters, but what it *is*. The poet is not writing as a scientist. He uses these words because the interests which the situation calls into play combine to bring them, just in this form, into his consciousness *as a means of ordering, controlling and consolidating* the whole experience. The experience itself, the tide of impulses sweeping through the mind, is the source and the sanction of the words. They represent this experience itself, not any set of perceptions or reflections, though often to a reader who approaches the poem wrongly they will seem to be only a series of remarks about other things. But to a suitable reader the words—if they actually spring from experience and are not due to verbal habits, to the desire to be effective, to factitious excogitation, to imitation, to irrelevant contrivances, or to any other of the failings which prevent most people from writing poetry—the words will reproduce in his mind a similar play of interests putting him for the while into a similar situation and leading to the same response.

Why this should happen is still somewhat of a mystery. An extraordinarily intricate concourse of impulses brings the words together. Then in another mind the affair in part reverses itself, the words bring into being a similar concourse of impulses. The words which seem to be the effect of the experience in the first instance, seem to become the cause of a similar experience in the second. A very odd thing to happen, not exactly paralleled outside communication. But this description is not quite accurate. The words, as we have seen, are not simply the effect in one case, nor the cause in the other. In both cases they are the part of the experience which binds it together, which gives it a definite structure and keeps it from being a mere welter of disconnected impulses. They are *the key,* to borrow a useful metaphor from Mc-Dougall, for this particular combination of impulses. So regarded, it is less strange that what the poet wrote should reproduce his experience in the mind of the reader.

CHAPTER III

WHAT IS VALUABLE?

ENOUGH perhaps as to the kind of thing a poem is, as to the general structure of these experiences. Let us now turn to the further questions 'Of what use is it?' 'Why and how is it valuable?'

The first point to be made is that poetic experiences are valuable (when they are) in the same ways as any other experiences. They are to be judged by the same standards. What are these?

Extraordinarily diverse views have been held upon this point. Very naturally, since such very different ideas have been entertained as to what kind of thing an experience is. For our opinions as to the differences between good and bad experiences depend inevitably upon what we take an experience to be. As fashions have changed in psychology men's ethical theories have followed suit. When a created, simple and eternal soul was the pivotal point, Good was conformity with the will of the creator, Evil was rebellion. When the associationist psychologists substituted a swarm of sensations and images for the soul, Good became pleasure and Evil became pain, and so on. A long chapter of the history of opinions has still to be written tracing these changes. Now that the mind is seen to be a hierarchy of interests, what will for this account be the difference between Good and Evil?

It is the difference between free and wasteful organization, between fullness and narrowness of life. For if the mind is a system of interests, and if an experience is their play, the worth of any experience is a matter of the degree to which the mind, through this experience, attains a complete equilibrium.

This is a first approximation. It needs qualifying and expanding if it is to become a satisfactory theory. Let us see how some of these amendments would run.

Consider an hour of any person's life. It holds out innumerable possibilities. Which of these are realized depends upon two main groups of factors:—the external situation in which he is living, his surroundings, including the other people with whom he is in contact; and, secondly, his psychological make-up. The first of these, the external situation, is sometimes given too much importance. We have only to notice what very different experiences different people undergo when in closely similar situations to recognize this fact. A situation which is dullness itself for one may be full of excitement for another. What an individual responds to is not the whole situation but a selection from it, and as a rule few people make the same selection. What is selected is decided by the organization of the individual's interests.

Now let us simplify the case by supposing that nothing which happens during this hour is going to have any further consequences either in our hypothetical person's life or in anyone else's. He is going to cease to exist when the clock strikes—but for our purposes he must be imagined not to know this—and no one is to be a whit better or worse whatever he thinks, feels or does during the hour. What shall we say it would be best for him, if he could, to do?

We need not bother to imagine the detail of the external situation or the character of the man. We can answer our question in general terms without doing so. The man has a certain definite instinctive make-up—the result of his past history, including his heredity. There will be many things which he cannot do which another man could, and many things which he cannot do in this situation, whatever it is, which he could do in other situations. But given this particular man in this particular situation, our question is, which of the possibilities open to him would be better than which others? How would we as friendly observers like to see him living?

Setting pain aside, we may perhaps agree that torpor would be the worst choice. Complete inertness, lifelessness, would be the sorriest spectacle—anticipating too nearly and unnecessarily what is to happen when the hour strikes. We can then perhaps agree, though here more resistance from preconceived ideas may be encountered, that the best choice would be the opposite of torpor, that is to say, the fullest, keenest, most active and completest kind of life.

Such a life is one which brings into play as many as possible of the *positive* interests. We can leave out the negative interests. It would be a pity for our friend to be frightened or disgusted even for a minute of his precious hour.

But this is not all. It is not enough that many interests should be stirred. There is a more important point to be noted.

> The Gods approve
> The depth and not the tumult of the soul.

The interests must come into play and remain in play with as little conflict among themselves as possible. In other words, the experience must be organized so as to give all the impulses of which it is composed the greatest possible degree of freedom.[3]

It is in this respect that people differ most from one another. It is this which separates the good life from the bad. Far more life is wasted through muddled mental organization than through lack of opportunity. Conflicts between different impulses are the greatest evils which afflict mankind.

The best life then which we can wish for our friend will be one in which as much as possible of himself is engaged (as many of his impulses as possible). And this with as little conflict, as little mutual interference between different sub-systems of his activities as there can be. The more he lives and the less he thwarts himself, the better. That briefly is our answer as psychologists, as outside observers abstractly describing the state of affairs. And if it is asked, what does such life feel like, how is it to live through? the answer is that it feels like and is the experience of poetry.

There are two ways in which conflict can be avoided or overcome. By conquest and by conciliation. One or other of the contesting impulses can be suppressed, or they can come to a mutual arrangement, they can adjust themselves to one another. We owe to psycho-analysis—at present still a rather undisciplined branch of psychology—a great deal of striking evidence as to the extreme difficulty of suppressing any vigorous impulse. When it seems to be suppressed it is often found to be really as active as ever, but in some other form, generally a troublesome one.

[3] See *The Foundations of Aesthetics,* by C. K. Ogden, James Wood and the author, pp. 74 ff. for a description of such experience.

Persistent mental imbalances are the source of nearly all our troubles. For this reason, as well as for the simpler reason that suppression is wasteful of life, conciliation is always to be preferred to conquest. People who are always winning victories over themselves might equally well be described as always enslaving themselves. Their lives become unnecessarily narrow. The minds of many saints have been like wells; they should have been like lakes or like the sea.

Unfortunately, most of us, left to ourselves, have no option but to go in for extensive attempts at self-conquest. It is our only means of escape from chaos. Our impulses must have some order, some organisation, or we do not live ten minutes without disaster. In the past, Tradition, a kind of Treaty of Versailles assigning frontiers and spheres of influence to the different interests, and based chiefly upon conquest, ordered our lives in a moderately satisfactory manner. But Tradition is weakening. Moral authorities are not as well backed by beliefs as they were; their sanctions are declining in force. We are in need of something to take the place of the old order. Not in need of a new balance of power, a new arrangement of conquests, but of a League of Nations for the moral ordering of the impulses; a new order based on conciliation, not on attempted suppression.

Only the rarest individuals hitherto have achieved this new order, and never yet perhaps completely. But many have achieved it for a brief while, for a particular phase of experience, and many have recorded it for these phases.

Of these records poetry consists.

But before going on to this new point let us return for a moment to our hypothetical friend who is enjoying his last hour, and suppose this limitation removed. Instead of such an hour let us consider any hour, one which has consequences for his future and for other people. Let us consider any piece of any life. How far is our argument affected? Will our standards of good and evil be altered?

Clearly the case now is, in certain respects, different; it is much more complicated. We have to take these consequences into account. We have to regard his experience not in itself alone, but as a piece of his life and as a probable factor in other people's situations. If we are to approve of the experience, it must not only be full of life and free from conflict, but it must be likely to lead to other experiences, both his own and those of other people, also full of life and free from conflict. And often, in actual fact, it has to be less full of life and more restricted than it might be in order to ensure these results. A momentary individual good has often to be sacrificed for the sake of a later or a general good. Conflicts are often necessary in order that they should not occur later. The mutual adjustment of conflicting impulses may take time, and an acute struggle may be the only way in which they learn to co-operate peacefully in the future.

But all these complications and qualifications do not disturb the conclusion we arrived at through considering the simpler case. A good experience is still one full of life, in the sense which we have explained, or derivatively one conducive to experiences full of life. An evil experience is one which is self-thwarting or conducive to stultifying conflicts. So far then, all is sound and shipshape in the argument, and we can go on to consider the poet.

CHAPTER IV

THE COMMAND OF LIFE

THE chief characteristic of poets is their amazing *command* of words. This is not a mere matter of vocabulary, though it is significant that Shakespeare's vocabulary is the richest and most varied that any Englishman has ever used. It is not the quantity of words a writer has at his disposal, but the way in which he disposes them that gives him his rank as a poet. His sense of how they modify one another, how their separate effects in the mind combine, how they fit into the whole response, is what matters. As a rule the poet is not conscious of the reason why just these words and no others best serve. They fall into their place without his conscious control, and a feeling of rightness, of inevitability is commonly his sole conscious ground for his certainty that he has ordered them aright. It would as a rule be idle to ask him why he used a particular rhythm or a particular epithet. He might give reasons, but they would probably be mere rationalizations having nothing to do with the matter. For the choice of the rhythm or the epithet was not an intellectual matter (though it may be capable of an intellectual justification), but was due to an instinctive impulse seeking to confirm itself, or to order itself with its fellows.

It is very important to realize how deep are the motives which govern the poet's use of words. No study of other poets which is not an impassioned study will help him. He can learn much from other poets, but only by letting them influence him deeply, not by any superficial examination of their style. For the motives which shape a poem spring from the root of the mind. The poet's style is the direct outcome of the way in which his interests are organized. That amazing capacity of his for ordering speech is only a part of a more amazing capacity for ordering his experience.

This is the explanation of the fact that poetry cannot be written by cunning and study, by craft and contrivance. To a superficial glance the productions of the mere scholar, steeped in the poetry of the past, and animated by intense emulation and a passionate desire to place himself among the poets, will often look extraordinarily like poetry. His words may seem as subtly and delicately ordered as words can be, his epithets as happy, his transitions as daring, his simplicity as perfect. By every intellectual test he may succeed. But unless the ordering of the words sprang, not from knowledge of the technique of poetry added to a desire to write some, but from an actual supreme ordering of *experience,* a closer approach to his work will betray it. Characteristically its rhythm will give it away. For rhythm is no matter of tricks with syllables, but directly reflects personality. It is not separable from the words to which it belongs. Moving rhythm in poetry arises only from genuinely stirred impulses, and is a more subtle index than any other to the order of the interests.

Poetry, in other words, cannot be imitated; it cannot be faked so as to baffle the only test that ought ever to be applied. It is unfortunately true that this test is often very difficult to apply. And it is sometimes hard to know whether the test has or has not been applied. For the test is this— that only genuine poetry will give to the reader who approaches it in the proper manner a response which is as passionate, noble and serene as the experience of the poet, the master of speech because he is the master of experience itself. But it is easy to read carelessly and shallowly, and easy to mistake for the response something which does not properly belong to it at all. By careless reading we miss what is in the poem. And in some states of mind, for example, when intoxicated, the silliest doggerel may seem sublime. What happened was not due to the doggerel but to the drink.

With these general considerations in mind we may turn now from the question—What can the dawning science of psychology tell us about poetry?—to the allied questions—How is science in general, and the new outlook upon the world which it induces, already affecting poetry, and to what extent may science make obsolete the poetry of the past? To answer these questions we need to sketch some of the changes which have recently come about in our world-picture, and to consider anew what it is that we demand from poetry.

CHAPTER V

THE NEUTRALISATION OF NATURE

THE poets are failing us, or we them, if after reading them we do not find ourselves changed; not with a temporary change, such as luncheon or slumber will produce from which we inevitably work back to the *status quo ante,* but with a permanent alteration of our possibilities as responsive individuals in good or bad adjustment to an all but over-whelming concourse of stimulations. How many living poets have the power to make such deep changes? Let us set aside youthful enthusi-asms; there is a time in most lives when, rightly enough, Mr. Masefield, Mr. Kipling, Mr. Drinkwater, or even Mr. Noyes or Mr. Studdert Ken-nedy may profoundly affect the awakening mind; it is being introduced to poetry. Later on, looking back, we can see that any one of a hundred other poets would have served as well or better. Let us consider only the experienced, the fairly hardened reader, who is familiar with a great deal of the poetry of the past.

Contemporary poetry which will, accidents apart, modify the attitudes of this reader must be such as could not have been written in another age than our own. It must have sprung in part from the contemporary situation. It must correspond to needs, impulses, attitudes, which did not arise in the same fashion for poets in the past, and criticism also must take notice of the contemporary situation. Our attitudes to man, to nature, and to the universe change with every generation, and have changed with unusual violence in recent years. We cannot leave these changes out of account in judging modern poetry. When attitudes are changing neither criticism nor poetry can remain stationary. To those who realise what the poet is this will be obvious; but all literary history bears it out.

It would be of little use to give a list of the chief recent intellectual revolutions and to attempt to deduce therefrom what must be happen-ing to poetry. The effects upon our attitudes of changes of opinion are too complex to be calculated so. What we have to consider is not men's current opinions but their attitudes—how they feel about this or that as part of the world; what relative importance its different aspects have for them; what they are prepared to sacrifice for what; what they trust, what they are frightened by, what they desire. To discover these things we must go to the poets. Unless they are failing us, they will show us just these things.

They will *show* them, but, of course, they will not state them. Their poetry will not be *about* their attitudes in the sense in which a treatise on anatomy is about the structure of the body. Their poetry will arise out of their attitudes and will evoke them in an adequate reader, but, as a rule, it will not mention any attitudes. We must, of course, expect occasional essays in verse upon psychological topics, but these should not mislead us. Most of the attitudes with which poetry is concerned are indescribable—because psychology is still in a primitive stage—and can only be named or spoken about as the attitude of this poem or that. The poem, the actual experience as it forms itself in the mind of the fit reader, controlling his responses to the world and ordering his impulses, is our best evidence as to how other men feel about things; and we read it, if we are serious, partly to discover how life seems to another, partly to try how his attitudes suit us, engaged as we also are in the same enterprise.

Although we cannot—for lack of a sufficient psychology—describe attitudes in terms which do not apply also to others which we are not considering, and although we cannot deduce a poet's attitudes from the general intellectual background, none the less, after reading his poetry, when his experience has become our own, we can sometimes profitably look round us to see why these attitudes should be so very different, in some ways, from those we find in the poetry of 100 or 1,000 years ago. In so doing we gain a means of indicating what these attitudes are, useful both for those who are constitutionally unable to read poetry (an increasing number), and for those victims of education who neglect modern poetry because they "don't know what to make of it."

What, then, has been happening to the intellectual background, to the world-picture, and in what ways may changes here have caused a reorganisation of our attitudes?

The central dominant change may be described as the *Neutralisation of Nature,* the transference from the Magical View of the world to the scientific, a change so great that it is perhaps only paralleled historically by the change, from whatever adumbration of a world-picture preceded the Magical View, to the Magical View itself. By the Magical View I mean, roughly, the belief in a world of Spirits and Powers which control events, and which can be evoked and, to some extent, controlled themselves by human practices. The belief in Inspiration and the beliefs underlying Ritual are representative parts of this view. It has been decaying slowly for some 300 years, but its definite overthrow has taken place only in the last 60. Vestiges and survivals of it prompt and direct a great part of our daily affairs, but it is no longer the world-picture which an informed mind most easily accepts. There is some evidence that Poetry, together with the other Arts, arose with this Magical View. It is a possibility to be seriously considered that Poetry may pass away with it.

The reasons for the downfall of the Magical View are familiar. It seems to have arisen as a consequence of an increase in man's knowledge of and command over nature (the discovery of agriculture). It fell through the extension of that knowledge of and command over nature. Throughout its (10,000 years?) reign its stability has been due to its capacity for satisfying men's emotional needs through its adequacy as an object for their attitudes. We must remember that human attitudes have developed always *inside* the social group; they are what a man feels, the mainsprings of his behaviour towards his fellow-men, and they have only a limited field of applicability. Thus the Magical View, being an interpretation of nature in terms of man's own most intimate and most important affairs, very soon came to suit man's emotional make-up better than any other view possibly could. The attraction of the Magical View lay very little in the actual command over nature which it gave. That Galton was the first person to test the efficacy of prayer experimentally is an indication of this. What did give the Magical View its standing was the ease and adequacy with which the universe therein presented could be emotionally handled, the scope offered for man's love and hatred, for his terror as well as for his hope and his despair. It gave life a shape, a sharpness, and a coherence that no other means could so easily secure.

In its place we have the universe of the mathematician, a field for the tracing out of ever wider and more general uniformities. A field in which intellectual certainty is, almost for the first time, available, and on an unlimited scale. Also the despondencies, the emotional excitements accompanying research and discovery, again on an unprecedented scale. Thus a number of men who might in other times have been poets are to-day in bio-chemical laboratories—a fact of which we might avail ourselves, did we feel the need, in defence of an alleged present poverty in poetry. But apart from these thrills, what has the world-picture of science to do with human emotions? A god voluntarily or involuntarily subjected to the General Theory of Relativity does not make an emotional appeal. So this form of compromise fails. Various emergent deities have been suggested—by Mr. Wells, by Professors Alexander and Lloyd Morgan—but, alas! the reasons for suggesting them have become too clear and conscious. They are there to meet a demand, not to make one; they do not do the work for which they were invented.

The revolution brought about by science is, in short, too drastic to be met by any such half-measures. It touches the central principle by which the Mind has been deliberately organised in the past, and no alteration in beliefs, however great, will restore equilibrium while that principle is retained. I come now to the main purport of these remarks.

Ever since man first grew self-conscious and reflective he has supposed that his feelings, his attitudes, and his conduct spring from his knowledge. That as far as he could it would be wise for him to organise himself in this way, with knowledge [4] as the foundation on which should rest feeling, attitude, and behaviour. In point of fact, he never has been so organised, knowledge having been until recently too scarce; but he has constantly been persuaded that he was built on this plan, and has endeavoured to carry the structure further on these lines. He has sought for knowledge, supposing that it would itself *directly* excite a right orientation to existence, supposing that, if he only knew what the world was like, this knowledge in itself would show him how to feel towards it, what attitudes to adopt, and with what aims to live. He has constantly called what he found in this quest, "knowledge," unaware that it was hardly ever pure, unaware that his feelings, attitudes, and behaviour were *already* orientated by his physiological and social needs, and were themselves, for the most part, the sources of whatever it was that he supposed himself to be knowing.

Suddenly, not long ago, he began to get genuine knowledge on a large scale. The process went faster and faster; it snowballed. Now he has to face the fact that the edifices of supposed knowledge, with which he has for so long buttressed and supported his attitudes, will no longer stand up, and, at the same time, he has to recognise that pure knowledge is irrelevant to his aims, that it has no *direct* bearing upon what he should feel, or what he should attempt to do.

For science, which is simply our most elaborate way of *pointing* to things systematically, tells us and can tell us nothing about the nature of things in any *ultimate* sense. It can never answer any question of the form: *What* is so and so? It can only tell us *how* so and so behaves. And it does not attempt to do more than this. Nor, indeed, can more than this be done. Those ancient, deeply troubling, formulations that begin

[4] *I.e.* thoughts which are both true and evidenced, in the narrower, stricter senses. For a discussion of some relevant senses of 'truth' and 'knowledge' see *Principles of Literary Criticism*, Chapters XXXIII and XXXIV.

with "What" and "Why" prove, when we examine them, to be not questions at all; but requests—for emotional satisfaction. They indicate our desire not for knowledge but for assurance,[5] a point which appears clearly when we look into the "How" of questions and requests, of knowledge and desire. Science can tell us about man's place in the universe and his chances; that the place is precarious, and the chances problematical. It can enormously increase our chances if we can make wise use of it. But it cannot tell us what we are or what this world is; not because these are in any sense insoluble questions, but because they are not questions at all.[6] And if science cannot answer these pseudo-questions no more can philosophy or religion. So that all the varied answers which have for ages been regarded as the keys of wisdom are dissolving together.

The result is a biological crisis which is not likely to be decided without trouble. It is one which we can, perhaps, decide for ourselves, partly by thinking, partly by reorganising our minds in other ways; if we do not it may be decided for us, not in the way we should choose. While it lasts it puts a strain on each individual and upon society, which is part of the explanation of many modern difficulties, the difficulties of the poet in particular, to come back to our present subject. I have not really been far away.

CHAPTER VI

POETRY AND BELIEFS

THE business of the poet, as we have seen, is to give order and coherence, and so freedom, to a body of experience. To do so through words which act as its skeleton, as a structure by which the impulses which make up the experience are adjusted to one another and act together. The means by which words do this are many and varied. To work them out is a problem for psychology. A beginning has been indicated above, but only a beginning. What little can be done shows already that most critical dogmas of the past are either false or nonsense. A little knowledge is not here a danger, but clears the air in a remarkable way.

Roughly and inadequately, even in the light of our present knowl-

[5] On this point the study of the child's questions included in *The Language and Thought of the Child* by J. Piaget (Kegan Paul, 1926) is illuminating.

[6] The remarks of Wittgenstein (*Tractatus Logico-Philosophicus*, 6.5, 6.52), which superficially resemble this, should be consulted, if only to show how important the *context* of a statement may be; for what is said above should lead not towards but away from all forms of mysticism.

edge, we can say that words work in the poem in two main fashions. As sensory stimuli and as (in the *widest* sense) symbols. We must refrain from considering the sensory side of the poem, remarking only that it is *not* in the least independent of the other side, and that it has for definite reasons prior importance in most poetry. We must confine ourselves to the other function of words in the poem, or rather, omitting much that is of secondary relevance, to one form of that function, let me call it *pseudo-statement*.

It will be admitted—by those who distinguish between scientific statement, where truth is ultimately a matter of verification as this is understood in the laboratory, and emotive utterance, where "truth" is primarily acceptability *by* some attitude, and more remotely is the acceptability *of* this attitude itself—that it is *not* the poet's business to make true statements. Yet poetry has constantly the air of making statements, and important ones; which is one reason why some mathematicians cannot read it. They find the alleged statements to be *false*. It will be agreed that their approach to poetry and their expectations from it are mistaken. But what exactly is the other, the right, the poetic, approach and how does it differ from the mathematical?

The poetic approach evidently limits the framework of possible consequences into which the pseudo-statement is taken. For the scientific approach this framework is unlimited. Any and every consequence is relevant. If any of the consequences of a statement conflicts with acknowledged fact then so much the worse for the statement. Not so with the pseudo-statement when poetically approached. The problem is— just how does the limitation work? The usual account is in terms of a supposed universe of discourse, a world of make-believe, of imagination, of recognised fictions common to the poet and his readers. A pseudo-statement which fits into this system of assumptions would be regarded as "poetically true"; one which does not, as "poetically false." This attempt to treat "poetic truth" on the model of general "coherence theories" is very natural for certain schools of logicians; but is inadequate, on the wrong lines from the outset. To mention two objections out of many; there is no means of discovering what the "universe of discourse" is on any occasion, and the kind of coherence which must hold within it, supposing it to be discoverable, is not an affair of logical relations. Attempt to define the system of propositions into which

"O Rose, thou art sick!"

must fit, and the logical relations which must hold between them if it is to be "poetically true"; the absurdity of the theory becomes evident.

We must look further. In the poetic approach the relevant consequences are not logical or to be arrived at by a partial relaxation of logic. Except occasionally and by accident logic does not enter at all. They are the consequences which arise through our emotional organisation. The acceptance which a pseudo-statement receives is entirely governed by its effects upon our feelings and attitudes. Logic only comes in, if at all, in subordination, as a servant to our emotional response. It is an unruly servant, however, as poets and readers are constantly discovering. A pseudo-statement is "true" if it suits and serves some attitude or links together attitudes which on other grounds are desirable. This kind of truth is so opposed to scientific truth that it is a pity to use so similar a word, but at present it is difficult to avoid the malpractice.[7]

This brief analysis may be sufficient to indicate the fundamental disparity and opposition between pseudo-statements as they occur in poetry and statements as they occur in science. A pseudo-statement is a form of words which is justified entirely by its effect in releasing or organising our impulses and attitudes (due regard being had for the better or worse organisations of these *inter se*); a statement, on the other hand, is justified by its truth, *i.e.* its correspondence, in a highly technical sense, with the fact to which it points.

Statements true and false alike do of course constantly touch off attitudes and action. Our daily practical existence is largely guided by them. On the whole true statements are of more service to us than false ones. None the less we do not and, at present, cannot order our emotions and attitudes by true statements alone. Nor is there any probability that we ever shall contrive to do so. This is one of the great new dangers to which civilisation is exposed. Countless pseudo-statements—about God, about the universe, about human nature, the relations of mind to mind, about the soul, its rank and destiny—pseudo-statements which are pivotal points in the organisation of the mind, vital to its well-being, have suddenly become, for sincere, honest and informal minds, impossible to believe. For centuries they have been believed; now they are gone, irrecoverably; and the knowledge which has killed them is not of a kind upon which an equally fine organisation of the mind can be based.

[7] For an account of the various senses of truth and of the ways in which they may be distinguished in discussion, cf. *The* *Meaning of Meaning*, by C. K. Ogden and the author, Chapters VII and X.

This is the contemporary situation. The remedy, since there is no prospect of our gaining adequate knowledge, and since indeed it is fairly clear that genuine knowledge cannot serve us here and can only increase our practical control of Nature, is to cut our pseudo-statements free from belief, and yet retain them, in this released state, as the main instruments by which we order our attitudes to one another and to the world. Not so desperate a remedy as may appear, for poetry conclusively shows that even the most important among our attitudes can be aroused and maintained without any belief entering in at all. Those of Tragedy, for example. We need no beliefs, and indeed we must have none, if we are to read *King Lear*. Pseudo-statements to which we attach no belief and statements proper such as science provides cannot conflict. It is only when we introduce illicit beliefs into poetry that danger arises. To do so is from this point of view a profanation of poetry.

Yet an important branch of criticism which has attracted the best talents from prehistoric times until to-day consists of the endeavour to persuade men that the functions of science and poetry are identical, or that the one is a 'higher form' of the other, or that they conflict and we must choose between them.

The root of this persistent endeavour has still to be mentioned; it is the same as that from which the Magical View of the world arose. If we give to a pseudo-statement the kind of unqualified acceptance which belongs by right only to certified scientific statements, if we can contrive to do this, the impulses and attitudes with which we respond to it gain a notable stability and vigour. Briefly, if we can contrive to believe poetry, then the world *seems,* while we do so, to be transfigured. It used to be comparatively easy to do this, and the habit has become well established. With the extension of science and the neutralisation of nature it has become difficult as well as dangerous. Yet it is still alluring; it has many analogies with drug-taking. Hence the endeavours of the critics referred to. Various subterfuges have been devised along the lines of regarding Poetic Truth as figurative, symbolic; or as more immediate, as a truth of Intuition, not of reason; or as a higher form of the same truth as reason yields. Such attempts to use poetry as a denial or as a corrective of science are very common. One point can be made against them all: they are never worked out in detail. There is no equivalent to Mill's *Logic* expounding any such view. The language in which they are framed is usually a blend of obsolete psychology and emotive exclamations.

The long-established and much-encouraged habit of giving to emotive utterances—whether pseudo-statements simple, or looser and larger wholes taken as saying something figuratively—the kind of assent which we give to established facts, has for most people debilitated a wide range of their responses. A few scientists, caught young and brought up in the laboratory, are free from it; but then, as a rule, they pay no *serious* attention to poetry. For most men the recognition of the neutrality of nature brings about—through this habit—a divorce from poetry. They are so used to having their responses propped up by beliefs, however vague, that when these shadowy supports are removed they are no longer able to respond. Their attitudes to so many things have been forced in the past, over-encouraged. And when the world-picture ceases to assist there is a collapse. Over whole tracts of natural emotional response we are to-day like a bed of dahlias whose sticks have been removed. And this effect of the neutralisation of nature is only in its beginnings. Consider the probable effects upon love-poetry in the near future of the kind of enquiry into basic human constitution exemplified by psycho-analysis.

A sense of desolation, of uncertainty, of futility, of the groundlessness of aspirations, of the vanity of endeavour, and a thirst for a life-giving water which seems suddenly to have failed, are the signs in consciousness of this necessary reorganisation of our lives.[8] Our attitudes and impulses are being compelled to become self-supporting; they are being driven back upon their biological justification, made once again sufficient to themselves. And the only impulses which seem strong enough to continue unflagging are commonly so crude that, to more finely developed individuals, they hardly seem worth having. Such people cannot live by warmth, food, fighting, drink, and sex alone. Those who are least affected by the change are those who are emotionally least removed from the animals. As we shall see at the close of this essay, even a considerable poet may attempt to find relief by a reversion to primitive mentality.

It is important to diagnose the disease correctly and to put the blame in the right quarter. Usually it is some alleged 'materialism' of science

[8] To those familiar with Mr. Eliot's *The Waste Land*, my indebtedness to it at this point will be evident. He seems to me by this poem, to have performed two considerable services for this generation. He has given a perfect emotive description of a state of mind which is probably inevitable for a while to all meditative people. Sec- ondly, by effecting a complete severance between his poetry and *all* beliefs, and this without any weakening of the poetry, he has realised what might otherwise have remained largely a speculative possibility, and has shown the way to the only solution of these difficulties. "In the destructive element immerse. That is the way."

which is denounced. This mistake is due partly to clumsy thinking, but chiefly to relics of the Magical View. For even if the Universe were "spiritual" all through (whatever that assertion might mean; all such assertions are probably nonsense), that would not make it any more accordant to human attitudes. It is not what the universe is made of but how it works, the law it follows, which makes knowledge of it incapable of spurring on our emotional responses, and further the nature of knowledge itself makes it inadequate. The contact with things which we therein establish is too sketchy and indirect to help us. We are beginning to know too much about the bond which unites the mind to its object in knowledge for that old dream of a perfect knowledge which would guarantee perfect life to retain its sanction. What was thought to be pure knowledge, we see now to have been shot through with hope and desire, with fear and wonder, and these intrusive elements indeed gave it all its power to support our lives. In knowledge, in the "How?" of events, we can find hints by which to take advantage of circumstances in our favour and avoid mischances. But we cannot get from it a *raison d'être* or a justification of more than a relatively lowly kind of life.

The justification, or the reverse, of any attitude lies, not in the object, but in itself, in its serviceableness to the whole personality. Upon its place in the whole system of attitudes, which is the personality, all its worth depends. This is true equally for the subtle, finely compounded attitudes of the civilised individual as for the simpler attitudes of the child.

In brief, experience is its own justification; and this fact must be faced, although sometimes—by a lover, for example—it may be very difficult to accept. Once it is faced, it is apparent that all the attitudes to other human beings and to the world in all its aspects, which have been serviceable to humanity, remain as they were, as valuable as ever. Hesitation felt in admitting this is a measure of the strength of the evil habit we have described. But many of these attitudes, valuable as ever, are, now that they are being set free, more difficult to maintain, because we still hunger after a basis in belief.

CHAPTER VII

SOME CONTEMPORARY POETS

IT is time to turn to those living poets through study of whose work these reflections have arisen. Mr. Hardy is for every reason the poet with whom it is most natural to begin. Not only does his work span the whole period in which what I have called the neutralisation of nature was finally effected, but it has throughout definitely reflected that change. Short essays in verse are fairly frequent among his *Collected Poems,* essays almost always dealing with this very topic; but these, however suggestive, are not the ground for singling him out as the poet who has most fully and courageously accepted the contemporary background; nor are the poems which are most definitely *about* the neutrality of nature the ground for the assertion. There is an opportunity for a misunderstanding at this point. The ground is the tone, the handling and the rhythm of poems which treat other subjects, for example *The Self Unseeing, The Voice, A Broken Appointment,* and pre-eminently *After a Journey.* A poem does not necessarily accept the situation because it gives it explicit recognition, but only through the precise mutation of the attitudes of which it is composed. Mr. Middleton Murry, against whose recent positions parts of this essay may be suspected by the reader to be aimed, has best pointed out, in his *Aspects of Literature,* how peculiarly "adequate to what we know and have suffered" Mr. Hardy's poetry is. "His reaction to an episode has behind it and within it a reaction to the universe." This is not as I should put it were I making a statement; but read as a pseudo-statement, emotively, it is excellent; it makes us remember how we felt. Actually it describes just what Hardy, at his best, does not do. He makes no reaction to the universe, recognising it as something to which no reaction is more relevant than another. Mr. Murry is again well inspired, this time both emotively and scientifically, when he says: "Mr. Hardy stands high above all other modern poets by the deliberate purity of his responsiveness. The contagion of the world's slow stain has not touched him; from the first he held aloof from the general conspiracy to forget in which not only those who are professional optimists take a part." These extracts (from a writer more agonisingly aware than others that some strange change has befallen man in this generation, though his diagnosis is, I believe, mistaken) indicate very well Mr. Hardy's place and rank in English poetry. He is the poet who has most steadily refused to be comforted. The comfort of forgetfulness, the comfort of beliefs, he has put both these away. Hence his singular preoccupation with death; because it is in the contemplation of death that the necessity for human attitudes, in the face of an indifferent universe, to become self-supporting is felt most poignantly. Only the greatest tragic poets have achieved an equally self-reliant and immitigable acceptance.

From Mr. Hardy to Mr. De la Mare may seem a large transition, though readers of Mr. De la Mare's later work will agree that there are interesting resemblances—in *Who's That* and in other poems in *The Veil* where Mr. De la Mare is notably less himself than when writing at his best. In his best poetry, in *The Pigs and the Charcoal Burner,* in *John Mouldy,* no intimation of the contemporary situation sounds. He is writing of, and from, a world which knows nothing of these difficulties, a world of pure phantasy for which the distinction between knowledge and feeling has not yet dawned. When in other poems, more reflective, in *The Tryst,* for example, Mr. De la Mare does seem to be directly facing the indifference of the universe towards "poor mortal longingness" a curious thing happens. His utterance, in spite of his words, become not at all a recognition of this indifference, but voices instead an impulse to turn away, to forget it, to seek shelter in the warmth of his own familiar thickets of dreams, not to stay out in the wind. His rhythm, that indescribable personal note which clings to all his best poetry, is a lulling rhythm, and anodyne, an opiate, it gives sleep and visions, phantasmagoria; but it does not give *vision,* it does not awaken. Even when he most appears to be contemplating the fate of the modern, "whom the words of the wise have made sad," the drift of his verse is still "seeking after that sweet golden clime" where the mental traveller's journey *begins.*

There is one exception to this charge (for in a sense it is an adverse criticism, though not one to be pressed except against a great poet), there is one poem in which there is no such reluctance to bear the blast —*The Mad Prince's Song* in *Peacock Pie.* But here the spirit of the poem, the impulse which gives it life, comes from a poet who more than most refused to take shelter; *The Mad Prince's Song* derives from *Hamlet.*

Mr. Yeats and Mr. Lawrence present two further ways of dodging those difficulties which come from being born into this generation rather than into some earlier age. Mr. De la Mare takes shelter in the dream-world of the child, Mr. Yeats retires into black velvet curtains and the visions of the Hermetist, and Mr. Lawrence makes a magnificent attempt to reconstruct in himself the mentality of the Bushman. There are other modes of escape open to the poet. Mr. Blundell, to name one other poet only, goes into the country, but few people follow him there in his spirit, whereas Mr. Yeats and Mr. Lawrence, whether they are widely read or not, do represent tendencies among the defeated which are only too easily observable.

Mr. Yeats' work from the beginning was a repudiation of the most active contemporary interests. But at first the poet of *The Wanderings of Usheen, The Stolen Child* and *Innisfree* turned away from contemporary civilisation in favour of a world which he knew perfectly, the world of folk-lore as it is accepted, neither with belief nor disbelief, by the peasant. Folk-lore and the Irish landscape, its winds, woods, waters, islets, and seagulls, and for a while an unusually simple and direct kind of love poetry in which he became something more than a minor poet, these were his refuge. Later, after a drawn battle with the drama, he made a more violent repudiation, not merely of current civilisation but of life itself, in favour of a supernatural world. But the world of the 'eternal moods,' of supernal essences and immortal beings is not, like the Irish peasant stories and the Irish landscape, part of his natural and familiar experience. Now he turns to a world of symbolic phantasmagoria about which he is desperately uncertain. He is uncertain because he has adopted as a technique of inspiration the use of trance, of dissociated phases of consciousness, and the revelations given in these dissociated states are insufficiently connected with normal experience. This, in part, explains the weakness of Mr. Yeats' transcendental poetry. A deliberate reversal of the natural relations of thought and feeling is the rest of the explanation. Mr. Yeats takes certain feelings—feelings of conviction attaching to certain visions—as evidence for the thoughts which he supposes his visions to symbolize. To Mr. Yeats the value of *The Phases of the Moon* lies not in any attitudes which it arouses or embodies but in the doctrine which for an initiate it promulgates.

The resort to trance, and the effort to discover a new world-picture to replace that given by science are the two most significant points for our purpose in Mr. Yeats' work. A third might be the singularly bitter contempt for the generality of mankind which occasionally appears.

The doctrinal problem arises again, but in a clearer form with Mr. Lawrence. But here (Mr. Yeats' promised treatise on the states of the soul has not yet appeared) we have the advantage of an elaborate prose exposition, *Phantasia of the Unconscious*, of the positions which so many of the poems advocate. It is not unfair to put the matter in this way, since there is little doubt possible that the bulk of Mr. Lawrence's published verse is prose, scientific prose too, jottings, in fact, from a psychologist's notebook, with a commentary interspersed. Due allowance being made for the extreme psychological interest of these observations, there remains the task of explaining how the poet who wrote the *Ballad of Another Ophelia* and *Aware,* and, above all, *The White*

Peacock, should have wandered, through his own zeal misdirected, so far from the paths which once appeared to be his alone to open.

Mr. Lawrence's revolt against civilisation seems to have been originally spontaneous, an emotional revulsion free from *ad hoc* beliefs. It sprang directly from experience. He came to abhor all the attitudes men adopt, not through the direct prompting of their instincts, but because of the supposed nature of the objects to which they are directed. The conventions, the idealisations, which come between man and man and between man and woman, which often queer the pitch for the natural responses, seemed to him the source of all evil. Part of his revolt was certainly justified. These idealisations—representative examples are the dogma of the equality of man and the doctrine that Love is primarily sympathy—are beliefs illicitly interpolated in order to support and strengthen attitudes in the manner discussed at length above. And Mr. Lawrence's original rejection of a morality not self-supporting but based upon beliefs, makes his work an admirable illustration of my main thesis. But two simple and avoidable mistakes deprived his revolt of the greater part of its value. He overlooked the fact that such beliefs commonly arise because the attitudes they support are already existent. He assumed that a bad basis for an attitude meant a bad attitude. In general, it does mean a forced attitude, but that is another matter. Secondly, he tried to cure the disease by introducing other beliefs of his own manufacture in place of the conventional beliefs and in support of very different attitudes.

The genesis of these beliefs is extremely interesting as an illustration of primitive mentality. Since the attitudes on which he fell back are those of a very early stage of human development, it is not surprising that the means by which he has supported them should be of the same era, or that the world-picture which he has worked out should be similar to that described in *The Golden Bough.* The mental process at work is schematically as follows: First, undergo an intense emotion, located with unusual definiteness in the body, which can be described as "a feeling *as though* the solar plexus were connected by a current of dark passional energy with another person." Those whose emotions tend to be localised will be familiar with such feelings. The second step is to say "I must trust my feelings." The third is to call the feeling an intuition. The last is to say "*I know* that my solar plexus is, etc." By this means we arrive at indubitable knowledge that the sun's energy is recruited from the life on the earth and that the astronomers are wrong in what they say about the moon, and so on.

The illicit steps in the argument are not quite so evident as they appear to be in this analysis. To distinguish an intuition *of* an emotion from an intuition *by* it is not always easy, nor is a description of an emotion always in practice distinguishable from an emotion. Certainly we must trust our feelings—in the sense of acting upon them. We have nothing else to trust. And to confuse this trusting with believing an emotive description of them is a mistake which all traditional codes of morality encourage us to commit.

The significance of such similar disasters in the work of poets so unlike and yet so greatly gifted as Mr. Yeats and Mr. Lawrence is noteworthy. For each the traditional scaffolding of conventional beliefs have proved unsatisfying, unworkable as a basis for their attitudes. Each has sought, in very different directions it is true, a new set of beliefs as a remedy. For neither has the world-picture of science seemed a possible substitute. And neither seems to have envisaged the possibility of a poetry which is independent of all beliefs, probably because, however much they differ, both are very serious poets. A great deal of poetry can, of course, be written for which total independence of all beliefs is an easy matter. But it is never poetry of the more important kind, because the temptation to introduce beliefs is a sign and measure of the importance of the attitudes involved. At present it is not primarily religious beliefs, in the stricter sense of the word, which are most likely to be concerned. Emphases alter surprisingly. University societies founded fifteen years ago, for example, to discuss religion, are usually found to be discussing sex to-day. And serious love poetry, which is independent of beliefs of one kind or another, traditional or eccentric, is extremely rare.

Yet the necessity for independence is increasing. This is not to say that traditional poetry, into which beliefs readily enter, is becoming obsolete; it is merely becoming more and more difficult to approach without confusion; it demands a greater imaginative effort, a greater purity in the reader.

We must distinguish here, however. There are many feelings and attitudes which, though in the past supported by beliefs now untenable, can survive their removal because they have other, more natural, supports and spring directly from the necessities of existence. To the extent to which they have been undistorted by the beliefs which have gathered round them they will remain as before. But there are other attitudes which are very largely the product of belief and have no other support. These will lapse if the changes here forecast continue. With their disappearance some forms of poetry—much minor devotional verse, for example—will become obsolete. And with the unravelling of the intellect *versus* emotion entanglement, there will be cases where even literature to which immense value has been assigned—the speculative portions of the work of Dostoevsky may be instanced—will lose much of its interest, except for the history of the mind. It was because he belonged to our age that Dostoevsky had to wrestle so terribly in these toils. A poet to-day, whose integrity is equal to that of the greater poets of the past, is inevitably plagued by the problem of thought and feeling as poets have never been plagued before.

A pioneer in modern research upon the origins of culture was asked recently whether his work had any bearing upon religion. He replied that it had, but that at present he was engaged merely in "getting the guns into position." The same answer might be given with regard to the probable consequences of recent progress in psychology, not only for religion but for the whole fabric of our traditional beliefs about ourselves. In many quarters there is a tendency to suppose that the series of attacks upon received ideas which began, shall we say, with Galileo and rose to a climax with Darwinism, has overreached itself with Einstein and Eddington, and that the battle is now due to die down. This view seems to be too optimistic. The most dangerous of the sciences is only now beginning to come into action. I am thinking less of Psycho-analysis or of Behaviourism than of the whole subject which includes them. It is very probable that the Hindenburg Line to which the defence of our traditions retired as a result of the onslaughts of the last century will be blown up in the near future. If this should happen a mental chaos such as man has never experienced may be expected. We shall then be thrown back, as Matthew Arnold foresaw, upon poetry. It is capable of saving us; it is a perfectly possible means of overcoming chaos. But whether man is capable of the reorientation required, whether he can loosen in time the entanglement with belief which now takes from poetry half its power and would then take all, is another question, and too large for the scope of this essay.

JOHN CROWE RANSOM

(1888–   )

JOHN CROWE RANSOM was born in Pulaski, Tennessee, on April 30, 1888. He was educated at Vanderbilt University and as a Rhodes Scholar at Oxford (B.A., 1913). He taught at Vanderbilt from 1914 to 1937, except for two years of military service with the A. E. F. His first book, *Poems about God,* was published in 1919; other poems were collected in *Chills and Fever* (1924) and *Two Gentlemen in Bonds* (1927). With Donald Davidson, Allen Tate, and others, he edited *The Fugitive* (1922–25) and the agrarian anthology *I'll Take My Stand* (1930). In 1937 he became Professor of English at Kenyon College, and editor of the *Kenyon Review* (1938–   ). He has published two volumes of literary criticism, *The World's Body* (1938) and *The New Criticism* (1941), and contributed numerous critical essays to magazines and anthologies. His *Selected Poems* appeared in 1945.

The cryptic title, *The World's Body,* indicates Ransom's preoccupation with a poetry and a criticism markedly divergent from the Romantic concepts of the arts. "I came late into an interest in poetry, after I had been stuffed with the law if not the letter of our modern sciences, and quickly I had the difficulty of finding a poetry which would not deny what we in our strange generation actually are: men who have aged in these pure intellectual disciplines, and cannot play innocent without feeling foolish. The expense of poetry is greater than we will pay if it is something to engage in without our faculties." [1] This demand for the use of all the faculties has led R. W. Stallman [in *The New Critics*] to describe Ransom's criticism as a "theory of poetry as knowledge. . . . Science and poetry present two different descriptions of the world. Science presents an abstract description, poetry attempts a total definition of the object. Poetry's representation of the world is an alternative to that pictured by science. The abstract structures of science sacrifice 'the body and substance of the world.' Poetry, by virtue of its concrete particulars, restores 'The World's Body.' "

Mr. Ransom's theories have been shared and extended by many modern critics. In *Reactionary Essays in Poetry and Ideas,* Allen Tate states that art, while proving nothing, "creates the totality of experience in its quality; and it has no useful relation to the ordinary forms of action." In "Tension in Poetry" [in *Reason in Madness*], Tate presents a definition that somewhat extends the concept: "Many poems that we ordinarily think of as good poetry—and

[1] Reprinted from the Preface to *The World's Body* by John Crowe Ransom. Copyright 1938 by Charles Scribner's Sons. Used by permission of the publisher.

some, besides, that we neglect—have certain common features that will allow us to invent, for their sharper apprehension, the name of a single quality. I shall call that quality tension. In abstract language, a poetic work has distinct quality as the ultimate effect of the whole, and that whole is the 'result' of a configuration of meaning which it is the duty of the critic to examine and evaluate. In setting forth this duty as my present procedure I am trying to amplify a critical approach that I have used on other occasions, without wholly giving up the earlier method, which I should describe as the analysis of the general ideas implicit in the poetic work."

These critical principles, as Ransom noted, must be worked out "in the constant company of the actual poems." Theories must be tested with close textual analyses, and re-shaped when they do not stand up under such close analysis. The critical theories must allow for various kinds of imperfections: as Robert Penn Warren puts it, "Poetry wants to be pure, but poems do not. At least, most of them do not want to be too pure. The poems want to give us poetry, which is pure, and the elements of a poem, in so far as it is a good poem, will work together toward that end, but many of the elements, taken in themselves, may actually seem to contradict that end, or be neutral toward the achieving of that end. Are we then to conclude that, because neutral or re-calcitrant elements appear in poems, even in poems called great, these elements are simply an index to human frailty, that in a perfect world there would be no dross in poems which would, then, be perfectly pure? No, it does not seem to be merely the fault of our world, for the poems include, de-liberately more of the so-called dross than would appear necessary. They are not even as pure as they might be in this imperfect world. They mar them-selves with cacophonies, jagged rhythms, ugly words and ugly thoughts, colloquialisms, clichés, sterile technical terms, head work and argument, self-contradictions, cleverness, irony, realism—all things which call us back to the world of prose and imperfection." [2]

Another friend of Ransom's, Cleanth Brooks, has approached the problem by stating ["The Language of Paradox," in *The Well Wrought Urn*] that "the language of poetry is the language of paradox. . . . It is the scientist whose truth requires a language purged of every trace of paradox; apparently the truth which the poet utters can be approached only in terms of paradox." Criticism of this kind, is, then, essentially concerned with the metaphysics of poetry. The critic is not dealing, when he considers a poem, with one simple problem; he is faced with a complex task. The critic's job, Mr. Ransom insists, is basically an ontological task, since poetry represents "a revolutionary de-parture from the convention of logical discourse. . . . The structure proper is the prose of the poem, being a logical discourse of almost any kind, and dealing with almost any content suited to a logical discourse. The texture, likewise, seems to be of any real content that may be come upon, provided it is so free, unrestricted, and large that it cannot properly get into the structure. One guesses that it is an *order* of content, rather than a *kind* of content, that distinguishes texture from structure, and poetry from prose." [3]

---

[2] Reprinted from "Pure and Impure Poetry" by Robert Penn Warren, *Kenyon Review*, Spring, 1943. Used by permission of the *Kenyon Review* and Mr. Warren.

[3] Reprinted from *The New Criticism* by John Crowe Ransom, New Directions, 1941. Used by permission of the publishers.

In "Criticism as Pure Speculation" [4] Ransom again emphasizes this key point in his concept of criticism: "A poem is a *logical* structure having a *local* texture. . . . The intent of the good critic becomes therefore to examine and define the poem with respect to its structure and its texture. If he has nothing to say about its texture he has nothing to say about it specifically as a poem, but is treating it only insofar as it is prose." This insistence on the inter-relation and the separation of structure and texture, on the need in poetry for logical irrelevance, leads back always to the need for a critic [*The Intent of the Critic*, p. 124] "to subscribe to an ontology. If he is a sound critic his ontology will be that of his poets; and what is that? I suggest that the poetic world-view is Aristotelian and 'realistic' rather than Platonic and 'idealistic.' He cannot follow the poets and still conceive himself as inhabiting the rational or 'tidy' universe that is supposed by the scientists."

POETRY: A NOTE IN ONTOLOGY *

(1934)

A POETRY may be distinguished from a poetry by virtue of subject-matter, and subject-matter may be differentiated with respect to its ontology, or the reality of its being. An excellent variety of critical doctrine arises recently out of this differentiation, and thus perhaps criticism leans again upon ontological analysis as it was meant to do by Kant. The recent critics remark in effect that some poetry deals with things, while some other poetry deals with ideas. The two poetries will differ from each other as radically as a thing differs from an idea.

The distinction in the hands of critics is a fruitful one. There is apt to go along with it a principle of valuation, which is the consequence of a temperament, and therefore basic. The critic likes things and intends that his poet shall offer them; or likes ideas and intends that he shall offer them; and approves him as he does the one or the other. Criticism cannot well go much deeper than this. The critic has carried to the last terms his analysis of the stuff of which poetry is made, and valued it frankly as his temperament or his need requires him to value it.

So philosophical a critic seems to be highly modern. He is; but this critic as a matter of fact is peculiarly on one side of the question. (The implication is unfavorable to the other side of the question.) He is in revolt against the tyranny of ideas, and against the poetry which celebrates ideas, and which may be identified—so far as his usual generaliza-

[4] Reprinted from *The Intent of the Critic*, edited by Donald A. Stauffer, Princeton University Press, 1941. Used by permission of the publishers.

* Reprinted from *The World's Body*, by John Crowe Ransom, copyright 1938 by Charles Scribner's Sons. Used by permission of the publishers.

tion may be trusted—with the hateful poetry of the Victorians. His bias is in favor of the things. On the other hand the critic who likes Victorian verse, or the poetry of ideas, has probably not thought of anything of so grand a simplicity as electing between the things and the ideas, being apparently not quite capable of the ontological distinction. Therefore he does not know the real or constitutional ground of his liking, and may somewhat ingenuously claim that his predilection is for those poets who give him inspiration, or comfort, or truth, or honest metres, or something else equally "worth while." But Plato, who was not a modern, was just as clear as we are about the basic distinction between the ideas and the things, and yet stands far apart from the aforesaid conscious modern in passionately preferring the ideas over the things. The weight of Plato's testimony would certainly fall on the side of the Victorians, though they may scarcely have thought of calling him as their witness. But this consideration need not conclude the hearing.

I. PHYSICAL POETRY

The poetry which deals with things was much in favor a few years ago with the resolute body of critics. And the critics affected the poets. If necessary, they became the poets, and triumphantly illustrated the new mode. The Imagists were important figures in the history of our poetry, and they were both theorists and creators. It was their intention to present things in their thinginess, or *Dinge* in their *Dinglichkeit;* and to such an extent had the public lost its sense of *Dinglichkeit* that their redirection was wholesome. What the public was inclined to seek in poetry was ideas, whether large ones or small ones, grand ones or pretty ones, certainly ideas to live by and die by, but what the Imagists identified with the stuff of poetry was, simply, things.

Their application of their own principle was sufficiently heroic, though they scarcely consented to be as extreme in the practice as in the theory. They had artistic talent, every one of the original group, and it was impossible that they should make of poetry so simple an exercise as in doctrine they seemed to think it was. Yet Miss Lowell wrote a poem on "Thompson's Lunch Room, Grand Central Station"; it is admirable if its intention is to show the whole reach of her courage. Its detail goes like this:

> Jagged greenwhite bowls of pressed glass
> Rearing snow-peaks of chipped sugar

> Above the lighthouse-shaped castors
> Of gray pepper and gray-white salt.

For most of us as for the public idealist, with his "values," this is inconsequential. Unhappily it seems that the things as things do not necessarily interest us, and that in fact we are not quite constructed with the capacity for a disinterested interest. But it must be noted even here that the things are on their good behavior, looking rather well, and arranged by lines into something approaching a military formation. More technically, there is cross-imagery in the snow-peaks of sugar, and in the lighthouse-shaped castors, and cross-imagery involves association, and will presently involve dissociation and thinking. The metre is but a vestige, but even so it means something, for metre is a powerful intellectual determinant marshalling the words and, inevitably, the things. The *Dinglichkeit* of this Imagist specimen, or the realism, was therefore not pure. But it was nearer pure than the world was used to in poetry, and the exhibit was astonishing.

For the purpose of this note I shall give to such poetry, dwelling as exclusively as it dares upon physical things, the name Physical Poetry. It is to stand opposite to that poetry which dwells as firmly as it dares upon ideas.

But perhaps thing *versus* idea does not seem to name an opposition precisely. Then we might phrase it a little differently: image *versus* idea. The idealistic philosophies are not sure that things exist, but they mean the equivalent when they refer to images. (Or they may consent to perceptions; or to impressions, following Hume, and following Croce, who remarks that they are pre-intellectual and independent of concepts. It is all the same, unless we are extremely technical.) It is sufficient if they concede that image is the raw material of idea. Though it may be an unwieldy and useless affair for the idealist as it stands, much needing to be licked into shape, nevertheless its relation to idea is that of a material cause, and it cannot be dispossessed of its priority.

It cannot be dispossessed of a primordial freshness, which idea can never claim. An idea is derivative and tamed. The image is in the natural or wild state, and it has to be discovered there, not put there, obeying its own law and none of ours. We think we can lay hold of image and take it captive, but the docile captive is not the real image but only the idea, which is the image with its character beaten out of it.

But we must be very careful: idealists are nothing if not dialectical. They object that an image in an original state of innocence is a delusion and cannot exist, that no image ever comes to us which does not imply the world of ideas, that there is "no percept without a concept." There is something in it. Every property discovered in the image is a universal property, and nothing discovered in the image is marvellous in kind though it may be pinned down historically or statistically as a single instance. But there is this to be understood too: the image which is not remarkable in any particular property is marvellous in its assemblage of many properties, a manifold of properties, like a mine or a field, something to be explored for the properties; yet science can manage the image, which is infinite in properties, only by equating it to the one property with which the science is concerned; for science at work is always *a science,* and committed to a special interest. It is not by refutation but by abstraction that science destroys the image. It means to get its "value" out of the image, and we may be sure that it has no use for the image in its original state of freedom. People who are engrossed with their pet "values" become habitual killers. Their game is the images, or the things, and they acquire the ability to shoot them as far off as they can be seen, and do. It is thus that we lose the power of imagination, or whatever faculty it is by which we are able to contemplate things as they are in their rich and contingent materiality. But our dreams reproach us, for in dreams they come alive again. Likewise our memory; which makes light of our science by recalling the images in their panoply of circumstance and with their morning freshness upon them.

It is the dream, the recollection, which compels us to poetry, and to deliberate æsthetic experience. It can hardly be argued, I think, that the arts are constituted automatically out of original images, and arise in some early age of innocence. (Though Croce seems to support this view, and to make art a pre-adult stage of experience.) Art is based on second love, not first love. In it we make a return to something which we had wilfully alienated. The child is occupied mostly with things, but it is because he is still unfurnished with systematic ideas, not because he is a ripe citizen by nature and comes along already trailing clouds of glory. Images are clouds of glory for the man who has discovered that ideas are a sort of darkness. Imagism, that is, the recent historical movement, may resemble a naïve poetry of mere things, but we can read the theoretical pronouncements of Imagists, and we can learn that Imagism is motivated by a distaste for the systematic abstractedness of thought. It presupposes acquaintance with science; that famous activity which is "constructive" with respect to the tools of our economic role in this world, and destructive with respect to nature. Imagists wish to escape from science by immersing themselves in images.

Not far off the simplicity of Imagism was, a little later, the subtler simplicity of Mr. George Moore's project shared with several others, in behalf of "pure poetry." In Moore's house on Ebury Street they talked about poetry, with an after-dinner warmth if not an early-morning discretion, and their tastes agreed almost perfectly and reinforced one another. The fruit of these conversations was the volume *Pure Poetry*. It must have been the most exclusive anthology of English poetry that had yet appeared, since its room was closed to all the poems that dallied visibly with ideas, so that many poems that had been coveted by all other anthologists do not appear there. Nevertheless the book is delicious, and something more deserves to be said for it.

First, that "pure poetry" is a kind of Physical Poetry. Its visible content is a thing-content. Technically, I suppose, it is effective in this character if it can exhibit its material in such a way that an image or set of images and not an idea must occupy the foreground of the reader's attention. Thus:

> Full fathom five thy father lies
> Of his bones are coral made.

Here it is difficult for anybody (except the perfect idealist who is always theoretically possible and who would expect to take a return from anything whatever) to receive any experience except that of a very distinct image, or set of images. It has the configuration of image, which consists in being sharp of edges, and the modality of image, which consists in being given and non-negotiable, and the density, which consists in being full, a plenum of qualities. What is to be done with it? It is pure exhibit; it is to be contemplated; perhaps it is to be enjoyed. The art of poetry depends more frequently on this faculty than on any other in its repertory; the faculty of presenting images so whole and clean that they resist the catalysis of thought.

And something else must be said, going in the opposite direction. "Pure poetry," all the same, is not as pure as it is claimed to be, though on the whole it is Physical Poetry. (All true poetry is a phase of Physical Poetry.) It is not as pure as Imagism is, or at least it is not as pure as Imagism would be if it lived up to its principles; and in fact it is significant that the volume does not contain any Imagist poems, which argues a difference in taste somewhere. Imagism may take trifling things for its material, presumably it will take the first things the poet encounters, since "importance" and "interest" are not primary qualities which a thing possesses but secondary or tertiary ones which the idealist attributes to it by virtue of his own requirements. "Pure poetry" as Moore conceives it, and as the lyrics of Poe and Shakespeare offer it, deals with the more dramatic materials, and here dramatic means human, or at least capable of being referred to the critical set of human interests. Employing this sort of material the poet cannot exactly intend to set the human economists in us actually into motion, but perhaps he does intend to comfort us with the fleeting sense that it is potentially our kind of material.

In the same way "pure poetry" is nicely metred, whereas Imagism was free. Technique is written on it. And by the way the anthology contains no rugged anonymous Scottish ballad either, and probably for a like reason; because it would not be technically finished. Now both Moore and De La Mare are accomplished conservative artists, and what they do or what they approve may be of limited range but it is sure to be technically admirable, and it is certain that they understand what technique in poetry is though they do not define it. Technique takes the thing-content and meters and orders it. Metre is not an original property of things. It is artificial, and conveys the sense of human control, even if it does not wish to impair the thinginess of the things. Metric is a science, and so far as we attend to it we are within the scientific atmosphere. Order is the logical arrangement of things. It involves the dramatic "form" which selects the things, and brings out their appropriate qualities, and carries them through a systematic course of predication until the total impression is a unit of logic and not merely a solid lump of thing-content. The "pure poems" which Moore admires are studied, though it would be fatal if they looked studious. A sustained effort of ideation effected these compositions. It is covered up, and communicates itself only on a subliminal plane of consciousness. But experienced readers are quite aware of it; they know at once what is the matter when they encounter a realism shamelessly passing for poetry, or a well-planned but blundering poetry.

As critics we should have every good will toward Physical Poetry: it is the basic constituent of any poetry. But the product is always something short of a pure or absolute existence, and it cannot quite be said that it consists of nothing but physical objects. The fact is that when we are more than usually satisfied with a Physical Poetry our analysis will probably disclose that it is more than usually impure.

The poetry of ideas I shall denominate: Platonic Poetry. This also has grades of purity. A discourse which employed only abstract ideas with no images would be a scientific document and not a poem at all, not even a Platonic poem. Platonic Poetry dips heavily into the physical. If Physical Poetry tends to employ some ideation surreptitiously while still looking innocent of idea, Platonic Poetry more than returns the compliment, for it tries as hard as it can to look like Physical Poetry, as if it proposed to conceal its medicine, which is the idea to be propagated, within the sugar candy of objectivity and *Dinglichkeit*. As an instance, it is almost inevitable that I quote a famous Victorian utterance:

> The year's at the spring
> And day's at the morn;
> Morning's at seven;
> The hill-side's dew-pearled;
> The lark's on the wing;
> The snail's on the thorn:
> God's in his heaven—
> All's right with the world!

which is a piece of transparent homiletics; for in it six pretty, co-ordinate images are marched, like six little lambs to the slaughter, to a colon and a powerful text. Now the exhibits of this poetry in the physical kind are always large, and may take more of the attention of the reader than is desired, but they are meant mostly to be illustrative of the ideas. It is on this ground that idealists like Hegel detect something unworthy, like a pedagogical trick, in poetry after all, and consider that the race will abandon it when it has outgrown its childishness and is enlightened.

The ablest arraignment of Platonic Poetry that I have seen, as an exercise which is really science but masquerades as poetry by affecting a concern for physical objects, is that of Mr. Allen Tate in a series of studies recently in *The New Republic*. I will summarize. Platonic Poetry is allegory, a discourse in things, but on the understanding that they are translatable at every point into ideas. (The usual ideas are those which constitute the popular causes, patriotic, religious, moral, or social.) Or Platonic Poetry is the elaboration of ideas as such, but in proceeding introduces for ornament some physical properties after the style of Physical Poetry; which is rhetoric. It is positive when the poet believes in the efficacy of the ideas. It is negative when he despairs of their efficacy, because they have conspicuously failed to take care of him, and utters his personal wail:

> I fall upon the thorns of life! I bleed!

This is "Romantic Irony," which comes at occasional periods to interrupt the march of scientific optimism. But it still falls under the category of Platonism; it generally proposes some other ideas to take the place of those which are in vogue.

But why Platonism? To define Platonism we must remember that it is not the property of the historical person who reports dialogues about it in an Academy, any more than "pure poetry" is the property of the talkers who describe it from a house on Ebury Street. Platonism, in the sense I mean, is the name of an impulse that is native to us all, frequent, tending to take a too complete possession of our minds. Why should the spirit of mortal be proud? The chief explanation is that modern mortal is probably a Platonist. We are led to believe that nature is rational and that by the force of reasoning we shall possess it. I have read upon high authority: "Two great forces are persistent in Plato: the love of truth and zeal for human improvement." The forces are one force. We love to view the world under universal or scientific ideas to which we give the name truth; and this is because the ideas seem to make not for righteousness but for mastery. The Platonic view of the world is ultimately the predatory, for it reduces to the scientific, which we know. The Platonic Idea becomes the Logos which science worships, which is the Occidental God, whose minions we are, and whose children, claiming a large share in His powers for patrimony.

Now the fine Platonic world of ideas fails to coincide with the original world of perception, which is the world populated by the stubborn and contingent objects, and to which as artists we fly in shame. The sensibility manifested by artists makes fools of scientists, if the latter are inclined to take their special and quite useful form of truth as the whole and comprehensive article. A dandified pagan worldling like Moore can always defeat Platonism; he does it every hour; he can exhibit the savor of his fish and wines, the fragrance of his coffee and cigars, and the solidity of the images in his favorite verse. These are objects which have to be experienced, and cannot be reported, for what is their simple essence that the Platonist can abstract? Moore may sound mystical but he is within the literal truth when he defends "pure poetry" on the ground that the things are constant, and it is the ideas which change—changing according to the latest mode under which the species indulges its grandiose expectation of subjugating nature. The things are constant in the sense that the ideas are never emancipated from the necessity of referring back to them as their original; and the sense that they are not altered nor diminished no matter which ideas may take off from them as a point of departure. The way to obtain the true *Dinglichkeit* of a formal dinner or a landscape or a beloved person is to approach the object as such, and in humility; then it unfolds a nature which we are unprepared for if we have put our trust in the simple idea which attempted to represent it.

The special antipathy of Moore is to the ideas as they put on their moral complexion, the ideas that relate everything to that insignificant centre of action, the human "soul" in its most Platonic and Pharisaic aspect. Nothing can darken perception better than a repetitive moral earnestness, based on the reputed superiority and higher destiny of the human species. If morality is the code by which we expect the race to achieve the more perfect possession of nature, it is an incitement to a more heroic science, but not to æsthetic experience, nor religious; if it is the code of humility, by which we intend to know nature as nature is, that is another matter; but in an age of science morality is inevitably for the general public the former; and so transcendent a morality as the latter is now unheard of. And therefore:

> O love, *they* die in yon rich sky,
>   *They* faint on hill or field or river;
> *Our* echoes roll from soul to soul,
>   And grow forever and forever.

The italics are mine. These lines conclude an otherwise innocent poem, a candidate for the anthology, upon which Moore remarks: "The Victorian could never reconcile himself to finishing a poem without speaking about the soul, and the lines are particularly vindictive." Vindictive is just. By what right did the Laureate exult in the death of the physical echoes and call upon his love to witness it, but out of the imperiousness of his savage Platonism? Plato himself would have admired this ending, and considered that it redeemed an otherwise vicious poem.

Why do persons who have ideas to promulgate risk the trial by poetry? If the poets are hired to do it, which is the polite conception of some Hegelians, why do their employers think it worth the money, which they hold in public trust for the cause? Does a science have to become a poetry too? A science is the less effective as a science when it muddies its clear waters with irrelevance, a sermon becomes less cogent when it begins to quote the poets. The moralist, the scientist, and the prophet of idealism think evidently that they must establish their conclusions in poetry, though they reach these conclusions upon quite other evidence. The poetry is likely to destroy the conclusions with a sort of death by drowning, if it is a free poetry.

When that happens the Platonists may be cured of Platonism. There are probably two cures, of which this is the better. One cure is by adversity, by the failure of the ideas to work, on account of treachery or violence, or the contingencies of weather, constitution, love, and economics; leaving the Platonist defeated and bewildered, possibly humbled, but on the other hand possibly turned cynical and worthless. Very much preferable is the cure which comes by education in the fine arts, erasing his Platonism more gently, leading him to feel that that is not a becoming habit of mind which dulls the perceptions.

The definition which some writers have given to art is: the reference of the idea to the image. The implication is that the act is not for the purpose of honest comparison so much as for the purpose of proving the idea by the image. But in the event the idea is not disproved so much as it is made to look ineffective and therefore foolish. The ideas will not cover the objects upon which they are imposed, they are too attenuated and threadlike; for ideas have extension and objects have intension, but extension is thin while intension is thick.

There must be a great deal of genuine poetry which started in the poet's mind as a thesis to be developed, but in which the characters and the situations have developed faster than the thesis, and of their own accord. The thesis disappears; or it is recaptured here and there and at the end, and lodged sententiously with the reader, where every successive reading of the poem will dislodge it again. Like this must be some plays, even some play out of Shakespeare, whose thesis would probably be disentangled with difficulty out of the crowded pageant; or some narrative poem with a moral plot but much pure detail; perhaps some "occasional" piece by a Laureate or official person, whose purpose is compromised but whose personal integrity is saved by his wavering between the sentiment which is a public duty and the experience which he has in his own right; even some proclaimed allegory, like Spenser's, unlikely as that may seem, which does not remain transparent and everywhere translatable into idea but makes excursions into the territory of objectivity. These are hybrid performances. They cannot possess beauty of design, though there may be a beauty in detailed passages. But it is common enough, and we should be grateful. The mind is a versatile agent, and unexpectedly stubborn in its determination not really to be hardened in Platonism. Even in an age of science like the nineteenth century the poetic talents are not so loyal to its apostolic zeal as they and it suppose, and do not deserve the unqualified scorn which it is fashionable to offer them, now that the tide has turned, for their performance is qualified.

But this may be not stern enough for concluding a note on Platonic Poetry. I refer again to that whose Platonism is steady and malignant. This poetry is an imitation of Physical Poetry, and not really a poetry. Platonists practise their bogus poetry in order to show that an image will prove an idea, but the literature which succeeds in this delicate mission does not contain real images but illustrations.

3. METAPHYSICAL POETRY

"Most men," Mr. Moore observes, "read and write poetry between fifteen and thirty and afterwards very seldom, for in youth we are attracted by ideas, and modern poetry being concerned almost exclusively with ideas we live on duty, liberty, and fraternity as chameleons are said to live on light and air, till at last we turn from ideas to things, thinking that we have lost our taste for poetry, unless, perchance, we are classical scholars."

Much is conveyed in this characteristic sentence, even in proportion to its length. As for the indicated chronology, the cart is put after the horse, which is its proper sequence. And it is pleasant to be confirmed in the belief that many men do recant from their Platonism and turn back to things. But it cannot be exactly a *volte-face,* for there are qualifications. If pure ideas were what these men turn from, they would have had no poetry at all in the first period, and if pure things were what they turn to, they would be having not a classical poetry but a pure imagism, if such a thing is possible, in the second.

The mind does not come unscathed and virginal out of Platonism. Ontological interest would have to develop curiously, or wastefully and discontinuously, if men through their youth must cultivate the ideas so passionately that upon its expiration they are done with ideas forever and ready to become as little (and pre-logical) children. Because of the foolishness of idealists are ideas to be taboo for the adult mind?

And, as critics, what are we to do with those poems (like *The Canonization* and *Lycidas*) which could not obtain admission by Moore into the anthology but which very likely are the poems we cherish beyond others?

The reputed "innocence" of the æsthetic moment, the "knowledge without desire" which Schopenhauer praises, must submit to a little scrutiny, like anything else that looks too good to be true. We come into this world as aliens come into a land which they must conquer if they are to live. For native endowment we have an exacting "biological" constitution which knows precisely what it needs and determines for us our inevitable desires. There can be no certainty that any other impulses are there, for why should they be? They scarcely belong in the biological picture. Perhaps we are simply an efficient animal species, running smoothly, working fast, finding the formula of life only too easy, and after a certain apprenticeship piling up power and wealth far beyond the capacity of our appetites to use. What will come next? Perhaps poetry, if the gigantic effort of science begins to seem disproportionate to the reward, according to a sense of diminishing returns. But before this pretty event can come to pass, it is possible that every act of attention which is allowed us is conditioned by a gross and selfish interest.

Where is innocence then? The æsthetic moment appears as a curious moment of suspension; between the Platonism in us, which is militant, always sciencing and devouring, and a starved inhibited aspiration towards innocence which, if it could only be free, would like to respect and know the object as it might of its own accord reveal itself.

The poetic impulse is not free, yet it holds out stubbornly against science for the enjoyment of its images. It means to reconstitute the world of perceptions. Finally there is suggested some such formula as the following:

Science gratifies a rational or practical impulse and exhibits the minimum of perception. Art gratifies a perceptual impulse and exhibits the minimum of reason.

Now it would be strange if poets did not develop many technical devices for the sake of increasing the volume of the percipienda or sensibilia. I will name some of them.

First Device: metre. Metre is the most obvious device. A formal metre impresses us as a way of regulating very drastically the material, and we do not stop to remark (that is, as readers) that it has no particular aim except some nominal sort of regimentation. It symbolizes the predatory method, like a sawmill which intends to reduce all the trees to fixed unit timbers, and as business men we require some sign of our business. But to the Platonic censor in us it gives a false security, for so long as the poet appears to be working faithfully at his metrical engine he is left comparatively free to attend lovingly to the things that are being metered, and metering them need not really hurt them. Metre is the gentlest violence he can do them, if he is expected to do some violence.

Second Device: fiction. The device of the fiction is probably no less important and universal in poetry. Over every poem which looks like a poem is a sign which reads: This road does not go through to action; fictitious. Art always sets out to create an "æsthetic distance" between the object and the subject, and art takes pains to announce that it is not history. The situation treated is not quite an actual situation, for science is likely to have claimed that field, and exiled art; but a fictive or hypothetical one, so that science is less greedy and perception may take hold of it. Kant asserted that the æsthetic judgment is not concerned with the existence or non-existence of the object, and may be interpreted as asserting that it is so far from depending on the object's existence that it really depends on the object's non-existence. Sometimes we have a certain melancholy experience. We enjoy a scene which we receive by report only, or dream, or meet with in art; but subsequently find ourselves in the presence of an actual one that seems the very same scene; only to discover that we have not now the power to enjoy it, or to receive it æsthetically, because the economic tension is upon us and will not indulge us in the proper mood. And it is generally easier to obtain our æsthetic experience from art than from nature, because nature is actual, and communication is forbidden. But in being called fictive or hypothetical the art-object suffers no disparagement. It cannot be true in the sense of being actual, and therefore it may be despised by science. But it is true in the sense of being fair or representative, in permitting the "illusion of reality"; just as Schopenhauer discovered that music may symbolize all the modes of existence in the world; and in keeping with the customary demand of the readers of fiction proper, that it shall be "true to life." The defenders of art must require for it from its practitioners this sort of truth, and must assert of it before the world this dignity. If jealous science succeeds in keeping the field of history for its own exclusive use, it does not therefore annihilate the arts, for they reappear in a field which may be called real though one degree removed from actuality. There the arts perform their function with much less interference, and at the same time with about as much fidelity to the phenomenal world as history has.

Third Device: tropes. I have named two important devices; I am not prepared to offer the exhaustive list. I mention but one other kind, the device which comprises the figures of speech. A proper scientific discourse has no intention of employing figurative language for its definitive sort of utterance. Figures of speech twist accidence away from the straight course, as if to intimate astonishing lapses of rationality beneath the smooth surface of discourse, inviting perceptual attention, and weakening the tyranny of science over the senses. But I skip the several easier and earlier figures, which are timid, and stop on the climactic figure, which is the metaphor; with special reference to its consequence, a poetry which once in our history it produced in a beautiful and abundant exhibit, called Metaphysical Poetry.

And what is Metaphysical Poetry? The term was added to the official vocabulary of criticism by Johnson, who probably took it from Pope, who probably took it from Dryden, who used it to describe the poetry of a certain school of poets, thus: "He [John Donne] affects the metaphysics, not only in his satires, but in his amorous verses, where nature only should reign. . . . In this Mr. Cowley has copied him to a fault." But the meaning of metaphysical which was common in Dryden's time, having come down from the Middle Ages through Shakespeare, was simply: supernatural; *miraculous.* The context of the Dryden passage indicates it.

Dryden, then, noted a miraculism in poetry and repudiated it; except where it was employed for satire, where it was not seriously intended and had the effect of wit. Dryden himself employs miraculism wittily, but seems rather to avoid it if he will be really committed by it; he may employ it in his translations of Ovid, where the responsibility is Ovid's and not Dryden's, and in an occasional classical piece where he is making polite use of myths well known to be pagan errors. In his "amorous" pieces he finds the reign of nature sufficient, and it is often the worse for his amorous pieces. He is not many removes from a naturalist. (A naturalist is a person who studies nature not because he loves it but because he wants to use it, approaches it from the standpoint of common sense, and sees it thin and not thick.) Dryden might have remarked that Donne himself had a change of heart and confined his miraculism at last to the privileged field of a more or less scriptural revelation. Perhaps Dryden found his way to accepting Milton because Milton's miraculism was mostly not a contemporary sort but classical and scriptural, pitched in a time when the age of miracles had not given way to the age of science. He knew too that Cowley had shamefully recanted from his petty miraculism, which formed the conceits, and turned to the scriptural or large order of miraculism to write his heroic (but empty) verses about David; and had written a Pindaric ode in extravagant praise of "Mr. Hobs," whose naturalistic account of nature seemed to render any other account fantastic if not contrary to the social welfare.

Incidentally, we know how much Mr. Hobbes affected Dryden too, and the whole of Restoration literature. What Bacon with his disparagement of poetry had begun, in the cause of science and protestantism, Hobbes completed. The name of Hobbes is critical in any history that would account for the chill which settled upon the poets at the very moment that English poetry was attaining magnificently to the fullness of its powers. The name stood for common sense and naturalism, and the monopoly of the scientific spirit over the mind. Hobbes was the adversary, the Satan, when the latter first intimidated the English poets. After Hobbes his name is legion.

"Metaphysics," or miraculism, informs a poetry which is the most original and exciting, and intellectually perhaps the most seasoned, that we know in our literature, and very probably it has few equivalents in other literatures. But it is evident that the metaphysical effects may be large-scale or they may be small-scale. (I believe that generically, or ontologically, no distinction is to be made between them.) If Donne and Cowley illustrate the small-scale effects, Milton will illustrate the large-scale ones, probably as a consequence of the fact that he wrote major poems. Milton, in the *Paradise Lost*, told a story which was heroic and miraculous in the first place. In telling it he dramatized it, and allowed the scenes and characters to develop of their own native energy. The virtue of a long poem on a "metaphysical" subject will consist in the dramatization or substantiation of all the parts, the poet not being required to devise fresh miracles on every page so much as to establish the perfect "naturalism" of the material upon which the grand miracle is imposed. The *Paradise Lost* possesses this virtue nearly everywhere:

> Thus *Adam* to himself lamented loud
> Through the still Night, not now, as ere man fell,
> Wholsom and cool, and mild, but with black Air
> Accompanied, with damps and dreadful gloom,
> Which to his evil Conscience represented

All things with double terror: On the ground
Outstretcht he lay, on the cold ground, and oft
Curs'd his Creation, Death as oft accus'd
Of tardie execution, since denounc't
The day of his offence. Why comes not Death,
Said hee, with one thrice acceptable stroke
To end me?

This is exactly the sort of detail for a large-scale metaphysical work, but it would hardly serve the purpose with a slighter and more natural-istic subject; with "amorous" verses. For the critical mind Metaphysical Poetry refers perhaps almost entirely to the so-called "conceits" that constitute its staple. To define the conceit is to define small-scale Meta-physical Poetry.

It is easily defined, upon a little citation. Donne exhibits two con-ceits, or two branches of one conceit in the familiar lines:

Our hands were firmly cemented
By a fast balm which thence did spring;
Our eye-beams twisted, and did thread
Our eyes upon one double string.

The poem which follows sticks to the topic; it represents the lovers in precisely that mode of union and no other. Cowley is more conventional yet still bold in the lines:

Oh take my Heart, and by that means you'll prove
    Within, too stor'd enough of love:
Give me but yours, I'll by that change so thrive
    That Love in all my parts shall live.
So powerful is this my change, it render can,
My outside Woman, and your inside Man.

A conceit originates in a metaphor; and in fact the conceit is but a metaphor if the metaphor is meant; that is, if it is developed so literally that it must be meant, or predicated so baldly that nothing else can be meant. Perhaps this will do for a definition.

Clearly the seventeenth century had the courage of its metaphors, and imposed them imperially on the nearest things, and just as clearly the nineteenth century lacked this courage, and was half-heartedly meta-phorical, or content with similes. The difference between the literary qualities of the two periods is the difference between the metaphor and the simile. (It must be admitted that this like other generalizations will not hold without its exceptions.) One period was pithy and original in its poetic utterance, the other was prolix and predictable. It would not quite commit itself to the metaphor even if it came upon one. Shelley is about as vigorous as usual when he says in *Adonais:*

> Thou young Dawn,
> Turn all thy dew to splendour. . . .

But splendor is not the correlative of dew, it has the flat tone of a Platonic idea, while physically it scarcely means more than dew with sunshine upon it. The seventeenth century would have said: "Turn thy dew, which is water, into fire, and accomplish the transmutation of the elements." Tennyson in his boldest lyric sings:

> Come into the garden, Maud,
> For the black bat, night, has flown,

and leaves us unpersuaded of the bat. The predication would be complete without the bat, "The black night has flown," and a flying night is not very remarkable. Tennyson is only affecting a metaphor. But later in the same poem he writes:

> The red rose cries, "She is near, she is near";
> And the white rose weeps, "She is late";
> The larkspur listens, "I hear, I hear";
> And the lily whispers, "I wait."

And this is a technical conceit. But it is too complicated for this author, having a plurality of images which do not sustain themselves individually. The flowers stand for the lover's thoughts, and have been prepared for carefully in an earlier stanza, but their distinctness is too arbitrary, and these are like a schoolgirl's made-up metaphors. The passage will not compare with one on a very similar situation in *Green Candles,* by Mr. Humbert Wolfe:

> "I know her little foot," gray carpet said:
> "Who but I should know her light tread?"
> "She shall come in," answered the open door,
> "And not," said the room, "go out any more."

Wolfe's conceit works and Tennyson's does not, and though Wolfe's performance seems not very daring or important, and only pleasant, he employs the technique of the conceit correctly: he knows that the miracle must have a basis of verisimilitude.

Such is Metaphysical Poetry; the extension of a rhetorical device; as one of the most brilliant successes in our poetry, entitled to long and thorough examination; and even here demanding somewhat by way of a more ontological criticism. I conclude with it.

We may consult the dictionary, and discover that there is a miraculism or supernaturalism in a metaphorical assertion if we are ready to mean what we say, or believe what we hear. Or we may read Mr. Hobbes, the naturalist, who was very clear upon it: "II. The second cause of absurd assertions I ascribe to the giving of names of 'bodies' to 'accidents,' or of 'accidents' to 'bodies,' as they do that say 'faith is infused' or 'inspired,' when nothing can be 'poured' or 'breathed' into anything but body . . . and that 'phantasms' are 'spirits,' etc." Translated into our present terms, Hobbes is condemning the confusion of single qualities with whole things; or the substitution of concrete images for simple ideas.

Specifically, the miraculism arises when the poet discovers by analogy an identity between objects which is partial, though it should be considerable, and proceeds to an identification which is complete. It is to be contrasted with the simile, which says "as if" or "like," and is scrupulous to keep the identification partial. In Cowley's passage above, the lover is saying, not for the first time in this literature: "She and I have exchanged our hearts." What has actually been exchanged is affections, and affections are only in a limited sense the same as hearts. Hearts are unlike affections in being engines that pump blood and form body; and it is a miracle if the poet represents the lady's affection as rendering her inside into man. But he succeeds, with this mixture, in depositing with us the image of a very powerful affection.

From the strict point of view of literary criticism it must be insisted that the miraculism which produces the humblest conceit is the same miraculism which supplies to religions their substantive content. (This is said to assert the dignity not of the conceits but of the religions.) It is the poet and nobody else who gives to the God a nature, a form, faculties, and a history; to the God, most comprehensive of all terms, which, if there were no poetic impulse to actualize or "find" Him, would remain the driest and deadest among Platonic ideas, with all intension sacrificed to infinite extension. The myths are conceits, born of metaphors. Religions are periodically produced by poets and destroyed by naturalists. Religion depends for its ontological validity upon a literary understanding, and that is why it is frequently misunderstood. The metaphysical poets, perhaps like their spiritual fathers the mediæval Schoolmen, were under no illusions about this. They recognized myth, as they recognized the conceits, as a device of expression; its sanctity as the consequence of its public or social importance.

But whether the topics be Gods or amorous experiences, why do poets resort to miraculism? Hardly for the purpose of controverting natural fact or scientific theory. Religion pronounces about God only where science is silent and philosophy is negative; for a positive is wanted, that is, a God who has his being in the physical world as well as in the world of principles and abstractions. Likewise with the little secular enterprises of poetry too. Not now are the poets so brave, not for a very long time have they been so brave, as to dispute the scientists on what they call their "truth"; though it is a pity that the statement cannot be turned round. Poets will concede that every act of science is legitimate, and has its efficacy. The metaphysical poets of the seventeenth century particularly admired the methodology of science, and in fact they copied it, and their phrasing is often technical, spare, and polysyllabic, though they are not repeating actual science but making those metaphorical substitutions that are so arresting.

The intention of Metaphysical Poetry is to complement science, and improve discourse. Naturalistic discourse is incomplete, for either of two reasons. It has the minimum of physical content and starves the sensibility, or it has the maximum, as if to avoid the appearance of evil, but is laborious and pointless. Platonic Poetry is too idealistic, but Physical Poetry is too realistic, and realism is tedious and does not maintain interest. The poets therefore introduce the psychological device of the miracle. The predication which it permits is clean and quick but it is not a scientific predication. For scientific predication concludes an act of attention but miraculism initiates one. It leaves us looking, marvelling, and revelling in the thick *dinglich* substance that has just received its strange representation.

Let me suggest as a last word, in deference to a common Puritan scruple, that the predication of Metaphysical Poetry is true enough. It is not true like history, but no poetry is true in that sense, and only a part of science. It is true in the pragmatic sense in which some of the generalizations of science are true: it accomplishes precisely the sort of representation that it means to. It suggests to us that the object is perceptually or physically remarkable, and we had better attend to it.

SUPPLEMENT

DIONYSIUS OF HALICARNASSUS

(*c.* 50–7 B. C.)

From

DE ANTIQUIS ORATORIBUS *

§§1–2

WE ought to feel very grateful to the times we live in, my dear Ammaeus, for improvement in many studies, and most particularly for the great advance made in political oratory. In the epoch before ours, the old philosophic type of Rhetoric, subjected to monstrous ill-treatment, was being destroyed. From the death of Alexander of Macedon she had gradually withered and declined, till in our own day she was almost gone. A new type of Rhetoric had supplanted her, an ill-bred, pretentious Rhetoric of intolerable effrontery, devoid of philosophy and every form of liberal education. Undetected by the ignorant and deluded mob, this new Rhetoric not only lived in greater wealth and luxury and magnificence than the other, but had actually attached to herself the posts of honour and political importance which should have belonged to her philosophic sister. She was a thoroughly vulgar and disagreeable person, and finally she made Greece resemble the house of a miserable debauchee. Just as in such a house the free-born, respectable wife sits deprived of all power over her possessions, while a giddy lady of pleasure, who is there to ruin the property, claims to rule the whole establishment, terrorizing the other and treating her like dirt: so it happened in every city in Greece, and, to crown all, in the educated ones as much as any. The ancient, indigenous Muse of Athens was reduced to a position of insignificance, expelled from her own possessions, while her rival, a parvenue from some Asiatic jail, some Phrygian or Carian or barbarian creature, claimed to administer Hellenic cities, driving the other out of

* Translated by W. Rhys Roberts (Cambridge, England: Cambridge University Press).

public life. Thus the ignoramus expelled the philosopher, the mad the sane.[1]

However, it is not only of just men that, as Pindar says: "time is the surest saviour," but of arts and studies and all else that is good. Our own day has proved that. Whether the initiative came from some god, or from nature's cycle bringing round the ancient order again, or from an impulse in mankind urging many people in the same direction: whichever it was, the present age has restored to the ancient, sober Rhetoric her former merited repute, and has compelled the new, silly Rhetoric to cease enjoying the fruits of a distinction to which she has no claim, and living luxuriously on the good things of another. Nor perhaps should we merely commend the present age, and the philosophers who aided it, for initiating a betterment of taste (though it is truly said that the beginning is half the whole), but also for effecting so swift a revolution and so striking an improvement. There are a few cities in Asia whose ignorance makes them slow to learn what is noble. But the rest of the world has stopped admiring vulgar, frigid and stupid oratory. Those who formerly prided themselves on such productions are learning shame, and are gradually deserting to the other side, except for a few incurables: while those who are just beginning their studies bring these speeches into contempt, and ridicule the idea of taking them seriously.[2]

---

[1] When the Romans began seriously to study prose writing and oratory (about 130 B. C.), they took as models the Asiatic. By 60 B. C., a reaction had set in. Quintilian (1st Century A. D.) wrote of this conflict: "From ancient times there has been the well-known division of Attic and Asiatic writers—the former being thought succinct and vigorous, the latter inflated and empty . . . a third division—the Rhodian—they would have to be a mean and mixture of the two." Quintilian wrote after the Atticists had largely triumphed; the century before, Cicero (who was Rhodian-trained) had attacked Asiatic excesses but fought the tendency to imitate particular Attic authors: he advised Romans [*Brutus*, XVII, 68] "not merely to copy the dry bones but also to imbibe the living spirit of their models." Quintilian pointed out the differing natures of Greek and Latin, in personality and language: the Greeks were more subtle and graceful, but the Romans stronger and weightier. This difference in character was not often considered. Men like Caecilius (friend of Dionysius and foe of Longinus) set about comparing Greek and Roman authors, recommending close imitations, and making elaborate attacks on the Asiatics. In the *Satyricon of T. Petronius Arbiter* [Burnaby's trans.], there is a statement which is undoubtedly typical of the Atticists' position: "This windy and irregular way of babbling came lately out of Asia into Athens; and . . . at once corrupted and put a period to all true Eloquence."

[2] Worth noting is the critical remark of Dionysius [*Early History of Rome*, i, 3]: "the style is the man." Better known, however, is Georges-Louis de Buffon's "Le style, c'est l'homme même."

MARCUS FABIUS QUINTILIANUS

(*c.* 35 A. D.–*c.* 100 A. D.)

From

INSTITUTIO ORATORIA X *

(96 A. D.)

II. FROM these authors [Homer, Virgil, Demosthenes, Cicero, etc.] and others worthy of being read must be gathered one's supply of words, variety of figures, method of composing; on the examples of excellencies the mind must be shaped. For it cannot be doubted that a great part of art is included in imitation (*imitatio*). As inventing (*invenire*) came first and is of greatest importance, so it is expedient to follow what has been well invented. It is a principle of universal application that what we approve in others we wish to do ourselves. So boys follow the shapes of letters, that they may acquire the practice of writing; so musicians take for models the voices of their teachers, painters the works of their predecessors, farmers the principles of agriculture that have been demonstrated. We may observe that the elements of every science are built to a design set out for it. We must be either like or unlike those who are good at it. Seldom does nature furnish the similarity; imitation does frequently. But this which renders the planning of everything so much easier for us than it was for those who had nothing to follow, proves an ill, unless it be embraced with caution and judgment. After all, imitation *per se* is not sufficient, if for no other reason, because the indolent content themselves with what have been invented by others. What would have happened in those times which were without models, if men had thought that nothing could be done or conceived except what had already been conceived? Certainly nothing would have been invented. Why, therefore, is it censurable for something to be devised by us which never was before?

·   •   •

* Translated by J. H. Smith.

Further, the greatest qualities of oratory are inimitable genius, invention, forcefulness, ease, and that something which art cannot transmit. Many, indeed, after they have excerpted certain words from orations or some particular rhythms of a composition, think that they have represented admirably what they have read; yet words become forgotten and revive with the times, the absolute standard for them being in usage, and they are not good or bad inherently (for in themselves they are only sounds), but according to whether they are opportunely and appropriately placed or not, and the arrangement adapted to the material, wherein variety is the most pleasing quality.

AELIUS DONATUS

(4th Century A. D.)

From

DE COMOEDIA ET TRAGOEDIA *

COMEDY deals with the various habits and customs of private and public affairs, from which one may learn what is of use in life, and what on the other hand must be avoided. . . . Cicero says that comedy is "a copy of life, a mirror of custom, a reflection of truth. . . ." [1] Livius Andronicus initiated comedy among us; he wrote "Comedy is a mirror of every-day life."

---

* Translated by Aileen Wells Parks.

[1] This remark has been quoted, translated, and paraphrased continually by later writers, with credit sometimes given to Donatus but more frequently to Cicero. It is possible that Cicero drew on Terence [*Adelphi,* 415], who has one character direct his son "to look into the lives of men, as it were into a mirror, and to take from them an example." Among the Renaissance critics who appealed to Cicero's authority by using these attributed words were Minturno, Tasso, Robortelli, Thomas Lodge (Gosson, answering Lodge, denied that the sentence could be found in Cicero's work), Lope de Vega, Cervantes—the list could easily be expanded. The best-known variation is Shakespeare's [*Hamlet,* III, 2], with reference to acting and the stage generally: "Suit the action to the word, the word to the action; with this special observance, that you o'erstep not the modesty of nature. For anything so overdone is from the purpose of playing, whose end, both at the first and now, was and is, to hold, as 'twere, the mirror up to nature; to show virtue her own feature, scorn her own image, and the very age and body of the time his form and pressure."

MANLIUS SEVERINUS BOETHIUS

(c. 470–524)

From

DE CONSOLATIONE PHILOSOPHIAE *

(c. 523)

WHEN she saw that the Muses of poetry were present by my couch giving words to my lamenting, she was stirred a while; her eyes flashed fiercely, and said she, 'Who has suffered these seducing mummers to approach this sick man? Never do they support those in sorrow by any healing remedies, but rather do ever foster the sorrow by poisonous sweets. These are they who stifle the fruit-bearing harvest of reason with the barren briars of the passions: they free not the minds of men from disease, but accustom them thereto. I would think it less grievous if your allurements drew away from me some uninitiated man, as happens in the vulgar herd. In such an one my labours would be naught harmed, but this man has been nourished in the lore of Eleatics and Academics; and to him have ye reached? Away with you, Sirens, seductive unto destruction! leave him to my Muses to be cared for and to be healed.'

SAINT THOMAS AQUINAS

(1225?–1274?)

From

THE "SUMMA THEOLOGICA" **

(Begun 1265)

FIRST PART

QUESTION I

THE NATURE AND EXTENT OF SACRED DOCTRINE

(In Ten Articles)

To place our purpose within proper limits, we first endeavour to investigate the nature and extent of this sacred doctrine. Concerning this there are ten points of inquiry:—

* Translated by W. V. Cooper.
** Literally translated by Fathers of the English Dominican Province.

(1) Whether it is necessary? (2) Whether it is a science? (3) Whether it is one or many? (4) Whether it is speculative or practical? (5) How it is compared with other sciences? (6) Whether it is the same as wisdom? (7) Whether God is its subject-matter? (8) Whether it is a matter of argument? (9) Whether it rightly employs metaphors and similes? (10) Whether the Sacred Scripture of this doctrine may be expounded in different senses?

·   ·   ·

TENTH ARTICLE

Whether in Holy Scripture a Word May Have Several Senses?
We proceed thus to the Tenth Article:—

Objection 1. It seems that in Holy Writ a word cannot have several senses, historical or literal, allegorical, tropological or moral, and anagogical. For many different senses in one text produce confusion and deception and destroy all force of argument. Hence no argument, but only fallacies, can be deduced from a multiplicity of propositions. But Holy Writ ought to be able to state the truth without any fallacy. Therefore in it there cannot be several senses to a word.

Obj. 2. Further, Augustine says (*De util. cred.* iii.) that *the Old Testament has a fourfold division as to history, etiology, analogy, and allegory.* Now these four seem altogether different from the four divisions mentioned in the first objection. Therefore it does not seem fitting to explain the same word of Holy Writ according to the four different senses mentioned above.

Obj. 3. Further, besides these senses, there is the parabolical, which is not one of these four.

On the contrary, Gregory says (*Moral.* xx., 1): *Holy Writ by the manner of its speech transcends every science, because in one and the same sentence, while it describes a fact, it reveals a mystery.*

I answer that, The author of Holy Writ is God, in whose power it is to signify His meaning, not by words only (as man also can do), but also by things themselves. So, whereas in every other science things are signified by words, this science has the property, that the things signified by the words have themselves also a signification. Therefore that first signification whereby words signify things belongs to the first sense, the historical or literal. That signification whereby things signified by words have themselves also a signification is called the spiritual sense, which is based on the literal, and presupposes it. Now this spiritual sense has a threefold division. For as the Apostle says (Heb. x., 1) the Old Law is a figure of the New Law, and Dionysius says (*Cœl. Hier* i.) *the New Law itself is a figure of future glory.* Again, in the New Law, whatever our Head has done is a type of what we ought to do. Therefore, so far as the things of the Old Law signify the things of the New Law, there is the allegorical sense; so far as the things done in Christ, or so far as the things which signify Christ, are types of what we ought to do, there is the moral sense. But so far as they signify what relates to eternal glory, there is the anagogical sense. Since the literal sense is that which the author intends, and since the author of Holy Writ is God, Who by one act comprehends all things by His intellect, it is not unfitting, as Augustine says (*Confess.* xii.), if, even according to the literal sense, one word in Holy Writ should have several senses.

Reply Obj. 1. The multiplicity of these senses does not produce equivocation or any other kind of multiplicity, seeing that these senses are not multiplied because one word signifies several things; but because the things signified by the words can be themselves types of other things. Thus in Holy Writ no confusion results, for all the senses are founded on one—the literal—from which alone can any argument be drawn, and not from those intended in allegory, as Augustine says (*Epist.* xlviii). Nevertheless, nothing of Holy Scripture perishes on account of this, since nothing necessary to faith is contained under the spiritual sense which is not elsewhere put forward by the Scripture in its literal sense.

Reply Obj. 2. These three—history, etiology, analogy—are grouped under the literal sense. For it is called history, as Augustine expounds (*loc. cit.*), whenever anything is simply related; it is called etiology when its cause is assigned, as when Our Lord gave the reason why Moses allowed the putting away of wives—namely, on account of the hardness of men's hearts; it is called analogy whenever the truth of one text of Scripture is shown not to contradict the truth of another. Of these four, allegory alone stands for the three spiritual senses. Thus Hugh of S. Victor (*Sacram.* iv., 4 *Prolog.*) includes the anagogical under the allegorical sense, laying down three senses only—the historical, the allegorical, and the tropological.

Reply Obj. 3. The parabolical sense is contained in the literal, for by words things are signified properly and figuratively. Nor is the figure itself, but that which is figured, the literal sense. When Scripture speaks of God's arm, the literal sense is not that God has such a member, but only what is signified by this member, namely, operative power. Hence it is plain that nothing false can ever underlie the literal sense of Holy Writ.

GIOVANNI BOCCACCIO

(1313–1375)

From

THE FOURTEENTH BOOK OF THE GENEALOGY OF THE GENTILE GODS *

(*c.* 1365)

VII. The Definition of Poetry, its Origin, and Function

THIS poetry, which ignorant triflers cast aside, is a sort of fervid and exquisite invention, with fervid expression, in speech or writing, of that which the mind has invented. It proceeds from the bosom of God, and few, I find, are the souls in whom this gift is born; indeed so wonderful a gift it is that true poets have always been the rarest of men. This fervor of poesy is sublime in its effects: it impels the soul to a longing for utterance; it brings forth strange and unheard-of creations of the mind; it arranges these meditations in a fixed order, adorns the whole composition with unusual interweaving of words and thoughts; and thus it veils truth in a fair and fitting garment of fiction. Further, if in any case the invention so requires, it can arm kings, marshal them for war, launch whole fleets from their docks, nay, counterfeit sky, land, sea, adorn young maidens with flowery garlands, portray human character in its various phases, awake the idle, stimulate the dull, restrain the rash, subdue the criminal, and distinguish excellent men with their proper meed of praise: these, and many other such, are the effects of poetry. Yet if any man who has received the gift of poetic fervor shall imperfectly fulfil its function here described, he is not, in my opinion, a laudable poet. For, however deeply the poetic impulse stirs the mind to which it is granted, it very rarely accomplishes anything commendable if the instruments by which its concepts are to be wrought out are wanting—I mean, for example, the precepts of grammar and rhetoric,

* Translated by Charles G. Osgood, *Boccaccio on Poetry* (Princeton, N. J.: Princeton University Press).

an abundant knowledge of which is opportune. I grant that many a man already writes his mother tongue admirably, and indeed has performed each of the various duties of poetry as such; yet over and above this, it is necessary to know at least the principles of the other Liberal Arts, both moral and natural, to possess a strong and abundant vocabulary, to behold the monuments and relics of the Ancients, to have in one's memory the histories of the nations, and to be familiar with the geography of various lands, of seas, rivers and mountains.

Furthermore, places of retirement, the lovely handiwork of Nature herself, are favorable to poetry, as well as peace of mind and desire for worldly glory; the ardent period of life also has very often been of great advantage. If these conditions fail, the power of creative genius frequently grows dull and sluggish.

Now since nothing proceeds from this poetic fervor, which sharpens and illumines the powers of the mind, except what is wrought out by art, poetry is generally called an art. Indeed the word poetry has not the origin that many carelessly suppose, namely *poio, pois,* which is but Latin *fingo, fingis;* rather it is derived from a very ancient Greek word *poetes,* which means in Latin exquisite discourse (*exquisita locutio*). For the first men who, thus inspired, began to employ an exquisite style of speech, such, for example, as song in an age hitherto unpolished, to render this unheard-of discourse sonorous to their hearers, let it fall in measured periods; and lest by its brevity it fail to please, or, on the other hand, become prolix and tedious, they applied to it the standard of fixed rules, and restrained it within a definite number of feet and syllables. Now the product of this studied method of speech they no longer called by the more general term poesy, but poem. Thus as I said above, the name of the art, as well as its artificial product, is derived from its effect.

Now though I allege that this science of poetry has ever streamed forth from the bosom of God upon souls while even yet in their tenderest years, these enlightened cavillers will perhaps say that they cannot trust my words. To any fair-minded man the fact is valid enough from its constant recurrence. But for these dullards I must cite witnesses to it. If, then, they will read what Cicero, a philosopher rather than a poet, says in his oration delivered before the senate in behalf of Aulus Licinius Archias, perhaps they will come more easily to believe me. He says: "And yet we have it on the highest and most learned authority, that while other arts are matters of science and formula and technique, poetry depends solely upon an inborn faculty, is evoked by a purely mental activity, and is infused with a strange supernal inspiration."

But not to protract this argument, it is now sufficiently clear to reverent men, that poetry is a practical art, springing from God's bosom and deriving its name from its effect, and that it has to do with many high and noble matters that constantly occupy even those who deny its existence. If my opponents ask when and in what circumstances, the answer is plain: the poets would declare with their own lips under whose help and guidance they compose their inventions when, for example, they raise flights of symbolic steps to heaven, or make thick-branching trees spring aloft to the very stars, or go winding about mountains to their summits. Haply, to disparage this art of poetry now unrecognized by them, these men will say that it is rhetoric which the poets employ. Indeed, I will not deny it in part, for rhetoric has also its own inventions. Yet, in truth, among the disguises of fiction rhetoric has no part, for whatever is composed as under a veil, and thus exquisitely wrought, is poetry and poetry alone.

MARCO GIROLAMO VIDA

(1480?–1566)

From

THE ART OF POETRY *

(1527)

BOOK III

What style, what language, suits the poet's lays,
To claim Apollo's and the Muses' praise,
I now unfold. To this last bound I tend,
And see my promised labors at an end.
First then, with care a just expression choose,
Led by the kind indulgence of the Muse
To dress up every subject when you write,
And set all objects in a proper light.
But lest the distant prospect of the goal
Should damp your vigor and your strength control,

---

* Translated by Christopher Pitt. (1724 ?)

Rouse every power, and call forth all the soul.
     ·   ·   ·

But now pursue the method that affords
The fittest terms and wisest choice of words.
Not all deserve alike the same regard,
Nor suit the godlike labors of the bard;
For words as much may differ in degree
As the most various kinds of poetry.
Though many a common term and word we find
Dispersed promiscuously through every kind,
Those that will never suit the heroic rage
Might grace the buskin and become the stage.
Their large, their vast variety explore
With piercing eyes, and range the mighty store.
From their deep fund the richest words unfold,
With nicest care be rich expression culled,
To deck your numbers in the purest gold;
The vile, the dark degenerate crowd refuse,
And scorn a dress that would disgrace the Muse.
   Then, to succeed your search, pursue the road,
And beat the track the glorious ancients trod;
To those eternal monuments repair,
There read, and meditate forever there.
If o'er the rest some mighty genius shines,
Mark the sweet charms and vigor of his lines;
As far as Phoebus and the heavenly powers
Smile on your labors, make his diction yours,
Your style by his authentic standard frame,
Your voice, your habit and address, the same.
With him proceed to cull the rest, for there
A full reward will justify your care;
Examine all, and bring from all away
Their various treasures as a lawful prey.
Nor would I scruple, with a due regard,
To read sometimes a rude unpolished bard.
Among whose labors I may find a line,
Which from unsightly rust I may refine,
And, with a better grace, adopt it into mine.
How often may we see a troubled flood

Stained with unsettled ooze and rising mud,
Which, if a well the bordering natives sink,   50
Supplies the thirsty multitude with drink;
The trickling stream by just degrees refines,
Till in its course the limpid current shines,
And, taught through secret labyrinths to flow,
Works itself clear among the sands below.
For nothing looks so gloomy, but will shine
From proper care and timely discipline;
If, with due vigilance and conduct, wrought
Deep in the soul, it labors in the thought.
Hence on the ancients we must rest alone;   60
And make their golden sentences our own;
To cull their best expressions claims our cares,
To form our notions and our styles on theirs.
See how we bear away their precious spoils,
And with the glorious dress enrich our styles,
Their bright inventions for our use convey,
Bring all the spirit of their words away,
And make their words themselves our lawful prey!
Unshamed in other colors to be shown,
We speak our thoughts in accents not our own.   70
But your design with modest caution weigh,
Steal with due care, and meditate the prey,
Invert the order of the words with art,
And change their former site in every part.
Thus win your readers, thus deceive with grace,
And let the expression wear a different face;
Yourself at last, the glorious labor done,
Will scarce discern his diction from your own.
Some, to appear of diffidence bereft,
Steal in broad day, and glory in the theft,   80
When with just art, design and confidence,
On the same words they graft a different sense,
Preserve the unvaried terms and order too,
But change their former spirit for a new,
Or, with the sense of emulation bold,
With ancient bards a glorious contest hold;
Their richest spoils triumphant they explore,

Which, ranged with better grace, they varnish o'er,
And give them charms they never knew before.
So trees that change their soils more proudly rise,   90
And lift their spreading honors to the skies;
And, when transplanted, nobler fruits produce,
Exalt their nature, and ferment their juice.
So Troy's famed chief the Asian empire bore,
With better omens, to the Latian shore,
Though from thy realm, O Dido, to the sea
Called by the gods reluctantly away,
Nor the first nuptial pleasures could control
The fixed, the stubborn purpose of his soul.
Unhappy queen! thy woes suppressed thy breath;   100
Thy cares pursued thee, and survived in death;
Had not the Dardan fleet thy kingdom sought,
Thy life had shone unsullied with a fault.
   Come then, ye youths, and urge your generous toils;
Come, strip the ancients, and divide the spoils
Your hands have won—but shun the fault of such
Who with fond rashness trust themselves too much.
For some we know, who, by their pride betrayed,
With vain contempt reject a foreign aid,
Who scorn those great examples to obey,   110
Nor follow where the ancients point the way.
While from the theft their cautious hands refrain,
Vain are their fears, their superstition vain,
Nor Phoebus' smiles the unhappy poet crown;
The fate of all his works prevents his own.
Himself his moldering monument survives,
And sees his labors perish while he lives;
His fame is more contracted than his span,
And the frail author dies before the man.
How would he wish the labor to forbear,   120
And follow other arts with more successful care?
   I like a fair allusion nicely wrought,
When the same words express a different thought;
And such a theft true critics dare not blame,
Which late posterity shall crown with fame;
Void of all fear, of every doubt bereft,

I would not blush, but triumph in the theft.
Nor on the ancients for the whole rely,
The whole is more than all their works supply;
Some things your own invention must explore,   130
Some virgin images untouched before.

.   .   .

When things are small the terms should still be so,
For low words please us when the theme is low.
But when some giant, horrible and grim,
Enormous in his gait, and vast in every limb,
Stalks towering on, the swelling words must rise
In just proportion to the monster's size;
If some large weight his huge arms strive to shove,
The verse too labors; the thronged words scarce move.
When each stiff clod beneath the ponderous plough   140
Crumbles and breaks, the encumbered lines march slow;
Nor less when pilots catch the friendly gales,
Unfurl their shrouds, and hoist the wide-stretched sails.

.   .   .

From every line to wipe out every blot,
Till the whole piece is guiltless of a fault,
Hard is the task, but needful, if your aim
Tends to the prospect of immortal fame.

.   .   .

But here, even here, avoid the extreme of such
Who with excess of care correct too much,
Whose barbarous hands no calls of pity bound,   150
While with the infected parts they cut the sound,
And make the cure more dangerous than the wound;
Till, all the blood and spirits drained away,
The body sickens, and the parts decay,
The native beauties die, the limbs appear
Rough and deformed with one continued scar.

.   .   .

BERNARDINO DANIELLO

(16th Century)

From

LA POETICA *

(1536)

Now, he continued, we should consider the poem, and it seems to me proper and necessary that we should first show briefly what the poetic faculty is and what the business and goal of the poet are; and afterwards we can discuss the poem and its parts. However, I say that not without excellent reason have the ancients and the most learned men compared poetry to painting and said that painting is nothing other than a silent and mute poem, and that poetry, on the other hand, is a speaking picture.[1] For just as the imitations of the pictorial artist are made with styluses, with pencils, and with a variety of colors (with which, imitating the nature, the deeds and the appearances of men or animals, he produces their images in a lively resemblance), so those of the poet are made with language and with the pen, with numbers and harmony. The poet's business, then, is the writing of things suitable and proper for instruction, and for delight. His goal is, by means of these writings, both to teach and to please. In the same way, the business of

* Translated by Calvin S. Brown, Jr.

[1] Minturno (De Poeta) agrees with this: "It would be superfluous to offer instructions for painting, for the painter is so close to the poet, that a poem is but a speaking picture, and a picture a silent poem." (Sidney probably draws from this source.) Tasso (Opere, XI) says, "the poet is a speaking painter," but Castelvetro disagrees sharply: "that which in poetry is first and of most account, the imitation of a human action as it ought to be, is the last in painting . . . in painting, the history or the plot is of no account." Charlton (Castelvetro's Theory of Poetry, 63–64) notes that to Castelvetro "the art of painting is like that of history, not that of poetry . . . the 'goodness' which the painter imitates is solely the goodness of the body, i. e., beauty, and that, says Castelvetro, is quite different from the goodness poets imitate, the goodness of the mind, i. e., character. . . . It is plain, then, that Castelvetro made the nature of the matter represented the basis of the distinction between poetry and painting. With truer insight, Lessing established it on consideration of the fundamental difference in the means of representation: painting uses forms and colours in space, poetry articulate sounds in time; hence, Lessing argues, bodies with their visible properties are the special subjects of painting, actions the special subjects of poetry. Castelvetro has nothing of this depth, but he does distinguish between poetry and painting. . . ." For other discussions on this point, see the selections from Reynolds and Lessing, and the introductions to their work.

the orator is speaking in a way apt and proper for persuasion. His goal is, by speaking aptly, to persuade. And the doctor's business is diligently to care for the sick man. His goal is, by this care, to cure him. And although the orator does not always convince the judges, and the doctor does not always cure his fevered patient, each of them can (without fear of correction) feel that he has achieved his goal—the former by having spoken well and elegantly, and the latter by having given the best treatment. But the poet's case is not at all a parallel. He who does not always teach and please either his audience or his readers cannot and should not consider himself worthy of the name of poet.

At present we will not stop to consider the types of poetry which are called active [dramatic], mixed (or common, if you prefer the term), and narrative. In the first of these the poet argues or narrates through the mouths of other characters; in the other two, he speaks sometimes partly in his own person and partly through his characters, or sometimes in his own person alone. Nor will we consider how, or when, or under what circumstances the inventors of tragedy and comedy first assigned to them their names, characters, choruses, prologues, and number of actors. These matters are all trivial and irrelevant, and not in keeping with our purpose.

Passing over these things, and speaking of the poem in general, I say that there are three principal elements to which the poem owes its condition and nature. The first is invention, or perhaps I should say discovery [*ritrovamento*]. Next comes disposition, or the arrangement of materials. Last comes the art of writing ornately the things already invented and arranged—an art which (to use a Latinized word) is called *elocution,* and which we call, in the vernacular, speaking smoothly and beautifully. Beginning, then, with the first of these three parts, I say that (in spite of what some think) no specific type of material is necessary for the poet. Hence he has full license (just as the painter can represent many and divers things, in divers ways) to discuss and write about all things which please him.[2] It is true, however, that he should always be careful to choose the most beautiful and loveliest flower of all, and then so to cultivate it with the living waters of his genius that neither cold nor hot seasons, nor injurious windy rains will be able

---

[2] Often quoted by Renaissance critics as justification for poetic license and the machinery of the heroic poem, were the remarks of T. Petronius Arbiter [*The Satyricon,* c. 60 A.D., W. Burnaby's trans.]: "for to relate past Actions, is not so much the business of a Poet, as an Historian; the boundless Genius of a Poet strikes through all Mazes, introduces Gods, and puts the Invention on the rack for Poetick Ornaments; that it may rather seem a Prophetick fury, than a strict relation, with witnesses of meer truth."

to cut it from its stem; but, safe from all these dangers, it will endure in perpetuity.

ANTONIO SEBASTIAN MINTURNO

(16th Century)

From

L'ARTE POETICA *

(1564)

[Vespesiano Gonzaga and Antonio Minturno]

M. . . . Hence such tales [as the romances] are very severely condemned, for in them we see many things inserted against verisimilitude and by no necessity—things such as usually fill our dreams.

V. You mean the loves and the famous deeds of the Paladins, which well deserve to be remembered by the noblest writers throughout eternity.

M. But do you not find in such books many episodes far removed from the principal action, and wide of the subject, introduced into them for no assignable reason; and are not their verses veritable crowds of romances?

V. But in spite of that, they are more eagerly sung, and any of the lays of the loves and deeds of Rinaldo or Orlando are more eagerly read, than any of the more graceful *Canzoni,* or the best sonnets of Petrarch.

M. True enough, but by whom? And with what judgment? By men of the common people, who do not know what poetry is, or what constitutes the excellence of a poet. I, for my part, value a sonnet of Petrarch more than all the romances; hence I consider the popular taste wrong.

V. But from the same material would it not be possible to make either poetic romances or a fine poem?

M. Why not? But with a different arrangement, different treatment,

* Translated by Calvin S. Brown, Jr.

and a different style.[1] Anyone who follows this discussion of ours will easily be able to see that.

V. Since we have come this far in our conversation, what is a romance?

M. I will not deny that it is an imitation of actions which are great, illustrious, and worthy of epic poetry. [A short explanation of the etymology of the foreign word, *romanzi,* follows.] This same word is used in Italy, since our writers have begun imitating the compositions of the outlanders. And since our people, as Cicero says, always improve the things which others invent, they have made the poetry of the romance more graceful and more beautiful—if it can be called poetry.

---

[1] Other critics did not hesitate to claim special liberties for new genres. Cinthio Giraldi (*Discorso dei Romanzi,* 1554) wrote a treatise to "show that the laws given by Aristotle do not extend save to the poems which are concerned with one action; but all the poetic compositions which contain deeds of heroes [i. e., Romances] are not included within the limits which Aristotle has set to writers of single-action poems." Although Cinthio wrote primarily to defend Ariosto, he was going beyond this; as Saintsbury paraphrases his words, "Kinds which the Ancients knew not, are free from the Ancients' laws." J. A. Symonds in his *Renaissance in Italy* quotes, as typical of this demand for freedom for new genres, from G. Cecchi's Prologue to his play, *La Romanesca* (1574): "The Farsa is a new third species between tragedy and comedy. It enjoys the liberties of both, and shuns their limitations; for it receives into its ample boundaries great lords and princes, which comedy does not, and, like a hospital or inn, welcomes the vilest and most plebeian of the people, to whom Dame Tragedy has never stooped. It is not restricted to certain motives; for it accepts all subjects—grave and gay, profane and sacred, urbane and crude, sad and pleasant. It does not care for time and place." In England, likewise, John Fletcher (Preface to *The Faithful Shepherdess,* 1609) claimed additional liberties: "A tragi-comedy is not so called in respect of mirth and killing, but in respect it wants deaths, which is enough to make it no tragedy, yet brings some near it, which is enough to make it no comedy, which must be a representation of familiar people . . . so that a god is as lawful in this as in a tragedy, and mean people as in a comedy." And in Spain Tirso de Molina, contemporary of Lope de Vega, argued against the unity of time (*Cigarrales de Toledo,* 1624), and in favor of new forms: "What can be more unreasonable than that a discreet character should fall in love with a modest lady in the morning . . . and marry her that night. . . . Does it matter if the drama varies the laws of ancient men, by ingeniously mingling tragedy with comedy and producing a pleasing type from these two opposite forms. . . ?"

LODOVICO CASTELVETRO

(1505–1571)

From

POETICS

(1570)

THE time of the representation and that of the action represented must be exactly coincident . . . and the scene of the action must be constant, being not merely restricted to one city or house, but indeed to that one place alone which could be visible to one person.

.   .   .

Tragedy ought to have for subject an action which happened in a very limited extent of place and in a very limited extent of time, that is, in that place and in that time, in which and for which the actors representing the action remain occupied in acting; and in no other place and in no other time. . . .

.   .   .

The time of the action ought not to exceed twelve hours.

.   .   .

There is no possibility of making the spectators believe that many days and nights have passed, when they themselves obviously know that only a few hours have actually elapsed; they refuse to be so deceived.

.   .   .

It is more marvelous when a great mutation of a hero's fortune is made, in a very limited time and in a very limited place, than when it is made in a longer time and in varied and larger places.

' Translated by H. B. Charlton.

LOPE DE VEGA

(1562–1635)

THE NEW ART OF WRITING COMEDIES IN THIS TIME *

(1609)

4. But, in truth, I discovered that comedies were not then written in Spain, as the first writers of comedy in the world thought they should be; but as many ignorant men devised them, so that they appealed to the crudeness of the populace; and thus were they first presented in such a form that he who today writes artistically dies without recognition or reward; for habit can do more among those who lack knowledge of art than can reason or force.

5. True, I have occasionally written in conformity to the art which few understand; yet, no sooner do I see from some other writer come those bizarre, over-decorated plays where the multitude gathers, and women patronize this sad art, than I hurry again to the old barbaric trade, and when writing a comedy I lock in the rules and precepts with six keys, and I banish Plautus and Terence from my study, that they may deride me not; for truth is wont to cry out, though imprisoned within dumb books; therefore, I compose plays by those precepts which were devised by those who sought the applause of all; since this mob pays for our comedies, we must talk foolishly to it in order to comply with its taste.

THOMAS CAMPION

(1566?–1620)

From

OBSERVATIONS IN THE ART OF ENGLISH POESIE

(1602)

THERE is no writing too breefe, that without obscuritie, comprehends the intent of the writer. These my late obseruations in English Poesy I

* Translated by Edd Winfield Parks.

haue thus briefely gathered, that they might proue the lesse trouble-some in perusing, and the more apt to be retayn'd in memorie. And I will first generally handle the nature of Numbers. Number is *discreta quantitas:* so that when we speake simply of number, we intend only the disseruer'd quantity; But when we speake of a Poeme written in number, we consider not only the distinct number of the sillables, but also their value, which is contained in the length or shortnes of their sound. As in Musick we do not say a straine of so many notes, but so many sem'briefes (though sometimes there are no more notes than sem'briefes) so in a verse the numeration of the sillables is not so much to be obserued, as their waite, and due proportion. In ioyning of words to harmony there is nothing more offensiue to the eare then to place a long sillable with a short note, or a short sillable with a long note, though in the last the vowell often beares it out. The world is made by Simmetry and proportion, and is in that respect compared to Musick, and Musick to Poetry: for *Terence* saith speaking of Poets, *artem qui tractant musicam,* confounding musick and Poesy together. What musick can there be where there is no proportion obserued? Learning first flourished in *Greece,* from thence it was deriued vnto the *Ro-maines,* both diligent obseruers of the number, and quantity of sillables, not in their verses only, but likewise in their prose. Learning after the declining of the *Romaine* Empire and the pollution of their language through the conquest of the *Barbarians,* lay most pitifully deformed, till the time of *Erasmus, Rewcline,* Sir *Thomas More,* and other learned men of that age, who brought the Latine toong again to light, redeem-ing it with much labour out of the hands of the illiterate Monks and Friers: as a scoffing booke, entituled *Epistolæ obscurorum virorum,* may sufficiently testifie. In those lack-learning times, and in barbarized *Italy,* began that vulgar and easie kind of Poesie which is now in vse throughout most parts of Christendome, which we abusively call Rime and Meeter, of *Rithmus* and *Metrum,* of which I will now discourse.

I am not ignorant that whosoeuer shall by way of reprehension ex-amine the imperfections of Rime must encounter with many glorious enemies, and those very expert, and ready at their weapon, that can if neede be extempore (as they say) rime a man to death. Besides there is growne a kind of prescription in the vse of Rime, to forestall the right of true numbers, as also the consent of many nations, against all which it may seeme a thing almost impossible, and vaine to contend. All this and more can not yet deterre me from a lawful defence of perfection,

or make me any whit the sooner adheare to that which is lame and
vnbeseeming. For custome I alleage, that ill vses are to be abolisht, and
that things naturally imperfect can not be perfected by vse. Old customes, if they be better, why should they not be recald, as the yet
florishing custome of numerous poesy vsed among the *Romanes* and
Grecians: But the vnaptnes of our toongs and the difficultie of imitation dishartens vs: againe, the facilitie & popularitie of Rime creates as
many Poets as a hot sommer flies. . . .

JOHN MILTON

(1608–1674)

From

LETTER TO SAMUEL HARTLIB
ON EDUCATION

(1644)

AND now, lastly, will be the time to read with them those organic arts,
which enable men to discourse and write perspicuously, elegantly, and
according to the fittest style, of lofty, mean, or lowly. Logic, therefore,
so much as is useful, is to be referred to this due place with all her
well-couched heads and topics, until it be time to open her contracted
palm into a graceful and ornate rhetoric, taught out of the rule of
Plato, Aristotle, Phalereus, Cicero, Hermogenes, Longinus. To which
poetry would be made subsequent, or indeed rather precedent, as being less subtile and fine, but more simple, sensuous, and passionate. I
mean not here the prosody of a verse, which they could not but have
hit on before among the rudiments of grammar; but that sublime art
which in Aristotle's poetics, in Horace, and the Italian commentaries
of Castelvetro, Tasso, Mazzoni, and others, teaches what the laws are
of a true epic poem, what of a dramatic, what of a lyric, what decorum
is, which is the grand masterpiece to observe. This would make them
soon perceive what despicable creatures our common rhymers and
play-writers be; and shew them what religious, what glorious and
magnificent use might be made of poetry, both in divine and human
things.

PREFACE TO PARADISE LOST

(1667)

THE measure is English heroic verse without rime, as that of Homer in Greek, and of Virgil in Latin—rime being no necessary adjunct or true ornament of poem or good verse, in longer works especially, but the invention of a barbarous age, to set off wretched matter and lame metre; graced indeed since by the use of some famous modern poets, carried away by custom, but much to their own vexation, hindrance, and constraint to express many things otherwise, and for the most part worse, than else they would have expressed them. Not without cause therefore some both Italian and Spanish poets of prime note have rejected rime both in longer and shorter works, as have also long since our best English tragedies, as a thing of itself, to all judicious ears, trivial and of no true musical delight; which consists only in apt numbers, fit quantity of syllables, and the sense variously drawn out from one verse into another, not in the jingling sound of like endings—a fault avoided by the learned ancients both in poetry and all good oratory. This neglect then of rime so little is to be taken for a defect, though it may seem so perhaps to vulgar readers, that it rather is to be esteemed an example set, the first in English, of ancient liberty recovered to heroic poem from the troublesome and modern bondage of riming.

PIERRE CORNEILLE

(1606–1684)

From

A DISCOURSE ON THE PURPOSEFULNESS AND THE PARTS OF THE DRAMATIC POEM *

(1660)

ALTHOUGH, according to Aristotle, the sole end of dramatic poetry is to please the spectators, and although most of these poems [1] have

---

* Translated by J. H. Smith.

[1] Corneille's own dramas, published with his *Discourses* for prefaces.

pleased them, I am perfectly willing to admit that many among them have not attained the end of art. "It is not to be demanded," says this philosopher, "that this kind of poetry give us every sort of pleasure, but only that proper to itself;" and to find the pleasure which is proper to it, and give that to the spectators, it is requisite to follow the precepts of art and to please them according to its rules. It is obvious that there are precepts, there being an art; but it is not obvious what they are. . . . The great subjects, those which stir the passions, and by opposing impetuosity to the laws of duty or the tendernesses of kinship, ought always to go beyond the verisimilar; they find credence among the hearers only if they be sustained either by the testimony of history, which convinces authoritatively, or by established opinion, which gives us these same hearers already quite persuaded. It is not verisimilar that Medea kill her children, that Clytemnestra assassinate her husband, that Orestes stab his mother; but history says it, and the representation of these great crimes finds none incredulous. It is neither true nor verisimilar that Andromeda, left to a sea-monster, was delivered from that peril by a knight who flew by means of wings on his feet; but that is a fiction which antiquity has accepted, and as it was transmitted so to us, no one is offended when he sees it in the theatre. It would not, however, be permissible to construct fiction on these examples. What truth or opinion might select would be rejected unless it had a foundation other than resemblance to that truth or that opinion. . . .

The centuries following have furnished us examples enough that we may go beyond these limits, and no longer follow in the footsteps of the Greeks; but I do not think that they have given us the liberty of setting aside their rules. We must, if we can, adjust ourselves to them, and apply them to ourselves. Our elimination of the chorus obliges us to fill our poems with more episodes than they did. This is a radical change, but one which ought not to go beyond their principles, although it go beyond their practice. . . .

What I advanced at the beginning of this discourse, that "dramatic poetry has for an end but the pleasing of the spectators," is not designed opinionatedly to confute those who hold for ennobling art by giving it for an object profit as well as pleasure. This dispute would seem to be bootless indeed, since it is impossible to please by following the rules unless utility be brought in. It is true that Aristotle, in the entire *Treatise on Poetics,* does not employ the word a single time; he attributes the origin of poetry to the pleasure we get in seeing the actions of men imitated; he places the part of the poem which deals with the plot above that which deals with manners, because the former contains what things most please, as *Recognitions* and the *Reversals of Intention;* he causes charm of discourse to enter into the definition of Tragedy; he rates it [tragedy] above the epic because it goes beyond it and involves decorative effect and music, which delight powerfully; and, being shorter and less diffuse, it gives one a more perfect pleasure. But it is nevertheless true that Horace advises us that we cannot please everybody unless we mix in the element of utility— that the grave and serious, the old, the lovers of virtue, will be annoyed if they do not find anything by which to profit:

> Those who are grave and serious
> Vote out the poems void of profit.
> [Horace: *Ars Poetica* 341.]

So, although utility enter only under the heading of the delectable, it does not fail to be necessary, and it is better to investigate in what manner it may find its place, than to argue, as I have said before, upon the useless question of the useful in the poem of this kind. . . .

I speak of the dramatic poem in general, although in treating of this same matter he [Aristotle] refers only to tragedy; because all that he says of it pertains also to comedy, and the difference of these two species of poetry consists only in the dignity of the characters and actions which they imitate, and not in the manner of imitating them, nor in the means used for that imitation. . . .

Comedy differs then in this from tragedy, that the latter wants for subject an action famous, extraordinary, serious: the former stops with an action which is usual and lively; the latter requires great dangers for its heroes; the former contents itself with the inquietude and the displeasures of those to whom it gives the first places among its actors. Both have this in common, that the action ought to be complete and thorough; that is to say, in the event which terminates it, the spectator ought to be so well informed of the feelings of all who have had any part that his mind is left in repose, doubting nothing.

From

A DISCOURSE ON TRAGEDY

IF the purgation of the passions takes place in tragedy, I hold that it ought to do so after the manner that I explain; but I doubt whether it ever does so, even in those plays which have the conditions which Aristotle demands. They occur in *le Cid,* and are the cause of its great success: Rodrigue and Chimène have the requisite probity submitted to passions, and these passions are their misfortune, for they are miserable only to the extent that they are enamoured of one another. They fall into distress by the human frailty of which we too are capable, like them; their misery arouses pity, and costs the spectators so many tears that this is incontestable. Our pity ought to give us fear of falling into like misfortune, and purge us of that over-plus of love which is the cause of their disaster, and makes us deplore them; but I do not know that it gives us that, or purges us, and I am afraid that the reasoning of Aristotle on this point is but a pretty idea. . . .

Nevertheless, whatever difficulty there be in considering this purgation of the passions by pity and fear effective and observable, we can still bring ourselves into accord with Aristotle. We need only say that it is not requisite that these two passions always serve together, and that it suffices, according to him, that one of the two bring about the purgation; with it understood, nevertheless, that pity does not arrive without fear, and that fear may be effective without pity. The death of the count does not produce any in *Le Cid,* and is able nevertheless better to purge us of the envy of another's glory than all the compassion that we have for Rodrigue and Chimène purges of the wild love which leaves them to be pitied. The audience could not have pity for Antiochus, for Nicodème, for Héroclitus; but if one stopped there and did not fear to fall into like misfortune, he could not be cured of any passion.

From

A DISCOURSE ON THE THREE UNITIES

I MAINTAIN, as I have previously said, that the unity of action consists, as to comedy, in a unity of intrigue, or of obstacle to the designs of the principal actors; as to tragedy, in a unity of peril, whether the hero succumb to it or escape. I do not mean that several perils may not be combined, in the latter, or several intrigues or obstacles, in the former, provided that one lead inevitably into another; the passing of the prime danger then does not complete the action, because it produces a secondary danger; and the clearing up of the one intrigue does not bring the actors into repose, since it embarrasses them with a new complication. My memory does not furnish me any ancient examples of this multiplicity of dangers bound together which does not destroy the unity of action; but I have marked as a fault the irrelative duality of plot in *Horace* and in *Théodore*, for it is not necessary in the former that the hero kill his sister immediately after his victory, or in the latter that the heroine martyr herself after having escaped prostitution. . . .

The dramatic poem is an imitation, or better yet, a portraiture of the actions of men; and it is beyond question that portraitures are more excellent in proportion as they better resemble the original. The [dramatic] representation lasts two hours, and would be a perfect resemblance if the action portrayed did not demand more to make it seem real. So let us not stop either with twelve or with twenty-four hours; but let us confine the action of the poem to the smallest space of time that we can, that the representation may better approach resemblance and perfection. . . .

As to the unity of place, I can find no precept regarding it either in Aristotle or Horace. This has brought some to think that the rule was established only in consequence of the unity of time, and to be persuaded that one might broaden the stage to include what distance a man might go and return in twenty-four hours. That opinion is somewhat libertine; if one were to have an actor travel by coach, the two sides of the theatre might represent Paris and Rouen. I should wish, in order not to annoy the spectator, that what is represented before him in two hours be able actually to take place in two hours, and that what he is shown on the stage (which does not change) be able to happen in a private room or salon, whichever might be desired; but often that is so awkward, not to say impossible, that some enlargement of place must of necessity be found, as also of time.

JOHN DENNIS

(1657–1734)

From

A LARGE ACCOUNT OF THE TASTE
IN POETRY

(1702)

.   .   .

But further, without the *Ridiculum* Comedy cannot subsist, for the design of Comedy is to amend the follies of Mankind, by exposing them. But the *Ridiculum* is a great deal more to be found in Humour, than it is in Love. For Love is so agreeable in its own nature, that it can never be made to appear Ridiculous, unless it is joyned with an Humour. Besides, Humour, if it is well writ, is always both delightful and instructive, it entertains and does good at the same time; whereas Love is very often agreeable without being instructive; nay, it very often gives a pernicious pleasure. For after all, it is a very great error in some Persons at present, to be so shy of Bawdy, and so fond of Love. For Obscenity cannot be very dangerous, because it is rude and shocking; but Love is a Passion; which is so agreeable to the movements of corrupted Nature, that by seeing it livelily touched and often represented, an Amorous disposition insensibly insinuates itself into the chastest Breast. Now as the design of every Art is to instruct and delight, it must be the design of Comedy; and therefore Humour which always both instructs and delights, must be more proper for Comedy than Love, which sometimes only barely delights, and sometimes is so far from instructing, that it insensibly corrupts an Audience.

JOSEPH ADDISON

(1672–1719)

From

SPECTATOR PAPERS

(1711–12)

From No. 62

. . .

As *true Wit* generally consists in this Resemblance and Congruity of Ideas, *false Wit* chiefly consists in the Resemblance and Congruity sometimes of single Letters, as in Anagrams, Chronograms, Lipograms, and Acrosticks: Sometimes of Syllables, as in Ecchos and Doggerel Rhymes: Sometimes of Words, as in Punns and Quibbles; and sometimes of whole Sentences or Poems, cast into the Figures of *Eggs, Axes* or *Altars:* Nay, some carry the Notion of Wit so far, as to ascribe it even to external Mimickry; and to look upon a Man as an ingenious Person, that can resemble the Tone, Posture, or Face of another.

As *true Wit* consists in the Resemblance of Ideas, and *false Wit* in the Resemblance of Words, according to the foregoing Instances; there is another kind of Wit which consists partly in the Resemblance of Ideas, and partly in the Resemblance of Words; which for Distinction Sake I shall call *mixt Wit.* This Kind of Wit is that which abounds in *Cowley,* more than in any Author that ever wrote. Mr. *Waller* has likewise a great deal of it. Mr. *Dryden* is very sparing in it. *Milton* had a Genius much above it. *Spencer* is in the same class with *Milton.* The *Italians,* even in their Epic Poetry, are full of it. Monsieur *Boileau,* who formed himself upon the Ancient Poets, has every where rejected it with Scorn. If we look after mixt Wit among the *Greek* Writers, we shall find it no where but in the Epigrammatists. There are indeed some Strokes of it in the little Poem ascribed to *Musaeus,* which by that, as well as many other Marks, betrays it self to be a modern Composition. If we look into the *Latin* Writers, we find none of this mixt Wit in *Virgil, Lucretius,* or *Catullus;* very little in *Horace*, but a great deal of it in *Ovid*, and scarce any thing else in *Martial*. . . .

Bouhours, whom I look upon to be the most penetrating of all the *French* Criticks, has taken Pains to shew, That it is impossible for any Thought to be beautiful which is not just, and has not its Foundation in the Nature of Things: That the Basis of all Wit is Truth; and that no Thought can be valuable, of which good Sense is not the Ground-work. *Boileau* has endeavoured to inculcate the same Notion in several Parts of his Writings, both in Prose and Verse. This is that natural Way of Writing, that beautiful Simplicity, which we so much admire in the Compositions of the Ancients; and which no Body deviates from, but those who want Strength of Genius to make a Thought shine in his own natural Beauties. Poets who want this Strength of Genius to give that Majestick Simplicity to Nature, which we so much admire in the Works of the Ancients, are forced to hunt after foreign Ornaments, and not to let any Piece of Wit of what Kind soever escape them. I look upon these Writers as *Goths* in Poetry, who, like those in Architecture, not being able to come up to the beautiful Simplicity of the old *Greeks* and *Romans*, have endeavoured to supply its Place with all the Extravagances of an irregular Fancy.

· · ·

From No. 409

After having thus far explained what is generally meant by a fine Taste in Writing, and shewn the Propriety of the Metaphor which is used on this Occasion, I think I may define it to be *that Faculty of the Soul, which discerns the Beauties of an Author with Pleasure, and the Imperfections with Dislike*. If a Man would know whether he is possessed of this Faculty, I would have him read over the celebrated Works of Antiquity, which have stood the Test of so many different Ages and Countries; or those Works among the Moderns, which have the Sanction of the Politer Part of our Contemporaries. If upon the Perusal of such Writings he does not find himself delighted in an extraordinary Manner, or if, upon reading the admired Passages in such Authors, he finds a Coldness and Indifference in his Thoughts, he ought to conclude, not (as is too usual among tasteless Readers) that the Author wants those Perfections which have been admired in him, but that he himself wants the Faculty of discovering them.

· · ·

From No. 416

I at first divided the Pleasures of the Imagination into such as arise from Objects that are actually before our Eyes, or that once entered in at our Eyes, and are afterwards called up into the Mind either barely by its own Operations, or on occasion of something without us, as Statues, or Descriptions. We have already considered the first Division, and shall therefore enter on the other, which, for Distinction sake, I have called the Secondary Pleasures of the Imagination. When I say the Ideas we receive from Statues, Descriptions, or such like Occasions, are the same that were once actually in our View, it must not be understood that we had once seen the very Place, Action, or Person that are carved or described. It is sufficient, that we have seen Places, Persons, or Actions in general which bear a Resemblance, or at least some remote Analogy, with what we find represented. Since it is in the Power of the Imagination, when it is once Stocked with particular Ideas, to enlarge, compound, and vary them at her own Pleasure.

.   .   .

Words, when well chosen, have so great a Force in them, that a Description often gives us more lively Ideas than the Sight of Things themselves. The Reader finds a Scene drawn in Stronger Colours, and painted more to the Life in his Imagination, by the help of Words than by an actual Survey of the Scene which they describe. In this Case the Poet seems to get the better of Nature; he takes, indeed, the Landskip after her, but gives it more vigorous Touches, heightens its Beauty, and so enlivens the whole Piece, that the Images which flow from the Objects themselves appear weak and faint, in Comparison of those that come from the Expressions. The Reason, probably, may be, because in the Survey of any Object, we have only so much of it painted on the Imagination, as comes in at the Eye; but in its Description, the Poet gives us as free a View of it, as he pleases, and discovers to us several Parts, that either we did not attend to, or that lay out of our Sight when we first beheld it. As we look on any Object, our Idea of it is, perhaps, made up of two or three simple Ideas; but when the Poet represents it, he may either give us a more complex Idea of it, or only raise in us such Ideas as are most apt to affect the Imagination.

From No. 418

The Pleasures of these Secondary Views of the Imagination, are of a wider and more universal Nature than those it has when joined with

Sight; for not only what is Great, Strange or Beautiful, but any Thing that is Disagreeable when look'd upon, pleases us in an apt Description. Here, therefore, we must enquire after a new Principle of Pleasure, which is nothing else but the Action of the Mind, which *compares* the Ideas that arise from Words, with the Ideas that arise from Objects themselves; and why this Operation of the Mind is attended with so much Pleasure, we have before considered. For this Reason therefore, the Description of a Dunghill is pleasing to the Imagination, if the Image be represented to our Minds by suitable Expressions; tho' perhaps, this may be more properly called the Pleasure of the Understanding than of the Fancy, because we are not so much delighted with the Image that is contained in the Description, as with the Aptness of the Description to excite the Image.

.   .   .

But because the Mind of Man requires something more perfect in Matter, than what it finds there, and can never meet with any Sight in Nature which sufficiently answers its highest Ideas of Pleasantness; or, in other Words, because the Imagination can fancy to it self Things more Great, Strange, or Beautiful, than the Eye ever saw, and is still sensible of some Defect in what it has seen; on this account it is the part of a Poet to humour the Imagination in its own Notions, by mending and perfecting Nature where he describes a Reality, and by adding greater Beauties than are put together in Nature, where he describes a Fiction.

He is not obliged to attend her in the slow Advances which she makes from one Season to another, or to observe her Conduct in the successive Production of Plants and Flowers. He may draw into his Description all the Beauties of the Spring and Autumn, and make the whole Year contribute something to render it the more agreeable. His Rose-trees, Wood-bines and Jessamines may flower together, and his Beds be covered at the same time with Lilies, Violets, and Amaranths. His Soil is not restrained to any particular Sett of Plants, but is proper either for Oaks or Mirtles, and adapts it self to the Products of every Climate. Oranges may grow wild in it; Myrrh may be met with in every Hedge, and if he thinks it proper to have a Grove of Spices, he can quickly command Sun enough to raise it. If all this will not furnish out an agreeable Scene, he can make several new Species of Flowers, with richer Scents and higher Colours than any that grow in the Gardens of Nature. His Consorts of Birds may be as full and harmonious, and his

Woods as thick and gloomy as he pleases. He is at no more Expence in a long Vista, than a short one, and can as easily throw his Cascades from a Precipice of half a Mile high, as from one of twenty Yards. He has his Choice of the Winds, and can turn the Course of his Rivers in all the variety of *Meanders,* that are most delightful to the Reader's Imagination. In a Word, he has the modelling of Nature in his own Hands, and may give her what Charms he pleases, provided he does not reform her too much, and run into Absurdities, by endeavouring to excel.

No. 419

——Mentis gratissimus error.—Hor.

There is a kind of Writing, wherein the Poet quite loses sight of Nature, and entertains his Reader's Imagination with the Characters and Actions of such Persons as have many of them no Existence, but what he bestows on them. Such are Fairies, Witches, Magicians, Demons, and departed Spirits. This Mr. *Dryden* calls *the Fairy Way of Writing,* which is, indeed, more difficult than any other that depends on the Poet's Fancy, because he has no Pattern to follow in it, and must work altogether out of his own Invention.

There is a very odd turn of Thought required for this sort of Writing, and it is impossible for a Poet to succeed in it, who has not a particular Cast of Fancy, and an Imagination naturally fruitful and superstitious. Besides this, he ought to be very well versed in Legends and Fables, antiquated Romances, and the Traditions of Nurses and old Women, that he may fall in with our natural Prejudices, and humour those Notions which we have imbibed in our Infancy. For, otherwise, he will be apt to make his Fairies talk like People of his own Species, and not like other Setts of Beings, who converse with different Objects, and think in a different manner from that of Mankind;

> *Sylvis deducti caveant, me judice, Fauni*
> *Ne velut innati triviis, ac pene forenses,*
> *Aut nimium teneris juvenentur versibus——.* —Hor.[1]

I do not say with Mr. *Bays* in the *Rehearsal,* that Spirits must not be confined to speak Sense, but it is certain their Sense ought to be a little

[1] "If the fauns are brought in from their forests, they should not, in my judgment, as though the public streets and almost the very forum were their habitat, make a display of the indiscretions of youth in their shallow verses." Horace: *Ars Poet.,* 244–46.

discoloured, that it may seem particular, and proper to the Person and Condition of the Speaker.

These Descriptions raise a pleasing kind of Horrour in the Mind of the Reader, and amuse his Imagination with the Strangeness and Novelty of the Persons who are represented in them. They bring up into our Memory the Stories we have heard in our Childhood, and favour those secret Terrors and Apprehensions to which the Mind of Man is naturally subject. We are pleased with surveying the different Habits and Behaviours of Foreign Countries; how much more must we be delighted and surprised when we are led, as it were, into a new Creation, and see the Persons and Manners of another Species? Men of cold Fancies, and Philosophical Dispositions, object to this kind of Poetry, that it has not Probability enough to affect the Imagination. But to this it may be answered, that we are sure, in general, there are many intellectual Beings in the World besides our selves, and several Species of Spirits, who are subject to different Laws and Oeconomies from those of Mankind; when we see, therefore, any of these represented naturally, we cannot look upon the Representation as altogether impossible; nay, many are prepossest with such false Opinions, as dispose them to believe these particular Delusions; at least, we have all heard so many pleasing Relations in favour of them, that we do not care for seeing through the Falshood, and willingly give our selves up to so agreeable an Imposture.

The Ancients have not much of this Poetry among them, for, indeed, almost the whole Substance of it owes its Original to the Darkness and Superstition of later Ages, when pious Frauds were made use of to amuse Mankind, and frighten them into a Sense of their Duty. Our Forefathers looked upon Nature with more Reverence and Horrour, before the World was enlightened by Learning and Philosophy, and loved to astonish themselves with the Apprehensions of Witchcraft, Prodigies, Charms and Enchantments. There was not a Village in *England* that had not a Ghost in it, the Church-yards were all haunted, every large Common had a Circle of Fairies belonging to it, and there was scarce a Shepherd to be met with who had not seen a Spirit.

Among all the Poets of this Kind our *English* are much the best, by what I have yet seen, whether it be that we abound with more Stories of this Nature, or that the Genius of our Country is fitter for this sort of Poetry. For the *English* are naturally Fanciful, and very often disposed by that Gloominess and Melancholy of Temper, which is so frequent in our Nation, to many wild Notions and Visions, to which others are not so liable.

Among the *English, Shakespear* has incomparably excelled all others. That noble Extravagance of Fancy, which he had in so great Perfection, thoroughly qualified him to touch this weak superstitious Part of his Reader's Imagination; and made him capable of succeeding, where he had nothing to support him besides the Strength of his own Genius. There is something so wild and yet so solemn in the Speeches of his Ghosts, Fairies, Witches and the like Imaginary Persons, that we cannot forbear thinking them natural, tho' we have no Rule by which to judge of them, and must confess, if there are such Beings in the World, it looks highly probable they should talk and act as he has represented them.

There is another sort of Imaginary Beings, that we sometimes meet with among the Poets, when the Author represents any Passion, Appetite, Virtue or Vice, under a visible Shape, and makes it a Person or an Actor in his Poem. Of this Nature are the Descriptions of Hunger and Envy in *Ovid,* of Fame in *Virgil,* and of Sin and Death in *Milton.* We find a whole Creation of the like shadowy Persons in *Spencer,* who had an admirable Talent in Representations of this kind. I have discoursed of these Emblematical Persons in former Papers, and shall therefore only mention them in this Place. Thus we see how many ways Poetry addresses it self to the Imagination, as it has not only the whole Circle of Nature for its Province, but makes new Worlds of its own, shews us Persons who are not to be found in Being, and represents even the Faculties of the Soul, with her several Virtues and Vices, in a sensible Shape and Character.

I shall, in my two following Papers, consider in general, how other kinds of Writing are qualified to please the Imagination; with which I intend to conclude this Essay.

HENRY FIELDING

(1701–1754)

From

PREFACE TO JOSEPH ANDREWS

(1742)

Now, a comic romance is a comic epic poem in prose; differing from comedy, as the serious epic from tragedy: its action being more extended an⋈ comprehensive; containing a much larger circle of incidents, and introducing a greater variety of characters. It differs from the serious romance in its fable and action, in this; that as in the one these are grave and solemn, so in the other they are light and ridiculous: it differs in its characters by introducing persons of inferior rank, and consequently, of inferior manners, whereas the grave romance sets the highest before us: lastly, in its sentiments and diction; by preserving the ludicrous instead of the sublime. In the diction, I think, burlesque itself may be sometimes admitted; of which many instances will occur in this work, as in the description of the battles, and some other places, not necessary to be pointed out to the classical reader, for whose entertainment those parodies or burlesque imitations are chiefly calculated.

But though we have sometimes admitted this in our diction, we have carefully excluded it from our sentiments and characters; for there it is never properly introduced, unless in writings of the burlesque kind, which this is not intended to be. Indeed, no two species of writing can differ more widely than the comic and the burlesque; for as the latter is ever the exhibition of what is monstrous and unnatural, and where our delight, if we examine it, arises from the surprizing absurdity, as in appropriating the manners of the highest to the lowest, or *è converso;* so in the former we should ever confine ourselves strictly to nature, from the just imitation of which will flow all the pleasure we can this way convey to a sensible reader. And perhaps there is one reason why a comic writer should of all others be the least excused for deviating from nature, since it may not be always so easy for a serious poet to meet with the great and the admirable; but life everywhere furnishes an accurate observer with the ridiculous.

I have hinted this little concerning burlesque, because I have often heard that name given to performances which have been truly of the comic kind, from the author's having sometimes admitted it in his diction only; which, as it is the dress of poetry, doth, like the dress of men, establish characters (the one of the whole poem, and the other of the whole man), in vulgar opinion, beyond any of their greater excellences: but surely, a certain drollery in stile, where characters and sentiments are perfectly natural, no more constitutes the burlesque, than an empty pomp and dignity of words, where everything else is mean and low, can entitle any performance to the appellation of the true sublime.

And I apprehend my Lord Shaftesbury's opinion of mere burlesque agrees with mine, when he asserts, There is no such thing to be found in the writings of the ancients. But perhaps I have less abhorrence than he professes for it; and that, not because I have had some little success on the stage this way, but rather as it contributes more to exquisite mirth and laughter than any other; and these are probably more wholesome physic for the mind, and conduce better to purge away spleen, melancholy, and ill affections, than is generally imagined. Nay, I will appeal to common observation, whether the same companies are not found more full of good-humour and benevolence, after they have been sweetened for two or three hours with entertainments of this kind, than when soured by a tragedy or a grave lecture.

But to illustrate all this by another science, in which, perhaps, we shall see the distinction more clearly and plainly, let us examine the works of a comic history painter, with those performances which the Italians call Caricatura, where we shall find the true excellence of the former to consist in the exactest copying of nature; insomuch that a judicious eye instantly rejects anything *outré,* any liberty which the painter hath taken with the features of that *alma mater;* whereas in the Caricatura we allow all licence—its aim is to exhibit monsters, not men; and all distortions and exaggerations whatever are within its proper province.

Now, what Caricatura is in painting, Burlesque is in writing; and in the same manner the comic writer and painter correlate to each other. And here I shall observe, that, as in the former the painter seems to have the advantage; so it is in the latter infinitely on the side of the writer; for the Monstrous is much easier to paint than describe, and the Ridiculous to describe than paint.

And though perhaps this latter species doth not in either science so strongly affect and agitate the muscles as the other; yet it will be owned, I believe, that a more rational and useful pleasure arises to us from it. He who should call the ingenious Hogarth a burlesque painter, would, in my opinion, do him very little honour; for sure it is much easier, much less the subject of admiration, to paint a man with a nose, or any other feature, of a preposterous size, or to expose him in some absurd or monstrous attitude, than to express the affections of men on canvas. It hath been thought a vast commendation of a painter to say his figures *seem to breathe;* but surely it is a much greater and nobler applause, *that they appear to think.*

But to return. The Ridiculous only, as I have before said, falls within my province in the present work. Nor will some explanation of this word be thought impertinent by the reader, if he considers how wonderfully it hath been mistaken, even by writers who have professed it: for to what but such a mistake can we attribute the many attempts to ridicule the blackest villanies, and, what is yet worse, the most dreadful calamities? What could exceed the absurdity of an author, who should write the comedy of Nero, with the merry incident of ripping up his mother's belly? or what would give a greater shock to humanity than an attempt to expose the miseries of poverty and distress to ridicule? And yet the reader will not want much learning to suggest such instances to himself.

Besides, it may seem remarkable, that Aristotle, who is so fond and free of definitions, hath not thought proper to define the Ridiculous. Indeed, where he tells us it is proper to comedy, he hath remarked that villany is not its object: but he hath not, as I remember, positively asserted what is. Nor doth the Abbé Bellegarde, who hath written a treatise on this subject, though he shows us many species of it, once trace it to its fountain.

The only source of the true Ridiculous (as it appears to me) is affectation. But though it arises from one spring only, when we consider the infinite streams into which this one branches, we shall presently cease to admire at the copious field it affords to an observer. Now, affectation proceeds from one of these two causes, vanity or hypocrisy: for as vanity puts us on affecting false characters, in order to purchase applause; so hypocrisy sets us on an endeavour to avoid censure, by concealing our vices under an appearance of their opposite virtues. And though these two causes are often confounded (for there is some difficulty in distinguishing them), yet, as they proceed from very different motives, so they are as clearly distinct in their operations: for indeed, the affectation which arises from vanity is nearer to truth than the other, as it hath not that violent repugnancy of nature to struggle with, which that of the hypocrite hath. It may be likewise noted, that affectation doth not imply an absolute negation of those qualities which are affected; and, therefore, though, when it proceeds from hypocrisy, it be nearly allied to deceit; yet when it comes from vanity only, it partakes of the nature of ostentation: for instance, the affectation of liberality in a vain man differs visibly from the same affectation in the avaricious; for though the vain man is not what he would appear, or hath not the virtue he affects, to the degree he would be thought to have it; yet it sits less awkwardly on him than on the avaricious man, who is the very reverse of what he would seem to be.

From the discovery of this affectation arises the Ridiculous, which always strikes the reader with surprize and pleasure; and that in a higher and stronger degree when the affectation arises from hypocrisy, than when from vanity; for to discover any one to be the exact reverse of what he affects, is more surprizing, and consequently more ridiculous, than to find him a little deficient in the quality he desires the reputation of. I might observe that our Ben Jonson, who of all men understood the Ridiculous the best, hath chiefly used the hypocritical affectation.

Now, from affectation only, the misfortunes and calamities of life, or the imperfections of nature, may become the objects of ridicule. Surely he hath a very ill-framed mind who can look on ugliness, infirmity, or poverty, as ridiculous in themselves: nor do I believe any man living, who meets a dirty fellow riding through the streets in a cart, is struck with an idea of the Ridiculous from it; but if he should see the same figure descend from his coach and six, or bolt from his chair with his hat under his arm, he would then begin to laugh, and with justice. In the same manner, were we to enter a poor house and behold a wretched family shivering with cold and languishing with hunger, it would not incline us to laughter (at least we must have very diabolical natures if it would); but should we discover there a grate, instead of coals, adorned with flowers, empty plate or china dishes on the sideboard, or any other affectation of riches and finery, either on their persons or in their furniture, we might then indeed be excused for ridiculing so fantastical an appearance. Much less are natural imperfections the object of derision; but when ugliness aims at the applause of beauty, or lameness endeavours to display agility, it is then that these unfortunate circumstances, which at first moved our compassion, tend only to raise our mirth.

The poet carries this very far:—

> None are for being what they are in fault,
> But for not being what they would be thought.

Where if the metre would suffer the word Ridiculous to close the first line, the thought would be rather more proper. Great vices are the proper objects of our detestation, smaller faults, of our pity; but affectation appears to me the only true source of the Ridiculous. . . .

FRIEDRICH SCHILLER

(1759–1805)

From

ON SIMPLE AND SENTIMENTAL POETRY [1]

(1795)

IF we think of that beautiful nature which surrounded the ancient
Greeks, if we remember how intimately that people, under its blessed
sky, could live with that free nature; how their mode of imagining, and
of feeling, and their manners, approached far nearer than ours to the
simplicity of nature, how faithfully the works of their poets express this;
we must necessarily remark, as a strange fact, that so few traces are
met among them of that *sentimental* interest that we moderns ever
take in the scenes of nature and in natural characters. I admit that the
Greeks are superiorly exact and faithful in their descriptions of nature.
They reproduce their details with care, but we see that they take no
more interest in them and no more heart in them than in describing a
vestment, a shield, armour, a piece of furniture, or any production of
the mechanical arts. In their love for the object it seems that they make
no difference between what exists in itself and what owes its existence
to art, to the human will. It seems that nature interests their minds and
their curiosity more than moral feeling. They do not attach themselves
to it with that depth of feeling, with that gentle melancholy, that char-
acterise the moderns. Nay, more, by personifying nature in its particular phenomena, by deifying it, by representing its effects as the acts
of free being, they take from it that character of calm necessity which
is precisely what makes it so attractive to us. Their impatient imagination only traverses nature to pass beyond it to the drama of human life.
It only takes pleasure in the spectacle of what is living and free; it
requires characters, acts, the accidents of fortune and of manners; and

[1] Of this essay, Goethe remarked: ". . .
we see how he [Schiller] plagued himself
with the design of perfectly separating sentimental from *naïve* poetry. For the former
he could find no proper soil, and this
brought him into unspeakable perplexity.
As if . . . sentimental poetry could exist
at all without the *naïve* ground in which,
as it were, it has its root." (*Conversations
of Goethe with Eckermann and Soret*,
Oxenford's trans.)

whilst it happens with *us,* at least in certain moral dispositions, to curse our prerogative, this free will, which exposes us to so many combats with ourselves, to so many anxieties and errors, and to wish to exchange it for the condition of beings destitute of reason, for that fatal existence that no longer admits of any choice, but which is so calm in its uniformity,—while we do this, the Greeks, on the contrary, only have their imagination occupied in retracing human nature in the inanimate world, and in giving to the will an influence where blind necessity rules.

Whence can arise this difference between the spirit of the ancients and the modern spirit? How comes it that, being, for all that relates to nature, incomparably below the ancients, we are superior to them precisely on this point, that we render a more complete homage to nature; that we have a closer attachment to it; and that we are capable of embracing even the inanimate world with the most ardent sensibility? It is because nature, in our time, is no longer in man, and that we no longer encounter it in its primitive truth, except out of humanity, in the inanimate world. It is not because we are more *conformable to nature*— quite the contrary; it is because in our social relations, in our mode of existence, in our manners, we are in *opposition with nature.* This is what leads us, when the instinct of truth and of simplicity is awakened —this instinct which, like the moral aptitude from which it proceeds, lives incorruptible and indelible in every human heart—to procure for it in the physical world the satisfaction which there is no hope of finding in the moral order. This is the reason why the feeling that attaches us to nature is connected so closely with that which makes us regret our infancy, for ever flown, and our primitive innocence. Our childhood is all that remains of nature in humanity, such as civilisation has made it, of untouched, unmutilated nature. It is, therefore, not wonderful, when we meet out of us the impress of nature, that we are always brought back to the idea of our childhood.

It was quite different with the Greeks in antiquity. Civilisation with them did not degenerate, nor was it carried to such an excess that it was necessary to break with nature. The entire structure of their social life reposed on feelings, and not on a factitious conception, on a work of art. Their very theology was the inspiration of a simple spirit, the fruit of a joyous imagination, and not, like the ecclesiastical dogmas of modern nations, subtle combinations of the understanding. Since, therefore, the Greeks had not lost sight of nature in humanity, they had no reason, when meeting it out of man, to be surprised at their discovery, and they would not feel very imperiously the need of objects in which nature could be retraced. In accord with themselves, happy in feeling themselves men, they would of necessity keep to humanity as to what was greatest to them, and they must needs try to make all the rest approach it; while we, who are not in accord with ourselves—we who are discontented with the experience we have made of our humanity—have no more pressing interest than to fly out of it and to remove from our sight a so ill-fashioned form. The feeling of which we are treating here is, therefore, not that which was known by the ancients; it approaches far more nearly that *which we ourselves experience for the ancients.* The ancients felt naturally; we, on our part, feel what is natural. It was certainly a very different inspiration that filled the soul of Homer, when he depicted his divine cowherd giving hospitality to Ulysses, from that which agitated the soul of the young Werther at the moment when he read the "Odyssey" on issuing from an assembly in which he had only found tedium. The feeling we experience for nature resembles that of a sick man for health.

As soon as nature gradually vanishes from human life—that is, in proportion as it ceases to be *experienced* as a *subject* (active and passive) —we see it dawn and increase in the poetical world in the guise of an *idea* and as an *object.* . . . The people who have carried farthest the want of nature, and at the same time the reflections on that matter, must needs have been the people who at the same time were most struck with this phenomenon of the *simple,* and gave it a name. If I am not mistaken, this people was the French. But the feeling of the simple, and the interest we take in it, must naturally go much farther back, and it dates from the time when the moral sense and the æsthetical sense began to be corrupt. This modification in the manner of feeling is exceedingly striking in Euripides, for example, if compared with his predecessors, especially Æschylus; and yet Euripides was the favourite poet of his time. The same revolution is perceptible in the ancient historians. Horace, the poet of a cultivated and corrupt epoch, praises, under the shady groves of Tibur, the calm and happiness of the country, and he might be termed the true founder of this sentimental poetry, of which he has remained the unsurpassed model. In Propertius, Virgil, and others, we find also traces of this mode of feeling; less of it is found in Ovid, who would have required for that more abundance of heart, and who in his exile at Tomes sorrowfully regrets the happiness that Horace so readily dispensed in his villa at Tibur.

It is in the fundamental idea of poetry that the poet is everywhere the *guardian* of nature. When he can no longer entirely fill this part, and has already in himself suffered the deleterious influence of arbitrary and factitious forms, or has had to struggle against this influence, he presents himself as the *witness* of nature and as its avenger. The poet will, therefore, be the *expression* of nature itself, or his part will be to *seek* it, if men have lost sight of it. Hence arise two kinds of poetry, which embrace and exhaust the entire field of poetry. All poets—I mean those who are really so—will belong, according to the time when they flourish, according to the accidental circumstances that have influenced their education generally, and the different dispositions of mind through which they pass, will belong, I say, to the order of the *sentimental* poetry or to *simple* poetry.

The poet of a young world, simple and inspired, as also the poet who at an epoch of artificial civilisation approaches nearest to the primitive bards, is austere and prudish, like the virginal Diana in her forests. Wholly unconfiding, he hides himself from the heart that seeks him, from the desire that wishes to embrace him. It is not rare for the dry truth with which he treats his subject to resemble insensibility. The whole object possesses him, and to reach his heart it does not suffice, as with metals of little value, to stir up the surface; as with pure gold, you must go down to the lowest depths. Like the Deity behind this universe, the simple poet hides himself behind his work; he is *himself* his work, and his work is *himself*. A man must be no longer worthy of the work, nor understand it, or be tired of it, to be even anxious to learn who is its author.

Such appears to us, for instance, Homer in antiquity, and Shakespeare among moderns: two natures infinitely different and separated in time by an abyss, but perfectly identical as to this trait of character. When, at a very youthful age, I became first acquainted with Shakespeare, I was displeased with his coldness, with his insensibility, which allows him to jest even in the most pathetic moments, to disturb the impression of the most harrowing scenes in "Hamlet," in "King Lear," and in "Macbeth," etc., by mixing with them the buffooneries of a madman. I was revolted by his insensibility, which allowed him to pause sometimes at places where my sensibility would bid me hasten and bear me along, and which sometimes carried him away with indifference when my heart would be so happy to pause. Though I was accustomed, by the practice of modern poets, to seek at once the poet in his works, to meet his heart, to reflect with him in his theme—in a word, to see the object in the subject—I could not bear that the poet could in Shakespeare never be seized, that he would never give me an account of himself. For some

years Shakespeare had been the object of my study and of all my respect
before I had learned to love his personality. I was not yet able to comprehend nature at first hand. . . .

Sentimental Poetry

I have previously remarked that the poet *is* nature, or he *seeks* nature.
In the former case, he is a simple poet, in the second case, a sentimental
poet.

The poetic spirit is immortal, nor can it disappear from humanity; it
can only disappear with humanity itself, or with the aptitude to be a
man, a human being. And actually, though man by the freedom of his
imagination and of his understanding departs from simplicity, from
truth, from the necessity of nature, not only a road always remains open
to him to return to it, but, moreover, a powerful and indestructible instinct, the moral instinct, brings him incessantly back to nature; and
it is precisely the poetical faculty that is united to this instinct by the
ties of the closest relationship. Thus man does not lose the poetic faculty
directly he parts with the simplicity of nature; only this faculty acts out
of him in another direction.

Even at present nature is the only flame that kindles and warms the
poetic soul. From nature alone it obtains all its force; to nature alone
it speaks in the artificial culture-seeking man. Any other form of displaying its activity is remote from the poetic spirit. Accordingly it may
be remarked that it is incorrect to apply the expression poetic to any of
the so-styled productions of wit, though the high credit given to French
literature has led people for a long period to class them in that category.
I repeat that at present, even in the existing phase of culture, it is still
nature that powerfully stirs up the poetic spirit, only its present relation
to nature is of a different order from formerly.

As long as man dwells in a state of pure nature (I mean pure and
not coarse nature), all his being acts at once like a simple sensuous
unity, like a harmonious whole. The senses and reason, the receptive
faculty and the spontaneously active faculty, have not been as yet separated in their respective functions: *à fortiori* they are not yet in contradiction with each other. Then the feelings of man are not the formless
play of chance; nor are his thoughts an empty play of the imagination,
without any value. His feelings proceed from the law of necessity; his
thoughts from *reality*. But when man enters the state of civilisation, and
art has fashioned him, this *sensuous* harmony which was in him dis-

appears, and henceforth he can only manifest himself as a *moral unity*, that is, as aspiring to unity. The harmony that existed as a *fact* in the former state, the harmony of feeling and thought, only exists now in an *ideal* state. It is no longer in him, but out of him; it is a conception of thought which he must begin by realising in himself; it is no longer a fact, a reality of his life. Well, now let us take the idea of poetry, which is nothing else than *expressing humanity as completely as possible*, and let us apply this idea to these two states. We shall be brought to infer that, on the one hand, in the state of natural simplicity, when all the faculties of man are exerted together, his being still manifests itself in a harmonious unity, where, consequently, the *totality* of his nature expresses itself in reality itself, the part of the *poet* is necessarily to imitate the real as completely as is possible. In the state of civilisation, on the contrary, when this harmonious competition of the whole of human nature is no longer anything but an idea, the part of the poet is necessarily to raise reality to the ideal, or what amounts to the same thing, *to represent the ideal*. And, actually, these are the only two ways in which, in general, the poetic genius can manifest itself. Their great difference is quite evident, but though there be great opposition between them, a higher idea exists that embraces both, and there is no cause to be astonished if this idea coincides with the very idea of humanity.

This is not the place to pursue this thought any further, as it would require a separate discussion to place it in its full light. But if we only compare the modern and ancient poets together, not according to the accidental forms which they may have employed, but according to their spirit, we shall be easily convinced of the truth of this thought. The thing that touches us in the ancient poets is nature; it is the truth of sense, it is a present and a living reality: modern poets touch us through the medium of ideas. . . .

Accordingly it would have been desirable not to compare at all the ancient and the modern poets, the simple and the sentimental poets, or only to compare them by referring them to a higher idea (since there is really only one) which embraces both. For, sooth to say, if we begin by forming a specific idea of poetry, merely from the ancient poets, nothing is easier, but also nothing is more vulgar, than to depreciate the moderns by this comparison. If persons wish to confine the name of poetry to that which has in all times produced the same impression in simple nature, this places them in the necessity of contesting the title of poet in the moderns precisely in that which constitutes their highest beauties, their greatest originality and sublimity; for precisely in the points where they excel the most, it is the child of civilisation whom they address, and they have nothing to say to the simple child of nature.

To the man who is not disposed beforehand to issue from reality in order to enter the field of the ideal, the richest and most substantial poetry is an empty appearance, and the sublimest flights of poetic inspiration are an exaggeration. Never will a reasonable man think of placing alongside Homer, in his grandest episodes, any of our modern poets; and it has a discordant and ridiculous effect to hear Milton or Klopstock honoured with the name of a "new Homer." But take in modern poets what characterises them, what makes their special merit, and try to compare any ancient poet with them in this point, they will not be able to support the comparison any better, and Homer less than any other. I should express it thus: the power of the ancients consists in compressing objects into the finite, and the moderns excel in the art of the infinite. . . .

From

ON THE USE OF THE CHORUS IN TRAGEDY

(1803)

. . .

ART has for its object not merely to afford a transient pleasure, to excite to a momentary dream of liberty; its aim is to make us absolutely free; and this it accomplishes by awakening, exercising, and perfecting in us a power to remove to an objective distance the sensible world; (which otherwise only burdens us as rugged matter, and presses us down with a brute influence;) to transform it into the free working of our spirit, and thus acquire a dominion over the material by means of ideas. For the very reason also that true Art requires somewhat of the objective and real, it is not satisfied with a show of truth. It rears its ideal edifice on Truth itself—on the solid and deep foundations of Nature.

But how Art can be at once altogether ideal, yet in the strictest sense real;—how it can entirely leave the actual, and yet harmonize with Nature, is a problem to the multitude:—and hence the distorted views which prevail in regard to poetical and plastic works; for to ordinary judgments these two requisites seem to counteract each other.

It is commonly supposed that one may be attained by the sacrifice of the other:—the result is a failure to arrive at either. One to whom Nature has given a true sensibility, but denied the plastic imaginative power, will be a faithful painter of the real; he will adapt casual appearances, but never catch the spirit of Nature. He will only reproduce to us the matter of the world, which, not being our own work, the product of our creative spirit, can never have the beneficent operation of Art, of which the essence is freedom. Serious, indeed, but unpleasing, is the cast of thought with which such an artist and poet dismisses us;—we feel ourselves painfully thrust back into the narrow sphere of reality by means of the very art which ought to have emancipated us. On the other hand, a writer, endowed with a lively fancy, but destitute of warmth and individuality of feeling, will not concern himself in the least about truth; he will sport with the stuff of the world, and endeavour to surprise by whimsical combinations; and as his whole performance is nothing but foam and glitter, he will, it is true, engage the attention for a time, but build up and confirm nothing in the understanding. His playfulness is, like the gravity of the other, thoroughly unpoetical. To string together at will fantastical images, is not to travel into the realm of the ideal; and the imitative reproduction of the actual cannot be called the representation of nature. Both requisites stand so little in contradiction to each other that they are rather one and the same thing; that Art is only true insomuch as it altogether forsakes the actual, and becomes purely ideal. Nature herself is an idea of the mind, and is never presented to the senses. She lies under the veil of appearances, but is herself never apparent. To the art of the ideal alone is lent, or rather, absolutely given, the privilege to grasp the spirit of the All, and bind it in a corporeal form.

Yet, in truth, even Art cannot present it to the senses, but by means of her creative power to the imaginative faculty alone; and it is thus that she becomes more true than all reality, and more real than all experience. It follows from these premises that the artist can use no single element taken from reality as he finds it—that his work must be ideal in all its parts, if it be designed to have, as it were, an intrinsic reality, and to harmonize with nature.

JOHANN WOLFGANG VON GOETHE

(1749–1832)

From

WILHELM MEISTER'S APPRENTICESHIP *

(1795)

"IN the novel as well as in the drama, it is human nature and human action that we see. The difference between these sorts of fiction lies not merely in their outward form; not merely in the circumstance that the personages of the one are made to speak, while those of the other have commonly their history narrated. Unfortunately many dramas are but novels, which proceed by dialogue; and it would not be impossible to write a drama in the shape of letters.

"But in the novel, it is chiefly *sentiments* and *events* that are exhibited; in the drama, it is *characters* and *deeds*. The novel must go slowly forward; and the sentiments of the hero, by some means or another, must restrain the tendency of the whole to unfold itself and to conclude. The drama on the other hand, must hasten, and the character of the hero must press forward to the end; it does not restrain, but is restrained. The novel-hero must be suffering, at least he must not in a high degree be active; in the dramatic one, we look for activity and deeds. Grandison, Clarissa, Pamela, the Vicar of Wakefield, Tom Jones himself, are, if not suffering, at least retarding personages; and the incidents are all in some sort modelled by their sentiments. In the drama the hero models nothing by himself; all things withstand him, and he clears and casts away the hindrances from off his path, or else sinks under them."

Our friends were also of opinion, that in the novel some degree of scope may be allowed to Chance; but that it must always be led and guided by the sentiments of the personages; on the other hand, that Fate, which, by means of outward unconnected circumstances, carries forward men, without their own concurrence, to an unforeseen catastrophe, can have place only in the drama; that Chance may produce

* Translated by Thomas Carlyle.

pathetic situations, but never tragic ones; Fate, on the other hand, ought always to be terrible; and is in the highest sense tragic, when it brings into a ruinous concatenation the guilty man, and the guiltless that was unconcerned with him.

These considerations led them back to the play of Hamlet, and the peculiarities of its composition. The hero in this case, it was observed, is endowed more properly with sentiments than with a character; it is events alone that push him on; and accordingly the piece has in some measure the expansion of a novel. But as it is Fate that draws the plan; as the story issues from a deed of terror, and the hero is continually driven forward to a deed of terror, the work is tragic in the highest sense, and admits of no other than a tragic end.

From

GOETHE'S CONVERSATIONS WITH ECKERMANN *

(1836–48)

A NEW expression occurs to me which does not ill define the state of the case. I call the classic *healthy,* the romantic *sickly.* In this sense, the Nibelungenlied is as classic as the Iliad, for both are vigorous and healthy. Most modern productions are romantic, not because they are new, but because they are weak, morbid, and sickly; and the antique is classic, not because it is old, but because it is strong, fresh, joyous, and healthy. If we distinguish "classic" and "romantic" by these qualities, it will be easy to see our way clearly.

.   .   .

From

SUPPLEMENT TO ARISTOTLE'S POETICS **

(1827)

EVERY one who has concerned himself to some extent about the theory of poetic art in general, but of tragedy in particular, will recall a passage

* Translated by John Oxenford.   ** Translated by Elizabeth L. Wenning.

from Aristotle which has given much trouble to commentators, without their having been able to agree entirely about its complete meaning. Upon a closer study of tragedy this great author seems to demand of it that it should by the stirring actions and events that arouse pity and fear purge the soul of the spectator from the so-called passions.

My ideas and conviction about the passage in question I believe can best be expressed by a translation of it. "Tragedy is the imitation of a significant and complete action, which has a certain extension and is presented in pleasing language and by distinct characters, each of whom plays his own role; and it is not presented through narration by some one person; but after a period of pity and fear the play ends with an adjustment of these passions."

By the preceding translation I feel I have made the passage hitherto regarded as obscure clear, and I add only the following. Could Aristotle in his way of indicating his object, because in actuality he speaks only of the technique of tragedy, think of the effect, and, what more, the remote effect, which tragedy would probably have on the spectator? By no means! He expresses it clearly and accurately: when tragedy has passed through a course of actions that arouse pity and fear, it should finally close on the stage with an adjustment and with a reconciliation of these passions.

He understands by catharsis this reconciling culmination which is really demanded of all drama, and in fact of all poetic works. In tragedy this takes place by a kind of human sacrifice; now it may really be achieved or, by intervention of a favoring deity, be fulfilled by a substitute, as in the case of Abraham and Agamemnon; enough, a reconciliation, a solution at the close is indispensable, if the tragedy is a complete poetical work. This solution, however, when accomplished by means of a favorable and desirable outcome, approaches a mediocre kind of art, as in the return of Alcestis: on the contrary in comedy usually to the solution of all difficulties, which quite evidently are of little importance in connection with fear and hope, marriage appears, which, even though it does not close life completely, still it does make an important and serious break therein. No one wishes to die, every one to marry, and in this lies the half-jesting, half-serious difference between tragedy and comedy in utilitarian aesthetics. . . .

Whoever advances on the path of a truly moral and spiritual self-cultivation, will feel and acknowledge that tragedies and tragic romances in no way soothe the mind, but rather put the spirit and that which we term the heart in a state of unrest, and induce a vague, uncertain frame of mind; youth loves this mood and is, therefore, passionately interested in such productions.

We return to the beginning and repeat: Aristotle speaks of the technique of tragedy, in as much as the poet, placing it as his objective, believes he can produce in a definite way something really attractive, worth seeing and worth hearing.

If the poet, for his part, has fulfilled his duty, raising important issues and worthily solving them, in that case the same takes place in the mind of the spectator; the complication will confuse him, the solution enlighten him, but he will go home none the better: he would, on the contrary, were he sufficiently observant, debate with himself that after getting home he finds himself just as frivolous as headstrong, just as violent as weak, just as lovable as loveless, as when he departed. Therefore, we believe we have said everything that concerns this matter until this subject can be made clearer by further investigation.

WILLIAM HAZLITT

(1778–1830)

From

ON POETRY IN GENERAL

(1818)

.   .   .

POETRY, then, is an imitation of nature, but the imagination and the passions are a part of man's nature. We shape things according to our wishes and fancies, without poetry; but poetry is the most emphatical language that can be found for those creations of the mind "which ecstasy is very cunning in." Neither a mere description of natural objects, nor a mere delineation of natural feelings, however distinct or forcible, constitutes the ultimate end and aim of poetry, without the heightenings of the imagination. The light of poetry is not only a direct but also a reflected light, that, while it shows us the object, throws a sparkling radiance on all around it: the flame of the passions, communicated to the imagination, reveals to us, as with a flash of lightning, the inmost recesses of thought, and penetrates our whole being. Poetry represents forms chiefly as they suggest other forms; feelings, as they suggest forms or other feelings. Poetry puts a spirit of life and motion into the universe. It describes the flowing, not the fixed. It does not define the limits of sense, or analyze the distinctions of the understanding, but signifies the excess of the imagination beyond the actual or ordinary impression of any object or feeling. The poetical impression of any object is that uneasy, exquisite sense of beauty or power that cannot be contained within itself; that is impatient of all limit; that (as flame bends to flame) strives to link itself to some other image of kindred beauty or grandeur; to enshrine itself, as it were, in the highest forms of fancy, and to relieve the aching sense of pleasure by expressing it in the boldest manner, and by the most striking examples of the same quality in other instances. Poetry, according to Lord Bacon, for this reason, "has something divine in it, because it raises the mind and hurries it into sublimity, by conforming the shows of things to the desires of the soul, instead of subjecting the soul to external things, as reason and history do." It is strictly the language of the imagination; and the imagination is that faculty which represents objects, not as they are in themselves, but as they are moulded by other thoughts and feelings, into an infinite variety of shapes and combinations of power. This language is not the less true to nature, because it is false in point of fact; but so much the more true and natural, if it conveys the impression which the object under the influence of passion makes on the mind. Let an object, for instance, be presented to the senses in a state of agitation or fear— and the imagination will distort or magnify the object, and convert it into the likeness of whatever is most proper to encourage the fear. "Our eyes are made the fools" of our other faculties. This is the universal law of the imagination,

> That if it would but apprehend some joy,
> It comprehends some bringer of that joy;
> Or in the night, imagining some fear,
> How easy is a bush suppos'd a bear!

When Iachimo says of Imogen,

> The flame o' th' taper
> Bows toward her, and would under-peep her lids
> To see the enclosed lights,

this passionate interpretation of the motion of the flame to accord with the speaker's own feelings, is true poetry. The lover, equally with the poet, speaks of the auburn tresses of his mistress as locks of shining gold. We compare a man of gigantic stature to a tower: not that he is anything like so large, but because the excess of his size beyond what we are accustomed to expect, or the usual size of things of the same class, produces by contrast a greater feeling of magnitude and ponderous strength than another object of ten times the same dimensions. The intensity of the feeling makes up for the disproportion of the objects. Things are equal, to the imagination, which have the power of affecting the mind with an equal degree of terror, admiration, delight, or love. When Lear calls upon the heavens to avenge his cause, "for they are old like him," there is nothing extravagant or impious in this sublime identification of his age with theirs; for there is no other image which could do justice to the agonizing sense of his wrongs and his despair!

THOMAS LOVE PEACOCK

(1785–1866)

From

THE FOUR AGES OF POETRY [1]

(1820)

A POET in our times is a semi-barbarian in a civilized community. He lives in the days that are past. His ideas, thoughts, feelings, associations, are all with barbarous manners, obsolete customs, and exploded superstitions. The march of his intellect is like that of a crab, backward. The brighter the light diffused around him by the progress of reason, the thicker is the darkness of antiquated barbarism, in which he buries him-

[1] According to Peacock, the first age of poetry was of iron, of the rude bards who rarely are known by name; the second age was of gold, Homeric in classical and Shaksperian in English poetry, with Milton standing between the ages of gold and of silver; the third age was of silver, represented classically by Virgil and, in English, "beginning with Dryden, coming to perfection with Pope, and ending with Goldsmith, Collins, and Gray;" the fourth age was of brass—"the best specimen of it . . . is the Dionysiaca of Nonnus, which contains many passages of exceeding beauty in the midst of masses of amplification and repetition;" in England, roughly, by the Lake Poets: Wordsworth, Coleridge, and Southey. The age of brass "by rejecting the polish and the learning of the age of silver, and taking a retrograde stride to the barbarisms and crude traditions of the age of iron, professes to return to nature and revive the age of gold. This is the second childhood of poetry."

self like a mole, to throw up the barren hillocks of his Cimmerian labours. The philosophic mental tranquillity which looks round with an equal eye on all external things, collects a store of ideas, discriminates their relative value, assigns to all their proper place, and from the materials of useful knowledge thus collected, appreciated, and arranged, forms new combinations that impress the stamp of their power and utility on the real business of life, is diametrically the reverse of that frame of mind which poetry inspires, or from which poetry can emanate. The highest inspirations of poetry are resolvable into three ingredients: the rant of unregulated passion, the whining of exaggerated feeling, and the cant of factitious sentiment: and can therefore serve only to ripen a splendid lunatic like Alexander, a puling driveller like Werter, or a morbid dreamer like Wordsworth. It can never make a philosopher, nor a statesman, nor in any class of life a useful or rational man. It cannot claim the slightest share in any one of the comforts and utilities of life of which we have witnessed so many and so rapid advances. But though not useful, it may be said it is highly ornamental, and deserves to be cultivated for the pleasure it yields. Even if this be granted, it does not follow that a writer of poetry in the present state of society is not a waster of his own time, and a robber of that of others. Poetry is not one of those arts which, like painting, require repetition and multiplication, in order to be diffused among society. There are more good poems already existing than are sufficient to employ that portion of life which any mere reader and recipient of poetical impressions should devote to them, and these having been produced in poetical times, are far superior in all the characteristics of poetry to the artificial reconstructions of a few morbid ascetics in unpoetical times. To read the promiscuous rubbish of the present time to the exclusion of the select treasures of the past, is to substitute the worse for the better variety of the same mode of enjoyment.

But in whatever degree poetry is cultivated, it must necessarily be to the neglect of some branch of useful study: and it is a lamentable spectacle to see minds, capable of better things, running to seed in the specious indolence of these empty, aimless mockeries of intellectual exertion. Poetry was the mental rattle that awakened the attention of intellect in the infancy of civil society: but for the maturity of mind to make a serious business of the playthings of its childhood, is as absurd as for a full-grown man to rub his gums with coral, and cry to be charmed to sleep by the jingle of silver bells.

As to that small portion of our contemporary poetry, which is neither descriptive, nor narrative, nor dramatic, and which, for want of a better name, may be called ethical, the most distinguished portion of it, consisting merely of querulous, egotistical rhapsodies, to express the writer's high dissatisfaction with the world and every thing in it, serves only to confirm what has been said of the semi-barbarous character of poets, who from singing dithyrambics and "Io Triumphe," while society was savage, grow rabid, and out of their element, as it becomes polished and enlightened.

Now when we consider that it is not the thinking and studious, and scientific and philosophical part of the community, not to those whose minds are bent on the pursuit and promotion of permanently useful ends and aims, that poets must address their minstrelsy, but to that much larger portion of the reading public, whose minds are not awakened to the desire of valuable knowledge, and who are indifferent to any thing beyond being charmed, moved, excited, affected, and exalted: charmed by harmony, moved by sentiment, excited by passion, affected by pathos, and exalted by sublimity: harmony, which is language on the rack of Procrustes; sentiment, which is canting egotism in the mask of refined feeling; passion, which is the commotion of a weak and selfish mind; pathos, which is the whining of an unmanly spirit; and sublimity, which is the inflation of an empty head: when we consider that the great and permanent interests of human society become more and more the main spring of intellectual pursuit; that in proportion as they become so, the subordinacy of the ornamental to the useful will be more and more seen and acknowledged; and that therefore the progress of useful art and science, and of moral and political knowledge, will continue more and more to withdraw attention from frivolous and unconducive, to solid and conducive studies: that therefore the poetical audience will not only continually diminish in the proportion of its number to that of the rest of the reading public, but will also sink lower and lower in the comparison of intellectual acquirement: when we consider that the poet must still please his audience, and must therefore continue to sink to their level, while the rest of the community is rising above it: we may easily conceive that the day is not distant, when the degraded state of every species of poetry will be as generally recognized as that of dramatic poetry has long been: and this not from any decrease either of intellectual power, or intellectual acquisition, but because intellectual power and intellectual acquisition have turned themselves into other and better channels, and have abandoned the cultivation and the fate of poetry to the degenerate fry of modern rhymesters, and their olympic judges, the magazine critics, who continue to debate and promulgate oracles about poetry, as if it were still what it was in the Homeric age, the all-in-all of intellectual progression, and as if there were no such things in existence as mathematicians, astronomers, chemists, moralists, metaphysicians, historians, politicians, and political economists, who have built into the upper air of intelligence a pyramid, from the summit of which they see the modern Parnassus far beneath them, and, knowing how small a place it occupies in the comprehensiveness of their prospect, smile at the little ambition and the circumscribed perceptions with which the drivellers and mountebanks upon it are contending for the poetical palm and the critical chair.

CHARLES LAMB

(1775–1834)

From

ON THE ARTIFICIAL COMEDY OF THE LAST CENTURY

(1822)

THE artificial Comedy, or Comedy of Manners, is quite extinct on our stage. Congreve and Farquhar show their heads once in seven years only, to be exploded and put down instantly. The times cannot bear them. Is it for a few wild speeches, an occasional license of dialogue? I think not altogether. The business of their dramatic characters will not stand the moral test. We screw everything up to that. Idle gallantry in a fiction, a dream, the passing pageant of an evening, startles us in the same way as the alarming indications of profligacy in a son or ward in real life should startle a parent or guardian. We have no such middle emotions as dramatic interests left. We see a stage libertine playing his loose pranks of two hours' duration, and of no after consequence, with the severe eyes which inspect real vices with their bearings upon two worlds. We are spectators to a plot or intrigue (not reducible in life to the point of strict morality) and take it all for truth. We substitute a real for a dramatic person, and judge him accordingly. . . .

I confess for myself that (with no great delinquencies to answer for) I am glad for a season to take an airing beyond the diocese of the strict conscience,—not to live always in the precincts of the law-courts—but now and then, for a dream-while or so, to imagine a world with no meddling restrictions—to get into recesses whither the hunter cannot follow me—

> Secret shades
> Of woody Ida's inmost grove,
> While yet there was no fear of Jove— [1]

I come back to my cage and my restraint the fresher and more healthy for it. I wear my shackles more contentedly for having respired the breath of an imaginary freedom. I do not know how it is with others, but I feel the better always for the perusal of one of Congreve's—nay, why should I not add even of Wycherley's—comedies, I am the gayer at least for it; and I could never connect those sports of a witty fancy in any shape with any result to be drawn from them to imitation in real life. They are a world of themselves almost as much as fairyland. . . .

Translated into real life, the characters of his—and his friend Wycherley's—dramas are profligates and strumpets,—the business of their brief existence the undivided pursuit of lawless gallantry. No other spring of action, or possible motive of conduct, is recognized; principles which, universally acted upon, must reduce this frame of things to a chaos. But we do them wrong in so translating them. No such effects are produced in *their* world. When we are among them, we are amongst a chaotic people. We are not to judge them by our usages. No reverend institutions are insulted by their proceedings,—for they have none among them. No peace of families is violated,—for no family ties exist among them. No purity of the marriage bed is stained,—for none is supposed to have a being. No deep affections are disquieted,—no holy wedlock bands are snapped asunder,—for affection's depth and wedded faith are not of the growth of that soil. There is neither right nor wrong,— gratitude or the opposite,—claim or duty,—paternity or sonship. . . .

The whole is a passing pageant, where we should sit as unconcerned at the issues, for life or death, as at a battle of the frogs and mice. But, like Don Quixote, we take part against the puppets, and quite as impertinently. We dare not contemplate an Atlantis, a scheme, out of which our coxcombical moral sense is for a little transitory ease excluded. We have not the courage to imagine a state of things for which there is neither reward nor punishment. We cling to the painful necessities of shame and blame. We would indict our very dreams. . . .

[1] Milton, "Il Penseroso," ll. 28–30.

SIR WALTER SCOTT

(1771–1832)

From

LIVES OF THE NOVELISTS

From *Fielding*

(1821)

IT is the object of the novel-writer to place before the reader as full and accurate a representation of the events which he relates as can be done by the mere force of an excited imagination, without the assistance of material objects. His sole appeal is made to the world of fancy and of ideas, and in this consists his strength and his weakness, his poverty and his wealth. He cannot, like the painter, present a visible and tangible representation of his towns and his woods, his palaces and his castles; but, by awakening the imagination of a congenial reader, he places before his mind's eye landscapes fairer than those of Claude, and wilder than those of Salvator. He cannot, like the dramatist, present before our living eyes the heroes of former days, or the beautiful creations of his own fancy, embodied in the grace and majesty of Kemble or of Siddons; but he can teach his reader to conjure up forms even more dignified and beautiful than theirs. The same difference follows him through every branch of his art. The author of a novel, in short, has neither stage nor scene-painter, nor company of comedians, nor dresser, nor wardrobe: words, applied with the best of his skill, must supply all that these bring to the assistance of the dramatist. Action, and tone, and gesture, the smile of the lover, the frown of the tyrant, the grimace of the buffoon, all must be told, for nothing can be shown. Thus the very dialogue becomes mixed with the narration, for he must not only tell what the characters actually said, in which his task is the same as that of the dramatic author, but must also describe the tone, the look, the gesture, with which their speech was accompanied—telling, in short, all which in the drama it becomes the province of the actor to express. It must, therefore, frequently happen that the author best qualified for a province in which all depends on the communication of his own ideas and feelings to the reader, without any intervening medium, may fall short of the skill necessary to adapt his compositions to the medium of the stage, where the very qualities most excellent in a novelist are out of place, and an impediment to success. Description and narration, which form the very essence of the novel, must be very sparingly introduced into dramatic composition, and scarce ever have a good effect upon the stage. Mr. Puff, in *The Critic,* has the good sense to leave out 'all about gilding the eastern hemisphere'; and the very first thing which the players struck out of his memorable tragedy, was the description of Queen Elizabeth, her palfrey, and her side-saddle. The drama speaks to the eye and ear, and when it ceases to address these bodily organs, and would exact from a theatrical audience that exercise of the imagination which is necessary to follow forth and embody circumstances neither spoken nor exhibited, there is an immediate failure, though it may be the failure of a man of genius. Hence it follows, that though a good acting play may be made, by selecting a plot and characters from a novel, yet scarce any effort of genius could render a play into a narrative romance. In the former case, the author has only to contract the events within the space necessary for representation, to choose the most striking characters, and exhibit them in the most forcible contrast, discard from the dialogue whatever is redundant or tedious, and so dramatise the whole. But we know not any effort of genius which could successfully insert into a good play those accessories of description and delineation which are necessary to dilate it into a readable novel. It may thus easily be conceived that he whose chief talent lies in addressing the imagination only, and whose style, therefore, must be expanded and circumstantial, may fail in a kind of composition where so much must be left to the efforts of the actor, with his allies and assistants the scenepainter and property-man, and where every attempt to interfere with their province is an error unfavourable to the success of the piece. Besides, it must further be remembered that in fictitious narrative an author carries on his manufacture alone, and upon his own account, whereas, in dramatic writing, he enters into partnership with the performers, and it is by their joint efforts that the piece is to succeed. Copartnery is called, by civilians, the mother of discord; and how likely it is to prove so in the present instance may be illustrated by reference to the admirable dialogue between the player and poet in *Joseph Andrews,* book III, chap. 10. The poet must either be contented to fail or to make great condescensions to the experience, and pay much attention to the peculiar qualifications of those by whom his piece is to be represented. And he who, in a novel, had only to fit sentiments, action, and character, to ideal beings, is now compelled to assume the much more difficult task of adapting all these to real existing persons, who, unless their parts are exactly suited to their own taste, and their peculiar capacities, have, each in his line, the means, and not unfrequently the inclination, to ruin the success of the play. Such are, amongst many others, the peculiar difficulties of the dramatic art, and they seem impediments which lie peculiarly in the way of the novelist who aspires to extend his sway over the stage.

VICTOR HUGO

(1802–1885)

From

PREFACE TO CROMWELL

(1827)

.   .   .

BEHOLD, then, a new religion, a new society; upon this twofold foundation there must inevitably spring up a new poetry. Previously . . . following therein the course pursued by the ancient polytheism and philosophy, the purely epic muse of the ancients had studied nature in only a single aspect, casting aside without pity almost everything in art which, in the world subjected to its imitation, had not relation to a certain type of beauty. A type which was magnificent at first, but, as always happens with everything systematic, became in later times false, trivial and conventional. Christianity leads poetry to the truth. Like it, the modern muse will see things in a higher and broader light. It will realize that everything in creation is not humanly *beautiful,* that the ugly exists beside the beautiful, the unshapely beside the graceful, the grotesque on the reverse of the sublime, evil with good, darkness with light. It will ask itself if the narrow and relative sense of the artist should prevail over the infinite, absolute sense of the Creator; if it is for man to correct God; if a mutilated nature will be the more beautiful for the mutilation; if art has the right to duplicate, so to speak, man, life, creation; if things will progress better when their muscles and their vigour have been taken from them; if, in short, to be incomplete is the best way to be harmonious. Then it is that, with its eyes fixed upon events that are both laughable and redoubtable, and under the influence of that spirit of Christian melancholy and philosophical criticism which we described a moment ago, poetry will take a great step, a decisive step, a step which, like the upheaval of an earthquake, will change the whole face of the intellectual world. It will set about doing as nature does, mingling in its creations—but without confounding them—darkness and light, the grotesque and the sublime; in other words, the body and the soul, the beast and the intellect; for the starting-point of religion is always the starting-point of poetry. All things are connected.

Thus, then, we see a principle unknown to the ancients, a new type, introduced in poetry; and as an additional element in anything modifies the whole of the thing, a new form of the art is developed. This type is the grotesque; its new form is comedy.

And we beg leave to dwell upon this point; for we have now indicated the significant feature, the fundamental difference which, in our opinion, separates modern from ancient art, the present form from the defunct form; or, to use less definite but more popular terms, *romantic* literature from *classical* literature. . . .

Thus, to sum up hurriedly the facts that we have noted thus far, poetry has three periods, each of which corresponds to an epoch of civilization: the ode, the epic, and the drama. Primitive times are lyrical, ancient times epical, modern times dramatic. The ode sings of eternity, the epic imparts solemnity to history, the drama depicts life. The characteristic of the first poetry is ingenuousness, of the second, simplicity, of the third, truth. The rhapsodists mark the transition from the lyric to the epic poets, as do the romanticists that from the lyric to the dramatic poets. Historians appear in the second period, chroniclers and critics in the third. The characters of the ode are colossi—Adam, Cain, Noah; those of the epic are giants—Achilles, Atreus, Orestes; those of the drama are men—Hamlet, Macbeth, Othello. The ode lives upon the ideal, the epic upon the grandiose, the drama upon the real. Lastly, this threefold poetry flows from three great sources—The Bible, Homer, Shakespeare.

Such then—and we confine ourselves herein to noting a single result —such are the diverse aspects of thought in the different epochs of mankind and of civilization. Such are its three faces, in youth, in manhood, in old age. Whether one examines one literature by itself or all literatures *en masse,* one will always reach the same result: the lyric poets before the epic poets, the epic poets before the dramatic poets. In

France, Malherbe before Chapelain, Chapelain before Corneille; in ancient Greece, Orpheus before Homer, Homer before Aeschylus; in the first of all books, *Genesis* before *Kings, Kings* before *Job;* or to come back to that monumental scale of all ages of poetry, which we ran over a moment since, The Bible before the *Iliad,* the *Iliad* before Shakespeare.

In a word, civilization begins by singing of its dreams, then narrates its doings, and, lastly, sets about describing what it thinks. It is, let us say in passing, because of this last, that the drama, combining the most opposed qualities, may be at the same time full of profundity and full of relief, philosophical and picturesque. . . .

We see how quickly the arbitrary distinction between the species of poetry vanishes before common sense and taste. No less easily one might demolish the alleged rule of the two unities. We say *two* and not *three* unities, because unity of plot or of *ensemble,* the only true and well-founded one, was long ago removed from the sphere of discussion. . . .

A final argument, taken from the very bowels of the art, would of itself suffice to show the absurdity of the rule of the two unities. It is the existence of the third unity, unity of plot—the only one that is universally admitted, because it results from a fact: neither the human eye nor the human mind can grasp more than one *ensemble* at one time. This one is as essential as the other two are useless. It is the one which fixes the view-point of the drama; now, by that very fact, it excludes the other two. There can no more be three unities in the drama than three horizons in a picture. But let us be careful not to confound unity with simplicity of plot. The former does not in any way exclude the secondary plots on which the principal plot may depend. It is necessary only that these parts, being skilfully subordinated to the general plan, shall tend constantly toward the central plot and group themselves about it at the various stages, or rather on the various levels of the drama. Unity of plot is the stage law of perspective. . . .

The critics of the scholastic school place their poets in a strange position. On the one hand they cry incessantly: "Copy the models!" On the other hand they have a habit of declaring that "the models are inimitable!" Now, if their craftsman, by dint of hard work, succeeds in forcing through this dangerous defile some colourless tracing of the masters, these ungrateful wretches, after examining the new *refacci-mento,* exclaim sometimes: "This doesn't resemble anything!" and sometimes: "This resembles everything!" And by virtue of a logic made for the occasion each of these formulae is a criticism.

Let us then speak boldly. The time for it has come, and it would be strange if, in this age, liberty, like the light, should penetrate everywhere except to the one place where freedom is most natural—the domain of thought. Let us take the hammer to theories and poetic systems. Let us throw down the old plastering that conceals the façade of art. There are neither rules nor models; or, rather, there are no other rules than the general laws of nature, which soar above the whole field of art, and the special rules which result from the conditions appropriate to the subject of each composition. The former are of the essence, eternal, and do not change; the latter are variable, external, and are used but once. The former are the frame-work that supports the house; the latter the scaffolding which is used in building it, and which is made anew for each building. In a word, the former are the flesh and bones, the latter the clothing, of the drama. But these rules are not written in the treatises on poetry. Richelet has no idea of their existence. Genius, which divines rather than learns, devises for each work the general rules from the general plan of things, the special rules from the separate *ensemble* of the subject treated; not after the manner of the chemist, who lights the fire under his furnace, heats his crucible, analyzes and destroys; but after the manner of the bee, which flies on its golden wings, lights on each flower and extracts its honey, leaving it as brilliant and fragrant as before.

The poet—let us insist on this point—should take counsel therefore only of nature, truth, and inspiration which is itself both truth and nature. . . .

But nature! Nature and truth!—And here, in order to prove that, far from demolishing art, the new ideas aim only to reconstruct it more firmly and on a better foundation, let us try to point out the impassable limit which in our opinion, separates reality according to art from reality according to nature. It is careless to confuse them as some ill-informed partisans of *romanticism* do. Truth in art cannot possibly be, as several writers have claimed, *absolute* reality. Art cannot produce the thing itself. . . .

We must admit, therefore, or confess ourselves ridiculous, that the domains of art and of nature are entirely distinct. Nature and art are two things—were it not so, one or the other would not exist. Art, in addition to its idealistic side, has a terrestrial, material side. Let it do what it will, it is shut in between grammar and prosody, between Vaugelas and Richelet. For its most capricious creations, it has formulae, methods of execution, a complete apparatus to set in motion. For genius there are delicate instruments, for mediocrity, tools.

It seems to us that someone has already said that the drama is a mirror wherein nature is reflected. But if it be an ordinary mirror, a smooth and polished surface, it will give only a dull image of objects, with no relief—faithful, but colourless; everyone knows that colour and light are lost in a simple reflection. The drama, therefore, must be a concentrating mirror, which, instead of weakening, concentrates and condenses the coloured rays, which makes of a mere gleam a light, and of a light a flame. Then only is the drama acknowledged by art. . . .

THOMAS DE QUINCEY

(1785–1859)

From

THE POETRY OF POPE

(1848)

. . . In that great social organ which, collectively, we call literature, there may be distinguished two separate offices that may blend and often *do* so, but capable, severally, of a severe insulation, and naturally fitted for reciprocal repulsion. There is, first, the literature of *knowledge;* and, secondly, the literature of *power.* The function of the first is—to *teach;* the function of the second is—to *move:* the first is a rudder; the second, an oar or a sail. The first speaks to the *mere* discursive understanding; the second speaks ultimately, it may happen, to the higher understanding or reason, but always *through* affections of pleasure and sympathy. Remotely, it may travel towards an object seated in what Lord Bacon calls *dry* light; but, proximately, it does and must operate,—else it ceases to be a literature of *power,*—on and through that *humid* light which clothes itself in the mists and glittering *iris* of human passions, desires, and genial emotions. Men have so little reflected on the higher functions of literature as to find it a paradox if one should

describe it as a mean or subordinate purpose of books to give information. But this is a paradox only in the sense which makes it honourable
to be paradoxical. Whenever we talk in ordinary language of seeking
information or gaining knowledge, we understand the words as connected with something of absolute novelty. But it is the grandeur of
all truth which *can* occupy a very high place in human interests that
it is never absolutely novel to the meanest of minds: it exists eternally
by way of germ or latent principle in the lowest as in the highest, needing to be developed, but never to be planted. To be capable of transplantation is the immediate criterion of a truth that ranges on a lower
scale. Besides which, there is a rarer thing than truth,—namely, *power,*
or deep sympathy with truth. What is the effect, for instance, upon
society, of children? By the pity, by the tenderness, and by the peculiar
modes of admiration, which connect themselves with the helplessness.
with the innocence, and with the simplicity of children, not only are
the primal affections strengthened and continually renewed, but the
qualities which are dearest in the sight of heaven,—the frailty, for instance, which appeals to forbearance, the innocence which symbolises
the heavenly, and the simplicity which is most alien from the worldly,
—are kept up in perpetual remembrance, and their ideals are continually
refreshed. A purpose of the same nature is answered by the higher literature, viz. the literature of power. What do you learn from "Paradise
Lost"? Nothing at all. What do you learn from a cookery-book? Something new, something that you did not know before, in every paragraph. But would you therefore put the wretched cookery-book on a
higher level of estimation than the divine poem? What you owe to
Milton is not any knowledge, of which a million separate items are
still but a million of advancing steps on the same earthly level; what
you owe is *power,*—that is, exercise and expansion to your own latent
capacity of sympathy with the infinite, where every pulse and each
separate influx is a step upwards, a step ascending as upon a Jacob's
ladder from earth to mysterious altitudes above the earth. *All* the steps
of knowledge, from first to last, carry you further on the same plane,
but could never raise you one foot above your ancient level of earth:
whereas the very *first* step in power is a flight—is an ascending movement into another element where earth is forgotten.

Were it not that human sensibilities are ventilated and continually
called out into exercise by the great phenomena of infancy, or of real
life as it moves through chance and change, or of literature as it re-
combines these elements in the mimicries of poetry, romance &c., it is

certain that, like any animal power or muscular energy falling into disuse, all such sensibilities would gradually droop and dwindle. It is in relation to these great *moral* capacities of man that the literature of power, as contradistinguished from that of knowledge, lives and has its field of action. It is concerned with what is highest in man; for the Scriptures themselves never condescended to deal by suggestion or co-operation with the mere discursive understanding: when speaking of man in his intellectual capacity, the Scriptures speak not of the understanding, but of *"the understanding heart,"*—making the heart, *i.e.* the great *intuitive* (or non-discursive) organ, to be the interchangeable formula for man in his highest state of capacity for the infinite. Tragedy, romance, fairy tale, or epopee, all alike restore to man's mind the ideals of justice, of hope, of truth, of mercy, of retribution, which else (left to the support of daily life in its realities) would languish for want of sufficient illustration. What is meant, for instance, by *poetic justice?*—It does not mean a justice that differs by its object from the ordinary justice of human jurisprudence; for then it must be confessedly a very bad kind of justice; but it means a justice that differs from common forensic justice by the degree in which it *attains* its object, a justice that is more omnipotent over its own ends, as dealing—not with the refractory elements of earthly life, but with the elements of its own creation, and with materials flexible to its own purest preconceptions. It is certain that, were it not for the Literature of Power, these ideals would often remain amongst us as mere arid notional forms; whereas, by the creative forces of man put forth in literature, they gain a vernal life of restoration, and germinate into vital activities. The commonest novel, by moving in alliance with human fears and hopes, with human instincts of wrong and right, sustains and quickens those affections. Calling them into action, it rescues them from torpor. And hence the pre-eminency over all authors that merely *teach* of the meanest that *moves,* or that teaches, if at all, indirectly *by* moving. The very highest work that has ever existed in the Literature of Knowledge is but a *provisional* work: a book upon trial and sufferance, and *quamdiu bene se gesserit.* Let its teaching be even partially revised, let it be but expanded,—nay, even let its teaching be but placed in a better order,—and instantly it is superseded. Whereas the feeblest works in the Literature of Power, surviving at all, survive as finished and unalterable amongst men. For instance, the *Principia* of Sir Isaac Newton was a book *militant* on earth from the first. In all stages of its progress it would have to fight for its existence: 1st, as regards absolute truth; 2dly, when that combat was over, as regards its form or mode of presenting the truth. And as soon as a La Place, or anybody else, builds higher upon the foundations laid by this book, effectually he throws it out of the sunshine into decay and darkness; by weapons won from this book he superannuates and destroys this book, so that soon the name of Newton remains as a mere *nominis umbra,* but his book, as a living power, has transmigrated into other forms. Now, on the contrary, the Iliad, the Prometheus of Æschylus, the Othello or King Lear, the Hamlet or Macbeth, and the Paradise Lost, are not militant, but triumphant for ever as long as the languages exist in which they speak or can be taught to speak. They never *can* transmigrate into new incarnations. To reproduce *these* in new forms, or variations, even if in some things they should be improved, would be to plagiarise. A good steam-engine is properly superseded by a better. But one lovely pastoral valley is not superseded by another, nor a statue of Praxiteles by a statue of Michael Angelo. These things are separated not by imparity, but by disparity. They are not thought of as unequal under the same standard, but as different in *kind,* and, if otherwise equal, as equal under a different standard. Human works of immortal beauty and works of nature in one respect stand on the same footing: they never absolutely repeat each other, never approach so near as not to differ; and they differ not as better and worse, or simply by more and less: they differ by undecipherable and incommunicable differences, that cannot be caught by mimicries, that cannot be reflected in the mirror of copies, that cannot become ponderable in the scales of vulgar comparison.

RALPH WALDO EMERSON

(1803–1882)

From

THE POET

(1844)

· · ·

THOSE who are esteemed umpires of taste are often persons who have acquired some knowledge of admired pictures or sculptures, and have an inclination for whatever is elegant; but if you inquire whether they are beautiful souls, and whether their own acts are like fair pictures, you learn that they are selfish and sensual. Their cultivation is local, as if you should rub a log of dry wood in one spot to produce fire, all the rest remaining cold. Their knowledge of the fine arts is some study of rules and particulars, or some limited judgment of color or form, which is exercised for amusement or for show. It is a proof of the shallowness of the doctrine of beauty as it lies in the minds of our amateurs, that men seem to have lost the perception of the instant dependence of form upon soul. There is no doctrine of forms in our philosophy. We were put into our bodies, as fire is put into a pan to be carried about; but there is no accurate adjustment between the spirit and the organ, much less is the latter the germination of the former. So in regard to other forms, the intellectual men do not believe in any essential dependence of the material world on thought and volition. Theologians think it a pretty air-castle to talk of the spiritual meaning of a ship or a cloud, of a city or a contract, but they prefer to come again to the solid ground of historical evidence; and even the poets are contented with a civil and conformed manner of living, and to write poems from the fancy, at a safe distance from their own experience. But the highest minds of the world have never ceased to explore the double meaning, or shall I say the quadruple or the centuple or much more manifold meaning, of every sensuous fact; Orpheus, Empedocles, Heraclitus, Plato, Plutarch, Dante, Swedenborg, and the masters of sculpture, picture and poetry. For we are not pans and barrows, nor even porters of the fire and torch-bearers, but children of the fire, made of it, and only the same divinity transmuted and at two or three removes, when we know least about it. And this hidden truth, that the fountains whence all this river of Time and its creatures floweth are intrinsically ideal and beautiful, draws us to the consideration of the nature and functions of the Poet, or the man of Beauty; to the means and materials he uses, and to the general aspect of the art in the present time.

The breadth of the problem is great, for the poet is representative. He stands among partial men for the complete man, and apprises us not of his wealth, but of the common wealth. The young man reveres men of genius, because, to speak truly, they are more himself than he is. They receive of the soul as he also receives, but they more. Nature enhances her beauty, to the eye of loving men, from their belief that the poet is beholding her shows at the same time. He is isolated among his contemporaries by truth and by his art, but with this consolation in his pursuits, that they will draw all men sooner or later. For all men live by truth and stand in need of expression. In love, in art, in avarice, in politics, in labor, in games, we study to utter our painful secret. The man is only half himself, the other half is his expression.

. . .

The sign and credentials of the poet are that he announces that which no man foretold. He is the true and only doctor; he knows and tells; he is the only teller of news, for he was present and privy to the appearance which he describes. He is a beholder of ideas and an utterer of the necessary and causal. For we do not speak now of men of poetical talents, or of industry and skill in metre, but of the true poet. I took part in a conversation the other day concerning a recent writer of lyrics, a man of subtle mind, whose head appeared to be a music-box of delicate tunes and rhythms, and whose skill and command of language we could not sufficiently praise. But when the question arose whether he was not only a lyrist but a poet, we were obliged to confess that he is plainly a contemporary, not an eternal man. He does not stand out of our low limitations, like a Chimborazo under the line, running up from a torrid base through all the climates of the globe, with belts of the herbage of every latitude on its high and mottled sides; but this genius is the landscape-garden of a modern house adorned with fountains and statues, with well-bred men and women standing and sitting in the walks and terraces. We hear, through all the varied music, the ground-tone of conventional life. Our poets are men of talents who sing, and not the children of music. The argument is secondary, the finish of the verses is primary.

For it is not metres, but a metre-making argument that makes a poem, —a thought so passionate and alive that like the spirit of a plant or an animal it has an architecture of its own, and adorns nature with a new thing. The thought and the form are equal in the order of time, but in the order of genesis the thought is prior to the form. The poet has a new thought; he has a whole new experience to unfold; he will tell us how it was with him, and all men will be the richer in his fortune. For the experience of each new age requires a new confession, and the world seems always waiting for its poet. . . .

Beyond this universality of the symbolic language, we are apprised of the divineness of this superior use of things, whereby the world is a temple whose walls are covered with emblems, pictures and commandments of the Deity,—in this, that there is no fact in nature which does not carry the whole sense of nature; and the distinctions which we make in events and in affairs, of low and high, honest and base, dis-

appear when nature is used as a symbol. Thought makes everything fit
for use. The vocabulary of an omniscient man would embrace words
and images excluded from polite conversation. What would be base,
or even obscene, to the obscene, becomes illustrious, spoken in a new
connection of thought. The piety of the Hebrew prophets purges their
grossness. The circumcision is an example of the power of poetry to
raise the low and offensive. Small and mean things serve as well as great
symbols. The meaner the type by which a law is expressed, the more
pungent it is, and the more lasting in the memories of men; just as we
choose the smallest box or case in which any needful utensil can be
carried. Bare lists of words are found suggestive to an imaginative and
excited mind; as it is related of Lord Chatham that he was accustomed
to read in Bailey's Dictionary when he was preparing to speak in Parliament. The poorest experience is rich enough for all the purposes of
expressing thought. Why covet a knowledge of new facts? Day and
night, house and garden, a few books, a few actions, serve us as well
as would all trades and all spectacles. We are far from having exhausted
the significance of the few symbols we use. We can come to use them
yet with a terrible simplicity. It does not need that a poem should be
long. Every word was once a poem. Every new relation is a new word.
Also we use defects and deformities to a sacred purpose, so expressing
our sense that the evils of the world are such only to the evil eye. In
the old mythology, mythologists observe, defects are ascribed to divine
natures, as lameness to Vulcan, blindness to Cupid, and the like,—to
signify exuberances.

For as it is dislocation and detachment from the life of God that
makes things ugly, the poet, who re-attaches things to nature and the
Whole,—re-attaching even artificial things and violation of nature, to
nature, by a deeper insight,—disposes very easily of the most disagreeable facts. Readers of poetry see the factory-village and the railway, and
fancy that the poetry of the landscape is broken up by these; for these
works of art are not yet consecrated in their reading; but the poet sees
them fall within the great Order not less than the beehive or the spider's
geometrical web. Nature adopts them very fast into her vital circles, and
the gliding train of cars she loves like her own. Besides, in a centred
mind, it signifies nothing how many mechanical inventions you exhibit. Though you add millions, and never so surprising, the fact of
mechanics has not gained a grain's weight. The spiritual fact remains
unalterable, by many or by few particulars; as no mountain is of any
appreciable height to break the curve of the sphere. A shrewd country-

boy goes to the city for the first time, and the complacent citizen is not satisfied with his little wonder. It is not that he does not see all the fine houses and know that he never saw such before, but he disposes of them as easily as the poet finds place for the railway. The chief value of the new fact is to enhance the great and constant fact of Life, which can dwarf any and every circumstance, and to which the belt of wampum and the commerce of America are alike.

The world being thus put under the mind for verb and noun, the poet is he who can articulate it. For though life is great, and fascinates and absorbs; and though all men are intelligent of the symbols through which it is named; yet they cannot originally use them. We are symbols and inhabit symbols; workmen, work, and tools, words and things, birth and death, all are emblems; but we sympathize with the symbols, and being infatuated with the economical uses of things, we do not know that they are thoughts. The poet, by an ulterior intellectual perception, gives them a power which makes their old use forgotten, and puts eyes and a tongue into every dumb and inanimate object. He perceives the independence of the thought on the symbol, the stability of the thought, the accidency and fugacity of the symbol. As the eyes of Lyncæus were said to see through the earth, so the poet turns the world to glass, and shows us all things in their right series and procession. For through that better perception he stands one step nearer to things, and sees the flowing or metamorphosis; perceives that thought is multiform; that within the form of every creature is a force impelling it to ascend into a higher form; and following with his eyes the life, uses the forms which express that life, and so his speech flows with the flowing of nature. All the facts of the animal economy, sex, nutriment, gestation, birth, growth, are symbols of the passage of the world into the soul of man, to suffer there a change and reappear a new and higher fact. He uses forms according to the life, and not according to the form. This is true science. The poet alone knows astronomy, chemistry, vegetation and animation, for he does not stop at these facts, but employs them as signs. He knows why the plain or meadow of space was strown with these flowers we call suns and moons and stars; why the great deep is adorned with animals, with men, and gods; for in every word he speaks he rides on them as the horses of thought. . . .

From

SHAKESPEARE; OR, THE POET

(1850)

GREAT men are more distinguished by range and extent than by originality. If we require the originality which consists in weaving, like a
spider, their web from their own bowels; in finding clay, and making
bricks, and building the house; no great men are original. Nor does
valuable originality consist in unlikeness to other men. The hero is in
the press of knights, and the thick of events; and, seeing what men
want, and sharing their desire, he adds the needful length of sight and
of arm, to come at the desired point. The greatest genius is the most
indebted man. A poet is no rattlebrain, saying what comes uppermost,
and, because he says everything, saying, at last, something good; but a
heart in unison with his time and country. There is nothing whimsical
and fantastic in his production, but sweet and sad earnest, freighted
with the weightiest convictions, and pointed with the most determined
aim which any man or class knows of in his times.

The Genius of our life is jealous of individuals, and will not have
any individual great, except through the general. There is no choice to
genius. A great man does not wake up on some fine morning, and
say, 'I am full of life, I will go to sea, and find an Antarctic continent:
to-day I will square the circle: I will ransack botany, and find a new
food for man: I have a new architecture in my mind: I foresee a new
mechanic power:' no, but he finds himself in the river of the thoughts
and events, forced onward by the ideas and necessities of his contemporaries. He stands where all the eyes of men look one way, and their
hands all point in the direction in which he should go. The church has
reared him amidst rites and pomps, and he carries out the advice which
her music gave him, and builds a cathedral needed by her chants and
processions. He finds a war raging: it educates him, by trumpet, in
barracks, and he betters the instruction. He finds two countries groping
to bring coal, or flour, or fish, from the place of production to the place
of consumption, and he hits on a railroad. Every master has found his
material collected, and his power lay in his sympathy with his people,
and in his love of the materials he wrought in. What an economy of
power! and what a compensation for the shortness of life! All is done to
his hand. The world has brought him thus far on his way. The human

race has gone out before him, sunk the hills, filled the hollows, and bridged the rivers. Men, nations, poets, artisans, women, all have worked for him, and he enters into their labours. Choose any other thing, out of the line of tendency, out of the national feeling and history, and he would have all to do for himself; his powers would be expended in the first preparations. Great genial power, one would almost say, consists in not being original at all; in being altogether receptive; in letting the world do all, and suffering the spirit of the hour to pass unobstructed through the mind.

. . .

Shakespeare is the only biographer of Shakespeare; and even he can tell nothing, except to the Shakespeare in us; that is, to our most apprehensive and sympathetic hour. He cannot step from off his tripod, and give us anecdotes of his inspirations. Read the antique documents extricated, analysed, and compared by the assiduous Dyce and Collier; and now read one of those skyey sentences,—aerolites,—which seem to have fallen out of heaven, and which, not your experience, but the man within the breast, has accepted as words of fate; and tell me if they match; if the former account in any manner for the latter; or which gives the most historical insight into the man. . . .

JAMES RUSSELL LOWELL

(1819–1891)

From

NATIONALITY IN LITERATURE

(1849)

THE poetry and romance of other nations are assumed to be national, inasmuch as they occupy themselves about local traditions or objects. But we, who never had any proper youth as a nation, never had our mythic period either. We had no cradle and no nursery to be haunted with such bugaboos. One great element of external and immediate influence is therefore wanting to our poets. They cannot, as did Goethe in his "Faust," imbue an old legend, which already has a hold upon the fancy and early associations of their countrymen, with a modern and philosophical meaning which shall make it interesting to their ma ture understandings and cultivated imaginations. Whatever be the cause, no race into whose composition so large a Teutonic element has entered, is divided by such an impassable chasm of oblivion and unbelief from the ancestral mythology as the English. Their poets accordingly are not popular in any true sense of the word, and have influenced the thought and action of their countrymen less than those of any nation except those of ancient Rome. Poets in other countries have mainly contributed to the creating and keeping alive of national sentiment; but the English owe theirs wholly to the sea which islands them. Chaucer and Spenser are Normans, and their minds open most fairly southward. Skelton, the Swift of his day, a purely English poet, is forgotten. Shakespeare, thoroughly English as he is, has chosen foreign subjects for the greatest of his dramas, as if to show that genius is cosmopolitan. The first thorough study, criticism, and consequent appreciation of him we owe to the Germans; and he can in no sense be called national except by accident of birth. Even if we grant that he drew his fairy mythology from any then living faith among his countrymen, this formed no bond of union between him and them, and was even regarded as an uncouthness and barbarism till long after every vestige of such faith was obliterated. If we concede any nationality to Milton's great poem, we must at the same time allow to the English an exclusive title to the localities where the scene is laid, a title which they would hardly be anxious to put forward in respect, at least, to one of them. When he was meditating a national poem, it was, he tells us, on the legend of Arthur, who, if he had ever existed at all, would have been English only in the same sense that Tecumseh is American. Coleridge, among his thousand reveries, hovered over the same theme, but settled at last upon the siege of Jerusalem by Titus as the best epical subject remaining. Byron, in his greatest poem, alludes only to England in a rather contemptuous farewell. Those strains of Wordsworth, which have entitled his name to a place on the selecter list of English poets, are precisely the ones in which England has only a common property with the rest of mankind. He could never have swum over Lethe with the sonnets to the river Duddon in his pocket. Whether we look for the cause in the origin of the people, or in their insular position, the English mind has always been characterized by an emigrating tendency. Their most truly national epic was the colonizing of America. . . .

The only element of permanence which belongs to myth, legend, or history, is exactly so much of each as refuses to be circumscribed by provincial boundaries. When once superstitions, customs, and historic personages are dead and buried in antiquarian treatises or county annals, there is no such thing as resurrection for them. The poet who encumbers himself with them takes just that amount of unnecessary burthen upon his shoulders. He is an antiquary, not a creator, and is writing what posterity will read as a catalogue rather than a poem. There is a homeliness about great genius which leads it to glorify the place of its "kindly engendure," (as Chaucer calls it), either by a tender allusion, or by images and descriptions drawn from that fairest landscape in the gallery of memory. But it is a strange confusion of thought to attribute to a spot of earth the inspiration whose source is in a universal sentiment. It is the fine humanity, the muscular sense, and the generous humor of Burns which save him from being merely Scotch, like a score of rhymesters as national as he. The Homers of Little Pedlington die, as their works died before them, and are forgotten; but let a genius get born there, and one touch of his nature shall establish even for Little Pedlington an immortal consanguinity which the whole world shall be eager to claim. The field-mouse and the mountain-daisy are not Scotch, and Tam o'Shanter died the other day within a mile of where we are writing. Measuring Burns by that which is best in him, and which insures to him a length of life coincident with that of the human heart, he is as little national as Shakespeare, and no more an alien in Iowa than in Ayrshire. There is a vast difference between truth to nature and truth to fact; an impassable gulf between genius, which deals only with the true, and that imitative faculty which patiently and exactly reproduces the actual. . . .

This demand for a nationality bounded historically and geographically by the independent existence and territory of a particular race or fraction of a race, would debar us of our rightful share in the past and the ideal. It was happily illustrated by that parochially national Gascon, who would have been edified by the sermon had it been his good fortune to belong to the parish. Let us be thankful that there is no court by which we can be excluded from our share in the inheritance of the great poets of all ages and countries, to which our simple humanity entitles us. No great poet has ever sung but the whole human race has been, sooner or later, the wiser and better for it. Above all, let us not tolerate in our criticism a principle which would operate as a prohibitory tariff of ideas. The intellect is a diœcious plant, and books are the bees which carry the quickening pollen from one to another mind. It detracts nothing from Chaucer that we can trace in him the influences of Dante and Boccaccio; nothing from Spenser that he calls Chaucer master; nothing from Shakespeare that he acknowledges how dear Spenser was to him; nothing from Milton that he brought fire from Hebrew and Greek altars. There is no degradation in such indebtedness. Venerable rather is this apostolic succession, and inspiring to see the *vitai lampada* passed thus from consecrated hand to hand.

JOHN RUSKIN

(1819–1900)

From

OF THE PATHETIC FALLACY

(*Modern Painters*, Vol. III, pt. 4)

(1856)

.   .   .

#4. Now, therefore, putting these tiresome and absurd words quite out of our way, we may go on at our ease to examine the point in question,—namely, the difference between the ordinary, proper, and true appearances of things to us; and the extraordinary, or false appearances, when we are under the influence of emotion, or contemplative fancy; false appearances, I say, as being entirely unconnected with any real power or character in the object, and only imputed to it by us.

For instance—

> "The spendthrift crocus, bursting through the mould
> Naked and shivering, with his cup of gold." *

This is very beautiful and yet very untrue. The crocus is not a spendthrift, but a hardy plant; its yellow is not gold, but saffron. How is it that we enjoy so much the having it put into our heads that it is anything else than a plain crocus?

It is an important question. For, throughout our past reasonings about art, we have always found that nothing could be good or useful, or ultimately pleasurable, which was *un*true. But here is something pleasurable in written poetry which is nevertheless untrue. And what is more, if we think over our favorite poetry, we shall find it full of this kind of fallacy, and that we like it all the more for being so.

* Holmes (Oliver Wendell), quoted by   ary Life.
Miss Mitford in her Recollections of a Liter-

5. It will appear also, on consideration of the matter, that this fallacy is of two principal kinds. Either, as in this case of the crocus, it is the fallacy of wilful fancy, which involves no real expectation that it will be believed; or else it is a fallacy caused by an excited state of the feelings, making us, for the time, more or less irrational. Of the cheating of the fancy we shall have to speak presently; but, in this chapter, I want to examine the nature of the other error, that which the mind admits when affected strongly by emotion. Thus, for instance, in Alton Locke—

> "They rowed her in across the rolling foam—
> The cruel, crawling foam."

The foam is not cruel, neither does it crawl. The state of mind which attributes to it these characters of a living creature is one in which the reason is unhinged by grief. All violent feelings have the same effect. They produce in us a falseness in all our impressions of external things, which I would generally characterize as the "Pathetic Fallacy."

6. Now we are in the habit of considering this fallacy as eminently a character of poetical description, and the temper of mind in which we allow it, as one eminently poetical, because passionate. But, I believe, if we look well into the matter, that we shall find the greatest poets do not often admit this kind of falseness,—that it is only the second order of poets who much delight in it.*

Thus, when Dante describes the spirits falling from the bank of

---

*I admit two orders of poets, but no third; and by these two orders I mean the Creative (Shakspeare, Homer, Dante), and Reflective or Perceptive (Wordsworth, Keats, Tennyson). But both of these must be *first*-rate in their range, though their range is different; and with poetry second-rate in *quality* no one ought to be allowed to trouble mankind. There is quite enough of the best,—much more than we can ever read or enjoy in the length of a life; and it is a literal wrong or sin in any person to encumber us with inferior work. I have no patience with apologies made by young pseudo-poets, "that they believe there is *some* good in what they have written: that they hope to do better in time," etc. *Some* good! If there is not *all* good, there is no good. If they ever hope to do better, why do they trouble us now? Let them rather courageously burn all they have done, and wait for the better days. There are few men, ordinarily educated, who in moments of strong feeling could not strike out a poetical thought, and afterwards polish it so as to be presentable. But men of sense know better than so to waste their time; and those who sincerely love poetry, know the touch of the master's hand on the chords too well to fumble among them after him. Nay, more than this; all inferior poetry is an injury to the good, inasmuch as it takes away the freshness of rhymes, blunders upon and gives a wretched commonalty to good thoughts; and, in general, adds to the weight of human weariness in a most woful and culpable manner. There are few thoughts likely to come across ordinary men, which have not already been expressed by greater men in the best possible way; and it is a wiser, more generous, more noble thing to remember and point out the perfect words, than to invent poorer ones, wherewith to encumber temporarily the world.

Acheron "as dead leaves flutter from a bough," he gives the most perfect image possible of their utter lightness, feebleness, passiveness, and
scattering agony of despair, without, however, for an instant losing
his own clear perception that *these* are souls, and *those* are leaves: he
makes no confusion of one with the other. But when Coleridge speaks of

> "The one red leaf, the last of its clan,
>   That dances as often as dance it can,"

he has a morbid, that is to say, a so far false, idea about the leaf: he
fancies a life in it, and will, which there are not; confuses its powerless-
ness with choice, its fading death with merriment, and the wind that
shakes it with music. Here, however, there is some beauty, even in the
morbid passage; but take an instance in Homer and Pope. Without the
knowledge of Ulysses, Elpenor, his youngest follower, has fallen from
an upper chamber in the Circean palace, and has been left dead, un-
missed by his leader, or companions, in the haste of their departure. They
cross the sea to the Cimmerian land; and Ulysses summons the shades
from Tartarus. The first which appears is that of the lost Elpenor.
Ulysses, amazed, and in exactly the spirit of bitter and terrified lightness
which is seen in Hamlet,* addresses the spirit with the simple, startled
words:

"Elpenor? How camest thou under the Shadowy darkness? Hast thou
come faster on foot than I in my black ship?"

Which Pope renders thus:—

> "O, say, what angry power Elpenor led
>   To glide in shades, and wander with the dead?
> How could thy soul, by realms and seas disjoined,
>   Outfly the nimble sail, and leave the lagging wind?"

I sincerely hope the reader finds no pleasure here, either in the nimbleness of the sail, or the laziness of the wind! And yet how is it that these
conceits are so painful now, when they have been pleasant to us in the
other instances?

7. For a very simple reason. They are not a *pathetic* fallacy at all,
for they are put into the mouth of the wrong passion—a passion which
never could possibly have spoken them—agonized curiosity. Ulysses
wants to know the facts of the matter; and the very last thing his mind
could do at the moment would be to pause, or suggest in anywise what

---

* "Well said, Old mole! can'st work i' the ground so fast?"

was *not* a fact. The delay in the first three lines, and conceit in the last, jar upon us instantly, like the most frightful discord in music. No poet of true imaginative power could possibly have written the passage. It is worth while comparing the way a similar question is put by the exquisite sincerity of Keats:—

> "He wept, and his bright tears
> Went trickling down the golden bow he held.
> Thus, with half-shut, suffused eyes, he stood;
> While from beneath some cumb'rous boughs hard by,
> With solemn step, an awful goddess came.
> And there was purport in her looks for him,
> Which he with eager guess began to read:
> Perplexed the while, melodiously he said,
> *'How cam'st thou over the unfooted sea?'* "

Therefore, we see that the spirit of truth must guide us in some sort, even in our enjoyment of fallacy. Coleridge's fallacy has no discord in it, but Pope's has set our teeth on edge. Without farther questioning, I will endeavor to state the main bearings of this matter.

8. The temperament which admits the pathetic fallacy, is, as I said above, that of a mind and body in some sort too weak to deal fully with what is before them or upon them; borne away, or over-clouded, or over-dazzled by emotion; and it is a more or less noble state, according to the force of the emotion which has induced it. For it is no credit to a man that he is not morbid or inaccurate in his perceptions, when he has no strength of feeling to warp them; and it is in general a sign of higher capacity and stand in the ranks of being, that the emotions should be strong enough to vanquish, partly, the intellect, and make it believe what they choose. But it is still a grander condition when the intellect also rises, till it is strong enough to assert its rule against, or together with, the utmost efforts of the passions; and the whole man stands in an iron glow, white hot, perhaps, but still strong, and in no wise evaporating; even if he melts, losing none of his weight.

So, then, we have the three ranks: the man who perceives rightly, because he does not feel, and to whom the primrose is very accurately the primrose, because he does not love it. Then, secondly, the man who perceives wrongly, because he feels, and to whom the primrose is anything else than a primrose: a star, or a sun, or a fairy's shield, or a forsaken maiden. And then, lastly, there is the man who perceives rightly in spite of his feelings, and to whom the primrose is for ever nothing else than itself—a little flower, apprehended in the very plain and leafy fact of it, whatever and how many soever the associations and passions may be, that crowd around it. And, in general, these three classes may be rated in comparative order, as the men who are not poets at all, and the poets of the second order, and the poets of the first; only however great a man may be, there are always some subjects which *ought* to throw him off his balance; some, by which his poor human capacity of thought should be conquered, and brought into the inaccurate and vague state of perception, so that the language of the highest inspiration becomes broken, obscure, and wild in metaphor, resembling that of the weaker man, overborne by weaker things.

.   .   .

11. Now so long as we see that the *feeling* is true, we pardon, or are even pleased by, the confessed fallacy of sight which it induces: we are pleased, for instance, with those lines of Kingsley's, above quoted, not because they fallaciously describe foam, but because they faithfully describe sorrow. But the moment the mind of the speaker becomes cold, that moment every such expression becomes untrue, as being for ever untrue in the external facts. And there is no greater baseness in literature than the habit of using these metaphorical expressions in cold blood. An inspired writer, in full impetuosity of passion, may speak wisely and truly of "raging waves of the sea, foaming out their own shame"; but it is only the basest writer who cannot speak of the sea without talking of "raging waves," "remorseless floods," "ravenous billows," &c.; and it is one of the signs of the highest power in a writer to check all such habits of thought, and to keep his eyes fixed firmly on the *pure fact,* out of which if any feeling comes to him or his reader, he knows it must be a true one.

HIPPOLYTE ADOLPHE TAINE

(1828–1893)

From

HISTORY OF ENGLISH LITERATURE *

(1856–59)

THE INTRODUCTION TO PART VI

I

HISTORY, within a hundred years in Germany, and within sixty years in France, has undergone a transformation, owing to a study of literatures.

The discovery has been made that a literary work is not a mere play of the imagination, the isolated caprice of an excited brain, but a transcript of contemporary manners and customs and the sign of a particular state of intellect. The conclusion derived from this is that, through literary monuments, we can retrace the way in which men felt and thought many centuries ago. This method has been tried and found successful.

We have meditated over these ways of feeling and thinking and have accepted them as facts of prime significance. We have found that they were dependent on most important events, that they explain these, and that these explain them, and that henceforth it was necessary to give them their place in history, and one of the highest. This place has been assigned to them, and hence all is changed in history—the aim, the method, the instrumentalities, and the conceptions of laws and of causes. It is this change as now going on, and which must continue to go on, that is here attempted to be set forth.

On turning over the large stiff pages of a folio volume, or the yellow leaves of a manuscript, in short, a poem, a code of laws, a confession of faith, what is your first comment? You say to yourself that the work before you is not of its own creation. It is simply a mold like a fossil shell, an imprint similar to one of those forms embedded in a stone by an animal which once lived and perished. Beneath the shell was an animal and behind the document there was a man. Why do you study the

* Translated by Henry Van Laun.

shell unless to form some idea of the animal? In the same way do you study the document in order to comprehend the man; both shell and document are dead fragments and of value only as indications of the complete living being. The aim is to reach this being; this is what you strive to reconstruct. It is a mistake to study the document as if it existed alone by itself. That is treating things merely as a pedant, and you subject yourself to the illusions of a book-worm. At bottom mythologies and languages are not existences; the only realities are human beings who have employed words and imagery adapted to their organs and to suit the original cast of their intellects. A creed is nothing in itself. Who made it? Look at this or that portrait of the sixteenth century, the stern, energetic features of an archbishop or of an English martyr. Nothing exists except through the individual; it is necessary to know the individual himself. Let the parentage of creeds be established, or the classification of poems, or the growth of constitutions, or the transformations of idioms, and we have only cleared the ground. True history begins when the historian has discerned beyond the mists of ages the living, active man, endowed with passions, furnished with habits, special in voice, feature, gesture, and costume, distinctive and complete, like anybody that you have just encountered in the street. Let us strive then, as far as possible, to get rid of this great interval of time which prevents us from observing the man with our eyes, the eyes of our own head. What revelations do we find in the calendared leaves of a modern poem? A modern poet, a man like De Musset, Victor Hugo, Lamartine, or Heine, graduated from a college and travelled, wearing a dress-coat and gloves, favored by ladies, bowing fifty times and uttering a dozen witticisms in an evening, reading daily newspapers, generally occupying an apartment on the second story, not over-cheerful on account of his nerves, and especially because, in this dense democracy in which we stifle each other, the discredit of official rank exaggerates his pretensions by raising his importance, and, owing to the delicacy of his personal sensations, leading him to regard himself as a Deity. Such is what we detect behind modern meditations and sonnets.

Again, behind a tragedy of the seventeenth century there is a poet, one, for example, like Racine, refined, discreet, a courtier, a fine talker, with majestic perruque and ribboned shoes, a monarchist and zealous Christian, "God having given him the grace not to blush in any society on account of zeal for his king or for the Gospel," clever in interesting the monarch, translating into proper French "the *gaulois* of Amyot," deferential to the great, always knowing how to keep his place in their

company, assiduous and respectful at Marly as at Versailles, amid the
formal creations of a decorative landscape and the reverential bows,
graces, intrigues, and finesses of the braided seigniors who get up early
every morning to obtain the reversion of an office, together with the
charming ladies who count on their fingers the pedigrees which entitle
them to a seat on a footstool. On this point consult Saint-Simon and the
engravings of Pérelle, the same as you have just consulted Balzac and
the water-color drawings of Eugène Lami.

In like manner, on reading a Greek tragedy, our first care is to figure
to ourselves the Greeks, that is to say, men who lived half-naked in the
gymnasiums or on a public square under a brilliant sky, in full view of
the noblest and most delicate landscape, busy in rendering their bodies
strong and agile, in conversing together, in arguing, in voting, in carrying out patriotic piracies, and yet idle and temperate, the furniture of
their houses consisting of three earthen jars and their food of two pots of
anchovies preserved in oil, served by slaves who afford them the time to
cultivate their minds and to exercise their limbs, with no other concern
than that of having the most beautiful city, the most beautiful processions, the most beautiful ideas, and the most beautiful men. In this respect, a statue like the "Meleager" or the "Theseus" of the Parthenon,
or again a sight of the blue and lustrous Mediterranean, resembling a
silken tunic out of which islands arise like marble bodies, together
with a dozen choice phrases selected from the works of Plato and
Aristophanes, teach us more than any number of dissertations and
commentaries.

And so again, in order to understand an Indian Purana, one must
begin by imagining the father of a family who, "having seen a son on
his son's knees," follows the law and, with axe and pitcher, seeks solitude
under a banyan tree, talks no more, multiplies his fastings, lives naked
with four fires around him under the fifth fire, that terrible sun which
endlessly devours and resuscitates all living things; who fixes his imagination in turn for weeks at a time on the foot of Brahma, then on his
knee, on his thigh, on his navel, and so on, until, beneath the strain of
this intense meditation, hallucinations appear, when all the forms of being, mingling together and transformed into each other, oscillate to
and fro in this vertiginous brain until the motionless man, with suspended breath and fixed eyeballs, beholds the universe melting away
like vapor over the vacant immensity of the Being in which he hopes
for absorption. In this case the best of teachings would be a journey
in India; but, for lack of a better one, take the narratives of travellers

along with works in geography, botany, and ethnology. In any event, there must be the same research. A language, a law, a creed, is never other than an abstraction; the perfect thing is found in the active man, the visible corporeal figure which eats, walks, fights, and labors. Set aside the theories of constitutions and their results, of religions and their systems, and try to observe men in their workshops or offices, in their fields along with their own sky and soil, with their own homes, clothes, occupations and repasts, just as you see them when, on landing in England or in Italy, you remark their features and gestures, their roads and their inns, the citizen on his promenades and the workman taking a drink. Let us strive as much as possible to supply the place of the actual, personal, sensible observation that is no longer practicable, this being the only way in which we can really know the man; let us make the past present; to judge of an object it must be present; no experience can be had of what is absent. Undoubtedly, this sort of reconstruction is always imperfect; only an imperfect judgment can be based on it; but let us do the best we can; incomplete knowledge is better than none at all, or than knowledge which is erroneous, and there is no other way of obtaining knowledge approximatively of bygone times than by seeing approximatively the men of former times.

Such is the first step in history. This step was taken in Europe at the end of the last century when the imagination took fresh flight under the auspices of Lessing and Walter Scott, and a little later in France under Chateaubriand, Augustin Thierry, Michelet, and others. We now come to the second step.

II

On observing the visible man with your own eyes what do you try to find in him? The invisible man. These words which your ears catch, those gestures, those airs of the head, his attire and sensible operations of all kinds, are, for you, merely so many expressions; these express something, a soul. An inward man is hidden beneath the outward man, and the latter simply manifests the former. You have observed the house in which he lives, his furniture, his costume, in order to discover his habits and tastes, the degree of his refinement or rusticity, his extravagance or economy, his follies or his cleverness. You have listened to his conversation and noted the inflections of his voice, the attitudes he has assumed, so as to judge of his spirit, self-abandonment or gayety, his energy or his rigidity. You consider his writings, works of art,

financial and political schemes, with a view to measure the reach and
limits of his intelligence, his creative power and self-command, to ascertain the usual order, kind, and force of his conceptions, in what way
he thinks and how he resolves. All these externals are so many avenues
converging to one centre, and you follow these only to reach that centre;
here is the real man, namely, that group of faculties and of sentiments
which produces the rest. Behold a new world, an infinite world; for
each visible action involves an infinite train of reasonings and emotions,
new or old sensations which have combined to bring this into light and
which, like long ledges of rock sunk deep in the earth, have cropped
out above the surface and attained their level. It is this subterranean
world which forms the second aim, the special object of the historian.
If his critical education suffices, he is able to discriminate under every
ornament in architecture, under every stroke of the brush in a picture,
under each phrase of literary composition, the particular sentiment out
of which the ornament, the stroke, and the phrase have sprung; he
is a spectator of the inward drama which has developed itself in the
breast of the artist or writer; the choice of words, the length or shortness
of the period, the species of metaphor, the accent of a verse, the chain of
reasoning—all are to him an indication; while his eyes are reading the
text his mind and soul are following the steady flow and ever-changing
series of emotions and conceptions from which this text has issued; he
is working out its psychology. Should you desire to study this operation,
regard the promoter and model of all the high culture of the epoch,
Goethe, who, before composing his "Iphigenia" spent days in making
drawings of the most perfect statues and who, at last, his eyes filled
with the noble forms of antique scenery and his mind penetrated by
the harmonious beauty of antique life, succeeded in reproducing internally, with such exactness, the habits and yearnings of Greek imagination as to provide us with an almost twin sister of the "Antigone"
of Sophocles and of the goddesses of Phidias. This exact and demonstrated divination of bygone sentiments has, in our days, given a new
life to history. There was almost complete ignorance of this in the last
century; men of every race and of every epoch were represented as
about alike, the Greek, the barbarian, the Hindoo, the man of the
Renaissance and the man of the eighteenth century, cast in the same
mold and after the same pattern, and after a certain abstract conception
which served for the whole human species. There was a knowledge
of man but not of men. There was no penetration into the soul itself;
nothing of the infinite diversity and wonderful complexity of souls had

been detected; it was not known that the moral organization of a people or of an age is as special and distinct as the physical structure of a family of plants or of an order of animals. History to-day, like zoölogy, has found its anatomy, and whatever branch of it is studied, whether philology, languages or mythologies, it is in this way that labor must be given to make it produce new fruit. Among so many writers who, since Herder, Ottfried Müller, and Goethe have steadily followed and rectified this great effort, let the reader take two historians and two works, one "The Life and Letters of Cromwell" by Carlyle, and the other the "Port Royal" of Sainte-Beuve. He will see how precisely, how clearly, and how profoundly we detect the soul of a man beneath his actions and works; how, under an old general and in place of an ambitious man vulgarly hypocritical, we find one tormented by the disordered reveries of a gloomy imagination, but practical in instinct and faculties, thoroughly English and strange and incomprehensible to whoever has not studied the climate and the race; how, with about a hundred scattered letters and a dozen or more mutilated speeches, we follow him from his farm and his team to his general's tent and to his Protector's throne, in his transformation and in his development, in his struggles of conscience and in his statesman's resolutions, in such a way that the mechanism of his thought and action becomes visible and the ever renewed and fitful tragedy, within which racked this great gloomy soul, passes like the tragedies of Shakespeare into the souls of those who behold them. We see how, behind convent disputes and the obstinacy of nuns, we recover one of the great provinces of human psychology; how fifty or more characters, rendered invisible through the uniformity of a narration careful of the properties, come forth in full daylight, each standing out clear in its countless diversities; how, underneath theological dissertations and monotonous sermons, we discern the throbbings of ever-breathing hearts, the excitements and depressions of the religious life, the unforeseen reaction and pell-mell stir of natural feeling, the infiltrations of surrounding society, the intermittent triumphs of grace, presenting so many shades of difference that the fullest description and most flexible style can scarcely garner in the vast harvest which the critic has caused to germinate in this abandoned field. And the same elsewhere. Germany, with its genius, so pliant, so broad, so prompt in transformations, so fitted for the reproduction of the remotest and strangest states of human thought; England, with its matter-of-fact mind, so suited to the grappling with moral problems, to making them clear by figures, weights, and measures, by geography and statistics, by texts and common sense; France, at length, with its Parisian culture and drawing-room habits, with its unceasing analysis of characters and of works, with its ever ready irony at detecting weaknesses, with its skilled finesse in discriminating shades of thought—all have ploughed over the same ground, and we now begin to comprehend that no region of history exists in which this deep sub-soil should not be reached if we would secure adequate crops between the furrows.

Such is the second step, and we are now in train to follow it out. Such is the proper aim of contemporary criticism. No one has done this work so judiciously and on so grand a scale as Sainte-Beuve; in this respect, we are all his pupils; literary, philosophic, and religious criticism in books, and even in the newspapers, is to-day entirely changed by his method. Ulterior evolution must start from this point. I have often attempted to expose what this evolution is; in my opinion, it is a new road open to history and which I shall strive to describe more in detail.

III

After having observed in a man and noted down one, two, three, and then a multitude of sentiments, do these suffice and does your knowledge of him seem complete? Does a memorandum book constitute a psychology? It is not a psychology, and here, as elsewhere, the search for causes must follow the collection of facts. It matters not what the facts may be, whether physical or moral, they always spring from causes; there are causes for ambition, for courage, for veracity, as well as for digestion, for muscular action, and for animal heat. Vice and virtue are products like vitriol and sugar; every complex fact grows out of the simple facts with which it is affiliated and on which it depends. We must therefore try to ascertain what simple facts underlie moral qualities the same as we ascertain those that underlie physical qualities, and, for example, let us take the first fact that comes to hand, a religious system of music, that of a Protestant church. A certain inward cause has inclined the minds of worshippers toward these grave, monotonous melodies, a cause much greater than its effect; that is to say, a general conception of the veritable outward forms of worship which man owes to God; it is this general conception which has shaped the architecture of the temple, cast out statues, dispensed with paintings, effaced ornaments, shortened ceremonies, confined the members of the congregation to high pews which cut off the view, and governed the thousand details of decoration, posture, and all other externals. This conception itself again proceeds from a more general cause, an idea of human conduct in general, inward and outward, prayers, actions, dispositions of every sort that man is bound to maintain toward the Deity; it is this which has enthroned the doctrine of grace, lessened the importance of the clergy, transformed the sacraments, suppressed observances, and changed the religion of discipline into one of morality. This conception, in its turn, depends on a third one, still more general, that of moral perfection as this is found in a perfect God, the impeccable judge, the stern overseer, who regards every soul as sinful, meriting punishment, incapable of virtue or of salvation, except through a stricken conscience which He provokes and the renewal of the heart which He brings about. Here is the master conception, consisting of duty erected into the absolute sovereign of human life, and which prostrates all other ideals at the feet of the moral ideal. Here we reach what is deepest in man; for, to explain this conception, we must consider the race he belongs to, say the German, the Northman, the formation and character of his intellect, his ways in general of thinking and feeling, that tardiness and frigidity of sensation which keeps him from rashly and easily falling under the empire of sensual enjoyments, that bluntness of taste, that irregularity and those outbursts of conception which arrest in him the birth of refined and harmonious forms and methods; that disdain of appearances, that yearning for truth, that attachment to abstract, bare ideas which develop conscience in him at the expense of everything else. Here the search comes to an end. We have reached a certain primitive disposition, a particular trait belonging to sensations of all kinds, to every conception peculiar to an age or to a race, to characteristics inseparable from every idea and feeling that stir in the human breast. Such are the grand causes, for these are universal and permanent causes, present in every case and at every moment, everywhere and always active, indestructible, and inevitably dominant in the end, since, whatever accidents cross their path, being limited and partial, end in yielding to the obscure and incessant repetition of their energy; so that the general structure of things and all the main features of events are their work, all religions and philosophies, all poetic and industrial systems, all forms of society and of the family, all, in fine, being imprints bearing the stamp of their seal.

IV

There is, then, a system in human ideas and sentiments, the prime motor of which consists in general traits, certain characteristics of thought and feeling common to men belonging to a particular race, epoch, or country. Just as crystals in mineralogy, whatever their diversity, proceed from a few simple physical forms, so do civilizations in history, however these may differ, proceed from a few spiritual forms. One is explained by a primitive geometrical element as the other is explained by a primitive psychological element. In order to comprehend the entire group of mineralogical species we must first study a regular solid in the general, its facets and angles, and observe in this abridged form the innumerable transformations of which it is susceptible. In like manner, if we would comprehend the entire group of historic varieties we must consider beforehand a human soul in the general, with its two or three fundamental faculties, and, in this abridgment, observe the principal forms it may present. This sort of ideal tableau, the geometrical as well as psychological, is not very complex, and we soon detect the limitations of organic conditions to which civilizations, the same as crystals, are forcibly confined. What do we find in man at the point of departure? Images or representations of objects, namely, that which floats before him internally, lasts a certain time, is effaced, and then returns after contemplating this or that tree or animal, in short, some sensible object. This forms the material basis of the rest and the development of this material basis is twofold, speculative or positive, just as these representations end in a general conception or in an active resolution. Such is man, summarily abridged. It is here, within these narrow confines, that human diversities are encountered, now in the matter itself and again in the primordial twofold development. However insignificant in the elements they are of vast significance in the mass, while the slightest change in the factors leads to gigantic changes in the results. According as the representation is distinct, as if stamped by a coining-press, or confused and blurred; according as it concentrates in itself a larger or smaller number of the characters of an object; according as it is violent and accompanied with impulsions or tranquil, and surrounded with calmness, so are all the operations and the whole running-gear of the human machine entirely transformed. In like manner again, according as the ulterior development of the representation varies, so does the whole development of the man vary. If the general conception in which this ends is merely a dry notation in Chinese fashion, language becomes a kind of algebra, religion and poetry are reduced to a minimum, philosophy is brought down to a sort of moral and practical common sense, science to a collection of recipes, classifications, and utilitarian mnemonics, the mind itself taking a wholly positive turn. If, on the contrary, the general conception in which the representation culminates is a poetic and figurative creation, a living symbol, as with the Aryan races, language becomes a sort of shaded and tinted epic in which each word stands as a personage, poesy and religion assume magnificent and inexhaustible richness, and metaphysics develops with breadth and subtlety without any consideration of positive bearings; the whole intellect, notwithstanding the deviation and inevitable weaknesses of the effort, is captivated by the beautiful and sublime, thus conceiving an ideal type which, through its nobleness and harmony, gathers to itself all the affectations and enthusiasms of humanity. If, on the other hand, the general conception in which the representation culminates is poetic but abrupt, is reached not gradually but by sudden intuition, if the original operation is not a regular development but a violent explosion—then, as with the Semitic races, metaphysical power is wanting; the religious conception becomes that of a royal God, consuming and solitary; science cannot take shape, the intellect grows rigid and too headstrong to reproduce the delicate ordering of nature; poetry cannot give birth to aught but a series of vehement, grandiose exclamations, while language no longer renders the concatenation of reasoning and eloquence, man being reduced to lyric enthusiasm, to ungovernable passion, and to narrow and fanatical action. It is in this interval between the particular representation and the universal conception that the germs of the greatest human differences are found. Some races, like the classic, for example, pass from the former to the latter by a graduated scale of ideas regularly classified and more and more general; others, like the Germanic, traverse the interval in leaps, with uniformity and after prolonged and uncertain groping. Others, like the Romans and the English, stop at the lowest stages; others, like the Hindoos and Germans, mount to the uppermost. If, now, after considering the passage from the representation to the idea, we regard the passage from the representation to the resolution, we find here elementary differences of like importance and of the same order, according as the impression is vivid, as in Southern climes, or faint, as in Northern climes, as it ends in instantaneous action as with barbarians, or tardily as with civilized nations, as it is capable or not of growth, of inequality, of persistence and of association. The entire system of human passion, all the risks of public peace and security, all the labor and action, spring from these sources. It is the same with the other primordial differences; their effects embrace an entire civilization, and may be likened to those algebraic formulae which, within narrow bounds, describe beforehand the curve of which these form the law. Not that this law always prevails to the end; sometimes, perturbations arise, but, even when this happens, it is not because the law is defective, but because it has not operated alone. New elements have entered into combination with old ones; powerful foreign forces have interfered to oppose primitive forces. The race has emigrated, as with the ancient Aryans, and the change of climate has led to a change in the whole intellectual economy and structure of society. A people has been conquered like the Saxon nation, and the new political structure has imposed on it customs, capacities, and desires which it did not possess. The nation has established itself permanently in the midst of downtrodden and threatening subjects, as with the ancient Spartans, while the necessity of living, as in an armed encampment, has violently turned the whole moral and social organization in one unique direction. At all events, the mechanism of human history is like this. We always find the primitive mainspring consisting of some widespread tendency of soul and intellect, either innate and natural to the race or acquired by it and due to some circumstance forced upon it. These great given mainsprings gradually produce their effects, that is to say, at the end of a few centuries they place the nation in a new religious, literary, social, and economic state; a new condition which, combined with their renewed effort, produces another condition, sometimes a good one, sometimes a bad one, now slowly, now rapidly, and so on; so that the entire development of each distinct civilization may be considered as the effect of one permanent force which, at every moment, varies its work by modifying the circumstances where it acts.

V

Three different sources contribute to the production of this elementary moral state, race, environment, and epoch. What we call race consists of those innate and hereditary dispositions which man brings with him into the world and which are generally accompanied with marked differences of temperament and of bodily structure. They vary in different nations. Naturally, there are varieties of men as there are varieties of cattle and horses, some brave and intelligent, and others timid and of limited capacity; some capable of superior conceptions and creations, and others reduced to rudimentary ideas and contrivances; some specially fitted for certain works, and more richly furnished with certain instincts, as we see in the better endowed species of dogs, some for running and others for fighting, some for hunting and others for guarding houses and flocks. We have here a distinct force; so distinct that, in spite of the enormous deviations which both the other motors impress upon it, we still recognize, and which a race like the Aryan people, scattered from the Ganges to the Hebrides, established under all climates, ranged along every degree of civilization, transformed by thirty centuries of revolutions, shows nevertheless in its languages, in its religions, in its literatures, and in its philosophies, the community of blood and of intellect which still to-day binds together all its offshoots. However they may differ, their parentage is not lost; barbarism, culture and grafting, differences of atmosphere and of soil, fortunate or unfortunate occurrences, have operated in vain; the grand characteristics of the original form have lasted, and we find that the two or three leading features of the primitive imprint are again apparent under the subsequent imprints with which time has overlaid them. There is nothing surprising in this extraordinary tenacity. Although the immensity of the distance allows us to catch only a glimpse in a dubious light of the origin of species,[1] the events of history throw sufficient light on events anterior to history to explain the almost unshaken solidity of primordial traits. At the moment of encountering them, fifteen, twenty, and thirty centuries before our era, in an Aryan, Egyptian, or Chinese, they represent the work of a much greater number of centuries, perhaps the work of many myriads of centuries. For, as soon as an animal is born it must adapt itself to its surroundings; it breathes in another way, it renews itself differently, it is otherwise stimulated according as the atmosphere, the food, and the temperature are different. A different climate and situation create different necessities and hence activities of a different kind; and hence, again, a system of different habits, and, finally a system of different aptitudes and instincts. Man, thus compelled to put himself in equilibrium with circumstances, contracts a corresponding temperament and character, and his character, like his temperament, are acquisitions all the more stable because of the outward impression being more deeply imprinted in him by more frequent repetitions and transmitted to his offspring by more ancient heredity. So that at each moment of time, the character of a

---

[1] Darwin, *The Origin of Species.* Prosper Lucas, *De l'Hérédité.*

people may be considered as a summary of all antecedent actions and sensations; that is to say, as a quantity and as a weighty mass, not infinite,[2] since all things in nature are limited, but disproportionate to the rest and almost impossible to raise, since each minute of an almost infinite past has contributed to render it heavier, and, in order to turn the scale, it would require, on the other side, a still greater accumulation of actions and sensations. Such is the first and most abundant source of these master faculties from which historic events are derived; and we see at once that if it is powerful it is owing to its not being a mere source, but a sort of lake, and like a deep reservoir wherein other sources have poured their waters for a multitude of centuries.

When we have thus verified the internal structure of a race we must consider the environment in which it lives. For man is not alone in the world; nature envelops him and other men surround him; accidental and secondary folds come and overspread the primitive and permanent fold, while physical or social circumstances derange or complete the natural groundwork surrendered to them. At one time climate has had its effect. Although the history of Aryan nations can be only obscurely traced from their common country to their final abodes, we can nevertheless affirm that the profound difference which is apparent between the Germanic races on the one hand, and the Hellenic and Latin races on the other, proceeds in great part from the differences between the countries in which they have established themselves—the former in cold and moist countries, in the depths of gloomy forests and swamps, or on the borders of a wild ocean, confined to melancholic or rude sensations, inclined to drunkenness and gross feeding, leading a militant and carnivorous life; the latter, on the contrary, living amidst the finest scenery, along-side of a brilliant, sparkling sea inviting navigation and commerce, exempt from the grosser cravings of the stomach, disposed at the start to social habits and customs, to political organization, to the sentiments and faculties which develop the art of speaking, the capacity for enjoyment and invention in the sciences, in art, and in literature. At another time, political events have operated, as in the two Italian civilizations: the first one tending wholly to action, to conquest, to government, and to legislation, through the primitive situation of a city of refuge, a frontier emporium, and of an armed aristocracy which, importing and enrolling foreigners and the vanquished under it, sets two hostile bodies facing each other, with no outlet for its internal troubles and rapacious instincts but systematic war-

[2] Spinosa, *Ethics,* part iv, axiom.

fare; the second one, excluded from unity and political ambition on a grand scale by the permanency of its municipal system, by the cosmopolite situation of its pope and by the military intervention of neighboring states, and following the bent of its magnificent and harmonious genius, is wholly carried over to the worship of voluptuousness and beauty. Finally, at another time, social conditions have imposed their stamp as, eighteen centuries ago, by Christianity, and twenty-five centuries ago by Buddhism, when, around the Mediterranean as in Hindostan, the extreme effects of Aryan conquest and organisation led to intolerable oppression, the crushing of the individual, utter despair, the whole world under the ban of a curse, with the development of metaphysics and visions, until man, in this dungeon of despondency, feeling his heart melt, conceived of abnegation, charity, tender love, gentleness, humility, human brotherhood, here in the idea of universal nothingness, and there under that of the fatherhood of God. Look around at the regulative instincts and faculties implanted in a race; in brief, the turn of mind according to which it thinks and acts at the present day; we shall find most frequently that its work is due to one of these prolonged situations, to these enveloping circumstances, to these persistent gigantic pressures brought to bear on a mass of men who, one by one, and all collectively, from one generation to another, have been unceasingly bent and fashioned by them, in Spain a crusade of eight centuries against the Mohammedans, prolonged yet longer even to the exhaustion of the nation through the expulsion of the Moors, through the spoliation of the Jews, through the establishment of the Inquisition, through the Catholic wars; in England, a political establishment of eight centuries which maintains man erect and respectful, independent and obedient, all accustomed to struggling together in a body under the sanction of law; in France, a Latin organization which, at first imposed on docile barbarians, then levelled to the ground under the universal demolition, forms itself anew under the latent workings of national instinct, developing under hereditary monarchs and ending in a sort of equalized, centralized, administrative republic under dynasties exposed to revolutions. Such are the most efficacious among the observable causes which mold the primitive man; they are to nations what education, pursuit, condition, and abode are to individuals, and seem to comprise all, since the external forces which fashion human matter, and by which the outward acts on the inward, are comprehended in them.

There is, nevertheless, a third order of causes, for, with the forces within and without, there is the work these have already produced together, which work itself contributes towards producing the ensuing work; beside the permanent impulsion and the given environment there is the acquired momentum. When national character and surrounding circumstances operate it is not on a *tabula rasa,* but on one already bearing imprints. According as this *tabula* is taken at one or at another moment so is the imprint different, and this suffices to render the total effect different. Consider, for example, two moments of a literature or of an art, French tragedy under Corneille and under Voltaire, and Greek drama under Æschylus and under Euripides, Latin poetry under Lucretius and under Claudian, and Italian painting under Da Vinci and under Guido. Assuredly, there is no change of general conception at either of these two extreme points; ever the same human type must be portrayed or represented in action; the cast of the verse, the dramatic structure, the physical form have all persisted. But there is this among these differences, that one of the artists is a precursor and the other a successor, that the first one has no model and the second one has a model; that the former sees things face to face, and that the latter sees them through the intermediation of the former, that many departments of art have become more perfect, that the simplicity and grandeur of the impression have diminished, that what is pleasing and refined in form has augmented—in short, that the first work has determined the second. In this respect, it is with a people as with a plant; the same sap at the same temperature and in the same soil produces, at different stages of its successive elaborations, different developments, buds, flowers, fruits, and seeds, in such a way that the condition of the following is always that of the preceding and is born of its death. Now, if you no longer regard a brief moment, as above, but one of those grand periods of development which embraces one or many centuries like the Middle Ages, or our last classic period, the conclusion is the same. A certain dominating conception has prevailed throughout; mankind, during two hundred years, during five hundred years, have represented to themselves a certain ideal figure of man, in mediæval times the knight and the monk, in our classic period the courtier and refined talker; this creative and universal conception has monopolized the entire field of action and thought, and, after spreading its involuntarily systematic works over the world, it languished and then died out, and now a new idea has arisen, destined to a like domination and to equally multiplied creations. Note here that the latter depends in part on the former, and that it is the former, which, combining its effect with those of national genius and surrounding circumstances, will impose their bent and their direction on new-born things. It is according to this law that great historic currents are formed, meaning by this, the long rule of a form of intellect or of a master idea, like that period of spontaneous creations called the Renaissance, or that period of oratorical classifications called the Classic Age, or that series of mystic systems called the Alexandrine and Christian epoch, or that series of mythological efflorescences found at the origins of Germany, India, and Greece. Here as elsewhere, we are dealing merely with a mechanical problem: the total effect is a compound wholly determined by the grandeur and direction of the forces which produce it. The sole difference which separates these moral problems from physical problems lies in this, that in the former the directions and grandeur cannot be estimated by or stated in figures with the same precision as in the latter. If a want, a faculty, is a quantity capable of degrees, the same as pressure or weight, this quantity is not measurable like that of the pressure or weight. We cannot fix it in an exact or approximate formula; we can obtain or give of it only a literary impression; we are reduced to noting and citing the prominent facts which make it manifest and which nearly, or roughly, indicate about what grade on the scale it must be ranged at. And yet, notwithstanding the methods of notation are not the same in the moral sciences as in the physical sciences, nevertheless, as matter is the same in both, and is equally composed of forces, directions and magnitudes, we can still show that in one as in the other, the final effect takes place according to the same law. This is great or small, according as the fundamental forces are great or small and act more or less precisely in the same sense, according as the distinct effects of race, environment and epoch combine to enforce each other or combine to neutralize each other. Thus are explained the long impotences and the brilliant successes which appear irregularly and with no apparent reason in the life of a people; the causes of these consist in internal concordances and contrarieties. There was one of these concordances when, in the seventeenth century, the social disposition and conversational spirit innate in France encountered drawing-room formalities and the moment of oratorical analysis; when, in the nineteenth century, the flexible, profound genius of Germany encountered the age of philosophic synthesis and of cosmopolite criticism. One of these contrarieties happened when, in the seventeenth century, the blunt, isolated genius of England awkwardly tried to don the new polish of urbanity, and when, in the sixteenth century, the lucid, prosaic French intellect tried to gestate a living poesy. It is this secret concordance of creative forces which produced the exquisite courtesy and noble cast of literature under Louis XIV and Bossuet, and the grandiose metaphysics and broad critical sympathy under Hegel and Goethe. It is this secret contrariety of creative forces which produced the literary incompleteness, the licentious plays, the abortive drama of Dryden and Wycherly, the poor Greek importations, the gropings, the minute beauties and fragments of Ronsard and the Pleiad. We may confidently affirm that the unknown creations toward which the current of coming ages is bearing us will spring from and be governed by these primordial forces; that, if these forces could be measured and computed we might deduce from them, as from a formula, the characters of future civilization; and that if, notwithstanding the evident rudeness of our notations, and the fundamental inexactitude of our measures, we would nowadays form some idea of our general destinies, we must base our conjectures on an examination of these forces. For, in enumerating them, we run through the full circle of active forces; and when the race, the environment, and the moment have been considered—that is to say the inner mainspring, the pressure from without, and the impulsion already acquired—we have exhausted not only all real causes but again all possible causes of movement.

GUSTAVE FLAUBERT

(1821–1880)

From

THE CORRESPONDENCE *

(Letter to Mlle. de Chantepe, 1857)

. . .

Madame Bovary is not fact. Its story is *entirely fictitious;* I have put into it nothing of my beliefs or of my experience. The deception (if there be one) comes, on the contrary, from the *impersonality* of the work. That is one of my principles: one simply must not *write himself* in.

The artist ought to be in his work like God in Creation, invisible and all-powerful; let him be felt everywhere but not seen.

And then art ought to raise itself above personal affections and nerv-

* Translated by Edd Winfield Parks.

ous susceptibilities! It is time that it be given, by a method which is unpitying, the precision of the physical sciences! The prime difficulty, for me, nevertheless remains—style, form, the indefinable beauty resulting from the conception itself, and which is the splendor of the true, as Plato said.

HENRY TIMROD

(1829–1867)

From

A THEORY OF POETRY

(*c.* 1859)

I DO not wish it to be supposed that I look at *Paradise Lost* as a perfect poem. It has many of the faults inseparable from all human productions. Indeed, I so far agree with Poe as to concede that by no possibility can a poem so long as *Paradise Lost* be all poetry (and Coleridge, the profoundest poetical critic of any age, says: It "ought not to be all poetry") from beginning to end. However noble the theme, there will be parts and aspects which do not admit of the presence of genuine poetry. Herein, however, I differ with Poe; inasmuch as I maintain that these parts may be raised so far above the ordinary level of prose by skillful verse as to preserve the general harmony of the poem and materially to insure its unity as a work of art. And in the distinction between poetry and the poem, between the spirit and its body, which Poe recognizes when he comes to develop his theory, but which he blinks or ignores altogether in his remarks upon *Paradise Lost,* I shall look for the justification of my position. I hold that the confusion of these terms, of the subjective essence with the objective form, is the source of most of the errors and contradictions of opinion prevalent upon this theme. The two should be carefully distinguished and should never in any critical discussion be allowed to mean the same thing.

What, then, is poetry? In the last century, if one had asked the question, one would have been answered readily enough; and the answer would have been the definition which I dismissed a little while ago as unworthy of minute examination. But the deeper philosophical criticism of the present century will not remain satisfied with such a surface view of poetry. Its aim is to penetrate to the essence, to analyze and comprehend those impressions and operations of the mind, acting upon and being acted upon by mental or physical phenomena, which when incarnated in language all recognize as the utterance of poetry and which affect us like the music of angels. That this is the aim of present criticism I need not attempt to show by quotation, since it looks out from the pages of the most popular writers of the day. Indeed, so very general has the feeling become that it is not of the forms of poetry that we need a description, that if you ask any man of common intelligence, who is not merely a creature of facts and figures, to define poetry, he will endeavor to convey to you his idea, vague, doubtless, and shadowy, of that which in his imagination constitutes its spirit. The poets who attempt to solve the question look rather into themselves than into the poems they have written. One, very characteristically, when his own poems are considered, defines it as "emotions recollected in tranquillity;" and another as "the best and happiest moments of the best and happiest minds." These definitions, if definitions they can be called, are unsatisfactory enough, but they indicate correctly the direction in which the distinctive principle of poetry is to be sought.

I think that Poe in his eloquent description of the poetical sentiment as the sense of the beautiful, and, in its loftiest action as a struggle to apprehend a supernal beauty above that which is about us, has certainly fixed with some definiteness one phase of its merely subjective manifestation. It is, indeed, to the inspiration which lies in the ethereal, the remote and the unknown, that the world owes some of its sweetest poems; and the poetry of words has never so strange a fascination as when it seems to suggest more than it utters; to call up by implication rather than by expression those thoughts which refuse to be embodied in language; to hint at something ineffable and mysterious of which the mind can attain but partial glimpses. But in making this feeling and this feeling only constitute the poetic sentiment, Poe simply verifies the remark of one of the most luminous critics of this century, that we must look as little to men of peculiar and original genius as to the multitude for broad and comprehensive critical theories. Such men have usually one faculty developed at the expense of the others; and the very clearness of their perception of one kind of excellence impairs their perception of other kinds. Their theories, being drawn from their own particular tastes and talents, just suffice to cover themselves and those who resemble them. . . .

It is then in the feelings awakened by certain moods of the mind, when we stand in the presence of Truth, Beauty, and Power, that I recognize what we all agree to call poetry. To analyze the nature of these feelings, inextricably tangled as they are with the different faculties of the mind, and especially with that great faculty which is the prime minister of poetry, imagination, is not absolutely necessary to the present purpose. Let us be satisfied with having ascertained the elements which excite in us the sentiment of poetry; and having thus in a measure fixed its boundaries, let us proceed to consider it as it appears when embodied in language. . . .

I look upon every poem strictly as a work of art, and on the poet, in the act of putting poetry into verse, simply as an artist. If the poet have his hour of inspiration, though I am so sick of the cant of which this word has been the fruitful source that I dislike to use it, this hour is not at all during the work of composition. A distinction must be made between the moment when the great thought strikes for the first time along the brain and flushes the cheek with the sudden revelation of beauty or grandeur and the hour of patient, elaborate execution. The soul of the poet, though constrained to utter itself at some time or other, does not burst into song as readily as a maiden of sixteen bursts into musical laughter. Many poets have written of grief, but no poet in the first agony of his heart ever sat down to strain that grief through iambics. Many poets have given expression to the first raptures of successful love, but no poet in the delirium of joy has ever bubbled it in anapests. Could this have been possible the poet would have been the most wonderful of improvisers; and perhaps a poem would be no better than what improvisations always are. . . .

. . . It must not be forgotten that my present aim is to show that a poem, without being all poetry from beginning to end, may be complete as a work of art. Now, there are two classes of poets, differing essentially in their several characters. The one class desires only to utter musically its own peculiar thoughts, feelings, sentiments, or passions, without regard to their truth or falsehood, their morality or want of morality, but in simple reference to their poetical effect. The other class, with more poetry at its command than the first, regards poetry simply as the minister, the highest minister indeed, but still only the minister, of Truth, and refuses to address itself to the sense of the beautiful alone. The former class is content simply to create beauty, and writes such poems as *The Raven* of Poe or *The Corsair* of Byron. The latter class aims to create beauty also, but it desires at the same time to mould this beauty into the shape of a temple dedicated to Truth. It is to this class that we owe the authorship of such poems as the *Paradise Lost* of Milton, the Lines at Tintern Abbey, and the *Excursion* of Wordsworth, and the *In Memoriam* of Tennyson.

The former class can afford to write brief and faultless poems, because its end is a narrow one; the second class is forced to demand an ampler field, because it is influenced by a vaster purpose. . . .

WALT WHITMAN

(1819–1892)

From

DEMOCRATIC VISTAS

(1870)

BEFORE proceeding further, it were perhaps well to discriminate on certain points. Literature tills its crops in many fields, and some may flourish, while others lag. What I say in these Vistas has its main bearing on imaginative literature, especially poetry, the stock of all. In the department of science, and the speciality of journalism, there appear, in these States, promises, perhaps fulfillments, of highest earnestness, reality and life. These, of course, are modern. But in the region of imaginative, spinal and essential attributes, something equivalent to creation is, for our age and lands, imperatively demanded. For not only is it not enough that the new blood, new frame of democracy shall be vivified and held together merely by political means, superficial suffrage, legislation, etc., but it is clear to me that, unless it goes deeper, gets at least as firm and as warm a hold in men's hearts, emotions and belief, as, in their days, feudalism or ecclesiasticism, and inaugurates its own perennial sources, welling from the center forever, its strength will be defective, its growth doubtful, and its main charm wanting. I suggest, therefore, the possibility, should some two or three really original American poets (perhaps artists or lecturers) arise, mounting the horizon like planets, stars of the first magnitude, that, from their eminence, fusing contributions, races, far localities, etc., together, they would give more compaction and more moral identity (the quality to-day most needed) to these States, than all its Constitutions, legislative and judicial ties, and all its hitherto political, war-like, or materialistic experiences. As, for instance, there could hardly happen anything that would more serve the States, with all their variety of origins, their diverse climes, cities, standards, etc., than possessing an aggregate of heroes, characters, exploits, sufferings, prosperity or misfortune, glory or disgrace, common to all, typical of it all—no less, but even greater would it be to possess the aggregation of a cluster of mighty poets, artists, teachers, fit for us, national expressers, comprehending and effusing for the men and women of the States, what is universal, native, common to all, inland and seaboard, northern and southern. The historians say of ancient Greece, with her ever-jealous autonomies, cities and states, that the only positive unity she ever owned or received, was the sad unity of a common subjection, at the last, to foreign conquerors. Subjection, aggregation of that sort, is impossible to America; but the fear of conflicting and irreconcilable interiors, and the lack of a common skeleton, knitting all close, continually haunts me. Or, if it does not, nothing is plainer than the need, a long period to come, of a fusion of the States into the only reliable identity, the moral and artistic one. For, I say, the true nationality of the States, the genuine union, when we come to a mortal crisis, is, and is to be, after all, neither the written law, nor (as is generally supposed) either self-interest, or common pecuniary or material objects—but the fervid and tremendous IDEA, melting everything else with resistless heat, and solving all lesser and definite distinctions in vast, indefinite, spiritual, emotional power.

GEORGE MEREDITH

(1828–1909)

From

AN ESSAY ON COMEDY *

(1877)

.   .

THE Comic poet is in the narrow field, or enclosed square, of the society he depicts; and he addresses the still narrower enclosure of men's intellects, with reference to the operation of the social world upon their characters. He is not concerned with beginnings or endings or surroundings, but with what you are now weaving. To understand his work and value it, you must have a sober liking of your kind and a sober estimate of our civilized qualities. The aim and business of the Comic

* Published by Charles Scribner's Sons, New York, N. Y.

poet are misunderstood, his meaning is not seized nor his point of view taken, when he is accused of dishonouring our nature and being hostile to sentiment, tending to spitefulness and making an unfair use of laughter. Those who detect irony in Comedy do so because they choose to see it in life. Poverty, says the satirist, has nothing harder in itself than that it makes men ridiculous. But poverty is never ridiculous to Comic perception until it attempts to make its rags conceal its bareness in a forlorn attempt at decency, or foolishly to rival ostentation. Caleb Balderstone, in his endeavour to keep up the honour of a noble household in a state of beggary, is an exquisitely comic character. In the case of 'poor relatives,' on the other hand, it is the rich, whom they perplex, that are really comic; and to laugh at the former, not seeing the comedy of the latter, is to betray dulness of vision. Humourist and Satirist frequently hunt together as Ironeïsts in pursuit of the grotesque, to the exclusion of the Comic. That was an affecting moment in the history of the Prince Regent, when the First Gentleman of Europe burst into tears at a sarcastic remark of Beau Brummell's on the cut of his coat. Humour, Satire, Irony, pounce on it altogether as their common prey. The Comic spirit eyes but does not touch it. Put into action, it would be farcical. It is too gross for Comedy.

Incidents of a kind casting ridicule on our unfortunate nature instead of our conventional life, provoke derisive laughter, which thwarts the Comic idea. But derision is foiled by the play of the intellect. Most of doubtful causes in contest are open to Comic interpretation, and any intellectual pleading of a doubtful cause contains germs of an Idea of Comedy.

The laughter of satire is a blow in the back or the face. The laughter of Comedy is impersonal and of unrivalled politeness, nearer a smile; often no more than a smile. It laughs through the mind, for the mind directs it; and it might be called the humour of the mind.

One excellent test of the civilization of a country, as I have said, I take to be the flourishing of the Comic idea and Comedy; and the test of true Comedy is that it shall awaken thoughtful laughter.

If you believe that our civilization is founded in common-sense (and it is the first condition of sanity to believe it), you will, when contemplating men, discern a Spirit overhead; not more heavenly than the light flashed upward from glassy surfaces, but luminous and watchful; never shooting beyond them, nor lagging in the rear; so closely attached to them that it may be taken for a slavish reflex, until its features are studied. It has the sage's brows, and the sunny malice of a faun lurks at the corners of the half-closed lips drawn in an idle wariness of half tension. That slim feasting smile, shaped like the long-bow, was once a big round satyr's laugh, that flung up the brows like a fortress lifted by gunpowder. The laugh will come again, but it will be of the order of the smile, finely tempered, showing sunlight of the mind, mental richness rather than noisy enormity. Its common aspect is one of unsolicitous observation, as if surveying a full field and having leisure to dart on its chosen morsels, without any fluttering eagerness. Men's future upon earth does not attract it; their honesty and shapeliness in the present does; and whenever they wax out of proportion, overblown, affected, pretentious, bombastical, hypocritical, pedantic, fantastically delicate; whenever it sees them self-deceived or hoodwinked, given to run riot in idolatries, drifting into vanities, congregating in absurdities, planning short-sightedly, plotting dementedly; whenever they are at variance with their professions, and violate the unwritten but perceptible laws binding them in consideration one to another; whenever they offend sound reason, fair justice; are false in humility or mined with conceit, individually, or in the bulk—the Spirit overhead will look humanely malign and cast an oblique light on them, followed by volleys of silvery laughter. That is the Comic Spirit.

. . .

WALTER PATER

(1839–1894)

From

THE RENAISSANCE

(1873)

CONCLUSION [1]

Λέγει που Ἡράκλειτος ὅτι πάντα χωρεῖ καὶ οὐδὲν μένει [2]

To regard all things and principles of things as inconstant modes or fashions has more and more become the tendency of modern thought.

[1] This brief "Conclusion" was omitted in the second edition of this book, as I conceived it might possibly mislead some of those young men into whose hands it might fall. On the whole, I have thought it best to reprint it here, with some slight changes which bring it closer to my original meaning. I have dealt more fully in *Marius the Epicurean* with the thoughts suggested by it.

[2] From Plato's *Cratylus:* "Heraclitus says that all things give way and nothing remains" (A. H. Gilbert, Trans.).

Let us begin with that which is without—our physical life. Fix upon it in one of its more exquisite intervals, the moment, for instance, of delicious recoil from the flood of water in summer heat. What is the whole physical life in that moment but a combination of natural elements to which science gives their names? But those elements, phosphorus and lime and delicate fibres, are present not in the human body alone: we detect them in places most remote from it. Our physical life is a perpetual motion of them—the passage of the blood, the waste and repairing of the lenses of the eye, the modification of the tissues of the brain under every ray of light and sound—processes which science reduces to simpler and more elementary forces. Like the elements of which we are composed, the action of these forces extends beyond us: it rusts iron and ripens corn. Far out on every side of us those elements are broadcast, driven in many currents; and birth and gesture and death and the springing of violets from the grave are but a few out of ten thousand resultant combinations. That clear, perpetual outline of face and limb is but an image of ours, under which we group them—a design in a web, the actual threads of which pass out beyond it. This at least of flame-like our life has, that it is but the concurrence, renewed from moment to moment, of forces parting sooner or later on their ways.

Or, if we begin with the inward world of thought and feeling, the whirlpool is still more rapid, the flame more eager and devouring. There it is no longer the gradual darkening of the eye, the gradual fading of colour from the wall—movements of the shore-side, where the water flows down indeed, though in apparent rest—but the race of the mid-stream, a drift of momentary acts of sight and passion and thought. At first sight experience seems to bury us under a flood of external objects, pressing upon us with a sharp and importunate reality, calling us out of ourselves in a thousand forms of action. But when reflexion begins to play upon those objects they are dissipated under its influence; the cohesive force seems suspended like some trick of magic; each object is loosed into a group of impressions—colour, odour, texture—in the mind of the observer. And if we continue to dwell in thought on this world, not of objects in the solidity with which language invests them, but of impressions, unstable, flickering, inconsistent, which burn and are extinguished with our consciousness of them, it contracts still further: the whole scope of observation is dwarfed into the narrow chamber of the individual mind. Experience, already reduced to a group of impressions, is ringed round for each one of us by that thick wall of personality through which no real voice has ever pierced on its way to us, or from us to that which we can only conjecture to be without. Every one of those impressions is the impression of the individual in his isolation, each mind keeping as a solitary prisoner its own dream of a world. Analysis goes a step farther still, and assures us that those impressions of the individual mind to which, for each one of us, experience dwindles down, are in perpetual flight; that each of them is limited by time, and that as time is infinitely divisible, each of them is infinitely divisible also; all that is actual in it being a single moment, gone while we try to apprehend it, of which it may ever be more truly said that it has ceased to be than that it is. To such a tremulous wisp constantly re-forming itself on the stream, to a single sharp impression, with a sense in it, a relic more or less fleeting, of such moments gone by, what is real in our life fines itself down. It is with this movement, with the passage and dissolution of impressions, images, sensations, that analysis leaves off—that continual vanishing away, that strange, perpetual weaving and unweaving of ourselves.

Philosophiren, says Novalis, *ist dephlegmatisiren, vivificiren.*[3] The service of philosophy, of speculative culture, towards the human spirit, is to rouse, to startle it to a life of constant and eager observation. Every moment some form grows perfect in hand or face; some tone on the hills or the sea is choicer than the rest; some mood of passion or insight or intellectual excitement is irresistibly real and attractive to us,—for that moment only. Not the fruit of experience, but experience itself, is the end. A counted number of pulses only is given to us of a variegated, dramatic life. How may we see in them all that is to be seen in them by the finest senses? How shall we pass most swiftly from point to point, and be present always at the focus where the greatest number of vital forces unite in their purest energy?

To burn always with this hard, gemlike flame, to maintain this ecstasy, is success in life. In a sense it might even be said that our failure is to form habits: for, after all, habit is relative to a stereotyped world, and meantime it is only the roughness of the eye that makes any two persons, things, situations, seem alike. While all melts under our feet, we may well grasp at any exquisite passion, or any contribution to knowledge that seems by a lifted horizon to set the spirit free for a moment, or any stirring of the senses, strange dyes, strange colours, and curious odours, or work of the artist's hands, or the face of one's friend. Not to discriminate every moment some passionate attitude in

---

[3] "To be a philosopher is to cease to be sluggish, to come alive" (A. H. Gilbert, Trans.). Novalis was Friedrich von Hardenberg's pseudonym.

those about us, and in the very brilliancy of their gifts some tragic dividing of forces on their ways, is, on this short day of frost and sun, to sleep before evening. With this sense of the splendour of our experience and of its awful brevity, gathering all we are into one desperate effort to see and touch, we shall hardly have time to make theories about the things we see and touch. What we have to do is to be for ever curiously testing new opinions and courting new impressions, never acquiescing in a facile orthodoxy of Comte, or of Hegel, or of our own. Philosophical theories or ideas, as points of view, instruments of criticism, may help us to gather up what might otherwise pass unregarded by us. "Philosophy is the microscope of thought." The theory or idea or system which requires of us the sacrifice of any part of this experience, in consideration of some interest into which we cannot enter, or some abstract theory we have not identified with ourselves, or of what is only conventional, has no real claim upon us.

One of the most beautiful passages of Rousseau is that in the sixth book of the *Confessions,* where he describes the awakening in him of the literary sense. An undefinable taint of death had clung always about him, and now in early manhood he believed himself smitten by mortal disease. He asked himself how he might make as much as possible of the interval that remained; and he was not biassed by anything in his previous life when he decided that it must be by intellectual excitement, which he found just then in the clear, fresh writings of Voltaire. Well! we are all *condamnés* as Victor Hugo says: we are all under sentence of death but with a sort of indefinite reprieve—*les hommes sont tous condamnés à mort avec des sursis indéfinis:* we have an interval, and then our place knows us no more. Some spend this interval in listlessness, some in high passions, the wisest, at least among "the children of this world," in art and song. For our one chance lies in expanding that interval, in getting as many pulsations as possible into the given time. Great passions may give us this quickened sense of life, ecstasy and sorrow of love, the various forms of enthusiastic activity, disinterested or otherwise, which come naturally to many of us. Only be sure it is passion—that it does yield you this fruit of a quickened, multiplied consciousness. Of such wisdom, the poetic passion, the desire of beauty, the love of art for its own sake, has most. For art comes to you proposing frankly to give nothing but the highest quality to your moments as they pass, and simply for those moments' sake.

From

POSTSCRIPT TO APPRECIATIONS *

(1889)

THE words, *classical* and *romantic,* although, like many other critical expressions, sometimes abused by those who have understood them too vaguely or too absolutely, yet define two real tendencies in the history of art and literature. Used in an exaggerated sense, to express a greater opposition between those tendencies than really exists, they have at times tended to divide people of taste into opposite camps. But in that *House Beautiful,* which the creative minds of all generations—the artists and those who have treated life in the spirit of art—are always building together, for the refreshment of the human spirit, these oppositions cease; and the *Interpreter* of the *House Beautiful,* the true æsthetic critic, uses these divisions, only so far as they enable him to enter into the peculiarities of the objects with which he has to do. The term *classical,* fixed, as it is, to a well-defined literature, and a well-defined group in art, is clear, indeed; but then it has often been used in a hard, and merely scholastic sense, by the praisers of what is old and accustomed, at the expense of what is new, by critics who would never have discovered for themselves the charm of any work, whether new or old, who value what is old, in art or literature, for its accessories, and chiefly for the conventional authority that has gathered about it—people who would never really have been made glad by any Venus fresh-risen from the sea, and who praise the Venus of old Greece and Rome, only because they fancy her grown now into something staid and tame.

And as the term, *classical,* has been used in a too absolute, and therefore in a misleading sense, so the term, *romantic,* has been used much too vaguely, in various accidental senses. The sense in which Scott is called a romantic writer is chiefly this; that, in opposition to the literary tradition of the last century, he loved strange adventure, and sought it in the Middle Age. Much later, in a Yorkshire village, the spirit of romanticism bore a more really characteristic fruit in the work of a young girl, Emily Brontë, the romance of *Wuthering Heights;* the figures of Hareton Earnshaw, of Catherine Linton, and of Heathcliffe—tearing open Catherine's grave, removing one side of her coffin, that he may really lie beside her in death—figures so passionate, yet woven

* Published by The Macmillan Co., New York, N. Y.

on a background of delicately beautiful, moorland scenery, being typical examples of that spirit. In Germany, again, that spirit is shown less in Tieck, its professional representative, than in Meinhold, the author of *Sidonia the Sorceress* and the *Amber-Witch*. In Germany and France, within the last hundred years, the term has been used to describe a particular school of writers; and, consequently, when Heine criticises the *Romantic School* in Germany—that movement which culminated in Goethe's *Goetz von Berlichingen;* or when Théophile Gautier criticises the romantic movement in France, where, indeed, it bore its most characteristic fruits, and its play is hardly yet over, where, by a certain audacity, or *bizarrie* of motive, united with faultless literary execution, it still shows itself in imaginative literature, they use the word, with an exact sense of special artistic qualities, indeed; but use it, nevertheless, with a limited application to the manifestation of those qualities at a particular period. But the romantic spirit is, in reality, an ever-present, an enduring principle, in the artistic temperament; and the qualities of thought and style which that, and other similar uses of the word *romantic* really indicate, are indeed but symptoms of a very continuous and widely working influence.

.   .   .

The charm, therefore, of what is classical, in art or literature, is that of the well-known tale, to which we can, nevertheless, listen over and over again, because it is told so well. To the absolute beauty of its artistic form, is added the accidental, tranquil, charm of familiarity. There are times, indeed, at which these charms fail to work on our spirits at all, because they fail to excite us. *"Romanticism,"* says Stendhal, "is the art of presenting to people the literary works which, in the actual state of their habits and beliefs, are capable of giving them the greatest possible pleasure; *classicism,* on the contrary, of presenting them with that which gave the greatest possible pleasure to their grandfathers." But then, beneath all changes of habits and beliefs, our love of that mere abstract proportion—of music—which what is classical in literature possesses, still maintains itself in the best of us, and what pleased our grandparents may at least tranquillise us. The "classic" comes to us out of the cool and quiet of other times, as the measure of what a long experience has shown will at least never displease us. And in the classical literature of Greece and Rome, as in the classics of the last century, the essentially classical element is that quality of order in beauty, which they possess, indeed, in a pre-eminent degree, and which impresses some minds to the exclusion of everything else in them.

It is the addition of strangeness to beauty, that constitutes the romantic character in art; and the desire of beauty being a fixed element in every artistic organisation, it is the addition of curiosity to this desire of beauty, that constitutes the romantic temper. Curiosity and the desire of beauty, have each their place in art, as in all true criticism. When one's curiosity is deficient, when one is not eager enough for new impressions, and new pleasures, one is liable to value mere academical proprieties too highly, to be satisfied with worn-out or conventional types, with the insipid ornament of Racine, or the prettiness of that later Greek sculpture, which passed so long for true Hellenic work; to miss those places where the handiwork of nature, or of the artist, has been most cunning; to find the most stimulating products of art a mere irritation. And when one's curiosity is in excess, when it overbalances the desire of beauty, then one is liable to value in works of art what is inartistic in them; to be satisfied with what is exaggerated in art, with productions like some of those of the romantic school in Germany; not to distinguish jealously enough, between what is admirably done, and what is done not quite so well, in the writings, for instance, of Jean Paul. And if I had to give instances of these defects, then I should say, that Pope, in common with the age of literature to which he belonged, had too little curiosity, so that there is always a certain insipidity in the effect of his work, exquisite as it is; and, coming down to our own time, that Balzac had an excess of curiosity—curiosity not duly tempered with the desire of beauty.

But, however falsely those two tendencies may be opposed by critics, or exaggerated by artists themselves, they are tendencies really at work at all times in art, moulding it, with the balance sometimes a little on one side, sometimes a little on the other, generating, respectively, as the balance inclines on this side or that, two principles, two traditions, in art, and in literature so far as it partakes of the spirit of art. If there is a great over-balance of curiosity, then, we have the grotesque in art: if the union of strangeness and beauty, under very difficult and complex conditions, be a successful one, if the union be entire, then the resultant beauty is very exquisite, very attractive. With a passionate care for beauty, the romantic spirit refuses to have it, unless the condition of strangeness be first fulfilled. Its desire is for a beauty born of unlikely elements, by a profound alchemy, by a difficult initiation, by the charm which wrings it even out of terrible things; and a trace of distortion, of the grotesque, may perhaps linger, as an additional element of expression, about its ultimate grace. Its eager, excited spirit will have strength, the grotesque, first of all—the trees shrieking as you tear off the leaves;

for Jean Valjean, the long years of convict life; for Redgauntlet, the quicksands of Solway Moss; then, incorporate with this strangeness, and intensified by restraint, as much sweetness, as much beauty, as is compatible with that. *Énergique, frais, et dispos*—these, according to Sainte-Beuve, are the characteristics of a genuine classic—*les ouvrages anciens ne sont pas classiques parce qu'ils sont vieux, mais parce qu'ils sont énergiques, frais, et dispos.* Energy, freshness, intelligent and masterly disposition:—these are characteristics of Victor Hugo when his alchemy is complete, in certain figures, like Marius and Cosette, in certain scenes, like that in the opening of *Les Travailleurs de la Mer,* where Déruchette writes the name of *Gilliatt* in the snow, on Christmas morning; but always there is a certain note of strangeness discernible there, as well.

The essential elements, then, of the romantic spirit are curiosity and the love of beauty; and it is only as an illustration of these qualities, that it seeks the Middle Age, because, in the overcharged atmosphere of the Middle Age, there are unworked sources of romantic effect, of a strange beauty, to be won, by strong imagination, out of things unlikely or remote.

. . . . . .

. . . In his book on *Racine and Shakspere,* Stendhal argues that all good art was romantic in its day; and this is perhaps true in Stendhal's sense. That little treatise, full of "dry light" and fertile ideas, was published in the year 1823, and its object is to defend an entire independence and liberty in the choice and treatment of subject, both in art and literature, against those who upheld the exclusive authority of precedent. In pleading the cause of romanticism, therefore, it is the novelty, both of form and of motive, in writings like the *Hernani* of Victor Hugo (which soon followed it, raising a storm of criticism) that he is chiefly concerned to justify. To be interesting and really stimulating, to keep us from yawning even, art and literature must follow the subtle movements of that nimbly-shifting *Time-Spirit,* or *Zeit-Geist,* understood by French not less than by German criticism, which is always modifying men's taste, as it modifies their manners and their pleasures. This, he contends, is what all great workmen had always understood. Dante, Shakspere, Molière, had exercised an absolute independence in their choice of subject and treatment. To turn always with that ever-changing spirit, yet to retain the flavour of what was admirably done in past generations, in the classics, as we say—is the problem of true romanticism. "Dante," he observes, "was pre-eminently the romantic poet. He adored Virgil, yet he wrote the *Divine Comedy,* with the episode of Ugolino, which is as unlike the *Æneid* as can possibly be. And those who thus obey the fundamental principle of romanticism, one by one become classical, and are joined to that ever-increasing common league, formed by men of all countries, to approach nearer and nearer to perfection."

Romanticism, then, although it has its epochs, is in its essential characteristics rather a spirit which shows itself at all times, in various degrees, in individual workmen and their work, and the amount of which criticism has to estimate in them taken one by one, than the peculiarity of a time or a school. Depending on the varying proportion of curiosity and the desire of beauty, natural tendencies of the artistic spirit at all times, it must always be partly a matter of individual temperament. The eighteenth century in England has been regarded as almost exclusively a classical period; yet William Blake, a type of so much which breaks through what are conventionally thought the influences of that century, is still a noticeable phenomenon in it, and the reaction in favour of naturalism in poetry begins in that century, early. There are, thus, the born romanticists and the born classicists. There are the born classicists who start with *form,* to whose minds the comeliness of the old, immemorial, well-recognized types in art and literature, have revealed themselves impressively; who will entertain no matter which will not go easily and flexibly into them; whose work aspires only to be a variation upon, or study from, the older masters. " 'Tis art's decline, my son!" they are always saying, to the progressive element in their own generation; to those who care for that which in fifty years' time every one will be caring for. On the other hand, there are the born romanticists, who start with an original, untried *matter,* still in fusion; who conceive this vividly, and hold by it as the essence of their work; who, by the very vividness and heat of their conception, purge away, sooner or later, all that is not organically appropriate to it, till the whole effect adjusts itself in clear, orderly, proportionate form; which form, after a very little time, becomes classical in its turn.

.   .   .

Classicism, then, means for Stendhal, for that younger enthusiastic band of French writers whose unconscious method he formulated into principles, the reign of what is pedantic, conventional, and narrowly academical in art; for him, all good art is romantic. To Sainte-Beuve, who understands the term in a more liberal sense, it is the characteristic of certain epochs, of certain spirits in every epoch, not given to the exercise of original imagination, but rather to the working out of refinements of manner on some authorised matter; and who bring to their perfection, in this way, the elements of sanity, of order and beauty in manner. In general criticism, again, it means the spirit of Greece and Rome, of some phases in literature and art that may seem of equal authority with Greece and Rome, the age of Louis the Fourteenth, the age of Johnson; though this is at best an uncritical use of the term, because in Greek and Roman work there are typical examples of the romantic spirit. But explain the terms as we may, in application to particular epochs, there are these two elements always recognisable; united in perfect art—in Sophocles, in Dante, in the highest work of Goethe, though not always absolutely balanced there; and these two elements may be not inappropriately termed the classical and romantic tendencies.

Material for the artist, motives of inspiration, are not yet exhausted: our curious, complex, aspiring age still abounds in subjects for æsthetic manipulation by the literary as well as by other forms of art. For the literary art, at all events, the problem just now is, to induce order upon the contorted, proportionless accumulation of our knowledge and experience, our science and history, our hopes and disillusion, and, in effecting this, to do consciously what has been done hitherto for the most part too unconsciously, to write our English language as the Latins wrote theirs, as the French write, as scholars should write. Appealing, as he may, to precedent in this manner, the scholar will still remember that if "the style is the man" it is also the age: that the nineteenth century too will be found to have had its style, justified by necessity—a style very different, alike from the baldness of an impossible "Queen Anne" revival, and an incorrect, incondite exuberance, after the mode of Elizabeth: that we can only return to either at the price of an impoverishment of form or matter, or both, although, an intellectually rich age such as ours being necessarily an eclectic one, we may well cultivate some of the excellences of literary types so different as those: that in literature as in other matters it is well to unite as many diverse elements as may be: that the individual writer or artist, certainly, is to be estimated by the number of graces he combines, and his power of interpenetrating them in a given work. To discriminate schools, of art, of literature, is, of course, part of the obvious business of literary criticism: but, in the work of literary production, it is easy to be overmuch occupied concerning them. For, in truth, the legitimate contention is, not of one age or school of literary art against another, but of all successive schools alike, against the stupidity which is dead to the substance, and the vulgarity which is dead to form.

WILLIAM DEAN HOWELLS

(1837–1920)

From

CRITICISM AND FICTION

(1891) *

· · ·

REALISM is nothing more and nothing less than the truthful treatment of material, and Jane Austen was the first and the last of the English novelists to treat material with entire truthfulness. Because she did this, she remains the most artistic of the English novelists, and alone worthy to be matched with the great Scandinavian and Slavic and Latin artists. It is not a question of intellect, or not wholly that. The English have mind enough; but they have not taste enough; or, rather, their taste has been perverted by their false criticism, which is based upon personal preference, and not upon principle; which instructs a man to think that what he likes is good, instead of teaching him first to distinguish what is good before he likes it. The art of fiction, as Jane Austen knew it, declined from her through Scott, and Bulwer, and Dickens, and Charlotte Brontë, and Thackeray, and even George Eliot, because the mania of romanticism had seized upon all Europe, and these great writers could not escape the taint of their time; but it has shown few signs of recovery in England, because English criticism, in the presence of the Continental masterpieces, has continued provincial and special and personal, and has expressed a love and a hate which had to do with the quality of the artist rather than the character of his work. It was inevitable that in their time the English romanticists should treat, as Señor Valdés says, "the barbarous customs of the Middle Ages, softening and disfiguring them, as Walter Scott and his kind did"; that they should "devote themselves to falsifying nature, refining and subtilizing sentiment, and modifying psychology after their own fancy," like Bulwer and Dickens, as well as like Rousseau and Madame de Staël, not to mention Balzac, the worst of all that sort at his worst. This was the natural course of the disease; but it really seems as if it

* The text used is that of the Library Edition (1910), which represents Howells' final version.

were their criticism that was to blame for the rest: not, indeed, for the performance of this writer or that, for criticism can never affect the actual doing of a thing; but for the esteem in which this writer or that is held through the perpetuation of false ideals. The only observer of English middle-class life since Jane Austen worthy to be named with her was not George Eliot, who was first ethical and then artistic, who transcended her in everything but the form and method most essential to art, and there fell hopelessly below her. It was Anthony Trollope who was most like her in simple honesty and instinctive truth, as un-philosophized as the light of common day; but he was so warped from a wholesome ideal as to wish at times to be like Thackeray, and to stand about in his scene, talking it over with his hands in his pockets, inter-rupting the action, and spoiling the illusion in which alone the truth of art resides. Mainly, his instinct was too much for his ideal, and with a low view of life in its civic relations and a thoroughly bourgeois soul, he yet produced works whose beauty is surpassed only by the effect of a more poetic writer in the novels of Thomas Hardy. Yet if a vote of English criticism even at this late day, when all continental Europe has the light of aesthetic truth, could be taken, the majority against these artists would be overwhelmingly in favor of a writer who had so little artistic sensibility that he never hesitated on any occasion, great or small, to make a foray among his characters, and catch them up to show them to the reader and tell him how beautiful or ugly they were; and cry out over their amazing properties.

ÉMILE ZOLA

(1840–1902)

From

THE EXPERIMENTAL NOVEL *

(1893)

IN my literary essays I have often spoken of the application of the ex-perimental method to the novel and to the drama. The return to nature, the naturalistic evolution which marks the century, drives little by little all the manifestation of human intelligence into the same scientific path.

* Translated by Belle M. Sherman.

Only the idea of a literature governed by science is doubtless a surprise, until explained with precision and understood. It seems to me necessary, then, to say briefly and to the point what I understand by the experimental novel.

I really only need to adapt, for the experimental method has been established with strength and marvelous clearness by Claude Bernard in his *Introduction à l'étude de la médecine expérimentale*. This work, by a savant whose authority is unquestioned, will serve me as a solid foundation. I shall here find the whole question treated, and I shall restrict myself to irrefutable arguments and to giving the quotations which may seem necessary to me. This will then be but a compiling of texts, as I intend on all points to intrench myself behind Claude Bernard. It will often be but necessary for me to replace the word "doctor" by the word "novelists," to make my meaning clear and to give it the rigidity of a scientific truth.

What determined my choice, and made me choose *L'Introduction* as my basis, was the fact that medicine, in the eyes of a great number of people, is still an art, as is the novel. Claude Bernard all his life was searching and battling to put medicine in a scientific path. In his struggle we see the first feeble attempts of a science to disengage itself little by little from empiricism,[1] and to gain a foothold in the realm of truth, by means of the experimental method. Claude Bernard demonstrates that this method, followed in the study of inanimate bodies in chemistry and in physics, should be also used in the study of living bodies, in physiology and medicine. I am going to try and prove for my part that if the experimental method leads to the knowledge of physical life, it should also lead to the knowledge of the passionate and intellectual life. It is but a question of degree in the same path which runs from chemistry to physiology, then from physiology to anthropology and to sociology. The experimental novel is the goal. . . .

Now, to return to the novel, we can easily see that the novelist is equally an observer and an experimentalist. The observer in him gives the facts as he has observed them, suggests the point of departure, displays the solid earth on which his characters are to tread and the phenomena to develop. Then the experimentalist appears and introduces an experiment, that is to say, sets his characters going in a certain story so as to show that the succession of facts will be such as the requirements of the determinism of the phenomena under examination call for. Here

[1] Zola uses empiricism in this essay in the sense of "haphazard observation" in contrast with a scientific experiment under- taken to prove a certain truth. (Trans- lator's note.)

it is nearly always an experiment *"pour voir,"* as Claude Bernard calls it. The novelist starts out in search of a truth. I will take as an example the character of the Baron Hulot, in *Cousine Bette,* by Balzac. The general fact observed by Balzac is the ravages that the amorous temperament of a man makes in his home, in his family, and in society. As soon as he has chosen his subject, he starts from known facts; then he makes his experiment, and exposes Hulot to a series of trials, placing him amid certain surroundings in order to exhibit how the complicated machinery of his passions works. It is then evident that there is not only observation there, but that there is also experiment; as Balzac does not remain satisfied with photographing the facts collected by him, but interferes in a direct way to place his character in certain conditions, and of these he remains the master. The problem is to know what such a passion, acting in such a surrounding and under such circumstances, would produce from the point of view of an individual and of society; and an experimental novel, *Cousine Bette,* for example, is simply the report of the experiment that the novelist conducts before the eyes of the public. In fact, the whole operation consists in taking facts in nature, then in studying the mechanism of these facts, acting upon them by the modification of circumstances and surroundings without deviating from the laws of nature. Finally, you possess knowledge of the man, scientific knowledge of him, in both his individual and social relations.

Doubtless we are still far from certainties in chemistry, and even physiology. Nor do we know any more the reagents which decompose the passions, rendering them susceptible of analysis. Often, in this essay, I shall recall in similar fashion this fact, that the experimental novel is still younger than experimental medicine, and the latter is but just born. But I do not intend to exhibit the acquired results, I simply desire to clearly expose a method. If the experimental novelist is still groping in the most obscure and complex of all the sciences, this does not prevent this science from existing. It is undeniable that the naturalistic novel, such as we understand it today, is a real experiment that a novelist makes on man by the help of observation.

Besides, this opinion is not only mine, it is Claude Bernard's as well. He says in one place: "In practical life men but make experiments on one another." And again, in a more conclusive way, he expresses the whole theory of the experimental novel:

When we reason on our own acts we have a certain guide, for we are conscious of what we think and how we feel. But if we wish to judge of the acts of another man, and know the motives which make him act, that is altogether a different thing. Without doubt we have before our eyes the movements of this man and his different acts, which are, we are sure, the modes of expression of his sensibility and his will. Further, we even admit that there is a necessary connection between the acts and their cause; but what is this cause? We do not feel it, we are not conscious of it, as we are when it acts in ourselves; we are therefore obliged to interpret it, and to guess at it, from the movements which we see and the words which we hear. We are obliged to check off this man's actions one by the other; we consider how he acted in such a circumstance, and, in a word, we have recourse to the experimental method.

All that I have spoken of further back is summed up in this last phrase, which is written by a savant.

I shall still call your attention to another illustration of Claude Bernard, which struck me as very forcible: "The experimentalist is the examining magistrate of nature." We novelists are the examining magistrates of men and their passions.

But see what splendid clearness breaks forth when this conception of the application of the experimental method to the novel is adequately grasped and is carried out with all the scientific rigor which the matter permits today. A contemptible reproach which they heap upon us naturalistic writers is the desire to be solely photographers. We have in vain declared that we admit the necessity of an artist's possessing an individual temperament and a personal expression; they continue to reply to us with these imbecile arguments, about the impossibility of being strictly true, about the necessity of arranging facts to produce a work of art of any kind. Well, with the application of the experimental method to the novel that quarrel dies out. The idea of experiment carries with it the idea of modification. We start, indeed, from the true facts, which are our indestructible basis; but to show the mechanism of these facts it is necessary for us to produce and direct the phenomena; this is our share of invention, here is the genius in the book. Thus without having recourse to the questions of form and of style, which I shall examine later, I maintain even at this point that we must modify nature, without departing from nature, when we employ the experimental method in our novels. If we bear in mind this definition, that "observation indicates and experiment teaches," we can even now claim for our books this great lesson of experiment.

The writer's office, far from being lessened, grows singularly from this point of view. An experiment, even the most simple, is always based on an idea, itself born of an observation. As Claude Bernard says: "The experimental idea is not arbitrary, nor purely imaginary; it ought always to have a support in some observed reality, that is to say, in nature." It is on this idea and on doubt that he bases all the method. "The appearance of the experimental idea," he says further on, "is entirely spontaneous and its nature absolutely individual, depending upon the mind in which it originates; it is a particular sentiment, a *quid proprium,* which constitutes the originality, the invention, and the genius of each one." Further, he makes doubt the great scientific lever. "The doubter is the true savant; he doubts only himself and his interpretations; he believes in science; he even admits in the experimental sciences a criterion or a positive principle, the determinism of phenomena, which is absolute in living beings as in inanimate bodies." Thus, instead of confining the novelist within narrow bounds, the experimental method gives full sway to his intelligence as a thinker, and to his genius as a creator. He must see, understand, and invent. Some observed fact makes the idea start up of trying an experiment, of writing a novel, in order to attain to a complete knowledge of the truth. Then when, after careful consideration, he has decided upon the plan of his experiment, he will judge the results at each step with the freedom of mind of a man who accepts only facts conformable to the determinism of phenomena. He set out from doubt to reach positive knowledge; and he will not cease to doubt until the mechanism of the passion, taken to pieces and set up again by him, acts according to the fixed laws of nature. There is no greater, no more magnificent work for the human mind. We shall see, further on, the miseries of the scholastics, of the makers of systems, and those theorizing about the ideal, compared with the triumph of the experimentalists.

I sum up this first part by repeating that the naturalistic novelists observe and experiment, and that all their work is the offspring of the doubt which seizes them in the presence of truths little known and phenomena unexplained, until an experimental idea rudely awakens their genius some day, and urges them to make an experiment, to analyze facts, and to master them.

V

. . . Let us clearly define now what is meant by an experimental novelist. Claude Bernard gives the following definition of an artist: "What is an artist? He is a man who realizes in a work of art an idea or a sentiment which is personal to him." I absolutely reject this definition. On this basis if I represented a man as walking on his head, I should

have made a work of art, if such happened to be my personal sentiments. But in that case I should be a fool and nothing else. So one must
add that the personal feeling of the artist is always subject to the higher
law of truth and nature. We now come to the question of hypothesis.
The artist starts out from the same point as the savant; he places himself before nature, has an idea apriori, and works according to this idea.
Here alone he separates himself from the savant, if he carries out his idea
to the end without verifying its truth by the means of observation and
experiment. Those who make use of experiment might well be called
experimental artists; but then people will tell us that they are no longer
artists, since such people regard art as the burden of personal error
which the artist has put into his study of nature. I contend that the personality of the writer should only appear in the idea apriori and in the
form, not in the infatuation for the false. I see no objection, besides, to
its showing in the hypothesis, but it is necessary to clearly understand
what you mean by these words.

It has often been said that writers ought to open the way for savants.
This is true, for we have seen in *L'Introduction* that hypothesis and
empiricism precede and prepare for the scientific state which is established finally by the experimental method. Man commenced by ventur-
ing certain explanations of phenomena, the poets gave expression to their
emotions, and the savants ended by mastering hypotheses and fixing the
truth. Claude Bernard always assigns the role of pioneers to the philosophers. It is a very noble role, and today it is the writers who should
assume it and who should endeavor to fill it worthily. Only let it be
well understood that each time that a truth is established by the savants
the writers should immediately abandon their hypothesis to adopt this
truth; otherwise they will remain deliberately in error without benefit-
ing anyone. It is thus that science, as it advances, furnishes to us writers
a solid ground upon which we should lean for support, to better enable
us to shoot into new hypotheses. In a word, every phenomenon, once
clearly determined, destroys the hypothesis which it replaces, and it is
then necessary to transport your hypothesis one step further into the
new unknown which arises. I will take a very simple example in order
to make myself better understood; it has been proved that the earth revolves around the sun; what would you think of a poet who should adopt
the old belief that the sun revolves around the earth? Evidently the
poet, if he wishes to risk a personal explanation of any fact, should
choose a fact whose cause is not already known. This, then, illustrates
the position hypothesis should occupy for experimental novelists; we

must accept determined facts, and not attempt to risk about them our personal sentiments, which would be ridiculous, building throughout on the territory that science has conquered; then before the unknown, but only then, exercising our intuition and suggesting the way to science, free to make mistakes, happy if we produce any data toward the solution of the problem. Here I stand at Claude Bernard's practical program, who is forced to accept empiricism as a necessary forerunner. In our experimental novel we can easily risk a few hypotheses on the questions of heredity and surroundings, after having respected all that science knows today about the matter. We can prepare the ways, we can furnish the results of observation, human data which may prove very useful. A great lyrical poet has written lately that our century is a century of prophets. Yes, if you wish it; only let it be well understood that these prophets rely neither upon the irrational nor the supernatural. If the prophets thought best to bring up again the most elementary notions, to serve up nature with a strange religious and philosophical sauce, to hold fast to the metaphysical man, to confound and obscure everything, the prophets, notwithstanding their genius in the matter of style, would never be anything but great gooses ignorant whether they would get wet if they jumped into the water. In our scientific age it is a very delicate thing to be a prophet, as we no longer believe in the truths of revelation, and in order to be able to foresee the unknown we must begin by studying the known.

The conclusion to which I wish to come is this: If I were to define the experimental novel I should not say, as Claude Bernard says, that a literary work lies entirely in the personal feeling, for the reason that in my opinion the personal feeling is but the first impulse. Later nature, being there, makes itself felt, or at least that part of nature of which science has given us the secret, and about which we have no longer any right to romance. The experimental novelist is therefore the one who accepts proven facts, who points out in man and in society the mechanism of the phenomena over which science is mistress, and who does not interpose his personal sentiments, except in the phenomena whose determinism is not yet settled, and who tries to test, as much as he can, this personal sentiment, this idea apriori, by observation and experiment.

I cannot understand how our naturalistic literature can mean anything else. I have only spoken of the experimental novel, but I am fairly convinced that the same method, after having triumphed in history and in criticism, will triumph everywhere, on the stage and in poetry even.

It is an inevitable evolution. Literature, in spite of all that can be said, does not depend merely upon the author; it is influenced by the nature it depicts and by the man whom it studies. Now if the savants change their ideas of nature, if they find the true mechanism of life, they force us to follow them, to precede them even, so as to play our role in the new hypotheses. The metaphysical man is dead; our whole territory is transformed by the advent of the physiological man. No doubt "Achilles' Anger," "Dido's Love," will last forever on account of their beauty; but today we feel the necessity of analyzing anger and love, of discovering exactly how such passions work in the human being. This view of the matter is a new one; we have become experimentalists instead of philosophers. In short, everything is summed up in this great fact: the experimental method in letters, as in the sciences, is in the way to explain the natural phenomena, both individual and social, of which metaphysics, until now, has given only irrational and supernatural explanations.

JOSEPH CONRAD

(1857–1924)

From

THE NIGGER OF THE NARCISSUS *

(1897)

PREFACE

A work that aspires, however humbly, to the condition of art should carry its justification in every line. And art itself may be defined as a single-minded attempt to render the highest kind of justice to the visible universe, by bringing to light the truth, manifold and one, underlying its every aspect. It is an attempt to find in its forms, in its colours, in its light, in its shadows, in the aspects of matter and in the facts of life what of each is fundamental, what is enduring and essential—their one illuminating and convincing quality—the very truth of their existence. The artist, then, like the thinker or the scientist, seeks the truth

---

* Preface to *The Nigger of the Narcis-*   Dent and Sons, Ltd. Used by permission of
sus by Joseph Conrad. Copyright J. M.   the publisher.

and makes his appeal. Impressed by the aspect of the world the thinker plunges into ideas, the scientist into facts—whence, presently, emerging they make their appeal to those qualities of our being that fit us best for the hazardous enterprise of living. They speak authoritatively to our common-sense, to our intelligence, to our desire of peace or to our desire of unrest; not seldom to our prejudices, sometimes to our fears, often to our egoism—but always to our credulity. And their words are heard with reverence, for their concern is with weighty matters: with the cultivation of our minds and the proper care of our bodies, with the attainment of our ambitions, with the perfection of the means and the glorification of our precious aims.

It is otherwise with the artist.

Confronted by the same enigmatical spectacle the artist descends within himself, and in that lonely region of stress and strife, if he be deserving and fortunate, he finds the terms of his appeal. His appeal is made to our less obvious capacities: to that part of our nature which, because of the warlike conditions of existence, is necessarily kept out of sight within the more resisting and hard qualities—like the vulnerable body within a steel armour. His appeal is less loud, more profound, less distinct, more stirring—and sooner forgotten. Yet its effect endures forever. The changing wisdom of successive generations discards ideas, questions facts, demolishes theories. But the artist appeals to that part of our being which is not dependent on wisdom; to that in us which is a gift and not an acquisition—and, therefore, more permanently enduring. He speaks to our capacity for delight and wonder, to the sense of mystery surrounding our lives; to our sense of pity, and beauty, and pain; to the latent feeling of fellowship with all creation—and to the subtle but invincible conviction of solidarity that knits together the loneliness of innumerable hearts, to the solidarity in dreams, in joy, in sorrow, in aspirations, in illusions, in hope, in fear, which binds men to each other, which binds together all humanity—the dead to the living and the living to the unborn.

It is only some such train of thought, or rather of feeling, that can in a measure explain the aim of the attempt, made in the tale which follows, to present an unrestful episode in the obscure lives of a few individuals out of all the disregarded multitude of the bewildered, the simple and the voiceless. For, if any part of truth dwells in the belief confessed above, it becomes evident that there is not a place of splendour or a dark corner of the earth that does not deserve, if only a passing glance of wonder and pity. The motive then, may be held to justify the matter of the work; but this preface, which is simply an avowal of endeavour, cannot end here—for the avowal is not yet complete.

Fiction—if it at all aspires to be art—appeals to temperament. And in truth it must be, like painting, like music, like all art, the appeal of one temperament to all the other innumerable temperaments whose subtle and resistless power endows passing events with their true meaning, and creates the moral, the emotional atmosphere of the place and time. Such an appeal to be effective must be an impression conveyed through the senses; and, in fact, it cannot be made in any other way, because temperament, whether individual or collective, is not amenable to persuasion. All art, therefore, appeals primarily to the senses, and the artistic aim when expressing itself in written words must also make its appeal through the senses, if its high desire is to reach the secret spring of responsive emotions. It must strenuously aspire to the plasticity of sculpture, the colour of painting, and to the magic suggestiveness of music—which is the art of arts. And it is only through complete, unswerving devotion to the perfect blending of form and substance; it is only through an unremitting never-discouraged care for the shape and ring of sentences that an approach can be made to plasticity, to colour, and that the light of magic suggestiveness may be brought to play for an evanescent instant over the commonplace surface of words: of the old, old words, worn thin, defaced by ages of careless usage.

The sincere endeavour to accomplish that creative task, to go as far on that road as his strength will carry him, to go undeterred by faltering, weariness or reproach, is the only valid justification for the worker in prose. And if his conscience is clear, his answer to those who in the fulness of wisdom which looks for immediate profit, demand specifically to be edified, consoled, amused; who demand to be promptly improved, or encouraged, or frightened, or shocked, or charmed, must run thus:— My task which I am trying to achieve is, by the power of the written word to make you hear, to make you feel—it is, before all, to make you *see*. That—and no more, and it is everything. If I succeed, you shall find there according to your deserts: encouragement, consolation, fear, charm —all you demand—and, perhaps, also that glimpse of truth for which you have forgotten to ask.

To snatch in a moment of courage, from the remorseless rush of time, a passing phase of life, is only the beginning of the task. The task approached in tenderness and faith is to hold up unquestioningly, without choice and without fear, the rescued fragment before all eyes in the light of a sincere mood. It is to show its vibration, its colour, its form; and through its movement, its form, and its colour, reveal the substance of its truth—disclose its inspiring secret: the stress and passion within the core of each convincing moment. In a single-minded attempt of that kind, if one be deserving and fortunate, one may perchance attain to such clearness of sincerity that at last the presented vision of regret or pity, of terror or mirth, shall awaken in the hearts of the beholders that feeling of unavoidable solidarity; of the solidarity in mysterious origin, in toil, in joy, in hope, in uncertain fate, which binds men to each other and all mankind to the visible world.

It is evident that he who, rightly or wrongly, holds by the convictions expressed above cannot be faithful to any one of the temporary formulas of his craft. The enduring part of them—the truth which each only imperfectly veils—should abide with him as the most precious of his possessions, but they all: Realism, Romanticism, Naturalism, even the unofficial sentimentalism (which like the poor, is exceedingly difficult to get rid of), all these gods must, after a short period of fellowship, abandon him—even on the very threshold of the temple—to the stammerings of his conscience and to the outspoken consciousness of the difficulties of his work. In that uneasy solitude the supreme cry of Art for Art itself, loses the exciting ring of its apparent immorality. It sounds far off. It has ceased to be a cry, and is heard only as a whisper, often incomprehensible, but at times and faintly encouraging.

Sometimes, stretched at ease in the shade of a roadside tree, we watch the motions of a labourer in a distant field, and after a time, begin to wonder languidly as to what the fellow may be at. We watch the movements of his body, the waving of his arms, we see him bend down, stand up, hesitate, begin again. It may add to the charm of an idle hour to be told the purpose of his exertions. If we know he is trying to lift a stone, to dig a ditch, to uproot a stump, we look with a more real interest at his efforts; we are disposed to condone the jar of his agitation upon the restfulness of the landscape; and even, if in a brotherly frame of mind, we may bring ourselves to forgive his failure. We understood his object, and, after all, the fellow has tried, and perhaps he had not the strength—and perhaps he had not the knowledge. We forgive, go on our way—and forget.

And so it is with the workman of art. Art is long and life is short, and success is very far off. And thus, doubtful of strength to travel so far, we talk a little about the aim—the aim of art, which, like life itself, is inspiring, difficult—obscured by mists. It is not in the clear logic of a triumphant conclusion; it is not in the unveiling of one of those heartless secrets which are called the Laws of Nature. It is not less great, but only more difficult.

To arrest, for the space of a breath, the hands busy about the work of the earth, and compel men entranced by the sight of distant goals to glance for a moment at the surrounding vision of form and colour, of sunshine and shadows; to make them pause for a look, for a sigh, for a smile—such is the aim, difficult and evanescent, and reserved only for a very few to achieve. But sometimes, by the deserving and the fortunate, even that task is accomplished. And when it is accomplished—behold!—all the truth of life is there: a moment of vision, a sigh, a smile—and the return to an eternal rest.

ANATOLE FRANCE

(1844–1924)

From

THE LITERARY LIFE

(1888)

I

THE ADVENTURES OF THE SOUL *

As I understand criticism it is, like philosophy and history, a kind of novel for the use of discreet and curious minds. And every novel, rightly understood, is an autobiography. The good critic is he who relates the adventures of his soul among masterpieces.

There is no such thing as objective criticism any more than there is objective art, and all who flatter themselves that they put aught but themselves into their work are dupes of the most fallacious illusion. The truth is that one never gets out of oneself. That is one of our greatest miseries. What would we not give to see, if but for a minute, the sky and the earth with the many-facetted eye of a fly, or to understand nature with the rude and simple brain of an ape? But just that is for-

* From *The Literary Life*, by Anatole France, translated by Ludwig Lewisohn, in *The Book of Modern Criticism*, The Mod-ern Library. Used by permission of Mr. Lewisohn.

bidden us. We cannot, like Tiresias, be men and remember having been women. We are locked into our persons as into a lasting prison. The best we can do, it seems to me, is gracefully to recognize this terrible situation and to admit that we speak of ourselves every time that we have not the strength to be silent.

To be quite frank, the critic ought to say:

"Gentlemen, I am going to talk about myself on the subject of Shakespeare, or Racine, or Pascal, or Goethe—subjects that offer me a beautiful opportunity."

I had the honor of knowing M. Cuvillier-Fleury, who was a very earnest old critic. One day when I had come to see him in his little house in the Avenue Raphael, he showed me the modest library of which he was proud.

"Sir," he said to me, "oratory, pure literature, philosophy, history, all the kinds are represented here, without counting criticism which embraces them all. Yes, the critic is by turn orator, philosopher, historian."

M. Cuvillier-Fleury was right. The critic is all that or, at least, he ought to be. He has occasion to show the rarest, most diverse, most varied faculties of the intellect. And when he is a Sainte-Beuve, a Taine, a Jules Lemaître, a Ferdinand Brunetière, he does not fail to do so. Remaining definitely within himself he creates the intellectual history of man. Criticism is the youngest of all the literary forms: it will perhaps end by absorbing all the others. It is admirably suited to a very civilized society with rich memories and long traditions. It is particularly appropriate to a curious, learned and polite humanity. For its prosperity it demands more culture than any of the other literary forms. Its creators were Montaigne, Saint-Evremond, Bayle, Montesquieu. It proceeds simultaneously from philosophy and history. It has required, for its development, an epoch of absolute intellectual liberty. It has replaced theology and, if one were to seek the universal doctor, the Saint Thomas Aquinas of the nineteenth century, of whom would one be forced to think but of Sainte-Beuve? . . .

According to Littré a book is a bound bundle of paper sheets whether hand-written or printed. That definition does not satisfy me. I would define a book as a work of magic whence escape all kinds of images to trouble the souls and change the hearts of men. Or, better still, a book is a little magic apparatus which transports us among the images of the past or amidst supernatural shades. Those who read many books are like the eaters of hashish. They live in a dream. The subtle poison that penetrates their brain renders them insensible to the real world and makes them the prey of terrible or delightful phantoms. Books are the opium of the Occident. They devour us. A day is coming on which we shall all be keepers of libraries, and that will be the end.

Let us love books as the mistress of the poet loved her grief. Let us love them: they cost us dear enough. Yes, books kill us. You may believe me who adore them, who have long given myself to them without reserve. Books slay us. We have too many of them and too many kinds. Men lived for long ages without reading and precisely in those ages their actions were greatest and most useful, for it was then that they passed from barbarism to civilization. But because men were then without books they were not bare of poetry and morality: they knew songs by heart and little catechisms. In their childhood old women told them the stories of the Ass's Skin and of Puss in Boots of which, much later, editions for bibliophiles have been made. The earliest books were great rocks covered with inscriptions in an administrative or religious style.

It is a long time since then. What frightful progress we have made in the interval! Books multiplied in a marvellous fashion in the sixteenth and eighteenth centuries. To-day their production has increased an hundredfold. In Paris alone fifty books are published daily without counting the newspapers. It is a monstrous orgy. We shall emerge from it quite mad. It is man's fate to fall successively into contradictory extremes. In the Middle Ages ignorance bred fear. Thus maladies of the mind reigned then which we no longer know. To-day, through study, we are hastening toward general paralysis. Would it not be wiser and more elegant to keep some measure?

Let us be lovers of books and let us read them: but let us not gather them with indiscriminate hands: let us be delicate: let us choose, and, like that lord in one of Shakespeare's comedies, let us say to our bookseller: "I would that they be well-bound and that they speak of love."

GEORGE MOORE

(1853–1933)

From

THE INTRODUCTION TO
AN ANTHOLOGY OF PURE POETRY *

(1924)

AND the reason may be stated why we are in these poems at the heart of poetry: because these poems were born of admiration of the only permanent world, the world of things. Ideas, thoughts, reflections, become common quickly; an idea is mine to-day, yours to-morrow, and the day after to-morrow it is on the barrel organs. Every ten years morality, patriotism, duty, and religion, take on meanings different from those they wore before, and that is why each generation, dissatisfied with the literature that preceded it, is inspired to write another literature round the new morality, the new patriotism, the new duty, the new religion, a literature which seems to the writers more permanent than the literature their fathers wrote, but which is destined to pass away as silently. Of the passing of literature there is no end; the world is littered with dead literature as with leaves, and the thought pursues us that the romantic movement which seemed as eternal as the hills thirty years ago is preparing to leave us. Mr. Gosse has climbed into the crow's-nest and thinks he discerns Pope and perhaps Cowper on the horizon. Last week he quoted:

> The poplars are fell'd; farewell to the shade,
> And the whispering sound of the cool colonnade,

lines that will be admired by men of letters and by whomsoever shall happen upon these lines, for there are always poplars in the world and men will always enjoy the whispering sound of a leafy avenue; but all that is essentially Cowper, his thoughts, his meditations, his ideas, have passed away, never to return. Wherefore the lines I have quoted do not undermine, rather do they uphold the belief that time cannot wither nor custom stale poetry unsicklied o'er with the pale cast of

* Reprinted from the Introduction to *An Anthology of Pure Poetry* by George Moore.   Boni and Liveright, 1924. Used by permission of Mr. C. D. Medley.

thought. Again we fall to thinking: Shakespeare never soiled his songs
with thought; we commit them to memory almost unconsciously; we
remember the objective passages of *The Ancient Mariner,* and no lines
of Keats are better known than:

> Deep in the shady sadness of a vale
> Far sunken from the healthy breath of morn,
> Far from the fiery noon, and eve's one star,
> Sat grey-haired Saturn, quiet as a stone,
> Still as the silence round about his lair;
> Forest on forest hung about his head
> Like cloud on cloud.

The poem as it proceeds becomes more reflective, and Keats may have
abandoned the subject for that reason, it seeming to him to lack the
innocency of a Greek poem, which he desired ardently whilst yielding
to pressure from without. The hub of an empire is not favourable
to innocency of vision, and it would need a robuster faith than ours to
believe that were Shakespeare's songs written by a modern poet they
would not be sneered at in the Press as art for art's sake and the poet
adjured to tell us instead large, noble and eternal truths about humanity.
Tennyson yielded to the large needs of humanity (we know with what
result), and many other poets might be named that have been devoured
one by one by the needs of the empire. Which shall it be, art or empire?
A grave subject for reflection this is, though the choice is not given to
us, and if it were, there is little doubt which would get the vote, a
fact that will not deter me from writing in this introduction that
what modern art lacks is not instruction (of that it has enough and
more than enough), but innocency of vision, a gift that our ancestors
retained from the cradle to the grave, but which is very soon quenched
in these modern times and derided in the newspapers as art for art's
sake, a phrase that probably dropped off the pen of some flippant, unthinking journalist, and which attained currency for no better reason
than that it supplied the tea-shop and the bus with a convenient catch-
word. It has been babbled for the last thirty or forty years, very few
caring to ask themselves if art could be produced for other than aesthetic
reasons, and the few that did fall to thinking do not seem to have
discovered that art for art's sake means pure art, that is to say, a vision
almost detached from the personality of the poet. So perhaps the time
has come for somebody to ask if there is not more poetry in things than
in ideas, and more pleasure in Gautier's *Tulipe* than in Wordsworth's
ecclesiastical, political, and admonitory sonnets.

BIBLIOGRAPHY

GENERAL

Aiken, Conrad, *Scepticisms*. New York, 1919.
Allen, G. W., and Clark, H. H., eds., *Literary Criticism, Pope to Croce*. New York, 1941.
Ascham, R., *The Scholemaster*, ed. E. Arber. London, 1870.
Atkins, J. W. H., *Literary Criticism in Antiquity*, Volume 1, Greek; Volume 2, Græco-Roman. Cambridge, 1934.
Babbitt, Brooks, Brownell, Boyd, Eliot, Mencken, Sherman, Spingarn, Woodberry, *Criticism in America*. New York, 1924.
Babbitt, Irving, *The Masters of Modern French Criticism*. Boston, New York, 1912.
Baldwin, Charles S., *Ancient Rhetoric and Poetic*. New York, 1924.
Belis, Alexandre, *La critique française à la fin du XIXe siècle*. Paris, 1926.
Blackmur, R. P., *The Double Agent*. New York, 1935.
Blackmur, R. P., *The Expense of Greatness*. New York, 1940.
Bond, Richmond P., *English Burlesque Poetry 1700–1750*, Chap. 2. Cambridge, Mass., 1932.
Borinski, Karl, *Die Poetik der Renaissance und die Aufänge der Litterarischen Kritic in Deutschland*. Berlin, 1886.
Bosanquet, Bernard, *A History of Aesthetic*. London, 1922.
Bourgoin, Auguste, *Les maîtres de la critique au XVIIe siècle*. Paris, 1889.
Bowman, James Cloyd, *Contemporary American Criticism*. New York, 1926.
Bradley, A. C., *Shakespearean Tragedy*, 2nd ed. London, 1905.
Bradley, A. C., *Oxford Lectures on Poetry*. London, 1909.
Bray, J. W., *A History of English Critical Terms*. Boston, 1898.
Bray, René, *La formation de la doctrine classique en France*. Lausanne, 1931.
Brewster, W. T., ed., *Specimens of Modern English Literary Criticism*. New York, 1907.
Bronson, Carleton, and Todd, O. J., trs., *Xenophon: Anabasis; Symposium; Apology* (Loeb Classical Library). New York, 1922.
Brooks, Cleanth, *Modern Poetry and the Tradition*. Chapel Hill, 1939.
Brooks, Cleanth, *The Well Wrought Urn*. New York, 1947.
Brunetière, Ferdinand, *Questions de critique*. Paris, 1889.
Brunetière, Ferdinand, *Nouvelles questions de critique*. Paris, 1890.
Brunetière, Ferdinand, *L'evolution des genres dans l'histoire de la litterature*. Paris, 1898.
Brunot, F., *La doctrine de malherbe d'après son commentaire sur desportes*. Paris, 1891.

Carton, Henri, *Histoire de la critique littéraire en France*. Paris, 1886.

Cinthio, Giraldi, *Scritti Estetici*. Milano, 1864.

Clark, Barrett H., *European Theories of the Drama*, rev. ed. New York, 1936.

Cline, Thomas Lucian, *Critical Opinion in the Eighteenth Century*. Ann Arbor, Mich., 1926.

Courthope, W. J., *History of English Poetry*. London, 1895–1905.

Dacier, A., *La poétique traduite en François*. Paris, 1692.

D'Alton, John F., *Roman Literary Criticism*. London, New York, 1931.

De Mille, George E., *Literary Criticism in America*. New York, Toronto, 1931.

Denniston, John Dewar, ed., *Greek Literary Criticism*. London, Toronto, 1924.

Dixon, W. M., *English Epic and Heroic Poetry*. London, 1912.

Donatus, Aelius, *Ars Poetica*. Bononiæ, 1659.

Durham, W. H., ed., *Critical Essays of the Eighteenth Century, 1700–1725*. New Haven, 1915.

Eliot, T. S., *The Sacred Wood*, London, 1932.

Empson, William, *Seven Types of Ambiguity*. London, 1930.

Foerster, E. M., *Aspects of the Novel*. New York, 1927, 1947.

Foerster, Norman, *American Criticism, a Study in Literary Theory from Poe to the Present*. Boston, New York, 1928.

Foerster, Norman, ed., *American Critical Essays, XIXth and XXth Centuries*. London, 1930.

Fracastoro, G., *Opera*. Genevae, 1621.

Frye, Prosser Hall, *Literary Reviews and Criticism*. New York, 1908.

Frye, Prosser Hall, *Romance and Tragedy*. Boston, 1922.

Gasté, Armand, *La querelle du cid*. Paris, 1898.

Gayley, Charles Mills, and Scott, Fred Newton, *An Introduction to the Methods and Materials of Literary Criticism*. Boston, 1899.

Gayley, Charles Mills, and Kurtz, B., *Methods and Materials of Literary Criticism*. Boston, 1920.

Gilbert, Allan H., ed., *Literary Criticism, Plato to Dryden*. New York, 1940.

Gordon, Caroline, and Tate, Allen, eds., *The House of Fiction*. New York, 1950.

Gosse, Edmund, *A History of Eighteenth Century Literature*. London, 1891.

Gosse, Edmund, *From Shakespeare to Pope*. Cambridge, England, 1885.

Gosson, S., *The Schoole of Abuse,* ed. E. Arber. London, 1868.

Heinsius, Daniel, *De Tragoediae Constitutione*. Leyden, 1611.

Housman, A. E., *The Name and Nature of Poetry*. Cambridge, England, 1933.

Isola, I. G., *Critica del Rinascimento*. Livorno, 1907.

Jones, Edmund David, ed., *English Critical Essays of the XIX Century*. London, 1922.

Klein, David, *Literary Criticism from the Elizabethan Dramatists*. New York, 1910.

Leavis, F. R., *Revaluation: Tradition and Development in Modern Poetry.* London, 1936.

Leavis, F. R., *The Great Tradition.* London, 1948.

Le Bossu, R., *Traité du poème épique.* Paris, 1675.

Lewisohn, Ludwig, ed., *A Modern Book of Criticism* (Modern Library). New York, 1919.

Lieder, P. R., and Withington, R., eds., *The Art of Literary Criticism.* New York, 1941.

Lounsbury, Thomas R., *Shakespeare as a Dramatic Artist.* New York, 1901.

Lounsbury, Thomas R., *Studies in Chaucer,* 3 vols. New York, 1892.

Lounsbury, Thomas R., *The Text of Shakespeare.* New York, 1906.

Lubbock, Percy, *The Craft of Fiction.* London, 1921.

Lyttleton, George, *Dialogues of the Dead,* 2nd ed. London, 1760.

McLaughlin, E. T., ed., *Literary Criticism for Students.* New York, 1893.

Miller, George Morey, *The Historical Point of View in English Literary Criticism from 1570–1770.* Heidelberg, 1913.

Monk, Samuel H., *The Sublime: A Study of Critical Theories in XVIII Century England.* New York, 1935.

More, Paul Elmer, *Shelburne Essays,* 7 vols. Cambridge, 1910.

Muir, Edwin, *The Structure of the Novel.* London, 1928.

Muir, Edwin, *Essays on Literature and Society.* London, 1948.

Nitchie, Elizabeth, *Vergil and the English Poets.* New York, 1919.

Oldmixon, John, *The Arts of Logic and Rhetoric.* London, 1728.

Patrizzi, F., *Della Poetica.* Ferrara, 1586.

Pelletier du Mans, Jacques, *L'art poétique.* Lyon, 1555.

Perrault, Charles, *Parallèle des anciens et des modernes,* 2 vols. Amsterdam, 1693.

Piccolomini, A., *Annotationi del Libro della Poetica d'Aristotele.* Vinegia, 1575.

Pontanus, Jacobus, *Poeticarum Institutionum Libri Tres.* Ingoldstadt, 1594.

Pusey, E. B., tr., *The Confessions of St. Augustine* (Everyman's Library). London, New York, 1910.

Rapin, René, *The Whole Critical Works of Monsieur Rapin.* . . . Newly translated into English by several hands. London, 1706.

Rhys, Ernest, *Literary Pamphlets, Chiefly Relating to Poetry, from Sidney to Byron.* London, 1897.

Rhys, Ernest, ed., *The Prelude to Poetry* (Everyman's Library). London, Toronto, New York, 1927.

Rigault, H., *Histoire de la querelle des anciens et des modernes.* Paris, 1856.

Roberts, W. Rhys, *Greek Rhetoric and Literary Criticism.* New York, 1928.

Robertson, J. G., *The French Academy.* New York, 1910.

Rymer, Thomas, *A Short View of Tragedy.* London, 1693.

Rymer, Thomas, *Tragedies of the Last Age.* London, 1678.

Saintsbury, George, *A History of Criticism and Literary Taste in Europe from the Earliest Texts to the Present Day.* Edinburgh, London, 1900–04.

Saintsbury, George, *A History of English Criticism* (Eng. chaps. of *History of Criticism*). 1911.

Saintsbury, George, *Loci Critici*. Boston, London, 1903.

Schelling, F. E., *Poetic and Verse Criticism of the Reign of Elizabeth*. Philadelphia, 1891.

Schorer, Mark; Miles, Josephine; and McKenzie, Gordon, eds., *Criticism, the Foundations of Modern Literary Judgment*. New York, 1948.

Sikes, E. E., *The Greek View of Poetry*. New York, 1931.

Smith, D. Nichol, *Eighteenth Century Essays on Shakespeare*. Glasgow, 1903.

Smith, G. G., ed., *Elizabethan Critical Essays*. Oxford, 1904.

Spender, Stephen, *The Destructive Element*. London, 1935.

Spender, Stephen, *Life and the Poet*. London, 1942.

Speroni, Sperone, *Opere*. Venezia, 1740.

Spingarn, Joel Elias, *History of Literary Criticism in the Renaissance*. New York, 1899.

Spingarn, Joel Elias, ed., *Critical Essays of the Seventeenth Century*. Oxford, 1908–09.

Stallman, R. W., ed., *Critiques and Essays in Criticism, 1928–1940*. New York, 1949.

Stauffer, Donald A., ed., *The Intent of the Critic*. Princeton, 1941.

Stauffer, Donald A., *The Nature of Poetry*. New York, 1946.

Tasso, T., *Opere, colle controversie sulla gerusalemme, per cura di G. Rosini*. Pisa, 1821–32.

Tate, Allen, *Reactionary Essays on Poetry and Ideas*. New York, 1936.

Tate, Allen, *Reason in Madness*. New York, 1941.

Tate, Allen, *On the Limits of Poetry*. New York, 1948.

Terrasson, Jean, *Dissertation critique sur l'Iliade*, 2 vols. Paris, 1715.

Thompson, G. A., *Elizabethan Criticism of Poetry*. Menasha, Wisconsin, 1914.

Tillyard, E. M. W., *Poetry Direct and Oblique*. London, 1934.

Tissot, Ernest, *Les evolutions de la critique française*. Paris, 1890.

Vaughan, C. E., ed., *English Literary Criticism* (Warwick Library). London, 1903.

Vaughan, C. E., *Types of Tragic Drama*. London, 1908.

Vial, Francisque, *Idées et doctrines littéraires du XVIIᵉ siècle*. Paris, 1906.

Vial, Francisque, *Idées et doctrines littéraires du XVIIIᵉ siècle*. Paris, 1909.

Vial, Francisque, *Idées et doctrines littéraires du XIXᵉ siècle*. Paris, 1918.

Vossler, Karl, *Mediaeval Culture*, Vols. 1 and 2 (tr. by W. C. Lawton). New York, 1929.

Vossler, Karl, *Poetische Theorien in der Italienischen Frührenaissance*. Berlin, 1900.

Walker, Hugh, *The Literature of the Victorian Era*. Cambridge, England, 1910.

Warren, A., and Wellek, R., *The Theory of Literature*. New York, 1949.

Wilson, Edmund, *Axel's Castle*. New York, 1931.

Wilson, Edmund, *To the Finland Station*. New York, 1940.

Wilson, Edmund, *The Wound and the Bow*. Boston, 1941.

Winters, Yvor, *In Defense of Reason*. New York, 1947.

Worsfold, William Basil, *The Principles of Criticism*. London, 1914.
Zabel, M. D., ed., *Literary Opinion in America*. New York, 1937.

ARISTOTLE

Breitinger, H., *Les unités d'Aristote avant le cid de Corneille*. Genève, 1895.
Butcher, S. H., tr., *Aristotle's Theory of Poetry and Fine Art*. London, New York, 1895.
Bywater, Ingram, tr., *On the Art of Poetry*. Oxford, 1920.
Cooper, Lane, *The Poetics of Aristotle*. Boston, 1923.
Cooper, Lane, *An Aristotelian Theory of Comedy*. New York, 1922.
Cooper, Lane, tr., *On the Art of Poetry*. Boston, New York, 1913.
Cooper, Lane, and Gudeman, Alfred, *A Bibliography of the Poetics of Aristotle*. New Haven, 1928.
Fyfe, W. H., tr., *Aristotle: The Poetics, Longinus: On the Sublime, Demetrius: On Style* (tr. by W. R. Roberts) (Loeb Classical Series). London, New York, 1927.
Lucas, F. L., *Tragedy in Relation to Aristotle's Poetics*. New York, 1928.
Robortelli, F., *In Librum Aristotelis de Arte Poetica Explicationes*. Florentiae, 1548.
Rymer, Thomas, tr., *Monsieur Rapin's Reflections on Aristotle's Treatise of Poesie*. London, 1694.
Twining, Thomas, tr., *Aristotle's Treatise on Poetry*. London, 1789.

MATTHEW ARNOLD

Arnold, Matthew, *Essays in Criticism* (First Series). London, Cambridge, 1865.
Arnold, Matthew, *Essays in Criticism* (Second Series). London, New York, 1888.
Trilling, Lionel, *Matthew Arnold*. New York, 1939.

BOCCACCIO

Osgood, Charles G., tr., *Boccaccio on Poetry*. Princeton, 1930.

NICOLAS BOILEAU-DESPRÉAUX

Albalot, Antoine, *L'art poétique de Boileau*. Paris, 1929.
Boileau-Despréaux, Nicolas, *Oeuvres diverse du sieur D****, *avec le traite du sublime ou de merveilleux dans le discours*, tr. du grec de Longin. Paris, 1685.
Clark, A. F. B., *Boileau and the French Classical Critics in England*. Paris, 1925.
Cook, A. S., *The Art of Poetry; The Poetical Treatises of Horace, Vida, and Boileau, with the Translations by Howes, Pitt, and Soame*. Boston, 1892.

CASTELVETRO

Castelvetro, L., *Poetica d'Aristotele vulgarizzata et sposta*. Basilea, 1576.
Castelvetro, L., *Opere Vaire Critiche*. Milano, 1727.
Charleton, H. B., *Castelvetro's Theory of Poetry*. Manchester, 1913.
Fusco, A., *La Poetica di Lodovico Castelvetro*. Napoli, 1904.

SAMUEL TAYLOR COLERIDGE

Ashe, T., ed., *Lectures and Notes on Shakespeare and other English Poets*, by S. T. Coleridge. London, 1890.
George, Andrew J., ed., *Coleridge's Principles of Criticism*. Boston, 1897.
Shawcross, J., ed., *Biographia Literaria*. Oxford, 1907.

JOSEPH CONRAD

Garnett, Edward, ed., *Conrad's Prefaces to His Works*. London, 1937.

PIERRE CORNEILLE

Croce, Benedetto, *Ariosto, Shakespeare and Corneille* (tr. by Douglas Ainslie). New York, 1920.

BENEDETTO CROCE

Croce, Benedetto, *The Poetry of Dante* (tr. by Douglas Ainslie). New York, 1922.
Croce, Benedetto, *Aesthetic* (tr. by Douglas Ainslie), 4th ed. London, 1929.
Croce, Benedetto, *The Defence of Poetry* (tr. by E. F. Carritt). Oxford, 1933.
Croce, Benedetto, *Poesia*. Bari, 1936.
Powell, A. E., *The Romantic Theory of Poetry, an Examination in the Light of Croce's Aesthetic*. New York, 1926.
Spingarn, J. E., *Creative Criticism*. New York, 1917.

SAMUEL DANIEL

Harrison, G. B., ed., *A Defense of Rime* (The Bodley Head Quartos). London, New York, 1925.

DANTE

Grandgent, C. H., *Dante*. New York, 1921.
Jackson, William Walrond, tr., *Dante's Convivio*. Oxford, 1909.
Latham, Charles Sterrett, tr., *Dante's Eleven Letters* (ed. by George Rice Carpenter). Boston, New York, 1892.
Lawton, William Cranston, tr., *Mediaeval Culture*, by Karl Vossler. New

York, 1921; Vol. 2, *An Introduction to Dante and His Times,* published in Germany as *Die Göttliche Komödie.*

Rossetti, Dante Gabriel, tr., *Dante and His Circle with the Italian Poets Preceding Him,* with a Preface by William M. Rossetti. London, 1908.

Smith, James Robinson, tr., *The Earliest Lives of Dante* (Yale Studies in English). New York, 1901.

B. DANIELLO

Daniello, B., *La Poetica.* Vinegia, 1536.

JOHN DENNIS

Dennis, John, *Remarks upon Mr. Pope's Translation of Homer.* London, 1717.

Dennis, John, *Select Works,* 2 vols. London, 1718–21.

Hooper, Edward Niles, ed., *The Critical Works of John Dennis,* Vol. 1. Baltimore, 1939.

THOMAS DE QUINCEY

Masson, David, ed., *The Collected Writings of Thomas De Quincey,* Vol. 11. London, 1897.

DIONYSIUS OF HALICARNASSUS

Roberts, W. Rhys, *Dionysius of Halicarnassus on Literary Composition.* London, 1910.

Roberts, W. Rhys, tr., *Dionysius of Halicarnassus. The Three Literary Letters.* Cambridge, 1901.

JOHN DRYDEN

Arundell, D. D., ed., *Dryden and Howard, 1664–1668.* Cambridge, 1929.

Dryden, John, *Dramatic Essays* (Everyman's Library). London, New York, 1912.

Eliot, T. S., *John Dryden: The Poet, The Dramatist, The Critic.* New York, 1932.

Frye, Prosser Hall, *Dryden and the Critical Canons of the Eighteenth Century,* Vol. 7, No. 1. Nebraska University Studies, 1907.

Hudson, W. H., ed., *Essay of Dramatic Poesie,* by John Dryden. London, 1903.

Ker, W. P., ed., *Essays of John Dryden.* Oxford, 1900.

Scott, Sir Walter, and Saintsbury, George, eds., *The Works of John Dryden.* Edinburgh, 1882–93.

THOMAS STEARNS ELIOT

Eliot, T. S., *The Sacred Wood: Essays on Poetry and Criticism.* London, 1920.
Eliot, T. S., *Homage to John Dryden.* London, 1924.
Eliot, T. S., *For Lancelot Andrewes: Essays on Style and Order.* London, 1928. New York, 1928.
Eliot, T. S., *Dante.* London, 1929.
Eliot, T. S., *Selected Essays: 1917–1932.* London, 1932. New York, 1932.
Eliot, T. S., *The Use of Poetry and the Use of Criticism.* Cambridge, England, 1933.
Eliot, T. S., *After Strange Gods: A Primer of Modern Heresy.* New York, 1934.
Eliot, T. S., *Essays Ancient and Modern.* London, 1936.
Eliot, T. S., *The Idea of a Christian Society.* London, 1939.
Eliot, T. S., *The Classics and the Man of Letters.* Oxford, 1942.
Eliot, T. S., *Notes towards the Definition of Culture.* New York, 1949.
Unger, Leonard, ed., *T. S. Eliot: a Selected Critique.* New York, 1948.

ANATOLE FRANCE

Evans, A. W., tr., *On Life and Letters.* London, 1911.
France, A., *La vie littéraire.* 4th ed., 4 vols. Paris, 1889–1892.

JOHANN WOLFGANG GOETHE

Norton, Charles Eliot, ed., *Correspondence Between Goethe and Carlyle.* London, New York, 1887.
Rönnfeldt, W. B., tr., *Criticisms, Reflections, and Maxims of Goethe.* London, n.d.
Saunders, Bailey, tr., *Maxims and Reflections.* London, 1892.

HORACE

Blakeney, E. H., tr., *Horace on the Art of Poetry.* London, 1928.
Cook, A. S., *The Art of Poetry; The Poetical Treatises of Horace, Vida, and Boileau, with the Translations by Howes, Pitt, and Soame.* Boston, 1892.
Fairclough, H. Rushton, tr., *Horace. Satires, Epistles and Ars Poetica* (Loeb Classical Library). London, 1929.
Fiske, George C., *Lucilius and Horace.* Madison, Wisconsin, 1920.
Goad, Caroline, *Horace in the English Literature of the Eighteenth Century.* New Haven, 1918.
Heinsius, Daniel, *Ad Horatii de Plauto et Terentio Judicium Dissertatio.* Leyden, 1612 (as notes to Heinsius' edition of Horace).

Rhys, Ernest, ed., *The Complete Works of Horace,* tr. by Various Hands. Pub. by J. M. Dent & Sons, London. Everyman's Library: *Art of Poetry* (tr. by The Earl of Roscommon). London, 1911.
Sellar, William, *Horace and the Elegiac Poets,* 2nd ed. Oxford, 1899.
Wickham, E. C., ed., *Horace. The Satires, Epistles, and De Arte Poetica.* Oxford, 1903.

WILLIAM DEAN HOWELLS

Howells, W. D., *Criticism and Fiction* (Library Edition, 1910). New York, 1891.
Howells, W. D., *Literature and Life.* New York, 1902.
Robertson, J. M., *Essays toward a Critical Method.* London, 1889.

HENRY JAMES

Blackmur, R. P., ed., *The Art of the Novel: Critical Prefaces.* New York, 1934.
James, Henry, *French Poets and Novelists.* London, 1878.
James, Henry, *Hawthorne.* London, 1879.
James, Henry, *Partial Portraits.* London, 1888.
James, Henry, *Notes on Novelists.* London, 1914.
Matthiessen, F. O., *Henry James: The Major Phase.* New York, 1946.
Roberts, M., ed., *Henry James's Criticism.* Cambridge, Mass., 1929.
Roberts, M., ed., *The Art of Fiction and Other Essays by Henry James.* New York, 1948.

SAMUEL JOHNSON

Bosker, A., *Literary Criticism in the Age of Johnson.* New York, 1930.
Brown, Joseph Epes, *The Critical Opinions of Samuel Johnson.* Princeton, 1926.
Houston, Percy H., *Doctor Johnson: A Study in Eighteenth Century Humanism.* Cambridge, Mass., 1923.
Johnson, Samuel, *Lives of the English Poets* (ed. by G. B. Hill), 3 vols. Oxford, 1905.

BEN JONSON

Jonson, Ben, *Discoveries* (The Bodley Head Quartos). London, New York, 1923.
Schelling, Felix, *Ben Jonson and the Classical School.* Baltimore, 1898.

GOTTHOLD EPHRAIM LESSING

Frothingham, Ellen, tr., *Laocoön.* Boston, 1874.
Robertson, J. G., *Lessing's Dramatic Theory.* New York, 1939.

LONGINUS

Briscoe, S., tr., *The Works of Dionysius Longinus, on the Sublime*. London, 1712.
Fyfe, W. H., and Roberts, W. R., trs., *Aristotle: The Poetics, Longinus: On the Sublime, Demetrius: On Style* (Loeb Classical Series). London, New York, 1927.
Havell, H. L., tr., *Longinus on the Sublime*. London, 1890.
Roberts, W. Rhys, tr., *Longinus on the Sublime*. Cambridge, 1899.
Smith, William, tr., *Dionysius Longinus on the Sublime*. London, 1752.

GEORGE MEREDITH

Cooper, Lane, ed., *George Meredith. An Essay on Comedy*. New York, 1918.

JOHN MILTON

Cook, Albert S., ed., *Addison. Criticism on Paradise Lost*. New York, 1926.
Havens, Raymond D., *The Influence of Milton in English Poetry*. Cambridge, Mass., 1922.

A. S. MINTURNO

Minturno, A. S., *De Poeta Libri Sex*. Venetiis, 1559.
Minturno, A. S., *L'Arte Poetica* (1564). Naples, 1725.

WALTER PATER

Child, R. C., *The Aesthetic of Walter Pater*. New York, 1940.
Pater, W., *Appreciations; with an Essay on Style* (Library Edition). London, 1910.
Pater, W., *The Renaissance* (Library Edition). London, 1910.

PLATO

Cooper, Lane, tr., *Plato: Phaedrus, Ion, Gorgias, and Symposium, with Passages from the Republic and Laws*. London, New York, Toronto, 1938.
Jowett, B., tr., *The Dialogues of Plato*, 5 vols. New York, London, 1892.

ALEXANDER POPE

Dennis, John, *Remarks upon Mr. Pope's Translation of Homer*. London, 1717.
Elwin, W., and Courthope, W. J., eds., *Works of Pope*, 10 vols. London, 1871–89.

Warburton, William, ed., *The Works of Alexander Pope*. London, 1751.
Warren, Austin, *Alexander Pope as Critic and Humanist*. Princeton, 1929.
Warton, Joseph, *An Essay on the Genius and Writings of Pope*. London, 1806.

EDGAR ALLAN POE

Foerster, Norman, *American Criticism, a Study in Literary Theory from Poe to the Present*. Boston, New York, 1928.
Krutch, Joseph Wood, *Edgar Allan Poe*. New York, 1926.
Moore, John Brooks, ed., *Selections from Poe's Literary Criticism*. New York, 1926.
Stedman, Edmund Clarence, ed., *The Works of Edgar Allan Poe*. Literary Criticism I, II. New York, 1927.

GEORGE PUTTENHAM

Willcock, Gladys D., and Walker, Alice, eds., *George Puttenham, The Arte of English Poesie*. Cambridge, 1936.

JOHN CROWE RANSOM

Ransom, J. C., *The World's Body*. New York, 1938.
Ransom, J. C., *The New Criticism*. New York, 1941.

SIR JOSHUA REYNOLDS

Hilles, F. L., *Literary Career of Sir Joshua Reynolds*. Toronto, 1936.
Malone, Edmund, ed., *Works of Sir Joshua Reynolds*. London, 1794.
Reynolds, Sir Joshua, *The Discourses* (World's Classics Series). London, New York, 1907.
Reynolds, Sir Joshua, *Fifteen Discourses Delivered in the Royal Academy* (Everyman's Library). London, 1907.

IVOR ARMSTRONG RICHARDS

Richards, I. A.; Ogden, C. K.; and Wood, James, *The Foundations of Aesthetics*. London, 1922.
Richards, I. A., and Ogden, C. K., *The Meaning of Meaning*. New York, 1923.
Richards, I. A., *Principles of Literary Criticism*. New York, 1925.
Richards, I. A., *Science and Poetry*. New York, 1926.
Richards, I. A., *Practical Criticism: A Study of Literary Judgment*. New York, 1929.
Richards, I. A., *Mencius on the Mind*. London, 1932.
Richards, I. A., *Coleridge on Imagination*. London, 1934.
Richards, I. A., *How to Read a Page*. New York, 1942.

CHARLES-AUGUSTIN SAINTE-BEUVE

Butler, A. J., tr., *Select Essays of Sainte-Beuve.* London, no date.
Lee, Elizabeth, tr., *Essays by Sainte-Beuve.* London, 189?.
MacClintock, Lander, *Sainte-Beuve's Critical Theory and Practice after 1849.* Chicago, 1920.

JULIUS CAESAR SCALIGER

Lintilhac, E. de J.-C., *Scaligeri Poetica.* Paris, 1887.
Padelford, F. M., tr., *Select Translations from Scaliger's Poetics.* New York, 1905.

FREDERICK SCHILLER

Dole, Nathan Haskell, ed., *The Works of Frederick Schiller. Aesthetical and Philosophical Essays.* New York, 1902.

PERCY BYSSHE SHELLEY

Brett-Smith, H. F., ed., *Peacock's Four Ages of Poetry; Shelley's Defence of Poetry; Browning's Essay on Shelley.* Oxford, 1923.
Cook, Albert S., ed., *Shelley. A Defence of Poetry.* Boston, 1890.
Dowden, Edward, *The Life of Percy Bysshe Shelley.* London, 1926.
Johnson, R. Brimley, ed., *Shelley—Leigh Hunt.* London, 1928.
Shawcross, John, ed., *Shelley's Literary and Philosophical Criticism.* London, 1909.
Solve, Melvin T., *Shelley. His Theory of Poetry.* Chicago, 1927.
White, Newman I., *The Unextinguished Hearth.* Durham, 1938.

PHILIP SIDNEY

Arber, Edward, ed., *An Apologie for Poetrie.* London, 1858.
Collins, J. Churton, ed., *Sidney's Apologie for Poetrie.* Oxford, 1907.
Cook, A. S., ed., *The Defense of Poesy.* Boston, 1890.

LEO TOLSTOY

Maude, Aylmer, tr., *What Is Art?* London, 1925.

MARCO GIROLAMO VIDA

Cook, A. S., *The Art of Poetry; The Poetical Treatises of Horace, Vida, and Boileau, with the Translations by Howes, Pitt, and Soame.* Boston, 1892.

WILLIAM WORDSWORTH

Barstow, M. L., *Wordsworth's Theory of Poetic Diction*. New Haven, 1917.
Beatty, Arthur, *William Wordsworth, His Doctrine and Art in Their Historical Relations*. Madison, 1922.
George, Andrew J., ed., *Wordsworth's Prefaces and Essays on Poetry*. Boston, 1892.
Grosart, A. B., *The Prose Works of William Wordsworth*. London, 1876.
Knight, William, ed., *Prose Works of William Wordsworth*. London, New York, 1896.
Smith, N. C., ed., *Wordsworth's Literary Criticism*. London, 1905.

ÉMILE ZOLA

Sherman, Belle M., tr., *The Experimental Novel and Other Essays*. New York, 1893.

INDEX